Handbook of Social Justice in Education

This *Handbook*—the first comprehensive review of social justice in education—examines, from multiple perspectives, education theory, research, and practice in historical and ideological context, with an emphasis on social movements for justice. It arrives at a moment when education and educators around the world are strained and in need of support for the deepest and most important purpose of education—to build societies in which people can learn, love, and imagine more and suffer less. Addressing current attacks on public education, it makes the theoretical and conceptual argument that social justice matters, and that it is the lens through which all of what happens in education should be refracted. Each of the nine sections explores a primary theme of social justice and education:

- Historical and Theoretical Perspectives
- International Perspectives on Social Justice in Education
- Race, Ethnicity, and Language: Seeking Social Justice in Education
- Gender, Sexuality, and Social Justice in Education
- Bodies, Disability, and the Fight for Social Justice in Education
- Youth and Social Justice in Education
- Globalization and Social Justice in Education
- The Politics of Social Justice Meets Practice: Teacher Education and School Change
- Classrooms, Pedagogy, and Practicing Justice

In moving from the rhetoric of despair to one of possibility and praxis, the *Handbook of Social Justice in Education* takes a first step in a lengthy journey—one that calls for abandoning the safe rhetoric of tolerance and engaging the entangled spaces of race, class, gender, sexuality, disability, and environment through an educational lens. It reflects what it means to work to fulfill such dreams.

William Ayers is Distinguished Professor of Education at the University of Illinois at Chicago.

Therese Quinn is Associate Professor of Art Education at The School of the Art Institute of Chicago.

David Stovall is Associate Professor of Educational Policy Studies and African-American Studies at the University of Illinois at Chicago.

Handbook of Social Justice in Education

Edited by

William Ayers
University of Illinois at Chicago

Therese Quinn
The School of the Art Institute of Chicago

David Stovall
University of Illinois at Chicago

Routledge
Taylor & Francis Group

NEW YORK AND LONDON

First published 2009
by Routledge
270 Madison Ave, New York, NY 10016

Simultaneously published in the UK
by Routledge
2 Park Square, Milton Park, Abingdon, Oxon OX14 4RN

Routledge is an imprint of the Taylor & Francis Group, an informa business

© 2009 Taylor & Francis

Typeset in Sabon by EvS Communication Networx, Inc.
Printed and bound in the United States of America on acid-free paper by Sheridan Books, Inc.

Library of Congress Cataloging in Publication Data
Handbook of social justice in education / editors, William
Ayers, Therese Quinn, [and] David Stovall.
p. cm.
Includes bibliographical references and index.
1. Education—Social aspects. 2. Social justice. I. Ayers,
William. II. Quinn, Therese. III. Stovall, David.
LC71.H364 2008
303.3'72—dc22
2008021343

1005890532

ISBN 10: 0-805-85927-6 (hbk)
ISBN 10: 0-805-85928-4 (pbk)
ISBN 10: 0-203-88774-3 (ebk)

ISBN 13: 978-0-805-85927-0 (hbk)
ISBN 13: 978-0-805-85928-7 (pbk)
ISBN 13: 978-0-203-88774-5 (ebk)

Contents

vi *Contents*

Preface

Generations do not cease to be born, and we are responsible to them because we are the only witness they have. The sea rises, the light fails, lovers cling to each other, and children cling to us. The moment we cease to hold each other, the moment we break faith with one another, the sea engulfs us and the light goes out.

James Baldwin, *The Price of the Ticket,* p. 393

In our dreams we have seen another world, an honest world, a world decidedly more fair than the one in which we now live. We saw that in this world there was no need for armies; peace, justice and liberty we so common that no one talked about them as far-off concepts, but as things such as bread, birds, air, water, like book and voice. This is how the good things were named in this world. And in this world there was reason and goodwill in the government, and the leaders were clear thinking people; they ruled by obeying. This world was not a dream from the past, it was not something that came to us from our ancestors. It came from ahead, from the next step we were going to take

Subcomandante Insurgente Marcos,
In Our Dreams We Have Seen Another World, p. 18

Not a Dream From the Past

Perhaps we've lost sight of the largest purposes of education in a democracy. Perhaps—as a society, as a citizenry—we've been temporarily blinded. If so, we should be forgiven—our blindness is in large measure understandable.

The dizzying dash to reform schools—the bump and run, the hoot and holler, the endless high-pitched clamor—can, after all, be exhausting. The thousands of consultants with their millions of concrete fixes for every perceived problem can be debilitating. And the steady drumbeat of criticism—often ideologically driven—falling on the heads of educators and parents and kids mostly can become deadening. And so if we've momentarily forgotten to focus upon those transcendent goals underlying the entire enterprise, perhaps we can forgive, even as we move now to right ourselves.

For education in a democracy is fundamentally an enterprise geared toward humanization—that is, it is always about human enlightenment and human liberation. Education invites us to know more and to be more, to see, to understand, to become more capable and more powerful, more courageous and more propulsive in the service of greater participation and more effective engagement in our work, our society, our lives. Education opens a path away from ignorance and prejudice, fear and backwardness, entanglement and confinement. Education opens doors—it is good for each of us, and it is good for all of us, for society, for democracy.

The mission of public education is to assist parents as they raise children and youth who can become thoughtful, strong, resilient, imaginative, and moral adults, people who can live productive, socially useful and individually satisfying lives. Classrooms and schools must become sites where young people envision, enact and renew democratic life. Democracy relies on neither rulers nor experts—it requires citizens capable of governing themselves, of running their own affairs, making up their own minds, inventing and creating, and building and re-building. Education for democracy is a popular undertaking—of, by, and for the people.

Education for social justice is not a new idea, nor is it just another reform proposal, an add-on to what already is. Rather, education for social justice is the root of teaching and schooling in a democratic society, the rock upon which we build democracy. We will have achieved a kind of Golden Age—enlightened and hopeful, civilized and advanced—when children are recognized as the foremost members of society, and when teaching is treated as the pre-eminent, transcendent enterprise it should be. While this may be contested in both policy and practice, it is rarely resisted rhetorically, in the open. We offer this text as a weapon in the battle to remind us all of its central, immutable place.

Living in a world of "high stakes accountability" places individuals concerned with social justice in education at a crossroads. At this intersection, those who wish to pose alternatives to school-based rhetoric and practices of fear are challenged to make conscious, proactive decisions for public education. We must operate within an overarching truth: public systems of education are increasingly threatened by moves toward privatization, and often serve as assembly lines for the status quo. To the purveyors of power—big city school systems, elected officials at local and national levels, multinational corporations, the military—"hard facts" and "tough choices" are the catch-phrases of the day. Within these logics, the hopes and aspirations of Baldwin and the Subcomandante are the reasons there's so much wrong with public education—too much "dreaming" and not enough "doing." However, we are faced with a parallel reality: if we do not continue and strengthen our efforts to critique, understand and create new systems by which to educate young people, we will continue to drown in defeat and the powerful will continue to argue for the destruction of our ability to dream and move on those dreams. This is what social justice education offers.

***

Social justice education rests on three pillars or principles: 1) *Equity*, the principle of fairness, equal access to the most challenging and nourishing educational experiences, the demand that what the most privileged and enlightened are able to provide their children must be the standard for what is made available to all children. This must also account for equitable outcomes, and somehow for redressing and repairing historical and embedded injustices. 2) *Activism*, the principle of agency, full participation, preparing youngsters to see and understand and, when necessary, to change all that is before them. This is a move away from passivity, cynicism and despair. 3) *Social literacy*, the principle of relevance, resisting the flattening effects of materialism and consumerism and the power of the abiding social evils of white supremacy, patriarchy, homophobia—nourishing awareness of our own identities and our connection with others, reminding us of the powerful commitment, persistence, bravery, and triumphs of our justice-seeking forebears, reminding us as well of the link between ideas and the concentric circles of context—economic condition, historical flow, cultural surround—within which our lives are negotiated.

Social justice education embraces these three R's: Relevant, Rigorous, and Revolutionary. We change our lives, we change the world.

***

We aspire here to an organic form featuring evocative phrases that are framed by commitment and possibility, and interludes by "non-traditional" expert voices. Each section that follows is organized around epigraphs taken from a wide range of activists, intellectuals, educators, and artists. Each epigraph was selected by the Handbook editors, not the section editors or chapter authors, and each is intended to be provocative and lateral rather than literal.

References

Baldwin, J. (1985). *The Price of the Ticket*. New York: St Martin's Press.

Subcomandante Insurgente Marcos. (2001). *In Our Dreams We Have Seen Another World*. In J. Ponce De Leon (Ed.). *The World is Our Weapon*. New York: Seven Stories Press.

Acknowledgments

The Handbook editors would like to thank Gabriela Fitz, Amos Kennedy, Beatriz Lopez, Grisel Martinez, Isabel Nuñez, Martin Ritter, and Bernardo Salazar for their help preparing the manuscript, cover art, and compiling resources.

Rick Ayers includes his thanks to Linda Christensen.

The project on which the chapter by Zvi Bekerman is based was funded by the Bernard Van Leer Foundation.

Ellen Brantlinger would like to thank and acknowledge Patricia Hulsebosch for her careful editing and helpful suggestions at various stages of chapter writing.

Julio Cammarota and Augustine Romero acknowledge the Social Justice Education Project, Lorenzo Lopez, Jose Gonzalez, Chiara Cannella, and Sean Arce.

Although the chapter by Rico Gutstein is single authored, the teaching, planning, assessment, and analysis involved in this story were collaboratively shared among three other people besides the author: Joyce Sia (teacher), Phi Pham (teacher), and Patricia Buenrostro (mathematics support staff). This research was partially supported by the National Science Foundation Grant # ESI-0424983. The views expressed in the chapter do not represent those of the funding agency.

Avi Lessing thanks Anna Deavere Smith for the courage to listen.

Pauline Lipman and Karen Monkman would like to thank Lisa Parker Short for her diligent editorial assistance and twelve colleagues who have generously reviewed the chapters in this section.

Cris Mayo expresses her thanks to Mara Sapon Shevin and Therese Quinn for their helpful and energetic editorial work and thanks to Stephanie Foote for her comments and engagement.

Morva McDonald and Ken Zeichner would like to thank Cap Peck for his comments on their chapter.

Julie Searle shares her "thanks and affection for the students who taught me so much in our year together."

Christine Sleeter would like to thank Joel Westheimer and Karen Suurtamm for some very helpful suggestions on an earlier draft of her chapter.

Andrew Smiler gives his thanks to Mara Sapon-Shevin and Barbara Garii for their comments on an earlier draft of his manuscript.

The following people were instrumental to the work of Laurence Tan: Kahelah Symmetric, Denise Pacheco, Benji Chang, the Phenomenal 5th Grade YoungStarZ, and the Watts Youth Collective.

Part 1

Historical and Theoretical Perspectives

Edited and Introduced by Kenneth J. Saltman

> If there is any purity left, it is in the stark understanding that social systems based on oppression imprint seemingly irresolvable conflicts onto every sphere of human endeavor. If there is a perspective shared by peoples around the world, it is that at this moment in history there are no easy solutions.
>
> (Glendinning, 2003)

> I don't expect to ever see a utopia. No, I think there will always be something that you're going to have to work on, always. That's why, when we have chaos and people say, "I'm scared. I'm scared. I'm concerned," I say, "Out of that will come something good." It will, too. They can be afraid if they want to, afraid of what is going to happen. Things will happen, and things will change. The only thing that's really worthwhile is change. It's coming.
>
> (Clark & Brown Stokes, 1990, p. 126)

The chapters in this section are unified by their recognition that people and groups struggle over the representation and retelling of history and that these representational contests over the meanings of the past are inextricably tied to broader material and symbolic struggles, forces, and structures of power. Though social justice does not have a unified or static meaning, these chapters are all concerned with elaborating a historical notion of social justice understood through the expansion of democratic values with regard to schooling, curriculum, pedagogy, policy, culture, politics, and economy. In different ways the contributors address the stakes involved for students, teachers, parents, and citizens in comprehending the past and in utilizing that comprehension to struggle for a more just and democratic future. These tasks could not be more pressing at the moment.

Educators, citizens, and activists committed to social justice face a recent history characterized by the radical rise of social injustice. In the United States an economic war against youth, the poor, the working class, and people of color has been waged in which child and family poverty have drastically increased at the same time that extreme wealth has been redistributed to the very top of the economy. Public goods and services including health care, public education, and public housing have been subject to decimation and privatization to turn them into an investment opportunity for those best off. As public schools across the United States in poor and working class communities are denied adequate funding and resources they are subject to punitive action including the denial of much needed funds, school closure, and privatization. These undemocratic upward material redistributions of wealth and resources are accompanied by an ongoing anti-democratic political and cultural onslaught by the political right.

Since 2001 the United States has endured a radical erosion of civil liberties and democratic constitutional protections and an amassing of executive power. The Bush administration, the Republican Party, and a largely complicit Democratic Party have undermined the democratic rights of habeus corpus, posse commitatus, right to privacy, right of assembly, freedom from search and seizure, freedom from cruel and unusual punishment, and more. Public democracy has been further assaulted by the production of a culture of fear and a culture hostile to critical dissent not to mention historical fact. A large part of this has been created through the ideological work of the mass media and the state that has, under the brand name, the Global War on Terror, instituted an historical amnesia. Within the fundamentalist thought of the "war on terror" not only are incompatible ideologies and values made interchangeable, and not only does the Big Enemy appear as a method of fighting, but to question the history leading to events appears treasonous in the current political climate.

History matters for democracy because it provides a form of intellectual self-defense for public citizens at a time when truth claims are increasingly legitimated by the power of the claimant. From the invasion of Iraq, to the cold war machinations that produced Al Qaeda and the Taliban, to the history of political liberalism and radicalism in the United States to grassroots social justice movements, public culture is increasingly subject to an eternal present and an active forgetting. This has, in part, to do with the commodification of knowledge and information as it is largely produced and circulated by corporate media with financial and ideological interests in selling fleeting spectacle for passive consumption. In fact public schooling remains one of the few places in a hypercommercialized society where knowledge and information can be investigated and debated as the basis for more complex and historically informed perspectives that can be the basis for greater individual and social understanding and public deliberation and action. Put differently, public schooling is a crucial site and stake in the struggle for the making of a democratic ethos. Yet in public schools, public democratic culture is under increasing assault by educational reforms that separate facts from underlying values and framing assumptions, that disconnect claims to truth from the interests and perspectives of those making them, that view knowledge as static discreet objects to be delivered to learners like units of commodity.

In short, the intensified positivism of constant standardized testing, "performance-based assessment," and standardization of curriculum undermine not only the curiosity and investigative powers of the student but also deny the dialogic nature of knowledge making. The new reforms see knowledge as exclusively needing to be enforced from above, determined by the experts—"the ones who know." Knowledge and schooling are alleged to be objective and neutral in this perspective. There is, of course, a politics in this denial of the politics of education as the values, interests, and ideological perspectives of "ones who know" are concealed under the guise of objectivity and neutrality fostered by standardized testing, tracking, and grading. The denial of underlying values and framing assumptions do more than threaten the development of critical individuals capable of critically interpreting the world in order to act and change it collectively. Such denials implicit in the positivist reforms also flatten history by falsely suggesting that consecrated knowledge is universally, transhistorically true. To recognize the partial, contextual nature of truth claims is not to deny objective reality but to recognize that truth claims are selected and mediated through subjectivity. The positivism of the new reforms posits a false objectivism in which the role of the subject in interpreting truth plays no part in shaping the object of knowledge itself.

How subjects come to particular claims to truth is historical. Objectivity is more closely approached by bringing the shaping historical force of subjectivity into the process of knowing the object of study. This is not an argument for relativism. On the contrary, subjects draw on historical traditions of thought to interpret and act on the world. The ahistorical tendency of the positivism of the new educational reforms is not only an epistemological matter but an ontological one as well. In seeking to bound knowledge for its standardization, knowledge and the material world are objectified such that changing material realities and changing knowledge appears as a threat to truth rather than as something to comprehend in relation to the forces that make change. But to teach is to make meanings, to produce culture, dialogically with others through exchange. Teaching is not a matter of delivering preordained guaranteed units of objectified truth. In fact, such a conception of education is really about dogma. While teachers inevitably exercise pedagogical and political authority, it is precisely the fallibilism, the nonguaranteed, relatively indeterminate nature of education, the possibility of interpretation that allows knowledge to be understood in relation to broader social issues, pressing matters of public import, and relations of power such that this interpretive knowledge can become the basis for social intervention.

These chapters are also linked by their focus on different aspects of the history of social movements in relation to education. Some chapters focus on broad-based social movements while others focus on social movements within institutional contexts. Deron Boyles, Tony Carusi, and Dennis Attick foreground the section by providing a historical overview of the philosophical origins of social justice with regard to education. Enora Brown provides an account of how education and the law were historically used as instruments of class and racial oppression and offers insights into what history tells us about contemporary neoliberal and antiaffirmative action educational policies and reforms. Sandra Mathison considers the historical struggle over the meaning of educational evaluation and the battle between public and private ideas of evaluation. Her chapter highlights the dangerous shift to a private notion of evaluation that presently services neoliberal ideology. Horace Hall recounts the history of the civil rights movement and the legacy of Brown to elaborate a contemporary theory of critical education. Like Mathison, Marc VanOverbeke provides an institutional history—a history of the higher education extension school movement. He raises a number of questions about the limited successes of this liberal mass education project aimed at the working class. David Gabbard considers the history of the anarchist movement to propose a radical emancipatory turn for public education. Gabbard's position breaks with the more prevalent Marxian tradition of radical education to call into question the very viability of compulsory state schooling as a means to achieve broad-based social justice. Pepi Leistyna offers a history of contemporary activist youth movements and argues for the centrality of theory and theorizing to achieve democratic social change.

References

Clark, S., & Brown Stokes, C. (1990). *Ready from within*. Lawrenceville, NJ: African World Press.

Glendinning, C. (2003). Introduction. In W. Churchill (Ed.), *On the justice of roosting chickens* (pp. 1–2). Oakland, CA: AK Press.

1 Public Good and Private Interest in Educational Evaluation

Sandra Mathison

If we share an apple, we can share a community

So reads the caption on a poster I received upon completion of an evaluation of an accelerated secondary school program. Over a six-month period I worked with this school and its stakeholders (including students, teachers, parents, school administrators, and graduates) to evaluate this accelerated program for precocious eighth and ninth graders. The evaluation was stakeholder based, the types of evidence collected evolved as the evaluation proceeded, the students became interested in the process and worked with me to develop data collection skills and then collect data themselves. The final report and where to go from the results was a collaborative effort among the stakeholder groups.

This is typically the kind of educational evaluation I do, although there is a wide range of approaches used in educational evaluation. But for this work, I did not get paid. The school has no money for evaluation. The school district has no money for evaluation. The evaluation approach the school wanted is not a priority or publicly funded.

Consider this quote from *Identifying and Implementing Educational Practices Supported by Rigorous Evidence: A User Friendly Guide*, published by the U.S. Department of Education (2003):

> Well-designed and implemented randomized controlled trials are considered the "gold standard" for evaluating an intervention's effectiveness, in fields such as medicine, welfare and employment policy, and psychology. This section discusses what a randomized controlled trial is, and outlines evidence indicating that such trials should play a similar role in education.

And so the stage for the current focus on educational evaluation is set by the U.S. Department of Education.

Educational Evaluation in Historical Context

Educational evaluation is by and large a public good—although evaluation occurs in many fields and in many contexts supported through many means, the genesis of educational evaluation is the stipulations in the Elementary and Secondary Education Act (ESEA) passed in 1965. Established as part of Lyndon Johnson's War on Poverty, the ESEA provides federal assistance to schools, communities, and children in need. With current funding of about $9.5 billion annually, the ESEA continues to be the single largest source of federal funding to K-12 schools. Through its many Title programs, especially Title I, ESEA has been a major force in focusing how and what is taught in schools, as well as the ways those activities are evaluated. With Johnson's conceptualization of ESEA, educational evaluation was seen to be a public good (just like education and schooling) that should serve the common public good. What I want to illustrate is that although educational evaluation remains a public good it increasingly serves private interests.

While the passage of ESEA marks the beginning of the formalization of educational evaluation, one prior event, the Eight Year Study, also played an important role in educational evaluation, although it is more often associated with developments in curriculum theory and design. The Eight Year Study involved 30 high schools dispersed throughout the United States and serving diverse communities (Aiken, 1942). Each school developed its own curriculum and each was released from government regulations, as well as the need for students to take college entrance examinations. With dissension early in the project about how its success should be evaluated, a young Ralph Tyler was brought on board to direct the evaluation, which was funded by the Rockefeller Foundation. Out of the Eight Year Study came what is now known as the "Tyler Rationale," the common-sense idea that what students were supposed to learn should determine what happened in classrooms and how evaluation should be done (Tyler, 1949).

Tyler's evaluation team devised many curriculum specific tests, helped to build the capacity for each school to devise its own measures of context specific activities and objectives, identified a role for learners in evaluation, and developed data records to serve intended purposes (including descriptive student report cards) (Smith & Tyler, 1942). All of these developments resonate with conceptual developments in evaluation from the 1970s to the present. The notion of opportunity to learn is related to the curriculum sensitivity of measures; the widespread focus on evaluation capacity building resonates with the Tylerian commitment to helping schools help themselves in judging the quality and value of their work; democratic and empowerment approaches, indeed all stakeholder based approaches, resonate with the learners' active participation in evaluation; and the naturalistic approaches to evaluation resonate with the use of behavioral descriptive data.

The Eight Year Study ended in 1941 and was published in five volumes in 1942, an event which was overshadowed by its unfortunate coincidence with U.S. troops taking an active role in World War II. Nonetheless, Ralph Tyler and the Eight Year Study evaluation staff provided a foundation, whether always recognized or not, for future education evaluators.

When ESEA was passed in 1965 (legislation which Ralph Tyler had a hand in as an educational advisor to the Johnson administration) the requirement that the expenditure of public funds be accounted for thrust educators into a new and unfamiliar role. Educational researchers and educational psychologists stepped in to fill the need for evaluation created by ESEA. But the efforts of practitioners and researchers alike were generally considered to be only minimally successful at providing the kind of evaluative information envisioned. The compensatory programs supported by ESEA were complex and embedded in the complex organization of schooling.

Since the federal politicians, especially ESEA architect Robert Kennedy, were primarily interested in accountability, evaluation requirements for ESEA, especially for Title I, which was the largest compensatory program, emphasized uniform procedures and comparable data at the state and national levels, a direction many evaluators found misdirected (Jaeger, 1978; Wiley, 1979). During this period, the advances in educational evaluation were, at least in part, over and against the federal approach to evaluation, especially Title I programs, primarily a focus on student achievement (expressed as "normal curve equivalents").

There is of course nothing wrong with knowing how well or how poorly a student performs. Yet schools, insofar as they are educational institutions, should not be content with performance. Education as a process is concerned with the cultivation of intellectual power, and the ability to determine what a student knows is not necessarily useful or sufficient for making the process more effective. (Eisner, 1979, p. 11)

The tension between meeting federally mandated reporting requirements and local needs for evaluative information was a significant part of the debate. School districts did the minimum to meet the federal reporting guidelines but at the same time often looked for guidance as to how to sincerely evaluate what was happening in local schools. While school districts may have needed only one person to meet the reporting mandate, a broader local interest led to the creation of evaluation departments in many and certainly all of the large school districts.

The late 1960s and into the 1980s were the gold rush days of educational evaluation. During this time, models of evaluation proliferated and truly exciting intellectual work was being done, especially in education. Often very traditionally educated educational psychologists experienced epiphanies that redirected their thinking about evaluation. For example, Robert Stake, a psychometrician who began his career at the Educational Testing Service, wrote a paper, "Countenance of Educational Evaluation," which reoriented thinking about the nature of educational interventions and what was important to pay attention to in determining their effectiveness (Stake, 1967). Egon Guba, a well known education change researcher abandoned the research, development, diffusion approach for naturalistic and qualitative approaches that examined educational interventions carefully and contextually (Lincoln & Guba, 1985). Lee Cronbach, psychometric genius, focused not on the technical aspects of measurement in evaluation, but on the policy-oriented nature of evaluation. This was an idea that led to a radical reconstruction of internal and external validity, which included separating the two conceptually and conceptualizing external validity in relation to usability and plausibility of conclusions, not as a technical feature of research or evaluation design (Cronbach, 1982).

While ESEA, now No Child Left Behind (NCLB), is the driving force in what counts as evaluation in education, other developments have occurred simultaneously and are important companion pieces to understanding the contemporary educational evaluation landscape. The National Assessment of Educational Progress (NAEP), sometimes referred to as the nation's report card, was created in the mid-1960s, building on and systematizing a much longer history of efforts to use educational statistics to improve and expand public education. Francis Keppel, the U.S. Commissioner of Education from 1962 to 1965 and a former dean of the Harvard School of Education, lamented the lack of information about the academic achievement of American students.

It became clear that American education had not yet faced up to the question of how to determine the quality of academic performance in the schools. There was a lack of information. Without a reporting system that alerted state or federal authorities to the need for support to shore up educational weakness, programs had to be devised on the basis of social and economic data.... (Keppel, 1966, pp. 108–109)

Under the direction of Ralph Tyler (Tyler's intellectual legacy in evaluation is huge, as noted by his continued involvement in pivotal events in educational evaluation), NAEP developed as a system to test a sample of students on a range of test items, rather than the simple testing of all students with the same test items. To allay fears that NAEP would be used to coerce local and state educational authorities the results were initially released for four regions only. NAEP has continued to develop, early on largely with the use of private funding from the Carnegie Corporation, and the early fears of superintendents and professional associations (such as the National Council for Teachers of English) turn out to be well founded. State level NAEP scores are indeed now available. This shift in the use of NAEP occurred during the Reagan administration with then Secretary of Education Terrel Bell's infamous wall chart. With a desire to compare states' educational performance, indicators available for all states were needed, and NAEP filled that bill. Southern states, such as Arkansas, under then governor Bill Clinton, applauded the use of such comparisons believing that they would encourage competition, a presumed condition for improvement.

During these halcyon years in educational evaluation, much evaluation was publicly funded, primarily by the U.S. Department of Education, but also by other federal agencies such as the National Science Foundation, in addition to many foundations, such as Carnegie, Rockefeller, Ford, and Weyerhaeuser. The dominance of public money and the liberal and progressive political era contributed significantly to the conceptualization of evaluation as a public good. Discussions of how best to judge if education and schooling are good contributed to a lively national debate about what counts as good education and schooling.

For example, the relatively small number of meta-evaluations conducted during this time focused primarily on whether the evaluation was fair and in the public interest. Two good examples of this are the meta-evaluation of Follow-Through (House, Glass, McLean, & Walker, 1978) (that thoroughly criticized economist Alice Rivlin's planned variation experiment as an evaluation method that did not do justice to the unique contributions of follow-through models for local communities) and the meta-evaluation of Push-Excel (House, 1988), Jesse Jackson's inspirational youth program that was undone by Charles Murray's evaluation that failed to consider the program on its own terms in the context of local communities (Murray was coauthor with Richard Herrnstein of *Bell Curve: Intelligence and Class Structure in American Life,* 1994).

The New Neoliberal Era and Educational Evaluation

The reauthorization of ESEA, now called No Child Left Behind (NCLB), reinforces the need for evaluation. But unlike the more general expectation for evaluation that typified the original ESEA evaluation mandate, NCLB is decidedly more prescriptive about how education should be evaluated, in part because of the inclusion of sanctions for failure to perform. While earlier versions of ESEA focused on student performance, NCLB did so by invoking the notion of "annual yearly progress" (AYP) and continued funding from the federal government was now dependent on each school making "continuous and substantial progress" toward academic proficiency by *all* students.

The 1965 authorization of ESEA, in spite of its emphasis on uniformity and standardization, opened new frontiers and contributed significantly to the discipline of evaluation, but NCLB has narrowed the scope of evaluation. Fewer federal funds are now spent on educational evaluation and the burden of evaluation has been shifted to the state and local levels through student testing. NCLB mandates what counts as evaluation (acceptable indicators, what counts as progress, consequences for lack of progress) but provides no funding to carry out the mandate. George W. Bush declared that with the reauthorization of NCLB, "America's schools will be on a new path of reform, and a new path of results." No one would disagree. Teaching has become less professional and more mechanical (Mathison & Freeman, 2003); business and profits for the test publishing and scoring companies has increased markedly, even though the testing is mostly misdirected (Popham, 2004); and schools chase unattainable goals out of fear (Linn, 2005). That the path is new does not necessarily mean it is the path best traveled.

The current narrow evaluation focus of NCLB (standardized tests for evaluating student learning and schools) evolved as a result of changes in political values. The current public and governmental neoliberalist sentiment (an ideology shared by Republicans and Democrats) has had major implications for government policies beginning in the 1970s but increasingly prominent since 1980. Neoliberalism deemphasizes government intervention in the economy, focusing instead on achieving progress (including social justice) by encouraging free market methods and fewer restrictions on business operations and economic development.

Concerns about and constructions of a crisis in American schools are formulated around constructs such as international competitiveness and work productivity. In other words, our schools are meant to serve the interests of the economy. *A Nation At Risk*, published in 1983, was the clarion call for educational reform: "The educational foundations of our society are presently being eroded by a rising tide of mediocrity that threatens our very future as a nation and a people.... We have, in effect been committing an act of unthinking, unilateral educational disarmament."

Although it took a few years, in 1989 President Bush and the state governors called an Education Summit in Charlottesville. That summit established six broad educational goals to be reached by the year 2000. President Clinton signed Goals 2000 into law in 1994. Goals 3 and 4 were related specifically to academic achievement and thus set the stage for both what educational evaluation should focus on and how.

In 1990, the federally funded procedures for moving the country toward accomplishment of these goals were established. The National Education Goals Panel (NEGP) and the National Council on Education Standards and Testing (NCEST) were created and charged with answering a number of questions: What is the subject matter to be addressed? What types of assessments should be used? What standards of performance should be set?

In 1996, a national education summit was attended by 40 state governors and more than 45 business leaders. They supported efforts to set clear academic standards in the core subject areas at the state and local levels and the business leaders pledged to consider the existence of state standards when locating facilities. Another summit followed in 1999 and focused on three key challenges facing U.S. schools—improving educator quality, helping all students reach high standards, and strengthening accountability—and agreed to specify how each of their states would address these challenges. And a final summit occurred in 2001, when state governors and business leaders met at the IBM Conference Center in Palisades, New York to provide guidance to states in creating and using tests, including the development of a national testing plan. The culminating event to this series of events beginning in the early 1980s was the passage of NCLB.

The heavy hand of business interests and market metaphors in establishing what schools should do and how we should evaluate what they are doing is evident in the role business leaders have played in the education summits. The infrastructure that supports this perspective is broad and deep. The Business Roundtable, an association of chief executive officers of U.S. corporations, and the even more focused Business Coalition for Education Reform, a coalition of 13 business associations, are political supporters and active players in narrowing evaluation of education to the use of standardized achievement tests.

With the passage of NCLB, the U.S. Department of Education simultaneously funds less evaluation. This is partly because of a much-narrowed definition of what the government now considers good evaluation and partly because the U.S. Department of Education sees itself as the judge of educational evaluation and research, rather than its sponsor.

The U.S. Department of Education recognizes four kinds of program evaluation: (1) continuous improvement (employing market research techniques); (2) program performance data (use of performance-based data management systems); (3) descriptive studies of program implementation (use of passive, descriptive techniques like surveys, self-reports, and case studies); and (4) rigorous field trials of specific interventions (field trials with randomized assignment). It is this last sort of evaluation that is the pièce de résistance, what are referred to as the "new generation of rigorous evaluations." It is this evaluation approach that permits entry to the What Works Clearinghouse (WWC) of the Institute of Education Sciences (IES), and thus an intervention, practice, or curriculum earns the governmental imprimatur of an "evidence-based best practice."

As reflected in the quote at the beginning of this chapter, evaluations must be randomized clinical trials, perhaps quasi-experimental or regression discontinuity designs. Few if any educational evaluations have been of this sort; indeed much of the work since the 1960s has been directed to creating different evaluation methods and models of evaluative inquiry (not just borrowed research methods) that answer evaluative questions. Questions about feasibility, practicability, needs, costs, intended and unintended outcomes, ethics, and justifiability are uniquely evaluative.

While neoliberalism clearly surrounds NCLB by the characterization of education as a commodity, the use of single indicators, and the promotion of market systems to improve the quality of schooling, the connection to the U.S. government mandate for randomized clinical trials is a little more tenuous. However, neoliberalism is characterized by a reliance on specialized knowledge and silencing or at least muting the voices of the populace. Unlike many approaches to evaluation that are built on the inclusion of stakeholders in directing and conducting the evaluation, experimental design is controlled by experts, and stakeholders (especially service providers and recipients) are conceived of more as anonymous subjects, and less as moral, sociopolitical actors.

By many accounts, the discipline of evaluation dealt with the role of experimental design in evaluation—it is potentially useful, most of the time impractical, and often limited in answering the array of evaluative questions invariably asked. It was unclear that the deep commitment to experimental design as the sine qua non of evaluation designs was only dormant, waiting for the political fertilizer to germinate and grow this commitment.

Evaluation Foci and Methods that Encourage Private Interests

Just as progressivism was the value context up to the late 1970s and even early 1980s, neoliberalism has been the value context that brings educational evaluation to where we are today. Schools are a business, education is a product, products should be created efficiently, and one should look to the bottom line in making decisions. Implicit in this neoliberal perspective are values (and rhetoric) that motivate action. The most obvious of these values are that accountability is good, that simple parsimonious means for holding schools accountable are also good, that choice or competition will increase quality, that it is morally superior to seek employability over other purposes of education. Econometrics drives thinking about what these simple parsimonious means are—the appeal of single indicators like standardized tests and the concept of value added now promoted in evaluating the teachers.

It is useful to look at two examples that illustrate this neoliberal focusing of evaluation.

Example 1: SchoolMatters

SchoolMatters describes its purpose thus: "SchoolMatters gives policymakers, educators, and parents the tools they need to make better-informed decisions that improve student performance. SchoolMatters will educate, empower, and engage education stakeholders."

It is a product of Standard and Poors, which is in turn owned by McGraw-Hill Companies—the biggest producer of educational tests; and it promises to provide, in one convenient location (schoolmatters.com), the following:

- Student Performance: national and state test results, participation, attendance, graduation, and dropout–promotion rates.
- Spending, Revenue, Taxes, and Debt: financial data for each school district, along with state and county comparisons.
- School Environment: class size, teacher qualifications, and student demographics.
- Community Demographics: adult education levels, household incomes, and labor force statistics.

And the highly interactive website delivers on this. A range of indicators are used: school size, reading scores, math scores, special needs (limited to information about English Language Learners), teacher–student ratios, ethnicity, income, and housing costs. But there is much about schools and education that SchoolMatters does not deliver, because it is considered unnecessary, or difficult to collect or aggregate data, or does not reflect a narrow conception of the purpose of schools to prepare skilled workers. Indicators you will not find: types of school programming, health and fitness, quality of physical plant, availability of resources such as books/paper/pencils, attrition rates, proportion of dropouts getting a GED, and levels of volunteerism or community involvement.

In addition, there is a decidedly different language used in the discussion of factors that are outside of school control versus those that are in school control. In the former case there are cautions about the importance of parents and communities in academic achievement.

> Research has shown that the education levels and contributions of parents are critical factors that impact a child's academic performance. To help all students reach their full potential, it is necessary that students, teachers, families, and communities collectively engage in efforts to improve student performance.

The implication here is that parents should get themselves educated and do something to contribute to the improvement of student performance—an essentially moral message to others.

This contrasts with a factor that is within the school's control, namely class size. When there is a potential change to the school that might improve student performance but at a cost, SchoolMatters advises caution.

> Smaller class sizes may improve student performance in certain settings; for example, research has shown that low-income students in early grades may benefit from smaller classes. Yet, there is less agreement on across-the-board benefits of small classes. Deciding to implement a policy to create smaller classrooms means that more teachers must be hired, and not all communities have a pool of qualified teachers from which to draw.

This selective presentation of research on the benefits of reducing class size serves other purposes—it diverts parents or educators from investing time in contemplating changes that might increase costs and therefore threaten the production of educational products at the lowest possible cost. Indeed, S&P promotes "improving the return on educational resources" rather than insuring there are adequate resources.

Example 2: What Works Clearinghouse

As mentioned earlier, the What Works Clearinghouse (WWC) promises "a new generation of rigorous evaluations" by specifying a single acceptable, desirable evaluation design, the randomized clinical trial (RCT). The WWC means to "identify studies that provide the strongest evidence of effects: primarily well conducted randomized controlled trials and regression discontinuity studies, and secondarily quasi-experimental studies of especially strong design."

With fewer resources for funding educational evaluation, the U.S. Department of Education has turned its attention via the WWC to evaluating research and evaluation.

> The WWC aims to promote informed education decision making through a set of easily accessible databases and user-friendly reports that provide education consumers with high-quality reviews of the effectiveness of replicable educational interventions (programs, products, practices, and policies) that intend to improve student outcomes.

The WWC standards for identifying studies that show what works are based on an examination of design elements only. The conclusions of studies that meet the design standards are those worth paying attention to, regardless of their substance.

Evaluation in Service of What?

These two examples demonstrate different but complementary ways that evaluation as a public good has come to serve private interests. Metaphorically, a database for rating schools created by a market rating firm implicitly reinforces and naturalizes the neoliberal market oriented values that inform what schooling is and how we evaluate it. And the narrowly defined and highly specialized conception of evaluation design promoted by the Institute for Education Science and manifest in the What Works Clearinghouse delineate what counts as evaluative knowledge and thus what counts as worth knowing about education and schooling.

These are powerful forces, and evaluators working within public school districts across the nation would agree they do little "evaluation" any more. They are too busy with NCLB's mandates for standardized testing of students and trying to figure out how, if at all, they can conjure up an RCT so as to obtain much needed money for local evaluation efforts (Mathison & Muñoz, 2004).

Educational evaluation has been and will continue to evolve. In its early days educational evaluation bore the mark of progressivism. Education and the evaluation of it were supported by public funding and defined as a public good, in the interest of all. Evaluation reflected these values (including efficiency, social justice, and democracy) and was financially supported with public funds. In the 1980s the values of progressivism gave way to the emerging values of neoliberalism. All evaluation requires the specification of the good-making qualities of what is being evaluated. And these good-making qualities are socially constructed; therefore the dominant approach to education evaluation reflects the current sociopolitical zeitgeist. In the current state of neoliberalism and neoconservatism, education and the evaluation of it increasingly reflect those values, including commodification, privatization, and Judeo-Christian morality. The practice of evaluation (like many social practices) is a reflection of the values, beliefs, and preferences of the time.

Some educational evaluators still follow in the footsteps of Tyler, Stake, Guba, and Cronbach and, although in small measure, continue to conduct evaluations that encourage broad understandings of quality in education and schooling. Participatory and stakeholder based approaches to educational evaluation can be found, approaches that recognize the importance of local context, the critical involvement of especially those who are most powerless in judgments of education supposedly in their best interests, the need to consider the complex purposes of schooling that include basic skills for employability but extend beyond to social development and citizenship (Mathison, in press). Evaluation capacity building, a strategy for helping people make their own judgments about the quality of their schools, is an underlying goal for a number of evaluators (King, 2005). And grassroots groups, such as the Massachusetts Coalition for Authentic Reform in Education (MassCARE), resist the narrow and singular criterion of academic achievement in considering the quality of education. There is still educational evaluation that builds on the explosive and exciting period of the 1970s and 80s—I still do it, but sometimes I get paid in posters.

References

Aiken, W. M. (1942). *The story of the Eight Year Study.* New York: Harper Brothers. Retrieved February 13, 2007, from http://www.8yearstudy.org

Cronbach, L. J. (1982). *Designing evaluations of educational and social programs.* San Francisco: Jossey-Bass.

Eisner, E. W. (1979). The use of qualitative forms of evaluation for improving educational practice. *Educational Evaluation and Policy Analysis, 1*(6), 11–19.

Herrnstein, R., & Murray, C. (1994). *The bell curve: Intelligence and class structure in American life.* New York: Free Press.

House, E. R. (1988). *The politics of charisma: The rise and fall of PUSH/Excel Program.* Boulder, CO: Westview Press.

House, E. R., Glass, G. V., McLean, L. D., & Walker, D. C. (1978). No simple answer: A critique of the follow-through evaluation. *Harvard Educational Review, 48,* 128–160.

Jaeger, R. M. (1978). *The effect of test selection of Title I project impact.* Paper presented at the annual meeting of the American Educational Research Association, Toronto.

Keppel, F. (1966). *The necessary revolution in American education.* New York: Harper & Row.

King, J. A. (2005). A proposal to build evaluation capacity at the Bunche-Da Vinci Learning Partnership Academy. In M. C. Alkin & C. A. Christie (Eds.), *New directions for evaluation, 106,* 85–98.

Lincoln, Y., & Guba, E. (1985). *Naturalistic inquiry.* Newbury Park, CA: Sage.

Linn, R. L. (2005). Conflicting demands of No Child Left Behind and state systems: Mixed messages about school performance. *Education Policy Analysis Archives, 13*(33). Retrieved February 13, 2007, from http://epaa.asu.edu/epaa/v13n33/

Mathison, S. (in press). Serving the public interest through educational evaluation: Salvaging democracy by rejecting neo-liberalism. In C. B. Cousins & K. Ryan (Eds.), *Handbook of educational evaluation.* Newbury Park, CA: Sage.

Mathison, S., & Freeman, M. (2003). Constraining the work of elementary teachers: Dilemmas and paradoxes created by state mandated testing. *Education Policy Analysis Archives, 11*(34). Retrieved February 13, 2007, from http://epaa.asu.edu/epaa/v11n34

Mathison, S., & Muñoz, M. (2004). Evaluating education and schools for democracy. In S. Mathison & E. W. Ross (Eds.), *Defending public schools: The nature and limits of standards based educational reform and testing* (pp. 71–81). Westport, CT: Greenwood Press.

Nation at Risk. (1983). http://www.ed.gov/pubs/NatAtRisk/index.html

Popham, J. (2004). Standards based education: Two wrongs don't make a right. In S. Mathison & E. W. Ross (Eds.), *Defending public schools: The nature and limits of standards based educational reform and testing* (pp. 1–26). Westport, CT: Greenwood Press.

Smith, E. R., & Tyler, R. W. (1942). *Appraising and recording student progress.* New York: Harper.

Stake, R. E. (1967). The countenance of educational evaluation. *Teachers College Record, 68*(7), 523–540.

Tyler, R. (1949). *Basic principles of curriculum and instruction.* Chicago: University of Chicago Press.

U.S. Department of Education. (2003). *Identifying and implementing educational practices supported by rigorous evidence: A user friendly guide.* Retrieved February 12, 2007, from http://www.ed.gov/rschstat/research/pubs/rigorousevid/index.html

Wiley, D. (1979). Evaluation by aggregation: Social and methodological biases. *Educational Evaluation and Policy Analysis, 1*(2), 41–45.

2 Educating the Democratic Citizen

Frederick Jackson Turner, History Education, and the University Extension Movement

Marc A. VanOverbeke

I

Frederick Jackson Turner, one of the most famous historians at the turn of the 20th century, argued that the American frontier and the continued availability of free land had driven the formation of a distinctive national identity. "The frontier is the line of most rapid and effective Americanization," he said at the 1893 World Columbian Exposition in Chicago, and its effect has been felt most "in the promotion of democracy." Turner concluded his address ominously by arguing that "the frontier has gone, and with its going has closed the first period of American history" (Turner, 1893/1994b, pp. 33, 53, 60). With the closing of the frontier, the development of large corporations and factories, the impressive growth of cities, and the striking stratification of social classes, the United States was in the midst of a profound transformation at the turn of the 20th century. Along with other scholars and reformers, Turner wondered how Americans would cope with such sweeping changes. What would stand in for the frontier and help Americans navigate the transition to a new century, Turner asked; and for much of his career he had been considering ways to foster democracy and an American identity in a country no longer teeming with free land. As a young history professor at the University of Wisconsin, Turner looked to mass education and the study of history as a way to deal with the challenges of a new century.

Turner believed that if Wisconsin's citizens understood the past and the role that their forebears had played in history they would have a greater comprehension of the present and of America, be able to use that knowledge to think critically about issues confronting society, and, thereby, play influential roles in maintaining democracy. To succeed in making history and education the foundation on which democratic citizenship existed, Turner championed a broadened focus for the discipline of history that included the common people that historians traditionally had neglected in favor of presidents, monarchs, and great inventors. He wanted Wisconsin's citizens to see themselves in the past and to gain strength from that past.

Expanding the scope of history, however, was not enough. Turner had to take this new conception of history directly to the people, and he turned to the university's extension program as part of the answer. Extension had the power, in Turner's view, to strengthen citizenship by taking rigorous, intellectually demanding courses—with the discipline of history in a commanding role—out of the university and into the communities and towns where people lived. His goal was to make knowledge available to all citizens so that they would have the information they needed to ensure that the country developed in ways that were harmonious, democratic, and just. In the process, Turner raised important questions about education that are at the heart of modern notions of social justice—who has access to it and can take advantage of that access; what is the connection between education and social action; and who determines what knowledge is most important?

II

To help Americans adapt to the sweeping events of the last decades of the 19th century, Turner looked to the university, and he was in the forefront of efforts that pushed the University of Wisconsin toward addressing the needs of the state's citizens. A native of Wisconsin, he earned his bachelor's and master's degrees at the state university in Madison and his doctorate from Johns Hopkins University in 1889, after which he returned to the University of Wisconsin as a professor of history. At Wisconsin, where he was an influential historian and a pivotal figure on campus, he joined other faculty in building one of the first extension or adult education programs in the country in 1891. What Turner and his colleagues developed was a fairly complex program of courses and credits that took knowledge to the state's citizens. Professors traveled throughout Wisconsin to offer classes that usually consisted of six lectures over a period of six weeks. Optional discussions followed each lecture and provided opportunities for in-depth consideration of relevant issues. Students electing to attend the lectures and discussions, finish weekly reading assignments, and complete an examination earned credit toward class work at the University of Wisconsin. In the program's initial year, Turner and his peers taught 47 courses in 34 cities and towns. They reached over 8,000 students, half of whom remained for the discussions that followed the lectures. They maintained this energetic pace over the next few years, and the number of courses given remained more or less the same. In building such a program, Wisconsin's professors were not unique, and other universities throughout the country developed similar programs in the last decade of the 19th century (Billington, 1973; Chamberlin, 1893; Curti & Carstensen, 1949a, b; Kett, 1994; Rudolph, 1968; Turner, 1893b).

These programs embraced a very precise notion of education. Thomas Chamberlin, Wisconsin's president, made the focus of extension clear when he inaugurated "University Extension of the English type" at Wisconsin. He was referring to an extension program that Cambridge University in England developed in 1873 that gave students "a thorough grasp of principles, and a real mental training" in courses "covering a range of subjects sufficiently wide to give a broad and liberal higher education" (Roberts, 1891, p. 123). As a result, Wisconsin's extension students took courses in the arts, humanities, and sciences, and on such varied topics as bacteriology and political economics, English literature and plant physiology, landscape geology and Scandinavian literature. Some of them enrolled in Turner's courses on North American colonization, American politics, American development, and the West and Revolution.

By offering these types of courses, the extension program built on, but was different from, the university's other outreach programs, including the farmers' institutes that had existed since 1885. These institutes focused on the utilitarian or practical side of life by training farmers in new agricultural techniques. The goal of the extension program, by contrast, was not a few lectures that focused on developing practical skills or appealing to mass interests, but a comprehensive program of study that was demanding and rigorous in scope. Extension courses exposed students to the liberal arts and sciences, and opened up to them the results of professorial research and expertise. At the turn of the 20th century, university professors were transforming academic disciplines in line with scientific principles of investigation and analysis, and Turner believed that the knowledge gained from such research had the power to improve people's lives and instill in them a sense of beauty and culture. The university professor, he argued, needed to share this valuable knowledge by being "the apostle of the higher culture to the community in which he is placed," and he approved of that "social impulse which has led university men to bring the fruits of their study home to the people" (Turner, 1891/1994a, p. 29).

In other words, extension lecturers would leave the ivied halls of the university, but their lecture notes would come with them (Brubacher & Rudy, 1968; Chamberlin, 1893; Curti & Carstensen, 1949a, b; Lucas, 1994; Rudolph, 1968; Thelin, 2004; Turner, 1890/1938, 1893b; Veysey, 1965; Wisconsin Teachers' Association, 1891).

Embracing a faith common to many reformers of the era that education would enhance democratic citizenship, Turner threw himself into establishing an academically rich extension program. He expected a lot from his extension students, many of whom probably had only a limited education, and his courses demanded that they think critically about history and consider evidence before drawing conclusions. In his course on the colonization of North America, for example, he asked his students to "trace the effects of Spanish discovery and colonization upon the English ideas of America in the sixteenth century." When discussing whether the "Norse voyages to America influenced Columbus," Turner encouraged his students to weigh the arguments for and against such an influence. Turning to slavery in the United States, he delved into the factors giving rise to slavery and debated with his students "the justice of excluding slavery from the territories" (Turner, n.d. [1892], 1893a, 1895).

True to his belief that extension courses should be demanding, Turner did not feed his students an easily digested menu of historical offerings. He refused to undermine the discipline of history by focusing solely on entertaining stories or by ignoring essential details and complexities for the sake of easy comprehension. He was not opposed to the compelling narrative or to making history interesting to his audiences, and he worked to include absorbing stories and anecdotes in his lectures, but he insisted that historical understanding be thorough in order to be valid. "An interesting style, even a picturesque manner of presentation, is not to be condemned," he reasoned, "provided that truthfulness of substance rather than vivacity of style be the end sought" (Turner, 1891/1994a, p. 12). His lectures did not gloss over subtleties or attempt to distort the truth, as he saw it, merely for the sake of a gripping narrative. Instead, he demanded the attention and intellectual concentration of those attending his extension lectures. Rather than sacrificing truth to a compelling narrative, he rejected a popular lecture style of simplified arguments and easy analyses. He would not democratize education simply by making it popular (Schafer, 1938).

While establishing a program that took knowledge directly to the masses, Turner championed a broader, more democratic version of knowledge, at least in his field of history. He argued for an expansive study of the past that moved beyond a traditional view that explored only the great heroes or that focused solely on religious struggles and the rise of political institutions. While historical research, he maintained, has had its focus on "intrigues of court, knightly valor, palaces and pyramids"—the "brilliant annals of the few," in other words—history had other tales to tell: "the degraded tillers of the soil, toiling that others might dream, the slavery that rendered possible the 'glory that was Greece,'" for example. History, he claimed, was "the biography of society in all its departments," and this biography needed to include "the great mass of the people" and not just the heroes or statesmen. Such a focus on the great masses reflected Turner's belief that average people had influenced the development of nations. The economic growth and social conditions of common people, the ownership of property, and the distribution of wealth, he asserted, had "been the secret of the nation's rise or fall." The tales of common laborers struggling to build nations and civilizations were the real stories for historians, "by the side of which much that has passed as history is the merest frippery," he thundered (Turner, 1891/1994a, pp. 15, 18).

When Turner talked about the biography of society, however, he was not ignoring the role of statesmen and rulers. Popes, kings, and presidents figured prominently in

Turner's courses. Columbus and Magellan made appearances, as did Washington and Jefferson. Martin Luther and the Reformation were present, as was George III. These were pivotal figures in the past. Ignoring them would have been as problematic as overlooking the common people. Yet, Turner did not concentrate on them to the exclusion of the average citizens. In his extension lectures, he addressed the role of the "tillers of the soil," the fur traders who explored Wisconsin, and the slaves in the southern regions of the country. His lectures included discussions of Indian civilizations and the architecture of the Pueblo cliff dwellings, the intertribal trade among Indians, and their interactions with early European settlers. When lecturing on the colonization of New England, Turner focused on the social distinctions of the original, "almost purely English" settlers. He discussed their schools and economic life and provided vignettes from various books, including official Massachusetts records, to highlight life in an early New England community. Additionally, as part of his lecture on westward expansion and settlement, Turner considered the importance of the Scotch-Irish frontiersmen to expansion (Turner, n.d. [1892], 1893a, 1895).

He wanted Wisconsin's citizens to see themselves in the extension courses he offered and in the past he opened up to them. Americans needed such knowledge, he contended, if they were to be strong, effective citizens. "Perhaps [history's] most practical utility to us, as public school teachers," he said at a summer lecture for teachers in 1890, "is its service in fostering good citizenship." For Turner, there was a direct connection between history education and citizenship, and he shared this view with other reformers then seeking to restructure education to include more American history courses. Historical knowledge and appreciation, he argued, would build a strong nation comprised of democratic citizens working to further strengthen the nation. But, Turner insisted, only by understanding the role of common people in history would Americans come to a full understanding of the past and, as he was linking it, the present. "The present," he said, "is simply the developing past, the past the undeveloped present" (Turner, 1891/1994a, pp. 19, 28).

Most Americans would never become statesmen or influential captains of industry. Still, as they always had, these citizens would help to define the character and identity of the nation. If they understood the past and the deeply crucial roles they had played, Turner declared, they would understand the fundamental role they needed to play in the present and, by implication, in the future. Historical knowledge, he professed, enables "us to realize the richness of our inheritance, the possibility of our lives, the grandeur of the present." It gives people "new thoughts and feelings, new aspirations and energies." These "thoughts and feelings," he said, then "flow into deeds," and such actions "create good politics" and improve society. Average Americans might not individually have the influence of presidents and kings, but collectively as an educated citizenry, they would define a country and its path toward democracy and justice (Curti, 1961; Reese, 1995; Reuben, 2005; Turner, 1891/1994a, pp. 23, 29).

For Turner, then, history had value, in part, because it furthered citizenship by demanding that people wade through complex historical events and consider their connection to the past and to the present. Connected with extension education, he claimed, such historical knowledge would be revolutionary. In a metaphor that likely resonated in the farming communities of Wisconsin, he asserted that university extension would be a means "for carrying irrigating streams of education into the arid regions of the State" (Turner, 1893b, p. 315). Extension gave him the chance to take history directly to the parched inhabitants of the state, and he reached his loftiest heights when he proclaimed that such a program would "work a real revolution in our towns and villages as well as in our great cities." Extension and history had the power to become revolutionary vehicles in the promotion of a modern democracy (Turner, 1891/1994a, p. 29).

Turner climbed the rhetorical heights of educational revolution to support the place of extension and history at a public university, but bringing about this revolution demanded more than grand phrases. He lectured exhaustively in an effort to make extension a statewide institution capable of taking an expanded conception of history to the people and awakening in them new ideas about their role in American society. Even with the energetic support of other extension lecturers and successive university presidents, however, the movement never materialized as Turner envisioned it would. The program began auspiciously with large audiences, but by the mid-1890s the courses were failing to consistently attract sizable audiences or to draw citizens from a variety of social classes and backgrounds. Extension was not a movement intended solely or even principally for the affluent. The important prerequisite to participation in extension work was not wealth or even prior preparation, but an interest in studying and learning. Even without the requirement of academic training, however, the movement failed to reach throughout the state and interest all of Wisconsin's residents. Turner found some mix of citizens in his lectures, with business and professional men, college students, and local teachers predominating, but most of the students were women and professionals.

As a result, the movement existed mainly as a series of lectures for a rather limited subsection of the common people that Turner desired to reach. He believed that average citizens, cognizant of their history, would carefully consider weighty issues confronting the state and help fuel social progress, but the failure to attract a diverse audience, especially from among the working classes, weakened the power of history as a tool for spreading good citizenship throughout Wisconsin and the nation. Extension work demanded significant time and effort from faculty in preparing courses, traveling to rural communities, and delivering lectures, but Turner was discovering that simply providing this educational opportunity did not mean that the people would flock to the courses and lectures offered. Disappointed with the limited interest and claiming that he needed more time for his own research, Turner completely ceased to lecture as part of the extension program in 1896, at a time when university extension programs were declining nationally (Billington, 1973; Birge, 1892; Chamberlin, 1893; Curti & Carstensen, 1949a; Kett, 1994; Mood, 1938; Powell, 1892; Rosentreter, 1957; Turner, 1893b; Veysey, 1965).

III

As Turner envisioned it, extension, by connecting education and history, would take knowledge directly to the people, imbue them with respect for the role of average people in shaping the character of the country, and encourage active citizenship. He was bringing the common people into the intellectual life of the university, and he was underscoring the pivotal role of such people in the formation of the country. He was uncovering their place in the past, while also giving them a way to access and think about that voice through extension education. As a number of scholars and historians have pointed out, Turner was successful in many of these efforts. He was one of the first historians to shift the focus of the discipline to deal with the problems of common people rather than solely with the works and times of great political leaders and powerful men. He was an influential historian who, along with other progressive historians, altered the discipline in powerful ways, and scholars continue to wrestle with his influence (see Billington, 1973; Cronon, 1991; Curti, 1961; Hofstadter, 1968; Novick, 1988). By expanding the discipline of history and by campaigning to improve educational opportunities through extension courses, Turner's efforts were a triumph for social justice ideals in a country in the midst of significant economic and social change. Once ignored by historians and by universities, the common people slowly were gaining a voice.

Yet, Turner's failure to sustain a thriving extension program at Wisconsin undermined the relationship between education, history, and democratic citizenship that he so elegantly espoused. This failure, along with Turner's very real successes, however, informed subsequent reforms. His efforts and the work of other reformers shaping education for a new century helped to establish a greater understanding of the connection between education and social justice. It is worth considering the questions and issues that Turner's experiences raised.

Turner assumed that people would take advantage of any access to knowledge and education, would reflect critically on what they were learning, and then would act in ways to benefit the nation as a whole as it navigated the transition to a new century. Turner seemed to think that creating the extension program and offering courses would be enough, and that students, sensing their own need for intellectual engagement, would flock to the lecture halls. The common people that Turner hoped to attract, however, may not have been interested in the courses and knowledge that Turner and the other lecturers offered, and the working classes especially often faced challenges—including long work days, limited leisure time, and poor academic preparation—that hindered their ability to take advantage of extension opportunities. These obstacles, combined with Turner's teaching style, likely discouraged attendance. Although Turner tried to find stories and anecdotes that he thought would interest his audiences, he struggled to find the right language and style to entertain and educate at the same time. His difficulty reflected the challenge of making complex knowledge accessible to an audience with varying educational backgrounds and interests. He espoused thoughtful academic arguments that influenced his field and by many accounts was a gifted orator, but he failed to find the language or approach to make history accessible and meaningful to a diverse audience.

As with many reformers of the era, Turner also never questioned that the masses might not be able to—or, might not want to—transform their thoughts and feelings into actions for the good of the nation. He was promoting action that furthered the needs of society as a whole rather than the needs of the individual, but there was no guarantee that the average citizens sitting in his courses would draw similar conclusions. The lessons of history, especially of individuals facing the frontier alone, could lead Americans to embrace actions and ideas that benefited them, even at the expense of others. Nor was there any guarantee that the average citizens—confronting large bureaucracies, powerful captains of industry, and monopolies—would even have the opportunity to advocate for themselves, much less others. Rather, Turner trusted that if "the degraded tillers of the soil" wrestled with the relationship of the past to the present and appreciated the role that people had played in shaping events, they would be able to use their new energies to shape the future and be better democratic citizens as a result. Turner's ultimate faith was that people, when given access to knowledge, would reflect on that knowledge and use it to act wisely for the benefit of the nation.

Turner's evangelical zeal and faith in the common people and extension went only so far, however. While he was bringing the common people into the life of the university and making such people a focus of historical research by asserting their active role in the formation of the nation, he increasingly carved out a separate space for the experts in making sense of that role. Democracy, while it may have rested on hardworking pioneers pushing across the frontier, now, in a time of profound change, required university-trained experts to help the common people understand and make sense of the nation and their place within it. By 1910, Turner was emphasizing the importance of prolonged study at the university as a basis for expertise and leadership and for a vibrant democracy. "By furnishing well-fitted legislators, public leaders and teachers, by graduating successive armies of enlightened citizens accustomed to deal dispassionately with the problems of modern life, able to think for themselves," he declared, "the State Universities will safeguard democracy" (Turner, 1910/1994c, pp. 115–116). These "dispassionate" leaders would have to spend long years in the university's libraries, seminar rooms, and lecture halls to gain expertise. The extension students would never reach such heights by attending one or two extension courses. They were getting a taste of an academic life, but this taste made it clear that they would not be the experts. Only prolonged exposure to debate and discussion and sustained reflection and engagement with ideas would prepare the leaders of the future.

By arguing that education and historical knowledge were central to democracy and by championing an extension program, Turner raised provocative questions that educators continue to wrestle with today: What obstacles prevent students of all ages from taking advantage of educational opportunities, and how can these obstacles be overcome? Are teachers able to reach out in meaningful ways to connect with their students? Does education lead to action, and to what kind of action? How much education is necessary to prepare students to become leaders and experts, and who determines what these experts need to know? When it comes to understanding the connection between education and citizenship, between education and opportunity, between education and social justice, Turner's ideas and work continue to inform, perhaps even to inspire, but certainly to raise questions worth considering and debating. For Turner, that may have been the ultimate goal of history and education: to raise ideas and questions, to bring all into the discussion in meaningful ways, and to debate solutions and actions for the good of society.

References

Billington, R. A. (1973). *Frederick Jackson Turner: Historian, scholar, teacher.* New York: Oxford University Press.

Birge, E. A. (1892). The university extension class. *Wisconsin Journal of Education, 22,* 256–257.

Brubacher, J. S., & Rudy, W. (1968). *Higher education in transition: A history of American colleges and universities, 1636–1968.* New York: Harper & Row.

Chamberlin. T. C. (1893). Report of the president. In *Biennial report of the Board of Regents of the University of Wisconsin for the fiscal year ending September 30, 1892* (pp. 44–45). Madison, WI: Democrat Printing Company.

Cronon, W. (1991). Turner's first stand: The significance of significance in American history. In R. Etulain (Ed.), *Writing western history: Essays on major western historians* (pp. 73–101). Albuquerque: University of New Mexico Press.

Crunden, R. (1982). *Ministers of reform: The progressives' achievement in American civilization, 1889–1920.* New York: Basic Books.

Curti, M. (1961). Frederick Jackson Turner. In O. L. Burnette, Jr., (Ed.), *Wisconsin witness to Frederick Jackson Turner: A collection of essays on the historian and the thesis* (pp. 175–204). Madison: The State Historical Society of Wisconsin.

Curti, M., & Carstensen, V. (1949a). *The University of Wisconsin: A history, 1848–1925* (Vol.1). Madison: University of Wisconsin Press.

Curti, M., & Carstensen, V. (1949b). *The University of Wisconsin: A history, 1848–1925* (Vol. 2). Madison: University of Wisconsin Press.

Gewirtz, S. (2001). Rethinking social justice: A conceptual analysis. In J. Demaine (Ed.), *Sociology of education today* (pp. 49–64). New York: Palgrave.

Greene, M. (1998). Introduction: Teaching for social justice. In W. Ayers, J. A. Hunt, & T. Quinn (Eds.), *Teaching for social justice: A democracy and education reader* (pp. xxvii–xlvi). New York: New Press/Teachers College Press.

Hofstadter, R. (1968). *The progressive historians: Turner, Beard, Parrington*. New York: Alfred A. Knopf.

Kett, J. F. (1994). *The pursuit of knowledge under difficulties: From self-improvement to adult education in America, 1750–1990*. Stanford, CA: Stanford University Press.

Lucas, C. J. (1994). *American higher education: A history*. New York: St. Martin's Press.

Mood, F. (1938). Introduction: Turner's formative period. In E. Edwards (Comp.), *The early writings of Frederick Jackson Turner* (pp. 1–39). Madison: University of Wisconsin Press.

Novick, P. (1988). That *noble dream: The "objectivity question" and the American historical profession*. Cambridge, UK: Cambridge University Press.

Powell, L. P. (1892). University extension and the public schools. *Wisconsin Journal of Education, 22*, 210–213.

Reese, W. J. (1991). Social justice through the lens of social history. In D. A. Verstegen & J. G. Ward (Eds.), *Spheres of justice in education* (pp. 35–52). New York: HarperBusiness.

Reese, W. J. (1995). *The origins of the American high school*. New Haven, CT: Yale University Press.

Reuben, J. (2005). Patriotic purposes: Public schools and the education of citizens. In S. Fuhrman & M. Lazerson (Eds.), *The public schools* (pp. 1–24). New York: Oxford University Press.

Roberts, R. D. (1888). *A new university*. London: C.F. Hodgson.

Roberts, R. D. (1891). *Eighteen years of university extension*. Cambridge, UK: Cambridge University Press.

Rosentreter, F. M. (1957). *The boundaries of the campus: A history of the University of Wisconsin extension division, 1885–1945*. Madison: The University of Wisconsin Press.

Rudolph, F. (1968). *The American college and university: A history*. New York: Alfred A. Knopf.

Schafer, J. (1938). Editorial comment: Turner's early writings. *The Wisconsin Magazine of History, 22*, 213–231.

Thelin, J. R. (2004). *A history of American higher education*. Baltimore: Johns Hopkins University Press.

Turner, F. J. (n.d. [1892]). *Syllabus of a university extension course of six lectures on the "Colonization of North America."* Madison: University of Wisconsin.

Turner, F. J. (1893a). *The colonization of North America from the earliest times to 1763: Syllabus of a course of six lectures*. Madison, WI: Tracy, Gibbs.

Turner, F. J. (1893b). The extension work of the University of Wisconsin. In G. F. James (Ed.), *Handbook of university extension* (pp. 311–324). Philadelphia: American Society for the Extension of University Teaching.

Turner, F. J. (1895). *American development, 1789–1829: Syllabus of a course of six lectures*. Madison, WI: Tracy, Gibbs.

Turner, F. J. (1938). Frederick Jackson Turner to H. B. Adams. In W. S. Holt (Ed.), *Historical scholarship in the United States, 1876–1901: As revealed in the correspondence to Herbert B. Adams* (pp. 144–145). Baltimore: Johns Hopkins Press. (Original work published December 8, 1890)

Turner, F. J. (1994a). The significance of history. In J. M. Faragher (Comp.), *Rereading Frederick Jackson Turner: "The significance of the frontier in American history" and other essays* (pp. 11–30). New York: Henry Holt. (Original work published 1891)

Turner, F. J. (1994b). The significance of the frontier in American history. In J.M. Faragher (Comp.), *Rereading Frederick Jackson Turner: "The significance of the frontier in American history" and other essays* (pp. 31–60). New York: Henry Holt. (Original work published 1893c)

Turner, F. J. (1994c). Pioneer ideals and the state university." In J. M. Faragher (Comp.), *Rereading Frederick Jackson Turner: "The significance of the frontier in American History" and other essays* (pp. 101–118). New York: Henry Holt. (Original work published 1910)

Tyack, D., & Hansot, E. (1982). *Managers of virtue: Public school leadership in America, 1820–1980.* New York: Basic Books.

Verstegen, D. A. (1991). Introduction: Justice and education. In D. A. Verstegen & J. G. Ward (Eds.), *Spheres of justice in education* (pp. 1–7). New York: HarperBusiness.

Veysey, L. (1965). *The emergence of the American university.* Chicago: University of Chicago Press.

Wiebe, R. (1967). *The search for order, 1877–1920.* New York: Hill & Wang.

Wisconsin Teachers' Association. (1891). Minutes from the thirty-eighth annual session of the Wisconsin Teachers' Association, Madison, December 29, 1890. *Wisconsin Journal of Education, 21,* 16.

3   Anarchist Movement and Education

David Gabbard

Writing for Salon.com, Gary Kamiya pondered how George W. Bush, in light of his administration's incessant abuses of power, has avoided impeachment. Bush's "problems go far beyond Iraq," Kamiya writes. "His administration has been dogged by one massive scandal after the other, from the Katrina debacle, to Bush's approval of illegal wiretapping and torture, to his unparalleled use of 'signing statements' to disobey laws that he disagrees with, to the outrageous Gonzales and U.S. attorneys affair" (Kamiya, 2007). So, why hasn't he been impeached?

For Kamiya, "the main reason is obvious" when viewed from the perspective of real-politik. The Democrats, with their narrow majority in Congress, do not have the political will to do so. In weighing the potential costs and benefits of such a move, they fear that impeachment could backfire on them. They prefer, it would seem, to give Bush enough rope to hang the Republican Party in the 2008 elections.

Kamiya, however, also identifies a deeper and more troubling reason that Bush has not and likely *will* not be impeached. This reason has less to do with either Bush or the Democratic Party, and more with us—the American people. "Bush's warmongering," Kamiya contends,

> spoke to something deep in our national psyche. The emotional force behind America's support for the Iraq war, the molten core of an angry, resentful patriotism, is still too hot for Congress, the media and even many Americans who oppose the war, to confront directly. It's a national myth. It's John Wayne. *To impeach Bush would force us to directly confront our national core of violent self-righteousness*—come to terms with it, understand it and reject it. And we're not ready to do that (emphasis added). (Kamiya, 2007)

In coming to terms with and understanding our national core of violent self-righteousness, we would have to acknowledge what underlies it. We would have to recognize, as Cornel West (2004) argues in *Democracy Matters*, that

> the American democratic experiment is unique in human history not because we are God's chosen people to lead the world, nor because we are always a force for good in the world, but because of our refusal to acknowledge the deeply racist and imperial roots of our democratic project. We are exceptional because of our denial of the anti-democratic foundation stones of American democracy. No other democratic nation revels so blatantly in such self-deceptive innocence, such self-paralyzing reluctance to confront the night-side of its own history. This sentimental flight from history—or adolescent escape from painful truths about ourselves—means that even as we grow old, grow big, and grow powerful, we have yet to grow up. (p. 41)

And whereas Kamiya (2007) simply asserts, "we need therapy," West (2004) offers a more specific prescription. West calls for the enactment of "democratic *paideia*—the cultivation of an active, informed citizenry—in order to preserve and deepen our democratic experiment" (p. 42), coupled with "*parrhesia*—frank and fearless speech—that is the lifeblood of any democracy" (West, 2004, p. 209). Such measures are necessary, he contends, if we are to escape "our self-deceptive innocence" and our "self-paralyzing reluctance to confront the night-side of [our] own history."

Educators committed to a pedagogy of social justice would eagerly answer West's call for fearless speech in service of what they hold to be one of the most important missions of America's schools—"the cultivation of an active, informed citizenry." Tragically, however, no one knows the sting of America's "violent self-righteousness" better than those same educators. Long before Bill O'Reilly of Fox News Channel, the official network of violent self-righteousness, launched the national demonization campaign against University of Colorado Professor Ward Churchill, the Monroe County Community Schools Corporation in Bloomington, Indiana declined to renew the contract of Deborah Mayer, an elementary school teacher. Mayer's transgression occurred while discussing the December 13th, 2002 issue *Time for Kids*, a children's version of *Time* magazine that was a regular part of the curriculum. That issue contained a story covering a peace march in Washington D.C. protesting the pending U.S. invasion of Iraq, which led a student to ask Mayer if she "would ever be in a peace march." Mayer informed the class that whenever she drove past marchers holding up signs asking motorists to "Honk for Peace" that she honked. She also told the children that she thought people "should seek peaceful solutions before going to war." The class then discussed a conflict resolution program at their own school, and they dropped the subject. Shortly afterward, however, a Bush-supporting parent brought a complaint against Mayer before the building principal, and the district later refused to renew her contract (Egelko, 2007).

Judge Sarah Evans Barker ruled against Mayer in her wrongful termination suit, arguing "teachers, including Ms. Mayer, do not have a right under the First Amendment to express their opinions during the instructional period" (Global Research, 2007). Later, in the United States Court of Appeals for the Seventh Circuit, famed neoliberal jurist and Chief Judge Frank H. Easterbrook upheld Barker's ruling. "Expression," Easterbrook wrote, "is a teacher's stock in trade, *the commodity she sells to her employer in exchange for a salary*" (emphasis added) (Egelko, 2007). Though she plans a further appeal, Mayer holds little optimism that the Supreme Court will take her case. If the decision stands, particularly in light of the neoliberal logic found in Easterbrook's ruling, we can abandon all but the slimmest of hopes that schools will ever become sites for pursuing social justice. In that case, perhaps the time has arrived for us to take the anarchist critique of education more seriously and recognize the futility of pushing for democratic educational reforms. Maybe we should begin considering the possibility that we might best pursue social justice, not by reforming schools, but by resisting state-controlled systems of compulsory schooling altogether.

The Anarchist Critique

When he published *What is Property?* (2003) in 1840, Pierre-Joseph Proudhon became the first person to call himself an anarchist. He was not, however, the first person to call for the abolition of the state. For this reason, scholarship traces the anarchist tradition back to William Godwin. Credited with developing the first comprehensive anarchist critique of government schools in his *Enquiry Concerning Political Justice* in 1793, Godwin viewed freedom of thought as fundamental to political liberty. As Joel Spring explains,

Godwin believed that "since people constantly improve their reasoning power and their understanding of nature, their understanding of the best form of government is constantly changing" (Spring, 1994, p. 42). While he recognized that education was crucial toward the development of individuals' powers of rational thought that would guide them in self-government, Godwin also, Spring notes, "considered national systems of education one of the foremost dangers to freedom and liberty" (Spring, 1983, p. 68). "Before we put so powerful a machine (education) under the direction of so ambiguous an agent (government)," Godwin warned, "it behooves us to consider well what it is we do. Government will not fail to employ it, to strengthen its hands, and perpetuate its institutions" (Godwin, 1946, p. 302, cited in Spring 1994, p. 42).

Indeed, Godwin's warning gives us good reason to question whether government-controlled schools can ever function as sites where students cultivate their powers of reasoning in the service of social justice. Furthermore, Godwin also provokes us to consider the extent to which schools, as instruments of state power, have contributed more to what Kamiya identifies as our "our national core of violent self-righteousness" than they have to cultivating the "active, informed citizenry" called for by Cornel West.

Echoing Godwin's concerns and armed with 200 years of historical hindsight, contemporary anarchist theorist Noam Chomsky describes "the basic institutional role and function of the schools" as providing "an ideological service: there's a real selection for obedience and conformity" (2003, pp. 37–28). In Chomsky's analysis, compulsory, government schooling brings children at a very early age into an indoctrination system "that works against independent thought in favor of obedience" with the goal of keeping people "from asking questions that matter about important issues that directly affect them and others" (Chomsky & Macedo, 2000, p. 24). In Deborah Mayer's case, of course, the important issue was the pending invasion of Iraq. Keep in mind that a *student* initiated the conversation concerning Mayer's participation in peace marches. Therefore, the decision of the school board and courts' rulings on that decision sent a clear message to students as well as teachers: "We don't discuss 'questions that matter' about issues that might interest *you*." That message, of course, underscores Chomsky's thesis that schools function to discourage independent inquiry and promote obedience and conformity.

Emma Goldman made similar observations early in the 20th century. "What, then, is the school of today?" she asked. "It is for the child what the prison is for the convict and the barracks for the soldier—a place where everything is being used to break the will of the child, and then to pound, knead, and shape it into a being utterly foreign to itself.... It is but part of a system which can maintain itself only through absolute discipline and uniformity"(n.d.).

Goldman's description of schools receives considerable support in the more heavily analytic writings of Michel Foucault. In books such as *Madness and Civilization* (1988) and *Discipline and Punish* (1995), Foucault points out for us a very peculiar historical oddity. Systems of government-sponsored compulsory schooling did, in fact, begin to emerge at the same point in history as the modern prison, and each was modeled on the Army barracks. Compulsory schooling of the masses has always had less to do with education and more to do with discipline. By "discipline," Foucault (1995) refers to a form of treatment that

> Increases the forces of the body (in economic terms of utility) and diminishes those same forces (in terms of political obedience). In short, it disassociates powers from the body; on the one hand it turns it into an "aptitude," a "capacity," which it seeks to increase; on the other hand, it reverses the course of the energy, the power that might result from it, and turns it into a relation of strict subjugation. If economic

exploitation separates the force of and the product of labor, let us say that disciplinary coercion establishes in the body the constricting link between an increased aptitude and an increased domination. (1995, p. 141)

Moreover, compulsory schooling functions to discipline individuals in a manner that increases the productive power that their bodies offer to the economic system while simultaneously diminishing their power to resist economic exploitation and the political system that initiates that exploitation by compelling students to attend school in the first place.

The writings of Benjamin Rush, a signer of the Declaration of Independence and recognized as the "father of American psychiatry," are particularly illuminative of how the early advocates of compulsory schooling viewed the importance of diminishing individuals' powers of resistance by building up their emotional attachments to the state. Rush wrote his "Thoughts Upon the Mode of Education Proper in a Republic" in 1786—just seven years before Godwin wrote his *Enquiry Concerning Political Justice*. Rush declared "the principle of patriotism stands in need of the reinforcement of *prejudice*, and it is well known that our strongest prejudices in favor of our country are formed in the first one and twenty years of our lives.... Our schools of learning," he argued, "by producing one general and uniform system of education, will render the mass of the people more homogeneous and thereby fit them more easily for uniform and peaceable government" (1786). The quotes below come from the same document:

> In order more effectually to secure to our youth the advantages of a religious education, it is necessary to impose upon them the doctrines and discipline of a particular church. Man is naturally an ungovernable animal, and observations on particular societies and countries will teach us that when we add the restraints of ecclesiastical to those of domestic and civil government, we produce in him the highest degrees of order and virtue....
>
> Let our pupil be taught that he does not belong to himself, but that he is public property. Let him be taught to love his family, but let him be taught at the same time that he must forsake and even forget them when the welfare of his country requires it....
>
> In the education of youth, let the authority of our masters be as *absolute* as possible. The government of schools like the government of private families should be *arbitrary,* that it may not be *severe*. By this mode of education, we prepare our youth for the subordination of laws and thereby qualify them for becoming good citizens of the republic. I am satisfied that the most useful citizens have been formed from those youth who have never known or felt their own wills till they were one and twenty years of age, and I have often thought that society owes a great deal of its order and happiness to the deficiencies of parental government being supplied by those habits of obedience and subordination which are contracted at schools....
>
> From the observations that have been made it is plain that I consider it as possible to convert men into republican machines. This must be done if we expect them to perform their parts properly in the great machine of the government of the state.

Noah Webster, known as "the schoolmaster of America," could not have agreed more. "Good republicans," Webster wrote, "are formed by a singular machinery in the body politic, which takes the child as soon as he can speak, checks his natural independence and passions, makes him subordinate to superior age, to the laws of the state, to town and parochial institutions." (quoted in Spring, 2005, pp. 48–49). Webster's real significance as a force in shaping the direction of American education and culture rests with his creation of a series of books that were the major school texts in 19th century America, selling over a million and a half copies by 1801 and 75 million copies by 1875. As Webster's biographer, Harry Warfel, characterized them,

> this series of unified textbooks effectually shaped the destiny of American education for a century. Imitators sprang up by the dozens, and each echoed the Websterian nationalism. The word "American became indispensable in all textbook titles; all vied in patriotic eloquence." (cited in Spring, 2005, p. 48)

We are able to trace, then, the roots of Kamiya's "national core of violent self-righteousness" right back to the very beginnings of America's experiment with compulsory schooling. "Our schools," wrote a veteran schoolteacher in 1910, "have failed because they rest on compulsion and constraint.... It is deemed possible and important that all should be interested in the same things, in the same sequence, and at the same time.... Under the circumstances [of 1910] teachers are mere tools, automatons who perpetuate a machine that turns out automatons" (Goldman, 1912).

Under the conditions of 2007, nearly a hundred years later, how little has changed. With Emma Goldman, we should recognize that under the enduring conditions of government-sponsored, compulsory schooling, "the child becomes stunted, that its mind is dulled, and that its very being is warped, thus making it unfit to take its place in the social struggle as an independent factor. Indeed, there is nothing so hated so much in the world today as independent factors in whatever line" (Goldman, 1912).

Room for Hope?

The anarchist critique of compulsory schooling leaves us little room for hope that our schools will ever promote social justice. Given the contemporary neoliberal push to privatize the management of schools, however, even that small glimmer of hope is fading quickly.

Rather than focusing our efforts to transform schools so heavily dependent on the direct empowerment of teachers, perhaps we should take a lesson from the playbook of the political right. They have grown effective in gaining control of democratically elected, local school boards. Educators interested in creating schools as democratic, public spheres for the advancement of social justice must begin working locally to change the face, as well as the democratic dispositions, of our local school boards to allow our teachers greater freedom to teach, and to allow our students greater freedom to learn.

As severe as the rulings of Judges Barker and Easterbrook may sound to our ears, they merely stated that teachers must adhere to the curricular policies set by their employer. Except in those districts where curricular decisions are now effectively controlled by private management firms—educational management organizations (EMOs)—that "employer" is a democratically elected school board. Only when local school boards begin recognizing and acknowledging the crucial link between education and democracy, through concrete policy decisions on curriculum and other matters, will schools ever be able to meaningfully address issue of social justice.

References

Chomsky, N. (2003). The function of schools: Subtler and cruder methods of control. In K. J. Saltman & D. A. Gabbard (Eds.), *Education as enforcement: The militarization and corporatization of schools* (pp. 27–28). New York: Routledge.

Chomsky, N., & Macedo, D. (2000). Beyond a domesticating education: A dialogue. In D. Macedo (Ed.), *Chomsky on miseducation* (p. 24). Lanham, MD: Rowman & Littlefield.

Egelko, B. (2007, May 14). "Honk for peace" case tests limits on free speech. *San Francisco Chronical*. Retrieved June 17, 2007, from http://www.sfgate.com/cgi-bin/article.cig?file=/c/a/2007/05/14MNG9PPQGVV1.DTL

Foucault, M. (1988). *Madness and civilization: A history of insanity in the age of reason*. New York: Vintage.

Foucault, M. (1995). *Disicpline and punish: The birth of the prison*. New York: Vintage.

Global Research. (2007). Judge rules teachers have no free speech rights in class. Center for Research on Globalization. Retrieved June 17, 2007, from http://www.globalresearch.ca/index.php?context=viewArticle&code=20061020&article1d=3551

Godwin, W. (1793). *An enquiry concerning political justice*. Charlottesville, VA: Electronic Text Center, University of Virginia Library. Retrieved June 17, 2007, from http://etext.virginia.edu/toc/modeng/public/GodJust.html

Goldman, E. (1912). The social importance of the modern school. Emma Goldman Papers, Manuscripts and Archives Division, The New York Public Library, Astor, Lenox, and Tilden Foundations. Retrieved June 17, 2007, from http://dwardmac.pitzer.edu/anarchist_archieves/goldman/socimportms.html

Kamiya, G. (2007, May 22). Why Bush hasn't been impeached. Salon.com. Retrieved June 17, 2007, from http://www.salon.com/opinion/kamiya/2007/05/22/impeachment

Proudhon, P.-J. (2003). *What is property: Or, an inquiry into the principle of right and of government*. Oshawa, Ontario: Mondo Politico. Retrieved June 17, 2007, from http://www.mondo-politico.com/library/pjproudhon/whatisproperty/toc.htm

Rush, B. (1786). Thoughts upon the mode of education proper in a republic. In *A plan for the establishment of public schools and the diffusion of knowledge in Pennsylvania, to which are added, thoughts upon the mode of education proper in a republic*. Retrieved June 17, 2007, from http://www.schoolchoices.org/roo/rush.htm

Spring, J. (1983, Spring). The public school movement vs. the libertarian tradition. *The Journal of Libertarian Studies, 7*(1), 68. Retrieved June 17, 2007, from http://www.mises.org/journals/jls7_1/7_1_3.pdf

Spring, J. (1994). *Wheels in the head: Educational philosophies of authority: Freedom and culture from Socrates to Paulo Freire*. New York: McGraw Hill.

Spring, J. (2005). *The American school 1642–2004*. New York: McGraw-Hill.

West, C. (2004). *Democracy matters: Winning the fight against imperialism*. New York: Penguin.

4 Historical and Critical Interpretations of Social Justice

Deron Boyles, Tony Carusi, and Dennis Attick

The term *social justice* seems to be in the ears and on the lips of educators who set as their task the fostering of a more democratic society through classroom practices. While generally well intended, the ways in which different educators go about defining social justice, and acting from those definitions, differ greatly. As a result, contradictory efforts emerge under the heading of social justice. With a diversity of meanings comes a diversity of understandings; and while diversity is necessary for a more democratic education, our goal is to help clarify the history and background of social justice. In doing so, our aim is to reveal the points of contestation over such competing definitions and to explore some of the ideological assumptions of the cultural and political interests from which specific parties operate. In other words, by providing an historical background to the concept of social justice we intend to bring into critical relief those underlying assumptions from which social justice proponents argue. Ultimately, engaging a critical history of social justice will provide a background to which and foundation from which educators interested in teaching for social justice can better interpret their own viewpoints in and among other positions.

The concept of social justice in education indicates that schools and society are, and always have been, replete with injustice. Some proponents of social justice see the term's enactment in our current meritocratic system of education. Other proponents understand it as directly opposed to such individualistic ideologies, encouraging instead a public education system that addresses the social inequities present in an already unjust society. This chapter understands public education as critical to engaging individuals as agents for social change in a participatory democracy complete with dissension, restructuring, and change. As such, this history of social justice in education addresses the shifts and differences in meanings this concept has undergone to better situate current debates calling for social justice in education. Said differently, there are groups promoting educational reform in order to perpetuate status quo norms of power and privilege acting in the name of social justice. Yet, and at the same time, there are other groups who wish to dismantle such privilege under the auspices of social justice.

Classical Ideas of Justice[1]

The different ways social justice is understood today can arguably be traced to their foundation in Plato's *Republic*, where Socrates questions what is meant by justice (Plato, 1991). Certainly many of the meanings and foci of justice have altered since antiquity, but in readdressing the idea of justice, and more specifically social justice, educators may encounter many similar problems as those found in and made by the *Republic*. Initially, Socrates and his interlocutors define justice as helping one's friends and harming one's enemies. As quickly as the definition is given, it is dispensed with because of the capability for one's friends to be unjust themselves. Examining the making and refuting of definitions of justice, Socrates decides to build his famous city in speech, *kallipolis*, in order to see the origins of justice and injustice writ large in civic life. In *kallipolis*, Socrates describes justice in terms of proportion according to a tripartite system of the appetites, passions, and reason. For Socrates, justice is achieved when the appropriate balance between these things, in the city-state and the soul, is maintained. After constructing the city, Socrates and his interlocutors spend the entirety of Book VII discussing the education necessary to maintain justice within the walls of *kallipolis*.

Plato sets his famous allegory of the cave as the stage on which education must act. The people within the cave are shackled, forced to watch a play of shadows on a wall. One of the prisoners looses his shackles, turns to see a blinding light, and realizes all these shadows before him are mere appearances—the light is their source. After traveling to the light, the freed cave dweller is compelled to return to the cave to release his fellow prisoners, so they, too, may see the light behind the shadows.

Plato ultimately argues that an aristocracy is the government that best provides education for the cave dwellers. While this chapter supports democracy over and above aristocracy, it is important to note such an early link between education and freedom (and the return to the cave as an act of justice) in order to develop a history of social justice in education without positing the emergence of such a concept ex nihilo. This also serves as a primary point for any history of social justice in that it takes as problematic any nostalgic look backwards to some mythological golden age of justice. In terms of this chapter's focus, we may say more specifically that any present day harkening back to such authoritarian ideals of justice, when done in the name of democracy, is suspect in its aim. Plato and Socrates are invaluable to the discussion of justice, but it is not the intent of this chapter to uphold an unchanging, eternal, or ahistorical notion of justice. As a corollary to problematizing an ahistorical rendering of justice, the use of the *Republic* as a starting point for a history of social justice should not be read as though Plato was a proponent of social justice. The actual concept is fairly recent in history, and unavailable to classical discussions of justice. The rise of social justice as a novel and unique idea is outlined below, but its conception emerged from inquiry into the meaning of justice. To this end, the *Republic* stands as Western society's first thoroughgoing treatment of justice and its involvement with education.

Picking up from Plato's discussion of justice in the *Republic*, Aristotle wrote extensively on the topic. His approach in the *Nicomachean Ethics* seeks to understand justice in its constituent parts. One key distinction he makes in kinds of justice is justice as distribution. This is important to note because distributive justice is often associated, if not conflated, with social justice by some contemporary writers. The relationship between social and distributive justice is addressed in its current formation more fully below. Aristotle, like Plato, did not have the idea of social justice available to him, but his coining of distributive justice has had much influence on proponents of social justice.

Justice as distributive, Aristotle explains, centers on property; for example, honors, wealth, and other material goods (Aristotle, 1999). Drawing upon a proportional sense of justice, as described above, distributive justice is the median between four terms: two people and the share belonging to each. In its mean, the share of property belonging to each person forms a ratio equal on both sides. Aristotle formulates, "Therefore, A:B = c:d and, by alternation, A:c = B:d. It also follows that one whole, (i.e., person plus share,) will stand in the same ration to the other (whole, as person stands to person). This is the union of terms that distribution (of honors, wealth, etc.) brings about, and if it is effected in this manner, the union is just" (p. 119).[2] Deviation from this ratio, in Aristotle's view, creates an unjust act, therefore injustice, where one person is afforded more than his or her just share and the other less than his or her just share. Important to this formula is its stress on property. The shares that belong to a person are either material, for example, wealth, or immaterial, for example, honors, but both are things which can be given or taken away; that is, distributed. While the giving and taking of material things is straightforward, those things that are immaterial, under distributive justice, must be reified, assumed as material, in order to understand them first as property and second as something that can be given and taken away. We bring this criticism to bear in full against contemporary notions of distributive justice later in this chapter. The point worth noting here is the tendency of definitions of distributive justice, as early as Aristotle's, to make immaterial things, such as performance and opportunity, more concrete by understanding them as quantifiable properties which can be distributed equally or otherwise.

The Rise of Social Justice

The idea of the social was never linked to justice in classical thought. The same holds for medieval thought. In fact, one of the largest figures of the Middle Ages, St. Thomas Aquinas, mostly appropriated Aristotle's thoughts on justice for a Christian theological perspective, distinguishing justice, along with Aristotle's distinctions, from charity and stressing its legalistic qualities.[3] If we follow Hannah Arendt's view, the concept of the social is something that arose out of modernity, after the Classical and Middle Ages (Arendt, 1998). Society, on her view, is the result of the collapse of classical distinctions between public and private realms into the modern notions of the social and the intimate. Corroborating this point is the first use of the term *social justice* in 1840 by a little studied Jesuit priest, Luigi Taparelli.

Taparelli took issue with the influence of Cartesian doubt during his lifetime. His concern was directed toward the ongoing unification of Italy. Should the radical doubt of Descartes, popular at the time, influence Italy's formation as a country, Taparelli foresaw the role of private interests dominating public integrity (Behr, 2003). In other words, a philosophy that values isolated reflection and doubt of everything outside of one's self necessarily leads, on Taparelli's view, to the valuing of one's own interests over and above any common interests which were always capable of being doubted. As a response, heavily steeped in Thomist philosophy, Taparelli composed a theory of society that focused on the relationship between authorities and subjects in various levels of society (Behr, 2003). Simply put, society is composed of other, smaller societies. These smaller societies, for example government and citizen groups, function to assist the common good of societies larger than them and so on until society at large is working toward the common good. As Behr (2003) notes, "'help' in this context is from the bottom up, not from the top down, as the inferior, mediating groups all participate in achieving the common good of the more perfect association" (p.105). Thus, social justice, as first defined by Taparelli, is achieved in a society ordered in this way so as to "[maximize] individual freedom to associate at all levels" (Behr, 2003, p. 114).

For its time, the focus of Taparelli's theory of social justice was quite unique in that society, on his view, became just from the unified efforts of the subjects working upwards to society at large, rather than the traditional top-down authoritative notions of justice exhibited in Platonic, Aristotelian, and, to a lesser degree, Thomist thought. His views may even sound familiar to current calls for "grassroots" movements in response to a political system heavily influenced by large corporate interests. But due to the conservative political climate in which Taparelli was writing, his reputation persisted "as a sophist and reactionary zealot" (Behr, 2003, p. 99). This is not to say, however, that had history lent a more sympathetic ear to Taparelli's idea of social justice there would be little argument over its meaning today. Nor is it to say that concepts of social justice should reappropriate Taparelli's distinctly Roman Catholic understanding of the common good. Instead, Taparelli affords us the origins of social justice as a specific concept, and brings forth an argument distinct from and engaged with the diverse but continuous history justice, and its corollary, social justice, have undergone.

While this section describes the origins of social justice as a term, Taparelli appears to have had little influence on the discussion of social justice in education, particularly in the United States. His works and the majority of the commentary on them remain in either Latin or Italian, with very few English translations. However, justice maintained its biblical grounding, albeit through Protestant rather than Catholic lineages, when it crossed from Europe over to the Americas. As European colonization began to take root in what would become New England, settlers, concerned with their children's education, put in motion laws that would eventually take shape as the current educational system in the United States.

Social Justice and American Education

As education of European settlers in the United States was initially grounded in the religiosity of Puritanism, its goal was to teach young people functional literacy so they could read The Bible, as well as develop a strong work ethic (Spring, 2001). The first law pertaining to education in the United States was *The Old Deluder Satan Law,* passed in Massachusetts in 1647. *Old Deluder Satan* mandated that all towns with more than 100 families establish a grammar school to teach young people to read and write while also instilling Christian values (Urban & Wagoner, 2003). These early grammar schools represent the earliest forms of structured education in the United States and the purpose of these schools was the maintenance of Christian traditions and the perpetuation of a strict social order (Spring, 2001).

Throughout the 18th and 19th centuries, education in the United States became more formal, although it was provided primarily for male children of elite, White families who could afford to send their sons to private academies (Urban & Wagoner, 2003). These private institutions slowly shed the religiosity of the early grammar schools by providing more secular instruction in the canon of Western literature and culture. However, these were private institutions exclusive to the male children of White, upper-class citizens, and therefore, social justice in terms of equal opportunity was not part of the agenda (Spring, 2001). In fact, even in the mid-1800s the idea of a "public" education system for *all* young people meant specifically all *White* young people, an idea which emerged as political leaders sought to maintain the country's burgeoning democracy (Lubienski, 2001; Osgood, 1997). It was this initial concept of public education, in the name of protecting and promoting the "common" good that led to the creation of common schools.

Horace Mann, the United States' first state Secretary of Education in Massachusetts, pioneered the idea of public schools for all young people with the development of his common schools. Mann's idea for common schools came to fruition as the country was experiencing rapid population growth, urbanization, and industrialization (Lubienski, 2001). Mann envisioned a system of state-administered public schools that would offer *all* American youth an equitable education rooted in the common experiences and values of 19th century life (Urban & Wagoner, 2003). As Robert Osgood (1997) argues, Mann's common school movement was both reformist and optimistic because Mann intended to alleviate friction between disparate social groups by uniting students through a common education.

Mann's vision for American schools represented the first attempt to educate mass numbers of a diverse population of students, but it remains debatable whether Mann's vision was realized. As Joel Spring argues,

> Common schooling was to create a common social class by the extension of a common class consciousness among all members of society. Mixing the rich and the poor within the same schoolhouse would cause social-class conflict to give way to a feeling of membership in a common social class and would thus provide society with a common set of political and moral values. (Spring, 2001, p. 113)

In this sense, the common schools were to unite *all* students by providing them with a common education which would eventually eliminate social inequity among disparate ethnic groups and socioeconomic classes.

While Mann's ideas for common schools invoke notions of distributive social justice, unsurprisingly, many of the subsequent practices ran counter to his ideals. First, while the common schools were supposed to educate *all* young people, the education provided by the common schools was grounded on the specific values and traditions of European Protestants. Second, there is no evidence that common schools ever remedied any of the social issues Mann held as problematic, including the unequal distribution of wealth and resources (Spring, 2001). Further, instead of alleviating inequities, common schools created formal structures such as standardized curricula and tracking, which have maintained inequality in schools throughout the last 150 years (Rogers & Oakes, 2005).

Common schools continued to proliferate throughout the early 20th century, but it was during this time that a growing number of progressive educators became more vocal in their critique of education's role in maintaining social injustices. John Dewey is perhaps the most prolific 20th century progressive philosopher and educator, and much of Dewey's philosophy informed notions of social justice in education. Throughout much of his early writings, Dewey argued that schools did not exist apart from society and that the chief responsibility of schools was to involve students in ongoing inquiry into real social issues (Dewey, 1900/1990, 1916/1944). In *Moral Principles in Education*, Dewey states that, "Apart from participation in social life, the school has no moral end nor aim" (Dewey, 1909/1975, p. 11). Dewey held that schools should be living, active communities where the deliberation over issues relating to social equality would replace the learning of isolated curricular information. In a Deweyan sense, schools were important in the degree to which they assisted students in becoming critical social beings who worked to create a more egalitarian society (Kliebard, 1994).

To Dewey, the creation of an equitable society had its genesis in democratic schools where individuals would freely engage with one another in ongoing inquiry that would inform current social practices. Dewey pushed for the creation of "joint spaces" where individuals would work together to reconstruct knowledge claims in the quest to fight inequality (Rogers & Oakes, 2006). In *Democracy and Education*, Dewey (1916/1944) argues

> Democracy is more than a form of government; it is primarily a mode of associated living; of conjoint communicated experience. The extension in space of the number of individuals who participate in an interest so that each has to refer his own action to that of others, and to consider the action of others to give point and direction to his own, is equivalent to the breaking down of those barriers of class, race, and national territory which kept men from perceiving the full import of their activity. (p. 89)

Again, for Dewey, social justice would be realized when individuals were free to participate in occupations of their choice, while also contributing to the welfare of their fellow citizens and society in general.

Throughout his writings on education, John Dewey advocated for an active public that would be educated in democratic schools, and would be free to engage in inquiry that was participatory and inclusive. To Dewey, a more just society could emerge only when the individuals most burdened by injustice were involved in actively working for social change. Again, we turn to *Democracy and Education*, where Dewey argues

> The desired transformation is not difficult to define in a formal way. It signifies a society in which every person shall be occupied in something which makes the lives of others better worth living, and which accordingly makes the ties which bind persons together more perceptible—which breaks down the barriers of distance between them. (1916/1944, p. 316)

To Dewey, the creation of a just society requires the active participation of all society's members in the democratic process. Further, while society was rife with injustices, Dewey held that schools were responsible not for reproducing the status quo, but for developing young people into active social beings who would work to ameliorate social injustices.

While the Reconstructionist movement in education was informed by much of Dewey's philosophy, both George Counts and Harold Rugg argued that the quest for a distributive social justice must be at the heart of the American curriculum (Kliebard, 1994). While Counts questioned the role of schools in perpetuating social inequity, Rugg focused his attention on the subject area of social studies. Despite their pedagogical differences, Counts and Rugg argued that economic and social disparities between rich and poor were harming the nation's democracy and suppressing opportunity (Stern & Riley, 2002). Through a focus on schools as social centers where issues of economic and social disparity could be questioned and critiqued, Counts and Rugg hoped to forge a new social order that was equitable and just.

Harold Rugg's efforts to instill elements of distributive social justice in American education were realized in his challenges to the American curriculum. Rugg extended Dewey's belief in an integrated curriculum in his critique of social studies as a curricular subject. Rugg argued that all curricula *were* social studies and all subject matter directly related to societal problems (Stern & Riley, 2002). In this sense, Rugg viewed the subject of social studies as the practice of critically examining social injustices, not a process of memorizing historical facts. Rugg held that teachers should act as facilitators working with students to critically evaluate current social problems. In a Ruggian curriculum, teachers and students would study "real world problems in the hope of preserving and building a more equitable democratic society in the United States" (Stern & Riley, 2002). Rugg believed that his approach to social studies would eradicate the passivity he saw in schools and inspire teachers and students to adopt an "active concern for social justice" (Kliebard, 1994).

Like his fellow Reconstructionists, George Counts was critical of the American education system's passivity regarding social injustice. Counts, who was an outspoken socialist in the 1920s, challenged teachers and schools to work together to create a society that was egalitarian (Kohl, 1980). Counts's ultimate goal was to replace the individualism embedded in America's schools with a new focus on issues of social justice (Kliebard, 1994). Counts argued that society would not become a socially just entity until students were taught to counter the conservative school order with a more radical education that promoted social change (Westbrook, 1991).

While the Reconstructionists were advancing schools as the key to ameliorating social injustice, African-American scholars, teachers, and students were fighting to gain access to education. It was during the years immediately following the end of the Civil War that schools established by ex-slaves began to emerge throughout the eastern United States (Spring, 2001). Throughout the last 25 years of the 19th century, African Americans fought to achieve equal access to education in hopes that literacy would lead to increased political power and economic prosperity. While African-American educational leaders made great strides in increasing educational opportunities for young people in the late 1800s, the fact remains that by 1900, most African-American children were educated in segregated schools that received little support from the White education establishment and were not adequately funded (Spring, 2001).

Two of the most important scholars leading the fight for equal access to education for African-American children during the late 19th century were W.E.B. Du Bois and Booker T. Washington. Washington was born a slave and was later educated at Hampton Institute, while Du Bois was born in Boston, MA and attended private schools (Newman, 2005; Urban & Wagoner, 2003). While each scholar fought for equal access to education for African Americans, the two educational leaders had disparate ideas for how best to educate young people so that they would become active in the struggle for social and economic equality.

Booker T. Washington advocated equal access to education for African Americans based in his belief that education should provide people with the skills needed to participate in an industrial society. To Washington, equality and justice would be realized when African Americans participated in the economy by holding jobs and earning a salary. To this end, Washington's sense of justice can be understood as distributive in that access to material possessions is equated with justice. Washington believed that

> the student shall be so educated that he shall be enabled to meet conditions as they exist now in the part of the South where he lives...that every student who graduates from the school shall have enough skill, coupled with intelligence and moral character, to enable him to make a living for himself and others; to make each one love labour instead of trying to escape it. (Washington, 1901/1995, p. 120)

Washington held that a strong work ethic, along with moral character would lead African Americans to equal standing in society.

W.E.B Du Bois promoted a different notion of education where schools would teach African-American children the skills needed to acquire social and political power while deepening their understanding of the struggle for equality (Spring, 2001). Unlike Washington, Du Bois shunned a distributive notion of justice in arguing that a just and democratic society required the recognition of each person's abilities and experiences (Seigfried, 1999). It was Du Bois's contention that all members of society had something to contribute and should have equal opportunity to use their strengths for the betterment of society. Du Bois argued that democracy is eroded when it "excludes women or Negroes or the poor or any class because of innate characteristics which do not interfere with intelligence..." (Du Bois, 1903/1994, p. 45). To this end, Du Bois supported full inclusion of all members of society in ongoing dialogues that would continue to reform and reshape a sense of social justice.

There is perhaps no greater example of distributive social justice in education than what was realized as a result of *Brown v. Board of Education of Topeka Kansas* in 1954. The landmark case, brought before the Supreme Court by the National Association for the Advancement of Colored People (NAACP), ended legally sanctioned segregation in public schools. The NAACP argued that "separate but equal has no place" in public education, and that separate schools, divided by race, are inherently unequal (Spring, 2001). While *Brown* overturned segregation in American schools, the case can be understood as an example of distributive justice. As the process of public education occurs within a larger social context, it cannot be seen merely as something to which people are granted equal access. If a true sense of social justice was realized, each individual would have the ability to influence the structural systems of power that grant or withhold access to things such as education.

Since the late 1970s, public education has continued to promote an understanding of social justice grounded in the ideals of distributive social justice. To this end, scholars and politicians have been able to claim that justice in education is something that is doled out to those who are in need of, or deemed worthy of, receiving it. As we have argued, the concept of justice is open to myriad interpretations, and privileging a distributive notion of justice allows dissimilar groups to claim that they are committed to promoting social justice in education.

Social Justice at Present

Discerning the meaning of social justice is challenging because of its disparate uses across diverse viewpoints. As described at the beginning of this chapter, due to such widely varied meanings, it is possible for different groups to act in opposition to another, yet each can do so under the aegis of social justice. In education, for instance, researchers such as Diane Ravitch (1994, 2005), Mortimer Adler (Adler & Paideia Group, 1982), Chester Finn, Jr. (1993), Hertling (1985), E. D. Hirsch, Jr. (Hirsch, Kett, & Trefil, 1988), and Ruenzel (1996) argue for a just society through assimilation, maintaining educational philosophies that serve to perpetuate the status quo of severely unbalanced power structures in the United States. At the same time, critical theorists, progressivists, and liberals are currently fighting for social justice in education with the specific goal of exposing and eradicating the same power structures their opposition seeks to preserve. How is it that groups with such different goals can both argue for social justice?

To begin to answer this question, the different senses of social justice that each of these groups utilizes must be explored. Iris Marion Young (1990), in her book, *Justice and the Politics of Difference*, explores the idea of social justice and brings to bear what she calls the "distributive paradigm," which she claims is designated by "a tendency to conceive social justice and distribution as coextensive concepts" (p. 16). Said differently, a person operating from the standpoint of the distributive paradigm argues for equality of distribution, and when this equality is met, their claims for justice are completely satisfied. Moreover, the distributive paradigm "assumes a single model for all analyses of justice: all situations in which justice is at issue are analogous to the situation of persons dividing a stock of goods and comparing the size of the portions individuals have" (p. 18). Given the earlier discussion of Aristotle, Young's definition of the distributive paradigm sounds very familiar. While much has happened to refine the idea of distributive justice since its inception, the primary tenet stated at its founding and rendered into the Aristotelian formula noted above, has held throughout all its revisions. For example, equal opportunity of education as understood by Mortimer Adler (Adler & Paideia Group, 1982), Finn (1993), Hirsch et al. (1988), and other "cultural literacy" proponents operates from the distributive paradigm by setting the goal of assuring students' equal access to the same materials (i.e., the cultural literacy curriculum). To step outside of this paradigm is to question the agenda of this curriculum of which each student has his or her just share.

Thus, by equating social justice with distributive justice, as many contemporary scholars are prone to do, problems arise. A conflation between two forms of justice, social and distributive, emphasizes the allocation of property, understood broadly, at the expense of less quantifiable qualities that society entails, such as virtues, actions, and ideas, each of which comprise in part the very "good" social justice seeks to attain. This is not to say distributive notions of justice should be removed or replaced. To be sure, a theory of social justice without a distributive corollary is undesirable because of the importance a fair allotment of resources has to education. What is important to note, though, is that one does not equal the other, nor does one cover the area of the other. As Young (1990) states when speaking of educational opportunity specifically,

> In the cultural context of the United States, male children and female children, working-class children and middle-class children, Black children and white children often do not have equally enabling educational opportunities even when an equivalent amount of resources has been devoted to their education. (p.26)

Distributive notions of justice find their strength in egalitarian ideals where each person has an equal share. While such dispensations are necessary to justice, absent from this egalitarian concept is the emancipatory emphasis found in social justice, an emphasis that seeks to free people from oppression. While distributive justice and social justice have areas that overlap in important ways, the latter becomes meager when equivocated with the former. The degree to which this is problematic in educational terms can be seen when those who argue for a distributive version of social justice reify knowledge as something which teachers deposit in their otherwise empty students, a process criticized by Paulo Freire as the "banking method" (2005). This reification of knowledge allows for people such as E. D. Hirsch, Jr., author of *Cultural Literacy* (Hirsch et al., 1988) and founder of the Core Knowledge Foundation, to claim they have a "social justice agenda" (Ruenzel, 1996) when constructing curricula in which a successful student is one who has memorized the preset list of facts for their grade level.

On the opposite side of the political spectrum from Hirsch, Kenneth Howe (1997), a staunch critic of Hirsch, presents a timely and extensive work on the role of social justice in equality of educational opportunity. In speaking against Hirsch's Core Knowledge program he argues, "Hirsch's proposal is worse than ineffectual. It constitutes an obstacle to equality of educational opportunity for those groups historically excluded from participation" (p.3). Recall the point above regarding the difficulties and contradictions that currently reside in debates on education with opposed views, both of which appeal to social justice as their goal. Howe obviously has a different agenda from Hirsch, yet both claim to work in the name of social justice. How does a teacher interested in the topic of social justice in education distinguish what Howe is calling social justice from Hirsch's use of the term?

Howe seems to slide between social justice as distributive justice, and social justice as something different from distributive justice. This is possibly due to his oftentimes traditionally grounded view of justice, which seems to understand distributive and social justice as interchangeable. For instance, in attempt to address oppression, something that, Young (1990) contends, falls outside of the "distributive paradigm," Howe (1997) calls for a principle of nonoppression, stating that, "nonoppression is rooted in the requirements of democracy. It must both be applied to and observed by all who make up a political community, which is to say it must be reciprocal" (pp. 69–70). While he bases this principle, at least in part, on Young's work (1990), the reciprocity (i.e., the give and take between groups) required by his principle slips too readily into a distributive model of justice that understands equal allocation of nonoppression between parties, for example "gay and lesbian youth versus Christian fundamentalists" (p. 70) as an attainment of social justice. Howe's work, in this sense, is indicative of much of the current work done by progressive scholars in the name of social justice. Given Young's (1990) criticism of the "distributive paradigm," the present chapter sees Howe's book as an example of the difficulties involved when writing about social and distributive justice in a way that fails to clearly distinguish the domain of each. It would be a misreading of Howe to understand him as arguing for the same social justice as Hirsch.

As a result, the following discussion of Howe follows two threads. First, his book serves as an extremely poignant criticism of ways which people interpret social justice to maintain status quo educational opportunity frameworks. For instance, he rightly criticizes as cultural imperialism "conservative" thinkers who emphasize the need for a uniform curriculum in order to maintain a uniform culture. Second, his use of social justice interchangeably with, and at times indistinguishable from, distributive justice reveals many of the difficulties the present chapter seeks to highlight as one of the primary historical problems which social justice in education currently faces. These threads, while organized individually, do not appear in Howe's text separately. In other words, the first thread, the criticism he offers of conservative educational opportunity is simultaneously subject to the second thread, the equivocation of social and distributive justice. While in agreement with the criticisms Howe (1997) makes of conservative educational ideologues such as Hirsch, Adler, Ravitch, and John Chubb, this chapter proceeds with a reading of Howe that points up the difficulties educators are subject to when failing to distinguish between social and distributive justice.

Howe (1997) recasts the ruling of *Brown v. Board of Education* stating, "even if, contrary to fact, resources were distributed equally among racially segregated schools, legally sanctioned segregation so stigmatizes and demoralizes segregated groups as to permanently disadvantage them" (p. 78). To extend his reasoning, this exhibits precisely the fault found in equating social and distributive justice. Imagine if, after the *Brown* ruling, schools were desegregated in such a way that all resources were made equal among desegregated schools. The conditions for just distribution would be met in accordance with Howe's request, but the oppression that comes in the forms of racism, classism, and sexism (among others) goes as much unaddressed in a segregated school as a desegregated one. Even when resources are distributed equally, including opportunity understood distributively, oppression continues to flourish. The concern of social justice, as it is conceived here, is ending that oppression. Again, this is not to say social justice operates outside of the distributive justice, or vice versa, but instead that social justice must act in tandem with distributive justice in education for a more just society. Additionally, an ongoing dialogue in which interlocutors, such as teachers, students, administrators, and parents actively address social justice as apart from and corollary to distributive justice can serve as an emancipatory practice by identifying and eradicating the institutional and individual constructs which work to oppress members of the school community.

Another difficulty we find in Howe (1997) is through the topics of recognition and self-respect. He concedes that even "[w]hen (full blown) equality of educational opportunity cannot be achieved…social justice still makes demands, including educational ones. In this vein, the participatory interpretation (of equal opportunity of education) has as one of its requirements that *all* persons be afforded recognition and secured self-respect" (p. 89). The "demands" social justice makes here are arguably outside the purview of a distributive form of justice. Neither recognition nor self-respect is a resource that can be distributed by a controlling body such as a school. Certainly, there are better and worse ways for a school to foster an environment for such qualities through equality of distribution, and this does much to emphasize the importance of distributive and social justice operating in tandem. But, we argue, recognition and self-respect are social interactions that are just or unjust in ways that distribution can only understand by its results. Without discounting this focus on results, it is only partial and does nothing to address the oppression inherent in many forms of recognition (e.g., recognizing a different race as inferior; and self-respect, understanding one's self in respect to racist worldviews). To reiterate, this is the point at which social justice can make the claim that particular forms of recognition are unjust, not by appealing to distributive results, but instead by exposing the oppression, in the examples above, inherent to racism.

These two examples express the injustice that can continue even when the demands of distributive justice are met in schools. In the first, racism can remain intact even if we agree to go along with Howe's thought experiment concerning *Brown v. Board of Education* because de jure desegregation does nothing to address the racism held by different groups equally distributed in the same school. In a related way, the second example shows how groups and individuals can internalize and externalize oppression in ways that can proceed unnoticed even when achieving equality of recognition and self-respect.

Conclusion

In this chapter we have provided a history of the concept and argued for a rethinking of the idea of social justice in education. It is our contention that over the last century educational theorists and scholars have conflated the idea of social justice with notions of distributive justice. By conceptualizing social justice as an ideal that exists within a distributive paradigm, scholars and education leaders, with ideologies that remain contrary to social justice, can claim to promote social justice by providing students equal access to education and participation in our meritocracy. Competing with these notions of distributive justice in education are those teachers, scholars, and leaders engaged in social justice education that attempts to bring about social change by addressing social injustice in schools and the greater community.

Currently, American education practices are grounded in notions of standardization and the preparation of young people for participation in a global economy. Realizing a nondistributive notion of justice in education is, arguably, an unattainable goal within an education system that promotes justice as existing when students are given equal access to education within an already stratified system. Further, preparing students for participation in a global economic system does not require that schools address issues of injustice; globalization requires only that schools offer students similar experiences within a meritocratic system. Current and future educators and leaders interested in education for social justice must consider how they can overcome notions of distributive justice so as to forge a democratic education for real social change.

Notes

1. The following section takes its starting point from Ancient Greek philosophy. While we understand Plato as a valuable contributor to discussions of justice, we do not take his philosophy as an ahistorical or acultural point of reference. His work in the *Republic* is useful as it pertains to justice and education, but we eschew a canonical or Eurocentric justification for his inclusion.
2. In this formula the terms *A* and *B* represent the persons, and the terms *c* and *d* represent their share.

3. For example, see St. Thomas Aquinas, *Summa Theologica* (London: Burns, Oates, and Washbourne, 1918), Qus 61 and 63 (vol. 10, pp. 157–167, 186–194).

References

Adler, M. J., & Paideia Group. (1982). *The paideia proposal: An educational manifesto.* New York: Macmillan.

Arendt, H. (1998). *The human condition* (2nd ed.). Chicago: University of Chicago Press.

Aristotle. (1999). *Nicomachean ethics* (M. Ostwald, Ed. & Trans.). Upper Saddle River, NJ: Prentice-Hall.

Behr, T. C. (2003). Luigi Taparelli D'azeglio, S. J. (1793–1862) and the development of scholastic natural-law thought as a science of society and politics. *Journal of Markets and Morality, 6,* 99–115.

Brown v. Board of Education of Topeka, 347 U.S. 483 (1954) and 349 U.S. 294 (1955).

Core Knowledge Foundation. (1999). *Core knowledge sequence: Content guidelines for grades K-8.* Charlottesville, VA: Core Knowledge.

Dewey, J. (1944). *Democracy and education.* New York: Simon & Schuster. (Original work published 1916)

Dewey, J. (1975). *Moral principles in education.* Carbondale: Southern Illinois Press. (Original work published 1909)

Dewey, J. (1990). *School and society.* Chicago: University of Chicago Press. (Original work published 1900)

Du Bois, W. E. B. (1994). *The souls of Black folk.* Mineola, NY: Dover. (Original work published 1903)

Finn, C. E., Jr. (1993). *We must take charge: Our schools and our future.* New York: The Free Press.

Freire, P. (2000). *Pedagogy of the oppressed* (30th anniversary ed.). New York: Continuum. (Original work published 1970)

Hertling, J. (1985, October 30). At senate hearing, advocates promote benefits of "choice." *Education Week.* Retrieved December 10, 2006, from http://www.edweek.org/ew/articles/1985/10/30/06280012.h05.html

Hirsch, E. D., Kett, J. F., & Trefil, J. S. (1988). *Cultural literacy: What every American needs to know.* New York: Vintage Books.

Howe, K. R. (1997). *Understanding equal educational opportunity: Social justice, democracy, and schooling.* New York: Teachers College Press.

Kliebard, H. (1994). *The struggle for the American curriculum.* New York: Routledge.

Kohl, H. (1980). Can the schools build a new social order? *Journal of Education, 3,* 57–66.

Lubienski, C. (2001). Redefining "public" education: Charter schools, common schools, and the rhetoric of reform. *Teachers College Record, 103,* 634–666.

Newman, J. W. (2005). *America's teachers: An introduction to education* (5th ed.). New York: Allyn & Bacon.

Osgood, R. L. (1997). Undermining the common school ideal: Intermediate schools and ungraded classes in Boston, 1838–1900. *History of Education Quarterly, 37*(4), 375–398.

Plato. (1991). *The republic of Plato* (2nd ed., A. D. Bloom Ed. & Trans.). New York: Basic Books.

Ravitch, D. (1994, Fall). Somebody's children. *Brookings Review,* 4–9.

Ravitch, D. (2005, November 7). Every state left behind. *The New York Times,* p. A23.

Rogers, J., & Oakes, J. (2005). John Dewey speaks to Brown: Research, democratic social movement strategies, and the struggle for education on equal terms. *Teachers College Record, 107,* 2178–2203.

Rogers, J., & Oakes, J. (2006). *Learning power: Organizing for education and justice.* New York: Teachers College Press.

Ruenzel, D. (1996, August). By the book. *Teacher Magazine,* 25–29.

Seigfried, C. H. (1999). Socializing democracy: Jane Addams and John Dewey. *Philosophy of the Social Sciences, 2,* 207–230.

Spring, J. (2001). *The American school: 1642–2000* (5th ed.). New York: McGraw-Hill.

Stern, B. S., & Riley, K. L. (2002). Linking Harold Rugg and social reconstructionism to "authenticity" in theory and practice. *Curriculum and Teaching Dialogue, 4,* 113–121.

Urban, W. J., & Wagoner, J. L. (2003). *American education: A history.* New York: McGraw-Hill.

Washington, B. T. (1995). *Up from slavery.* Mineola, NY: Dover. (Original work published 1901)

West, C. (2004). *Democracy matters: Winning the fight against imperialism.* New York: Penguin Press.

Westbrook, R. B. (1991). *John Dewey and American democracy.* Ithaca, NY: Cornell University Press.

Young, I. M. (1990). *Justice and the politics of difference.* Princeton, NJ: Princeton University Press.

5 Tensions, Ironies, and Social Justice in Black Civil Rights
Lessons from Brown and King

Horace R. Hall

When studying history, ideally we come to the conclusion that it is not random, nor is it a result of mishaps. History is a decision that we make with our lives, and by gaining a richer understanding of it, we become more aware of how individual choices impact the lives of others. Moreover, history informs us of the deep-seated structural inequities persistent in our society and the ways in which we can continue challenging them based upon past struggles. In his book *Living Black History* (2006), Manning Marable writes:

> Knowledgeable civic actors can draw important lessons from history, which does incrementally increase civic capacity. Historical amnesia blocks the construction of potentially successful social movements. As the gap between the past, present, and future diminishes, individuals can acquire a greater sense of becoming the "makers" of their own history. Thus, for the oppressed, the act of reconstructing history is inextricably linked to the political practices, or *praxis*, of transforming the present and future. (p. 37)

Noting Marble's commentary, historians, sociologists, and legal scholars have all drawn and extensively documented lessons from *Brown v. Board of Education of Topeka, Kansas* (1954/1955) and the *Civil Rights movement* (1955–1968)—lessons that can surely advance *civic capacity* and, if heeded, assist present-future social movements in avoiding *historical amnesia*. The following discussion, however, is not a comprehensive historical review of these milestones. Rather, I choose to reflect on these events, using political–historical research, with the hope of expanding the discourse that seeks to deepen our senses of history and increase our capacity for civic action. Thus, for the sake of organization, I will present a synopsis of some of the social tensions catalyzed by these events. I will then discuss significant ironies that emerge out of each. Finally, I will close with some brief thoughts on the meaning of these tensions and ironies within the conceptual framework of social justice education, specifically underscoring the individual's role in initiating personal and institutional change through the practice of *social perspective-taking*.

Brown (Desegregating Schools with Segregated Minds)

Brown v. Board of Education was a class action suit comprised of five cases from segregated school districts in Kansas, Delaware, South Carolina, Virginia, and Washington, D.C. The National Association for the Advancement of Colored People (NAACP), the most important civil rights organization at that time, used these cases in consolidation in order to magnify the unconstitutionality of maintaining separate school facilities and to bring school segregation to an end altogether (Brown, 2004). The *Brown* decision overturned almost 60 years of "separate-but-equal" policies under *Plessy v. Ferguson* (1896) (Franklin & Moss, 1988). *Brown I* (1954) declared that segregated educational facilities were "inherently unequal" and violated the Equal Protection Clause assured by the Fourteenth Amendment (Franklin & Moss, 1988). *Brown II* (1955) reargued the issue of relief to the plaintiffs in *Brown* I, citing that dismantling of separate school systems must be initiated "with all deliberate speed" (Brown, 2004). Over the next 30 years, "all deliberate speed" became somewhat of a relative term. As the Court gave state and local school authorities primary control in organizing desegregation, there was only gradual progress toward making this happen, particularly in areas of the country not aligned with public opinion or court decree (Butler, 1996; Mack, 2005).

In the 1960s, massive White resistance to desegregation, at the state and local level, often took the form of procedural delays and school transfers (Mawdsley, 2004). In one extreme case, Prince Edward County, Virginia had abolished public schools entirely. Much of the open antipathy toward school desegregation occurred in the Old South, where in a decade after the *Brown* decision "only 2.14% of African American children in 7 of 11 southern states attended desegregated schools (Horowitz & Karst, 1969)" (Mawdsley, 2004, p. 246). While the Civil Rights Act of 1964 provided more incentives for school districts to comply with school desegregation (as federal dollars would go to these districts), the 1970s and 80s witnessed a surge in White flight, where White families left urban centers for suburban life (Kruse, 2005). During this period, the courts used busing to advance "all deliberate speed," as well as to establish more racially balanced schools in urban communities. However, Black children were primarily bussed to those schools nearest to their home. In this instance, White flight proved to be the most effective oppositional tool to school integration as the courts could not control residential segregation (Andrews, 2002; Brown, 2004).

Other societal tensions roused by *Brown* can be found in the paradoxes emerging out of it. Two of the more notable ironies of the case are the links between "equal access" and Black identity development. The NAACP contended that legal segregation had a negative psychological effect on Black children, and thus school desegregation was the principal method for ensuring healthy Black identities, as well as harmonious future relationships between Blacks and Whites (Martin, 1998). With regard to the latter point, *Brown*, as previously stated, sparked intense White resistance to integration as witnessed in school transfers and White flight—two dynamics still in effect today in the form of school vouchers and regentrification. Yet, to the former point, mass school desegregation might have incurred another form of detriment on Black students than what was alleged by the NAACP. The idea of equal access for Blacks was embodied and pursued in the legalism of "separate educational facilities are inherently unequal." Hence, the initial course of action taken by the courts was *not* to financially equalize Black schools (via school curricula, teacher salaries, and building infrastructure) or to merge White students into them. Instead, the view of the Court was that wherever Black students were coming from was racially inferior and that the spaces they sought to occupy were culturally superior (Butler, 1996). And so witnessed were mandated thrusts of Black students into White academic arenas, which for some were tremendously hostile and violent (Martin, 1998; Ogletree, 2004). Bell (2004) points out, Black children "were shuffled in and out of predominantly white schools" and "all too often met naked race-hatred and a curriculum blind to their needs" (p. 112). Furthermore, the courts' misguided approach to equal access and the alleged fostering of healthy Black identities came at the cost of Black school closings and consolidations, the loss of employment and status of Black teachers and principals in their respective communities, and the removal of Black students from their cultural spaces of connection, esteem, and self-knowledge, which was negligently replaced with White curriculum and ideology (Karpinski, 2006; Ogletree, 2004).

The impact of the above is still felt today as Black and Latino students continue to struggle with the lingering effects of community dislocation, and the reality of attending disproportionately segregated schools that are poorly resourced, overcrowded, standards driven, and exceptionally punitive in disciplinary measures (Conchas, 2001; Hall, 2006; Noguera, 2003; Stevens, 2002). As civic actors, we should understand that the limitation of the *Brown* case was that the notion of "equality" was ill-defined at the outset. Though *Brown* sought to level the playing field by destroying legal segregation (via skin color), arguably it did so, but in principle only. Equality, most assuredly, must also be linked to economic parity. Racial integration alone cannot eliminate concentrated sections of poverty, much less transform minds bent on segregation. In the NAACP's quest for social justice, the goal of equality was lost in litigation as it was obfuscated by the political rhetoric of "sameness" (i.e., the norms of Whiteness by which all other racial groups are judged). Nonetheless, with all its shortcomings, *Brown* should still be seen as a victory. It confronted a brutally White supremacist system embedded in nearly 300 years of slavery, Jim Crow, and racial violence. While it did fall short of social equity and educational opportunity, the *Brown* decision produced a ripple effect which compelled others toward change in multiple aspects of social life. The next segment looks at the Civil Rights Movement and its central figure, Dr. Martin Luther King Jr.

King (and the Civil Rights Movement)

The legacy of the Civil Rights Movement is founded in its struggle to emancipate and develop the lives of marginalized groups through the intersection of legal and educational efforts. Largely viewed as an integrationist movement, its accomplishments include the passage of key civil rights and antipoverty legislation. The origin of the movement arguably was an outgrowth of the discontentment that Black citizens, predominantly in the South, felt toward the prolonged, legal approaches to desegregation assumed by the NAACP (Lehman, 2006). Although Black communities acknowledged the triumph of *Brown*, they continued to wrestle with second-class citizen status in areas of housing, employment, voting rights, and segregated public facilities, which still included schools. As an alternative to litigation, small Black grassroots organizations in the South began to employ tactics of civil disobedience. One notable example, and the stimulus for the Civil Rights Movement, was the Montgomery, Alabama Bus Boycott of 1955. Initiated by the arrest of Rosa Parks (an active NAACP member at the time), organized by E. D. Nixon (president of the Montgomery NAACP chapter), and led by an inexperienced and reluctant Dr. King, the one-year boycott involved a community of hundreds. As it gained national attention, in part due to a significant number of protestor arrests that included King, the federal government, pressured to intervene, finally passed a city-wide injunction that brought an end to the segregation of buses (Gordon, 2000). The success of the boycott propelled King into the role of leader and spokesperson of the Civil Rights Movement. It also served to galvanize other locally based organizations (e.g., the Student Nonviolent Coordinating Committee; SNCC) to take part in nonviolent protests which took the form of sit-ins, pray-ins, read-ins, and freedom rides (Miller, 2004). The media associated many of these campaigns, often student organized, with King, in spite of the fact that these groups sought to operate relatively independent of his top-down leadership (Fairclough, 1987; Lawson & Payne, 2006).

Just as *Brown* was an impetus of enormous racial discord and opposition through legislative pressure, the Civil Rights Movement, with its hand in multiple social settings, heightened racial tensions exponentially. One significant aspect of the movement is that it comprised a number of national (NAACP and the Congress of Racial Equality; CORE), regional (King's Southern Christian Leadership Conference; SCLC) and local grassroots organizations. Based mainly in southern states, the mobilization of these groups helped to unmask White hostility and, with the use of media outlets, position it on a national stage (Lawson, 1997; Levy, 1998). Thus, communities all across America were able to witness the explosion of White resistance to Black nonviolent protest. Television, newspapers, and magazines captured horrendous images of White private citizens, police officers, fire fighters, and other public officials engrossed in hate speech and terrorist retaliation against demonstrators. For King, the attention of the media was integral to the civil rights agenda because organizing and mobilizing in and of itself could not generate change—a national conscience had to be evoked (Washington, 1986). And indeed it was, as the face of the oppressor and of the oppressed were rendered in daily news stories such as the Little Rock Nine, where Black students entered into the fiercely contested Little Rock Central High School in Arkansas (1957); the lunch counter sit-ins in Tallahassee, Florida, Atlanta, Georgia, Greensboro, North Carolina, and Nashville, Tennessee where Black college students protested eating facilities slow to desegregate (1960); the March on Birmingham, Alabama, where fire hoses and police dogs were turned on high school students and teachers opposing biased voter registration (1963); the March on Seattle, contesting unfair hiring practices in retail stores (1963); the bombing of the Sixteenth Street Baptist Church in Birmingham, a frequent meeting place for civil rights organizers, where 20 church members were injured and four young girls were killed (1963); the Marches from Selma to Montgomery (also known as Sunday Bloody Sunday), where thousands of protestors converged on the state's capitol disputing intimidation tactics in Black voter registration only to be met with billy clubs, bull whips, and tear gas (1965) (Lawson, 1997; Levy, 1998). The appallingly inhumane responses that demonstrators faced were magnified tenfold by news images, which swayed mainstream sentiment toward the movement, weakening White Southern business structures and pressuring political powers to intercede (Lee, 2002).

An intriguing paradox that surfaces from the Civil Rights Movement concerns the intersection between King, the media, and the movement itself. As previously stated, the media linked King to virtually every organized nonviolent protest. Though these news reports served organizers by bringing national attention to the movement, they also inflated the public perception of King's power and position. While he embraced the efforts (e.g., the mass sit-ins in the South) of independently acting groups, King was mostly unaware of their planning and outcomes (Garrow, 1986). Even so, the press perceived King as the head coordinator, much to the resentment of other national and local protest organizers. In *Debating the Civil Rights Movement, 1945–1968*, Lawson and Payne (2006) write,

> King, many of them complained, would come into a town where SNCC or CORE had done the dangerous, thankless work of getting something off the ground, give some speeches to the adoring masses and the fawning press and then fly off to the next place, leaving others to deal with the letdown.... He was a mobilizer, not an organizer, good at involving large numbers of people in short-term, media oriented events but never in one place long enough to see that a local infrastructure got created that could carry the struggle on with or without him. (p. 115)

The intention here is not to minimize the extraordinary leadership of Dr. King, but rather to point out how media sensationalized him, influencing the public mindset of the time. News reports and public perceptions fitted comfortably within the pervasive American ethos of *rugged individualism*, which accordingly minimized the organizational efforts of other grassroots campaigns. This, in turn, later constructed a skewed, more widely established history of King *as* the Civil Rights Movement—its creator, hero, and martyr (Lawson & Payne, 2006). The oddity of this is that while King and the movement used media to emphasize its struggles, the process inadvertently deemphasized the foundation of the movement itself. Its roots had been grounded in the actions of everyday, individual citizens unified with the shared desire and commitment for social change. Yet today, school history books implicitly tell students that for people to mass mobilize a great and omnipresent leader must emerge to engage them. This idea runs counter to the reflective, activist spirit that the Civil Rights Movement espoused in the first place and induces a kind of mental paralysis that subconsciously tells citizens that they cannot act with fire and fervency (as witnessed in the actions of Rosa Parks and others) unless a centralized, larger figure is present to spur and control their "movement."

The celebrated achievement of the Civil Rights Movement was that it produced a series of antidiscriminatory legislation that fundamentally changed U.S. social policies in voting, housing, employment, and immigration. With the passage of these various acts followed the assumption, like *Brown*, that "integration as equality" would settle racial tensions and improve the lives of *all* Black folks (Carnoy, 1994). Yet, the intersection of race and class plays a pivotal role in discerning which Black folks benefited most from civil rights legislation. Marable (1998) contends that, in a capitalist society, social class arrangements have everything to do with "ownership of capital, material resources, education, and access to power" (p. 151). While civil rights statutes offered greater access for middle/working class Blacks (those comparatively more integrated into the system), for Blacks unemployed, illiterate, poor, and homeless (those by and large invisible to the system), these enactments did not translate in the same manner (Marable, 1998). Though integration was unmistakably a significant factor in helping Black citizens carve out a sociopolitical space in American society, it offered them little by way of full economic engagement (Levy, 1998). Hence, the benefits of civil rights legislation mostly impacted those who previously had a "bootstrap" to pull up by and could more easily meld into the White social order. In one respect, the gains of the movement were conciliatory and on the conditions of White society (Lawson & Payne, 2006). The message being, "We'll give you access and maybe some privileges, but power is a thing you will never have." Quite aptly, these terms were part and parcel to the same rugged individualist ideology that enveloped perceptions of the movement. And, over the past three decades, this pervasive ideology has functioned to shift public opinion, subtlety dismantle the rewards of the Civil Rights Movement, and manipulate policy outcomes that stress individualism, competition, and privatization (Bonilla-Silva, 2001). Today, we observe this as disproportionate numbers of working class folk find themselves overtaxed and underemployed and public educational institutions are being inexorably subjected to nationalized accountability and privatized control and conformity (Bell-McKenzie & James, 2004; Saltman, 2000).

Social Perspective-Taking (Equality versus Equity)

Perhaps, we can best understand the tensions and ironies of *Brown* and the Civil Rights Movement by first undertaking the notion of "equality." Though integration served as a means of maximizing social equality and minimizing racial conflict, it deceptively transmuted into mass assimilation. Stated differently, "integration as equality" actually meant the absorption of Black minds into the dominant group's ideology—their norms, standards, and mores. Thus, Black identities, represented by infinite epistemologies, cosmologies, and ontologies, have been relentlessly measured and defined by the yardstick of another culture. In turn, Black folks have been left with biased moral and cultural interpretations that frame their individual problems as group pathologies and deficits. While being able to integrate into the larger system may be necessary for the benefit of exploiting resources to address one's needs, full incorporation into it comes at the cost of losing one's humanity, as well as the capacity to see others as fully human. Therefore, as civic actors and social justice educators, an additional lesson we may be able to draw from *Brown* and the Civil Rights Movement lies in discerning the concept of equality. Gordon (1999) differentiates between equality and equity this way: "equality requires sameness, but equity requires treatments be appropriate and sufficient to those characteristics and needs of those treated...for educational equity to be served, treatment must be specific to one's functional characteristics and sufficient to the realities of one's condition" (p. xiv). So the question becomes: How do we come to know one another as human beings for the purpose of one, recognizing individual needs and conditions, and two, transforming and humanizing the workings of oppression from the personal to the institutional level?

In answering the above query, I propose the use of social perspective-taking as an extension of our pedagogical practice. As humans, it is enormously difficult to separate our personal theories about the traits of others from our views on how to relate to them (Selman, 1980). In this instance, social perspective-taking works to develop new cultural schemas that help individuals reevaluate the deeply internalized subjectivities of race, class, ethnicity, and gender, and those biases (and even hatreds) that are attached to them. Through narrative, poetry, oral history, and spoken word, this self-defining activity invites us into the lives of others. It offers us a glimpse into their world and informs us of far more than their skin color, the community in which they live, or the statistic that the larger society attempts to make them. Social perspective-taking encourages classroom participants to rethink and reconstruct their personal theories about other social groups, in relation to themselves, and provoke critical dialogue around oppression and the ways in which it can be altered at multiple levels. When educators take on this practice, Rios and others (Rios, Trent, & Vega-Castaneda, 2004) claim that "'Teaching otherness' connects teachers' lives to difference and similarity," whereby they come to "understand, embody, and become advocates for social justice and in turn, transfer this perspective to their students as a way of understanding and improving society" (p. 6). Social justice, in this regard, becomes more than just about theoretical declarations of egalitarianism. It is also fused with genuine inflection that serves to revolutionize and nurture our human existence.

In our labor to embrace and transform humanity, we must first come to understand the intimate and unbounded nature of it. Unearthing stories of triumph and defeat, of ignorance and awareness, of hate and love help us in understanding our shared human thread. Such stories hold the potential for desegregating minds that operate to keep our world segregated and the marginalized excluded from possessing power. Social perspective-taking as a small, but critical piece of social justice, compels us to stare deep into ourselves and acknowledge that we may be both the oppressor and the oppressed, but that change is possible. As we are exposed to the narratives of others, made aware of their life history and the choices that they make, we become more cognizant of how smaller, seemingly inconsequential, personal histories can impact our collective future. It is at this point that we truly discover what equality and equity is, realizing that it looks different from person to person and from community to community.

References

Andrews, K. T. (2002). Movement–countermovement dynamics and the emergence of new institutions: The case of "White flight" schools in Mississippi. *Social Forces, 80*(3), 911–936.

Bell, D. (2004). *Silent covenants: Brown v. Board of Education and the unfulfilled hopes for racial reform*. Oxford: Oxford University Press.

Bell-McKenzie, K., & James, J. S. (2004). The corporatizing and privatizing of schooling: A call for grounded critical praxis. *Educational Theory, 54*(4), 431–444.

Bonilla-Silva, E. (2001). *White supremacy and racism in the post-civil rights era*. Boulder, CO: Lynn Reiner.

Brown, F. (2004). The road to Brown, its leaders, and the future. *Education and Urban Society, 36*, 255–265.

Butler, J. S. (1996). The return of open debate. *Society, 33*(3), 11–18.

Carnoy, M. (1994). *Faded dreams: The politics and economics of race in America*. Cambridge, UK: Cambridge University Press.

Conchas, G. Q. (2001). Structuring failure and success: Understanding the variability in Latino school engagement. *Harvard Educational Review, 71*(3), 475–505.

Fairclough, A. (1987). *To redeem the soul of America: The Southern Christian Leadership Conference and Martin Luther King, Jr.* Athens: University of Georgia Press.

Franklin, J. H., & Moss, A. A., Jr. (1988). *From slavery to freedom: A history of Negro Americans* (6th ed.). New York: McGraw-Hill.

Garrow, D. J. (1986). *Bearing the cross: Martin Luther King, Jr., and the Southern Christian Leadership Conference*. New York: Morrow.

Gordon, E. W. (1999). *Education and justice: A view from the back of the bus*. New York & London: Teachers College Press.

Gordon, J. U. (2000). Black males in the civil rights movement. *The Annals of the American Academy of Political and Social Science, 569*(1), 42–55.

Hall, H. (2006). *Mentoring young men of color: Meeting the needs of African-American and Latino students*. Lanham, MD: Rowman & Littlefield.

Karpinski, C. F. (2006). Bearing the burden of desegregation: Black principals and Brown. *Urban Education, 41*, 237–276.

Kruse, K. M. (2005). *White flight: Atlanta and the making of modern conservatism*. Princeton, NJ: Princeton University Press.

Lawson, S. F. (1997). *Running for freedom: Civil rights and black politics in America since 1941* (2nd ed.). New York: McGraw-Hill

Lawson, S. F., & Payne, C. M. (2006). *Debating the civil rights movement, 1945–1968*. Lanham, MD: Rowman & Littlefield.

Lee, T. (2002). *Mobilizing public opinion: Black insurgency and racial attitudes in the civil rights era*. Chicago: University of Chicago Press.

Lehman, C. P. (2006). Civil rights in twilight: The end of the Civil Rights movement era in 1973. *Journal of Black Studies, 36*(3), 415–428.

Levy, P. B. (1998). *The civil rights movement*. Westport, CT: Greenwood Press.

Mack. K. W. (2005). Rethinking civil rights lawyering and policies in the era before *Brown*. *The Yale Law Journal, 115*(256), 256–354.

Marable. M. (1998). *Black leadership: Four great American leaders and the struggle for civil rights*. New York: Columbia University Press.

Marable, M. (2006). *Living Black history: How reimagining the African-American past can remake America's racial future*. New York: Basic Books.

Martin, W. E., Jr. (1998). *Brown v. Board of Education: A brief history with documents*. Boston & New York: Bedford/St. Martin's.

Mawdsley, R. D. (2004). A legal history of Brown and a look to the future. *Education and Urban Society, 36*, 245–254.

Miller, J. (2004). *Sit-ins and freedom rides: The power of nonviolent resistance*. New York: PowerKids Press.

Noguera, P. A. (2003). Schools, prisons, and social implications of punishment: Rethinking disciplinary practices. *Theory into Practice, 42*(4), 341–350.

Ogletree, C. J., Jr. (2004). All deliberate speed. *Reflections on the first half-century of Brown v. Board of Education.* New York: W. W. Norton.

Rios, F., Trent, A., & Vega-Castaneda, L. (2004). Social perspective taking: Advancing empathy and advocating justice. *Equity and Excellence in Education, 36*(1), 5–14.

Saltman, K. J. (2000). *Collateral damage: Corporatizing public schools—A threat to democracy.* Lanham, MD: Rowman & Littlefield.

Selman, R. (1980). *The growth of interpersonal understanding.* New York: Academic Press.

Stevens, J. W. (2002). *Smart and sassy: The strengths of inner-city Black girls.* New York & Oxford: Oxford University Press.

Washington, J. M. (Ed.). (1986). *A testament of hope: The essential writings of Martin Luther King, Jr.* San Francisco: Harper & Row.

Young, I. M. (1990). *Justice and the politics of difference.* Princeton, NJ: Princeton University Press.

6 Preparing for Public Life
Education, Critical Theory, and Social Justice

Pepi Leistyna

> The public education system in America is one of the most important foundations of our democracy. After all, it is where children from all over America learn to be responsible citizens, and learn to have the skills necessary to take advantage of our fantastic opportunistic society.
>
> (George W. Bush, May 1, 2002)

While this statement is an obvious slip of the tongue, and sadly a sign of a semiliterate man, creating responsible citizens really demands that members of society collectively participate in maintaining healthy public institutions and restraining rather than nurturing those opportunistic forces that have great contempt for public life and an undying love for the monopolization of knowledge and profit.

Given that public schools in any democracy are always intended to be agencies of civic mindedness and responsibility, and that the well-being of young people is the pretext for almost every political movement on the planet, these institutions should be used to encourage youth to recognize their power to act upon the world via critical awareness.

In every country on every continent, young people have always played a critical role in struggles for social justice. In the last 500 years alone—certainly since the advent of the European university in the Middle Ages, societies have witnessed social transformation on a grand scale, which has been mobilized, or at least in part energized, by young people (Boren, 2001; Sherrod, Flanagan, Kassimir, & Syvertsen, 2005).

With the ratification of the Convention on the Rights of the Child on November 20, 1989 the United Nations took the first steps to institutionally realize the active participation of youth in global affairs:

Article 12: States Parties shall assure to the child who is capable of forming his or her own views the right to express those views freely in all matters affecting the child, the views of the child being given due weight in accordance with the age and maturity of the child.

Article 15: States Parties recognize the rights of the child to freedom of association and to freedom of peaceful assembly.

In order to embrace youth activism, it is essential to move beyond the simplistic notion that kids inhabit a land of innocence. From birth on, as children are being initiated into values and beliefs—what it means to be an integrated member of a particular group—they come to occupy an inherently ideological and thus political space, whether or not they are aware of it. It's important to ask: What kinds of cultural practices are they being apprenticed into, what notions of youth are they subjected to, and what effects can young people have on such processes?

Unfortunately, youth, especially the poor and racially subordinated, are far too often left out of drafting history, describing social realities, and debating social policies and practices. In fact, conservatives in the United States have worked relentlessly to dismantle participatory democratic spaces that nurture their potential to come to voice. Pertaining to public schools, Noam Chomsky (1999) elaborates:

> It starts in kindergarten: The school system tries to repress independence; it tries to teach obedience. Kids and other people are not induced to challenge and question, but the contrary. If you start questioning, you're a behavior problem or something like that; you've got to be disciplined. You're supposed to repeat, obey, follow orders.... (p. 117)

Even in the well-intentioned calls to "empower" and "give voice" to students, young people are mostly heard about but rarely from. What many educators fail to realize is that even the most progressive and concerned pedagogue can't empower kids. On the contrary, it is both objectifying and patronizing to assume that teachers can simply tap any given child on the shoulder with a magical epistemological wand, abstracted from the critical process of active engagement and meaning making. This critique also applies to the notion of "giving voice." It is presumptuous to claim to possess the ability to bequeath the power of expression. Since all people already have voices—often critical ones at that—the real challenge is for educators to be willing to create dialogical spaces where all lived experiences and worldviews can be heard. In other words, will teachers be able and willing to create the necessary self-empowering conditions that allow kids of all walks of life to explore, theorize, reveal, and act upon the truths behind the worlds that they inhabit?

There are certainly plenty of reasons for young people to work for social change in the United States. Nationally, one-in-five children grow up poor; 9.2 million children currently lack health insurance; 3.9 million people are homeless (a number projected to increase 5% each year) and 1.3 million (or 39%) of them are children. The nation ranks 17th of all industrialized countries in efforts to eradicate poverty among the young, and 23rd in infant mortality. In addition to these economic hardships, young people are experiencing a great deal of discrimination along the lines of race, language, disability, religion, gender, and sexuality.

The government's response to the growing problems that youth in this country face is the implementation of a standardized curriculum, high stakes testing, accountability schemes, English-only mandates, strict zero-tolerance policies, and Draconian budget cuts. In this era of No Child Left Behind—conversely referred to as "the war against the young"—6 million children have thus far been left in the wake. Meanwhile, millions of students are being drugged into conformity and complacency in the name of Attention Deficit Disorder, and public schools are now largely controlled by private interests such as pharmaceutical, publishing, and food companies, for-profit education management organizations, and corporate lobbyists.

While the title *No Child Left Behind* connotes fairness, compassion, and equity and the instigators of testing mania promise academic and professional success for the nation's children, they virtually disregard why inequities exist in the first place. As these advocates of a corporate model of schooling hide behind notions of science, objectivity, and universal knowledge, what is largely missing from national debates and federal and state policies—and what should be central to any good teacher education program and public school classroom—is recognition and analysis of how racism, the structures of social class, and other oppressive and malignant ideologies inform actual educational practices and institutional conditions. These factors play a much more significant role in students' academic achievement than whether or not they have access to abstract content, a monolingual setting, and constant evaluation.

In this political climate where conservatives readily blame progressive educational programs, democratic social policies, and organized labor for the country's problems, K-12 students need to learn how to be more effective agents of change. In order to be active "subjects" of history rather than passive "objects" to be acted upon, manipulated, and controlled, literacy development should work in a way that helps people read the economic, social, and political realities that shape their lives in order to develop the necessary critical consciousness to name, understand, and transform them (Freire & Leistyna, 1999).

In order to work toward youth liberation as part of the formal curriculum, educators can help mobilize students into organized political bodies (critical communities of struggle) so that they are able to voice their concerns and realize their own goals. This is precisely what the U.S. Constitution protects—not the mandates of a Wall Street agenda. Such political participation requires praxis—the ongoing relationship between theory and practice. Educators can mentor students into critical inquiry and theory. Not to be confused with what's traditionally thought of as the "higher order thinking skills," *critical* in this sense implies being able to understand, analyze, pose questions, and affect the sociopolitical and economic realities that shape people's lives. Developing critical consciousness isn't an exercise to get people to think in a certain way; rather it is intended to get them to think more deeply about the issues and relations of power that affect them.

In this spirit of ongoing reflection and action, theory embodies how people interpret, analyze, and make generalizations about why the world works the way that it does. It is the why and how of what has been happening around us, and not simply a focus on what is occurring and how to effectively respond. While theory provides existing explanations of the whys and hows of the world, theorizing is the ability to actively engage bodies of knowledge and human practices for the logics and sociohistorical conditions that inform them so that they can be reworked. It encourages individuals to evaluate, based on their own experiences, expertise, and insight, the strengths and weaknesses of any conceptual and practical movement and recontextualize and reinvent its possibilities for their own predicaments. As an integral part of any political project, theorizing presents a constant challenge to imagine and materialize alternative political spaces and identities and more just and equitable economic, social, and cultural relations. It makes possible consciousness raising, coalition building, resistance, activism, and structural change.

As part of their apprenticeship into theorizing, students could gain a great deal of theoretical and practical insight from the study of social movement and action research, which documents the power of movements and their impact on people, public discourse, policy, institutions, and governments. It looks at the ways in which activists understand and make use of the cracks of agency made possible by shifting economic, political, and cultural relations, and how organizations and networks develop, mobilize, and change. Action research has also always had a political and transformative agenda explicitly woven into its theoretical and empirical fabric. Advocates of this exploratory model embrace the idea of doing research with others rather than on them in an effort to understand and consequently change any given situation. Students should not only learn about these areas of inquiry but they should be encouraged to engage in their own empirical projects.

In such undemocratic times, it's not surprising that this type of critical practice is often discouraged. The youth of the world can certainly be looked to as a democratizing force capable of dismantling the structured inequalities in societies. It is for this very reason that conservatives vigilantly work to contain and control them. Reactionary educators in the United States like Diane Ravitch, Lynne Cheney, and William Bennett—omnipresent spokespersons for the Republican Party and capitalist interests—have argued and continue to argue that attempts to reveal the underlying values, interests, and power relationships that structure educational and other social policies and practices have corrupted the academic environment. Such efforts to depoliticize the public's understanding of social institutions, especially schools, in the name of neutrality are obviously a reactionary ploy to maintain the status quo.

In other words, this assault on theorizing is in part connected to ways in which public schools have been used as an indoctrinating force to deskill students by working to mold them into uncritical receivers and consumers of existing theory, but rarely viewing them as active and creative participants in the generative process of understanding. This is especially evident as globally public schools are falling prey to the kinds of corporate logic that package thought as a commodity for exchange in the marketplace rather than inspiring the kinds of inquiry that probe that very logic and use of public energy and space. Within these corporate models of public education the production of technicians in all disciplines (areas of study which are artificially disconnected from one another) comes at the expense of transdisciplinary thinkers and producers of social knowledge about the world. As students of all levels are distracted or lured away from critically reading historical and existing social formations, especially those that maintain abuses of power, they often become the newest wave of exploited labor power and reproducers, whether they are conscious of it or not, and the target of oppressive social practices. It is precisely this lack of inquiry, analysis, and agency that a critical and activist-based philosophy of learning and teaching should work to reverse.

Social Justice in the Classroom: Lessons from History

As part of their formal educational experience, it would be enormously invaluable to expose students to the history of activist efforts to change the world. There are plenty of examples to choose from out of the vast historical pool of grassroots organizing, intercultural, and intergenerational cooperation, and international solidarity. The curriculum could include the exploration of the labor movement in the United States, and youth participation therein: it should investigate important events like the Newsboy Strike in 1899, the 1903 "Children's Crusade," and the development of the American Youth Congress in the 1930s. Students could also examine efforts to desegregate schools in the 1950s and the work of the Student Nonviolent Coordinating Committee. They could find a great deal of inspiration for their own political projects in the Civil Rights movement of the 1960s and the college campus activism that was mobilized by groups such as Students for a Democratic Society. There are also lessons to be learned from government efforts to mobilize youth involvement in public policy such as the National Commission on Resources for Youth in the 1970s (see Wikipedia for an elaboration of each of these). Students need to be apprenticed into conducting archival research so as to be able to tap into this vast history.

The youth of this nation have also inherited an immense legacy of radical thought, research, and action (Duncombe, 2002; Tilly, 2004). An indispensable part of praxis is to make use of existing theory and research in order to study historically significant events and the actors and organizations therein that have worked toward economic and social justice. To name a few of these individuals and groups: the Abolitionists, the First and Second Internationals, the Cuban, Mexican, and Russian revolutions, anarcho-syndicalism, experiments in social democracy, first and second-wave feminism, and anticolonial, civil rights, indigenous, and antiwar movements. There is also much to learn from the histories of trade union revivals, labor and environmental coalitions, antinuclear protests, and the global networks that have developed in the fight against AIDS.

It is important to note that such research needs to go beyond an introduction to the primary personalities that led many of these movements, and move into the world of everyday people struggling for change, struggles that set the stage for the emergence of great leaders.

Students could also learn from the ways that movements have critically appropriated from the past. Take for example the sociohistorical underpinnings of the 1999 Battle for Seattle. Largely coordinated by the Direct Action Network (DAN), this multi-interest decentralized manifestation was the product of years of political reinvention (Kauffman, 2002). Seattle protestors found strength in the history of the peace movement, the civil rights activism of the 1950s and 60s, antinuclear and environmental movements beginning in the early 1970s, the actions against U.S. intervention in Central America in the 1980s, and decades of anticolonial, feminist, queer, and antiracist theory, research, and activism.

Many of the techniques and strategies used in Seattle, such as affinity groups, spokescouncils, consensus building and the use of nonviolence, also have historical roots. Affinity groups—small protest units that choose targets and tactics—are derived from the Iberian Anarchist Federation in Spain which used this underground organizing structure in the 1930s during the Spanish Civil War. It was later reinvented by chapters of Students for a Democratic Society (SDS) and other civil rights and antiwar activist groups in the late 1960s and early 1970s in the United States (Kauffman, 2002). Spokescouncil meetings have descended from the early Soviets of the Russian revolution. Internationally, the "No Nukes" protestors of the 1970s critically appropriated this format so that representatives of affinity groups could meet, dialogue, and develop action plans. The idea of consensus decision making was handed down by the Quakers and enhanced by feminist movements that have also valued voice, inclusion, and dialogue. Nonviolent civil disobedience was inspired by Mahatma Gandhi's struggle to liberate India from British colonial rule, and later by the Civil Rights Movement in the United States under the guidance of Martin Luther King, Jr.

The forces that made Seattle possible were also influenced by the anti-Vietnam war movement in the early 1970s that implemented small and decentralized operational strategies as opposed to many of the massive and unwieldy organizational structures of the 1960s.

In addition, many protestors in Seattle benefited from the work of the organization ACT UP, a radical coalition of activists that got its start in the late 1980s in the fight against AIDS. Its members were tired of typical party politics, the divisiveness of identity politics, and the general ineffectiveness of endless lectures at fixed protest sites. "Through innovative use of civil-rights-era nonviolent civil disobedience, guerrilla theatre, sophisticated media work, and direct action, ACT UP helped transform the world of activism" (Shepard & Hayduk, 2002, p. 1). Rejecting the binarism between artistic expression and social responsibility and borrowing aspects of the carnivalesque approach to politics that have been around since the Middle Ages (Bakhtin, 1984), contemporary activists have made effective use of technology, street theater, puppets, block parties, art, music, and dance.

Many of the activists fighting for economic and social justice in Seattle also learned about coalition building from the anti-IMF agitation of the mid-1970s, efforts to bring down the apartheid government in South Africa, battles against the North American Free Trade Agreement (NAFTA), the Zapatista revolution, the WTO protests in 1995, the shutdown of the Multilateral Agreement on Investments of 1998, and the anti-World Economic Forum (WEF) demonstration in Davos that same year.

The intent of exploring the history of activism is not to generate nostalgia in these conservative times, nor does it offer up a recipe book to be followed to the last grain of salt; rather, it is a way to inspire youth to engage in the critical appropriation and reinvention of revolution as these struggles offer theoretical, empirical, and practical springboards for contemporary efforts. Such lessons should be part of any public education system that hopes to prepare students for public life.

Not only do students readily express an interest in their own lives and what they are deeply connected to, but they also generate a great deal of interest in education and the state of society if allowed to connect in substantive and politically influential ways to the very world around them. When given the opportunity to speak, youth are more than willing and able—as they have always been—to analyze social injustice and come up with solutions to such problems. Youth movements in the past two decades provide a great deal of evidence of this. Students of all ages and grade levels have taken up such causes as education reform, immigrant rights, AIDS awareness, environmental protection, animal rights, antiwar activism, civil liberties, and gay, disability, and women's rights. They have battled against sweatshop labor, racism, police brutality, poverty, and the rise in incarceration. There have been a plethora of recent protests against discriminatory and abusive social and educational policies such as in California against the passage of Propositions 187, 209, and 21 led by organizations like the Critical Resistance Youth Force and Youth Organizing Communities. In fact, there is a vast array of organizations that merit investigation of the likes of Youth on Board, the Youth Activism Project, the Freechild Project, and the National Youth Rights Association (see Wikipedia for an elaboration of each of these).

But it's important to note that social justice has no fixed definition. Not only are there conservative claims to social justice, but empowered communities from across the ideological spectrum could in fact result in the rule of an oppressive majority. Youth should be exposed to and learn from cases where feminist movements, working class struggles, Gay and Lesbian groups, antiracist efforts, and antiglobalization movements have experienced discriminatory and conservative tendencies; and where some struggles for national sovereignty have turned fascist, mass revolutions have become totalitarian, or social democracies have capitulated to capitalist demands.

If progressive educators and community activists wish to continue to do the important work of creating civic-minded students that are prepared to actively participate in a vibrant public sphere, then kids should also be exposed to how the art of organizing is undergoing radical changes as a result of the ways that activists have been making effective use of new interactive technologies. Youth are often technologically literate with such innovations, but not in the ways that they have been used to mobilize social justice projects.

First, students should explore how media have always played a pivotal role in activist efforts—with the advent of printing, newspapers, telephones, radio, TV, film, and so on. It is then much easier to understand how the power of cultural production and circulation has taken on new life with digital, multimedia, and wireless technologies, and especially with the Internet. Helping individuals and organizations mobilize is a wireless, multimedia palette that includes notebook computers, personal digital assistant (PDA) devices, cell phones (with digital cameras built in), text messaging, pagers, global GPS positioning systems, and digital camcorders. These technologies facilitate organizing and coordinating efforts. Along with the aforementioned tools, and often in connection to them, the Internet has ushered in a revolution in cultural activism. Unlike the activists of yesteryear who accomplished so much with so little, the new hybrid "smart mobs" have access to e-mail, blogs, podcasts, computer-faxes, listservs, hyperlinks, chat rooms, and downloadable street posters with tear-off instructions. These and other cybertools are all used for educating the public on pertinent issues, building and mobilizing communities, coordinating events locally, nationally, and internationally, and influencing policy initiatives both locally and globally. They can also be used to transcend the language divide with software that instantly translates messages. Making effective use of webcasting, news outlets offer access to Internet radio and video feeds, information and photo archives, and frequently updated news reports. There is an abundance of hyperorganization websites that keep the public up to date on current events, that support real-life mobilization, and that connect activists to other like-minded organizations through hyperlinks. And, there is an endless stream of electronic information that is readily available through e-journals, online zines, and info-pages.

These innovative technologies have also made possible the reinvention of many traditional methods of activism into electronic civil disobedience in the form of online petitions, boycotts, blockades, sit-ins, hacktivism, and other kinds of cyberprotest.

Perhaps the most revolutionary contribution that these technologies have made is that they've radically advanced social networking. The Internet allows people, with relative facility, to cross geographical, political, and professional boundaries. As cyberculture helps groups transcend traditional borders, develop cross-interest coalitions, and forge collaborative knowledge, it simultaneously opens the door to more inclusive and effective political struggle. Students can be apprenticed into how such efforts have been coordinated and encouraged to experiment for themselves how to implement these practices.

In this era of globalization, in which no society is entirely isolated and untouched by neoliberal economic policies and practices, and any local action has a global impact and vice versa, any constructive cross-disciplinary, multidimensional approach to youth activism has to have an international component. Of the 6.3 billion people that currently live on this planet, almost half are under the age of 25. Half the world's 1 billion poor are children. Victims of the residue of a brutal history of colonial rule, sustained racism and patriarchy, and now the imperial grasp and draconian mandates of deregulation and structural adjustment, 11 million of these kids under the age of 5 die annually because of malnutrition, dirty water or a lack thereof, disease, and poor housing. Hundreds of millions of youth around the world are not getting a formal education and millions are trapped in the sex trade and sweatshops or caught up in military conflicts where they are often forced into fighting someone else's economic and ideological wars.

Students in the United States need to be exposed to the global justice movement's innovative efforts to work simultaneously through a politics of location (i.e., area-specific conditions, traditions, and economic interests) and a politics of global unity. The goal has been and should continue to be to search out new forms of democratic and revolutionary identification, to recognize differences and commonalities within struggles for economic and social justice, and to work through dialogue and action to sustain what has become a "movement of many movements." In this way, youth in the United States can more effectively walk on to the political stage in solidarity with other young people from around the world.

If "the public education system in America is one of the most important foundations of our democracy...where children from all over America learn to be responsible citizens," as the president claims, then teaching social justice should be a fundamental component of the curriculum.

References

Bakhtin, M. (1984). *Rabelais and his world*. Bloomington: Indiana University Press.
Boren, M. E. (2001). *Student resistance*. New York: Routledge.

Chomsky, N, (1999). Demystifying democracy: A dialogue with Noam Chomsky. In P. Leistyna (Ed.), *Presence of mind: Education and the politics of deception* (p. 117). Boulder, CO: Westview.

Duncombe, S. (Ed.). (2002). *Cultural resistance reader.* London: Verso.

Freire, P., & Leistyna, P. (1999). A dialogue with Paulo Freire. In P. Leistyna (Ed.), *Presence of mind: Education and the politics of deception* (p. 46). *Boulder, CO: Westview.*

Kauffman, L. A. (2002). A short history of radical renewal. B. Shepard & R. Hayduk (Eds.), *From Act Up to the WTO: Urban protest and community building in the era of globalization* (p. 207). London: Verso.

Shepard, B., & Hayduk, R. (Eds.). (2002). *From Act Up to the WTO: Urban protest and community building in the era of globalization.* London: Verso.

Sherrod, L. R., Flanagan, C. A., Kassimir, R., & Syvertsen, A. K. (Eds.). (2005). *Youth activism: An international encyclopedia* (2 vols.). Westport, CT: Greenwood Press.

Tilly, C. (2004). *Social movements, 1768–2004.* Boulder, CO: Paradigm.

7 Education and the Law
Toward Conquest or Social Justice

Enora R. Brown

Introduction

> ...the state tends to create and maintain a certain type of civilization and of citizen (and hence of collective life and individual relations), and to eliminate certain customs and attitudes and to disseminate others...the Law will be its instrument for this purpose (together with the school system, and other institutions and activities). (Gramsci, 1971, p. 246)

Public education is under siege, and the hard-won gains of past generations are being eroded by judicial decisions and neoliberal government policies. For the past 150 years, social movements and the cumulative efforts of individuals, within and across African-American, Latino, Native-American, and selective White communities, have been instrumental in struggling for/attaining the legal, social, and economic rights to insure equality in education at all levels. These historic gains—from the establishment of Freedmen's Bureau Schools and universal public education in the late 1800s, and mandated desegregation of public schools via *Brown vs. Board of Education* in 1954, to the Civil Rights movement of the 1960s, including the enactment of the Bilingual Education Act in 1968 and implementation of affirmative action policies throughout the 1970s—are systematically being rescinded in courts of law, and this is being justified by retrograde market-driven, color-blind ideology. Current legislation is undermining past *legal* mandates: No Child Left Behind Act (NCLB, 2001) privatizes public education, Proposition 209 in California in 1996, the Hopwood Decision in Texas (1996), *Regents of the University of California* v. *Bakke* (1978), *Grutter v. Bollinger* (2003) in Michigan, and other cases bolster the elimination of affirmative action. Proposition 227 and local mandates require English-only instruction, dismantle bilingual education, or delegitimate languages other than English. The most recent judicial assault on democratic efforts to attain equal, desegregated education was the Supreme Court decision on June 28th, 2007. This ruling limits, prohibits, and revokes the right to use race or ethnicity to implement voluntary integration plans in educational institutions, and will have devastating consequences on the long-term amelioration of racial inequality.

The temporary provision and strategic rollback of social policy, however, is not new. It is endemic to the history of the United States that the scions of wealth have benefited from their use of *the law*—both legal and extralegal forms—to provide, extend, withhold, and rescind public education and other social goods, and their use of *public education* as a means to secure, indoctrinate, and divide the labor force, to discard a reserve army of the unemployed, and to insure the expansion of capital at all costs, on both domestic and global fronts. Though education is revered as the great leveler and the law is revered as a guarantor of equality, the history of the federal and state use of public education and the law reveal that both have served to build and maintain a stratified society (Brown et al.,

2003). This history has implications for current efforts toward social justice in education, and the strategic use of education and the law to realize equality.

This chapter chronicles how the state's strategic use of *education and sanctions of the law* has complemented *force* in the historic conquest of Native Americans, subjugation of Mexican Americans, and enslavement of African Americans, to create and sustain a racialized, class stratified society. It addresses the legalized racial segregation and exploitation of conquered peoples that enabled colonization, westward expansion, and industrialization, and chronicles the acquisition of land and labor that relied on education, religious conversion, and a "commonsense" racial ideology to "naturalize" the consolidation of economic and political power. This chapter draws on the work of Antonio Gramsci and Cheryl Harris. Gramsci posits that *education* and *the law,* are the respective dimensions of twin arms of the state, *civil society* and *political society*, which "exercise hegemony" in the dominant culture through *consent* and *force.* Cheryl Harris's critical analysis of the law posits that the social meanings constructed by and embodied in the law institutionalize racial and economic hierarchies of power and structures of domination in society. This chapter argues that legal mandates and protection by law are necessary, but not sufficient means to attain or insure equality in education, and that social justice efforts must be directed toward and challenge the societal structures and dominant ideologies that constitute the systemic roots of race–class hierarchy in the United States.

The first section of the chapter examines the gains and losses for African Americans, Native Americans, and Latinos in the wake of *Brown v. Board of Education* and related civil rights legislation. The next section, Foundations of Power: Land, Labor and Racial Ideology, provides a historical overview of legal mandates and education/religious conversion efforts from 16th-18th century that fostered racial subjugation and building *American* capitalism—the seizure of Native American and Mexican land, creation of a labor force based on African enslavement, and construction of an accompanying racial ideology embedded in the nation's Constitution. The third section, Sources of Power: U.S. Expansionism and Social Resistance, addresses the politics of westward expansion, including the annexation of Mexico, and growing resistance to slavery and racial oppression. Section Four, Consolidation of Power: The Ascendance of Industrial Capitalism, discusses the exercise of *force* and *consent* through war and other means that ended slavery and reinstated white supremacy, secured the conquest of Native Americans, and instituted a public education system consonant with industrial capitalism. The chapter concludes with a discussion of the implications that this legacy has for current social justice efforts in the context of neoliberal educational reform and anti-affirmative action legislation, and posits the liberatory possibilities of public education as a democratic right and as a source of opposition to social inequality.

I. *Brown vs. Board of Education*—Two Steps Forward, Two Steps Back and Counting

> The law masks as natural what is chosen; it obscures the consequences of social selection as inevitable. The result is that the distortions in social relations are immunized from truly effective intervention, because the existing inequities are obscured and rendered nearly invisible. The existing state of affairs is considered neutral and fair, however unequal and unjust it is in substance. (Harris, 1995, p. 287)

The Supreme Court 5-4 decision on June 28, 2007, set the clock back to the pre-*Brown vs. Board of Education* years of legalized segregated, unequal education. As Cheryl

Harris suggests in the above quote, the ruling denies the inherent structural inequalities in society, by mandating "color-blindness," thereby legitimating the pervasive resegregation of schools that was catalyzed by NCLB. This decision equates *discussions of race* with *promoting discrimination,* as captured in the statement by Chief Justice Roberts, one of the majority opponents of voluntary integration: "The way to stop discrimination on the basis of race is to stop discriminating on the basis of race" (*New York Times*, June 29, 2007, p. 1). Roberts's view undergirds the court ruling and the increasingly popular notion that racial equality has been attained and that the Civil Rights Act of 1964 ended racism and discrimination—at least for the few who are worthy. From this perspective, there is no need to redress social inequality through race-conscious measures such as integration, affirmative action, bilingual education, or to provide social support services for the poor and people of color. Nothing could be farther from the truth.

Legislation that grew out of the Civil Rights Movement did make a difference, temporarily. It came on the heels of World War II and the emergence of the United States as a strong capitalist nation advocating democracy, but the victory was short-lived (Anderson, 2004, 2007; Brown, 2005; Clofelter, 2004). On the one hand, the movement proffered significant changes in school desegregation, dropout/graduation rates, bilingual education, and college attendance by race between 1970 and 1991. African-American attendance at desegregated schools rose dramatically from 1% to 44% in the South, after the Civil Rights Act of 1964 enforced *Brown v. Board of Education* (Orfield, 2006, p. 13; Langemann, 1996). Bilingual education made considerable gains after the Bilingual Education Act of 1968 and *Lau v. Nichols* case in 1974 required affirmative action in accord with the 1964 Civil Rights Act (Darder, 1997; Ruiz, 1997). School dropout rates declined between 1972 and 1998, from: 30% to 20% for African Americans; 30% to 28% for Latinos and sharply increase to 40% in 1979; and Native Americans sustained the highest dropout rate at 36% in 1991 (Whites 17–11%) (Hauser, Simmons, & Pager, 2004; Reyhner & Eder, 2004). Affirmative action prompted a marked increase in the admittance and attendance of students of color at colleges and universities from the late 1960s to late 1970s, before the *Bakke* case. On the other hand, *Brown v. Board of Education* catalyzed massive closings of African-American schools and job loss for thousands of African-American teachers and principals in the South (Anderson, 2005; Russell & Hawley, 1983). Desegregation for Latinos was tepidly enforced, and their attendance at segregated schools increased from 42% to 80% in the West from 1969 to 2001. For Native-American students, there was little change in their segregated status on reservations and attendance at indigenous schools.

Within 10 years of the Civil Rights Act the legislative rollback had begun. The *Milliken v. Bradley* decisions I and II (1974, 1978) (Street, 2005; Orfield, 2004, 2005), disputed education as a constitutional right, blocked desegregation across city–suburban lines, and encouraged White flight. Assertions in the 1978 *Bakke* case of "reverse discrimination," "preferential treatment," and violation of the 14th Amendment initiated the dismantling of affirmative action, and by 1991, the *Oklahoma v. Dowell* case officially ended desegregation, allowing students to return to neighborhood schools. Hayakawa's proposal in 1984 and the English Language Empowerment Act in 1996 initiated successive legislative efforts to declare English the official language of the United States, while Propositions 227 (1998), 203 (2000), and 31 (2001) eliminated bilingual education in California, Arizona, and Colorado. These and other rulings began to corrode the compensatory antidiscrimination measures passed, and precipitated the return to pre-1970 levels of racial disparities in education—glaring resegregation of schools, shrinking bilingual education, and declining graduation and college attendance rate Macedo, 1997; Orfield, 2005).

The legislation had a profound impact on students of color in schools. By 2001, almost 50 years after *Brown*, African-American students attending multiracial schools fell precipitously from 44% to 30%, 65% of Black and Latino students were in Black and Latino schools, and 79% of White students were in White schools (Orfield & Lee, 2004, p. 16), and those in multiracial schools were: Whites, 12%; Asians, 42%; Latinos, 27%; African Americans, 23%; Native Americans, 20% (Orfield, 2006). Structured English immersion, the "sink-or-swim approach" mandated by NCLB, reduced enrollments in bilingual education from 29.1% to 5.5% in California between 1998 and 2007, and contributed to the increasing dropout rate across the country (Crawford, 2007; Gonzalez, 1997; Yzaquirre & Kamasaki, 1997). High school graduation rates in 2001 were: African American, 50.2%; Native American, 51.1%; Latino, 53.2%; Asian, 76.8%; White, 74.9%, with a 22% to 25% gap between Whites and students of color. Fewer male students of color graduated: African American (43%), Native American (47%), Latino (48%) (Orfield, 2004, p. 17). Many students drop out/are being pushed out by school exclusion policies and high stakes testing and discouraged by grade retention and the poor quality of education (Darling-Hammond, 2005, 2007; McNeil, 2000; Mishel & Roy, 2006). They end up in the military or school-to-prison pipeline, given the newly approved military recruitment of school dropouts, cash bonuses, and 600% increase in criminal justice spending versus 25% real dollar increase in public education spending (Alvarez, 2007; Darling-Hammond, 2005; Philpott, 2006; Silent Epidemic, 2007). College entrance for African-American students declined steadily throughout the mid-1980s and 1990s, due to drastic tuition increases and financial aid cuts (Dobbs, 2004; Moore, 2005; Orfield & Miller, 1998). This trend was exacerbated by the split Supreme Court decision in June 2003 on college admissions at the University of Michigan, which precipitated a 26% to 32% decline in African-American student admissions to public and private universities and colleges, while White student admissions from alumni families rose; for example, affirmative action at prestigious universities (Katznelson, 2005).

With the legislative rollback, *savage inequalities* in current school funding, quality of education, teacher preparation, and pedagogical and capital resources have persisted and are worsening (Darling-Hammond, 1998; Darling-Hammond & Berry, 1999; Street, 2005; Wise, 2005). Per pupil funding disparities rose 50% in select cities to a 2:1 ratio from 1989 to 2002; for example, $17,291:$8,482 (2002) in Chicago between wealthy White suburbs and poor urban areas with majority Black and Latino students (Kozol, 1991, 2005), and continue to be exacerbated by NCLB's charter schools, test score sanctions, and inadequate funding. College preparatory magnet schools in cities freed from consent decrees and federal desegregation mandates, have been placed disproportionately in White communities, thereby creating increasingly segregated schools (Allensworth & Rosenkrantz, 2000). The new, least educated teachers from abbreviated alternative certification programs tend to be sent to low income schools of color, teach outside of their area of expertise, and have the lowest retention rates after three years (Darling-Hammond & Berry, 1999). Despite these glaring disparities, Secretary of Education, Margaret Spellings's online videos and Fact Sheets, *How No Child Left Behind Benefits African Americans, Hispanic Americans, American Indians*, perpetuate the illusion that all is well. All is not well. As James Anderson states, in *A Tale of Two Browns*, the 1954 ruling constitutes "a heritage of constitutional equality and…[a] legacy of unequal public schooling…" (2005, p. 16).

These data are indicative of the quick reversion to legalized inequality, possible because *Brown v. Board of Education*, civil rights legislation, and other rulings did not/could not rectify or overhaul the foundational structures of inequality in society at large. Despite the hopeful promise of educational equality for people of color, these measures were subject to mercurial renunciation, when they were deemed no longer relevant, necessary, or desirable. They were not intended to upend the race–class hierarchy as a system of rule in this country, which was/is in place and maintained in education through segregated housing, property tax-based school funding, White flight, school choice, location of magnet schools, and an underlying commitment to racial inequality. Their benefits to the poor and people of color are often the *temporary* byproducts of measures that maintain basic structures of inequality. In addition, the strategic rollback of social policy and exacerbation of social inequality is grounded in a national history of legislative mandates and educational policies and practices that have been used by those in power to acquire land/natural resources, to maintain a labor force, and to accumulate capital, under the banners of "manifest destiny," "civilizing the heathens," or "democracy for all" (Takaki, 1993; Woodson, 2004; Zinn, 1980). Though this history is obscured and systematically denied by Roberts and other proponents of color-blind legislation in the name of equality, there are threads of continuity between the past and present uses of the law, education, and racial ideologies, which reveal shifting, often deceptive efforts to preserve inequality, *towards which our social justice efforts must be directed*. Persistent patterns emerge in 21st century forms of race and class oppression that are anchored in, or are reversions to, this country's early years of *conquest, accumulation, and consolidation of capital*. The following sections in this chapter provide a historical overview of the ways in which the subjugation of Native Americans, African Americans, and Latinos was aided and abetted by the passage of certain laws and provision or prohibition of education, and their exploitation was instrumental in acquiring the *land*, cultivating the *work force,* and promoting the lubricant of *racial ideology* to create and maintain the machinery of American capitalism.

Foundations of Power: Land, Labor, and Racial Ideology

Early Conquest: Stakes in Native American Land and Racialization

> The "normal" exercise of hegemony on the now classical terrain of the parliamentary regime is characterized by the combination of force and consent, which balance each other reciprocally, without force predominating excessively over consent. (Gramsci, 1971, p. 80)

The acquisition of land as a source of capital, the creation of a labor force, and the infusion of racial ideology characterized the beginnings of European colonial rule and established the roots of social and economic inequality in the Americas. Prior to 1492, the indigenous people of the Caribbean had free access to their land, and had established communal ways of life, education, religion, and systems of social law that sustained and promoted their survival. Columbus' arrival from Spain, bearing disease and visions of colonization, disrupted the Arawak economic, political, and cultural life, marking the advent of the genocidal plunder, enslavement, and conquest of Native Americans' land, lives, and labor in the Western Hemisphere. In 1521, the Spaniards colonized indigenous people in Mexico and imported African slaves in 1527 to work the cocoa plantations and silver mines, and build the colony they ruled for 300 years (Churchill, 1997; Menchaca, 2001). Though free Afro-Phoenician navigators reached the Atlantic coast of North America prior to Europeans in about 750 BC, Spaniards were the first Europeans to bring Africans as slaves in 1526 to South Carolina to supplement the forced labor of enslaved Native Americans (Loewen, 1995; Van Sertima, 1976). African slaves revolted along with the indigenous population, forcing the Spanish to abandon their settlement efforts, until they wrested St. Augustine, Florida from the Native Americans and French Protestants in 1565, and extended their mission to the Southwest into present-day New Mexico in 1598. The Spaniards initiated European colonization in the "New World," using instruments of rule that would endure long after their departure.

The racialized acculturation and religious conversion of the Native American and Mexican peoples to Catholicism were central to Spanish colonization (Churchill, 1997; Menchaca, 2001; Reyhner & Eder, 2004; Samora & Simon, 2007; Spring, 1994). Education and the law became pivotal tools of consent and force in this process. The Law of Burgos (1512) legislated the Hispanicization of indigenous peoples in Mexico, requiring owners of over 50 enslaved Indians on encomiendas, their land grants from the king, to provide for the "salvation of Indian souls and conservation of their lives" (quoted in Reyhner & Eder, 2004). Toward this end, schools and missions were established by Jesuits and other Catholic orders, under various forms of "ecclesiastical slave" conditions for the indigenous people. Complementarily, the colonists instituted a rigid and elaborate hierarchical *caste system* of "race"—class assignation from Spaniards to mixed Africans—Peninsulares/Criollas, Mestizos, Indians, Afromestizos, and in 1575 added anti-miscegenation laws. Grounded in an emergent system of social and economic privilege, Mexicans, Africans, and Indians became a source of free labor in agriculture, deemed "necessary resources" for the colonists' survival. The incipient racialization of the conquered laborers by the Spaniards presaged that of the English colonists who arrived a century later. The English would ultimately triumph over the French, Spanish, and Portuguese in their ruthless seizure of land from the indigenous peoples in Mexico and North America, and would give new meanings to physical differences, that is, race, that became foundational in the "permanence" of their acquisition of land and labor.

The foundation for the American capitalist labor system began to take shape in the 17th century, after Protestant missionaries established the first permanent English colonies in Jamestown, Virginia (1607) and Plymouth, Massachusetts (1620). Acquiring land through relationships with the indigenous peoples was the priority, and as James Loewen (1995) suggests, *syncretism* and *cultural imperialism* framed the hierarchical relations that emerged between the colonists and Native Americans. Initially, White colonists coexisted, traded, and intermingled with indigenous people, dependent on their guidance in adjusting to the new land. Once acclimated, the colonists pursued their aggressive plan of land acquisition, and gained military and cultural ascendance over the indigenous people. Within two years, the first Anglo-Powhatan War's (1609–1613) steady encroachment precipitated a successful counteroffensive by the Wahunsonacock Nation. The second Anglo-Powhatan War resulted in the forced submission of the Wahunsonacock Nation to colonists' rule. Anticipating Native-American resistance to "foreign" invasion, from earlier failed colonial efforts, the English used open combat and covert operations as means of conquest; for example, firearms, destruction of farms, incineration of cornfields, slaughter of whole villages, starvation, marauding pillage, torture, leveling of towns, and diseased "trade blankets," poison, deception, and duplicitous treaties. The press for and resistance to land acquisition continued in a new form. The New England Confederation (1643) united northeastern colonies against "Indian attacks" by using *education and religious conversion* as alternative strategies of conquest.

By the mid-1600s, colonists were establishing schools in Protestant "Praying Towns" to isolate, contain, educate, and "civilize" the Indians apart from the "pagan others"; that is, to "change their whole Habit of thinking and acting...raise them...into...civil industrious and polish'd People...[instill] Vertue and Piety...and introduce the English Language among them instead of their own imperfect and barbarous Dialect" (quoted from Reyhner & Eder, 2004, p. 29), as part of their continuing aggressive campaign of conquest. Amidst profound resistance to forced conversion efforts, the colonists threatened annually to execute Native Americans who failed to comply and demonized long hair and other Native-American cultural norms (Spring, 1994). Conversion efforts included the establishment of Harvard's Indian College (1636), which provided printings of the Bible in Algonquian language, and William and Mary College (1693) (Reyhner & Eder, 2004). Colonists' efforts to pacify and indoctrinate indigenous people through education and religious conversion accompanied the continuous wars over the land, despite the opposition of Quakers and others to the colonists' pillage. Armed with entitlement and belief that "God was on their side," the seeds of "Manifest Destiny" and White supremacy were being sewn as the colonists sought to dispossess and systematically dislocate Native Americans, that is, to "...destroy them...[and] enjoy their cultivated places... [to] be inhabited by us" (quote in W. Churchill, 1997, p. 147). Savage wars, religious conversion, and deceptive treaties were resisted, as for example, the annihilation of the Pequot Nation and its dissolution in the 1636 Treaty of Hartford prompted the retaliatory destruction of the "praying towns" by the Narragansett and Wampanoag Nations in the 1676 "King Philip's War" (Loewen, 1995; Reyhner & Eder, 2004). While the 17th century was characterized by colonists' engagement in military and ideological warfare, that is, education and religion, against Native Americans to set stakes upon their land, it was also characterized by their efforts to secure a labor force.

Slavery: Free Labor, the Law, and White Supremacy

It was the interaction between conceptions of race and property which played a critical role in establishing and maintaining racial and economic subordination.... Through slavery, race and economic domination were fused.... Slavery produced a peculiar, mixed category of property and humanity—a hybrid with inherent instabilities that were reflected in its treatment and ratification by the law. (Harris, 1995, pp. 277–278)

Initially, the colonists used the "unending supply" of enslaved Native Americans and the influx of European indentured servants in 1616 to produce the labor-intensive and lucrative cash crop, tobacco. The European laborers were impoverished, unemployed workers and former convicts, who became the bonded property of the master/employer in payment for their transatlantic voyage, food, clothing, and shelter. Initially, these English, German, and Scottish servants worked alongside of Native American and African slaves, and indentured servants, experienced branding, public flogging, and other cruel punishments, and revolted together against the punitive and harsh working and living conditions of the four to seven plus years of bonded labor (Article, 1640). If they survived, the servants, some of whom were apprenticed, were "free" to build a life in the colony after indenture. Native Americans, otherwise healthy, had no immunities to European-borne disease, and were decimated by both the onslaught of smallpox and other European epidemics from livestock and from the effects of forced labor (Loewen, 1995). Though the press for labor created an immigrant population comprised of 80% to 85/90% White indentures, the short-term status and declining life expectancy of Native Americans and European servants was not cost effective. Africans were imported to sustain the labor supply. Increasingly, Black slaves were replacing White indentured servants, with numbers increasing from 150 to 3,000 slaves from 1640 to 1680, as those for Whites decreased. Gradually, distinctions were made between European and African indentured servants, on the basis of religion. Though conversion to Christianity was an explicit goal of and justification for English colonization, the initial religious discrimination of non-Christian

African servants, was gradually supplanted by discrimination on the basis of "racial" or physical differences, resulting in the extension of servitude, differential punishments, and the forced conversion of Africans from temporary servant to lifelong slave. The permanent enslavement of Africans was passed on to or inherited by their children, providing an unending, far more productive and profitable source of labor.

It also became clear to Southern landowners that the creation of a material and psychological wedge between White and Black laborers would establish a hierarchy pivotal to the maintenance of slavery as a source of wealth. White servants outnumbered Black slaves by more than five to one in 1668, and joined forces with them in their opposition to landowners' exploitation in the Bacon Rebellion of 1676. This show of class unity between Black and White laborers and the threat of further uprisings hastened the transition to slavery and contributed to the drastic inversion in Black slave–White indentured servant ratio of five to one by 1700. As the transatlantic slave trade rose, European immigration levels declined until their rise again in the late 18th and 19th centuries. Since African slaves were geographically isolated from their homeland, estranged from Europeans by language, easily distinguished physically, and highly productive laborers—they were a profitable human investment, rivaled only by the dividends from the transatlantic slave trade itself. The slave trade created burgeoning lucrative business in the regional economies of the North, such as the shipping industry, raw material production, foreign rum trade, artisans' and craftsmen's work, textile industries, emergent insurance companies, and legal and bookkeeping enterprises, which were as essential to the profits of slavery as the daily exploitation of the free labor of Africans (Murphy, 2005).

With the securing of land and labor well underway, the passage of laws was an indispensable instrument for the institution of a racialized hierarchy amidst the laboring masses/classes. Those laws were the Slave Codes passed from 1660 to 1705, which gradually codified racialized distinctions between servitude and slavery (Franklin, 1994; Higginbotham, 1978). These legal mandates institutionalized the subjugated status of slaves, through harsh controls; for example, slave passes curtailed movement, the forbiddance of groups of four slaves curtailed freedom to congregate, prohibition of slave testimonies in court or right to trade rescinded civilian status and economic independence. In 1661, Virginia recognized slavery with the passage of a fugitive slave law and a year later, mandated distinctions between slaves and indentured servants, based on length of servitude and children's heritability of slavery vs. freedom. By 1670, laws across various states ruled that Christian conversion did not alter one's slave status, that slaves were subject to corporal punishment and unprotected by law, and that free Blacks and Native Americans could not own Christians, that is, White indentured servants or enter free Whites' homes "unaccompanied." Slave owners fear of and retribution for slave resistance and revolts prompted the anti-insurrection laws of 1680 and 1682, which prohibited slaves from bearing arms or traveling without a certificate or owner (1687) and stipulated the requisite punishment. In 1691, antirunaway laws were enacted with the creation of "informal" slave patrols of poor slaveless Whites and others, which targeted "Negroes, mulattoes, and other slaves," and initiated the use of race in the law. Also, interracial marriages were banned, sanctions were levied against White women with mixed-race children, Black women's mixed race children were relegated to slavery, and strict conditions were established for the manumission of slaves. Decisive, however, were the Slave Codes of 1705 passed by the Virginia General Assembly, which institutionalized slavery and sealed the status and classification of Africans as property and Whites as human:

> All servants imported and brought into the country...who were not Christians in their native country...shall be accounted and be slaves. All Negro, mulatto and

Indian slaves within this domain...shall be held to be real estate. If any slave resist his master... correcting such slave, and shall happen to be killed in such correction... the master shall be free of all punishment...as if such accident never happened. (Hening, 1809, p. 447)

Thus, at the advent of the 18th century, chattel slavery was instantiated by law and woven into the social and economic fabric of the colonies—reifying the commonsense notion of the inferiority of African slaves. The harshness and subhuman atrocities of enslavement are well documented; that is, subhuman living conditions, whipping, branding, torturous work, rupture of families, slave auctions, slave breeding, the rape of African women. Africans tried to run away in search of their families, despite the consequences, and as chattel, they were treated as thieves who had stolen their master's property. Slavery in the North was no less brutal or morally depraved, but neither climate nor economic conditions allowed for the development of large-scale agrarian plantations, and the Puritans in Massachusetts had a somewhat mollifying effect on its expansion. The slave resistance, such as work stoppage, property damage, assault, escape, and slave rebellions persisted as a continual threat (intense circle of violence) and an increasing reality for slave owners and northern colonists (e.g., the Revolt in Virginia in 1663, New York Revolt of 1712) (Aptheker, 1983; Doak, 2006). As stated by John Hope Franklin, "Perhaps the greatest impact runaways had on the peculiar institution, was in their defiance of the system. Masters and slaves knew that there were blacks who were willing to do almost anything to extricate themselves from bondage" (Franklin & Schweninger, 2000, p. 293). The slave owners responded with increased repression, violence, and the formation of paid slave patrols from 1704 to 1754. The Stono Rebellion of 1739 in South Carolina prompted the decisive passage of the Comprehensive Slave Act in 1740, which forbade slaves to learn to read or learn English and mandated penalties for violators of the law.

The Comprehensive Slave Act was the first in a series of comparable state laws (until 1819) that was decisive in structuring slavery by forbidding the education of Africans. The denial of education to slaves in the South was considered a deterrent to slaves' "uppity ideas about freedom and equality" that would incite slave revolts (e.g., Gabriel Prosser in 1800, Denmark Vesey in 1820), and it amplified the social distance between former indentured servants, who were now split into free White laborers and chattel slaves of White landowners. In addition, Christianity was viewed as a means to increase the morality, reduce the resistance, and gain better control of those in slavery. Thus, "education without letters," listening to but not reading the Bible, was embraced by slave owners to inculcate religion without literacy. Despite the laws and sanctions, African slaves clandestinely educated themselves, were educated by free Blacks and Whites and by some landowners who wanted to enhance work efficiency. Religion was also used by enslaved Africans as a source of personal refuge and social resistance to slavery.

While the provision of education was initially deemed the civilizing handmaiden of Native American conquest, it was denied to African Americans to create a schism between poor Blacks, Whites, and Native Americans, who had already risen up against a common oppressor, and to forestall the insurrectionary yearnings of Africans for freedom. This bifurcation would settle into a racialized hierarchy, moored by material and ideological White-skinned privilege, which would bolster the economic and political power/ hegemony of the slave owning oligarchy and the imminent industrial capital. As such, the Black Codes and other mandates restricting the education of African slaves created fertile ground for the entrenchment of slavery, marked by the invention of the cotton gin in 1793. The cotton gin rapidly increased cotton production by 50-fold for export, increased the demand for and price of slaves, intensified the slave trade and related textile and shipping industries, and was accompanied by the introduction of the first federal Fugitive Slave Law and insurance on slaves to protect Northern and Southern financial investments. The cotton gin further entrenched the institution of slavery and the degradation of African Americans, as their families were ripped asunder with the dissemination of "surplus" slave men and women to neighboring states, leaving their children behind. While the free labor of slaves was instituted as a prime source of profit for the North and South, and as the foundation for a racially stratified working class, the quest for land as a source of capital continued. Both land and labor were fundamental to the private accumulation of wealth and the development of the propertied versus the laboring class.

A New Democracy: Constitution and Legal Foundations for Inequality

> The assumption of American law as it related to Native Americans was that conquest did give rise to sovereignty. Indians experienced the property laws of the colonizers and the emergent American nation as acts of violence perpetuated by the exercise of power and ratified through the rule of law. At the same time, these laws were perceived as custom and "common sense" by the colonizers. (Harris, 1995, p. 280)

> The dual and contradictory character of slaves as property and persons was exemplified in the Representation Clause of the Constitution. (Harris, 1995, p. 278)

Throughout the late 17th and 18th centuries, the struggle over possession of the land intensified and expanded for Native Americans, as the institution of slavery settled in as a way of life. Native American tribes and nations often joined forces to resist English and other European encroachments on their land; for example, the Peach Tree War in New York (1655), Esopus War against the Dutch in New Jersey (1663), Yamasee War in South Carolina (1715), Dummer's War in Vermont (1723–1727), despite English colonists' passage and renewal of the Scalp Act (1722, 1747–1880), which made bounty hunting a lucrative business (Churchill, 1997). Intermittently, they allied with the French and English during the four Intercolonial or "French and Indian Wars" between 1689 and 1763 (Churchill, 1997), which culminated in the English colonists ousting the French. Native Americans retaliated in the Pontiac's Rebellion (1763–1766) against English colonists' unbridled rule after their defeat of the French, which was a successful campaign until they received blankets infected with smallpox. War expense and England's focus on seaboard mercantilism prompted the Royal Proclamation (1763), forbidding colonists to settle west of the Appalachian Mountains or to purchase land independent of the Crown. It incurred the vengeful slaughter of Native Americans by the "Paxton Boys" and colonists who had already taken land out west, and the revolt against England in the ensuing Revolutionary War (Reyhner & Eder, 2004).

The War of Independence in 1776 temporarily shifted the colonists' attention from appropriating land from the indigenous people to defeating England, and induced the cry for freedom, equality, and inalienable rights. Toward this end, the colonists solicited support from Native Americans and African slaves to fight the English, but received disparate responses from them, given the history of mistreatment and broken agreements they had experienced at the hands of the colonists. Though many Native Americans eschewed participation in yet another European conflict, the promise of manumission and the opportunity to weaken the enslavers drew some to fight for the British. Though some African slaves and indigenous people fought for the colonists, voluntarily and by force, their lot after the war worsened and their resistance heightened. The final campaign to extinguish Native Americans was launched with increased fervor, and the grip of chattel slavery intensified with the cotton gin's invention 17 years later in 1792. However, this occurred amidst the new national discourse of "democracy for all" which emerged after the colonies' independence from England.

The Constitution of 1787 embodied the rhetorical call for democracy, ironically, drawn from Native Americans' democratic principles of governance, as a basis for the formation of the nation. In the context of slavery, as a national institution and investment, the Constitution's single reference to equality was intended for White men and for the equal representation of all states in the legislature (Anderson, 2005, 2006). However, the letter of the law established to govern the United States, "equality for all," converged with the genuine democratic strivings of the free and the enslaved, and incurred a dramatic increase in runaway slaves, the economic- and morality-induced stirrings of abolitionism, and Mum Bett's successful lawsuit for freedom from slavery in New York in 1781. In addition, the Constitution's "Three-Fifths Clause" reduced each African-American slave to the equivalent of "3/5 of a man," which served the propertied interests of the Southern slave owners, limited the power of the Southern vote in Congress and increased its taxes, and along with the Fugitive Slave Clause, instantiated the notion of African Americans as property and as less than human in social life and in the American psyche. In 1788, a Fugitive Slave Clause was added to the Constitution. The incongruity within the Constitution and national ambivalence, about whether equality should be for all or for some, were also manifested by seven Northern states that officially ended slavery—*by law*—from 1777 to 1804, but took a quarter to a half century to end slavery *in practice*. Concerns about "assimilating" former slaves into society, fear of a massive influx of African American fugitive slaves from the South, resentments against African Americans "taking" the jobs of poor White laborers, and an ingrained commitment to maintain a segregated Black population not only deterred the actual end of Northern slavery, but incurred Northern violence against African Americans and the passage of numerous laws to exclude these free men and women from economic, political, and social spheres of life in the newly-formed U.S. These racial concerns extended to limitations placed on immigrants, with the passage of the Naturalization Act of 1790, which reserved the right of U.S. citizenship to "free White persons" of "good moral character." The hierarchical relations that were being forged amongst White colonists, Native Americans, and African Americans, and eventually Mexican Americans along class lines were being codified in the first laws of this new nation.

Independent of England and with Constitution in hand, the former colonists were unfettered by British rule, free to pursue the further conquest of the Native American land and people. However, the toll that the War exacted on the colonies led the U.S. government to pursue less taxing, nonmilitary strategies of coercion and isolation to extract more land from the indigenous people. This took the form of an *acculturation–acquisition plan* for the peaceful negotiation of land through treaties and civilization/ education programs. "Binding" treaties, laws, and other strategies became essential tools to secure previous gains made and to establish policy that would facilitate the procurement of new land, without the expense of war (Avalon Project, 2007). From 1778 to 1889, over 400 treaties were signed with the Native Americans, constituting "diplomatic" efforts to coexist, take the land, and confine the indigenous people to reservations. Treaties were often used as "gradual steps" in the land acquisition process, from the designation of "Indian land," to confinement on reservations, to outright appropriation or encroachment. Treaties often deceptively turned the land over to the "settlers," or more often, the agreements establishing terms of exchange or protection for Native Americans' rights were disregarded, ignored, or broken by the government. A case in point is the Northwest

Ordinance (1787), which illegally created slave-free territory from Native American land "won from England," eventually becoming Ohio, Indiana, Illinois, Michigan, Wisconsin, and Minnesota. The Ordinance promised Native Americans "good faith" in honoring their "property, rights, and liberty," one of many promises broken with indifference. In peace talks, the Shawnee rejected the U.S. definition of them as "a conquered people" allied with the British and their offers of payment for the land. They formed a confederation to stop the acquisition of ceded lands and U.S. military advancement, waging devastating battles against the army. With a vengeance, the army retaliated and won at Fallen Timbers, followed by the signing of the Greenville Treaty in 1795, which ceded the land. Though Native Americans resisted at every turn, often refusing the ultimate compromise of land-for-education exchanges proposed in the treaties, duplicitous agreements ceded almost a billion acres of their land to the United States in exchange for education and other "goods" (Spring, 1994).

During this postwar period, education and other persuasive strategies were central to the U.S. *acculturation–acquisition plan*. The government established "trading houses," or "factories," as convenient places for Native Americans to sell their land for cash from White settlers. Through this factory system, they hoped to lure the indigenous people to the marvels of money and consumption of goods, to inculcate their desire for wealth accumulation, and to persuade them to value the "superiority" of private property, over their customary practice of sharing resources. In addition, government agents were sent as emissaries to "Indian land" to set up schools for Native Americans to educate and convince them to abandon their hunting practices for husbandry, agriculture, and "domesticity." Their goal was to reduce indigenous people's "need" for hunting land, so that Whites could take over the huge tracts of "unused territory." The government's plan to convert Native Americans to European Americans' economic, political, and social ways of life in order to take their land with the least resistance, was no "easy sell" (Spring, 1994). Native Americans valued their own way of life and disdained the "White man's" destructive ways of being. Their distrust of White Americans had been well earned over the past 200 years, having experienced settlers' intentions rarely matching the implementation of their avowed plans or treaties. A classic example is that of Rev. Samson Occom, a Native American Christian convert, who raised funds in England for Indian education. The money was used by missionaries to found Dartmouth College in 1769, which since its inception has served primarily White students, as have many schools set up for Native Americans; for example, Harvard College and William and Mary College (Reyhner & Eder, 2004; Spring, 1994).

U.S. "Indian" policy in the late 18th century, consisting of treaties, trading houses, and strategies of persuasive education, backed by war, was framed by a U.S. Constitution that espoused democracy in the nation, but institutionalized inequality by law. This provided the context for the government's dismissive negotiations with Native Americans and seizure of their land. Though the Constitution's 3/5 Clause explicitly "excluded Indians," it set the precedent for relegating a people to subhuman status, justifying their mistreatment, and positioning them "outside of the law of moral obligation." The government's temporary shift to diplomacy after the War of Independence did not belie its intractable, unrelenting campaign to acquire land, to decimate the indigenous people, and to accumulate capital. By 1800, the population of over five million Native Americans was reduced by 95% to 600,000 (Churchill, 2004) and encroachment on their land progressed. Important inventions in the 18th century catalyzed the production of goods, including the move from water to steam power (1780s), cotton industry-spinning in textile mills (1783), iron smelting replacing coal, potting and stamping (1786), and steam power locomotive (1804). The decimation of the Native Americans, the massive profits accrued from slavery, and the emergent mechanization paved the way for eventual emergence of large scale industrial production.

Sources of Power: U.S. Expansionism and Social Resistance

The Politics of Westward Expansion: Education and the Law

> ...Educative pressure [is] applied to single individuals so as to obtain their consent and their collaboration, turning necessity and coercion into "freedom"...Classified as "legally neutral",...civil society...operates without "sanctions" or compulsory "obligations", but...exerts a collective pressure and obtains objective results in the form of an evolution of customs, ways of thinking and acting, morality, etc.... The Law is the repressive and negative aspect of the entire positive, civilizing activity undertaken by the State.... (Gramsci, 1971, pp. 242, 247)

> The inherent contradiction between the bondage of blacks and republican rhetoric that championed the freedom of "all" men was resolved by positing that blacks were different. (Harris, 1995 p. 286)

> Because the law recognized and protected expectations grounded in white privilege... the dominant and subordinate positions within the racial hierarchy were reified in law...Whiteness as racialized privilege was then legitimated by science and was embraced in legal doctrine as "objective fact." (Harris, 1995, pp. 281, 283)

The first half of the 19th century was marked by important social and political developments toward consolidating land, labor, and racial ideology—the building blocks for an emergent U.S. industrial capitalist democracy. They included: (1) an acculturation–acquisition process embodied in the passage of the Civilization Fund Act (1819), the Indian Removal Acts (1830) following the Gold Rush, and federal compromises on slavery (1820–1850); (2) the emergence of scientific racism and mounting resistance to conquest and slavery by Native Americans, African Americans, and White abolitionists (1829–1853); and (3) Mexico's independence from Spain, the Mexican-American War, and culminating Treaty of Guadalupe Hidalgo (1821–1848). Education and the law played a key role in forging U.S. expansionism in the North American continent and creating a workforce free to sell its labor.

Armed with the taste of freedom, the entitlement of "Manifest Destiny," and unquenchable thirst for wealth and power, the government spurred new laws and it was federal policy to "civilize" the remaining Native Americans through education, clear them from desired land, and enact their removal to the west. Education was deemed an important palliative for the Native Americans and a primary source of the ideological indoctrination needed to secure the U.S. government's land "investments" and the position of Native Americans within the nation's social hierarchy. The Civilization Fund Act (1819) provided financial support for religious groups and others to educate Native Americans, convince them of the benevolence and wisdom of U.S. government policy, teach English to them, and convert them to Christianity. As declared by a House Committee, "In the present state of our country, one of two things seems to be necessary: either that these sons of the forest should be moralized or exterminated" (from Reyhner & Eder, 2004). Since the "Indian problem" was an official priority for the U.S. government, the Office of Indian Affairs was created in 1824 and was placed within the War Department to manage war, schools, and trade, and to oversee treaties and funding for Native Americans

(Churchill, 2002; Travel and History, 2007, www.u-shistory.com/pages/h3577.html). Its strategic placement in the War Department positioned Native Americans as potential "enemies of the state," upon whom war or requisite military action could be unleashed at any time.

The 1928 Georgia Gold Rush heightened the drive for the accumulation of land and wealth, and catalyzed The Indian Removal Act (1830). President Jackson's view was, "Build a fire under them. When it gets hot enough, they'll move" (quoted in Heidler & Heidler, 2007). This decisive Act mandated the forced relocation of the Cherokee Nation from the state of Georgia to west of the Mississippi River, and guards were placed at the gold mines for protection from the inhabitants of the land. This dispossession–relocation process was further supported in the final version of the Indian Trade and Intercourse Act (1790, 1802, 1834), which identified "Indian land" and restricted trade with and travel by Native Americans on this land, and terminated federal support for mission education east of the Mississippi. The government appointed leaders for land negotiations, who "voluntarily ceded" territory, and effectively reduced Native Americans to protectorates without rights. As stated in the Supreme Court ruling of 1831, the indigenous people are "dependent nations...in a state of pupilage...resembl[ing]...a ward to his guardian" (Reyhner & Eder, 2004; Spring, 1994). In response, Native Americans fought numerous battles to protect their homes, amidst the invaders' incessant decimating ravage of communities, corn, hunting grounds, and lives (Churchill, 1997). They resisted valiantly in the Black Hawk Wars of 1832 and in the Seminole Wars (1832, 1835–1842), where Black Seminoles and African slaves joined on the heels of their largest slave rebellion in the United States (1835–1838) (Aptheker, 1983; Bird 2005). The onslaught of the militia caused some Native Americans to accept small tracts of land in exchange for millions of ceded acres, while other Africans and Seminoles emigrated to slave-free Mexico. The tragic removal process began with deceptive, violated treaties between President Jackson and the Cherokee Nation, and culminated with the stockade housing of 18,000 Cherokees and their deadly "Long Walk" under the force of 7,000 military troops on the "Trail of Tears" in 1838, and their forced dislocation from Georgia to Oklahoma.

After the Removal, Cherokees established a national school system in the 1840s with funds from ceded land, as did Cheeks and Choctaws with eastern missionaries. However, many rejected Christianity, governmental indoctrination, and the promotion of White supremacy by school officials, because they sought education and literacy for their own survival and well-being (Reyhner & Eder, 2004; Spring, 1994). Their relative peace was short-lived as expansionist settlers sought new territory, as seekers of gold in the Rushes of 1848 and 1859 pursued wealth, as a burgeoning new wave of European immigrants sought land in the 1820s, and as the Irish fled poverty and death from the English-induced Potato Famine (1846–1850). In 1849, the Office of Indian Affairs was renamed the Bureau of Indian Affairs with its transfer from the War Department to the Department of the Interior, signaling the shift in policy to "civilize" the Indians through the reservation system. The Fort Laramie Treaties of 1851/1868 promised Native Americans exclusive rights to the Great Plains and Black Hills (Sioux, Blackfoot, Assinaboin, Crow Nations, and the Gros Ventre, Cheyennes, and Arapahoes), provided "mission" education for the children, sought "peace" between Whites and indigenous people, exchanged prospectors' safe road passage to gold mines and the West in exchange for 50-year annuities and reparations. What ensued, however, were brutal attacks by the flood of Whites to this territory and land gained in the illegal Louisiana Purchase (1803) from the French.

As the influx of White settlers grew in the western territories and new states were being formed, the issue of slavery came to the fore. By 1804, though slavery was officially abolished in seven Northern states, and the slave trade to the United States was ended in

1808, slavery and the slave trade continued in the South. North and South were monitoring the number of slave versus free states admitted to the union, to maintain a relative regional balance of power in Congress. Thus, three compromises and a court decision were reached, not on the basis of the morality of slavery, but in the interest of equalizing/gaining state representation and "preserving the Union." The Missouri Compromise (1820) admitted Maine as a free state and slavery was illegal in the Louisiana territory, except for Missouri. In the Compromise of 1850, California was admitted as a free state, while Utah and New Mexico could determine their status. The Dred Scott Decision of 1854 denied citizenship and the right to sue to Blacks, and reversed the restrictions on slave territories in the Missouri Compromise. These rulings were indicative of mounting economic and political tensions between the North and South over slavery.

Scientific Racism and Social Resistance

Growing resistance to slavery and rising tensions over the morality of slavery had begun to surface in the late 1820s. The seeds of scientific racism were sewn in fertile ground to justify slavery. The early theories of Carolus Linnaeus, a botanical taxonomist, classified and hypothesized the differing mental, moral, and physical capabilities of "the races," Black, White, Yellow, and Red people in 1763. Edward Long also created a simple classification of race in 1774, and his monogenism thesis attributed all mankind to the same origin, while others believed in polygenism, positing that the "races" had different origins. Finally, Arthur de Gobineau, from France published his famous work, *The Inequality of Human Races,* in 1853, hierarchically ranking the "races" and advocating the maintenance of racial integrity/purity and preservation of the social order. These theories of racial inferiority-superiority reaffirmed the subhuman treatment of Africans and Native Americans and justified racial discrimination. They bolstered craniometry and other efforts to document the existence of and inherent differences between "races." Scientific racism reinforced the American Colonization Society's (1817) belief in the providential inferiority of Africans, underlying the formation of Liberia (1822) and their efforts to assist African-American emigration to Africa. As an ideological weapon, scientific racism laid the foundation for the eugenics movement and undergirded the institutionalization of racism as a cornerstone of American industrial capitalism. While it strove to naturalize racial inequality, it also fueled heightened resistance and revolts against slavery.

Resistance to slavery was manifest in the mid-1800s with a marked rise in slave rebellions, runaways, and full-scale collaborative revolts between African Americans and Native Americans (Aptheker, 1983; Doak, 2006; Franklin & Schweninger, 2000). David Walker, a free Black man, led the resistance with his famous *Appeal,* published in 1829. He called for the armed rebellion of slaves against their slave owners, arguing that, "America is more our country than it is the Whites—we have enriched it with our *blood and tears...* will they drive us from our property and homes, which we have earned with our *blood?*" He spoke to Whites' fear, not only of educating Blacks, noting: "The Whites... know that they have done us so much injury, they are afraid that we, being men, and not brutes, will retaliate, and woe will be to them" (1829). Two years later, in 1831, Nat Turner, a slave, led 40 other slaves in a highly organized revolt in Southampton, Virginia, killing over 50 slave owners. As a result, slave codes were severely tightened, and the abolitionist movement took off. Henry Highland Garnet, a prominent ex-slave, escaped slavery with his family, eventually attended Oneida Theological Institute, and delivered the famous, "A Call to Rebellion" in 1843. He was known for his rousing oration, staunch political activism, and radical organizing, juxtaposed against William Lloyd Garrison, the leading White abolitionist who formed the Anti-Slavery Society in 1831, was editor of the

Liberator, and favored moral suasion. Abolitionists became more visible in their advocacy and effected the rescue of runaway slaves by means of courtroom trials.

In the spirit of the slave uprisings of Gabriel Prosser and Denmark Vesey, slave rebellions spread throughout the South. In the Seminole Slave Rebellion of 1835 to 1838 in Florida, John Horse led hundreds of slaves in their flight from the plantations to the Seminoles, their allies against the colonists in 1776. After the Seminoles and African slaves swiftly destroyed 21 of the most developed plantations, some plantations surrendered and some slaves moved west to freedom. This was the largest, most prolonged, and successful slave revolt—typically left out of historical accounts. Two outstanding revolts also occurred on slave ships. In 1839, slaves on the Spanish slave trader ship *Amistad* mutinied under the leadership of Cinque. The ship was steered to the United States where the slaves were tried, rigorously supported by abolitionists, and granted freedom by the U.S. Supreme Court in 1841. After the *Amistad* mutiny, slaves aboard the *Creole,* en route from Hampton, Virginia to New Orleans, Louisiana, took over the ship and sailed to freedom in the Bahamas. The mounting thirst for freedom was embodied in the voice of Sojourner Truth, an avid Black female abolitionist, who suffered unspeakable cruelty as a domestic slave in New York. She escaped slavery with one of her children, was eventually "called by the Spirit" to fight, began to lecture around the country in 1842, and sought free land from the government for former slaves out west. She is known for her rousing speech, "Ain't I a Woman," delivered at the Ohio Women's Rights Convention in 1851. Harriet Tubman, renowned ex-slave, and courageous "conductor" of the Underground Railroad, freed her family in 1850 and escorted hundreds of slaves to the North and Canada until slavery ended. Supported by many White abolitionists with "stops on the line," she was close to John Brown, who led the famous attack on Harpers Ferry in 1859. However, scientific racism and resistance to slavery fueled a backlash: the Dred Scott decision (1857) reified that Blacks, as property, could not be citizens or sue in court and rescinded the Missouri Compromise restrictions on slave territories; the harsh retrenchment and expansion of the slave codes occurred; and a wave of White violence was unleashed in cities; for example, the police-sanctioned burning and terrorizing rampage of Black neighborhoods in Philadelphia in 1838. The fight for freedom continued until the abolition of slavery in 1865.

The Annexation of Mexico and Racialized Displacement

These strivings for freedom in the United States were paralleled by Mexico's independence from Spain in 1821. The Mexican provisional government immediately dismantled Spain's racial order, gradually closed the missions, and established economic policies to address the 300-year impact of the *casta* system. The *Plana de Iguala* was instituted making it illegal to bar Indians, Mestizos and free Afromestizos from the citizenship rights enjoyed by Whites. Acculturation through education, religion, and language exchanges became strategies employed to "win" over the subjugated populations. Though ostensibly, Mexico was moving towards slave-free status, the enslavement of indigenous people—Mayans/Pueblo Indians/Native Americans—still existed. In 1824, the new Constitution prohibited the slave trade and declared free any enslaved U.S. émigrés to Mexico (Menchaca, 2001), and The General Law of Colonization reorganized the land to rectify the *casta* system's positioning of Native Americans.

However, shortly after independence, the Mexican government sought help in "managing" the resistance of the non-Christian Native Americans, by liberalizing the immigration policies and welcoming a flood of European American settlers. These settlers became the real beneficiaries of land reorganization, and though illegal, brought slaves to the present-day Southwest in Texas. When Mexico's President Vicente Guerrero issued the Emancipation Proclamation, declaring all former slaves free Mexican citizens, the settlers rebelled. Having grown to a majority in Texas, they ignored the Proclamation, demanded as much land as Mexican citizens, and eventually began separatist movements. The settlers waged war against Mexico, seceded Texas in 1836, and sought annexation to the United States in 1837. Following deliberations about slavery in Texas and potential war with Mexico, the United States annexed Texas as a slave state in 1845. Disputes that emerged between Mexico and the United States over Texas' boundaries, led to the Mexican-American War of 1846. The War ended with a U.S. victory and the Treaty of Guadalupe Hidalgo in 1848, promising to protect the rights of the conquered population. The ensuing Gadsen Treaty's (1854) land purchase shifted the U.S. boundaries south, providing ample land for the eventual building of the transcontinental railroad in the mid-1860s, and significantly reduced the U.S. debt to Mexico, undermining Mexico's financial viability. By 1854, the United States had acquired present-day California, Arizona, New Mexico, Texas, and parts of Nevada, Utah, Colorado, Oklahoma, Kansas, and Wyoming from Mexico through "annexation, conquest, and purchase" (Menchaca, 2001, p. 216), which intensified the power struggle between the North and South over the creation of free or slaves states. The acquisition of Mexico reinforced the Monroe Doctrine's "benevolent" pledge in 1824, to protect newly independent Latin American republics from European colonization, and fulfilled U.S. claims to the "manifest destiny" of U.S. domination both within and outside its expanding borders. For the indigenous population, the acquisition of Mexico had serious implications.

Though all inhabitants of Mexico were assured their rights as full citizens and protection under the Monroe Doctrine, the U.S. government violated the agreements within a year of signing. The United States reinstituted a racialization system, comparable to that created by the Spanish, and confiscated Mexicans' property. Since Mexicans were "White," they were entitled to full rights, while the blood quantum of Mestizos, Native Americans, Afromestizos, and Blacks determined that they were not. Since U.S. legislators of the ceded territories had the right to determine eligibility for citizenship, Native Americans were excluded and restrictions were placed on the rights of Mexicans. The California Gold Rush of 1848 intensified the drive to stake claims on the land and precipitated the massive influx of White prospectors to the West, barring indigenous people from their camps, and invoking illegal rules to pursue the invaders' right to get rich. The California Land Act of 1851 established a Board of Commissions to review land claims and exorbitant taxes were levied against Mexicans in order to expropriate their land and property, and the Anti-Vagrancy Act of 1855 deemed Mexicans to be "aliens," in order to prohibit them from owning land or silver and gold mines. Another Act in 1855 negated the state's constitutional requirement for laws to be printed in Spanish. These Acts were enforced by numerous lynchings of Mexicans between from 1848 and 1928, which violently pushed them off the land and revoked their citizenship rights. Starvation and minimal existence resulted. Evicted from their homes and dispossessed of their land, Mexicans were forced to be low-paid workers on the land, in mines, railroads, canneries, and in service positions, and were pushed onto the fast track of economic decline that continues to be sustained to this day. In this familiar saga of U.S. exploits, Mexico's independence from Spain made it a prime target for the unbridled expansionism that completed the U.S. occupation of the North American continent.

Simultaneously, freed Blacks and Native Americans in the West were being evicted, dispossessed of their land, and subjected to forced labor through various Acts. Provisions from the Indian Intercourse Act of 1834 confined Native Americans on reservations with the threat of death for fleeing, and the Northwest Ordinance was invoked to deny Native Americans property rights to their own land. The Preemptive Act of 1853 declared all "Indian lands" public domain, open for squatting, and the Homestead Act of 1862 allowed citizens, that is, White settlers, to claim the newly designated "public land," which dispossessed Native Americans in the West and Mexicans, barring them from land grant allotments. The Kansas-Nebraska Act of 1854 revoked the Missouri Compromise and allowed states to determine their slave/free status, forcing Blacks to emigrate from their homes or be enslaved. The passage of the Indentured Act of 1860 in California allowed Whites to make Native Americans indentured servants in the West, and allowed a Native American to be placed in bondage or sold at an auction, if a White person filed a complaint against him or her for unacceptable public behavior (Menchaca, 2001). Claiming to have "stabilized" California, White settlers demanded and received privileges in land allotments, while Mexicans, Native Americans, and African Americans were being converted from "small farmers into landless wage workers" (Menchaca, 2001).

"Manifest Destiny" was well under way as the size of the United States doubled through westward expansion, the acquisition of Oregon Territory from Britain (1846), and annexation of the entire northern half of Mexico. On the one hand, education, the law, and scientific racism facilitated and justified the U.S. appropriation of land and the forced relegation of subjugated people to the laboring class. On the other, the democratic ideals embraced by the peoples of the land and the burgeoning needs of an emergent industrial capitalism forged mounting resistance to slavery, racial oppression, and inequality. The stage set by the early 19th century fight for domination versus equality framed the consolidation of power and ascendance of American capitalism in the second half of the century.

Consolidation of Power: The Ascendance of Industrial Capitalism

The last half of the 19th century was marked by the politics of war that resulted in the end of slavery and retrenchment of White supremacy, the final acquisition of Native American land and former Spanish colonies, and the institutionalization of a public education system consonant with industrial capitalism.

The Great Rollback: End of Slavery and Reconstruction

The military battles fought during this time—the Civil War, Wounded Knee, and the Spanish American War—accomplished the initial victories of land acquisition and the creation of a "free" racialized labor force. These military gains were solidified with the passage of laws and creation of educational institutions, which instantiated forms of racial discrimination that would remain virtually unchanged until the mid-20th century Civil Rights movement. The first major battle was the Civil War.

Tensions between the North and the South exploded around the issue of the expansion of slavery when Lincoln was elected President in 1860. Following his election, the South seceded from the Union, formed the Confederacy in 1861, and created a constitution endorsing slavery. Though the issue of slavery was a moral rallying point, the Civil War (1861–1865) was fought to preserve the Union. Lincoln was skillful in his strategic issuance of the 1863 Emancipation Proclamation before the war was over, because it drew international support for the North, but did not free the slaves. In the meantime, the Fugitive Slave Act was upheld and reinforced, as were states' rights to abolish or sustain slavery. Though the Union would not fight to abolish slavery in its own right, it galvanized the energies of the democratic-minded to put an end to slavery. In 1865, the South's surrender ended the Civil War, slavery was officially abolished by the 13th

Amendment, and Reconstruction began with the Bureau of Refugees, Freedmen, and Abandoned Lands. The Freedmen's Bureau, though underfunded, was created to provide food, clothing, housing, assistance with property, and to administer justice and establish schools for ex-slaves.

African Americans were jubilant, though ex-slaves were sobered by the challenges of finding their families, setting up their lives, and facing the beginnings of the horrific White backlash, marked by Mississippi's enactment of the Black Codes in 1865 and the founding of the Ku Klux Klan in 1865–1866, and designed to violently resist the abolition of slavery and to terrorize African Americans. On the one hand, Reconstruction brought many advances for Blacks, though terribly short-lived, from the election of first Black senator, Hiram R. Revels (one year)/Blanche Kelso Bruce (full 6 year term), and other public officials, the ascendance of educational opportunities to the passage of significant legal mandates. The 14th Amendment guaranteed citizenship and equal protection under the law, overturning the Dred Scott decision; the Civil Rights Bill of 1866 gave full citizenship rights to African Americans (excluding Native Americans). Reconstruction Acts were passed in 1867 with conditions for the South's readmission to the Union, including the enfranchisement of ex-slaves. The 15th Amendment secured the right to vote in 1870, the Civil Rights Act of 1871, aka Ku Klux Klan Act, was passed to enforce the 14th Amendment and provide civil remedy against the abuses against Blacks in the South. The Civil Rights Act of 1875 guaranteed equal rights to African Americans in public accommodations and jury duty. Some Northerners went South to support the Freedmen's Bureau's efforts toward racial equality during Reconstruction, while others sought to enrich themselves through corruption and opportunistic land grabbing (Stampp, 1967). Many of the historically Black colleges and universities (HBCUs) were established for the industrial education of African Americans, including Howard University (1867), Hampton Institute (1868), Florida Agricultural and Mechanical University (1873), and Tuskegee Institute (1881). As W.E.B. DuBois stated, "The greatest success of the Freedmen's Bureau [and Reconstruction] lay in the planting of the free school among Negroes, and the idea of free elementary education among all classes in the South" (DuBois & Lewis, 1935/1998).

On the other hand, Reconstruction brought the passage of the Black Codes, which effectively overrode the 13th Amendment, reaffirmed White supremacy in the South, and restricted African Americans' civil and legal rights, such as the right to marry, own/rent/ lease property, work independently, raise crops, and reside in towns. They were established to control Blacks, to secure them as agricultural workers, and were brutally reinforced from 1865 until the end of Reconstruction in 1877, by the illegal hand of force and terror. Poll taxes, literacy tests, and property requirements were instituted to disenfranchise Blacks. Sundown towns quickly populated the North and South (many of which exist to this day), forcing Blacks to leave town before sundown, under threat of violence (Loewen, 2006). Vigilante violence escalated along with a rage of White race riots and savage mob assaults on whole Black communities, including the Memphis Massacre, police massacres in New Orleans, the founding of the KKK, the Opelousas Massacre in Louisiana, the Clinton Massacre in Mississippi, and a series of ravaging attacks in South Carolina, ended only by the federal troops. Ultimately, the illegal hand of force was officially sanctioned by the state with the abolition of the Freedmen's Bureau and passage of the Amnesty Act (restoring full rights to confederate states) in 1872, and the withdrawal of troops from the South in 1877, ending Reconstruction. The ultimate Compromise of 1877 was made with the South: Rutherford B. Hayes (Republican) became President in exchange for the withdrawal of federal troops from the South.

The reign of terror and vigilante justice moved into full gear as an auxiliary arm of the state, with massive police-sanctioned lynchings, documented from 1882 through the mid-20th century. Intimidation, fraud, and violence enabled plantation owners to restore themselves to power, and expressed the rage of many poor Whites over their own tentative economic status and resentment toward Blacks for ostensibly "taking their jobs." Lynching targeting African Americans reached epidemic proportions, and abolitionists, Mexicans in the newly formed Southwest, Native Americans in the West, Chinese, and some other immigrants were also killed at random in these "spectacle" events of "entertainment." Land redistribution was nullified with the rejection of Sumner's proposed "40 acres and a mule law," and "possessory titles" to abandoned land in the South given to former slaves during the war were summarily revoked to preserve the sanctity of private property. Dispossessed of their land, African Americans were forced to work for former slave owners, become sharecroppers or wage earners. While free labor was necessary for industrial capitalism to advance, at least temporarily, both the South and the North wanted Blacks in the cotton fields to sustain the export of cotton. With disenfranchisement, social, educational, and employment discrimination, and the peonage system instituted against Blacks, the retrenchment of White supremacy and a laboring class was being secured. The Black Codes and reign of terror paved the way for the Jim Crow era, which began officially when the Supreme Court decision in 1883 overturned the Civil Rights Act of 1875 and rendered it constitutional to discriminate in public places. It institutionalized "separate but equal" status for African Americans. In 1896, *Plessy v. Ferguson* upheld the constitutionality of racial discrimination, based on the doctrine of "separate but equal," asserting that the 14th Amendment forbade states, not citizens from discriminating. Further, the *Cumming v. County Board of Education* case in 1899 stipulated that separate schools were allowed, even if comparable facilities across race were not available. Second-class citizenship was institutionalized for African Americans.

Final Conquest of Native American Land

Throughout the Civil War, the smoldering battle for Native American land continued, escalating with the passage of the Homestead Act of 1862. It facilitated the final acquisition of Native American land, by unleashing a flood of settlers to each claim of 160 acres on Native American land. The intensified quest for land fueled brutal onslaughts throughout the Civil War, such as the execution of Sioux men after the Sioux Uprising in Minnesota (Santee War) (1862), and the dispersal of mercenaries to eradicate Native Americans who were in the way; for example, Sand Creek (1864) and Washita (1868), massacres of peaceful men, women, and children, which ceded the Colorado Territory. In 1866, the post-Civil War 9th and 10th Calvary Regiments, better known as the African American Buffalo Soldiers, were formed as "peacetime" units. Despite opposition to the mistreatment of Native Americans by Black Senator Blanche Kelso Bruce, the Buffalo Soldiers were used as accessories to the U.S. government's expansionist displacement of indigenous people in the West. Revered for their discipline, leadership, and bravery, the Buffalo Soldiers were pitted in classic fashion against the Native American peoples—their allies against a common oppressor. In 1862, Congress passed a bill authorizing the building of a transcontinental railroad to promote western settlement. The Gadsen Treaty's renegotiation of the Mexican border enabled this project to take place. As many White workers abandoned railroad construction to pursue gold in the West, the Irish potato famine, Chinese immigration during the Gold Rush, the imminent end of slavery, and the land-dispossessed Mexican people provided available sources of labor for this massive project. In 1865, Union and Central Pacific Railroad Companies began construction with the labor of the Irish, Chinese, Mexicans, African Americans, and other European immigrants. Railroad construction was a disaster for Native Americans, resulting in the loss of territory, massive killing of buffalo to feed the railroad workers, removal of cattle from the land, and the incursion of troops to "protect" the railroad from the indigenous people (Reyhner & Eder, 2004; Takaki, 1993). By 1867, most Native Americans from the east were in "Indian Territory" and those from the west were confined to reservations. The U.S. government sought the respite of "relative peace" with Native Americans during this early post-Civil War period, though Massacre on the Marias (1870) and other retaliatory slaughters continued to occur.

The Peace Commission was established in 1867 to settle treaties and to quell Native Americans' growing "hostility" and resistance to "settlers'" violence, rapid encroachment, wanton slaughter of over 40 million buffalo, and to the intrusion of the railroads. Coinciding with the aims of Reconstruction's Freedmen's Bureau for former slaves, the Commission's goal was to expedite Native Americans' acculturation so that they could eventually assimilate into society. Even if desired, this was an impossible feat without equality. Foremost amongst their strategies was the provision of education in English to replace the indigenous languages. In addition, the Peace Commission proposed that the destruction of Native American culture and allegiance to the U.S. government would help resolve the hostilities between Whites and Native Americans and facilitate acculturation (Spring, 1994). The government set aside funds in 1870 to support industrial and other schools on reservations. The repeal of the Civilization Fund Act in 1873 and increased federal funding reflected a policy shift from private missionary-based education to centralized federally funded education for Native Americans through the Office of Indian Affairs. The centralization of education coincided with the decision in 1871 that independent indigenous Nations were no longer recognized and that all treaties required the approval of both Houses of Congress (Churchill, 2004). This marked shift in policy—from the *relocation* of Native Americans as independent nations (epitomized by the Trail of Tears), to their *confinement on reservations* as government wards—lasted until 1953.

The government's "relative peace" and disregard for Native Americans, sequestered on the "barren" western plains, shifted dramatically with the discovery of gold in 1874 on Paha Sapa, sacred Native American land in California's Black Hills. Hordes of miners were unleashed to invade and illegally ravage the land for gold, with no "courtesy" notification given to the indigenous people. Though the U. S. government had signed the second Treaty of Laramie in 1868, promising this land to the Sioux, the discovery of gold precipitated their violation of the Treaty and efforts to remove the Cheyenne and Sioux Nations from their land, as they had done to the Cherokees in Georgia. Their offers to buy the land were refused in 1875, so the government exerted pressure by cutting funds allocated to the region, and in 1876 issued the ultimatum that Sioux who were not on their reservation would be considered hostile. George Custer's military detachment to the area was annihilated in 1876 by Sitting Bull and the Sioux Nation in the Battle of Little Big Horn. Subsequent defeats ended the Great Sioux Wars, though battles continued to rage for the next 14 years, well after the Paha Saba was confiscated in 1877. Political maneuvers by the government repositioned and discredited Native Americans; for example, the Manypenny Agreement in 1877 confiscated Paha Sapa, over 900,000 acres, and confined the Nations to reservations, and a Commission Report's official discreditation of the Office of Indian Affairs led to its reorganization. In addition, the first police force of Native Americans was established in 1878 to supplement "domestic enforcement" by the military on reservations.

The passage of the Dawes Severalty Act of 1887, or General Allotment Act, was the political coup de grace. It reduced the landholdings of Native Americans by allotting 160 acres to heads of Indian families and 80 acres to individuals, and racialized the land ownership process by basing allotments on Native Americans' "blood quantum" level. Under the guise of acculturating Native Americans to the merits of private property ownership, the Dawes Act relegated them to bounded acreage, while the remaining "surplus lands" were open to settlement by Whites who were moving west. Over 4.5 million Whites moved to the west from 1877 to 1887, creating a 1:40 ratio of Native Americans to Whites. In 1889, 2 million acres was opened to over 100,000 settlers in the Oklahoma District, statehood was granted to Montana, North and South Dakota, and Washington, and, in 1890, Idaho and Wyoming were awarded statehood. Though Native American battles of resistance to the intrusion continued throughout the 1890s, the U.S. military assault at Wounded Knee 1890 was decisive in "settling" the West. Under the guise of routing the Ghost Dance religion of the Sioux Nation, the 9th Calvary massacred over 250 men, women, children at Pine Ridge, and confiscated the Dakota Territory (Spring, 1994; Churchill, 1997). In 1898, the Curtis Act "officially abolished" the Native American courts and governments in the Oklahoma Territory, subjected the Five Tribes to the Dawes Act's land allotment process from which they had been exempt, and laid the groundwork for Oklahoma to attain statehood in 1907, officially ending the existence of Indian Territory. U.S. expansionism of the 19th century peaked with the acquisition of Puerto Rico, Guam, and Philippines after the Spanish-American War of 1898.

Universal Education: Towards Acculturation, Stratification, and/or Social Mobility

The last half of the 19th century was marked by the introduction of a racialized education system for African Americans, Native Americans, and Mexicans, instituted as the U.S. government consolidated its continental acquisition of land and labor, and prepared for the ascendance of industrialization. Launched in the 1830s, the Common School Movement focused on Whites and pushed forward the development of public education in an effort to "civilize" the growing number of Irish immigrants, over 2 million by 1854, and other European immigrants in the mid- to late-1800s. Prior to any federal commitment to the education of African Americans, slaves and free Blacks had operated schools clandestinely during slavery, like the school run by Deveaux, a Black female teacher in Savannah, Georgia from 1833 to 1865, and they established schools at their own expense before the establishment of the Freedmen's Bureau during Reconstruction. Mary Peake was one of the first teachers to set up a Black school in 1861 in Fortress Monroe, Virginia. These early efforts to educate African Americans expanded after the war. W.E.B. DuBois stated: "Public education for all at public expense was in the South, a Negro idea" (Quoted in James Anderson, 1988, p. 6). Ex-slaves were the first "native" Southerners to struggle for universal, state-supported public education in the *classical liberal tradition*, in defense of emancipation and against the planters' regime.

However, in the late 1860s, "White architects of Black education," a contingent of Northern and Southern White entrepreneurs, social scientists, and philanthropists, crafted a special form of *industrial education* for Blacks to substitute older, cruder methods of socialization, coercion, and control, and to support the demand for an efficient, organized agricultural sector to supplement the emergent industrial nation's trade with England (Watkins, 2001). The "architects'" advocacy and financial support for an industrial education for Blacks and classical liberal education for Whites afforded marginal material and psychological privilege to White workers; that is, racial privilege would compensate for their social class disadvantage. This stratified public education would address the educational and ideological needs of a growing industrial society; while subjugating Black and White laborers in relation to the owners of wealth. The statements of William Baldwin, Northern philanthropist and universal public education advocate, capture the sentiment guiding the formation of schools for African Americans:

·The potential economic value of the Negro population properly educated is infinite and incalculable.... Time has proven that he is best fitted to perform the heavy labor.... This will permit the southern white laborer to perform the more expert labor, and to leave the fields, the mines, and the simpler trades for the Negro. (quoted in Anderson, 1988, p. 82)

The union of white labor, well organized, will raise the wages beyond a reasonable point, and then the battle will be fought, and the Negro will be put in at a less wage, and the labor union will either have to come down in wages, or Negro labor will be employed. (quoted in Anderson, 1988, p. 91)

Except in the rarest of instances, I am bitterly opposed to the so-called higher education of Negroes. (quoted in Anderson, 1988, p. 247)

Baldwin's and other advocates' financial support for public education was contingent on a brand of industrial education for Blacks, the Hampton-Tuskegee Idea, which was not equivalent to higher education for Whites, and would divide the working poor in the interests of the burgeoning industrial capitalists. This brand of education was embodied in the formation of Hampton (1868) and Tuskegee (1881) Institutes, and other schools for Blacks created during this era. Despite their differences, the economic motives of the "White architects of Black education" dovetailed with those of Southern White planters who opposed public education, fearing that education would fuel workers' economic and political aspirations. Both agreed on Black disfranchisement, segregation, and economic subordination. As the "architects" instituted a brand of universal public education integral to the development of a capitalist democracy, they also "ignored" their opponents' funding of widespread vigilante violence by the Ku Klux Klan and other terrorist groups, which forced freedmen and freedwomen back to slave status, secured a wedge between them and poor Whites, and reestablished the rule of a White slave owning oligarchy (Zinn, 1980). The architects and their opponents protected the economic interests of the wealthy in the North and South, through both legal and extralegal forms of coercion. In concert, the industrial education "for" and the reign of terror against Blacks served to maintain the social and economic order, reinforced by legal segregation mandated by *Plessy v. Ferguson* in 1896. Public education that would undergird the creation of a stratified working class and would promote the acculturation of subjugated peoples was the order of the day.

Choctaw, Cherokee, and other indigenous Nations maintained their own schools prior to European invasion and strove to preserve their culture and language in schools after confinement on reservations. The U.S. government had other educational aims— the Americanization, acculturation, and assimilation of Native Americans into Western culture through the suppression of their religion, language, and way of life. Towards this end, government day schools, contract mission schools, and industrial (trade) boarding schools were established with rigid disciplinary practices. In 1878, Native American students were sent under federal contract to Hampton Institute with African Americans, until the funding was stopped in 1923. They were not permitted to receive books until they spoke English, and academic study was minimized to prevent their being "distracted from Christianity and hard work." In 1879, Carlisle Indian Industrial School (1879–1918) was established as the first government-run boarding school for the acculturation of Native American children, set up by Lt. Pratt in an old army barracks in Pennsylvania. Carlisle's philosophy of cultural genocide was: "Kill the Indian, Save the Man," a supposed advancement over the adage: "The only good Indian is a dead Indian." Initially, some parents wanted their children to learn English to better negotiate with Whites, and sent them "voluntarily." Increasingly, however, Indian police and U.S. troops used night raids and other means to force children to go to boarding school with "the foreigners." The promise of education was far from the reality. Under harsh and abusive conditions, children were "reclothed, regroomed, and renamed," forced to abandon their language, values, dress, names, beliefs, and ways of life for those of "the White man" (Reyhner & Eder, 2004). Students were limited to vocational training, often in obsolete trades like tinsmithing, harness making, or blacksmithing that were being replaced by mass production in factories. Children were subjected to severe discipline, hard labor, difficult lessons, and Outing—the placement of students with White families as cheap servants. Both the lives and the spirits of children were lost at Carlisle. They were force-fed Christianity and English to, as Pratt stated: "Civilize the Indian, get him into civilization. To keep him civilized, let him stay" (Reyhner & Eder, 2004). Upon the children's return home, they were alienated from their families, their Nations, and from themselves. The horrors of this school and others led parents to endure prison sentences rather than subject their children to life at the boarding schools. St. Labre (1884), Holy Rosary (1888) on Pine Ridge Reservation, and other Indian mission schools followed similar models. The government's three-pronged approach to the "Indian problem" was to offer education and Christianity, confine Native Americans on reservations and land allotments, and use military force to secure their goals. During The Indian Removal, compulsory education at nonreservation schools was not mandatory. After Wounded Knee, however, and the creation of six states in the West, compulsory education was instituted as national policy for Native American children and was enforced by truant officers from 1892 to 1897.

Conclusions: The Significance of History and Social Justice

By the 20th century, the former land of indigenous populations constituted the United States of America, a labor force had been created, and the racial ideology of White supremacy was codified under the aegis of the U.S. government. The decimated Native American population was securely sequestered away on reservations, elevated from "ward status," and incorporated into the fold of American citizenry in 1924. With the annexation of Northern Mexico, Mexicans were forced to be low-wage workers for Whites in commercial agriculture and industry in the North and West, but the Deportation Act (1929) initiated their repositioning as "illegal aliens" on their own land; Enslaved African Americans moved from chattel slavery to free labor and migrated North to populate the burgeoning factories, along with the continuous influx of European immigrants, Mexican Americans, Native Americans, and other people of color. To maintain their forceful acquisition of land and labor, European settlers and the U.S. government relied on education, the law, and the infusion of racial ideology.

Colonialists strategically offered or withheld education to manufacture hegemonic *consent* to domination through acculturation or appeasement amongst Native Americans or through stratified division of African and White laborers. As industrialization emerged, the U.S. government instituted compulsory education to Americanize the multiracial/ethnic workforce being forged in large scale, assembly line production of auto, steel, and coal. The two separate and racially stratified systems, industrial and classical liberal education, would sustain the racial divide that was established in the labor force during slavery, and continues in the current form of privatized charter versus magnet schools for the racialized poor and wealthy. The Civil Rights Act and *Brown vs. Board of Education* temporarily ended separate unequal education, but this legislation could not dismantle society's long-standing economic and political commitment to a racially class stratified society—the source of glaring disparities in education. The founding laws of this country, backed by federal and state force protect the economic imperative to sustain social inequality.

The guise of true democracy has been an inherent contradiction since the "founding" of this country (Foner, 1998). On the one hand, the law—in the form of treaties, Slave/ Black Codes, and a plethora of Acts, mandates, and legislative rulings—was indispensable in annexing land, in educational and religious conversion, and in the physical, social, and ideological subjugation of designated populations. The law facilitated the economic and political power that grew out of U.S. colonization, westward expansion, and industrialization. As Cheryl Harris stated: "...dominant and subordinant positions within the racial hierarchy [are]...reified in law (1995, p. 283). On the other hand, the fledging United States passed democratic laws that supported entrepreneurs' competition in commerce and political participation in civic life, were embraced by the general populace. While the U.S. Constitutional government advocated democracy for all, that is, White men, it legislated racial inequality and violated numerous treaties for land acquisition, annexation, and westward expansion to land and labor for economic gain. Similarly, though the 13th, 14th, and 15th Amendments ended slavery, guaranteed citizenship across race, and the right to vote, these mandates were violently rolled backed with the termination of Reconstruction. These democratic rights were sacrificed in the service of the developing industrial economy and "preservation of the nation." Ultimately, the rule of force secured the de facto law of inequality. Historically, the State has fought to preserve or rescind democratic rights based on their ability to protect the economic and political interests of the ruling elite and to thwart/appease/buy off the resistance of the working masses. Thus, for example, the democratic legislation that grew out Reconstruction and out of the social uprisings and political activities of the Civil Rights Movement were swiftly followed by violent retrenchment—Klan violence, law and order, and a return to de facto segregation and social inequality buoyed by White supremacist ideology.

Historically, the ideological and material division along racial/ethnic lines has secured the position of the workforce as a laboring class, by thwarting its movement toward united opposition against corporate industrialists (Roediger, 2005). The "commonsense" ideology of White supremacy justified racial segregation in education, housing, and societal institutions (Fredrickson, 1971; Oliver & Shapiro, 2006). It bolstered the sentiments of Irish and other European immigrants who were "becoming White" and resented African-American and other workers of color, who took "their jobs" and dreamed of equality after serving in World War I. The resentment and imperative to sustain the racial hierarchy through terror culminated in the Red Summer of 1919. This rampage of urban lynchings (e.g., the worst was in Chicago in 1919), mirrored attacks that occurred after northern Mexico was annexed, after Reconstruction, and throughout the confiscation of Native American land. Racial scapegoating and the entitlement backlash are powerful hegemonic tools, rendering the reversion to inequality as a "common sense" return to the "natural order."

This history has implications for current social justice efforts in education. The state has used education, the law, and racial ideology simultaneously to manufacture consent and to exercise force in the divisive oppression of subjugated peoples and to serve the democratic-minded interests of an American capitalist republic. The dual use and function of these dimensions of the state apparatus also provide possibilities and limitations for their use in the struggle for equality in education and the broader society. The law has recognized, protected, and reified the dominant interests of the ruling elite in society, and has provided important, though potentially transient democratic rights that are worth fighting for and preserving. It is important to consider that such democratic legislation is vitally necessary in daily life, but not sufficient to secure true democracy, a level of equality that is divergent with the interests of the ruling elite. Thus, affirmative action efforts are worthy of struggle in order to preserve a modicum of hope and possibility for poor children to access the opportunity structure in the United States. Also worthy of struggle are legal efforts to preserve public education, to provide equal funding and human resources for all children, and to insure that students receive health and nutritional supports for learning. Simultaneously, we must distinguish between the emancipatory possibilities of public education and enslaving function of race-class stratified education.

It is paramount for our social action, curricular, and theoretical efforts to protect the democratic goal of education—to think critically, challenge assumptions, and create possibilities for the poor and subjugated populations. We should examine, question, and expose dominant ideologies that bolster the systemic roots of race–class hierarchy in the United States; for example, color-blind ideology, White supremacy, meritocracy, diminution of the private over public resources, reverence of individual versus the social good. In other words, we should fight to preserve our civil rights and liberties, to protect those genuine efforts within a capitalist democracy that may level the playing field temporarily, and to provide an alternative worldview to destructive "commonsense" notions that prevail. However, we must not lose sight of the other side of the equation—that legislation, education, and opposition to racial ideology within the system cannot alone attain broad based social mobility, achieve true equality, or undo the history of subjugation. Social action and social movements have a cherished place in the historical struggle for democracy. As current neoliberal policies dismantle public education, replace social services with the privacy of individual choice, ignore past/present social inequalities, propagate color-blindness to deny the social significance of race, we must remember that, "… [the] State tends to create and maintain a certain type of civilization and of citizen…the Law will be its instrument for this purpose…with the school system…(Gramsci, 1971, p. 246). Thus, we must create new possibilities, strategies, and structures to attain true democracy, while carefully analyzing and utilizing the current legal, educational, and ideological resources bequeathed to us.

References

Allensworth, E., & Rosenkrantz, T. (2000). *Access to magnet schools in Chicago.* Chicago: Consortium on Chicago School Research.

Alvarez, L. (2007, February 14). Army giving more waivers in recruiting, *New York Times.*

Anderson, J. (1988). *The education of Blacks in the South, 1860–1935.* Chapel Hill: University of North Carolina Press.

Anderson, J. (2004, July). Crosses to bear and promises to keep: The Jubilee anniversary of Brown v. Board of Education. *Urban Education, 39*(4), 359–373.

Anderson, J. (2005). *Looking back: Historical perspectives on Brown v. Board of Education.* Ch. 1 – A tale of two Browns: Constitutional equality and unequal education.

Anderson, J. (2006, January/February). Still desegregated, still unequal: Lessons from up North. *Educational Researcher, 35*(1), 30–33.

Anderson, J. (2007, June/July). Race-conscious educational policies versus a "color-blind Constitution": A historical perspective. *Educational Researcher, 36*(5), 249–257.

Aptheker, H. (1983). *American Negro slave revolts.* NewYork: International Publishers.

Avalon Project. (2007). Control by treaties: Law/policy, 1778–1994. Retrieved from http://www.yale.edu/lawweb/avalon/ntreaty.htm

Bird, J. B. (2005). The largest slave rebellion in U.S. history. Retrieved from http://www.johnhorse.com/highlights/essays.htm

Blumer, H. (1990). *Industrialization as an agent of social change.* New York: Aldine de Gruyter.

Board of Education of Oklahoma City Public Schools v. Dowell, 498 U.S. 237 (1991).

Brown v. Board of Education of Topeka Kansas, 347 U.S. 483 (1954)

Brown, K. (2005). *Race, law, and education in the post-desegregation era: Four perspectives on desegregation and resegregation*. Durham, NC: Carolina Academic Press.

Brown, M. Carnoy, M., Currie, E., Duster, T., Oppenheimer, D., Shultz, M., & Wellman, D. (2003). *White-washing race: The myth of a color-blind society*. Berkeley: University of California Press.

Churchill, W. (1997). *A little matter of genocide: Holocaust and denial in the Americas 1492 to the present*. San Francisco: City Lights Books.

Churchill, W. (2002). *Struggle for the land: Native North American resistance to genocide, ecocide, and colonization*. San Francisco: City Lights Books.

Churchill, W. (2004). *Kill the Indian, save the man*. San Francisco: City Lights Books.

Clotfelter, C. (2004). *After Brown: The rise and retreat of school desegregation*. Princeton, NJ: Princeton University Press.

Crawford, (2007). A diminished vision of civil rights: No Child Left Behind and the growing divide on how educational equity is understood. *Education Review, 6*, 1.

Cumming v. Richmond County Board of Education, 175 U.S. 528.

Darder, A., Torres, R., & Gutierrez, H. (Eds.). (1997). *Latinos and education: A critical reader*. New York: Routledge.

Darling-Hammond, L. (1998). Unequal opportunity: Race and education. *Brookings Review, 16*(2), 28–32.

Darling-Hammond, L. (2005). No Child Left Behind and high school reform. Retrieved from http://www.qualityednow.org/statelegresource/conference2005/session6-HSReform.pdf

Darling-Hammond, L. (January, 2007). A Marshall Plan for teaching: What it will really take to leave no child behind. *Education Week, 26*(18), 28, 48.

Darling-Hammond, L., & Berry, B. (1999). Recruiting teachers for the 21st century: The Foundation for Educational Equity. *Journal of Negro Education, 68*(3), 254–279.

De Gobineau, A. (1853/1999). *The inequality of human races*. Brooklyn, NY: Howard Fertig.

Doak, R. (2006). *Slave rebellions*. New York: Chelsea House.

Dobbs, M. (2004, November 22). Universities record drop in Black admissions. *Washington Post*, p. A01.

DuBois, W. E. B., & Lewis, D. L. (1998). *Black Reconstruction in America, 1860–1880*. New York: The Free Press. (Original work published 1935)

Foner, E. (1998). *The story of American freedom*. New York: W.W. Norton.

Franklin, J. H. (1994). *From slavery to freedom: A history of African Americans* (7th ed.). New York: McGraw Hill.

Franklin, J. H., & Schweninger, L. (2000). *Runaway slaves: Rebels on the plantation*. New York: Oxford University Press.

Fredrickson, G. (1971). *The Black image in the white mind: The debate on Afro-American character and destiny, 1817–1914*. Hanover, NH: Wesleyan University Press.

Gonzalez, G. (1997). Culture, language, and the Americanization of Mexican children. In A. Darder, R. Torres, & H. Gutierrez (Eds.), *Latinos in education: A critical reader* (pp. 158–173). New York: Routledge.

Gramsci, A. (1971). *Selections from the prison notebooks of Antonio Gramsci*. New York: International Publishers.

Grutter v. Bollinger, 539 U. S. 306 (2003).

Harris, C. (1995). Whiteness as property, In K. Crenshaw, N. Gotanda, G. Peller, & K. Thomas (Eds.), *Race theory: The key writings that formed the movement* (pp. 276–291). New York: The New Press.

Hauser, R., Simmons, S., & Pager, D. (2004). High school dropout, race-ethnicity, and social background from the 1970s to the 1990s. In G. Orfield (Ed.), *Dropouts in America: Confronting the graduation rate crisis* (pp. 85–106). Cambridge, MA: Harvard Education Press.

Heidler, D., & Heidler, J. (2007). *Indian removal*. New York: W.W. Norton.

Hening, W. W. (1809). *The Statutes at large: Being a collection of all the laws of Virginia from the First Session of the Legislature in the Year 1619* (V. 3).

Higginbotham, A. L. (1978). *In the matter of color: Race and the American legal process: The colonial period.* New York: Oxford University Press.

Hopwood v. State of Texas, 78F.3d 932 (5th Circuit, 1996).

Katznelson, I. (2005). *When affirmative action was white: An untold history of racial inequality in 20th century America.* New York: W. W. Norton.

Kozol, J. (1991). *Savage inequalities: Children in America's schools.* New York: Harper Perennial.

Kozol, J. (2005). *Shame of the nation: The restoration of apartheid schooling in America.* New York: Three Rivers Press.

Langemann, E., & Miller, L. (Eds.). (1996). *Brown v. Board of Education: The challenge of today's schools.* New York: Teachers College Press.

Lau v. Nichols, 414 U.S. 563 (1974)

Loewen, J. (1995). *Lies my teacher told me: Everything your American history textbook got wrong.* New York: Touchstone Books.

Loewen, J. (2006). *Sundown towns: A hidden dimension of American racism.* New York: Touchstone Books.

Macedo, D. (1997). English only: The tongue-tying of America. In A. Darder, R. Torres, & H. Gutierrez (Eds.), *Latinos in education: A critical reader* (pp. 269–278). New York: Routledge.

McCarthy, C. (1998). *The uses of culture: Education and the limits of ethnic affiliation.* New York: Routledge.

McNeil, L. (2000). *Contradictions of school reform: Educational costs of standardized testing.* New York: RoutledgeFalmer.

Menchaca, M. (2001). *Recovering history, constructing race: The Indian, Black and White roots of Mexican Americans.* Austin: University of Texas Press.

Milliken v. Bradley, 418 U.S. 717 (1974).

Mishel, L., & Roy, J. (2006). Rethinking high school graduation rates and trends, Economic Policy Institute: Research for Broadly Shared Prosperity. Retrieved from, http://www.epi.org/content.cfm/book_grad_rates

Moore, J. (2005). *Race and college admissions: A case for affirmative action.* Jefferson, NC: McFarland.

Murphy, S. (2005, Winter). Securing human property: Slavery, life insurance, and industrialization in the Upper South. *Journal of the Early Republic, 25,* 615–623.

Oliver, M. & Shapiro, T. (2006). *Black wealth/White wealth: A new perspective on racial inequality.* New York: Routledge.

Orfield, G. (Ed.). (2004). *Dropouts in America: Confronting the graduation rate crisis.* Cambridge, MA: The Civil Rights Project.

Orfield, G. (2005). Why segregation is inherently unequal: The abandonment of Brown and the continuing failure of Plessy, New York Law School. *Law Review, 49,* 1041–1052.

Orfield, G. (2006). *Racial transformation and the changing nature of segregation.* Civil Rights Project. Cambridge, MA.: Harvard University Press.

Orfield, G., & Lee, C. (2004). *Brown at 50: King's dream or Plessy's nightmare?* (pp. 1–54). Cambridge, MA: The Civil Rights Project. http://www.civilrightsproject.ucla.edu/research/reseg04/brown50.pdf

Orfield, G., Losen, D., Wald, J., & Swanson, C. (2004, March). Losing our future: How minority youth are being left behind by the graduation rate crisis—*Executive Summary.* President and Fellows of Harvard College (p. 2).

Orfield, G., & Miller, E. (1998). *Chilling admissions: The affirmative action crisis and the search for alternatives.* Cambridge, MA: Harvard Education Publishing Group.

Philpott, T. (November 22, 2006). Army signs more dropouts. Retrieved from http://www.military.com/features/0,15240,119382,00.html

Plessy v. Ferguson, 163 U.S. 537 (1896).

Regents of the University of California v. Bakke, 438 U.S. 265 (1978).

Reyhner, J., & Eder, J. (2004). *American Indian education: A history.* Norman: University of Oklahoma Press.

Roediger, D. (2005). *Working toward whiteness: How America's immigrants became white.* New York: Basic Books.

Ruiz, R. (1997). The empowerment of language-minority students. In A. Darder, R. Torres, & H. Gutierrez (Eds.), *Latinos in education: A critical reader* (pp. 319–330). New York: Routledge.

Russell, C., & Hawley, W. (Eds.). (1983). *The consequences of school desegregation.* Philadelphia, PA: Temple University Press.

Samora, J., & Simon, P. (200). A history of the Mexican-American People http://www.jsri.msu.edu/museum/pubs/MexAmHist/chapter1-22.html

Silent Epidemic. (2007). Why students drop out; Statistics and facts about high school drop out rates. Retrieved from http://www.silentepidemic.org/epidemic/statistics-facts.htm

Spellings, M. (August, 2005). *How No Child Left Behind Benefits African Americans, Hispanic Americans, American Indians.* Washington, D.C.: U.S. Department of Education. Retrieved October 29, 2006, from http://www.ed.gov/nclb/accountability/achieve/edpicks.jhtml?src=az

Spring, J. (1994). *Deculturalization and the struggle for equality: A brief history of the education of dominated cultures in the United States.* New York: McGraw-Hill.

Stampp, K. (1967). *The era of Reconstruction, 1865–1877.* New York: Vintage Press.

Street, P. (2005). *Segregated schools: Educational apartheid in post-civil rights America.* New York: Routledge.

Takaki, R. (1993). *A different mirror: A history of multicultural America.* New York: Back Bay Books.

Travel and History (2008). Bureau of Indian Affairs. Retrieved from http://www.u-s-history.com/pages/h3577.html

Van Sertima, I. (1976). *The African presence in ancient America: They came before Columbus.* New York: Random House.

Watkins, W. (2001). *The White architects of Black education: Ideology and power in America, 1865–1954.* New York: Teachers College Press.

Watkins, W. (2005). *Black protest thought and education.* New York: Peter Lang.

Wise, T. (2005). *Affirmative action: Racial preference in Black and White.* New York: Routledge.

Woodson, C. G. (2004). *The education of the Negro prior to 1861: A history of the education of the Colored People of the United States from the beginning of slavery to the Civil War.* Whitefish, MT: Kessinger Publishing.

Yzaguirre, R., & Kamasaki, C. (1997). *The Latino civil rights crisis. The Civil Rights Project.* Berkeley, CA: UCLA

Zinn, H. (1980). *A people's history of the United States.* New York: Harper Perennial.

Response to Part 1

Education and Social Justice Movements

Anthony Arnove

Movements for social justice in the United States historically have concerned themselves with education in two fundamental senses. Every self-conscious movement for reform and for deeper social change has undertaken efforts to educate its own membership, a process that has meant challenging the dominant ideas of the time about the content and form of "proper" education. And social justice movements have sought to change the institutional norms of education, often coming to challenge the dominant understanding of education entirely. From its inception in the United States, education has been a contested terrain and remains so today.

Consider the abolitionist movement. Slaves in the United States risked their lives to learn to read and write. In the *Narrative of the Life of Frederick Douglass,* Douglas recalls:

> Very soon after I went to live with Mr. and Mrs. Auld, she very kindly commenced to teach me the A, B, C. After I had learned this, she assisted me in learning to spell words of three or four letters. Just at this point of my progress, Mr. Auld found out what was going on, and at once forbade Mrs. Auld to instruct me further, telling her, among other things, that it was unlawful, as well as unsafe, to teach a slave to read.... "Now," said he, "If you teach that nigger (speaking of myself) how to read, there would be no keeping him. It would forever unfit him to be a slave. He would at once become unmanageable, and of no value to his master. As to himself, it could do him no good, but a great deal of harm. It would make him discontented and unhappy...." From that moment, I understood the pathway from slavery to freedom.... Though conscious of the difficulty of learning without a teacher, I set out with high hope, and a fixed purpose, at whatever cost of trouble, to learn how to read. The very decided manner with which he spoke, and strove to impress his wife with the evil consequences of giving me instruction, served to convince me that he was deeply sensible of the truths he was uttering.... What he most dreaded, that I most desired. What he most loved, that I most hated. That which to him was a great evil, to be carefully shunned, was to me a great good, to be diligently sought; and the argument which he so warmly urged, against my learning to read, only served to inspire me with a desire and determination to learn. (p. 48)

While Douglass here describes a process of self-education, through newspapers like *The North Star*, secret study circles, and eventually alternative schools, the abolitionist movement sought to collectively educate its own members and to change an education system that was rooted in a racist social order that denied the humanity of African Americans.

During the industrial revolution, women in the mills of Lowell, Massachusetts, formed reading circles and began to write and circulate their own newspapers in the process of challenging sexist ideas about women's "natural" place in society. In an 1841 article called "A New Society" in *The Lowell Offering*, "Tabitha" (Betsy Chamberlain) describes an imaginary organization whose bylines included the following provisions:

1. *Resolved,* That every father of a family who neglects to give his daughters the same advantages for an education which he gives his sons, shall be expelled from this society, and be considered a heathen.
2. *Resolved,* That no member of this society shall exact more than eight hours of labor, out of every twenty-four, of any person in his or her employment.
3. *Resolved,* That, as the laborer is worthy of his hire, the price for labor shall be sufficient to enable the working-people to pay a proper attention to scientific and literary pursuits.
4. *Resolved,* That the wages of females shall be equal to the wages of males, that they may be enabled to maintain proper independence of character, and virtuous deportment. (p. 209)

The Lowell women wrote of the need to empower women *and* men and sought to develop the full potential of working people to express their creative capacities.

In the 1960s and 1970s, the women's rights, gay rights, civil rights, and antiwar movements all undertook processes of internal education, organizing teach-ins, setting up study circles, and creating an alternative networks of newspapers, books, and other publications. Many in these movements also began to question a capitalist education system that sought to create a docile labor force, rather than independent, critical thinkers. They showed how most textbooks and curricula reinforced stereotypes about women and other oppressed people, denied the history of the violent dispossession of Native Americans, excused the horrors of slavery, ignored the struggles of working people, and distorted the history of U.S. military interventions.

These are not merely historical concerns, however. Today, these struggles continue in the movement to challenge an education model of "teaching to test" that constrains teachers and reinforces rote rather than critical learning; in the efforts to stave off the growing privatization of the public school system; in the struggles to reverse the rapid resegregation of the U.S. school system; and in new social movements that fight for a world based on people rather than profit. Education will continue to be a critical battlefield where people imagine and fight for an alternative present and future.

References

Chamberlain, B. (1997). *The Lowell offering: Writings by New England mill women (1984–1845)*. New York: W.W. Norton. (Original published 1841)

Douglass, F. (1997). *Narrative of the life of Frederick Douglsas*. New York: Signet Classics.

Part 2

International Perspectives on Social Justice and Education

Edited and Introduced by Fazal Rizvi

> That is why it is very important for you to have the right kind of education. For this, the educator must be rightly educated, so that he will not regard teaching as merely a means of earning a livelihood but will be capable of helping the student to put aside all dogmas and not be held by any religion or belief.
>
> (J. Krishnamurti, 2004, p. xxvii)

> The materialist doctrine that men are products of circumstances and upbringing, and that, therefore, changed men are products of changed circumstances and changed upbringing, forgets that it is men who change circumstances and that the educator must himself be educated. Hence this doctrine is bound to divide society into two parts, one of which is superior to society. The coincidence of the changing of circumstances and of human activity or self-change [Selbstveränderung] can be conceived and rationally understood only as revolutionary practice.
>
> (Marx, 1845/1924)

The title of this section of the Handbook, "International Perspectives on Social Justice and Education," suggests a number of interrelated questions. How might international perspectives contribute to a better understanding of the idea of social justice and its relationship to education? Is a universal definition of social justice in education possible? To what extent are its expressions the same around the world? And if they are different, what does this difference consists in? What can we learn from the ways in which different educational systems have addressed social justice? To what extent has globalization made it more difficult to realize the goals of social justice in education? In a world increasingly characterized by global interconnectivity and interdependence, how are the various forms of injustice changing, both within and across nation-states? And how should education be structured as an instrument for promoting global justice? These are just some of the questions that are explored by the five papers in this section. They are designed to promote a dialogue about the meaning and significance of thinking about social justice in terms that are not only critical and reflexive but also comparative and transnational.

Any comparative and international analysis of social justice and education indicates the impossibility of a universal definition. While, as an ideal, social justice may be universally applicable and aspired to, its expressions vary across different cultural and national traditions. Indeed, its meaning is historically constituted and is a site of conflicting and divergent political endeavors. It does not refer to a single set of primary or basic goods, conceivable across all moral and material domains. Having said this, it needs to be acknowledged, however, that injustice does have a material reality that is readily recognized by those who experience it. Those who are hungry or poor, or homeless, do not need abstract philosophical discussions in order to realize that they are subjected to marginalization, discrimination, and oppression. The idea of justice thus points to something real and tangible, and represents a moral blight on communities that do not attempt to do their best to mitigate its worst effects.

In the political realm, however, social justice is an essentially contested notion, and the search for its realization arises from the meeting of a particular kind of authority with political aspirations and activism located in particular historical circumstances. In the past few decades, for example, policy thinking around the notion of social justice in most Western countries has revolved around three distinct philosophical traditions: liberal-humanism, market-individualism and social-democratic. A liberal-humanist notion of social justice, associated most notably with the ideas of John Rawls (1972), conceptualizes social justice in terms of fairness, implying principles of individual freedom, as well as the idea that the state has a major responsibility in creating policies and programs directed toward removing barriers arising from unequal power relations that prevent access, equity, and participation.

Market-individualism, on the other hand, invokes not so much the idea of fairness as what people deserve. It suggests that the state has no right to distribute the private goods that people have produced through their own efforts. Highlighting the importance of the market in economic and social exchange, this tradition of thinking rejects redistributive notions, and suggests that it is unjust for the state to transfer property owned by individuals without their consent. Social democratic notions of justice, in contrast, reject this individualism, and stress the needs people have within a community. It views "need" as a primary rather than a residual category. In this way, its interpretation of needs is different from the charity-based arguments about the "needy," which are perfectly compatible with both the fairness and desert principles.

It is important to note then that market-individualism and social democracy rest on a very different understanding of the nature between social justice and the market. In the former, the market is seen as crucial in facilitating social exchange and the exercise of individual choice, while the social democratic view suggests that the idea of justice is not entirely compatible with markets unless they are controlled in a sufficiently rigorous manner. The former view is based on an assumption about "property rights" that individuals possess and are able to exchange in the market. In contrast, the social democratic perspective emphasizes "person rights" involving equal treatment of citizens, freedom of expression and movement, equal access to participation in decision making, and reciprocity in relations of power and authority.

A comparative analysis of social justice shows how in policy different countries have emphasized different aspects of these traditions in thinking about social justice. In Scandinavian countries, for example, social democratic principles have, until recently at least, been dominant, exercised by the Keynesian welfare state. The state has sought to provide equality of educational opportunity for all through various redistributive programs. In the postcolonial developing world, the project of nation-building has necessarily required a commitment to the principles of social democracy, designed to increase levels of literacy and educational participation. The United States has, in contrast, leaned more toward market-individualism, encapsulated in education most notably in policies of choice and accountability, especially since the so-called Reagan economic revolution.

Since the late 1980s, market-individualism has become increasingly hegemonic in educational policy development around the world. This seemingly global convergence toward neoliberal thinking in education has occurred within a broader discourse about the changing nature of the global economy, which is characterized as "knowledge-based," and which is assumed to require greater levels of education and training than ever before. In this way, the idea of social justice in education, couched narrowly as access, and the politics of globalization have become inextricably linked. The purposes of education are now increasingly conceived in human capital terms, encouraging individuals, organizations, and even nations to consider investment in education largely in economic terms. This has encouraged educational administration to be viewed in a particular way, centered on the new public management notions of individual choice and system accountability.

What is clear then is that globalization has transformed the ways in which educational policy, often couched in a language of reform, have been set, invoking the idea of "global imperatives." But their effects of globalization on different groups and communities have varied greatly, creating considerable disparities around the world, with some communities benefiting enormously from globalization, while others have encountered major disruptions to their economic and cultural lives. Globalization has moreover transformed the discursive terrain within which educational priorities are developed and enacted. This terrain is increasingly informed by a range of neoliberal precepts that do not only affect the ways we think about the governance of education but also about its basic purposes. As a particular way of interpreting globalization has become globally hegemonic, it has undermined, in various ways, stronger social democratic claims to educational justice.

Globalization has moreover weakened the authority of the state in promoting stronger redistributive policies and programs. Traditional ways of thinking about social justice in education assumed a strong role for the state in bringing about greater equality of access, opportunities, and outcomes. It was the state to which the claims for greater redistribution of resources were addressed. And it was the state that was expected to develop programs designed to ensure conditions that reflected desert or fairness principles. But in a global economy, the choices any state can make have become somewhat restricted, with an increasingly preference for a minimalist state, concerned to promote the instrumental values of competition, economic efficiency and choice. National policy mechanisms have become increasingly interconnected. A new logic of networks has demanded their restructuring. Yet not all countries have restructured the state in the same way, highlighting once again the importance of looking at issues of social justice from international perspectives, both in terms that are comparative but also relational.

The state is, however, not the only site of struggle over social justice. The contemporary social movements, often working at the global level, have underscored a new politics of difference around issues not only of class but also of gender, ethnicity, race, disability, sexuality, and religion, as well as their complex articulations with each other. As Nancy Fraser (1997) has pointed out, the struggle for recognition is fast becoming the paradigmatic form of political conflict, and that therefore heterogeneity and pluralism must now become the norms against which the demands for justice are articulated. In this way, group identity has supplanted class conflict as the chief medium of political mobilization. Of course, material injustices have not disappeared but are now linked to the demands for recognition of difference, and for representation on the institutions of both local and national as well as global decision making.

What this suggests is that the distributive paradigm, as Young (1990) calls it, that informed the three major traditions of thinking about social justice is no longer sufficient to capture the complexities of global interconnectivity and interdependence on the one hand and of contemporary identity politics on the other. The distributive paradigm is concerned with the morally proper distribution of benefits and burdens among all members of a society. But this logic clearly applies to the distribution of material goods, such as wealth and income, it is inadequate in fully accounting for nonmaterial resources such as respect, recognition, rights, opportunities, and power, because injustice can also be rooted in social patterns of representation, interpretation, and communication. In this way, while concerns of distribution, located within the economic structure of a society, are important, then so are the issues of identity, difference, and cultural recognition and exploitation.

These issues are highly relevant to the concerns of justice in education because it is in education that students learn to develop their sense of self-worth and acceptable modes of social communication. These cultural facts are, of course, interpreted differently in different communities, and therefore require an understanding not only of difference but also of relationalities that link considerations of justice in one place to most others. The emphasis on relationalities points to the importance of cosmopolitan sensibilities needed to negotiate differences that are now resulting from the increased volume and intensity of cultural interactions produced by the global flows of people, ideas and technologies.

References

Fraser, N. (1997). *Justice interruptus*. London: Routledge.

Krishnamurti, J. (2004). *This matter of culture*. Chennai, India: KFI.

Marx, K. (2002). *Theses on Feuerbach* (Vol. 3; C. Smith, Trans., based on work done jointly with D. Cuckson). Moscow: Institute of Marxism-Leninism in Marx-Engels Archives. Book 1. (Original work published 1845/1924)

Young, I. M. (1990). *Justice and the politics of difference*. Princeton, NJ: Princeton University Press.

8 Moving Abjection

Jane Kenway and Anna Hickey-Moody

This chapter draws on a wider study of the intersections between the changing social and cultural base of place and identities as they are increasingly caught up in, and also attempt to stand apart from, globalizing flows.[1] The focus is on mobility and stasis in places beyond the city in Western first world countries and their implications for relationships and inequalities.

Appadurai (1996, 2000) considers mobility through his notion of scapes. Ethnoscapes are:

> ...landscapes of persons who constitute the shifting world in which we live: tourists, immigrants, refugees, exiles, guest workers, and other moving groups and individuals [that] constitute an essential feature of the world and appear to affect the politics of (and between) nations to a hitherto unprecedented degree. (2000, p. 95)

Lived cultures of ethnoscapes are reconfigured in global ideoscapes (moving political ideas) and mediascapes (moving electronic images). These "scapes" come together to form imagined worlds. Such worlds are "multiple [and]...constituted by the historically situated imaginations of persons and groups spread around the global" (Appadurai, 1996, p. 2).

We read global ideoscapes and mediascapes in terms of Giroux's (1999) assumption that culture plays a central role in producing narratives, metaphors, and images that exercise a powerful pedagogical force over how people think of themselves and their relationship to others.

We add political and affective edge to the pedagogical potential of Appadurai's "scapes" and "imagined worlds" through Bauman's (1998a, 1998b) work on "global hierarchies of mobility" and Kristeva's (1982) notion of the "abject." These concepts allow us to think through the ways in which young Aboriginal masculinities are produced as abject. We show how this localized process is entangled with global flows of people, ideas, and images. Bringing this range of theoretical resources together also assists us in highlighting contemporary inflections of longstanding social and cultural prejudices.

Our concern in this chapter is the unjust politics of the interlaced scapes associated with Aboriginal people in Australia. We begin with a brief elaboration of what we call "scapes of abjection." We then consider the abject dynamics of the ways in which tourist ideoscapes and mediascapes construct Aboriginal people. Throughout, we note the implications of such noxious politics for masculinity and gender dynamics. This chapter focuses on one Australian locality—Coober Pedy (a tourist and opal mining desert town). We call our approach to identifying, gathering, and reading data for this study "place-based global ethnography" (see Kenway, Kraack, & Hickey-Moody, 2006, pp. 35–59). This methodology links Appadurai's global scapes to Burawoy et al.'s (2000) notion of global ethnography, and is concerned with flows through places. The ethnographic fieldwork involved in-depth semistructured interviews with 36 young people. For six weeks, 24 males were each interviewed weekly and 12 females were interviewed every two weeks. Loosely structured focus and affinity group discussions were held with mothers, fathers, community members, teachers, and youth and welfare service providers. Informal conversations were held with a wide range of local people. All participants have been rendered anonymous. Field research also involved time at a variety of community and youth-specific locales (e.g., the school, beach, and main street) and events (e.g., sporting matches, discos, and local carnivals). Bringing these localized texts together with global media and ideoscapes, we identified and analyzed popular discourses in film, television, print media and Internet media about places beyond the metropolis.

Mediascapes and Ideoscapes as Public Pedagogies

Giroux (1999) argues that pedagogy can no longer be considered as confined to the site of schooling. It needs to be understood as applying to everyday political sites in "which identities are shaped, desires mobilized, and experiences take on form and meaning." Such sites are, arguably, those that Appadurai considers global mediascapes and ideoscapes—cultural mores of thought, image, and patterns of association. Giroux's concept of "public pedagogy" draws on his belief that scholarly communities need to:

> ...acknowledge the primacy of culture's role as an educational site where identities are being continually transformed, power is enacted, and learning assumes a political dynamic as it becomes not only the condition for the acquisition of agency but also the sphere for imagining oppositional social change. (2004b, p. 60)

For Giroux, culture is pedagogical. We learn about ourselves and understand our relations to others through our position in lived cultures. A more explicit consideration of how culture influences identity production and relations of power is, for Giroux, one of the intended outcomes of considering culture as pedagogical. In demonstrating culture's educational role, Giroux hopes that we will become more cognizant of the myriad effects associated with consumer-media culture. For Giroux, this is an important task because such knowledge of the role of culture is intrinsic to acquiring agency and "imagining... social change" (2004b, p. 60).

For example, in his essay, "Education after Abu Ghraib," Giroux (2004a) draws attention to how the nature of photographs and the technologies that produce them enable particular meanings; how these meanings connect with broader discourses and relations of power; how these sites allow or disallow resistance and challenge. In this chapter, we analyze local and global media and ideoscapes as forms of public pedagogy. Vernacular and Internet depictions of Aboriginal people, celebrated ghosts of Aboriginal elders forever on the move, public figures and private beliefs fold together as media and ethnoscapes produce evolving, pedagogical depictions of Australian Aboriginal people.

Scapes of Noxious Mobility and Immobility

Fraser (2005) argues that there are two main forms of injustice, "socioeconomic" and "cultural or symbolic." These two profound forms of social injustice are affected by global movements. The former refers to experiences of economic exploitation, marginalization, and deprivation. The latter involves cultural domination, nonrecognition, and disrespect. She observes that although some social groupings suffer injustices that are primarily economic these may also involve cultural devaluation, and the reverse. In globalizing circumstances in which "the world is on the move" as Appadurai says, notions of material and cultural injustice are usefully complemented by ideas associated with the unjust politics of mobility, immobility, and affect.

One of the ways these unjust ethnoscapes are linked is through global ideo- and mediascapes of abjection. In the early 1980s Kristeva (1982) theorized the corporeal, psychological, and social processes associated with the abject. She identified three main forms of abjection associated with food, waste, and sexual difference. The abject has since come to be associated with those bodily fluids, people, objects, and places that are couched as unclean, impure, and even immoral. The abject disturbs "identity, system, order" (Kristeva, 1982, p. 4) and provokes the desire to expel the unclean to an outside, to create boundaries in order to establish the certainty of the self. It involves the production of social taboos and individual and group psychic defenses. Insofar as the abject challenges notions of identity and social order it "must" be cast out. Abjection involves the processes whereby that or those named unclean are reviled, repelled, and resisted. But the "abject" does not respect such expulsions and boundaries and so constantly threatens to move across them and contaminate. It is thus understood as a threat to "the pure and the proper." Grosz (1989) observes, that the abject "can never be fully obliterated but hovers at the borders of our existence, threatening the apparently settled unity of the subject with disruption and possible dissolution" (p. 71).

Scapes of abjection circulate globally and seep into national and local geometries of power and affect. As we will show, they reinvigorate such things as the ugly history of colonization and the geopolitical relationships between the metropolis and its othered spaces. They justify injustice, draw attention away from social suffering, and thus deny the social reality of the marginalized. They are woven through neoliberal economic and social ideologies and help to legitimate the more insidious aspects of global economic restructuring. They provide a justification for the diminishment of state welfare support for those who suffer the economic and cultural consequences of the noxious politics of mobility. The associated social tensions come to be expressed in the language of disgust and it becomes accepted that certain social groups, the Black welfare poor particularly, can justifiably be treated as trash. Scapes of abjection can also be entangled with the long chains of commodification associated with global ethnoscapes. In such cases, we go on to explain, the processes of abjection take on an even more complex configuration as culture is navigated for profit.

Abjectifying Aboriginality

Explaining the historical and spatial processes of abjection, McClintock (1995) argues:

> Abject peoples are those whom industrial imperialism rejects but cannot do without: slaves, prostitutes, the colonized, domestic workers, the insane, the unemployed, and so on. Certain threshold zones become abject zones and are policed with vigor: the Arab Casbah, the Jewish ghetto, the Irish slum, the Victorian garret and kitchen, the squatter camp, the mental asylum, the red light district and the bedroom. (p. 71)

The various processes whereby the abject is expelled, restricted to "abject zones" and returns to "haunt" are all evident in the complex history of the abjection of Aboriginal Australians. These processes of abjection are integral to Australia's colonial and neocolonial history and have been rearticulated in recent discourses of "downward" envy associated with the abject positioning of Aboriginal welfare recipients. They are also rearticulated in the ideoscapes and mediascapes related to the tourist industry.

The noxious politics of mobility and associated processes of abjection are a characteristic of the treatment of Australia's original inhabitants by the British occupying power in the 18th and 19th century. Cast out and treated as nonhuman contaminants, Aboriginal Australians were dispossessed of their land, denied their laws and customs, refused citizenship, and usually treated brutally and exploited by White settlers (Broome, 2001; Reynolds, 1999). Australia's colonial history involves the dispossession, denial, and exploitation of Aboriginal peoples who continue to experience well-documented, indisputable economic injustice and widespread social exclusion, cultural denial, and denigration. Such injustices are integral to their mobility, which has included not just voluntary movement but also being forcibly moved (Haebich, 2001).

The life chances and opportunities of Aboriginal males are severely circumscribed. According to the *National Strategic Framework for Aboriginal and Torres Straight Islander Health* (NATSIHC; 2003, p. 10) significant numbers of Aboriginal men have very poor physical and mental health, suffer from alcohol and substance abuse, and are involved in family violence. Fifty-three percent die before they reach 50 years of age. Such men commit suicide more often than non-Aboriginal men and they are more often imprisoned. They are less likely to have educational qualifications and employment than non-Aboriginal Australian men and their personal and household income is particularly low. These patterns for older males arise early in life. Aboriginal boys have far less educational success than their non-Aboriginal peers. Indeed, completing primary and secondary schooling and attaining a higher education qualification are much less likely for Aboriginal boys than non-Aboriginal boys. Twenty-two percent of Aboriginal males are unemployed, compared to 8% of non-Aboriginal males (Australian Bureau of Statistics [ABS], 2003, p. 25). Aboriginal boys living in remote or regional areas do not have access to the same housing and environmental health facilities that other Australian boys take for granted. Such facilities include safe drinking water, continuous power supplies, effective sewerage systems, housing and transport (ABS, 2003, p. 35).

Various forms of government welfare support seem little able to alter this situation and, equally, varied approaches to reconciliation seem unable to end racist sentiment. Interwoven with this situation is a racialized version of abjection in which the White working poor and the White welfare poor join forces to abjectify Aboriginal people who come to be seen as privileged, undeserving, and ungrateful.

There is quite a common belief in Coober Pedy that Aboriginal people "get it easy" because of the government subsidies and allowances allotted to them. Take the case of schooling. Systems have been put in place to try to encourage Aboriginal young people to regularly attend school. For example, those schoolchildren living in the Umoona Community (a settlement outside the main township) are bussed to the school every day, while local White students walk (most live much closer to the school). The State government also subsidizes school fees and the costs of extracurricula activities for Aboriginal students. This extra financial assistance is the focus of much resentment. Indeed, the provision of government benefits more generally is central to the local White residents' abjectification of local Aboriginal people. Stefani Moulder, age 14, holds this dominant view:

> When school camps come up,—we had to pay $200 and the Aboriginals only had to pay $20. That is because the government pays for them, and I think that is stupid.... They [Aboriginal people] think that they own this place but they don't.

Stefani's logic is that everyone in financial difficulty should be entitled to the same financial subsidies and allowances. At a "commonsense" level this seems reasonable enough, but it denies the history and current difficulties of Aboriginal people. Like most residents, Stefani does not agree that such benefits are a justifiable means of addressing the broader social, cultural, and political denial of Aboriginal people in Australia. The common view is that the local poor Whites are more in need and deserving of assistance. Further, Stefani's comment that "They think that they own this place but they don't" is a rather poignant reminder that while they once did, they now do not. Welfare benefits seem little compensation for the loss of their land and independence and the attacks on their identities and pride. Stefani's view is also that Aboriginal people should not be so "pushy," should not act as if "they own the place."

Such "pushy" assertions of Aboriginality have been "shaped within a long-standing, but now vigorously contested subordination" (Cowlishaw, 2004, p. 11). They include an assertion of self-respect and a denial of an "ever-abject state of being." This state of being is implied in the "permanent victim status" associated with a politics whose "central motif" is "injured and suffering Aboriginal people" (Cowlishaw, 2004, p. 52). Who represents whom, how, and with regard to what, are central and highly contentious questions within and beyond Aboriginal communities and come to the fore in relation to the Indigenous tourist industry.

The Tourist Gaze

The cultural and economic dynamics of abjectifying Indigenous peoples now feature prominently in global tourist ideoscapes and mediascapes. Bauman calls people who are on the move by choice and who accept few territorial responsibilities as they travel, "tourists." "They stay and move at their heart's desire. They abandon a site when new untried opportunities beckon elsewhere" (1998a, p. 92). Bauman's notion of the tourist is one of many "metaphors of mobility" (Urry, 2000, p. 27), in current social thought and his tourist metaphor is applied largely to the mobile winners of globalization, "the global businessman, global culture managers, or global academics" for instance, those who are "emancipated from space" (Bauman, 1998a, pp. 89–93) because of the resources at their disposal. Amongst Bauman's "tourists" are actual tourists—those who combine leisure and travel in search of "experience" (MacCannell, 1999).

Tourism has become a key economic renewal strategy among many nonurban communities around the world. It involves branding place. It is about the identification and promotion of difference, where differentiation marks a place as unique. It is also about the construction and promotion of marketable differences within places. Aboriginal culture has become a highly marketable feature of the Australian tourist industry, particularly to those sorts of tourists whom Cohen and Kennedy (2000, p. 219) call "alternative tourists" (as opposed to mass tourists). These people require adventure, contact with nature, spiritual renewal, or experiences of authenticity. As Cohen and Kennedy (2000, p. 221) observe, they yearn to "sample exotic cultures," seek the "curative properties of wilderness, remote regions," the "off beat and unusual." They "are disposed to interact directly with locals and show interest in traditional culture."

The contemporary ideoscapes and mediascapes that frame our discussion are certain global, national, state, and local tourist texts constructed to tantalize the palate of such tourists. These texts and some of their associated spatial practices involve complex abjection processes of selective recognition and erasure. Aboriginality with all its complexity (Cowlishaw, 2004) is spilt in two; certain aspects become cultural embellishments to the tourist industry while other aspects are denied. Denials and erasures occur when features of Aboriginality are found lacking in market value or when they detract from the image of place. These are eliminated by restricting them to abject zones beyond the "tourist gaze" (Urry, 1990). Alternatively, marketable aspects of Aboriginal identity become tourist "zirconia": culturally fabricated gems—the tourist glaze.

Aboriginal Australians have their own disparate and evolving cultures and histories, which continue to be significant despite past and present injustices. But it is highly selected aspects of Aboriginal culture and history that have become Australia's cultural tourist zirconia. These aspects are the acceptable and commodifiable parts of the abject split. Included here are Aboriginal cultural knowledge, ancient art, connections to the land, and experiences of spirituality. These are allocated a tourist patina. Such processes of commodification and exoticization can be understood as contemporary examples of Aboriginal abjection. They involve a stage-managed set of comfortable images that White populations want to see. They suggest that Australia has now exorcised the ghosts of the trauma of White invasion and injustice and become reconciled. As culturally objectified zirconias, Aboriginal identities become bound to a colonial past and a neocolonial present.

In appealing to the tourist demographic, marketing Australian places beyond the metropolis often involves the historical and spatial fixing of Aboriginal Australian people. They may thus, for instance, be conflated with Australian bushscapes. They may be used to make nonmetropolitan places seem especially interesting and profound. But they are likely to ignore the fact that many present-day Aboriginal people live in the metropolis and that urban Aboriginal people and sites might be of tourist interest. The consumer-driven psychology here is that tourists will feel there is something tantalizing, almost sensual, about Aboriginal histories. In order to relate to such ancient powers, one must travel and get close to the land, as the soil holds traces of such "mythical peoples." Subtly implied within these ideoscapes are particular tropes of Aboriginal masculinity. Authentic Aboriginal masculinity is sutured to timeless ideas of the wise tribal elder, the purveyor of spiritual wisdom, the skilful hunter and tracker with spears or sticks in hand, the pensive player of the didgeridoo, the seminaked, body-decorated and scarified ceremonial dancer. Such cultural character is, in its very synthesis, simultaneously put forward as fascinating but ultimately impractical. It is a reason to visit a place, but not a way of life that will be useful for "getting on" in an economically driven world. Many examples of such temporal and spatial fixity and exotic imagining can be found in online tourist mediascapes. The examples to follow are collectively emblematic of abject splitting processes.

Texts produced by the Lonely Planet publishers are a significant feature of contemporary global tourist mediascapes and ideoscapes and have important implications for out of the way places around the world. They support "adventure on demand" (Friend, 2005, p. 20). *Journeys to Authentic Australia* is written as a guide to what the Lonely Planet suggests is "Authentic Australia." The Lonely Planet has declared the left-hand side of Australia is its "authentic" region. From Mount Gambier in South Australia, via Alice Springs in Central South Australia, to Darwin and the top of the Northern Territory, and down along the coast of Western Australia via Albany and Esperance back to South Australia, the Lonely Planet maps out the "real heart and soul" of the country. Indeed, according to their advice, traveling this land is a way of "accessing Australia's heart and soul" (The Lonely Planet, 2005). A key aspect of this "authentic" Australia is ancient Aboriginal culture, which lends the land particular desirability:

> Away from Australia's eastern seaboard lies a treasure-trove of superb beaches, mind-
> blowing natural features, authentic outback experiences, world-class wines and gour-

met fare, ancient Aboriginal cultures, rare and precious fauna, and, of course, the resilient and welcoming people who have made this part of Australia the intriguing and unforgettable place that it is. (Lonely Planet, 2005)

Through the use of the word *ancient*, Aboriginal culture is positioned as temporally distinct from "the resilient and intriguing people" (some of whom are Aboriginal) "who have made this part of Australia the intriguing and unforgettable place that it is." Here, ideoscapes of abjection deploy what McClintock (1995, p. 37), drawing on Foucault, calls "panoptical time." Panoptical time is an "image of global history consumed—at a glance—in a single spectacle from a point of privileged invisibility" (McClintock, 1995, p. 37). Panoptical time makes invisible the full history of colonized peoples but also makes hypervisible, indeed turns into a tourist spectacle, those historical features that can be exoticized.

Sadly, Aboriginal sensibilities do not play a major role in most tourist constructions of Aboriginal Australia. They certainly do not resonate with Coober Pedy's construction of itself as a tourist destination. Coober Pedy's District Council's promotional online site is aimed at showcasing Coober Pedy to a "World Wide" audience. The District Council invokes a selective, past tense notion of Aboriginal people that imagines them only in relation to landscape. Indeed, the following quote is one of three past-tense references made to Aboriginal people or communities on this particular page of the website. There are no present tense references to Aboriginal peoples on this page. It reads:

> For thousands of years Aboriginal people walked across this area. Because of the desert environment, these people were nomadic hunters and gatherers who traveled constantly in search of food and water supplies as well as to attend traditional ceremonies. (District Council of Coober Pedy, 2005)

According to this website, the land around Coober Pedy is steeped with the sacred significance of ancient nomadic knowledges of Aboriginal people. But no connection is made between these "nomadic hunters and gatherers" and the existing, large Aboriginal population in Coober Pedy. It is as if contemporary lived cultures of Aboriginal local people are being imagined into extinction. By focusing only on the past, it is easier to erase them from the present.

Alongside the construction of Aboriginal people as spirits that infuse the landscape with qualities of desirability, they are positioned as charming zirconias to be consumed alongside fine local produce, live art, and scenic tours. For instance, the South Australian Tourist Commission (STAC) suggests that tourists with "special interests" in backpacking or four wheel driving may like to sample some Indigenous Culture. The backpackers' page of the South Australian Tourist Commission's website (2005) features images of didgeridoos and a link to the Commission's page on Indigenous Culture, which also discusses Aboriginal people mainly in historical terms, or positions them as the special ingredient that makes Australian landscape worthy of tourist consumption. This retrospective/consumed by landscape discursive continuum is broken by a single reference to seeing the "city through the eyes of the Kaurna people" and learning to play the didgeridoo. Interestingly, none of the Commissions' "special interest" tourist groups are Aboriginal people— nor are there images of Aboriginal people in representations of "special interest" groups, which include Family, Gay, and Lesbian, with Pets, Disability, Backpacker, and Self-Drive.

The SATC (2005) publicity website suggests the tourist might like to:

...see the world's largest collection of Aboriginal artifacts at the South Australian Museum, get tips on how to play the didgeridoo at Tandanya, or take a guided Tauondi tour to experience the city through the eyes of the Kaurna people. Coorong National Park, south of Adelaide, was declared a Wetland of International Importance in 1975. For thousands of years it's been home to the Ngarrindjeri Aboriginal peoples—their ancient middens (rubbish and fire mounds) strewn with cockle shells and heating stones can still be found at sheltered spots throughout the sand dunes. The Ngarrindjeri gave the region its name of Karangh, meaning "long narrow neck", and today share their culture at Camp Coorong on Lake Alexandrina. Stay in simple accommodation and learn about the environment, food, traditional life and Dreaming stories of the Coorong. In 1929, a 7000-year-old skeleton of a young boy was discovered on the Murray River in Ngaut Ngaut Conservation Park. Today, you can take a guided tour of the archaeological site and listen as tribal elders unearth Dreamtime legends of the region. (South Australian Tourism Commission, 2005)

No mention is made of who these "tribal elders" are. Contemporary Aboriginal creative practices or art forms, and contemporary Aboriginal engagements with the ways their cultural histories are commodified are also excluded from this discussion of Aboriginal culture. No reference is made to where the proceeds of these cultural tours go, who owns the land being promoted, and who owns the companies that facilitate tourists being able to "stay in simple accommodation and learn about...Dreaming stories of the Coorong."

Erasure and Spatial Purification

Another example in which historicized imaginings of Aboriginal Australians are deployed to market place can be found in the media corporation Fairfax Digital's international tourist website. This website is called the *Walkabout Australian Travel Guide* (2005). "Walkabout" is the name given to the wanderings of Aboriginal people and has deep cultural resonance. But what we see here is the deployment of the concept as a linguistic gimmick rather than a comprehensive engagement with contemporary Aboriginal cultures. Indeed, in relation to Coober Pedy, the *Walkabout Australian Travel Guide* textually erases the town's Aboriginal people. It does so via a discussion of the town's multicultural population:

At the moment there are about 4000 people living in and around the town and over 45 nationalities are represented. The majority of the population is Greek, Yugoslav and Italian (the town has a remarkable similarity to a dusty Mediterranean village) with many Chinese buyers of opals. (Fairfax Digital, 2005)

Aboriginal people are not mentioned here even though they constitute 11.8% of the total population of Coober Pedy (ABS, 2001). This is a notably higher percentage than the Greek population (4.0%; ABS, 2001) and the Yugoslav (2.8%; ABS, 2001) population. Only 1.4 % of Coober Pedy residents were born in China. The Italian population of Coober Pedy is so small that it is not listed by the Australian Bureau of Statistics.

As this example suggests, tourism results in the development of artificial authenticities. These conceal those things that are seen to detract from "best face," including place-based divisions, stratifications, and conflicts. The packaging and selling of place by the tourist industry is not just about mobilizing marketable differences but also about willing away certain unpalatable differences. In Coober Pedy such willing-away has involved a form of "spatial purification," an attempt to provide a "clean space" (Sibley, 1995, p.

77) for tourists. Here many local Aboriginal people are made invisible in order to attract tourists.

The development of the Coober Pedy tourist industry has resulted in an increased focus on the image of the town. Even some of the young non-Aboriginal people see the presence of Aboriginal people in the main street as detrimental to this image. Pailin Rieflin, age 13, observes "They [Aboriginal people] make the place look messy. The street is ruined by the drunken Aboriginals." Chuck Clinton, age 14, agrees:

> They look like flies hanging around. They used to drink booze up and down the street, and I have even seen them throw bricks at each other.... A bit of that still goes on. It is not quite as bad but you still do get the occasional people who hang around the streets and do bad things and make Coober Pedy look bad.

Flies are an abject symbol. Aboriginal people in the street are marked as dirty and dangerous. Their public alcohol consumption is seen as a particular issue. Indeed, Aboriginal people are often constructed as a constantly drunk public spectacle. "It is not really something you want to see or you want your children seeing everyday" says Mario Ciccone, age 16. Steps have been taken to remove them from the main street; the establishment of a "dry zone" being the most notable.

The town applied to the Attorney General's office to make its streets alcohol free. Anybody caught drinking in the street could be moved. Given that mainly Aboriginal people drink outdoors, this change was clearly racist in its intent. It also came to mean that any aboriginal residents who were found drinking in town were dumped in Umoona, whether they resided there or not. This caused such subsequent problems as increased violence and property damage. It also led to a clash between what Cowlishaw (2004, p. 191) calls "respectable and disreputable Aboriginality." The Umoona community then applied to become a dry area. This move was met by significant opposition from other Coober Pedy townspeople, who realized that they could not so easily sweep public drunkenness out of view to the abject zone of Umoona and neither could they use this excuse to create a "clean space" for the tourist gaze.

Kristeva explains, "that word, 'fear'...no sooner has it cropped up than it shades off like a mirage and permeates all...with a hallucinatory ghostly glimmer" (1982, p. 6). The deployment of abject splitting keeps Aboriginal identity and culture both erasable and marketable. But it also means that the tourist industry constantly "shades off" into a "hallucinatory ghostly glimmer" of fear that the erased will return to "haunt" the industry. A particular fear is associated with what we call "abject agency" (drawing on Cowlishaw, 2004). Such agency arises from "chronic discontent" and "continuing and unresolved rage and resentment which has resulted from past injustices" (Cowlishaw, 2004, pp. 75, 189). It is derived from the derogatory symbolic codes used to abjectify the group in the first place. "Abject agency" involves "taking up an abject position" (Cowlishaw, 2004, p. 158), mocking and exaggerating it through defiance and disrespect, and hurling it back at the original perpetrator. Cowlishaw talks of the ways in which some young Aboriginal men participate in this process. As a result, say, of being noisy or fighting in the street or throwing stones at shop windows, or drinking or chroming (sniffing gasoline), many come into direct contact with the White legal system. She explains how:

> Anger and abjection are performed in the court and in the street, using language which confounds, disconcerts and embarrasses the White audience.... [and] seem to confirm the grotesque images of deformed Aboriginality. (2004, p. 74)

Cowlishaw then suggests that: "Experiences and actions that Whites despise can be displayed as triumphant defeat of attempted humiliation" (Cowlishaw, 2004, p. 192). As a consequence, such young men may be treated "like champions" with cries of "Good on you brother." This form of "desperate excess' (Cowlishaw 2004, p. 163) is designed to evoke extreme discomfort, disgust or dismay in the dominant White population. It can thus be argued that "spatial purification" for the tourist gaze may create precisely the sorts of behaviors it seeks to hide.

Kristeva explains:

> ...abjection is elaborated by a failure to recognize its kin...hence before they are signifiable—[the subject in question] drives them out...and constitutes his own territory edged by the abject.... Fear cements his compound.... (1982, p. 6)

The splitting of abject Aboriginal people and culture into "compounds" of the desirable and the undesirable can be read in Kristeva's (1982, p. 6) terms as a refusal to let a population solidify and become fully recognizable to itself and to others; to be understood and to understand itself in all its complexity and ambiguity. So, for Aboriginal boys growing up in Coober Pedy, tourism has a range of different significances, not the least being its abject refusal of their full selfhood.

Moving Abjection?

We look to create possibilities for moving scapes of abjection. We do so by adding spatial, political, and affective density to Appadurai's global scapes. These scapes intersect with local geometries of race, poverty, and gender. Even minor mobilities within the nation state can be modulated through noxious global ideoscapes and media scapes of abjection. We have illustrated how ethno- and mediascapes abjectify "local" populations in contradictory ways. We have put further flesh on ideas associated with the disjunctive flows of the global cultural economy by offering examples of such flows in and through marginalized places. Further, we developed the notion of "scapes of abjection" to show how affect and abjection work on and in the imagination. They have flow-on effects on economically and culturally marginalized and stigmatized populations of Australian Aborigines. Long-standing injustices are rescripted and reinscribed through their links with contemporary scapes of abjection, highlighting the noxious politics of movement and stasis and the infectious ill-feelings they provoke. At local and global levels, education seems the most critically equipped social process available to move scapes of abjection. Classroom contexts and popular pedagogies such as film, television, radio, Internet, and print media, need to be mobilized as devices for speaking back to, and intercepting, the processes of abjection produced by local and global scapes of abjection.

Note

1. This wider study (Kenway, Kraack, & Hickey-Moody, 2006) considers youthful masculinities and gender relations in marginalized, stigmatized, but also sometimes romanticized and exoticized places beyond the metropolis in the so-called developed West. We thank the Australian Research Council for funding this three-year study, Anna Kraack for her contributions to this chapter, and Palgrave for permission to reprint selections from Kenway, Kraack, and Hickey-Moody (2006).

References

Appadurai, A. (1996). *Modernity at large: Cultural dimensions of globalization*. Minneapolis: University of Minnesota Press.

Appadurai, A. (2000). Disjuncture and difference in the global cultural economy. In F. J. Lechner & J. Boli (Eds.), *The globalization reader* (pp. 322–300). Oxford: Blackwell.

Australian Bureau of Statistics. (2001). Updated Coober Pedy stats 2001 census. Retrieved December 2, 2005, from http://www.abs.gov.au/

Australian Bureau of Statistics. (2003). *The health and welfare of Australia's Aboriginal and Torres Straight islander peoples*. Report 4704.0, Retrieved August 11, 2005, from http://www.abs.gov.au/

Bauman, Z. (1998a). *Globalization: The human consequences*. Cambridge: Polity.

Bauman, Z. (1998b). *Work, consumerism & the new poor*. Buckingham: Open University Press.

Burawoy, M., Blum, J. A., George, S., Gille, Z., Gowan, T., Haney, L., et al. (Eds.). (2000). *Global ethnography: Forces, connections, and imaginations in a postmodern world*. Berkeley: University of California Press.

Broome, R. (2001). *Aboriginal Australians: Black responses to White dominance, 1788–2001* (3rd ed.). St. Leonards, NSW: Allen & Unwin.

Cohen, R., & Kennedy, P. (2000). *Global sociology*. New York: New York University Press.

Cowlishaw, G. (2004). *Blackfellas, Whitefellas and hidden injuries of race*. Oxford: Blackwell.

District Council of Coober Pedy. Retrieved July 9, 2005 from http://www.opalcapitaloftheworld.com.au/history.asp

Fairfax Digital Media. (2005).*Walkabout Australian travel guide*. Retrieved July 8, 2005, from http://walkabout.com.au/index.shtml

Fraser, N. (2005, November-December). Reframing justice in a globalizing world. *New Left Review, 36*. Retrieved September 12, 2006, from http://www.newleftreview.net/?page=article&view=2589

Friend, T. (2005, August 13). He's been everywhere, man. *The Good Weekend, The Age Magazine*, 20–24.

Giroux, H. (*1999)*. Cultural studies as public pedagogy making the pedagogical more political. *Encyclopaedia of philosophy of education*. Retrieved May 15, 2005, from http://www.vusst.hr/ENCYCLOPAEDIA/main.htm

Giroux, H. (2004a). Education after Abu Ghraib: Revisiting Adorno's politics of education. *Cultural Studies, 18*, 779–815.

Giroux, H. (2004b). Cultural studies, public pedagogy, and the responsibility of intellectuals. *Communication and Critical Cultural Studies, 1*(1), 59–79.

Grosz, E. (1989). *Sexual subversions: Three French feminists*. Sydney, Australia: Allen & Unwin.

Haebich, A. (2001). *Broken circles: Fragmenting indigenous families 1800–2000*. Fremantle, Australia: FACP.

Kenway, J., Kraack, A., & Hickey-Moody, A. (2006). *Masculinity beyond the metropolis*. New York: Palgrave Macmillan.

Kristeva, J. (1982). *Powers of horror*. New York: Columbia University Press.

Lonely Planet, The. (n.d./a) *Journeys to authentic Australia*. Retrieved July 8, 2005, from http://www.lonelyplanet.com

Lonely Planet, The. (n.d./b). *Guide to Aboriginal Australia*. Retrieved July 8, 2005 from http://www.lonelyplanet.com

MacCannell, D. (1999). *The tourist: A new theory of the leisure class*. Berkeley: University of California Press.

McClintock, A. (1995). *Imperial leather: Race, gender and sexuality in the colonial contest*. New York: Routledge.

National Aboriginal & Torres Straight Islander Health Council (NATSIHC). (2003). National strategic framework for Aboriginal and Torres *Strait islander health: Framework for action by governments*. Canberra: NATSIHC.

Reynolds, H. (1999).*Why weren't we told? A personal search for the truth about our history.* Ringwood, Victoria: Penguin.

Sibley, D. (1995). *Geographies of exclusion: Society and difference in the west.* London: Routledge.

South Australian Tourist Commission, The (STAC). Retrieved July 8, 2005 from http://www.southaustralia.com

Urry, J. (1990). *The tourist gaze.* London: Sage.

Urry, J. (2000). *Sociology beyond societies: Mobilities for the twenty-first century.* New York: Routledge.

9 Global Politics, Gender Justice, and Education
Contemporary Issues and Debates

Amanda Keddie and Martin Mills

Introduction

Despite the institution of global social equity imperatives such as those represented in the 1948 Universal Declaration of Human Rights, gender justice remains an elusive ideal. Indeed, in spite of the long time focus on women and gender equity within international policy (see UNIFEM, 2005–2006) and a specific emphasis on girls in the sphere of education (e.g., the frameworks in Dakar, 2000; Jomtein, 1990; UNESCO, 2006) women's position in relation to poverty and oppression has, by some accounts, barely improved (Tikly, 2004). While other accounts contend that the situation for women and girls worldwide has slowly, albeit inconsistently, improved since the institution of such global imperatives, it is clear that girls as a group continue to face extensive issues of disadvantage in relation to education. In many "developing" countries girls are denied even the most basic education; in others where they do obtain access to schooling, many are the victims of sexual harassment and abuse; in many locations girls' high illiteracy and poor retention rates are alarming, as is the quality of the education that some receive at school when compared with that provided to boys.

Prevailing social and cultural traditions, particularly in "developing" countries invariably compound these gender disparities. Cultural traditions that position boys' schooling participation as more important than that of girls have become more pronounced and the situation has been exacerbated by issues of poverty and the rising costs associated with schooling. Of concern in recent times, and fortifying the barriers to closing such inequities in many non-Western contexts, particularly those in the Islamic world, are the enduring tensions associated with the imposing of Western ideologies of "development." Certainly, the ideological conflicts between the West and Islam, as we argue in this chapter, do little to militate against the existing broader cultural barriers that constrain girls' progress in terms of education.

The situation for girls in the "developed" world is somewhat different. Against a resource rich backdrop and decades of feminist reform, girls as a group in many Western countries generally fare much better than their non-Western counterparts. From the late 1970s, there has been a concerted focus in many Western countries on national equity policy to raise girls' schooling achievement, which has generated substantial improvements in girls' general academic attainment. However, from the early 1990s, a backlash context against feminist gains in education has meant the downstreaming of gender reform for girls (Blackmore, 1999; Hayes, 2003). Girls' equity issues are now sidelined or ignored alongside an aggressive recuperative politics of "What about the boys?" (Lingard, 2003).

In this chapter we locate such trends in gender priorities within the globalizing processes of neoliberalism and the new international politics post-September 11. The chapter begins by tracking the regressive impacts of the global neoliberal agenda. We articulate here how the masculinist and neoimperialist regimes embedded in this agenda constrain women's economic, social, and physical well-being and narrow educational priorities in ways that distort gender justice goals. We consider these issues in light of the changed global politics post-September 11, and thus draw attention to the ways in which new narratives of national security, antagonistic relations between the West and Islam, and resurgent nationalism (Rizvi, 2004) pose particular problems for gender equity. Principally, we express concern about how these narratives constrain gender justice through shutting down dissent and championing a return to conservative or fundamental values.

In exploring the localized gendered effects of these global narratives, we draw particular attention to some of the gender equity and schooling trends in Australia and Egypt. We do not suggest that each is representative of Western and non-Western contexts, rather, that each provides a means of illuminating particular dominant "turns" taking place within the global field of gender justice and education. The selection of these two contexts enables a discussion of the global implications of gender policies constructed within a neoliberal paradigm, whilst at the same time enabling a discussion of the ways in which recent tensions between, and within, countries allied with the United States and countries influenced by Islam are impacting upon the educational gender agenda.

Globalization, Neoliberalism, and Gender

The valorized Western-led discourses of neoliberalism have acquired hegemonic status within global politics since the mid- to late 1980s. The dominant norms of efficiency and an "ethic" of cost-benefit analysis have served to venerate the "market" as the organizing principle of public policy (e.g., Apple, 2005). Within understandings that markets are driven and regulated by consumer choice and demand, neoliberal discourses construct an unquestioning faith in their essential fairness and justice in terms of their capacity to work in ways that will distribute resources efficiently and fairly according to effort. However, as many commentators have consistently argued, far from creating fair and equitable societies, these economizing and depoliticizing strategies actually exacerbate the inequitable distribution of resources and power along racialized, gendered, and classed lines (Apple, 2005; Eisenstein, 1998; Mohanty, 2003).

There has been much debate about how the global expansion of neoliberal or capitalist discourses impact on non-Western or "developing" contexts. Many commentators understand this expansion as an imperialist project that works to homogenize culture in unidirectional ways from "the West" to "the Rest" (Giroux, 2002; Rizvi, 2004). From the underlying premise that global capital needs local states to ensure the social cohesion and economic growth necessary for capital accumulation (Rizvi, 2004), this process works to construct and perpetuate vast global inequities through incorporating so-called developing nations into regimes that render them economically useful and politically docile (Tikly, 2004). Tikly (2004), and others (Goldman, 2005; Hardt & Negri, 2001), contend that this agenda "...serves to secure the interests of the USA, its Western allies and of global capitalism more generally" (p. 173).

Along these lines, Tikly (2004) notes the often conflicting ideologies relating to social change or development in Western and non-Western traditions. He is especially critical of how Western ideas of progress, imposed on alternative cultural traditions, perpetuate bias in defining underdevelopment simplistically, in terms of "lack." Such disciplinary paradigms highly restrict the capacities of developing countries to determine their own social agendas (Chabbott, 2003; Tikly, 2004). Exploring these issues, Blackmore (2000) talks about the Western "mantras" of efficiency and economy embedded in structural adjustment and conditional lending policies instituted by organizations such as the World Bank. These regulatory policies are not only seen as limiting the autonomy of "developing" nations but also as compromising social equity goals within these contexts (Abouharb & Cingranelli, 2006; Goldman, 2005; Mohanty, 2003) including progressivist agendas seeking to reduce poverty and women's oppression (Blackmore, 2000).

Invariably, this is because the neoliberal ideals of individualism, independence, and freedom underpinning these economic-centric policies are inherently masculinist in their endorsement of gender inequities. Such ideals, it is well established, tend only to acknowledge the masculinized self of the public sphere and thus "...obscure a fundamental source of power and inequality in relations between the sexes" (O'Connor, Orloff, & Shaver, 1999, p. 45). These principles have generated a global environment of increased privatization and deregulation of public services and a weakening of the welfare state that has compounded gender disadvantage. In Western and non-Western contexts alike, poverty levels have increased since the 1970s for many women, and other disadvantaged groups, through neoliberalism's whittling away of affirmative, protectionist, and welfare policies (Blackmore, 2000; Bulbeck, 1994; Hatem, 1994). Such protectionist and welfare policies are, of course, imperative to pursuing the goals of gender justice in a global climate where:

> ...women and girls are still 70 percent of the world's poor and the majority of the world's refugees; [where] girls and women comprise almost 80 percent of displaced persons of the ["developing world" and where] women own less than one-hundredth of the world's property, while they are the hardest hit by the effects of war, domestic violence and religious persecution. (Mohanty, 2003, p. 234)

Clearly constraining in terms of any hope of beginning to remedy these stark gender inequities, Blackmore (2000, p. 475) argues, that in subsuming political imperatives with the market, "...gender equity is [generally] perceived to be a luxury that democratic states, new and old, cannot afford...." Within this paradigm, as she points out, gender equity policies can only be justified if linked to productivity.

Such links between women and issues of productivity are key characteristics within the discourses that surround the policies and initiatives of multilateral agencies concerning women in the developing world (Tikly, 2004). Developing and integrating women's productive capabilities more effectively into national and international economies are central poverty remedying strategies of the World Bank. Another remedy for addressing issues of poverty concerns the Bank's discourses around women's reproductive capacities. Here concerns about overpopulation and issues of increased poverty, have resulted in various initiatives aimed at controlling women's fertility in low-income contexts. Such economic-centric initiatives are strongly condemned as disciplining women in neoimperialist and bioracist ways (Tikly, 2004; Wangari, 2002). In particular, they ignore the gross disparities in the consumption patterns between populations in low and high-income contexts and "...the effects of economic globalisation on poverty and the local environment" (Tikly, 2004). Most significantly perhaps, the justification of gender equity policy through neoliberal regimes of efficiency and economy imposes:

> ...a western conception [and homogenous worldview] of women's empowerment based on the notion of individual rights, sex equality and the nature of sisterhood... [that] fails to connect either with the unique forms of oppression and power relationships experienced by many women in low-income contexts, [or the] alternative, more

collectively orientated and indigenous forms of struggle organised around an alternative view of basic needs as constituting "rights."' (Tikly, 2004, p. 184)

While by some accounts these Western conceptions of women's empowerment have changed some women's positions in countries of the developing world for the better in terms of improved socioeconomic conditions, many other accounts point to the failure of initiatives based on these conceptions to reduce poverty and redress women's oppression (Keddie, 1991; Mohanty, 2003; Tikly, 2004). Keddie (1991) for instance, tells of the suffering particularly poorer women have endured under these broader imperatives, such as substandard working conditions, poorly paid employment, and removal from the security of rural life.

Neoliberalism, Education, and Gender Equity

Globally, neoliberal discourses have had a major impact upon public institutions such as education. In endorsing the core relationship between education and capitalism, these discourses resonate with a vision of students as human capital (Apple, 2005). Here resource provision for educational reform agendas in Western and non-Western contexts alike, have tended to be driven by concerns that ensure states are globally competitive. Such concerns are based on the need to ensure that students are appropriately educated as future workers in order that they can be productive in an ever increasing and intensely competitive global economy. While, as Apple (2005) points out, the educational initiatives arising from neoliberal concerns with human capital growth are varied, many have focused on increasing policy and practice around education for employment and work-related education programs and involve a stress on higher academic standards and more rigorous testing.

Taylor and Henry suggest that the ascendancy of these tenets, and in particular, the "...increasing emphasis on markets to drive educational provision...[and] a focus on outcomes rather than inputs as a policy and funding lever..." (2000, pp. 1–2) is highly regressive for social equity. They argue that a deregulated environment of competition, reduced funding, and the pressure of "market advantage" is incongruent with producing enhanced equity outcomes (see also Gillborn & Youdell, 2000). The cultures of performativity generated in schools by these pressures have resulted in an obsession with academic results and the measurement of specific aspects of education, principally, easily quantifiable and measurable literacy and numeracy outcomes. Such a focus is seen as narrowly defining success and achievement and delimiting measures of school effectiveness in ways that sideline broader social concerns (Mahony, 1999; Pallotta-Chiarolli, 1997). To these ends, critical educational issues, especially those that impact negatively on girls, such as the perpetuation of gender dualisms through schools' masculinist infrastructures (Mahony, 1999), and the level of violence and sexist harassment in schools, tend to be overlooked (Kenway, Willis, Rennie, & Blackmore, 1998; Pallotta-Chiarolli, 1997). Moreover, and particularly regressive for groups of students who are marginalized through gender or other identity relations, such as class or race, these cultures of performativity have produced a schooling climate where teachers generally place greater emphasis on efficiency and basic skills rather than social justice outcomes (Lingard, 2003).

Amplified within a backlash context against feminist gains in education, these broader discourses, in Western contexts such as Australia, have shifted gender equity concerns from a social justice focus on girls in the 1970 and 1980s to a selective emphasis on standards and the current overwrought concerns with boys' schooling performance (Lingard, 2003; Mills, 2003). Indeed, the rearticulation of equity in education to stress literacy outcomes, has enabled a re-presentation of boys as educationally disadvantaged and provided impetus for many large-scale government funded programs, such as the A\$19.4 million *Success for Boys* initiative in Australia, aimed at improving boys' educational outcomes. The broader context within which such initiatives are generated has been extensively criticized as hindering the pursuit of gender justice goals. This climate reflects a counterproductive "competing victims approach" to issues of gender justice; sidelines the significance of class and ethnicity in compounding educational disadvantage for many boys *and* girls; ignores any recognition of boys' and men's relative economic and social advantage beyond the school; and is particularly hostile in terms of disregarding the issues of disadvantage that continue to be experienced by many girls (Collins, Kenway, & McLeod, 2000; Francis & Skelton, 2005; Lingard, 2003).

Priorities associated with academic standards and the school-to-work nexus resonate in many ways with the schooling concerns of countries within the developing world and can be associated with the alignment of education in these contexts with the global imperative of economic growth. Underpinned by a view of education as a key factor in economic development—a view adopted by the United Nations in 1960—human capital theory has dominated much of the literature on education in the developing world (Resnik, 2006). Indeed, raising human capital for the purposes of sustaining the economic growth of developing nations remains a central platform of World Bank discourses about education and remains a key policy area for the multilateral development agencies (Little, 2003; Schultz, 1971; Tikly, 2004). To these ends, agencies like the World Bank have significant disciplinary power in relation to shaping the educational agenda of developing nations through social intervention and discretion over resource provision (Chabbott, 2003; Jones, 1998). Tikly (2004) refers here to initiatives such as the extension and expansion of education and training along Western lines.

Such initiatives are criticized as promoting an integrated world system along market lines (Jones, 1998). While Tikly (2004) and others (Stiglitz, 2002) are cognizant of the relatively recent shifts that associate the resource provision of multilateral agencies with addressing social concerns such as the development of global citizenship through education, they also align this shift with broader neoimperialist imperatives that view social cohesion within nation states as central to the sustainability of global capitalism. While such shifts can clearly be seen as reflecting benevolent concerns for human rights, Ball (1998) contends that organizations such as the World Bank see equity as a residual concern of governments and as such the social and welfare purposes of education are systematically played down.

Notwithstanding these interpretations, such priority areas continue to enable a focus on girls as a disadvantaged group that requires affirmative action and special treatment—unlike the focus on boys in the West. The World Bank, for example, supports the *Millennium Development Goals*, one of which is to promote gender equity and empower women, another of which is to achieve universal primary education (UNESCO, 2005). A current innovative program supported by the Bank to achieve these two goals in the developing world is a stipend initiative to reward parents for allowing their daughters to attend school. This stipend helps families in abject poverty with the costs of schooling and compensates for girls being away from home (World Bank, 2006). Global social movements around such gender justice goals, as Rizvi argues (2004), exemplify the generative principles of a cosmopolitan global solidarity. While addressing gender equity issues within a Western led neoliberal paradigm is far from unproblematic, as the above discussion points out, this focus on girls has made some inroads to reducing gender injustices in the developing world and is thus undoubtedly positive in terms of global equity.

Nonetheless, the regressive impacts of the global neoliberal agenda on gender justice and schooling goals in both Western and non-Western contexts are marked. The emphasis on performative cultures that prioritize the market over social justice concerns has worked against the interests of girls in the West in distorting gender equity priorities to produce a focus on boys as an equity group. Outside the West some aspects of the neoliberal agenda (in generating a focus on women and girls as equity groups), can be interpreted as progressive for gender justice. While not wishing to detract from this, the valorization of the West in terms of imposing a particular homogenized view of women's and girls' empowerment remains problematic in its cultural exclusivity.

We now turn to a discussion of the new global narratives post-September 11, namely those associated with security, resurgent nationalism, and increased antagonism between the West and Islam. In particular, we draw on, and juxtapose, some of the educational debates in Australia with those in Egypt to illuminate some of what we suggest pose major impediments to gender justice.

Gender in the Post-September 11 Context

Global narratives espousing a concern for national security have dominated the political agenda in many Western countries since the terrorist attacks in the United States on September 11, 2001. Such security concerns, fed by a culture of fear, particularly in Western countries allied with the United States, have fueled a resurgent nationalism and increasing demonization of those who associate with Islam (Rizvi, 2004). Resurgent nationalism in contexts influenced by Islam, conversely, has been shaped by an anti-U.S./Western sentiment. The shutting down of dissent associated with the nationalistic imperatives produced by the global "war on terror" that champion a return to conservative or fundamental values, signify potentially deleterious implications for gender equity worldwide.

The various Western responses to the September 11 attacks in the United States, alongside wars instigated against Afghanistan and Iraq, have seen a greater policing and surveillance of marginalized local, usually Muslim, communities within countries such as Australia, the United States, Canada, and Britain (Rizvi, 2004). This concern with national security has also worked to stifle critical debates about matters relating to social justice. As with many wars, the "war on terror" has seen nationalist discourses being deployed in ways that seek to unify nations' residents into an "us" who is opposed to a "them." The achievement of an "us" requires the absence of dissent, an adherence to a common set of values (read in the West, values that align with White, conservative, Anglocentrism), and a fear and distrust of "them." The "them," within the current climate are Muslims who threaten "our" way of life, and "our" fear of them has been used to justify the oppression of Muslim communities, and has worked to construct those opposed to so-called Western values as undermining the "war effort." Such nationalistic discourses, fed by the simplistic moral certainty of broader political rhetoric, have hindered democratic debate (Giroux, 2002; hooks, 2003; Rizvi, 2004). Commentators, for example, hooks (2003), express particular concern about this stifling of critical debate post September 11:

> In a matter of months many citizens ceased to believe in the value of living in diverse communities, of anti-racist work, of seeking peace. They surrendered their belief in the healing power of justice. Hardcore White-supremacist nationalism reared its ugly voice and spoke openly, anywhere. Individuals who dared to dissent, to critique, to challenge misinformation were and are labelled traitors. As time passed, we wit-

nessed a mounting backlash against any individual or group who dared to work for justice, who opposed domination in all its forms. (p. 10)

Fed by the neoconservative narratives associated with the right-wing politics of the Western alliance against the "war on terror"—the so-called "coalition of the willing," this upsurge in uncritical and morally righteous nationalism along White supremacist and patriarchal lines has impacted on schools and schooling in highly regressive ways in terms of social justice. Particularly, as hooks (2003) suggests, because such nationalism serves to stifle socially critical pedagogies and heighten surveillance in relation to what is taught in schools and how it is taught. In Australia, for example, neoconservative imagery along Anglocentric and masculinist lines has framed the federal government's agenda for national values education. This agenda has been accompanied by a flag pole initiative in schools to develop a nationalist pride amongst young people and a call for more rigorous teaching of Australian history (usually with a focus on Australia's British heritage rather than on its development as a multicultural society). Such initiatives have been accompanied by overt suspicion of Islamic schools, in terms of government surveillance of curriculum and pedagogy, as well as attempts to police particular cultural traditions. For example, there have been in Australia, as in other places, most notoriously France, ministerial calls for a banning of Muslim girls' wearing the hijab at public schools—this symbol of Islam is seen as a sign of "iconic defiance" to the "Australian" way of life. In the United Kingdom, there are plans to bring Islamic schools under the control of the local educational authorities. Ironically, in a country that prides itself on its commitment to free speech, some teachers in the United States who have criticized its war effort in Afghanistan and Iraq, or have sought to examine the reasons behind the September 11 attacks, have been fired from their jobs (Giroux, 2002).

These broader trends are clearly damaging for the gender equity project. It is well established that the social critique and debate of dominant ideologies are cornerstones to facilitating pedagogies of gender justice in schools (Alloway, 1995; Davies, 1993; Martino & Pallotta-Chiarolli, 2005). Stifling such questioning and debate in the area of identity politics and sociocultural justice, particularly within a schooling context where performative cultures have already skewed equity concerns and sidelined social outcomes, is likely to be constraining for gender justice. Such trends will do little to disrupt the masculinist discourses within and beyond schools that continue, for example, to silence the misogynistic regimes that undergird the sexual harassment and cultural marginalization of females endemic in school cultures.

At the very least, these trends can be seen as fueling the current widespread and highly vocal political backlash against progressive education. Endemic in the "back to basics" approach of conservative politics, this backlash has sought to suppress the critical agenda of particular curriculum materials that promote debate concerning the exploration of contentious political and cultural issues. Such progressive agendas are regularly attacked in the Australian media. *The Australian* newspaper, for instance, has taken a particularly resolute stance against critical literacy—frequently condemning such practice as excessively nihilistic, excessively critical of Eurocentrism, nationalism, and conservatism or ridiculing it along the lines of "destructive postmodern claptrap" (Donnelly, 2006). More broadly, such neoconservative trends, particularly given the antifeminist politics within Western countries like Australia, the United Kingdom, and the United States (indeed, the then Prime Minister of Australia, John Howard, implied the irrelevance of feminism, publicly commenting that he believed Australia to be in a "postfeminist era"), would seem likely to further amplify the gender disparities of an already regressive neoliberal environment where conservative ideologies of women and the family have taken a firm hold in government policy and public consciousness.

In non-Western contexts such as Egypt, the new global narratives post-September 11, also pose significant problems for the pursuit of gender justice. This is principally because, as Mazawi (2002) points out, as a response to global Western culture, "...there has been a worldwide revival of fundamentalism in its myriad forms" (p. 60). Within a context of increasing anti-Western sentiment in Egypt, and ever growing concern and resentment associated with how Western/liberal ideologies are eroding and undermining Egyptian identity, heritage, and tradition, this revival in fundamentalism is unlikely to be tempered. This is particularly so given that the new rhetoric of security has enabled the United States to reassert its global authority and preeminence in international relations (Rizvi, 2004).

Nonetheless, containing religious fundamentalism, and more specifically militant Islamic fundamentalism, and promoting social stability in Egypt, are key imperatives underpinning the development and aid agenda of the major international donor agencies. Certainly, this nation's geopolitical characteristics mean that it is an important ally of the United States and Western European countries—particularly post-September 11, given the perceived threat that instability in the Middle East and North Africa regions continues to pose for Western interests (Sayed, 2005).

Within broader discourses of national security, the public education system in Egypt is positioned as one of the central ways that this stability can be generated. Indeed, as Cook (2000) argues, public schooling is seen to be the primary means of combating Egypt's most dangerous threat—Islamic extremism. To these ends, considerable aid has assisted Egypt's endeavors to modernize their nation along Western development lines, and more specifically to expand secular schooling (Cook, 1999, 2000). Many Egyptians, however, according to Cook (1999, 2000), and others (see Mazawi, 2002; Sayed, 2005), are highly critical of secular schooling, principally because its antireligious and liberal tenets are seen to fundamentally conflict with Islamic tradition and philosophy. Cook (2000) argues that many in the Islamic world align secularized schooling with "educational apartheid" and see it as representing the epitome of Muslim decline. Furthermore, as Cook (2000) points out, a prevailing and far from uncommon view is that secularist educational policies and Egypt's blind imitation of the West, are responsible for Egypt losing its identity.

Amid heightened antagonism post September 11 and disillusionment toward Western approaches to development that have done little to remedy Egypt's enduring poverty and hardship and within a broader global climate of resurgent nationalism that has intensified Egypt's search for a national identity distinct from the West, Islamic militant groups have managed to develop strong and growing alliances with the general Egyptian public (Sayed, 2005). Of significance, these groups have been able to tap into the public's general disdain toward secular schooling and are increasingly providing educational alternatives for poor and disenfranchised communities (where religious fundamentalism is likely to be most prevalent) based on conservative Islamic values (Sayed, 2005). Such trends, especially within a context where gender disparities are considerable, throw up particular concerns along the trajectory to meeting such gender equity and primary education imperatives as those within the *Millennium Development Goals*.

While under the global *Education-for-All* umbrella (UNESCO, 1994), concerted efforts have been made by Egypt's Ministry of Education to improve the situation for girls, particular sociocultural barriers continue to hinder their attendance, attainment, and training. Exacerbating the gender gap, these barriers are associated with, for example, parental concerns with protecting their daughters' modesty and security; a lack of enforcement of compulsory education policies; issues of poverty and the rising costs associated with schooling and basic school supplies; prevailing attitudes that families feel that it is a better investment to educate their sons; cultural expectations in terms of girls' domestic responsibilities and parental reluctance to send their girls to coeducational schools; and the association between girls' early marriage and their elevated school dropout rates (World Bank, 2003).

It is contended here that the cultural and socioeconomic barriers hindering girls' schooling attainment are likely to be exacerbated within Egypt's current climate of tension between the perceived Westernization of schooling and a resurgent nationalism founded on particular Islamic principles. Much has been written, especially by feminists, about the ways in which conservative or fundamentalist readings of Islam are particularly oppressive to women (Ghoussoub, 1987; Kazemi, 2000; Keddie, 1991). Such oppressions are generally seen to relate to how the Quran represents women in ways that emphasize and rigidify gender difference and where unequal practices (related to, for example, political representation and economic security) are justified on a perception of men's and women's different natures and needs (Keddie, 1991). The amplification of women's oppressions in nations such as Egypt in the more recent past has been attributed to increased anti-Western sentiment and more specifically, Muslim resistance to Western-sanctioned change and Western views of women's empowerment. Against this backdrop, as Keddie (1991) argues, the home has become the last bastion against the cultural, political, and economic offensive of the West and thus attempts to retain the Islamization of women's roles have been concerted because this is a touchstone of Islam. As Keddie (1991) further points out, this is partly because: "...a return to Quranic injunctions on dress, polygamy, and so forth are a highly visible way to show one is a good Muslim" (p. 17). And in the current context of anti-Western, or more precisely anti-U.S. feelings in these locations, being a "good Muslim" can be constructed as an act of defiance and resistance to a perceived Western cultural imperialism.

When considering that many of the barriers that constrain girls' school attendance and performance are cultural barriers that would be further fortified through conservative readings of the Quran, the future trajectory in terms of reaching the *Millennium Development Goals* for women, equity, girls and schooling, does not look bright. Certainly, for example, it would seem that the cultural traditions that hinder girls' attendance and attainment at school would likely be further reinforced within the fundamental interpretations of Islam which have burgeoned in the post-September 11 context.

Conclusion

In this chapter we have explored some of the gender equity implications that are associated with the globalizing processes of neoliberalism. In particular we have drawn attention to the ways in which the regimes of efficiency and economy embedded in these processes are at odds with creating an environment conducive to pursuing gender justice goals. Within an ethos where politics becomes subsumed by market imperatives, and where notions of democracy shift from political to economic concepts, the inequitable distribution of resources and power along gendered (as well as racial and class) lines becomes increasingly pronounced. The decline in social policy and reduction of welfare services, as a product of such imperatives, has had particularly adverse effects, to varying extents, on women worldwide. In the non-West or developing world the imperialism of these imperatives, particularly in terms of imposing homogenized views of women and empowerment, has in many ways compounded issues of disadvantage for many women and girls.

In articulating how these regimes adversely impact on the sphere of equity in education, we foregrounded key issues of gender injustice. We highlighted here how the limited academic, and more specifically literacy, outcomes focus of performative cultures within many Western schooling contexts, skews gender equity concerns to position boys as a disadvantaged group and to silence key injustices that continue to characterize the schooling experience of many girls. In discussing how these regimes tend to impact on the sphere of gender equity and education in non-Western contexts, while acknowledging how some aspects of the global neoliberal agenda have made inroads to improving the lifeworlds of many girls and women, we expressed concern about the ways in which these regimes are unresponsive to the cultural specificities of non-Western environments.

Drawing on these concerns, we explored some of the gender debates and issues in countries such as Australia and Egypt, within the context of the changed imperatives for education, post-September 11. We argued here that the new narratives of resurgent nationalism, security, and increased antagonism between the West and Islam, that have pervaded the global education agenda, pose particular problems for pursuing the goals of gender equity. Such narratives were seen as intersecting with some of the key educational trends in Australia and Egypt to further exacerbate some of the negative byproducts of the neoliberal agenda. Constraining gender justice in many Western countries, and in particular, Australia, we argued that the new narratives post September 11 served to stifle the socially critical and progressive agenda in schools and to strengthen the Anglo-centric resolve of the conservative/neoliberal politics already seen as highly regressive to the gender equity project. The debates in Egypt, a non-Western context seen as reflective of the educational experience of many other Muslim countries, were similarly juxtaposed with the narratives post-September 11, to propose a highly regressive trajectory for gender justice. Here we foregrounded the ways in which heightened antagonism and disillusionment toward imposed Western approaches to development, including education, in Egypt, intensified through the "war on terror," has strengthened the grip of Islamic fundamentalism in many parts of this country. This state of affairs was argued as further compounding the many cultural barriers that continue to constrain the gender justice possibilities for girls and women in the Egyptian context. The current upsurge in anti-Western sentiment, fueling the revival of Islamic fundamentalism, conservative readings of the Quran, and the amplifying of women's and girls' oppressions, is far from conducive to generating the cosmopolitan trajectory necessary to realizing the gender equity and schooling Millennium Development Goals.

In pursuing the goals of a global gender justice, it is clear that these negative trajectories in both Western and non-Western contexts need to be disrupted. In taking up struggles against the neoliberal discourses that drive the global capitalist juggernaut, much has been written in the area of social equity and antiglobalization about ways in which such disruptions might take place (e.g., Giroux, 2002; McLaren, 2000). However, despite, as we have articulated in this chapter, girls and women bearing the brunt of globalization, gender analyses have tended to be absent from such writing (Mohanty, 2003). Within the masculinizing discourses of globalization, on the one hand, and the masculinization within antiglobalization movements, on the other, Mohanty draws attention to the urgency of making feminist agendas and projects explicit. Her call for a feminism without borders that proposes a global feminist solidarity organized against capitalism, that exposes and makes visible the various, overlapping forms of subjugation of women's lives and reenvisions forms of collective social resistance for women, offers a trajectory of hope. In a world where global capitalism, while destroying possibilities for social action, also opens up new possibilities, she urges a transnational feminist solidarity "...across the divisions of place, identity, class, work, belief..." (2003, p. 250). The reimagining of liberatory politics, she proposes, is possible through a solidarity that is attentive to both the micropolitics of everyday life as well as the macropolitics of global economic and political processes. Such solidarity that works against repressive politics will be central to challenging and transforming the increasingly brutal cultural landscape post September 11 (Mohanty, 2003).

References

Abouharb, M., & Cingranelli, D. (2006). The human rights effects of World Bank structural adjustment, 1981–2000. *International Studies Quarterly, 50*, 233–262.

Alloway, N. (1995). *Foundation stones: The construction of gender in early childhood*. Carlton, Australia: Curriculum Corporation.

Apple, M. (2005). Are markets in education democratic? Neoliberal globalism, vouchers, and the politics of choice. In M. Apple, J. Kenway, & M. Singh (Eds.), *Globalizing education: Policies, pedagogies, and politics* (pp. 209–230). New York: Peter Lang.

Ball, S. (1998) Big policies/small world: An introduction to international perspectives in education policy. *Comparative Education, 34*(2), 119–130.

Blackmore, J. (1999). *Troubling women: Feminism, leadership and educational change*. Buckingham, UK: Open University Press.

Blackmore, J. (2000). Warning signals or dangerous opportunities? Globalisation, gender, and educational policy shifts. *Educational Theory, 50*(4), 467–486.

Bulbeck, C. (1994). Where to now? The contemporary loss of faith in feminism's transformative power. *Social Alternatives, 12*(4), 10–14.

Chabbott, C. (2003). *Constructing education for development: International organisations and education for all*. New York: RoutledgeFalmer.

Collins, C., Kenway, J., & McLeod (2000). *Factors influencing the educational performance of males and females in school and their initial destinations after leaving school*. Canberra: DEETYA.

Cook, B. (1999). Islamic versus western conceptions of education: Reflections on Egypt. *International Review of Education, 45*(3/4), 339–357.

Cook, B. (2000). Egypt's national education debate. *Comparative Education, 36*(4), 477–490.

Davies, B. (1993). *Shards of glass*. St. Leonards, Australia: Allen & Unwin.

Donnelly, K. (2006, September 23–24). The literacy debate: Subject for complaint. *The Weekend Australian*, 24.

Eisenstein, Z. (1998). *Global obscenities: Patriarchy, capitalism, and the lure of cyberfantasy*. New York: New York University Press.

Francis, B., & Skelton, C. (2005). *Reassessing gender and achievement*. London: Routledge.

Ghoussoub, M. (1987). Feminism or the eternal masculine in the Arab world? *New Left Review, 161*, 3–18.

Gillborn, D., & Youdell, D. (2000). *Rationing education: Policy, practice, reform and equity*. Buckingham, UK: Open University Press.

Giroux, H. (2002). Democracy, freedom and justice after September 11th: Rethinking the role of educators and the politics of schooling, *Teachers College Record, 104*(6), 1138–1162.

Goldman, M. (2005). *Imperial nature: The World Bank and struggles for social justice in the age of globalisation*. London: Yale University Press.

Hardt, M., & Negri, A. (2001). *Empire*. London: Harvard University Press.

Hatem, M. (1994). Egyptian discourses on gender and political liberalisation: do secularist and Islamist views really differ? *The Middle East Journal, 48*(4), 661–676.

Hayes, D. (2003). Mapping transformations in educational subjectivities: Working within and against discourse. *International Journal of Inclusive Education, 7*(1), 7–18.

hooks, b. (2003) .*Teaching community: A pedagogy of hope*. New York: Routledge.

Jones, P. W. (1998). Globalization and internationalism: Democratoc prospects for world education. *Comparative Education, 34,* 143–155.

Kazemi, F. (2000). Gender, Islam and politics. *Social Research, 67*(2), 453–475.

Keddie (1991). Deciphering Middle Eastern women's history. In N. Keddie & B. Baron (Eds), *Women in middle eastern history.* London: Yale University Press.

Kenway, J., Willis, S., Rennie, L., & Blackmore, J. (1998). *Answering back.* London: Routledge.

Lingard, B. (2003). Where to in gender theorising and policy after recuperative masculinity politics? *International Journal of Inclusive Education, 7*(1), 33–56.

Little, A. (2003). Motivating learning and the development of human capital. *Compare, 33*(4), 437–452.

Mahony, P. (1999). Girls will be girls and boys will be first. In D. Epstein, J. Elwood, V. Hey, & J. Maws (Eds.), *Failing boys: Issues in gender and achievement* (pp. 37–55). London: Open University Press.

Martino, W., & Pallotta-Chiarolli, M. (2005). *Being normal is the only way to be: Adolescent perspectives on gender and school.* Sydney: UNSW Press.

Mazawi, A. (2002). Educational expansion and the mediation of discontent: The cultural politics of schooling in the Arab states. *Discourse: Studies in the cultural politics of education, 23*(1), 59–74.

McLaren, P. (2000) *Che Guevara, Paulo Freire and the pedagogy of revolution.* Oxford: Rowman & Littlefield.

Mills, M. (2003). Shaping the boys' agenda: The backlash blockbusters. *International Journal of Inclusive Education, 7,* 57–73.

Mohanty, C. (2003). *Feminism without borders.* Durham, NC: Duke University Press.

O'Connor, J., Orloff, A., & Shaver, S. (1999). *States, markets, families: Gender, liberalism and social policy in Australia, Canada, Great Britain and the United States.* Cambridge, UK: Cambridge University Press.

Pallotta-Chiarolli, M. (1997). We want to address boys' education but... In J. Kenway (Ed.), *Will boys be boys?* (pp. 17–21). Deakin West: Australian Curriculum Studies Association.

Resnik, J. (2006). International organizations, the "education-economic growth" black box, and the development of world education culture. *Comparative Education Review, 50*(2), 173–195.

Rizvi, F. (2004). Debating globalisation and education after September 11. *Comparative Education, 40*(2), 157–171.

Sayed, F. (2005, Spring,). Security, donors' interests and education policy making in Egypt. *Mediterranean Quarterly,* 66–84.

Schultz, T. (1971). *Investment in human capital.* New York: Free Press.

Stiglitz, J. (2002). *Globalisation and its discontents.* London: W. W. Norton.

Taylor, S., & Henry, M. (2000). Challenges for equity policy in changing contexts. *The Australian Educational Researcher, 27*(3), 1–15.

Tikly, L. (2004). Education and the new imperialism. *Cambridge Journal of Education, 40*(2), 173–198.

United Nations Development Fund for Women (UNIFEM). (2005–2006). *UNIFEM annual report: 30 years of challenge/30 years of change.*New York: Author.

United Nations Educational Scientific and Cultural Organisation (UNESCO). (1994). *Monitoring Education-for-All goals: Focussing on Learning Achievement* (Joint UNESCO–Unicef Project). Paris: Author.

United Nations Educational Scientific and Cultural Organisation (UNESCO). (2005). *Millennium Development Goals.* Retrieved September 10, 2006, from http://www.un.org/millenniumgoals/

United Nations Educational Scientific and Cultural Organisation (UNESCO). (2006). Education for All International Coordination. Retrieved October 1, 2006, from http://portal.unesco.org/education/

Wangari, E. (2002). Reproductive technologies: A third world women's perspective. In K. Saunders (Ed), *Feminist post-development thought: rethinking modernity, post-colonialism and representation* (pp. 298–312). London: Zed.

World Bank. (2006). *Stipend program rewarded with success.* Retrieved October 9, 2006 from http://web.worldbank.org

World Bank, Social and Economic Development Group. (2003). *Arab Republic of Egypt, gender assessment.* Washington, D.C.: Author.

10 Social Justice in African Education in the Age of Globalization

Leon Tikly and Hillary Dachi

Introduction

The aim of this chapter is to consider the possibilities and limitations for realizing social justice goals in African education in the global era. It will do this through reviewing the social justice implications of a range of initiatives that have emerged at the regional level. We have focused on sub-Saharan Africa because as a region it is most at risk of being left behind by the globalization process (World Bank, 2006; Economic and Social Research Council [ESRC], 2006). The decision to focus on the regional level is because of the increasing significance that is attached to this level by African governments, donors and nongovernmental organizations (NGOs) (see Robertson et al., 2007). This is exemplified by the launch of the New Partnership for African Development (NEPAD)[1] and the more recent Commission for Africa (CFA).[2] There has also been a proliferation of other regional initiatives, all of which have implications for social justice and education.[3] The chapter will start by setting out a theoretical framework for understanding social justice and a broad overview of the wider context of social justice and education in sub-Saharan Africa. The chapter will then focus on five inter-related themes that together exemplify the possibilities and limitations for realising social justice goals on the continent.

Toward a Framework for Understanding Social Justice in the African Context

The American political scientist Nancy Fraser provides a thought provoking analysis of social justice in relation to globalization. She argues that:

> Until recently, most theorists of justice have tacitly assumed the Westphalian sovereign state as the frame of their inquiry. Today, however, the acceleration of globalization has altered the scale of social interaction. Thus, questions of social justice need to be reframed. Whether the issue is structural adjustment or indigenous land claims, immigration or global warming, unemployment or homosexual marriage, the requirements of justice cannot be ascertained unless we ask: Who precisely are the relevant stakeholders? Which matters are genuinely national, which local, which regional, and which global? Who should decide such questions, and by what decision-making processes? (Fraser, 2006, p. 1)

Here Fraser draws attention to the complexities of social justice debates in the global era in a way that we suggest has relevance for Africa. For example, she highlights the limited applicability of the Western state model (the Westphalian state) as a framework for considering non-Western contexts. She also draws attention to another feature of the debate, namely, that understanding issues of social justice requires taking account of the broader economic, political, and social contexts. Fraser's ideas have the following implications. First, rather than assuming that issues of education and social justice will take a similar form to those in the West, we need to base our argument on an analysis of the African context. Second, just as important as the issues themselves is an understanding of the *process* by which some voices get heard in educational debates whilst those of others remain marginalized.

Fraser usefully draws attention to three dimensions of social justice. The first, "redistribution" relates to access to resources which in our case equates with access to a quality education and the potential outcomes that arise from this. Here we find Sen's concept of capabilities to be useful in terms of understanding the range of cognitive and affective outcomes that contribute to a person's well-being; namely, what enables learners to become economically productive, healthy, secure, and active citizens (Sen, 1999). Access to and ideas about what counts as a quality education, however, are contested in the context of neoliberalism and the increasing marketization of education as we will argue. The second dimension, that of "recognition," means that we need to first identify and then acknowledge the claims of historically marginalized groups. In the African context these include women, rural dwellers, victims of HIV/AIDS, orphans and vulnerable children refugees, cultural, linguistic, religious, racial, and sexual minorities and indigenous groups. In this chapter, issues of recognition roughly equate to the extent to which the needs of these groups are catered for in understandings of the quality of education, including the formal and overt curriculum and the way that schools are resourced. The third dimension, "participatory justice," includes the rights of individuals and groups to have their voices heard in debates about education and to actively participate in decision making. Importantly, for Fraser and indeed for the argument of this chapter, this is a prerequisite for realizing issues of redistribution and recognition.

Before proceeding, a few riders are necessary. Careful consideration needs to be given before applying the concept of social justice to the African context. The origins of the term lie outside of Africa in the European Enlightenment and in the development of Western humanism. These events coincided with particularly brutal periods in African history, including the advent of Western colonialism and the slave trade.[4] It is important to acknowledge this history whilst also recognizing that indigenous understandings of justice have been present on the continent since precolonial times (Ramose, 2006) and how ideas of social justice have often lain at the heart of struggles against colonialism and slavery. Indeed, there has been a recent upsurge in interest in social justice as a concept on the continent and this is reflected in a range of new initiatives and publications.[5] It is also important to acknowledge the enormous diversity of views around social justice issues in Africa and, as is the case elsewhere in the world, their often contested and contradictory nature.[6] A third caveat in applying a social justice framework to Africa relates to the relative predominance of redistributive issues over those of recognition and participation compared to similar debates in the West. In this respect Susan George (2003) has argued that the deepening of poverty and inequality under globalization is the most profound obstacle to realizing global rights. In the African context we argue that whilst issues of redistribution are clearly central, they are inseparable from those of recognition and participation.

The Context of Social Justice in Africa

The aim of this section is to highlight elements of the broader context of social justice in the African context as a basis for understanding education's role in realizing social justice

- With 11 percent of the world's population (700 million people), Sub Saharan Africa accounts for only about 1 percent of the global gross domestic product (GDP) (World Bank 2005: xx)
- Africa has seen its share of world trade fall from 6% in 1980 to less than 2% in 2002. Africa has suffered because developed countries restrict Africa's ability to sell its products in their countries as well as other 'supply side' barriers. (CFA, 2005)
- Share of world exports that dropped from more than 3.5 percent in 1970 to about 1.4 percent at the end of 2002 (World Bank 2005: xx)
- Flows to investment in Africa by foreign investors are average for all low-income countries if measured as a percentage of Africa's income (2-3%) but are low in absolute terms. It is strongly focused on high value resource-based industries like oil and diamonds. (CFA, 2005)
- Large sums of money depart Africa in the form of capital flight estimated at $15 billion a year. About 40% of the stock of African savings is held outside the continent. (CFA, 2005)
- As a percentage of GDP, Africa's share of remittances is higher than that of either the East Asia or Pacific region or the Europe or Central Asia region. However, in cash terms, Africa receives less in remittances than does any other low-income region. (CFA, 2005)

Figure 10.1 Africa in a globalised world integration of African countries in the global economy.

goals. Figure 10.1 provides a summary of some key facts that highlight Africa's position in economic, political, and human development terms in the global era.

These stark facts shed light on the multifaceted nature and magnitude of Africa's marginalization from the globalization process. Developing policies and programs to tackle poverty through changing Africa's position in the global economy is one focus for debates relating to social justice. However, whilst the majority of Africa's population is impoverished and excluded in global terms, this should not mask the fact that some groups are more excluded than others. The Commission for Africa makes these points as shown in Figure 10.2.

Different explanations are offered to explain Africa's predicament and for the nature and causes of social injustice on the continent. The Commission for Africa (CFA, 2005), for instance, identifies a range of political causes that includes poor governance and civil conflict linked to structural issues, and also a poor investment climate; a continuing dependency on primary commodities; high transport costs; a weak transport infrastructure going back to the colonial legacy; and, late entry into manufacturing. These structural factors are exacerbated by environmental ones, such as low agricultural productivity and the impact of climate change; and by a range of human factors including the impact of poor health and low levels of education coupled with the pressures of population growth and urbanization. The CFA also mentions a range of factors associated with Africa's relationship with the outside world including low levels of foreign direct investment (FDI), a changing aid environment, and Africa's lack of control over world markets.

An alternative analysis written from the perspective of the Namibian labor movement, exemplifies a more radical tradition of thought on the continent dating back to the work of Walter Rodney (1972) and Kwame Nkrumah (1965) and incorporating recent analyses

- Although women head one in five households and are responsible for 80 per cent of agricultural production and all of the household production, they are systematically excluded from institutions and have fewer opportunities to generate income. They accumulate more of the burden of care and are less likely to attend school. They are subject to harassment and violence and when widowed lose their assets (CFA, 2005).
- Africa is also the continent with the highest proportion of young people. Stagnant economies with high unemployment combined with HIV and AIDS have left this large generation especially vulnerable. And this vulnerability is particularly evident in the urban slums, where youth unemployment was 38 per cent in Ethiopia in 1999 and 56 per cent in South Africa in 2000 (CFA, 2005).
- Rapid urbanisation is also seeing growing numbers of street children, for example, in Nairobi numbers have risen from 4,500 to 30,000 in three years, many of whom are also orphans. The growing orphan crisis is one of the critical challenges emerging. Africa had 43 million orphans in 2003—one third more than in 1990, many due to conflict and a growing proportion of them due to AIDS. By 2010 the numbers will reach 50 million (CFA, 2005).
- There are 50 million disabled people in sub-Saharan Africa. In Uganda, disabled people are 38 per cent more likely to be poor than those without disabilities, and this does not take into account the extra costs incurred due to being disabled.
- Other people often regarded as excluded are indigenous peoples and ethnic minority groups, even to the point of being considered to have no rights, like the Batwa of the Great Lakes.

Figure 10.2 Social exclusion in Africa. *Source:* Commission for Africa (2005).

of Africa's problems by some radical critics of globalization (Amin, 1997; Bond, 2001; Chossudovsky, 2001; Hoogvelt, 1997). From this perspective Africa's current position is principally explained in terms of the legacy of the slave trade and extraction of natural resources by Europeans, which culminated in the colonization of the continent and more recently by neocolonialism, which has been exacerbated by neoliberal globalization; the impact of the Cold War which fueled many foreign funded wars and conflicts; the continued material, financial, and intellectual dependency of Africa on her former colonizers; the Bretton Woods institutions (IMF/World Bank), and the use of foreign aid as instruments through which the West continues to dictate—often to the detriment of the African people—policy and governance in Africa; and, poor leadership by most African leaders who are preoccupied with their positions of power and self-enrichment with only a minority of African leaders prepared to voluntarily relinquish power (Labour Resource and Research Institute [LaRRI], 2003).

At the heart of these more radical critiques is an analysis of the impact of neoliberal ideas on the development agenda in Africa linked to powerful donor and international interests and the implications of these for poverty and inequality on the continent. In a recent state of the art literature review (Robertson et al., 2007) the authors trace the development of neoliberal ideas from the 1980s to the present. Although there have been shifts in the form these ideas have taken and in their relative influence, they have remained a powerful shaping force on policy discourses. Exponents of neoliberalism have often opposed the very idea of social justice emphasizing instead the role of the individual entrepreneur within a free market as the basis for freedom and prosperity.[7] As Ndoye (1997) and others have argued, these ideas sit uncomfortably with the collective and communal basis on which many grass roots organizations have historically labored in Africa.

Debates about social exclusion and injustice in Africa are also linked to demands for greater democracy and voice for marginalized groups and for more accountability of political leaders. Many commentators have questioned the credentials of some of the leaders and regimes associated with regional bodies such as the African Union (AU) and initiatives such as the New Partnership for Africa's Development (NEPAD; Bond, 2001; LaRRI, 2003) and the CFA. There was criticism of the CFA, for example, because of an apparent hesitation to name the ruling class oppression which exists in many places (with women, the rural poor, migrants, and refugees among principal victims), and the divisive role of ethnicity, tribalism, religion, and regionalism (CFA secretariat, 2005, p. 1). These criticisms must be seen in the context of a discussion of the form of the nation-state that has emerged in Africa. Debates about the state in the West assume the predominance of the ideal of the so-called Westphalian state model.[8] The form of state in Africa, however, is more commonly characterized as a postcolonial state. Whereas nations based on the Westphalian model emerged from preexisting empirical entities, the borders that territorially defined postcolonial African states were arbitrarily drawn by colonizers. Unlike in the Westphalian model, the mode of rule in postcolonial states has variously been described as "personal rule," "elite accommodation," and "belly politics," and as a "shadow" or "neopatrimonial state" (see Bøås, 2003 for a summary).

Some commentators, whilst recognizing the validity of some of these criticisms point out that NEPAD and the CFA also contain commitments to peace, security, democracy, and social justice, but that these aspects need to be further strengthened. Some also suggest that "good governance" should not necessarily rely on Western models (Ake, 1998; Cheru, 2002; Cornwell, 1998). Cornwell argues that greater accountability of African leaders ought to involve "the creation of voluntary neighbourhood governments and rural grass roots movements that produce alternative institutions of decision making, drawing on customary notions of justice, fairness and political obligation" (1998, p. 14). Cheru (2002), has identified a series of grass roots, civil society organizations, such as peasants' organizations, informal economy and self-help associations, the human rights movement, trade unions, and religious organizations, prodemocracy forces, women's movements, environmentalists, and other civil society movements, including those with an educational focus.

Access to Education

We have suggested that access to a quality education is a fundamental aspect of redistributive social justice in African education because so many continue to be denied such access. Basic education provision has been correlated with an improved economic growth and productivity including agricultural productivity (Appleton & Balihuta, 1996) and individual economic welfare (Hannum & Buchmann, 2005). Education is seen to have a critical role to play within local communities through providing access to information that can support the feasibility and diversity of sustainable livelihoods and can give communities access to their rights (Lawrence & Tate, 1997). Many of the regional initiatives provide support for the Dakar framework[9] and for the Millennium Development Goals (MDGs) relating to education, namely:

- Ensure that all boys and girls complete a full course of primary schooling;
- Eliminate gender disparity in primary and secondary education preferably by 2005, and at all levels by 2015.

Figure 10.3 provides some facts and figures concerning access to education. Although lack of access is a general issue affecting hundreds of thousands of African children, the situation is worse for some groups than for others. For example, it is alarming that in Africa girls can expect to stay in school for only six years compared to eight years for boys (UNESCO, 2002). Poor educational outcomes and low participation rates become more pronounced at the secondary and tertiary levels and in vocational education. The focus of the *Millenium Development Goals* (MDGs) on the access of girls and women to education is not only a question of recognizing their equal rights. It is also perceived to have wider benefits to health and welfare, including the fight against HIV/AIDS and greater control by women over their own fertility (see also Benefo, 2005; Department for International Development [DfID], 2000a; Hannum & Buchmann, 2005; Lloyd, Mensch, & Clark, 2000). Citing recent research (Abu-Ghaida & Klasen, 2004), the CFA, for example, argues that

> Countries which are not on track to meet the gender parity MDG target in education (and nearly half of those are in Africa) will have child mortality rates one and a half per cent worse than countries with better education systems, and they will also have two and a half per cent more underweight children. (CFA, 2005, p. 181)[10]

Educating women and girls can also contribute to their alleviation from poverty and can have wider economic benefits.[11] It has a positive effect on overall labor supply through increasing the amount of time women work (UNESCO, 2003). Finally, educating mothers

- African has the lowest school life expectancy of any region. A child in Africa can expect to attend school (including primary, secondary and tertiary education) for 7.8 years compared to a world average of 10.5 and an average for all low income countries of 9.9 years (UNESCO, 2005: 38).
- The gross enrolment ration (GER) in pre-primary education is the lowest for any region at 5.6% compared to a global average of 48.6% and an average for low income countries of 34.3% (UNESCO, 2005: 302).
- The region has the lowest GER in primary education of any region at 91% in 2002 with the largest number of children primary school age out of school children (40, 370). Primary education on the continent has the highest drop out rate for any region (40.5% compared to 25.5% for all low income countries) and the lowest transition rate to secondary education (53.8% compared to 84.5% for all low income countries) (UNESCO, 2005: 44).
- Africa also has the lowest GER for any region in secondary education at 28.4% and in 2002 compared to a global average of 65.2% and an average for all low income countries of 58.3% (UNESCO, 2005: 342). At 2.5% Africa has the lowest GER of any region in tertiary education. This compares with a global average of 21.2% and an average for low income countries of 11% (UNESCO, 2005: 350).

Figure 10.3 Participation in education and training in Africa.

through adult literacy programs has been linked with improving their children's attendance and performance at school (UN Millenium Project, 2005).

Those with special education needs, including physical disabilities, are often excluded as already overstretched and underresourced schools fail to meet their needs (UNESCO, 2005). Orphans (including AIDS orphans) and other vulnerable children are more likely to be excluded. A death of a parent has been related to a delay in starting primary education and girls' lowered school attendance (Ainsworth, Beegle, & Koda, 2002). The conflicts that have blighted the continent in recent years have had a big impact on issues of access and social justice (see Robertson et al., 2007).[12] A UN Development Programme (UNDP; 2005) report, for example, observed that half of all primary schools were closed or destroyed during Mozambique's civil war between 1976 and 1992. Furthermore, the UNDP states that countries in conflict are likely to spend less on education, and parents are less likely to send girls to school for fear of violence (Kirk, 2004). Similarly, poor children are far more likely to be deprived of education and affected by conflict than wealthier children (Seitz, 2004).

The debate, however, is wider than access to primary education. Tackling youth and adult illiteracy through adult literacy programmes is also important for realizing social justice goals (UNESCO, 2005). There is much debate in the literature over the precise meaning of literacy[13] although there is less dispute over its benefits. It is seen not only as a fundamental human right but as central to economic growth, sustainable development, individual and community empowerment, and the fostering of democracy. Thus it is tragic that whereas in most other parts of the world the number of illiterates has declined, in Africa there has been an increase from 108 million in 1970 to 141 million in 2004, and that of the 30 countries most at risk of not achieving the target of ending illiteracy by 2015, 21 are in Africa (UNESCO, 2006). Part of the reason for this is the relatively low priority accorded to literacy programs and adult education in government and donor spending priorities.

Similarly there are pressures for increasing access to preprimary education where the foundations for learning in later life are laid. Africa currently has the lowest enrolment in this sector of any region (see Figure 10.3 above). There are also growing demands for access to secondary and tertiary education given the role these levels can play in supporting sustainable development, including the provision of middle and higher order skills. In the case of higher education the development of an indigenous capacity for research is considered essential for tackling Africa's problems and breaking the chains of dependency on the West (African Union [AU], 2005; Tikly et al., 2004). Furthermore, as we have seen, globalization has contributed to the informalization of labor. In Africa, as Afenyadu et al. (1999), Tikly et al. (2003), and King and McGrath (2002) point out, a very significant proportion of school leavers are likely to enter into the *jua kali* informal sector which is the mainstay of many local economies. In this respect, these authors ask whether some basic vocational skills ought to be included under the heading of basic education. Similar arguments are advanced about access of children and adult learners to basic agricultural and other livelihood skills such as various kinds of crafts. What is emerging is the need for a holistic and balanced approach to funding education for all across the various sectors and levels of education and training, taking into account differences in local realities and priorities across the continent.

The Quality of Education

The issue of access, however, does not stop at getting learners into formal education. A key feature of social injustice in education on the continent is the poor quality of education that is experienced by many learners. However, as Ilon (1994) has argued, there is a growing gulf in educational opportunities between emerging global elites and the rest of the population: "a national system of schooling is likely to give way to local systems for the poor and global systems for the rich" (p. 99). Within this highly differentiated environment, a top tier will benefit from a private education that will make them globally competitive; a middle tier will receive a good but not world class education, whilst the majority, the third tier, will have a local, state education that will make them "marginally competitive for low-skill jobs" (p. 102).

The quality of education is important for several reasons. For example, there is evidence from the wider literature that improvements in the quality and relevance of education can ultimately have a beneficial impact on enrolments and on continuation rates (Bergmann, 1996; Lloyd et al., 2000; UNESCO, 2005). Improvements in the quality of education are associated with improved cognitive and affective outcomes that can contribute both to economic growth and to social cohesion.

The poor quality of education is related to a range of factors, chief amongst which are an underqualified, poorly paid, and poorly motivated teaching force (which has also been depleted due to the impact of HIV/AIDS) (e.g., AU, 2005; CFA, 2005); a lack of basic resources that include teaching materials and textbooks; large class sizes (a problem which has been exacerbated by recent growth in enrolments); a perceived lack of relevance of the curriculum (see below); the prevalence of teacher centered and authoritarian teaching; a poor; infrastructure that includes a lack of electricity, potable water, and basic sanitary facilities; and a lack of leadership skills and low levels of community involvement. Issues of quality in higher education are further exacerbated by the brain drain and a poor research infrastructure. A key issue relating to education quality in the global era is the need to address the growing digital divide in African education. Africa significantly lags behind the rest of the world in terms of popular access to technology (UN, 2005b).[14] There is a growing consensus about the potential benefits of information and communication technology (ICT) use in supporting a more student centered, problem based, and collaborative approaches to teaching and learning and to assessment (Haddard & Draxler, 2000; Hawkins, 2002; World Bank, 2004). However, to achieve these benefits and to transform learning, ICT use has to be integrated into national policy and into practice in schools. In this respect, according to UNESCO, most African countries are still at the "emerging" stage of development (Farrell & Wachholz, 2003) and the upshot is that many learners continue to be denied access to even basic ICT skills.[15]

Other issues relating to quality are less widely recognized but are also important from a social justice perspective. Bush and Saltarelli (2000) describe how education has two faces, and its negative side can promote rather than reduce the chances of violent conflict. The authors argue that the negative face shows itself in the uneven distribution of education to create or preserve privilege, the use of education as a weapon of cultural repression, and the production or doctoring of textbooks to promote intolerance (Bush & Saltarelli, 2000, p. vii). Davies (2004) discusses the multiple ways that school systems might reproduce social inequalities, increase tension, and be a catalyst for war. One example of this relationship is pointed out by the UNDP which highlights how school exclusion as a result of poverty contributed in Sierra Leone to young people joining the rebel armies.[16] Furthermore, girls and women are more likely to experience gendered abuse in African schools (Forum for African Women Educationalists [FAWE], 2003; Leach, Fiscian, Kadzamira, Lemani, & Machakanja, 2003) and teenage girls may expose themselves to sexual risk in order to fund their education (Vavrus, 2003, 2005). Girls also face particular difficulties in accessing some areas of the curriculum, such as science and mathematics and technology education (Swainson, 1998). Children, who suffer abuse and neglect at home, may be especially vulnerable to bullying and abuse by teachers or fellow students in school (Leach et al., 2000). AIDS orphans are more likely to fall into this category as well as suffering, together with learners, who are HIV positive, the stigma attached to the disease.

Both NEPAD and the CFA make several recommendations to improve education quality (e.g., CFA, 2005). Chief amongst these is the need to improve the quality of teachers, the curriculum and pedagogy, a better supply of textbooks and other learning materials, greater accountability, and community involvement. NEPAD, in particular, makes proposals to address the digital divide and there are several NEPAD initiatives in the area of ICTs as well as a range of similar initiatives.[17] Some commentators have argued that the curriculum needs to become more girl friendly; for example, by emphasizing subjects more accessible to females and by paying greater heed to women's strengths and custodial roles in African culture (Mazrui, 1999). A key issue is the lack of women in senior positions within institutions and at a national policy making level. An important consideration for teenage girls is the availability of appropriate sanitary facilities (UNESCO, 2005). For organizations such the Federation of African Women in Education (FAWE), which champions the education of girls and women on the continent, gender issues need to be tackled in a holistic way and must be mainstreamed into all areas of policy and practice (FAWE, 2003b). The CFA document refers in particular to the need for support for orphans and vulnerable children. For example, those living in remote rural areas are more likely to attend schools with a poor infrastructure. A growing area for curriculum reform is the development of life skills programs that include the provision of HIV/AIDS education and the teaching of citizenship. The quality of education with respect to the practice and teaching of human rights and citizenship is particularly important for refugees and those living in contexts of violence.

The African Cultural Renaissance and the Burning Language Question

Issues of education quality in Africa are intimately tied up with culture and language. For example, the CFA argues that "Education systems are often based on inherited curriculum content that is limited to conventional academic subjects.... Curricula should be designed with regional histories, cultures and languages in mind" (CFA, 2005, p. 187). Elsewhere in the report there is a suggestion that development must be African-led and informed by African values. A view of the "collectivism/communalism" of African culture is counterposed against the "individualism" of Western understandings of what development entails, and this has been a consistent aspect of African humanist thought and in thinking about the African Renaissance—a concept that provides much of the political and intellectual inspiration behind NEPAD and in turn the CFA. Whilst these ideas fit with some of the earlier perspectives outlined, they need to be more adequately developed. For example, no consideration is given to what cultural values ought to be selected, given that Africa itself represents a wide range of cultural traditions, languages, and religions, nor to which norms and values ought to be transmitted where they are associated with the oppression of other groups.

With respect to the language question, the CFA report (2005) explains that the problem of identifying and implementing a suitable medium of instruction policy is intimately tied up with the way that colonial boundaries were drawn in the past. A key tension is around whether African-led development is best served by using indigenous or European languages as the medium of instruction (Association for the Development of Education in Africa [ADEA], 2005). On the one hand, the use of a global language as a medium of instruction can help to diffuse ethnic tensions through providing a lingua franca.

Furthermore, the acquisition of English in particular is recognized by many as important for gaining access to power and prosperity. English as a medium of instruction is favored by many parents, as evidenced by the growth of English medium private schools. It is also cheaper to obtain suitable learning materials in English and it is sometimes seen as a "neutral" medium in a multilingual setting (ADEA, 2005, p. 1). On the other hand, no country has successfully advanced scientifically without significantly developing indigenous language/s; examples here include global success stories such as Japan and Korea (Mazrui, 1999). Furthermore, there are pedagogical and psychological benefits to learning in one's own language, especially in the early years. These advantages feed into more critical perspectives which see the spread of European languages as vehicles for Western consumer culture and as an aspect of neocolonialism (e.g., Brocke-Utne, 2001; Brocke-Utne, Desai, & Quorro, 2004; Moodley, 2000; Pennycook, 1995; Phillipson, 1999; Watson, 1999).

Language rights are becoming ever more complex in the global era. For Phillipson (1999), the complexity is around the use and recognition of different dialects and forms of English, besides Standard English. For Rassool (1999) it is about recognizing language rights in transnational settings, such as the language rights of refugees or migrants. Speakers of minority languages may be particularly disadvantaged by blanket language policies that promote either a global language or a local majority language (Brock-Utne et al., 2004; Trudell, 2005). They may perceive learning in these languages as a threat to their culture (Aikman, 1995) and certain ethnic groups, including pastoralists and nomads, find formal education alien and even hostile to their culture (e.g., Dyer, 2001; Tshireletso, 1997).

Faced with conflicting perspectives and complexity, African countries are increasingly adopting a phased bilingual or even trilingual approach, favoring indigenous languages in the early years and global languages such as English in the later years (Heugh, 2005). In some countries, such as South Africa, choice of languages for learning is left up to individual school communities within broad national guidelines. The Great Lakes Initiative (GLI; 2004) has specifically identified overcoming the deep ethnic divisions caused in part by the legacy of the colonial language issue as fundamental to securing regional co-operation and peace. Many regional initiatives, including the CFA, NEPAD, and the AU, are committed to developing and promoting African languages but shy away from detailed policy recommendations about how this commitment can be realized in practice. The problem is that the resources, training, and political will required to support such a policy are often lacking (Brock-Utne et al., 2004) and schools often to revert to English as the default medium.

The Privatization and Marketization of Education

Debates about access to quality education are bound up with the privatization and marketization of education on the continent. Privatization and marketization has been a feature of education policy in low-income countries since the 1980s (Bullock & Thomas, 1997; Whitty, Power, & Halpin, 1998), although the degree of marketization has varied considerably across the continent (Bennell, 1997). The increase in privatization is related to the influence of neoliberal ideas in contemporary globalization. In most African countries, marketization has involved encouraging the policy of charging user fees, a proliferation of private schools and universities, and the development of a limited notion of "choice" for some students in the urban areas.

The CFA initiative provides support for partnerships in the provision of education and training. It points out that non-state actors, including faith-based organisations, civil society, the private sector and communities, have historically provided much education in Africa. Some of these it claims, are excellent, but others (often aiming at those who cannot afford the fees common in state schools) are without adequate state regulation and are of a low quality. (CFA, 2005, p. 186)

The CFA is supportive of public/private partnerships, particularly in relation to secondary and tertiary education provision. Privatisation has major implications for social justice in education. For example, the introduction of user fees had disastrous consequences for primary and secondary school enrolments during the 1980s and early 1990s in many countries. Private education has also been associated with growing educational inequality in countries such as Tanzania (Lassibille, Tan, & Sutra, 1998) and the quality of private schools compared to government schools in Africa has been extremely variable (Kitaev, 1999). The policy of encouraging private provision in secondary and tertiary education since the 1980s has led to only a modest increase in enrolments at these levels throughout sub-Saharan Africa (secondary school enrolment, for example has only slightly risen from 20.1% in 1991 to 24.3% in 2000) (UNESCO, 2002). The African Union argues that the privatization of higher education poses risks for what it describes as the "fulfillment of the broad mission of a university, spanning critical thinking, knowledge generation, innovation, production of different skills, 'an enlightened citizenry', laying the foundation for democracy, nation building, and social cohesion" (AU, 2005, p. viii).

The proposed marketization of higher education through the introduction of a General Agreement on Trade in Services has proved controversial in many low income countries (Tikly, 2003b). The implication of African countries signing up to such an agreement would be to open up the provision of education to a range of international suppliers with Western, industrialized countries having a distinct market advantage. The recently adopted Accra Declaration on GATS and the Internationalization of Higher Education in Africa calls for an internationalization process that is mutually beneficial. It called on African governments to exercise caution on further GATS commitments in higher education until a more informed position is arrived at on how tradable, transnational education can best serve national and regional development priorities. In the same vein, higher education institutions, expressed concern (Association of African Universities [AAU], 2004) that market forces alone are inadequate to ensure that cross-border education contributes to the public good and by implication social justice.

Leadership, Governance and the Representation of Marginalized Groups

All of the initiatives emphasize the importance of education's role in relation to leadership and governance. These issues are important for our purposes because they impact on the third aspect of Fraser's framework, namely the rights of marginalized groups to be represented and to have their voices heard in policy debates. Some of the regional initiatives make specific recommendations relating to "good governance" that are echoed in the wider literature (e.g., Ashton & Green, 1996; Carnoy, 1999; Cheru, 2002). However, it is also important to recognize that implementing change requires going beyond developing the technical capacity of leaders to effect change. We have seen in relation to the earlier discussion on the postcolonial state that a key issue in advancing African social justice relates to creating greater accountability. For the CFA (2005), education has an important role to play in this regard because it is argued that a more educated citizenry is better able to make leaders accountable to them.

However, the emphasis in most of the initiatives is on developing leadership capacity in government (i.e. developing top-down leadership). Little, if any, attention is given to the need to develop leadership capacity outside of government within civil society. In this respect there is a tension between the commitment in NEPAD and the CFA toward developing democratic institutions and providing training for civil society organizations that would allow them to effectively engage in policy advocacy and policy making. For some critics there is also a tension between developing effective and accountable indigenous leadership and the continued dominance of donor led agendas in determining policy (e.g., Sogge, 2002; Samoff 1992, 1999).

Conclusion

Social justice issues in education in Africa are multilayered. They are overdetermined by the realities of poverty and inequality on the continent and by Africa's worsening position in relation to the global economy. Many of the issues we identified relate to a lack of resource. In this respect the CFA recommends that "donors and African governments should meet their commitments to Education for All, ensuring that every child in Africa goes to school. Donors should provide an additional U.S.\$7 to 8 billion per year as African governments develop comprehensive national plans to deliver quality education" (CFA, 2005, p. 184). However, perhaps the largest risk facing the CFA and the other initiatives is that the international community will fail to find funds to meet their commitments, particularly in a global context where development funding is increasingly being diverted away from Africa to support the U.S. led "war on terror" (see Robertson et al, 2007). There is also a silence in the initiatives concerning the relative priority that African governments themselves should give to education funding over other areas of government expenditure such as support for armed conflicts. Finally, it has been suggested that drawing too sharp a line between the three elements of social justice represents something of a false distinction and that redistribution of educational opportunities, recognition of the rights of marginalized and socially excluded groups, and their participation in determining policy priorities are mutually reinforcing objectives.

Notes

1. NEPAD was adopted by African Heads of State in October 2001. It is the official development project of the newly fledged African Union (AU). NEPAD is an integrated development plan with the goals of achieving sustainable economic growth, eradicating poverty, and ending Africa's marginalization from the globalization process (NEPAD, 2001a).
2. It is conceived as a commitment on the part of Africa's leaders to their people and as a framework of partnership between Africa and the rest of the world. The Commission for Africa was launched by then British Prime Minister Tony Blair in February 2004 with the aim of taking a fresh look at Africa's past and present and the international community's role in its development path. Although it was established in part to respond to NEPAD and other initiatives on the African continent, it was also designed to take advantage of the United Kingdom's chairmanship of both the G8 and, in the second half of the year, the European Union, and to target recommendations at these bodies as well as other wealthy countries and African countries.
3. Although some reference is made to these in the text, these are outlined in more detail elsewhere (Robertson et al., 2007).
4. Specifically, the origins of social justice lie in the thinking of writers such as John Rawls who himself drew on a longer tradition going back to the Jesuits and encompassing the liberalism of John Locke, the utilitarianism of Jeremy Bentham and John Stuart Mill, and the moral philosophy of Emmanuel Kant.

5. See for example, *Pambazuka News* which is a pan-African imitative that provides a weekly forum for discussing social justice issues on the continent, including educational issues! Retrieved April 11th, 2007, from http://www.pambazuka.org/en/

6. For example, just as some Western norms and values sit uneasily with some principles of social justice so too do some African ones. This is evident, for example, in the practice of female circumcision, in patriarchal attitudes to women, in homophobia, and in the suppression of indigenous and other minority groups. Further, some individuals and groups who may support some social justice goals, for example, racial equality, may hold deeply conservative views in relation to other issues, such as the role of women in society.

7. We are thinking here in a particular about neoliberal thinkers such as Hayek and, famously Margaret Thatcher who actively opposed the very category of "the social."

8. A particular "ideal type" model of the state as a sovereign authority associated with the peace agreement in Westphalia in 1648 that is characterized by a demarcation between the public and private institutions; the autonomy of the state which lies in its control over economic resource and a monopoly on violence; the assumption that the rule of law is based on popular support; and, that the state is a nation-state, in the sense that it is governed by an in-group based on common cultural and ethnic heritage.

9. The Framework was adopted by the World Education Forum Dakar, Senegal, April 26–28th, 2000. It sets out global and regional frameworks for achieving a quality education for all. Retrieved May 1st, 2007, from http://unesdoc.unesco.org/images/0012/001211/121147e.pdf

10. Following in the same vein, the CFA recommends that "in their national plans African governments must identify measures to get girls as well as boys into school with proper allocation of resources. Donors should meet these additional costs" (CFA, 2005, p. 185).

11. Providing girls with one extra year of education has been estimated to boost their eventual wages by 10 to 20% (Dollar & Gatti, 1999).

12. Two thirds of the African countries affected by conflicts had enrolment rates of less than 50% during the time of the conflict (Watkins, 2000). According to a DfID commissioned report (Smith & Vaux, 2003, p. 9), 82% of the reported 113 million children out of school were from crisis and postcrisis countries.

13. The definition offered here is that adopted by the UNESCO (GMR) team (UNESCO, 2006, p. 30): "A person is functionally literate who can engage in all those activities in which literacy is required for effective functioning of his group and community and also for enabling him to continue to use reading, writing and calculation for his own and the community's development."

14. In this regard, as Butcher (2001) has pointed out, of the 818 million people in Africa, 1 in 4 have a radio; 1 in 13 have a television; 1 in 35 have a cell phone; 1 in 40 have a fixed line telephone; 1 in 130 have a personal computer; 1 in 160 use the Internet; 1 in 400 have pay TV.

15. Related to the above point is that older, nondigital ICTs also have an important role to play in supplementing teacher knowledge and providing increased opportunities for disadvantaged learners. Whilst digital technologies might transform education in the longer term, an exclusive focus on newer ICTs is likely to disproportionately benefit elites who have access to them and have the effect of exacerbating the digital divide at least in the short term.

16. A survey of ex-combatants in Sierra Leone found that an overwhelming majority of those who joined the brutal rebellions were youths who had been living in difficult conditions prior to the onset of the war and that half had left school because they could not afford the fees or because the school had shut down (UNDP, 2005, p. 159).

17. Besides the NEPAD e-school initiative there are several other initiatives: *Catalyzing access to ICT in Africa* (CATIA) (http://www.catia.ws); *Global E-school and Community Initiative* (http://www-wbweb4.worldbank.org/disted/); Leland Initiative-Africa Global Initiative (retrieved from http://www.usaid.gov/regions/afr/lelnad/).

References

Abu-Ghaida, D., & Klasen, S. (2004). *The costs of missing the millennium development goal on gender equity* Institute for the Study of Labour (IZA Discussion Paper 1031). Bonn, Germany.

Afenyadu, D., King, K., McGrath, S., Oketch, H., Rogerson, C., & Visser, K. (1999). *Learning to compete: Education, training and enterprise in Ghana, Kenya and South Africa.* Department for International Development, UK (DfID) (Education Paper 42). London: DfID.

African Union (AU). (2005). *Revitalizing higher education in Africa: Synthesis report.* Accra, Ghana: Department of Human Resources, Science and Technology.

Aikman, S. (1995). Language, literacy and bilingual education: An Amazon people's strategies for cultural maintenance. *International Journal of Educational Development, 15*(4), 411–422.

Ainsworth, M., Beegle, K., &Koda, G. (2002). *The impact of adult mortality on primary school enrolment in North Western Tanzania.* Washington, D.C.: The World Bank.

Ajulu, R. (2001). Thabo Mbeki's African renaissance in a globalising world economy: The struggle for the soul of the continent. *Review of African Political Economy, 87,* 27–42.

Ake, C. (1988). Building on the indigenous. In P. Fruhling (Ed.), *Recovery in Africa: A challenge for development co-operation in the 1990s* (pp. 19–21). Stockholm: SIDA.

Alphonce, N. R (1998, July 8–10th). *Tertiary education reforms in Tanzania and New Zealand and the vocational extolation.* Paper presented at the Higher Education Research and Development Society of Australasia (HERDSA) Conference, Auckland, New Zealand.

Amin, S. (1997). *Capitalism in the age of globalization.* London: Zed Books.

Appleton, S., & Balihuta, A. (1996). Education and agricultural productivity: Evidence from Uganda. *Journal of International Development, 8,* 415–444.

Ashton, D., & Green, F. (1996). *Education, training and the global economy.* Cheltenham, UK: Edward Elgar.

Association of African Universities (AAU). (2004, 27th–29th April). *Accra declaration on GATS and internationalization of higher education in Africa. Participants' Declaration, at the Workshop on the Implications of WTO/GATS for Higher Education in Africa.* Accra, Ghana: AAU.

Association for the Development of Education in Africa (ADEA). (2005). Learning, but in which language? *ADEA Newsletter, 17*(2), 1.

Atkinson, T. (2002). Is rising income inequality inevitable? A critique of the transatlantic consensus. In P. Townsend & D. Gordon (Eds.), *World poverty: New policies to defeat an old enemy* (pp. 25–53). Bristol, UK: The Policy Press,.

Benefo, K. D. (2005). Child schooling and contraceptive use in rural Africa: A Ghanaian case study. *Population Research and Policy Review, 24*(1), 1–25.

Bennell, P. (1997). Privatisation in sub-Saharan Africa: Progress and prospects during the 1990s. *World Development, 25*(11), 1785–1804.

Bergmann, H. (1996). Quality of education and the demand for education—Evidence from developing countries. *International Review of Education 42*(6): 581–604.

Bøås, M. (2003). Weak states, strong regimes: Towards a "real" political economy of African regionalization. In J. A. Grant & F. Söderbaum (Eds.), *The new regionalism in Africa* (pp. 31–46). Aldershot, UK: Ashgate.

Bond, P. (Ed.). (2001). *Fanon's warning: A civil society reader on the new partnership for Africa's development.* Trenton, NJ: Africa World Press.

Brock-Utne, B. (2001). Education for all—In whose language? *Oxford Review of Education, 27*(1), 115–134.

Brock-Utne, B., Desai, Z., & Quorro, M. (2004). *Researching the language of instruction in Tanzania and South Africa.* Oxford: One world.

Bullock, A., & Thomas, H. (1997). *Schools at the centre: A study of decentralisation.* London: Routledge.

Bush, K. D., & Saltarelli, D. (2000). The two faces of education in ethnic conflict: Towards a peace-building education for children. Florence: Innocent Research Cemtre, UNICEF. Retrieved January 1, 2008, from http://www.unicef-icdc.org/publications/pdf/insight4.pdf

Butcher, N. (2001). *Technological infrastructure and use of ICT in education in Africa: An overview*. Paris: Association for the Development of Education in Africa.

Carnoy, M. (1999). *Globalization and educational reform: What planners need to know*. Paris: UNESCO.

Cheru, F. (2002). *African renaissance: Roadmaps to the challenges of globalization*. London: Zed ·Books.

Chinkin, C. (2002). *Gender and globalization. Way forward. Quarterly Report of the World Youth Foundation.* Retrieved January 7th, 2006, from http://www.worldassemblyofyouth. org/way-forward/may_issue/gender.htm

Chisholm, L. (2005). The politics of curriculum review and revision in South Africa in regional context. *Compare, 35*(1), 35–100.

Commission for Africa (CFA). (2005). *Our common interest: Report of the Commission for Africa.* Retrieved November 11th, 2006, from http://www.commissionforafrica.org/english/ home/newsstories.html

Commission for Africa (CFA), Secretariat. (2005*). Summary of main points emerging from consultation.* Retrieved January 7th, 2006, from http://www.commissionforafrica.org/french/ consultation/consultation-dfs/review_of_consultation.pdf

Cornwell, R. (1998, Winter). The African renaissance: "The art of the state." *Indicator South Africa*, 9–14.

Davies, L. (2004). *Education and conflict: Complexity and chaos*. London: RoutledgeFalmer.

Department for International Development (DfID). (2000a). *Eliminating world poverty: Making globalization work for the poor, white paper on international development.* Retrieved January 7th, 2006, from http://www.dfid.gov.uk/Pubs/files/whitepaper2000.pdf

Department for International Development (DfID). (2000b). *Poverty alleviation and the empowerment of women.* London: Author.

Dollar, D., & Gatti, R. (1999). *Gender inequality, income, and growth: Are good times good for women?* World Bank Policy Research Report on Gender and Development (Working Paper Series No.1).Washington, D.C.: World Bank.

Dyer, C. (2001). Nomads and education for all: Education for development or domestication? *Comparative Education, 37*(3), 315–327.

Economic and Social Research Council (ESRC). (2006). *Africa after 2005: From promises to policy.* Retrieved January 7th, 2006, from http://www.esrc.ac.uk/ESRCInfoCentre/Images/ africa_after_2005_tcm6-13210.pdf

Farrell, G., & Wachholz, C. (Eds.). (2003). *Meta-survey on the use of technologies in education in Asia and the Pacific (2003–2004).* Bangkok: UNESCO. Retrieved January 7th, 2006,from http://www.unescobkk.org/ips/ebooks/documents/metasurvey/

Forum for African Women Educationalists (FAWE). (2000, March). FAWE strategic plan. *FAWE News.* Nairobi: FAWE.

Forum for African Women Educationalists (FAWE). (2002). *The ABC of gender responsive education policies.* Nairobi: FAWE.

Forum for African Women Educationalists (FAWE). (2003, January–June). *Engendering EFA: Is Africa on track?* FAWE News, 11. Nairobi: FAWE.

Fraser, N. (2006).Retrieved November 11th, 2006, from http://www.newschool.edu/GF/polsci/ faculty/fraser/

Galabawa, J. C. J. (2004,26th–27th August). Implications of the World Trade Organization (WTO)'s GATS on higher education delivery in Tanzania. Paper presented at the Workshop on the Role of Higher Education in the Development of Tanzania: Prospects and Challenges, organized by the Higher Education Accreditation Council (HEAC), Dar es Salaam.

George, S. (2003). Globalizing rights? In M. Gibney (Ed.), *Globalizing rights* (pp. 15–33). Oxford: Oxford University Press.

Great Lakes Initiative (GLI). (2004). Retrieved November 11th, 2006, from http://www.aglion-line.org/

Haddad, W. D., & Draxler, A. (2002). *Technologies for education: Potential, parameters and prospects.* Paris: UNESCO/Washington, D.C.: The Academy for Educational Development.

Hannum, E., & Buchmann, C. (2005). Global educational expansion and socio-economic development: An assessment of findings from the social sciences. *World Development, 33*(3), 333–354.

Hawkins, R. (2002). *Ten lessons for ICT in education in the developing world.* Cambridge, MA: Harvard CID. Retrieved January 7th, 2006, from http://www.cid.harvard.edu/cr/pdf/gitrr2002_ch04.pdf

Held, D., McGrew, A., Goldblatt, D., & Perraton, J. (1999). *Global transformations: Politics, economics and culture.* Cambridge, UK: Polity Press.

Heugh, K. (2005). The case for additive bilingual/multilingual models.*ADEA Newsletter, 17*(2), 11–12.

Hoogvelt, A. (1997). *Globalization and the postcolonial world: The new political economy of development.* London: Macmillan.

Independent, The.(2005, December 27th). Bracelets and pop concerts can't solve our problems. Retrieved November 11th, 2006, from http://news.independent.co.uk/world/africa/article335183.ece

Ilon, L. (1994). Structural adjustment and education — adapting to a growing global market. *International Journal of Educational Development, 14*(2), 95–108.

International Labor Organization (ILO). (2004). *A fair globalization: Creating opportunities for all. Report of the World Commission on the Social Dimensions of Globalization.* Geneva: ILO.

Keller-Herzog, A. (1998). *Globalization and equality between women and men.* Stockholm: SIDA.

Khor, M. (2002). *Rethinking globalization: Critical issues and policy choices.* London: Zed Books.

King, K., & McGrath, S. (2002). *Globalization, enterprise and knowledge: Education, training and development in Africa.* London: Springer.

Kirk, J. (2002, November). Promoting a gender-just peace: The roles of women teachers in peacebuilding and reconstruction. *Gender and Development,* 50–59. Retrieved January 7, 2008, from, http://www.oxfam.org.uk/what_we_do/resources/downloads/gender_peacebuilding_and_reconstruction_kirk.pdf

Kitaev, I. (1999). *Private education in sub-Saharan Africa: A re-examination of theories and concepts related to its development and finance.* Paris: UNESCO.

Labor Resource and Research Institute (LaRRI). (2003). *Nepad: A new partnership between rider and horse?* Windhoek: Author. Retrieved January 7th, 2006, from http://www.sarpn.org.za/documents/d0000406/index.php

Lassibille, G., Tan, J., & Sumra, S. (1998). *Expansion of private secondary education: Experiences and prospects for Tanzania.* (Working Paper Series on Impact Evaluation of Education Reforms 12). Washington, D.C.: World Bank.

Lawrence, J., & Tate, S. (1997). *Basic education for sustainable livelihoods: The right questions.* New York: United Nations Development Programme.

Leach, F., Fiscian, V., Kadzamira, E., Lemani, E., & Machakanja, P. (2003). *An investigative study of the abuse of girls in African schools* (Education Research Report No. 54). London: Department for International Development.

Lloyd, C. B., Mensch, B. S., & Clark, W. (2000). The effects of primary school quality on school dropout among Kenyan girls and boys. *Comparative Education Review, 44*(2), 113–147.

Mazrui, A. (1999, November 23rd). *The African renaissance: A triple legacy of skills, values and gender.* Paper presented to The African Renaissance—From Vision to Reality Conference, The Barbican Centre, London.

Mittelman, J. (2000). *The globalization syndrome.* Princeton, NJ: Princeton University Press.

Mohan, G., Brown, E., Milward, B., & Zack-Williams, A. B. (2000). *Structural adjustment: Theory, practice and impacts.* London: Routledge.

Moodley, K. (2000). African renaissance and language policies in comparative perspective. *Politikon, 27*(1), 103–115.

Ndoye, M. (1997). Globalization, endogenous development and education in Africa. *Prospects*, 27(1), 79–84.

New Partnership for Africa's Development (NEPAD). (2001a). The new partnership for Africa's development. Retrieved January 7th, 2006, from http://www.avmedia.at/nepad/indexgb.html

New Partnership for Africa's Development (NEPAD). (2001b). *Reversing the brain drain*. Retrieved January 7th, 2006, from http://www.nepad.org/2005/files/health.php, last accessed 07/01/06.

New Partnership for Africa's Development (NEPAD). (2001c). *Bridging the education gap*. Retrieved January 7th, 2006, from http://www.nepad.org/2005/files/health.php

New Partnership for Africa's Development (NEPAD). (2001d) *Skills development*. Retrieved January 7th, 2006, from http://www.nepad.org/2005/files/health.php

New Partnership for Africa's Development (NEPAD). (2001e) *Integrating higher education*. Retrieved January 7th, 2006, from http://www.nepad.org/2005/files/health.php

Nkrumah, K. (1965). *Neo-colonialism: The last stage of imperialism*. London: Panaf.

Obidegwu, C. (2004). *Post-conflict peace building in Africa: The challenges of socio-economic recovery and development* (Africa Region Working Paper Series, No. 73). Washington, D.C.: World Bank. Retrieved May 11th, 2005, from http://www.worldbank.org/afr/wps/wp73.pdf

Ogot, B. A. (2004). The marketing of international education: Lessons from Australia and Africa. In D. K. Some & B. M. Khaemba (Eds.), *Internationalization of higher education: The African experience and perspective* (pp. 5–14). Eldoret, Kenya: Moi University Press.

Pennycook, A. (1995). English in the world/The world in English. In J. Tolleffson (Ed.), *Power and inequality in language education* (pp. 17–26). Cambridge, UK: Cambridge University Press.

Phillipson, R. (1999). The globalization of dominant languages. *Education in Africa, 8*, 199–216. Oslo: Institute for Educational Research.

Ramose, M (2006). An African perspective on justice and race. Retrieved November 11th, 2006 http://them.polylog.org/3/frm-en.htm

Rassool, N. (1999). *Literacy for sustainable development in the age of information*. Clevedon, UK: Multilingual Matters.

Robertson, S. Novelli, M. Dale, R., Tikly, L, Dachi, H., & Alphonce, N. (2007). *Globalization education and development: Ideas, actors and dynamics*. London: Department for International Development.

Rodney, W. (1972). *How Europe underdeveloped Africa*. London: Bogle-L'Ouverture.

Rose, P. (2003). Community participation in school policy and practice in Malawi: Balancing local knowledge, national policies and international agency priorities. *Compare, 33*(1), 47–64.

Samoff, J. (1992). The intellectual/ financial complex of foreign aid. *Review of African Political Economy, 53*, 60–87.

Samoff, J. (1999). Education sector analysis in Africa: Limited national control and even less national ownership. *International Journal of Education Development, 19*, 249–72.

Scholte, J. A. (2006). *Globalization: Crucial choices for Africa in ESRC.Africa after 2005: From promises to policy*. Swindon, UK: Economic and Social Research Council.

Sen, A. (1999), *Development as freedom*. Oxford: Oxford University Press.

Seitz, K. (2004). Education and conflict: The role of education in the creation, prevention and resolution of societal crises — Consequences for developmental cooperation. German Technical Cooperation/Duetsche Gessellschaft fur Technische Zusammenarbeit (GTZ).

Simon, D. (2003). Deteriorating human security in Kenya: Domestic, regional and global dimensions. In J. A. Grant & F. Söderbaum (Eds.), *The new regionalism in Africa*. Aldershot, UK: Ashgate.

Sogge, D. (2002). *Give and take: What's the matter with foreign aid*. London: Zed Books.

Southern African Development Community (SADC). (1997). *Protocol on education and training*. Retrieved January 7th, 2006, from http://www.sadc.int/

Swainson, N. (1998). *Promoting girls' education in Africa—The design and implementation of policy interventions* (Education Research Paper No. 25). London: Department for International Development.

Tikly, L. (2003a). The African renaissance, NEPAD and skills formation: Policy tensions and priorities. *International Journal of Educational Development, 23*(5), 543–564.

Tikly, L. (2003b, May 29). GATS, globalization and skills for development in low-income countries. In R. Carr-Hill, K. Holmes, P. Rose, & T. Henderson (Eds.), *Education and the general agreement on trade in services: What does the future hold?* (Report of the Fifteenth CCEM preliminary Meeting). London: Commonwealth Secretariat.

Tikly, L., Lowe, J., Crossley, M., Dachi, H., Garrett, R., & Mukabaranga, B. (2003). *Globalization and skills for development in Rwanda and Tanzania*. London: Department for International Development.

Trudell, B. (2005). Language choice, education and community identity. *International Journal of Educational Development, 25*(3), 237–251.

Tshireletso, L. (1997). "They are the government's children." School and community relations in a remote area dweller (Basarwa) settlement in Kweneng District, Botswana. *International Journal of Educational Development, 17*(2), 173–188.

United Nations. (2005a) *The inequality predicament: Report on the world social situation 2005*, UN Department of Economic and Social Affairs. Retrieved July 1st, 2006, from http://www.un.org/esa/socdev/rwss/rwss.htm

United Nations. (2005b*). Understanding knowledge societies*. New York: Author.

United Nations Development Programme. (2005). *Human development report 2005: International cooperation at a crossroads: Aid trade and security in an unequal world*. New York: Author. Retrieved January 7th, 2006, from http://hdr.undp.org/reports/global/2005

United Nations Educational, Scientific and Cultural Organization (UNESCO). (2002). *Is the world on track? Global monitoring report 2002*. Paris: Author.

United Nations Educational, Scientific and Cultural Organization (UNESCO). (2003). *EFA global monitoring report 2003/4: Gender and education for all: The leap to equality*. Paris: Author.

United Nations Educational, Scientific and Cultural Organization (UNESCO). (2005). *Education for all: The quality imperative—EFA global monitoring report 2005*. Paris: Author.

United Nations Millennium Project. (2005) *Investing in development: A practical plan to achieve the millennium development goals*. Retrieved July 10th, 2006, from http://www.unmillenniumproject.org/reports/fullreport.htm

Vavrus, F. (2003). *Desire and decline: Schooling amid crisis in Tanzania* New York: Peter Lang.

Vavrus, F. (2005). Adjusting inequality: Education and structural adjustment policies in Tanzania. *Harvard Educational Review, 75*(2), 174–201.

Watkins, K. (2003). *The Oxfam educational report*. Oxford: Oxfam International.

Watson, K. (1999). Language, power, development and geopolitical changes: Conflicting pressures facing plurilingual societies. *Compare, 29*(1), 5–22.

Whitty, G., Power. S., & Halpin, D. (1998). *Devolution and choice in education: The school, the state and the market*. Buckingham, UK: Open University Press.

Wolfensohn, J. (1999). *Education and development*. Washington, D.C.: World Bank.

World Bank. (2004). *Technology in schools: Education, ICT and the knowledge society*. Washington, D.C.: World Bank. Retrieved January 7, 2006, from http://www1.worldbank.org/education/pdf/ICT_report_oct04a.pdf

World Bank. (2005). Africa—Development indicators. Washington, D.C.: World Bank.

World Bank. (2006). *World development report—Equity and development*. Washington, D.C.: World Bank.

World Development Movement (WDM). (2005, April 29th). Press Release, 2004. WDM.

Young, R. (1992). Colonialism and humanism. In J. Donald & A. Rattansi (Eds.), *"Race", culture and difference* (pp. 243–251). London: Sage.

11 Social Justice, Identity Politics, and Integration in Conflict-Ridden Societies
Challenges and Opportunities in Integrated Palestinian–Jewish Education in Israel

Zvi Bekerman

Introduction

The arguments I put forward in the following chapter have been in the making for a long time. Put succinctly, I claim that it is mainly class interests and not multicultural interests that guide even well-intentioned, bottom-up, educational initiatives declaratively geared toward recognition, inclusion, and coexistence. As such, these educational settings are shown to further social justice only for those who already enjoy it. These arguments stem from seven years of ethnographic research in an outstanding educational initiative in Israel. This initiative attempts to educate a new generation of students toward mutual recognition, coexistence, and reconciliation through the creation of integrated bilingual schools where Palestinians (Palestinians living in the State of Israel) and Jews learn together. The insights I offer here do not contradict previous findings. Rather, they add to their complexity and emphasize the importance of longitudinal research in education and the need to account for ever expanding contexts within which to situate our interpretations.

One of the primary issues I have had to confront as a result of my research is the realization that the way I look at these schools and their functioning in Israeli society is tinted by macropolitical formations, such as the nation-state. These formations fix our gaze in ways we are not always "aware" of. For example, I have come to realize how easy it is to overlook class issues in a national context because we are thirsty for cultural and identity categories. I have also come to realize how easy it is to fall prey to romantic approaches which focus on the meeting of, so called, different and conflicted national/cultural/ethnic groups while losing sight of subgroups within these categories—groups that might want to maneuver themselves out of such categorizations or of other structural differences that, if accounted for, expand our understanding and might help us offer better advice.

In my recent publications I have dealt with issues related to bilingualism and multiculturalism, identity formation and stakeholder's expectations as they are exposed in the daily practices of the schools (Bekerman, 2002, 2003c, 2004, 2005a, 2005b; Bekerman & Horenczyk, 2004; Bekerman & Shhadi, 2003). Using previously gathered data, I deal here with larger issues related to the possibility of educational reform as a means to advance social justice in general and, more specifically, within conflict ridden societies. I believe that an analysis based on this particular case, as opposed to those based on "regular" schools, brings sophistication to arguments against the declared aspirations of national frameworks to promote further recognition and social justice through mass education. Israel is a society full of cleavages (Shafir & Peled, 2002), in which segregation among ethnic/national groups reigns in the educational system and in which most top-down reform efforts have been implemented in the Jewish educational realm. So, more specifically, in the Israeli case, it is of utmost importance to inquire into bottom-up integrated reform which can easily be exploited by the hegemonic powers to their own benefit while co-opting them to show their attempts to alleviate the suffering of its minorities.

Before bringing this introduction to an end, I want to mention my Jewish background. Such a mention is made out of a sensibility toward theoretical perspectives which emphasize the relevance of the researcher's sociocultural and historical trajectories in the performance of any research activity (Denzin & Lincoln, 2000; Haraway, 1991). This sensibility should be doubled in the case of this study, which is conducted in an area engaged in one of the most intractable conflicts of modern times (Bar-Tal, 2000). Indeed, ethnic, national, and religious identities operate in the lives of people by connecting them with some individuals and dividing them from others (Appiah & Gates, 1995). Still, individuals negotiate their identities while constituting and being constituted by them (Harre & Gillett, 1995; Sampson, 1993). Though in present conditions my Jewishness might be a given, I want to believe that throughout my many years of life experiences and theoretical training in a variety of sociohistorical perspectives, I have come to sustain a critical perspective on myself and the circumstances of my research. This has never been an easy task; suspicion (self and that of others) has been everywhere (Bekerman, 2003b). Thus, in addition to my own reflective and critical position, I have made sure throughout the research process to be assisted by figures fully identified with those groups which might not have initially trusted my "ethnic/national/cultural" presence.

On Educational Reform and Paradigmatic Gaze

Education is central to the preservation of the nation-state machinery by helping it shape a national consciousness and ideology. Education is also the main conduit for mobility. As such, it comes as no surprise that education and its goals become the focus of agitated debates. These debates are full of conflicts and compromises among social groups which hold different perspectives of the "good." Even when in sync about meaning, they do not necessarily share a vision of how the "good" is to be realized. The arguments are often organized around either class, national, or ethnic distinctions. Though not all citizenry is involved in these disputes, all pay the price or make a cent participating, or not participating, in the deliberation.

Those in power see with clarity the lack of achievement of the underprivileged. However, in order to keep their power they need to show an interest in the fate of the deprived and try to advance them. Since the central sphere for the advancement of the destitute in modernity has been the state-instituted, mass educational establishment, suggesting its reform is parallel to taking a true interest in reforming society toward the "good," or so we are asked to believe.

In short, the three main assumptions behind educational reform are: (1) that equality can be achieved through reforms in the educational system; (2) that inequality in the educational system is a product of ignorance as opposed to bad will; and (3) that when considering the above, investing in teacher training will remedy the present situation and education will foster the implementation of social justice for all (Rogers & Oaks, 2005).

These assumptions rest on a second set of cultural assumptions. In the case of Israel, for example, this second set of assumptions presupposes that the very basic values of the Jewish civilization deny racist perspectives while emphasizing love and recognition of "otherness." If so, and in the absence of unexpected obstacles, the Jewish civilization can produce only justice and Jews can work only for the good. Given this, reform efforts simply need to achieve technical changes such as the reorganization of curriculum, the adding of hours to the school schedule, and the training of teachers. All these are supervised by specialists informed by strong positivist research.

Still, it has become increasingly clear that, save for a few exceptions, educational reform has failed to deliver the goods. Even if educational reform would, in any measure, succeed, we would have to deal with the efforts invested by the middle upper class to sustain the existing gaps so as to secure the future well-being of their children. The middle upper classes will, without doubt, be successful in achieving educational reform, once again letting us realize that what education is asked to correct, has little to do with education and a lot to do with the world in which schools exist, the very world they are asked to support. For better or for worse, present research supports this critique showing that reforms developed in Western countries in the last half-century have achieved little, if anything, in the way of bettering the chances of the destitute (Anyon, 1995; Apple, 1999; Berliner, 2006; Hirschland & Steinmo, 2003; Ravitch, 2000; Sarason, 1990; Tyack & Cuban, 1995). Similar results have been documented for Israel (Shye & Zion, 2003).

The views expressed above with their emphasis on just distribution and care for the destitute easily become identified as some kind of communist plot for they challenge myths about the power of education to effect change. Indeed, they have been voiced by Marxist influenced educational theoreticians such as Willis (1977), Bernstein (1970), Wexler (1992), Apple (1982), and others, but this does not make them less relevant.

As previously mentioned, arguments concerning educational reform organize around more than simply class issues. With the development of postmodern theorizing, the traditional effort of ignoring or diminishing the potential influence of class has been reinforced and class, as an analytical category, seems to have receded to back stage with categories related to culture and identity taking its place. Much of present educational thinking points in this direction, including calls for reform. It is enough to mention the numerous academic publications dealing with multicultural issues in educational reform (Banks & Banks, 1995). Their chief arguments align with the writings of philosophers who have challenged self-centered perspectives such as Taylor (1994), communitarian perspectives such as those represented by Kymlika (1995), feminist traditions identified with names such as Benhabib (1992) and Fraser (1997), and in the political sciences with thinkers such as Walzer (1984, 1997) and Young (1990, 2000). Such arguments call for the need to overcome individual centered perspectives which dominate the West in all that relates to social and political rights legislation. Even those within this tradition who have to struggle to maintain a balance between class/recognition, individual/universal categories find difficulties in their conceptualizations. For example, Fraser's bifocal approach focuses our attention on both economic redistribution and cultural recognition while trying to prevent the reduction of one category into the other. Benhabib believes her deliberative model offers built-in protection against the discursive tyranny of the majority but her emphasis on "rationality" seems, at times, to sustain the same universal perspective she wishes to overcome. Young points to the limits of understanding alterity; she stresses the fundamental asymmetry of subject positions. In her view, communication does not necessarily allow for communion. From Young's perspective, there is no place for universal presuppositions. She calls for a renegotiation of political and socioeconomic impediments so as to secure the active and effective participation of marginal groups (including their right to veto majoritarian decisions unacceptable to them). Still, and though commendable, her project has difficulty challenging social movements that act in nonpluralistic fashions.

It is not just an issue of personal choice in deciding which of these perspectives to adopt. In my introduction, I have hinted that one of my main realizations while involved in the research had to do with understanding how macropolitical formations such as the nation-state fix our gaze in ways we are not always "aware" of. Adopting a class or a cultural and identity perspective is not just the reflection of one's own ideological inclinations.

The adoption of individualized perspectives and the development of cultural and identity categories are strongly related to the development of the nation-state (Elias, 1998; Porter, 1997; Watt, 1997; Williams, 1961). From whatever theoretical position one opts to look at nationalism, either as the awakening of a dormant force (Smith, 1998) or as the consequence of a new form of social organization (Gellner, 1997), it seems nationalism is "the most successful ideology in human history" (Birch, 1989), one that shapes our present perspective. Regardless of nationalism's assumed components, whether civic or ethnic, nation-states have struggled to homogenize their population through the development of institutional practices (the most powerful of which is education) creating for their inhabitants a sense of uniqueness (individual identity) and togetherness (cultural identity) which, by now, we all assume to be natural.

Class was so displaced within the national scheme that for the most part we have been raised to think of class and cultural and ethnic differences as existing in isolation from each other. Reviews of theories of nationalism (Hutchinson & Smith, 1994) have largely overlooked class categories, and, though for different reasons related to our following critique, within the Marxist tradition class and ethnicity have traditionally been considered polar opposites (Connor, 1972).

The social sciences and their social analysis seem to have been influenced by nation-state structures as well. Reicher and Hopkins (2001) and Billig (1995), among others, have urged the social sciences to recognize the crucial influence of national structures in shaping our understandings of group identities. Our flattened perspectives, on issues such as identity or ethnic belonging, do not seem to reflect the dynamics of human experience and though allowing for fast analysis, might not further our understanding of complexity.

These issues are echoed in some of the recent arguments sustained within critical and feminist circles around issues of social justice and education. The discourses of distribution and recognition align themselves easily with the problems expounded above. Even when theoreticians, such as those mentioned above, do not deny social class as a relevant category for social analysis but ask us to add cultural and identity categories which, in their case, cannot be easily criticized for falling prey to essentialist perspectives of identity and culture, as is the case with most multiculturalist theorizing (Arvizu & Saravia-Shore, 1990; Bekerman, 2003a; Hoffman, 1996; Urciuoli, 1999).

When considering the above, we should be able to understand why my first interpretative efforts at the integrated bilingual schools rested on theoretical cultural identity frameworks. The one thing we seem to fix on when visiting or just hearing about these schools is that social class categories, though important, might not be the only ones through which to try to understand the schools. Other categories make their appearance; national, ethnic, and cultural categories burst into the picture. These categories, as they are revealed in the setting, raise doubts regarding the potential of class theorizing to serve as a rich enough foundation upon which to base socioeducational analysis. Still, during the years of fieldwork, when I probed deeper into the picture, I found theoretical frameworks focusing on culture and identity to be lacking and expressive of a gaze fixed by the larger sociopolitical contexts within which participants and researchers were functioning. It is around these multiple paths that my argument will evolve when considering issues related to social justice and educational reform as they are played out in the schools.

For the sake of those not fully acquainted with Israel's realities, I now offer a short historical review of the sociopolitical context.

The Political, Sociocultural, and Educational Background of the Bilingual Initiative

Since its inception, and as stated in its Declaration of Independence, Israel has been committed to full political and social equality for all its citizens irrespective of religion or ethnic affiliation. Still, for the most part, Israel as an ethnic democracy (Smooha, 1996) has not welcomed the active participation in political, cultural, or social spheres of any other than its legitimate invented community (Anderson, 1991) of Jews. Though officially offered full rights as citizens, Israeli Palestinians, a 20% of the population, have chronically suffered as a putatively hostile minority. They have little political representation and a debilitated social, economic, and educational infrastructure (Ghanem, 1998). In general, the Palestinian Israeli population is geographically segregated and institutionally and legally discriminated against (Al-Haj, 1995; Kretzmer, 1992).

In spite of Israel's declared goals of offering equal opportunity to all its citizens through the educational system, a gap remains between the Jewish and Arab sectors. For example, in 1980, the proportion of high school students between the Arab and the Jewish sector was 0.64. In 1990, the proportion increased to 0.69 and in 2002, an additional decrease of the gap is evident as the proportion reached 0.84 (Shye & Zion, 2003). The improvement is also evident in the rate of children who pass the matriculation examinations. In 1991, 45.4% Arab and 67.3% Jewish children earned a matriculation diploma, while in 2001, the percentage increased to 59.1% and 69.7% respectively (Central Bureau of Statistics [Israel], 2002), reflecting that the gap between sectors remains.

Not only are the school systems segregated, but so too are the curricula. The Jewish curriculum focuses on national Jewish content and Jewish nation-building and the Palestinian curriculum is sanitized of any national Palestinian content (Rouhana, 1997). While Jewish students are called to engage in the collective Jewish national enterprise, Palestinian students are called on to accept the definition of Israel as a Jewish democratic state (Al-Haj, 2002; Gordon, 2005). They are not allowed to choose freely their own narratives concerning issues related to their cultural and national histories. Lastly, it is worth mentioning some features of the Palestinian educational system in Israel which reflect the unique sociocultural background of this population (Abu-Nimer, 1999). Among these is an authoritarian model of student–teacher relationships, a very traditional frontal pedagogical approach, and, for teachers, a sense of conflict regarding their loyalty toward their employer, the Ministry of Education, and their loyalty toward their Palestinian community. The security principal traditionally used by Israeli officialdom to restrict teacher appointments was canceled only in 1994 (Kretzmer, 1990; Rouhana, 1997). All in all, the Arab educational system in Israel lacks the preferential support given by the government to the Jewish educational system, thus creating an enormous gap and leaving the Arab educational system behind.

Main Findings

As mentioned in our introduction, my arguments presented here are built on data collected through a longitudinal ethnographic study which I have been conducting since 1999. Those interested in the specifics of the methodologies adopted are encouraged to consult my previously published work (Bekerman, 2002, 2003c, 2004, 2005a, 2005b; Bekerman & Horenczyk, 2004; Bekerman & Shhadi, 2003). Space limitations force me not only to skip methodological details but also to present the descriptive materials in brief. These do not do justice to the richness of the data gathered throughout the many years of research. The publications previously mentioned may satisfy readers interested in more detailed accounts of the events described.

The Center for Bilingual Education, the NGO behind the initiative was established in 1997, with the aim of fostering egalitarian Palestinian–Jewish cooperation in education, primarily through the development of bilingual and multicultural coeducational institutions (Bekerman, 2004). The first school opened in 1998 in Misgav, a Jewish settlement, situated in the northern part of Israel. The second school opened a year later as part of the experimental "open" school, the bastion of liberal education in Jerusalem. Within a year, the school was moved to an independent site as an experiment (the integrated school) within an experiment (the experimental school) was too much of an experiment, or so the parents said, when explaining why the bilingual school needed to move into a new site. The third and most recent school opened in 2004 in Kfar Kara. Undoubtedly, this was a surprising turn given that Kfar Kara is a segregated Muslim Palestinian village. For the first time, Jewish parents were asked to send their children to school in a solely Palestinian populated area.

The schools are recognized as nonreligious schools supported by the Israeli Ministry of Education. For the most part, they use the standard curriculum of the Jewish nonreligious school system, the main difference being that both Hebrew and Arabic are used as languages of instruction.

The educational initiative has to confront what Spolsky and Shohamy (1999) have characterized as a Type 1 monolingual society: one in which a sole language (Hebrew) is associated with national identity while other languages (i.e., Arabic), though officially recognized as second languages for education and public use (Koplewitz, 1992; Spolsky, 1994), have been marginalized.

The schools have adopted what has been characterized as a strong additive bilingual approach, emphasizing symmetry between both languages in all aspects of instruction (Garcia, 1997). The schools are also distinct in that they reflect a strong egalitarian structure that attempts to sustain symmetry in multiple aspects of activity. The schools are directed by two coprincipals a Palestinian and a Jew. Each classroom has two co-homeroom teachers, a Palestinian and a Jew, a balanced body of students half Palestinian and half Jewish, and also a well-balanced parents' committee with equal representation of Palestinians and Jews

Regarding their educational practices, the schools seem to be faring well when their educational achievements are compared to other, segregated educational institutions. Though not all the needed assessments have been made, it seems that in some cases Palestinian students are doing better when compared to Palestinian students in segregated Palestinian schools.

Like many bilingual programs, the bilingual schools suffer from somewhat contradictory practices, perspectives, and expectations in relation to their goals. Despite serious efforts by the entire staff, the attempt to sustain full symmetry through the implementation of bilingual educational practices fails. Even when the language policy shifted toward an even stronger support for Arabic, the introduction of English and Israel's rather low tolerance toward multicultural educational approaches and its homogenic context renders the bilingual efforts mostly ineffective with regard to the Jewish population at school, at least for now (Amara, 2005; Bekerman, 2005b). While teachers and the NGO see this as a serious obstacle to achieving their declared goals, both Jewish and Palestinian parents seem less worried. Jewish parents support bilingualism as long as it does not harm educational excellence. They seem satisfied with an educational initiative that allows them to substantiate their liberal positions and to offer their children cultural understanding and sensitivity toward the other. Palestinian parents seem to be after the best education available given the present Israeli sociopolitical context. As apparent from the interviews we conducted, Israel's present sociopolitical conditions make it almost impossible for parents to dream about a soon-to-arrive top-down multicultural, multilingual policy and given their educational aspirations for their children, they prefer an English lingua franca and high Hebrew literacy.

With the introduction of English into the school curriculum Jewish parents and their children increasingly questioned either the absolute need to study Arabic, or the amount of time invested in the study of Arabic. Palestinian parents also expressed positive feelings toward increasing the time allotted to English. In the larger context, where Hebrew is the local dominant language and English potentially offers a free pass into a global reality, Arabic risks being completely undermined. Such a context may be too powerful, even for the most well-intentioned bilingual initiatives.

Though central to the ideological aims of the schools, bilingualism is not the only sphere which needs to be confronted. All well intentioned teachers and parents are committed to acknowledging alterity. However, for alterity to be acknowledged, it must first be shaped and thus essentialized. Israel is a fertile cradle for the, at times, violent shaping of identity and its inseparable twin, culture. But the "fact" is that Jews are recognized by the Palestinians, willingly or not, if only because of their irreducible power, putting Palestinians in the unfortunate situation of being the only ones in need of recognition. At school, Palestinians again have to recognize Jews, for the sake of symmetry (the basis of the school's declared educational goals) while this time being thankful that they are recognized back. Palestinians seem to stand at that place which Arendt (1979) and Agamben (1998) identify as "the place of non-citizens," thus in need of human rights.

Recognition for the nation-state implies the recognition of nationhood and culture and these become the two spheres in which recognition is wrestled with in the schools. Wrestling with religion, while at times accommodating and at times co-opting particular meanings, is rather easy. Parents emphasize the need to know and understand the other's culture better, and believe that the schools are achieving this goal. Teachers emphasize similar goals and educational activities/celebrations (i.e., the study of holy texts, Hanukkah, Christmas, and Idel-Fiter celebrations, etc.) around these issues appear to be conducted with ease and in fruitful collaboration. These celebrations carry a strong religious emphasis. In fact, it could be said that religious aspects are disproportionately emphasized given that the majority of the Jewish parents belong to secular sectors of Israeli society and the Muslim populations, though more traditionalist, are also mostly nonreligious (Bekerman, 2004). While at times, Jewish parents express concerns and ambivalence about this religious emphasis, they also seem to find solace in the religious underpinning of cultural activities given their (mostly unarticulated) fear that their children's Jewish identity will be eroded as a result of participation in a binational program.

The ethnographic data suggest that issues of national identity have become the ultimate educational challenge for parents and educational staff alike (Bekerman & Maoz, 2005). National issues are compartmentalized into a rather discrete period in the school year corresponding, in the Jewish Israeli calendar, to Memorial Day and Israel's Independence Day, and in the Arab calendar, to the Day of the Nakba (Bekerman, 2002, 2004). In accordance with the policy of the Ministry of Education, all three schools hold a special ceremony for the Jewish cohort on Memorial Day, which the Palestinian cohort need not attend. Depending on the schools' (complex) relations with the surrounding community and the Ministry of Education's supervision, a separate ceremony is conducted for the Palestinians in commemoration of the Nakba. Though Jews at the schools clearly represent the politically liberal, center-left segments of Israeli society, Palestinian national expression does not always fall within the limits of legitimate expression as delineated by liberal Jews. For most liberal Jews, Israeli Palestinian cultural and religious expression in school is legitimate. However, national identification with the Palestinian Authority is not welcomed, and neither are perspectives which would in any way try to deny the right of Israel to be a Jewish state.

For the Palestinian group, tensions are apparent, particularly among the teachers, who see themselves at the forefront of the struggle to safeguard the Palestinian national narrative which remains unrecognized by Israeli educational officialdom. Though truly trying, and at times achieving the best possible outcomes, the schools find themselves in awkward positions. During these ceremonial occasions, Jews meet the limits of their liberalism. The Palestinians, pragmatists not necessarily by choice, accept the limits of their partial resignation to national recognition, knowing well that the other option is to forfeit hope for their children's better education, the key to a better future. When choosing to retreat, they once again endanger their position within their own community which does not easily accept their crossing the borders of segregated education into integrated settings. Treason is not an easily digested accusation.

The parents' backgrounds and perspectives ultimately reveal the centrality of class categories. Last year for one of the schools, 55% of the Palestinian children and over 80% of the Jewish children came from families where at least one parent held an academic degree (similar numbers have been confirmed, though informally, for the other schools). Undoubtedly, and maybe as expected, families sending their children to the bilingual schools belong to the middle/middle-upper class.

From the many interviews I conducted with these parents, it becomes apparent that their main interests regarding school do not revolve around social order change, particularly as it pertains to distributive justice or recognition. While they do support liberal views regarding majority–minority relations in Israel, parents ultimately seem concerned with the school functioning in a manner that will secure their children a place of preference in Israeli society. Securing the social mobility of their children is the parental main interest. While many of the parents might not have sent their children to the school in the absence of some of the egalitarian practices previously discussed, they are not after emancipatory education for their children.

All issues related to identity and culture are secondary to the aim of mobility. This does not mean participating parents lack an interest in their own cultures or identities. Rather, they see these issues as related to private spheres and not to the school's environment and by extension the public sphere. The main problem that arises is that the schools develop within the nation-state context, ever so thirsty for identity and culture, and are thus not able, or allowed, to put these issues to rest.

Finally, but of no less importance, our observations show children as the ultimate challenge. Watching them carefully, we become easily aware that each of them knows exactly where they belong. At the same time, we become aware of the fact that the younger the children are, the less these groups of belonging matter in their daily activity. From the children's perspective, other differences usurp identity or culture. Sports, games, fashion, preferences and or choice of music, TV programs, or behavioral idiosyncrasies might be better differences to pay attention to when chasing alliances and friendships. The children are alert to their surroundings and the presence of their adults. They will ultimately come to resemble them at a later stage. Until then, they will complain about the emphasis adults put on national identity and cultural differences realizing that the efforts at interethnic parity, themselves, reconfirm the boundaries of ethnicity. Children constantly show us that the world can be organized according to categories which differ from the ones present political systems have made so salient.

Discussion

Israel's sociopolitical context seems to invite theoretical perspectives like those mentioned in our opening section. Such perspectives challenge the aptness of class based theories to serve as the only analytical tool for understanding social context and the potential success of educational reform. The descriptive materials present an educational environment which, in spite of a rather difficult and conflicted sociopolitical context, is able to successfully implement educational practices guided by culture-sensitive strategies which help develop a bottom-up reform project in an area whose official educational policies seem to have no interest in developing such initiatives.

A combination of outstanding entrepreneurship, with a rather positive political atmosphere and the educational and ideological needs of a sector of the majority and minority population, allowed for the creation of such an educational experiment. This endeavor crosses tabooed boundaries and opens spheres of trust and fairness for groups suffering from intractable conflict. As described above, the schools' structure illustrates the possibility of creating egalitarian social settings even in conflict ridden societies such as Israel; structures in which Jews and Palestinians can live happily, for the most part, and together. Through the creation of symmetry among the groups they show that structural change can indeed take us a long way toward equity and social justice. From this viewpoint, the bilingual integrated initiative is indeed an unprecedented success.

But there is more in the descriptions we rendered. Further investigation introduces us to a much more complex picture. The efforts invested toward recognition and inclusion through the bilingual, culture-sensitive, and inclusive curriculum, though recognized for their unprecedented reality, seem not to be faring well. Nevertheless, given Israel's present policies, there is no way they can be considered a failure. In spite of the partial success, stakeholders seem unhappy. The context that surrounds these educational efforts configures stakeholders to maintain essentialist understandings of culture and identity. They shape them in ways which reify and misrepresent culture and identity, strengthening at times stereotypical perspectives or making salient aspects which do not necessarily benefit their understandings of themselves or serve their goals. In spite of their relative malfunction, we might assume that lacking these strategies, the schools would not allow for the participation of representatives of both groups. Lacking strong observable efforts toward inclusion in the school curriculum, parents would not find it easy to justify sending their children to these settings and would fear their communities' reprisal. It is important to point out that parents seem to express different concerns regarding the bilingual and multicultural policies implemented at the schools. They seem to hold both public and private concerns, mostly the minority parents' group. Privately, they do not seem to be particularly concerned with issues related to recognition and inclusion; it seems as if they would have sent their children to the bilingual school even if these would have not been part of the curriculum in as much as the schools would not embody open prejudiced views. In a society thirsty for identity and cultural differences, the fact that the schools explicitly adopt an inclusive perspective helps parents justify their choice on the public level.

The schools attract rather homogeneous sectors of both Jewish and Palestinian populations. This is understandable given that the schools, in order to allow for a fully bilingual curriculum in line with their symmetry policies, need parents' fees to supplement coverage from the Ministry of Education. The schools receive support from the Ministry of Education comparable to the amount regular segregated schools receive. In a sense, the middle upper classes use multicultural ideologies to further their mobility chances, their class mobility. To reference Bourdieu (1991), it can be said that in general they are after cultural capital relevant to the Israeli marketplace and not reformation of the marketplace.

Palestinian parents, on the whole and mainly because of contextual conditions, can rest assured that their children's Arabic skills are safeguarded while concurrently gaining Hebrew literacy. This literacy will serve their children in the future and help them succeed in a variety of institutional frameworks on their path toward upward mobility. Paradoxically, the bilingual schools' emphasis on sustaining parity between the languages through affirmative action toward Arabic could endanger Palestinian aspirations toward upward mobility within the Israeli Hebrew-speaking society. Jews, while rhetorically supportive of bilingual parity, are satisfied with an educational initiative that allows them to substantiate their political liberal stands and to offer their kids the opportunity to know the "other's" culture and tradition better. They might enjoy having their children learn Arabic, but this is not deemed as ultimately necessary. The Jewish parents are well aware that Arabic is not the key to any upward mobility, particularly given present circumstances. However, the symbolic value of participating in a seemingly just, educational initiative, with the added value of its standing as an excellent learning institution, was enough to justify their children's attendance.

All in all, it is class interests that seem to guide parents in their decision to enroll their children in the bilingual schools. If so, then it seems that the bilingual schools will not further social justice in Israel except for those who already enjoy distributive justice and, moreover, for those that enjoyed it before joining the schools.

Bottom up reforms, though relatively successful when compared to the ones imposed from above by the reigning hegemony (in our case of the dominant group with its needs to incorporate some limited segments of the minority agenda into their own position so as to sustain their position of power), seem to achieve reform only for a particular segment of the society, mostly those whose values comply with the present hegemony (Apple, 2001). Reform in whatever direction seems always to be co-opted to benefit those in power.

Conclusion

Traditional, theoretically based, neo-Marxist perspectives which point toward the impossibility of institutionalized educational reform to achieve its declared goals to offer equality for all, were doubted at the beginning of our work. This was because of the salient cultural/identity features of the sociopolitical context. Rescue was sought in more recent theoretical perspectives which emphasize the need to account for cultural recognition and a politics of identity. These, though seemingly active and successful in the educational initiative under study, seemed not to be essential to its development and, at times, to interfere with its goals as these are interpreted by the stakeholders. Even culture-sensitive theories, which are not essentialist or reify cultural categories, seem to offer, in the best case, answers to questions not asked, or, in the worst case, serve to cover up what indeed stands at the basis for change—material benefits and the basis on which these resources are allocated.

Thus, it seems that schools (institutionalized education) have not been, are not, and will not become arenas where the struggle for social justice can or should be fought. Schools might be places where such struggles should be supported, but they can never be expected to become the arenas where the "war" for social justice can be won. The struggle has more to do with the allocation of resources than with the recognition of identity and culture; the arena for these struggles is political and not educational. This does not mean education is not political, it always is, it just means that as in many other cases our schools, though working through a rhetoric of "political change" seem for the most part to support the existing asymmetries. Schools cannot reallocate resources and seem not to be able to prepare masses to relocate themselves in the allocation system. When adopting cultural sensitivities and multicultural strategies, they seem, at the most, to replicate the social system.

We need to be suspicious of any argument which raises identity and cultural issues, even those which, like the ones submitted in our introduction, seem to be free from essentialist reified cultural underpinnings. Staying uncritically attached to them hides the fact that at present culturally and linguistically sensitive educational projects seem primarily to serve class and political agendas, within the realm of the nation-state, in a world where national boundaries no longer represent clear-cut national identities. For whatever the reasons, these initiatives seem, in the best cases, not to be accomplishing their goals, and in the worst cases, to be oblivious to the reasons for their failure.

We need to continue the critical work initiated by Elias (1998) and Williams (1961) in trying to uncover the complex connections between the development of the concepts of culture and identity and the development of the modern nation-state. In our analysis, we need to emphasize the search for strategies and practices implemented by the hegemonic powers to achieve their goal. Moreover, these studies need to help us to critically approach present sociopsychological perspectives which stand at the basis of present theorizing regarding educational reform, multiculturalism, and so forth.

What ultimately needs to be addressed is the deeply entrenched, paradigmatic perspective that supports nation-state ideology and its traditional massive socializing tool—schools—which sustain its power. The nation-state monologic stance denies otherness through the representation of culture as unitary (Bauman, 1999; Billig, 1995; Gellner, 1983) and schools and national curriculums serve a central task in imprisoning individuals in these monolithic perspectives which have little tolerance for difference. If a dialogue about the epistemological basis which substantiates this attitude is not initiated, I doubt whether educational initiatives, even the best intentioned of them, will ever be able to help support change toward equality.

In no way do I want these remarks to reflect a critique of the minority or majority behavior. Judging them would be too easy and unfair when considering that what they are doing is what most of us would do when trying to secure a better future for our children. Moreover, elitist initiatives may have a positive impact on the surrounding context by helping start a process of reformulation of present categories and practices which may, in the future, influence larger sectors of the population as well as policy makers.

At this point, given Israel's present realities, the integrated schools present a partially egalitarian option unheard off in the surrounding context and as such serve as an example of how "things" could look even in deeply conflicted societies. We might not want to support a large bottom-up reform project which serves only to further the mobility of those already mobile even if they are mixed Palestinian–Jewish groups. However, as a small project it might contribute to a change of rhetoric which might inspire others to follow. The schools once again raise questions as to what the purpose of national educational systems should be. Schools might need to restrict themselves to teaching competence in multiple literacy and not to creating a homogenized citizenry. That said, we do understand the difficulties and realize education is never neutral or free of ideological underpinnings. Still, we could choose to support environments which implement serious structural change (as our schools do), working toward symmetry and equality while trying not to be too attentive to or supportive of cultural and identity differentiations.

My emphasis on the primacy of class in social analysis should not be understood as a denial of other relevant categories. Edward Said (1993) has argued that we are never one thing. It is clear to me that I might need to further my analysis so as to again include culture and ethnicity, but not as mutually exclusive; and while inquiring in depth from all involved, about the motivations for exclusion or inclusion of certain categories and not others.

The children at the bilingual schools seem to know this option well and manage it with ease. The only question that remains is whether we, the adults, are ready to pay attention to their profound understanding and let them live. I doubt we will.

Acknowledgments

The research on which this paper is based was funded first by the Ford Foundation (Grant Number: 990-1558) and for the last three years by the Bernard Van Leer Foundation. I want to thank Vivienne Burstein and Julia Schlam for their critical insights and assistance when editing the manuscript.

References

Abu-Nimer, M. (1999). *Dialogue, conflict, resolution, and change: Arab-Jewish encounters in Israel*. Albany: SUNY.

Agamben, G. (1998). *Homo Sacer: Sovereign power and bare life* (D. Heller-Roazen, Trans.). Stanford, CA: Stanford University Press.

Al-Haj, M. (1995). *Education, empowerment, and control: The case of the Arabs in Israel*. Albany, NY: SUNY Press.

Al-Haj, M. (2002). Multiculturalism in deeply divided societies: The Israeli case. *International Journal of Intercultural Relations, 26,* 169–183.

Amara, M. H. (2005). *Summary report: The bilingual model*. Jerusalem: Hand in Hand-The Center for Arab Jewish Education in Israel.

Anderson, B. (1991). *Imagined communities: Reflections on the origins and spread of nationalism*. London: Verso.

Anyon, J. (1995). Race, social class, and educational reform in an inner-city school. *Teachers College Record, 97*(1), 69–94.

Appiah, K. A., & Gates, H. L. (1995). *Identities*. Chicago: University of Chicago Press.

Apple, M. W. (1982). *Education and power*. Boston: Routledge & Kegan Paul.

Apple, M. W. (1999). Rhetorical reforms: Markets, standards and inequality. *Current Issues in Comparative Education, 1*(2), 6–18.

Apple, M. W. (2001). Educational and curricular restructuring and the neo-liberal and neo-conservative agendas: Interview with Michael Apple. *Curriculo sem Fronteiras, 1*(1), i–xxvi.

Arendt, H. (1979). *The origins of totalitarianism*. New York: Harcourt Brace Jovanovich.

Arvizu, S., & Saravia-Shore, M. (1990). Cross-cultural literacy: An anthropological approach to dealing with diversity. *Education and Urban Society, 22*(4), 364–376.

Banks, J. A., & Banks, C. A. M. (Eds.). (1995). *Handbook of research on multicultural education*. New York: Macmillan.

Bar-Tal, D. (2000). From intractable conflict through conflict resolution to reconciliation: Psychological analysis. *Political Psychology, 21*(2), 351–365.

Bauman, Z. (1999). *Culture as praxis*. London: Sage.

Bekerman, Z. (2002). Can education contribute to coexistence and reconciliation? Religious and national ceremonies in bilingual Palestinian-Jewish schools in Israel. *Peace and Conflict: Journal of Peace Psychology, 8*(3), 259–276.

Bekerman, Z. (2003a). Hidden dangers in multicultural discourse. *Race Equality and Teaching* (formerly *MCT-Multicultural Teaching*), *21*(3), 36–42.

Bekerman, Z. (2003b). Never free of suspicion. *Cultural Studies—New Methodologies, 3*(2), 136–147.

Bekerman, Z. (2003c). Reshaping conflict through school ceremonial events in Israeli Palestinian-Jewish co-education. *Anthropology & Education Quarterly, 34*(2), 205–224.

Bekerman, Z. (2004). Multicultural approaches and options in conflict ridden areas: Bilingual Palestinian-Jewish education in Israel. *Teachers College Record, 106*(3), 574–610.

Bekerman, Z. (2005a). Are there children to educate for peace in conflict-ridden areas? A critical essay on peace and coexistence education. *Intercultural Education, 16*(3), 235–246.

Bekerman, Z. (2005b). Complex contexts and ideologies: Bilingual education in conflict-ridden areas. *Journal of Language Identity and Education, 4*(1), 1–20.

Bekerman, Z., & Horenczyk, G. (2004). Arab-Jewish bilingual coeducation in Israel: A long-term approach to intergroup conflict resolution. *Journal of Social Issues, 60*(2), 389–404.

Bekerman, Z., & Maoz, I. (2005). Troubles with identity: Obstacles to coexistence education in conflict ridden societies. *Identity, 5*(4), 341–358.

Bekerman, Z., & Shhadi, N. (2003). Palestinian Jewish bilingual education in Israel: Its influence on school students. *Journal of Multilingual and Multicultural Development, 24*(6), 473–484.

Benhabib, S. (1992). *Situating the self: Gender, community and postmodernism in contemporary ethics.* New York: Routledge.

Berliner, D. C. (2006). Our impoverished view of educational reform. *Teachers College Record, 108*(6), 949–995.

Bernstein, B. (1970). Education cannot compensate for society. *New Society, 15*(387), 344–347.

Billig, M. (1995). *Banal nationalism.* London: Sage.

Birch, A. H. (1989). *Nationalism and national integration.* London, UK: Unwin Hyman.

Bourdieu, P. (1991). *Language and symbolic power.* Cambridge, MA: Harvard University Press.

Central Bureau of Statistics [Israel]. (1995). *Statistical abstract of Israel.* Jerusalem: Author.

Connor, W. (1972). Nation-building or nation-destroying. *World Politics 24,* 319–355.

Denzin, N. K., & Lincoln, Y. S. (Eds.). (2000). *Handbook of qualitative research* (2nd. ed.). London: Sage.

Elias, N. (1998). Civilization, culture, identity: "Civilization" and "Culture": Nationalism and nation-state formation: An extract from the Germans. In J. Rundell & S. Mennell (Eds.), *Classical readings in culture and civilization* (pp. 225–240). New York: Routledge.

Fraser, N. (1997). *Justice interruptus: Critical reflections on the "postsocialist" condition.* New York: Routledge.

Garcia, O. (1997). Bilingual education. In F. Coulmas (Ed.), *The handbook of sociolinguistics* (pp. 405–420). Oxford: Blackwell.

Gellner, E. (1983). *Nations and nationalism.* Oxford: Basic Blackwell.

Gellner, E. (1997). *Nationalism.* New York: New York University Press.

Ghanem, A. A. (1998). State and minority in Israel: the case of ethnic state and the predicament of its minority. *Ethnic and Racial Studies, 21*(3), 428–448.

Gordon, D. (2005). History textbooks, narratives, and democracy: A response to Majid Al-Haj. *Curriculum Inquiry, 35*(3), 367–376.

Haraway, D. J. (1991). *Simians, cyborgs, and women: The revision of nature.* New York: Routledge.

Harre, R., & Gillett, G. (1995). *The discursive mind.* London: Sage.

Hirschland, M. J., & Steinmo, S. (2003). Correcting the record: Understanding the history of federal intervention and failure in securing U.S. educational reform. *Educational Policy, 1,* 343–364.

Hoffman, D. M. (1996). Culture and self in multicultural education: Reflexions on discourse, text, and practice. *American Educational Research Journal, 33*(3), 545–569.

Hutchinson, J., & Smith, A. D. (1994). Introduction. In J. Hutchinson & A. D. Smith (Eds.), *Nationalism* (pp. 3–13). Oxford & New York: Oxford University Press.

Koplewitz, I. (1992). Arabic in Israel: The sociolinguistic situation of Israel's linguistic minority. *International Journal of the Sociology of Language, 98,* 29–66.

Kretzmer, D. (1990). *The legal status of the Arabs in Israel.* Boulder, CO: Westview.

Kretzmer, D. (1992). The new basic laws on human rights: A mini-revolution in Israeli constitutional law? *Israel Law Review, 26*(2), 238–249.

Kymlicka, W. (1995). *Multicultural citizenship: A liberal theory of minority rights.* Oxford: Clarendon Press.

Porter, R. (1997). Introduction. In R. Porter (Ed.), *Rewriting the self histories from the Renaissance to the present* (pp. 1–17). London: Routledge.

Ravitch, D. (2000). *Left back: A century of failed school reforms.* New York: Simon & Schuster.

Reicher, S., & Hopkins, N. (2001). *Self and nation.* London: Sage.

Rogers, J., & Oaks, J. (2005). John Dewey speaks to Brown: Research, democratic social movement strategies, and the struggle for education on equal terms. *Teachers College Record, 107*(9), 2178–2203.

Rouhana, N. N. (1997). *Palestinian citizens in an ethnic Jewish state.* New Haven, CT: Yale University Press.

Said, E. (1993). *Culture and imperialism.* New York: Vintage.

Sampson, E. E. (1993). *Celebrating the other: A dialogic account of human nature.* Hemel Hempstead, UK: Harvester Wheatsheaf.

Sarason, S. B. (1990). *The predictable failure of educational reform: Can we change course before it's too late?* San Francisco, CA: Jossey-Bass.

Shafir, G., & Peled, Y. (2002). *Being Israeli: The dynamics of multiple citizenship.* Cambridge: Cambridge University Press.

Shye, A., & Zion, N. (Eds.). (2003). *Education and social justice in Israel: On equality in educational opportunities* (Vol. 4). Jerusalem: The Van Leer Institute (in Hebrew)

Smith, A. (1998). *Nationalism and modernism.* London: Routledge.

Smooha, S. (1996). Ethno-democracy: Israel as an archetype. In P. Ginosar & Bareli (Eds.), *Zionism: A contemporary polemic* (pp. 277–311). Jerusalem: Ben-Gurion University (Hebrew).

Spolsky, B. (1994). The situation of Arabic in Israel. In Y. Suleiman (Ed.), *Arabic sociolinguistics: Issues and perspectives* (pp. 227–236). Richmond, UK: Curzon Press.

Spolsky, B., & Shohamy, E. (1999). Language in Israeli society and education. *International Journal of the Sociology of Language, 137,* 93–114.

Taylor, C. (1994). The politics of recognition. In D. T. Goldberg (Ed.), *Multiculturalism: A critical reader* (pp. 75–106). Oxford: Blackwell.

Tyack, D., & Cuban, L. (1995). *Tinkering toward Utopia: A century of public school reform.* Cambridge, MA: Harvard University Press.

Urciuoli, B. (1999). Producing multiculturalism in higher education: Who's producing what for whom? *Qualitative Studies in Education, 12*(3), 287–298.

Walzer, M. (1984). *Spheres of justice: A defense of pluralism and equality.* New York: Basic Books.

Walzer, M. (1997). *On toleration.* New Haven, CT: Yale University Press.

Watt, I. (1997). *Myths of modern individualism: Faust, Don Quixote, Don Juan, Robinson Crusoe.* Cambridge, UK: Cambridge University Press.

Wexler, P. (1992). *Becoming somebody: Toward a social psychology of school.* New York: Routledge.

Williams, R. (1961). *Culture and society, 1780–1950.* Hardmondsworth, UK: Penguin Books.

Willis, P. (1977). *Learning to labor: How working class lads get working class jobs.* New York: Columbia University Press.

Young, I. M. (1990). *Justice and the politics of difference.* Princeton, NJ: Princeton University Press.

Young, I. M. (2000). *Inclusion and democracy.* Oxford: Oxford University Press.

12 Beyond the Justice of the Market

Combating Neoliberal Educational Discourse and Promoting Deliberative Democracy and Economic Equality

David Hursh

What public education should be for and how it should be organized has been contested from its inception. One of the central debates has been over whether education is primarily a means to increase the nation's economic productivity or to develop well-rounded democratic citizens. In the early 1900s, some educators built on Frederick Winslow Taylor's (1911) publications on "scientific management," which promoted efficiency in the workplace through standardization, accountability, rewards, and punishments (Kanigel, 2005). For example, David Snedden, an influential Commissioner of Education, built explicitly on Taylor's ideas and reconceived education to aid "the economy to function as efficiently as possible" (Wirth, 1977, p. 163). For Snedden, schools should not only serve corporate interests but also be organized like factories; both literally and figuratively— what was good for business was good for education. Snedden, in "Education for a World of Team Players and Team Workers" (1924), compared society to a crew on a submarine, with a commander, a few officers, and numerous subordinates, and asserted that schools should prepare a few students to be leaders, while training the vast majority "to follow." Fortunately, stated Snedden, deciding which students to select as leaders only required knowing students' "probable destinies," which coincided with students' gender, race, and class. A few white males would be tracked into leadership positions; the rest were consigned to subordinate roles. Schools were to be assessed on how much they contributed to economic growth and not on whether they promoted economic equality or critical citizenship. A democratic society was one in which leaders made decisions that others accepted uncritically. Social justice was achieved when everyone was prepared for and accepted his or her "proper" place.

In contrast, John Dewey opposed proponents of social efficiency such as Snedden, arguing that a primary purpose of education was the development of critical democratic citizens. For Dewey, all social institutions, including workplaces, should facilitate personal growth and be judged on the "contribution they make to the all-around growth of every member of society" (Dewey, 1919/1950, p. 147). Dewey and Snedden publicly debated one another in *The New Republic,* where Dewey disagreed with the idea that students were to be prepared for the needs of business and stated that the kind of education in which he was interested was "not one which will 'adapt' workers to the existing industrial regime," but, instead, one which would "alter the existing industrial system, and ultimately transform it" (Dewey, 1915, p. 42). Dewey wanted schools to create citizens who would force workplaces to become democratic. For Dewey, institutions should be assessed based on their contribution to human development rather than to "a senseless pursuit of profits" (Wirth, 1977, p. 169).

For Dewey (1987), schools were essential to developing the "democratic habits of thought and action" necessary for effective participation in the democratic process (p. 225). Dewey's conception of freedom differed from conceptions in which freedom is the right to do what one pleases (see Dewey's *Experience and Education*, 1934). Rather, for Dewey, freedom exists only in relationship with others; with whom, as a community, people engage in the task of improving themselves and society. Achieving this goal requires that individuals deliberate with one another and practice habits of "open-mindedness, tolerance of diversity, fairness, rational understanding, respect for truth, and critical judgment" (Olssen, Codd, & O'Neill, 2004, p. 269). In sum, Dewey believed schooling was essential for the development of deliberative democracy.

While David Snedden and others who promoted social efficiency seem, a century later, to be too easily convinced of the superiority of business and overly pessimistic regarding human abilities, their ideals reappear within the current push to adopt neoliberal economic and education policies. Neoliberalism similarly privileges the economy by assuming that the "economic system works best when individuals are allowed to seek their private interest. The pursuit of self-interest will foster free enterprise, and the operation of the market will always lead to superior outcomes to those achieved through government planning" (Lauder, Brown, Dillabough, & Halsey, 2006, p. 26). For neoliberals, societies work best when individuals are free to pursue their private interests without governmental intervention through public funding of either institutions or individuals. Increasingly, cities, states, and the federal government are restructuring education around the notion that market principles of competition and quantitative measurement best promote educational efficiency and social justice.

This chapter, then, aims to reveal and challenge the current neoliberal ideals and policies that are redefining social justice and reshaping American schools and society. It is crucial that as educators, we understand that different conceptions of society are founded on different assumptions about the nature of social justice. We must determine which conceptions make sense to us and use them as a basis to form the kinds of institutions, including schools, that we desire. I will suggest that neoliberal policies increase economic and social inequality, and degrade the social and natural environment. In short, neoliberal conceptions of social justice harm people and the world around them, and are therefore unjust.

I begin by describing the social democratic liberalism that preceding neoliberalism so that we can appreciate the ways in which neoliberalism redefines the essential characteristics of society. I then show how neoliberal principles of individualism, equality, markets, and choice currently form the basis of recent educational policies at the district (Chicago), state (New York), and federal (No Child Left Behind) levels. I conclude by suggesting some ways in which we might strengthen conceptions of social justice that emphasize equity and deliberative democracy.

The Attack on Social Democratic Liberalism by Neoliberals

Prior to the rise of neoliberalism in the 1970s, social democratic liberalism dominated, arising in the United States in the 1930s during the Franklin D. Roosevelt administration. Social democratic liberal policies were themselves a response to then prevalent laissez-faire social and economic policies in which the state did little to ensure individual and social welfare. Roosevelt, in his 1935 address to Congress, made clear his view that excessive market freedoms had led to the economic and social problems of the Depression (Harvey, 2005). In contrast, his social democratic liberal policies focused on ensuring individuals at least the necessities for human survival and growth. Roosevelt argued for a liberal conception of social justice, which could be achieved if the state and civil society allocated "its resources to eradicate poverty and hunger and to assure security of livelihood, security against the major hazards and vicissitudes of life, and the security of decent homes" (Harvey, 2005, p. 183). Roosevelt ultimately envisioned providing more than the basic necessities and in 1944 proposed a second Bill of Rights, which included

> the right to a useful and remunerative job...the right to earn enough to provide adequate food and clothing and recreation...the right of every family to a decent home; the right to adequate medical care and the opportunity to achieve and enjoy good health; the right to adequate economic protection from the economic fears of old age, sickness, accident and unemployment; [and] the right to a good education. (quoted in Sunstein, 2004, p. 13)

Roosevelt's policies arose both out of necessity and from political pressure. Clearly, laissez-faire policies would not alleviate the problems of the Depression. The poor, the unemployed, and other citizens were clamoring for solutions. In response, Roosevelt implemented social democratic policies that included deficit-financed job creation, government regulation of banking policy, social security, and other welfare programs. Later, World War II increased state intervention into the everyday economic life of the nation as part of its war effort.

Because governmental planning was central to economic recovery and to victory in World War II, citizens in the United States and Western Europe pressed for continued state intervention and public welfare (Judt, 2005). Furthermore, postwar growth in individual incomes provided for increasing corporate profits, satisfying both citizens and corporations. The decades after the war, then, were characterized by "the historic compromise" between capital and labor. In exchange for improving wages, labor consented not only to capitalist control of the workplace, but also to capitalist control of investment and growth, primarily by multinational corporations.

However, efforts to expand personal and political rights were not uncontested. Social security was denied to many African Americans when Congress surrendered to demands of Southern politicians to exclude agricultural and domestic household workers, jobs typically filled by African Americans (Katznelson, 2005). Even the now venerated G.I. Bill for returning veterans "roused the ire of all but the most moderate business leaders... [who] disliked the liberal agenda and felt that the New Deal traditions associated with the Labor movement and the Democratic Party continued to appeal to American workers" (Fones-Wolfe, 1994, p. 7). Similarly, Roosevelt's Second Bill of Rights was quickly forgotten and now seems utopian.

Social democratic liberalism, then, was never secure and in the later 1960s increasingly attacked as businesses' net profits began to fall (Parenti, 1999, p. 118). Because falling profits were attributed primarily to the inability of businesses to pass increasing wage costs on to consumers in an increasingly competitive and open world economy, part of the solution for emerging neoliberals was to squeeze workers' wages. In 1979, the head of the Federal Reserve Bank, Paul Volcker, stated that "the average wage of workers has to decline" (cited in Bowles & Gintis, 1986, p. 60). Volcker instituted policies that increased the Federal Reserve's interest rates, leading to a "long, deep recession that would empty factories and break unions in the U.S. and drive debtor countries to the brink of insolvency, beginning the long era of structural readjustment" (Henwood, 2003, p. 208), and a decrease in workers' real wages.

In the late 1970s and early 1980s, Ronald Reagan in the United States and Margaret Thatcher in Britain began to systematically implement neoliberal policies, turning back social democratic liberalism by reducing state responsibility for individual welfare. Neoliberalism, in contrast to social democratic liberalism, is "a theory of political economic practices that proposes that human well-being can best be advanced by liberating individual entrepreneurial freedoms and skills within an institutional framework characterized by strong private property rights, free markets, and free trade" (Harvey, 2005, p. 2). In a neoliberal economic order, the state is limited to creating and preserving "an institutional framework appropriate to such practices" (p. 2). Thus, nongovernmental organizations such as the World Bank and the International Monetary Fund are permitted to pressure national governments to eliminate trade barriers and reduce social spending.

For neoliberals, the market is essential.

> The market introduces competition as the structuring mechanism through which resources and status are allocated efficiently and fairly. The "invisible hand" [as in Adam Smith's *The Wealth of Nations*, 1976/1776] of the market is thought to be the most efficient way of sorting out which competing individuals get what. (Olssen et al., 2004, pp. 137–138)

Moreover, neoliberal policies emphasize "the deregulation of the economy, trade liberalization, the dismantling of the public sector, [including, education, health, and social welfare], and the predominance of the financial sector of the economy over production and commerce" (Tabb, 2002, p. 7). Neoliberalism stresses

> the privatization of the public provision of goods and services—moving their provision from the public sector to the private—along with deregulating how private producers can behave, giving greater scope to the single-minded pursuit of profit and showing significantly less regard for the need to limit social costs for redistribution based on nonmarket criteria. The aim of neoliberalism is to put into question all collective structures capable of obstructing the logic of the pure market. (Tabb, 2002, p. 29)

Neoliberalism not only changes social structures but also changes the relationship between the individual and society. Under social democratic liberal policies, social inequality is a social responsibility. Social justice requires that inequalities be minimized through social programs and the redistribution of resources and power (Levitas, 1998, p. 14). Under neoliberal policies, inequality is the product of individual choice and should not be remedied by social welfare programs, but by individuals taking more responsibility and striving to become productive members of the workforce. Neoliberal governments accept little responsibility for the welfare of individuals; the individual is held to be the author of his or her own (mis-)fortune. As Margaret Thatcher famously stated, "There is no such thing as society...there are individual men and women, and there are families. And no government can do anything except through people, and people must look after themselves first" (Thatcher, 1993, pp. 626–627).

Neoliberal societies aim to create competitive, instrumentally rational individuals who can compete in the marketplace (Peters, 1994). They are to become entrepreneurs responsible for themselves, their progress, and their position. Lemke (2002) describes neoliberalism as seeking:

> to unite a responsible and moral individual and an economic-rational individual. It aspires to construct responsible subjects whose moral quality is based on the fact that they rationally assess the costs and benefits of a certain act as opposed to other alternative acts. (p. 59)

Individuals are transformed into "entrepreneurs of themselves" (Foucault, 1979, cited in Lemke, 2001), who operate within a marketplace that includes commodities such as education, health care, and pensions.

Social Democratic Liberalism, Neoliberalism and Education

During the decades immediately after World War II, education in the U.S. and Western Europe, guided by social democratic polices, expanded to serve more students at more grades. States aimed to increase their secondary school graduation rates and to enroll more students in expanding state supported higher education systems. Education was perceived as a necessary, though insufficient, condition for social justice. Until recently, few people doubted that public education was a public responsibility.

However, neoliberals reject the notion that education should be provided by the State. In their view, education should, as much as possible, be privatized or forced to compete in an open marketplace. Private schools, charter schools, and voucher systems are among the results. Milton Friedman (1995) called for education to be transformed from a "government" (used pejoratively) to a "market system":

> Our elementary and secondary system needs to be radically restructured. Such a reconstruction can be achieved only by privatizing a major segment of the educational system—i.e., by enabling a private, for profit industry to develop that will provide a wide variety of learning opportunities and offer effective competition to public schools. (p. 1)

Under the market system advocated by neoliberals, schools should be assessed using standardized measures and curriculum standards, so that "consumers" can compare one school to another in making a choice. Neoliberal policies now implicitly or explicitly inform the foundation of education policies at the district, state, and federal levels and call for standards, standardized tests, and accountability. The neoliberal faith in markets and privatization provides the basis for pushing for educational systems in which public funding would go to private business corporations and religious organizations.

Recent reforms in Chicago, New York, and at the federal level with No Child Left Behind (NCLB) reflect the prevalence of neoliberalism in education. An examination of the rationale for these reforms reveals the extent to which neoliberals have changed not only how we talk about and organize education, but also how we think about social justice.

Pauline Lipman, in *High Stakes Education: Inequality, Globalization, and Urban School Reform* (2004), situates her analysis of Chicago's recent education reforms within the rise of neoliberalism globally, showing how these reforms further efforts by corporate and political elites to remake Chicago into a global financial and tourist center. Neoliberal policies privilege international finance over labor, and promote individual self-interest pursued through markets in all spheres of economic and social life. Chicago's education policies employ "a corporate, regulatory regime centered on high stakes tests, standards, and remediation" (p. 36).

In its efforts to attract and retain the professional workforce required by a global city, the Chicago City School District has implemented many new programs, including International Baccalaureate and College Prep Programs, to prepare children of the middle and upper classes for university. At the same time, most students of color and children from the working class are being prepared for service and retail jobs through programs that focus on "vocational education, restricted (basic skills) curricula, and intensified regimentation of instruction and/or control of students" (p. 49). Lipman maps out where the different programs started, showing how those that are more academically rigorous tend to be situated in or draw students from upper-income and gentrifying neighborhoods, and those using direct instruction or preparing students for low paying service jobs or the military are situated in low-income African-American and Latina/o neighborhoods.

Lipman (2004) also describes how testing policies, including publicly reporting standardized test scores by school, further legitimize program differences by forcing schools with low test scores (those composed primarily of students of color and students living in poverty) to institute more regimented methods of instruction. She argues that the college prep programs act as an incentive for middle-class families to live in the city and provide a veneer of equal opportunity in a vastly unequal system (p. 56). Although presented as reforms that decrease inequality, the Chicago programs exacerbate inequality and heighten economic and social disparity. She concludes:

> The policy regime that I have described is producing stratified knowledge, skills, dispositions, and identities for a deeply stratified society. Under the rubric of standards, the policies impose standardization and enforce language and cultural assimilation to mold the children of the increasingly linguistically and culturally diverse workforce into a most malleable and governable source of future labor. This is a system that treats people as a means to an end. The "economizing of education" and the discourse of accounting reduce people to potential sources of capital accumulation, manipulators of knowledge for global economic expansion, or providers of the services and accessories of leisure and pleasure for the rich. Students are reduced to test scores, future slots in the labor market, prison numbers, and possible cannon fodder in military conquests. Teachers are reduced to technicians and supervisors in the education assembly line—"objects" rather than "subjects" of history. This system is fundamentally about the negation of human agency, despite the good intentions of individuals at all levels. (p. 179)

More recently, Lipman (2005) explains how the Chicago mayor's newly enacted "Renaissance 2010" policy makes a bad situation worse, as schools for the poor are taken over and administered by a corporate-dominated board. Renaissance 2010 "calls for closing 60 public schools and opening 100 small schools, two-thirds of which will be charter or contract schools run by private organizations" using nonunion teachers and school employees (Lipman, 2005, p. 54). Schools will not be governed by the Local School Councils, to which teachers, parents, and community members are elected, but rather by New Schools for Chicago, a board constituted by corporate and Chicago Public School leaders appointed by the Commercial Club of Chicago, an organization representing the city's corporate and political elite. New Schools for Chicago will use current corporate models to evaluate schools by developing "performance contracts" based on student test scores. By undermining democratic control of schools, further deprofessionalizing teachers, and transferring public funds to private for-profit corporations, Renaissance 2010 is a renaissance only for some.

Lipman's (2004) research demonstrates how neoliberal discourse used by policymakers "shifts responsibility for social inequality produced by the state onto parents, students, schools, communities and teachers" (pp. 171–172). Chicago's policymakers, like those in New York and in the Bush administration (Hursh, 2005), promote their neoliberal agenda by asserting that standardized testing and accountability increase equity and fairness, "holding all students to the same high standards." However, as Lipman shows, schools in Chicago prepare most students for retail and service jobs, or for the military.

Moreover, in the push to raise test scores, schools cannot develop curricula that build on students' culture. Consequently, low-income students and students of color are unlikely to do well, not only because of low expectations, but also because the curriculum does not connect to their experience. Yet because policymakers portray all students as being provided the same opportunities, student failure is blamed on individual lack of effort. Lipman shows how the policies shift the blame for student failure away from the failure to provide academically challenging schools and the necessary economic and cultural resources, and onto individual students.

New York state along with federal education officials have followed Chicago in promoting testing, accountability, markets, and choice by arguing that within an increasingly competitive global economy, neoliberal reforms are necessary to ensure that all students and the nation succeed. They link the discourse of the "necessity" of increased educational and economic productivity with a discourse that blames teachers for inadequately instructing and assessing students, a strategy also used by the proponents of No Child Left Behind (NCLB). Beginning in the 1990s, the New York State Board of Regents and the Commissioner of Education implemented standards-based assessment and a standardized testing regime, making graduation contingent on passing five statewide standardized exams, and requiring that secondary students enroll in state-regulated Regents courses to graduate, thereby eliminating locally developed courses. While new testing requirements were being developed, the state also passed legislation establishing up to 100 charter schools, usually administered by for-profit business corporations, siphoning students and funds from public schools.

Former New York Chancellor of Education Carl Hayden (1999, cited in Cala, personal communication to Deputy Commissioner of Education, New York, 2000) and current Commissioner of Education Richard Mills justify the new regime on the grounds that standards and standardized testing are the only way to ensure that all students, including students of color and those living in poverty, have an opportunity to learn. They argue that it is these same students who, because of the end of industrialization and the rise of globalization, can no longer be permitted to fail. All students must succeed educationally to ensure that the individual and the nation succeed economically. Hayden (personal communication to Richard Brodsky and Richard Green, New York State Assembly, 2001) described the testing requirement as a means to improving life prospects for "poor and minority children who in the past would have been relegated to a low standards path. Too often, such children emerged from school without the skills and knowledge needed for success in an increasingly complex economy" (p. 1). Furthermore, both Hayden and Mills argue that the curriculum standards were objectively determined and that standardized tests provide a valid and reliable means of assessing student learning. Such objective methods are required, they say, because teachers and administrators cannot be trusted to assess student learning objectively and accurately (Hayden, 1999, 2001).

At the federal level, the No Child Left Behind Act requires states to develop standardized tests and assessment systems in order to determine whether schools are making "adequate yearly progress" (AYP). NCLB became law because it, like the standards, testing, and accountability movement on which it builds, ostensibly aims to improve education, especially for those students who have historically been disadvantaged, including students of color and students living in poverty. President Bush promoted NCLB as a means of replicating at the national level the "success" achieved by reforms in some states. Rodney Paige, former Secretary of Education, has even described NCLB as an extension of the Civil Rights Movement of the 1960s, building on the legacy of Martin Luther King, Jr.

Forty-four years ago, Dr Martin Luther King, Jr. said, "The great challenge facing the nation today is to solve segregation and discrimination and bring into full realization the ideas and dreams of our democracy." The No Child Left Behind Act does that. The law creates the conditions of equitable access to education for all children. It brings us a step closer to the promise of our constitution. (Paige & Jackson, 2004)

It is Paige and Jackson's aim to position opponents to NCLB as anti-civil rights. To this discourse of equality Paige adds the two other discourses prominent in New York's and Chicago's reform arguments: testing provides more objective assessments and global economic competition requires education reform. In *What to Know and Where to Go: A Parents' Guide to No Child Left Behind* (U.S. Department of Education, 2002), Paige conveys to the public the purported benefits of NCLB. He informs readers that standardized tests provide a valid and reliable means of assessing student learning, and this approach improves on teacher-generated assessments. The parent guide informs parents that NCLB "will give [parents] objective data" through standardized testing (U.S. Department of Education, 2002, p. 12). Further, objective data from tests are necessary because in the past "many parents have children who are getting straight As, but find out too late that their child is not prepared for college. That's just one reason why NCLB gives parents objective data about how their children are doing" (p. 12). Teachers, he implies, have neither rigorously enforced standards nor accurately assessed students, thereby covering up their own failures and those of their students.

However, federal and state education reforms have failed to achieve the goals of improved student assessments and increased educational equality. In New York almost every standardized exam has been criticized for poorly constructed, misleading, or erroneous questions; or for using a grading scale that either over- or understates student learning. Critics have charged that the level of difficulty for a standardized exam depends on whether the State Education Department (SED) wants to increase graduation rates or wants to appear rigorous and tough. The passing rate for any exam can be increased or decreased simply by adjusting the cut score, turning a low percentage of correct answers into a pass or a high percentage of correct answers into a failure. On exams that students are likely to take as part of their graduation requirement, the SED makes it easier for students to pass by lowering the cut score. Conversely, the exams for the advanced, non-required courses, such as physics and chemistry, have been made more difficult (Winerip, 2003).

Furthermore, sometimes an unusually low or high failure rate may not be intentional but the result of incompetence. The June 2003 Math A exam (also a test students are likely to take to meet the graduation requirement) was so poorly constructed that all the test scores had to be discarded. Statewide, only 37% of students received a passing score (Arenson, 2003). At Rochester's Wilson Magnet High School, an urban school with an International Baccalaureate Program, then ranked 49th in the nation by *Newsweek*, all 300 students who took the exam failed (Rivera, personal communication, 2003).

Moreover, educational inequality has increased as a result of these neoliberal reforms. Quantitative evidence from New York suggests that high-stakes testing has harmed educational achievement. Fewer students, especially students of color and students with disabilities, are completing high school. From 1998 to 2000, the dropout rate increased by 17%. A report from the Harvard Center for Civil Rights concluded that New York now has the lowest graduation rate of any state for African-American (35%) and Latino/a (31%) students (Orfield, Losen, Wald, & Swanson 2004). Haney (2003) reported that New York's graduation rate currently ranks 45th in the nation. Standardized tests have negatively affected English language learners, the highest diploma-earning minority in 2002 (Monk, Sipple, & Killen, 2001). Lastly, dropouts among students with disabilities increased from 7,200 in 1996 to 9,200 in 2001.

NCLB has been criticized for numerous reasons, most significantly for failing to achieve its stated goal of decreasing educational inequality and its more likely goal of discrediting public schools so as to privatize them. Orfield (2006), in the foreword to a study by the Civil Rights Project at Harvard University concluded that:

> neither a significant rise in achievement, nor closure of the racial achievement gap is being achieved…. The reported state successes are artifacts of state testing policies which lead to apparent gains on state tests [which] do not show up on an independent national test, the National Assessment of Educational Progress. (p. 5)

While recent neoliberal education reformers may not have achieved their ostensible goal of improving educational outcomes for all students, their reforms have significantly altered the discourse and the organization and provision of public education. Education, which is generally perceived as key to economic growth, is being reorganized to develop workers with the skills necessary for their ultimate vocational position. Furthermore, because schools should not only serve businesses but also be exposed to the same market competition as businesses, corporate executives promote themselves as better equipped than educators to organize and run the public education system. Consequently, corporations play a larger role in determining education policy, as evidenced by the Commercial Club's central role in shaping Chicago's education policies and the role of corporations and conservative think tanks in developing and passing the NCLB Act (DeBray, 2006). Standardized testing, accountability, auditing, and choice now dominate educational policy discourse.

Furthermore, while neoliberal ideology promotes markets as free from governmental intervention, as Thrupp and Wilmott (2003) pointed out above, all markets require oversight and control. Educational choice, as in Chicago and under NCLB, is a result of corporate and governmental intervention, undermining parent and community control. However, because neoliberals do not control schooling by intervening directly in the daily lives of teachers, but instead indirectly through standards, tests, and markets, makes their interference less noticeable. Standardized tests and other accountability mechanisms allow governing entities to intervene in the classroom indirectly, to focus on output while leaving the means to achieving these goals to the school. Ball (1990) describes this strategy as "steering from a distance," whereas others have described it as the rise of the "audit" or "evaluative" state (Clarke & Newman, 1997; Gerwitz, 2002; Whitty, Powers, & Halpin, 1998). Consequently, under neoliberalism, control over schools has shifted away from the local level towards state and federal levels (Ball, 1994; Rose, 1999). Parents and students are marginalized as their input into education is restricted to what schools they choose.

Neoliberalism, by incorporating market discourses and systems, has transformed how we think about and engage in democracy. The emphasis on markets replaces deliberative forms of democracy with aggregative democracy. Aggregative forms of democracy focus on tallying individual preferences; families chose which schools they prefer and based on those preferences some schools flourish while others fail and may ultimately close. Such systems, Young (2000) argues, focus on individual choices but ignore the reasons for those choices. She states that "There is no account for their origins, how they might have been arrived at…no criteria for determining the quality of the preferences by either content, origin, or motive…preferences are seen as exogenous to the political process" (p.

20). For example, under NCLB parents and students may be given the choice of attending another school based on schools' standardized test scores, scores that may largely reflect not the quality of the school but the socioeconomic status of the students. Since such choices are individual family choices, "individuals never need to leave the private realm of their own interest," that is, they can choose without engaging others regarding the consequences of the choice beyond their own family. Such decision making "lacks any distinct idea of a public formed from the interaction of democratic citizens and their motivation to reach some decision" (p. 20). Gutmann and Thompson (2004) add:

> Aggregative democracy is seriously flawed, and cannot serve as a principled basis for democratic decision-making. By taking existing or minimally corrected preferences as given, as the base line for collective decisions, the aggregative conception fundamentally accepts and may even reinforce existing distributions of power in society. These distributions may or may not be fair, but aggregative conceptions do not offer any principle by which they can decide. Even more important, they do not provide any process by which citizens' views about these distributions might be changed. (p. 16)

Debate over what the purposes of schools should be and how those goals should be achieved and assessed has been eliminated. In contrast, deliberative democracy requires that people participate "in the decisions and processes that affect" their lives and use their knowledge and skills to affect those around them (Young, 2000, p. 156). For Young, like Dewey, social institutions, especially schools, should promote individual growth and change through "communication among citizens, and between citizen and public officials, where issues are discussed in an open and critical fashion" (p. 167). Similarly, Dewey (1916) described democracy as "a mode of associated living, of conjoint communicative experience" (p. 87). Mathison (2000), in writing about Dewey's notion of deliberative democracy, states that this requires that people collectively decide what and how to be and what to do: "Differences of opinion must therefore be settled through deliberation, not by coercion, appeal to emotion, or authority" (p. 236). This does not guarantee resolution but "members of a community can disagree as long as they are willing to engage in discussion about their beliefs, as long as their beliefs are consistent with the best available evidence, and as long as they are open-minded about their beliefs" (p. 237).

The deliberative model provides places in which people can present justifications for their preferences, listen to others, and, where possible, work out new understandings and compromises. Such discussion and debate has the positive outcome of deepening people's understanding of the purposes and processes of schooling as they engage in defense of their own views and listen to the views of others The process of setting social and educational goals becomes an educative process in itself as citizens work to refine their views in light of increased understanding. Further, it is important for Young and Dewey that civil society be strengthened and remain relatively autonomous from government, making it possible to "limit state power and make its exercise more accountable and democratic" (Young, 2000, p. 159).

Reinstituting Rights and Deliberation Into Education Social Justice

That neoliberals have failed to deliver on promises of increased equality should not be surprising given neoliberalism's primary goal of increasing economic and corporate growth, and the concomitant weakening of the welfare state so that individuals are alone responsible for their well-being. Nor should it be surprising that neoliberalism undermines civic participation in democratic decision making when, as in Chicago and Washington, D.C., corporate leaders direct educational policies for the private rather than the public good.

Yet neoliberalism persists in part because its proponents frame their reforms as inevitable in a global economy. Sociologist Pierre Bourdieu (1998) noted:

> A whole set of propositions are being imposed as self evident: it is taken for granted that maximum growth, and therefore productivity and competitiveness, are the ultimate and sole goal of human actions; or that economic forces cannot be resisted. Or again—a presupposition which is the basis of all the presuppositions in economics—a radical separation is made between the economic and the social, which is left to one side...as a kind of reject. (p. 31)

In response, we need to examine the dangers of neoliberal reforms to democratic institutions and to reinstate deliberative forms of democracy that support individual rights beyond the right to choose. For neoliberals, social justice merely requires that individuals be given access to markets. If they fail to achieve educational and economic success, then individuals only have themselves to blame.

Instead, we need to reaffirm the principles of social justice on which Roosevelt based his Second Bill of Rights, such as the right to a job, home, medical care, economic protection from the economic fears of old age, sickness, accident and unemployment, and, most importantly, "a good education" (Sunstein, 2004, p. 13). Harvey, in *A Brief History of Neoliberalism* (2005), extends the list to incorporate rights we need to consider in an age of increased globalization:

> The right to life chances, to political association and "good" governance, for control over production by the direct producers [workers], to the inviolability and integrity of the human body, to engage in critique without fear of retaliation, to a decent and healthy living environment, to collective control of common property resources, to the production of space [to move in and reconstruct the environment], to difference, as well as rights inherent in our status as species beings [that is, to become fully human]. (p. 204)

How these rights should be defined and how we might work toward them needs to be deliberated. We also need, as Dewey wrote, to rethink how all social institutions, particularly schools, promote conceptions of social justice in which such rights might be recognized. Schools should be places in which the rational capacities of children are cultivated; places where children think critically about the kind of persons they would like to be and the kind of society in which they would like to live. Social justice requires critiquing neoliberalism for the way in which it exacerbates inequality, and radically rethinking society and public schooling to promote deliberation, democratic engagement, and individual autonomy.

References

Arenson, K. (2003, August 27). New York math exam trials showed most students failing. *New York Times*, C12.

Ball, S. (1990). *Politics and policymaking in education: Explorations in policy sociology*. London: Routledge.

Ball, S. (1994). *Education reform: A critical and post-structural approach*. Buckingham, UK: Open University Press.

Bourdieu, P. (1998). *Act of resistance: Against the tyranny of the market*. New York: The New Press.

Bowles, S., & Gintis, H. (1986). *Democracy and capitalism: Property, community and the contradictions of modern thought*. New York: Basic Books.

Clarke, J., & Newman, J. E. (1997). *The managerial state*. Thousand Oaks CA: Sage.

Debray, E. (2006). *Politics, ideology, and education: Federal policy during the Clinton and Bush administrations*. New York: Teachers College Press.

Dewey, J. (1915, May 5). *The New Republic, 3*, 40.

Dewey, J. (1916). *Democracy and education*. New York: Free Press.

Dewey, J. (1934). *Experience and education*. New York: Macmillan.

Dewey, J. (1950). *Reconstruction in philosophy*. New York: The New American Library/Mentor Books. (Original work published 1919)

Dewey, J. (1987). Democracy and educational administration. In J. A. Boysdon (Ed.), *John Dewey: The later works, 1925–1953*. Carbondale & Edwardsville: Southern Illinois University Press. (Original work published 1937)

Fones-Wolfe, E. (1994). *Selling free-enterprise: The business assault on labor and liberalism 1945–1960*. Urbana: University of Illinois Press.

Friedman, M. (1995, June 23). *Public schools: Make them private*. Briefing paper no. 23. Retrieved from http://www.cato.org/pubs/briefs/bp-023.html

Gerwitz, S. (2002). *The managerial school: Post-welfarism and social justice in education*. New York: Routledge.

Gutmann, A., & Thompson, D. (2004). *Why deliberative democracy?* Princeton, NJ: Princeton University Press.

Haney, W. (2003, September 23). *Attrition of students from New York schools*. Invited testimony at a public hearing "Regents Learning Standards and High School Graduation Requirements" before the New York Senate Standing Committee on Education, Senate Hearing Room, New York.

Harvey, D. (2005). *A brief history of neoliberalism*. Oxford: Oxford University Press.

Henwood, D. (2003). *After the new economy*. New York: The New Press.

Hursh, D. (2005). The growth of high-stakes testing in the USA: Accountability, markets and the decline of educational equality. *British Educational Research Journal, 31*(4), 605–622.

Judt, T. (2005). *Postwar: A history of Europe since 1945*. New York: Penguin.

Kanigel, R. (2005). *The one best way: Frederick Winslow Taylor and the enigma of efficiency (Sloan technology)*. Cambridge, MA: MIT Press.

Katznelson, I. (2005). *When affirmative action was White: An untold history of racial inequality in twentieth-century America*. New York: W. W. Norton.

Lauder, H., Brown, P., Dillabough, J., & Halsey, A. H. (2006). *Education, globalization, and social change*. Oxford: Oxford University Press.

Lee, J. (2006). *Tracking achievement gaps and assessing the impact of NCLB on the gaps: An in-depth look into national and state reading and math outcome trends*. Boston: The Civil Rights Project of Harvard University.

Lemke, T. (2001). "The birth of bio-politics": Michel Foucault's lecture at the Collège de France on neo-liberal governmentality. *Economy and society, 30*(2), 198.

Lemke, T. (2002). Foucault, governmentality, and critique. *Rethinking Marxism. 14*(3), 49–64.

Levitas, R. (Ed.). (1986). *The ideology of the new right*. Cambridge, UK: Polity Press.

Lipman, P. (2004). *High-stakes education: Inequality, globalization, and urban school reform*. New York: Routledge Falmer.

Lipman, P. (2005). We're not blind. Just follow the dollar sign. *Rethinking Schools, 19*(4), 54–58.

Mathison, S. (2000). Promoting democracy through evaluation. In D. Hursh & E. W. Ross (Eds.), *Democratic social education: Social studies for social change* (pp. 229–241). New York: Falmer Press.

Monk, D., Sipple, J., & Killen, K. (2001). *Adoption and adaptation: New York States school districts' responses to state imposed high school graduation requirements: An eight-year retrospective*. New York: Education Finance Research Consortium. Retrieved from http://www.albany.edu/edfin/CR01_MskReport.pdf

Olssen, M., Codd, J., & O'Neill, A. M. (2004). *Education policy: Globalization, citizenship and democracy*. Thousand Oaks, CA: Sage.

Orfield, G. (2006). Forward. In J. Lee (Ed.), *Tracking achievement gaps and assessing the impact of NCLB on the gaps: An in-depth look into national and state reading and math outcome trends*. Boston: The Civil Rights Project of Harvard University.

Orfield, G., Losen, D., Wald, J., & Swanson, C. (2004). *Losing our future: How minority youth are being left behind by the graduation rate crisis*. Cambridge, MA: The Civil Rights Project at Harvard University.

Paige, R., & Jackson, A. (2004, November 8). Education: The civil rights-issue of the twenty-first century. *Hispanic Vista*. Retrieved (Dec.11, 2007) from http://www.hispanicvista.com/HVC/Opinion/Guest_Columns/1108Road_Paige-Alphonso_Jackson.htm

Parenti, C. (1999). Atlas finally shrugged: Us against them in the me decade. *The Baffler, 13*, 108–120.

Peters, M. (1994, June). Individualism and community: Education and the politics of difference. Discourse: Studies in the cultural politics of education, *14*(2), 65–78.

Rose, N. (1999). *Powers of freedom: Reframing political thought*. Cambridge, UK: Cambridge University Press.

Snedden, D. (1924, November). Education for a world of team players and team workers. *School and Society, 20*, 554–556.

Sunstein, C. (2004). *The second Bill of Rights: FDR's unfinished revolution and why we need it more than ever*. New York: Basic Books.

Tabb, W. (2002). *Unequal partners: A primer on globalization*. New York: New Press.

Taylor, F. W. (1911). *The principles of scientific management*. New York: Harper Brothers.

Thatcher, M. (1993). *The Downing Street years*. London: HarperCollins.

Thrupp, M., & Wilmott, R. (2003). *Education management in managerialist times: Beyond the textual apologists*. Maidenhead, UK: Open University Press.

U.S. Department of Education, Office of the Secretary. (2002, April) *What to know and where to go: A parents' guide to No Child Left Behind*. Washington, D.C.: Author.

Whitty, G., Powers, S., & Halpin, D. (1998). *Devolution and choice in education: The school, the state, and the market*. Philadelphia: Open University Press.

Winerip, M. (2003, March 12). Passing grade defies laws of physics. *New York Times*, A22, B7.

Wirth, A. (1977). Philosophical issues in the vocational-liberal studies controversy (1990–1991): John Dewey vs. the social efficiency philosophers. In A. Bellack & H. M. Kliebard (Eds.), *Curriculum and evaluation* (pp. 161–172). Berkeley, CA: McCutcheon Press.

Young, I. M. (2000). *Inclusion and democracy*. Oxford: Oxford University Press.

Response to Part 2

International Perspectives on Social Justice in Education

Lisa Lee

Jane Addams, the first (and only) U.S. woman to win the Nobel Peace Prize—in 1931—served for three exhilarating terms on the Chicago Board of Education. For Addams, the importance of securing education for youth was entangled with the furious struggle to establish a broad system of social welfare. Although she was most famous for her work to end militarism abroad, Addams passionately believed that there could be no peace without justice and that justice would not exist until we created the conditions for peace to flourish at home, in our own communities and neighborhoods. These conditions included public housing, public health, living wages for all people, playgrounds and green spaces in all neighborhoods, and vibrant art and music programs in our schools to ensure the unleashing of imagination and creativity in young people from all backgrounds.

Also of critical importance at this time, was her support for the founding of the nation's first Juvenile Justice Court in 1899, a building that stood directly across the street from the Hull House Settlement where Addams lived and worked. Instead of incarcerating the youth that were found "uneducable," she insisted instead that we consider the following question, a question that would become the title of one of her most famous essays, "How Shall We Respond to the Dreams of Youth?"

If we directed our efforts to asking and answering this question of our public institutions and ourselves, we might help to insure the welfare of our common good. Although frightening, it is also worth asking ourselves how is it that just a few short generations after the death of Jane Addams, there has been such a profound and disastrous reversal in the meaning of "welfare"? What has happened to our sense of peace, justice, and solidarity with other human beings so that we no longer see all of the issues listed above as inextricably linked with the education of our youth?

Reference

Addams, J. (1994). How shall we respond to the dreams of youth? In *The spirit of youth and the city streets*. Edison, NJ: Transaction Press.

Part 3

Race, Ethnicity, and Language

Seeking Social Justice in Education

Edited and Introduced by Annette Henry

> The brutal truth is that the bulk of white people in America never had any interest in educating Black people, except as this could serve white purposes. It is not the Black child's language that is in question, it is not his language that is despised: It is his experience. A child cannot be taught by anyone who despises him, and a child cannot afford to be fooled. A child cannot be taught by anyone whose demand, essentially, is that the child repudiate his experience, and all that gives him sustenance, and enter a limbo in which he will no longer be Black, and in which he knows that he can never become white. Black people have lost too many children that way.
>
> (Baldwin, 1979)

> Ethnic identity is twin skin to linguistic identity—I am my language. Until I can take pride in my language I cannot take pride in myself...while I still have to speak English or Spanish when I would rather speak Spanglish, and as long as I have to accommodate the English speakers rather than having them accommodate me, my tongue will be illegitimate.
>
> (Anzaldúa, 1987)

> The white fathers told us: I think, therefore I am. The Black mother within each of us—the poet—whispers in our dreams: I feel, therefore I can be free.
>
> (Lorde, 1984, p. 100)

The chapters in this section represent a range of thinking about language, race, culture, equity, and justice. The pursuit of social justice necessitates "probing, exposing and interrogating how a sense of what counts as justice is produced through conceptual categories, frameworks and social problematics that constitute dimensions of the transdisciplinary terrain of critical educational inquiry," writes philosopher Grace Livingston (in press). These chapters challenge the very discourses upon which certain epistemic understandings rest. Each presents a case or cases, such as one's teaching, a particular linguistic or historical event, or cultural group.

Two chapters explore bilingualism, civil rights, and human rights for oppressed cultural and linguistic minorities. In chapter 13, Shelley Taylor and Tove Skutnabb-Kangas examine the case of Kurds, their language, identity, and oppression in particular Western countries, to illustrate their arguments about Linguistic Human Rights (LHRs). Questions of minority languages, bilingualism, and language rights in the United States are contentiously political and emotionally charged. Along with all the chapters in this section, Taylor and Skutnabb-Kangas denounce the lack of justice for all members of society. They brilliantly argue that the same lack of cultural and linguistic human rights encountered by Kurdish minorities in Europe welters in the historical and contemporary United States. The case of the Kurds resonates with language communities globally and locally who, through state-sanctioned institutions, find themselves in unjust situations: dispersed, oppressed, colonized, rendered invisible, minoritized, and in some instances killed. Consider the ways that the United States has treated indigenous peoples, African slaves, and "unwelcome" Latino/a immigrants. And, consider the ways in which the languages of these groups have been suppressed or even obliterated. Taylor and Skutnabb-Kangas critique the contemporary subtractive, dominant-language only policies in the United States. Their critique is timely, as we note that America continues indeed to espouse the myth of monolingualism (Edwards, 2004). One example, a consequence of the No Child Left Behind Act, is that the former Office of Bilingual Instruction is now called the U.S. Office of English Language Acquisition and Language Instruction (Spring, 2005). This English Only view contributes not only to the loss of the mother tongue intergenerationally, but also to linguistic genocide. We have to think more deeply about how language is not only a record of cultural practices, but a syntactic and semantic representation of what is important or salient in that culture (Tsuda, 1985).

Helen Thumann and Laurene Simms (chapter 14), educators at Gallaudet University, give a historical context for understanding the struggle for deaf self-determination regarding identity, culture, language, curricula, and research. They discuss audism—a hegemonic practice of the hearing community. Hearing researchers and practitioners have perpetuated a normative model of deficiency/deviance to studies of deafness and deaf education. While the deaf community is far more heterogeneous than discussed in their chapter (Padden & Humphries, 1988), Thumann and Simms argue for a deaf educational research by, for, and with deaf people, and from counterhegemonic frames of reference. Again with examples from their own sociopolitical lives at the now famous Gallaudet University, they illustrate how social justice entails self-empowerment, which is the only true empowerment (Marable, 1990). Truly, as Jesse Jackson, uttered, during the week long protest staged by deaf students at Gallaudet in 1988 to elect their first deaf president, "the problem is the hearing world does not listen" (Gannon, 1989, p. 88).

The final three chapters analyze aspects of race. Both Ricky Lee Allen (chapter 15) and Zeus Leonardo (chapter 16) discuss issues of Whiteness in the research literature and in their own classroom practice. Their chapters can be read in tandem, as they both explicate and complicate aspects of Mills's (1997) racial contract thesis through their antiracist work with prospective teachers. They draw upon cases from their own pedagogy to theorize how Whiteness operates in North American culture and to theorize White racial knowledge. Indeed, Leonardo argues that although White people evade discussions and analyses of racism, they do not lack racial knowledge. They are indeed full participants in racialization.

Leonardo writes: "The concept of racism is central to understanding the American landscape and history" (p. 241). One of the most difficult challenges in teacher education programs is to help (mostly White and female) students think about race and racism as more than statistics and events of no consequence to them (Berlak & Moyenda, 2001; Chapman, 2007). For White students, as scholars tell us (Cochran-Smith, 2004; Henry, 2005), it is difficult to grapple with race as constitutive of American social formations and even more difficult to grapple with what Charles Mills (1997) has called the "epistemology of ignorance" (p. 19) and the historical and contemporary practices of White supremacy as a system and one's own participation in it. The classroom, then, can be a place to imagine and work for social transformation; it is also a highly contested and contentious site for educators who are pushing the boundaries and trying to "decenter the white patriarchal gaze" (Dash, 1992). Allen further complicates notions of Whiteness by arguing against the homogeneity often attributed to Whiteness. Using examples from the research literature, his teaching, and from his Appalachian background, he deconstructs the realities of "nonpoor Whites" and "low-status Whites." Allen examines how Whites, especially middle class Whites or "nonpoor" Whites, show their allegiance to White hegemony, but also how poor Whites also benefit and show their allegiance to the White racial polity. Like Leonardo, Allen's project is set in a vision of curricular and pedagogical transformation, indeed, education for critical consciousness (Freire, 1970). Allen calls for heterogeneity in understanding Whites' relations in the political and societal structures.

In chapter 17, Amanda Lewis, Carla O'Connor, and Jennifer Mueller employ the case of African Americans to argue that educational research on achievement and Black youth has undertheorized race most often as a variable or as culture. They demonstrate that researchers have failed to examine fully intersectionalities such as gender, class, and country of origin. They illustrate the conceptual limitations within these analytic traditions and advance alternative conceptual lenses with "more fruitful starting points" for a reorientation with more explanatory power. Lewis, O'Connor, and Mueller explore several multidimensional and ecological ways of arriving at theoretically informed understandings of race and other related constructs in understanding the everyday social, material, and educational lives of youth.

As educators who desire transformation, we must be mindful of the ways that injustices have been historicized and naturalized through everyday current theories, policies, and practices. Moreover, even though each chapter herein explores one aspect or group, we have to work against a "one-sided" model of social justice (Henry, in press), and acknowledge its intersectionality, as Lewis, O'Connor, and Mueller also warn. Indeed, Alexander writes (2005), "Race is always gendered, class is always racialized, sexuality is always experienced through race, and so on" (p. 156). This intersectionality is a place where we can help teacher education students become critical readers of their worlds and insatiable workers for social justice.

References

Alexander, M. J. (2005). *Pedagogies of crossing: Meditations on feminism, sexual politics, memory, and the sacred*. Durham, NC: Duke University Press.

Anzaldúa, G. (1987). *Borderlands/la frontera: The new mestiza*. San Francisco: Aunt Lute Books.

Baldwin, J. (1979, July 29). If Black English isn't a language, then tell me, what is? *New York Times*.

Berlak, A., & Moyenda, S. (2001). *Taking it personally: Racism in the classroom from kindergarten to college*. Philadelphia: Temple University Press.

Chapman, T. (2007). *"I feel like I don't have the right to lord it over them": A White teacher's attempts at critical multiculturalism*. Paper presented at the Annual Conference of the American Educational Research Association. Chicago, IL.

Cochrane-Smith, M. (2005). *Walking the road: Race, diversity, and social justice in teacher education*. New York: Teachers' College Press.

Dash, J. (1992). *Daughters of the dust. The making of an African American women's film*. New York: The New Press.

Edwards, V. (2004). *Multilingualism in the English-speaking world*. Malden, MA: Blackwell.

Freire, P. (1970). *Pedagogy of the oppressed*. New York: Continuum.

Gannon, J. (1989). *The week the world heard Gallaudet*. Washington D.C.: Gallaudet University Press.

Henry, A. (2005). Black feminist pedagogy: Critiques and contributions in W. Watkins (Ed.), *Black protest thought and education* (pp. 89–106), New York: Peter Lang.

Henry, A. (in press). Feminist theory. In S. Tozer, B. Gallegos, & A. Henry (Eds.), *Handbook of research in the social foundations of educations*. Mahwah, NJ: Erlbaum.

Livingston, G. (in press). Historical memory and the foundations of the critical categories of justice in education. In S. Tozer, B. Gallegos, & A. Henry (Eds), *Handbook of research in the social foundations of education*. Mahwah, NJ: Erlbaum.

Lorde, A. (1984). *Sister outsider: Essays and speeches*. Trumansburg, NY: Crodding Press.

Marable, M. (1990, May). Toward Black American empowerment. *African Commentary*, 16–21.

Mills, C. (1997). *The racial contract*. Ithaca, NY: Cornell University Press.

Padden, C., & Humphries, T. (1988). *Deaf in America: Voices from a culture*. Cambridge, MA: Harvard University Press.

Spring, J. (2005). *American education* (11th ed.). New York: McGraw-Hill.

Tsuda, Y. (1985). *Language, inequality and distortion*. Amsterdam: John Benjamins.

13 The Educational Language Rights of Kurdish Children in Turkey, Denmark, and Kurdistan (Iraq)[1]

Shelley K. Taylor and Tove Skutnabb-Kangas

Linguistic Human Rights in Education: An Overview

Research on educational performance indicates that linguistic minority (LM) children taught through the medium of a dominant language in submersion (sink-or-swim) programs[2] often perform considerably less well than native dominant-language-speaking children in the same class, both in general and on tests of (dominant) language and school achievement. They suffer from higher levels of push-out rates, stay in school fewer years, have higher unemployment, and, for some groups, drug use, criminality, and suicide figures, and so forth. There would appear to be a strong argument that such children do not benefit from the right to education to the same extent as children whose mother tongue is the teaching language of the school, and that this distinction is based on language—see Skutnabb-Kangas (2000), for educational and sociological arguments, and for the human rights instruments that embody some linguistic human rights; for legal arguments, see also de Varennes (1996); Magga, Nicolaisen, Trask, Dunbar, and Skutnabb-Kangas (2005), for a summary of the arguments.

Given what we know about the educational benefits of mother tongue medium (MTM) education and, as importantly, the educational harm, with resulting impact on employment prospects, mental and physical health, and life chances generally, of education of LM children mainly through another language, it can be forcefully argued that only MTM education, at least in primary school, is consistent with the provisions of several human rights documents (see Magga et al., 2005, for an elaboration; see also http://www.tomasevski.net (n.d.), the website of the late Katarina Tomasevski, the UN Special Rapporteur on the Right to Education from 1998 to 2004, for reports on the right to education). No other form of education seems to guarantee the full development of the human personality and the sense of its dignity, nor does it enable children who are subject to non-MTM education to participate as effectively in society. Those research findings are thus taken for granted in this article which state that maintenance-oriented MTM education (with good teaching of a dominant language as a second language, with bilingual teachers) is often the best way to enhance LM children's high-level bilingualism, school achievement, a positive development of identity, and self-confidence.

In this article we are going to use a "particular case," namely Kurds in Turkey, Iraq, and Denmark, to elucidate a general phenomenon of presence or absence of Linguistic Human Rights (LHRs).

Why Kurds? Why Comparisons?

Kurds have often been called the world's largest people without a state. Since none of the states where the Kurds have lived for centuries (Syria, Azerbaijan, Iran, Turkey, and Iraq) have census figures based on language or ethnicity, the figures for the numbers of

Kurds vary between 25 and over 40 million, depending on the reliability of the source (McDowall, 2004). For instance, Kemal Burkay (n.d.), the General Secretary of the Kurdistan Socialist Party, and Wikipedia (n.d.-c) end up with similar total upper figures for Kurds in Iran, Iraq, Syria, and Turkey (36.5 and 37.5 million, respectively; in addition, there are a minimum of 1.5 million Kurds in diaspora in other countries).[3] Turkey has the largest Kurdish population, a minimum of 15 million, probably much more. Statistics provided by the Central Intelligence Agency (CIA; 2007) document the Kurdish population as accounting for some 20% of the total population of Turkey.[4]

Most Kurds see themselves as one people. The borders of Kurdistan (the land of the Kurdish people where they have lived for centuries, often interspersed with other peoples but in most cases as the majority in their own areas) are likewise unclear and contested, but there is agreement about what the "core" Kurdish areas are, except maybe among the most ideologically anti-Kurdish politicians. In Turkey, even the very existence of Kurds has been denied until very recently. The Turkish Law No. 2820 on Political Parties, section 81, from 22 April 1983, had the following (close to surrealistic) formulation: "It is forbidden to claim that there exist minorities in Turkey. It is forbidden to protect or develop non-Turkish cultures and languages." The second part indirectly admits that minorities do in fact exist—no law would be needed to deny protection and development of something that does not exist. The law was repealed on April 12th, 1991, the same day as a new Law to Combat Terrorism (No. 3713) came into force. This law prohibits claims of minority existence equally efficiently but more covertly (see Skutnabb-Kangas, 2000, pp. 517–518). And the latest denial of the existence of Kurds is embedded in Article 301 of the Turkish Penal Code, where all expressions of Kurdishness, including use of the Kurdish colors in clothes, is forbidden (see below). How can children, whose ethnicity, language, and very existence are denied, be granted linguistic human rights in education?

When these children or their parents immigrate to some democratic Western country, in our case Denmark, is it easier for them to enjoy these rights? Official European Union (EU) policies celebrate multilingualism and claim to support it—but is this valid also for Kurds in the EU?

And when Kurds can decide for themselves how to educate their own children, do they rush for English-medium, as many Asian parents do (Hong Kong, Singapore, parts of India), or do they opt for another big international language, Arabic? Do Kurdish children under the Kurdistan Regional Government in Iraq have educational language rights? Have the Kurds in Iraq learned anything from the oppression that they have experienced, most recently under Saddam Hussain[5]—do the Kurds in their turn now oppress linguistic minorities such as Assyrians or the Turkomen in Iraqi Kurdistan? We believe that there are lessons of more general relevance for social justice to learn from how the three countries concerned are treating Kurds.

(Lack of) Educational Language Rights in North West Kurdistan (Turkey)

This part could, sadly, consist of one sentence: As of early spring 2008, Kurds in Turkey have no educational language rights.

All education is through the medium of Turkish. Children are not allowed to study Kurdish as a subject in schools. There is no Kurdish medium education in day care, kindergarten, or schools. In theory, some teaching of Kurdish as a subject to teenagers and adults is allowed, but the rules around this teaching have so far made it more or less impossible.

The following examples from 2002 to 2006 are from court cases where the Kurdish language and expressions of Kurdish culture are either overtly prohibited, or prohibited on the basis of being labeled "terrorist activities" which fall under the vague definition of terrorism in the Turkish Penal Code, Article 301.

> A case has begun before the state security court in Diyarbakir against 27 children aged between 11–18, because they had demanded the right to native [Kurdish] language tuition…. The state prosecutor…accused the children and adolescents of "aiding [i.e. "sponsoring"] a terrorist organization" through their demands, and has called for prison terms of 3 years and 9 months.[6]

> In 2002, student petitions calling for the right to merely receive some optional instruction in the Kurdish language were incriminated "on grounds of being instrumental to the ["terrorist"] PKK's efforts to establish itself as a political organisation. State Prosecutors were briefed by the Ministry of the Interior in January, 2002, to bring charges of "membership in a terrorist organization" punishable with 12 years' imprisonment against any students or parents who lodge[d] petitions demanding optional Kurdish lessons. By 23rd January 2002, a total of 85 students and more than 30 parents ha[d] been imprisoned and over 1,000 people (among them some juveniles) detained" for merely "having demanded optional first language education in Kurdish."[7]

Even today, as Turkey is engaged in the EU "accession process," "programmes in Kurdish for children on radio or TV" remain "prohibited."[8] An August 2005 BIA News Centre report described the following restrictions that were in place:

> Local media groups who seek [to] broadcast programs in languages and dialects other than Turkish"—i.e. Kurdish—"…will [need to] present…an *affidavit*" clarifying their intentions and behaviour, "stating that they will not broadcast…programmes with the aim of teaching that language.[9]

Teachers who have sought to simply "learn the Kurdish language" in preparation for a time when they might be allowed to teach it in schools, have also been targeted by the "Anti-Terror Police" and tortured by them for their seemingly "terrorist inspired" activities: "12 people, of whom 11 were teachers", we are told, for instance, "were allegedly tortured while being detained by police after having been arrested in Kiziltepe for learning Kurdish together."[10]

The Swedish news agency TT reported on the 25th of August, 2006, the Turkish authorities in Istanbul have seized 1,208 Kurdish versions of books about Pippi Långstrump (Pippi Longstocking), the world-famous fictional children's character. They were sent on the August 7th from Sweden by an organization that runs an education project for Kurds. The books had been sent for delivery to libraries in five Kurdish villages. As it is well known, Astrid Lindgren's books about Pippi Longstocking have been translated into 85 languages and published in more than 100 countries.[11]

The Article that has been criticized most intensely in the negotiations regarding Turkish EU membership is Article 301 from the Turkish Penal Code. We quote some of the parts that are most relevant for our language-related concerns here, together with a short extract from one of the most respected critics, Martin Scheinin. Article 301, on the denigration of Turkishness, the Republic, and the foundation and institutions of the State, was introduced with the legislative reforms of June 1, 2005. It states in its first two Articles the following:

1. Public denigration of Turkishness, the Republic or the Grand National Assembly of Turkey shall be punishable by imprisonment of between six months and three years.
2. Public denigration of the Government of the Republic of Turkey, the judicial institutions of the State, the military or security structures shall be punishable by imprisonment of between six months and two years.

Even if Article 4 states that "Expressions of thought intended to criticize shall not constitute a crime," we note the following in the lists of "Offences committed for terrorist purposes" (from its Articles 5 and 6):

> A person who makes the propaganda of the terrorist organisation or its purposes shall be punished with a prison sentence of one to three years.... The below stated acts shall also be punished according to the provisions of this paragraph:
> a) Carrying the emblem or the signs of the terrorist organisation in a way to demonstrate that s/he is a member or supporter of the organisation, wearing clothes that [are reminiscent of] the uniforms on which such emblems and signs are placed, or covering the face partly or completely during demonstrations and rallies in order to conceal one's identity,
> b) Carrying posters, banners, placards, pictures, signboards, equipment and materials, chanting slogans or using audio devices for the purposes of the organization.

A letter, sent on May 21, 2006, to the Parliament Justice Committee by Martin Scheinin, UN Special Rapporteur on the Promotion and Protection of Human Rights and Fundamental Freedoms while Countering Terrorism, informed Turkey that the new anti-terrorism law

> ...fails to meet the requirement of proportionality in the use of force by security forces, introduces "improper restrictions on freedom of expression" and reflects the danger of punishing civilians not involved in violence. This danger is exacerbated by the very broad definition of terrorism that is being used and the very long and wide list of terrorist offences. (Fernandes, 2006b)

Similar sentiments are also expressed in the protest letter by Article 19, the NGO monitoring freedom of expression (Mendel, 2006).

In the U.S. backed "war" against "PKK terrorists," it has become apparent that "one line of reasoning" currently used "in Turkish legal practice is," indeed, *guilt by association*" (Rud, 2005, p. 57). An example of this reasoning is from the education field:

1. The terrorist organisation the PKK is making propaganda for the right to use the Kurdish language, including in education.
2. Consequently, anyone who advocates the right to use the Kurdish language is guilty of supporting ("aiding and abetting," Article 169 of the Turkish Penal Code) a terrorist organization.

(Lack of) Educational Language Rights for Kurds in Denmark

It is presently estimated that 1.3 million Kurds live in Europe where they settled as guest workers and refugees (Council of Europe, 2006). Denmark recruited many foreign workers from the 1960s until it permanently closed its borders to immigration in 1973. By

1995 the largest group of Denmark's 195,000 foreign citizens was from Turkey (Just Jeppesen, 1995). The 35,000 Turks residing in Denmark in 1995 made up 30% of foreign citizens from third world countries. In January 1991, 18,056 immigrant children were enrolled in Danish schools, of which 7,148 were "Turks" (i.e., Turks or Kurds) (Holmen & Jørgensen, 1993). Like Germans, Danes lump third world immigrants together as "Turks" even though many "Turks" are Kurds (Leggewie, 1996, p. 79). In fact, as early as 1981, it was estimated that from 60 to 70% of all "Turks" residing in Denmark were Kurds (Skutnabb-Kangas, 1981). This misclassification has had ramifications on the educational language rights of ethnic Kurdish children in Denmark for the past 40 years. The children and grandchildren of the guest workers who begun arriving in the 1960s are now enrolled in the Danish public school system, and are referred to as second and third generation immigrants, or *efterkommere* (literally "those who come after"—it is not said after whom), and there is a separate category in official Danish census figures for *efterkommere*.

The overall population of Denmark was close to 5.5 million (5,427,459) in January 2006, according to *Danmarks statistikbank* (Statistics Denmark) (2006). Of this overall population, 31,008 were listed as Turkish "immigrants"; 24,542 were listed in a separate category as Turkish *efterkommere*.[12] The distinction made in official documents between children born to ethnic Danes versus those born to other ethnic groups is noteworthy, given that ethnic Kurds, for example, have resided in Denmark for up to 40 years and three generations. This distinction is indicative of extant social divisions between ethnic groups in Denmark, divisions that play themselves out in how access to mother tongue education is prioritized for some, rather than a right for all, thus pitting ethnic groups against each other in a divide and rule manner. Following recent changes to educational language policies in Denmark, Danish municipalities are now only obliged to provide free mother tongue instruction (as a subject, not a medium of instruction) to school-aged children whose parents come from the Danish territories of Greenland and the Faeroe Islands, and member countries of the European Union (Kristjánsdóttir, 2003). The change left the municipalities free to charge immigrant groups a fee for their children to receive mother tongue instruction – or to organize it themselves. A further complication to ethnic Kurdish children exercising educational language rights by gaining access to mother tongue instruction existed long before the more recent limitation cited above. Various European Community (EC) now European Union (EU) countries interpreted the EC 1977 Directive on the education of the children of migrant workers differently, on the basis of what they thought was implied by the term *a national language.* The different interpretations resulted in different policies as to which language(s) migrant workers' children had the right to receive mother tongue (MT) instruction in.

Informants in a longitudinal ethnographic study on ethnic Kurdish children's educational experiences in Denmark (Taylor, 2001; in press) had different interpretations of how the directive applied to Kurds residing in the EU. Some believed that EU countries such as Denmark were obliged to provide MT instruction in Kurdish because it was a national language in Turkey. Others believed that ethnic Kurds in Denmark should receive MT instruction in Turkish since Kurdish was a (much disputed) national language, but not an official language in Turkey. Still others believed that by not providing MT instruction in Kurdish, Denmark was tacitly respecting Turkish national language policy of the time ("No language other than Turkish may be taught as a native language to citizens of Turkey in instructional and educational institutions," Turkish Constitution, Article 42/9, quoted in Skutnabb-Kangas & Bucak, 1995, p. 355). Yet others believed that ignoring the fact that not all Turks were "Turks" suited Denmark's policy of nondecision on the matter of Kurdish language rights in Turkey as minority language rights in Denmark are an unpopular (Achilles heel) issue with Danes who view maintaining minority languages as un-Danish, therefore no priority (Taylor, 2001). In that sense, speaking Kurdish or other minority languages was and is seen as denigrating Danishness in Denmark, just as much as speaking Kurdish in Turkey is seen as denigrating Turkishness. However, while daring to request Kurdish MT instruction in Turkey or Denmark is in violation of the Turkish Penal Code, Article 301 (3. "denigration of Turkishness is committed by a Turkish citizen in another country the punishment shall be increased by one third") in Turkey, it is not (yet!) in violation of the Danish Penal Code.

The Taylor (2001; in press) study revealed that a Danish–Turkish bilingual/bicultural program that featured equal numbers of ethnic Danish and Turkish students also featured a (hidden) Kurdish population: half of all students classified as "Turks" were, in fact, Kurds. The key question that arose in the study was: How could such a misclassification error occur, and continue? There were many layers to the answer. For one, both Turkish and Kurdish students were registered in the program on the basis of their citizenship, as either Danish or Turkish. As Kurdish children in the diaspora are made invisible by virtue of being members of the world's largest people without a state, they were classified as "Turks." A policy document from the program inception phase, however, revealed that the bilingual–bicultural program planning committee did recognize the potential for (Turkish/Kurdish) error (Helkiær, 1987). Section 4.4 of the report, "Turkish and Kurdish children" (*Tyrkiske og kurdiske børn*), deals specifically with population variables. It states:

> Since there are two school-entry choices for Turkish and Kurdish pupils in this municipality—that is, bicultural and parallel groups—on a practical level, it would be feasible to divide the two groups up. There is no doubt that [this arrangement] would be preferable from a linguistic point of view. But obviously the issues involving Turkish and Kurdish peoples involve much more than language. The committee's assessment of the situation was that if we were to propose such a clear division of the two groups, we would be meddling in a politically and emotionally charged matter and, as Danes, would have a hard time imagining the consequences of such an action. (p. 15)

Therefore, Denmark respected Turkish domestic language policy even for ethnic Kurds residing in the diaspora, on Danish soil.

This raises the further question of why Kurdish parents residing in Denmark did not object vociferously then, and do not now. Again turning to the Turkish Penal Code, Article 301, which even prohibits instruction in the Kurdish language in the diaspora, Article 3 is informative. For a Kurd residing in Denmark ("a Turkish citizen in another country") to request Kurdish MT instruction, which could be construed as the "denigration of Turkishness," the punishment is not only steep: punishment "shall be increased by one third." Data deriving from interviews with Kurdish parents, and Turkish and Kurdish educators in Denmark (Taylor, 2001) revealed that Kurdish parents greatly feared negative repercussions for seeking Kurdish-medium MT instruction in Denmark. They feared for themselves as they frequently returned to Turkey for summer holidays, and they feared for their loved ones residing in Turkey. In 1981, when the first course was offered that taught Kurdish teachers from Turkey to read and write Kurdish, there were threats toward the participants from the Turkish Embassy. During the course, there was a burglary in the locality where the course was held, and the only thing that disappeared was a list of the participants. When we (the course organizers, including Tove Skutnabb-Kangas) complained to the relevant Danish Ministry about obstruction in relation to a legal activity in Denmark (to learn how to read and write a language), there was no reply.

Article 301 shows that this threat still exists, effectively limiting Kurdish parents' ability to decide for themselves how to educate their own children by limiting the Kurdish MT option. Therefore, the Danish case shows that children whose ethnicity, language, and very existence are denied in one country (Turkey) do not readily have access to and may be severely limited in their ability to exercise their right to linguistic human rights in education even when their parents or grandparents immigrated to a democratic Western country such as Denmark. Their Kurdishness is still "forbidden" due to their membership in a people without a state, and because of a combination of ethnic Danes viewing the maintenance of non-Danish MTs as denigrating Danishness in Denmark and Kemalists (i.e., supporters of Kemal Atatürk's ideologies) in Turkey viewing maintenance of Kurdish as an MT as denigrating Turkishness. Combined, this accounts for Kurdish children's lack of educational language rights in Denmark.

Educational Language Rights in South Kurdistan (Iraq)

In South Kurdistan (northern Iraq), with a population of 5.5 million, where Kurds form a large majority, the situation today is completely different. The area of South Kurdistan (approximately 80,000 square kilometers, around 18% of the total area of Iraq, is comprised of the governorates of Arbil, Sulaimania, Dohuk, Kirkuk, and parts of Dyala and Nineva. Two thirds of the 5 million Kurds in Iraq live in the first three provinces (Kurdistan Democratic Party [KDP], n.d.-a). These are under the administration of the Kurdistan Regional Government (KRG; 2006). The rest are still administered by Iraq.

All education in South Kurdistan, including university education, is free. In the last report that Tomasevski (2006) submitted to the United Nations as Special Rapporteur on the Right to Education, she examined 170 countries in terms of the extent to which they offered education free or for-fee. Even primary education is for-fee in more than half the countries examined (see Table 25 in Tomasevski's document). The global pattern of economic poverty-based exclusion from primary school is part of the global strategies for "no poverty reduction." Education is often priced out of the reach of the poor. The trend has been a transition from free-and-compulsory to market-based education where the costs of even primary education have been transferred from governmental to family budgets. In view of this, South Kurdistan is remarkable. The "Educational Ladder" in Iraqi Kurdistan consists of "2 years pre-school education for the 4–5 years age group (not compulsory); 6 years compulsory primary education for 6–11 years; 6 years of secondary education of 2 cycles of 3 years each and higher education of 2–6 years" (KDP, n.d.-b).

During Saddam Hussain's regime, all education in South Kurdistan—where it existed in the first place—was in Arabic; however, Kurds have themselves had the administrative control of education since 1991 when the "safe haven" (no-fly zone) was created. Article 4 of the new Constitution of Iraq, which was ratified on October 15th, 2005, states:

> First: The Arabic language and the Kurdish language are the two official languages of Iraq. The right of Iraqis to educate their children in their mother tongue, such as Turkomen, Syriac, and Armenian shall be guaranteed in government educational institutions in accordance with educational guidelines, or in any other language in private educational institutions. Wikipedia (n.d.-a)

Today Kurdish children in Kurdistan have Kurdish as their medium of education in all subjects. Abdulaziz S. Faris, Director General (DG) of Primary Schools and Kindergartens in South Kurdistan's Ministry of Education, informed the second author in

Hawler/Erbil that Kurdish children also learn English as an obligatory subject in primary school (personal communication, March 2006). Faris (personal communication, 2006) further commented that: Assyrian-, Turkomen-, and Arabic-speaking children are taught through Assyrian/Syriac, Turkomen, and Arabic in Kurdistan; they learn Kurdish and English as second/foreign languages, and minorities have their own departments in the Ministry of Education, each with their own director general (DG). Additional meetings between the second author and Fakhradin Bahaddin, DG of Turkoman Education, and Nazar Hana Khizo, DG of Assyrian Education (personal communication, March 2006) in the Ministry of Education in Hawler/Erbil gave her the impression that these DGs were very satisfied with the position of minority groups in education, as compared to the period before the new Constitution came into effect. There are obviously also critical voices (for Assyrian education, see Odisho, 2004).

Assyrian/Syriac, Armenian, Chaldean, Turkoman, and Arabic are taught as mother tongues. All these languages are also taught as elective subjects to those who want to learn them, while English (and Kurdish for non-Kurdish speakers) are obligatory as second/foreign languages. During a private dinner that the second author attended with the former Minister of Education, Abdul-Aziz Taib, he said: "Every child in the world has the right to education through the medium of their mother tongue" (personal communication, March 15th, 2006).[13] Abdul-Aziz Taib (personal communication, March 2006) reiterated this comment during a private dinner that the second author attended with the former Minister and his brother Mueyed Taib, a lawyer.[14] Thus, in (Iraqi) Kurdistan, basic linguistic human rights are respected, for both Kurdish children (an earlier minority), and for most minority children.

There are, of course, problems too. Nimrod Raphaeli, Senior Analyst of the Middle East Media Research Institute/MEMRI's Middle East Economic Studies Program, claims (2006):

> [In the] Middle East Economic Studies Program Kurdish and English will be the two leading languages, while Arabic, like the languages of other minorities, will be an elective subject. It is no secret that a whole new Kurdish generation, including many who studied at Kurdish universities, has little or no proficiency in Arabic. That situation raises a serious question about their future integration into a federated Iraq. (n.p.)

While signs of prosperity are palpable across Kurdistan, there are also signs of corruption, nepotism and, generally, poor governance. Also, as in the rest of Iraq, there are shortages of electricity and gasoline, which are causing a lot of hardship to large segments of the Kurdish population. Further, there is the issue of poverty. Despite rapid economic growth generated by local and foreign investments, many families still live below the poverty line. All this influences children's health, including food availability and intake.

School resources and supplies, including teaching materials, are still poor. Teacher training is traditional and often authoritarian and inadequate, despite good intentions. Teaching through the medium of languages that have never or seldom been used in schools requires time, effort, and training. There is no training as yet in language planning. Both corpus planning and acquisition planning are badly needed. There is also a risk of inappropriate "advice" from American and British publishers and other bodies being accepted both of necessity and because of lack of awareness of research on various aspects of languages and education research and experience elsewhere. *But* the good intentions and motivation are palpable. Children's literature is very much in evidence and it includes children's magazines.

A Short History of the Kurds and Their Language(s) in Iran, Iraq, Syria, Turkey, and the Former Soviet-Union

The Kurds are amongst the oldest inhabitants of the Middle East, and Kurdistan was an ancient Mesopotamian civilization (Skutnabb-Kangas & Bucak, 1995). The Kurdish language has a rich legacy. It has been spoken for at least 3000 years, and the oldest Kurdish literary text predates the Islamization of Kurdistan (Skutnabb-Kangas & Bucak, 1995). Following the signing of the Treaty of Lausanne in 1923, Kurdistan was divided between five countries: Turkey, Iran, Iraq, Syria, and the former Soviet Union (Chaliand, 1993; Mauriès, 1967), leaving the Kurdish language community divided and dispersed. Since then, the Kurds have been subjected to colonial rule in four states, Turkey, Iran, Iraq, and Syria, and hundreds of thousands of Kurds have been deported or internally displaced from Kurdistan to other parts of the occupying states or forced to move to other countries. Thus it has been, and still is, difficult for the Kurds to develop their language in any way similar to what occurs in closely knit nondispersed language communities (Skutnabb-Kangas & Bucak, 1995, p. 351).

Kurdish has four dialect groups, but two main dialects (Hassanpour, 1992). Kurmanji (the northern dialect of Kurdish), is spoken in the northern half of Iraqi Kurdistan, the Caucasus, Turkey, Syria, and northwestern Iran. Kurdi or Sorani (the central dialect), is spoken in western Iran and central Iraqi Kurdistan. Kurmanji is the most commonly spoken dialect, especially in Turkey, and 75% of all Kurds worldwide are estimated to speak Kurmanji (Chyet, 1992, p. xix). Kurds forcibly moved from the Kurdish-dominant provinces into the interior of Turkey over a hundred-year period did not experience a total disappearance of the language, but their Kurdish was altered. Due to the Turkification policy of deportations from the eastern provinces to the interior, widespread borrowing occurred, and "Kurdish vocabulary...evolved in different directions in different parts of Kurdistan" (Skutnabb-Kangas & Bucak, 1995, p. 352). Another side effect of the Turkification policy was that Kurds denied linguistic human rights such as Kurdish-medium instruction never learned to read or write their mother tongue.

As of 1972, 82% of all Kurds worldwide who self-identified as Kurds were concentrated in the eight Kurdish dominant provinces along the (south-)eastern frontiers of Turkey (Bulloch & Morris, 1993, p. 180; Kendal, 1993, p. 39; McDowall, 1991, 2004). Hassanpour's (1992, p. 22) "Map 9" illustrates that Kurmanji- and Zaza-[15] (or *Dimili*-) speakers are concentrated in two areas encompassed by those Kurdish-majority provinces. This means that using both Kurmanji and Zaza as instructional languages would be a viable alternative; however, while instruction via the medium of high-status languages (e.g., English) is offered, Kendal's (1993, p. 75) statement is still true: "there is not one school where teaching is carried out in Kurdish, the language spoken by about one-quarter of the population" of Turkey.

Because the borders between languages and dialects are hazy, not linguistically but politically defined, it is also impossible to tell whether there is one Kurdish language, with several dialects, or several Kurdish languages. Nonetheless, Wikipedia (n. d.-b) lists the following as subdialects of Kurdish: Kermanshahi, Laki, Gorani, and Zazaki (Dimilî). Though clarity is lacking about whether languages or dialects such as Zaza belong under the label "Kurdish," most Zaza-speakers seem to identify themselves as Kurds and their language as a dialect of Kurdish. For example, the author of an online Kurdish school for Kurmanji, Sorani, and Dimilî (Diljen, 2006) describes Dimilî (Zazakî) as a Kurdish dialect spoken by 3 million Kurds.

The Treaty of Lausanne also left Kurdish writing systems divided and dispersed. For example, the Kurdish alphabet is a modified version of the Arabic alphabet in Iraq and

Iran; a modified Latin alphabet is used in Turkey and Syria, and a modified Cyrillic alphabet is used by Kurds residing in the former USSR (Wikipedia, n.d.-b).

Comparison and Lessons from the Comparisons

We can start analyzing children's educational linguistic human rights by looking at the extent to which:

1. their mother tongues are accepted and respected;
2. they learn their mother tongues fully (it is their main teaching language):
3. they are not forced to shift languages;
4. they learn an official language;
5. they can profit from education, regardless of what their mother tongue is (see Skutnabb-Kangas, 2000, pp. 501–505 for details).

It is clear from the three descriptions that Kurdish children in South Kurdistan (and to a large extent also Assyrian and Turkoman children) are granted these basic LHRs in education.

On the other hand, both Turkey and Denmark violate Kurdish children's LHRs. Turkey does it brutally and visibly, with the help of fear, threats, open prohibition, imprisonment, and torture. Denmark does it in more sophisticated and invisible ways, with hidden prohibition and naturalizing the nonexistence of the Kurdish language in education. Both states *glorify* their own official language and culture (Turkish and Danish) and *stigmatize* Kurdish language and culture (and, in Denmark, other minority languages; for example, Arabic, and cultures and religions, especially Islam).

This was how Atatürk, the founder of the Republic of Turkey and its first President,[16] saw the Turkish language:

> The Turkish language is one of the most beautiful, rich and easy languages in the world. Therefore, every Turk loves his language and makes an effort to elevate its status. The Turkish language is also a sacred treasure for the Turkish nation because the Turkish nation knows that its moral values, customs, memories, interests, in short, everything that makes it a nation was preserved through its language despite the endless catastrophes it has experienced. (Virtanen, 2003, p. 15)

The glorifying claims about Danishness presented by several MPs of Dansk Folkeparti, the extreme right-wing supporting party of the Danish Centre-right government (Spring 2007) are to a large extent similar, as one can see if one runs a search for the word *sprog* (language) on the party's home page (Dansk Folkeparti, n.d.).

Stigmatizing Kurdish is done somewhat differently in Turkey and Denmark. In Turkey, it has long been claimed that Kurds are mountain Turks. When the possibility of "Kurdish" existing arises in Turkey, it is not seen a separate language but as a dialect of Turkish; however, in actual fact, Kurdish is Indo-European in origin and Turkish is not—the two languages are unrelated. The following examples underscore the suppression and oppression of the Kurdish language and the very Kurdish nation.

> "We have no ethnic minorities," a "high official in Ankara" told Alan Cowell of the *New York Times* in February 1990.
>
> In May 1989, the National Security Council launched a campaign denying the existence of a distinct Kurdish nation and a Kurdish language. Pamphlets were issued

and distributed to schools in the south-east, claiming that Kurdish is not a distinct language, but a dialect of Turkish.

> There is no such thing as the Kurdish people or nation. They are merely carriers of Turkish culture and habits. The imagined region proposed as the new Kurdistan is the region that was settled by the proto-Turks...Kurdish is a border dialect of Turkish"—Professor Dr. Orhan Turkdogan. (all quoted in Fernandes, 2006a)

In Denmark, on the other hand, all immigrant minority languages are seen as useless by most center and right wing politicians (hence, the policy of nondecision), and as preventing the learning of Danish. Danish is even claimed to be the mother tongue of the "second generation"; that is, the children of immigrant minorities:

> It is self-evident that refugees who are only going to be in Denmark during a short period should maintain their mother tongue. But when one is born and has grown up in Denmark and will have one's whole existence here, then *the mother tongue is Danish—full stop.* (Svend Erik Hermansen, Social Democrat Party, quoted in Skutnabb-Kangas 2000, p. 109; emphasis added)

In both countries, the relationship between the two languages *is rationalized* so as to make enforced linguistic and cultural assimilation seem useful or the only sensible possibility for the minority—it is claimed to happen for their own good, and the state educational authorities are "helping" the children. It is interesting that both countries, despite not being settler colonies, are following the example of the United States. Just as the United States killed off or forcibly assimilated the indigenous peoples, in order to profit from their land, water, and material resources, Turkey wants to eliminate, physically or linguistically and culturally the Kurds *as a nation*. In the same way as the United States does not tolerate other languages and cultures and sees them as "un-American," and a threat to "Americanness," Turkey and (many politicians in) Denmark see other languages and cultures as a threat to the integrity of the state and as denigrating its "Turkishness"/"Danishness." While the United States aggressively supports the Turkish state's war against "PKK terrorists," that is, all Kurdish people (see Skutnabb-Kangas & Fernandes, 2008), the Turkish and Danish ideologies of genocide vis-á-vis Kurds fit the old and present-day U.S. physically genocidal (indigenous peoples) and culturally and linguistically genocidal assimilationist (immigrant) policies extremely well. Change "immigrant" to "Kurdish," "American" to "Turkish/Danish," and "English" to "Turkish/Danish" in the Theodore Roosevelt (1919/1926) quote below, and we have post-1923 to present-day Turkish ideologies and present-day Danish ideologies:

> In the first place, we should insist that if the immigrant who comes here in good faith becomes an American and assimilates himself to us, he shall be treated on an exact equality with everyone else, for it is an outrage to discriminate against any such man because of creed, or birthplace, or origin. But this is predicated upon the person's becoming in every facet an American, and nothing but an American.... There can be no divided allegiance here. Any man who says he is an American, but something else also, isn't an American at all. We have room for but one flag, the American flag.... We have room for but one language here, and that is the English language...and we have room for but one sole loyalty and that is a loyalty to the American people. (p. 554)[17]

The parallels between the above quote by Roosevelt (1919) and Atatürk's (1931) quote, which follows, is astounding:

> Language is one of the essential characteristics of a nation. Those who belong to the Turkish nation ought, above all and absolutely, to speak Turkish…. Those people who speak another language could, in a difficult situation, collaborate and take action against us with other people who speak other languages. (Mustafa Kemal [Atatürk], quoted in Meiselas, 1997, p. 145)

Here we have one of the main global reasons behind enforced assimilation: the false hypothesis that the existence of minorities necessarily leads to the disloyalty and the disintegration of what one, also falsely, claims to be a nation-state, with one nation and one language. In fact, it is often precisely a lack of human rights, including minority rights and linguistic and cultural human rights that, in situations where ethnic and linguistic differences match economic and political injustices, leads to conflict and the desire to secede.

Global Comparison: Assimilation Is Not Freely Chosen if the Choice Is between One's Mother Tongue and One's Future

Assimilationist education of minorities is genocidal, according to the United Nations (1948) Genocide Convention's definitions. Turkey is guilty of systematically treating Kurds in ways which fall under each of the five definitions of genocide in its Article 2:

> In the present Convention, genocide means any of the following acts committed with intent to destroy, in whole or in part, a national, ethnical, racial or religious group, as such:
>
> (a) Killing members of the group;
> (b) Causing serious bodily or mental harm to members of the group;
> (c) Deliberately inflicting on the group conditions of life calculated to bring about its physical destruction in whole or in part;
> (d) Imposing measures intended to prevent births within the group;
> (e) Forcibly transferring children of the group to another group. (United Nations, 1948, E793)

Education offered to Kurdish children in both Turkey and Denmark is specifically guilty of genocide according to the definitions II(e): "forcibly transferring children of the group to another group"; and II(b): "causing serious bodily *or mental* harm to members of the group"; (emphasis added). In the following, we give a few examples from other parts of the world of how education may contribute to genocide according to these two definitions (for more, see Skutnabb-Kangas, 2000).

Pirjo Janulf's (1998) longitudinal large-scale study of Finnish children in grade 9 in Sweden is one. All their education was through the medium of Swedish—there were no Finnish-medium classes at that point. After 15 years Janulf went back to as many of her original Finnish subjects in Sweden as she could find. *Not one* of them spoke *any* Finnish to their own children (Janulf, 1998, p. 2). Even if they themselves might not have forgotten their Finnish completely, their children were forcibly transferred to the majority group, at least linguistically. This is what both Turkish and Danish education attempts to do to Kurdish children.

A Canadian report from 1998 ("Kitikmeot Struggles to Prevent Death of Inuktitut") cited in Martin (2000a) discusses what happens to Inuit children who have only experienced English-medium instruction throughout their educational careers: Once teenagers, they can no longer converse fluently with their grandparents. This also happens with many Kurdish children in Turkey and Denmark. Assimilationist education is genocidal because it transfers children forcibly from their own group to another group, linguistically and culturally.

In an African study Williams (1993, p. 24) conducted in Zambia and Malawi, some 1,500 students in grades one through seven were observed and tested. The Zambian students had all their education in English, from day one, whereas the children in Malawi were taught in local languages, frequently their mother tongues, during their first four years of schooling, with English as a subject. The children in Malawi switched over to English-medium instruction from grade five onwards. Large numbers of Zambian pupils "have very weak or zero reading competence in two languages," Williams (1995) states, whereas the children in Malawi had slightly better test results even in the English language than the Zambian students. In addition, the children from Malawi learned to read and write their own languages. Williams (1998) concluded that there was a clear risk that the policy of using English as a vehicular language could contribute to stunting, rather than promoting, children's academic and cognitive growth. This constitutes "causing serious mental harm" in the Genocide Convention's (1948) sense. Education of many Kurdish children in Turkey (and also in Denmark) is also very likely to stunt rather than promote their cognitive and academic growth.

Another Canadian report about Inuit children in English-medium education, "Keewatin Perspective on Bilingual Education," by Katherine Zozula and Simon Ford 1985 (cited in Martin 2000a), discusses Inuit students who are neither fluent nor literate in English or Inuktitut, and who only perform at a fourth grade level of achievement after nine years of schooling. Mick Mallon and Alexina Kublu (1998, cited in Martin 2000b) confirm this observation, noting that many Inuit young people are not fully fluent in either language, and are apathetic. This is also likely to be the case with many Kurdish children in Turkey and also some in Denmark.

As for the United States, the same lack of LHRs for minorities that we see in Turkey and Denmark is also a major factor in preventing members of U.S. minorities from achieving, and high-stakes testing and other measures included in the No Child Left Behind (NCLB) legislation do not help. Baker (2006) observes that, in essence, the NCLB "makes states, districts, and schools accountable for the performance of LEP [limited English proficient] students" (p. 198). Indeed, the intention of NCLB is to "punish failure to show progress in annual English assessments"; hence, its emphasis on the rapid acquisition of English (Edwards, 2004, p. 120).[18] In fact, NCLB legislation has missed its mark with regard to enhancing the performance of English-language learners.

Neither has NCLB improved students' math or reading scores in general. Stephen Krashen (2007a; Information disseminated on Krashen's e-mail list krashen@sdkrashen.com, March 4, 2007) cites research that documents how far NCLB has missed its mark: two major reports by Lee (2006), published by the Harvard Civil Rights Project, and Fuller and colleagues (2006) at the Policy Analysis for California Education research center at Berkeley, note that there is

> no improvement on national tests of reading since NCLB was passed, and the rate of growth in math was the same as it was before NCLB. Lee's report also concluded, contrary to White House statements, that gaps among racial groups and high and low poverty groups are mostly unchanged.

If, as Baker (2006) suggests, the purpose of NCLB legislation was to enhance the performance of English-learners, and if, as Krashen (2007a, 2007b) reports, gaps among dominant and minority group children have not changed, what motivation could the government have had in formulating, and currently reauthorizing, NCLB legislation?

Crawford (2000) outlines links between the push for subtractive, dominant-language-only-medium, submersion education and the English Only movement in the United States. Ideologically, the English Only movement is linked to Roosevelt's (1919/1926) views and the way he mixes his vision of equality and loyalty to allegiance to one nation. To Roosevelt, Atatürk, many Danes, and Americans that sympathize with the English Only movement, allegiance to one nation—be it the United States, Turkey, or Denmark—is symbolized by speaking only one language: English, Turkish, or Danish, as the case may be. Crawford (2000) suggests that for people with an English Only mentality, provision of MT instruction may only represent one accommodation to societal diversity, but is viewed as a dangerous accommodation; one that may lead dominant group members down a "slippery slope" to "social equality? fewer advantages for white Anglo-Americans? linguistic human rights for everyone? These are nightmarish prospects for the privileged and the powerful, and for those who share their worldview" (p. 28). Substitute Turkish or Danish for English in English Only, and the parallels are overwhelming.

While the fears of adversaries of linguistic accommodation for LM children may seem exaggerated, when translated into state educational language policy, these fears have deleterious effects. Subtractive, dominant-language-only-medium, submersion education may cause serious mental harm to indigenous, minority, or dominated group students, and attempts, often successfully, to forcibly transfer them to another linguistic group. This is linguistic genocide.

To qualify as genocide, an act has to be intentional. Have states had an intention to "forcibly transfer children of the group to another group"; and "cause serious bodily or mental harm to members of the group"? *YES*, unfortunately they have. As many examples show (e.g., Fernandes 2006a, 2006b, in press-a, in press-b, Skutnabb-Kangas & Fernandes, 2008), Turkey has certainly had (and has) the intention to kill the Kurdish language and identity. This intention has been and is still openly expressed in countless documents. Denmark has been less open about the genocidal intentions. But it is possible to read the intentions from effects.

Dominant-language-only submersion programs "are widely attested as the least effective educationally for minority language students" (May & Hill, 2003; May, Hill, & Tiakiwai, 2003, a thorough two-volume survey of bilingual education research). This is the model Turkey is using for Kurdish children. The negative results of subtractive teaching were already known at the end of the 1800s. States and educational authorities (including churches) have had this information (Hough & Skutnabb-Kangas, 2005) for a very long time. "Modern" research results regarding the organization of indigenous and minority education have been available for at least 50 years, since the publication of the UNESCO (1953) expert group book: *The Use of Vernacular Languages in Education*. If states, despite this, and despite very positive results from properly conducted additive teaching, have continued and continue to offer subtractive education, with no alternatives, knowing that the results are likely to be negative and thus to "transfer children" and "cause serious mental harm," this must be seen as intentional.

What should Turkey and Denmark do instead? We know from research that the longer indigenous and minority children in a low-status position have their own language as the main medium of teaching, the better they also become in the dominant language, provided, of course, that they have good teaching in it, preferably provided by bilingual teachers. If the Turkish/Danish states want Kurdish children to learn Turkish/Danish well, the best method would be to use Kurdish as the main teaching language, and to teach Turkish/Danish as a subject, using bilingual teachers who know both Turkish/Danish and Kurdish. While a reason frequently offered for *not* providing bilingual education is that students' backgrounds are too diverse for MT provision to be feasible, this paper has shown how Kurdish MT instruction is not even offered in settings with sufficient numbers of Kurdish children for the provision of bilingual education to be a sound, feasible option for parents (e.g., in the eight Kurdish dominant provinces along the [south-] eastern frontiers of Turkey). While Turkey and Denmark are remarkably short-sighted in this respect, focusing on the supposed denigration of their official state language, (Iraqi) South Kurdistan is remarkably visionary.

While the (Iraqi) South Kurdistan system is still far from reaching its goal, it has envisioned and implemented a system aimed at providing education that promotes trilingualism. This could be compared with the Indian three-language formula (with successes and failures) (see, e.g., Annamalai, 1995, 1998, 2001, 2003, 2005; Mohanty, 2000, 2006). If such vision can be translated into policy and practice in a region with as many logistical and political challenges as there are in (Iraqi) South Kurdistan, schools in both Turkey and Denmark should *minimally* aim at school-aged children gaining competence in three languages:

1. for all: *mother tongue* (Arabic, Armenian, Danish, Kurdish, Turkish, etc);
2. for all minorities: *the dominant state language* (Turkish or Danish); for native Turkish or Danish-speakers: *a domestic minority language*;
3. for all: English (or some other major international language).

Schools in both Turkey and Denmark have the resources to realize (Iraqi) South Kurdistan's vision for a trilingual educational system that enables minority children to maintain their language and identity and to have the educational benefits of MTM education. What Denmark and Turkey lack are South Kurdistan's good intentions and motivation to act on behalf of its linguistic minority children. They value linguistic chauvinism at the cost of the heightened employment prospects, mental and physical health, life chances, and social justice that MTM education brings. There is a lesson here for all countries with indigenous peoples, minorities, and oppressed majorities. The Organization for Security and Cooperation in Europe (OSCE), which has 55 member states, including Canada and the United States, has a High Commissioner on National Minorities whose main task is to prevent ethnic conflict. Max van der Stoel (1997), OSCE's first High Commissioner, has reported that the two main demands of the many minorities he has consulted with have been: more political and economic rights, and mother tongue medium education. When launching *The Hague Recommendations Regarding the Education Rights of National Minorities* (Foundation for Inter-Ethnic Relations, 1996), authoritative guidelines for minority education, interpreting standards in international law, van der Stoel (1997) stated:

>...in the course of my work, it had become more and more obvious to me that education is an extremely important element for the preservation and the deepening of the identity of persons belonging to a national minority. It is of course also clear that education in the language of the minority is of vital importance for such a minority. (p. 153)

The Hague Recommendations (1996) advocate for mainly MTM education in elementary and secondary schools, and for bilingual teachers who know the LM children's MT and the official (or "State") language as a second language. The *Explanatory Note* to *The Hague Recommendations* (1996) states:

[S]ubmersion-type approaches whereby the curriculum is taught exclusively through the medium of the State language and minority children are entirely integrated into classes with children of the majority are not in line with international standards. (p. 5)[19]

The United Nation's (2004) Human development report links cultural liberty to language rights and human development and argues that there is:

...no more powerful means of "encouraging" individuals to assimilate to a dominant culture than having the economic, social and political returns stacked against their mother tongue. Such assimilation is not freely chosen if the choice is between one's mother tongue and one's future. (p. 33)

Minimal social justice requires that children do not need to choose between their mother tongue and their future; however, the three cases outlined in this chapter suggest that Kurdish children must choose between their MT and their future in Denmark and Turkey because there is no provision for Kurdish MT instruction in those countries. While the educational system in (Iraqi) South Kurdistan is not ideal and has many logistical and political challenges, it envisions, implements, and provides education that promotes trilingualism. Thus, the case of (Iraqi) South Kurdistan may serve as an example for Denmark, Turkey, and other countries, not only for providing for Kurdish children's educational language rights, but for striving for social justice in education for all LM children. Therefore, while this chapter emphasizes how the three countries concerned are treating Kurds, it also presents lessons of general relevance to all educators concerned with linguistic and cultural justice.

Notes

1. Shelley K. Taylor is mainly responsible for the Danish data, based on Taylor (2001) and updates; Tove Skutnabb-Kangas is mainly responsible for the Turkish and Iraqi data, some of which is from Skutnabb-Kangas and Fernandes (2008). The rest was composed jointly. We would like to thank Hongfang Yu for her conscientious, diligent assistance in formatting this text.
2. The submersion (sink-or-swim) metaphor refers to LM children (e.g., ethnic Kurds in Denmark) who begin receiving instruction through the medium of a dominant language (e.g., Danish is the dominant language in Denmark) without prior knowledge of the language of instruction. They do not receive MTM instruction or MT support, but are left to sink, struggle, or swim; hence, the image of being thrown off a diving board into the deep end of the pool without knowing how to swim, without swimming lessons, and without a life preserver (Baker, 2006).
3. Hassanpour (1992) reports that, since the 1970s, Kurdish diasporas have emerged in Europe, North America, Oceania, Lebanon, Japan, and other countries. See McDowall (2004) for further discussion of the Kurdish diaspora in Europe.
4. Exact figures are not available for the total number of Kurds worldwide since (a) Kurds have not been included in any census as Kurds and ethnic or mother tongue questions have not been asked; (b) respondents fear reprisals for self-identifying as Kurds; and (c) Middle Eastern authorities prefer to minimize numbers of Kurds (Hassanpour, 1992, p. 12; Kendal, 1993, p. 39; Yassin, 1995, p. 37). However, the country report updated by the CIA (2007) on April 17th, 2007 and Kurdologists concur with McDowall's (1991, p. 9) earlier estimate that some 20 to 25% of the population of Turkey is Kurdish.
5. Please note that spellings of Kurdish and Arabic names often vary as transliteration produces many ways to spell them (see note 14 below for a related point).

6. *Hurriyet* (2002, June 11). "27 children brought before Diyarbakir's State Security Court," as reproduced by IMK Weekly Information Service, June 17th to June 28th, 2002, no. 160. Retrieved from http://www.kurds.dk/english/2000/news107.html); here quoted from Fernandes (2006a), retrieved January 3, 2007 from http://www.variant.randomstate.org/.

7. Aram (2002). *Conspiracy and crisis: Turkey and the Kurdish question: From the nineties to the present day*—Written by a collective of journalists and researchers on behalf of Aram Publisher. Aram, Istanbul, January 2002. Retrieved October 16, 2006 from, http://www.zmag.org/content/ForeignPolicy/aram0122.cfm.

8. Rud (2005, p. 65). See also Hassanpour (2006a).

9. BIA News Centre (2005). Ten local TVs queued for Kurdish broadcast. BIA News Centre, August 25th, 2005; here quoted from Fernandes (2006a). Retrieved January 3, 2007 from, www.variant.randomstate.org/.

10. Yedinci Gundem (2002). Kurdish tuition as grounds for torture, May 12th, 2002, as reproduced in IMK Weekly Information Service, May 13th to May 24th, 2002, No. 156. Retrieved from http://www.kurds.dk/english/2000/news102.html); here quoted from Fernandes (2006a), retrieved January 3, 2007 from www.variant.randomstate.org/.

11. *Kurdish Linguistic Rights Report* (2006), submitted to the Translation and Linguistic Rights Committee of the International PEN at the Ohrid Conference, Republic of Macedonia, September 14th–17th. Retrieved July 16, 2008 from http://www.info_turk.be/338.htm.

12. For sake of comparison, figures listed for *efterkommere* from other countries in the January 2006 census included 1,690 from Norway, 336 from Canada, and 4,189 from Vietnam.

13. The official Ministry interpreter translated the former Minister of Education, Abdul-Aziz Taib's comment to Tove Skutnabb-Kangas from Kurdish to English.

14. During the second dinner, the lawyer acted as a Kurdish–Swedish interpreter.

15. Most things Kurdish (e.g., place names, language/dialect names) have both a Kurdish name and a Turkish/Iraqi/Iranian/Syrian name. Thus, Zaza is the Turkish term while Dimilî is the Kurdish term. The unofficial capital of North Kurdistan (Turkish Kurdistan) is Diyarbakir in Turkish, but Amed in Kurdish. We use the Turkish names if these are used in our references. Furthermore, as noted in note 4 above, the spelling of place and language/dialect names often varies.

16. For further information on Atatürk, see Wikipedia (n.d.-d).

17. This same quote is also cited in Urban Legends and Folklore (n.d.). Roosevelt. Theodore Roosevelt on Immigrants—Netlore Archive. Retrieved at from http://urbanlegends.about.com/ library/bl_roosevelt_on_immigrants.htm [16 October 2006]

18. For a summary of NCLB requirements, see Baker (2006, pp. 198–199).

19. See earlier definition/explanation of the term in note 2 above.

References

Annamalai, E. (1995). Multilingualism for all—An Indian perspective. In T. Skutnabb-Kangas (Ed.), *Multilingualism for all* (pp. 215–220). Lisse, The Netherlands: Swets & Zeitlinger.

Annamalai, E. (1998). Language choice in education: Conflict resolution in Indian courts. In P. Benson, P. Grundy, & T. Skutnabb-Kangas (Eds.), *Language rights* [Special issue]. *Language Sciences, 20*(1), 29–43.

Annamalai, E. (2001). *Managing multilingualism in India*. New Delhi: Sage.

Annamalai, E. (2003). Medium of power: The question of English in education in India. In J. W. Tollefson & A. B. M. Tsui (Eds.), *Medium of instruction policies. Which agenda? Whose agenda?* (pp. 177–194). Mahwah, NJ: Erlbaum.

Annamalai, E. (2005). Nation-building in a globalised world: Language choice and education in India. In A. M. Y. Lin & P. W. Martin (Eds.), *Decolonisation, globalization, language-in-education policy and practice* (pp. 20–37). Clevedon, UK: Multilingual Matters.

Baker, C. (2006). *Foundations of bilingual education and bilingualism* (4th ed.). Clevedon, Avon, UK/Toronto: Multilingual Matters.

Bulloch, J., & Morris, H. (1993). No friends but the mountains: The tragic history of the Kurds. New York: Penguin Books.

Burkay, K. (n.d.). The Kurdish question—its history and present situation. Retrieved October 26th, 2006, from http://members.aol.com/KHilfsvere/Kurds.html

Chaliand, G. (1993). Introduction. In G. Chaliand (Ed.), A people without a country: The Kurds & Kurdistan (pp. 1–10). New York: Olive Branch Press.

Chyet, M. (1992). Foreword. In A. Hassanpour (Ed.), Nationalism and language in Kurdistan, 1918–1985 (pp. xix–xxi). San Francisco: Mellen Research University Press.

Central Intelligence Agency (CIA). (2007). The world fact book. Turkey. Retrieved April 19th, 2007, from https://www.cia.gov/cia/publications/factbook/geos/tu.html

Council directive on the education of the children of migrant workers [77/48610]. (1977, July 25th). Brussels: European Community.

Council of Europe. (2006). The cultural situation of the Kurds. Retrieved January 3rd, 2007, from http://assembly.coe.int/Main.asp?link=/Documents/WorkingDocs/Doc06/EDOC11006.htm

Crawford, J. (2000). At war with diversity: US language policy in an age of anxiety. Clevedon, UK: Multilingual Matters.

Danmarks statistikbank (Statistics Denmark). (2006). Befolkning og valg (Population and elections). Retrieved January 3rd, 2007, from http://www.statistikbanken.dk/statbank5a/default.asp?w=800.

Dansk Folkeparti (n. d.). Retrieved October 16th, 2006, from http://www.danskfolkeparti.dk/

de Varennes, F. (1996). Language, minorities and human rights. The Hague, Boston: Martinus Nijhoff.

Diljen, H. (2006). Dibistana kurdî (The Kurdish school). Retrieved January 6th, 2007, from http://www.dibistanakurdi.com/modules.php?name=Content&pa=showpage&pid=1

Edwards, V. (2004). Multilingualism in the English-speaking world. Malden, MA: Blackwell.

Fernandes, D. (2006a). Turkey's US-backed war on terror: A cause for concern? Variant, 27 (Winter 2006). Retrieved January 6th, 2007, from http://www.variant.randomstate.org/

Fernandes, D. (2006b, October). A step backwards: The effects of the new anti-terror law on fundamental rights and freedoms. Plenary paper presented at the Third International Conference on EU, Turkey, and the Kurds. European Parliament: EU Turkey Civic Commission.

Fernandes, D. (in press-a) Colonial genocides in Turkey, Kenya and Goa. Stockholm: Apec Press.

Fernandes, D. (in press-b). The Kurdish genocide in Turkey. Stockholm: Apec Press.

Foundation for Inter-Ethnic Relations. (1996, October). The Hague recommendations regarding the education rights of national minorities & explanatory note. The Hague: Author. Retrieved October 26th, from http://www.osce.org/documents/hcnm/1996/10/2700_en.pdf

Fuller, B., Gesicki, K., Kang, E., & Wright, J. (2006). Is the No Child Left Behind Act Working? The reliability of how states track achievement. University of California, Berkeley: Policy Analysis for California Education.

Hassanpour, A. (1992). Nationalism and language in Kurdistan, 1918–1985. San Francisco: Mellen Research University Press.

Hassanpour, A. (2006). Kurdish on death row. Ideas: The Arts & Science Review, 3(2), 33–35. (Faculty of Arts & Science, University of Toronto)

Helkiær, L. (1987). Tokulturel 1. klasse i Høje-Taastrup [Bicultural Gr. 1 in Høje-Taastrup]. Høje-Taastrup, Denmark: Høje-Taastrup Kommune.

Holmen, A., & Jørgensen, J. N. (1993). Tosprogede børn i Danmark [Bilingual children in Denmark]. Viborg, Denmark: Hans Reitzels Forlag.

Hough, D. A., & Skutnabb-Kangas, T. (2005). Beyond good intentions: Combating linguistic genocide in education. In AlterNative—An International Journal of Indigenous Scholarship, 1, 114–135.

Janulf, P. (1998). Kommer finskan i Sverige att fortleva? En studie av språkkunskaper och språkanvändning hos andragenerationens sverigefinnar i Botkyrka och hos finlandssvenskar i Åbo [Will Finnish survive in Sweden? A study of language skills and language use among second generation Sweden Finns in Botkyrka, Sweden, and Finland Swedes in Åbo, Fin-

land]. Acta Universitatis Stockholmiensis, Studia Fennica Stockholmiensia (Serial No. 7). Stockholm: Almqvist & Wiksell International.

Just Jeppesen, K. (1995). *Etniske minoriteter–ved vi nok ?* [*Ethnic minorities in Denmark: Do we know enough?*]. De fremmede i Danmark Series No. 6 [Foreigners in Denmark]. Copenhagen: Socialforskningsinstituttet.

Kendal. (1993). Kurdistan in Turkey. In G. Chaliand (Ed.), *A people without a country: The Kurds and Kurdistan* (pp. 38–94). New York: Olive Branch Press.

Krashen, S. (2007a, March 4th). Preserve "core" of No Child Left Behind Act, Bush urges. [Letter to the editor] *Los Angeles Times.*

Krashen, S. (2007b, April 25th). Reading list for a less rosy view of NCLB effects [Letter to the editor]. *Education Week, 26*(34), 33–34.

Kurdistan Democratic Party (KDP). (n.d-a). *Kurdistan: General info.* Retrieved October 26th, 2006, from http://www.kdp.se/

Kurdistan Democratic Party. (n.d-b). *Kurdistan: Education.* Retrieved October 26th, 2006, from http://www.kdp.se/

Kurdistan Regional Government (KRG). (2006). About the Kurdistan regional government. Retrieved May 9th, 2006, from http://www.krg.org/articles/article_detail. asp?showsecondimage=&RubricNr=9 &ArticleNr=48

Kristjánsdóttir, B. (2003). Viljen til undervisning i tosprogede elevers modersmål [The will to provide instruction in bilingual children's mother tongue]. In C. Horst (Ed.), *Interkulturel pædagogik: Flere sprog—problem eller ressource? [Intercultural pedagogy: Many languages—problem or resource?*] (pp. 85–111). Vejle, Denmark: Kroghs Forlag.

Lee, J. (2006). *Tracking achievement gaps and assessing the impact of NCLB on the gaps: An in-depth look into national and state reading and math outcome trends.* Cambridge, MA: The Civil Rights Project at Harvard University.

Leggewie, C. (1996, Summer). How Turks became Kurds, not Germans (K. Winston, Trans.). *Dissent,* 79–83.

Magga, O. H., Nicolaisen, I., Trask, M., Dunbar, R., & Skutnabb-Kangas, T. (2005). *Indigenous children's education and indigenous languages.* New York: United Nations/United Nations Permanent Forum on Indigenous Issues.

Martin, I. (2000a). *Aajjiqatigiingni* [Language of instruction research paper]. Report to the Government of Nunavut. Department of Education: Iqaluit, Nunavut, Canada. Unpublished manuscript.

Martin, I. (2000b). *Sources and issues: A backgrounder to the discussion paper on language of instruction in Nunavut schools.* Iqaluit, Nunavut, Canada: Department of Education. Unpublished manuscript.

May, S., & Hill, R. (2003). *Bilingual/immersion education: Indicators of good practice* (Milestone Report 2). Hamilton, New Zealand: Wilf Malcolm Institute of Educational Research, School of Education, University of Waikato.

May, S., Hill, R., & Tiakiwai, S. (2003). *Bilingual/Immersion education: Indicators of good practice* (Milestone Report 1). Hamilton, New Zealand: Wilf Malcolm Institute of Educational Research, School of Education, University of Waikato.

Mauriès, R. (1967). *Le Kurdistan ou la mort* [Kurdistan or death]. Paris: Robert Laffont.

McDowall, D. (1991). *The Kurds.* London: Minority Rights Group.

McDowall, D. (2004).A modern history of the Kurds (3rd ed.). London: I. B. Tauris.

Meiselas, S. (1997). *Kurdistan: In the shadow of history.* Random House: New York.

Mendel, T. (2006). Article 19 global campaign for free expression. Retrieved December 10th, 2006, from http://www.article19.org/pdfs/letters/turkey-amendments-to-terror-law.pdf

Mohanty, A. K. (2000). Perpetuating inequality: The disadvantage of language: Minority mother tongues and related issues. In A. K. Mohanty & G. Misra (Eds.), *Psychology of poverty and disadvantage* (pp. 104–117). New Delhi: Concept.

Mohanty, A. K. (2006). Multilingualism of the unequals and predicaments of education in India: Mother tongue or other tongue? In O. García, T. Skutnabb-Kangas, & M. Torres-Guzmán

(Eds.), *Imagining multilingual schools. Languages in education and glocalization* (pp. 262–283). Clevedon, UK: Multilingual Matters.

Odisho, E. Y. (2004). Assyrian (Aramaic): A recent model for its maintenance and revitalization. In A. Panaino & A. Pries (Eds.), *Melammu Symposia IV* (pp. 183–196). Milan.

Raphaeli, N. (2006, October 25th). Kurdistan: The quest for statehood. The Middle East Media Research Institute/MEMRI. *Inquiry & Analysis Series, 298.* Retrieved November 25th, 2006, from http://memri.org/bin/articles.cgi?Page=archives&Area=ia&ID=IA29806

Roosevelt, T. (1926). *Works* (memorial ed.). New York: Charles Scribner's. (Original work published 1919)

Rud, J. (2005). Turkey's implementation of European human rights standards—Legislation and practice. In M. Muller, C. Brigham, K. Westrheim, & K. Yildiz (Eds.), *EU Turkey Civic Commission: International Conference on Turkey, the Kurds and the EU,* European Parliament, Brussels, November 22–23, 2004—Conference Papers. GB, KHRP, 53–70.

Skutnabb-Kangas, T. (1981). *Bilingualism or not: The education of minorities.* Clevedon, UK: Multilingual Matters.

Skutnabb-Kangas, T. (2000). *Linguistic genocide in education—Or worldwide diversity and human rights?* Mahwah, NJ: Erlbaum.

Skutnabb-Kangas, T., & Bucak, S. (1995). Killing a mother tongue: How the Kurds are deprived of linguistic human rights. In T. Skutnabb-Kangas & R. Phillipson (Eds.), *Linguistic human rights: Overcoming linguistic discrimination* (pp. 347–370). Berlin/New York: Mouton de Gruyter.

Skutnabb-Kangas, T., & Fernandes, D. (2008). Kurds in Turkey and in (Iraqi) Kurdistan—A comparison of Kurdish educational language policy in two situations of occupation. *Genocide Studies & Prevention, 3*(1), 43–73.

Taylor, S. K. (2001). *Trilingualism by design? An investigation into the educational experiences of Kurdish children schooled in Denmark.* Doctoral dissertation, Ontario Institute for Studies in Education at the University of Toronto, Toronto, ON.

Taylor, S. K. (in press). Right pedagogy, wrong language, and caring in times of fear: Issues in the schooling of ethnic Kurdish children in Denmark. *The International Journal of Bilingual Education and Bilingualism, 12*(3).

Tomasevski, K. (2006). *The state of the right to education worldwide. Free or fee: 2006 global report.* Retrieved October 26th, 2006, from http://www.katarinatomasevski.com

tomasevski.net. (n.d.). Katarina Tomasevski. Retrieved October 26, 2006, from http://www.tomasevski.net/

United Nations General Assembly. (1948). *International convention on the prevention and punishment of the crime of genocide.* New York: United Nations.

United Nations. (2004). *Human development report 2004.* Retrieved October 26th, 2006, from http://hdr.undp.org/reports/global/2004/

UNESCO. (1953). *The use of the vernacular languages in education.* Paris: Author.

van der Stoel, M. (1997). Introduction to the seminar. Education Rights of National Minorities [Special]. *International Journal on Minority and Group Rights, 4*(2), 153–155.

Virtanen, Ö. E. (2003). Recent changes in Turkey's language legislation. (*Mercator Working Paper, 11*). Retrieved October 15th, 2006, from http://www.ciemen.org/mercator

Wikipedia (n.d.-b). Kurdish language. Retrieved December 19th, 2006, from http://en.wikipedia.org/wiki/Kurdish_language

Wikipedia (n.d.-c). Kurdish people. Retrieved December 19th, 2006, from http://en.wikipedia.org/wiki/Kurdish_people

Wikipedia (n.d.-a). Constitution of Iraq—Basic principles, Article 4. Retrieved December 19th, 2006, from http://en.wikipedia.org/wiki/Constitution_of_Iraq#Sections_and_Articles

Wikipedia (n.d.-d). Mustafa Kemal Atatürk. Retrieved December 19th, 2006, from http://en.wikipedia.org/wiki/Mustafa_Kemal_ Atat%C3%BCrk

Williams, E. (1998). *Investigating bilingual literacy: Evidence from Malawi and Zambia.* Education Research. London: Department for International Development.

Yassin, B. A. (1995). *Vision or reality? The Kurds in the policy of the Great Powers, 1941–1947.* Lund, Sweden: Lund University Press.

14 Who Decides for Us, Deaf People?

Helen R. Thumann and Laurene E. Simms

Introduction

The purpose of this chapter is to examine certain perspectives and present a defensible analysis of the research that has shaped the destiny of a people who are categorized by society-at-large as being "disabled" or "hearing impaired": the Deaf.[1] Specifically, this chapter attempts to compare educational and social research emerging from pathological versus cultural viewpoints. Given our identities as members of the Deaf community and culture, fluent American Sign Language (ASL) users, former teachers of Deaf children, and current faculty members of Gallaudet University's Department of Education, we have observed and experienced how Deaf people and the Deaf community have been viewed and regarded as "less than." By deconstructing the patriarchal assumptions of Deaf people as deficient, we will address implications of viewing Deaf people through cultural and sociolinguistic perspectives versus medical perspectives. Our intent is to depathologize "Deafness" by showing how a lack of cultural recognition has influenced research on Deaf people. Finally this chapter will discuss implications for researchers when the Deaf community[2] is recognized as a linguistic and cultural minority with a rich and unique heritage that is just as valid as the mainstream culture in which they are expected to try to participate.

Anthropologically, heritage and cultures cannot be rated as one being more or less superior than another. In this view, the difference between Deaf and Hearing people can be seen as cultural differences, not as deviations from a Hearing norm (Woodward, 1982). This also represents a development in research toward the understanding of Deaf society and culture in the United States and toward an understanding of why Hearing society in the United States has been so slow to give up the idea of "Deafness" as a pathological condition and Deaf people as handicapped or disabled individuals.

Historical Treatment of Deaf People: Pathological View versus Cultural View

Pathological View

Historically, Deaf people have been viewed though the lens of a medical model and therefore have been labeled as deviants with a pathology (i.e., hearing loss) that must be remediated. This pathological perspective has shaped Deaf education for several centuries and is an outgrowth of more general beliefs about people who are different, which has resulted in labels such as "normal" for those who are not perceived to be disabled versus "handicapped" for those who deviate from the medical model's standards. This view has historically been held by the majority of able-bodied persons who interact with disabled people and parallels how other language minority people such as Native Americans and

Mexican Americans have been viewed in the educational system (Ballin, 1930; Davidson, 1996; Lane, 1992; Spindler & Spindler, 1990). The widely held majority view that Deaf people have a medical problem has prohibited the acceptance of American Sign Language as a separate language from English and Deaf Culture as a culture separate from the majority culture (Lane, 1992; Woodward, 1982). The underlying principle of this pathological view is to "fix" Deaf people and Deaf children in particular. The pathological view perpetuates the belief that the ultimate educational goal for Deaf children is to "pass as Hearing."

Deviation from the norm is likely to entail a stigma (Baker & Cokely, 1980; Lane, 1992) which in turn serves to reinforce the paternalistic and patriarchal, colonial assumptions of the political and economical elite (Reinharz, 1992). Critical theory (Freire, 1992; Wink, 2000) challenges these traditional Western assumptions and permits one to deconstruct the pathological view and demonstrate its similarity to patriarchal assumptions found in many other situations involving majority/minority interactions (Woodward, 1982).

However, up to now, critical theory has not impacted the pathological/clinical views of Deaf people held by the Hearing culture. At the 1880 Conference on the Education of the Deaf in Milan, Italy, the pathological view was codified in the field of Deaf education when Hearing participants voted to forbid the use of sign language in the education of Deaf people. This decision not only forbade the use of sign language in schools, it also led to the expulsion of Deaf teachers from classrooms (Gannon, 1981). Prior to this conference about 50% of the teachers of the Deaf in the United States were Deaf (Gannon, 1981). One can still see the long-lasting impact of this decision when looking at the current percentage of Deaf teachers, roughly 16% (Andrews &Franklin, 1996–1997). This numerical change has resulted in Deaf people having practically no input into how Deaf children were and continue to be educated. The central idea put forth at the conference was that speaking, referred to as oralism by the Deaf community, was superior to manual communication or sign language. As a result, school policies and questions about which method of communication to use in the classrooms for Deaf children have been continuously and heatedly debated over the last 170 years. The pathological view has been perpetuated by researchers and educators who have attempted to understand how Deaf people differ from Hearing people and then to provide remediation to eliminate these differences; that is, to have Deaf people communicate orally rather than use sign language.

As we argue in what follows, society's view of the Deaf is pathological; the Deaf self-view is cultural. The pathological view has carried over time to influence: (1) education and language planning for Deaf children; (2) training of teachers of the Deaf; and (3) educational and social research involving Deaf children and adults. The origin of this pathological view can be discovered by analyzing the historical treatment of Deaf individuals, and other individuals, who are "different" for whatever reasons, by the Hearing society at large.

Society's view of the Deaf is an outgrowth of more general binary beliefs about people with differences; for example, "normal" vs. "handicapped." The pathological/clinical view takes the behaviors and values of the majority as the "standard" or "norm" and then focuses on how disabled people deviate from the norm. This view has been historically and traditionally held by the majority of able-bodied persons who interact on a professional basis with people with disabilities. This deviation from the "norm" is likely to entail a stigma (Lane, 1992), which in turn serves to reinforce the patriarchal, colonial assumptions of the political and the economical elite (Reinharz, 1992). Ladd (2003) in defining the colonization of the Deaf community, explains that the Hearing majority colonizes the Deaf community linguistically (as opposed to economically) by imposing

Table 14.1 Chronology of the Historical Treatment of Deaf people

355 B.C.	Aristotle says those "born deaf become senseless and incapable of reason."
800 B.C.–500 A.D.	Deaf newborns in Greece and Sparta were cast out in pursuit of being "perfect, normal, and healthy."
To 500 A.D.	In Christianity, people believed that Deaf individuals were possessed by the devil.
	The views of the Church held out no hope for deaf people, for the apostle Paul had written that "faith cometh by hearing." (Van Cleve, 1993 p. 7)
1485	Rudolphus Agricola (1443–1485) wrote about a deaf-mute who learns to read and write.
1500	Girolamo Cardàno (1501–1576), the first physician to recognize the ability of the deaf to reason.
1600s	Juan Pablo Bonet (1579–1620) published the first book on education of the deaf in Madrid, Spain.
	John Wallis (1616-1703) published *De Loquela,* reported to be the first publication describing a successful method for teaching English and Speech to deaf children.
	Johann Amman (1699–1724), a Swiss medical doctor developed and published methods for teaching speech and lipreading to the deaf called *Surdus Loquens.*
1755	Samuel Heinicke (1712–1790) establishes the first oral school for the deaf in the world in Germany.
	Charles Michel Abbe de l'Epee (1712–1789) establishes the first free school for the deaf in the world in Paris, France.
1800s	On Martha's Vineyard Deaf and Hearing people use sign language to communicate with each other on a daily basis, even during business hours (Groce, 1985).
1817	The first permanent school for the deaf was founded and taught by the first Deaf teacher, Laurent Clerc, in Hartford, Connecticut.
1840's	William Willard, Deaf founder of the Indiana School for the Deaf and graduate of the American School, documented his early analysis of sign language.
1864	Congress founds Gallaudet College (later University) as the first institute of higher education for deaf students.
1880	Birth of the National Association of the Deaf and Deaf Movement; Conference on the Education of the Deaf in Milan, Italy where Hearing participants voted to forbid the use of signs in the education of Deaf people threatening the learning freedom of deaf children and the employment of Deaf teachers.
1891	Gallaudet College adds teacher training program.
1960	William Stokoe's research provided evidence that American Sign Language (ASL) is a true language.
1970's	Birth of English-based sign systems controlled by non-deaf professionals.
1988	The first Deaf president of Gallaudet University, the only Liberal Arts University for deaf and hard of hearing students, was selected. This marks a significant milestone in the civil rights of deaf and disabled individuals.
1990's	Birth of the Bilingual/Bicultural educational movement using ASL and English in the classroom.

Source: Adapted from Gannon, 1981.

"the colonizer's language (in this case English)...on the colonized" (p. 25). Conversely, the cultural view focuses on the language experiences and values of a particular group of people who happen to be different from the "norm."

This brief chronology shows a gradual shift from viewing Deaf people as "incapable of reason" to capable of learning, and most recently, capable of leading. The pathological/clinical views of Deaf people held by the Hearing culture seem not to have changed significantly over time while the views held by the Deaf Community have changed to a cultural perspective. The most explicit example of this progression can be taken from the history of Deaf Education in the United States.

Oral versus Manual Controversy

School policies and questions about which methods of communication to use in the classrooms for Deaf children have been a subject of controversy over the last 170 years. Until the late 1960s, the debate over language use in teaching had always been between the proponents of the oral (spoken language) method and the manual (sign) method. In 1817 the first school for Deaf children in the United States was founded in Hartford, Connecticut. Students were taught by a Deaf teacher, Laurent Clerc, who used sign language as the method of communication. The trend toward oralism was codified by the 1880 Conference on the Education of the Deaf in Milan, Italy where Hearing participants voted to forbid the use of signs in the education of Deaf people. Gannon (1981) explains that Deaf people are still smarting from the indignity they suffered at that international meeting in 1880 which banned the use of sign language in the teaching of Deaf children and led to the expulsion of Deaf teachers from classrooms. As a result, Deaf people had practically no say in how Deaf children were educated. The oral method of teaching quickly became widespread across both the United States and Europe. The shift to oralism had a profound impact on Deaf teachers, who were considered inferior speech models for their students. Prior to the Milan Conference in 1880, about 50% of the teachers of the Deaf were Deaf. Today only 11% of the teaching force is Deaf. The oral-only method continues to be greatly favored as the method of instruction in the United States and worldwide (Nover, 1993).

Efforts of Alexander Graham Bell

Alexander Graham Bell, inventor of the telephone, which was intended for his Deaf wife, was one of the biggest proponents of the oral movement. In 1883 he presented a paper, "Upon the Formation of a Deaf Variety of the Human Race," before the National Academy of Science in New Haven, Connecticut. Bell wrote, "Those who believe as I do, that the production of a defective race of human beings would be a great calamity to the world, will examine carefully the causes that lead to the intermarriages of the deaf with the object of applying a remedy" (cited in Gannon, 1981, p. 75). He would have razed all residential and day schools for the deaf. Bell believed that "herding" Deaf children under one roof was a cruel thing to do. He broached the possibility of forbidding Deaf–Deaf marriages by law arguing that such marriages would produce Deaf offspring (Gannon, 1981, pp. 75–76). Years later, Mindel and Vernon (1971) challenged Bell's theory by demonstrating that 90 to 95% of Deaf people are born of "normal" Hearing parents and have Hearing children.

George W. Veditz, a Deaf teacher and former President of the National Association of the Deaf (NAD), a political organization, called Alexander Graham Bell the American most feared by Deaf people, saying "...he comes in the guise of a friend, and [is], therefore, the most to be feared enemy of the American Deaf, past and present" (quoted in Gannon, 1981, p. 77). As a result of the oral movement, which was greatly influenced by Bell, the manual (sign) method was banned from the classroom and the Hearing perspective dominated the education of the Deaf.

Recognition of American Sign Language

By the 1960s the majority of Deaf schools in the United States and worldwide employed the oral method for educating Deaf children. Children who were unsuccessful using the oral method and communicated using ASL were seen as failures, regardless of their intellectual ability. In 1960 William C. Stokoe was the first non-Deaf linguist to apply linguistic science to the study of ASL. He recognized ASL as one of the legitimate human languages. (Only recently have universities, such as the University of Arizona, accepted ASL as fulfillment for the foreign language requirement for graduation.) Also during the 1960s, the Civil Rights Movement, along with advocacy and community groups such as the National Association of the Deaf and Deaf Pride, spurred government action targeting the Deaf and other "handicapped" groups. These groups used ASL as their symbol of Deaf pride and culture in order to campaign for "Deaf awareness/heritage" as well as greater government action in an area where, up to then, little attention had been paid. Recognition of ASL as a language as well as the political empowerment of the Deaf community renewed the struggle for the power to decide their language. However, Hearing, nonnative ASL-using educators still dominate the educational process and seriously affect the lives of Deaf children by denying them the use of ASL in the classroom.

ASL versus English-Based Sign System

The oral–manual controversy moved into a new phase in the 1970s. The issue moved from whether or not to sign with Deaf students to what kind of signing to use. Rather than make use of ASL, groups of researchers and educators (primarily Hearing) created "English-based sign systems" which attempted to make spoken English more visible (Stedt & Moores, 1990). This exemplifies how control of language policy has been in the hands of nonDeaf professionals. The use of ASL was seen as insufficient and ineffective for teaching Deaf children. Bornstein, Hamilton, and Sornier (1983) make this view clear:

> Can most deaf children get enough information from these signals (ASL) to learn English well? The answer to this question is a clear and very well documented no. Most deaf children do not learn English well, recent surveys of the educational achievement of older deaf children indicate that, on the average, they equal the reading performance of hearing fourth or fifth graders. Not all deaf students do that well. (p. 2)

Since Stokoe's demonstration that ASL is indeed a true language, more and more signed-language researchers and scholars have made significant contributions to the study of language acquisition. In addition, a number of books on sign languages such as ASL, French Sign Language, British Sign Language, and others have appeared along with a myriad of Deaf-related books on such topics as linguistics, sociolinguistics, language acquisition, second language learning, English as a second language (Andrews, Leigh, & Weiner, 2004; Chamberlain, Morford, & Mayberry, 2000; Ladd, 2003; Lucas, 1989, 2006; Lucas, Bayley, & Valli, 2001, 2003; Metzger, 2000).

Unfortunately, the outcome of the 1880 Milan Conference still profoundly affects daily life in the American Deaf community. Prejudice and discrimination were inherently expressed by parents as well as non-Deaf educators in the decision made at the conference to forbid participation by Deaf educators. The ideas put forth at the conference, that is, that oralism is superior to manual communication, fosters the illusion that Deaf people are in agreement with the concept that every Deaf child should be given a chance to be like a "Hearing, normal child"; this classic bias against ASL is a clear formulation of the hegemony of English and an English-based manual system promoted in schools for the Deaf (Bornstein et al., 1983).

The history of Deaf education indicates that audism, in which a higher value is placed on Hearing and oral/aural perspectives and parallels ableism (Lane, 1992), hearization, which is similar to assimilation in nondominant communities, and domination significantly affects the educational and linguistic lives of Deaf people. An examination of the parties who are playing significant roles in the development of Deaf education reveals exactly what ideology controls this institution. In addition, history indicates that those in Deaf education have not been effective in addressing the concerns of the Deaf community regarding Deaf education (Lane, Hoffmeister, & Bahan, 1996). Language planning is still under the control of Hearing educators. In recent years, some programs, such as Texas School for the Deaf, New Mexico School for the Deaf, Metro Deaf School in Minnesota, and Marathon High School in Los Angeles have adopted a bilingual and bicultural approach. Yet, they are still very controversial and do not easily replace the institutionalized Hearing orientation to Deaf education.

Where do Deaf people stand now? What has been the impact of this history on Deaf education and the quality of life for Deaf children? Where do Deaf people begin the "attack" to change this situation? Unfortunately, the pathological perspective is much more deeply ingrained in the Hearing world than we may realize. It pervades the foundations of education and research.

Pathological Perspective Maintained Through Education and Research

In Nover's (1993) discussion of the current state of the education of the Deaf, he points out that most textbooks used in training programs for teachers of the Deaf are written by those who view Deaf people as outsiders and who believe that Deaf children and adolescents should behave like Hearing persons. These courses include many terms that denote pathology, such as: *Hearing impaired, special education, disorders of the language development, diagnosis, correction, improvement, hearing loss, and adaptations of regular curriculum.* Nover further explains that a majority of the courses represent the promotion of an English-only philosophy, which is auditory-based, along with a pathological orientation toward Deaf children. He found that classes could be categorized into three areas: English-only centered orientation (75%); Deaf-centered orientation (e.g., those emphasizing ASL; 12%); and nonrelevant (13%).

Nover (1993) argues that a Deaf-centered orientation would include, for example, courses such as teaching English as a second language, teaching reading skills in a second language, second language writing, language transfer, ASL literature, Deaf culture, Deaf history, cross-cultural issues, bilingual education, and first and second language acquisition and teaching.

The majority of researchers who conduct various studies on the Deaf community have been trained and exposed only to literature that emphasizes the English-only, pathological, and non-Deaf orientation. The pathological perspective is still being perpetuated in the majority of teacher training programs as well as by many of the researchers who study Deaf people.

There is a growing number of researchers who have conducted their research from a Deaf culture perspective. The following section will compare several researchers from both the cultural and pathological perspective in order to clarify the differences between the two groups.

Research in the Field of Deaf Education

For nearly 200 years the focus of research and education has been Deaf children's inability to hear. From this pathological view, social scientists like Alexander Graham Bell, Bornstein, Ling, and others have looked at Deaf people as a deviant group with hearing loss and they have consistently compared Deaf students to Hearing "normal" counterparts. To study how one becomes "deviant," social scientists assign labels to demoralize a particular group or individual when behavior is marked as abnormal (Gamson, 1991). Thus, such social scientists who study Deaf people make it clear that Deaf people are not normal and are categorized as deviants from the Hearing society because they do not possess what Hearing people possess: the ability to hear. Gamson and Schiffman point out that the attempts to use labels of abnormalities foster the process of stigmatization (Burawoy et al., 1991). Social scientists assign such labels to Deaf people, and thereby continue to control the stigmatizing and demoralizing power over Deaf people.

Further, in Lane's book, *The Mask of Benevolence* (1992), he argues that so-called "experts" in the scientific, medical, and education fields, while claiming to help Deaf people and their community in fact do them great harm. In other words, social scientists look at themselves as the experts on Deafness while Deaf people see themselves as inferior and are "trained" to become dependent on Hearing people. The majority of the social scientists with the colonizing and pathological attitudes toward Deaf people are still making decisions about Deaf people and enabling the Deaf to depend on them because of the hold over and control they have over so many aspects of the lives of the Deaf. Lane (1992) argues that paternalism and money are inseparable in this transaction. For example, these social scientists with pathological views of Deaf people write the textbooks and materials for use in the teacher education programs for teachers preparing to teach Deaf children. The books on methods of instruction for the Deaf are written by researchers who in turn receive recognition for their expertise and profits for their work. Bornstein's attitude about Deaf children can be seen in his text as he (1990) attempts:

> to offer an authoritative description of manual communication as it is used in the United States. It is designed for professionals who work with Deaf and language-delayed children and adolescents (including some who may hear). It should also be useful for teachers-in-training and interested parents. (p. 253)

Students in teacher preparation programs are taught a pathological view through the books written by Hearing researchers. When these students become teachers of the Deaf, they bring attitudes and a mind-set that Deaf people are, to quote social scientists, "deviants." The main point is that social scientists aim to maintain the professional authority over the description of education and communication. The focus is that the social scientists do not want to relinquish their power over Deaf people.

Thus, while numerous statistical and quantitative studies have documented the failures of Deaf students (Allen, 1986; Braden, 1994; Schirmer, 2003; Trybus & Karchmer, 1977) the work of these social scientists has been used to hinder advancement in education of Deaf children by reinforcing the concept of ableism as well as disability. The pathological perspective is perpetuated in research being conducted by social scientists using traditional approaches from a Hearing orientation. Shapiro (1993) noted that in research nondisabled people use "prettifying euphemisms" (Shapiro, 1993, p. 33) and rely on the stereotype that disabled persons should be an inspiration in their efforts to overcome challenges. To the contrary, Blackwell (1993) in her narrative about her experiences growing up Deaf, considered herself not handicapped and was angry that Deaf people were allowed to believe they were handicapped. Bahan (cited in Wilcox, 1989) proclaims that it is the Hearing world that tells us we are handicapped and disabled. Educators trained to think of Deaf children as handicapped and disabled continue to lower the educational expectations and achievements of Deaf children. In turn, these attitudes encourage Deaf children to believe they are handicapped and disabled in the eyes of the majority of Hearing people and thus will never equalize themselves with Hearing peers.

In contrast to this mainstream view, the work of linguistic and anthropological social scientists in American Sign Language and Deaf Culture has facilitated new perspectives on Deaf people (Baker & Battison, 1980; Baker & Cokely, 1980; Erting and Woodward, 1979; Groce, 1985; Klima & Bellugi, 1979; Liddell & Johnson, 1989; Lucas, 1989; Padden & Humphries, 1988; Stokoe, Casterline, & Croneberg, 1965; S. Supalla, 1990; T. Supalla, 1986; Van Cleve & Crouch, 1989). Johnson, Liddell, and Erting (1989) noted that the low average academic achievement levels are not results of loss of Hearing or learning deficits inherently associated with being Deaf but with the problems in the communication practices of the students' teachers. In her study on teacher communication competency, Baker (1978) stated that teachers using sign language and spoken English simultaneously did not provide comprehensive and complete linguistic input for Deaf children during the instructional time. In contrast, Moores (1991) wrote an editorial in the *American Annals of the Deaf* on teacher morale:

> Teachers of the deaf typically deal with a situation in which their children have normal intellectual potential but academic progress is constrained by limited English and other communication skills. Teachers may see only small incremental growth in standardized test scores from year to year and may mistakenly, in my opinion, hold themselves responsible for what they perceive to be an unsatisfactory rate of progress. (p. 243)

Corbett and Jensema (1981) indicated that the majority of teachers of the Deaf were White, Hearing, and female. Teacher training programs offer courses from a medical perspective as illustrated earlier. Therefore, with the majority of White, Hearing females being responsible for the language and instruction of Deaf children, it is anticipated that those people are already trained in a pathological view of Deaf children. Hence, many educational programs for Deaf children described earlier are still employing old research theories regarding learning English as the first language and espousing a paternalistic attitude toward Deaf people.

In a survey, Woodward and Allen (1987) studied 609 elementary teachers. Eighty-five percent of this predominantly Hearing and female group had minimal skills in ASL. In general the research suggests that the educational programs for the Deaf are being dominated by Hearing educators whose communication has been shown to be insufficient as a means to convey information through instruction. Certified teachers of the Deaf may have had only two or fewer classes in sign language during their teacher education program (Maxwell, 1985). As a result, some Deaf children were put in the position of having to teach ASL to their teachers; therefore, the instructional time for Deaf children often is replaced with teachers learning from the children. Additionally, when teachers (and future teachers) of Deaf children do know how to sign, often their ASL fluency is lacking.

One example of this occurred in March 1992. Gallaudet University placed four student teachers at a residential school for the Deaf in the Midwest where the Bilingual and Bicultural program is used. These four student teachers included three White Hearing women and one who identified herself as Hearing impaired. After observing these student teachers working with children in the class, the teachers and principal at the school determined that the student teachers' sign skills were insufficient. As a result the student teachers were asked to cease their practicum at the school. After returning to Gallaudet they were transferred to another school, one that presumably had lower expectations of the sign skills of their teacher interns. This action helped to convince faculty and administrators at Gallaudet University to change its graduate studies program to include more cultural and linguistic aspects of Deaf people and require students to become knowledgeable and proficient in both areas before they could participate in their practicum. The faculty at Gallaudet changed the curriculum of the Deaf Education program to include a demonstration of sign proficiency for students planning to teach. However, state and professional requirements for obtaining a teacher's license in Deaf Education include coursework that emphasizes the pathological view, not a cultural and linguistic view. In spite of new cultural and linguistic theories that emerged in 1960 and thereafter on ASL and Deaf Culture, only a few schools (e.g. Texas School for the Deaf, California School for the Deaf, Metro Day School for the Deaf) and universities (e.g., Gallaudet University, Lamar University, Boston University) have adopted a cultural and linguistic view as the basis for instruction and hire Deaf people who are trained as ASL and Deaf studies instructors.

Deaf People as Researchers

Lane (1988) proposed that psychologists involve Deaf people themselves at all levels of research undertaken. Deaf people need to be recruited and trained, and researchers should turn to the Deaf community as advisors and collaborators in collecting analyzing, interpreting, and disseminating results. Kurzman (1991) stated that the ideal is to give subjects a voice in the research; however, he warned that the complex sentences and eloquent works in the researchers' writings may remind the subjects of their inability to communicate in the Deaf individual's way. He suggests that we allow subjects to provide input to correct any mistakes the researcher might have made; to create a sense of cooperation between subjects and researcher in the quest to understand the subjects' world; to empower subjects by making them active members in their own analysis; and to keep writings clear in order to keep the subjects' possible reactions in mind as the research unfolds. Padden and Humphries (1988) note in the introduction to their book, *Deaf in America: Voices from a Culture*, that the traditional way of writing about Deaf people is to focus on their condition, the fact that they do not hear, and to interpret all other aspects of their lives as consequences of this fact. In contrast, a sociolinguistic or cultural approach to research focuses on "normalization" of Deaf people as a linguistic and cultural group.

Lane (1980) reviewed existing literature and found over 350 textbooks and reports that reveal paternalistic attitudes toward Deaf people. Though no similar study has been conducted on the research done on or about Deaf people, such a study would likely reveal the preponderance of Hearing researchers and few (though growing) numbers of Deaf researchers or Deaf/Hearing teams. The perspectives of Hearing researchers may differ from those of Deaf researchers or even those of collaborative groups including both Hearing and Deaf researchers. If the number of research studies done by Deaf social scientists were to increase or surpass the number of studies by Hearing social scientists, would a Deaf perspective eventually reflect a new change in the picture of Deaf people?

Although an increasing number of Deaf researchers with higher levels of sophistication have contributed to the field, we still have to deal with enduring stereotypes, negative interpretations, and inappropriate pathological theoretical suggestions already imposed on Deaf people. When social scientists proclaim their theories, the results are often in conflict with a Deaf perspective. For example researchers continue to compare the English ability of Deaf children with Hearing children for reading and writing competencies, while they ignore ASL as literacy. So, the validity of tests and measurements in English for Deaf children is being challenged by the linguistic and cultural theories. What a researcher in one framework may consider to be problematic and require a remedial solution may count as healthy independence to someone looking from a different perspective. Researchers who hold pathological views would consider the importance of teaching English in the classroom to improve the linguistic and grammatical skills, whereas Deaf people find that they could achieve their learning of English through ASL. Lane (1984) adds "But the deaf did not have, do not have, the final word (in research). The final word as always came from their Hearing benefactors" (p. 413).

While some researchers have included Deaf people in their research (both as participants and collaborators) the involvement of those Deaf people has been greatly restricted. Kannapell (1980), a Deaf researcher in Deaf Studies, in discussing her experience working with Signed English developers (Bornstein et al., 1983) expressed that she was disillusioned by the oppression she experienced from the researchers with whom she worked. She eventually resigned from this work, after she discovered her identity as a Deaf person and began a new endeavor, establishing Deaf Studies at Gallaudet University where she retired as a professor. She was a pioneer in recognizing the ambivalence of Deaf people regarding their own identity and language, which was the subject of her doctoral dissertation. It is possible that Deaf researchers who collaborate with Hearing researchers are either not aware of their rights or accept the fact that they have little or no power over the work. Paternalism can corrupt some members of an oppressed minority, forming a class that conspires with the authority to maintain the status quo (Lane, 1992). Indeed, researchers are likely to approach Deaf people with paternalistic attitudes. The failure to involve Deaf people as active participants in research has been a longstanding issue. However, we are seeing more works of linguistic and anthropological researchers involving Deaf people as collaborative researchers, assistants, and subjects (L. Erting & Pfau,1993; C. Erting, Prezioso, & Hynes,1990; Lucas & Valli, 1990; Padden & Ramsey,1997; T. Supalla & Newport, 1978). For example, in the 1990s two proposals for Deaf research projects were funded by the U.S. Department of Education, Office of Special Education and Rehabilitative Services. Both proposals were submitted by collaborative Deaf and Hearing researchers; Padden and Ramsey and Supalla and Singleton. Both worked with Deaf professionals at different residential schools for the Deaf. Additionally, research projects like the Signs of Literacy (SOL) and the Visual Language, Visual Learning (VL2) research projects at Gallaudet University bring Deaf and Hearing researchers together to examine issues of language development, education of Deaf children, and literacy.[3]

Reinharz (1992, p. 260) noted that feminist researchers draw on a new "epistemology of insider-ness" that sees life and work as intertwined. Feminist research aims at the following goals: "1) to document the lives and activities of women, 2) to understand the experience of women from their own point of view, and 3) to conceptualize women's behavior as an expression of social contexts" (Reinharz, 1992, p. 51). The research on women contributes significantly to rethinking perspectives of Deaf people. With this new influence on the Hearing perspective of Deaf people, the patriarchal attitudes and stigmatization of Deaf people can perhaps be eradicated. Researchers as experienced insiders are able to understand what Deaf people have to say in a way that no outsider could.

Reinharz also points out that there may be a danger of overgeneralizing women's experiences when researchers fail to differentiate their own experiences from those of other women (p. 262). She suggests that feminist researchers include their personal experiences as an asset for their research, using objectivity and subjectivity to serve each other.

Anthropological research has shown diversity among Deaf people (Lane, 1992; Lucas, 1989; Padden & Humphries, 1988). Deaf researchers may already or will draw on their own personal and cultural experiences to do research, but at the same time carefully differentiate their own experience from the experience of other Deaf people (Kannapell, 1980; Stone-Harris & Stirling, 1987; Suppala, 1992). This is a departure from the traditional homogenizing model of Hearing researchers working on Deaf people and a new approach between Hearing and Deaf researchers as collaborators as well as the Deaf as individual researchers. This emerging trend (Andrews, Leigh, & Weiner, 2004; Kuntze, 2004; Ladd, 2003) will give the opportunity to bring in more Deaf perspectives than the traditional model and will offer more valid descriptions of Deaf people.

In order to depathologize the Deaf community and deconstruct the inherent patriarchal assumptions, it has become necessary to develop new strategies such as revising language and eradicating stigmatizing terms. Woodward (1982) discusses the commonly "take for granted" term, *handicapped,* and notes:

> For if we look more closely at the notion of "handicapped" and its ramifications, we come to a rather unpleasant logical conclusion. *The American Heritage Dictionary* (1976) defines handicapped as a "deficiency, or especially an anatomical, physiological or mental efficiency, that prevents or restricts normal achievement." (p. 133)

If we follow the traditional handicapped classification of Deaf people, they are doomed to failure because they will never achieve (nor do they always want to "achieve") the "normality" of becoming a Hearing person. Most Deaf people will then remain deficient (i.e., according to Hearing society's norms), that is "lacking an essential quality or element; incomplete; defective."

Moreover, another controversial term, *Hearing impaired,* is for Hearing people, a more acceptable and tolerable term, but it is a euphemism for "Deaf." The term *Hearing impaired* has a negative connotation and is no longer an acceptable usage among the World Federation of the Deaf and other organizations, such as the National Association of the Deaf (NAD) and the Registry of Interpreters for the Deaf (RID). Bienvenu (1989) points out that "Hearing impaired" defines Deaf people solely in terms of broken or defective ears and this term tends to be preferred by most of the professionals in the audiological and rehabilitation field who take a narrow medical view of Deaf people. Furthermore, Bienvenu challenges the lack of acceptance and misuse of the term *Deaf* as she asks; "Why is it so hard to accept the word 'deaf'? Is it because it sounds like 'death' which is commonly misused by Hearing people?" (Bradford, 1993).

In *The Bicultural Center Newsletter,* April 1991, Bienvenu considers the use of the term *Deafness* (as in "the field of Deafness") as equally ridiculous and a nonhuman entity. She notes that there is no such thing as the "field of womanness" for women and "field of blackness" for Black people (p. 1) but the "field of deafness" has been seen as acceptable. There is nothing horrible or undignified about the term *Deaf,* so no sophisticated or polite substitute is needed. Even that cringe-inducing term is less debasing than *non-Hearing.* Perhaps the terms *Deaf* and *non-Deaf* should be something to consider (Bradford, 1993). Bradford further explains that in referring to Deaf people as "non-Hearing" is rather like saying "non-Whites" to describe Blacks; it appears to reduce Deaf people to a sterile, subaverage population.

From within the Deaf community, new vocabularies have emerged for shaping theories. Though many of these terms have been commonly used for several centuries by the Deaf, they need to be replaced for the aforementioned negative connotations. In order to promote better understanding and sustain an endogenous cultural view, the term *Deaf* is preferred over any other as a powerful term, presenting a positive identify, and as another way of being human. "Deaf" implicates a language and culture (Padden & Humphries, 1988). "Deaf" is inclusive. The entry "Deaf" reads in the American Heritage Dictionary of the English language (1992):

> Adj. 1 Partially or completely lacking in the sense of Hearing. 2. Deaf. Of or relating to the Deaf or their culture. 3. Unwilling, refusing to listen: heedless: *was deaf to our objections.* N. (used with a plural verb). 1. Deaf people considered as a group 2. Deaf. The community of deaf people who use American Sign Language as a primary means of communication. (p. 368)

To contrast, from a Deaf perspective, ASL is considered as the primary, dominant language. English should be considered a second language for Deaf people in the United States (Grosjean, 1982). Furthermore, Nover and Ruiz (1992) contend that there is a great need to develop more Deaf-centered or Deaf-informed aspects among such disciplines as psychology, education, anthropology, sociology, and the like before researchers will have accurate and acceptable cultural information regarding Deaf people.

Results and Effects of the Pathological View in the Education of Deaf People

The historical treatment of Deaf people has resulted in a number of detrimental effects on the Deaf Community. To justify the need for a change in Deaf education, however, one only needs to look at a long list of studies by researchers in the field of Deaf Education (Allen, 1994; DiFrancesca, 1972; Hoffmeister, 2000; Padden & Ramsey, 1997; Prinz & Strong 1998; Traxler, 2000; Trybus & Karchmer, 1977; Vernon & Andrews, 1990). These studies showed that 30% of Deaf students in the United States left school functionally illiterate (at grade 2.8 or below on education achievement tests); 60% read at grade levels between 5.3 and 2.9 (DiFrancesca, 1972; Trybus & Karchmer, 1977); and only 5% achieved a 10th-grade level or above (Jensema & Trybus, 1978). Approximately one-half of Deaf high school students were unable to meet the academic requirements for a diploma, exiting instead with a certificate or less (Schildroth et al., 1991). Those who dropped out or aged out of high school programs accounted for 29% of those leaving while only 29% of Deaf students graduated with high school diplomas (Bowe, 2003; Schildroth et al., 1991). Students who did graduate often went on to be unemployed or underemployed when compared to Hearing counterparts (Garay, 2003; Punch, Hyde, & Creed, 2004).

This situation with the education of Deaf individuals has had a severe impact on their ability to make the transition from school to employment, and then to independent living. The importance of education was highlighted by Jones (2004) who found no evidence of significant differences in earnings between Deaf and Hearing individuals, *except* for those with lower levels of educational attainment. A series of surveys conducted by

MacLeod (1983, 1984, 1985) revealed employment trends among Deaf/hard-of-Hearing graduates of residential and mainstreamed public school programs. Persons responding to those surveys experienced rates of unemployment higher than the norm for Hearing persons; if employed, they typically found work in blue-collar occupations where they earned a lower salary, demonstrated little upward mobility, and tended to stay at the same job for a long period of time. Furthermore, Dr. Frank R. Turk, former director of North Carolina's Division of Deaf and Hard of Hearing Services, claimed approximately 70% of the nation's Deaf-school graduates receive Supplemental Security Income (SSI). These poor educational and work history outcomes point to an ongoing crisis in the state of Deaf education in the United States.

After this long history of linguistic, cultural, and educational oppression and its resultant impacts on the success of members of the Deaf Community, a grassroots change began. This change, beginning in the Civil Rights era of the 1960s, had its roots in the recognition that the signs that Deaf people were using were not simply visual representations of the local spoken language but, in fact, consisted of a rich language with its own grammar, syntax, history, and culture. This recognition of ASL coincided with the Civil Rights Movement, and the sense of Deaf Civil Rights emerged. The resultant empowerment of the Deaf community sparked a change in how Deaf people saw themselves and led to a critical look at the educational methods used in schools and universities throughout the United States. This growing empowerment continued through the 1980s with the Deaf President Now[4] movement at Gallaudet University. In the 1990s the ASL/English Bilingual Education movement began. These changes reflected a shift from a pathological to a cultural view of Deaf people.

Implications for Research

Through our discussion of opposing perspectives on Deaf people (cultural as compared to pathological), the resultant oppression of Deaf people, and the impact of that oppression on the education of Deaf and hard of hearing children, we have argued that there needs to be more Deaf influence and perspective in the education of Deaf and hard of hearing children. Though there is a growing movement toward ASL/English bilingual education, there continues to be a tremendous need for promoting more Deaf focused research in language use and planning, education, and culture. This research should include exploring the attitude and relations between non-Deaf professionals and the Deaf community in order to gain a better understanding and come to a resolution of this conflict of perspectives (Clifford, 1991; Nover, 1993). Kurzman (1991) notes that it is absurd for social scientists to debate subjects' situations without letting them speak for themselves, even though it has been an historical reality for the Deaf community. For Deaf people to gain more control over the research on Deaf lives, the Hearing people in control should relinquish some of their power by hiring more Deaf researchers and collaborating with them when necessary, to maintain a Deaf perspective in their work. Deaf people should have the right to see and comment on Hearing researchers' work especially in the early stages. Though not all perspectives can be addressed and satisfied by any one project, researchers will gain support from the Deaf community for their projects if the work is shared and criticized by Deaf people as part of the project itself.

Hearing social scientists hiring Deaf people only as assistants for their research perpetuate colonization and perpetuate the current power structure through dominant/dominated relationships. Also, "hiring" implies a power differential, that the Deaf people are doing the "dirty work" and that the research design is Hearing oriented. Collaboration of Deaf and Hearing researchers may contribute to an eradication of pathological views to develop relevant, explanatory theories uniquely fitted to what we are studying and to lived realities of Deaf people. Traditional, antiquated theories may explain a particular view of phenomena colored by biases of researchers. We need to refute these erroneous theories with valid arguments and evidence. Experts in the scientific, medical, and education establishments who purport to serve the Deaf in fact do them great harm when they address the realities of our lives, and portray Deaf people as disabled. Woodward (1982) points out that it is very improbable that Deaf people will even achieve equality unless the Hearing society depathologizies Deafness; that is, unless Hearing society rejects the handicapped classification of Deaf people. After all, Deaf people, like all other human beings simply want liberty, equality, and the pursuit of happiness.

Notes

1. Many authors use capital "D" Deaf to refer to those who are members of the American Deaf culture and lower case "d" deaf to refer to the audiological condition.
2. In using the term *Deaf culture* or *Deaf community* we do not mean to imply that all Deaf people believe, act, or support the same ideas and beliefs. As with any culture or community, the Deaf community is varied and diverse. With this in mind, however, interviews and research on identity in the Deaf community often find members of the Deaf community as identifying themselves first as Deaf. For example in a survey of Deaf lesbians, it was found that these women consistently identified themselves as Deaf first then as women or lesbians.
3. For additional information on the Signs of Literacy project go to http://sol.gallaudet.edu. For information about the Visual Language, Visual Learning project go to http://vl2.gallaudet.edu.
4. In 1988, the Board of Trustees at Gallaudet University selected Elizabeth Zinser, a Hearing woman with no experience working with the Deaf community, to be the President of Gallaudet. The two other candidates were Deaf men who had long histories of working both at Gallaudet and in the Deaf community. This resulted in a protest which included Gallaudet students, faculty, staff, as well as members of the larger Deaf community. The protesters demanded a Deaf president for Gallaudet and 51% Deaf representation on the Board of Trustees. After a week of protests the Board of Trustees chose I. King Jordan as the first Deaf president of Gallaudet. For a detailed account of the Deaf President Now Movement see Christiansen and Barnartt (1995) and Gannon (1989).

References

Allen, T. (1986). Patterns of academic achievement in hearing-impaired students: 1974 and 1983. In A. Schlidroth & Karchmer, M. (Eds.), *Deaf children in America* (pp. 161–206). San Diego, CA: College-Hill Press.

Allen, T. (1994). *Who are the deaf and hard of hearing students leaving high school and entering postsecondary education?* Gallaudet University Center for Assessment and Demographic Studies, Washington, D.C. Unpublished manuscript.

Andrews, J., & Franklin, T. (1996–1997, August). Why hire deaf teachers? *Texas Journal of Audiology and Speech Pathology, 22*(1), 120–131.

Andrews, J., Leigh, I., & Weiner, M. (2004). *Deaf people: Evolving perspectives from psychology, education and sociology.* Boston, MA: Pearson Education.

Baker, C. (1978). How does "sim com" fit into a bilingual approach to education? In F. Caccamise & D. Hicks (Eds), *Proceedings of the second National Symposium in Sign Language Research and Training.* Silver Spring, MD: National Association of the Deaf.

Baker, C., & Battison, R. (Eds.). (1980). *Sign language of the Deaf Community: Essays in honor of William C. Stokoe.* Silver Spring, MD: National Association of the Deaf.

Baker, C., & Cokely, D. (1980). *American Sign Language: A teacher's resource text on grammar and culture.* Silver Spring, MD: T.J. Publishers.

Ballin, A. (1930). *The Deaf Mute howls.* Los Angeles, CA: Grafton

Bienvenu, M. J. (1989, October). An open letter to alumni, students of Gallaudet and friends. *The Bicultural Center News, 18.*

Bienvenue, M. J. (1991, April). *The Bicultural Center Newsletter, 21.*

Blackwell, L.R. (1993). Going beyond the anger. In M. Garretson (Ed.), *Deafness: 1993–2013.* Silver Spring, MD: National Association of the Deaf.

Bornstein, H. (1990). *Manual communications: Implications for education.* Washington, D.C.: Gallaudet University Press.

Bornstein, H., Hamilton, L., & Saulnier, K. (1983). *The comprehensive signed English dictionary.* Washington, D.C.: Gallaudet University Press.

Bowe, F. (2003). Transition for deaf and hard of hearing students: A blueprint for change. *Journal of Deaf Studies and Deaf Education, 8* (4), 485–493.

Braden J. P. (1994). *Deafness, deprivation and IQ.* New York: Plenum.

Bradford, S. (1993, May). What do we call ourselves? *Deaf Life,* 22–26.

Burawoy, M., Burton, A., Arnett Ferguson, A., Fox, K., Gamson, J., Gartrell, N., et al. (1991). *Ethnography unbound: Power and resistance in the modern metropolis.* Berkeley, CA: University of California Press.

Chamberlain, C., Morford, J., & Mayberry, R. (Eds.). (2000). *Language acquisition by eye.* Mahwah, NJ: Erlbaum.

Christiansen, J. and Barnartt, S. (1995). *Deaf President Now! The 1988 revolution at Gallaudet University.* Washington, D.C.: Gallaudet University Press.

Clifford, J. (1990). Notes on (field) notes. In R. Sanjek, (Ed.), *Fieldnotes: The making of anthropology* (pp. 47–70). Ithaca, NY: Cornell University Press.

Corbett, E. , & Jensema, C. (1981). *Teachers of the hearing impaired: Descriptive profiles.* Washington, D.C.: Gallaudet University Press.

Davidson A. (1996). *Making and molding identity in schools.* Albany, NY: State University of New York Press.

DiFrancesca, S. (1972). *Academic achievement test results of a national testing program for hearing impaired students, United States, 1971.* Washington, D.C.: Office of Demographic Studies, Gallaudet College.

Erting, C., Prezioso, C., & Hynes, M. (1990). The interactional context of Deaf mother–infant communication. In V. Voltera & C. Erting (Eds.), *From gesture to language in hearing and deaf children.* Washington, D.C.: Gallaudet University Press.

Erting, C., & Woodward, J. (1979). Sign language and the deaf community. *Discourse Processes, 2,* 183–300.

Erting, L., & Pfau, J. (1993, June). *Becoming bilingual: Facilitating English literacy development using ASL in preschool.* Paper presented at CAID/CEASD Convention, Baltimore.

Freire, P. (1992). *Pedagogy of the oppressed.* New York: Continuum.

Gamson, A. (1991). Silence, death, and the invisible enemy: AIDS activism and social movement "newness." In M. Burawoy, A. Burton, A. Arnett Ferguson, K. Fox, J. Gamson, N A. Gartrell et al. (Eds.), *Ethnography unbound: Power and resistance in the modern metropolis* (pp. 35–57). Berkeley, CA: University of California Press.

Gannon, J. (1981). *Deaf heritage: A narrative history of Deaf America.* Silver Spring, MD: National Association of the Deaf.

Gannon, J. (1989). *The week the world heard Gallaudet.* Washington, D.C.: Gallaudet University Press.

Garay, S. (2003). Listening to the voices of Deaf students: Essential transition issues. *Teaching Exceptional Children, 35*(4), 44–48.

Groce, N. (1985). *Everyone here spoke sign language: Hereditary deafness on Martha's Vineyard.* Cambridge: MA: Harvard University Press.

Grosjean, F. (1982). *Life with two languages: An introduction to bilingualism.* Cambridge, MA: Harvard University Press.

Hoffmeister, R. (2000). A piece of the puzzle: ASL and reading comprehension in deaf children. In C. Chamberlain, J. P. Morford, & R. I. Mayberry (Eds.), *Language acquisition by eye* (pp. 143–164). Mahwah, NJ: Erlbaum.

Jensema, C., & Trybus, J. (1978, August). *Communicative patterns and educational achievement of hearing impaired students* (Series T, Number 2). Washington, D.C.: Gallaudet College, Office of Demographic Studies.

Johnson, R. B., Liddell, S., & Erting, C. (1989). *Unlocking the curriculum: Principles for achieving access in Deaf Education* (GRI Working Paper Series, No. 89-3). Washington, D.C.: Gallaudet Research Institute.

Jones, D. (2004, Fall). Relative earnings of deaf and hard-of-hearing individuals. *Journal of Deaf Studies and Deaf Education, 9,* 459–461.

Kannapell, B. (1980). Personal awareness and advocacy in the Deaf Community. In C. Baker & R. Battison (Eds.), *Sign language of the Deaf Community: Essays in honor of William C. Stokoe* (pp. 105–116). Silver Spring, MD: National Association of the Deaf.

Klima, E., & Bellugi, U. (1979). *The signs of language.* Cambridge, MA: Harvard University Press.

Kuntze, M. (2004). *Literacy acquisition and deaf children: A study of the interaction between ASL and written English.* Doctoral dissertation, Stanford University, Stanford, California.

Kurzman, C. (1991). Convincing sociologists: Values and interests in the sociology of knowledge. In M. Burawoy A. Burton, A. Arnett Ferguson, K. Fox, J. Gamson, N. Gartrell, et al. (Eds.), *Ethnography unbound: Power and resistance in the modern metropolis* (pp. 250–270). Berkeley, CA: University of California Press.

Ladd, P. (2003). *Understanding Deaf culture: In search of Deafhood.* Clevedon, UK: Multilingual Matters.

Lane, H. (1980, Spring). *Some thoughts on language bigotry.* A presentation at Gallaudet University.

Lane, H. (1984). *When the mind hears: A history of the Deaf.* New York: Random House.

Lane, H. (1988, February). *Is there a psychology of the Deaf?* A presentation at Gallaudet University.

Lane, H. (1992). *The mask of benevolence: Disabling the Deaf Community.* New York: Alfred A. Knopf.

Lane, H., Hoffmeister, R., & Bahan, B. (1996). *A journey into the Deaf-World.* San Diego, CA: Dawn Sign Press.

Liddell, S., & Johnson, R. (1989). American Sign Language: The phonological base. *Sign Language Studies, 64,* 195–277.

Lucas, C. (Ed.). (1989). *The sociolinguistics of the Deaf Community.* San Diego, CA: Academic Press.

Lucas, C. (Ed.). (2006). *Multilingualism and sign languages: From the Great Plains to Australia.* Washington, D.C.: Gallaudet University Press.

Lucas, C., Bayley, R., & Valli, C. (2001). *Sociolinguistic variation in American Sign Language.* Washington, D.C.: Gallaudet University Press.

Lucas, C., Bayley, R., & Valli, C. (2003). *What's your sign for pizza? An introduction to variation in American Sign Language.* Washington, D.C.: Gallaudet University Press.

Lucas, C., & Valli, C. (1990). Predicates of perceived motion in ASL. In S. Fischer & P. Siple (Eds.), *Theoretical issues in sign language research* (pp. 153–166). Chicago: University of Chicago Press.

MacLeod, J. (1983). *Secondary school graduate follow-up program of the hearing impaired: Fourth annual report.* Rochester, NY: National Technical Institute for the Deaf.

MacLeod, J. (1984). *Secondary school graduate follow-up program of the hearing impaired: Fifth annual report.* Rochester, NY: National Technical Institute for the Deaf.

MacLeod, J. (1985). *Secondary school graduate follow-up program of the hearing impaired: Sixth annual report.* Rochester, NY: National Technical Institute for the Deaf.

Maxwell, M. (1985). Sign language instruction and teacher preparation. *Sign Language Studies. 47,* 173–180.

Metzger, M. (Ed.). (2000). *Bilingualism and identity in Deaf communities.* Washington, D.C.: Gallaudet University Press.

Mindel, B., & Vernon, M. (1971). *They grow in silence: The Deaf child and his family.* Washington, D.C.: American International Printing.

Moores, D. (1991). Teacher morale. *American Annals of the Deaf, 136*(3), 243.

Nover, S. (1993, June). *Our voices. our vision: Politics of Deaf education.* Paper presented at the AID/CEASD Convention, Baltimore.

Nover, S., & Ruiz, R. (1992, June 4–6). *ASL and language planning in Deaf education.* Paper presented at the International Symposium in Celebration of the Centennial of Teacher Education. Gallaudet University, Washington, D.C.

Padden, C., & Humphries, T. (1988). *Deaf in America: Voices from a culture.* Cambridge, MA: Harvard University Press.

Padden, C., & Ramsey, C. (1997*). Deaf students as readers and writers: A mixed mode research approach. Final Report to U.S. Department of Education.* University of California, San Diego. Unpublished manuscript,

Prinz, P. M., & Strong, M. (1998). ASL proficiency and English within a bilingual deaf education model of instruction. *Topics in Language Disorders, 18*(4), 47–60.

Punch, R., Hyde, M., & Creed, P. (2004). Issues in the school-to-work transition of hard of hearing adolescents. *American Annals of the Deaf, 149*(1) 28–38.

Reinharz, S. (1992). *Feminist methods in social research.* New York: Oxford University Press.

Schildroth, A., Rawlings, B, & Allen, T. (1991). Deaf students in transition: Education and employment issues for deaf adolescents. *The Volta Review, 93, 5.*

Schirmer, B. R. (2003, Spring). Using verbal protocols to identify the reading strategies of students who are deaf. *Journal of Deaf Studies and Deaf Education, 8*(2), 157–170.

Shapiro, J. (1993). *No pity: People with disabilities forging a new Civil Rights Movement.* New York: Random House.

Spindler, G., & Spindler, L. (1990). *The American cultural dialogue and its transmission.* New York: Falmer Press.

Stedt, F., & Moores, D. (1990). Manual codes of English and American Sign Language: Historical perspectives and current realities. In H. Bornstein (Ed.), *Manual communications: Implications for education.* Washington, D.C.: Gallaudet University Press.

Stokoe, W. C., Casterline, D., & Croneberg, C. G. (1965). *A dictionary of American Sign Language on linguistic principles.* Washington, D.C.: Gallaudet College Press.

Stone-Harris, R., & Stirling, L. (1987). Developing and defining an identity: Deaf children of Deaf and Hearing parents. In *Proceedings of Social Change and the Deaf. Proceedings of the Second Research Conference on the Social Aspects of Deafness.* Washington, D.C.: Gallaudet University Press.

Supalla, S. (1992). *The book of name signs: Naming in American Sign Language.* San Diego, CA: Dawn Sign Press.

Supalla, T. (1986). The classifier system in American Sign Language. In C. Craig (Ed.), *Noun classification and categorization.* Philadelphia: J. Benjamins.

Supalla, T., & Newport, E. (1978). How many seats in a chair? The derivation of nouns and verbs in American Sign Language. In P. Siple (Ed.), *Understanding language through sign language research.* New York: Academic Press.

Traxler, C. B. (2000). Measuring up to performance standards in reading and mathematics: Achievement of selected deaf and hard-of-hearing students in the national norming of the ninth edition Stanford Achievement Test. *Journal of Deaf Studies and Deaf Education, 5,* 337–348.

Trybus, R. J., & Karchmer, M. A. (1977). School achievement scores of hearing impaired children: National data on achievement status and growth patters. *American Annals of the Deaf, 122,* 62–69.

Van Cleve, J. (1993). *Deaf history unveiled: Interpretations from the new scholarship.* Washington, D.C.: Gallaudet University Press.

Van Cleve, J., & Crouch, B. (1989). *A place of their own: Creating the Deaf Community in America.* Washington, D.C.: Gallaudet University Press.

Vernon, M., & Andrews, J. (1990). *The psychology of deafness.* New York: Longman.

Wink, J. (2000). *Critical pedagogy: Notes from the real world* (2nd ed.). New York: Addison Wesley Longman.

Woodward, J. (1982). *How you gonna get to heaven if you can't talk to Jesus?* Silver Spring, MD: T.J. Publishers.

Woodward, J., & Allen, T. (1987). Classroom use of ASL by teachers. *Sign Language Studies, 54*, 1–10.

15 "What About Poor White People?"

Ricky Lee Allen

I have been teaching about Whiteness at the university level since 1997. As a veteran of antiracist[1] education, I have become quite familiar with the highly predictable White responses to my (and others') critique of White privilege. White responses typically contain racialized sayings or phrases that are common to White subjectivity. For example, when I talk with nonpoor Whites[2] about White racism as a structural phenomenon that gives all Whites psychological and material advantages, their common refrain is "What about poor White people?" The first time I heard this from a nonpoor White person I was surprised. Growing up around poor Whites (see note 1), I had heard *them* raise this question with one another in discussions about race. But I did not expect *nonpoor* Whites to do the same, especially in a way that seemed to express concern for poor Whites. I was skeptical about their concern because in my own experience I had never known nonpoor Whites to show any serious commitment to ending poverty for poor Whites. Instead, experience told me that nonpoor Whites look down on poor Whites. So this sudden outpouring of concern for poor Whites was perplexing to me.

Out of all the different tactics that nonpoor Whites use to avoid responsibility for their White privilege, "What about poor White people?" is the one that I think about the most, maybe because I grew up as a poor White person, or maybe because I have long thought that it says more about the workings of race in the United States than most people realize. Time after time, nonpoor White education students interject "What about poor White people?" into the conversation when the subject of White privilege is on the table. Yet, they are otherwise curiously silent about the plight of poor Whites both before and after uttering this phrase. It is as though nonpoor Whites think that there is no need to talk about poor Whites unless Whiteness is the main topic of discussion. What this suggests to me is that nonpoor Whites' evocation of poor Whites through the phrase "What about poor White people?" warrants further examination because it appears to be a type of self-interested racial tactic.

In my earlier years of antiracist teaching, I reacted to "What about poor White people?" as if it was just one more of those sayings, or "semantic moves"[3] (Bonilla-Silva, 2003; Bonilla-Silva & Embrick, 2006), that we White people use to avoid the spotlight of racial criticism. Even though the phrase really bothered me, I minimized my gut feeling and considered "What about poor White people?" to be functionally similar to other problematic racial sayings like "I don't see color" or "Everyone gets an equal chance in America." To me, they were all semantic moves that prevented Whites from having to deal with the realities of racial injustice in a system of White supremacy.

However, in more recent years I have come to believe that this one particular semantic move is categorically different from the others that nonpoor Whites employ in that its rhetoric is as much *intraracial*[4] as interracial. In fact, it is one of the few semantic moves nonpoor Whites use that contains overtly intraracial language. It enters into the conversation the notion of a different kind of Whiteness (i.e., poor Whites) in order to make a point about the alleged inadequacy of critical race analyses for identifying and understanding the social and economic differences between Whites and people of color. The implication is that privilege cannot be assigned to all members of a particular group because some members of that group, in this case poor Whites, are not privileged. There-fore, privilege must be considered at the level of the individual, not the group. Since non-poor Whites are usually not really concerned about poor Whites, most nonpoor Whites who use this phrase are actually suggesting that they should be treated as individuals and not assigned White privilege simply because they are White. If these nonpoor Whites were more direct, they would ask instead, "How do you know me well enough to know that I am privileged?"

But they are not more direct because "What about poor White people?" does more than express a desire for an individualistic notion of racism. It also signifies that poor and nonpoor Whites share a close bond; nonpoor Whites stand up for poor Whites when poor Whites are not around to represent themselves. But do poor and nonpoor Whites actually interact with one another in a positive and unified way? Are nonpoor Whites really acting in the interest of poor Whites when they use "What about poor White people?" Do poor and nonpoor Whites share a hidden or normalized social bond that prevents us from better understanding the significance and ramifications of "What about poor White people?"

As I argue in this chapter, the signification of poor Whites by nonpoor Whites provides a window into the internal political organization[5] of the White race, which has yet to be adequately theorized in race-based terms. Toward this end, my hope is to shed light on the internal machinations of the White race by looking at the hegemonic[6] alliance that exists between poor and nonpoor Whites. Although this alliance has tremendous strength and is arguably the primary mortar holding together White supremacist structure, it has a number of cracks and crevices that need to be exposed and widened in the hope of bring-ing the whole structure crashing down. In other words, political alliances, such as the alliance that holds together what we know as the White race, can be undone in ways that work towards real social justice.[7] Garvey and Ignatiev (1997) make an important critique when they say,

> The "social construction of race" has become something of a catchphrase in the academy, although few have taken the next step. Indeed, we might say that until now, philosophers have merely interpreted the white race; the point is to abolish it. (p. 346)

If a race can be made, then it can also be unmade. Understanding how the White race is held together is the first step toward the ultimate goal of breaking it apart so as to disassemble the political alliances that keep White supremacy in place. Thus, it is my belief that a critical examination of "What about poor White people?" can add a new dimension to the ongoing debate around the most accurate and strategic way to theorize the intersection between race and class in the United States.

I teach in the field of education. Most of my students are (future) teachers or aspiring education scholars. The majority of these students are White, much like the U.S. teacher workforce. Data gathered in 2001 by the National Center for Educational Statistics shows that 90% of all public school teachers in the United States are White (National Collab-orative on Diversity in the Teaching Force, 2004). While I am most disturbed by and focused on the problematic beliefs that my White students hold about students of color, I am also highly troubled by the problematic beliefs that my nonpoor White students hold about poor Whites, which they will take with them to the classroom or research site. Therefore, another goal of this chapter is to look at the social justice implications of poor and nonpoor White relations for poor White students. For example, how does "What about poor White people?" perpetuate pedagogical approaches that see the poor White student as someone who does not have privilege relative to people of color or as someone who is more racist than nonpoor Whites? How does a lack of attention to the racialization of poor Whites work toward reproducing the racial order that encompasses us all? How does the racialization of poor Whites shape the politics of their schooling? And, how should an antiracist education for poor Whites be conceptualized? Drawing from my critique of what I am calling the *White hegemonic alliance* (which I describe later in this chapter), I will address these questions and outline a social and political context of schooling for poor Whites that takes into account the dynamics of the White hegemonic alliance.

Occasionally in this chapter, I will look at White Appalachians as my example of a poor White subgroup, mainly because as a group member I am more familiar with their history, experiences, and positionality.[8]

The Racial Politics of "What About Poor White People?"

For those of us who see the education of Whites as a vital component of the larger antiracist project, we need to closely examine what may seem at first glance to be "critical" responses to "What about poor White people?" For example, one could argue from a class-based perspective that race critique has its limitations in that although it can show us the construction of power and difference between racial groups it cannot shed light on the construction of power and difference within racial groups. What we would need, or so the logic goes, are class-based or Marxist analyses to sort out intraracial class hierarchies such as the one between poor and nonpoor Whites. The problem with this approach is that it implies that the racialization of White people is monolithic and there are no political struggles within the White race that could be explained by different yet related racialization processes for poor and nonpoor Whites. It assumes that race-based analyses have little or nothing to contribute to understanding and disrupting intraracial stratification. It also naturalizes and minimizes the racial alliance between poor and nonpoor Whites in that it only pays attention to their class-based public tensions (e.g., the exploitation of coalminers by mining corporations) and not their tacit race-based agreements (e.g., remaining silent about the normativity of White privilege). The inherent, teleological assumption being made is that poor and nonpoor Whites *should* be aligned, and class conflicts divert attention from the racial agreements that hold them together.

In the class-based approach, it is as if somehow those people we know as "White" were not politically and historically constructed; they are allegedly natural biological allies. This perspective wrongly assumes that somehow the amalgamation of the White racial polity out of various groups with different status levels had nothing to do with the construction of the "White race," its rise to power, and its persistence in domination. In other words, we must consider whether the initial and ongoing differences in power between subgroups that we now think of as White were and are essential to the life of the White racial polity. My assertion is that the White race *requires* an internal hierarchy in order for it to exist, meaning that those at the bottom of this hierarchy must be willing to submit to the authority of those on the top. I will come back to this point later in the chapter.

Coming from a Whiteness studies approach, another example of a seemingly critical response to "What about poor White people?" is that one could simply argue that all

Whites have more privilege than people of color, regardless of the White person's class status. So, there is no need to waste time distinguishing between poor and nonpoor Whites. This position is also problematic. Recent critical studies of Whiteness have tended to lump all Whites into one group monolithically privileged by Whiteness (e.g., McIntosh, 1997; McIntyre, 1997; Tatum, 2003). I believe that this trend arose—justifiably so—as a reaction to the difficulty of keeping folks, especially White folks, engaged in a sustained, transformative dialogue on Whiteness. I have heard numerous antiracist educators say that Whites often try to shift the conversation away from race and toward class when the focus is on Whiteness. They also say, and I would agree, that it is difficult to prevent the shift to class, especially when semantic moves like "What about poor White people?" are made. So, I do understand why an antiracist educator might simply avoid discussing the differences in structural privilege between poor and nonpoor Whites. But avoiding the reality of poor Whites' lower status relative to nonpoor Whites ultimately weakens the overall effort to create cross-racial solidarity and end White supremacy because an opportunity to expose and disrupt the troubling racial alliance between poor and nonpoor Whites is lost.

In the Whiteness studies approach, it is the avoidance of discussing poor Whites, both on the part of the educator and the students, that gives "What about poor White people?" much of its power. Although I agree that relative to people of color all Whites are privileged by a system of White supremacy, clearly White supremacy does not privilege all Whites equally (Heilman, 2004). And while class, culture, and language certainly operate to reproduce the multigenerational poverty of poor Whites, we are missing their racialization, which situates them in a different experiential realm and political position within the White group (Hartigan, 2004). Unless we unpack the racialization of poor Whites, we will fail to recognize that the power of the White group lies in the dominant subgroup's (i.e., nonpoor Whites') ability to maintain a tightly defended and seemingly natural allegiance among all group members. A critical understanding of the role of racialization in the formation of the White racial polity holds the key to opening the door to racial justice because it emphasizes the need to disrupt the unnatural solidarity of the White race so as to disband it.

To move beyond the limited analytical vision of undifferentiated-White-privilege versus Marxist-analysis-to-the-rescue, what I suggest is a critical race exegesis of "What about poor White people?" A critical race exegesis is an interpretation of a text or social phenomenon that is rooted in critical race theory (CRT). CRT is a relatively new way of making sense of the social world in explicitly racial terms (Allen, 2006; Delgado & Stefancic, 2001). While its more recent growth can be traced to legal studies, its roots go back at least to the work of W. E. B. DuBois (1868–1963) and Franz Fanon (1925–1961). As it has grown, it has also branched out into disciplines beyond legal studies. Scholars in various social science disciplines have taken up CRT in ways that take from, add to, and go beyond the theorization of CRT by legal scholars. In education, there are now numerous authors who participate in CRT scholarship (e.g., Delgado Bernal & Villalpando, 2002; Dixson & Rousseau, 2005; Ladson-Billings, 1999; Ladson-Billings & Tate, 1995; Love, 2004; Lynn, 1999; Parker & Stovall, 2004; Solorzano & Yosso, 2002; Tate, 1997; Taylor, 1999).

Limited space prevents me from giving an adequate overview of CRT.[9] However, a brief explanation of two general CRT tenets is important for the inquiry at hand. First and foremost, White supremacy is an endemic and structurally determining social system in which we all live (Allen, 2001, 2006; Bonilla-Silva, 1996, 2001). White supremacy is a system of oppression that both parallels and intersects with other systems of oppression, such as capitalism and patriarchy (Bonilla-Silva, 1996, 2001). This means that White supremacy is not subsumed within capitalism or patriarchy, but rather is a related yet distinct social system.

Second, CRT moves the definition of race beyond the older notion of a biologically defined group and the newer notion of a socially constructed group. Instead, CRT sees races as political constructions as opposed to the more passive, and politically neutral notion of a social construction (Mills, 1997). In this view, races are political groups, or polities, with particular political interests that derive in large part from their situatedness within White supremacist racial hierarchies (Mills, 1997). Race membership is based largely on racialized, and thus political, perceptions of the body, or what Fanon (1952/1967) referred to as "body schema." Racial group members act, consciously or not, as political representatives of their racial polity (Mills, 1997). In other words, races are seen as forms of human organization mired in group conflict over status and power.

At the top of the White supremacist hierarchy, the White racial polity is invested in its dominant status and will only give political concessions to people of color when they are pressured from multiple sides to do so and, most importantly, stand to benefit the most from what appears to many as racial progress for people of color. Bell (1980, 1992) calls this White supremacist phenomenon the "interest convergence principle." His primary example is the *Brown* decision in 1954. He argues that the Cold War with the Soviet Union and Black radicalism in the United States pressured White leaders to support ending formal segregation. On the international front, White America needed the support of "Third World" people of color in the fight against communism, but the U.S. system of racial apartheid scared away potential allies. On the domestic front, White America was feeling threatened by growing Black radical and communist movements (Bell, 1980). Although the *Brown* decision appeared to be a victory for people of color, White America gained a larger victory, ultimately, in achieving global domination and breaking apart the Soviet Union. Also, the *Brown* decision did little, if nothing, to disrupt the U.S. racial hierarchy. And once the Soviet Union broke apart, White America quickly turned against civil rights gains like affirmative action and bilingual education.

An exegesis of "What about poor White people?" that is rooted in CRT assumes that texts created by Whites must be scrutinized for their political race implications. As Leonardo (2002) argues, it is crucial that we "dismantle discourses of whiteness" by "disrupting...and unsettling their codes" (p. 31). Does a certain discursive text further the dominant status of Whites? Does it strengthen political alliances that maintain White power? Does it set the agenda, acting as a talking point for the White racial polity? When it comes to "What about poor White people?" I believe that the answer is "Yes" to all of these questions. Let me explain further.

On one level of analysis, it is fair to say that "What about poor Whites?" is less about nonpoor Whites' concern for poor Whites and more about their discomfort with their own Whiteness.[10] To avoid discomfort, they have learned that this semantic move can remove them from the spotlight of critique and accountability by shifting the discussion to a group that most "educated" folks have not spent much time thinking about: poor White people. Consequently, they avoid dealing in more positive ways with their pent up feelings of guilt and defensiveness (which nearly all Whites have, even those of us who think of ourselves as antiracist) emanating from their denial of the unearned privilege and status that a White supremacist social system affords them (Allen, 2004; Helms, 1993). Of course, this semantic move never leads to any serious discussion about why poor White people are poor because the speaker rarely has any serious interest in exploring the social, economic, and political situatedness of poor Whites. The speaker's greater concern seems to be about silencing the conversation on Whiteness. Once that happens, it is as if they see the issue of poor Whites as resolved.

Before moving on, I want to point out that indeed there are nonpoor Whites who appear to express genuine concern for poor Whites. Unfortunately, much of their discourse about poor Whites is scripted by a fundamental lack of understanding of the race-based problem at hand. These folks tend to come from a class-based perspective and do not seem to understand the importance of analyzing in structural terms the racialization of poor Whites. So despite the fact that a few of those who ask "What about poor Whites?" may really be concerned about poor Whites, it is my contention that despite their good intentions they are still guided by, consciously or not, a White supremacist ideology that works to not only maintain White domination over people of color but also, ironically, the domination of nonpoor over poor Whites.[11]

Also, I want to make it clear that examining the poverty of White people, especially the entrenched, generational poverty of certain White subcultures, is critical because poor Whites are *in a relational sense* oppressed people who do face institutional and everyday forms of dehumanization. Ignoring their situation leaves behind many potential antiracist allies who are in a position to disrupt the seemingly natural solidarity between poor and nonpoor Whites. In *Racism Without Racists*, Bonilla-Silva (2003) says that in his study of White people's racial beliefs working class White women were the ones most likely to exhibit signs of being racially progressive. In my experience as an antiracist educator, Whites who have grown up poor or working class have been much more likely than nonpoor Whites to embrace an antiracist agenda that places White supremacy at the center of critique. Though these examples do not qualify as definitive evidence, they do suggest that the commonsense notion that nonpoor Whites are more likely than poor Whites to be racially progressive may be erroneous and needs of further study.

One of the ways that poor Whites are dehumanized is through stereotypes. Many of the prevalent slurs used against them directly communicate their lower status in the White group. Yet, stereotypes of poor Whites are not the same as stereotypes of people of color. As Smith (2004) explains,

> Depictions of "rednecks" and "crackers" demean white (male) workers by endowing them with inherent brutality and ignorance; ironically, their sub-human state is also commonly signified by an irredeemably violent racism. This twisted racial logic does *not* mean, however, that white workers are actually victims of racism. Rather, their derogatory representation may be seen as a product of the disjuncture between their racial privilege and class disadvantage, which it serves to explain and legitimate. As whites degraded by class exploitation, they can never be quite white enough. As working-class whites, they must not be good enough to be truly white, i.e., self-evidently (by virtue of color) superior and deservedly privileged. (p. 46)

Although I agree that poor Whites are not the victims of racism, I disagree with the notion that their denigration stems primarily from class exploitation. Notions of race and the internal racial politics of the White race are also to blame. The "White but not quite"[12] positionality of poor Whites is perpetuated not just by attitudes toward their economic status or alleged cultural dysfunction but also by beliefs about their biological inferiority. To this day, there are many nonpoor Whites who believe that the generational poverty of White Appalachians is due to the role inbreeding has played in creating their allegedly damaged gene pool[13] (Smith, 2004). Beliefs about genetic inferiority have made their way into the media. Comedic actors on TV often portray White Appalachians who marry or have sex with their siblings or cousins, creating children with exaggerated birth defects.

Moreover, stereotypes of poor Whites are often rooted in racial notions. For example, negative images of poor Southern Whites' racism, backwardness, and biological corruption are often juxtaposed against images of the educated, genteel White Southerner who supposedly embodies civility and protects seemingly defenseless Blacks from the violent racism of poor Whites (Smith, 2004). In the 1996 film *A Time to Kill*, a trio of White lawyers, two Southern males and one Northern female, defend a Black man who killed the working-class Southern White men who raped his daughter. *A Time to Kill* conveys a common message that says educated White Southerners are the friends of people of color whereas uneducated poor White Southerners are their enemies. The film fails to depict any poor Whites in a positive light, as if somehow all poor White Southerners are incapable of antiracist thought and action. Consistent with the film's message, the over-the-top ending shows a huge mob of crazed, racist poor Whites shooting up the courthouse in protest of the defendant's acquittal. Meanwhile, the victorious lawyers are presented as the antiracist heroes, saving the South from poor Whites' racism one court case at a time.

While some poor White Southerners do in fact live out the stereotype of the uneducated, virulent racist, the problem is that portrayals of poor White Southerners by seemingly antiracist filmmakers leave nonpoor White Southerners looking as though they are the only members of the White group who work for racial progress. These images communicate to an audience that "redneck hillbillies" or "White trash" are the racists that people should despise the most, not nonpoor White Southerners, or for that matter, nonpoor Whites in general. The fact that White politicians, business people, educators, and policymakers from mostly nonpoor backgrounds have been the primary perpetrators of institutional and structural racism gets obscured. Poor Whites are hated more, even though they do not have as much institutional and economic power as nonpoor Whites. The point is that nonpoor White Southerners require a distortion of the image of poor White Southerners in order to distort their own image. In other words, they need a White "Other" in order to justify their sense of superiority. I am suggesting that the same is true for all nonpoor Whites. They necessitate an image of the racist poor White to pass themselves off as nonracist.

Given that nonpoor Whites are the main group that distorts the image of poor Whites, one would think that poor Whites would harbor a lot of animosity toward nonpoor Whites. Such is not the case. It is as if poor Whites do not care if they are depicted as crazed racists. In fact, they may have internalized this image of themselves, believing that it is true. My suspicion is that most poor Whites think that they are more racist than nonpoor Whites. However, I am not sure that they would admit it publicly. In my experience as an antiracist educator, rarely do poor White students make comments that suggest that they think nonpoor Whites are more racist than poor Whites. Yet, they rarely express the belief that they are more racist than nonpoor Whites. This does not necessarily mean that poor Whites do not believe that they are more racist. They might be embarrassed to admit what they really think. Nonpoor White students do not exhibit any turmoil over expressing who is the most racist. Without hesitation, they usually say that they are less racist than poor Whites. They say it as though it is commonsense. But commonsense can often mask reality. In this case, it can mask the truer beliefs of poor Whites, and maybe even nonpoor Whites. It can also mask the objective reality: nonpoor Whites are more racist in the sense that their elevated status means that they are in positions of greater power, which they can use to perpetuate or disrupt White supremacy. Research needs to be conducted that examines poor Whites' dispositions toward nonpoor Whites, and vice versa. In particular, researchers should look at how members of each group perceive their own level of racism as well as the other group's level of racism.

Although nonpoor Whites' depiction of poor Whites as virulent racists does not make poor Whites angry, nonpoor Whites' economic exploitation of poor Whites has created animosity. For example, many White Appalachians have a general distrust of wealthy White people due to centuries of economic exploitation by Northeastern corporations. I know that I was raised to distrust business people, especially if they were strangers or worked for a corporation. I have also seen how coalmining companies have exploited some of my relatives, tossing them aside when they contracted black lung. I internalized this animosity even though I grew up in a small town in northern Indiana. My father's family had moved away from the mountains as part of the Appalachian migration to the Midwest after World War II (see note 2). I can only imagine the level of animosity that exists among White Appalachians that still reside in the mountains. Smith (2004) argues that nonpoor Whites sense White Appalachian's animosity, causing them to fear that White Appalachians might someday retaliate.

What this means is that nonpoor White perceptions of and interactions with poor Whites, particularly with members of subgroups like White Appalachians, are largely guided by a combination of fear (of retaliation) and revulsion (toward their genetic inferiority). Also, poor Whites seem to care about how they have been economically exploited, but their anger does not cause them to want to break free of the White group. Instead, they want to be more respected White people, in the eyes of nonpoor Whites, as opposed to leaving the White group altogether.

Although poor Whites experience systemic dehumanization, they are as much oppressors as they are the oppressed. They are invested in Whiteness and receive the benefits of White privilege, even if their returns on their investments are not as great as the returns for nonpoor Whites. Returning to the example of White Appalachians, it may be a surprise to some, as it was for me, that the field of Appalachian Studies has often depicted Appalachia as a place of racial innocence (Billings, Pendarvis, & Thomas, 2004), which is nearly the complete opposite of the more common image in popular media of Appalachia as a place of extreme racism. Appalachia Studies scholars have studied the region as if only poor Whites and coalmines inhabit it. Rarely is Appalachia discussed as a multiracial place[14] (Hayden, 2004). And even more rarely is the Whiteness of Appalachia considered an important arena of study (Smith, 2004). For example, critical studies of Whiteness in Appalachia are just beginning to systematically reveal why there are not more people of color living in Appalachia. In other words, Appalachia is mostly White for a reason. As Smith (2004) explains,

> If whites are the only people left in many parts of the region, then there are no "race relations," hence no enduring relevance to race. The contemporary predominance of whites in Appalachia becomes a benign demographic fact, rather than a product of active practices characterized in part by persistent white supremacy. Racial innocence is preserved. (p. 43)

The racial innocence narrative erases the fact that slavery existed in the mountain South. And after slavery ended, Kentucky created laws that made it difficult for Blacks to settle there (Smith, 2004). In the Tennessee cities of Knoxville and Chattanooga, laws "prohibited blacks from selling groceries and dry goods" (Smith, 2004, p. 43). These are two examples of the many ways that White supremacy created better opportunities for those raced as White by driving away competition from members of other racial groups, especially Blacks.

What I have discussed thus far is a pretext for understanding "What about poor White people?" Moving to a deeper level of critical race analysis, we need to look at how the racialization of poor Whites is part and parcel of their structural relationship with nonpoor Whites. To study racialization is to analyze "the social relations in order to comprehend how [racial] groups of people see other [racial] groups in relation to themselves and to each other" (Hartigan, 2004, p. 61). In the case of poor and nonpoor White relations, we also need to look at how intraracial perceptions, interactions, and identity politics reproduce the larger racial order, that is, the racial hierarchy of the U.S. White supremacist social system (Allen, 2007; Bonilla-Silva, 1996).

To better read "What about the poor Whites?" we need to consider the history of the formation of the U.S. White racial polity. After all, the White race has not always existed and its membership has changed over time. One fundamental question seems to guide much of the study of poor Whites and the making of the White race: Why have poor Whites seemingly gone against their own economic interests by siding with higher-status members of the White race and not people of color?

One answer is that nonpoor Whites wanted assistance in repressing the large numbers of Native and African people, groups that Whites considered to be not just as inferior people but also as political and economic adversaries who must be controlled. In the early 1800s, White leaders saw what happened to French colonialists and slaveholders in the Haitian Revolution (1791–1804) and that drove them to seek out and bring in more Whites from Europe to act as a buffer against a similar slave revolt in the United States (DuBois, 1935). The Whites they brought in by the millions were most often members of lower-status European ethnic groups, such as the Irish, Slavs, Jews, and southern Europeans (DuBois, 1935; Jacobson, 1998). Since the history of White supremacy suggests that the White racial polity operates in a self-interested way, I am curious about why U.S. nonpoor Whites would have brought in groups that they saw as inferior. U.S. nonpoor Whites must have perceived a threat to the normative order of White supremacy, such as the possibility of a slave revolt, and were therefore willing to open up the ranks of the White racial polity in order to preserve White domination.

But what did poor Whites, whether they were new immigrants or historically marginalized subgroups, have to gain from a political organization where they were not the top group within their own race? What was available to them in the United States was a multiracial White supremacist society where they could receive what DuBois (1935) called "the public and psychological wages of whiteness." In Europe, they were on the bottom of the social status ladder. In the United States, they were not. White supremacy created a White opportunity structure where the wages of Whiteness were doled out in both de jure and de facto ways (DuBois, 1935; Roediger, 1999). Nonpoor Whites gave these White immigrants—at least the males—certain voting and property rights not offered to others (Roediger, 1999). Also, poor Whites had the opportunity to rise up the economic and social status ladder in ways not open to people of color (Ignatiev, 1995; Jacobson, 1998; Sacks, 1994). And even though many of these Whites did not achieve the "American Dream" (i.e., middle-class status or higher), more poor Whites than people of color did "succeed," which must have reinforced in poor Whites the value of the White opportunity structure in a multiracial society (DuBois, 1935).

Although many poor Whites were not completely happy with this arrangement, as evidenced by their complaints about the limited permeability of the opportunity structure and what they saw as the privileges (i.e., food and shelter) enslaved Blacks received from their masters (DuBois, 1935), they understood that they occupied a higher social status than people of color (Roediger, 1999). I believe that this White supremacist context taught them that they were superior to people of color. In what had to have been a harsh and dangerous society for Blacks enduring enslavement and Indigenous people suffering land loss and genocide, my assumption is that nonpoor Whites' relative favoritism toward poor Whites must have solidified a hegemonic yet unequal alliance among poor and nonpoor Whites and made the stranglehold of the White racial polity over social and economic life in the United States that much greater. Both now and then, the politically interesting aspect of the hegemonic alliance between poor and nonpoor Whites is that while White privilege extends to all of those perceived as White some reap fewer benefits than others. Yet, the unequal rewards do not seem to deter those who get the least, that is, poor Whites, from being staunch defenders of a pro-White agenda.

In our contemporary context, I see "What about poor White people?" as a coded representation of the long-standing hierarchical and hegemonic alliance within the White racial polity. In this hegemonic alliance, poor Whites agree *not* to become race traitors and disrupt the normativity of a White supremacist system. In other words, they agree to support a skewed, racialized opportunity structure that gives them advantages over people of color (Mills, 1997). And, most importantly for the argument I am making here, they comply, whether actively or passively, with being used as the archetypal image of a racist, thus serving to deflect critical racial scrutiny away from those Whites who benefit the most from a White supremacist system, namely nonpoor Whites. Even those White Appalachians who are openly critical of and work against the consuming image of the "racist redneck" often do so in a way that does not name who the most institutionally powerful racists are, which if we follow this line of logic leaves us with the curious situation of having a racist social order but seemingly no racists. As I suggested earlier, too many poor Whites accept the notion that nonpoor Whites are less racist. In fact, I cannot recall a single time I have heard a poor White person say, "I wish those nonpoor Whites would not depict us as the poster-children of racism. They are the real racists, you know." I am not suggesting that poor Whites are not racist. Poor Whites engage in both individual and systemic acts of racism against people of color and they rarely hold themselves accountable for their complicity with a White supremacist social system that most harms people of color. What I am suggesting is that when we say the phrase "racist" whose face is the first to pop-up in your head? And, why do I suspect that in the minds of most Whites, even poor Whites, it is not the face of a nonpoor White, such as a White soccer mom or White professor?

The benefit that dutiful poor Whites receive for playing the role of decoy is the current manifestation of the public and psychological wages of Whiteness. They receive race-based benefits that people of color do not receive (McIntosh, 1997; Oliver & Shapiro, 1997) for allowing themselves to be the distraction that is necessary for nonpoor Whites to evade a high level of scrutiny. Poor Whites would have to organize and publicly protest their depiction as the stereotype of the ultimate racist in order to change their current situation. They would have to join with people of color in denouncing White supremacy as a social system. In effect, they would have to be willing to commit "race suicide" in order to lose their White benefits and gain their humanity (Allen, 2004). But I do not believe that most poor Whites, at least at this juncture in history, are ready to even consider a commitment to end White supremacy; they are in a Weberian sense "rationally" invested in Whiteness (Bobo, 1983; Lipsitz, 1998). They can see how the game is stacked, and they have decided to play the mediocre hand they have been dealt rather than trying to change the game. Maybe poor Whites actually *are* acting in their economic interest, but selling their soul in the process.

What is the benefit of this hegemonic intraracial arrangement for nonpoor Whites? This question needs to be explored because why would higher-status Whites want to be aligned in any way with people they see as "backwards," "rednecks," "hillbillies," and "trailer trash"? After all, nonpoor Whites have defined Whiteness however they have wanted in order to suit their own political and economic interests (Haney Lopez, 1997). And they have been able to keep those perceived as non-European out of the White group.

So why would they not redefine "White" such that those "inferior" Whites are no longer considered White?

I think that the reason nonpoor Whites do not expel poor Whites from the White group is that the benefits of the White hegemonic alliance are even greater for those on the higher-status side. Extending DuBois' (1935) framework for thinking critically about poor Whites and nonpoor Whites, my argument is that they gain a buffer group (i.e., poor Whites), a shield between themselves and people of color, and thus a divide and conquer victory. If we step outside of a monolithic view of the White group, we will see that nonpoor Whites need a political alliance with some large part of the population so as to protect their unearned wealth and status against the political force of those who wish to have a more equitable and humanizing situation (e.g., many people of color). They desperately want to avoid becoming equals, let alone subordinates, to people of color. In short, Whiteness itself, as a form of racialized property with high market value, has been offered to poor Whites throughout the history of the U.S. as a political quid pro quo (Harris, 1995; Roediger, 1999).

If there is one novel point I am making in this chapter it is this: higher-status, nonpoor Whites will never want all Whites to be economically equal because there would be no device left to divert attention away from the racism and White racial privilege of nonpoor Whites. To reiterate, nonpoor Whites need a White other who is at once a stereotype of the ultimate racist and a dutiful ally in the White hegemonic alliance. For poor Whites, "ultimate racist" and "dutiful White ally" have become two sides of the same coin, each side working in dialectical relation with the other side to create poor Whites' social identity and political positionality. Together, the two sides of the coin work to elevate the intraracial status of nonpoor Whites. In other words, nonpoor Whites would no longer be able to say "What about poor White people?" if all Whites were nonpoor and considered equally nonracist; in other words, if there were no poor White people. Nonpoor Whites do not want to lose their White other because their White privilege would be too obvious. Although poor Whites would still be supporters of White supremacy in this scenario, people of color would have a more coherent target to organize against. *Therefore, poor Whites will never achieve social justice as long as they are practicing members of the White racial alliance.* Their investment in a unified White racial polity and unwillingness to meaningfully challenge the ultimate racist stereotype prevents cross-racial solidarity between themselves and people of color against the more absolute dominance of nonpoor Whites. Clearly, nonpoor Whites have much to gain by claiming that the situation of poor Whites is about class and not race.

Rather than having people of color do all of the antiracist work, we poor Whites need to be the ones who challenge nonpoor Whites during discussions about race when they ask, "What about poor White people?" I have seen too many poor Whites remain silent and let nonpoor Whites do the dirty work of the White hegemonic alliance, but sometimes we poor Whites join them in this semantic move and support more actively the White racial cause. And we do this because we think our interests are being served and to do otherwise, to speak out against the alliance, would be to commit a type of race treason that we seem to be unwilling to do because we fear losing our unearned and immoral benefits, even though the reward would be a more humanizing way of life. We need to break away from this White hegemonic alliance. In short, we need a divorce! (Not to mention, we need to find a healthier relationship!) I am not naïve about how difficult it would be to persuade poor Whites to speak out against the individual and collective racism of nonpoor Whites, take responsibility for their White privilege, and create meaningful, trusting, and powerful antiracist alliances with people of color. But, it is an antiracist strategy that deserves serious consideration.

What About Poor White Students?

The major educational implication of my critique of "What about poor White people?" is that social justice approaches to teaching and researching poor White students need to pay attention to their racialization within the White racial polity and in relation to other racial groups. Absent a curriculum that provides poor White students with an opportunity to unlearn their submission to nonpoor Whites, investment in Whiteness, and learned superiority relative to people of color, the future of poor Whites will most likely resemble their past since they will not be able to forge meaningful and transformative political alliances with people of color. A social justice approach would intervene in this cycle by empowering poor Whites to more forcefully challenge nonpoor Whites. But more importantly, they would first have to acknowledge and be accountable for their relative White privilege and investment in White supremacy. They would have to become solidary[15] in authentic ways with people of color by taking responsibility for their group privilege and gaining the trust of people of color (Allen, 2002, 2004). With poor Whites in alliance with people of color, the movement against nonpoor Whites' investment in White supremacy would be powerful and unlike anything seen before in the United States.

Unfortunately, we are far from achieving this vision. The White hegemonic alliance overdetermines the educational experiences of poor White students. Likewise, their schooling covertly, and sometimes overtly, teaches poor Whites to be agents in the perpetuation of White dominance. We should expect schooling to play a key role in reproducing the White hegemonic alliance. Since nonpoor Whites need poor Whites as their racial other, we should not expect most nonpoor Whites to work toward making sure poor Whites get a well funded, transformative, and antiracist education. To keep the alliance alive, poor Whites need to learn political complacency and internalize a sense of inferiority relative to nonpoor Whites. And their schooling facilitates this lesson.

Complacency is taught in a number of ways. Given that nonpoor Whites typically see White Appalachians as culturally corrupt (i.e., "rednecks," "trailer trash," and "hillbillies) or biologically damaged (i.e., "inbred"), we should expect most nonpoor White teachers, as well as poor White teachers who act, consciously or not, as supporters of the White hegemonic alliance, to see White Appalachian students from a deficit model. Referring to her research on White Appalachian students in the Midwest, Heilman (2004) reports,

> One elementary school principal, known for her support for progressive curriculum and multiculturalism quite unselfconsciously reported, "We have a big group of trailer trash in this school," when orienting a new group of preservice teachers. Similarly, an urban Indianapolis teacher insidiously confided, "These city hillbilly kids are the *real* bottom of the barrel, if you know what I mean." (p. 67)

Since stereotypes about poor White Appalachians abound, it is fair to assume that nonpoor White teachers internalize messages that say that the problems of poor White Appalachians are caused by dysfunctional families, violent neighborhoods, alcoholism, child abuse, teen pregnancy, virulent racism, welfare dependency, and so on.

With a deficit view firmly entrenched, it is hard to imagine that nonpoor White educators see White Appalachian students as possessing particular forms of knowledge, experience, and wisdom that are insightful and valuable. Moreover, it is doubtful that nonpoor White teachers see themselves as members of the group most responsible for creating the negative learning conditions for poor Whites and people of color. We should not expect then that nonpoor White teachers are teaching poor Whites ways of gaining a positive sense of self through learning how to challenge the White hegemonic alliance. This would go against the normative role that nonpoor White social actors are taught to play. Instead, we should expect nonpoor Whites to be teaching White Appalachian students as if they are just like all other White people, and we should expect them to chastise White Appalachians for not living up to the model of the "nonpoor White."

Of course, some White Appalachians, such as myself, will be seen as successful exceptions to the rule and used as examples to put down the others. Without a critical discourse to reveal the myth of the achievement ideology, a good many White Appalachians will experience self-hate and blame themselves or others of their group for their predicament. As a relative of mine once told me, "I tell my kids that if they study hard like Ricky then they will be successful." The reality is that I did not study hard in high school, mainly because I did not have to. Additionally, I seriously doubt that the quality and quantity of study habits explains why less than 10% of my nearly all White high school class went on to a four-year college. I think a better explanation is that we were taught relative to the norm of nonpoor Whites as the model of humanity and success. We were never engaged in discussions of what it meant to be poor Whites or Appalachian Whites. We were never taught about White privilege or how systemic racism affected people of color. Consequently I am sure that many of my classmates did not critically understand that they were being educated to fill their prescribed role in the White hegemonic alliance.

Despite the educational woes of poor Whites, it would be a mistake to suggest that poor Whites, such as White Appalachians, are in the same social and educational situation as students of color. This is not the case. Although poor White students are racialized, they are not "racial minorities." Since race operates as a castelike system, White Appalachians can pass into the middle-class, much as I have, in ways that people of color cannot because our bodies are perceived as White. Also, to say that White Appalachians are racial minorities is to grossly underestimate the current horrendous state of systemic and institutional racism in the United States and its consequences for people of color (Smith, 2004). Sometimes White educational scholars use the notion of White Appalachians as a racial minority in order to make the case that their oppression is equal to that of people of color. For example, Heilman (2004) discusses how White Appalachians are prone to joining overt White supremacist organizations. To keep them from joining groups like the KKK, she says that they should learn about processes of marginalization and injustice for various oppressed groups, not just White Appalachians. While I agree that they should learn about other oppressed groups, she goes too far when she says, "This understanding would instead promote solidarity and social action among different marginalized 'races'" (p. 77). The implication is that White Appalachians are one of the "marginalized races." While White Appalachians are surely marginalized, they do not constitute a separate race because they are seen as White regardless of their lower status within the White polity. With the exception of a few melungeons (see note 14), I do not know of any White Appalachians who have been asked, "What is your race?" In other words, actual social practice does not suggest that White Appalachians are seen as a separate race, or even a race within a race.

Sometimes, it seems to me that White scholars think that they have to show that poor Whites experience oppression that is close, if not equal, to that which people of color face in order for others to pay attention to their plight. But painting a false or overstated picture of reality can have the opposite effect by demonstrating a lack of accountability for White privilege, creating doubt about whether poor Whites are trustworthy in the minds of antiracist people of color. Ultimately this distances poor Whites from the antiracist imagination. As Smith (2004) states,

> The argument for hillbillies-as-an-oppressed-minority-whose-disparagement-exceeds-that-of-other-racial-groups pulls up the drawbridge even further, and guards Appalachian distinctiveness against the possibility that hillbilly stereotypes largely represent the ugly ideology of racism turned against poor and working class whites. (p. 51)

The benefits of being White and Appalachian are highly evident when looking at educational attainment. According to the 2000 Census, White Appalachians have significantly higher graduation rates than Appalachians of color. For White Appalachians, 77.5% have high school diplomas and 17.9% have college degrees. For Black Appalachians, 69.9% have high school diplomas and 12.2% have college degrees. For Hispanic Appalachians, 51.4% have high school diplomas and 13.0% have college graduation degrees (Shaw, DeYoung, & Rademacher, 2004). Assuming U.S. patterns hold for Appalachia, we could further speculate that the economic return for the degrees that Appalachians earn vary by race (and gender), meaning educational attainment disparities have an amplified material effect in the job market that makes the real benefits of White privilege that much greater (Fine, 1991).

I agree with Heilman's (2004) contention that educational researchers have overlooked the struggles of White Appalachian students. However, we need to be careful about how we explain this omission. Although groups like Blacks and Latinos are now often the object (for better or worse) of educational research, they used to be overlooked, too. The attention given to students of color is a recent historical phenomenon. It is not, as some may believe, a natural state of affairs but rather a contemporary construction that is in large part the result of organized social justice efforts to pressure researchers, educators, and policymakers to pay greater attention to students of color. If the educational struggles of people of color are "noticed" and not "hidden," it is because they have made themselves noticed, risking the wrath of White supremacy in an attempt to better their schooling experiences. And the risk is real. One could argue that Whites have in fact retaliated against people of color by creating a public discourse that depicts the problems of students of color as the result of their alleged cultural deficits, which in turn leaves White students looking superior.

The point is that if the struggles of poor Whites are hidden then it is due to their situatedness within the White hegemonic alliance. Poor Whites seem unwilling to create an organized social movement to bring to the public's attention the problems that poor White students face. I think that a major reason that they have not organized is that they do not want to anger nonpoor Whites and risk losing White benefits. Given the current racial climate, the only way that they might be willing to organize is if they claim that "reverse racism" is the reason that poor Whites have been overlooked. In other words, educational scholars' inattention to poor White groups such as White Appalachians is seen through a White supremacist ideology as a form of discrimination against White people. The reverse racism approach would perpetuate a pro-White politics and thus appease nonpoor Whites, but ultimately nonpoor Whites would undermine any gains for poor Whites that may derive from this strategy because they do not want to lose their White other. A more likely scenario is that groups like White Appalachians will continue with the status quo, meaning that their educational struggles will continue to be overlooked.

Poor Whites' learned sense of inferiority relative to nonpoor Whites is only half of the story. For the other half, we need to think about the benefits that poor Whites receive for not engaging in an antiracist social movement to change the dehumanizing education that they are offered. Through the hidden curriculum of Whiteness, poor Whites are taught a sense of superiority relative to people of color. Yet, they do not receive all of the benefits that nonpoor Whites get. Plus, nonpoor Whites often interact negatively with poor Whites. One would think that this would be enough to cause poor Whites to protest. But this has not happened on a broad, organized level. I do not believe that it is a natural characteristic of any group to silently accept mistreatment. There has to be coercion, persuasion, or some combination of the two to create a condition of complicity and complacency. My argument is that nonpoor Whites offer poor Whites an educational concession in order to keep the peace and maintain the White hegemonic alliance. While the education of poor Whites is denigrating, it cannot be so denigrating as to make poor Whites think that they would be better off if they were students of color. Currently, poor Whites do not believe that they are worse off than people of color. Sure, there are poor Whites who will say that they think affirmative action gives people of color an unfair advantage. But my sense is that these same folks do not really believe that they, as a group, are worse off than people of color, as a group. Just try asking a group of poor Whites if they would want to trade places *as a racial group* (not as individuals) with any other racial group, that is, White people would take on the racial situation of, say, Blacks. I doubt there would be any takers. I have never found any when I ask them this question. To be educated into the White hegemonic alliance, poor White students need to exit schooling believing that although they may have had it bad at least they have had it better than most Blacks and Latinos. And, my guess is that schooling is "successful" at instilling this belief in poor Whites, although an empirical study of this hypothesis is necessary and would be quite interesting.

It is also important for the maintenance of White supremacy that poor Whites leave school believing that their worldviews and knowledge systems are superior to those of people of color (Mills, 1997). Indeed, they must leave believing, at some level of consciousness, that they *are better people* than people of color. Although, as mentioned above, some White Appalachians feel victimized by affirmative action programs and other forms of so-called "reverse racism,"[16] it would be a mistake to think that their feelings of victimization have a positive correlation to feelings of inferiority relative to people of color. If there were a positive correlation, they would not feel so angry about "reverse racism" because they would have internalized that they belong in a lower status than people of color and taken a more complacent role, as they have relative to nonpoor Whites. Instead, what they are more likely to feel is that they are being cheated out of opportunities that should be rightfully theirs as faithful, superior White people. Anger is more likely to result from this psychosocial condition. Thus, poor Whites are more likely to blame people of color because they perceive people of color as inferior people who will allegedly squander scarce opportunities. Also, poor Whites are less likely to blame nonpoor Whites because they are perceived as a natural ally, even though poor Whites harbor conflicted feelings about nonpoor Whites' deceptiveness and superiority.

Although White Appalachians and other poor Whites are taught to feel superior to people of color through the hidden curriculum of Whiteness, educating against the White hegemonic alliance means that we need to stop seeing poor Whites as little more than racists in the making. Rather, they need to be seen as racialized subjects situated within both intraracial and interracial hierarchies. It is important to understand and create pedagogy around their racialization so as to maximize their social justice potential. They need to be seen as possible antiracist allies who, with the proper education, can transform their complicity with the White hegemonic alliance so as to not only better their own lot but also to better the lot of those who have even less social power.

We also need to avoid class-based approaches that see race as an empty ideology (Leonardo, 2005) and stop imagining poor Whites primarily, if not solely, as victims of capitalist exploitation. These class-based approaches do not take into account that White supremacy itself is an opportunity structure that Whites are invested in and are not going to give up easily because there are serious psychological and material benefits to being White, even to being a poor White. Class-based approaches say nothing about how the White hegemonic alliance operates through social institutions, such as schools, to maintain the U.S. racial order.

In "Walking the Dance: Teaching and Cross-Cultural Encounter," Gilbert Valadez (2004), a self-identified gay Latino, offers a powerful narrative about how he taught White Appalachians in a teacher education course. He writes candidly about how he had internalized the stereotype of the "racist hillbilly." The positive interactions he had with the students, which were partly fostered through the transformative pedagogy he brought to the classroom, changed his perception of White Appalachians. Reflecting upon the course, he says,

> I gained many insights into the lives of White Appalachians. Indeed, many of them live with injustice, prejudice, poverty, and pain. As time passed, the differences between us mattered less than did the process of coming to mutual understandings. Mostly, my students were able to conceptualize the notions of white identity and white privilege. They also were more able to articulate central issues surrounding inequity and inequality in education. (p. 163)

Valadez taught these students as people who occupy an in-between social status, that is, as both oppressor and oppressed. As White Appalachians, they occupied a lower social status than nonpoor Whites. Many had experienced material hardship and psychological trauma that needed to be shared, contextualized, and debated. They also occupied a higher social status than people of color. Valadez engaged them in critical dialogues about their White privilege and asked them to think about ways in which they contributed to a system of White racism. In other words, he did not see them solely as racist oppressors or solely as economic victims. Instead, what he offered was a humanizing pedagogy that reflected some of the complex realities of their social location.

That said, I do have a criticism of his approach. It can leave poor Whites with the misunderstanding that their oppressor position as Whites and their oppressed position as poor Whites are unrelated, or at least, vaguely related. If they are taught to believe that their oppression as poor Whites is due to their class status, as seemed to be the case in Valadez's classroom, then they have a less likely chance of understanding how their alliance with nonpoor Whites oppresses and dehumanizes not only people of color but also themselves. They may still believe that their membership in the White race is a natural and permanent condition. Poor White students need to learn about how the White hegemonic alliance functions, what their role in it has been, and what they can do to end it.

A critical race pedagogy of the White hegemonic alliance must be directly and explicitly taught. Indirect attempts to teach about it are likely to fail. Poor Whites need to see how nonpoor Whites are not just the main beneficiaries of a capitalist system but also of a White supremacist system. Although they certainly need to learn how to unlearn their investment in White domination, they also need to be able to differentiate between how they participate in a White supremacist system versus how nonpoor Whites participate in a White supremacist system. They need to talk with one another about how to break away from nonpoor Whites and how to form solidary relations with people of color. They need to figure out how to muster the courage to confront both the racism and classism of nonpoor Whites. Their loyalty to Whiteness is a dehumanizing condition that requires intervention. As Garvey and Ignatiev (1997) say, "Treason to whiteness is loyalty to humanity." A critical race pedagogy of the White hegemonic alliance should help poor Whites gain their humanity by learning how to be disloyal to the White race and loyal to the antiracist project, and thus, to humanity itself. In short, I am saying that poor Whites should be taught to be effective race traitors.

Conclusion

Nowadays, I react differently when a nonpoor White person asks, "What about poor White people?" I spend a lot of time talking about the workings of the White hegemonic alliance, and I believe that I have become a more effective antiracist educator as a result. I am now able to disarm "What about poor White people?" and turn it into a teachable moment. My hope is that the unveiling of the White hegemonic alliance becomes a focus of the field of social justice education. For social justice education to play an effective role in abolishing White supremacy, it needs to be able to transform poor Whites into race traitors. It needs to be bold enough to seek to dismantle the White race. Some may argue that we can retain the races so long as there are no power differences between them. But as I have argued, races are politically constructed groups. The White race cannot be salvaged because the real problem is how it is constructed. The only real way to abolish White supremacy is to dismantle the coalition of subgroups that comprise the White race. Although Whites' investment in White power and privilege is a serious concern that deserves the attention of social justice educators, the deeper issue is Whites' investment in the White hegemonic alliance.

Acknowledgments

I would like to thank Dr. Annette Henry for her insightful suggestions.

Notes

1. Racism is an ideology that works to perpetuate a social system of racial domination, which in the United States means domination by those raced as White (Bonilla-Silva, 1996). The racialized social system endemic to the United States is White supremacy. Although White people are most responsible for White supremacy, people of color may also support White supremacy through internalized racism (i.e., a learned sense of inferiority about one's own racial identity or racial group) and interethnic racism (i.e., a learned sense of superiority relative to another non-White race). The term *antiracist* refers to those efforts that seek to undo White supremacy by transforming White racism, internalized racism, and interethnic racism.

2. It would take a whole chapter to sort through the debates around how to define "poor" and "nonpoor" Whites, not to mention my reasons for using "poor" and "nonpoor" versus "working class," "middle class," and "upper class." Instead, I offer here a brief description of my position. By using "nonpoor" in a U.S. context, I am primarily referring to upper-, middle-, and even some working class Whites who were raised in nonpoor families. A key point is that not all working class Whites are poor, or are imagined as poor. One reason that I am using the term *poor* is that it is the word contained in the phrase that I am critiquing. I think that the use of the term *poor* is purposeful. My assumption is that when people use the phrase "What about poor White people?" they are referring to all of those Whites who are poor and not necessarily all of those who are working class. So, the term *poor* for me is more contextually precise, even though it may be difficult, if not impossible, to define an exact dividing line between who is or is not poor. That said, it is important not to be paralyzed by debates over the imprecision of the term. My preference is to proceed with a definition that

may in fact be dichotomous and incomplete, but it at least provides a starting point to begin the larger discussion of the relations between poor and nonpoor Whites that perpetuate White supremacy. Moving to a working definition, nonpoor White families have little or no experience with multigenerational poverty. They or their families have wealth levels closer to the norm for most Whites. The more difficult subgroups to categorize are White immigrant families, such as those from the former Soviet Union, who might experience a lack of wealth and income for the first generation or two, but ultimately they may become mostly nonpoor as they assimilate into a U.S. construct of Whiteness, as was the case previously for many Jews, Irish, and Slavs. In other words, for some White immigrants we do not yet have any evidence that their condition persists over time, meaning that they may or may not experience *on a group level* a condition of multigenerational poverty, making it unclear whether they fit the definition of nonpoor. Conversely, "poor" Whites are those people who come from families and communities that have experienced entrenched, multigenerational poverty, such as that experienced by many White Appalachians.

3. Bonilla-Silva (2003) describes semantic moves as the "linguistic manners and rhetorical strategies," or more simply as the "race talk," of a racial ideology. Semantic moves are stylistic maneuvers used during dialogical moments of ideological conflict in an attempt to gain legitimacy for the racial ideology supported by the speaker. They are ideological performances that, if considered effective, are repeated time and time again by multiple actors as they are passed from one ideological subscriber to another.

4. "Intraracial" refers to social phenomena that occur between individuals or subgroups within a particular race whereas "interracial" refers to social phenomena that occur between different racial groups or between individuals of different racial groups.

5. "Political organization" refers to the way in which power and status are created within a social identity group, in this case the White race. Through a complex web of conflicts and alliances between subgroups, the whole group achieves cohesion and social power, even as power and status are hierarchically arranged on an internal (or in this case, intraracial) level.

6. "Hegemonic" is an adjective used to describe those phenomena that contribute to a system of hegemony. Allen (2002) defines hegemony as "a social condition in which relationships of domination and subordination are not overtly imposed from above, but are part of consensual cultural and institutional practices of both the dominant and the subordinate" (p. 106). A hegemonic alliance is a political bond formed between dominant and subordinate groups. Consciously or not, the subordinate group participates in the perpetuation of its own lower status by going along with beliefs and behaviors that maintain the hegemonic system and thus the higher status of the dominant group. Hegemony works more on the level of ideological control than repressive force.

7. "Social justice" refers to a societal condition that is egalitarian and humanizing because it is free from oppressive structures such as White supremacy, patriarchy, heterosexism, and capitalism. Also, the term implies that such a society does not currently exist and efforts must be made to work toward a socially just society.

8. I think of myself as both an insider and outsider to the White Appalachian group. I feel like an outsider in that I did not grow up in Appalachia. Instead, I grew up in a small town in northern Indiana called Medaryville. My father is from Appalachia, and like many others his family moved to Indiana during the mid-1900s to look for better job opportunities. I also have come to feel like an insider as I learn more and more about how my Appalachian heritage has shaped my views and experiences. In the town where I am from, there were many families that had moved there from Appalachia. The non-Appalachian kids looked down on us because we spoke differently and did not have much money. They called us the "Grits."

9. See Richard Delgado and Jean Stefancic's (2001) *Critical Race Theory: An Introduction* for a good overview of CRT.

10. Whereas White supremacy is a social *system* that perpetuates White domination, Whiteness is a social *identity* that shapes and is shaped by White supremacy. As a social identity, Whiteness is a form of individual and collective self-presentation. It is the meaning made from the

experience of being a White person and a member of a White group as well as a particular way of being in the world. Like Blackness or Asianness, Whiteness is not a monolithic form of expression and being, though definite patterns of subjectivity and behavior exist. Many Whites are ashamed of their Whiteness because they have learned to be defensive or guilty about White privilege. They have not yet learned how to model their Whiteness after antiracist Whites who offer a more socially and politically positive way of being White in a White supremacist system (Helms, 1993; Tatum, 2003), though this is an intermediate stage since, as I argue in this chapter, the ultimate goal is to disband the White race altogether.

11. From recent work in sociology we know that race is critical for understanding wealth and class in the United States since the average White household has nearly ten times the net financial assets as the average Black household (Oliver & Shapiro, 1997). In fact, even working-class Whites have, on average, more accumulated wealth than middle-class Blacks (Oliver & Shapiro, 1997). In other words, terms like *working class* are deceptive in that they more accurately signify income, job status, and educational attainment rather than the more crucial aspect of wealth. Thus, there are large wealth gaps between, say, the White working class and the Black working class that get erased when the two are referred to as being of the same "class."

12. I think phrases like "never be White enough," "not quite White," "not fully White," or "not truly White" are problematic in that they do not make it clear that poor Whites are in fact Whites who receive White benefits. Using phrases that depict their White status as only partial can create a slippery slope to where they are constructed by some as non-White since they are "not fully White." But by saying "White but not quite," as I am suggesting, their status as Whites is indexed from the beginning because "White" is the first word. Then "but not quite" references their lower social status within the White group. There is also the problem of confusion with terminology used to describe individuals or groups of color who really do lie on the borderline between being seen as White or as a person of color (e.g., light-skinned Latinos or some multiracials with White heritage). Some may refer to these folks as "not quite White" or "not fully White" because they are perceived as having non-European heritage or features that negate their claim to Whiteness.

13. Alleged genetic inferiority is depicted differently for poor Whites and people of color. For poor Whites, their genetic inferiority is depicted as the result of "good genes gone bad" due to inbreeding and isolation in the mountains. In other words, this type of racist logic assumes that their genetic stock was originally good because it was European but dysfunction and corruption ruined it. For people of color, their genetic makeup is depicted as inherently inferior because they have been perceived historically by Whites as less evolved subpersons. In other words, their genetic makeup was never good, or so the racist "logic" goes.

14. Blacks, Indigenous peoples, Hispanics/Latinos, and mixed-race or "melungeon" folks also inhabit Appalachia. Overall, people of color makeup 11.2% of the Appalachian population (Hayden, 2004). Although race relations in Appalachia have not received enough academic attention, the recent interest in interracialism promises to make race relations a more vital area of interest in Appalachian Studies. The history of race mixture in Appalachia is not widely known. The mixed-race people of Appalachia are often referred to as "melungeons." Melungeons typically have Black, Indigenous, and European ancestry. Many melungeons are accepted as White, although those with darker pigmentation are more likely to be subject to racist ridicule and seen as having a lower status. My own family, on my father's side, is melungeon. Our ancestry includes people who were African, Indigenous, and European. With a couple of exceptions, most of us look White, identify as White, and are treated as White. The existence of melungeons calls into question notions of White racial purity in Appalachia. Also, it would be interesting to look into how Whiteness became constructed in Appalachia given the historical presence of race mixture.

15. "Solidary" is a state of being in solidarity with others. Those who are solidary share common political interests and goals and take part in communal responsibilities.

16. The concept of "reverse racism" against Whites is highly problematic since it is not supported by data (James, 1995).

References

Allen, R. L. (2001). The globalization of white supremacy: Toward a critical discourse on the racialization of the world. *Educational Theory, 51*(4), 467–485.

Allen, R. L. (2002). Wake up, Neo: White consciousness, hegemony, and identity in *The Matrix*. In J. Slater, S. Fain, & C. Rossatto (Eds.), *The Freirean legacy: Educating for social justice* (pp. 104–125). New York: Peter Lang.

Allen, R. L. (2004). Whiteness and critical pedagogy. *Educational Philosophy and Theory, 36*(2), 121–136.

Allen, R. L. (2006). The race problem in the critical pedagogy community. In C. Rossatto, R. L. Allen, & M. Pruyn (Eds.), *Reinventing critical pedagogy: Widening the circle of anti-oppression education* (pp. 3–20). Lanham, MD: Rowman & Littlefield.

Allen, R. L. (2007, April). *Schooling in white supremacist America: How schooling reproduces the racialized social system*. Paper presented at the annual meeting of the American Education Research Association, Chicago, Illinois.

Bell, D. (1980). *Brown v. Board of Education* and the interest-convergence dilemma. *Harvard Law Review, 93*(3), 518–533.

Bell, D. (1992). *Faces at the bottom of the well: The permanence of racism*. New York: Basic Books.

Billings, D., Pendarvis, E., & Thomas, M. K. (2004). From the editors. *Journal of Appalachian Studies, 10*(1–2), 3–6.

Bobo, L. (1983). Whites' opposition to busing: Symbolic racism or realistic group conflict? *Journal of Personality and Social Psychology, 45*(6), 1196–1210.

Bonilla-Silva, E. (1996, June). Rethinking racism: Toward a structural interpretation. *American Sociological Review, 62*, 465–480.

Bonilla-Silva, E. (2001). *White supremacy and racism in the post-civil rights era*. Boulder, CO: Lynne Rienner.

Bonilla-Silva, E. (2003). *Racism without racists*. Lanham, MD: Rowman & Littlefield.

Bonilla-Silva, E., & Embrick, D. (2006). Racism without racists: "Killing me softly" with color blindness. In C. Rossatto, R. L. Allen, & M. Pruyn (Eds.), *Reinventing critical pedagogy: Widening the circle of anti-oppression education* (pp. 21–34). Lanham, MD: Rowman & Littlefield.

Brown v. Board of Education, 3247 U.S. 483 (1954).

Delgado, R., & Stefancic, J. (2001). *Critical race theory: An introduction*. New York: New York University Press.

Delgado Bernal, D., & Villalpando, O. (2002). An apartheid of knowledge in academia: The struggle over the "legitimate" knowledge of faculty of color. *Equity & Excellence in Education, 35*(2), 169–180.

Dixson, A., & Rousseau, C. (2005). And we are still not saved: Critical race theory in education ten years later. *Race, Ethnicity and Education, 8*(1), 7–27.

DuBois, W. E. B. (1935). *Black Reconstruction in America (1860–1880)*. New York: Simon & Schuster.

Fanon, F. (1967). *Black skin, white masks* (C. L. Markmann, Trans.). New York: Grove Press. (Original work published 1952)

Fine, M. (1991). *Framing dropouts: Notes on the politics of an urban high school*. Albany, NY: SUNY Press.

Garvey, J., & Ignatiev, N. (1997). Toward a new abolitionism: A race traitor manifesto. In M. Hill (Ed.), *Whiteness: A critical reader* (pp. 346–349). New York: New York University Press.

Haney Lopez, I. (1997). *White by law: The legal construction of race* (rev. ed.). New York: New York University Press.

Harris, C. (1995). Whiteness as property. In K. Crenshaw, N. Gotanda, G. Peller, & K. Thomas (Eds.), *Critical race theory: The key writings that formed the movement* (pp. 276–291). New York: New Press.

Hartigan, J. (2004). Whiteness and Appalachian studies: What's the connection? *Journal of Appalachian Studies, 10*(1–2), 58–72.

Hayden, W., Jr. (2004). Appalachian diversity: African-American, Hispanic/Latino, and other populations. *Journal of Appalachian Studies, 10*(3), 293–306.

Heilman, E. (2004). Hoosiers, hicks, and hayseeds: The controversial place of marginalized ethnic whites in multicultural education. *Equity & Excellence in Education, 37*(1), 67–79.

Helms, J. (1993). *Black and white racial identity.* Westport, CT: Praeger.

Ignatiev, N. (1995). *How the Irish became white.* New York: Routledge.

Jacobson, M. (1998). *Whiteness of a different color: European immigrants and the alchemy of race.* Cambridge, MA: Harvard University Press.

James, C. E. (1995). "Reverse racism": Students' response to equity programs. *Journal of Professional Studies, 3*(1), 48–54.

Ladson-Billings, G. (1999). Preparing teachers for diverse student populations: A critical race theory perspective. *Review of Research in Education, 24,* 211–247.

Ladson-Billings, G., & Tate, W. (1995). Toward a critical race theory of education. *Teachers College Record, 97*(1), 47–68.

Leonardo, Z. (2002). The souls of white folk: Critical pedagogy, whiteness studies, and globalization discourse. *Race, Ethnicity and Education, 5*(1), 29–50.

Leonardo, Z. (2005). Through the multicultural glass: Althusser, ideology and race relations in post-civil rights America. *Policy Futures in Education, 3*(4), 400–412.

Lipsitz, G. (1998). *The possessive investment in whiteness: How white people profit from identity politics.* Philadelphia: Temple University Press.

Love, B. (2004). *Brown* plus 50 counter-storytelling: A critical race theory analysis of the "majoritarian achievement gap" story. *Equity & Excellence in Education, 37,* 227–246.

Lynn, M. (1999). Toward a critical race pedagogy: A research note. *Urban Education, 33*(5), 606–626.

McIntosh, P. (1997). White privilege and male privilege. In R. Delgado & J. Stefancic (Eds.), *Critical white studies: Looking behind the mirror* (pp. 291–299). Philadelphia: Temple University Press.

McIntyre, A. (1997). Constructing an image of a white teacher. *Teachers College Record, 98*(4), 653–681.

Mills, C. (1997). *The racial contract.* Ithaca, NY: Cornell University Press.

National Collaborative on Diversity in the Teaching Force. (2004, October). *Assessment of diversity in America's teaching force: A call to action.* Washington, D.C.: Author.

Oliver, M., & Shapiro, T. (1997). *Black wealth/white wealth: A new perspective on racial inequality.* New York: Routledge.

Parker, L., & Stovall, D. (2004). Actions following words: Critical race theory connects to critical pedagogy. *Educational Philosophy and Theory, 36*(2), 167–182.

Roediger, D. (1999). *Wages of whiteness: Race and the making of the American working class* (Rev. ed.). New York: Verso.

Sacks, K. B. (1994). How did Jews become white folks? In S. Gregory & R. Sanjeck (Eds.), *Race* (pp. 78–102). New Brunswick, NJ: Rutgers University Press.

Shaw, T. C., DeYoung, A. J., & Rademacher, E. W. (2004). Educational attainment in Appalachia: Growing with the nation, but challenges remain. *Journal of Appalachian Studies, 10*(3), 307–329.

Smith, B. E. (2004). De-gradations of whiteness: Appalachia and the complexities of race. *Journal of Appalachian Studies, 10*(1–2), 38–57.

Solorzano, D., & Yosso, T. (2002). A critical race counterstory of race, racism, and affirmative action. *Equity & Excellence in Education, 35*(2), 155–168.

Tate, W. F. (1997). Critical race theory in education: History, theory, and implications. *Review of Research in Education, 22,* 195–250.

Tatum, B. D. (2003). *"Why are all the Black kids sitting together in the cafeteria?" and other conversations about race* (5th ed.). New York: Basic Books.

Taylor, E. (1999). Critical race theory and interest convergence in the desegregation of higher education. In L. Parker, D. Deyhle, & S. Villenas (Eds.), *Race is...race isn't: Critical race theory and qualitative studies in education* (pp. 181–204). Boulder, CO: Westview Press.

Valadez, G. (2004). Walking the dance: Teaching and cross-cultural encounter. *Journal of Appalachian Studies, 10*(1–2), 152–166.

16 Reading Whiteness
Antiracist Pedagogy Against White Racial Knowledge

Zeus Leonardo

In studies of race, the idea that Whites do not know much about race is generally accepted. By virtue of their life experiences, White students and teachers are portrayed as subjects of race without much knowledge of its daily and structural features (Dalton, 2002; Kincheloe & Steinberg, 1997; McIntosh, 1992; McIntyre, 1997). It has been suggested that Whites do not grow up with a race discourse, do not think of their life choices in racial ways, and do not consider themselves as belonging to a racial group. Gary Howard (1999) puts it best when he suggests that Whites "can't teach what they don't know," an appropriation of a statement from Malcolm X to mean that White educators cannot teach about race if they do not have knowledge of it. As a result of this oblivion and apparent lack of race knowledge, many White educators and researchers avoid studying racialization because "Race is not 'their' project" (Greene & Abt-Perkins, 2003), a sentiment that Aanerud (1997) rejects when she claims that race affects and is fundamental to all our lives, including White lives. The challenge is often posed as the transformation of Whites into knowledgeable people about race.

Arguing that Whites are initially ignorant of race is helpful within certain parameters because it exposes their nonchalance and lack of urgency about its processes. Taken too far, it has unintended, but problematic consequences, one of which is that it promotes the "innocence" of Whites when it comes to the structures of race and racism. It constructs them as almost oblivious to the question of race and therefore obscures their personal and group investment in Whiteness (Lipsitz, 1998), as if racial oppression happens behind their backs rather than on the backs of people of color (Leonardo, 2005). This essay, however, argues that Whites do know a lot about race in both its everyday sense as a lived experience and its structural sense as a system of privilege. It attempts to "make race visible" (Greene & Abt-Perkins, 2003), with the specific goal of "making Whiteness visible." A critical reading of Whiteness means that White ignorance must be problematized, not in order to expose Whites as simply racist but to increase knowledge about their full participation in race relations. It also means that the racial formation must be read into the practices and texts that students and teachers negotiate with one another (Harris, 1999) as a move to affirm educators' power to question narratives that have graduated to common sense or truth (Bishop, 2005), like the "fact" of White racial ignorance.

That Whites enter race discourse with a different lens than people of color, such as a "color-blind" discourse (Leonardo, 2006; Schofield, 2001), sometimes called "new racism" (Bonilla-Silva, 2005), "laissez-faire racism" (Bobo & Smith, 1998), or "symbolic racism" (Kinder & Sears, 1981), should not be confused with the idea that Whites lack racial knowledge. Moreover, that they consistently evade a racial analysis of education should not be represented as their nonparticipation in a racialized order. In fact, it showcases precisely how they do perpetuate the racial order by turning the other cheek to it or pretending it does not exist. Constructing Whites as knowledgeable about race has two advantages: one, it holds them self-accountable for race-based decisions and actions; two, it dismantles their innocence in exchange for a status as full participants in race relations. If constructing Whites as knowledgeable about race means they are full participants in racialization, then this means that race knowledge is shared between people of color and Whites as opposed to the idea that the former are the fundamental "race knowers" whereas the latter are "race ignorant." This essay attempts to build a conceptual apparatus by which to understand White racial knowledge. It offers suggestions for antiracist practices in education that Whites as well as educators of color may appropriate when teaching, particularly about race. I argue that antiracist pedagogy cannot be guided by White racial knowledge for reasons I hope to make clearer.

The following account is an attempt to describe White racial knowledge, which is different from taking an inventory of *White people's racial knowledge*. Following Roediger (1994), we may assert that White racial knowledge is not only false and oppressive, it is *nothing but* false and oppressive. If this smacks of "conspiracy theory," David Gillborn (2006) reminds us that perpetuating racism does not require a conspiracy. If educators conduct schooling as usual, the results are predictable and consistent with racial stratification. If this sketch paints White racial knowledge into a corner and as seeming sinister, then it is in line with the argument that Whiteness and anything that comes with it, is violent and bogus. Its history is filled with stories of genocide, enslavement, and the general process of othering. Its way of knowing partitions the world for racial domination; therefore, White epistemology is caught up in a regime of knowledge that is inherently oppressive. Willis and Harris (2000) enter the battle over epistemology in the field of literacy by remarking,

> The importance of the role that epistemology has played in the intersection of politics and reading research cannot be ignored. It serves as an explanation for how elite powerful groups, with shared interest in maintaining their status, have worked together to determine how literacy should be conceptualized, defined, taught, and assessed. Understanding the role of epistemology also helps to explain how these groups have worked to convince others of the veracity of their claims by suggesting that alternative ways of viewing the role of literacy in society are invalid because they fall outside of their ideological conceptions. (p. 77)

As an epistemology, Whiteness and its hirsute companion, White racial knowledge, seem to contain little hope. They are bound up with a White ideology that simultaneously alludes to and eludes a critical understanding of racial stratification. Against the suggestion that Whiteness be reconstructed, the neo-abolitionist movement suggests the complete dismantling of Whiteness, finding little redeeming value in it (hooks, 1997; Ignatiev & Garvey, 1996; Roediger, 1991). Here, I am using ideology in the classical Marxist sense as an evaluative, rather than a neutral or descriptive, concept in order to assess group belief systems; that is, concrete forms of social thought (Shelby, 2003). In terms of a study of Whiteness, this *critical moment of ideology* allows for a race critique that highlights not just the descriptive properties of White racial knowledge but its *functions* and *consequences*.

However, White people's racial knowledge is not synonymous with White racial knowledge. As concrete and thinking subjects of history, White people have some choices to make regarding how they will come to know the world. Sometimes, this knowledge comes in the form of endarkened epistemologies (Dillard, 2000; Scheurich & Young, 1997; Wright, 2003), as ways of knowing that are generated from the historical experiences of people of color and then appropriated by Whites. We often see this happen with antiracist Whites who, while acknowledging their own White privilege, denounce White racism (Wise, 2002). Working against the invidious effects of White racial knowledge supports "teachers' ability to create a professional community [that] is integral to improving teaching and student learning" (Ladson-Billings & Gomez, 2001, p. 676), which makes the problem of Whiteness central to the search for a countercommunity. In this journey, we give up hope in Whiteness as an oppressive racial epistemology but retain hope in White people as concrete subjects in the struggle against racial oppression.

White educators' epistemological framework is not *determined* by their Whiteness, although there is certainly a preponderance of White people who interpret social life through White racial knowledge. For this reason, Whites are the usual suspects of White racial knowledge, the usual subjects for its discourse. That said, even people of color may embody White racial knowledge. Through his comparative studies of Brazilian and U.S. race relations, Jonathan Warren (2002) found that many Black Brazilians espouse a color-blind perspective that resembles that of many White Americans, despite the fact that their structural positions in society differ greatly. This is a compelling argument against the notion that while certainly a powerful influence on one's epistemology, structural position *does not determine* how a person ultimately makes sense of that structure. Thus, the following argument is less an indictment of Whites and more a challenge, a gift that requires a countergift as response.[1]

White Racial Knowledge: What Do Whites Know about Race?

It is understandable that studies of Whiteness have evolved in a way that constructs Whites as quite unknowledgeable about race, especially in light of the fact that they benefit from racial structures. In this sense, uncritical studies of Whiteness have fallen victim to a hegemonic assumption about race, in this case, that Whites do not know much about race and therefore must be taught about it. Usually, this means that people of color become the tutors for Whites, the ones "tapping Whites on the shoulder" to remind them how they have "forgotten" about race once again. Nieto (2003) proclaims, "White educators need to make the problem of racism *their* problem to solve" (p. 203; italics in original). White racial knowledge is an epistemology of the oppressor to the extent that it suppresses knowledge of its own conditions of existence.

It works to make Whiteness visible against White racial knowledge's insistence on maintaining its own invisibility. It comes with the realization that "even though no one says it, race matters [sic]" (Enciso, 2003, p. 156). In her study of fourth and fifth grade classrooms, Enciso finds that "the real is mediated." Her evidence supports the idea that race is a structuring principle that must be interpreted in classroom interactions, not as a naturally occurring phenomenon but part of the assumptions that ultimately inform how people construct their world. Furthermore, she resists the individualistic rendition of race as explainable ultimately through interpersonal relations and places it rightly in "systematic constructions of dichotomies, coherences, repetitions, and rationales" (p. 162), a condition that is additive to White students' education but subtractive for most minority youth (Valenzuela, 1999, 2002). Freire (1970/1993) has insisted that when groups are involved in relations of oppression, the beneficiaries of their structures perpetuate a system whereby they are absolved of any holistic understanding of its processes. However, Freire asks educators to be critical of such myths in one of the first steps toward a "pedagogy of the oppressed."

As beneficiaries of racism, Whites have had the luxury of neglecting their own development in *racial understanding*, which should not be confused with *racial knowledge*. Whites forego a critical understanding of race because their structural position is both informed by and depends on a *fundamentally superficial grasp* of its history and evolution (Mills, 1997). This fact does not prevent Whites from *realizing* their position of privilege, which is a pedagogical task. It points out the possibility of being "pulled up short" (Gadamer's phrase) when life events "interrupt our lives and challenge our self-understanding in ways that are painful but transforming" (Kerdeman, 2003, p. 294; Gadamer, 1975). Taken racially, I am arguing that Whites may experience being pulled up short in order that they experience a "loss [that] can be an opening to recognize perspectives that [they] tend to dismiss or ignore when life is going [their] way" (Kerdeman, 2003, p. 297). Racially pulled up short, Whites realize that they have forsaken a "clearer, more honest, and deep understanding" of race in exchange for a delusionary "condition of self-inflation." To appropriate Kerdeman, pulled up short counters a certain White *hidalguismo* (Rimonte, 1997), or son of God status, and opens them to the humble condition of human fallibility.

This pedagogical realization is arguably what makes McIntosh's description of White privilege so powerful. Its value lies in its ability to engage, even to surprise Whites in realizing the fact of their racial power. I would argue that many Whites are surprised not because they did not know their power, but they did not realize that people of color knew it as well. That Whites then understand and name the basis of racial power in White supremacy is another matter altogether, which requires an epistemology of color to the extent that this is possible for Whites. A deep engagement of race and racism by Whites contradicts their ability to enforce efficiently the differential treatment of people of color. Otherwise, Whites would have to consider their benefits as unearned and arbitrary, and at the expense of people of color. Of course, this does not speak for all Whites, but for the collectivity known as Whiteness. As utilized in this essay, the term *Whiteness* refers to a collective racial epistemology with a history of violence against people of color.

Whites are the subjects of Whiteness, whereas people of color are its objects. All Whites benefit from racist actions whether or not they commit them and despite the fact that they may work against them. Bonilla-Silva (2004) uses the term *White* to denote "traditional" Whites, such as established Euro-Americans, but also includes more recent White immigrants, and increasingly, assimilated White or light-skinned Latinos, and certain Asian groups. We may take issue with Bonilla-Silva's classifications, but he complicates the category of "White" by pointing out its flexibility to include and exclude groups based on the historical conjuncture of Whiteness. One only needs to consider how Irish and British in the United States live in relative racial harmony despite their longstanding ethnic animosities toward each other (Ignatiev, 1995). Consider also the racial position of Arab Americans, currently classified by the U.S. census as White, but whose racial affiliation has witnessed a shift since 9/11. In short, Whiteness is an objective yet flexible racial force that is supraindividual and "destabilizing the category 'White' [sic] shakes the very foundation on which racial differentiation and inequality is built" (Dutro, Kazemi, & Balf, 2005, p. 102).

Whiteness is also vulnerable when knowledge about its unspoken structures is formulated and used to subvert its privileges. Such knowledge can come from Whites themselves, but is not generated from their social position or experience. Rather, it comes from the experiences of people of color. This point does not suggest that people of color are "right" by virtue of their identity but that racial analysis begins from their objective social location. Even when racial analysis centers Whiteness, it must do so from the analytics of the racially oppressed (Leonardo, 2005). Because White racial knowledge comes from a particular point of privilege, it is often evasive, which leads Margaret Hunter (2002) to assert that, "Whites' unspoken knowledge works as a barrier to antiracist education because it denies the reality of racism and it maintains the invisibility of whiteness as a racial identity" (p. 257).

As White children are socialized into everyday life and schooling, they learn their place in the racial hierarchy. They begin to *know who* they are. By "knowing," I do not suggest a conscious, self-present mode of thinking, but rather a social condition of knowledge, sometimes buried in the unconscious, sometimes percolating to the level of consciousness. It is less an act by the knowing White subject and more of an awareness of one's racial condition that may escape critical scrutiny. For example, White children learn but rarely question history books that speak almost exclusively of their accomplishments, distorted as these accounts may be (Loewen, 1995), that literature breathes their civilized culture (Takaki, 1993), and that science verifies their superiority as a people (Stepan, 1990). Very quickly, they build a racial cosmology where they assume a place of selfhood whereas people of color pose as the other or as interlopers. From this learning, Whites gain valuable knowledge about the racial order, such as with whom they should associate, play, and later date or marry. Whites' racial knowledge develops into a particular racial self-understanding that begins with a sense of belonging in two ways. One, Whites are born into a world that is racially harmonious with their sense of self. In the film *Color of Fear*, Loren remarks that Whites do not have to think about their place in society because they exist in a world that tells them who they are, from day one. They do not experience the self-doubts about identity that many people of color go through in their search for belonging. Growing up White in America has its own challenges, but it is a development rarely bound up with the question, "What does it mean to be White?" because to be White means to belong. Two, it does not take long for White children to recognize that the world belongs to them, in the sense that Whites feel a sense of entitlement or ownership of the material and discursive processes of race (Van Ausdale & Feagin, 2001). From the means of production to the meanings in everyday life, Whites enjoy a virtual monopoly of institutions that make up the racial landscape.

White knowledge is also about *knowing where* to traverse the social landscape. They know that Blacks live in ghetto spaces, that barrios are replete with Latinos, if not Mexicans (in the case of Los Angeles), and that Chinatown has good "ethnic" foods. Often, Whites avoid such spaces altogether either out of fear of crime or discomfort with a different cultural (sometimes third-worldish) repertoire. In the former, Whites rationalize their fear of ghettos and barrios due to their higher crime rates compared with suburbs. In the latter, Whites feel anxious about the "strange" sounding syllables of Asian languages or the informal economy of ethnic enclaves. They are indeed a long way from the confines of The Gap and Starbucks.

During a class exercise led by a group of my students, the presenters asked their peers, "What are the advantages to your racial identity?" Significantly, Whites answered that they experience freedom in mobility. By and large, they confessed that they felt little prohibition from travel or neighborhood selection on the basis of racial considerations or fear of racial violence. White racial knowledge is the ability to imagine oneself in any space, untethered by the concern, "Will there be people like me (other Whites) living there?" Of course, many Whites cannot afford to purchase a house in particular neighborhoods or travel to expensive resorts, but these are economical, not racial, reasons. Furthermore, when it concerns White fears of minority violence, be it in the form of drive-by shootings or random crime, we have to consider the fact that such fears have little basis in fact since most violent crimes are intraracial, such as Black-on-Black gang or drug activity.

Likewise, my students of color saw advantages to their identity, such as the ability to speak a language besides English in the case of Latinos and the strength of a group to withstand centuries of oppression in the case of African Americans. However, it was noted that although these examples are personally felt advantages, they are not necessarily structural advantages. In the case of bilingualism, a wave of antibilingual education initiatives is cresting over the nation, led arguably by California's Proposition 227. Latinos are constantly told where they can speak their language, from the workplace to public schools. In the case of slavery and its legacies, for Blacks there is no structural advantage attached to it. They are victims of explicit racial profiling and implicit cultural rules of etiquette and social behavior, such as interracial dating. Students of color recognized that self and group pride do not equate with structural advantage.

White racial knowledge is *knowing how* the world works in racially meaningful ways, but avoiding naming it in these terms. Whites know how to talk about race without actually having to mention the word, opting instead for terms such as "ethnicity," "nationality," "background," asking questions like "What are you?" or that most veiled of all euphemisms, "Where are you from?" When a person of color names a state (e.g., New York), the question is restated as, "No, where are you *really* from?" Moreover, knowing how to invoke the concept of racism without having to utter the word is a trademark of even the liberal White discourse. Manning Marable (2002) found common substitutions, like "'the country's racial picture,' 'the overall racial climate,' 'relations between Americans of different races and ethnic backgrounds,' 'racial matters,' 'the race theme,' 'an incendiary topic,' 'this most delicate and politically dangerous of subjects'...'the state of race relations,' 'the racial front,' 'black-white relations'" (p. 46). In fact, Whites spend a lot of time talking about race, often coded/coated in apparently racially neutral, or color-blind, terms (Myers &Williamson, 2001; Schofield, 2003). In Bonilla-Silva's (2001) surveys of Black and White racial attitudes in the Detroit area, he concludes that "[W]hites avoid using direct racial references and traditionally 'racist' language and rely on covert, indirect, and apparently nonracial language to state their racial views" (p. 153). Moreover, his research team found, "Only a handful of white respondents did not say something that was problematic at some point in their interview" (p. 143).

Of course, things may change when Whites are exclusively around other Whites. David Roediger (1991) says as much when he describes his childhood experience in the Introduction to *The Wages of Whiteness*,

> Even in an all-white town, race was never absent. I learned absolutely no lore of my German ancestry and no more than a few meaningless snatches of Irish songs, but missed little of racist folklore. Kids came to know the exigencies of chance by chanting "Eany, meany, miney, mo/Catch a nigger by the toe" to decide teams and first batters in sport. We learned that life—and fights—were not always fair: "'Two against one, nigger's fun." We learned not to loaf: "Last one in is a nigger baby." We learned to save, for to buy ostentatiously or too quickly was to be "nigger rich." We learned not to buy clothes that were bright "nigger green." (p. 3)

Roediger's suggestion is that White racial knowledge exists and is a particular way of knowing—rather than the absence of it—that is intimate with what it means to be White. White racial knowledge is comprised of a constellation of metaphors used to define Whites' sense of self and group in opposition to a denigrated other: in this case, Blacks (see also Giroux, 1997).

In Michael Moore's award winning documentary about gun violence, *Bowling for Columbine*, Charlton Heston reasoned that we have such high rates of violence in the United States because of a long history of ethnic differences. Curiously, the NRA spokesman found that gun homicides were a result of ethnic differences, rather than a product of a fundamentally, racially divided society. To Heston, the existence of these differences was the root of such problems, with fantasies of a homogeneous White society coming through loud and clear. This episode also shows another aspect of White racial knowledge. While they may claim that they know very little about race, Whites suddenly speak volumes about it when their racial ideology is challenged. This happens in university courses where Whites become animated about race and assert their knowledge when their perceptions of the world are questioned. It may surprise the educator that for a group that claims racial ignorance, Whites can speak with such authority and expertise when they do not like what they hear. Of course, as this essay argues they are indeed experts and authorities on race.

Knowing how to act in racially "acceptable" ways is a form of knowledge that Whites develop in their everyday life. For example, it is often touted that people of color "play the race card." When Johnny Cochran invoked the issue of race during the O. J. Simpson trial, Whites were aghast at the suggestion that the case had anything at all to do with race, or at least that it was tangential to the proceedings. Cochran was accused of making the case racial when race was apparently irrelevant. However, one does not have to look farther than the *Loving v. Virginia* case of 1967 to understand that miscegenation, or interracial marriage, is a racially charged issue with (Funderberg, 1994) most Whites. Inscribed by a history of antimiscegenation, the Simpson case was already racial; Cochran did not have to make it so (Leonardo, 2003a). Whites reacted in racially significant ways to the case, which showcased their racial knowledge. They projected racialism onto people of color, removing themselves as alibis, or nonracial spectators, rather than participants in the racialization process. In other words, Whites often play the race card as a sign of their investment in Whiteness and as a way to direct the public discourse in terms acceptable to them (Lipsitz, 1998).

In my courses, through much dialogue my students and I have discovered that Whites live with race everyday of their lives. As in the movie, *American History X*, some White students admit that they learn racial lessons in their daily interaction with the world, usually with their family. The challenge is to find a condition whereby this knowledge is made visible. In response to our readings of Toni Morrison's *The Bluest Eye* (1970), Frederick Douglass's (1982) autobiography, or Peggy McIntosh's (1992) essay on White privilege, White students confessed that they have memories of race that they rarely speak about or analyze. Given the discursive space, Whites tell narratives about moments when dating a Black man, for example, brought out the worst in their friends and family. That is, what was otherwise a "nonracial" home discourse became racial when a person of color was introduced as a potential, albeit unwelcome, visitor. In her essay, one student wrote a poignant story about having left her school and then receiving a letter from one of her former classmates, informing her that a "nigger" now sits in her old seat. Not to worry, the friend added, because the class would make sure she never felt comfortable. A selective group of White students reflected on their own investment in, experience with, and knowledge of race. However, not all Whites respond to racial analysis in such an embracing way. Usually, resistance and evasion are more common.

In what might be called an "ideal type" in Max Weber's (1978) sense of it, a White student played the race card in the most prototypical way. During a class discussion, the student confessed to me that she had been feeling unaffirmed because of her peers' negative reactions to her ideas about race. She concluded that she felt this slight was due to her being a "nonminority," that is, her status as a White person. After I addressed her observations and offered some advice, she decided to complain publicly to the class during a subsequent session, the main thrust being that her thoughts about race were not treated seriously because she was White. She saw this as a problem if sensitivity about diversity included White participation. On this last point, she was on the right track. Based on this incident and the concerns I have about White racial knowledge, I would like to offer some analysis.

First, the student should be commended for feeling empowered to confront her peers and communicate her feelings and observations about race. Dialogues about race are never easy and entrance to them is most awkward for Whites. Her desire to publicly confront her peers is not a problem in and of itself. Second and more problematically, her racial assumptions are symptomatic of the way that many Whites play the race card, an aspect of White racial knowledge. In this particular case, throughout the semester this student received criticisms from peers of all races. In fact, her most vocal critic was another, albeit radical, White student. That the student in question interpreted her "victimization" as resulting from her peers' racialization of her as a White woman begs some questions, one of which is, Why did she fail to observe that other White students in the class did not feel victimized on the basis of their race? In other words, how was she somehow singled out on the basis of her race, whereas other Whites were not?

To address this question, it is important to remember that when *personally* confronted with a negative situation, Whites interpret it as racial prejudice against the *group*. My student may have overlooked the more obvious reason for her peers' disagreements with her, that is, they found her ideas problematic. Her discursive reversal is not hard to imagine when we consider that Whites, for example, oppose affirmative action based on the perception that it disadvantages them, rather than defining it as a historical form of corrective intervention. Whites are comfortable with constructing racial knowledge when they feel threatened. Racial knowledge here means that the person perceives the group victimized by another group (even if this may not be the case) and speaks out in explicitly racial ways. In other words, this incident is an instance of throwing the White race card. However, when situations are positive and preserve group power, Whites claim that their advantages stem from individual merit, that is, nonracial, deserving, and neutral. This suggests that Whites *know when* to invoke race in a manner that maintains their "innocence." In fact, it is at this point when White racial knowledge mysteriously transforms into racial ignorance. Whites suddenly become oblivious to the racial formation.

This case also points out another important element in White racial knowledge. When dialogue is without tension, Whites are willing to enter racial dialogue. For example, they enjoy discussions about diversity. What educator wants to be perceived as antidiversity these days? When discussions become tense or uncomfortable and people of color show some anger or outrage, Whites' racial resolve wanes and opting out of race dialogue becomes convenient. It becomes too difficult, too much of a strain, and too dangerous. Their participation becomes strenuous and the journey arduous. People of color do not enjoy the same choice because understanding racism and formulating accurate racial knowledge are intimate with the search for their own humanity. As Hurtado (1996) has found, Whites selectively participate in racial dialogue when it serves their needs, which is more often driven by the desire "not to look racist" than by a real commitment to end racism through honest race work.

When threatened, Whites play the "generalization card." That is, they challenge sociological knowledge of race with the notion that not all Whites benefit from racism or that talks of White supremacy paint an otherwise complex group with too broad of a stroke. They may play the "exception-to-the-rule" card, or elevating individual people of color who have "made it" (Rains, 1997). They personalize what is at heart an institutional analysis. In these instances where race is named, Whites transform into many of the charges they make against people of color (e.g., irrational, emotional, and using identity politics). In the beginning of a course, instructors may remind students that sociological analysis is not about them per se, as I do; but when discussions become tense yet insightful, Whites perceive generalizations to be about them, as individual persons. Students of color also personalize institutional knowledge, preventing them from apprehending the racial totality, but the consequences are different when Whites derail knowledge of racial patterns. When minorities resist sociological knowledge of race, they further their own oppression; when Whites resist, they further their own supremacy.

In order to maintain their previous knowledge of race, Whites may disrupt radical discussions of racism with exceptions-to-the-rule in efforts to redirect race discourse from an institutional knowledge base to a personal one. As a result, White racial knowledge constructs the formation on its head rather than on its feet. Rather than speak of patterns, it would speak of exceptions. Thus, it fails to understand the racist and pervasive underpinnings of White society. Rather than use generalizations as evidence of a significant, and sometimes growing, problem, White racial knowledge would characterize generalizations as part of the problem. Generalizations are branded "politically incorrect" since they smack of stereotyping. And rather than scrutinize specific forms of racism that need to be combated, colorblind Whites would rather offer examples of "racial progress," as if the interrogation of racism were on the opposite side of progress. The most common instance of this last point is Whites' refusal to engage seriously the legacy of slavery because it ended over a century ago. Although American society has indeed changed and slavery is now outlawed, White knowledge fails to grasp the devastating effects of slavery on Black communities, psyche, and lack of material prosperity today.

In order for White racial knowledge to free itself of erroneous assumptions, Whites must be self-critical on a couple of fronts. First, they must disinvest in the notion that they do not know much about race. Second, they can critically decode much of what comes across as "race free" discourse and analyze the racial underpinnings of White knowledge. Third, Whites must learn to be racially sensitive about contexts when race seems a legitimate theme to invoke and ask why it was relevant to them then and not other times. Finally, Whites can participate in building an antiracist pedagogy against White mystifications, and displacing White racial knowledge from its privileged position as the center of classroom discourse.

Notes on Antiracist Pedagogy: Decentering White Racial Knowledge in the Classroom

Antiracist pedagogy is informed by a constellation of discourses and sets of concepts. It also inheres several targets for analysis, one of which is White racial knowledge. Although it certainly comes with teaching methods, antiracism should not be thought of as a method, just as Ana-Maria Freire and Donaldo Macedo (1998) warn against treating Paulo Freire as a method. By portraying antiracism as a discourse, I am suggesting that it comes with a certain family of concerns organized into an overarching project. Antiracism makes White supremacy and its daily vicissitudes a central concern for educators of any racial background. In effect, antiracism is the recognition and critique of White racial knowledge. It is informed by Hunter's (2002) suggestion of decentering the often White and male standpoint guiding courses on race and ethnicity (see also Hunter & Nettles, 1999).

White supremacy is a specific form of modern racism and is the inscribing force that makes other forms of racism thrive; that is, Whites benefit from race relations in absolute ways. Non-White racism is certainly a problem but to equate it with White supremacy is to forget that Euro-White American hegemony is global and remains unmatched by either Japan's imperialist history or China's economic power in Asia. We can say that understanding White supremacy and undercutting White racial knowledge form the problematic of antiracist analysis and pedagogy. Antiracism is first and foremost a political project such that it is a particular form of work and commitment. In other words, its essence is not a method, a profession, or a curriculum unit. Antiracism is a project of negation to the extent that its main target of critique is the condition that makes White supremacy a structured, daily possibility for many students of color (Leonardo, 2003b).

Whiteness should not be confused with *White ethnic cultures*, some forms of which may be benign or even critical (see Leonardo, 2002). By contrast as a racial collective, Whiteness is associated with colonization, takeover, and denial. We may go a long way with the White neo-abolitionist movement in asserting that the greatest problem of our time is the White race but find it necessary to qualify Roediger's (1997) assertion that the White race does not have a culture (see also Ignatiev, 1997). A *White racial culture* exists, which is intimately linked with a certain way of knowing. Whites as a race appear to have a culture, if by culture, we accept Geertz (1994) and Erickson's (2005) definition that it signifies the combination of material rituals, symbolic meanings, and sense-making strategies that a group shares. It is summed up in this essay as a way of knowing the world, an epistemology. We only have to point out that people do not seem to question the existence of Black or Latino culture, but have a more difficult time naming *White racial culture*.

When we recall lynching practices in the United States, we name White racial culture whereby Whites from young to old gathered to pose for pictures eerily circulated like postcards. From this cultural practice, it is convenient for White children and their parents and grandparents to read the event from the perspective of White racial knowledge; along with partitioning the material world, Whites have also divided the epistemological world and segregated counterknowledge from White common sense. It does not mean that Whites do not harbor contradictory feelings about these and similar events like them in history, such as photos of boarding schools for Native Americans, but that the totality of White uptake of race relations informs and creates White racial culture and knowledge.

The concept of racism is central to understanding the American landscape and history. However, because of the distorting effects of Whiteness I have found through teaching that it is paradoxically both underused and overused in education classroom discourse. It is underused for the reasons stated above, that is, guided by White racial knowledge race is perceived as divisive and therefore should be downplayed. In general, White students avoid it, fearing that it would make them a target for criticism from people of color. That said, after having established a level of rapport with my students and peeling away the stigma attached to the term, I noticed that it quickly becomes overused. By this, I mean that anything racist becomes branded as a form of *racism without distinctions*. In these instances, analysis of racism is stripped of its radical, objective thrust and differences between its forms are leveled and equated with one another.

For example, Latinos are deemed racist when they exhibit hostility toward Whites; that is, racial hatred. Asians are deemed racist when they express stereotypical assumptions about Blacks; that is, racial prejudice. Blacks are said to be racist when they argue for Afrocentric schools; that is, racial segregation. As a result, every group is constructed as an equal opportunity racist and racism becomes the problem of all racial groups, not just Whites. Of course, these situations represent symptoms of a racist society that educators must mediate and problematize. In my courses, I have found it helpful to make distinctions between "interminoritarian politics," minority-to-majority attitudes, and White supremacy in order to avoid confusing differences in kind with differences in degrees. White racial knowledge seduces students to equate these historical forms and antiracist pedagogy differentiates them. White-to-minority racism is different in kind from the struggles found between groups of color or animosity from minorities to Whites.

I make it clear to my students that although Latinos may harbor hostilities toward Whites based on race, Latinos do not own the apparatuses of power to enforce these feelings. Of course, a critical educator would mediate these animosities in a historically sensitive manner by acknowledging their root sources. Likewise, I point out that when Asians express racial prejudice against Blacks, although these actions must be denounced, it must be remembered that this is a result of the middleman social position that Asians occupy as a buffer within the historic Black–White anxiety (see Leonardo, 2000). In other words, as the "model minority" Asians are often used as a foil to discipline the Black and Latino population. Last, Afrocentric or Native American-based schools are compromises within a public school system that fails to meet their needs. It would be inaccurate to call their attempts to address their own community's needs as a form of segregation, as many White students are wont to do.

If segregation represents a group's institutional attempts to maintain power relations, then efforts by racial minorities to address their own community issues through self-separation cannot be called "self-segregation" or "reverse segregation." Minority-based schools do not promote the same segregation we saw earlier when Whites segregated Blacks into their ghettoized neighborhoods and prevented them from integrating into the nation's schools (Kozol, 1991; Massey & Denton, 1993). If segregation is an action perpetrated by a group on another in order to maintain group power, then it is difficult to claim that Blacks are segregating Whites through Afrocentric schools in order to maintain Black power. In the same light, Native American nations, Latino-based organizations, or Asian-American ethnic enclaves do not represent attempts by these communities to segregate Whites into their own sectors, let alone ghettoize them.

This colorblind sentiment is showcased in a statement made by Sharon Browne, the leading attorney for the California-based Pacific Legal Foundation concerning a Seattle lawsuit that has reached the Supreme Court (see Blanchard, 2006). The suit involves parents who question the school district's use of race as one of the determining factors in students' access to particular neighborhood schools. Browne remarks, "By using race as a factor…they're teaching our kids that race matters. That is just plain wrong, and it's not the type of teaching that our school districts should be doing" (p. A8). Only White racial knowledge could suggest that "race doesn't matter" and in the same suit invoke the Civil Rights discourse as a line of defense against using racial considerations in public policy. It takes the word, as opposed to the spirit, of the Civil Rights Movement to suggest the very opposite of its intent that race matters. In the same school district, Seattle director of the Office of Equity and Race Relations, Dr. Caprice Hollins constructs a color-conscious website that names "cultural racism" as the normalization of rugged individualism and Standard English, among other things (Carlton, 2006). She receives criticism from Andrew Coulson, director of the Cato Institute's Center for Educational Freedom, for challenging one of the "founding principles" of the U.S. nation: mainly individualism. One wonders if the Institute would also consider slavery and genocide as founding principles of U.S. nation creation.

Through my teaching, I have found that the concept of White supremacy is helpful in making distinctions between different forms of racism. For instance, whereas racism has been relativized to mean any form of racial animus stripped of its comparative basis, White supremacy is less ambiguous at the level of terminology. This does not mean abandoning the concept of racism altogether, but points out the usefulness of invoking White supremacy in particular contexts. I go a long way with David Gillborn (2005), who deems education policy that does not make central the problem of racism as an act of White supremacy. He explains,

> This critical perspective is based on the recognition that race inequity and racism are central features of the education system. These are not aberrant nor accidental phenomena that will be ironed out in time, they are fundamental characteristics of the system. *It is in this sense that education policy is an act of white supremacy.* (pp. 497–498; italics in original)

The concept of White supremacy names the group in question. It is unequivocal in its political capacity to name Whites as the group enforcing its racial power. In contrast, the notion of Black, Asian, or Latino supremacy lacks any solid historical reference. There is no such thing. Two, supremacy is also unambiguous; it signifies a group's attempt to establish absolute control. It is clearly a representation of both personal value systems and institutional behavior because it invokes images of Klan activity and White racial riots, but also Whites' daily feelings of superiority. Here again, White racial knowledge becomes a challenge, for it constructs White supremacy as a thing of the past, or at least as insignificant as Strom Thurmond's outdated beliefs.

Concerning White privilege, it is common to argue that Whites benefit from race structures in differing degrees. Because of other intersecting systems or relations, it is not unusual to argue that Whites do not benefit equally from race (Leonardo, 2005; Mills, 1997; Newitz & Wray, 1997). On the level of empirical knowledge, this seems harmless enough. For example, there are poor Whites, White women, and gay and lesbian Whites who suffer oppression. However, it is conceptually misleading to suggest that certain White subgroups benefit *less* from race than their counterparts who are rich Whites, White men, and heterosexual Whites. It seems even more questionable to suggest that "White trash" is somehow a racist insult, as Newitz and Wray (1997) claim.

By contrast, I argue that *all Whites benefit equally from race and racism, but they do not all benefit equally from other social relations.* People are instantiations of many relations grafted all at once on their bodies, which creates a nexus of power relations, an interdependent system of forces. Given this state of affairs, it is still helpful to invoke a language of causality. Thus, we are warranted to suggest that White women, for example, are not less advantaged than White men with respect to race, but with respect to gender, which affects their overall relation to the totality of forces. That is, it is not White women's place in race relations that causes their oppression but rather their place in gender relations. Likewise, the phrase "White trash" is a denigration of poor Whites' economic and cultural location rather than a term of derision based on racial positionality. It is true that "White trash" contains a racial component. But structurally speaking, the exploitation that working-class Whites suffer is ameliorated by what DuBois (1935/1998) once called their "public and psychological wages" (see also Roediger, 1991). No doubt social relations intersect one another and a shift in one alters the overall relation of forces. Failing to provide students with a language of causality, educators forsake a compelling explanation for the particular benefits and burdens that a racial structure produces. This distinction is different from arguing that Whites do not benefit equally from race.

Another point that I teach my students is that antiracism is historically self-reflective. It fully appreciates the role that history plays in shaping today's milieu. The legacy of slavery, Apartheid, anti-Coolie laws, immigration exclusion acts, territorial takeovers, and other crimes against racialized subjects of history are events from a hundred years ago that are regarded as if they happened yesterday. As antiracist educators, my students understand that our racialized present was not dropped from above by a Euclidian observer, but rather that our current conditions were made possible by continuities in White treatment of people of color. On this point, I often take sports as an example. More than ever, today's Black inner city youth are seduced by the spectacle of success in sports (see James, 2005). Many kids believe they can "be like Mike" (Jordan), move like Randy Moss, and swing like Sammy Sosa. In my courses on diversity, I link sports with slavery by explaining that during slavery, Africans were treated as depositories of White anxieties. Fearing carnal desires, the White imaginary invested the African body with sexual prominence and promiscuity. This spectacularization of the Black body happened in conjunction with the exploitation of African labor. During Jim Crow, Blacks filled Whites' void by assuming the stage with White faces in minstrel shows. Again, Blacks provided a convenient spectacle for White audiences. Today, basketball, baseball, and football are no minstrel show but they function in similar ways to showcase the spectacle we know as the Black body.

Critical scholars and pedagogues face particular issues when teaching about race and antiracist work. They understand teaching antiracism to be a social condition that they navigate aggressively and yet tenderly. Aggressively confronting the theme of racism is important because it does both student and instructor a disservice when we fail to name its contours in the most direct and demystifying way, much like White racial knowledge. Thus, in my courses I try to enter the discourse of race and critique its consequences with plain talk. By that, I do not suggest a discourse of transparency (see Aoki, 2000; Giroux, 1995; Lather, 1996). Instead, it is time to suggest that it is quite normal to overtly discuss race, over dinner at the restaurant to activities in the classroom, from the home to home-room. For too long, race discussions have been stifled because of the conservative and even liberal notion that any talk of race is, by default, recreating the problem of race; that is, it reifies what is at heart a social construction. Of course, this is a mystification in itself because it mistakes invoking race with its fetishization. Discussions of race may fetishize the concept, but this is a risk worth taking and on which any critical work reflects.

Whenever I discuss the topic of race, I make sure that I do not stammer or speak in a hesitating manner, whisper when I say "Black" or "White," or act incredulous when I cite or hear examples of racism as if surprised that certain acts of hatred persist in our post-Civil Rights era. Like other academic subjects, race is part of normal classroom discourse: as normal as Newton in physics or Shakespeare in English. I have tried to remove the "controversial" stigma that White racial knowledge puts on race discourse. Whether or not I have been successful is another matter. However, I have also noticed that it means something different for a scholar of color to invoke race and this is where certain distinctions would help. When a minority scholar speaks plain talk about race, she may be constructed as militant, as needlessly angry about relations that are, after all, "on their wane." Thus, White racial knowledge constructs scholars who speak with such plainness about an *existing* problem as part of the problem because it assumes that the most functional way to deal with the situation is to focus on the "positive" relations between the races, not their insidious past.

Because race taps into students' affective investments, I have found that it touches tender histories in their lives. This is what I mean when I say that I tread tenderly on the topic of race at the same time that I aggressively analyze it. For White students, it should be painful to hear that the White race has colonized and constructed a world after its own image. It is not easy for them to read that, as Massey and Denton (1993) assert in their book, *American Apartheid*, Whites have *intentionally* segregated and ostracized Black people into ghettos. Many White students in education consider themselves decent, egalitarian people who believe in racial equality. However, they also frequently have a superficial understanding of race. Likewise, students of color are surprisingly deprived of a classroom discourse that extends beyond essentialisms. That said, students of color have the experiential basis to understand the effects of race on their lives in a way that White students, who often claim no racial affiliation or knowledge, do not. The various examples mentioned here are hard for students of color to hear as well because they jog memories passed down from their parents and communities. Sometimes they may even resist Massey and Denton's argument that Blacks have been ghettoized in such a complete and enduring manner like no other group in American history for two reasons.

First, they refuse to be classified as "ghetto," the image of which has been source of shame and embarrassment when spoken outside of certain Black contexts. Second, because they are college or graduate students, they are a selective group of people who have "made it out of the ghetto" and believe it is a discrete possibility for others who work hard. Of course, we know from Kozol's (1991) *Savage Inequalities* that housing segregation leads to paltry material conditions in schools for predominantly Black populated areas. We can extend a similar argument for Latino *barrios*, and inner cities with Asian refugees. Here we see that teaching antiracism necessitates a simultaneous sensibility for class relations, or race's material cognate, especially when we recognize that capitalism has wreaked havoc on people of color.

Race is completely socially constructed, but we have invested it with material institutions. In its modern sense, race does not mean "group," although some students would like to construct it that way. If the concept of race were to equate with the notion of group—the idea being that groups have always oppressed each other throughout history—this would effectively cancel out the particularities of our current racial formation. If race were to equate with the commonsense understanding of it as "group difference," then the Trojans were another race from the Greeks, the Romans just another race of people. In its modern sense, race is the creation of what many race scholars refer to as skin color stratification. That is, although it is possible to refer to race as a trope in biblical times, this is not its modern sense. The basic question of "What is race?" must be asked, something that White racial knowledge assumes is a relatively settled issue. Race is not just a figment of the imagination, but what Ruben Rumbaut (1996) calls a *pigment of the imagination*. Its genealogy is coterminous with the creation of science and its eugenics movement, its "enlightenment" philosophy of the other from Kant to Kierkegaard, its cultural imperialism of orientalist proportions, its colonization of the Americas and Africanization of slavery, and its global exploitation of non-White labor for unimaginable profits (see Allen, 2002; Mills, 1997; Said, 1979). In order to discuss race in its specific and historical form, this modern sense of racialization is what my students and I first try to understand. Any talk of visions of race must initially discuss its propensity for divisions. That is, Whites created race in order to divide the world, to carve it up into enlightened and endarkened continents, and to delineate the White subject from the Black object of history.

That race divides the U.S. nation as well as others around the world certainly can be proven. After all, race was a White European concept created for the benefit of Whites and burden of non-Whites. However, this insight provides little guidance into the workings of race relations or how it worked out that Whites have benefited from racism in an absolute way. That is, if race divides the world, how did Whites come out as the subjects of its specious history? Marxist struggle against capital should complement any antiracist work, but we must also be reflective about its inadequacy for explaining why—outside of Japanese exceptionalism—Euro and American Whites have exploited the international labor force, frequently made up of third world non-White people. It is easy to see that the race-divides-the-nation thesis is more of an evasion and mystification of White privilege rather than an honest analysis of it, because "We cannot prepare realistically for our future without honestly assessing our past (Bell, 1992, p. 11). White racial knowledge fails to ask why history worked out the way it did, what actions White Europeans took to secure their domination, or the hegemonic assumptions about the goodness of Whiteness in everyday discourse. Race invests skin color with meaning and erects institutions around it to modernize its processes and establishes a hierarchy based on skin color, or what Bonilla-Silva (2004) calls "pigmentocracy" (p. 226). In order to transcend current race relations, which is a concrete possibility, we must first go *through* race in order to have any hopes of going *beyond* it.

Note

1. The gift concept was offered by Marcel Mauss (1967) based on his ethnographic studies of the Melanesian islands where he found an economy based on gift-giving as a form of challenge. In *The Gift*, Mauss documented the process whereby Melanesian natives obligated each other through gifts, instituting power in favor of the giver. In order to cancel out the gift, the receiver must respond with a different and deferred gift, usually raising the stakes and obligating the original giver. This process goes on and on in order to balance power relations. The gift concept has since been appropriated by several theorists, among them Georges Bataille, Pierre Bourdieu, and Jean Baudrillard. In education, McLaren, Leonardo, and Allen (2000) applied the gift concept to the study of Whiteness.

References

Aanerud, R. (1997). Fictions of whiteness: Speaking the names of whiteness in U.S. literature. In R. Frankenberg (Ed.), *Displacing whiteness* (pp. 35–59). Durham, NC: Duke University Press.

Allen, R. L. (2002). The globalization of white supremacy: Toward a critical discourse on the racialization of the world. *Educational Theory, 51*(4), 467–485.

Aoki, D. (2000). The thing never speaks for itself: Lacan and the pedagogical politics of clarity. *Harvard Educational Review, 70*(3), 345–369.

Bell, D. (1992). *Faces at the bottom of the well: The permanence of racism.* New York: Basic Books.

Bishop, R. S. (2005). Working together for literacy: Faces of hope. In B. Hammond, M. Hoover, & I. Mcphail (Eds.), *Teaching African American learners to read: Perspectives and practices* (pp. 105–114). Newark, DE: International Reading Association.

Blanchard, J. (2006, June 6). Supreme Court to hear Seattle schools race case. *Seattle Post-Intelligencer,* p. A1, A8.

Bobo, L., & Smith, R. (1998). From Jim Crow racism to laissez-faire racism: The transformation of racial attitudes. In W. Katkin, N. Landsman, & A. Tyree (Eds.), *Beyond pluralism: The conception of groups and group identities in America* (pp. 182–220). Urbana: University of Illinois Press.

Bonilla-Silva, E. (2001). *White supremacy and racism in the post-Civil Rights era.* Boulder, CO: Lynne Rienner.

Bonilla-Silva, E. (2004). From biracial to tri-racial: The emergence of a new racial stratification system in the United States. In C. Herring, V. Keith, & H. Horton (Eds.), *Skin/deep: How race and complexion matter in the "color-blind" era* (pp. 224–239). Urbana: University of Illinois Press.

Bonilla-Silva, E. (2005). "Racism" and "new racism": The contours of racial dynamics in contemporary America. In Z. Leonardo (Ed.), *Critical pedagogy and race* (pp. 1–35). Malden, MA: Blackwell.

Carlton, D. (2006, June 2). School district pulls website after examples of racism spark controversy. *Seattle Post-Intelligencer,* p. B1.

Dalton, H. (2002). Failing to see. In P. Rothenberg (Ed.), *White privilege* (pp. 15–18). New York: Worth.

Dillard, C. (2000). The substance of things hoped for, the evidence of things not seen: Examining an endarkened epistemology in educational research and leadership. *Qualitative Studies in Education, 13*(6), 661–681.

Douglass, F. (1982). *Narrative of the life of Frederick Douglass, an American slave.* New York: Penguin. (Original work published 1845)

DuBois, W. E. B. (1998). *Black Reconstruction in America, 1860–1880.* New York: The Free Press. (Original work published 1935)

Dutro, E., Kazemi, E., & Balf, R. (2005). The aftermath of "You're only half": Multiracial identities in the literacy classroom. *Language Arts, 83*(2), 96–106.

Enciso, P. (2003). Reading discrimination. In S. Greene & D. Abt-Perkins (Eds.), *Making race visible: Literacy research for cultural understanding* (pp. 149–177). New York: Teachers College Press.

Erickson, F. (2005). Culture in society and in educational practices. In J. Banks & C. Banks (Eds.), *Multicultural education: Issues and perspectives* (pp. 31–60). New York: Wiley.

Freire, P. (1993). *Pedagogy of the oppressed* (M. Ramos, Trans.). New York: Continuum. (Original work published 1970)

Freire, A., & Macedo, D. (1998). Introduction. In A. Freire & D. Macedo (Eds.), *The Paulo Freire reader* (pp. 1–44). New York: Continuum.

Funderberg, L. (1994). *Black, White, other.* New York: Quill.

Gadamer, H-G. (1975). *Truth and method.* New York: Seabury Press.

Geertz, C. (1994). Ideology as a cultural system. In T. Eagleton (Ed.), *Ideology* (pp. 279–294). London: Longman.

Gillborn, D. (2005). Education as an act of White supremacy: Whiteness, critical race theory and education reform. *Journal of Education Policy, 20*(4), 485–505.

Gillborn, D. (2006). Public interest and the interests of White people are not the same: Assessment, education policy, and racism. In G. Ladson-Billings & W. F. Tate (Eds.), *Education research in the public interest: Social Justice, action, and policy* (pp. 173–195). New York: Teachers College Press.

Giroux, H. (1995). Language, difference, and curriculum theory: Beyond the politics of clarity. In P. McLaren & J. Giarelli (Eds.), *Critical theory and educational research* (pp. 23–38). Albany: SUNY Press.

Giroux, H. (1997). *Channel surfing.* New York: St. Martin's Press.

Greene, S., & Abt-Perkins, D. (2003). How can literacy research contribute to racial understanding? In S. Greene & D. Abt-Perkins (Eds.), *Making race visible: Literacy research for cultural understanding* (pp. 1–31). New York: Teachers College Press.

Harris, V. (1999). Applying critical theories to children's literature. *Theory into Practice, 38*(3), 147–154.

hooks, b. (1997). Representing whiteness in the black imagination. In R. Frankenberg (Ed.), *Displacing whiteness* (pp. 165–179). Durham, NC: Duke University Press.

Howard, G. (1999). *We can't teach what we don't know.* New York: Teachers College Press.

Hunter, M. (2002) Decentering the white and male standpoint in race and ethnicity courses. In A. Macdonald & S. Sanchez-Casal (Eds.) *Twenty-first century feminist classrooms: Pedagogies of identity and difference* (pp. 251–279). New York: Palgrave.

Hunter, M., & Nettles, K. (1999, October). What about the white women? Racial politics in a women's studies classroom. *Teaching Sociology, 27,* 385–397.

Hurtado, A. (1996). *The color of privilege.* Ann Arbor: University of Michigan Press.

Ignatiev, N. (1995). *How the Irish became White.* New York: Routledge.

Ignatiev, N. (1997). *The point is not to interpret whiteness but to abolish it.* Talk given at the Conference on The Making and Unmaking of Whiteness. University of California, Berkeley. Retrieved July 26, 2007, from http://www.racetraitor.org)

Ignatiev, N., & Garvey, J. (1996). Abolish the White race: By any means necessary. In N. Ignatiev & J. Garvey (Eds.), *Race traitor* (pp. 9–14). New York: Routledge.

James, C. E. (2005). *Race in play: Understanding the socio-cultural worlds of student athletes.* Toronto: Canadian Scholars' Press.

Kerdeman, D. (2003). Pulled up short: Challenging self-understanding as a focus of teaching and learning. *Journal of Philosophy of Education, 37*(2), 293–308.

Kincheloe, J., & Steinberg, S. (1997). Addressing the crisis of whiteness: Reconfiguring white identity in a pedagogy of whiteness. In J. Kincheloe, S. Steinberg, N. Rodriguez, & R. Chennault (Eds.), *White reign* (pp. 3–29). New York: St. Martin's Griffin.

Kinder, D., & Sears, D. (1981). Prejudice and politics: Symbolic racism versus racial threats to the good life. *Journal of Personality and Social Psychology, 40*, 414–431.

Kozol, J. (1991). *Savage inequalities.* New York: Harper Perennial.

Ladson-Billings, G., & Gomez, M. L. (2001). Just showing up: Supporting early literacy through teachers' professional communities. *Phi Delta Kappan, 82*(9), 675–680.

Lather, P. (1996). Troubling clarity: The politics of accessible language. *Harvard Educational Review, 66*(3), 525–545.

Leonardo, Z. (2000). Betwixt and between: Introduction to the politics of identity. In C. Tejeda, C. Martinez, & Z. Leonardo (Eds.), *Charting new terrains of Chicana(o)/Latina(o) education* (pp. 107–129). Cresskill, NJ: Hampton Press.

Leonardo, Z. (2002). The souls of White folk: Critical pedagogy, whiteness studies, and globalization discourse. *Race Ethnicity & Education, 5*(1), 29–50.

Leonardo, Z. (2003a). Race. In D. Weil & J. Kincheloe (Eds.), *Critical thinking and learning: An encyclopedia* (pp. 347–351). Westport, CT: Greenwood.

Leonardo, Z. (2003b). Institutionalized racism. In D. Weil & J. Kincheloe (Eds.), *Critical thinking and learning: An encyclopedia* (pp. 341–347). Westport, CT: Greenwood.

Leonardo, Z. (2005). The color of supremacy: Beyond the discourse of "White privilege." In Z. Leonardo (Ed.), *Critical pedagogy and race* (pp. 37–52). Malden, MA: Blackwell.

Leonardo, Z. (2006). Through the multicultural glass: Althusser, ideology, and race relations in post-Civil Rights America. *Policy Futures in Education, 3*(4), 400–412.

Lipsitz, G. (1998). *The possessive investment in whiteness.* Philadelphia: Temple University Press.

Loewen, J. (1995). *Lies my teacher told me.* New York: New Press.

Marable, M. (2002). The souls of White folk. *Souls, 4*(4), 45–51.

Massey, D., & Denton, N. (1993). *American apartheid.* Cambridge, MA: Harvard University Press.

Mauss, M. (1967). *The gift.* United States: W.W. Norton.

McIntosh, P. (1992). White privilege and male privilege: A personal account of coming to see correspondences through work in women's studies. In M. Andersen & P. H. Collins (Eds.), *Race, class, and gender: An anthology* (pp. 70–81). Belmont, CA: Wadsworth.

McIntyre, A. (1997). *Making meaning of whiteness.* Albany, NY: SUNY Press.

McLaren, P., Leonardo, Z., & Allen, R. L. (2000). Epistemologies of whiteness: Transforming and transgressing pedagogical knowledge. In R. Mahalingam & C. McCarthy (Eds.), *Multicultural Curriculum: New directions for social theory, practice, and policy* (pp. 108–123). New York: Routledge.

Mills, C. (1997). *The racial contract.* Ithaca, NY: Cornell University Press.

Morrison, T. (1970). *The bluest eye.* New York: Plume Books.

Myers, L., & Williamson, P. (2001). Race talk: The perpetuation of racism through private discourse. *Race and Society, 4*(1), 3–26.

Newitz, A., & Wray, M. (1997). What is "White trash"? Stereotypes and economic conditions of poor Whites in the United States. In M. Hill (Ed.), *Whiteness: A critical reader.* New York: New York University Press.

Nieto, S. (2003). Afterword. In S. Greene & D. Abt-Perkins (Eds.), *Making race visible: Literacy research for cultural understanding* (pp. 201–205). New York: Teachers College Press.

Rains, F. (1997). Is the benign really harmless? Deconstructing some "benign" manifestations of operationalized White privilege. In J. Kincheloe, S. Steinberg, N. Rodriguez, & R. Chennault (Eds.), *White reign* (pp. 77–101). New York: St. Martin's Griffin.

Rimonte, N. (1997). Colonialism's legacy: The inferiorizing of the Filipino. In M. Root (Ed.), *Filipino Americans* (pp. 39–61). Thousand Oaks, CA: Sage.

Roediger, D. (1991). *The wages of whiteness*. New York: Verso.

Roediger, D. (1994). *Towards the abolition of whiteness*. New York: Verso.

Rumbaut, R. (1996). Prologue. In S. Pedraza & R. Rumbaut (Eds.), *Origins and destinies: Immigration, race, and ethnicity in America* (pp. xvi–xix). Belmont, CA: Wadsworth.

Said, E. (1979). *Orientalism*. New York: Random House.

Scheurich, J., & Young, M. (1997). Coloring epistemologies: Are our research epistemologies racially biased. *Educational Researcher, 26*(4), 4–16.

Schofield, J. (2005). The colorblind perspective in school: Causes and consequences. In J. Banks & C. Banks (Eds.), *Multicultural education* (pp. 265–288). New York: Wiley.

Shelby, T. (2003). Ideology, racism, and critical social theory. *The Philosophical Forum, 34*(2), 153–188.

Stepan, N. (1990). Race and gender: The role of analogy in science. In D. Goldberg (Ed.), *Anatomy of racism* (pp. 38–57). Minneapolis: University of Minnesota Press.

Takaki, R. (1993). *A different mirror*. Boston: Little, Brown.

Valenzuela, A. (1999). *Subtractive schooling: U.S.-Mexican youth and the politics of caring*. Albany: State University of New York Press.

Valenzuela, A. (2002). Reflections on the subtractive underpinnings of education research and policy. *Journal of Teacher Education, 53*(3), 235–241.

Van Ausdale, D., & Feagin, J. (2001). *The first R: How children learn race and racism*. Lanham, MD: Rowman & Littlefield.

Warren, J. (2002). Critical race studies in Latin America: Recent advances, recurrent weaknesses. In D. T. Goldberg & J. Solomos (Eds.), *A companion to racial and ethnic studies* (pp. 538–560). Malden, MA: Blackwell.

Weber, M. (1978). The three pure types of authority. In G. Roth & C. Wittich (Eds.), *Economy and society* (Vol. 1, pp. 215–216). Berkeley: University of California Press.

Willis, A., & Harris, V. (2000). Political acts: Literacy learning and teaching. *Reading Research Quarterly, 35*(1), 72–88.

Wise, T. (2002). Membership has its privileges: Thoughts on acknowledging and challenging whiteness. In P. Rothenberg (Ed.), *White privilege* (pp. 107–110). New York: Worth.

Wright, H. (2003). An endarkened feminist epistemology? Identity, difference and the politics of representation in educational research. *Qualitative Studies in Education, 16*(2), 197–214.

17 Discrimination, Culture, or Capital?

The Challenges of Underconceptualizing Race in Educational Research

Amanda Lewis, Carla O'Connor, and Jennifer Mueller

Introduction

Concerns about racial inequity are central to conversations about the role of education in promoting social justice as well as in promoting more just educational outcomes and experiences. In this chapter we examine how race is typically deployed in educational research and raise a number of concerns about its underconceptualization in the literature. Specifically, at the same time that race serves as a commonplace marker for deciphering group-based distinctions in school experience, it has been undertheorized as a social construct (Lynn & Adams, 2002; Pollock, 2004). As we will elaborate upon below, our failure to attend to race with greater conceptual (and by implication methodological) precision, impinges upon our ability to develop more exact interpretations of how and why students fare in school as they do.

In order to make our argument both concrete and clear, we particularly focus our attention in this chapter on how race has been deployed in trying to understand and explain the educational experiences of one group—African Americans. African Americans[1] represent the most often-studied minority group in educational research. While much of this research has invoked White Americans (explicitly and implicitly) as a comparative referent for measuring, interpreting, and explaining the educational experiences of African Americans, researchers have also examined how the schooling experiences of African Americans compare with those of other minority groups. Accordingly, researchers have marked and subsequently analyzed the underachievement of African Americans relative to how other groups (e.g., White Americans, Asian Americans, Latinos, immigrants) perform on a wide variety of measures (e.g., standardized test scores; rates of high school attrition and graduation; cumulative grade point averages; enrollment in advanced vs. remedial vs. special education courses). Work that examines African-American students who beat the odds for failing in school is often implicitly concerned with understanding why these students compete favorably with White Americans in academic effort or educational outcomes. And, research that explores the promise of culturally relevant pedagogy and other interventions (pedagogical or reform) designed to raise the achievement performance of African Americans is implicitly concerned with eradicating group-based (especially Black-White) differences in educational opportunity and outcomes. Clearly, the larger problem is the lack of conceptual clarity about race and a similar set of analyses could (and should) be applied to the study of experiences of other groups. Here, however, we wanted to focus on arguably the most studied and discussed group in order to illustrate several larger patterns.

Our discussion will begin by reporting on the patterns by which race has been captured as a social category in contemporary educational literature. Focusing on research produced within the last 40 years, we will emphasize the work that has been concerned with the elementary and secondary schooling of African Americans. Within this area of research, we have identified two dominant traditions and one emerging focus, by which educational researchers have sought to invoke the significance of race. In terms of the dominant traditions, researchers have operationalized race most often either as a variable or as culture.

We will elaborate upon the nature and conceptual limitations of the two primary traditions. More precisely, we will discuss the following: (1) how these approaches (when taken in total) confound causes and effects in the estimation of when and how race is "significant" to Black achievement performance; (2) how they underanalyze the influence of institutionalized inequities and racial discrimination; and (3) the ways in which they mask the heterogeneity of the African-American experience, and its accordant relationship to the differentiated school performance of Black youth. These stated limitations effectively cloud our ability to interpret with precision when and how race is implicated in the educational experiences, achievement, and outcomes of Black students.

We will subsequently discuss how future studies on African Americans' educational experiences might account for these limitations at different stages in the research process. More specifically, we will recommend productive directions in which researchers might reorient their empirical and analytical foci. We identify the emergent focus on race as capital as one of several fruitful starting points for this reorientation. Our call for reorientation necessarily warrants shifts in research design and methodology. Consequently, we will also elaborate upon the ways in which this reorientation might be supported via the use of ethnographic methods and mixed methods approaches.

Race As an Undertheorized Social Construct

Research on the educational achievement, outcomes, and experiences of African American youth must necessarily attend to race. However, undertheorized, oversimplified, or inaccurate conceptualizations of race can serve to create as many problems as they solve. We must, consequently, pursue more accurate and precise ways of capturing race as a social phenomenon.

Toward this end, we must first account for how contemporary educational discourse has circumscribed our understanding of how race is implicated in how Black students experience and perform in school. As aforementioned, we will focus the discussion on the categories that emerged in our examination of the research (i.e., race as a variable, race as culture, and race as capital). It is important to point out that these categories are not mutually exclusive. That is, while they represent different ways that race has been captured or conceptualized in educational discourse on African Americans, these different conceptualizations of race are sometimes reflected in, or alluded to, within a single text, study, or article. Our discussion begins by elaborating upon the most common pattern by which race has been captured in the literature—that being when race operates as a variable.

Race as a Variable

In most instances (particularly within sociological and psychological studies of education), little effort is made to theorize or conceptualize race as social category or as a social phenomenon. Typically, race is incorporated as one of many "control" variables, but often without any clear theoretical articulation of what it is imagined to be capturing. As Zuberi (2001) argues:

Researchers typically use selected variables [race being amongst them] in a statistical model that purports to correspond to a poorly explained substantive theory. They then use some data to estimate the parameters of the model, and these parameter estimates and their functions give the effects of interest. However, this strategy makes too many unsubstantiated assumptions. (p. 123)

This work is often short on theoretical detail, and becomes a data-driven process intending to identify which variables are significant for explaining observed variance. The problems are several. First, race is typically included in statistical models as an individual attribute that is stable (doesn't change across time or space). Second race cannot be, in the way that is often implied, a "cause" for social outcomes (Zuberi, 2001). While racial discrimination, for example, may be a cause of some specified outcome, race itself is merely a marker of social location. It is an ascribed characteristic and a political classification system. Race as a variable, thus, functionally serves as place-marker—a proxy—for an unspecified "something else" that is difficult to measure or quantify. While in some cases that imagined relevance is articulated, (e.g., Morgan, 1996), often it is the case that race is found to be significant without a discussion of why it is likely to have an association with the phenomenon under question (e.g., Dauber, Alexander, & Entwisle, 1996).[2]

This is not, by any means, to suggest that we should not collect or analyze racial data. As Zuberi (2001) states, "Racial data are necessary for viewing the effects of racial prejudice" (p. 119) on such things as socioeconomic status, individual well-being, and educational experiences and outcomes. This kind of data is essential for tracking continuing racial inequalities, and for charting racial progress. However, it should not be used as a proxy for "traits" (such as intelligence or criminality) that are imagined to be innate or culturally engrained. There are several practical challenges of using race as a variable, including how to interpret the findings of racial "significance," and how to avoid underestimating the effect of racial discrimination through the use of misspecified models. We will discuss these challenges in turn.

(Mis)Interpreting Significance

When studies suggest that "race" is a significant variable with regard to African Americans' educational outcomes, what, in fact, does this mean? "African American" (or for that matter "Black") is not a biological or genetic category. It is a social group united by a long history of racialized experiences within the United States. However, researchers regularly fail to pay attention to this when they interpret findings of statistical significance. Scholars from Herrnstein and Murray (1994), who treat race as genetic category, to those whose arguments constitute what William Darity (2002) has called a kind of "cultural determinism," treat race as if it captures or identifies something deficient within individuals or groups. Race here is a proxy for bad genes or a lack of the "cultural 'right stuff'" (Darity, 2002, p. 1). While "race as biology" has been entirely disproved in biological and anthropological literature, its more recent replacement, the "biologization of culture" (as it is termed by Bonilla-Silva, 2001) or the "culture as destiny" arguments (so named by Darity, 2002) are not all that different. These arguments suggest a mostly intractable set of cultural traits (sometimes reinterpreted as deficiencies) that lie within an imagined, coherent "Black" community, which are supposed to, at least partially, explain racial inequality.

Importantly, while there are studies where the focus has been unilaterally placed on documenting the cultural deficiencies of African Americans, these researchers have been unable to substantiate their presumptions. For example, Graham (1994) noted that "motivation research on African Americans has been guided less by general theoretical principles than by the relationship of particular constructs to socioeconomic status, the ease with which comparisons could be made, and [for the purposes of our discussion] the availability of explanations to account for presumed motivational deficits in Blacks" (p. 2).[3] But while researchers expected that motivational deficits would account for why Blacks performed poorly in school, their findings generally contradicted their presumption that Blacks had low expectations, felt hopeless, marginalized the importance of individual effort, gave up in the face of failure, and expressed low self-esteem (Graham, 1994).

Additionally, the notion of an homogeneous Black community that embodies a set of intractable (and deficient) traits has also been challenged by studies that show that family wealth or child socioeconomic status are much more important predictors of educational outcomes than supposed "cultural" measures such as family values (Conley, 1999; Darity, Dietrich,& Guilkey, 2001; Mason, 1996, 1999). For example, Dalton Conley (1999) found that once family wealth was controlled, African-American school performance and outcomes were equivalent if not superior to White outcomes. This is no small issue when thinking about educational success and failure. The cumulative consequences of several centuries of systematic racism in the United States have left some communities collectively with far more wealth than others (Johnson, 2006; Oliver & Shapiro, 1995; Shapiro, 2004; Wolfe, 1994). The parallel developments of White supremacy and capitalism in this country meant that even after emancipation, Black workers were limited to the worst and lowest paying jobs, blocked from access to union jobs, once admitted into unions were often the first fired in bad times because they were the last hired (Marable, 1983; Takaki, 1993). Urban Black communities forged in the context of virulent segregation were devastated by urban renewal programs, red lining, and other public and private practices (Drake & Cayton, 1993; Massey & Denton, 1993; Sugrue, 1996). One result is that today, even controlling for income and education, Blacks on average have far less wealth than Whites (Oliver & Shapiro, 1995; Wolfe, 1994).

While today, income differences persist generally and at all education levels (Table 17.1), they aren't nearly as dramatic as wealth differences (Table 17.2). Wealth gaps are the effects of congealed effect of centuries of racial hierarchy and are almost entirely explained by intergenerational transfers (Wolff, 2000). As shown in Table 17.2, differences in median net wealth show Blacks on average with 2 to 3% of the median net wealth of White households.[4] Recent studies indicate that wealth does more for you educationally than income (Conley 1999; Johnson & Shapiro 2003; Orr 2003; Shapiro 2004). However, we do not have good measures of wealth in most analyses of school

Table 17.1 Median Income in 2002 by Educational Attainment of Population 18 yrs. older (full time year roud)

Educational level	White	Black	Ratio
<HS Diploma	$25,254	$19,859	.79
HS Diploma	$30,875	$25,311	.82
Some College	$36,361	$30,270	.83
College Graduate	$51,024	$42,048	.82
MA Degree	$60,480	$49,078	.81
Professional Degree	$96,767	$52,457	.54

Source: U.S. Census.

Table 17.2 Average Net Worth by Race (1984, 1989, 1994)

All Familes	Mean Values			Medium Values		
	Whites	African Americans	Ratio	Whites	African Americans	Ratio
1984	139.8	25.2	.81	51.8	0.1	0.02
1989	179.0	34.2	.19	52.6	1.3	0.03
1994	180.7	32.4	.18	57.2	1.1	0.02

Source: Wolff, 2001.

achievement. This is no small issue when thinking about educational success and failure. As detailed in the careful work of Shapiro (2004), Johnson and Shapiro (2003), and Johnson (2006) intergenerational transfers of even small amounts of wealth provide a whole range of educational options to those who have access to them.

When resources are pooled so inequitably across communities, there are potentially multiple kinds of collective consequences—especially when those communities tend not to live and attend school together (Massey & Denton, 1993; Orfield, 1996; Orfield & Gordon, 2001). As Gary Orfield and colleagues' work has shown, most White children, even poor White children, don't attend high poverty schools (Orfield & Gordon, 2001; Orfield & Yun, 1999). But most Black and Brown children, even middle class ones, attend high poverty schools. Segregation in housing is key here and such segregation is, as Yinger (1995) points out "an outcome of a complex system in which prejudice, segregation, discrimination, and racial or ethnic economic dispartities are simultaneously determined. Each one of these phenomena influences the other" (p. 122). Using longitudinal data, Roslyn Mickelson (2001) found that attending a racially isolated Black elementary school had both direct and indirect negative effects on achievement and track placement even with controls for numerous individual and family indicators. This measure is often not available and thus is not usually included in analyses, but given persistently high levels of school segregation it might well be one thing typically captured in the variable "race." Studies that do not include measures of wealth, segregation, or related issues too often attribute to race a significance it does not have, and ignore meaning it does have. The second challenge of treating race as a variable provides a good example of this.

Underanalyzing Racial Discrimination

As *opposed* to our previous account of how certain meanings, which do not hold, are attributed to race, there are other examples where the effect of race on African-American educational outcomes is underappreciated. While culture has dubious significance in explaining educational outcomes (as will be elaborated upon further in the next section of the chapter), race does have an effect, particularly in the way it functions to shape access to resources (Johnson, Boyden, & Pittz, 2001; Johnson, Libero, & Burlingame, 2000; Lewis, 2003b). Specifically, large disparities have been documented in the quality of K-8 educational experiences between White students and students of color (Carter, 1995; Darling-Hammond & Sclan, 1996; A. A. Ferguson, 2000; Lewis, 2003b; Mickelson, 2003; Nettles & Perna, 1997; Rist, 1970). There is substantial evidence that these gaps are often the result of widespread institutionalized racism in our national school system. Researchers continue to document differential disciplinary rates and teacher expectations, continuing and increasing patterns of racial segregation within schools, racially stratified academic placement systems, differential teacher expectations, or unequal funding for minority schools (Ainsworth-Darnell & Downey, 1998; Ayers, Dohn, & Ayers, 2001; Bonilla-Silva & Lewis, 1999; Feagin, Vera, & Imani, 1996; Ferguson, 1998a, 1998b, 2000; Johnson, Boyden, & Pitz, 2001; Orfield & Gordon, 2001; Orfield & Yun, 1999; Roscigno & Ainsworth-Darnell, 1999; Valenzula, 1999).

However, in using undertheorized racial constructs, researchers are unable to account for this differential access to educational opportunities. A good example of this comes from studies that measure an association between race and some school outcome after "controlling for previous achievement" (most often operationalized as test scores or grades). Such work fails to recognize that "previous achievement" may well serve as a proxy for racial discrimination. That is, "previous achievement" may, in fact, measure, in part, "previous institutional racism in educational opportunities." For example, Dauber et al. (1996) discuss the way the effects of social background factors (race, SES, etc.) can be masked as "objective academic qualifications." In their research on track placements they found that sixth grade course placement (i.e., advanced, regular, or remedial) was the main predictor of eighth grade course placements. However, they then found that the main predictors of sixth grade course placement included social background factors—race being one of the most significant. They state:

> This finding suggests that social-background differences in eighth-grade course enrollments can be explained, to a large extent, by associated differences in students' academic histories. However, the power of this explanation should be tempered by knowledge of social-background differences in initial sixth-grade placements, since the latter placements have large effects on eighth-grade assignments...by the eighth-grade, social-background differences in mathematics are almost entirely hidden by their strong association with sixth-grade placements. (p. 300)

This illustrates how using seemingly "objective" academic outcomes, from early in a student's career, as controls in analyzing later academic outcomes can mask other effects. Specifically, in sixth grade, African-American students were much less likely than similar White peers to be placed in a higher track class and were more likely than similar White peers to be placed in low-track classes. Those patterns held in eighth grade, but any analysis that used sixth-grade placement as an objective measure of prior achievement would find almost no race effects—as they were almost entirely captured by the variable "sixth-grade placement."

Similarly, studies that draw on large, longitudinal national data sets may well often underestimate the effects of institutional racism on educational outcomes by including measures of "previous achievement" as if they are good controls for academic ability or proclivity rather than of measures of "previous opportunity." For example, Morgan (1996) used a measure of "cognitive skill," a composite of students' performance on a variety of standardized tests, which he described as "not an IQ measure of innate ability. Instead it measures the ability to succeed in postsecondary education and, as such, is a composite of unknown portions of innate intelligence and prior academic preparation" (pp. 309–310). As Oakes (1988), Dauber et al. (1996), Persell (1977), and others have argued, and as Morgan even seems to acknowledge in his description, such measures are not, as they are often used, direct measures of student ability.

Generally, findings that include such measures of "prior achievement," but suggest that race is not "significant," potentially have misspecified models with clear endogeneity problems. That is, by including race and prior achievement in a regression model it implies, temporally, that they occur or have effect at the same time, when, in fact, race (as a proxy for institutionalized racism) has causal significance in shaping prior achievement (e.g., sixth grade track placement).

Thus we need more conceptual clarity both in terms of how race is included in statistical models and how we interpret its significance.

Variation within the Category "Black"

Finally, how are we to interpret the election of individuals into the category of Black or African American on social surveys? Survey research accounts for individuals' self-identification (or parental identification depending on who is responsible for filling out the survey questionnaire) with the category Black/African American, over the other racial categories featured on the questionnaire. However, it does not account for how the context of administration and the design of the survey impinged upon the respondents' choice of label. Depending on how demographic questions are asked, the range of available options, and the context in which the asking is happening, we may well get different responses to "racial/ethnic questions" (Harris & Sim, 2000; Rodriguez, 1991, 1992, 2000; Rodriguez & Cordero-Guzman, 1992).[5]

Additionally, surveys regularly prevent "Hispanics" from claiming a racial designation. Thus the racial and ethnic options provided on a given survey often situates "Hispanic" as a category that lies alongside "Black not of Hispanic origin" and "White not of Hispanic origin." By defining racial and ethnic "choices" in this way, we blur the distinction between race and ethnicity and deny respondents the ability to claim (if they are so inclined) an ethnic as well as a racial affiliation. It is important to note that even when surveys enable "Hispanics" to claim a racial designation,[6] the choices—to the chagrin of many Hispanics—are dichotomized (i.e., White vs. Black) (Rodriguez, 2000). And even when this racial data (however limited) is available to researchers, they rely on "Hispanic" as the default social categorization and avoid race-related analyses.

Additionally, while place of birth on these same surveys can signal the ethnic affiliations of Blacks (e.g., African vs. West Indian) researchers have rarely taken advantage of this data.[7] Thus, with the few exceptions (e.g., Farley & Allen, 1989; Sowell, 1978; Waldinger, 1996; Waters, 1994, 1999), the ethnic differentiation amongst Blacks and its relation to their educational outcomes and experiences is not studied. The need to explore ethnic differentiation becomes exceptionally intriguing in light of findings that indicate that the differences in the achievement performance of native and immigrant Blacks has shifted over time (Waldinger, 1996). Additionally, there is evidence that immigrant Blacks are both the most and the least competitive students in America's schools (Waters, 1999).

Often when researchers situate Blacks by birthplace, the focus is on their status as immigrants and not as members of ethnic groups. Moreover, the impact of race is often left unexamined. Such tensions are suggested in Portes and MacLeod's (1996) examination of the educational progress of children of immigrants from Cuba, Vietnam, Haiti, and Mexico. The importance of the Portes and MacLeod study rests with its conceptual attention to how the context of reception is implicated in the differential performance of these immigrant groups. However, the researchers did not attend to how the race of their immigrants might have moderated, in part, the nature of that reception. For example, they noted that Cuban and Vietnamese refugees, compared to the Haitian and Mexican immigrants, were "received sympathetically by the U.S. government and were granted numerous forms of federal assistance" (p. 260). The authors indicated that Cubans and Vietnamese then used these subsidies to "create solidary and dynamic entrepreneurial communities" that framed, in part, their more competitive achievement performance.

However, Portes and MacLeod then pointed out that earlier waves of Cubans received generous governmental assistance that was denied subsequent arrivals. While the researchers register how social class distinguished the earlier and the later waves of Cubans, they silence the fact that the first wave was not only of higher social class origins, but was disproportionately "White" (Pedraza & Rumbaut, 1996). In contrast, the latter waves were not only of lower class origins, but were primarily "Black" and "Brown" (Pedraza & Rumbaut, 1996). The analyses, therefore, fail not only to conceptualize how "race," as it is signaled by phenotype, might be implicated in institutionalized access to resources, but how it intersects with social class in the determination of that access.

The survey design and application issues discussed above raise the following questions: (1) About whom are we speaking, precisely? (2) Who is being captured within and being excluded by the category "African American" or "Black"? (3) How does this impinge upon our comparative analyses of African-Americans vis-à-vis others? While some of this can be addressed with the use of control variables (e.g., socioeconomic status, region, place of birth), some of this variation is often left out because of limitations in data collection.

Traditional survey approaches also constrain our ability to assess how the participants make sense of the racial options with which they were provided (i.e., emically rather than etically). While an etic approach privileges researcher imposed categories and interpretations, an emic approach enables the participants to introduce and offer interpretations of categories that were unanticipated by the researcher (Watson & Watson-Franke, 1985). By committing ourselves to more emic approaches, we can design surveys with the intent of examining how respondents understand their selected racial option in relation to researcher-selected parameters of interest.

For example, Sellers and his colleagues (Sellers, Smith, Shelton, Rowley, & Chavous, 1998) have developed the Multi-Dimensional Model of Racial Identity survey (MMRI), which has made a significant contribution to our understanding of the multidimensionality of Black racial identity. Use of the MMRI allows us to gauge the following: (1) the extent to which "being Black" is central to the identity of the person under study; (2) whether the person assesses being Black in positive or negative terms, or believes this racial designation is regarded publicly in positive or negative terms; (3) when and under what conditions she or he imagines that being Black is especially salient to his or her experiences; and (4) whether this self-designation as Black is aligned with a specific racial ideology.

Like other surveys, however, the MMRI necessarily restricts the respondents' ability to impose categories unanticipated by the researcher. Consequently, we are unable to assess dimensions of racial identity that were not targeted a priori. Nor can we make adequate sense of those dimensions that are represented via performance (e.g., style, dress, language) rather than cognition, and would be better captured via observation.

The substantive variation with which African Americans can perform their racial identity has been most recently and compellingly captured in John Jackson's (2001), Harlem World. Educational researchers have additionally developed ethnographic insight into the variation with which African Americans can perform their Blackness (e.g., Ogbu, 1989). Sometimes these variations are performed via the intersections of class and gender (Carter, 2005; Cousins, 1999; Fordham, 1996; Horvat & Antonio, 1999; Kenny, 1999; O'Connor, 1999; Tyson, 2002). The complexity of such performances is, however, outside the scope of survey research.

The forced choice nature of survey research also prevents respondents from providing commentary that would qualify their responses in significant ways. This is true both for how students might identify racially (Harris & Sim, 2001), and true for the nature of their answers to substantive questions. For example, in a mixed-method study, Bonilla-Silva and Forman (2000) found that respondents' answers to survey items differed significantly from the elaborations they provided in interviews.

Additionally, we are unable to explore how the social construction of these categories (via macro- and microdynamics; historical and contemporary forces) informs the development and reflection of these categories, and constrain or frame, in part, the participant's election into one category rather than another (Cornell, 1996; Hall, 1990; Ignatiev, 1995). For example, researchers (e.g., Bashi & McDaniel, 1997; Vickerman, 1999) have found that immigrants of dark phenotype, who had not previously imagined themselves as "Black," come to claim this identity upon their stay in the United States, given the power with which skin color operates as signifier of race and ethnicity within this context.

Our failure to attend to the methodological and conceptual issues elaborated upon above has substantive implications for how we make sense of the statistically robust relationships that are regularly reported on in research that features race as variable. That is, while this work is often focused on identifying correlates for Black achievement performance and educational attainment (especially in relationship to educational "gaps" that exist between racial groups) it does not allow us to interpret the way that race as a social phenomenon is implicated in these relationships. For example, when a researcher finds that income and occupation are less robust predictors of achievement performance for Blacks than for Whites, we cannot discern (i.e., empirically) if this relationship is a function of: (1) the ways in which Blacks across social class groups might similarly make sense of and display what it means to "be" Black within the school setting; (2) how frames or meanings of Blackness are imposed upon Black bodies, by schooling agents and others, in ways that diminish the significance of social class; (3) how social class as signaled by income and occupation marks culture, and determines opportunity differently and less powerfully than when it is signaled by wealth, and it is the similar wealth deficits African Americans experience across income and occupation categories that account for their performance in school; or (4) some interaction of the aforementioned.

The tendency to ignore variation within the category "Black," and the inadequate attention to how institutions and their agents are active agents in the racializing of African-American youths, also marks the limitations in the second way race is deployed in educational research on African Americans—race as culture.

Race as Culture

Within this tradition, researchers have historically interpreted culture as either the norms and values, or the competencies and practices that distinguish one racial group from another. Subsequent efforts have then been made to make sense of the academic underperformance of African Americans relative to other racial groups—especially White Americans. These efforts have often taken the direction of documenting a disjuncture between the cultural norms, values, competencies, and practices that marked individuals as Black, and those norms, values, competencies, and practices that frame the organization and expectations of America's schools.

Our review of the literature reveals that contemporary educational discourse has generally evolved from the notion that culture operates as the norms and values that distinguish African Americans from other racial groups. While this notion has not generally fallen out of favor in other academic arenas (particularly in relation to intellectual debates on welfare reform), educational researchers have increasingly shied away from this analytical orientation. This avoidance is due, in part, to the ardent criticisms that, having situated Whites as the normative referent, Black culture has thus been interpreted from a deficit perspective, power has been stripped from the analysis, and a "blame the victim" orientation has been cultivated. Critics have additionally emphasized that this early work did not, in fact, capture culture at all. Rather, it captured traits, activities, and behaviors. More precisely, those like Valentine (1968) indicated that cultural deprivation theorists, having isolated select behaviors (or "nonbehaviors") of the (Black) poor, imposed their own meaning on these behaviors (or their absence) and, in the process, obfuscated the native understanding of what was being "said" by engaging in or eschewing these actions. [8]

The above criticisms did cause researchers to refrain from examining Black culture via the prism of norms and values. However, work continues to be conducted where culture is conceptualized in terms of the practices or competencies that presumably mark individuals as Black.[9] This notion of culture is commonly reflected in work that examines the empirical or theoretical promise of "culturally relevant pedagogy," as well as efforts to analyze how race-specific practices are implicated in the achievement performance of African Americans. In accordance with this orientation, researchers have been especially sensitive to how African-American discourse practices, learning styles. and social dispositions are at odds with the norms and expectations of America's schools.[10]

In contrast to the emphasis on norms and values that had been privileged two generations earlier, and had interpreted registers of African-American culture (however inappropriate) via a deficit paradigm, work on the competencies and practices of African Americans is generally critical of how schools and their agents have failed to incorporate Black practices and competencies as scaffolds to academic learning (Ladson-Billings, 1995; Villegas, 1988). Despite this advance, this work too has been criticized for not attending specifically to the meaning that undergirded the practices and competencies that were documented as "Black." For example, John Ogbu (1999) in response to the national discourse on AAVE (or Ebonics) and the education of African American youth stated that:

> ...the national discourse focused almost exclusively on differences in dialects per se. Some people agreed...that the academic problems [of African Americans] are caused by large differences between Black students' home dialect and school standard English. Others contended that the differences are not large enough to cause problems. The two groups, however, missed the point: It is not only the degree of differences in dialects per se that counts. What also seems to count is the cultural *meanings* of those dialect difference. (p. 148; authors' emphasis)

Fordham (1999) similarly claimed that we cannot limit our analyses to how Ebonics "parallels or deviates from...standard dialect" but must examine "the meaning of the linguistic practices of African American youths" (p. 272). More specifically, she stressed the extent to which these language practices might operate as *marker[s] of Black identity*," and elucidate "*imagined* cultural traditions and practices" that facilitate the recognition and resistance to the imposition of White power (Fordham, 1999, p. 274; authors' emphasis).

In alignment with these claims, contemporary scholars have sought to examine how Blackness is articulated via meaning-making rather than objectified competencies and practices. In accordance with this orientation, Blacks are distinguished from other racial groups in light of how they "take up" or make sense of publicly available tools or symbols. This conceptual emphasis is consistent with larger trends in both sociology and anthropology to characterize culture "by the publicly available symbolic forms through which people experience and express meaning" (Swidler, 1986, p. 273). Through this emphasis on meaning-making, researchers have attempted to map, conceptually and empirically, how people interpret, act upon, and produce material (e.g., art forms, tools, books), as well as social texts (e.g., language, social interaction, ideology, rituals, moral codes; ceremonies, strategies for action, identity).

As suggested by our previous reference to Fordham (1999), researchers are especially focused on understanding how Black youths take up (or perform), make sense of (or perceive), act upon (or act within) race and school (two common symbolic referents within the American context). More specifically, researchers continue to examine the following: (1) how African American youths interpret themselves and others as racial subjects; (2) how they construct these understandings in relation to the perceived utility of school; and (3) how such meaning-making is implicated in how they act and subsequently achieve in school. John Ogbu's cultural ecological model (CEM) provides us with not only the most cited, but also the most influential conceptual framework within this tradition (Jencks & Phillips, 1998).

According to CEM, Black youths, via the experiences and narratives of family members and other Black adults, learn about the historical and contemporary subjugation of African Americans. In response, they not only generate theories of "making it" which contradict dominant notions of status attainment and produce disillusionment about the instrumental value of school, but develop substantial distrust for school and its agents, which then suppresses commitment to school norms. Moreover, youth develop an oppositional cultural identity. Situating schooling as a White domain that requires Blacks to "think" and "act" White in exchange for academic success, Black youth are said to limit their efforts in school because they do not want to compromise their own racial identity or risk affiliation with the Black community (Ogbu, 1987).

Ogbu's framework has provided the impetus for continued investigations of how Black youths contend with what it "means" to be and act Black. Some of this work substantiates Ogbu's claims (e.g., Fordham, 1996; Gibson, 1991; Solomon, 1991). For example, Fordham (1996) offers us insight into how Black students resist their peers' normative interpretations of what it means to be Black, and consequently strive to assume a raceless persona in their pursuit of high achievement. Other work requires us to contend with the ways in which Ogbu's framework might homogenize and essentialize the subjectivity and performances of Black youths (Ainsworth-Darnell & Downey, 1998; Carter, 1999; Cook & Ludwig, 1998; O'Connor, 1997, 1999; Tyson, 1998). For example, Carter found that the Black youth in her study imagined that Blackness was reflected through a variety of statuses, preferences, and practices (e.g., affiliating with and respecting other Black folk; being able to speak Black English; dressing in popular urban youth attire), but never in opposition to school achievement. In response to these findings, Carter (2001) like others (e.g., Ainsworth-Darnell & Downey, 1998; Cook & Ludwig, 1998), argues that we should more carefully examine how schools situate Black subjects and "culture" in our effort to better understand the academic performance of Black youths.

Educational researchers' efforts to contend with the limitations of Ogbu's framework and develop ever more complex renderings of culture in relation to race and schooling, are first attempts to escape what Walter Ben Michaels (1992) refers to as the "anticipation of culture by race" (p. 677). Such anticipation occurs when we presume, "To be [Black] you have to do [Black] things, but you can't really count as doing [Black] things unless you already are [Black]" (p. 677).[11] When we anticipate culture by race, we not only reify race as a stable, objective, and measurable category, but for the purposes of our immediate discussion, link it deterministically to culture. When race is operationalized in this way we lose sight of Black heterogeneity, underconceptualize intersectionalities of various identity markers, and silence the extent to which Blackness is not only reflected in the meanings students bring with them to school, but the meanings that are imposed upon them by school structures and officials. Omi and Winant (1994) have long claimed that "[t]he effort must be made to understand race as an unstable and 'decentered' complex of social meanings constantly being transformed by political struggle" (p. 55). In the next section of the chapter, we consequently examine, more closely, the need for exploring Black heterogeneity, class, and gender intersectionalities, and the impact of institutionalized constructions of race that are articulated via political struggles that occur in school.

The Circumscription of Black Heterogeneity

Whether reporting on norms and values, competencies and practices, or subjectivity and meaning-making, researchers are usually reporting on findings that are specific to a particular segment of the Black community who are specifically framed by a host of social influences, including, but not limited to, race. While researchers often allude to these other influences via their elaborated descriptions of the research participants (e.g., by referring to the gender or social class of the Blacks under study) and the research setting (e.g., by referring to the demographics, organization, and location of the site in which the study was conducted), these influences are rarely invoked analytically, and the findings reported on are often attributed solely to the race of the participants. For example, while the majority of studies which have situated race as culture have focused expressly on lower income African Americans in contemporary urban spaces, the ways in which social class and place may have shaped these reported expressions of "Black" culture are often stripped from the analyses. Thus, in one stroke, researchers have not only cast the Black poor as a homogenous social category, but have silenced the ways in which space, time, and social class likely moderated the experience of being Black, and the consequent norms, values, competencies, practices, and subjectivity that derived from that experience.

Focusing first on the subject of space, there is already ample evidence that Black life in large urban cities in the Northeast, Midwest, and South is marked more profoundly by both race and social class segregation than life in the West (Massey & Eggers, 1990). Additionally, researchers continue to document how the Black experience varies from one school system to the next, in part as a consequence of how the economic and labor market influences differentially frame the demographics and funding of school systems (e.g., Anyon, 1997; Hertert, 1994; Kozol, 1991; Rubenstein, 1998). At more microlevels, scholars have documented how the specifics of neighborhood (e.g., MacLeod, 1995; Patillo-McCoy, 1999) and school (e.g., Bryk, Lee, & Holland, 1993; Comer & Haynes, 1999; Hemmings, 1996; Sizemore, 1998; Tyson, 1998; Wang, Haertel, & Walberg, 1994) impact Black life.

Racial experiences are additionally marked by historical time. However, with few exceptions (e.g., MacLeod, 1995; O'Connor, 2002; Siddle-Walker, 1996), educational researchers operate as if race related constraints and opportunities do not vary from one historical period to another to differentially shape the experience of being Black. To provide one example, John Ogbu's cultural ecological model denies the dynamism with which Blacks have been subjugated across time. Instead the model operates as if there is only one story to be told about Black subjugation and it is *this* tale that is reiterated through the narratives of Black adults to frame Black youth's renderings of opportunity, and their consequent performance in school. Sociologists, however, continue to mark critical shifts in Black people's experiences with oppression. Sociologists have discerned shifts from "economic racial oppression" to "class subordination" (Wilson, 1978); from "overt" racism to "color blind racism" (Bonilla-Silva, 2001); and, from "traditional" to "laissez fair" racism (Bobo, Kluegel, & Smith, 1997). Operating within the logic of Ogbu's model, then, we would expect that Black adults coming of age in particular eras would generate distinct narratives about Black opportunity. This would, then, differentially affect how different cohorts of Black youths come to interpret their life chances and subsequently how they respond to school. Unfortunately, the failure to attend to how the contexts and demands of particular environments (marked both by space and time) are implicated in the norms, practices, and meaning-making of Black youth is not an uncommon phenomenon. As indicated by Spencer, Swanson, and Cunningham (1991), with few exceptions, "studies that explore contextual effects are seldom conducted on minority youth" (p. 368).

Moving beyond the subjects of time and space, Blacks are additionally classed. The importance of social class as a moderating influence might be growing in significance in light of the income polarization that has occurred amongst African Americans. This polarization, which is defined by "proportionate declines in the middle class, and sharp increases in the proportions of both the affluent and the poor," suggests that the experience of Black "haves" and "have-nots" has become more differentiated (Massey & Eggers, 1990). Further, political scientists and sociologists continue to document distinctions in how Black "haves" and "have-nots" not only interpret their life chances, but how they define their interests and ideologies (Hochschild, 1995; Reed, 1999).

But, we must also recognize the differentiation that occurs amongst African Americans when they are similarly classed and are operating within the same space and time. For example, O'Connor (1997) documents how African Americans who share the same class standing, and operate within the same social spaces, vary considerably in their social encounters, worldviews, and social identities. Additionally, gender as a differentiating experience amongst Blacks is especially understudied (O'Connor, 2002). But, the nature of this understudy is not simply a function of whether researchers have attended to the educational experiences of Black males and Black females (because they have), but whether they have examined the subject of race and gender intersectionalities with conceptual depth. The same would hold true for race and class intersectionalities, or the intersectional triumvirate of race, class, *and* gender. Before elaborating upon the subject of intersectionalities more specifically, we will discuss how the general failure to attend to Black heterogeneity has hampered our ability to make sense of the educational outcomes and experiences of African-American youths.

In the absence of accounting analytically for Black heterogeneity, we construct a seamless and necessarily oversimplified notion of what it means to be Black, and, in the process, mask our ability to make sense of the substantive variation in achievement performance that occurs amongst African Americans. Despite overarching accounts of Black underperformance in school, researchers have documented considerable distinctions in how Blacks have performed in school both within and across time. For example, the differences between Black and White educational attainment narrowed during the 1970s, but by the mid-1980s the gap in Black and White matriculation to college began to grow (Nettles & Perna, 1997). Similarly, researchers documented the dramatic narrowing of the Black–White test score gap during the 1970s, which leveled off during the 1980s, and then began to reverse itself on some measures (e.g., reading and science scores) (Grissmer, Flanagan, & Williamson, 1998; Hedges & Nowell, 1998).

Moving to the subject of space, across this same span of time, Black test score gains were somewhat larger in the Southeast and smallest in the Northeast (Grissmer et al., 1998). Researchers have additionally pointed out that while Black students in suburban (read racially integrated) settings tend to outperform their urban (and racially segregated) counterparts on some measures (e.g., SAT scores), they lag behind them in others (e.g., enrollment in Advanced Placement courses). And within the same vein, Black students at Catholic and Effective Schools outperform Blacks in public and unreformed neighborhood schools (Bryk et al., 1993; Wang et al., 1994).

At the level of Black subgroups, while middle class Blacks are generally conceived of as having an academic advantage over poor Blacks, in some contexts poor(er) Blacks outperform their Black peers who are middle class (O'Connor, 2001b). And, while Black boys now lag behind Black girls on the rates at which they matriculate to and complete college (Hawkins, 1996; Nettles & Perna, 1997), this was not always the case. Prior to the 1960s and mid-1970s Black males had outperformed Black females on measures of educational attainment (Cross & Slater, 2000; U.S. Department of Commerce, 1940, 1960, 1980). In the 1970s in New York City, Black West Indians were significantly more likely than native born Blacks to be college graduates, and equally likely to have less than a high school education. By 1990, Black West Indians were almost as likely as Native Blacks to have attained a college education, and were more likely to be amongst the least educated (Waldinger, 1996).

Our account of the variation in Black school performance, both within and across space and time, is not exhaustive. These findings, nevertheless, signal the need to focus specifically upon which Blacks are being studied and the conditions under which they are operating. But this focus cannot stop with the naming and description of who, when, and where, but must analyze and theorize how these specificities are implicated procesurally in the cultural formations we attach to Black achievement performance. We must, however, stress that in our struggle to establish analytical and theoretical links between the heterogeneity of the African-American experience and the heterogeneity in African-American achievement and attainment, we must contend more substantively with the subject of intersectionalities.

The Underconceptualization of Class and Gender Intersectionalities

As conveyed above, African Americans are not only raced. They are positioned by gender, as well as by social class. In accord with this recognition, researchers have conducted studies that contrast the experiences of Black females versus Black males (e.g., Cross & Slater, 2000; Grant, 1984; Hawkins, 1996; Hubbard, 1999; Waters, 1999). Other studies have focused expressly on Black males or Black females, or otherwise used Whites or other ethnic groups of the same gender category as a comparative referent (e.g., Ferguson, 2000; Fordham, 1993, 1996; Holland & Eisenhart, 1990; Taylor, Gilligan, & Sullivan, 1995). Similarly, there have been some attempts to account for the experience of middle class, working class, or poor Blacks (Heath, 1983; Hemmings, 1996; Lareau & Horvat, 1999). Still others have sought to examine the intersections of race, class, and gender (Cousins, 1999; Horvat & Antonio, 1999).

Much of this work, however, stops short of actually examining intersectionalities in any substantive way (see Carter, 1999; Carter, Sellers, & Squires 2002; Frazier-Kouassi, 2002; O'Connor, 2001a for further discussion). In some instances researchers who compare Blacks of different genders or social classes, or Whites and Blacks of the same gender and social classes, simply *list* the differences in the groups' educational experiences, achievement, or outcomes. They do not offer a concomitant analysis regarding how the social class location or gender location of their participants interfaces with their race location to explain the noted differences. When such analyses are attempted, the researchers often privilege one group position over the other(s). To provide one example, Holland and Eisenhart (1990), in their study of Black and White women in college, identify distinctions in how the two groups of women negotiate the culture of femininity in relation to how they achieve in and experience college. While noting that the culture of femininity and its accordant relationship with the women's college achievement and experiences is differentially framed, partly as a consequence of the peer cultures that are found at their respective colleges, the authors offer no analysis regarding how race shapes these differences. The evident marginalization of race as an analytical (as opposed to a descriptive category) in this explicitly gendered analysis is not only highlighted by the fact that some of the women are Black and others are White. Additionally, the Black women are attending an historically Black college, while the White women are attending a predominantly White college.

The work of feminist scholars, however, warns us against emphasizing one social position over another, or establishing cumulative or hierarchal relationships between social positions (e.g., Collins, 1990, 1998; Crenshaw, 1991, 1992; King, 1998). Rather, they compel us to examine how these positions are "inextricably intertwined and circulate together in the representations [or structuring] of subjects and experiences of subjectivity (Ferguson, 2000, pp. 22–23). Researchers, however, have been hesitant to attend conceptually to the relevance of class and gender out of concern that the significance of race gets trumped in the process. Indeed, some researchers who have sought to attend to this relevance have been sorely criticized for their efforts (e.g., Wilson, 1978). But, by examining these positions as intertwined, rather than as "isolated and independent," we evade the risk of displacing the significance of race, or placing it in competition with gender and social class.

The Silencing of Institutionalized Productions of Race

Within the tradition of examining race as culture, the latest emphasis on interpreting culture as racialized meaning-making has made some strides in reporting on intersectionalities. For example, Fordham (1993) examined how gender and race intersect in the production of Black women's conception of womanhood, and how these conceptions are subsequently implicated in their pursuit of competitive academic outcomes. Alternatively, Lareau and Horvat (1999) examined, in part, how the race and social class of the Black parents in their study simultaneously (though not singularly) framed how they gauged the racial terrain of their child's school, and how they then went about advocating on their child's behalf.

Works like these provide us with growing insight into how Black individuals, who are simultaneously positioned by gender or class, produce classed and gendered interpretations (enacted via subjectivity and performance) of themselves as racial subjects. These interpretations are implicated in how these individuals then think about and act in school to affect their own achievement performance (writ large) or, that of their children. But, while this work is generally focused on making sense of the racialized (but not wholly raced) productions Black youths bring with them to school, very little of this work makes a concomitant effort to explore the racial productions that are generated as a consequence of the structuring of schools and the practices of schools' agents. That is, race is not only a product of how African Americans make sense of themselves as racial subjects, and then enact this sense-making in relation to school, it is also a consequence of how schools and their agents racialize African-American subjects (Davidson, 1996; Dolby, 2001; Ferguson, 2000; Lewis, 2003a; Pollock, 2003).

For example, in Ferguson's (2000) study, Black and White boys were both apt to perform their masculinity (or their position as males) through the transgression of school rules. Having identified some differences in how White and Black boys performed their masculinity, she stressed that Black boys more often found themselves in trouble because of how their performances were interpreted, rather than how they actually performed. More specifically, Ferguson found that when White boys transgressed, school officials presumed that "boys will be boys," attributed "innocence to their wrong doing," and believed that "they must be socialized to fully understand the meaning of their acts" (p. 80). In contrast, when Black boys transgressed their acts were "adultified." That is "their transgressions [were] made to take on a sinister, intentional, fully conscious tone that is stripped of any element of naivete" (p. 83). Having framed them as "not children," the interpreters (most of whom were White and constituted authority and, therefore, power in the school setting) were necessarily directed toward treatment "that punish[ed] through example and exclusion rather than through persuasion and edification, as [was] practiced with the young White males in the school" (p. 90). Too often we have treated race, and even racial subjectivities, as something that students bring with them to school, rather than understanding race and racial subjectivities as *coproduced* in relation to educational practices and processes.

Race as Capital

Researchers such as Ferguson (2000) (cited above) are just beginning to address the ways that race can function as a source of capital in educational settings. As outlined by Pierre Bourdieu, "Capital" is those resources that serve to advance one's position or status within a given context (Bourdieu, 1977; Bourdieu & Passeron, 1990). Bourdieu discussed four types of capital: *economic* (money and property); *social* (connections, social networks); *cultural* (cultural knowledge, educational credentials); and *symbolic* (symbols of prestige and legitimacy). Each form of capital can be converted into the others in order to enhance or maintain positions in the social order (Connolly, 1996: Swartz, 1997). Race can function as capital in several ways. First, race has shaped historic access to economic resources, particularly wealth (Oliver & Shapiro, 1995), such that it influences who has access to what kind of schooling (Kozol, 1991; Orfield, 1996). Second, race affects how cultural resources are responded to and rewarded in schools (Carter, 1999; Lareau & Horvat, 1999; Tyson, 1998). Third, patterns of racial segregation impact social networks and, thus, access to social capital (Massey & Denton, 1993; Orfield, 1996). And, fourth, race or skin color can serve as symbolic capital. Because of racist presumptions and stereotypes, race functions at a conscious or subconscious level to shape interactions. In relation to classroom experiences, Connolly (1998) states, "It is clearly the case that White skin, for instance, can represent symbolic capital in certain contexts. Some teachers may be influenced (whether directly or indirectly) by a set of racist beliefs, which encourages them to think of White children as being more intelligent and well behaved than Black children" (p. 21).

There remains a hole in the literature on African-American educational experiences with regard to systematic studies of everyday practices and experiences in schools. The work of authors such as Ferguson (2000), Horvat, Weininger, and Lareau (2003), Lewis (2003b), and Lareau and Horvat (1999) in elementary school; Davidson (1996), Dolby (2001), Fergus (2004), Jewett (2006), Kenny (1999), O'Connor (2001b), Peterson-Lewis and Bratton (2004), and Pollack (2001) in middle and high schools; and Feagin et al. (1996) in college settings are significant contributions toward this end. However, the everyday practices within the Black box of schooling, which illuminate the subtle but powerful ways that race shapes interactions and opportunities, and serve as symbolic capital for some, remain far too scarce.

Multilevel Ecological Analyses

An ecological analysis requires us to link microprocesses (e.g., student subjectivity and actions; student–teacher interactions; peer interactions; familial relations and involvement in school) with more meso- (e.g., school and district level policies, practices, demographics, and organization) and macro- (e.g., the economic forces, system of racial hierarchy, and federal policies that are specific to the "time" in which the study is being conducted) influences. For example, recent advances in quantitative methods provide one useful tool for enabling statistical modeling of data on multiple levels (Bryk & Raudenbush, 1992; Frank, 1998). By establishing empirical and analytical links between these levels of (inter) action and influence, we generate precise assessments of how the specificity of context is implicated in the educational realities of African Americans operating within a specific place and historical time (Spencer, Dupree, & Hartmann, 1997; Swanson, Spencer, & Peterson, 1998). Such multilevel and historically specific studies are essential to the task of unpacking why Black students operating within one space and time have distinct educational experiences and outcomes compared to Black students operating within a different space and time.

Institutional and Everyday Racism

Just as importantly, a multilevel analysis establishes the groundwork for exploring, with more conceptual rigor, the impact and operation of institutional racism on the achievement, attainment, and experiences of Blacks in school. As Holt (1995) argues, the analysis of racism requires us to resolve the "linkage" between the "individual actor" and the "social context." In other words, we must analyze "the levels of the problem" such that we establish "continuity between behavioral explanations sited at the individual level of human experience and those at the level of society and social force" (p. 7). Holt, therefore, conceives of "everyday" acts of racism as "minor links in a larger historical chain of events, structures, and transformations anchored in slavery and the slave trade." Holt's use of the term *anchored*, however, conveys that slavery and the slave trade do not operate deterministically to frame contemporary expressions of racism but only provide a root for its reflection. Consequently, educational researchers must explore how contemporary social forces nourish the racial knowledge, structures, and practices that sustain and reward everyday racism (Essed, 1991). As Holt (1995) outlines:

> ...it is at...[the] level [of the everyday]...that race is reproduced via the marking of the racial Other and that racist ideas and practices are naturalized, made self-evident, and thus seemingly beyond audible challenge. It is at this level that race is reproduced long after its original historical stimulus—the slave trade and slavery—have faded. It is at this level that seemingly rational and ordinary folk commit irrational and extraordinary acts. (p. 7)

The irrational and extraordinary acts to which Holt directs our attention should not be imagined simply as traditional and explicit forms of racism, but the many complicated social processes whereby educational opportunities are circumscribed for some racial subjects and fostered for others. Within this frame, then, we can explore more subtle forms of racism that are not readily signaled by overt behavior (Forman, 2001). Thus, like Ferguson (2000) did, we can study how the interpretations and responses of individual school actors shape Black students' experiences in schools in ways that systemically deny them privilege and educational access. In this way we not only come to understand

Orienting Future Research

Our analysis of research on African Americans' educational experiences yields
specific recommendations for future efforts. We suggest the following: (1) a fo
school processes and racial meaning making; (2) more multilevel ecological appro
(3) additional examination of the operation of institutional and everyday racis
attention to the intersections of race class and gender; (5) multiple method stra
and (6) more theoretically robust understandings of important constructs such a
culture, and self-esteem.

School Processes and Meaning Making

Research on African Americans and education must pay attention to school prc
and issues of racial meaning-making. This kind of research would go far in addr
some of the shortcomings in current research raised above, including the way rac
fact, a product of educational settings, as much as it is something that students '
with them" to school, the way educational outcomes are impacted by everyday in
tions and practices in schools, and the way students make sense of their racialized
locations through their schooling experiences. This work could help to unveil the w
which schools produce race as a social category.

One research strategy that will be especially important to consider here is e
graphic or participant observation research. Ethnographic research involves ente
social setting and getting to know the people who move within it. It thus holds the p
ise of also addressing the varying roles of different school contexts for African-Ame
students. As Emerson (1983, p. 25) articulates, ethnography proceeds on the assum
that "context is not an obstacle to understanding but a resource for it." Ethnograph
also provide "empirical and theoretical gains in understanding larger social comple
actors, actions, and motives" (Feagin, Orum, & Sjoberg, 1991, p. 8). Thus, ethnog
has the potential to provide insight into how race shapes interactions in schools, o
it is that disciplinary patterns differ across race and gender categories. Ethnography
permits the study of relationships as they happen and develop, rather than abstra
people from their lives and treating them as if they live, act, and believe "in isolation
one another" (Feagin, Orum, & Sjoberg, 1991, p. 8). Here it has the potential to ill
nate what race means for particular African-American students in particular cont
and how their understandings of themselves and others develop in relation to parti
people or locations. Especially in the study of race and race relations, this kind of rese
is crucial for capturing the workings of complex social processes and for capturing
consistencies or inconsistencies between what people say and do.

Researchers have previously indicated that "[s]ome of the most insightful and
vocative data in the area of race and race relations have been obtained via the me
of participant observation" (Dennis, 1988, p. 44). We argue that this tradition
provide us with robust insight into how race shapes the educational experience
outcomes of African Americans if it is wed to multilevel ecological analyses, an
focused on uncovering the "everydayness" of racism and the dynamism of intersect
alities. In short, we need more ethnographic and ecologically grounded studies of l
race is implicated in the education of African Americans, including how the impac
race is realized via institutional racism and informed by race, class, and gender in
sectionalities. Below we elaborate upon the promise of each of these methodolog
orientations.

how culture can operate as structure (Hays, 1994; also see Gould, 1999 for further discussion), but we establish an analytical lens for revealing the meso- and macrolevel forces that legitimize, reinforce, and institutionalize these actions.

Intersections of Race, Class, and Gender

African-American educational research needs to take seriously how race intersects with social class, gender, and other markers of identity. This includes paying attention not only to variation in Black school experiences, but to how and why class and gender might shape African-American school experiences differently from the way they shape other groups' experiences. As aforementioned, it is essential that work of this kind examine race, class, and gender as intertwined and not isolated and independent social positions. As indicated by McCarthy and Crichlow (1993) you cannot interpret the educational experiences of minority groups "from assumptions about race pure and simple" because different gender and class interests and identities within minority groups often "cut at right angles" to racial politics and identities (p. xxvii). Ideally, however, analyses of intersectionalities should be conducted in accord with the kind of multilevel analysis we discussed above. Here, examining "levels of the problem" is warranted because "the relative significance of race, sex, or class in determining the conditions of [people's] lives is neither fixed nor absolute, but rather is dependent on the sociohistorical context and the social phenomenon under consideration" (King, 1998, p. 49).

Multimethod Research Strategies

In our effort to make better sense of the education of African Americans we must additionally take advantage of the natural complement of quantitative and qualitative methodologies, and more aggressively and effectively pursue mixed-methods studies toward this end. For example, challenges abound in understanding fully why we continue to have racial gaps in achievement. Some recent research has shown that students often come into kindergarten with different skill sets. Rather than narrowing, however, these gaps in skills increase in the first couple of years in school (Denton & West, 2002; Phillips, Crouse, & Ralph, 1999). We are only now beginning to fully understand how this process unfolds over time, and why it is that African-American students are being undereducated (Tyson, Darity, & Castellano 2005). This issue, along with other important research questions about African-American educational experiences, can only be fully addressed with productive pairings between quantitative and qualitative methodology. The pairing of survey research and qualitative interviewing is an especially productive option. Young (1999) argues that qualitative interviews provide the entrée to what Erving Goffman (1973) identified as "schemata of interpretation. These are the meanings that actors formulate about their social encounters and experiences." Consequently, when coupled with individuals' "forced choice" selection, we are provided with a phenomenological framing of the responses they provided.

The aforementioned pairing not only provides possibilities for clarification and elaboration of survey findings, but also can provide an important corrective function. For example, recent studies on racial issues, both in school and beyond, have found important inconsistencies between survey and qualitative data. For example, Bonilla-Silva and Forman (2000) found gaps between people's responses to abstract survey items about race (e.g., whether they approve of interracial marriage in general) and their expanded responses in an in-depth interview (e.g., how they felt about interracial marriage and whether they would ever marry someone of a different race). Additionally, in recent school research, one of the coauthors found inconsistencies between teachers and parents reported views, and the way they acted when in direct relation to someone of another racial group (Lewis, 2001). These are not mere "contradictions" but provide more complex information about how race works in and across settings.

Conclusion

As stated at the beginning of this chapter, the problems we have identified with the deployment of race in educational issues shapes our understanding not just of African-American students' educational outcomes but those for all racial/ethnic groups. For example, much research on Latino/a and Asian-American educational outcomes does not give enough attention to phenotypic variation, ignores bimodal distributions in group success or failure, or reifies culture in an effort to explain aggregate group achievement. Throughout this paper we have focused on research on African Americans' educational experiences in order to make the general case for the need to develop more theoretically informed understandings of race, in particular, but also of other related constructs such research includes (e.g., culture, racism, self-esteem). The question of what meaning race has for Black students' educational outcomes is one that must be theorized, not assumed or implied. Our ability to develop more accurate interpretations of how and why students fare in school as they do, depends at least in part on our ability to attend to race with greater conceptual (and by implication methodological) precision. This challenge is relevant to a range of methodological issues that include the productive framing of research questions, the proper specification of statistical models in quantitative analyses, and the appropriate selection of research design.

Our emphasis on developing more theoretically informed relationships between key constructs, such as race, and research design and methodology is not simply an academic matter. Educational research can impact life outcomes via the policy implications that emerge. For example, work that suggests that African-American students' underperformance in school is a function of individual or group deficiencies leads to very different policy proposals than work that suggests that school policies and practices are responsible. Moreover, work that suggests that African Americans are a monolithic cultural group facing the same issues across space, time, and context flattens out the complex topography of Black life in the United States, and misses important variation in educational experiences. The stakes are, therefore, substantial. Our failure to establish more theoretically rigorous relationships between central concepts, such as race, and research design and methodology will not only deny us the ability to improve educational opportunity for African Americans, but will likely impinge negatively on Black people's already narrowed educational chances.

Notes

1. In this paper we generally use the terms *African American* and *Black* interchangeably. However, as later discussion will reveal, we recognize that the term Black references a variety of ethnic groups that comprise the African Diaspora. We, therefore, specify when we are referring to Blacks who are not ethnically American.
2. Here we are not citing examples that are particularly egregious or exemplary. Rather, we have selected some examples from a major social science education journal (Sociology of Education) that are quite interesting and important articles but which, nevertheless, have possible shortcomings in this arena.
3. This review included research that examined more specifically Blacks' (a) need for achieve-

ment; (b) locus of control; (c) causal attributions for success and failure;(d) expectancy beliefs; and (e) self-esteem and self-concept of ability.

4. Median values are often better indicators than "Mean values" as means can be skewed upwards by very few very wealthy individuals at the top of the distribution.

5. For example, in a recent analysis of national data, Harris and Sim (2000) found that multi-racial students responded differently to questions about their racial identification depending on the mode of the questioning—self-administered survey or interview—and the location of the questioning—school vs. home.

6. For example, when the NELS survey asks Hispanics to "mark one" of the following in response to the question "What is your race?"—Black Hispanic; White Hispanic; Other Hispanic.

7. It should be noted, however, that items which reveal place of birth provide inadequate proxies for ethnicity, as some Blacks claim ethnic affiliations that are not signaled by where they are born (e.g., Blacks who claim West Indian identity but were born in Britain or the United States) (Waters, 1990).

8. For example, researchers like Deutsch (1967) maintained that the "implicit value system of the poor" (especially the Black poor) was communicated via the structure, interactions, and activities of their homes. In accord with this presumption, he concluded that the Black poor devalued "intellectual activity" in light of having limited if any "dinner" conversation, books in the home, and trips to the museum, library, and zoo.

9. For another recent example see Stephen and Abigail Thernstrom's *No Excuses* (Thernstrom & Thernstrom, 2005).

10. More specifically, researchers have examined the mismatch between African-American Vernacular English (AAVE), and the privileging of Standard English in America's schools, but reported on disjunctures between the style, tone, and nuance of "Black" talk and that of teacher discourse (e.g., Delpit, 1988). Researchers additionally documented the devaluation of "Black" students' everyday experiences and the knowledge that accompanies them (Asante, 1991; Ladson-Billings, 1994; Willis, 1995). Contrasts have been established between Black students' orientations toward interdependence and collective survival, in contrast to schools' emphasis on independence and individuality (Ward, 1995). And still other work focused explicitly on "learning styles," argued that, while African Americans could be characterized as "field dependent" (i.e., learners who are more impulsive, unreflective, and reliant on the social environment and authority figures), instruction in America's school is designed for field independent learners (i.e., learners who are more conceptual and analytical in orientation detached, goal oriented, and self-aware) (see review by Irvine & York, 1995).

11. We have substituted the term Black where Michaels (1996) had previously used the term Navajo.

References

Ainsworth-Darnell, J. W., & Downey, D. B. (1998). Assessing the oppositional culture explanation for racial/ethnic differences in school performance. *American Sociological Review, 63*(4), 536–553.

Anyon, J. (1997). *Ghetto schooling: A political economy of urban educational reform.* New York: Teachers College Press.

Asante, M. K. (1991). The Afrocentric idea in education. *Journal of Negro Education, 60*(2), 170–180.

Ayers, W., Dohrn, B., & Ayers, R. (2001). *Zero tolerance: Resisting the drive for punishment in our schools.* New York: The New Press.

Bashi, V., & McDaniel, A. (1997). A theory of immigration and racial stratification. *Journal of Black Studies, 27,* 668–682.

Bobo, L., Kluegel, J. R., & Smith, R. A. (1997). Laissez faire racism: The crystallization of a "kinder, gentler" anti-Black ideology. In S. A. Tuch & J. K. Martin (Eds.), *Racial attitudes in the 1990s: Continuity and change* (pp. 15–42). Westport, CT: Praeger.

Bonilla Silva, E. (2001). *White supremacy and racism in the post-civil rights era*. Boulder, CO: Lynne Rienner.

Bonilla Silva, E., & Forman, T. A. (2000). "I am not a racist, but...": Mapping college students racial ideology in the United States. *Discourse and Society, 11*, 50–85.

Bonilla Silva, E., & Lewis, A. (1999). The new racism: Racial structure in the United States, 1960s–1990s. In P. Wong (Ed.), *Race, ethnicity, and nationality in the United States* (pp. 55–101). Boulder, CO: Westview.

Bourdieu, P. (1977). *Outline of a theory of practice*. Cambridge, UK: Cambridge University Press.

Bourdieu, P., & Passeron, J.C. (1990). *Reproduction in education, society and culture*. Beverly Hills, CA: Sage.

Bryk, A. S., Lee, V. E., & Holland, P. B. (1993). *Catholic schools and the common good*. Cambridge, MA: Harvard University Press.

Bryk, A. S., & Raudenbush, S. (1992). *Hierarchical linear models*. Newbury Park, CA: Sage.

Carter, P. (1999). *Balancing "Acts": Issues of identity and cultural resistance in the social and educational behaviors of minority youth*. Doctoral dissertation, Columbia University, New York.

Carter, P. (2001, April). *African American and Latino youths' perspectives on achievement and socioeconomic mobility: What "Acting White" really means to them*. Paper Presented at the Annual Meeting of the American Educational Research Association, Seattle, WA.

Carter, P. (2005). *Keepin' it real*. New York: Oxford University Press

Carter, P., Sellers, S. L., & Squires, C. (2002). Reflections on race/ethnicity, class and gender inclusive research. *African American Research Perspectives, 8*(1), 111–124.

Carter, R. L. (1995). The unending struggle for equal educational opportunity. *Teachers College Record, 96*(4), 19–26.

Collins, P. H. (1990). *Black feminist thought: Knowledge, consciousness, and the politics of empowerment*. Boston, MA: Unwin Hyman.

Collins, P. H. (1998). *Fighting words: Black women and the search for justice*. Minneapolis, MN: University of Minnesota Press.

Comer, J., & Haynes, N. (1999). The dynamics of school change: Response to the article, "Comer's school development program in Prince George's County Maryland: A theory based evaluation," by Thomas D. Cook et al. *American Educational Research Journal, 36*(3), 599–607.

Conley, D. (1999). *Being Black, living in the red: Race, wealth, and social policy in America*. Berkeley, CA: University of California Press.

Connolly, P. (1998). *Racism, gender identities, and young children: Social relations in a multiethnic, inner-city primary school*. New York: Routledge.

Cook, P. J., & Ludwig, J. (1998). The burden of "Acting White": Do Black adolescents disparage academic achievement? In C. Jencks & M. Phillips (Eds.), *The Black–White test score gap* (pp. 375–400). Washington, D.C.: Brookings Institution Press.

Cornell, S. (1996). The variable ties that bind: Content and circumstance in ethnic processes. *Ethnic and Racial Studies, 19*(2), 266–289.

Cousins, L. H. (1999). "Playing between classes": America's troubles with class, race, and gender in a Black high school and community. *Anthropology & Education Quarterly, 30*(3), 294–316.

Crenshaw, K. (1991). Mapping the margins: Intersectionality, identity, politics and violence against women of color. *Stanford Law Review, 43*, 1241–1299.

Crenshaw, K. (1992). Whose story is it anyway? Feminist and antiracist appropriations of Anita Hill. In T. Morrison (Ed.), *Race-ing justice, en-gendering power* (pp. 402–436). New York: Pantheon.

Cross, T., & Slater, R. B. (2000). The alarming decline in the academic performance of African-American men. *The Journal of Blacks in Higher Education, 27*, 82–87.

Darity, W. A. (2002). *Intergroup disparity: Why culture is irrelevant*. Chapel Hill, NC. Unpublished manuscript,

Darity, W. A., Dietrich, J., & Guilkey, D. K. (2001). Persistent advantage or disadvantage? Evidence in support of the intergenerational drag hypothesis. *The American Journal of Economics and Sociology, 60*(2), 435–470.

Darling-Hammond, L., & Sclan, E. (1996). Who teaches and why? In J. Sikula (Ed.), *Handbook of research on teacher education* (pp. 67–101). New York: Macmillan.

Dauber, S., Alexander, K., & Entwisle, D. (1996). Tracking and transitions through middle grades: Channeling educational trajectories. *Sociology of Education, 69*, 290–307.

Davidson, A. (1996). *Making and molding identity in schools: Student narratives on race, gender, and academic engagement.* Albany, NY: SUNY Press.

Dennis, R. M. (1988). The use of participant observation in race relations research. *Race and Ethnic Relations, 5*, 25–46.

Denton, K., & West, J. (2002). *Children's reading and mathematics achievement in kindergarten and first grade* (NCES 2002125).Washington, D.C.: National Center for Educational Statistics, U.S. Department of Education.

Deutsch, M. (1967). *The disadvantaged child.* New York: Basic Books.

Dolby, N. (2001). *Constructing race: Youth, identity, and popular culture in South Africa.* Albany, NY: SUNY Press.

Drake, S., & Cayton, H. (1993). *Black metropolis.* Chicago: Chicago University Press.

Emerson, R. M. (1983). *Contemporary field research: A collection of reading.* Boston, MA: Little, Brown.

Essed, P. (1991). *Understanding everyday racism: An interdisciplinary theory.* Newbury Park, CA: Sage.

Farley, R., & Allen, W. R. (1989). *The color line and the quality of life in America.* New York: Oxford University Press.

Feagin, J. R., Orum, A. M., & Sjoberg, G. (1991). *A case for the case study.* Chapel Hill: University of North Carolina Press.

Feagin, J. R., Vera, H., & Imani, N. (1996). *The agony of education: Black students at White colleges and universities.* New York: Routledge.

Fergus, E. (2004). *Skin color and identity formation: Perceptions of opportunity and academic orientation among Mexican and Puerto Rican youth.* New York: Routledge.

Ferguson, A. A. (2000). *Bad boys: Public schools in the making of Black masculinity.* Ann Arbor, MI: University of Michigan Press.

Fordham, S. (1993). "Those loud Black girls": (Black) women, silence, and gender "passing" in the academy. *Anthropology & Education Quarterly, 24*(1), 3–32.

Fordham, S. (1996). *Blacked out: Dilemmas of race, identity, and success at Capital High.* Chicago: University of Chicago Press.

Fordham, S. (1999). Dissin' "the standard": Ebonics as guerilla warfare at Capital High. *Anthropology & Education Quarterly, 30*(3), 272–293.

Forman, T. A. (2001). Social determinants of White youth's racial attitudes. *Sociological Studies of Children and Youth, 8*, 173–207.

Frank, K. (1998). Quantitative methods for studying social context in multilevels and through interpersonal relations. *Review of Research in Education, 23*, 171–216.

Frazier-Kouassi, S. (2002). Race and gender at the crossroads: African American females in school. *African American Research Perspectives, 8*(1), 151–162.

Gibson, M. (1991). Ethnicity, gender and social class: The school adaptation patterns of West Indian youths. In M. Gibson & J. Ogbu (Eds.), *Minority status and schooling: A comparative study of immigrant and voluntary minorities* (pp. 169–203). New York: Garland.

Gould, M. (1999). Race and theory: Culture, poverty, and adaptation to discrimination in Wilson and Ogbu. *Sociological Theory, 17*, 171–200.

Goffman, E. (1973). *The presentation of self in everyday life.* Woodstock, NY: Overlook Press.

Graham, S. (1994). Motivation in African Americans. *Review of Educational Research, 64*(1), 55–117.

Grant, L. (1984). Black females' "place" in desegregated classrooms. *Sociology of Education, 57*(2), 98–111.

Grissmer, D., Flannagan, A., & Williamson, S. (1998). Why did the Black–White score gap narrow in the 1970s and the 1980s? In C. Jencks & M. Phillips (Eds.), *The Black–White test score gap* (pp. 182–228). Washington, D.C.: The Brookings Institution.

Hall, S. (1990). Cultural identity and diaspora. In J. Rutherford (Ed.), *Identity: community, culture, and difference* (pp. 222–237). London: Lawrence & Wishart.

Harris, D. R., & Sim, J. J. (2000). *Who is mixed race? Patterns and determinants of adolescent racial idenity.* Ann Arbor: University of Michigan Press.

Hawkins, D. B. (1996). Gender gap: Black females outpace Black male counterparts at three degree levels. *Black Issues in Higher Education, 13*(10), 20–22.

Hays, S. (1994). Structure and agency and the sticky problem of culture. *Sociological Theory, 12,* 57–72.

Heath, S. B. (1983). *Ways with words: Language, life, and work in communities and classrooms.* New York: Cambridge University Press.

Hedges, L.V., & Nowell, A. (1999). Changes in the black–white gap in achievement test scores. *Sociology of Education, 72*(2), 111–135.

Hemmings, A. (1996). Conflicting images? Being Black and a model high school student. *Anthropology & Education Quarterly, 27*(1), 20–50.

Herrnstein, R. J., & Murray, C. (1994). *The Bell curve: Intelligence and class structure in American life.* New York: Free Press.

Hertert, L. (1994). School financing inequities among the states: The problem from a national perspective. *Journal of Education Finance, 19*(3), 231–255.

Hochschild, J. L. (1995). *Facing up to the American dream: Race, class, and the soul of the nation.* Princeton, NJ: Princeton University Press.

Holland, D. C., & Eisenhart, M. A. (1990). *Educated in romance: Women, achievement, and college culture.* Chicago: University of Chicago Press.

Holt, T. C. (1995). Marking: Race, race making, and the writing of history. *American Historical Review, 100*(1), 1–20.

Horvat, E. M., & Antonio, A. L. (1999). "Hey, those shoes are out of uniform": African American girls in an elite high school and the importance of habitus. *Anthropology & Education Quarterly, 30*(3), 317–342.

Horvat, E.M., Weininger, E., & Lareau, A. (2003). From social ties to social capital: class differences in the relations between schools and parent networks. *American Educational Research Journal, 40*(2), 319–351

Hubbard, L. (1999). College aspirations among low-income African American high school students: Gendered strategies for success. *Anthropology & Education Quarterly, 30*(3), 363–383.

Ignatiev, N. (1995). *How the Irish became White.* New York: Routledge.

Irvine, J. J., & York, D. E. (1995). Learning styles and culturally diverse students: A literature review. In J. A. Banks & C. A. M. Banks (Eds.), *Handbook of research on multicultural education* (pp. 484–497). New York: Macmillan.

Jackson, J. L. (2001). *Harlem world: Doing race and class in contemporary Black America.* Chicago: University of Chicago Press.

Jencks, C., & Phillips, M. (Eds.). (1998). *The Black–white test score gap.* Washington, D.C.: Brookings Institute Press.

Jewett, S. (2006). "If you don't identify with your ancestry, you're like a race without a land": Constructing race at a small urban middle school. *Anthropology and Education Quarterly, 37*(2), 144–161

Johnson, H. B. 2006. *The American dream and the power of wealth.* New York: Taylor & Francis.

Johnson, H. B., & Shapiro, T. (2003). Good neighborhoods, good schools: Race and the "good choices" of White families. In A. W. Doane & E. Bonilla-Silva (Eds.), *White out: The continuing significance of race* (pp. 173–188). New York: Routledge.

Johnson, T., Boyden, J. E., & Pittz, W. J. (2001). *Racial profiling and punishment in US public schools.* Oakland, CA: Applied Research Center.

Johnson, T., Libero, D. P., & Burlingame, P. (2000). *Vouchers: A trap, not a choice.* Oakland, CA: Applied Research Center.

Kenny, L. (1999). *Daughters of suburbia*. New Brunswick, NJ: Rutgers University Press.

King, D. (1998). Multiple jeopardy, multiple consciousness: The context of Black feminist ideology. *Journal of Women in Culture and Society, 14*, 42–72.

Kozol, J. (1991). *Savage Inequalities: Children in America's schools*. New York: HarperCollins.

Ladson-Billings, G. (1994). *The dreamkeepers: Successful teachers of African American children*. San Francisco, CA: Jossey-Bass.

Ladson-Billings, G. (1995). Toward a theory of culturally relevant pedagogy. *American Educational Research Journal, 32*(3), 465–491.

Lareau, A., & Horvat, E. M. (1999). Moments of social inclusion and exclusion: Race, class, and cultural capital in family-school relationships. *Sociology of Education, 72*(1), 37–53.

Lewis, A. E. (2001). There is no "race" in the schoolyard: Colorblind ideology in an (almost) all White school. *American Educational Research Journal, 38*(4), 781–812.

Lewis, A. E. (2003a). Everyday race-making: Navigating racial boundaries in schools. *American Behavioral Scientist, 47*(3), 283–305.

Lewis, A. E. (2003b). *Race in the schoolyard: Reproducing the color line in school*. New Brunswick, NJ: Rutgers University Press.

Lynn, M., & Adams, M. (2002). Introductory overview. [Special Issue: Critical race theory and education: Recent developments in the field]. *Equity and Excellence in Education, 35*(2), 87–92

MacLeod, J. (1995). *Ain't no makin' it: Aspirations and attainment in a low-income neighborhood*. Boulder, CO: Westview Press.

Marable, M. (1983). *How capitalism underdeveloped Black America*. Boston: South End Press.

Mason, P. L. (1996). Race, culture, and the market. *Journal of Black Studies, 26*, 782–808.

Mason, P. L. (1999). Family environment and intergenerational well-being: Some preliminary results. In W. Spriggs (Ed.), *The state of Black America*. Washington, D.C.: National Urban League.

Massey, D. S., & Denton, N. A. (1993). *American apartheid: Segregation and the making of the underclass*. Cambridge, MA: Harvard University Press.

Massey, D. S., & Eggers, M. L. (1990). The ecology of inequality: Minorities and the concentration of poverty, 1970–1980. *American Journal of Sociology, 95*(11), 53–1188.

McCarthy, C., & Crichlow, W. (1993). Introduction: Theories of identity, theories of representation, theories of race. In C. McCarthy & W. Crichlow (Eds.), *Race, identity, and representation in education* (pp. xiii–xxix). New York: Routledge.

Michaels, W. B. (1992). Race into culture: A critical genealogy of cultural identity. *Critical Inquiry, 18*, 655–685.

Mickelson, R. A. (2001). Subverting Swann: First and second-generation segregation in the Charlotte-Mecklenburg schools. *American Educational Research Journal, 38*(2), 215–252.

Michelson, R. A. (2003). When are racial disparities in education the result of racial discrimination? A social science perspective. *Teachers College Record, 105*(6), 1052–1086.

Morgan, S. (1996). Trends in Black-White differences in educational expectations: 1980–92. *Sociology of Education, 69*, 308–319.

Nettles, M. T., & Perna, L. W. (1997). *The African American education data book*. Fairfax, VA: Frederick D. Patterson Research Institute of the College Fund.

Oakes, J. (1988). Tracking in mathematics and science education: A structural contribution to unequal schooling. In L. Weis (Ed.), *Class, race, and gender in American education* (pp. 106–125). Albany, NY: SUNY Press.

O'Connor, C. (1997). Dispositions toward (collective) struggle and educational resilience in the inner city: A case of six American high school students. *American Educational Research Journal, 34*(4), 593–629.

O'Connor, C. (1999). Race, class, and gender in America: Narratives of opportunity among low-income African American youths. *Sociology of Education, 72*, 137–157.

O'Connor, C. (2001a). Making sense of the complexity of social identity in relation to achievement: a sociological challenge in the new millennium [Special issue]. *Sociology of Education*, 159–168.

O'Connor, C. (2001b, October). *Being Black in a White high school: Re-examining the relationship between racial identity and school performance.* Paper presented at the 2001 National Academy of Education/Spencer Foundation Postdoctoral Fellows' Fall Forum, Berkeley, California.

O'Connor, C. (2002). Black women beating the odds from one generation to the next: How the changing dynamics of constraint and opportunity affect the process of educational resilience. *American Educational Research Journal, 39*(4), 855–903.

Ogbu, J. (1987). Variability in minority school performance: A problem in search of an explanation. *Anthropology and Education Quarterly, 18*(4), 312–333.

Ogbu, J. (1989). The individual in collective adaptation: A framework for focusing on academic underperformance and dropping out among involuntary minorities. In L. Weis, E. Farrar, & H. G. Petrie (Eds.), *Dropouts from school* (pp. 181–204). Albany, NY: SUNY Press.

Ogbu, J. (1999). Beyond language: Ebonics, proper English, and identity in a Black-American speech community. *American Educational Research Journal, 36*(2), 147–184.

Oliver, M. L., & Shapiro, T. M. (1995). *Black wealth/White wealth: A new perspective on racial inequality.* New York: Routledge.

Omi, M., & Winant, H. (1994). *Racial formation in the United States: From the 1960s to the 1990s.* New York: Routledge.

Orfield, G. (1996). *Dismantling desegregation: The quiet reversal of Brown v. Board of Education.* New York: New Press.

Orfield, G. & Yun, J. T. (1999). *Resegregation in American schools.* The Civil Rights Project. Cambridge, MA: Harvard University.

Orfield, G. and Gordon, N. (2001). *Schools more separate: Consequences of a decade of resegregation.* The Civil Rights Project. Cambridge, MA: Harvard University.

Orr, A. J. 2003. Black-White differences in achievement: The importance of wealth. *Sociology of Education, 76*(4), 281–304.

Patillo-McCoy, M. (1999). *Black picket fences: Privilege and peril among the Black middle class.* Chicago: University of Chicago Press.

Pedraza, S., & Rumbaut, R. G. (1996). *Origins and destinies: Immigration, race, and ethnicity in America.* Belmont, CA: Wadsworth.

Persell, C. (1977). *Education and inequality.* New York: Free Press.

Peterson-Lewis, S., & Bratton, L. M. (2004). Perceptions of "Acting Black" among African American teens: Implications of racial dramaturgy for academic and social achievement. *The Urban Review, 36*(2), 81–100.

Phillips, M., Crouse, J., & Ralph, J. (1999). Does the Black–White test score gap widen after children enter school? In C. Jencks & M. Phillips (Eds.), *The Black–White test score gap* (pp. 229–272). Washington D.C.: Brookings Institution Press.

Pollock, M. (2001). How the question we ask most about race in education is the very question we most suppress." *Educational Researcher, 30*(9), 2–11.

Pollock, M. (2003). *Colormute.* Princeton, NJ: Princeton University Press.

Pollock, M. (2004). Race wrestling: Struggling strategically with race in educational practice and research. *American Journal of Education, 111*, 25–43.

Portes, A., & MacLeod, D. (1996). Educational progress of children and immigrants: The roles of class, ethnicity, and school context. *Sociology of Education, 69*(4), 255–275.

Reed, A. (1999). *Stirrings in the jug: Black politics in the post-segregation era.* Minneapolis, MN: University of Minnesota Press.

Rist, R. (1970). Student social class and teacher expectations: The self-fulfilling prophecy in ghetto education. *Harvard Educational Review, 40*(3), 411–451.

Rodriguez, C. E. (1991). *Puerto Ricans: Born in the U.S.A.* Boulder, CO: Westview Press.

Rodriguez, C. E. (1992). Race, culture, and Latin "otherness" in the 1980 Census. *Social Science Quarterly, 73*, 930–937.

Rodriguez, C. E. (2000). *Changing race: Latinos, the census, and the history of ethnicity in the United States.* New York: New York University Press.

Rodriguez, C. E., & Cordero-Guzman, H. (1992). Placing race in context. *Ethnic and Racial Studies, 15*, 523–542.

Roscigno, V. J., & Ainsworth-Darnell, J. W. (1999). Race, cultural capital, and educational resources: Persistent inequalities and achievement returns. *Sociology of Education, 72*(3), 158–178.

Rubenstein, R. (1998). Resource equity in the Chicago public schools: A school-level approach. *Journal of Negro Education, 23*(4), 68–89.

Rutledge, D. (1988). The use of participant observation in race relations research. *Race and Ethnic Relations, 5*, 25–46.

Sellers, R. M., Smith, M. A., Shelton, J. N., Rowley, S. A. J., & Chavous, T. M. (1998). Multidimensional model of racial identity: A reconceptualization of African American racial identity. *Personality & Social Psychology Review, 2*(1), 18–39.

Shapiro, T. (2004). *The hidden cost of being African American: How wealth perpetuates inequality.* New York: Oxford University Press.

Siddle-Walker, V. (1996). *Their highest potential: An African American schoolcommunity in the segregated South.* Chapel Hill: University of North Carolina Press.

Sizemore, B. (1998). The Madison Elementary School: A turnaround case. *Journal of Negro Education, 57*, 243–266.

Solomon, R. P. (1991). *Black resistance in high school.* Albany, NY: SUNY Albany Press.

Sowell, T. (1978). Three Black histories. In T. Sowell (Ed.), *Essays and data on American ethnic groups* (pp. 7–64). Washington, D.C.: The Urban Institute.

Spencer, M. B., Dupree, D., & Hartmann, T. (1997). A phenomenological variant of ecological systems theory (PVEST): A self-organization perspective in context. *Development and Psychopathology, 9*, 817–833.

Spencer, M. B., Swanson, D. P., & Cunningham, M. (1991). Ethnicity, ethnic identity, and competence formation: Adolescent transition and cultural transformation. *Journal of Negro Education, 60*(3), 366–387.

Sugrue, T. (1996). *The origins of the urban crisis.* Princeton, NJ: Princeton University Press.

Swanson, D., Spencer, M. B., & Peterson, A. (1998). Identity formation in adolescence. In K. Borman & B. Schneider (Eds.), *The adolescent years: Social influences and educational challenges, 97th yearbook for the National Society for the Study of Education—Part 1* (pp. 18–44). Chicago: Chicago University Press.

Swartz, D. (1997). *Culture and power: The sociology of Pierre Bourdieu.* Chicago: University of Chicago Press.

Swidler, A. (1986). Culture in action: Symbols and strategies. *American Sociological Review, 51*(2), 273–286.

Takaki, R. (1993). *A different mirror: A history of multicultural America.* Boston, MA: Little, Brown.

Taylor, J. M., Gilligan, C., & Sullivan, A. M. (1995). *Between voice and silence: Women and girls, race and relationship.* Cambridge, MA: Harvard University Press.

Thernstrom, A., & Thernstrom, S. (2004). *No excuses: Closing the racial gap in learning.* New York: Simon and Schuster.

Tyson, C. (1998). *Debunking as persistent myth: Academic achievement and the burden of "Acting White" among Black students.* Paper presented at the American Sociological Association, San Francisco, CA.

Tyson, K. (2002). Weighing in: Elementary-age students and the debate on attitudes toward school among Black students. *Social Forces, 80*(4), 1157–1189.

Tyson, K., Darity, W., & Castellino, D. (2005). "It's not "a Black thing": Understanding the burden of acting White and other dilemmas of high achievement. *American Sociological Review, 70*(4), 582–605

U.S. Department of Commerce. (1940). *Statistical abstract of the United States 1940* (No. 62). Washington, D.C.: Government Printing Office.

U.S. Department of Commerce. (1960). *Statistical abstract of the United States 1960* (No. 82). Washington, D.C.: Government Printing Office.

U.S. Department of Commerce. (1980). *Statistical abstract of the United States 1980* (No. 101). Washington, D.C.: Government Printing Office.

Valentine, C. (1968). *Culture and poverty: Critique and counter-proposals.* Chicago: University of Chicago Press.

Valenzula, A. (1999). *Subtractive schooling: US–Mexican youth and the politics of caring.* Albany, NY: SUNY Press.

Vickerman, M. (1999). *Crosscurrents: West Indians immigrants and race.* New York: Oxford University Press.

Villegas, A. M. (1988). School failure and cultural mismatch: Another view. *Urban Review, 20*(4), 253–265.

Waldinger, R. (1996). *Still the promised city? African Americans and new immigrants in postindustrial New York.* Cambridge, MA: Harvard University Press.

Wang, M. C., Haertel, G. D., & Walberg, H. J. (1994). Educational resilience in inner cities. In M. C. Wang & E. Gordon (Eds.), *Educational resilience in inner-city America* (pp. 45–72). Hillsdale, NJ: Erlbaum.

Ward, J. V. (1995). Cultivating a morality of care in African American adolescents: A culture-based model of violence prevention. *Harvard Educational Review, 65*(2), 175–188.

Waters, M. C. (1994). Ethnic and racial identities of second generation Black immigrants in New York City. *International Migration Review, 28,* 795–820.

Waters, M. C. (1999). *Black identities: West Indian immigrant dreams and American realities.* Cambridge, MA: Harvard University Press.

Watson, L. C., & Watson-Franke, M. B. (1985). *Interpreting life histories: An anthropological inquiry.* New Brunswick, NJ: Rutgers University Press.

Willis, A. I. (1995). Reading the world of school literacy: Contextualizing the experience of a young African American male. *Harvard Educational Review, 65*(1), 30–49.

Wilson, W. J. (1978). *The declining significance of race: Blacks and changing American institutions.* Chicago: University of Chicago Press.

Wolff, E. N. (2001). *Racial wealth disparities: Is the gap closing?* (No. 66, Levy Economic Institute). Annandale-on-Hudson, NY: Bard College.

Yinger, J. 1995. *Closed doors, opportunities lost.* New York: Russell Sage.

Young, A. A. (1999). The (non)accumulation of capital: Explicating the relationship of structure and agency in the lives of poor Black men. *Sociological Theory, 17*(2), 201–227.

Zuberi, T. (2001). *Thicker than blood: How racial statistics lie.* Minneapolis, MN: University of Minnesota Press.

Response to Part 3

Race, Ethnicity, and Language

Salim Muwakkil

I am often asked to speak at various educational institutions during Black History Month, which comes each February. A few years ago, I made a decision to reject those invitations because too many commemorations had become desiccated rituals. I since have changed my mind. Even rituals are better than nothing. Most Americans know next to nothing about the context of our current racial dilemma.

For instance, few Americans know how slavery so thoroughly distorted the cultural narratives of 22 generations of African-Americans and crippled their future. Were Americans better educated about slavery's damaging legacy, they would better understand the genesis of the racial disparities that mar the United States today.

Whatever audience I address during the year's shortest month, I make the point that African Americans as a distinct ethnic variation in the African diaspora were created by slavery. This stark conclusion often sparks dissent, so I explain that millions of Africans were kidnapped to America solely because they were needed for a slave economy. This process forged a new people that had to be dehumanized and dishonored in a society dependent on their labor as slaves. The maintenance of this economic arrangement demanded a rigid and pitiless racial hierarchy.

At this point, many students begin to grasp the powers of these structural barriers, but they often are surprised about an even more insidious aspect of slavery's legacy: African-Americans were socialized by a culture dependent on their debasement; they have viewed themselves through the perceptions of a culture of white supremacy. The scholar/activist W. E. B. DuBois most famously diagnosed this quandary in his formulation of "double consciousness" contained in his 1903 book *The Souls of Black Folk*. In it, DuBois described "...a peculiar sensation, this double-consciousness, this sense of always looking at one's self through the eyes of others, of measuring one's soul by the tape of a world that looks on in amused contempt and pity."

Invariably someone responds that Black people are still regarded with amused contempt and pity and I take this opportunity to urge a national commitment to acknowledge slavery's damage to the progeny of enslaved Africans and make it an integral part of the nation's general curricula. Without some historical context of our racial history, most Americans see contemporary racial disparities as a state of nature.

One glaring example of this attitude is Americans' tolerance of a criminal justice system replete with dramatic racial disparities. African Americans make up about 13% of the U.S. population and black men near 6%. How can Americans accept the reality that this 6% of the population totals about 50% of all the nation's inmates? We accept it because we have been socialized (hypnotized?) to deny these disparities. This cultural denial is as old as the nation's founding; the logical fallacy of being simultaneously the "land of the free" *and* the home of the slave would have been too jarring a contradiction without the balm of denial.

This denial of our biased assumptions is deeply embedded and can be extricated only by a concerted campaign to make comprehensive corrections in the nation's educational curricula. Because that project seems unlikely, at worst, and distant at best, I do my share during Black History Month.

Part 4

Gender, Sexuality, and Social Justice in Education

Edited and Introduced by Mara Sapon-Shevin

Imagine living in a world where there is no domination, where females and males are not alike or even always equal, but where a vision of mutuality is the ethos shaping our interaction. Imagine living in a world where we can all be who we are, a world of peace and possibility. Feminist revolution alone will not create such a world; we need to end racism, class elitism, imperialism. But it will make it possible for us to be fully self-actualized females and males able to create beloved community, to live together, realizing our dreams of freedom and justice, living the truth that we are all "created equal."

(hooks, 2000, p. x)

We have been raised to fear the *yes* within ourselves, our deepest cravings.... The fear of our desires keeps them suspect and indiscriminately powerful, for to suppress any truth is to give it strength beyond endurance.

(Lorde, 1984, p. 57)

One Dead Canary Is One Dead Bird Too Many

If one enters a toy store and states, "I'd like to buy a present for a 9-year old," the first question is "Boy or girl?" rarely "What is the child interested in?"

The majority of mothers in the United States now ask to know the sex of their unborn child, stating that they need to know how to "prepare" (pink or blue, dolls or footballs) for their child's birth and that it helps them bond with the fetus. In the past two weeks I have seen these four T-shirts: "Future Trophy Wife," "With tits like this, who needs brains?" "Boys suck, throw rocks at them," and "He's gay" (with an arrow pointing sideways).

We live in a highly gendered and gender-troubled world. Thirty-five years after the publication of the "X: A Fabulous Child's Story" by Lois Gould (http://www.trans-man. org/baby_x.html) in which parents refused to tell people the gender of their child—and were assailed by distress and confusion—we continue to live in a state of categories. Ambiguity—because a child is intersexed, or transgendered, or simply doesn't "act like a girl" or "look like a boy"—shakes many people to their core. There is clearly something very frightening about those who challenge gender categories and norms and those who do often pay a painful (sometimes) deadly price for confusing others. Treating people with dignity and respect because they are human beings is obviously too challenging— we must know about their genitals, their sexual experiences and behaviors, and what they call themselves so that *we* can know what to call them and how to treat them.

The chapters in this section make us look hard—and it's a painful exploration—at rigidities, rules, and boundaries—and what happens to those who cross them. Although "sexism" and "heterosexism" are often presented as separate categories, they are actually tightly woven together, and the narratives here are proof of that. One of the section authors, Andrew Smiler, explores gender roles, expectations, and conformity and shows us that the lessons come fast and hard; even a teacher's daily greeting, "Good morning boys and girls," enforces that there are two kinds of children. Those who fail to learn their place are instantly corrected.

If we unpack the common critique, "He's acting like a girl," we find powerful subtexts: There are ways boys behave and he's not doing it right; to behave as a girl, if you're a girl or especially if you're a boy, is a bad thing; to be a girl is be of less value; to act outside one's assigned role is a dangerous act, a sin, a violation of our cultural/religious/societal standards. The discussion rarely allows us to ask, "And this [transgression of gender roles] would be a problem why?"

Another section author, Elizabeth Payne, points out, you don't even have to *be* gay or lesbian to experience homophobic bullying, you simply have to look weird or be seen as "homosexual." Students begin policing their own behavior and that of others, on the lookout for indications of gender transgression. People begin to bend and twist, to create themselves differently, to hide, to enforce. Heterosexism gives us the lens to lay sexism bare.

Although four of the six chapters in this section deal explicitly with issues of lesbian, gay, bisexual, transgendered, and queer youth (LGBTQ), this should not be interpreted as meaning that there are two kinds of problems in schools, those relating to gender and heterosexuality and those relating to homosexuality. What is true, is that what happens to LGBTQ youth tells us much more about the institutions in which they function (or don't) than it does about the students; the lessons are important for everyone, not simply those with a particular gender/sexual identity.

Eric Rofes, to whom this section is dedicated, helps us ask broader questions about queer youth in schools:

> What is it about our current system of schooling that produces the conditions in which bullies thrive? How do the ways we conceptualize, recruit, and prepare teachers create conditions in which a system that oppressively categorizes, sorts and assigns young people is perpetuated and strengthened? How does the contemporary position of children and youth in our culture serve to drive scapegoating, harassment, and persecution? Is much of our work on gay issues in schools ultimately focused on assimilation and reform, rather than on authentic cultural pluralism and radical social change? (Rofes, 2005, p. 17)

The lives of LGBTQ youth can be read in two ways, one more traditional and the other more radical. The first perspective is to read the narratives of queer youth as victims, showing us what happens to those who dare to transgress, and how little we seem to care.

Consider the analogy of the canaries in the coal mine:

> Because early coal miners didn't have the special equipment we now have to measure dangerous gasses in the air, they used canaries to test the air quality in the mines. The canaries would chirp and sing and make noise all day, but because the birds are very sensitive to carbon monoxide, if the level of the poisonous gas rose to a dangerous level, the canaries would have trouble breathing, and maybe even die. This would alert the miners to the immediate need to leave the coal mines.

In many ways, LGBT youth are our canaries in the coal mine; the experiences of gender-and-sexuality nonconforming youth tell us much about the school culture and climate in general—the air quality, if you will—for all kids. We should look at what happens to nonconforming students and know that we have a serious problem. We should know that there are dangerous poisonous gasses in our schools and in our society. We should worry a lot about air quality.

There is a well-known statistic that 30% of queer youth attempt suicide, and yet, we do little about it. If 30% of National Merit Scholars, for example, or 30% of varsity athletes attempted to kill themselves, there would be an immediate response of outrage and action. What does it mean that this doesn't happen when it is gay youth who are self-harming, quitting school, abusing drugs and alcohol, and otherwise damaging their life chances? Schools' responsiveness (or nonresponsiveness) to the often-horrifying school experiences of LGBT youth is an indication of how frequently we are willing to sacrifice youth who are viewed as surplus population or marginalized outsiders. In blunt terms, we don't care that much about dead canaries.

Many schools have mounted massive antibullying campaigns, yet in many of these same schools, gay bullying is still permitted, and sometimes modeled by the teachers as well. One 15-year-old male student reported that when a classmate called him a "Stupid faggot," the teacher's response was: "You know we don't use the word *stupid* in this classroom."

A young man, Brian, speaking at a conference on Teaching Respect for All, told the audience about his school experiences. He was called names in the hallways, his artwork ripped off the walls and urinated on, tied up in a volleyball net and thrown in the trash, and the school's response was to tell him that *he* needed to alter his appearance and gender performance so that he wouldn't be such a target. The tormentors and bullies remained unsanctioned.

Even within these victim narratives, however, we could move from sadness and regret to indignation and anger. We could declare the current state of affairs completely unacceptable—a state of emergency. Why don't we act with more power and agency? What should be happening differently?

It is possible to change the schools, but it is not without complexity. Cosier describes schools that have become safe havens for LGBTQ youth, and responds to the debate between changing "typical" schools and removing targeted youth to separate facilities. We begin to think about what it would take to make schools safe for everyone, or whether we should just give up and give in and remove students who are so badly targeted. Payne asks us to "imagine a school without fear and isolation" and, truly, that is hard. To some, this sounds like stating, "Imagine a prison without fear and isolation." The level of transformation required on so many levels is overwhelming. Mayo points to Gay–Straight Alliances as possible sites of empowerment and change, but the level of adult surveillance makes even these potential sites of safety and power jeopardized spaces. McReady shows us that even school solutions designed to help marginalized youth often fail to take into account multiple identities; safe havens for some are still alien spaces for others. The chapters by Blanchett and Smiler, as well as the McReady chapter force us to examine the complexity of identities that students bring to school (gender, race, disability, and class) and to recognize that reform will need to take into account multiple positionalities and power relationships to be effective.

Although some of the chapters in this section evidence the pain and challenge experienced by those who operate outside traditional boundaries, they are also deeply hopeful. We have evidence of individuals, schools, and communities that recognize that the rigid restraint of tradition and rules—that living in fear—damages everyone. This is what makes radical reform of gender expectations a broad social justice issue. This is the second possible lens through which we can view the experiences of queer youth in schools. We can see these youth as brave, courageous fighters for a different reality, as evidence that it is possible to transform yourself and those around you.

Rofes asks us:

> Have our efforts of the past quarter-century done anything to ensure that young people have greater autonomy and authority in the world, freed them from the constraints of their families, or provided them with the kind of empowerment to step beyond the usual boundaries of social propriety?
>
> ... If schools are about preparing people to become activist citizens in a democracy, then schools must be reorganized as models of authentic participatory democracy. (p. 138)

The good news is that this is not a zero-sum game. Making life better for LGBTQ youth will not make things "worse" for students who identify as heterosexual or for those with other identities related to race, ethnicity, religion, or language. Indeed, if we don't make it right for everyone, then we've made it wrong for everyone, even those who don't know it!

There are sites of struggle, sparks of possibility, acts of great courage and transformation: Smiler's work illuminates the limitations that rigid gender roles place on everyone, including those assumed to be in more dominant or protected roles. He makes very clear that it is in everyone's best interest to move away from categories that conflict and constrain our breadth and our possibilities.

Black, gay students speak to McReady about the ways in which they are learning to navigate through complex identity issues, seeking solidarity as well as individuation. From them we learn that work against homophobia isn't enough if it doesn't also include attention to other issues such a Black masculinity and societal power structures.

The alternative schools described by Cosier show us that it is possible to create environments in which students can actually devote themselves to learning without the constant fear of ill-treatment. She describes the difference between rule-bound schools with a focus on policing behavior, and principled school cultures that attempt to foster a school climate that supports social justice. From this we learn that the school culture makes a huge difference.

In Payne's chapter, we learn about personal and institutional courage. When a parent who was a major funder of the school threatened to remove her daughter from the Catholic school she attended if the school made lesbian students welcome, the administrator told her, "I hope you find a good school for your daughter."

The students in the GSAs described by Mayo had to examine not only issues of gender and sexuality, but were also forced to confront their own racism within the group. We learn from these stories how complicated it is to learn to become an ally, but also what happens when students begin to think of themselves as powerful change agents in the school and beyond.

Blanchett helps us to see that disrespecting the rights of anyone to become sexually responsible and safe affects the possibilities for everyone: Injustice to one is an injustice to all.

Rofes (2005) argues strongly that

> ...the radical reforms needed to transform the educational experiences of queer and gender-nonconforming youth are precisely those reforms that might best benefit all marginalized populations—and privileged populations as well. (p. 139)

If the school culture is rigid, unaccepting, harsh, and punitive for students who do not conform to gender and sexuality norms, then we must realize, as in the coal mining analogy, that the air is toxic. In a more perfect world, we would thank those students who show us just how unacceptable schools are—recognizing that their painful experiences are a warning, a litmus test of all that must be addressed. And we would applaud those who struggle, who push back, who courageously define and redefine their lives, refusing to accept others' definitions and limitations. And it is all shared air; environmental pollution is difficult to contain. Lives are distorted and potential lost even for those who feel somehow protected from the poison. A world in which any person is unsafe because of gender identity, performance, or appearance, is not completely safe for anyone. The amount of energy spent trying to fit in, hide or make oneself acceptable to others is energy lost from far more important personal and professional endeavors. Hiding is exhausting. This is not an esoteric issue, but one at the core of social justice for all. And, from a more positive perspective, efforts to change school culture—to widen the circle—benefit all of us. Pete Seeger reminds us that "Either we all make it over the rainbow or none of us do." This is a time for radical courage and transcendent reform. Let us keep struggling.

Author's Note

This section is lovingly dedicated to the memory and work of Eric Rofes, a radical thinker and advocate for all youth. His vision, his hard work, and his energy improved the world for many. May we continue to pursue work that honors his big vision of world change.

References

hooks, b. (2000). *Feminism is for everybody: Passionate politics.* Cambridge, MA: South End Press.

Lorde, A. (1984). *Sister outsider: Essays and speeches by Audre Lorde.* Berkeley, CA: The Crossing Press.

Rofes, E. (2005). *Status quo or status queer? A radical rethinking of sexuality and schooling.* Lanham, MD: Rowman & Littlefield.

18 Creating Safe Schools for Queer Youth

Kimberly Cosier

A school can make a difference in a young person's life. More precisely, the people in a school can make a difference. For kids who don't fit neatly into rigid social norms, schools can be alienating and hostile places. Every child has a right to a safe and supportive learning environment, yet the school experiences of children and youth who are negatively impacted by gender and sexuality-based issues can be fraught with trouble, even danger. Because such children and young people are diverse, I begin this chapter with a section devoted to brief descriptions of who I mean when I say "queer[1] youth."

To describe the range of problems that can arise for queer kids, I discuss ways schools have traditionally done a poor job of protecting queer students from discrimination. I argue that school experiences need not be negative for queer kids, and appeal for help from educators who are committed to working for social justice. My appeal is situated within stories about my own experiences as a queer student, teacher, and researcher.

As a way to celebrate the possibilities of social justice for all, I highlight two safe public schools: New Dawn Alternative High School[2] and Alliance High School. Educators must meet their obligation to provide safe, supportive places for all kids to learn about themselves and the world around them. The stories of the kids, who found homes at New Dawn and Alliance after they had faced roadblocks to equal education in traditional schools, will help make the case for that. Finally, in order to support such change, I provide helpful resources for concerned educators including: a list of 10 action points developed by the Gay, Lesbian, Straight Education Network (GLSEN), a glossary of terms, and web resources.

Understanding the Problem: Who Is At Risk?

Children and young people whose lives are impacted by LGBT issues are far from homogeneous. Therefore, "queer youth," as a population, must be conceptualized and theorized quite broadly. About the difficulties of this endeavor, Sears (2006) writes, "it is apparent that there is no consensus on…what it means to be a queer adolescent" (p. 2). When we factor in younger children, who may be gender variant, or who have lesbian or gay parents, our scope becomes wider still.

In this context, I use the word *queer* as an umbrella term to encompass all children and youth who are impacted by their own and other people's reactions to lesbian, gay, bisexual, transgender, intersex, and queer/questioning issues. A queer kid might be someone who has a gay dad, someone who is straight but whom others perceive to be a lesbian; or the term might refer to someone who is saving up money from a job at a burger joint for sex reassignment surgery. The possibilities are numerous, fluid, and wide-ranging. That said, I'll attempt to categorize the uncategorizable.

Lesbian, Gay, and Bisexual Youth (and Those Perceived to Be So)

> Claire: There are some out people at my high school, but they're treated like lepers. I don't really care if people call me names; it's the physical abuse I couldn't take. And believe me, our school has been reported numerous times for the violence against my friends. But that's all—they get reported and then it's hushed up and nothing gets done. (*Young Gay America*, 2006)[3]

Perhaps the first people to come to mind, when we think of queer youth, are those who are lesbian, gay, or bisexual. Today, there are growing numbers of kids who come out to their peers or school personnel as lesbian, gay, or bisexual (Owens, 1998; Savin Williams, 2001). Gay–Straight Alliances are springing up in schools across the country. This phenomenon is astonishing to me. When I was in high school in the 1970s, I would have never dreamed of coming out! I was aware of being attracted to other girls, but I knew that while I was at my high school I had to play a game of fitting in with the prevailing heterosexual norm—or risk being teased, ostracized, or worse (I was successful at the game to the point of being a runner up homecoming queen, which people who know me now find quite funny). A great deal of progress has been made with regard to lesbian, gay, and bisexual kids, but as a later section on research in schools will reveal, many still face dangerous challenges in schools.

In addition to students described above, there are also kids who are perceived to be queer. They may actually be gay, lesbian, or bisexual but not out of the closet (perhaps not even to themselves) or they may not be gay, lesbian, or bisexual but are still perceived to be, or accused of being, queer for a variety of reasons. Students in this group often deviate from heterosexual social norms; for doing so, they are censured by their peers. This can take a variety of forms, but one example would be a girl who is unreceptive to boys' sexual advances who is then stigmatized and labeled a "dyke" or "lezzie." In one such case, Emily, a sweet girl whom I met through my work at Alliance High School, experienced bullying due to the perceptions of her peers at her former, traditional high school. A survivor of sexual abuse by an uncle, she had lashed out at a group of male student athletes when they grabbed at her as she tried to pass them in the hallway. The boys began calling her "dyke" and other names; before long, many of her classmates were bullying her.

Gender Variant and Transgender Youth (and Those Perceived to Be So)

> Katherine: My third grade teacher was very fond of boy-versus-girl activities. I guess that's because everybody, but me, got so into it. I didn't like it. Why did we have to compete with everything: spelling bees, math problem races to the board, etc, etc, etc? Why'd I have to get stuck on the "boy" team when most of my friends were on the "girl" team? I'd even asked if I could switch teams. But the reply was the laughter of students and my teacher's scolding not to cause trouble. Third grade was the first time I was clearly in the "outgroup." (YouthResource, 2006)

Other young people are at risk of harassment, or worse, because of issues associated with gender identity. In our culture, gender behavior is split into a heavily regulated, false binary system. The policing of this system begins at a very early age. There are toys for girls and toys for boys. Even colors are policed; I have seen boys who choose pink or violet crayons reprimanded by kindergarten classmates! Children who are gender variant do not fit neatly into one of the two categories that are typical of boys and girls in our society. Gender variant children are often a source of great anxiety for parents and teachers. Negative reactions of parents, teachers, and other adults in their lives, as well as teasing and bullying from their peers can take a toll on kids with atypical gender behaviors (Menvielle & Tuerk, 2006).

I was fortunate to hear Catherine Tuerk and Edgardo Menvielle, MD speak at a conference on gender variant children in 2005. They run a clinic at Children's National Medical Center (CNMC) in Washington, D.C. At this time, it is the only clinic dedicated to the well-being of gender variant children and their families. According to Tuerk and Menvielle, boys who behave in ways that are considered in our culture to be typically feminine are at considerable risk at a very early age. The vast majority of the families who participate in the CNMC program do so out of concern for gender variant boys (Menvielle et al., 2006).

"Tomboys" or girls who behave in ways that are typically regarded as masculine (preferring to play contact sports over playing with dolls for example) have traditionally been tolerated more readily than gender-variant boys (Menvielle et al., 2006). Recently, in my visits to elementary schools, however, I have noticed that tolerance for young tomboys is evaporating. It may be a phenomenon that is limited to the particular schools I have visited; however, it seems plausible that as children become increasingly sophisticated in their knowledge of gender and sex roles at earlier ages, they become less tolerant of girls' gender difference. In any case, when girls reach an age of sexual maturity, they are no longer free to behave in ways reserved for males because at adolescence, tomboys become a threat to the status quo (Halberstam, 1998).

Transgender individuals are gender variant to the degree that they feel their biological gender is incorrect. According to YouthResource (2006), a website "by and for gay, lesbian, bisexual, transgender, and questioning (GLBTQ) young people":

> Transgender people feel that the gender to which they were born, or assigned at birth, does not fit them.... Transgender people also include people who identify as "genderqueer", gender neutral, and/or gender-free—people who may not identify as either male or female. Transsexual people are those who choose to medically transition to the gender that is right for them. (http://youthresource.com/living/content/trans/brochure.htm)

Most transgender people are born with biological sex characteristics that are typically male or typically female. There are some people, however, who are born intersexed. There is a growing understanding of intersex, which can manifest in wide-ranging ways. Some children are born with obvious genital variations, while others have only chromosomal differences that may never visibly emerge. According to the Intersex Society of North America (2006):

> Intersex is a relatively common anatomical variation from the "standard" male and female types; just as skin and hair color vary along a wide spectrum, so does sexual and reproductive anatomy. Intersex is neither a medical nor a social pathology. (http://www.isna.org/compare)

In many cases, intersex conditions do not impact a child's educational life, However, those whose gender identity is different from the one assigned at birth can experience some of the same challenges faced by other gender variant kids. A great resource for understanding the public and private life of a person who is intersexed is *Middlesex: A Novel* by Jeffery Eugenides (2002).

Children and Youth with Queer Families

> Joshua: I live with my two moms in Louisiana. I am very lucky to have my family because they give me great things like lots of love and support and security. We take care of each other and take turns making dinner. We play games, make up silly songs in the car, and like to go fishing.... The hardest thing about having lesbian parents is that people make fun of my family but you get used to it because it doesn't matter what other people think. It only matters what I think and I like it. (*Young Gay America*, 2006)

Finally, some children experience bias in schools because they have gay, lesbian, bisexual, or transgender parent(s) or other family members. For these children, problems often arise due to unexamined heteronormativity, which can be defined as the social and institutional support of a compulsory heterosexual worldview (Warner, 1991). Although these children can be the victims of overt bullying and discrimination, it is often the case that they suffer as much from unexamined assumptions on the parts of school personnel. One can imagine, for example, that Father's Day can be fraught with complications and emotional stress when a child has two moms and "dad" is an anonymous sperm donor.

In sum, not all queer kids are the same, nor do they all come from similar home situations. Some queer kids take everything life hands them in stride, while others suffer from depression and anxiety as a result of their own or others' fears and biases. The one thing all queer kids share is a need for supportive, caring, and ethical school personnel. Sadly, these needs quite often go unmet. As the following research reveals, queer students can be at great risk of social aggression, even violence in schools (Bontempo & D'Augelli, 2002; Russell, Franz, & Driscoll, 2001). To make matters worse for some queer kids, they may also be rejected or abused at home by family members (D'Augelli & Grossman, 2006; Savin Williams, 2001). Caring educators need to make a difference.

Research on School Experiences

> Freddie Fuentes, a student in the Morgan Hill Unified School District in California, endured years of abuse at school—and even ended up in the hospital after a group of students beat him while shouting "faggot" in the presence of a school bus driver. (GLSEN, 2005, p. vii)

> Emily sat alone and depressed at a lunch table in the cafeteria of her former school. A nearby group of students began taunting her, calling her "lesbian" and "bulldyke" She ran out of the building after they threw opened cartons of milk at her. Such abuse was a regular feature of her life in her former school. Though she had gone to them for help, school officials had done nothing to stop the bullies. This is why, she says, she came to Alliance High School. (personal communication, 2006)

> Jim came to New Dawn after two years of taunting by a group of boys at his former school. Though Jim didn't identify as gay, the bullies had decided that he was a "faggot" and set out to make his life miserable. When he was cornered in the shower after gym class one day he became fearful of going to school altogether. He began skipping school regularly and his grades fell. Jim's mother heard about New Dawn and encouraged him to apply. If not for the principal, teachers, and students of the New Dawn community, Jim believes he would have dropped out school and thrown away his future. (personal communication, 2000)

Sadly, such stories of harassment, violence, and neglect are not rare (American Association of University Women, 2004; Harris Interactive & GLSEN, 2005; Human Rights Watch, 2001). Research shows that social aggression, or bullying, is extremely common in schools. Twemlow, Fonagy, and Sacco write, "[s]chool violence continues to be a major menace, ranking with cancer and heart disease among America's most serous public health problems" (2002, p. 304). According to Harris Interactive and GLSEN (2005) "overall, two-thirds of middle and high school students reported that they have been harassed or assaulted in the past year at school because of their appearance, gender, sexual orientation, gender expression, race/ethnicity, disability or religion" (p. 4).

Harassment that is connected to queer issues is nearly ubiquitous (Baker, 2002; Harris Interactive & GLSEN, 2005; Human Rights Watch, 2001; Macgillivray, 2004). The 2003 and 2005 GLSEN studies of school climate found that "[a]ctual or perceived sexual orientation is one of the most common reasons that students are harassed by their peers, second only to physical appearance" (Harris Interactive & GLSEN, 2005, p. iii). Kosciw (2003) writes:

> Violence, bias, and harassment directed at LGBT students continue to be the rule— not the exception—in American schools...The bottom line remains that more that 4 out of 5 LGBT students reported being verbally harassed at school because of their sexual orientation, and more than 9 out of 10 reported hearing homophobic remarks such as "faggot," "dyke" or "that's so gay" frequently or often. (p. 5)

According to Kosciw, LGBT students are over three times more likely than non-LGBT students to report that they feel unsafe at school.

Teachers' Perceptions of the Problem

In addition to surveying students, the Harris Interactive and GLSEN (2005) study also investigated secondary school teachers' perceptions of bullying and harassment in their schools. Half of teacher respondents said they believed that bullying "is a serious problem at their school" (p. 4). A majority of the teachers surveyed said they felt it was their responsibility to ensure the safety and well-being of LGBT students, with only a very small minority of teachers saying they did not believe it was their responsibility to help make schools safe for queer kids. Most teachers said they would feel comfortable intervening if they heard students making homophobic slurs or other bullying behaviors.

Student Perceptions of Teachers' Ability and/or Willingness to Respond

Unfortunately, there is a discrepancy between what teachers reported about supporting queer kids, and what students themselves believed to be true. The majority of students reported that they felt teachers would *not* intervene. If they did step in when trouble arose, students felt that teachers would be powerless to change a hostile situation. Thus, most students do not report bullying and harassment to school personnel. According to the GLSEN study:

> Despite the fact that only nine percent of the teachers who participated in the study said they disagreed with the view that they have an obligation to ensure a safe learning environment for gay, lesbian, bisexual and transgender students, these kids do not tend to go to teachers for help. Most of these students (57%) never report this harassment or assault to a teacher, principal or other school staff person. One in ten

students do not report these incidents because they believe the teachers or staff are powerless to improve the situation. (Harris Interactive & GLSEN, 2005, p. 80)

This finding suggests that there is a need to address the "gap between the support that teachers say they would provide to students and students' perceptions of teachers' willingness to take action" (Harris Interactive & GLSEN, 2005, p. 80).

Queer kids know they are less likely than others to be able to depend on the majority of school personnel to intervene when problems arise. Some teachers, staff, and administrators feel that it goes against their religious beliefs to support the needs of LGBT children and youth. Parents or students may also claim that their rights are being violated by not being allowed to express negative attitudes about homosexuality, but "there is no constitutional right to bully or intimidate other students" (Kosciw, 2003, p. 12). While all school community members have a right to express their views, particularly where religious beliefs are concerned, they cannot do so in a way that makes LGBT students feel unsafe or feel as if their education is being imperiled.

As noted, only 9% of the teachers surveyed stated that they did not believe they were responsible to ensure a safe learning environment for queer kids. Most others simply do not understand the problem. They blame the victims of antiqueer bullying and harassment rather than working to fix the problem. Or they underestimate the degree to which such bullying can affect queer children and youth. It is the responsibility of every educator to help create an emotionally healthy, safe, and equitable learning environment for all students, including queer youth (National Education Association, 2006). Caring teachers, who are committed to social justice, must develop strategies to identify themselves as resources for students experiencing harassment.

An Uphill Battle

My own experience as a teacher supports student perceptions that school personnel will not take steps to make schools queer friendly, as the following story reveals. Though I work at a university now, I was once a middle school art teacher. A couple of years prior to my time there, the Strategic Planning Committee had conducted a school climate survey through which they found that a substantial number of students were fearful of passing in the hallways, using the restrooms, and so forth. A smaller but significant number of students reported that they found the whole school to be an unsafe place. To address the problem, school officials took steps, which ranged from encouraging teachers to engage positively with students in the hallways between classes, to hiring a tough (but fair) ex-marine as an assistant principal.

By the time I started teaching there the school was, on the whole, a nice place to be. There was one thing, however, that remained distressing. At this school, as in many others (Harris Interactive & GLSEN, 2005; Human Rights Watch, 2001) homophobic slurs were used constantly. Why, if I had a nickel for every time I heard the word *faggot* I swear I could have retired early! So far as I know, there were no kids at our school who openly identified as lesbian, gay, bisexual, transgender, or any other queer category. I knew that they were out there, just the same (either in the closet, as I had been, or not yet able to name their difference). I also believed that hate speech hurts *everyone* in a community, so I tried to do what I could to stop the use of such ugly slurs. I found myself, like Sisyphus, toiling under impossible circumstances.

My fellow teachers told me I was being "too sensitive." I knew that my colleagues meant this as a warning to me—"We like you kid, don't push your luck!" Still I pressed on (being young and stubborn). At one point, I got myself in a pot of considerably hot water because I refused to ignore a homophobic slur. I gave Mitch, a boy whose parents were prominent citizens in the community, an after-school detention when he kept taunting a classmate by calling him a "fag" after I told him to stop. The next day, his mother dropped by my classroom: She said her son was "very upset" and felt the disciplinary action I had taken was "unfair." I explained the situation to her, telling her that I had clearly warned him of the consequences he would face should he continue to use the word *fag* in our classroom. Since he disregarded my warning and disrespected his classmate again, I said that I felt my actions were appropriate.

She did not agree and suggested that I was letting my "personal feelings" cloud my judgment (implying a threat, of course). I held fast to my decision. The matter was taken to the principal, who gave Mitch a perfunctory talk about respecting teachers and classmates and let him go. As Mitch and his mother left the office, he smirked at me. After they left, the principal made it clear, through her apple cheeked smile, that she would prefer it if I would just let these things go. She said I "must understand that the district is family oriented" and that I had better think about "choosing my battles." At that point, I did not feel that I was ready to lose my job over this particular battle, so I let it go.

The Impact of Social Aggression on Academic Achievement

The large-scale research studies noted above, as well as the American Association of University Women's *Hostile Hallways* reports (1993, 2001), all found "a direct linkage between academic performance and experiences of harassment and an unsafe learning environment in school" (cited in Harris Interactive & GLSEN, 2005, p. 3). Queer students were four to five times more likely to report having skipped school in the last month because of safety concerns than the general population of students (Harris Interactive & GLSEN, 2005; Kosciw, 2003). Queer students who experience frequent physical harassment were more likely to report they did not plan to go to college and their grade point averages were half a grade lower than their counterparts who were not physically harassed (Bontempo & D'Augelli, 2002; Russell, Franz, & Driscoll, 2001; Russell, Serif, & Truong, 2001). If nothing else, the academic performance of all students should be seen as every educator's responsibility; therefore, making schools safe for queer kids to learn is everybody's business.

Reversing the Negativity Narrative

Queer young people are at risk of any number of social problems, including poor academic performance, skipping or dropping out of school, and homelessness. They use drugs and alcohol at higher rates than their straight peers and engage in risky sexual behaviors (Kissen, 2002; Mallon, 1998; Padilla, Neff, Rew, & Crisp, 2006). Most alarmingly, LGBT youth also have significantly higher rates of suicidal thoughts and kill themselves at a much higher rate than heterosexual youth (D'Augelli, Hershberger, & Pilkington, 2001). In one study, "a very high proportion of GLB youth, 60%, reported that they had seriously thought about suicide, and 60% believed that their sexual orientation will be an obstacle in their life" (Padilla et al., 2006, p. 1).

Certainly such dismal reports are valuable. Those of us who work with, and on behalf of, queer youth must document the bullying and abuse they endure in order to make a case for the need to support them. Yet, I believe that this persistent focus on the negative places queer young people, and anyone who cares about them, in a psychologically and emotionally precarious place. With the danger always lurking "in the hallways" (Human Rights Watch, 2001) as well as in most publications about queer youth, there is little place for them to see positive images of people like themselves. About the challenges of conducting research on queer issues in schools, Quinlivan (2006) writes:

> The process of labeling queer students within a deficit framework…[is] problematic. It ran the risk of the students being attributed with a set of characteristics that pathologised and abnormalised them in relation to what was assumed to be the heterosexual norm. (p. 13)

Dwelling on the negative does not celebrate the many contributions young, queer people are making in their communities. It does little to support queer kids, beyond engendering pity among some people who could potentially offer help. It makes parents and their children feel that they are doomed to a dismal and dangerous life if they don't fit within the heteronormative paradigm. The negativity narrative does not offer hope to a kid who thinks she or he is the only person on the face of the earth to feel the way she or he feels. It asks them (borrowing from W. E. B. Dubois), "How does it feel to be a problem?" Therefore, positive stories for queer youth are sorely needed.

Two Schools that Make a Difference for Queer Kids

In the following sections, I offer narrative vignettes from my experiences in two public alternative schools that were created for kids who did not fit in the rigid social structures of traditional schools. These stories each begin in the negative but move forward, toward hope.

New Dawn Alternative High School

Passing through the glass doors that lead inside New Dawn Alternative High School, I was immediately struck by an absence of institutional frigidity. The secretary's office was directly to the right of the entrance. I stopped at the door and peered in. Sandy, the very busy school secretary, greeted me warmly. A little unsure of myself on my first visit, I explained that I was there to see Noel, the art teacher. "Oh yes," she said smiling, "Noel said you would be coming by today. If you wait just a minute, I can take you to her room."

As I waited, a girl emerged from a large room, which I would later learn was called "The Commons." The girl asked Sandy if she could use the phone to call her mother to inquire about adopting a kitten. Sandy, who was feverishly looking for something in a stack of papers on her desk, recognized the girl by the sound of her voice alone. Still rifling through the pile of forms, she didn't miss a beat saying, "You can use the one in the conference room Samantha." She quickly glanced up from her work, saw the kitten and exclaimed, "Oh my, what a sweetheart!"

The girl, who was holding the little creature tenderly in her arms, was tiny herself. Her clothing was strangely incongruous with her delicate features, which were almost obscured by heavy black eyeliner and lipstick. She wore a huge army surplus coat that seemed to enshroud her diminutive frame. Under the coat she had on an outrageously short patent leather skirt and a black spandex shirt that had been ripped up and stitched back together with about 57 safety pins. Her outfit was completed with a thick, spiked, black leather dog collar, torn fishnet stockings, and black, knee-high Doc Marten boots. I guessed that her fashion sense was one reason she had not fit in at her former school.

Shortly, a boy joined the girl and the kitten. He wrapped his long arms around her. The dark girl with the kitten leaned backward into the newcomer's embrace. The boy was tall, well over 6 feet, with a fresh scrubbed, baby face and a shock of spiky, bleached blonde hair. He wore a pink, cap sleeved Rainbow Bright® T-shirt atop a baggy pair of orange cargo pants. As his long arms encircled the girl, the contrast of multicolored bangles against her black and olive drab clothing was striking. The tall boy bent and rested his head on the tiny shoulder of the girl and said (about the kitten) "I hope we get to keep her."

I learned the stories of these two kids, and many other misfits, during the year I spent at New Dawn doing fieldwork for my dissertation. It turned out that Samantha and Caleb had become friends at a larger, more traditional high school prior to coming to New Dawn. While there, both had been harassed for being different. Samantha was routinely called a "Satanist" and other names because of the way she looked. Caleb faced even tougher treatment, being harassed on a regular basis and sometimes physically assaulted for being gay. The two had formed a false romantic union in order to try to protect one another from the other students; a scheme that had met with limited success. Thus, when they heard about an alternative school that welcomed kids who didn't fit in traditional schools, they both jumped at the chance to apply (New Dawn is a public alternative school, but students must submit a written application to be considered for enrollment).

Once they both settled in at New Dawn, Samantha and Caleb were able to forego their charade. They were free to be themselves. Over the year I spent at New Dawn, I found that the caring and supportive environment purposefully created by the principal, teachers, other school employees, and students of New Dawn was incredibly important to nearly all of its kids. Like Sandy, the school secretary who knew Samantha by the sound of her voice alone, students knew they could count on members of the New Dawn community to "see what makes them tick," For Caleb, and others, this caring community turned out to be a lifesaver. After I was at the school for several months, Caleb told me that if it wasn't for the people at New Dawn, he was sure he would have killed himself by then. Caleb was not the only student who expressed such feelings to me while I was at New Dawn. Schools, and the people in them, can make a difference.

Alliance High School

Billed as the first school for kids who have been bullied and harassed in other schools, the Alliance School of Milwaukee has garnered wide-ranging interest on local, national, and international levels. One of the unintended outcomes of this media attention has been a public debate about bullying. There were talk radio jocks calling it a school for "losers;" some even declared such a school to be the end of democracy. For example, a professor of public interest law at George Washington University was quoted in an article about the school as saying:

> High schools are often the last opportunity to instill basic citizenship values, including tolerance for a pluralistic society, and removing victims from that environment is, in many ways, a concession. If these administrators cannot guarantee a healthy and safe environment, the solution is to get new administrators, not create a new school. (Carr, 2006, p. 1)

While I agree with the heart of this statement, the reality is this: some students don't have the time to wait! For many of the kids at New Dawn and Alliance bullying and harassment were simply too dangerous in the moment for them to wait for adults to reach such long-range and complex goals. Emily didn't have the time to wait for adults to fix this enormous societal problem when she was being called "dyke" at her former school and having cartons of milk thrown at her in the cafeteria. She had to leave, to find a place where she could safely get her education. Fortunately, for Emily and others in the Milwaukee area, there is Alliance.

In the fall of 2005, opening day of Alliance High School was abuzz with jittery, expectant energy. Many students arrived well before the first class was to begin. Though some tried not to show it, everyone there seemed to have high hopes and expectations for the school. Collectively, the student body looked like it sailed over from the Island of Misfit Toys. They stood outside the building anxiously waiting for their lives to be transformed.

Though the school was not exclusively for queer students, it was not surprising to see so many students who appeared to be so. I knew some of the kids from work I had done at Project Q, a youth-led LGBT community center in Milwaukee. A group, which appeared to be mostly young transgender women shrieked each time they saw someone they knew. One little guy, who apparently had not been prepared for the gender (and other forms of) diversity was visibly shaken. I watched, relieved, as the lead teacher and founder of the school, Tina Owen, walked over, gently put her arm around him and spoke to him quietly about his obvious fears. This school was for everyone.

The doors finally opened. We had some time to mingle before classes began. I sat down next to a 6'4" Goth kid, named Chris, who I had never met before. He was sitting, hunched and alone, trying very hard to put out "don't f**k with me" vibes. Chris's ghastly makeup, heavy black eyeliner and lipstick expertly teased at the corners of his mouth into sharp, downward points, was worn like protective mask. He had on a variation of the Goth uniform that Samantha had worn at New Dawn—mostly black clothing with lots of zippers, safety pins and other menacing, bondage and vampire-inspired accessories. Undaunted by his appearance and demeanor, I cheerily chatted him up. I found, as I suspected, that he was actually quite sweet and vulnerable.

At his former school, I learned, Chris had been a football player but his grades slipped and he wasn't able to stay on the team. Then he became interested in Goth culture. He told me he considered himself a "genderqueer," which meant that he wanted to be free of gender labels and stereotypes—not that he wanted to be a girl. With his newly minted identity, he began to be taunted cruelly by his former teammates, which was why he had left his former school. On opening day of Alliance High School, with a double-edged look of defiance and dejection in his black-rimmed eyes, Chris grumbled that he hated school and he didn't hold out much hope that this school would be any different.

Later that year, during their final all-school community meeting before winter recess, I was moved to tears when Chris stood and addressed the Alliance school community. With a huge smile on his black lipsticked face, he dramatically swept his arm around the room and thanked his fellow students and teachers for making him feel welcomed at Alliance. He seemed on the verge of tears himself, when he said with absolute conviction that he knew Alliance had saved him from dropping out of school and that it might have even stopped him from taking his own life. This sort of talk was common in both school settings.

Emily (the girl who had milk cartons thrown at her) was equally connected to the Alliance community. By the time she worked with me on an art project in the spring of 2006, she told me she felt part of a school community for the first time since elementary school. She said she loved Alliance because the teachers showed that they cared about her and other kids by really listening to them and sticking with them to make sure they were learning. "Sometimes it feels like they want to get on your nerves," she said, "but you know its 'cause they want you to do good and succeed." Emily also said that she thought it was very important that the students had a voice in the way the school was run. The weekly community meetings were important to her because it was a time and place where you could speak your mind to the whole school. Emily thought that Alliance being based on an antibullying, social justice mission made it a safe place for everyone.

By that spring, Emily was no longer afraid to be herself. Though she told me she had become very shy and "shut down" during the time she was being bullied at her former school, Emily was very open and talkative during the afternoons we spent working on huge banners for the school's entrance. Since coming to Alliance, Emily had come out as bisexual. She was in a relationship with Jake, a talented graffiti and "zine" artist and self-styled punk anarchist. Emily said she liked Jake because he was "funny—and just as pretty as a girl."

With his foot-tall Mohawk and punk clothing, Jake tried hard to look tough, but Emily is right, in spite of his efforts he is pretty. For his art project, Jake made a couple of banners but my favorite was a huge painting in the form of a comic strip. It featured his signature graffiti character, Morty the Rat. In the painting, Morty is walking along, happy with his new "Liberty Spikes" (which I learned are what you call those spiky Mohawks). In the next frame, his happiness is squashed when he gets "stuff" thrown at him by some frat boys. Later, Morty finds a brochure for Alliance that intrigues him. He goes to investigate the school and discovers a home among other misfits. For Jake, who tries to be a tough guy, this was the highest form of praise for Alliance, which got a little more publicity when the piece was shown at an exhibition at the Gay Arts Center.

For Chris, Emily, Jake, as well as for other kids who did not fit within the social structures of their former schools, teachers who take time to listen to their students can make a difference. Listening means more than offering a shoulder to cry on: It means designing a curriculum that reflects diversity, and attends to the needs and interests of the students. It means being willing to talk frankly about social issues, using students' experiences as a jumping off point. It means acknowledging students' alternative romantic and sexual desires and honoring gender diversity. Accepting sexual, gender, and other forms of identity diversity can contribute greatly to the well-being of kids who might otherwise fall through the cracks, or worse. For some kids caring teachers may actually save lives.

A First Step Toward Justice: Antidiscrimination Policies

Inclusion of sexual orientation and gender identity in school antidiscrimination policies has been found to have a positive effect on school climate for queer kids (Harris Interactive & GLSEN, 2005). Unfortunately, unlike students who are members of other groups who may experience bias and hostility in schools, queer youth cannot always count on being included in such policies (Harris Interactive & GLSEN, 2005). Hence, queer kids are often an invisible minority where official policy is concerned. Research shows that working to get sexual orientation and gender identity included in policy is an important first step toward equity.

A Framework for Change

I believe that understanding the interdependence of school structure and student/teacher relationships is vital to the creation of school cultures that support kids who do not fit the norm. In my research at New Dawn, three themes emerged, which are also appropriate to the school community at Alliance. The theme of *Rule-Bound School Cultures versus Principled School Cultures* helps explain differences in the ways schools structure themselves and how those structures impact students (Cosier, 2001, 2004).

Schools that are rule-bound focus on policing behavior. As a result, rather than foster-ing a caring community based on principles of social justice, rule-bound schools tend to be inhospitable to difference. They are, therefore, usually not safe spaces for queer kids. Principled school cultures, on the other hand, are built upon a small number of over-arching principals rather than laundry lists of rules. As a result of a broader notion of school governance, these schools tend to be more open to difference and place the onus of behavior on the students. Student voice emerged as an enormously important feature of governance of both New Dawn and Alliance. This approach has the effect of empowering students and fostering a school climate that supports social justice.

A second theme, *Bureaucratic Pedagogy versus Relational Pedagogy*, explains differ-ences in the ways teachers and students relate to one another within the systems described in the first theme. In a rule-bound school, teachers tend to be placed in the role of rule enforcers. They become servants of standard procedure, bureaucrats who are unlikely to approach teaching as a mutually beneficial relationship between an educator and her or his pupils. Principled school cultures are much more amenable to relational teaching. There are teachers who manage to take a relational teaching stance, even in the most rule-bound school. Relational teaching is arguably the single most important factor for at-risk student attachment and resilience.

The third theme, *Student Alienation versus Student Attachment*, explains differen-tial outcomes that occur for individual students as a result of the interplay of the first two themes. When the students I met at New Dawn and at Alliance were in rule-bound schools they had mostly bureaucratic teachers and became alienated from school. Many of the students I came to know had been considered to be problems in their former schools. When they switched to schools that were based on principles, and centered on relational teaching, these students became incredibly attached to the new school com-munity and became less likely to be "problem students." In fact, many of them grew into strong, positive leaders.

No school culture is either wholly rule-bound or completely principled. Teacher/stu-dent relationships are all comprised of varying degrees of bureaucratic and relational ele-ments, and from day to day, an individual student's feelings of alienation or attachment to a school community can fluctuate. Overall, New Dawn and Alliance lean heavily toward being principled and relational; the students' affection for the schools is proof. Students knew that they could count on their teachers to be open about topics often swept under the rug in rule-bound schools. As part of being principled, New Dawn and Alliance teachers allowed students access to "dangerous knowledge" (Britzman, 1999, p. 2). That is, teachers and students talk about gender variance and sexuality in a frank and honest manner. Diversity was treated as an asset rather than a violation of standard conduct.

Conclusion

In my work in New Dawn I found that queer students enrolled in the school because they had been targets of bullying and harassment by students, teachers, and administrators at their former schools (Cosier, 2001). This bullying seems to be rooted in both homophobia (the irrational fear and hatred of all things queer) and misogyny (the irrational fear and hatred of all things female). The same is true at Alliance. Though they came to Alliance and New Dawn from many schools, their negative experiences were surprisingly similar. Equally similar were their reasons for attachment to their new school communities: a principled school structure and relational teaching. Students in both alternative schools told me they stayed in school because they felt they had a voice in the school and that they felt valued and cared for by all members of the new school communities. A number of them reported that when they joined the school communities, they felt safe in school for the first time in their lives.

Though New Dawn and Alliance are small, alternative high schools, I believe the principles that made them work for queer kids (and others who did not fit in) are simple and could work in more traditional school settings, either on a school-wide or individual classroom basis. Traditional schools do not have to be scary places; people in school communities can decide to make a change.

Even if a whole school is not moving toward acceptance of sexual and gender diversity, individual teachers can still make a difference. Before starting Alliance, Tina Owen had made her classroom a safe space in a huge, urban high school. Because of the stories her students shared with her over the years, Tina was inspired to start a different kind of school for kids who had been bullied and harassed. One or two teachers can make a difference. According to Harris Interactive and GLSEN (2005), "the presence of supportive staff contributed to a range of positive indicators including greater sense of safety, fewer reports of missing days of school, and a higher incidence of planning to attend college" (p. 12). So please, be bold and make your classroom a safe haven for queer kids and other misfits.

If your whole school *is* willing to make a change, then all players must understand the process to be broad and systematic. A schoolwide policy against discrimination based on sexual orientation and gender identity is a start. Restructure your school to become more principled and to support relational teaching—it is an ongoing, messy, democratic process—stick with it! Student participation in the development of curriculum and the governance of the school or classroom is also vital. Rules should be few but meaningful, for example, at Alliance and New Dawn, kids were not punished for letting the occasional swear word slip out so long as they were not "cussing out" another member of the school community. In order to truly feel safe in a school, young people must be allowed and encouraged to speak their minds, without fear of reprisal by school officials.

It takes courage, integrity, and committed effort on the parts of teachers who want to support queer kids. Educators who wish to work against the alienation many queer kids feel in school must recognize that listening is a key ingredient, as noted above. With these simple (not easy) qualities in place, New Dawn Alternative High School and Alliance High School can serve as models for safe schools for queer kids, even schools that are larger and more traditional in nature. Though not all schools can, or should, look exactly like either of the schools I have described, all schools should look more like them than they do at present. It is vital to the health and well-being of our youth that bullying and harassment be taken on as the public health crisis it has been shown to be. This can only be done when school people take seriously their responsibility to educate *all* children and youth equally and fairly.

Helpful Resources for Concerned Educators

GLSEN's Ten Things Educators Can Do To Ensure That Their Classrooms Are Safe Spaces for ALL Students

1. *Do Not Assume Heterosexuality.* The constant assumption of heterosexuality renders gay, lesbian, bisexual, and transgender (LGBT) people invisible. Such invisibility is devastating to the individual's sense of self. Both the school as an institution and its professionals must be inclusive in their language and attitudes. By reminding themselves that LGBT people are found on every staff, in every classroom, and on every team, faculty can "unlearn" heterosexism.

2. *Guarantee Equality.* LGBT members of the school community need to know that their schools value equality and that they are protected against discrimination. Schools should add sexual orientation and gender identity to their nondiscrimination and harassment policies. In addition, sexual orientation and gender identity and gender expression should be included in multicultural and diversity statements as a way to communicate a commitment to equal treatment for all.

3. *Create a Safe Environment.* It is the school's obligation to take proactive measures to ensure that all members of its community have a right to participate without fear of harassment. Schools must make it clear that neither physical violence nor harassing language like "faggot" and "dyke" will be tolerated. Creating a "Safe Zone" program—displaying posters, stickers, and other literature encouraging acceptance—is a great way to communicate that your school is a safe environment for all.

4. *Diversify Library and Media Holdings.* The library is frequently the first place to which students turn for accurate sexuality and gender information. Too often, few or no works on LGBT issues are found there. Librarians and media specialists need to be sure their holdings are up to date and reflect the diversity of our world.

   Materials that reflect LGBT themes and authors should be prominently displayed and easily accessible to students seeking them. The library and media center should reflect LGBT holidays and events in their programming, and should strive to make sure that individual classroom libraries are similarly inclusive. The GLSEN Bookstore is a great online "one-stop shopping" resource for LGBT materials.

5. *Provide Training for Faculty and Staff.* School staff need to be equipped to serve all the students with whom they work, including LGBT students and children from LGBT families. Understanding the needs of LGBT youth/families and developing the skills to meet those needs should be expected of all educators regardless of their personal or religious beliefs.

6. *Provide Appropriate Health Care and Education.* While being LGBT is not only a "health issue," health education on sexuality and sexually transmitted diseases should sensitively address the issues of LGBT people. Counselors and health staff should be particularly careful to make their sensitivity to LGBT issues clear. By educating themselves about related support services and agencies, and making pamphlets and other literature available, health professionals can provide for the needs of the LGBT students and families with whom they work.

7. *Be a Role Model.* Actions speak louder than words. The most effective way to reduce anti-LGBT bias is to consistently behave in ways that appreciate all human beings and condemn discrimination of any kind. Though both straight and LGBT students will benefit from having openly LGBT educators, coaches, and administrators, staff members need not be "out" or LGBT themselves in order to be good role models. By demonstrating respectful language, intervening during instances of anti-LGBT harassment, and bringing diverse images into the classroom in safe and affirming ways, all staff members can be model human beings for the students with whom they work.

8. *Provide Support for Students.* Peer support and acceptance is the key to any student's feeling of belonging in the school. Gay-Straight Alliances (GSAs) offer students this sense of belonging as well as the chance to effect positive change in their schools. GSAs welcome membership from any student interested in combating anti-LGBT bias and raising awareness of heterosexism and diverse gender/sexual identities. There are currently over 1,200 GSAs registered with GLSEN and countless more across the nation. Consider being a GSA advisor and helping students in your com-

munity to form a club that provides support, understanding and an avenue for promoting equality and school change.

9. *Reassess the Curriculum.* Educators need to integrate LGBT issues throughout the curriculum—not just in classes such as health education, but in disciplines such as English, History, Art, and Science. Preexisting curricula should be broadened to include LGBT images where appropriate (such as in studies of the Holocaust and Civil Rights Movement). Current events, popular music and film, and other media that include LGBT people and issues should be regularly discussed in class. Classroom libraries, story times, and assigned reading should be thoughtfully structured to include the full range of human diversity. Finally, educators should take advantage of "teachable moments," treating questions, comments, and instances of name-calling as opportunities to educate students about LGBT people and issues. Children spend the majority of their time in class. As long as LGBT issues are seen as "special" and outside the classroom, students will continue to see LGBT people as marginal.

10. *Broaden Entertainment and Extracurricular Programs.* Extracurricular activities often set the tone for the community. Programs such as assemblies, film nights, and school fairs should regularly include content that reflects the diversity of our world. Special LGBT events and holidays such as LGBT History Month (October) and Pride Month (June) should be incorporated into schoolwide celebrations. Guest speakers and lectures that can inform the school community about the unique needs and accomplishments of LGBT people should be a regular part of school programming (GLSEN, 2005).

Glossary of Queer Terms

Androgyny: having both masculine and feminine characteristics, as in appearance, attitude, or behavior.

Bisexual: persons who are attracted to partners of either (or any) gender.

Biological Sex: determined by our chromosomes (XX for females; XY for males); our hormones (estrogen/progesterone for females, testosterone for males); and our internal and external genitalia (vulva, clitoris, vagina for females, penis and testicles for males).

Gender dysphoria: A psychological term for being unhappy with your gender (physically, anatomically). Full-blown gender dysphoria syndrome is the same as transsexualism.

Gender identity: This is an individual's innermost concept of self as "male or "female" what we perceive and call ourselves. Most people develop a gender identity that is aligned with their biological sex. For some, however, their gender identity is different from their biological sex.

Genderqueer: A person who identifies as a gender other than "man" or "woman," or someone who identifies as neither, both, or some combination thereof.

Gender role: The set of socially defined roles and behaviors assigned to females and males. This can vary from culture to culture. Our society recognizes basically two distinct gender roles.

Homophobia: Refers to a fear or hatred of homosexuality, especially in others, but also in oneself (internalized homophobia). Transphobia is a newer and related term having to do with fear and hatred of Trans people.

Heterosexism: Bias against nonheterosexuals based on a belief in the superiority of heterosexuality. Heterosexism does not imply the same fear and hatred as homophobia.

Heteronormativity: The practices and institutions "that legitimize and privilege heterosexuality and heterosexual relationships as fundamental and 'natural' within society" (Cohen, 2005, p. 24).

Intersex (or intersexual): People who are born with the full or partial sex organs or chromosomes of both sexes, or with underdeveloped or ambiguous sex organs. This word replaces the politically incorrect hermaphrodite.

LGBT/GLBTQ/GLBTIQ (and so on): a variety of acronyms are used by to refer to queer people the order of the letters and number of initials varies by user. The letters refer to (L)esbian, (G)ay, (B)isexual, (T)ransgender, (I)ntersex, (Q)ueer/or (Q)ueer and (Q)uestioning: Now you see why I use the word *queer*, right?

Out/Coming Out/Coming Out of the Closet: To be "in the closet" means to hide one's identity. Many LGBT people are "out" in some situations and "closeted" in others. To "come out" is to publicly declare one's identity, sometimes to one person in conversation, sometimes to a group or in a public setting. Coming out is a life-long process—in each new situation a person must decide whether or not to come out. Coming out can be difficult for some because reactions vary from complete acceptance and support to disapproval, rejection, and violence.

Queer: Historically a negative term used against people perceived to be LGBT, "queer" has more recently been reclaimed by some people as a positive term describing all those who do not conform to rigid notions of gender and sexuality. Queer is often used in a political context and in academic settings to challenge traditional ideas about identity ("queer theory").

Questioning: Refers to people who are uncertain as to their sexual orientation or gender identity. They are often seeking information and support during this stage of their identity development.

Sexual identity: The label used to identify oneself such as "lesbian," "gay," "bisexual," "bi," "queer, " "questioning," "undecided," "undetermined," "heterosexual," "straight," "asexual," and others.

Sexual orientation: This is determined by whom we are sexually and romantically attracted to.

Straight Ally: Any nonqueer person who supports and stands up for the rights of LGBT people.

Transgender: People who are inclined to cross the gender line, differs from genderqueer in that transgender individuals present as the "opposite" gender rather than trying to be gender free.

Transition: The process of changing sex, including hormones, cross-living (see above), and finally surgery. A practical minimum for this process is about two years, but usually it takes longer, sometimes much longer.

Transsexual: Anyone who (1) wants to have, (2) has had, or (3) should have a sex-change operation.

Definitions adapted from GLESN: http://www.glsen.org/cgi-bin/iowa/all/library/record/1278.html

Runaway Hotlines

Many young people are turned out of their homes when parents discover they are queer. For those youth, these numbers may come in handy: National Network of Runaway and Youth Services at 202-783-7949 or the National Runaway Switchboard at 1-800-621-4000 (or 1-800-621-0394 TDD for the hearing impaired).

Web Resources

Gay, Lesbian, Straight Education Network (GLSEN). http://www.glsen.org/cgi-bin/
iowa/home.html

Downloadable documents from GLSEN

*Dealing with Legal Matters Surrounding Students' Sexual Orientation and Gen-
der Identity.* http://www.glsen.org/cgi-bin/iowa/all/library/record/1742.html

From Teasing to Torment: New National Report on School Bullying. http://www.
glsen.org/cgi-bin/iowa/all/library/record/1859.html

PFLAG http://www.pflag.org/ Parents, Families, and Friends of Lesbians and Gays.
About transgendered children and their families. A FAQ sheet from the PFLAG-
Talk/TGS-PFLAG Virtual Library HYPERLINK http://www.critpath.org/pflag-
talk/tgKIDfaq.html

Online Bibliography of Books for Parents, Supporters, and Caregivers of Sexual
Minority Youth http://www.bidstrup.com/parbiblio.htm

My Child is GAY! Now What Do I Do? http://www.bidstrup.com/parents.htm A website for parents of LGBT youth.

Intersex Society of North America http://www.isna.org/

Online Communities for Queer Kids. There are some new venues for youth that are
positive!

Coalition for Positive Sexuality (http://www.positive.org). This girl-friendly site
also has a lot of queer-friendly images.

Mogenic (http://www.mogenic.com) touts itself as "the world's biggest gay and lesbian youth online community."

Youth Pride (http://www.youthpride-ri.org/youth/default.asp) YPI provides support, advocacy, and education for youth and young adults impacted by sexual
orientation and gender identity/expression.

Outright (http://www.outright.org/) Outright's mission is to create safe, positive,
and affirming environments for young gay, lesbian, bisexual, trans, and questioning people ages 22 and under. Outright aspires to a youth-driven philosophy
in which youth needs and beliefs form decisions, and a collaboration of youth
and adults provides support, education, advocacy, and social activities.

Youth TIES (http://www.youthgenderproject.org/)

Youth Trans & Intersex Education Services (Youth TIES) is a youth-led organization advocating for trans, gender-variant, intersex, and questioning (TGIQ)
youth.

Notes

1. I acknowledge that the term *queer* is problematic and politically charged (Macgillivray,
   2004), but because there are so many children and youth who fall under this rubric, I am
   most comfortable with the general term *queer*. I have found many young people who use it
   freely and it is much easier to say than LGBTIIQ.
2. Pseudonyums are used for New Dawn and its students. I do not use pseudonyms for Alliance
   because it has been extensively covered by local and national media, Chris was interviewed
   in the local paper and other students have been featured in national magazines.
3. Since this chapter was written, one of the two founders of Young Gay American (YGA) has
   undergone a religious conversion and renounced his gay identity and his queer-positive work.
   Young Gay America, the magazine, is in the process of renewal under new management.
   Readers are, therefore, advised to use resources other than UGA at this time.

References

American Association of University Women. (1993). *Hostile hallways*. Washington, D.C.: American Association of University Women Educational Foundation.

American Association of University Women. (2001). *Hostile hallways: Bullying,teasing, and sexual harassment in schools*. Washington, D.C.: American Association of University Women Educational Foundation.

American Association of University Women. (2004). *Harassment-free hallways: How to stop sexual harassment in school*. Washington, D.C.: American Association of University Women Educational Foundation.

Baker, J. M. (2002). *How homophobia hurts children: Nurturing diversity at home, at school, and in the community*. Binghamton, NY: Harrington Park Press.

Bontempo, D. E., & D'Augelli, A. R. (2002). Effects of at-school victimization and sexual orientation on lesbian, gay, or bisexual youths' health risk behavior. *Journal of Adolescent Health, 30,* 364–374.

Britzman, D. P. (1998). *Lost subjects, contested objects: Towards a psychoanalyutic inquiry of learning*. Albany: State University of New York Press.

Carr, S. (2006, May 7th). Embracing and accepting. *Milwaukee Journal Sentinal.* Retrieved March 15, 2006 from, http://www.jsonline.com/story/index.aspx?id=4202887

Cohen, C. J. (2005). Punks, bulldaggers, and welfare queens: The radical potential of queer politics. In E. P. Johnson & M. G. Henderson (Eds.), *Black queer studies*.(pp. 21–51). Chapel Hill, NC: Duke University Press.

Cosier, L. (2001). *From the outside, in: An ethnograohic case study of an art classroom in an alternative high school for at-risk students*. Unpublished PhD dissertation, Indiana Universitry.

Cosier, L. (2004). Anarchy in the art classroom: A proposal for meaningful art education. In D. Smith-Shank (Ed.), *Semiotics and visual culture: Sights, signs, and significance* (pp. 48–50). Reston, VA: National Art Education Association.

D'Augelli, A. R., & Grossman, A. H. (2006). Researching lesbian, gay, and bisexual youth: Conceptual, practical and ethical considerations. *Journal of Gay and Lesbian Issues in Education, 3*(2/3), 35–56.

D'Augelli, A. R., Hershberger, S. L., & Pilkington, N. W. (2001). Suicidality patterns and sexual orientation-related factors among lesbian, gay, and bisexual youths. *Suicide and Life-Threatening Behavior, 31,* 250–274.

Eugenides, J. (2002). *Middlesex*. New York: Picador.

Gay, Lesbian, & Straight Education Network (GLSEN). (2005). *Ten things educators can do to ensure that their classrooms are safe spaces for ALL students*. Retrieved August 20th, 2006 from, http://www.glsen.org/cgi-bin/iowa/all/library/record/1796.html

Harris Interactive & GLSEN. (2005). *From teasing to torment: School climate in America, a survey of students and teachers*. New York: GLSEN.

Halberstam, J. (1998). *Female masculinity*. Durham, NC and London: Duke University Press.

Human Rights Watch. (2001). *Hatred in the hallways: Violence and discrimination against lesbian, gay, bisexual and transgender students in U.S. schools*. New York: Human Rights Watch.

Intersex Society of North America. (2006). Shifting the paragigm of intersex treatment. Retrieved March 20, 2006, from http://www.isna.org/compare

Kissen, R. M. (Ed.). (2002). *Getting ready for Benjamin: Preparing teachers for sexual diversity in the classroom*. Lanham, MD: Rowman & Littlefield.

Kosciw, J. G. (2003). *The 2003 National School Climate Survey: The school-related experiences of our nation's lesbian, gay, bisexual and transgender youth*. New York: GLSEN.

Macgillivray, I. K. (2004). *Sexual orientation and school policy: A practical guide for teachers, administrators, and community activists*. Lanham, MD: Rowman & Littlefield.

Mallon, G. P. (1998). *We don't exactly get the welcome wagon: The experiences of gay and lesbian adolescents in the child welfare systems*. New York: Columbia University Press.

Menvielle, E., & Tuerk, C. (2006). *To the beat of a different drummer: The gender-variant child.* Retrieved September 6, 2006 from, http://www.patientcarenp.com/pcnp/article/articleDetail.jsp?id=162480

National Education Association. (2006). *Safe schools for everyone:Gay, lesbian, bisexual, and transgendered students.* Retrieved December 27, 2006 from, http://www.nea.org/school-safety/glbt.html

Quinlivan, K. (2006). Affirming sexual diversity in two New Zealand secondary schools: Challenges, constraints and shifting ground in the research process. *Journal of Lesbian and Gay Studies in Education, 3*(2,3), 5–33.

Owens, R. E. (1998*). Queer kids: The challenges and promise for gay, lesbian and bisexual youth.* Binghamton, NY: Harrington Park Press.

Padilla, Y. C., Neff, J. A., Rew, L., & Crisp, C. (2006). *Social risk factors associated with substance abuse among gay and lesbian youth.* Retrieved August 28, 2006 from, http://www.utexas.edu/research/cswr/nida/Padillapage.html

Russell, S. T., Franz, B. T., & Driscoll, A. K. (2001). Same-sex romantic attraction and experiences of violence in adolescence. *American Journal of Public Health, 91,* 903–906.

Russell, S. T., Serif, H., & Truong, N. L. (2001). School outcomes of sexual minority youth in the United States: Evidence from a national study. *Journal of Adolescence, 24,* 111–127.

Savin Williams, R. C. (2001). *Mom, Dad, I'm gay: How families negotiate coming out.* Washington, D.C.: American Psychological Association.

Sears, J. T. (2006). Editor's note. *Journal of Gay & Lesbian Issues in Education, 3*(2/3), 1–4.

Twemlow, S. W., Fonagy, P., & Sacco, F. C. (2002). Feeling safe in school. *Smith Studies in Social Work, 72*(2), 303–326.

Warner, M. (1991). Introduction: Fear of a queer planet. *Social Text, 9*(4 [29]) 3–17).

Young Gay America. (2006). Retrieved March 10, 2006 from, http://www.ygamag.com

YouthResource. (2006). *Trangender youth.* Retrieved March 26, 2006 from, http://youthresource.com/living/trans.htm

19 Stand Up, Keep Quiet, Talk Back
Agency, Resistance, and Possibility in the School Stories of Lesbian Youth

Elizabethe C. Payne

People just looked at you different in the hallways. It's so hard to go in day-in and day-out and know people are looking at you based on something that you can't help. And it's like "dyke this, dyke that." You're just that—a stereotype—and not who you are. —Linda

The opening quotation provides a glimpse into the inhospitable environment many young lesbians experience school to be. Schools are typically heterosexist and homophobic institutions where all members of the school culture are presumed to be heterosexual, expected to conform to rigid gender role stereotypes, and punished for doing otherwise (Blackburn, 2004; Macgillivray, 2000; Payne, 2007). Heterosexism is "one of the most significant realities of adolescents' day-to-day experiences in schools" (van Wormer & McKinney, 2003, p. 409). Possibilities outside the "norm" of heterosexuality are not officially acknowledged in school curricula (Macgillivray, 2000) and rarely acknowledged through school sanctioned programming (Payne, 2007). The existence of these "silences" also goes unacknowledged (Loutzenheiser & MacIntosh, 2004, p. 152). Such schooling practices reproduce heterosexuality and the gender performances associated with it as "normal," "morally superior," "dominant," and "privileged" (Loutzenheiser & MacIntosh, 2004, p. 152) over other ways of experiencing sexuality and gender. The silences surrounding nonhetero sexualities often leave lesbian students feeling "invisible" (Quinlivan & Town, 1999) and alone (Payne, 2002a) while simultaneously marking lesbian identities and the young women who claim them as "Other" (Youdell, 2005).

Adolescent girls who refuse to conform to the sexual and gendered expectations of heterosexuality often face isolation and ridicule (Thurlow, 2001; Wyss, 2004) in school. Girls without social status are accused of being lesbian (Duncan, 2004; Durham, 2002), as are girls who exhibit less interest in their own physical appearance or in heterosexual romance (Eckert, 1994) than their (presumably) heterosexual peers. Also named "lesbian" are young women who continue to compete in athletics (Chambers, Tinckell, & Van Loon, 2004; Shakib, 2003). Once named as lesbian, a young woman is "socially and politically marginalized" (Loutzenheiser & MacIntosh, 2004, p. 152). Fear of being called "dyke" limits the behaviors of many young women in school (Macgillivray, 2000; Shakib, 2003) and shapes the responses of many young lesbians to their homophobic school environments. Those who are taunted as "lesbian" usually "lack the protection" of teachers or other school staff (van Wormer & McKinney, 2003, p. 410). Teachers become so accustomed to hearing the name calling that they rarely react (Macgillivray, 2000), further reinforcing the heterosexist culture of school and "sanctioning the culture of intolerance" (van Wormer & McKinney, 2003, p. 410).

With curricular and institutional silences and an "othered" identity, how do lesbian adolescents experience school? Little is actually known about adolescent lesbians' lives as they are living them. The majority of research focused on adolescent lesbians has utilized adult recollection to examine adolescent sexual identity development (Boxer & Cohler, 1989) rather than exploring the stories of young lesbians. Additionally, little research has been done on the discrimination experienced by lesbian youth or on reducing heterosexism in schools (Loutzenheiser & MacIntosh, 2004; van Wormer & McKinney, 2003).

This chapter utilizes portions of a broader life history study with adolescent lesbians, conducted in a large metropolitan area in Texas, to explore their experiences of school and their resistance to its heteronormalizing culture. Their stories demonstrate not only the "ways in which heterosexual identities are constructed as normal while lesbian...identities are constructed as outside acceptability" within schools (Youdell, 2005, p. 251), but the creative strategies these young women employed to "stick it out" (Lindsey) and stay in school. These young lesbian women coped with the stresses and institutional silences around their nonhetero genders and sexualities by choosing their own silence, attempting to blend in, addressing the homophobia directly, and through telling their stories.

Method

Participants

The participants in this life history research were eight white, middle class, lesbian-identified women, ages 18 to 21, who had attended or were attending high school in a large metropolitan area in Texas. At the time of the research, two were in high school, one had recently graduated high school and was working, and five were in college. None of the young women attended the same high school. The two high school students and one working high school graduate were accessed through the local LGBT youth support group. The college students learned of the study through campus postings on several campuses or through contact with the researcher as a former instructor. All of the participants in this study self-selected. Because the young women in this study were in late adolescence at the time of the interviews, they were still within the period they were being asked to recall, and could share stories not yet fully reconstructed through adult experiences (Payne, 2002a; Wyss, 2004).

For this study, self-labeling as lesbian during high school, attending high school in the area of Texas where the research was conducted, being born with the attributed sex of "female," and age were the only criteria for research participation. There were no racial criteria for participation in this study. The lower age limit was set by IRB at 18. All of the young women who participated claimed a lesbian identity, but it is not assumed in this research that all attached the same meaning to the label "lesbian," that "lesbian" is a stable category, or that it has ever had a singular meaning. No research participants claimed the identity of "queer."

As adolescents self-labeling as lesbian within the same sociohistoric period in the same geographic area, these young women encountered similar systemic pressures related to gender and sexuality and had similar resources (or lack thereof) available to them. Encountering these same systemic pressures from similar social positions (adolescent white middle class female) during the same sociohistoric time frame created similarities in experiences. These young women should not, however, be seen as "representative" of young lesbians from this or any other historic moment. Their experiences are best understood by examining the structural elements and systemic pressures that they encountered as adolescent women in the early 21st century. Shared elements between these stories and the stories of older generations of American lesbians highlight the marginalized positions LGBTQ people and women continue to hold within American culture, and the deep unchangedness of sex and gender expectations, despite advances from the feminist and LGBT rights movements (Payne, 2002a).

Subjectivity

In my last two years of teaching high school, I participated with a group of students in starting an AIDS awareness club they called SAAV, Students for AIDS Awareness and Volunteerism. There was no GSA in this high school and the SAAV meetings also served as sites of acceptance for lesbian, gay, bisexual, and questioning students. Through the club, I met Lissa. Lissa was a sophomore in high school who had experienced a relationship with another young woman in her freshman year when she was 14. Her parents had read her diary describing this relationship and punished her severely. She was threatened with eviction from her home if she didn't renounce all things lesbian. Her every move was monitored both in and out of school, and her parents forced her to quit SAAV when they learned of her involvement. I remained a source of adult support for Lissa and she would sometimes come to my classroom at the end of the school day to talk. I was in awe of Lissa throughout her high school experience. Her strength and determination to succeed, despite a painful family life, were moving, as was her conviction that it was the rest of the world—not her—that had a problem. Through Lissa, I became interested in adolescent lesbian self-labeling and in the agency and resilience of young lesbian women. I changed my research and professional focus to explore the lives of young lesbians. I remain most interested in the ways in which young lesbians "make sense" of their experiences of gender and sexuality and in self-labeling. The high school, while not my primary research focus, often provides the stage for these identity processes.

Interview Method and Analysis

Carspecken's (1996) method of critical qualitative research was applied to life story methodology, based upon the work of Linde (1993). Life history method and its variants can be well-suited to giving "voice" to individuals and has held particular appeal among feminist researchers interested in exploring and representing women's lives, but the traditional forms of life history lack the critical potential to locate that voice within a larger sociopolitical context. By adding critique to life history method, the process of articulating hierarchical structures which devalue groups of people, limit voice and power, and locate processes which undermine or weaken subjects' opportunities to fully recognize potential is facilitated.

The interview format was fully open-ended with all interviews beginning with the same lead-off question requesting descriptions of high school experience: "Describe a high school experience that really stands out for you." The immediate responses of five of the young women to the "lead off" question reveals the difficult time they had in high school:

> I hated it until senior year (Nicky).
> I was like in a big depression for several years (CiCi).
> I had some really horrible experiences (Lindsey).
> I don't think I've had a great experience in high school (Amy).
> I hated going to school. I just hated it. I didn't want to be there. I felt like crying everyday (Linda, on her freshman year).

The participants continued to talk about their lives until they became tired. The interviews averaged 3 hours and 25 minutes in length. Questions specifically about sexuality were asked only in the form of probes after the participant had introduced the topic as central to an area of her story.

A life story is a constantly changing narration of self bound by cultural contexts. The "truth" of the story is in the meaning it holds for the individual who tells the story and the navigation through social situations made possible by the story. The "validity" of the events and whether or not they "really" happened as reported and were "really" causal in the experiences of the teller is not the focus of this methodology. For example, a participant recalls a teacher making a specific statement regarding homosexuality in school. Whether or not the young woman remembers the teacher's comment "correctly" is less important than how she presents the event as pertinent to her story.

Note: All words or phrases within quotation marks in the data sections of this chapter reflect the words of the research participants.

Hanging in There Until You Can "Get the Hell Out"

Some of the young women in this research were "out" by choice, some had been "outed," and others had chosen not to disclose their sexuality, keeping it a carefully guarded secret. All of the young women in this research experienced the verbal and emotional abuse of a homophobic school environment. Each young woman developed her own form of resistance, her own way to survive in school as a lesbian student. All but one of these young women felt alone in her efforts to cope with her heterosexist school environment. Each of the experiences these young women described offers us the opportunity to ask what might have been done differently by a teacher, a counselor, or an administrator that could have made a positive difference in the lives of these lesbian students. Through their stories we are given the opportunity to imagine a school without the fear and isolation experienced by these young women, to imagine change and possibility.

Agentic Silence

Amy, CiCi, and Nicky were not "out" at their high schools but that did not protect them from the homophobia of their school environments. Hurt by the curricular and institutional silences of school and aware of the dangers they could face if their lesbian identities were discovered, each young woman chose her own silence as protection, keeping her sexual identity a carefully guarded secret from fellow students and teachers. Silence is often seen as inaction and framed in opposition to agency. Here, silence is a strategic choice carefully made based upon these young women's assessment of their high school scenes.

Amy attended a large suburban high school where she never heard anything positive about LGBTQ people, and she knew she could not disclose her sexuality:

> ...that [homosexuality] was never [officially] talked about in high school. If it was talked about, it was negative—very negative—like, in different people's, you know, conversations or, um, people calling each other "fags" or, or especially, like, I don't know, just difference in people's conversations. And I heard no one say anything positive about homosexuals. [*It made me feel*] very bad. It made me—like, because I wouldn't say anything when people would talk about stuff like that. I was very hurt because—in a way—because they were talking about me, but they didn't know that. And some of the things they said were just really hurtful and, um, I took it straight to heart.

When Amy heard other students telling "gay jokes" and calling each other "fags," she wanted to speak out—she wanted to defend others and herself—but she was afraid to do so. At Amy's school, there was an assumption that all students were heterosexual—and students were careful not to act against this assumption. Amy said: "Some people, some people who are, like friends, like Nancy, who are defending homosexuality, it's like 'They must be gay.'" Students who spoke out against the homophobic language were marked as homosexual. Teachers who heard these comments did nothing.

Homosexuality was not mentioned in Amy's school except through the pejorative name calling. She felt alone and without allies and she felt bad about herself for not speaking up, but she knew that to speak up was to risk being named. Amy tried to blend in and though she never "lied" about her sexuality or talked about boyfriends she didn't have, she wanted others to assume she was straight. Amy attended the prom with a male friend, and many of her peers assumed they were dating. On the night of prom, she disclosed her sexuality to her date. He was the first and only person she had told in her school. Though "he said he was OK with it, he was fine and all with it," she was "really extremely nervous" that this information might now spread in her high school. She was one month from graduation at the time of the interview and hoping that the month passed without her becoming the subject of the rumor mill. Her silence had protected her for three years and she was afraid she had made a mistake in confiding in her prom date.

Amy knew of no one at her school that was "out." She said, "For all I knew, I thought I was, like, the only gay person in the state, you know. I think I actually thought that for a while, but there's not many of us, and I thought I was the only one in high school." Amy's coping strategy, to withdraw from most social interactions, created a space for her where she felt both isolated and insulated. She ate lunch with other members of her sports teams, but never associated with them outside of school. She limited what she would discuss over lunch to the activities of the sports team or class assignments. She did not develop close friendships with other students. She said "I was pretty much a loner." Though she was a strong student and "made good grades," she rarely spoke in class. Amy's silence was her shield.

CiCi also attended a large suburban high school and chose not to "come out" at school. She said, "I wasn't going to encourage getting my butt kicked." CiCi felt her high school was a dangerous place to be "out." She had already experienced verbal harassment from other students for "being different" and for "being from California." Though she feared she might be physically harmed if her sexuality were discovered, she was uncomfortable with directly lying about it. If someone called her "a dyke" she recalled "I didn't say yes and I didn't say no. I just left it. If someone thought I was, well I wasn't going to tell them I wasn't, but I'm not going to confirm it either." The teachers in her school did nothing to punish homophobic comments and CiCi often felt they sided with the abusers. In the cafeteria one day, boys were

> throwing food at one another. Then they started calling each other "fag" and they said, "Oh, I've got AIDS," and the teachers weren't doing anything about it. They weren't saying anything to them. One of the teachers I saw watching it with a kind of smirk on their face heard me say the word "bastard" later that day and said, "We don't talk like that here." I was like "Oh, the word *faggot* is completely acceptable," and so I just found it to be a big joke and dumb. But, I mean, it sure wreaked hell on my self-esteem, you know?

She learned not to trust teachers and did not report incidents of harassment she witnessed or experienced.

CiCi's response to the homophobic climate was to "not think about school." When she wasn't in class, most of her time while on campus was spent reading in the library. She said "So, I started getting really into reading…I'd spend lunch, free period [*in the library*]. A couple of times I skipped class. I just stayed in the library." CiCi did not make friends at her high school. She said: "I didn't hang out really with anyone. I just did a lot of reading." CiCi resisted the homophobic climate of her high school by removing herself from it to the extent that she could. She felt safe in the quiet of the library and says "books were (her) friends."

The heterosexist climate of Nicky's large suburban high school made it clear to her that she needed to hide her lesbian identity and she felt very alone. She says: "In high school, I think I knew gay people existed out there, but I still thought I was like the only one…. There weren't any [*gay people*] at my school." Nicky carefully crafted an entertaining school personality. It was important to her that no one suspect she was struggling with her sexuality and her feelings of isolation. She said:

> I didn't really open up to anybody because I knew they wouldn't understand, you know. Like, well, why should I tell this person this, because, I mean, they wouldn't understand. So I was more like the class clown to like cover it up, and, like, crack comments to just make people laugh or just to be stupid…I'd be like happy-go-lucky you know, so people aren't going "Oh, so what's wrong?" or "Is something bothering you?" I just wouldn't want to put myself in that situation where they would ask or they would want to know. And so I just put this act on, and I wouldn't talk to anybody. I didn't want to show anything other than the happy-go-lucky perky. I kept everything bottled up inside. And that's not good. I would, I would like lie in bed late at night and I would just cry…. This was pretty much all of high school, actually.

Nicky said when she got to college:

> It was great because I didn't have to censor myself, you know, whereas in high school, like, I had to watch every little thing I said and really worried about it. I could talk about things and say "Oh, that girl's cute" or whatever. In high school, I'd have to watch—I just couldn't say that. It was so different, like, in college I could say whatever and not really care, you know, not really have to worry about it. Nothing [bad] would, would like, happen to me. It was great. I was like that was really cool.

Nicky was careful to "mask" her "true" identity as lesbian to protect herself throughout high school. She was "always playing a role" as class clown and as straight. She gave herself regular pep talks to help her keep up the front: "I was like, 'Oh, you don't have to be yourself. You can do this, you can,' you know?" She felt "secondary, like a second class citizen" in high school because she was not free to express who she "really was." Nicky was afraid that something would "happen" to her if her sexuality was discovered. This fear led to the creation of an elaborate coping strategy that often placed Nicky at the center of attention. Though people laughed and joked with Nicky, she did not consider them friends. She developed a small friendship group in her senior year of high school but chose to keep her sexuality secret until she entered college. She said of high school, "I was just ready to get the hell out."

Rather than have their gender and sexuality questioned and risk naming, some young women strive to conform to the expectations of heteronormativity (Shakib, 2003) or to give the illusion of doing so through constructing a "false heterosexual self" (O'Conor, 1993). This silence and masking around their sexuality is often associated in the "coming out" literature with "shame" or a lack of "pride" (Payne, 2002b). Amy, CiCi, and Nicky all chose forms of silence to help them cope with school. These acts of silence are not borne of shame but rather are agentic choices made by young lesbians operating in the heterosexist culture of school. These strategies were well thought out by each of these young women based upon her evaluation of her school environment. Amy and Nicky presented themselves as straight, though neither lied about relationships with or interest in boys. Each felt that being perceived as straight increased her personal and social safety in school. CiCi, while not actively creating a straight persona, believed that claiming a nonhetero identity would put her in danger of "getting (her) butt kicked." All three young women chose forms of isolation as protection from other students getting too close and perhaps discovering their sexuality. These choices, which these young women felt necessary to help them cope with school, allowed them to feel that they had some power in their respective situations and that they could regulate the abuse they suffered through these strategies.

Broken Silence

Silence is not always an option, and sometimes young women are named "lesbian" before they have fully claimed that identity or thought about revealing it to others. This was the case for Lindsey. Lindsey attended a large, prestigious magnet school for the arts where she says "You'd have thought they'd be OK with it (*lesbian identities*), but it was really, really bad." Lindsey began to experience verbal assaults her freshman year of high school after she was unexpectedly "outed." The ramifications were devastating to her. Lindsey felt she was under constant assault and that no one would help her. She said:

> I was outside eating lunch and all these guys came over and, like, started reading Bible verses and telling me how wrong I was and all this kind of stuff, and so I went into the counselor's office, which was right at the front of the school. I ran in there and I said, "Look, these guys are taunting me and I can't get them to stop," and she said "Well what did you do to provoke them?" I didn't have a response for that at first. I said—I think I started crying actually—and I said, "I don't know."

Lindsey received no support from the school counselor after she disclosed her sexual identity. In fact, the counselor called Lindsey's parents—without her knowledge—and told them about her sexuality, creating a new set of problems for Lindsey at home. Lindsey says she was "taunted every day in school." "I was a little girl; it was easy to pick on me." "God, it was horrible. Everybody was talking about me. Everybody." She shifted her strategy:

> In order to completely disarm people that were taunting me, it was easier to say—instead of hiding—when they would, if they had said, "You're a faggot" or whatever, if I had said "No," then that would have given them more to play with. Instead, when they, like, called me "dyke" and "faggot" or whatever, I'd say, "Yeah, I am. Do you have a problem with it?" And I'd just get really defensive and try to disarm them so they couldn't come at me more than they already had.

Lindsey spent her first two years of high school aggressively defending herself and being "really, really mad." She was "the only 'out' person in the entire school." She had no help from faculty or school counselors, though many were aware of her experiences. She stated "My high school career was tainted from the beginning because people didn't see me as Lindsey anymore. They saw me as a lesbian and that's that." She cried nearly every day. "Everybody (*at school*) hated me." After two years of school that she described as "so horrible," her father moved her to a new school in the suburbs. In preparation for her move, Lindsey "grew (her) hair out" so that "no one would know (she) was gay." She felt she needed "time off" from the harassment. Lindsey acted "straight" when she got to her new school, successfully hiding her identity. She concentrated on her music and didn't socialize with other students. She allowed other students to assume that she and her only friend, a young man who sat next to her in band, were dating. "It was just easier," she said. "I needed that time." She came out at her new high school during the second semester of her senior year when she developed a crush on a classmate. She said, "I wanted to be as out as possible and as outlandish as possible because I had been in the closet for a long time." She began boldly wearing "freedom rings" and said, "I was almost done [*with school*]. I figured I could stick it out." Lindsey believed that her teachers treated her differently in those last months of high school, that she was graded more harshly, and that she was given less opportunity to be creative in her work. She said, "my grades dropped from As to Bs and the quality of my work never wavered."

Lindsey chose three strategies, each one matched to the school situation in which she found herself. When she could not gain support from school administration, faculty, or staff in her first high school, she chose to become verbally assertive in defending herself. She tried to shut down her attackers by claiming the pejoratives they threw at her. It was constant work and it drained her. By the end of her sophomore year, Lindsey said, "I was exhausted. I just couldn't take it anymore." When she had the opportunity to "start over" Lindsey chose a different strategy: silence. She removed all the markers of lesbian identity she had embraced as her defense in her first two years of high school. She let her hair grow, "took off (her) thumb ring," and got a new binder that "didn't have Melissa Etheridge stickers on it." For a year and a half, she told no one she was lesbian and preferred others assume she was straight. In her senior year when there were just three and a half months of school left, she chose to "come out" using an offensive, rather than defensive, approach. Though the response from her school was not positive, she was determined to "stick it out." As Lindsey struggled to find strategies to deal with the heterosexist environments in which she was trying to get her education, teachers and staff remained silent or contributed to her difficulties. No one helped her.

Standing Up, Speaking Out

Silence is one strategy for dealing with heterosexism in schools. Sometimes young women feel, as Lindsey did at her first high school, that they must actively stand up for themselves and address those who are harassing them. As with silence, these strategies take many forms. Melanie played sports throughout her childhood but as she entered adolescence, her athleticism led to accusations and taunts with peers calling her "butch" and "lezzie." Teachers in her suburban junior high school often heard the remarks, but did nothing. Melanie felt that if she altered her appearance and dressed "more girlie," she could continue her sports activities with less attention. With the help of her mother, Melanie recreated herself to conform to "girlie" expectations of appearance, wearing "girl" clothes, "sometimes dresses and skirts," a "little makeup," and carrying a purse. The taunts continued. The teachers remained silent. One boy particularly tormented her and wouldn't let up.

So I, like, go to school and I'm there and he starts laying into me. He says "Oh, look what we have here," and he picks up my purse and he starts ridiculing me to the whole room of people…. And he's just talking away, and I get up and I just run over and slug him. And I just start beating him up, and I beat him up wearing a dress….

Melanie was taken to the principal's office and received punishment for her actions. The boy did not. After the incident, Melanie stopped trying to be "girlie" and returned to her "comfortable" clothes that supported her "sporty" lifestyle. Though the name calling continued behind her back, the boys no longer taunted her directly. Melanie decided she could not rely on the teachers to stop others from harassing her and would have to rely on herself. She chose first to try to stop the harassment through active gender conformity and when that strategy failed, she quieted the mockery through asserting her physical strength. Melanie let it be known that she was not going to be openly ridiculed.

June and Linda were out by choice in their high schools and each experienced verbal assaults and discrimination directly. The young women asserted their resistance to the homophobia they experienced in school by speaking up to acknowledge the homophobic climate or trying to educate for tolerance.

June attended a large city high school where sports were emphasized. She thought the school would be a good place for her because of her athletic abilities, but she found she didn't "fit in." June believed that other people knew she was "gay" before she did because she's "just like more masculine than most people." Though June has long hair and does not present herself in a way immediately identifiable as "masculine," she felt that people "just knew about (her)" and that it affected the way she was treated even before she came out. Once she "came out," the taunts and prejudice became overt. June felt that teachers were not supportive of her in classes, and that she could not get the academic help she needed because the teachers "didn't like (her)" because she was "gay." June also attributed the difficulty she had with a sports coach to homophobia. In addition to her basketball, June played volleyball, until she "got kicked off."

> Last year I came out and she [the coach] didn't like homosexuals and she was very against it. I soon found out, and she told me to my face—kicked me off because of it. She comes up to me, she was like, "You want to know the reason I kicked you off?" "Yeah, tell me." "Because you're gay."

June felt more accepted when she moved onto the varsity basketball team, but her sexuality remained a topic for comment and gossip. There was a girl on her team who "preached" to June about her sexuality while they were on a bus together. "She was sitting there on the bus 'Oh God, help this person.' And I'm going 'God, get her away, get her away.'" June also had trouble in the locker room with teammates after she came out to her basketball team. Though she felt helpless to change the strained situation, she also felt compelled to verbally acknowledge the treatment she received from them. She explained:

> A couple of girls got really uncomfortable especially, like, in the locker room. They were hiding [behind] their clothes. I said "Don't worry; I'm not looking at you." And they were still uncomfortable. I knew I was making them like that so I took the liberty of like going to my own little aisle of lockers and stuff and changing. And when I would do that I knew—I wasn't going to just like leave and not say anything to them, but when I go outside I have to go by that little strand of lockers where they all dress, and I said "Hey guys, I'm going outside now. You can actually dress now." And they kind of looked at me like "What do you mean?" "You know what I mean.

You're so uncomfortable around me that it's not even funny, I mean I can cut the tension in the room."

Though she heard taunts of "butch" and "dyke" in the school hallways, it was the homophobia from her teammates that most impacted June. Though her teammates praised her skill on the court, they chose not to interact with her outside of practice or games. She continued to have trouble with her teammates in the locker room yet continued to assert her right to be there. She says "They like me when I make the shots."

I love always making the shots and always getting the ball because I'm the one like right underneath the goal. It's kind of like a little power surge, you know. I always make the shots.... But they don't want me in there [the locker room].

June felt alone in dealing with the tensions on the team but she continued to verbally acknowledge that she was being treated differently. She says, "I wasn't going to just not say anything you know, like about how they were (treating her). So I did. I said, you know." June believed her basketball coach was aware of the situation and the tension between June and the other players, and chose to "stay out of it." June speculated that this might be related to the coach's own identity, which June suspected was lesbian.

June initially dealt with the homophobia she experienced in school by trying to ignore it. She didn't respond to the name-calling she heard in the hallways and she didn't speak with teachers about the ways in which she felt she was treated differently. Her strategy was to "not egg 'em on." She hoped that the ridicule would stop if she did not escalate it. But June was not comfortable with this strategy in all arenas of her high school life. June's athletics were more important to her than her academics, and her identity as a valuable team member was central for her. It is here that she felt she had to speak out. She wanted to be known for her athletic skill—not for her sexuality. She felt that it was unfair that she was ostracized from the team despite her contributions on the court. And she said so.

Linda had her first girlfriend in her senior year. Though they were "out" at her Catholic all-girls school, they always kept a physical distance between them. Linda said: "Michelle was my best friend also, she wasn't just my girlfriend, and I was scared to death to hug her in the hallways if she was crying, because I was so scared of the ramifications. It was hard." Though Linda experienced discrimination and homophobia at school from the other girls, she was not alone. Several young women "came out" in senior year, and some of them "hung out" together. For the first time in her school experiences, Linda felt supported. The rampant homophobia sparked by the visibility of these out young women showed itself through "fears," "myths," and "rumors" that impacted the way in which the young women labeling as lesbian were treated by others. "Women who I'd see in the halls and talked to [in the past] and who I'd sat next to [during] freshmen orientation would smile and would just move on and things like that." But the discrimination experienced by Linda and her friends went beyond the silent treatment.

A lot of them [other students] had come from very small private schools and weren't comfortable with sexuality and lesbianism, so there were rumors all over the place. They said we had orgies in the halls. I wasn't invited to any of them (smiles and giggles).

"Misconceptions" about the lesbian young women were rampant.

> Where we sat, we sat between the gym and the cafeteria every morning for no other
> reason than it was a comfortable place to sit—and people would be scared to walk
> in the cafeteria in the morning, because people, I don't know, they'd think we'd jump
> them.

The rumors about these young women created a picture of lesbians as not only deviant
in desire, but deviant in their supposed promiscuity, having "orgies in the halls," and as
predators, waiting to "jump" innocent heterosexual girls. Being able to spot the dangerous lesbian became important.

> Two of the women who were jocks wore white baseball caps and so people at my
> school were convinced that if you were gay you wore a white baseball cap. And there
> were all these other myths going around.

The rumor grew so that any one wearing any color baseball cap was suspect. Soon,
girls were afraid to wear any baseball caps for fear of being labeled lesbian. Jewelry, hair-
cuts, and ear piercing styles also were interpreted as markers of lesbianism. Linda says
many of the rumors were "really silly," but also painful.

For many of the students at her school, this was their "first exposure" to lesbians and
they were not happy about it and felt that they should be "protected" from "people like
us." One young woman approached Linda and said "I don't like you, I don't like who you
are, and I think you are detestable." Having eight "out" lesbians was "a really big issue
for a lot of the women at (her) school. And they went to the principal and complained."

Not only did students complain to the administration about the "out" young women
wanting the administration to "do something," parents also complained:

> This woman who gave a lot of money to the school—and because it was a private
> school they rely heavily on donations and things like that—and this woman gave a
> lot of money to the school. And she told Sister Mary Grace, who was my principal, to
> "Kick out the lesbians or I'm taking my daughter out along with the funding."

Additionally, the boys' school next door provided frequent abuse for the young
women.

> There was an all guys' school next door and that was a really big problem for a lot
> of my friends. I would be driving out of the parking lot and people would scream,
> "dyke," at me and they would throw things at my friends' cars.

Linda's friend "was driving out and, this guy, like, half-way, like, literally, like, jumped
into her window and started screaming and, like, throwing things at her."

The physical abuse from the Catholic boys' school next door pushed the administration of Linda's school to respond. Given the negative stance taken by the Roman Catholic
Church on homosexuality, a Catholic girl's school seems an unlikely site for promoting
the tolerance of nonhetero identities. This school, however, began a systematic response
to educate parents and students and to reduce the abuse.

> The woman who was in charge of ministries at my school, who was disconcerted
> by this, and she asked to have a panel discussion at the senior retreat, so we did,
> and essentially the point was to dispel myths and, I don't know, just say that there's
> more—there was more to us than our sexuality.

Linda sat on that panel and felt empowered by the experience. For the first time she had the opportunity to talk about the abuse she and the other young women had experienced, and to state that she was "more than just a lesbian." She said, "It was the first time I had ever stood up for who I was and I had ever said flat out this is who I am and I'm not scared to tell anyone. It was so empowering and so scary."

The administration also offered "informational sessions for parents about homosexuality, about lesbianism. There was more information. They really emphasized educating people and tolerance." The parent who had threatened Sister Mary Grace that she would take her daughter out of the school if the lesbians were not kicked out was told: "I hope you can find a good school for your daughter." Though Linda acknowledged that the story was "hearsay," she was proud of her principal's response. Faculty began monitoring the halls for derogatory language and reprimanded students for homophobic remarks. The administration posted faculty in the school parking lot to watch the boys' school and took down license plate numbers of cars and names of boys involved in harassing behavior. Linda's school worked with the adjacent Catholic boys' school to "promote tolerance" and increase security.

Though Linda felt hurt by the way other young people treated her, she also felt supported by the administration and bonded with others through the experience. She felt she had "made a difference" by sharing her feelings of marginalization on the panel. She said:

> The point of being up there [on the panel] was to try and teach them a little bit more and to make them not scared because there's nothing to be scared of…. There are just so many misconceptions and so much fear and so much hatred, and that just couldn't go on.

Linda's strategy to cope with the homophobic environment of her school was to work with the administration to help educate the student body on nonhetero sexualities, issues of injustice and discrimination, and to advocate for tolerance through school programming. While she was nervous about the public forum in which she agreed to speak, she wanted other students to understand the "pain and that it was really bad" for many of the out young women who had been tormented in school. She hoped that through her participation, she could reduce fear and educate others to see that she was "more than just a lesbian." She hoped to make her school a better place for herself and for others.

Each of the young women in this study assessed the homophobic situation she faced in her school and responded by developing various coping strategies. All but one did so without any support from her school. While these stories are the stories of homophobia, harassment, and the neglect of lesbian students, they are also stories of young women's agency in creating strategies to allow their survival in these homophobic environments. LGBTQ youth have a high school drop-out rate three times the national average (GLSEN) and yet all of the young women in this study graduated high school—a testament to the success of their various strategies. These strategies were not, however, employed without high cost. Amy, CiCi, and Nicky chose to conceal their lesbian identities but feared the discovery of their sexuality every school day. Efforts to maintain their secrets were taxing and included distancing themselves from peers and a choice not to develop friendships with other students. High school was a lonely and isolating place for them. Lindsey was left exhausted after two school years of aggressive verbal defense of her sexuality; Melanie came to believe that it was only through her physical strength that she could be safe at school. June and Linda, though they spoke up about the unequal treatment they received, were not immune from the damaging effects of that treatment. For each of these young women, being lesbian and a high school student meant great expenditure of time and energy aimed at surviving school as a lesbian student. How might that energy have been otherwise directed if these young women had experienced school as a supportive and affirming environment? While we cannot know the answer for these students, through their stories we can see possibilities for creating a more affirming educational environment for lesbian and other nonhetero identifying students now and in the future.

Conclusion

Public schools have an obligation to treat all students equally and in a socially just manner. This obligation requires providing not only a physically safe environment, but an environment where the emotional safety and self-esteem of all young people can be nurtured. Typically, high school is not an easy place for most young people—regardless of sexual identity, but the discrimination experienced by LGBTQ youth and the lack of support and resources available to them in the school setting make their high school experiences particularly difficult. The stories told by the young women in this research reveal missed opportunities for school administration and teachers to move their schools toward greater safety and equality for LGBTQ youth. Each young woman in this research could have been positively impacted by a teacher or school administrator who demonstrated awareness that not all students are heterosexual, who challenged the harassment of LGBTQ youth, who included LGBTQ content in the curriculum in ways that did not further marginalize lesbian students, and who stood up for the rights of LGBTQ youth to equal education.

So invisible were nonhetero identities in their schools that Amy and Nicky were convinced they were the "only gay people" there (each of their high schools had an enrollment of over 2,600 students, so it is highly doubtful that they were indeed the only ones). If these schools had offered Gay–Straight Alliances (GSAs), these young women would have been able to see that they were not alone, even if they chose not to participate in the clubs. Gay–Straight Alliances have been shown to positively impact not only the self-esteem of LGBTQ youth, but their academic performance as well (Lee, 2002).

The stories of unchecked verbal gay bashing told by Amy, CiCi, and Lindsey provided missed opportunities for teachers to step in and to make clear to the students involved that harassment based upon sexual or gender identity and derogatory language about LGBTQ people would not be tolerated, just as such harassment based upon race or ethnicity would not be tolerated. Lindsey's high school experience might have been less painful for her if the school counselor from whom she requested help in her freshman year had actually provided support and assistance to her. So too might Melanie's school experience have been more positive if her teacher had stopped the harassment she was experiencing and talked with the class about gender diversity. The messages received by the other students in Melanie's class would have been very different if both Melanie and the boy who tormented her had been made to visit the principal's office after their altercation.

June and Lindsey speak of discrimination experienced directly from school faculty or staff members. A coach removed June from a sports team once she disclosed her sexuality. Lindsey feels her course work was differently evaluated by her teachers after she "came out" in her senior year. Unfortunately, teacher and school counselor preparation programs have been slow to include issues of sexuality in their courses. New teachers and school counselors often enter schools having never considered that they will be working with nonhetero identifying students and not knowing how to provide affirming learning environments for them. Districts rarely include sessions on LGBTQ inclusive curriculum or the experiences of LGBTQ youth in their continuing education programs. Teachers need opportunities to challenge their own homophobia and to learn ways in which they can support all youth.

June's difficulty with her sports team was exacerbated, she believed, by her coach hiding her own sexual identity. June believed that her coach was unwilling to work with the team to address the issues introduced by June's sexuality for fear that her own sexuality might be implicated. Research has shown that many teachers fail to intervene on behalf of LGBTQ youth in schools because of this fear and the threat of job loss. Most states do not protect teachers from employment discrimination based upon sexual or gender identity, though individual cities or counties can offer that protection. Having strong nondiscrimination policies in educator employment can provide LGBTQ teachers with the safety they need to be open about their own nonhetero sexual identities, to serve as role models for youth, and to advocate for the well-being and equal treatment of lesbian youth in schools.

Many teachers perceive "stopping anti-gay peer harassment as too risky an endeavor to undertake" and "fear retribution" for acknowledging lesbian issues in the classroom (Macgillivray, 2000, p. 320). Teachers who have "remained silent" (van Wormer & McKinney, 2003, p. 412) need support in speaking out. Clearly written school and district policies supporting efforts to end harassment of lesbian students would empower teachers and administrators to take effective action. Taking action requires schools to acknowledge the presence of lesbian youth in schools and challenges us all to question the heteronormativity that shapes our schools (Loutzenheiser & MacIntosh, 2004). We must all question how that heteronormativity systematically excludes lesbian and other nonhetero identifying youth, and ask how it might be made different. These young women's stories provide us with clear examples of how individual educators can act and how school systems can begin to provide more affirming learning environments for all students regardless of their sexual orientation or gender performance: acknowledge their presence; address the discrimination they experience; advocate for their inclusion in school life and curriculum.

References

Blackburn, M. (2004). Understanding agency beyond school sanctioned activities. *Theory into Practice, 43*(2), 102–110.

Boxer, A., & Cohler, B. (1989). The life course of gay and lesbian youth: An immodest proposal for the study of lives. *Journal of Homosexuality.*

Carspecken, P. F. (1996). *Critical ethnography in educational research: A theoretical and practical guide.* New York: Routledge.

Chambers, D., Tincknell, E., & Van Loon, J. (2004). Peer regulation of teenage sexual identities. *Gender and Education 16*(3), 397–415.

Duncan, N. (2004). It's important to be nice, but it's nicer to be important: Girls, popularity and sexual competition. *Sex Education, 4*(2), 137–151.

Durham, M. G. (2002). Girls, media, and the negotiation of sexuality: A study of race, class, and gender in adolescent peer groups. In C. Williams & A. Stein (Eds.), *Sexuality and gender.* (pp. 332–348). Malden, MA: Blackwell.

Eckert, P. (1994). *Entering the heterosexual marketplace: Identities of subordination as a developmental imperative* (Working Papers on Learning and Identity No. 2.). Palo Alto, CA: Institute for Research on Learning.

Eckert, P. (1997, November). *Gender, race and class in the preadolescent marketplace of identities.* Paper presented at the annual meeting of the American Anthropological Association, Washington, D.C.

Eder, D. (1985). The cycle of popularity: Interpersonal relations among female adolescents. *Sociology of Education, 58*(3), 154–165.

Gay, Lesbian, Straight Education Network (GLSEN). (n.d.). http://www.glsen.org

Lee, C. (2002, February/March). Impact of belonging to a high school Gay–Straight Alliance. *The High School Journal, 85(3)*, 13–26.

Linde, C. (1993). *Life stories: The creation of coherence.* New York: Oxford University Press.

Loutzenheiser, L. W., & MacIntosh, L. B. (2004). Citizenships, sexualities, and education. *Theory into Practice, 43*(2), 151–158.

Macgillivray, I. (2000). Educational equity for gay, lesbian, bisexual, transgendered and queer/questioning students: The demands of democracy and social justice for America's schools. *Education and Urban Society, 32*(3), 303–323.

O'Conor, A. (1993, October/November). Who gets called queer in school? *The High School Journal, 77,* 7–12.

Payne, E. (2002a). *Adolescent females self-labeling as lesbian and the gender binary: A critical life story study.* Doctoral Dissertation, University of Houston, Texas.

Payne, E. (2002b). *A critical examination of homosexual identity development models and their applicability to adolescent lesbian development.* Paper presented at American Education Research Association (AERA), New Orleans, LA.

Payne, E. (2007). Heterosexism, perfection, and popularity: Young lesbians' experiences of the high school social scene. *Educational Studies, 41*(1), 60–79.

Quinlivan, K., & Town, S. (1999). Queer pedagogy, educational practice and lesbian and gay youth. *Qualitative Studies in Education, 12*(5), 509–524.

Rivers, I., & D'Augelli, A. (2001). The victimization of lesbian, gay, and bisexual youths. In A. D'Augelli & C. Patterson (Eds.), *Lesbian, gay, and bisexual identities and youth: Psychological perspectives.* New York. Oxford University Press.

Shakib, S. (2003). Female basketball participation: Negotiating the conflation of peer status and gender status from childhood through puberty. *American Behavioral Scientist, 46*(10), 1405–1422.

Thurlow, C. (2001). Naming the "outsider within": Homophobic pejoratives and the verbal abuse of lesbian, gay and bisexual high-school pupils. *Journal of Adolescence, 24,* 25–38.

van Wormer, K., & McKinney, R. (2003). What schools can do to help gay/lesbian/bisexual youth: A harm reduction approach. *Adolescence, 38* (151), 409–420.

Wyss, S. (2004). "This was my hell": The violence experienced by gender non-conforming youth in U.S. high schools. *Journal of Qualitative Studies in Education, 17,* 5.

Youdell, D. (2005). Sex-gender-sexuality: How sex, gender and sexuality constellations are constituted in secondary schools. *Gender and Education, 17*(3), 249–270.

20 Access and Obstacles

Gay–Straight Alliances Attempt to Alter School Communities

Cris Mayo

...if students are to speak to students they must do so where students gather—at school. (Sen. Denton, 1983, during discussion of Equal Access Act)

Gay–Straight Alliances (GSAs) highlight the ethical and political work public school students engage in to improve school climate for sexual minority youth and allies, even when traditional sources of authority, such as school leaders, policy, teachers, and curricula fail to do so (Lee, 2003; Mayo, 2004; Perrotti & Westfield, 2001; Walker, 2004). Although there is substantial legal precedent supporting the right of their groups to organize in public schools, GSAs may still find themselves initially without school support and so spend much of their time organizing to change school and district policies in order to ensure that they may continue to meet. GSAs, then, provide sexual minority and ally students with space in the school but also remind them of how much work they have to do to make the entire school community supportive of LGBT-related social justice issues.

While many schools may initially be unsupportive of GSAs, official school programs are partially responsible for why GSAs are organized. As students learn from even minimal curricular lessons about diversity and political responsibility, they are encouraged to find space to engage in their own forms of political and identity-related association. GSAs, then, are born of increasing interest in sexual minority issues and also a long tradition of voluntary association in public schools. There has been some concern by democratic and liberal theorists that, in addition to supporting the development of democratic civic culture, voluntary associations, especially those that organize around minority identities, pose challenges to democracy by turning members away from diverse, public, civic culture and encouraging them instead to focus their energies on building community among like-minded or identified groups. But as Amy Gutmann (2003) notes, voluntary associations organized around identities help provide the support, influence, and opportunity for members to work to improve civic life for all. This concern with the potential divisiveness of identity-based or voluntary associations arises at roughly the same time that writing about identity has moved to looking at how identity categories are constructed. Rather than thinking about identity simplistically, recent theories grapple with how identities come to be formed, how they form communities, and how associations across difference challenge older notions of insider/outsider. Especially given the pervasive effects of homophobia on all students, alliances across sexual orientations are particularly necessary. GSAs are part of that turn toward associational identity and alliance. While all GSAs may not focus on social justice as their intended goal—some organize to socialize—all GSAs do raise the visibility of minority sexualities in public schools and so contribute to working against the presumption that all students are heterosexual. This chapter begins with an analysis of policies and court cases that have enabled GSAs to meet, and more recent policy and legal challenges they face. It then turns to accounts of student interactions in GSAs that point to internal challenges GSAs continue to face regarding racial and ethnic diversity, sexism, and the tensions of allying across differences. It will be clear that students in GSAs are working actively for social justice in their schools, but like other social justice groups also create exclusions that replicate the raced and classed context in which they form (McCready, 2004).

While most student-led social justice groups organize without controversy, GSAs are often an exception. Part of the hostility is simple homophobia, but there are also concerns about the schools' responsibilities for students who have not yet developed a sexual identity and whether schools should be the place where students critically consider their sexuality. In addition, administrators and teachers worry that if students think about their sexuality and decide they are gay, they will organize their lives entirely around that sexuality, ghettoizing themselves and removing themselves from the school community. More troubling, sometimes GSAs do not receive school support because administrators and other school officials may simply presume that there are no sexual minority students and thus they do not need to care about homophobia (Kozik-Rosabal, 2000).

Especially in the case of associational groups of young people, the identity or issue around which they organize may be more of an open question than it is for adults. In part, students join associational organizations because they are curious about their own sexual identities or curious to see what it would be like to be involved in a community with others who are LGBT, questioning, or ally. In other words, GSAs are not only about coming out, but also about forming communities of difference that engage in critical questioning about identity formations and as such, like other challenges to homophobia, they benefit students of all sexual orientations (Schneider & Owens, 2000). Part of what associations across difference may do is to broaden one's sense of one's ethical community: if other people are involved in the same kinds of critical questioning, even if they do not come up with the same answer, those questions help form community. While groups do not necessarily require particular identities, they shift the ethical relationship of one's identity toward that of others. Group members need not share identity, but they do identify with the struggles against homophobia, heterosexism, and heteronormativity. Rather than identifying *as* gay, for instance, group members identify *with* the work for social justice for sexual minorities.

Alliances are different from identity groups in that they are made up of diverse people who may be particularly concerned about issues relating to a few identities, but are not necessarily members of those identity groups themselves. Unlike other forms of alliance, GSAs may run into difficulties in school districts when parents or administrators feel that any discussion of sexual minorities implies an unacceptable critique of local values. In these cases, adults are objecting to students seeing the possibility of rethinking attitudes about sexual minorities—even to the point of deciding to become a member of sexual minority group. The problem of the alliance is thus not just a problem of associating with sexual minority students, but also challenging dominant ideas about the unacceptability of sexual minority people. The fact that students other than out sexual minority students might be willing to associate with those out students also may indicate a fair degree of "play" in the concept of sexuality. For conservative parents, the fact that their children are willing to engage in any kind of curious reconsideration of local norms is itself a problem and a powerful wedge in disrupting false binaries and oppression.

Access to School Space

The growing popularity of GSAs attest to their relevance for students, especially in a broader cultural climate that is at the very most ambivalent about sexual orientation. GSAs meet in about 2,500 schools nationwide, according to the Gay, Lesbian, and Straight Education Network (GLSEN), a group that has been critical in providing resources for organizing groups. In a cultural climate where many still believe homosexuality and bisexuality to be unethical, these alliances of gay, straight, bisexual, transgender, questioning, and heterosexual students are important reminders of the central role of social justice in forming and maintaining communities. GSAs also mark an interesting turn in identity-based political movements because they underscore the degree to which identity is a social process of recognition and negotiation. For instance, people are not simply heterosexual: they must act in particular ways or they will be criticized as being "gay" or "queer"; they must associate with other socially recognized heterosexuals or their own sexual orientation will be called into question; they must also act in "correctly" gendered ways.

Because they are made up of diverse students, GSAs are a curious assortment of groups that do not necessarily have more than the press of normalizing power in common. That is, many students who join GSAs are concerned about the pressures they face to conform, whether or not those pressures are specifically directed at sexuality, gender, or some other issue in their lives. Students who feel themselves to be outcast from "normal" find GSAs to be comfortable spaces in which to converse with others who also feel more comfortable in nonnormative identities. For instance, GSAs are increasingly incorporating analysis and critique of dominant forms of gender as transgender students and their allies work to ensure they are not excluded from school communities. Sexual orientation may be the central concern for some students, though other students may find gender expression more pressing (Boldt, 1996; Grossman & D'Augelli, 2006; Haynes, 1999). Students who want only to have gay people respected because they are just like heterosexuals are sometimes initially surprised that other students do not want to live their lives within the dominant bounds of gender. In short, for some, alliances provide a context in which to critique normative sexuality. For others, they are a place to critique normative gender, and for others any combination of critique and stability. By centering curiosity in their ethical project, alliance groups understand the positive value of difference and the possibilities that difference and innovation open up for new forms of identity and relations. More than a few young women when they explained how they first came to join one particular GSA, for instance, realized that though they had initially joined because they had a friend who was thinking about coming out, they then realized that they themselves had unacknowledged crushes on other girls. One pointed out that in retrospect she had tried to keep herself from thinking about her own sexuality by telling herself she was in the group to help another young woman through her questioning period. Other students have also remarked, especially after Trans Awareness Day, that they had never really thought about being critical about gender norms and realized they had unexamined biases against trans and gender nonconforming people that they needed to challenge. Understanding their own personal stakes in improving school climate has helped some students to broaden their understandings of the pressures and obstacles other people face. And, understanding the struggles that friends are going through has also helped some students see that they share similar, unacknowledged struggles with sexuality.

The Equal Access Act (EAA) of 1984 provides legal justification for most GSAs to meet in public schools. Initially crafted as an act to protect religious liberties, debate in Congress and revisions to the act opened its coverage to all political, philosophical, and religious organizations. According to the EAA, if a school provides access for some student extracurricular groups, it must do so for all groups that do not violate the law or substantially disrupt the school community. When GSAs have had to go to court to demand that schools allow them space and the courts have accepted that equal access is the main issue, GSAs have won the right to meet in public schools (Buckel, 2000).

Legal justification alone has not been the only factor in the ability of GSAs to successfully find a place in the school community. Sympathetic administrators (Capper, 1999), faculty, parents, and community members have all been part of efforts to improve the school experiences of sexual minority youth and secure school space for GSAs. In perhaps the most egregious attempt to circumvent the requirements of the EAA, the Salt Lake City school board decided to cancel all extracurricular groups rather than allow GSAs to meet. Mass demonstrations of students from a vast array of extracurricular groups were part of the political and legal pressure brought to bear on the ultimately unsuccessful school board maneuver, showing not only that students were angry that their own groups had been cancelled but that they recognized the injustice done to the GSA in particular.

Obstacles to Alliance: Parental Notification and Obscenity

While GSAs have met with notable success in organizing in many public schools, obstacles remain. Laws protecting sexual orientation and gender identity vary from state to state (Elliott & Bonauto, 2005) and this inconsistency alone makes it difficult for students to know how best to frame their request for a group. Because GSAs are extracurricular groups, they are not tied to official school support. Though they have access to meeting places in schools, they are also subject to regulations that attempt to curtail their membership. Primary among these is a recent trend toward requiring that either the school notify parents of their children's extracurricular activities or parents notify schools about which extracurricular activities they do not want their children to participate in. In Georgia, the legislature has passed a law requiring local boards of education to provide parents with information about their children's club membership or extracurricular activities. An early version of the bill said that, "each local school system shall comply with the written notification from a parent or guardian who has withheld permission for a child to join a club or participate in an activity" (Georgia 148th General Assembly, 2005). Debate over the word *permission* and opposition from the Georgia State Board of Education (Fields, 2006) led to a change in wording to "notify," though the means of notification remain unspecified. While the Christian Coalition of Georgia, one of the bills strongest supporters, maintains that GSAs are not the target of the bill, one of the legislators, Representative Len Walker stated, "I don't know about you but when I was in school there was no need for this kind of legislation...because the clubs and organizations...were honorable and were right for kids" (For god's sake, is this still going on?, 2004). Clearly policies like this are intent on removing all sources of support from sexual minority youth and their allies. Without curricular information in schools, sexual minority and questioning students have no space to learn about themselves from adults. Extracurricular groups are one way that youth have to try to learn and organize in safety—they are already at school, they know members of their school community, and can find support from sponsoring faculty members. But legislation intent on driving GSAs out of school can take away the one place where young people can organize and learn together.

Another strategy to prohibit GSAs has been to argue that any advocacy or discussion of homosexuality is inherently obscene and in violation of community standards, as well as against abstinence-only educational policy. In one of the few cases that rejected the right of a GSA to form in a public school, *Caudillo v. Lubbock Independent School District* started out seemingly well situated. The Supreme Court had just outlawed antisodomy laws in a case that decided that Texas's antisodomy law was unconstitutional. The *Lawrence v. Texas* decision came down on June 26th, 2003; the case contending that Lubbock High School's GSA had the right to meet was filed on July 8 (Lambda Legal,

2003). While Lambda Legal Defense had already successfully argued two cases whose rulings set the precedent for justifying GSAs under the Equal Access Act, Brian Chase, the lawyer for Lambda filing this case noted the context of *Lawrence*:

> When it struck down Texas's "Homosexual Conduct" law, the Supreme Court called for gay people to be given full respect, equality and dignity from government institutions. Lubbock High School runs afoul of that by treating this group differently simply because it supports gay students. (Lambda Legal, 2003)

While all state laws now protect an adult right to privacy, including the right to engage in same-sex sexual activity in private, the Lubbock school district policy prohibits the *discussion* of sodomy—or any sexual activity—in student groups (*Caudillo v. Lubbock*, 2004). Because the group asked for permission to post flyers in the school and the flyers had their web address that originally linked to a site that itself had links to a site that discussed sex, the case hinged not on their right to associate but on the fact that they were discussing sex. The group removed the link before asking permission a second time, but the fact that they had had such a link stayed a key point in the legal case. The court ruled against the GSA in a decision that, in effect, paralleled the decision in *Lawrence*, albeit for different reasons and to a different end. The Supreme Court decision in *Lawrence* argued that sodomy was not a reprehensible act; it is one among many acts that bring people together and allow them to maintain their intimate ties to one another. In the Lubbock case, the relationship between gay identity and sexual acts are turned on their head. The court ruling argues, essentially, that gay youth are gay because they can engage in sodomy, so just being gay means that sodomy must be part of the discussion and thus their right to associate is essentially a right to have sodomy, which as youth they do not have, so they also do not have a right to associate because the topics they would be discussing are obscene. A Christian athlete group that had discussions about abstinence from sex that did involve some discussion of sex were not similarly prohibited from meeting because the goal of their discussion was abstinence and thus not obscene.

In Arizona, following the precedent set out in the Lubbock-based *Caudillo* case, a bill has been introduced to the State Senate that would reinforce the basic message of the Equal Access Act, but adds the requirement that public postsecondary student organizations not be "obscene" (Arizona 47th Legislature, 2006). In Utah, the "Student Clubs Act" adds clubs to the list of school organizations that must make activity disclosure statements and forbids clubs from "advocating or engaging in sexual activity outside of legally recognized marriage or forbidden by state law, presenting or discussion or information relating to the use of contraceptive devices or substances, regardless of whether the use is for purposes of contraception or personal health" (Utah 56th Legislature, 2006). Further, the bill allows the school to deny any club that does not "protect the physical, emotional, psychological, or moral well-being of students and faculty" or involves "human sexuality" (Utah 56th Legislature, 2006). Referred to widely as the "Gay Club Ban," Utah S.B. 97, too, is also intent on using *Caudillo* to get around the previous court ruling that cited the EAA to demand the district recognize the GSA. In other words, these bills that purport to be interested in parental rights are very clearly being designed to challenge students' rights under federal law. Because federal law recognizes that students do need the freedom to meet with other students to discuss diverse social and political issues—especially those not covered by official curricula—laws intent on constraining what little freedom of inquiry students have are especially pernicious. For students who are members of nongenerational minority groups, that is, students whose minority status is not part of their family background, being able to meet with other similarly situated students is all the more important. Student groups are crucial spaces for learning how to articulate social justice claims with others, learning how to organize and cooperate across differences, and spaces to begin to develop strategies for working toward justice. These are all the goals of the EAA, in fact, goals that underscore the important role that students can play in improving their school and broader community.

Because extracurricular groups are one starting place for young people to build their own versions of community, they are particularly fraught spaces for an older generation more interested in maintaining the heteronormative status quo than addressing homophobia and exclusion. While the advocates of student religious groups pointed to the importance of having such groups in schools because that is where the students are, opponents to GSAs want them out of schools and away from where the students are. Opponents further do not want GSAs drawing in allies, not only because they do not want their children in spaces where they might be recruited into a minority sexuality, but also because they do not want alliance to come close to implying acceptance. Especially for youth who already feel isolated from their families and communities, alliance groups can provide necessary support, even support to help them begin to find strategies for educating their families and communities. In addition, because GSAs are groups that organize across different sexualities, genders, races, and ethnicities, they also provide students with the opportunity to work closely in common cause with others who are different from them. In short, GSAs are a remarkable resource for all members of school communities because they show that justice is an evolving concept—new groups, new issues, and new identities may arise and change the kind of conversations that need to happen. Student groups working toward social justice need to have spaces that encourage them to be open to potential innovations in identities, to critique problematic norms constraining possibilities for gender and sexuality, and to organize to improve their communities. Without space in school and the kind of visibility that school groups provide, those changes will be more difficult to achieve.

Varying Levels of Alliance

Conservative external forces are not the only barriers to GSA attempts to organize for social justice in schools. This next section turns to questions about internal divisions within groups that limit their ability to extend justice to all group members or all members of the school community. GSAs are, to a large extent, notable for their mixed membership, particularly along lines of differences in sexuality. These alliances complicate earlier forms of identity politics, complicating exactly who it is that ought to be concerned about bias against queers and coming up with the answer "all of us." Emphasizing alliance is also, of course, a way to open a safe space for thinking about queer life without having to publicly identify as queer or even ever have to consider thinking about oneself as possibly queer.

Before turning to some of the complications to identity and association observed in GSAs, it is important to point out that even attempting to do research on GSA members raises important social justice issues. Institutional Review Boards generally prefer that parents give active consent for their children to participate in research projects. There are many compelling reasons to demand that parents have a say in the kind of research involving their children, but like parental notification laws directed at limiting GSA membership, more than a few students have said they do not want their parents to know that they are questioning their sexuality or that they support members of minority sexualities, and this may mean that research on LGBTQ youth cannot be done (Donelson & Rogers, 2004). Even straight-identified youth have said that as much as they want to be able to challenge homophobia in schools, they would not feel comfortable with their parents' knowing that they are GSA members. Students who are questioning have said that the GSA is the only safe space for them to be with other questioning, queer, and ally students and that any hint to their parents that they are gay would put them at risk. Even out gay students have said that as much as they are out at school, their sexuality is still an undiscussed issue at home and sending home a note requesting parental consent for research would likely turn into an occasion for full-scale confrontation with their parents. Students who are members of minority racial, ethnic, or immigrant communities may find the potential loss of support of their home community an impossible resource to lose. Granted all youth depend on families, but for youth of color, wanting to maintain strong ties to home and community in order to help confront racism may also provide additional reason not to risk rejection (Duncan, 2005; Leck, 2000). Some research suggests that communities of color are less homophobic than White communities, but that "coming out," especially when one's sexuality is already an open secret, is taken as an affront to community solidarity (Ross, 2005). So while parental consent is meant to help parents protect their children from unethical research practices, many GSA members perceive parental notification as potentially dangerous because it would out them to parents. With high rates of homelessness among sexual minority youth, it is not surprising that they have these concerns. A few students I've approached about getting parental consent for research on GSAs have said they could not risk it: they were afraid parents would withdraw financial support for college or kick them out of the house.

It is important to remember that fear of homophobic reaction from parents and peers is experienced by straight, gay, and questioning youth alike. In other words, the pressures of homophobia affect youth of all sexualities. Because GSAs may have very few (or even no) out queer members, they can be groups that advocate for other people's rights, not their own. But it is also often the case that students initially join GSAs thinking that they do not know someone gay and then find out a close friend who never felt comfortable coming out to them is actually gay. Or they may join thinking they themselves are not gay and then find themselves questioning their sexual identity. Still, there are plenty of GSA members who are straight and simply find homophobia intolerable and identify with the struggles of sexual minority students, even if they themselves do not experience the limitations imposed by homophobia in the same way.

In part, GSAs are a space to think critically about gender and sexuality, replacing feminist groups that had often also been places to discuss the problems of gender norms and the need to critically evaluate concepts like sexual identity and gender relations. This use of GSAs has its own complications. In one GSA, whenever the female president would try to lead a conversation, two young out gay men would turn up a DVD player and drown her out. The gay young men interrupted other young women when they tried to speak and generally evinced attitudes of disrespect for women. Partially this was motivated by a belief that the women were not gay. From talking to the young women it became clear that while they were not out, neither would they label themselves as heterosexual. The young women expressed frustration at the gender dynamics in the group but when I asked young women why they did not organize feminist groups to discuss sexual harassment and gender inequality, more than a few responded that people would think they were lesbians if they belonged to a feminist group. Does this seeming contradiction point to a dislike of the term *feminist*? Or is the implication that there are different forms of being gay? Perhaps the old stereotype of the angry lesbian feminist is more negative than the new stereotype that all members of GSAs are gay? Further, the gender antagonism in the group has to be put in a context of antagonism over sexuality as well. Even though the young women self-described themselves as not straight, publicly they passed as heterosexual.

The young men were clearly quite irritated by this, but rather than expressing their critique by reference to sexuality, they chose instead to direct their hostility toward women. Clearly this example points to the overlapping complications involved in any alliance group. Gender bias and sexuality bias overlap, and without explicit conversations among the members about the different forms of privilege that attach to normative sexuality and dominant gender, the antagonisms will remain unaddressed.

GSAs also act as liberal alliance groups, where members can mark their progressiveness to one another by addressing a bias issue that may not seem to implicate them. While race remains a difficult issue for White students to situate themselves in relation to, gayness is sometimes less difficult. Because Whiteness and White privilege operate by removing a sense of responsibility from White students, beginning to think critically about race means that they have to confront their own participation in structures that maintain racial hierarchy. At least in my observations, heterosexual privilege does not seem to elicit "heterosexual guilt" to the same extent that "White guilt" seems to be elicited by serious conversations about race. More troublingly, White students seem adept at avoiding conversations about race, likely to dodge around the responsibility they may know they ought to feel. In one GSA meeting, students decided they wanted to have group t-shirts and began discussing designs, all of them agreeing that the public representation of the group's mission had to be a central part of the design. One young Black woman suggested that the club use a kaleidoscope-like design that another group she had been involved with had used. In this case, she suggested that the design would represent both the rainbow colors and the idea that the group was multiracial. She explained that she had joined the group because she wanted to support LGBTQ people because as an African American, she had seen the importance of having cultural groups. She explained that she had heard that when the school's African-American cultural group started, it was very small and that other people besides African-American students had supported it and helped it to grow. A young White woman responded that she thought that design would make the group seem like a "diversity club" and she did not want to represent the group that way.

This discussion happened only one week after the group had been told by the principal that they could be an official school group if they backed off from being called a "gay–straight alliance" and instead agreed to call themselves the "diversity club." The group had decided instead to stick with its original name "gay–straight alliance" and to forego status as an official school club. While they were still disappointed at becoming a group "neither endorsed nor supported" by the district, they felt it was important to be clear about being a gay–straight alliance. But the discussion about the t-shirt design showed a willingness to remove race from consideration in defining the group's identity. On the one hand, one could argue this was a tactical decision to centralize sexuality, but on the other hand, it also meant that the group decided not to simultaneously recognize that the racial diversity of their members was an important issue, neglecting the interlocking ways oppressions based on race, class, gender, and sexuality work (Collins, 2004; Kumashiro, 2003). They decided on a design where a series of bathroom-sign figures, lined up in couples: boy-boy, boy-girl, girl-girl with the words underneath "It's all the same to me." The group's decision, then, was to maximize their similarity to one another rather than point to internal diversity, but by so doing they also chose to silence a group discussion on race. Especially in a group dedicated to examining sexual and gender diversity, this lack of attention to race is all the more troubling and points to the possibility that gender and sexual associations may find some forms of diversity relatively easy to discuss and others still too much of a challenge for many members.

The next year, at another gay–straight alliance, the same young Black woman who had just transferred schools ran into a similar obstacle to raising race as an issue for the gay–straight alliance she had just joined. She had been attending for a few weeks when, a conversation started between two group members, an Asian-American young woman and a South-Asian young woman about the different versions of Asian culture they were familiar with. They both agreed that they shared the experience of being part of communities that were extremely interested in their academic achievements and their social interactions. When the young Black woman tried to join the conversation to invite them to the African-American literature club, that line of conversation stopped, and the South Asian woman, who was also the group leader, shifted the topic to a discussion of the misuses of the word *gay*. Shared experience of "cultural" difference was a topic the group apparently could manage but the introduction of racial difference jolted them into silence.

Sometimes, though, racial/ethnic identity is discussed in order to diffuse tension over sexual identity. In the midst of a discussion of the heterosexual questionnaire (Rochlin, 1995, p. 407), for instance, the group began their discussion pointing out that the questionnaire could be reversed and it would look like the sort of thing people ask gay people. Clearly, of course, that was the point, and the fact that the group spent several conversational volleys describing the task of the questionnaire rather than answering the questions, as the group leader had asked them to, was striking. Even as they discuss how heterosexual is presumed to be a "default" identity, their discussions sometimes showed that they did not feel particularly implicated in its dominance. The discussion about the heterosexual questionnaire was essentially 45 minutes of self-identified straight students being actively unwilling to discuss how their affectional lives were framed by heterosexual privilege. Each time the group leader asked another question from the questionnaire: How long have you known you were straight? Do you ever think that you just need to have a good experience with a member of the same sex? and so on, the group members replied that the questions were too personal. The group leader tried to explain that the point of the exercise was to examine how heterosexuality is presumed and how gay people need to be constantly justifying themselves, but no one was willing to engage in a critical discussion, despite the fact that they could see that the questionnaire was meant as a reversal.

They further dodged the issue when a young White woman asked one of the Asian-American woman, in reference to that woman's having brought noodles from home for lunch, "Why do Asians get all the really good food?" The Asian-American woman replied, "Because Asia's really big." The group spent the next five minutes discussing whether the probability of good food versus bad food depended on the size of the continent and then moved to a discussion of probability in general. The faculty advisor, quite used to the tendency of the group to wander, pulled them back to the questionnaire and though the conversation continued for the rest of the group's meeting time, no one in the group answered any of the questions designed to have them confront heterosexual privilege. This incident may also point to challenges that remain for GSAs as they try to get members to think more critically about their own lives, in addition to giving them conceptual tools to challenge homophobia in general. It is easier, of course, to advocate for someone else without fully taking responsibility for one's own racial, sexual, or gendered privileges, but GSAs do need to also work on those important internal issues in order to successfully address the biases they find in their school communities.

While many GSA members may be curious about what it means to be gay and how processes of gay life proceed (coming out, trying to figure out whom to date, negotiating one's sexual identity across a variety of contexts, and so on), organizing as an alliance sets up a task for the group that often involves, not the creation of a considered alliance across difference, but an attempt to alter the environment of the school. The fact that the group is already an alliance means that it begins its work as if the group itself already agreed on the issues and then moves the site of struggle to the space outside the group. GSAs, in other words, think of themselves as definitionally safe spaces because they are in opposition to schools that are not. So the identity of someone in such an alliance is not based on sexual orientation but rather orientation toward a political goal that supports freedom of sexual orientation. The point of the group, then, is not necessarily to explore the issues around sexual identities, but to develop group cohesion against homophobic bias. They emphasize working against homophobia, rather than working toward sexual identity in part because they are often told very explicitly that they may not discuss sexuality.

To the extent that it is possible to work against homophobia without examining the particularities of sexualities and their experiences in the world, GSAs do show us that work against bias can be done without centralizing sexual identity. Avoidance of sexuality as a topic for discussion has fairly major pitfalls, but responses from members of school communities not in GSAs show that the very presence of the group stands as a marker of the importance of addressing homophobia and acknowledging queer presence. For instance, queer kids who do not belong to GSAs still report how important it was for them to know there was someone in school who might "have their back" if something went wrong. As one student put it, "I was the gum on the bottom of everyone's shoe" before a group of other students started to work on a GSA. While their experience was not without conflict—their principal objected that there were no gay students in the school, their posters were torn down, and their members harassed—the fact that there was even a small group of students interested was enough to give her hope. Another student in a college gay group remarked that the sight of the GSA poster in high school, though she was never brave enough to actually show up to the meetings, gave her a sense of future and the feeling that there were other people like her that she could meet if she ever really felt she had to. Other research shows LGBT students say they would feel better just knowing about a group, especially when they are faced with family crisis or harassment (Ginsberg, 1998). Though many teachers believe either that homophobia is not an important issue in their school or that other forms of bias, like racism and sexism, are more pressing (Ferfolja & Robinson, 2004; McConaghy, 2004), some teachers report that their attitudes about public displays of queer affection have changed just since seeing posters about GSAs (personal communication, 2005). In that case, the teacher said that seeing a poster advertising a GSA jolted her out of her visceral dislike of same gender demonstrations of affection and reminded her that there were colleagues and students who thought about homophobia. That thought, in turn, led her to challenge what she began to see was the uninterrogated homophobia that was structuring her visceral response. School leaders have reported that the presence of the GSA reminds them that kids that they care about are affected by homophobia; a particularized understanding of the issue helps them to counter conservative attempts to disband GSAs. During a difficult conversation with a local minister, who wanted to pray over the GSA group, one principal was able to remain committed to protecting the GSA by being able to visualize the members of the group. She explained that as she thought about what the kids' reaction to such a prayer would be, it was easier to explain to the minister patiently and carefully that she thought he could understand that the kids would not take his intervention as a gesture of kindness but rather one of affront. (Interestingly enough, quite a number of school leaders have reported the same situation.) In a certain sense, then, for some in the community, GSA members, regardless of their particular sexual orientations, are all in traitorous relationship to heterosexuality and normalcy. Situations such as these also act as important reminders of the kind of support GSA members and sexual minority students need from school community members as they try to negotiate their way through potentially hostile relationships with others inside and outside the school community (Muñoz-Plaza, Quinn, & Rounds, 2002). Even in schools where homophobia is not the central issue, GSAs provide students with important skills to help them address homophobia in the broader community and help students to become educated on sexual and gender minority issues. In one GSA with a very supportive principal and liberal school climate, students remarked that local homophobia was not really their focus. Instead they kept up with national politics and worked with students in GSAs at less liberal schools to alter policies and educate one another. GSAs, in other words, are laboratories for democracy, places where young people can learn how to be critically aware of social justice issues and learn strategies for confronting bias from one another. In some states, GSA members actively lobby state legislatures to challenge bills intent on restricting extracurricular clubs. In other areas, GSA members join with adult LGBT community members to demonstrate on local antidiscrimination efforts. Many GSAs also educate themselves on issues missing from the curricula, a reminder that schools themselves remain sadly lacking in academic content on sexuality and gender.

Gay–straight alliances also work to strategically forestall objections to a group that would only focus on queer life. Here we get into some of the difficulties of alliance groups that often must justify themselves on the basis of their address to dominant group members and not on the needs of minority group members. It is much easier for GSA advocates to talk to people who object to gay–straight alliances and point out to them that they are objecting as much to straight people as they are to gay people. It is strategically easier to talk about the necessity of countering homophobic bias and not bring up the particularities of queer life. In short, it is easier to talk about the problem of homophobic harassment and violence and considerably less easy to talk about the actual presence of queer students. Now that queer studies has shifted the focus from recovery of gay and lesbian lives to an examination of the process of queering sexuality, thinking about who matters becomes more complicated. But the tendency to dodge around sexual minority youth continues, no matter the disciplinary shift. On the one hand, GSA members are queer to the extent that they are all deeply concerned with the damaging effects of homophobia. They are also possibly queer because their studied lack of attention to identity seems to suggest that as long as all members are potentially victims of homophobia and definitely advocates for queer people, they share some sort of queer identity. On the other hand, kids who are GSA members and not out as gay tend more to say they are not queer, rather they identify as progressive or radical. But they do have something of a "queer eye" as most of the members of GSAs demonstrate their ability to analyze the problematic dominance of heterosexuality in daily experience, curricula, media, and the news. In other words, they are adept at reading for overt homophobic responses and more normalized forms of heterosexism.

But just because they engage in projects of critical reading and intervention does not mean that they can easily imagine the full range of what queer lives are like—of course, this is a problem that extends to out queer youth as well who may have no or little contact with adult queers and thus no strong sense of how to negotiate their sexuality in adulthood. So while the groups may be able to sustain an alliance on the basis of concern about bias, the fact that they do not sufficiently engage with the identity experiencing the bias means that a crucial piece of their understanding is missing. When legislation intent on providing students with critical forums in which to discuss philosophical, political, and religious differences are challenged by laws intent on keeping those differences out of schools, students lose freedom of association and with it, the chance to imagine their futures differently.

References

Arizona 47th Legislature. (2006). AZ S.B.1153.

Boldt, G. M. (1996). Sexist and heterosexist responses to gender bending in an elementary classroom. *Curriculum Inquiry, 26*(2), 113–131.

Buckel, D. S. (2000). Legal perspective on ensuring a safe and nondiscriminatory school environment for lesbian, gay, bisexual, and transgendered students. *Education and Urban Society, 32*(3), 390–398.

Capper, C. A. (1999). (Homo)sexualities, organizations, and administration: Possibilities for in(queer)y. *Educational Researcher, 28*(5), 4–11.

Caudillo v. Lubbock Independent School District, et al. No. 03-165 (N.D. Tex. March 3, 2004).

Collins, A. (2004). Reflections on experiences in peer-based anti-homophobia education. *Teaching Education, 15*(1), 107–112.

Denton, J. A., Sen. (1983, February 3rd). *Congressional Record, 129,* 1645.

Donelson, R., & Rogers, T. (2004). Negotiating a research protocol for studying school-based gay and lesbian issues. *Theory Into Practice, 43*(2), 128–135.

Duncan, G. A. (2005). Black youth, identity, and ethics. *Educational Theory, 55*(1), 3–22.

Elliott, R. D., & Bonauto, M. (2005). Sexual orientation and gender identity in North America: Legal trends, legal contrasts. *Journal of Homosexuality, 48*(3/4), 91–106.

Ferfolja, T., & Robinson, K. H. (2004). Why anti-homophobia education in teacher education? Perspectives from Australian teacher educators. *Teaching Education, 15*(1), 9–25.

Fields, S. (2005). Keeping the faith action alert. Retrieved March 16th, 2006 from, http://www.gachristiancoalition.org/action.htm

For god's sake, is this still going on? (2006, February 18th). Retrieved February 19th, 2006, from majikthise.typepad.com/majikthise_/2006/02/for_gods_sake_i.html

Georgia 148th General Assembly. (2005). GA S.B.149.

Ginsberg, R. W. (1998, Winter). Silences voices inside our schools. *Initiatives, 58,* 1–15.

Grossman, A. H., & D'Augelli, A. R. (2006). Transgender youth: Invisible and vulnerable. *Journal of Homosexuality, 51*(1), 111–128.

Gutman, A. (2003). *Identity in democracy.* Princeton, NJ: Princeton University Press.

Haynes, F. (1999). More sexes please? *Educational Philosophy and Theory, 31*(2), 189–203.

Kozik-Rosabal, G. (2000). "Well, we haven't noticed anything bad going on," said the principal: Parents speak about their gay families and schools. *Education and Urban Society, 32*(3), 368–389.

Kumashiro, K. (2003). Queer ideals in education. *Journal of Homosexuality, 45*(2–4), 365–367.

Lambda Legal. (2003). Lambda Legal files lawsuit today on behalf of students at Lubbock High School barred from forming Gay Straight Alliance. Retrieved March 7th, 2006, from http://www.lambdalegal.org/cgi-bin/iowa/news/press.html?record=1284

Lawrence et al. v. Texas 539 U. S. 558 (2003).

Leck, G. M. (2000). Heterosexual or homosexual? Reconsidering binary narratives on sexual identities in urban schools. *Education and Urban Society, 32*(3), 324–348.

Lee, C. (2003). The impact of belonging to a high school gay/straight alliance. *The High School Journal* (Feb./March), 13–26.

Mayo, C. (2004). *Disputing the subject of sex: Sexuality and public school controversy.* Boulder, CO: Rowman and Littlefield.

McConaghy, C. (2004). On cartographies of anti-homophobia in teacher education and the crisis of witnessing rural teacher refusals. *Teaching Education, 15*(1), 63–79.

McCready, L. T. (2004). Understanding the marginalization of gay and gender non-conforming Black make students. *Theory Into Practice, 43*(2), 136–143.

Muñoz-Plaza, C., Quinn, S. C., & Rounds, K. A. (2002). Lesbian, gay, bisexual, and transgender students: Perceived social support in the high school environment. *High School Journal,* 52–63.

Perrotti, J., & Westfield, K. (2001). *When the drama club is not enough: Lessons from the Safe Schools Program for gay and lesbian students.* Boston: Beacon Press.

Rochlin, M. (1995). The heterosexual questionnaire. In M. Kimmel & M. Messner (Eds.), *Men's lives*. Rocklin, CA: Hazelden Press.

Ross, M. (2005). Beyond the closet as raceless paradigm. In E. P. Johnson & M. G. Henderson (Eds.), *Black queer studies: A critical anthology* (pp. 161–189). Durham, NC: Duke University Press.

Schneider, M. E., & Owens, R. E. (2000). Concern for lesbian, gay, and bisexual kids: The benefits for all children. *Education and Urban Society, 32*(3), 349–367.

Utah 56th Legislature. (2006). UT S.B.97.

Walker, R. (2004). "Queer"ing identity/ies: Agency and subversion in Canadian education. *Canadian On-Line Journal of Queer Studies in Education, 1*(1), 1–19.

21 Social Justice Education for Black Male Students in Urban Schools
Making Space for Diverse Masculinities

Lance T. McCready

Introduction

Urban education is the field of study that focuses on teaching and learning in K–12 urban schools. The research literature on urban education has tended to focus on the problems of low-status minority groups, the complexity of urban school systems, and the financing and governance of such systems (Gordon, 2003). Progressive teacher-educator Joe Kincheloe argues that

> Urban education teachers and educators need a rigorous, inter/multidisciplinary understanding of urban education. They need to draw on a number of disciplines and transdisciplines such as history, cognitive studies, philosophy, political science, economics geography, and others to help them understand the complex context in which urban education takes place. In this way teachers and educators gain unique and powerful insights into research on educational policy, pedagogy, and the lives of children living in densely populated urban settings.

While Kincheloe (2004) and others assert that urban educators need a "rigorous, inter/multidisciplinary understanding of urban education," gender and sexuality studies are rarely if ever included in lists of "disciplines and transdisciplines" (p. 14) urban educators need to draw on.

Typically, subject areas that emphasize race, class, and political economy dominate urban education, as a field of study (Anderson, 1992; Anyon, 1997; Kunjufu, 1982/1986; Meier, Stewart, & England, 1989; Noguera, 1996; Rothstein, 2004; Wilson, 1987). I speculate there are a host of reasons why gender and sexuality issues are left out of the discourse of urban education. There might be a fear of tainting discussions of race and class with sexuality since historically homosexuality and women's issues have served as "wedge" issues in communities of color (Pharr, 1996). Moreover, recognizing the way gender and sexuality inform issues and problems in urban education inevitably leads to more, not less, complexity.

From a policymaking perspective, too much complexity seemingly weakens the possibility that educational policies can provide solutions to the problems of urban education. Both of these concerns are understandable, however, using them to guide the practice of social justice in urban education is highly problematic because they lead educators to overlook the ways in which gender intersects with other identities and how these intersections contribute to unique experiences of oppression and privilege. In this chapter, I focus on one of the most pressing social justice issues facing urban educators in the United States: race–gender gaps (or disparities by race and gender) in achievement, discipline, and participation (Lopez, 2003). Using a case study of Black male students' experience of marginalization in an urban high school in Northern California, I argue that urban educators undertheorize masculinity in their conceptualization of race–gender gaps. I begin this discussion with the conceptual framework that has most influenced my thinking about social justice in urban education: intersectionality.

Intersectionality

Intersectionality is a feminist theory that starts from the premise that people live multiple, layered identities derived from social relations, history, and the operation of structures of power (Association for Women's Rights in Development [AWID], 2004). Intersectional analysis uncovers multiple identities and therefore reveals different types of discrimination and disadvantage that occur as a consequence of the combination of identities. For example, sociologist Patricia Hill Collins uses a feminist intersectional analysis to understand the experiences of working class African-American women, in particular, how multiple forms of oppression have been used to disempower Black women and deny them citizenship (Collins, 1990). From Collins's perspective, "Assuming that each system (of oppression) needs the others in order to function creates a distinct theoretical stance that stimulates the rethinking of basic social science concepts" (p. 222).

The importance of rethinking basic social science concepts such as race–gender gaps from feminist intersectional perspectives became evident to me while I was working on a school–university collaborative action research project (CARP) at a California High School (CHS) located in a small urban community in the Bay Area of California.[1] Teachers, parents, graduate students, and professors had come together under the auspices of CARP to address race and class disparities in achievement and racial segregation within school programs and activities. Working together with approximately 10 other members of the Core Team, CARP's steering committee, our task was to strategize how to explain the goals of CARP and recruit teachers at the next staff development meeting.

"How should we explain the goals of the Project?" asked Joyce,[2] a Japanese-American woman in her late 30s who taught Ethnic Studies. "Why don't we just say that the D-F rate[3] for Black and Latino students is higher than any other racial or ethnic group of students?" offered Don, a White, male math teacher in his mid-50s. "But, that's not entirely true," I countered, "because Black and Latino males are failing at a higher rate than their female counterparts. Shouldn't we bring up the gender dimension as well?" Several teachers and graduate students nodded their heads in agreement after I made this statement. After a brief pause during which time it seemed as if everyone was thinking about how to explain the goals of CARP in a way that incorporated gender issues, a faculty member suggested, "Let's just stick to our original agenda of race and class disparities in achievement and hold off on the gender issue; we don't want to make things too complicated too soon." Everyone nodded in agreement, seemingly relieved that we found a way to sidestep the "complicated" gender dimension of the achievement gap at CHS.

I wanted to challenge this faculty member, but felt, in the absence of vocal support from my colleagues, that my concerns would be interpreted as personal rather than integral to the political agenda of the project. While the Core Team seemed to appreciate knowing I was gay, and that I had strong interest in women and gender studies, I never received any encouragement to share insights from either a feminist or queer perspective. My sexuality made the Core Team more diverse, but it was not expected this added diversity would have an impact on the political agenda of CARP. In addition, the faculty member who encouraged us to "hold off" on gender issues was charismatic and well-respected. So, even though I was outraged at the ease with which we sidestepped gender issues, at that moment I felt pushing a feminist intersectional perspective could weaken my ties on CARP and within the school. I decided to investigate the way gender and sexuality oppression affects disparities in achievement and participation on my own.

Key Questions and Issues

During the four years I worked on CARP, between 1996 and 2000, I was drawn to questions of why students from the poorest sections of the city consistently had the lowest grade point averages, or why Black male students represented the majority of students in the school's discipline system, or why in a school where over 60% of the students were non-White, the social/support group for lesbian, gay, bisexual, and transgender students tended to be White female students. Two other graduate student members of CARP and I conducted in-depth interviews with 10 Black male students as part of CARP's Taking Stock and Class of 2000 collaborative inquiry teams.

The data we collected revealed that Black male students were marginalized within the school's institutional structure, meaning they felt isolated from mainstream programs, were concentrated in low-track classes, and underrepresented in most extracurricular activities. The specific experiences of three gay and gender nonconforming Black male students that I present in this chapter, however, indicate a need for urban educators to understand the way multiple forms of oppression contribute to the marginalization of Black male students. Intersectionality can help urban educators make sense of the identities and circumstances of Black male students, and help us understand the ways in which Black male students develop a sense of their gender and sexual identities in relation to their race, class, and ability identities, and the complex ways their identities affect school participation. Out of this complexity emerge new ways of envisioning social justice education for Black male students that expand the boundaries of gender expression (for both male and female students) and open up the potentialities of gender identity and sexuality for everyone.

Gay and Gender Nonconforming Black Male Students at CHS

David

During the fall semester 1997 I interviewed David, a Black gay male senior at CHS. David was 17 years old when I interviewed him. He was a lanky 6'4" with skin the color of honey. He had large, earthy brown eyes, meticulously arched eyebrows, and usually dressed in jeans, sneakers, a T-shirt, and a hooded sweatshirt. Occasionally, I saw him wear something flashier such as a Hawaiian print shirt, but most times he wore standard Gap-inspired clothes with either a baseball or wool-knit cap, depending on how cold it was outside. The combination of David's light brown skin color, height, and what some students viewed as feminine appearing eyes, marked him as gender nonconforming and thus made him a target of abuse from his peers.

I was rapt with attention as David recounted multiple incidents of harassment he received in elementary and middle school. "I had long curly hair," he said, "so people used to think I was a girl and I used to get teased a lot because of that." When David got to CHS the harassment became more physical. "...People eventually started throwing things at me and shit." David approached Mr. Jones, a Black man in his mid-40s and the director of CHS security, about the harassment he was receiving, particularly from his Black male peers. Mr. Jones asked, "Well, what did you do to deserve it [the harassment]?" David replied, "I was walking out of the library and these [Black] boys threw a magazine at me and called me names." Mr. Jones replied, "Oh, well, usually someone does something to someone first before they're going to throw some books at you."

Besides the fact that Mr. Jones was clearly "blaming the victim," his response reflects the way certain forms of violence and harassment that maintain the masculine status quo are seemingly sanctioned by members of the school community. When Mr. Jones asks "What did you do to deserve it?" And later says, "usually someone does something to someone first before they're going to throw some books at you," he is letting David know that he must have provoked the harassment by doing something inappropriate. Mr. Jones doesn't name David's gender expression explicitly, he implies it through coded language ("something") and his skepticism of David's innocence.

As a result of this harassment during the fall semester of his junior year, David no longer felt safe at CHS and decided, after much pleading with his mother, to finish high school in Independent Studies, a self-directed high school diploma program administered by the continuation high school in the school district. It is important to understand that David's decision to leave was not based solely on the harassment he experienced because of his gender nonconformity. Rather, his gender nonconformity exacerbated the marginalization he experienced emanating from multiple dimensions of his identity. For example, in my interview with David I learned he had been identified as a "gifted" student in elementary school. For most of his time in school David was in a separate academic track from the majority of Black students. According to David, participating in gifted and talented programs was hard because he was one of the few students of color in his classes and his Black peers felt his participation in these programs symbolized that he was trying to "act White" (Fordham & Ogbu, 1986). In addition, David was biracial; his mother was White, his father Black. At times, David believed his skin color combined with his gender nonconformity, seemed to position him outside the "boundaries of blackness" in the eyes of his Black peers. Finally, David was becoming more aware of his gay identity and did not think there was an adult at CHS with whom he could discuss his feelings.

Although David experienced enormous personal growth during his year on Independent Studies (he developed close friendships with other gay, lesbian, and gender nonconforming students of color) his academic progress was less than stellar. After giving it much thought he decided to confront his fear of failure and give CHS a second chance. When he returned to CHS, however, David found it difficult to find a peer group that met his social and emotional needs. Even though he openly identified as gay, he felt alienated from the group of White female students who participated in Project 10. According to David, "It's (Project 10) about four or five girls who all know each other. They're all out, you know, within that group. And they go there I guess for social support." David felt that it was more difficult for guys, guys of color in particular, to "come out" and feel comfortable attending a queer support group. He attributed the difficulty of students of color openly identifying as gay or lesbian to cultural differences in the ways homophobia and heterosexism are expressed in Black communities

In addition to possible cultural differences in identifying as gay, David's experiences seem to reflect the tendency of White female students, like their Black peers, to socialize with one another around a distinct set of racially defined concerns, rather than build coalitions with students from different racial backgrounds who may have an entirely different set of interests. For example, in *Women Without Class* (Bettie, 2003), Julie Bettie describes how White, middle-class female students, "preps," developed intricate social networks that allowed them to control participation in the student government, a class where students learned "leadership skills" that translated into the management of other students they considered subordinate.

Fran Thompson, the faculty advisor for CHS Project 10, believed that the strong participation of White female students was related to the fact that they were the most concerned about encountering discrimination for being openly queer. In contrast, queer students of color seemed to relate more to groups outside of CHS such as Lavender, which was a more racially diverse support group run by a local lesbian and gay community center. Admitting that "diversifying the ethnic composition of the group is very complicated," Fran questioned her own ability to fully understand the multitude of pressures queer students of color face. Her limited understanding of multiple dimensions of social/support needed by queer youth of color may have unintentionally alienated David, encouraging him and others to seek resources outside the school. In this way Project 10 and other queer youth programs in segregated school environments may privilege White students and marginalize queer youth of color.

From a feminist intersectional perspective, David's gender nonconformity and academic status seemed to be the primary causes of harassment from his Black peers. His marginalization from Project 10, however, seemed to stem from his racial identity. More specifically, the White female participants in Project 10 were unaware of how to construct the group's activities around the identities of LGBT students of color like David. Through examining David's multiple identities and the various forms of discrimination he faced, urban educators can begin the difficult work of developing more comprehensive approaches to social justice education. As we turn to the next student narrative, we see how Black male students' class identity can affect their experience of marginalization.

Jamal

At the time of the interview, Jamal was a trim 5'10", dark brown skinned African-American young man with a mustache and goatee. His sparkling light brown eyes complemented his short afro which he often wore in twists, at the time a common urban style for African-American youth. He also liked to experiment with his dress, one day wearing a hip hop outfit, the next day wearing platform black shoes, tight black pants, and a tight fitting, dark blue shirt with long lapels.

> Growing up in my house, it was totally different. Just because of like who my family is and stuff. So, it's like I don't know I think I compare it to like being I guess um, maybe being interracial? Having a Black parent and a White parent. It's like cause you're living like this kinda double existence. So, it's like I lived in the ghetto, but my life was different than my neighbors. Like I had summer vacations and I had everything I wanted and if anything the other kids thought I was…. Cause I was also an only child, so anything I wanted I got….I'd say, I'd say, I mean, if it's, if middle-class is based off of education I'd say, I mean my mom has two master's degrees. Everybody [in my family] has an education. I think I've lived a middle-class life, just in the 'hood.

Jamal's likening of his middle-class status to Whiteness demonstrates the complex ways he identifies as Black and how his sense of authenticity as a young Black man is intimately tied to his socioeconomic status. By comparing his living situation to that of an interracial person, Jamal shows how he is struggling to reconcile his sense that in some situations, acting middle-class would be perceived as being less Black, or White, by his economically poor Southside neighbors.

In addition to socioeconomic status, Jamal's identity as Black was influenced by his gender. More specifically, Jamal felt his masculinity was different from the majority of his

Black male peers, which inadvertently called into question his Blackness. Both in school and in his neighborhood, Jamal remembered having different interests from most boys his age:

> This guy [Durrell], like we were friends from fourth grade until age 13. But I mean like, like there was a difference. I was doing things differently. Like he was popping wheelies on his bicycle and I wasn't interested in popping wheelies. Or he would learn to play, he would learn to, um ride his skateboard and I stuck with the skates, and skates were considered, they weren't considered as like macho.... And like, I don't know, but that, I guess...I guess I started to feel different toward like fourth, fifth grade. But I don't know, 'cause I was fat in the fifth, sixth, and seventh grade. So I don't know if it was because I was fat or because I, I like...Like I hated sports and PE... and I didn't dress like the other kids. Like I would come in tight like um...Not exactly leggings, but I mean, you know, like tight, like I wasn't into other fifth, sixth, seventh, eighth grade boys styles. And like I would bring my Diana Ross tourbooks to school and they were probably into what? Um, what was popular then? That was when rap was starting to emerge. They were probably, yeah they were, I remember this. They were like idolizing LL Cool J and I was like idolizing Diana and Janet you know? Even just, that was just an example as far as music goes of the difference between me and them.

As Jamal's interests grew apart from most of his Black male peers, their inclinations toward certain performances of gender also diverged. Jamal's Black male peers idolized LL Cool J, a popular rapper from New York City whose Kangol hats, muscular body, womanizing, and aggressive style of rapping won him the stamp of approval from throngs of Black male youth who perceived him as authentically Black, male, urban, and heterosexual. Jamal, on other hand, idolized Diana Ross who epitomized Black people who were "living well." By idolizing Diana Ross, a wealthy Black woman who clearly had made it out of the ghetto, the authenticity of Jamal's Blackness was again called into question. In seventh grade, however, Jamal figured out that certain masculine identity markers could garner him power, prestige, and respect:

> I remember in the seventh grade it was like this big thing when somebody.... We were playing kickball and I like, I was in the outfield or whatever and like I caught the ball and everybody was like "Jamal caught a ball!" because I was not known for my athletic ability. No, it was like a big thing. Like it was around the school, like "Jamal caught a ball!" It was a big, I'm telling you it was a big thing that I caught a ball. Everybody was surprised, nobody ever expected me to catch a ball ever in my life.

Jamal's experience of catching the ball seemed like a critical turning point in early adolescence when he realized that participating and excelling in certain extracurricular activities, particularly athletic ones, could win the approval of his Black peers.

This strategy would come in handy at CHS where being middle-class and high-achieving set him apart from the majority of Black students who, if not poor and underachieving, would at least posture as such. White students occupied the college-bound academic tracks, while Black students were overrepresented in low-level classes. I asked Jamal how he managed to make his way around or through the formidable social boundaries between Black students and non-Black students, especially since he had been in the college-bound track and was somewhat of a gender nonconformist. Jamal responded with the familiar strategy of participating in the extracurricular activities that were valued by his peers. For example, at CHS he was class secretary for student government. This position gave him influence since student government organized proms and other important social events.

In addition to being involved in student government, Jamal maintained his racial authenticity and influence by deemphasizing his gayness. More specifically, he stayed away from Project 10 because he knew participating in this activity would damage his reputation among Black students. In short, to align oneself with Project 10 meant to invite harassment. According to Jamal, these dynamics were particularly evident when students read announcements in class for Project 10 from the Bulletin, the daily publication for school-wide events:

I: What do you remember about Project 10?

J: Just that they used to have announcements in the Bulletin, "Are you gay, bisexual, queer, questioning?" And then like I guess there would always be a designated reader for the class Bulletin everyday. So then I mean sometimes, it was interesting though, it was interesting because when I would have a predominantly White class in the morning second period when the Bulletin was read, like they would read it, they would read it. And people were just kinda like, just listen to it. There might be little side comments here and there, but they would listen and like, "That's a club in the school." But in the Black classes that I had, that same period? Ohhh my god, they would skip over it like the club did not exist. They would either speak through it [the announcement], or it was just treated differently than the other club announcements, which is interesting. People always, there was a running joke at school like people wanted to go and actually see who actually went to the club. Like they wanted to go and stand outside the door just to see who went.

Why didn't Jamal express anger or indignation that his peers dismissed the importance of Project 10 and actually made it difficult for him and other LGBT students to attend? His nonchalant tone suggests he could not even conceive how the group could benefit a student like himself who identified as Black, gay, and middle class. In addition, avoiding Project 10 may have served as a way for Jamal to show solidarity with his peers who thought it served no purpose for Black students. His concern about his Black peers' reaction can be traced to his experience of being identifiably middle class in a Black community where the majority of residents were poor and working class. The fact that Jamal's class status differed from the majority of his peers made him incredibly aware of how his racial authenticity was being judged. His peers served as human "panopticons" for Project 10—living, breathing technologies of surveillance that govern students' every move and gesture (Foucault, 1984). Under the gaze of his panoptic Black peers, Jamal feared the social consequences of being seen at a Project 10 meeting. Jamal assessed the risk of openly identifying with a predominantly White group of LGBT students and made a cool, pragmatic decision not to attend because of the way it might sever his already tenuous ties to homophobic Black peers.

Jamal's marginalization both converges with and diverges from David's in interesting ways. Both young men seemed to experience marginalization as a result of their gender identity; however, Jamal's class identity positioned him differently with respect to Project 10. Jamal, unlike David, never even attended a Project 10 meeting because the class differences he experienced in the Black community influenced the way he negotiated his gender and sexual identities. For Jamal, attending a Project 10 meeting could potentially call into question his already fragile relationships with his Black peers, most of whom were homophobic and did not identify as middle class.

From a feminist intersectional perspective, Jamal's narrative complicates the notion of marginalization by showing how class identity can affect Black male students' experience of marginalization. Jamal chose to avoid Project 10 altogether to maintain his ties with the Black community. Interestingly, both young men were harassed and marginalized by members of their own racial group, which raises a question of intragroup marginalization (Cohen, 1999). It seems that social justice education for Black male students would have to address the way various forms of oppression lead to the marginalization of Black male students both between *and* within racial groups. As we turn to Antoine's narrative, the theme of intragroup marginalization returns, as well as a heretofore unmentioned social identity that holds the potential to marginalize Black male students in urban schools: ability.

Antoine

At 18 years old, 5'7" and 150 pounds, Antoine was smaller than most of his Black male peers. His medium brown skin, prominent nose, light brown eyes (from contact lenses), textured dark brown hair (with a bronze tuft in the front), and a slightly nasal, lispy, baritone voice gave him a feminine air. Despite these qualities he dressed in the uniform worn by most of his Black male peers: baggy jeans, T-shirt under an oxford-type shirt, plain baseball cap, pierced left ear, boots, and a backpack with a single arm sling. His clothing reflected his desire to fit in rather than to call attention to the ways his voice, stature, hairstyle, openly gay sexual identity, and participation in dance set him apart as gender nonconforming.

When Antoine came to CHS in the ninth grade he lacked confidence. "I wasn't really good at like holding your head up and smiling and stuff like that," he said. When he met with a counselor about his class schedule the counselor brought up the physical education. Antoine asserted that "I'm not interested in any kind of sports or nothing like that so don't put me in that." The counselor suggested Afro-Haitian dance, which at CHS fulfills the P.E. requirement. Antoine agreed to "give it a shot." During his first semester of the Afro-Haitian Dance Program (ADP) he was nervous and danced in the back. Second semester he began to warm up, and by sophomore year he remembered, "I was fine...and I gradually started coming to the front [of the class]."

Although participating in ADP gave Antoine a newfound celebrity, he continued to be socially reserved due in part to openly identifying as gay and, as I later learned, being a special education student. The disproportionate representation of Black students in special education programs has been well documented, Black students are disproportionately referred to and placed in the high-incidence special education categories of mental retardation, emotional or behavioral disorders, and learning disabilities, and once labeled are educated in segregated, self-contained settings with little or absolutely no exposure or access to their nondisabled peers or to the general curriculum (Blanchett, 2006). Given overrepresentation of Black students in special education, it makes sense that the stigma of being a special education student made Antoine extremely self-conscious of his status relative to his peers, all of whom were Black, but not special education students. He had difficulty accepting his academic shortcomings and routinely skipped his special education classes to serve as an informal teaching assistant in beginning ADP classes. Even though Mama Mwingu, the director of ADP, knew he was skipping academic classes, she empathized with his desire to fit in with Black students who were labeled disabled.

In addition to marginalization caused by his status as a special education student, Antoine, like David and Jamal, experienced harassment for being gender nonconforming. Some of the heterosexual-identified Black male dancers liked to tease him by punching him on the arm, slapping him upside the head, or expressing their disgust with homosexuality. When I asked Antoine about this negative behavior he suggested it could be a form of flirting or same-sex desire:

> I think everybody has thought about it in a negative or positive way, being with the same sex. And when I say a negative way, if I was straight and I was like, "Ooh, I can't see myself doing it to another dude" or "I can't see myself being with a dude." That's still thinking about it!

From my perspective, Antoine's nonconfrontational reaction to the harassment was a way of keeping the peace with Black male students with whom he wanted to remain friends. For instance, I often observed Chris, another Black male dancer in ADP, jokingly hit Antoine upside the head during rehearsal. On another occasion I observed Darrell, a CHS graduate who had been hired as one of the official drummers for ADP, hit Antoine repeatedly as Antoine yelled, "Stop!" at the top of his lungs. Antoine chuckled after both incidents.

When I witnessed these incidents I was baffled as to why Antoine did not seem excessively bothered by his peers' aggressiveness. After reflecting on my observations and interviews, one possible explanation I deduced was that Antoine liked the attention his heterosexual peers showed him, regardless of whether or not it was violent, because it made him feel like one of the guys. It allowed him to interact with his peers and counteracted the marginalization that could result from openly identifying as gay or being a special education student. I wonder, however, what kind of social environment such coping styles create in urban schools. As a matter of social justice, shouldn't urban educators attempt to facilitate school climates that affirm a range of masculine identities and work against both intergroup and intragroup marginalization? In the final section of this chapter I consider three necessary conceptual tools for enabling urban educators to create such environments.

Conceptual Tools for Social Justice Education in Urban Schools: Intersectionality, Multiple Masculinities, Antihomophobia Education

The narratives of gay and gender nonconforming Black male students presented in this chapter have important implications for social justice education in urban schools, particularly with respect to the way urban educators understand the marginalization of Black male students evidenced by race–gender gaps in achievement, participation, and discipline. Rather than making specific policy-driven recommendations, I present the implications as conceptual tools that hold the possibility for several different kinds of practices and interventions.

Conceptual Tool 1: Intersectionality

As stated at the beginning of this chapter, feminist intersectional perspectives grew out of the particular situation of women of color who experienced marginalization based on multiple social identities including their race, class, gender, and sexuality identities. Women's social justice organizations such as the Canadian Research Institute for the Advancement of Women (CRIAW) use intersectional feminist frameworks (IFF) to bring together the visions, directions, and goals of women from diverse experiences and different perspectives (see http://www.criaw-icref.ca/indexFrame_e.htm). IFF fosters an understanding of the many circumstances that combine with discriminatory social practices to produce and sustain inequality and exclusion.

Overall, as a theoretical framework, feminist intersectional perspectives or "intersectionality" emphasize both general patterns of exclusion and particular experiences of marginalization. Focusing on the particular experiences of gay and gender nonconforming Black male students enable urban educators to uncover multiple identities and reveal different types of marginalization that occur among Black male students in general. While the narratives of gay and gender nonconforming Black male students presented in this chapter reveal how Black male students' marginalization can be traced to their race, class, gender, sexuality, or ability identities, a thread that runs throughout all of the narratives is experiencing harassment due to gender nonconformity. The experience of harassment, I argue, reflects a general intolerance for nonnormative gender identities which points to the need for urban educators to incorporate conceptual tools that allow them to develop policies and practices that affirm a range of gender identities for Black male students. Two such conceptual tools are multiple masculinities and antihomophobia.

Conceptual Tool 2: Multiple Masculinities

Sociologist R. W. Connell uses the term *multiple masculinities* to describe the variety of masculine gender identities that exists (Connell, 1993). Imms (2000) describes four key characteristics of the multiple masculinities approach:

1. Masculinity is a multiple entity.
2. Gender is constructed by individuals as well as societal forces. Individuals do not automatically adopt predetermined gender roles; they are continually, active in building, negotiating, and maintaining perceptions of their gender.
3. Gender is a relational construct. Thus, boys do not construct their versions of masculinity apart from the influences of femininity or other men.
4. Multiple masculinities diversify hegemonic power structures, rendering them more accessible to rehabilitation.

The multiple masculinities approach is an important conceptual tool for urban educators because it provides a framework for understanding how Black male students' gender identities are constantly being built, negotiated, and maintained. Moreover, the multiple masculinities approach calls attention to the existence of nonhegemonic masculinities (masculinities that are subordinated, or repressed) like those of gay and gender nonconforming Black male students. Multiple masculinities approaches are beginning to be used to develop "boy-centered programs" in Germany, England, and Australia (Connell, 1996).

As a matter of social justice, it is crucial that urban educators affirm nonhegemonic masculinities of Black male students not only because these masculinities are known to invite harassment, but also because they hold the potential for conceptualizing Black male student identity in ways that resist institutional- and peer-driven forces of marginalization. Consider, for example, the way Antoine used dance, thought by many to be a feminine activity, to counteract the marginalization he experienced in special education. From my perspective, what seems to prevent urban educators from seeing the possibilities of nonhegemonic masculinities is homophobia, the fear of homosexuals based on societal norms of masculinity/femininity and a belief in biologically-based innate sex differences. For this reason, I believe antihomophobia education is a controversial, yet

342   *Lance T. McCready*

crucial conceptual tool for urban educators who want to address the marginalization of Black male students.

Conceptual Tool 3: Antihomophobia Education

Antihomophobia education is a controversial field of social justice work that challenges both the fear and the ideas underlying the fear of homosexuality. Antihomophobia education is both dynamic and volatile because it invites students and educators to confront and negotiate a range of complex and contradictory subject positions associated with politics and gender identity and sexuality (Robinson, Ferfolja, & Goldstein, 2004). Although metropolitan areas are home to some of the most politically vibrant and visible LGBT communities, urban educators, as a group, are ambivalent about the relevance of antihomophobia to their social justice work in urban schools, perhaps because historically race, class, political economy, and immigration issues have dominated the landscape of urban education. Or maybe urban educators' own homophobia has prevented them from taking gender and sexuality issues seriously. While these issues are without a doubt critical, at the end of the day gender and sexuality oppressions remain overlooked as significant structural and cultural forces in urban communities, which in turn leads to their undertheorization in urban education (McCready, 2001).

Antihomophobia education in the United States has been taken up somewhat erratically by professional organizations such as the Queer Studies special interest group in the American Educational Research Association, LGBT youth organizations such as the Hetrick-Martin Institute in New York City and Horizons Youth Program in Chicago, and LGBT education-advocacy organizations such as Project 10 and Gay Lesbian Straight Education Network (GLSEN). GLSEN has been particularly successful at galvanizing antihomophobia work at the local level through providing technical assistance to teachers and students who want to start gay–straight alliances (GSAs) in their schools. It is unclear, however, to what extent GSAs are present in urban schools, and whether or not these organizations serve the needs of students of color (remember David's experience in Project 10) (McCready, 2004).

Antihomophobia education is crucial for urban educators helping Black male students "make space" for diverse masculinities that resist marginalization. The writings of Black gay men can serve as a template for this work of reimagining Black manhood. For example, in the book *Brother to Brother: New Writings by Black Gay Men* (Hemphill, 1991) a variety of writers such as Isaac Julien, Essex Hemphill, Marlon Riggs, and Kobena Mercer confront their fear of being openly gay, gender nonconforming, profeminist, and authentically Black. Similarly, from my perspective, much of the refusal to explore new definitions of Black masculinity stem from the fear that profeminist, antiheterosexist conceptions of Black manhood threaten the stability of the Black community. It is clear, however, from the lives of the Black gay male students depicted in this chapter that gender oppression (Connell, 2000) and compulsory heterosexuality (Rich, 1980) create more, rather than less trouble for Black male students in urban schools. Given these problems, urban educators should consider using intersectionality, multiple masculinities, and antihomophobia education to address issues of social justice for Black male students in urban schools.

Notes

1. CARP was a six-year project comprised of collaborative inquiry teams of teachers, students administrators, parents, professors, and graduate students who investigated the reasons

behind two problems CHS has faced since it voluntarily desegregated over 50 years ago: the race–class academic achievement gap and racial segregation in academic and extracurricular programs.

2. In accordance with the recommendations from the UCB Protection of Human Subjects Committee, the names of all people associated with CHS and DP, including teachers, students, faculty, graduate students, and staff have been changed to protect their identities.

3. Until recently, the CHS administration published a annual report of the number of Ds and Fs given to students, disaggregated by race and ethnicity. Black and Latino students always received the higher numbers of Ds and Fs compared to White and Asian-American students. Teachers and administrators often used the D-F rate report to highlight racial disparities in achievement at CHS.

References

Anderson, E. (1992). *Streetwise: Race, class, and change in an urban community.* Chicago: University of Chicago Press.

Anyon, J. (1997). *Ghetto schooling: A political economy of urban educational reform.* New York: Teachers College Press.

Association for Women's Rights in Development (AWID). (2004). Intersectionality: A tool for economic and social justice. *Women's Rights and Economic Change, 9,* 1–8.

Bettie, J. (2003). *Women without class.* Berkeley, CA: University of California Press.

Blanchett, W. (2006). Disproportionate representation of African American students in special education: Acknowledging the role of whiteprivilege and racism. *Educational Researcher, 35*(6), 24–28.

Canadian Research Institute for the Advancement of Women (CRIAW). Retrieved December 29th, 2006, from http://www.criaw-icref.ca/indexFrame_e.htm

Cohen, C. (1999). *The boundaries of blackness: AIDS and breakdown of blackness.* Chicago: University of Chicago Press.

Collins, P. (1990). *Black feminist thought.* New York: Routledge.

Connell, R. W. (1987). *Gender and power.* Stanford, CA: Stanford University Press.

Connell, R. W. (1993). Disruptions: Improper masculinities and schooling. In L. Weis & M. Fine (Eds.), *Beyond silenced voices: Class, race, and gender in United States schools* (pp. 191–208). Albany, NY: SUNY.

Connell, R. W. (1996). Teaching the boys: New research on masculinity and gender strategies for schools. *Teachers College Record, 98,* 206–235.

Connell, R. W. (2000). *The men and the boys.* Berkeley, CA: University of California Press.

Fordham, S., & Ogbu, J. U. (1986). Black students' school success: Coping with the "burden of acting White." *Urban Review, 18,* 176–206.

Foucault, M. (1984). The means of correct training. In P. Rabinow (Ed.), *The Foucault reader* (pp. 188–205). New York: Pantheon.

Gordon, E. (2003). Urban education. *Teachers College Record, 105*(2), 189–207.

Hemphill, E. (Ed.). (1991). *Brother to brother: New writings by Black gay men.* Boston: Alyson.

Imms, W. D. (2000). Multiple masculinities and the schooling of boys. *Canadian Journal of Education, 25*(2), 152–165.

Kincheloe, J. (2004). Why a book on urban education? In S. Steinberg, & J. Kincheloe (Eds.), *19 Urban Questions: Teaching in the City.* New York: Peter Lang.

Kunjufu, J. (1986). *Countering the conspiracy to destroy black boys* (Vol. 2, Rev. ed.). Chicago: African American Images. (Original work published 1982)

Lopez, N. (2003). *Hopeful boys, troubled girls: Race and gender disparity in urban education.* New York: Routledge.

McCready, L. T. (2001). When fitting in isn't an option: Black queer students experience racial separation at a California high school. In K. Kumashiro (Ed.), *Troubling intersections of race and sexuality* (pp. 37–53). Lanham, MD: Rowman & Littlefield.

McCready, L. T. (2004). Some challenges facing queer youth programs in urban high schools: Racial segregation and de-normalizing whiteness. *Journal of Gay and Lesbian Issues in Education, 1(3)*, 37–51.

Meier, K. J., Stewart, J., & England, R. E. (1989). *Race, class, and education: The politics of second-generation discrimination.* Madison, WI: University of Wisconsin Press.

Noguera, P. (1996). Responding to the crisis confronting California's Black male youth: Providing support without furthering marginalization. *Journal of Negro Education, 65(2)*, 219–236.

Pharr, S. (1996). *In the time of the right: Reflections on liberation.* Little Rock, AK: Women's Project.

Robinson, K., Ferfolja, T., & Goldstein, T. (2004). [Special issue: Anti-homophobia teacher education]. *Teaching Education, 15(1)*, 3–8.

Rothestein, R. (2004). *Class and schools: using social, economic, and educational reform to close the black–white achievement gap.* New York: Economic Policy Institute.

Seidman, S. (2002). *Beyond the closet: The transformation of gay and lesbian life.* New York: Routledge.

Wilson, W. J. (1987). *The truly disadvantaged: The inner city, the underclass, and public policy.* Chicago: University of Chicago Press.

22 HIV/AIDS Prevention and Sexuality Education for *All* Students

Critical Issues in Teaching for Social Justice

Wanda J. Blanchett

Notwithstanding many calls (e.g., Blanchett, 2000; Blanchett & Prater, 2006; Pardini, 2002–2003; Rodriguez, Young, Renfro, Asencio, & Haffner, 1996; Skripak & Summerfield, 1996) for all students to receive developmentally appropriate comprehensive school health education including HIV/AIDS prevention education, many students are still not consistently educated in this area, and the idea of contextualizing these issues within the larger context of social justice is even more foreign for some educators. In recent years much attention has been given to the importance of infusing social justice philosophy into education and the professional preparation of educators (Cochran-Smith, 2004; Gay, 2000; Murrell, 2006). The social justice discussions, however, have primarily centered on preparing educators to teach for social justice with little attention given to issues of sexuality. Surprisingly, despite so much emphasis having been placed on teaching for social justice since the mid- to late 1990s, rarely has the field of education embraced or even recognized comprehensive school health education, including HIV/AIDS prevention and sexuality education, as critical elements in the quest to teach for social justice.

Comprehensive health education is aimed at increasing students' quality of life by preventing some of the most serious health problems and issues associated with youth. Thus, comprehensive health education is designed to prevent youth from experiencing lifelong consequences associated with their youthful and unhealthy living behaviors including sexual, unintentional, and intentional injury and death, tobacco, alcohol, and other substance use and addiction, sexual risk activities that result in unintended pregnancy and sexually transmitted infections, unhealthy dietary patterns, and lack of physical activity (Frauenknecht, 2003). To ensure that all students do indeed have access to developmentally appropriate HIV/AIDS prevention and sexuality education, educators and the public alike must embrace these issues as components of the larger social agenda of teaching for social justice and adequately prepare educators to meet the challenge of educating all students, including students with disabilities, in these areas. Because of the vulnerabilities associated with their learning characteristics and social positioning within the larger society, students with disabilities must be included in any social justice agenda to ensure that all students receive HIV/AIDS prevention and sexuality education.

Access to information such as HIV/AIDS prevention and sexuality education that allows one to take control over one's life and to make informed decisions is a basic component of social justice in a democratic society. As illustrated above, comprehensive health education encompasses a wide range of content and targets a variety of skills and behaviors, but for the purpose of this chapter, my discussion of comprehensive health education will be limited to the HIV/AIDS prevention and sexuality education components of comprehensive school health education. Also, for the purposes of this chapter, social justice is defined as "…a disposition toward recognizing and eradicating all forms of oppression and differential treatment extant in the practices and policies of institutions"

(Murrell, 2006, p. 81). The focus of this chapter is the institutional practice of teacher preparation programs, and I will situate the need to provide HIV/AIDS prevention and sexuality education to all students including students with disabilities within the larger context of teaching for social justice. To do this, I will discuss why HIV/AIDS prevention and sexuality education is important for all students and especially students with disabilities. Second, I will provide an overview of the current state of teacher preparation in the area of HIV/AIDS prevention and sexuality education. Third, I will provide an overview of general and special educators' preparation to teach HIV/AIDS prevention education to students with disabilities as a component of social justice. Lastly, strategies for infusing HIV/AIDS prevention and sexuality education into teacher preparation as a component of social justice preparation for all educators will be offered.

Why is HIV/AIDS Prevention and Sexuality Education Important for All Students?

Comprehensive school health education is both a social justice issue and it is critically important for all students because today's youth have a number of risk factors and behaviors that may increase the likelihood that they experience future health problems and potentially a decreased quality of life. These risk factors and behaviors include but are not limited to substance abuse, family and social violence, sexual activity, and teenage pregnancy (Baker, 2005; Frauenknecht, 2003). Although the percentage of American youth who are sexually active decreased slightly from 54% in 1991 to 45.6% in 2001, a large percentage of youth are still sexuality active prior to adulthood and it appears that many of them may not be receiving the information that they need to make safe and informed decisions (Pardini, 2002). Despite a decline in young people's sexual activity, birth, pregnancy, and abortion rates, disaggregated data for cities and school districts highlight the need for continued concern. For example, in 2001, while the national rate of sexual activity was down from slightly over 50% to 45.6%, 57% of Milwaukee public high school students reported having had sexual intercourse at least once (Pardini, 2002). What is even more starling is the fact that only slightly over half of sexually active youth reported using condoms in previous studies of risk behavior (Kann et al., 1996). The findings of these sexual risk behavior studies highlight the need to consistently provide developmentally appropriate comprehensive health education including HIV/AIDS prevention and sexuality education to all students as a component of their PK-12 curriculum. Because "comprehensive school health education can help youth obtain the greatest benefits from education and become healthy and productive adults," (Frauenknecht, 2003, p. 2) the Department of Health and Human Services, through its Healthy People 2010 campaign is trying to increase the proportion of all high schools that provide comprehensive health education to their students (Frauenknecht, 2003). Unfortunately, even with such targeted campaigns, due to their social positioning in our society students with disabilities are often not included.

For more than a decade, several articles (e.g., Colson & Carlson, 1993; Prater, Serna, Sileo, & Katz, 1995) have appeared in the special education professional literatures that have called attention to students with disabilities as a group for whom HIV/AIDS prevention and sexuality education should be provided. Students with disabilities are believed to be more vulnerable for not only HIV infection but also for other sexually transmitted diseases, sex abuse, and teen pregnancy than their peers without disabilities (Council for Exceptional Children, 1991). Particularly, many students with disabilities (1) lack knowledge and information about their bodies and sexuality; (2) are misinformed because many of them are unable to distinguish between reality and unreality; (3) limited social skills;

(4) are easily influenced by others; and (5) exercise poor judgment that may increase their health risks. Despite acknowledgment of specific learning characteristics of students with disabilities that may increase their susceptibility to HIV infection, little has been done to educate them about prevention.

Indeed, research suggests that comprehensive sexuality education is not offered consistently to this population nor does it always include HIV/AIDS prevention education (Blanchett, 2000). Additionally, students' with learning disabilities access to HIV/AIDS prevention seems to be related to where they receive their educational services. Students with learning disabilities who are in general education classrooms for 75% or more of the day are more likely to receive HIV/AIDS education than their peers who spent 25% or more of their time in special education classes (Blanchett, 2000). The fact that students' access to HIV/AIDS education is indeed linked to their access to the general education classroom further highlights the importance of continuing to advocate for general education placements for all students with disabilities as a social justice strategy to eradicate these inequities. Furthermore, when students with disabilities are exposed to HIV/AIDS prevention education it is rarely tailored to address their unique learning characteristics, learning styles, or preferences. Needless to say, providing these students with appropriate HIV/AIDS prevention education is critically important but it must be linked to the whole notion or philosophy of teaching for social justice. Placing students with disabilities in general education settings will likely increase their access to this information.

Given that there is still no known cure for the human immunodeficiency virus (HIV) which causes AIDS, effective HIV/AIDS prevention and sexuality education and subsequent appropriate risk reduction are the only weapons available to prevent the spread of HIV. Since we know that not all students have access to HIV/AIDS prevention and sexuality education, it must become a component of teaching for social justice. HIV is spread through the transmission of bodily fluids. Although the virus can be transmitted through a number of modes (e.g., contaminated needles, intravenous drug use, blood transfusions), the most common mode of transmission is by far through sexual activity. To halt the rate of infection and the spread of HIV/AIDS, the Centers for Disease Control and Prevention established guidelines for the delivery of HIV/AIDS Prevention Education in 1988 (Centers for Disease Control & Prevention, 1988). According to the Centers for Disease Control and Prevention (CDC), HIV/AIDS prevention education is most effective when it is aligned with the developmental levels and risk behaviors of the targeted group. Second, HIV/AIDS prevention education is most effective when it is offered as a component of a comprehensive health education program. Third, and most importantly, HIV/AIDS education is most effective when it is taught by qualified teachers. Qualified teachers can be defined as teachers who not only know the crucial and relevant content but are also comfortable teaching such content and are capable of selecting and implementing curricula that are tailored to their students' developmental levels and sexual risk behaviors.

Why Is HIV/AIDS Prevention Education Important for Students with Disabilities?

Students with disabilities have an elevated risk for contracting HIV because they may be more vulnerable than their peers to sexual abuse and drug abuse. Their vulnerability is attributed partially to characteristics of increased impulsivity, lack of resistance to peer pressure, and deficient problem-solving strategies (Prater et al., 1995). Some data indicate that students with disabilities might actually contract HIV/AIDS at greater rates than their peers. For example, a study of more than 8,000 Medicaid beneficiaries with HIV infection identified a larger percentage of individuals diagnosed with mental retardation than are present in the general population (Walker, Sambamoorthi, & Crystal, 1999). Transmission of HIV to these individuals cannot be pinpointed, but drug abuse most likely played a role, as most subjects in the group were substance abusers with a "registry-based injection drug use...classification" (Walker et al., p. 360).

Of course, individuals with disabilities may be more susceptible to HIV/AIDS than their nondisabled peers due to their limited exposure to school-based prevention curricula. Professionals do not always agree about their responsibility for teaching HIV/AIDS prevention to students with and without disabilities. Most educators believe HIV prevention should be taught by a health instructor, school nurse, or other trained medical specialist (Lavin et al., 1994). However, other school personnel, including physical education, science, and social studies teachers, have also been identified as appropriate instructors (Prater et al., 1995). This disagreement about who should or should not teach HIV/AIDS prevention education has likely contributed to students' inconsistent access and educators' lack of preparation in this area.

Segregated teacher preparation programs compound the confusion about which teachers are responsible for teaching HIV/AIDS prevention and sexuality education content. Currently, many programs are dual systems in which general and special educators are prepared separately (Carroll, Forlin, & Jobling, 2003). A potential outgrowth of segregated systems is that general educators are not prepared to work with diverse learning populations. They often perceive that they are prepared inadequately to work with students with disabilities (Lombard, Miller, & Hazelkorn, 1998). If general educators are responsible for teaching HIV/AIDS prevention to all students, they also must have the skills to select and adapt appropriate curriculum and instructional strategies for students with special needs.

The whole notion of teaching for social justice is in some ways paradoxical when it comes to students with disabilities for a number of reasons including, but not limited to, the fact that many individuals with disabilities unfortunately still have low social status in our society. They are also perceived to be asexual, despite a significant body of literature that suggests that this misperception is inaccurate (Blanchett, 2002; Colson & Carlson, 1993; Prater, Sileo, & Black, 1995). Additionally, despite a noteworthy push in recent years to ensure that all students with disabilities, regardless of the severity of their disabilities, are indeed fully included in general education classrooms, many students with disabilities, a disproportionate percentage of whom are African American, continue to be educated in segregated, self-contained classrooms with limited exposure to their nondisabled peers and to the general education curriculum (Blanchett, 2006). Also, few teacher preparation programs have adopted a social justice philosophy that centers on helping candidates to develop knowledge, skills, and dispositions that accord with teaching for social justice, and that also include addressing issues of sexuality for all students, including those with disabilities. Given that students with disabilities are a growing population and the fact that some of them are more likely to be included in the general education setting today than in the past, this reality is unacceptable. Excluding students with disabilities from HIV/AIDS prevention and sexuality education is unacceptable and socially unjust because it denies these students an opportunity to gain the knowledge and skills needed to participate in all aspects of life and to protect themselves against HIV infection and other sexually transmitted diseases.

Many teacher preparation programs have yet to fully understand and embrace social justice even in its most basic form of preparing candidates to confront and deconstruct their own privilege, racism, sexism, classism, and biases around issues of sexuality (Ferri & Conner, 2005). Needless to say, even fewer programs, whether they are general or special education teacher preparation programs, have infused issues of sexuality that include HIV/AIDS prevention education into their curriculum as a component of teaching for social justice. Thus, it is reasonable to conclude that even in those rare instances when issues of sexuality are infused into teacher education curriculum and programs, these issues are not addressed within the larger context of teaching for social justice. Lastly, notwithstanding the need for interdisciplinary preparation of educators to ensure that they have the skills necessary to engage in effective collaboration as practitioners, many general and special education teacher preparation programs continue to prepare their respective candidates in isolation with few opportunities to interact with relevant professionals from other disciplines (Carroll, Forlin, & Jobling, 2003). This is also true for the field of health education where health educators tend to go through their programs with a lot of attention given to content mastery and little interaction with general and special educators about how to meet the needs of students with varying learning characteristics and instructional needs.

Current State of Teacher Preparation in HIV/AIDS Prevention and Sexuality Education

Although educators agree that the most effective way to prevent the spread of HIV infection is to provide comprehensive health education to all students prior to them becoming sexually active and no later than seventh grade, it appears that teachers might not be equipped to meet this challenge, due to their poor preparation in this area. For example, even though elementary health education is most commonly provided by regular classroom teachers, only 31 states require elementary teachers to complete health coursework for certification (Stone & Perry, 1990, as cited in Skripak & Summerfield, 1996) and it seems that few teacher preparation programs are even addressing this issue in their program curriculum. In their study of 169 teacher education programs, Rodriquez, Young, Renfro, Asencio, and Haffner (1996) found that only 14% required a health education class for all of their preservice teachers and none of the programs required a sex education class for all preservice teachers. Additionally, only 61% of programs studied required their health education certification students to take sexuality courses and only 12% offered courses that even mentioned HIV/AIDS in the class at all (Rodriquez et al., 1996).

General educators play a critical role in teaching skills and concepts associated with HIV/AIDS prevention and sexuality education. In elementary schools, general education classroom teachers bear primary responsibility for providing health education to all students (Hausman & Ruzek, 1995), including those with disabilities. In a study of elementary teachers' techniques in responding to student questions related to sexuality, researchers found that only 34% of teachers reported receiving formal training related to sexuality education (Price, Drake, Kirchofer, & Tellijohann, 2003). These researchers also found that the most common questions that students asked pertained to sexually transmitted diseases (STDs), puberty, homosexuality, abortion, and pregnancy. Teachers' willingness to answers their students' questions related to these issues during class time ranged from 73% to 14%. Teachers in this study also reported that they experienced difficulty responding to questions that related to homosexuality, abortion, masturbation, and the male genitals. In secondary education settings, health education is often provided by specialized health and physical educators; however, as illustrated above few health educators are adequately prepared and even fewer secondary teachers are prepared to reinforce health education skills and concepts. Only one in six teacher preparation programs require health education courses for preservice secondary teachers who do not specialize in health or physical education (Rodriguez et al., 1997). If teachers prepared in general education programs lack training in health or HIV/AIDS prevention and sexuality education, it is unlikely that they will be able to teach this content to any students, let alone students with disabilities with a wide range of learning characteristics and abilities.

Special Educators' Preparation in HIV/AIDS Prevention and Sexuality Education

Teachers' lack of preparation compounds the challenges already facing students with disabilities regarding HIV/AIDS prevention and sexuality education. Although special educators' lack of preparation to provide sexuality education is well documented, few attempts have been made to improve their training. Surveys of preservice preparation programs suggest that only 50% provide special education teacher candidates with coursework related to HIV/AIDS prevention, sex education, and drug abuse (May & Kundert, 1996; May, Kundert, & Akpan, 1994). More importantly, most preservice programs do not require such coursework as a curricular component. Some 41% of special education programs in the May and Kundert (1996) study did not include any sex education in their curricula. When health or sex education content is included in special education teacher preparation, it is not required consistently.

In this same study, about 66% of programs indicated that sex education was covered in a required course, and 14% in an elective course; 20% did not answer the question. When asked where students receive sex education coursework, 11% of respondents indicated a separate special education course, and 19% reported a separate course offered by another department. May and Kundert (1996) found that there was more coverage of sex education in required special education courses in the 1990s than the 1980s. However, the total time allotted to sex education in special education classes decreased, although the time increased in courses offered by other departments. The average amount of time per semester devoted to sex education content in special education courses and those offered by other departments was 3.6 hours and 7.7 hours, respectively.

Studies in the 1990s of special educators who state that preservice preparation did not prepare them to meet students' needs regarding sex education support the belief that special education programs provide limited health education training (Foley, 1995; Foley & Dudzinski, 1995; Rabak-Wagener, Ellery, & Stacy, 1997). Three later studies provide additional evidence that special education teachers do not receive adequate preparation in this area. First, Ubbes et al. (1999) reported that only three states require health education certification for elementary teachers. Second, in a study that examined what and how risk-related content is addressed in special education teacher preparation programs, Prater, Sileo, and Black (2000) found that HIV/AIDS was one of the topics least likely to be covered. Third, an analysis of textbooks providing an introduction to exceptionalities, which are used in courses usually required of all general and special education majors, revealed that only one of 11 texts provided comprehensive coverage of HIV/AIDS and disabilities; one text did not address the topic at all (Foulk, Gessner, & Koorland, 2001).

Although there are a number of issues that impede students' access to HIV/AIDS education, the lack of preparation of general and special education teachers to address issues of sexuality with all students are among the most frequently cited (e.g., Blanchett & Prater, 2005; Rodriguez, Young, Renfro, Asencio, & Haffner, 1997). While one might be inclined to believe that general education teachers are bettered prepared, as illustrated above, it appears that neither group of teachers receives the preparation needed because the curriculum in few teacher preparation programs addresses sexuality in any form and even fewer addresses HIV/AIDS. If we are to really embrace HIV/AIDS prevention and sexuality education as components of our larger agenda of teaching for social justice, we must examine current practices in teacher education to ensure that all teacher candidates are indeed exposed to content and knowledge, skills, and dispositions that will enable them to be effective.

What Does It Mean to Prepare Teacher Education Candidates to Address HIV/AIDS Prevention Education as a Component of Teaching for Social Justice?

In order for educators to provide HIV/AIDS prevention education to students with disabilities as a component of teaching for social justice, their teacher education programs must address this critically important issue. Therefore, in this section, I will discuss what teacher preparation programs must do to better prepare their candidates to provide HIV/AIDS education to all students, including students with disabilities, as a component of teaching for social justice. Addressing HIV/AIDS prevention and sexuality education as a social justice component requires the following: (1) Teacher preparation programs must commit to preparing all candidates to teach for social justice. (2) Teacher preparation must require coursework to ensure that all candidates have sufficient knowledge and to help candidates deconstruct their own sexuality, HIV/AIDS, and disability-related perceptions, misperceptions, and biases to become comfortable addressing these issues. (3) Candidates must be provided with opportunities to reflect on how issues of racism, class, culture, gender, disability, sexual orientation, and multiple identities or affiliations impact their students' access to appropriate information. (4) Teacher preparation programs need to retool or retrain their faculty and staff. (5) National and state professional standards should address HIV/AIDS prevention and sexuality education as a component of teaching for social justice. and (6) Attention must be given to the relative isolation in which professional educators are currently prepared and interdisciplinary collaboration must be explored.

Teacher preparation programs need to adopt a philosophy of teaching for social justice that includes addressing issues of sexuality and HIV/AIDS prevention education for all students. Once adopted, teacher preparation programs' philosophy of teaching for social justice should guide and direct their curriculum and subsequent candidate experiences. Teacher preparation programs need to infuse issues of sexuality including HIV/AIDS prevention education into their curriculum in a deliberate and meaningful way that connects these issues to their overall effort to teach for social justice (Blanchett, 2002).

While there a number of ways to ensure that candidates develop essential knowledge, skills, and dispositions to teach HIV/AIDS prevention education as a component of social justice, at a minimum programs need to challenge students' perceptions, misperceptions, and biases regarding sexuality, gender, and issues of sexual expression. To do this, teacher education programs need to provide candidates with a safe and nonthreatening environment to interrogate their personal beliefs pertaining to sexual roles, gender roles, sexual communication comfort, and sexual power structures. Candidates also need to be offered opportunities to deconstruct their perceptions, misperceptions, and biases related to sexual expression and HIV/AIDS. Within the context of such deconstructions and critiques, there is also a need for discussions of sexuality as it relates to individuals with disabilities. Because issues of power and oppression are also associated with issues of sexuality and sexual expression, it is important for candidates to de-construct these issues as well and to examine the impact of other social justice issues such as race, class, disability, and culture on their own perceptions as well as society's treatment of marginalized groups when it comes to issues of sexuality. Addressing HIV/AIDS prevention and sexuality education for students with disabilities is but one of many manifestations of power and oppression that must be thoroughly and consistently address in our quest to teach for social justice.

Candidates should also be afforded opportunities to reflect on how issues of racism, class, culture, gender, disability, sexual orientation, and multiple identities or affiliations might also impact their students' access to appropriate sexuality and HIV/AIDS prevention education and to some extent their sexual behavior and level of risk for sexually transmitted diseases. I underscore the importance of understanding how students' multiple identities impact access to appropriate prevention education because we saw issues of race, gender, sexual orientation, class, and culture played out in very interesting ways with White middle class gay men and Black gay men during the beginning of the HIV/AIDS epidemic in this country.

For example, because the face of HIV/AIDS at that time was believed to be White males, HIV/AIDS prevention education employed strategies that were grounded in White middle class gay male cultural values and included billboards of sexy White middle class men advocating for safe sex and the use of condoms and an aggressive White gay male bar safe sex outreach campaign. Although this strategy was very successful in curtailing the HIV/AIDS risk behaviors of White middle class gay men and resulted in a significant decrease in the rate of new infection, when this same strategy was employed in the Black gay male community, a disproportionate percentage of whom lived significantly below the middle class standard of living, it failed miserably. Some wondered how a campaign that had been so successful in one community could fail so badly in another. The answer to this question is quite simple, the campaign failed in the African-American gay male community because it did not address African-American gay male cultural beliefs, values, behaviors, gender norms, and expectations that are also influenced by social class standing. In sum, in order for HIV/AIDS prevention education to be most effective, educators need to know and understand the learning characteristics and behaviors of their intended audience, and consideration must be given to issues of race, ability, disability, social class, culture, and gender.

Teacher preparation programs need to retool or retrain their faculty and staff to ensure that they have the knowledge and content expertise needed to effectively prepare candidates to address HIV/AIDS prevention and sexuality education with a wide range of PK-12 students, including those with disabilities and others that might not learn in traditional ways, including students of color (Blanchett & Prater, 2005). Most teacher educators were not exposed to issues of sexuality during their professional preparation so it is likely that many of these teacher educators themselves lack a minimum level of comfort in discussing issues of sexuality in general let alone HIV/AIDS with their candidates. Even when teachers are comfortable discussing issues of sexuality and HIV/AIDS prevention education, the extent to which they are indeed content area experts is questionable, so it seems that professional development in this area would increase their capacity to address this critically important issue in their programs. Just as most professional organizations (e.g., American Association of Colleges for Teacher Education [AACTE], American Educational Research Association [AERA]) offer a wide range of professional development workshops that center on current important topics (e.g., candidate assessment, value-added models, diversity, student achievement) that proceeds or are offered in conjunction with their annual conference program, it is important for these organization to also embrace issues of sexuality as a social justice issue and to offer sessions that center on issues of sexuality and HIV/AIDS prevention education. Void of attention given to the retooling of teacher educators, it is highly unlikely that they will develop the skills needed to actually infuse issues of sexuality and HIV/AIDS prevention education into their teacher education curriculum as a component of social justice even if they desire to do so.

In recent years, it seems that to some extent the field of teacher education has been successful in identifying an essential body of knowledge, skills, and dispositions that all teacher education candidates ought to mastery in order to effectively teach in today's schools (Cochran-Smith, 2004). Increasingly, despite a recent setback, teacher education accrediting bodies that include the National Council for Accreditation of Teacher Educators (NCATE) and Teacher Education Accreditation Council (TEAC) have been leaders in insisting that their members comply with these agreed upon standards around the professional preparation of teachers. Ironically, their respective national accreditation standards address a wide range of professional knowledge, skills, and dispositions and each state also has standards that teacher preparation programs must address in order to obtain state level approval. However, most of these professional expectations, whether they are at the national or state level, do not address issues of sexuality and HIV/AIDS prevention education in any deliberate or clear manner. To make matters worst, NCATE, supposedly under governmental pressure, recently dropped its social justice standard. Thus, an initial step in holding teacher preparation programs accountable for infusing sexuality and HIV/AIDS education into their curriculum would be to not only add a social justice standard but to also ensure that such a standard included HIV/AIDS prevention education standards at both the national and state accreditation or program approval level. There is much debate right now about whether or not NCATE and TEAC are the appropriate accrediting bodies for teacher education programs to allow the general public to have confidence that there is indeed an essential body of knowledge for teachers. More importantly, the debate is around whether or not our national accrediting process reflects "best practice"; so since this debate is already occurring, now is a particularly good time to revisit our definition of "best practice" in the 21st century. Such a step might also increase the likelihood that teacher educators in general, special, and health education give serious thought to interdisciplinary preparation of educators.

Even though much has been written about the need to collaboratively prepare general, special, and health educators to ensure that all have the content knowledge, skills, and dispositions needed to effectively providing HIV/AIDS prevention education to all students (e.g., Blanchett & Prater, 2005; Ellery, Rabak-Wagener, & Stacy, 1997), these programs continue to prepare their respective candidates in relative isolation (Carroll et al., 2003). To move forward in this direction would require professional education programs to think outside of the box and to actually redesign their programs to ensure that candidates take classes together and have the benefit of working across disciplines while still in their programs. Research teacher education and collaboration suggests that candidates who are exposed to cross- and interdisciplinary experiences while in training are more likely to engage in such collaboration as practitioners (Blauton, Griffin, Winn, & Pugach, 1997).

As stated previously, when it comes to HIV/AIDS prevention education, few teacher educators have the content and background expertise to assist their students in mastery of this content (Rodriquez et al., 1997). Similarly, most health educators have extensive content and background knowledge related to HIV/AIDS prevention education but few have the pedagogical skills needed to reach students with diverse learning characteristics and students for whom English is not their first language, so collaboration seems to be the answer to developing appropriate education for all students (Hausman & Ruzek, 1995). Adopting an interdisciplinary or cross-disciplinary approach to the preparation of general, special, and health educators would also require the culture of higher education to change to reward educators for the labor intensive curriculum redesign and collaboration that is necessary to transform how educators are currently prepared. The current culture in higher education actually supports preparing professionals in isolation rather than in more collaborative and innovative ways.

Teaching HIV/AIDS Education as a Component of Teaching for Social Justice (What Does It Look Like?)

Although the notion of expanding our conceptualization of social justice to be inclusive of issues of sexuality, including HIV/AIDS prevention education, might be a stretch for some classroom teachers and even some teacher educators, it is a natural fit. However, if we are to reengage educators in thinking more broadly about our philosophies and commitment to social justice the time is now because some of our most vulnerable students continue to be short changed when it comes to having access to information that they need to make safe and responsible sexuality decisions. Embracing sexuality and HIV/AIDS education as a component of a social justice philosophy will require teacher education and health education programs to rethink how they do business by doing the following:

1. General, special, and health education programs need to commit to a philosophy of social justice that includes addressing issues of sexuality and HIV/AIDS education.
2. Teacher preparation programs need to infuse issues of sexuality into their curriculum in a deliberate and meaningful way and health education programs need to focus specific attention on meeting the needs of diverse students including students with disabilities and students of color.
3. Professional preparation programs in general, special, and health education need to retool their faculty and staff to ensure that they have the content expertise, pedagogy, and dispositions to effectively prepare candidates to address HIV/AIDS education with a diverse student population that includes those with disabilities and students of color.
4. Professional accreditation bodies and states need to hold professional preparation programs in general, special, and health education accountable for addressing issues of sexuality and HIV/AIDS education as a social justice concern.
5. General, special, and health educators need to adopt either a cross- or interdisciplinary approach to preparing their respective candidates to ensure that candidates have an opportunity to see collaboration at work in their programs prior to becoming practitioners.
6. Professional education programs must expose their candidates to a model sexuality and HIV/AIDS education curriculum that is responsive to other social justice issues including but not limited to race, gender, culture, social class, and sexual orientation that impacts both students' access to information and risk behaviors.

In addition to a solid overall understanding of what it means to teach for social justice in its broadest sense, teacher educators and teacher education candidates alike need specific knowledge about the characteristics of all students including students with disabilities as well as curricular and instructional modifications. Teacher educators also need fundamental understanding of these issues to prepare future general, health, and special educators. Building upon Blanchett and Prater (2006), I propose that classroom teachers and teacher educators must be knowledgeable about eight major areas in the context of teaching sexuality and HIV/AIDS prevention to all students as a component of social justice:

1. Understand the importance of addressing the HIV/AIDS prevention education needs of all students, including students with disabilities, as a component of teaching for social justice.
2. Know the learning characteristics of all students, including those with disabilities, and their particular HIV/AIDS risk factors and behaviors as well as how disabilities can affect HIV/AIDS prevention instruction.
3. Understand how issues of race, class, culture, and gender can impact all students, including sexuality risk behaviors of students with disabilities and their access to appropriate HIV/AIDS prevention education.
4. Be comfortable discussing and addressing issues related to HIV/AIDS prevention such as death and dying, sexuality, disability, and the intersection of sexuality with disability, race, class, and culture.
5. Be familiar with developmentally appropriate HIV/AIDS curriculum and instruction for all students.
6. Gain expertise with adapting and modifying HIV/AIDS prevention education curricula and instructional materials and strategies for students with varying abilities.
7. Develop skills in forming and maintaining collaborative relationships with professionals essential to educating all students.
8. Be willing to deconstruct their own bias and perceptions regarding students' and issues of sexuality including students with disabilities.

If social justice is indeed, as Powers and Faden (2006) claim, the moral foundation of public health and health policy, it is reasonable to expect that a concerted effort would be made to ensure that those most vulnerable, marginalized, least privileged, and most in need would have access to appropriate health education, services, and resources.

References

Baker, J. L. (2005). Accountability issues in adolescent sexuality. *Sexual Science, 46*, N–O.

Blanchett, W. J. (2000). Sexual risk behaviors of young adults with LD and the need for HIV/AIDS education. *Remedial and Special Education, 21*(6), 336–345.

Blanchett, W. J. (2002). State of professional preparation of special educators in health education. In *Proceedings of the National Preservice Forum: Implications for professional preparation of special education teachers in health education* (pp. 10–12). Fairfax, VA: American Association for Health Education/American Alliance for Health, Physical Education, Recreation, and Dance.

Blanchett, W. J. (2006). Disproportionate representation of African Americans in special education: Acknowledging the role of White privilege and racism. *Educational Researcher (ER), 35*(6), 24–28.

Blanchett, W. J., & Prater, M. A. (2006). HIV/AIDS, Sexuality, & Disability. In L. M. Summerfield & C. A. Grant (Eds.), *Humanizing pedagogy through HIV and AIDS prevention: Transforming teacher knowledge. Coordinated by the American Association for Colleges of Teacher Education (AACTE)*. Boulder, CO: Paradigm.

Blauton, L. P., Griffin, C. G., Winn, J., & Pugach, M. C. (1997). *Teacher education in transition: Collaborative programs to prepare general and special educators*. Denver, CO: Lore Publishing.

Carroll, A., Forlin, C., & Jobling, A. (2003). The impact of teacher training in special education on the attitudes of Australian preservice general educators towards people with disabilities. *Teacher Education Quarterly, 30*(3), 65–79.

Centers for Disease Control and Prevention. (1988). Guidelines for effective school health education to prevent the spread of AIDS. *Morbidity and Mortality Weekly Report, 37*(S–2), 1–14.

Cochran-Smith, M. (2004). Defining the outcomes of teacher education: What's social justice got to do with it? *Asia-Pacific Journal of Teacher Education, 32*(3), 193–212.

Colson, S. E., & Carlson, J. K. (1993). HIV/AIDS education for students with special need. *Intervention in School and Clinic, 28*(5), 262–274.

Council for Exceptional Children. (1991). *HIV prevention education for exceptional youth: Why HIV prevention education is important* (ERIC Digest No. E507). Reston, VA: ERIC Clearinghouse on Handicapped and Gifted Children. (ERIC Document Reproduction Service No. ED340151)

Ellery, P. J., Rabak-Wagener, J., & Stacy, R. D. (1997). Special educators who teach health education: Their role and perceived ability. *Remedial and Special Education, 18,* 105–112.

Ferri, B. A., & Conner, D. J. (2005). Tools of exclusion: Race, disability, and (re)segregated education. *Teachers College Record, 107, 453–474.*

Foley, R. M. (1995). Special educators' competencies and preparation for the delivery of sex education. *Special Services in the Schools, 19*(1), 95–112.

Foley, R. M., & Dudzinski, M. (1995). Human sexuality education: Are special educators prepared to meet the educational needs of disabled youth? *Journal of Sex Education and Therapy, 21*(3), 182–191.

Foulk, D., Gessner, L. J., & Koorland, M. A. (2001). Human Immunodeficiency Virus/Acquired Immune Deficiency Syndrome (HIV/AIDS) content in introduction to exceptionalities textbooks. *Action in Teacher Education, 23*(1), 47–54.

Frauenknecht, M. (2003). *The need for effective professional preparation of school-based health educators.* Washington, D.C.: ERIC Clearinghouse on Teaching and Teacher Education. (ED482701)

Gay, G. (2000). *Culturally responsive teaching: Theory, research, and practice.* New York: Teachers College Press.

Hausman, A. J., & Ruzek, S. B. (1995). Implementation of comprehensive school health education in elementary schools: Focus on teacher concerns. *The Journal of School Health, 65,* 81–86.

Kann, L., Warren, C. W., Harris, W. A., Collins, J. L., Williams, B. I., Ross, J. G., & Kolbe, L. J. (1996, September 27). Youth risk behavior surveillance—United States, 1995. *Morbidity and Mortality Weekly Report. CDC Surveillance Summaries, 45*(SS-4), 1–83.

Lavin, A. T., Porter, S. M., Shaw, D. M., Weill, K. S., Crocker, A. C., & Palfrey, J. S. (1994). School health services in the age of AIDS. *Journal of School Health, 64,* 27–31.

Lombard, R. C., Miller, R. J., & Hazelkorn, M. N. (1998). School-to-work and technical preparation: Teacher attitudes and practices regarding the inclusion of students with disabilities. *Career Development for Exceptional Individuals, 21,* 161–172.

May, D. C., & Kundert, D. K. (1996). Are special educators prepared to meet the sex education needs of their students? A progress report. *The Journal of Special Education, 29*(4), 433–441.

May, D., Kundert, D., & Akpan, C. (1994). Are we preparing special educators for the issues facing schools in the 1990s? *Teacher Education and Special Education, 17*(3), 192–199.

Murrell, P. C. (2006). Toward social justice in urban education: A model of collaborative cultural inquiry in urban schools. *Equity & Excellence in Education, 39,* 81–90.

Pardini, P. (2002–2003). Abstinence-only education continues to flourish. *Rethinking Schools: An Urban Educational Journal, 17*(2), 14–17.

Powers, M., & Faden, R. (2006). *Social justice: The moral foundations of public health and health policy.* New York: Oxford University Press.

Prater, M. A., Serna, L. A., Sileo, T. W., & Katz, A. R. (1995). HIV disease: Implications for special educators. *Remedial and Special Education, 16,* 68–78.

Prater, M. A., Sileo, T. W., & Black, R. S. (2000). Preparing educators and related school personnel to work with at-risk students. *Teacher Education and Special Education, 23,* 51–64.

Price, J., Drake, J., Kirchofer, G., & Tellijohann, S. (2003). Elementary school teachers' techniques of responding to student questions regarding sexuality issues. *Journal of School Health, 73*(1), 9–14.

Rabak-Wagener, J., Ellery, P. J., & Stacy, R. D. (1997). An analysis of health education provided to students with disabilities in Nebraska. *Journal of Health Education, 28*, 165–170.

Rodriguez, M., Young, R., Renfro, S., Asencio, M., & Haffner, D. W. (1996). Teaching our teachers to teach: A SIECUS study on training and preparation for HIV/AIDS prevention and sexuality education. *SIECUS Report, 28*(2).

Rodriguez, M., Young, R., Renfro, S., Asencio, M., & Haffner, D. W. (1997). Teaching our teachers to teach: A study on preparation for sexuality education and HIV/AIDS prevention. *Journal of Psychology and Human Sexuality, 9*(3/4), 121–141.

Skripak, D., & Summerfield, L. (1996). *HIV/AIDS education in teacher preparation programs.* Washington, D.C.: ERIC Clearinghouse on Teaching and Teacher Education. (ED403264)

Ubbes, V. A., Cottrell, R. R., Ausherman, J. A., Black, J. M., Wilson, P., Gill, C., & Snider, J. (1999). Professional preparation of elementary teachers in Ohio: Status of K-6 health education. *Journal of School Health, 69* 17–21.

U.S. Department of Education. (2002). *To assure the free appropriate public education of all children with disabilities. Twenty-fourth annual report to Congress on the implementation of the Individuals with Disabilities Education Act.* Washington, D.C.: Author.

Walker, J., Sambamoorthi, U., & Crystal, S. (1999). Characteristics of persons with mental retardation and HIV/AIDS infection in a statewide Medicaid population. *American Journal on Mental Retardation, 104*, 356–363.

23 Unintentional Gender Lessons in the Schools

Andrew P. Smiler

For most children, schooling represents their first contact with a governmental institution of social control. As such, schools provide an important setting for transmitting socially held values. These social values include beliefs about gender-appropriate behavior, and most of these lessons are transmitted informally through school structures, teachers' comments, curricula, and students themselves. These gender lessons are particularly important in America, where gender is an organizing cultural principle (Bem, 1993) that influences academic and vocational performance and choices, family roles, sexual behavior, and other aspects of daily life such as "polite" behavior. Within a patriarchal and heterosexist society that purports to have prohibited gender-based discrimination and sexual harassment, we might question what lessons students learn about gender and how they do so.

In this chapter, gender is defined as a set of socially constructed expectations about the roles and behaviors that are identified as "appropriate"[1] and "expected" for girls and boys.[2] For American girls, these expectations include being kind, caring, deferring to others, focusing on their appearance, enacting a passive or reactive approach to dating and sexuality, and, eventually, becoming primary caregivers in their families. By contrast, boys are expected to be independent and unemotional, seek status and power, take an active or agentic role in the dating and sexual realms, and become the primary bread-winners in their families. The result of these paired expectations is that members of the population are encouraged to focus on only certain gender-appropriate aspects of their personality and their interests, while abandoning others because they are "inappropriate." For educators, this may translate into differences in classroom participation rates (i.e., girls deferring to boys) as well as course preferences and encouragements (e.g., for girls in English courses, for boys in math). Ultimately, this might lead to later vocational and occupational differences such as women's "choice" to leave the workforce to be an at-home parent and the "wage gap." Taken to the extreme, the combination of female passivity and reactivity along with male status and violence may lead to situations that facilitate domestic violence. Creation of a just society requires that these discrepancies—based upon American preferences related to biology—be addressed and eliminated so that individuals have the opportunity to make life-choices that will help them achieve their full potential without being restricted by cultural assumptions about gender.

In this chapter, I explore the ways in which schools contribute to and reinforce these gender roles, as well as ways in which schools can counter these messages. Particular attention is given to the ways in which gender roles are highlighted and enforced by the school structure and students, as well as the outcomes of conformity and non-conformity to gender roles. I begin with a more detailed discussion of the "content" of femininity and masculinity and children's adherence to these ideals, followed by the ways in which schools, teachers, and children highlight, maintain, and enforce these boundaries and the consequences for those who violate gendered expectations. Discussion then shifts to two specific sites of interaction between the school and students. The first of these sites explores the gender-typed messages in extracurricular activities, especially athletics, and the second focuses on adolescents' romantic and sexual relationships. The chapter ends with a brief discussion of challenges to the institutionalized binary conception of gender. Each section of the chapter includes ways in which gendered-expectations might be minimized and equality achieved.

Gender Content and (Non-)Conformity

At present, American culture places pleasing others at the center of cultural expectations of femininity. Accordingly, girls and women are taught to prioritize personal relationships, express emotion, defer to others, be nice, and be physically attractive (i.e., be visually pleasing) while also remaining virginal (to please their future husband) (Mahalik et al., 2005; Tolman & Porche, 2000). Combinations of these directives instruct girls to avoid direct interpersonal conflict and to privilege others' feelings and perspectives over their own. Boys and men receive a cultural message that emphasizes being not-feminine. They are directed to be unemotional, take risks, be in charge/make decisions, be tough, and be sexually promiscuous (Connell, 1995; David & Brannon, 1976; O'Neil, Helms, Gable, David, & Wrightsman, 1986). Combinations of these directives instruct boys to control women. Directives for girls and boys influence individual beliefs, traits, and behaviors. It is important to note that these gender ideals have changed over time in the United States (Kimmel, 1996; Stearns, 1994); vary across cultures (Connell, 1995; Gilmore, 1990; Herdt, 1994); and limit the gender options to two (Gilmore, 1990; Herdt, 1994).

In the United States, these conceptions of femininity and masculinity are often conceived of as opposites (Bem, 1993), although they may be better understood as complements. This positioning contributes to the idea that homosexuality represents "gender inversion" (see Bem, 1993 for discussion) and the stereotyping of gay men as "effeminate." Scientific investigation, as well as anecdotal evidence (e.g., "lipstick lesbians"), indicate that gender is separate from sexual orientation (L. Diamond, 2003; M. Diamond, 2002).

From the time children enter elementary school until their midteens, the average child tends to show greater conformity to gendered notions of appropriate behavior; there is a slight decline in gender-appropriate behavior among older teens (Galambos, Almeida, & Petersen, 1990; Liben & Bigler, 2002; McHale, Updegraff, Helms-Erikson, & Crouter, 2001). Theoretical and empirical approaches have highlighted the input of parents and other family members, age-mates, schools, and the media through explicit teaching (e.g., "boys don't cry") and children's observations of sex-segregated activities (e.g., Bem, 1993; Eckes & Trautner, 2000; Gelman, Taylor, & Nguyen, 2004). It is important to note that most youth also demonstrate a low to moderate level of gender-inappropriate behavior during this time (Chu, Porche, & Tolman, 2005; Liben & Bigler, 2002; Pleck, Sonenstein, & Ku, 1993, 1994; Tolman & Porche, 2000) and that some youth are more nonconforming than conforming (Striepe & Tolman, 2003).

Thorne's (1993) ethnography provides a detailed examination of children's gendered behavior within schools. Over the course of two years at two different elementary schools, she observed children before, during, and after the school day. Children rewarded each other's gender conformity through social acceptance, inclusion, and higher status (e.g., popularity). She observed that gender enforcement was particularly common among students whose teachers highlighted gender, especially through comparisons between girls and boys. Thorne also noted that the importance and attention to gender varied throughout the day and could shift from one moment to the next. She described, for example, an occasion when a boy and a girl were playing tennis against each other and had not mentioned their gender; they were simply playing against each other. After several other children joined the game and the configuration eventually became two girls playing against two boys, the children then described the game as girls against boys. This label arose only after the active players fit the categories.

Although the importance of gender varies throughout the day, children consistently notice both gender-appropriate and gender-inappropriate behavior. Children and adolescents who violate gender norms often find themselves excluded and ridiculed by both same-sex and other-sex peers (Bartlett, Vasey, & Bukowski, 2002; Bem, 1993; Striepe & Tolman, 2003; Thorne, 1994), and boys are often punished more harshly than girls (Bartlett et al., 2002; Maccoby, 1998). Some gender nonconforming children are eventually diagnosed with Gender Identity Disorder (GID) (American Psychiatric Association, 1994), which is indicated by strong and persistent cross-gender identification, including preference for clothing and activities typically associated with the other gender. Depression and poor self-esteem are also common, but are not indicative of GID. When brought to treatment, these children typically complain about the reactions of family, peers, and others to their behavior; they are rarely disturbed by their own "gender-discrepant" behavior (Bartlett et al., 2002; Bradley & Zucker, 1997). Treatment emphasizes the acquisition of gender-typical behavior and the reduction of gender-atypical behavior (Bradley & Zucker, 1997). Although these children receive a psychiatric diagnosis, their "problem" is one of not being accepted by the people in their environment and their "cure" is conformity.

Overall, children experience an environment that prioritizes conformity to cultural expectations over individual preferences. Pressure is transmitted through social exclusion and ostracism, which appears to lead to low self-esteem and depression. Moreover, the mental health system is complicit in enforcing these norms (by identifying nonconformity as a diagnosable illness and prescribing conformity) and may further stigmatize those who are now officially "different." This system of gender enforcement leads to a restriction of individual preferences and maltreatment of those who violate social gender norms.

Things may be changing, however. GID has recently been questioned as a valid diagnostic category (e.g., Bartlett et al., 2002). Evidence indicates that less than 10% of GID diagnosed children maintain this diagnosis into adolescence or adulthood but more than 60% of GID diagnosed children self-identify as gay men, lesbians, or bisexuals during adolescence or adulthood (Bartlett et al., 2002, 2003; Bradley & Zucker, 1997, 1998). This long term evidence suggests that the childhood GID diagnosis is an excellent predictor of later homosexuality. Because homosexuality is no longer considered a mental illness, some have argued that GID should also lose its status as a mental illness. It seems likely that the GID diagnosis is being used to "catch" gay youth and force them into therapy; GID treatment may be directed at changing sexual orientation (Pickstone-Taylor, 2002), a treatment goal that the American Association of Pediatrics, the American Psychological Association, and the National Association of Social Workers, among others, have deemed unacceptable (Just the Facts, n.d.).

Extracurricular Activities

From the summer of 2004 through its settlement in the spring of 2005, American sports fans and other news watchers received regular updates on the sexual harassment charges filed against basketball star Kobe Bryant. For many observers, the most unique aspect of the case was the fact that criminal charges were filed against an elite player; criminal trials of lower-status professional athletes had become commonplace. Such crimes have also been committed by high school athletes, perhaps the most shocking of which was the gang rape of a developmentally delayed adolescent girl by the all-male Glen Ridge, New Jersey high school football team (Lefkowitz, 1998). Accordingly, we might then ask what it is about male athletics and athletes that fosters these behaviors. (To my knowledge, there have been no accusations of this sort against female athletes.)

Examinations of high school athletics are particularly important because extracurricular activities (of all types) provide an important context for adolescent development (Eccles, Barber, Stone, & Hunt, 2003). Surveys consistently show that 70 to 80% of adolescents report participating in at least one extracurricular activity (Brown & Theobald, 1998). One sample of upper-middle class American high school students reported a 93% participation rate in extracurricular activities, with an average of 7.7 hours per week in school-based athletic activities (and 4.9 hours per week in non-school-based athletics) (Fuligni & Stevenson, 1995).

It is important to note that these settings are not value free, and that adolescents can and do acquire value messages from these settings. James Youniss has been particularly interested in how adolescents' values are related to and influenced by their experiences. His review of the literature indicates that adolescents who participate in "service" or "prosocial" activities (e.g., volunteering) tend to be more motivated by moral and political beliefs and values than their peers. Volunteering typically reinforces these beliefs and values and tends to increase the differences between adolescents who volunteer and those who do not (Yates & Youniss, 1996). More importantly, these activities emphasize "feminine" characteristics such as care for others and cooperation, values that underlie many social justice movements.

By contrast, athletics provide a different set of values. The most obvious of these is competition, which is inherent in any athletic contest. Interviews with retired professional, semiprofessional, and amateur (e.g., collegiate, Olympic) male athletes revealed that athletes also competed with teammates and friends in a variety of realms outside of their sport, including competition for girlfriends (Messner, 1992). At the cultural level, the most prominent American men's team sports (e.g., football, basketball) have been described as homophobic and sexist (Adams & Bettis, 2003; Messner, 1992). One ethnographic study of Little League baseball revealed this pattern of sexism and antihomosexuality among the boys and some of their male coaches; less-skilled boys and boys who violated social norms were called "sissies," "girly," or "fags" (G. Fine, 1987). In addition, (professional) media tend to disproportionately emphasize men's sports, discuss women's personality characteristics and appearance (but not men's), and otherwise minimize or deemphasize women's abilities (Billings, Halone, & Denham, 2002; Sabo & Jansen, 1992). Overall, athletics and its media presentation emphasizes many aspects of the currently dominant image of masculinity (see also David & Brannon, 1976; G. Fine, 1987; Messner, 1992; Smiler, 2006).

Collectively, these findings suggest that participation in extracurricular activities leads to greater adoption of the values associated with those activities. Volunteer activities, not surprisingly, promote values such as cooperation and caretaking that are associated with many social justice movements, whereas athletics tend to promote patriarchal values. Because these values are also consistent with cultural notions of femininity and masculinity, service is likely perceived as less valuable than athletics and may be less appealing to many youth. If these implicit values translate into later beliefs and behaviors, then they set the stage for women to be overrepresented in service-oriented professions and overrepresented at (less competitive) lower levels of the corporate ladder. In addition to maintaining the imbalance of men in powerful positions, these "outcomes" would also lead to lower wages for women and would thus maintain women's financial dependence on men.

There are several ways in which extracurricular activities might be altered or examined that could diminish these effects. One approach would be to minimize the prominence of sports over other activities. A quick examination of my own high school yearbook, as well as the current yearbook of my local school district, reveals a substantially greater number of pages (and presumably faculty positions) devoted to athletic activities than all other activities (combined). I suspect that high school newspapers and other vehicles for informing students are similarly biased toward athletics, and do not routinely mention other activity groups. And to the extent that student-run news sources (e.g., newspaper, radio) mimic professional media, the presentation may be biased in favor of male over female athletes (Billings et al., 2002; Sabo & Jansen, 1992). Accordingly, school staff responsible for these media could promote equality (of activities) by requiring parity in coverage of athletic and nonathletic activities, as well as equal coverage of women and men.

The classroom is another potential site of intervention. Here, students could be helped to think critically about the "texts" that accompany professional sports. Differences in the amount and placement of text in local newspapers are obvious; differential treatment in the use of first names (a diminutive, for women) and surnames (respectful, for men) and the focus on personality and appearance would likely become apparent with relatively little effort. Questions could also be directed to often undiscussed topics, such as the relative paucity of media coverage of women's sports, the presentation of women as sexual objects (e.g., *Sports Illustrated*'s swimsuit edition), or the participation of sexual minority members (and the lack of televised images of the partners of gay male athletes). This deconstruction process would help students recognize the narratives employed and their associated values, and is a necessary first step in questioning the status quo.

This deconstruction could also be used to illuminate distinctions based on ethnicity and social class. Messner's (1992) interviews suggested that children's and adolescents' choice of sport are guided in direct and subtle ways based on the youth's ethnicity and social class; non-Whites and members of lower classes tended to be steered toward more violent sports (e.g., boxing, football). In addition, descriptions of ethnic minority group members likely differ across sections of the newspaper (e.g., sports, local news). The influence of social class could also be examined, particularly as it relates to a child or adolescent's ability to pay for equipment, league fees, and training/coaching. Examination of these patterns would help students challenge stereotypes and identify systemic inequalities regarding access.

Dating and Sex

More than half of American high school seniors report voluntary experience with coitus prior to their high school graduation (Centers for Disease Control and Prevention, 2005). Many more report voluntary experiences of oral sex (especially fellatio) and the vast majority (>90%) report passionate (or "French") kissing (Darling & Davidson, 1987; Horne & Zimmer-Gembeck, 2005; O'Sullivan, 2005). These activity rates are broadly similar to other industrialized countries, such as England, France, and Sweden (Haggstrom-Nordin, Hanson, & Tyden, 2002; Hofstede, 1998; Ponton & Judice, 2004), but American adolescents report a substantially greater proportion of pregnancy, abortion, and sexually transmitted infections (STIs) (Hofstede, 1998). Gendered behavior plays a key role in this. Adolescent boys who report greater adherence to masculine norms tend to view dating as more adversarial, report greater levels of control of their girlfriends, are less likely to use condoms, and are more likely to believe that their girlfriends have primary responsibility for birth control (Chu et al., 2005; Pleck et al., 1993, 1994). At the same time, adolescent girls who report greater adherence to feminine norms report greater difficulty discussing birth control with their partners and are less likely to use birth control (Tolman, 2002; Ward & Wyatt, 1994). These are important issues for schools not only because they affect the health and potential life courses of adolescents, but also because most adolescents find dating and sexual partners within school-based face-to-face (vs. online) social networks (Wolak, Mitchell, & Finkelhor, 2002).

Most adolescents begin to date during adolescence, and the age at which this behavior begins is more closely related to the adolescents' social maturity than to biological puberty (Zimmer-Gembeck, Siebrenbrunner, & Collins, 2004). Data on heterosexual activity from adolescents and undergraduates suggest that an individual's first romantic kiss typically occurs before age 14 (O'Sullivan, 2005; Smith & Udry, 1985) and first voluntary intercourse occurs around age 17 (Oliver & Hyde, 1993; Smiler, Ward, Caruthers, & Merriwether, 2005). Less is known about youth with same-sex attractions, but the data suggest that first voluntary same-sex genital sexual activity also occurs around age 17 (Savin-Williams, 2005).

As with any "new" behavior, adolescents begin with no direct experience. In contrast to many (all?) other adult-sanctioned behaviors for adolescents, adults provide adolescents with relatively little guidance either before or after they start dating. Research with high school students and undergraduates reveals that parents typically provide "not" messages (e.g., "do not have intercourse," "do not get pregnant or impregnate anyone") and stress the importance of love (Smiler et al., 2005; Ward & Wyatt, 1994). American schools provide similar messages, when they address the issue at all (Irvine, 2002; Levine, 2002). This pattern indicates that adults are withholding information from adolescents (a form of "adultism"). The lack of information does not seem to prevent adolescents from experiencing coitus, but appears to inhibit their ability to use or access items that would prevent disease transmission and pregnancy. Potential results include unwanted pregnancies and STIs, including herpes and HIV, all of which could potentially be avoided if adults provided adolescents with the necessary knowledge and resources.

When adolescents are provided with sex education in schools, it typically consists of an "abstinence-only" curriculum that presents abstinence as the only method of disease and pregnancy prevention, emphasizes the failure rates of contraceptive devices, addresses only heterosexual behavior, and reinforces gendered notions of sexuality (sexually driven males and gatekeeping females). Since the mid-1990s, American schools that accept federal funds have been increasingly required to adopt this curriculum (Irvine, 2002; Levine, 2002). Unfortunately, the evidence suggests that these programs have little effect on the general adolescent population (Rostosky, Regenerus, & Comer-Wright, 2003; see review by Ponton & Judice, 2004). These programs may only benefit adolescents who were comparatively more religious than their peers; religious adolescents are more likely to abstain or defer their first coitus (Miller, Norton, Fan, & Christopherson, 1998; Rostosky, Wilcox, Comer-Wright, & Randall, 2004). Reviews of methodologically rigorous empirical studies rely on a relatively small number of published findings and indicate that students who receive abstinence-only sex education have less contraceptive knowledge and may be more likely to become pregnant or impregnate someone (Bennett & Assefi, 2005; DiCenso, Guyatt, Willan, & Griffith, 2002).

Desirous of information, adolescents may then turn to the Internet. Here, they may also find abstinence oriented websites, as well as websites that adopt a "comprehensive" approach such as Columbia University's "Go ask Alice" (www.goaskalice.com). These websites include instruction on the use and success rates of contraceptive devices, discuss relationship issues, and (typically) address sexual minority issues (Bay-Cheng, 2001; see also M. Fine, 1988). However, these websites may be difficult to separate from the pornographic websites also identified by search engines (Bay-Cheng, 2001; M. Smith, Gertz, Alvarez, & Lurie, 2000). Adults who hope to prevent adolescents from accessing pornography or encountering "obscene" language on the Internet through the use of filtering software may also prevent adolescents from accessing these sites, and may again deny information to adolescents.

Given the general lack of information from parents and schools, it should be no surprise that adolescents tend to identify their peers and the media as the two most important sources of sexual information (Sutton, Brown, Wilson, & Klein, 2002). Popular media, which provide demonstrations of how to behave in romantic and sexual situations, may be consulted privately, repeatedly, and with little/no fear of embarrassment, and thus are a particularly important source of information. Unfortunately, mainstream media are heavily stereotyped and present an image of male sexuality that is natural, promiscuous, and power-oriented alongside an image of female sexuality that is sexually appealing, sexually chaste, and responsible for limiting men's sexuality; discussions of pregnancy and disease protection are extremely rare (Carpenter, 1998; Kunkel, Eyal, Finnerty, Biely, & Donnnerstein, 2005; Ward, 1995). Recent evidence has revealed that adolescents who are exposed to greater amounts of sexual content on television, as well as greater amounts of degrading musical lyrics, report an earlier age of first intercourse and a faster progression through "precoital" behaviors (e.g., petting; oral sex) (Collins et al., 2004; Martino et al., 2006).

Collectively, these findings suggest that the minimal and largely stereotypical portrayal of dating and sexuality to which American adolescents are exposed does little to prepare them for the realities of sexual behavior and likely contributes to an environment where STIs and pregnancy, both of which are easily preventable, occur with greater frequency than they otherwise might. This situation places the health and the future of adolescents in jeopardy, and it does so simply because adults refuse to provide adolescents with the information and materials they need to care for themselves.

The most obvious—and most controversial—solution would be for schools to provide more substantive sexual education. This would allow schools to provide adolescents with the information they need; that is, schools could genuinely educate adolescents about sexuality. Moreover, if schools were to adopt a normative or "positive" approach to sexual development and behavior (Haffner, 1998; Russell, 2005), they could acknowledge that sexual development is part of growing up and that individuals vary in the rate and ways in which they demonstrate their sexuality. Further, educators could contextualize sexuality within a relational and health-promoting framework that would highlight the importance of values, decision-making, mutual respect, and responsibility. The Sexuality Information and Education Center of the United States website (http://www.siecus.org), includes a "clearinghouse" of sexuality education curricula that have been empirically validated.

Less obvious, but still highly useful, would be for teachers to help students think critically about the sexualized "texts" they see in the media. Here, students might analyze the content of popular magazines such as *Seventeen* or popular television shows and deconstruct the portrayals of ever-present male sexual desire and women's roles as gatekeepers (e.g., Carpenter, 1998; Ward, 1995). Critical examination of these stories would help students recognize this particular portrayal of sexuality, which likely does not match their own experience. Omitted stories, such as safer sex discussions and techniques, homosexuality, female sexual desire, and male refusal could also be discussed in the classroom. This broadening of the conversation would provide students with a wider range of behaviors to choose from, alleviate pressure to conform to gendered patterns of sexual behavior, and would be more inclusive of sexual minorities. As a result, students with varying experiences would likely see a connection between their own experiences and the curriculum, thus facilitating learning. More importantly, it would emphasize the diversity of actual experience.

Binary Constructions of Gender and School Structure

Around the United States, schools are increasingly being challenged on policies based on the binary American gender system that identifies many activities as either "feminine" or "masculine" and prohibits individuals from crossing these boundaries. The current challenges are very different from the push for equality in offerings in the 1970s. In the last few years, children, adolescents, and their parents, occasionally with legal representation, have sought to violate American gender norms. In one instance, a Finnish adolescent boy residing in the United States was not allowed to play field hockey because his high school categorized it as a women's sport; in his native Finland, the game is played by both women and men (Kadaba & Shea, 2005; see also "ACLU wants boys allowed in high school cheer tourney," 2006). Greater controversy is raised in instances where a child sees her- or himself as a member of the other sex ("transgendered") and wishes to be treated as such (Pfeiffer & Daniel, 2000; Reischel, 2002). In the typical case, a biological male who identifies as female wants permission to function as a girl, including being recognized by a different name than appears on his birth certificate, wearing girls' clothing (which may violate school policy), and in some cases, using the girls' bathroom and (physical education) changing rooms. Schools are also asked to protect these children from gender and sexual harassment.

Schools could expand harassment differences to include gender-based insults. Perhaps more effective would be the elimination of gender comparative processes within schools. Thorne's (1994) research revealed that children in classrooms where teachers did not highlight sex differences were less likely to use this categorization themselves. Recently, Rebecca Bigler (2006) has drawn parallels between efforts to end gender prejudice and discrimination and earlier efforts to end racial prejudice and discrimination. Noting that any teacher who began class with "Good morning Whites and Blacks" would quickly be fired and potentially jailed, she has asked why teachers should be allowed to begin with "Good morning girls and boys"? Similarly, teachers might ask children to form two lines based on color of footwear (e.g., light vs. dark) instead of sex.

Finally, lessons on gender could be explicitly incorporated into the curriculum. Although many such lessons exist, from discussions of gender-specific expectations as they relate to literature to the influence of the women's movements on U.S. history, they typically focus on the outcomes of gender differentiation. Lessons that question the idea that there are only two genders (and two biological sexes) would help students develop critical thinking skills, while also acknowledging the transgendered and intersexed populations, who are presently ignored (for examples, see Gilmore, 1990; Herdt, 1994). Lessons that identify occasions where gender is and is not important, highlight findings that most children and adolescents display only moderate levels of enactment of gender norms, and emphasize similarities between women and men would facilitate equality and minimize belief that there is a "battle of the sexes." Discussion of the ways in which gender roles limit different aspects of human functioning, especially when combined with cross-cultural examples (e.g., emotionally expressive Italian men and emotionally stoic American men) would facilitate students' understanding of culture and the ways in which cultures construct gender. Broadly, attention to these topics would likely increase the range of acceptable behavior for girls and boys and minimize the "naturalness" of gender.

If our goal is to create a truly just society, we must explicitly address gender in a meaningful way in schools. Ideally, this would occur through explicit inclusion and discussion of gender as part of the curriculum. Curricular changes are not sufficient, however. Teachers, administrators, and other involved adults must also demonstrate greater tolerance for those who transcend strict American gender categories, much as they accepted and encouraged women's struggles for greater access to education and prestigious occupations in the 1970s. As such, educational institutions must demonstrate greater tolerance for gender "atypical" behavior and support a broader diversity of genders within the school. Ultimately, schools should become a place where gender categories (and their associated biological categories) become irrelevant to the day to day lives of students, teachers, and staff. Elimination of these subtle sources of gender bias, combined with explicit examination of beliefs about gender, will allow children to achieve their full potential without having to struggle against restrictive cultural assumptions about gender.

Notes

1. Throughout this chapter, I will discuss (gender-)appropriate and (gender-)inappropriate behavior. This choice is consistent with much of the literature on children's gender-related behavior. However, because the appropriateness of such behaviors is determined by our culture, more accurate terms might be "culturally desired gender-related behavior" or "culturally appropriate gendered behavior." These terms should be understood as equivalent.
2. Although I speak of only two biological sexes, female and male, humans are not sorted into only these two biological categories. Intersexuality has become increasingly recognized since the early 21st century, largely as the result of biologist Anne Fausto-Sterling's (2000) *Sexing the Body* and the activism of Cheryl Chase, who founded the Intersexual Society of North America. Fausto-Sterling argues that there are (at least) five sexes.

References

ACLU wants boys allowed in high school cheer tourney. (2006, June 24). *Chicago Tribune.* Retrieved June 24, 2006, from http://www.chicagotribune.com/news/local

Adams, N., & Bettis, P. (2003). Commanding the room in short skirts: Cheering as the embodiment of ideal girlhood. *Gender and Society, 17,* 73–91.

American Psychiatric Association. (1994). *Diagnostic and statistical manual of mental disorders* (4th ed.). Washington, D.C.: Author.

Bartlett, N. H., Vasey, P. L., & Bukowski, W. M. (2002). Is gender identity disorder in children a mental disorder. *Sex Roles, 43,* 753–785.

Bartlett, N. H., Vasey, P. L., & Bukowski, W. M. (2003). Cross-sex wishes and gender identity disorder in children: A reply to Zucker (2002). *Sex Roles, 49,* 191–192.

Bay-Cheng, L. Y. (2001). Sexed.Com: Values and norms in web-based sexuality education. *Journal of Sex Research, 38,* 241–251.

Bem, S. L. (1993). *The lenses of gender.* New Haven, CT: Yale University Press.

Bennett, S. E., & Assefi, N. P. (2005). School-based teenage pregnancy prevention programs: A systematic review of randomized controlled trials. *Journal of Adolescent Health, 36,* 72–81.

Bigler, R. (2006, April 22). *Viva la difference or vanquish la difference.* Panel discussant at the Second Gender Development Research Conference, San Francisco, CA.

Billings, A. C., Halone, K. K., & Denham, B. E. (2002). "Man, that was a pretty shot": An analysis of gendered broadcast commentary surrounding the 2000 men's and women's NCAA final four basketball championships. *Mass Communication & Society, 5,* 295–315.

Bradley, S. J., & Zucker, K. J. (1997). Gender identity disorder: A review of the past 10 years. *Journal of the American Academy of Child and Adolescent Psychiatry, 36*, 872–880.

Bradley, S. J., & Zucker, K. J. (1998). Gender identity disorder. *Journal of the American Academy of Child and Adolescent Psychiatry, 37*, 244–245.

Brown, B. B., & Theobald, W. (1998). Learning contexts beyond the classroom: Extracurricular activities, community organizations and peer groups. In K. Borman & B. Schneider (Eds.), *The adolescent years: Social influences and educational challenges* (pp. 109–141). Chicago: University of Chicago Press.

Carpenter, L. M. (1998). From girls into women: Scripts for sexuality and romance in *Seventeen* magazine, 1974–1994. *Journal of Sex Research, 35*, 158–168.

Centers for Disease Control and Prevention. (2005). Youth risk behavior surveillance—United States, 2005. *Morbidity and Mortality Weekly Report, 55*(SS-5). Atlanta, GA: Author.

Chu, J. Y., Porche, M. V., & Tolman, D. L. (2005). The adolescent masculinity ideology in relationships scale: Development and validation of a new measure for boys. *Men and Masculinities, 8*, 93–115.

Collins, R. L., Elliott, M. N., Berry, S. H., Kanouse, D. E., Kunkel, D., Hunter, S. B., et al. (2004). Watching sex on television predicts adolescent initiation of sexual behavior. *Pediatrics, 114*, e280–e289.

Connell, R. W. (1995). *Masculinities*. Berkeley, CA: University of California Press.

Darling, C. A., & Davidson, S., J. K. (1987). The relationship of sexual satisfaction to coital involvement: The concept of technical virginity revisited. *Deviant Behavior, 8*, 27–46.

David, D., & Brannon, R. (1976). The male sex role: Our culture's blueprint for manhood and what it's done for us lately. In D. David & R. Brannon (Eds.), *The forty-nine percent majority: The male sex role* (pp. 1–48). Reading, MA: Addison-Wesley.

Diamond, L. M. (2003). New paradigms for research on heterosexual and sexual-minority development. *Journal of Clinical Child and Adolescent Psychiatry, 32*, 490–498.

Diamond, M. (2002). Sex and gender are different; sexual identity and gender identity are different. *Clinical Child Psychology and Psychiatry, 7*, 320–334.

DiCenso, A., Guyatt, G., Willan, A., & Griffith, L. (2002). Interventions to reduce unintended pregnancies among adolescents: Systematic review of randomised controlled trials. *British Medical Journal, 324*, 1426–1430.

Eccles, J. S., Barber, B. L., Stone, M., & Hunt, J. (2003). Extracurricular activities and adolescent development. *Journal of Social Issues, 59*, 865–889.

Eckes, T., & Trautner, H. M. (2000). Developmental social psychology of gender: An integrative framework. In T. Eckes & H. M. Trautner (Eds.), *The developmental social psychology of gender* (pp. 3–32). Mahwah, NJ: Lawrence Erlbaum.

Fausto-Sterling, A. (2000). *Sexing the body*. New York: Basic Books.

Fine, G. A. (1987). *With the boys: Little League baseball and preadolescent culture*. Chicago: University of Chicago press.

Fine, M. (1988). Sexuality, schooling, and adolescent females: The missing discourse of desire. *Harvard Educational Review, 58*, 29–53.

Fuligni, A. J., & Stevenson, H. W. (1995). Time use and mathematics achievement among American, Chinese and Japanese high school students. *Child Development, 66*, 830–842.

Galambos, N. L., Almeida, D. M., & Petersen, A. C. (1990). Masculinity, femininity, and sex role attitudes in early adolescence: Exploring gender intensification. *Child Development, 61*, 1905–1914.

Gelman, S. A., Taylor, M. G., & Nguyen, S. P. (2004). Mother–child conversations about gender. *Monographs of the Society for Research in Child Development, 60*(1, Serial No. 275).

Gilmore, D. D. (1990). *Manhood in the making: Cultural concepts of masculinity*. New Haven, CT: Yale University Press.

Haffner, D. W. (1998). Facing facts: Sexual health for American adolescents. *Journal of Adolescent Health, 22*, 453–459.

Haggstrom-Nordin, E., Hanson, U., & Tyden, T. (2002). Sex behavior among high school students in Sweden: Improvement in contraceptive use over time. *Journal of Adolescent Health, 30*, 288–295.

Herdt, G. (Ed.). (1994). *Third sex, third gender: Beyond sexual dimorphism in culture and history*. New York: Zone Books.

Hofstede, G. (1998). Comparative studies of sexual behavior: Sex as achievement or as relationship? In G. Hofstede (Ed.), *Masculinity and femininity: Taboo dimensions of national culture* (pp. 153–178). Thousand Oaks, CA: Sage.

Horne, S., & Zimmer-Gembeck, M. J. (2005). Female sexual subjectivity and well-being: Comparing late adolescents with different sexual experiences. *Sexual Research and Social Policy: Journal of NSRC, 2*, 25–40.

Irvine, J. M. (2002). *Talk about sex: The battles over sex education in the United States*. Berkeley, CA: University of California Press.

Just the facts about sexual orientation and youth: A primer for principals, educators, and school personnel. (n.d.). Retrieved December 3, 2006 from, http://www.apa.org/pi/lgbc/publications/justthefacts.html#2

Kadaba, L. S., & Shea, K. B. (2005, October 21st). Boys on girls' teams drive gender debate. *Philadelphia Inquirer*. Retrieved October 21, 2005 from, http://www.philly.com/mld/philly/sports/high_school/12960553.htm

Kimmel, M. (1996). *Manhood in America: A cultural history*. New York: The Free Press.

Kunkel, D., Eyal, K., Finnerty, K., Biely, E., & Donnerstein, E. (2005). *Sex on TV* (Vol. 4). Menlo Park, CA: Henry J. Kaiser Family Foundation.

Lefkowitz, B. (1998) *Our guys*. New York: Vintage Books.

Levine, J. (2002). *Harmful to minors: The perils of protecting children from sex*. Minneapolis: University of Minnesota Press.

Liben, L. S., & Bigler, R. S. (2002). *The developmental course of gender differentiation*. Conceptualizing. measuring, and evaluating constructs and pathways. Preview Monographs of the Society for Research in Child Development, 67(2), vii–147.

Maccoby, E. E. (1998). *The two sexes: Growing up apart, coming together*. Cambridge, MA: Belknap Press.

Mahalik, J. R., Morray, E. B., Coonerty-Femiano, A., Ludlow, L. H., Slattery, S. M., & Smiler, A. P. (2005). Development of the conformity to feminine norms inventory. *Sex Roles, 52*, 417–435.

Martino, S. C., Collins, R. L., Elliott, M. N., Strachman, A., Kanouse, D. E., & Berry, S. H. (2006). Exposure to degrading versus nondegrading music lyrics and sexual behavior among youth. *Pediatrics, 118*, 430–441.

McHale, S. M., Updegraff, K. A., Helms-Erikson, H., & Crouter, A. C. (2001). Sibling influences on gender development in middle childhood and early adolescence: A longitudinal study. *Developmental Psychology, 37*, 115–125.

Messner, M. A. (1992). *Power at play: Sports and the problem of masculinity*. Boston, MA: Beacon Press.

Miller, B. C., Norton, M. C., Fan, X., & Christopherson, C. R. (1998). Pubertal development, parental communication and sexual values in relation to adolescent sexual behaviors. *Journal of Early Adolescence, 18*, 27–52.

Oliver, M. B., & Hyde, J. S. (1993). Gender differences in sexuality: A meta-analysis. *Psychological Bulletin, 114*, 29–51.

O'Neil, J. M., Helms, B. J., Gable, R. K., David, L., & Wrightsman, L. S. (1986). Gender-role conflict scale: College men's fear of femininity. *Sex Roles, 14*, 335–350.

O'Sullivan, L. F. (2005). The social and relationship contexts and cognitions associated with romantic and sexual experiences of early-adolescent girls. *Sexual Research and Social Policy: Journal of NSRC, 2*, 13–24.

Pfeiffer, S., & Daniel, M. (2000, October 13). Court rules Brockton boy can dress as girl at school. *Boston Globe*, p. A1.

Pickstone-Taylor, S. D. (2002). Children with gender nonconformity. *Journal of the American Academy of Child and Adolescent Psychiatry, 42*, 266.

Pleck, J. H., Sonenstein, F. L., & Ku, L. C. (1993). Masculinity ideology: Its impact on adolescent males' heterosexual relationships. *Journal of Social Issues, 49*, 11–29.

Pleck, J. H., Sonenstein, F. L., & Ku, L. C. (1994). Attitudes toward male roles: A discriminant validity analysis. *Sex Roles, 30,* 481–501.

Ponton, L. E., & Judice, S. (2004). Typical adolescent sexual development. *Child and Adolescent Psychiatric Clinics of North America, 13,* 497–511.

Reischel, J. (2006, May 30). See Tom be Jane. *The Village Voice.* Retrieved June 15, 2006, from http://www.villagevoice.com/2006-05-30/news/see-tom-be-jane

Rostosky, S. S., Regenerus, M. D., & Comer-Wright, M. L. (2003). Coital debut: The role of religiosity and sex attitudes in the Add Health survey. *Journal of Sex Research, 40,* 358–367.

Rostosky, S. S., Wilcox, B. L., Comer-Wright, M. L., & Randall, B. A. (2004). The impact of religiosity on adolescent sexual behavior: A review of the evidence. *Journal of Adolescent Research, 19,* 677–697.

Russell, S. T. (2005). Conceptualizing positive adolescent sexuality development. *Sexual Research and Social Policy: Journal of NSRC, 2,* 4–12.

Sabo, D., & Jansen, S. C. (1992). Images of men in sport: The social reproduction of gender order. In S. Craig (Ed.), *Men, masculinity and the media* (pp. 169–184). Newbury Park, CA: Sage.

Savin-Williams, R. C. (2005). *The new gay teenager.* Cambridge, MA: Harvard University Press.

Sexuality Information and Education Center of the United States. (n.d.). http://www.siecus.org

Smiler, A. P. (2006). Living the image: A quantitative approach to masculinities. *Sex Roles, 55,* 621–632.

Smiler, A. P., Ward, L. M., Caruthers, A., & Merriwether, A. (2005). Pleasure, empowerment, and love: Factors associated with a positive first coitus. *Sexual Research and Social Policy: Journal of NSRC, 2,* 41–55.

Smith, E. A., & Udry, J. R. (1985). Coital and noncoital sexual behaviors of white and black adolescents. *American Journal of Public Health, 75,* 1200–1203.

Smith, M., Gertz, E., Alvarez, S., & Lurie, P. (2000). The content and accessibility of sex education information on the Internet. *Health Education & Behavior, 27,* 684–694.

Stearns, P. N. (1994). *American cool: Constructing a twentieth-century emotional style.* New York: New York University Press.

Striepe, M. I., & Tolman, D. L. (2003). Mom, dad, I'm straight: The coming out of gender ideologies in adolescent sexual-identity development. *Journal of Clinical Child and Adolescent Psychology, 32,* 523–530.

Sutton, M. J., Brown, J. D., Wilson, K. M., & Klein, J. D. (2002). Shaking the tree of knowledge for forbidden fruit: Where adolescents learn about sexuality and contraception. In J. D. Brown, J. R. Steele, & K. Walsh-Childers (Eds.), *Sexual teens, sexual media: Investigating media's influence on adolescent sexuality* (pp. 25–55). Mahwah, NJ: Erlbaum.

Thorne, B. (1993). *Gender play: Girls and boys in school.* New Brunswick, NJ: Rutgers University Press.

Tolman, D. L. (2002). *Dilemmas of desire: Teenage girls talk about sexuality.* Cambridge, MA: Harvard University Press.

Tolman, D. L., & Porche, M. V. (2000). The adolescent femininity ideology scale: Development and validation of a new measure for girls. *Psychology of Women Quarterly, 24,* 365–376.

Ward, L. M. (1995). Talking about sex: Common themes about sexuality in the prime-time television programs children and adolescents view most. *Journal of Youth and Adolescence, 24,* 595–615.

Ward, L. M., & Wyatt, G. E. (1994). The effects of childhood sexual messages on African-American and white women's adolescent sexual behavior. *Psychology of Women Quarterly, 18,* 183–201.

Welsh, D. P., Haugen, P. T., Widman, L., Darling, N., & Grello, C. M. (2005). Kissing is good: A developmental investigation of sexuality in adolescent romantic couples. *Sexuality Research and Social Policy: A Journal of NSRC, 2,* 32–41.

Williams, J. E., & Best, D. L. (1990). *Sex and psyche: Gender and self viewed cross-culturally.* Newbury Park, CA: Sage.

Wolak, J., Mitchell, K. J., & Finkelhor, D. (2002). Close online relationships in a national sample of adolescents. *Adolescence, 37,* 441–455.

Yates, M., & Youniss, J. (1996). A developmental perspective on community service in adolescence. *Social Development, 5,* 85–111.

Zimmer-Gembeck, M. J., Siebrenbruner, J., & Collins, W. A. (2004). A prospective study of intraindividual and peer influences on adolescents' heterosexual romantic and sexual behavior. *Archives of Sexual Behavior, 33,* 381–394.

Response to Part 4

Outing the Profession's Fear of Teaching Like a Girl

Erica R. Meiners and Therese Quinn

After a few years on the social justice educational conference circuit, we observe that despite the feminization of teaching, apparently no one wants to be perceived as *teaching like a girl*. For us, the evidence is clear: pre-service teacher education programs that routinely ignore gender; critical pedagogues who neglect to mention feminist and queer contributions to movements for educational justice; and the erasure of a gender, sexuality, race and power analysis from our nation's obsessive discussions about academic success of boys are just three of what could be many examples. Girls, feminisms and queers are not just left behind in education, we are the toxic outsiders.

But, let's face it—talking about how gender shapes our lives, even in a profession that is 80% plus female, is out of favor? Who wants to be You Tube's "Nice White Lady" or risk being confused with Hillary Swank from *Freedom Writers* or Michelle Pfeiffer from *Dangerous Minds*? Who wants to be mistaken for one of those fresh-faced modern day missionary gals—recruited at only the best Ivy League universities and exclusive liberal arts colleges by Teach for America, of course—who, with a summer's "training" are sent off to the schools to spend a few years saving poor people? Just like throwing like a girl—all limp-wristed wind-up and no sure aim—these representations offer depictions of lady teachers as naïve, duped, and way too earnest to know that social justice means organizing and acting up.

We propose that given the current political and cultural backlash against women and queers, and Hollywood's persistent snow job on the profession of teaching, it is past time to reclaim our radical justice seeking-and-making *lady* teachers and their sissy and tranny colleagues—those who are often rendered invisible by overt discriminatory laws and policies and the ever present fear of the queer in schools. The riotous and revolutionary experiences of these outspoken activist teachers—Ellen Gates Starr, Mary McLeod Bethune, Margaret Haley, Septima Clark, Mary Church Terrell, Virginia Uribe, Eric Rofes, and so many others—must be invoked whenever we talk about social justice in education.

Calling up this history of feminist teaching, queer organizing, *passing* for survival and resistance, education as linked to civil rights movements, more clearly demonstrates that to teach and organize *like a girl,* is about radical and risky work in the public sphere, not private or charitable actions in the classroom.

This is a co-authored work with equal contributions from each of us and no first author. The order in which we are listed is based on a rotation we use in our publishing collaborations.

Part 5

Bodies, Disability, and the Fight for Social Justice in Education

Edited and Introduced by Patricia Hulsebosch

Culture, the great enabler, is disabling. Culture is generally taken to be a positive term. If there is anything people do naturally, it is that they live culturally, in groups, with goals, rules, expectations, abstractions, and untold complexities. Culture, as we say in our lectures, gives all we know and all the tools with which to learn more. Very nice, but every culture, we must acknowledge, also gives, often daily and eventually always, a blind side, a deaf ear, a learning problem, and a physical handicap. For every skill people gain, there is another not developed; for every focus of attention, something is passed by; for every specialty, a corresponding lack. People use established cultural forms to define what they should work on, work for, in what way, and with what consequences; being in a culture is a great occasion for developing abilities, or at least for having many people think they have abilities. People also use established cultural forms to define those who do not work on the "right" things, for the "right" reason, or in the "right" way. Being in a culture is a great occasion for developing disabilities, or at least for having many people think they have disabilities. Being in a culture may be the only road to enhancement; it is also very dangerous.

(McDermott & Varenne, 1995)

Gender reaches into disability; disability wraps around class; class strains against abuse; abuse snarls into sexuality; sexuality folds on top of race...everything finally piling into a single human body.

(Clare, 1999, p. 123)

"Disabled": surely that's a category that's clear, unambiguous, and not open to interpretation. We all know what it means to be disabled. Either you have what it takes—ability—or you don't. And if you don't, then you must be disabled. And if you're disabled, you need to be learning in a special place, under special conditions, with a special teacher, with others who are like you. And the rest of society—"normal people"—need not accommodate to your problems. Those are some of the assumptions underlying disability labels in education.

But wait a minute: What ability is it that we're discussing? Is it the ability to walk? To hold a pencil? To speak? To see? To communicate? Is it the ability to make new friends? To repair broken machines? Is it the ability to find your way home when you're lost? Or perhaps to stay calm and unemotional in oppressive and neglectful situations? Or to not draw attention to yourself, your differences, your needs, no matter what else you do or do not do? Which among these are the essential abilities that mark a person as able-bodied or, in their absence, as disabled? Exactly which abilities in what societies or situations will earn the label of disabled person? Where is the line that, once crossed, marks someone as disabled?

Ten years ago the fax arrived from the adoption agency, showing a round-faced girl with deep brown eyes and an ice cream bowl haircut. My partner Lynda and I had found Ariana on a Listserv sponsored by the Deaf Adoption News Service (DANS). DANS was set up by a deaf adoptive mother in order to help others locate deaf children who were waiting to be adopted around the world. While there was some controversy about the parents who sought out the DANS list (talk of people adopting deaf children only to try to make them hearing by having them cochlear implanted), many of the parents were themselves immersed in Deaf[1] culture or Deafhood (Ladd, 2003). Some were deaf themselves, while others had deaf family members, or worked in the deaf community as interpreters. Lynda is Deaf, with several generations of Deaf folks in her family, including her father who was one of the first deaf trial lawyers in the country. We wanted to bring Ariana into the Deaf community and a long, proud line of deaf people.

We had carefully combed the lists of children waiting to be adopted considering who might be a good fit for us. Ariana was the daughter we asked for, and we were eager to know as much about her as we could long-distance. The fax contained a brief statement: "The orphanage says she's a 'scrapper.'" Hmmm, Deaf, Latino, female. Sounds like being a scrapper will be a good thing for her. We went on to talk about how we would value and support Ariana for the qualities that had helped her be a survivor. We knew she was likely to be "determined," but of course, not "stubborn." We expected her to be "energetic," but not "hyperactive." And, of course, she would be Deaf, not "hearing-impaired." But, here we were, 10 years later in a meeting with all of the "support" people on the seventh grade team at Ariana's school, and none of them were very appreciative of the "scrapper" in her.

It was all a bit ironic. We had moved to an area so that Ariana could attend a school with a strong visual learning environment. This was a school in which her audiological status was in the background, being a Deaf learner was the norm, and all of the school's staff were fluent in American Sign Language (Ariana's first language).

When we had moved and Ariana had entered first grade at a new school, her teachers described her as confident and curious; eager to learn and a leader among her peers. Perhaps as important, she worked independently, followed rules, and got along well with others. But she just wasn't mastering the tools of learning so critical for access to the broader world. Slowly, over the years, we noticed that she wasn't often reading more complex texts that were beyond a primer level, and she wasn't understanding mathematical and scientific concepts. We did notice, however, that when the topic was animals she would go to great lengths to use the tools she had: to read the books, or solve the problems. When there was a real reason for reading or computing, her capabilities seemed much stronger. At home she was writing daily in her journal, and sitting with us, book in hand, as we enjoyed the latest best-seller.

The teachers agreed that Ariana could and should be able to do more than she was in school. But they also said there were just too many students for them to be able to fit their teaching to Ariana's interests or needs. So my partner and I became advocates for her rights to services and support. After all, if the classroom teachers didn't have enough time, then maybe more people (tutors, occupational therapists, curriculum coordinators), with the right skills who weren't working with the entire class of seven children would solve the problem. When we asked if support staff could be brought into the classroom we were told, "Sorry, we don't have resources to support individual students who aren't making progress."

Now my partner and I, like so many other parents who run out of tools for influencing a school, resorted to the very tool we had so adamantly avoided: labels. We knew that there are laws that, given the right test results and the right label (i.e., a "documented disability"), would require the school to find the resources to support Ariana's learning. Off we went to a private psychologist who, sure enough, identified a documented learning disability in Ariana. Back we went to the Individualized Education Planning (IEP) meetings with "proof" that we thought would require the school to change their approach to teaching. "Sorry we don't have the resources to support students with learning disabilities (LD). None of our teachers are qualified to teach LD children."

Being educators, we assumed that building the capacity of the school and of the teachers would help to build on her strengths and respond to her weaknesses. We described strategies and times of success at home. We brought in articles about inclusive practices: differentiated instruction, peer teaching, cooperative learning. We suggested more of a contextualized and scaffolded approach. Eventually we hired a consultant to work with the teachers on formative assessment and strategies for varying their instruction. But try as we might to expand teachers' notions of their classroom practice, year after year teachers could not envision a different kind of classroom that could include in meaningful ways a learner like Ariana. Meanwhile, Ariana's academic progress languished as she worked again and again on the same math problems, practiced the same Dolch words, and read and reread the same Accelerated Reader computerized worksheets. In sharp contrast to years gone by, teachers began to note Ariana's lack of motivation and desire to learn, and the descriptions of her in her newest IEP's were stark in their omission of any description of strengths.

Five years later we're sitting in a room full of support staff at the school, dreading a hearing for her to reenter the school after a suspension. The day of the meeting, the principal met us at the office and ushered us into a bare room where two other administrators were waiting for us around a table. "So 'the team' has met and discussed how to help Ariana make this transition back into school. We've decided she should see her counselor more often, and move to a different Math class. And we're working with the teachers to add more structure to her day. In fact, it's clear that Ariana's disability now means that everything must change in all of her programming." I thought "Disability, what disability do you mean?"

Another administrator continued: "Right, everything needs to change for Ariana. Clearly, now she fits the ED [Emotionally Disturbed] category, and we want to include that in her new IEP we're currently writing." I was stunned. My first thoughts were about the stigma attached to the "ED" label, especially in schools, and even more so in schools for Deaf kids which are often trying to maintain the appearance that Deaf kids are all alike. We had, for example, already been told that the other Deaf school in the area routinely denies admission to deaf children labeled ED. Then I was confused. For four years we had been suggesting, then asking, then demanding from the school that they teach Ariana in a way that we support her to learn. Every year for the past seven years at this school, teachers ended the year saying that Ariana seemed "bright," capable, and, until the last year or so, very engaged in school. But surprisingly, she wasn't making progress on any of the measures they were using; she wasn't learning to read, write, and do mathematics. We, in response, asked the school to vary its strategies and structures from its one-size-fits-all approach. But in spite of individualized education plans, teachers again and again told us, "I have seven students in my class. I can't change my teaching to fit one child." And administrators told us, "Sorry, we just don't have the resources."

In my confusion I asked, "What's different now? What's different about Ariana now? What do you mean when you say that 'everything must change in all of her programming?' How can that be true when for five years you've said that nothing could change to help her to learn? Why the change? What's different now?" A short pause, a stuttered response: "Well, to be honest...we have resources for ED support, but we don't have the resources to support LD programming." Incredulously I responded, "So you're saying you have the resources to support deaf children to be 'crazy', but not to be smart?"

And so it seemed that over the course of five years Ariana had been transformed from being an ordinary Deaf kid, with learning strengths and needs that no one in the school could see or respond to, to one her parents had worked to have labeled as learning disabled in order to provide some extraordinary support, to being a child who, instead of being truly seen, was now seen as what Bèrubè (1996, p. xi) calls "an instance of a category": "emotionally disturbed."

Who decides who we "are?" Whose interests are served by disability identities in general, and by particular disability labels? Why do some schools or districts seem to have an overabundance of "LD" students, while in others children are labeled disturbed? How do learners gain access to supports, services, and approaches that best fit their strengths and needs, without acquiescing to crippling categories that stigmatize? How do humans manage to see and be seen clearly in this society, with all their intricacies, especially in our educational systems?

Social justice education, with its focus on the oppression, marginalization, powerlessness, and inequities that people experience on the basis of group membership, offers possibilities for understanding why events, such as those in Ariana's education, unfold the way they do. This section of the Handbook brings together authors who write about concepts such as hierarchy, imposed identity, and the intersection of race and disability, that are core to understanding the question, "What does social justice have to do with disabilities in education?" Here you'll read about well-meaning individuals working within pervasive systems of cultural practices and institutional structures that result in daily misperceptions of children. You'll read about educational systems, often based in paternalistic and so-called "benevolent" desires that fail in their attempts to support children's learning—and, even worse, make children less than they are. These authors urge a reexamination of the bases for our institutional structures and full attention to the resources that communities, families, and individuals themselves bring to education.

Note

1. We use the D/d distinction that has become conventional to differentiate members of a cultural group.

References

Bèrubè, M. (1996). *Life as we know it.* New York: Vintage Books.

Clare, E. (1999). *Exile and pride: Disability, queerness, and liberation.* Cambridge, MA: South End Press.

Ladd, P. (2003). *Understanding deaf culture: In search of deafhood.* Bristol, UK: Multingual Matters.

McDermott, R., & Varenne, H. (1995). *Culture as disability. Anthropology & Education Quarterly, 26*(3). Retrieved October 7, 2007, from http://links.jstor.org/sici?sici=0161-7761%28199509%2926%3A3%3C324%3AC%22D%3E2.0.CO%3B2-B

24 Theorizing Disability

Implications and Applications for Social Justice in Education

Susan L. Gabel and David J. Connor

From Hope to Criticism

Any reference to disability in education in the United States immediately draws associations with special education. Perhaps this makes some sense given special education's historical claim on disabled young people. In fact, special education in the United States once offered hope to so many families whose disabled children remained at home or languished in institutions because until 1975 the public schools were not required or expected to educate them (Safford & Safford, 1996). Yet now special education is implicated in resegregating schools (Losen & Orfield, 2002), watering down curriculum (Brantlinger, 2006), and stigmatizing difference (Reid &Valle, 2004). In the United States, we find ourselves in an era different from the one in which Public Law 94-142, now the Individuals with Disabilities Educational Improvement Act (IDEIA) (NICHCY, 1996; U.S. Department of Education, 2005), first became federal law—an era of new technologies; values and beliefs about difference and diversity; notions about what counts as "an education," who "gets an education," or who gets a rigorous academic curriculum; and, finally, ideas about the possibilities and promises of an inclusive society.

Today, many critical scholars question the very foundations of the field of special education (and by extension general education when it comes to educating disabled students), including its basis in positivism (Danforth, 1999, 2004; Gallagher, 2001); its dehumanization of people with significant cognitive impairments (Erevelles, 2000; Taylor & Bogdan, 1989) or autism (Biklen, 1992), as well as its widespread low expectations of them; and the professionalization of failure or what Phil Ferguson (2002) refers to as the impetus to blame disabled people for the failure of expert intervention. Commonplace policies and practices that have been taken for granted are now in contention or disrepute, including segregated special education classrooms (Allan, 1999a, 1999b), overreliance on intervention aimed at specific deficits (Hehir, 2005), developmental curriculum (Brantlinger, 2005), intelligence testing (see classic critique by Gould, 1981), and the medicalization of disabled people (Abberley, 1987; Barton, 1996; Donoghue, 2003). These critiques resonate with those of the past, including Lous Heshusius's (1989, 1995), Iano's (1986; 1990), and Skrtic's (1995) criticisms of positivism and its influences on pedagogy in special education; Skrtic's (1991) deconstruction of professionalization in special education, and Robert Bogdan and Steve Taylor's (1989) description of the dehumanization of people who have significant cognitive impairments.

The bottom line for many teachers, critical special educators, and scholars has become the question of how to avoid stigmatizing difference and how to combat ableism in schools while simultaneously creating access to equal educational opportunity. This bottom line focuses attention on a systemic unit of analysis in contrast with special education's traditional focus on the individual student. Yet situating disability within a broader sociological context and implicating society in the disablement of people proves to be provocative and radical, particularly where special education is concerned. An exploration of the traditional special education literature in which these sociological critiques are decried demonstrates just how disruptive they are (Kauffman & Hallahan, 2005; Kauffman & Sasso, 2006a, 2006b; Sasso, 2001). For example, James Kauffman and Gary Sasso refer to such critiques as "foppery" (Kauffman & Sasso, 2006b, p. 109) that "give license to demagogues of the extreme left and the extreme right, to fundamentalists and oppressors who define the truth according to their particular orthodoxy" (p. 111). While such tensions between critical and traditional standpoints exist and have been heatedly debated (Brantlinger, 1997; Danforth, 1997, 2004; Gallagher, 1998, 2001, 2006; Gallagher, Heshusius, Iano, & Skrtic, 2004; Heshusius, 1994; Kauffman & Hallahan, 2005; Kauffman & Sasso, 2006a, 2006b; Rice, 2005), we urge that they be nurtured and seen as a site of productive dialogue (Andrews et. al., 2000; Gallagher, 2006) rather than claiming an impasse between paradigms (Kauffman & Sasso, 2006a, 2006b).

One field that has emerged as a result of criticisms of special education is disability studies in education (DSE). Many educators view disability studies as offering theoretical frameworks, ideas, and values that respond to the criticisms described previously and that speak to their discomfort with the dominant paradigm in education. In the next three sections of this chapter we describe some of the fundamental ideas of disability studies in education. Later we discuss the ways in which disability studies in education intersect with other educational fields and we conclude with ideas for incorporating disability studies into teaching, curriculum, and educational policy.

Disability Studies in Education

The interdisciplinary field of disability studies has steadily flourished for over three decades within the social sciences, arts, and humanities, but education is a relative latecomer to the field. The establishment of the DSE special interest group (SIG) of the American Educational Research Association (AERA) a full two decades after the founding of the Society for Disability Studies (SDS, n.d.) in the United States reflects this time lag. DSE's earliest documents define and outline what its founders consider to be the application of disability studies to educational theory, research, and practice as follows:

> Disability studies is an emerging and interdisciplinary field of scholarship that critically examines issues related to the dynamic interplays between disability and various aspects of culture and society. [It] unites critical inquiry and political advocacy by utilizing scholarly approaches from the humanities, humanistic/post-humanistic social sciences, and the arts. [A]pplied to educational issues, it promotes the importance of infusing analyses and interpretations of disability throughout all forms of educational research, teacher education, and graduate studies in education. (DSE, 2004, ¶1)

Our chapter offers an admittedly contemporary American account of the emergence of a distinct field called disability studies in education, yet U.S. and U.K. educational researchers have been engaged with disability studies for years prior to the founding of the SIG and the institution of a name for the field. For example: Len Barton (1996), Dan Goodley and Lathom (2005), in England; Julie Allan (1996, 1999a, 1999b) in Scotland; Roger Slee (1996, 1997) in Australia and now London; and Phil Ferguson (1994), Steve Taylor and Robert Bogdan (1989), Doug Biklen (1992), and Susan Peters (1996) in the United States. Furthermore, prior to the founding of the SIG, North American special educators were producing work quite consistent with disability studies in education and some of them later became founding members of the SIG: Lous Heshusius (1989, 1994, 1996), Ellen Brantlinger (1997), Scot Danforth (1997, 1999), and Deborah Gallagher (1998).

Given its emergence in the disability studies arena, we are often asked how disability studies in education should best be characterized. Answering this question promises to be contentious, but in brief, disability studies seeks to challenge limited understandings that often view disability as a medical or clinical condition characterized by individual deficiency, dysfunction, or disorder, and sometimes even portray it as a tragedy awaiting a "fix," a cure, treatment, or remediation (Brantlinger, 2004; Danforth & Smith, 2005; Garland-Thomson, 1997; Shakespeare, 1994). Simi Linton confronts this problem in *Claiming Disability* (1998) when she writes that,

> [s]ociety, in agreeing to assign medical meaning to disability, colludes to keep the issue within the purview of the medical establishment, to keep it a personal matter and "treat" the condition and the person with the condition rather than "treating" the social processes and policies that constrict disabled people's lives. (p. 11)

Instead of casting disability as an individual deficit, disability studies recognizes it as a natural form of human variation—one difference among many human differences—and better understood as the results of an interplay between the individual and society and through analyzing social, political, cultural, and historical frameworks (Allan, 1996; Corker & Shakespeare, 2002; Ferri & Connor, 2006; Oliver, 1996; Russell, 1998). Most importantly, DSE is critical of beliefs and practices that produce inequalities in the social conditions of schooling. These beliefs and practices constitute ableism, a phenomenon Laurel Rauscher and Michael McClintock (1996) define as

> A pervasive system of discrimination and exclusion that oppresses people who have mental, emotional, and physical disabilities.... Deeply rooted beliefs about health, productivity, beauty, and the value of human life, perpetuated by the public and private media, combine to create an environment that is often hostile to those whose physical, mental, cognitive, and sensory abilities...fall out of the scope of what is currently defined as socially acceptable. (p. 198)

To be sure, we are making a clear case for disability studies in education as a definitive field of study that is both distinct from and intersecting with special education and other fields. In later sections we demonstrate some of these connections with other fields yet it must be recognized that DSE seems to be of great interest to those whose work is defined in relation to disability—special educators. Many of the founding and current members of the DSE SIG are special educators. To date, all of the awards granted by the SIG have gone to people who identify as special educators and who represent the majority membership of the SIG. There is a desire for expanding the SIG membership to include anyone who shares the SIG's concerns, and, of course, there are those who identify with or are identified with disability studies in education who can be found in curriculum studies (Baker, 2002; Selden, 2000), educational foundations (Erevelles, 2000), educational sociology (Michalko, 2002; Titchkosky, 2001), and many other subfields. In addition, one certainly can find special educators who do not identify with disability studies but who share many of the goals of those of us in disability studies. For example, Thomas Hehir (2002) has consistently focused attention on ableism in schools.

Many educators who do not identify with disability studies share similar concerns. Using the SIG's founding description of disability studies in education as an example, there are traditional special educators who are concerned about "the dynamic interplay between disability and various aspects of culture and society," particularly those ways in which racism disables students and produces overrepresentation of African-American and Hispanic youth in special education (Ferri & Connor, 2005; Losen & Orfield, 2002). Some of the finest socially conscious work has come from those who have demonstrated that the promise of special education has been turned on its head by using it to further racial segregation (Blanchett, 2006; Harry & Klingner, 2006; McDermott, Goldman, & Varenne, 2006; O'Connor & Fernandez, 2006; Reid & Knight, 2006). Nevertheless, it remains important to emphasize that disability studies in education is not the same field as special education, although its differences and similarities have yet to be mapped in a way that brings any kind of consensus.

What Is Disability?

One basic feature that distinguishes disability studies from other fields that engage in the study of disability is its critical stance toward the master narrative of disability. This radical departure is represented by two fluid strands of thought—one originating in the U.S. (minority group model of disability) and one from the U.K. (social model of disability). In reality, scholars on both sides of the Atlantic and around the world have eclectic ways of understanding and representing disability.

The minority group model of disability emerged in the late 1970s as an offshoot of the U.S. Civil Rights Movement. In 1977 Robert Bogdan and Doug Biklen also borrowed from the Civil Rights Movement to coin the term *handicapism* (consistent with the popular use of "handicap" at that time) to refer to "a set of assumptions and practices that promote the differential and unequal treatment of people because of apparent or assumed... differences" (p. 15). The minority group model holds that "the problems faced by disabled citizens are essentially similar to the difficulties encountered by other minorities" (Hahn, 2002, p. 171). Harlan Hahn observes that, like other minorities, disabled people

> have been plagued by...high rates of unemployment, poverty, and welfare dependency; school segregation; inadequate housing and transportation; and exclusion from many public facilities that appear to be reserved exclusively for the non-disabled majority. (pp. 171–172)

While Hahn references the social conditions facing disabled Americans in the 1970s and 80s, his claim remains valid even as we near the end of the first decade of the 21st century.

The origin of the social model of disability often is traced back to the *Fundamental Principles of Disability* (Union of Physically Impaired Against Segregation [UPIAS], 1975), a document published by the UK Disability Rights Movement, then composed primarily of people with physical impairments. The Principles state:

> In our view, it is society which disabled physically impaired people. Disability is something that is imposed on top of our impairments by the way we are unnecessarily isolated and excluded from full participation in society. Disabled people are therefore an oppressed group in society. (p. 3)

This emphasis on the distinction between impairments (functional limitations) and disability (social oppression) is the hallmark of the strong social model of disability (Abberley, 1987; Humphrey, 2000; Oliver, 1990; Shakespeare & Watson, 1997, 2001).

Today, the social model is recognized globally as a way to understand disability within its historical, material, and social contexts. It is referred to in government documents in Great Britain (e.g., Birmingham City Council, 2006; Manchester City Council, 2005), Canada (e.g., Government of Canada, 2004; Provincial Health Ethics Network, 2001), and the United States (National Institute of Disability Research and Rehabilitation [NIDRR], 1999). Although it has wide recognition in the international Disability Rights Movement and among disability studies researchers, it has had little influence over U.S. legislation, educational policy, or the general public, a situation Donoghue (2003) describes in his analysis of the Americans with Disabilities Act (U.S. Congress, 1990). He argues that while the ADA attempts to alter social barriers to inclusion (something the social model would applaud), it adheres to a medical model definition of disability—a definition that aims its lens at individual pathology and interventions that cure or remediate individual difference. In contrast, the social model focuses on the disabling consequences of social exclusion and isolation and interventions that attempt to restructure society so that disabled people are fully included in all aspects of social life.

The strong social model that draws a clear distinction between disability and impairment recently is under debate. Some have argued that the full diversity of individual experience needs to be recognized and understood (Corker & Shakespeare, 2002; Shakespeare & Watson, 2001) within social interpretations of disability while Vic Finkelstein (2003) has argued that it is not a model after all and that it has been appropriated away from the Disability Rights Movement by academicians who use it for elitist purposes, thereby rendering it impotent as a tool for activism. Thus, a model of disability that has produced many successful legislative outcomes has become a contentious and amorphous idea that may have outlived its time (Gabel & Peters, 2004; Shakespeare & Watson, 2001; Thomas & Corker, 2002; Tremain, 2002).

In addition to the epistemological debate surrounding the social model, its meaning and application seems to be in flux. Susan Gabel and Susan Peters' (2004) examination of a decade of disability studies literature reveals that although the strong social model falls within a historical–materialist epistemology, scholars across paradigms (e.g., interpretivism, postmodernism, poststructuralism) reference the social model but are not necessarily assigning it the same meaning. In fact, the only thing these authors appear to have in common is the study of disability within its social contexts and resistance to the medical model of disability's functionalist paradigm. These more amorphous standpoints are often referred to as social interpretations of disability (Finkelstein, 2003; Gabel, 2005). With time, the use, misuse, or demise of a social model of disability will become clear, but until then, we are cautioned to search for clarity when reading or writing "from a social model perspective" or, for that matter, "from a disability studies perspective."

Regardless of (1) the stance taken on the idea of disability and (2) whether one claims to adhere to the minority group model or the social model or some other social interpretation of disability, those who identify with disability studies in education remain concerned with inequities in society that exist for disabled people. What is troubling in particular are the ways in which cultural values, assumptions, and ideas about difference, and the practical consequences of these, can be disabling. This concern results in a preference for and encouragement of dialogue and debate about many complex issues and problems related to disability. By calling attention to ableist beliefs and practices in the educational system and the world in which it exists, a goal of disability studies in education is to ensure that people with disabilities have *access* to the same opportunities afforded to nondisabled citizens including education, community living, recreational possibilities, family life, freedom of expression (including sexual expression), and employment options. Finally, DSE holds close a mantra of the Disability Rights Movement: "Nothing About Us Without Us" (Charlton, 1998/2002), signifying a commitment to engage in research and publication side-by-side with disabled people and the allies who work *with* them in forging social change.

The importance of scholarly and political leadership by disablec people is, in fact, one of the basic tenets of disability studies, as defined by the U.S. Society for Disability Studies. Other tenets hold that disability studies: (1) is inter-/multidisciplinary; (2) should challenge the notion that disability is an individual deficit that can be remediated by experts; (3) studies disability across the broadest contexts possible (e.g., historical periods, national and international contexts); and (4) "actively encourage participation by disabled students and faculty" and assure access (SDS, n.d., section 5).

Intersections with Other Fields of Study

Because disability studies is both eclectic and interdisciplinary, there are many potential intersections with other fields of inquiry that are founded upon the quest for equity and social justice, including multicultural studies, critical race studies, and queer studies (as well as feminist studies, class studies, etc.). Like disability studies, all of these fields challenge the dominant paradigm of mainstream thinking and seek to expand restrictive notions of normalcy by centering a difference that is usually placed in the margins. While many other intersections exist and could be explored, we limit ourselves to examining three areas of overlap with disability studies.

Multicultural studies

The concept of multicultural education is that of "...a broad interdisciplinary field that focuses on a range of racial, ethnic, and cultural groups as well as both genders" (Banks, 1995, p. 274). Like disability studies in education, multiculturalism is concerned with issues of equity and social justice, aiming to transform mainstream curriculum into one that truly embraces a plurality of perspectives. James Banks (1995) has suggested five dimensions of multicultural education: (1) diversity must be integrated into the content, and not an additive approach; (2) the origins and construction of knowledge is openly addressed, including the influence on scholars; (3) a proactive approach is used to reduce prejudice and helps students develop positive attitudes to different groups; (4) equitable pedagogy is employed, encouraging diverse forms of interaction such as cooperative learning; (5) and an empowering school culture and social structure is consciously cultivated. Used together, these dimensions support a transformative approach to education, encouraging plurality in perspective, and acknowledge the epistemological contributions of formerly marginalized groups. Calling upon Robert Merton's (1972) idea that all groups have insiders and outsiders, Banks (1995) notes that, "...insiders and outsiders often have different perspectives on the same events, and both perspectives are needed to give the total picture of social and historical reality" (p. 8). It is clear that as a group, disabled people are often positioned at the margins or even outside of the social realm and are thus able to contribute knowledge that marginal/outsider status brings—knowledge that often contradicts traditional or mainstream understandings of phenomena. When incorporating the voices and perspectives of disabled people in their teaching, educators use them as tools to critique widespread misunderstandings of disability prevalent throughout all aspects of society (history, culture, structures, the media, everyday interactions, etc.). By interrogating "commonplace" and accepted notions of disability, educators actively teach *against* widespread misinformation. Instead, the "problem" of disability is significantly recast, sharply illustrating examples of social injustice by focusing on ways in which practices, regulations, representations, and attitudes contribute toward limiting access to all spheres of society.

When applying the tenets of multiculturalism to disability studies, existing curricula designed to facilitate the teaching of disability is scrutinized, including the use of disability simulations. While these are some of the most commonplace methods of teaching about disability—for example, blindfolding students and making them walk around the building to experience the world of Helen Keller—such simulations are misleading in that nondisabled people are "playing" with disability, experiencing a loss of function for a short period of time and reinforcing commonplace notions that disability is a difference to be avoided at nearly all cost. Disability activists have suggested that refusing to enter inaccessible buildings, always sitting in designated and often less desirable areas marked for "handicapped" or "disabled," and discussing why some people believe there are many positive aspects to the experience of being disabled, exemplify more accurate understandings of how individuals with a disability function in society (Blaser, 2003).

Furthermore, when scholars theorize toward a different society, one in which diversity is valued instead of devalued, ignored, or feared, it must be a world welcoming and supportive of disability. Bearing this in mind, the world of multiculturalism allows the possibility of integrating disability culture. Disability culture has been described by a variety of scholars and activists (Davis, 1995; Fleischer & Zames, 2001; Linton, 2006; Peters, 2000), and can be used to inform a curriculum negligent of disability-related issues by promoting teaching practices that bring these issues into the classroom (Linton, 1998) and infuse them throughout the curriculum in relevant, meaningful ways. A documentary useful for educating teachers about disability culture is David Mitchell and Sharon Snyder's (1997) *Vital Signs: Crip Culture Talks Back*.

Finally, as Banks notes (1995), by recognizing and critically analyzing the other (be it disability, race, ethnicity, etc.), it becomes apparent that "...the Other often becomes essential for the in-group to create its own identity" (p. 22). Thus, transformative teaching and learning can occur as students come to recognize that "[r]ace [like disability] is a human invention constructed by groups to differentiate themselves from other groups, to create ideas about the 'other,' to formulate their identities, and to defend the disproportionate distribution of rewards and opportunities within society" (p. 22). Once disability and race are realized as inventions rather than scientific facts—inventions that became collective, deeply ingrained, enduring historical beliefs—the damage that such concepts have wreaked can begin to be undone.

Critical Race Studies

Like multiculturalism, critical race studies emerged from Black scholarship, specifically "the development of African-American thought in the post-civil rights era: the 1970s to the present" (Tate, 1997, p. 206). Just as multiculturalism expanded to become multivoiced, incorporating increasingly diverse perspectives, critical race studies grew from the original grounding in the African-American experience to incorporate critical perspectives on race from Latinos (Delgado & Stefanic, 2001), Asian Americans (Teranishi, 2002), Native Americans (Snipp, 1998), and European Americans (Marx, 2004).

Matsuda, Lawrence, Delgado, and Crenshaw's (1993) acknowledgment that race and racism are organizing principles of society highlights how ability and ableism operate in a similar manner. Their six tenets of critical race theory hold that: (1) racism is endemic to American life; (2) dominant legal claims of neutrality, objectivity, color-blindness (sic), and meritocracy must be openly challenged; (3) contextual/historical analysis of the law is needed to demonstrate that racism has contributed to all contemporary manifestations of groups advantage and disadvantage along racial lines; (4) the experiential knowledge of people of color and their communities of origin must be recognized in analyzing law and society; (5) the field is interdisciplinary; and (6) it works toward the end of eliminating racial oppression as part of the broader goal of ending all forms of oppression. Comparing this list to the Society for Disability Studies guidelines for disability studies, one can see many similarities on points 2, 3, 4, 5, and 6 above. On point 1, we might add that disability studies would claim that ableism is endemic to American life.

Critical race studies and disability studies appear to have even more commonalities. As disciplines, their evolution has occurred over the same period of time. William Tate (1997) has described critical race studies as being "interdisciplinary and eclectic by nature" (p. 198) and having "academic and activist goals" (p. 198). The same can be said for disability studies (Corker & Shakespeare, 2002; Linton, 1998). Both seek to challenge existing practices in society that devalue and marginalize people based on socially constructed characteristics. Furthermore, both foreground the voices of disenfranchised groups, insist that they be heard from historically subjugated positions, and explicitly challenge dominant practices that have positioned them as inferior.

The tenets of critical race theory, like those of disability studies, can be incorporated into school curricula and classroom pedagogy. In terms of curricula, Gloria Ladson-Billings and William Tate (1995) have urged critical race theory be used to: reinterpret ineffective civil rights law, understand ways in which racism is endemic and deeply ingrained in American life, and challenge claims of neutrality, objectivity, color-blindness [sic] and meritocracy. In addition, Ladson-Billings' calls for "culturally relevant pedagogy" (1995, p. 465) in which history, race, ethnicity, and class are factored into important teaching decisions made about content, methods, and expected outcomes. Other scholars have encouraged the exploration of student knowledge, history, and experience in the world as a foundation for meaningful, respectful, teaching and learning, oftentimes cultivating student knowledge and experiences as "counterstories" to contrast with mainstream knowledge (Solorzano & Yosso, 2002).

On another note, while only recently has disability studies begun to seriously contemplate racism from within (Bell, 2006), critical race studies has yet to fully acknowledge the political aspect of disability. In contrast, scholars in disability studies in education have been more inclined to use critical race theory in intersectional scholarship, looking at the intersection of disability and race in legislation (Beratan, 2006), overrepresentation of students of color in special education (Ferri & Connor, 2006), school violence (Watts & Erevelles, 2004), living at the intersections of being Black and disabled (Mitchell, 2006), as well as being Black, disabled, and working class (Connor, 2006), and the history of race and disability in schooling (Erevelles, 2006). To a large degree their work foregrounds an intersectional approach in which human existence is seen as multidimensional, with each aspect of identity potentially informing the other(s).

Queer Studies

The term *queer* has been used as an inclusive sociopolitical umbrella, a subversive worldview of sorts, outside the heteronormative mainstream. As such, the word has been reclaimed, by many members of the gay, lesbian, bisexual, asexual, transgender, and heterosexual communities—shifting significantly from insult to moniker of pride. This appropriation can be seen on many fronts, from the growth of queer studies recognized within the academy (formerly gay and lesbian studies) to its presence within popular culture as evident, for example, in the television show *Queer Eye for the Straight Guy*, in which five queer men solve fashion, design, and relationship dilemmas for straight men who have requested their help. The disability community, too, has embraced terms once used to denigrate its members—crip, gimp, disabled—and has incorporated them into its identity lexicon (Mitchell & Snyder, 1997).

Like multiculturalism and critical race studies, queer studies seeks to trouble the status quo in society, specifically by calling attention to endemic heterosexism experienced by gay, lesbian, bisexual, asexual, transgender, and heterosexual people. Michael Warner (1993) reminds us that:

> Every person who comes to a queer self-understanding knows in one way or another that her stigmatization is connected with gender, the family, notions of individual freedom, the state, public speech, consumption and desire, nature and culture, maturation, reproductive politics, racial and national fancy, class identity, truth and trust, censorship, intimate life and social display, terror and violence, health care, and deep cultural norms about the bearing of the body. Being queer means fighting about these issues all the time, locally and piecemeal but always with consequences. (p. xiii)

Stigmatization and general mistrust of queers remains entrenched at every level of society from national debates about antigay marriage amendments to the U.S. Constitution, to state constitutional amendments and Supreme Court rulings against gay marriage, to local gay bashing, and, even worse, hate crimes (e.g., Matthew Shepherd; see Gabay & Kaufman, *The Laramie Project*, 2002). In a survey of almost 1,000 college students who were asked which group would have the hardest time "fitting in" to a campus school, gays and lesbians were identified as the number one group (80%), followed by international students (57%), students with disabilities (43%), and finally African Americans (30%) (Globetti, Globetti, Brown, & Smith, 1993).

Queer studies—like disability studies and critical race studies—challenges stereotypic, negative notions of homosexuality or queerness. In doing so, it critiques the naturalized discourse of majority-enforced heterosexuality by calling upon "the necessarily and desirably queer nature of the world" (Warner, 1993, p. xxi). That queerness has been pervasively repressed in blatant and subtle ways—elimination by death, imprisonment, subjugation and silencing via humor and ridicule, discrimination against gay families, deprivation of civil and human rights—testifies to the "danger" it poses, including the recognition and acceptance of different ways of knowing, understanding, loving, living, and being—thereby challenging many existing assumptions.

One such assumption is the commonplace notion of binary thinking. As Diana Fuss (1991) describes, "Queer, as a term, signals not only the disruption of the binary of heterosexual normalcy on one hand and homosexual defiance on the other, but desires to bring the hetero/homo opposition to the point of collapse" (cited in Luhman, 1998, p. 145). However, in demythologizing "normal" homo/hetero oppositions, the precedent is set for actively questioning the predictability and stability of *all* categories. Susanne Luhmann (1998) sees this as opening the door for "...the refusal of any normalization, be it racist, sexist, or whatever, necessarily has to be part of the queer agenda" (p. 151).

Thus, queer studies and disability studies share an interest in resisting "normalcy," by destabilizing the solidity of its foundations. Intersectional work in disability studies and queer studies has been manifest in several ways, including: the First International Queerness and Disability conference held in San Francisco in 2002; a special edition of

Gay and Lesbian Quarterly edited by Robert McRuer and Abby Wilkerson (2003); auto-biographical accounts (Clare, 1999; Fries, 1998), refereed articles (Solis, 2007); and a volume on crip theory that explores "cultural signs of queerness and disability" (McRuer, 2006). Just as queer theory desires a queerer world in which pleasurable and gratifying aspects of queerness are acknowledged, disability studies seeks a world in which the knowledge that living with disability brings can be seen as an asset (Mooney & Cole, 2000; O'Connor, 2001). Finally, queer and disabled students face similar dilemmas in schools: both groups are more likely to be victimized and bullied; both often do not see themselves realistically portrayed in the curriculum; issues around queerness and disability are often seen as "private" matters rather than "public" issues (Sedgwick, 1990); and both groups may in fact be subject to a barrage of negative associations reflected in the language of the school playground; for example, "Gay," "Fag," "Dyke," "Retard," "Spastic," "Nut Case, etc." that adults often do not act upon.

Applications for Social Justice Education

Earlier we demonstrated that the project of DSE is a radical one that irritates tradition through its critiques of educational inequity and questioning of the commonplace. We have offered examples of the intersections of disability studies in education with other fields of inquiry including multicultural studies, critical race studies, and queer studies. There are, of course, other intersections. We have provided examples of how disability studies could be incorporated into the thought and research of intersecting fields, and now we urge colleagues in intersecting fields to incorporate disability into their theorizing and ideas about practice and policy in order to engage in dialogue and debate with disability studies in education so that we learn from one another. In this section we illustrate some ways in which educational practice and policy can be transformed by disability studies in education by focusing on three areas: curriculum, teaching, and educational policy.

Curriculum Content

Banks (1995) claims that "[m]ulticultural education is trying to help unify a deeply divided nation, not to divide one that is united" (p. 8). With this in mind, we offer ways in which the study of disability can help unify through illuminating the ways in which: disability discrimination is related to other forms of discrimination; the social construction of disability is related to and serves some of the same social purposes as does the social construction of other marginalities; and like other marginalized groups, in spite of their status, disabled people have contributed to our cultural and political landscape. This follows the SDS guideline that disability should be studied in the broadest contexts possible and across all disciplines.

When thinking about curriculum, two major issues are present: the content of the curriculum and access to that content. Consistent with multicultural studies, disability studies compels us to analyze whether or not and how disabled people are represented in the curriculum. In doing so, teachers can consider which representations accurately portray disabled people's lives, which reinforce stereotypes, and which are available at each grade (Ayala, 1999; Blaska & Lynch, 1998; Connor & Bejoian, 2006).

Art educators will find many opportunities to incorporate disability representations and disability culture into the curriculum. For example, two statues of people with disabilities placed in general prominence—one in the United States one in Britain—have provoked dynamic debates about recognition, understanding, and acceptance of disability within a national context. In Washington, DC, arguments have raged about whether or not to depict former president Franklin D. Roosevelt in a wheelchair, even though he carefully maintained a public image that hid his disability. In the UK, a large statue of a heavily pregnant woman born with shortened arms due to the drug Thalidomide was temporarily installed in Trafalgar Square amid much controversy and discussions of taste. She juxtaposes interestingly with Lord Nelson's in the same public space, a depiction calling attention to his arm lost in battle and giving rise to conversations about disability in relation to gender, sexuality, reproduction, and war. In addition to sculpture, disability is present—although not necessarily acknowledged—in iconic paintings such as Andrew Wyeth's *Christina's World*—the young woman who twists her body to gaze into the distance was his neighbor who did not walk.

The stunning autobiographical works of Frida Kahlo explicitly chronicle life with physical disabilities, and beg the important question: In what ways does disability inform an artist's work? Kahlo is arguably the world's most famous female painter, and clearly much of her work exists *because of* her disability—from sketches of the initial accident to bold canvases in which she openly shares her bodily experience, physical and psychological. In other examples—without wanting to sound clichéd—artists who have lived with what have been termed "depression" and "schizophrenia," such as Vincent Van Gogh and Beauford Delaney, have produced pioneering original works. Indeed, disability has allowed many artists to create in innovative ways, including Manet's abstract-like *Water Lillies*, and Matisse's colorful boldly shaped collages, creations by individuals actively functioning with visual impairments. Disability confronts the viewer head on in Riva Lehrer's *Circle Stories* (Lehrer, n.d.) which are richly symbolic and vivid portraits of disabled people, including Riva herself, a woman with spina bifida who paints her own portrait in two parts—a top third and bottom third without a midsection, where she positions her spina bifida.

In terms of disability culture, the *values* within the traditional canon of Western art can be examined with view to social and cultural notions of physicality. Ancient Greek and Roman ideals still exert a powerful influence on what constitutes desirable images of perfect bodies. Yet, as Lennard Davis (1995) points out with great irony, we must question a world that will culturally enshrine and accord great beauty to *The Venus de Milo*, but will have the opposite reaction when faced with a real nude woman without arms. In another instance, the act of creating art with body parts considered nonconventional—such as sculpting with feet, painting with a brush in the mouth, can serve to rethink how often narrowly defined are the ways in which we use our bodies for *all* tasks. Finally, there has been a recent interest in Outsider Art as evidenced in annual national exhibitions such as that held at the Puck Building in New York City. Outsider Art values the creative work of people who have not been formally schooled in art techniques, but rather have developed their own distinctive style. Interestingly, many of the artists are disabled and have lived in institutions. As such, Outsider Art can be seen as art from the margins, symbolic of life at the margins, and of epistemological value.

Social studies teachers can use biographies of the artists listed above as well as other famous disabled people including Albert Einstein, Stephen Hawkings, Muhammad Ali, Adrienne Rich, or Stevie Wonder. Social studies is also a good place to learn about the various ways in which disability is socially constructed—by inaccessible schools, social segregation, intolerance of difference, for example—and the ways in which students, themselves, can combat disability discrimination—by speaking out against taunts and hate speech, intentionally including disabled peers in social activities, joining a local disability rights organization, and participating in social action. Similar to critical race studies' call for acknowledging the endemic presence of racism and queer studies' argument for including studies of heterosexism and homophobia in the curriculum, disability studies would urge the study of ableism in the curriculum. History teachers can incorporate disability history into the curriculum: as an offshoot of the Civil Rights Movement (Fleischer & Zames, 2001) and response to systemic ableism; as manifest in other times of history such as the Holocaust (Stiker, 1999); as an outcome of war, particularly any current war; and in national cultural debates as in the Terry Schiavo case (Stolz, 2006). One striking documentary about the Holocaust is Snyder and Mitchell's (2002) *A World Without Bodies*, a film that describes the Nazi campaign to murder disabled people in addition to Jews and other social groups. Given its gruesome contents, the film should be used with older students. When studying culture and ethnicity, it is important to be sure to include disability culture as an example of culture, as well as the ways in which disability and ethnicity intersect (e.g., every ethnic group includes disabled members). These can be studied through art, literature, music, language, and behavior.

The English and language arts curriculum can include fiction or nonfiction reading and writing about disability. Linda Ware (2001) has explored the concept of disability in an English language arts classroom by having students consider people who are not fully included in society. This results in rich discussions among students, and acknowledgment by teaching staff of their own previously unexamined prejudices and areas of discomfort. The unit ends with students creating poetry and prose that foregrounds the theme of disability in relation to contemporary social practices and cultural values. In another example, students with learning disabilities in the self-contained class of Santiago Solis have created illustrated autobiographical portraits in story book form and shared them at interactive exhibitions (Solis & Connor, 2007). While these examples emphasize actual and perceived understandings of the disability experience(s), both the traditional and nontraditional canons of literature offer ample opportunities to analyze how disability is portrayed, largely in inauthentic and misleading ways (Mitchell & Snyder, 2001).

Given the influence of the media in the lives of today's youth, teachers across subject areas can use media studies to help students critically examine popular culture messages that perpetuate disability stereotypes, use media to understand disability, and construct their own media to confront ableism (e.g., making documentaries about disabled family members or classmates; creating music videos that explore disability themes, writing reviews of movies that deal with disability, sending letters to the editor related to current events). Films like the academy award nominees *Autism is a World* (Bedingfield & Wurzberg, 2004) and *King Gimp* (Hadary & Whiteford, 1999), and novels such as *Stuck in Neutral* (Trueman, 2001) and *Freak the Mighty* (Philbrick, 1995) can be used to debate and discuss relevant issues while also meeting state standards (Connor & Bejoian, 2006; Kates, 2006). It is also useful to tap into those films that students see in theaters and that are likely to dispel myths and undermine stereotypes; for example, documentaries like *Murderball* (Shapiro & Rubin, 2005), about athletes who play wheelchair rugby, and movies like *Rory O'Shea Was Here* (Flynn & O'Donnell, 2004), about young adults struggling to choose where they live and with whom. The Farrelly brothers often produce films that end up being controversial in the disability community and can create lively debates about disability stereotypes and the ethics and meanings of representation. These include most recently *The Ringer* (Farrelly, Farrelly, & Blaustein, 2005), about a nondisabled man who pretends to have mental retardation in an attempt to infiltrate and win the Special Olympics.

Today's teacher has been given a monumental task that includes pressure to bring all students to grade level in literacy and math while adhering to state learning standards. When it is suggested that disability be integrated into the curriculum, the response is often, "I don't have time to add anything else to the curriculum." However, there are teachers who have found this is possible (Dinaro, 2006; Kates, 2006; Stolz, 2006). Innovative educators realize that many state standards clarify performance outcomes but avoid dictating the materials used to achieve the outcomes. Whether or not district policy requires the use of particular textbooks, teachers usually have the flexibility to select materials of their own choosing while still adhering to state standards. Finally, teachers often wonder how to make decisions about what curriculum materials are appropriate, and there are many resources available to help, including the *Ragged Edge Online* (formerly *Disability Rag*), the Disability is Natural website (2006), Disability Studies: Information and Resources (Taylor, Shoulz, & Walker, 2003), and the website Disability Studies for Teachers (Syracuse University, 2004).

Access to Curriculum

Another tenet of disability studies holds that programs should be accessible to all students. Access to the curriculum requires much more than merely physically placing disabled students in the general education classroom—an unfortunate and all too common response to the call for inclusion. Sitting in the classroom but having no means of understanding concepts, accessing text or conversations, or demonstrating what one knows or has learned does not represent inclusion. Access to the curriculum requires significant changes in the way curriculum is offered to students and the way in which students are given opportunities to demonstrate learning. One way of achieving this is through universal design for learning (UDL), also called university design for instruction (UDI) (Hackman & Rauscher, 2004; Pliner & Johnson, 2004; Scott, McGuire, & Shaw, 2003), and sometimes abbreviated as universal design (UD). The universal design literature echoes many of the principles of differentiated instruction but universal design deemphasizes documentation and labeling (proving eligibility for specific accommodations), particularly at the higher education level, and emphasizes the creation of environments accessible to the greatest number of people possible without regard to disability status (Burghstahler & Corey, 2008). Resources can be found at the University of Washington (n.d.), National Council on Disability (2004), and in various other publications (Pisha & Coyne, 2001; Preiser & Ostroff, 2004; Rose & Meyer, 2002).

In the last few years, interest in universal design has increased dramatically. IDEIA now requires the application of universal design principles to the education of disabled students in terms of access to assistive technology and the general education curriculum (U.S. Congress, 2004, Sect. 674). The President's Commission on Excellence in Special Education (U.S. Department of Education, 2002) recommended the use of UD in general *and* special education instruction. The Commission specifically stated that "all measures used to assess accountability and educational progress be developed according to principles of universal design" (U.S. Department of Education, 2002, Sect. 2, ¶ 24). It remains to be seen how schools and districts navigate the tensions between the medical model of the IDEIA in light of its call for the use of universal design in curriculum and assessment.

Numerous online resources are available for teachers, including: The Universal Design Education Project (University of Oregon, n.d.), the DO-IT project (University of Washington, 2006), Universal Design Education Online (UDE Online, 2004), and the Ivy Access Initiative (Brown University, 2002) which is a site intended for a higher education audience but it has specific examples of UD in subject matter curriculum as well as useful and specific how-to's.

Teaching

Mara Sapon-Shevin (2000) has noted that "[e]ducators need to transcend discussions of diversity as a classroom problem and regard it as [a] natural, desirable, and inevitable occurrence that enriches educational experiences for both teachers and students" (p. 34). Critical race studies has been instrumental in helping teachers understand race in this light by creating awareness about the importance of racial self-reflection and White privilege. Queer studies and disability studies can help teachers recognize the artifacts of hetero- and ability-privilege, although they have been less effective at this task. Ability privilege plays out in the classroom through ability grouping, segregated classrooms, student leadership roles, playground taunts, and subtle verbal and nonverbal interactions with teachers. Teachers sensitive to the ways in which ability privilege marks some students as disabled while it advantages others can choose teaching strategies and make instructional decisions that minimize the effects of these social processes.

Phil Ferguson (2001) has published an excellent resource for teachers for the Office of Special Education Programs that is available online and includes practical ideas for infusing disability studies into the curriculum: (1) have disabled adults come to the class to talk about their lives; (2) have students do accessibility surveys; (3) have students write stories about disability; (4) incorporate and discuss stories that have disability themes; (5) have children do interviews with disabled people; (6) have students write an essay on stereotypes; (7) show students informational videos about eugenics; (8) have students write biographies of individuals with disabilities; (9) have students learn American Sign Language signs; (10) have students learn the alphabet in Braille; (11) take students to a museum and look for things about disability; (12) have students prepare photo essays; (13) teach students about different brain functions; (14) have students design assistive devices; (15) have students surf the web for disability resources; and (16) have students design a new graphic symbol to signify disability.

Educational Policy

DSE has focused too little on educational policy (Gabel, 2008). A major obstacle to policy work in disability studies in education is the fact that U.S. educational policy—federal, state, and local—uses the medical model of disability. Within this model, policy interventions focus on curing, correcting, or caring for disabled people (Finkelstein, 1996; Longmore, 2003). In other words, the medical model of disability produces intervention models that aim to remediate or fix disabled people and, in turn, take care of them. As Longmore (2003) has noted, "cure or correction has been viewed as the only possible means by which people with disabilities could achieve social acceptance and social assimilation" (p. 217). "Those who are cured or corrected," he continues, "have been relegated to invalidism" (p. 217). This patronizing orientation has been criticized widely in disability studies as a means to oppress disabled people by keeping them subordinate to clinical experts and caretakers (Abberley, 1987; Ferguson, 1994, 2002; van Drenth, 2008). Contrastingly, the social model of disability, according to Finkelstein, produces intervention models that put disabled people in charge of their lives and construct experts as resources to be accessed as consumers. If policy is an attempt to find solutions to social problems, then one must ask whether or not the medical model produces solutions to the problems resulting from the challenging social conditions under which disabled people live their lives. Christopher Donoghue's (2003) analysis of the purposes and outcomes of the ADA are an excellent response to this conundrum. He demonstrates that while the groups advocating for the ADA hoped for policy interventions that would transform social conditions by eliminating discrimination in facilities, programs, and jobs, the federal definition of disability as a medical condition tied the hands of the courts when disabled people sought litigation. Judiciary logic required the application of medical definitions of disability categories to determine if someone was eligible for consideration under the ADA. Of course few impairments, particularly those that are intermittent and invisible, meet strict medical guidelines. Therefore, many disabled litigants have found themselves declared nondisabled and ineligible for protection under the ADA.

Since educational policy follows medical model definitions of disability, students who struggle in school face similar roadblocks to justice. They, too, often face discrimination by virtue of how or how quickly they learn, whether or not they speak Standard English, whether or not they behave or look "normal." The sole recourse of most struggling students and their families is to appeal to special education—a system guided by the IDEIA and that adheres to the same model of disability as does the ADA. If these students are found eligible for special education, they may receive interventions but these interventions, unfortunately, are too often aimed at fixing the individual student—an outcome that flows logically from medical model definitions of disability. When this is the case, the social conditions that produce disability (e.g., inaccessible curriculum or instruction, ability privilege, social isolation, etc.) receive little or no attention.

In 1975, P.L. 94-142 (now the IDEIA) was heralded as civil rights legislation and, to be sure, disabled children have benefited from many of the protections in the law. Yet because the IDEIA also provides the means to discriminate (i.e., segregate) against students based on race, language, behavior, and body function, it can be difficult to argue solidly for maintaining the IDEIA if one adheres to a social model or social interpretation of disability (Beratan, 2006). However, Gabel (2008) has demonstrated that the IDEIA requires states to incorporate universal design for learning in state assessments and curriculum as a means toward student achievement of learning standards. Perhaps this is where disability studies in education can influence policy. First, DSE can advocate for the application of UDL principles in all curriculum and assessment practices. Second, DSE can propose alternatives to the IDEIA. How could we shape policy that protects equal access and opportunity in inclusive learning communities, particularly for the most vulnerable disabled—students with very significant functional limitations? What might that policy look like, what might be its intended and unintended consequences, and how can we be ready with such alternatives when the time is right and policy windows open?

In the meantime, we propose four things that can be done by those interested in these issues: (1) actively pursue research agendas that illuminate the inherent problems with IDEIA, ADA, Section 504 (U.S. Congress, 1973), and any other educational legislation or policy applied to education; (2) disseminate descriptions of efforts by local educators to creatively build inclusive school communities in spite of legislation built on the medical model, including efforts that utilize universal design; (3) disseminate policy alternatives that protect equal access and free appropriate public *inclusive* education but that adhere to a social model or social interpretation of disability; (4) do numbers 1 through 3 in collaboration with the disability rights community and disability studies researchers.

A Way Forward

In *Challenging Orthodoxy*, Gallagher (2004b) notes that "for more than a decade a vigorous discussion has taken place among educators in special education and disability studies...that, despite its importance, has had relatively few participants" (p. vii). Continuing, she claims that "this conversation is of crucial importance because it confronts the fundamental frameworks within which the debates over full inclusion, disability definitions, labeling, and the like are deliberated" (p. vii). We would broaden her claim to point out that while few scholars, practitioners, or policy analysts outside special education have shown an interest in the rights of disabled people in schools, the issue raised by Gallagher extends beyond special education and disability studies. We have attempted to show that there are connections between the issues facing disabled people and those facing people identified by race, sexual orientation, and culture—job and housing discrimination, poverty, suppression of their right to choose who to love and live with, to give some examples.

First and foremost, disability intersects each of these other social groups through the lives of members of those groups and through their shared experiences with discriminatory social arrangements. As Eli Clare (1999) has so eloquently put it: "Gender reaches into disability; disability wraps around class; class strains against abuse; abuse snarls into sexuality; sexuality folds on top of race...everything finally piling into a single human body" (p. 123). Recognizing this as the reality complicates things but also offers interesting challenges both inside and outside the field of education, challenges that are only beginning to be explored (Danforth & Gabel, 2007). "Deliberations on ideas," suggests Gallagher (2004a), and, we would add, deliberations on curriculum, teaching, and policy, need to be "deeply and broadly informed. And this requires...the opportunity to explore disciplines of study outside the confines of [one's] own field" (p. 371). We propose that any movement forward in social justice must integrate disability studies and that this integration deepens and broadens what can be understood and accomplished.

Notes

1. We are using this form to be consistent with the international Disability Rights Movement. Simi Linton (1998) writes that although there is some disagreement about disability language, "[t]he terms *disability* and *disabled people* are most commonly used by disability rights activists" (p. 10). See Titchkosky (2001) for critique of people-first language that points out the ontological problems with its use.
2. For a discussion of two common disability stereotypes—Tiny Tims and supercrips—see Doris Fleischer and Frieda Zames (2001) and the Education for Disability and Gender Equity Curriculum (EDGE) (n.d.).

References

Abberley, P. (1987). The concept of oppression and the development of a social theory of disability. *Disability, Handicap, and Society, 2*(1), 5–19.

Allan, J. E. (1996). Foucault and special educational needs: A "box of tools" for analyzing children's experiences of mainstreaming. *Disability and Society, 11*(2), 219–233.

Allan, J. E. (1999a). *Actively seeking inclusion: Pupils with special needs in mainstream schools.* London: Falmer.

Allan, J. E. (1999b). I don't need this: Acts of transgression by pupils with special educational needs. In K. Ballard (Ed.), *Inclusive education: International voices on disability and justice* (pp. 67–80). London: Falmer.

Andrews, J. E., Carnine, D. W., Coutinho, M. J., Edgar, E. B., Forness, S. R., Fuchs, L. S., et al. (2000). Bridging the special education divide. *Remedial and Special Education, 21*(5), 258–267.

Ayala, E. C. (1999). "Poor little things" and "brave little souls": The portrayal of individuals with disabilities in children's literature. *Reading Research and Instruction, 39*(1), 103–116.

Baker, B. (2002). The hunt for disability: The new eugenics and the normalization of school children. *Teachers College Record, 104*, 663–703.

Banks, J. A. (1995). The historical reconstruction of knowledge about race: Implications for transformative teaching. *Educational Researcher, 24*(2), 15–25.

Barton, L. (Ed.). (1996). *Disability and society: Emerging issues and insights*. London/New York: Longman.

Bedingfield, S. (Producer), & Wurzberg, G. (Director). (2004). *Autism is a world*. [Documentary]. CNN.

Bell, C. (2006). Introducing white disability studies: A modest proposal. In L. J. Davis, (Ed.), *The disability studies reader* (2nd ed., pp. 275–282). New York: Routledge.

Beratan, G. (2006). Institutionalizing inequity: Ableism, racism, and IDEA 2004. *Disability Studies Quarterly,* March. Retrieved May 4th, 2005, from http://www.dsq-sds.org/_articles_html/2006/spring/beratan.asp

Biklen, D. (1992). *Schooling without labels: Parents, educators, and inclusive education*. Philadelphia: Temple University Press.

Birmingham City Council. (2006). Implementing the social model of disability. Retrieved June 2nd, 2006, from http://www.birmingham.gov.uk/GenerateContent?CONTENT_ITEM_ID=1196&CONTENT_ITEM_TYPE=0&MENU_ID=1815

Blanchett, W. (2006). Disproportionate representation of African American students in special education: Acknowledging the role of white privilege and racism. *Educational Researcher, 35*(6), 24–28.

Blaser, A. (2003). Awareness days: Some alternatives to simulation exercises. Retrieved July 9th, 2006, from http://www.ragged-edge-mag.com/0903/0903ft1.html

Blaska, J. K., & Lynch, E. C. (1998). Is everyone included? Using children's literature to facilitate the understanding of disabilities. *Young Children, 53*(2), 36–38.

Bogdan, R., & Bicklen, D. (1977). Handicapism. *Social Policy, 7*(5), 14–19.

Bogdan, R., & Taylor, S. (1989). Relationships with severely disabled people: The social construction of humanness. *Social Problems, 36*(2), 135–147.

Brantlinger, E. A. (1997). Using ideology: Cases of nonrecognition of the politics of research and practice in special education. *Review of Educational Research, 67*(4), 425–459.

Brantlinger, E. A. (2004). Confounding the needs and confronting the norms: An extension of Reid & Valle's essay. *Journal of Learning Disabilities, 37*(6), 490–499.

Brantlinger, E. A. (2005). Slippery shibboleths: The shady side of truisms in special education. In S. L. Gabel (Ed.), *Disability studies in education: Readings in theory and method* (pp. 125–138). New York: Peter Lang.

Brantlinger, E. A. (Ed.). (2006). *Who benefits from special education? Remediating (fixing) other people's children*. Mahwah, NJ: Erlbaum.

Brown University. (2002). Ivy access initiative. Retrieved December 16th, 2006, from http://www.brown.edu/Administration/Dean_of_the_College/uid/html/what_uid.shtml.

Burghstahler, S., & Corey, R. (2008). Postsecondary education: From accommodation to universal design. In S. L. Gabel & S. Danforth (Eds.), *Disability studies in education: An international reader*. New York: Peter Lang.

Charlton, J. (2000). *Nothing about us without us: Disability oppression and empowerment*. Berkeley/Los Angeles: University of California Press.

Clare, E. (1999). *Exile and pride: Disability, queerness and liberation*. Cambridge, MA: South End Press. (Original work published 1998)

Connor, D. J. (2006). Michael's story: "I get into so much trouble just by walking": Narrative knowing and life at the intersections of learning disability, race, and class. *Equity and Excellence in Education, 39*(2), 154–165.

Connor, D. J., & Bejoian, J. (2006). Pigs, pirates, and pills: Using film to teach the social context of disability. *Teaching Exceptional Children, 39*(2), 52–60.

Corker, M., & Shakespeare, T. (Eds.). (2002). *Disability/postmodernity*. London: Continuum.

Danforth, S. (1997). On what basis hope? Modern progress and postmodern possibilities. *Mental Retardation, 35*(2), 93–106.

Danforth, S. (1999). Pragmatism and the scientific validation of professional practices in American special education. *Disability and Society, 14*(6), 733–751.

Danforth, S. (2004). The "postmodern" heresy in special education: A sociological analysis. *Mental Retardation, 42*(6), 445–458.

Danforth, S., & Gabel, S. L. (2007). *Vital questions for disability studies in education.* New York: Peter Lang.

Danforth, S., & Smith, T. J. (2005). *Engaging troubling students: A constructivist approach.* Thousand Oaks, CA: Corwin Press.

Davis, L. J. (1995). *Enforcing normalcy: Disability, deafness and the body.* London: Verso.

Delgado, R., & Stefancic, J. (2001). *Critical race theory: An introduction.* New York: New York University Press.

Dinaro, A. (2006). *Students' understandings: "Special education is where students with disabilities learn to be normal."* Paper presented at the annual meeting of Society for Disability Studies, Bethesda, MD.

Disability is Natural. (2006). Retrieved October 2nd, 2006, from http://www.disabilityisnatural.com/

Disability Studies in Education (DSE). (2004). Objectives. Retrieved July 10th, 2004, from http://ced.ncsu.edu/2/dse

Donoghue, C. (2003). Challenging the authority of the medical definition of disability: An analysis of the resistance to the social constructionist paradigm. *Disability and Society, 18*(2), 199–208.

Education for Disability and Gender Equity (EDGE). (n.d.). Retrieved December 5th, 2006, from http://www.disabilityhistory.org/dwa/edge/curriculum/cult_contenta1.htm

Erevelles, N. (2000). Educating unruly bodies: Critical pedagogy, disability studies, and the politics of schooling. *Educational Theory, 50*(1), 25–47.

Erevelles, N. (2006). How does it feel to be a problem? Race, disability, and exclusion in educational policy. In E. A. Brantlinger (Ed.), *Who benefits from special education? Remediating (fixing) other people's children* (pp.77–99). Mahwah, NJ: Erlbaum.

Farrelly, P., & Farrelly, B. (Producers), & Blaustein, B. W. (Director). (2005). *The ringer.* [Motion picture]. Los Angeles: Fox Searchlight Pictures.

Ferguson, P. (1994). *Abandoned to their fate: Social policy and practice toward severely retarded people in America, 1920–1920.* Philadelphia: Temple University Press.

Ferguson, P. (2001). *On infusing disability studies into the general curriculum. On point... Brief discussions of critical issues.* Washington, D.C.: Special Education Programs (ED/OSERS). Retrieved July 25th, 2006 from, http://www.urbanschools.org/pdf/OPdisability.pdf?v_document_name=On%20Infusing%20Disability%20Studies

Ferguson, P. (2002). Notes toward a history of hopelessness: Disability and the places of therapeutic failure. *Disability, Culture and Education, 1*(1), 27–40.

Ferri, B. A., & Connor, D. J. (2005). Tools of exclusion: Race, disability, and (re)segregated education. *Teachers College Record, 107*(3), 453–474.

Ferri, B. A., & Connor, D. J. (2006). *Reading resistance: Discourses of exclusion in the desegregation and inclusion debates.* New York: Peter Lang.

Finkelstein, V. (1996). *Modeling disability.* Retrieved July 28, 2006 from, http://www.leeds.ac.uk/disability-studies/archiveuk/finkelstein/models/models.htm

Finkelstein, V. (2003). *The social model of disability repossessed.* Retrieved September 15th, 2004 from, http://www.leeds.ac.uk/disability-studies/archiveuk/finkelstein/soc%20mod%20repossessed.pdf

Fleischer, D. Z., & Zames, F. (2001). *The disabilities rights movement: From charity to confrontation.* Philadelphia: Temple University Press.

Flynn, J. (Producer), & O'Donnell, D. (Director). (2004). *Rory O'Shea was here.* [Motion picture]. Focus Features.

Fries, K. (1998). *Body, remember.* New York: Plume.

Fuss, D., (Ed.). (1991). *InsideOut: Lesbian theories, gay theories.* New York: Routledge.

Gabay, R. (Producer), & Kaufman, M. (Director). (2002). *The Laramie project.* [Documentary]. HBO.

Gabel, S. L. (2008). A model for policy activism. In S. L. Gabel & S. Danforth (Eds.), *Disability studies in education: An international reader.* New York: Peter Lang.

Gabel, S. L. (2005). Introduction: Disability studies in education. In S. L. Gabel (Ed.), *Disability studies in education: Readings in theory and method* (pp. 1–20). New York: Peter Lang.

Gabel, S. L., & Peters, S. (2004). Presage of a paradigm shift? Beyond the social model of disability toward a resistance theory of disability. *Disability and Society, 19*(6), 571–596.

Gallagher, D. J. (1998). The scientific knowledge base of special education: Do we know what we think we know? *Exceptional Children, 64*(4), 493–502.

Gallagher, D. J. (2001). Neutrality as a moral standpoint, conceptual confusion and the full inclusion debate. *Disability and Society, 16*(5), 637–654.

Gallagher, D. J. (2004a). Moving the conversation forward: Empiricism versus relativism reconsidered. In D. J. Gallagher, L. Heshusius, R. P. Iano, & T. M. Skrtic (Eds.), *Challenging orthodoxy in special education: Dissenting voices* (pp. 363–376). Denver, CO: Love.

Gallagher, D. J. (2004b). Preface. In D. J. Gallagher, L. Heshusius, R. P. Iano, & T. M. Skrtic (Eds.), *Challenging orthodoxy in special education: Dissenting voices* (p. ix). Denver, CO: Love.

Gallagher, D. J. (2006). If not absolute objectivity, then what? A reply to Kauffman and Sasso. *Exceptionality, 14*(2), 91–107.

Gallagher, D. J., Heshusius, L., Iano, R. P., & Skrtic, T. M. (2004). *Challenging orthodoxy in special education: Dissenting voices.* Denver, CO: Love.

Garland-Thompson, R. (1997). *Extraordinary bodies.* New York: Columbia University Press.

Globetti, E., Globetti, G., Brown, C. L., & Smith, R. E. (1993). Social interaction and multiculturalism. *NASPA, 30*(3), 209–218.

Goodley, D., & Lathom, R. (2005). *Disability and psychology: Critical introductions and reflections.* New York: Palgrave Macmillan.

Gould, S. J. (1981). *The mismeasure of man.* New York: W. W. Norton.

Government of Canada. (2004). Defining disability. Retrieved July 18th, 2006 from, http://www.sdc.gc.ca/asp/gateway.asp?hr=/en/hip/odi/documents/Definitions/Definitions003.shtml&hs=oxf

Hackman, H. W., & Rauscher, L. (2004). A pathway to access for all: Exploring the connections between universal instructional design and social justice education. *Equity and Excellence in Education, 37*, 114–123.

Hadary, S. H. (Producer), & Whiteford, W. A. (Director). (1999). *King gimp.* [Documentary] HBO Films.

Hahn, H. (2002). Academic debates and political advocacy: The U.S. disability movement. In C. Barnes, M. Oliver, & L. Barton (Eds.), *Disability studies today* (pp. 162–189). Cambridge, UK: Polity Press.

Harry, B., & Klingner, J. (2006). *Why are so many minority students in special education?* New York: Teachers College Press.

Hehir, T. (2002). Eliminating ableism in education. *Harvard Educational Review, 72*(1). Retrieved September 20th, 2004 from, http://www.gse.harvard.edu/hepg/hehir.htm

Hehir, T. (2005). *New directions in special education: Eliminating ableism in policy and practice.* Cambridge, MA: Harvard University Press.

Heshusius, L. (1989). The Newtonian mechanistic paradigm, special education, and contours of alternatives: An overview. *Journal of Learning Disabilities, 22*(7), 403–415.

Heshusius, L. (1994). Freeing ourselves from objectivity: Managing subjectivity, or turning toward a participatory mode of consciousness? *Educational Researcher, 23*(3), 15–22.

Heshusius, L. (1995). Holism and special education: There is no substitute for real life purposes and processes. In T. M. Skrtic (Ed.), *Disability and democracy: Reconstructing (special) education for postmodernity* (pp. 166–189). New York: Teachers College Press.

Heshusius, L. (1996). *From positivism to interpretivism and beyond: Tales of transformation in educational and social research: The body–mind connection.* New York: Teachers College Press.

Humphrey, J. C. (2000). Researching disability politics, or, some problems with the social model in practice. *Disability and Society, 15*(1), 63–85.

Iano, R. (1986). The study and development of teaching: With implications for the advancement of special education. *Remedial and Special Education, 75*(5), 50–61.

Iano, R. (1990). Special education teachers: Technicians or educators? *Journal of Learning Disabilities, 23,* 462–465.

Johnson, J. R. (2004). Universal instructional design and critical (communication) pedagogy: Strategies for voice, inclusion, and social justice/change. *Equity and Excellence in Education, 37,* 145–153.

Kates, B. (2006). *There's no such thing as normal.* Paper presented at the annual meeting of Society for Disability studies, Bethesda, MD.

Kauffman, J. M., & Hallahan, D. P. (2005). *The illusion of full inclusion: A comprehensive critique of a current special education bandwagon.* Austin, TX: Pro-Ed.

Kauffman, J. M., & Sasso, G. M. (2006a). Toward ending cultural and cognitive relativism in special education. *Exceptionality, 14*(2), 65–90.

Kauffman, J. M., & Sasso, G. M. (2006b). Certainty, doubt, and the reduction of uncertainty. *Exceptionality, 14*(2), 109–120.

Ladson-Billings, G. (1995). Toward a theory of culturally relevant pedagogy. *American Educational Research Journal, 32*(3), 465–491.

Ladson-Billings, G., & Tate, W. F. (1995). Toward a critical race theory of education. *Teachers College Record, 97*(1), 47–68.

Lehrer, R. (n.d.). Circle stories. retrieved December 6, 2006, from http://home.earthlink.net/~rivalehrer/circlestories/csframesest.html

Linton, S. (1998). *Claiming disability.* New York: New York University Press.

Linton, S. (2006). *My body politic: A memoir.* Ann Arbor: University of Michigan Press.

Longmore, P. K. (2003). *Why I burned my book and other essays on disability.* Philadelphia: Temple University Press.

Losen, D., & Orfield, G. (2002). *Racial inequity in special education.* Cambridge, MA: Harvard University Press.

Luhmann, S. (1998). Queering/querying pedagogy? Pedagogy is a pretty queer thing. In W. Pinar (Ed.), *Queer theory in education* (pp. 141–155). Mahwah, NJ:Erlbaum.

Manchester City Council. (2005). The social model of disability. Retrieved May 10th, 2006 from, http://www.manchester.gov.uk/disability/policies/model.htm

Marx, S. (2004). Regarding whiteness: Exploring and intervening in the effects of white racism in teacher education. *Equity and Excellence in Education, 37*(1), 31–43.

Matsuda, M. J., Lawrence, C. R., Delgado, R., & Crenshaw, K. W. (1993). *Critical race theory, assaultative speech, and the First Amendment.* Boulder, CO: Westview Press.

McDermott, R., Goldman, S., & Varenne, H. (2006). The cultural work of learning disabilities. *Educational Researcher, 35*(6), 12–17.

McRuer, R. (2006). *Crip theory: Cultural signs of queerness and disability.* New York: New York University Press.

McRuer, R., & Wilkerson, A. L. (2003). Introduction. Desiring disability: Queer theory meets disability studies. *Journal of Gay and Lesbian Studies, 9*(1–2), 1–23.

Merton, R. K. (1972). Insiders and outsiders: A chapter in the sociology knowledge. *American Journal of Sociology, 78*(1), 9–47.

Michalko, R. (2002). *The difference that disability makes.* Philadelphia: Temple University Press.

Mitchell, D., & Snyder, S. (Directors). (1997). *Vital signs: Crip culture talks back.* [Documentary]. Brace Yourself Productions.

Mitchell, D., & Snyder, S. (2001). *Narrative prosthesis: disabilities and the dependence of discourse.* Ann Arbor: University of Michigan.

Mitchell, D. D. (2006). Flashcard: Alternating between visible and invisible identities. *Equity and Excellence in Education, 39*(2), 154–165.

Mooney, J., & Cole, D. (2000). *Learning outside the lines.* New York: Simon & Schuster.

National Center for Children and Youth with Disabilities (NICHCY). (1996). The education of children and youth with special needs: What do the laws say? Retrieved July 15th, 2006 from, http://www.nichcy.org/pubs/outprint/nd15txt.htm

National Council on Disability. (2004). *Design for inclusion: Creating a new marketplace.* Washington, D.C. Retrieved July 30th, 2006 from, http://www.ncd.gov/newsroom/publications/2004/online_newmarketplace.htm#afbad

National Institute on Disability Research and Rehabilitation (NIDRR). (1999). *Long range plan for fiscal years 1999–2003.* Retrieved April 20th, 2005 from, http://www.ncddr.org/new/announcements/nidrr_lrp/lrp_bg.html#1di

O'Connor, C., & Fernandez, S. DeL. (2006). Race, class, and disproportionality: Reevaluating the relationship between poverty and special education placement. *Educational Researcher, 35*(6), 6–11.

O'Connor, G. (2001). Bad. In P. Rodis, S. Garrod, & M. L. Boscardin (Eds.), *Learning disabilities and life stories* (pp. 62–72). Needham Heights: Allyn & Bacon.

Oliver, M. (1990). *The politics of disablement.* Basingstoke, UK: Macmillan.

Oliver, M. (1996). *Understanding disability: From theory to practice.* New York: St. Martin's Press.

Peters, S. (1996). The politics of disability identity. In L. Barton (Ed.), *Disability and society: Emerging issues and insights* (pp. 215–246). London/New York: Longman.

Peters, S. (2000). Is there a disability culture? A syncretisation of three possible world views. *Disability & Society, 15*(4), 583–601.

Philbrick, P. (1995). *Freak the mighty.* New York: Scholastic.

Pisha, B., & Coyne, P. (2001). Smart from the start: The promise of universal design for learning. *Remedial and Special Education, 22*(4), 107–203.

Pliner, S. M., & Johnson, J. R. (2004). Historical, theoretical, and foundational principles of universal instructional design in higher education. *Equity and Excellence in Education, 37,* 105–113.

Preiser, W. F. E., & Ostroff, E. (Eds.). (2004). *Universal design handbook.* New York: McGraw-Hill.

Provincial Health Ethics Network. (2001). Disability and the allocation of health care resources: The case of Connor Auton. Retrieved July 18th, 2006, from http://www.phen.ab.ca/materials/het/het12-01b.htm.

Ragged Edge Online. (n.d.). Retrieved October 2nd, 2006, from http://www.ragged-edge-mag.com/

Rauscher, L., & McClintock, J. (1996). Ableism and curriculum design. In M. Adams, L. A. Bell, & P. Griffen (Eds.), *Teaching for diversity and social justice* (pp. 198–231). New York: Routledge.

Reid, D. K., & Knight, M.G. (2006). Disability justifies exclusion of minority students: A critical history grounded in disability studies. *Educational Researcher, 35*(6), 18–23.

Reid, D. K., & Valle, J. (2004). The discursive practice of learning disability: Implication for instruction and parent school relations. *Journal of Learning Disabilities, 37*(6), 466–481.

Rice, N. (2005). Guardians of tradition: Presentations of inclusion in three introductory special education textbooks. *International Journal of Inclusive Education, 9*(4), 405–429.

Rose, D. H., & Meyer, A. (2002). *Teaching every student in the digital age: Universal design for learning.* Alexandria, VA: Association for Supervision and Curriculum Development.

Russell, M. (1998). *Beyond ramps: Disability at the end of the social construct.* Monroe, ME: Common Courage.

Safford, P. L., & Safford, E. J. (1996). *A history of childhood and disability.* New York: Teachers College Press.

Sapon-Shevin, M. (2000). Schools fit for all. *Educational Leadership, 58*(4), 34–39.

Sasso, G. M. (2001). The retreat from inquiry and knowledge in special education. *The Journal of Special Education, 34*(4), 178–193.

Scott, S. S., McGuire, J. M., & Shaw, S. F. (2003). Universal design for instruction: A new paradigm for adult instruction in postsecondary education. *Remedial and Special Education, 24*(6), 369–370.

Sedgwick, E. K. (1990). *The epistemology of the closet.* Berkeley: University of California Press.

Selden, S. (2000). Eugenics and the construction of merit, race, and disability. *Journal of Curriculum Studies, 32*(2), 235–252.

Shakespeare, T. (1994). Cultural representations of disabled people. *Disability and Society, 9*(3), 283–299.

Shakespeare, T., & Watson, N. (1997). Defending the social model. *Disability & Society, 12*(2), 293–300.

Shakespeare, T., & Watson, N. (2001). The social model of disability: An outdated ideology? In S. Barnartt & B. Altman (Eds.), *Exploring theories and expanding methodologies: Where we are and where we need to go* (pp. 9–28). Oxford, UK: Elsevier Science.

Shapiro, D. A. (Producer), & Rubin, H. A. (Director). (2005). *Murderball.* [Documentary]. United States: Think Film.

Skrtic, T. M. (1991). *Behind special education: A critical analysis of professional culture and school organization.* Denver, CO: Love.

Skrtic, T. M. (1995). Theory/practice and objectivism: The modern view of the professions. In T. M. Skrtic (Ed.), *Disability and democracy: Reconstructing (special) education for postmodernity* (pp. 3–24). New York: Teachers College Press.

Slee, R. (1996). Clauses of conditionality: The "reasonable" accommodation of language. In L. Barton (Ed.), *Disability and society: Emerging issues and insights* (pp. 107–122). London/New York: Longman.

Slee, R. (1997). Imported or important theory? Sociological interrogations of disablement and special education. *British Journal of Sociology of Education, 18*(3), 107–119.

Snipp, C. M. (1998). The first Americans: American Indians. In M. L. Anderson & P. H. Collins (Eds.), *Race, class, and gender* (pp. 357–364). Belmont, CA: Wadsworth.

Snyder, S., & Mitchell, D. M. (Producers, Directors). (2002). *A world without bodies* [Documentary]. Chicago: Brace Yourself Productions.

Society for Disability Studies (SDS). (n.d.). Guidelines for disability studies. Retrieved January 7, 2006 from, http://www.uic.edu/orgs/sds/generalinfo.html

Solis, S., & Connor, D. J. (2007). Theory meets practice: Disability studies and personal narratives in school. In S. Danforth & S. Gabel (Eds.), *Vital questions facing disability studies in education* (pp. 103–120). New York: Peter Lang.

Solis, S. (2007.) Snow White and the seven "dwarfs"—Queercripped. *Hypatia: A Journal of Feminist Philosophy, 22*(1), 114–131.

Solorzano, D. G., & Yosso, T. J. (2002). Critical race methodology: Counter-storytelling as an analytical framework for education research. *Qualitative Inquiry, 8*(1), 23–44.

Stiker, H. J. (1999). *A history of disability.* Ann Arbor, MI: Love.

Stolz, S. (2006). *Confronting ableist conceptions in the high school classroom.* Paper presented at the annual meeting of Society for Disability Studies, Bethesda, MD.

Syracuse University. (2004). Disability studies for teachers. Retrieved October 2nd, 2006 from, http://www.disabilitystudiesforteachers.org

Tate, W. F. (1997). Critical race theory and education: History, theory, and implications. *Review of Research in Education, 22,* 195–247.

Taylor, S., & Bogdan, R. (1989). On accepting relationships between people with mental retardation and non-disabled people: Towards an understanding of acceptance. *Disability, Handicap, & Society, 4*(1), 21–36.

Taylor, S., Shoultz, B., & Walker, P. (Eds.). (2003). Disability studies: Information and resources. Retrieved October 2nd, 2006 from, http://thechp.syr.edu/Disability_Studies_2003_current.html

Teranishi, R. T. (2002). Asian Pacific Americans and critical race theory: An examination of school racial climate. *Equity and Excellence in Education, 35*(2), 144–154.

Thomas, C., & Corker, M. (2002). A journey around the social model. In M. Corker & T. Shakespeare (Eds.), *Disability/postmodernity* (pp. 18–31). New York/London: Routledge.

Titchkosky, T. (2001). Disability: A rose by any other name? "People-first" language in Canadian society. *Canadian Review of Sociology and Anthropology, 38*(2), 125–140.

Tremain, S. (2002). On the subject of impairment. In M. Corker & T. Shakespeare (Eds.), *Disability/postmodernity* (pp. 32–47). New York/London: Routledge.

Trueman, T. (2001). *Stuck in neutral*. New York: HarperCollins.

Union of Physically Impaired Against Segregation (UPIAS). (1975). *Fundamental principles of disability*. Retrieved July 5, 2004 from, http://www.leeds.ac.uk/disability-studies/archiveuk/UPIAS/fundamental%20principles.pdf

U. S. Congress. (1973). *Rehabilitation Act,* P.L. 93-112. Retrieved July 13th, 2005 from http://www.usdoj.gov/crt/ada/pubs/ada.txt

U.S. Congress. (1990). *Americans with Disabilities Act,* P.L. 101-336. Retrieved July 1, 2006 from from, http://www.usdoj.gov/crt/ada/pubs/ada.txt

U.S. Congress. (2004). *Individuals with Disability Educational Improvement Act,* 108-446. Washington, DC: Author.

U.S. Department of Education. (2002). *President's commission on excellence in special education report: A new era: Revitalizing special education for children and their families.* Washington, D.C.: Author.

U.S. Department of Education. (2005). *IDEA reauthorization.* (Federal Register). Retrieved July 13, 2005 from, http://a257.g.akamaitech.net/7/257/2422/01jan20051800/edocket.access.gpo.gov/2005/pdf/05-11804.pdf

Universal Design Education Online. (2004). Retrieved December 16th, 2006, from http://www.udeducation.org/

University of Oregon. (n.d.). Universal Design Education Project. Retrieved December 16th, 2006, from http://www.uoregon.edu/~sij/udep/index.htm

University of Washington. (2006). DO-IT. Retrieved December 16th, 2006 from, http://www.washington.edu/doit/

van Drenth, A. (2008). Caring, power and disabled children: The rise of the educational élan in the United States and Europe, in particular in Belgium and the Netherlands. In S. L. Gabel & S. Danforth (Eds.), *Disability studies in education: An international reader.* New York: Peter Lang.

Ware, L. (2001). Writing, identity, and the other: Dare we do disabilities studies? *Journal of Teacher Education, 52*(2), 107–123.

Warner, M. (1993). *Fear of a queer planet: Queer politics and social theory.* Minneapolis: University of Minnesota Press.

Watts, I. E., & Erevelles, N. (2004). These deadly times: Reconceptualizing school violence by using critical race theory and disability studies. *American Education Research Journal, 41*(2), 271–299.

25 Impediments to Social Justice

Hierarchy, Science, Faith, and Imposed Identity (Disability Classification)

Ellen Brantlinger

In this chapter, I discuss how school hierarchy and imposed disability identity are products of a (social) science that refuses ethics as a grounding for actions. Observing that the special education faith community touts the science of classifying children and applying evidence-based practices as an enhancement of classified students' lives, I counter that such scientific "progress" interferes with social justice for students caught in the burgeoning and sticky web of disability labels and specialized placements. I take a hard look at what science actually does as it tinkers in the realm of reifying student distinctions. I explore the historical braiding of science and disability, and challenge professionals who fixate on science to understand that for there to be social justice in school and society, they must infuse a social reciprocity morality into their practice. I briefly review evidence of the historical dangers of relying on science without considering the ethics of practice. I account for how traditional scientists can lose their intellectual edge in understanding authentic human problems. I also focus on theories of hierarchy production and social class to explain how stratified school and social class systems affect identity formation and democratic governance.

Eying the Prize: Infusion of Social Reciprocity Ethics in Social Actions

Based on his meta-analysis of anthropological studies, Brown (1991) concludes that social hierarchy is a human universal; that is, people in all societies construct stratified social relations around such characteristics as race, gender, appearance, and family affiliation. Although Brown points to hierarchy's intractability, he more optimistically reports that the universal people also proclaim a social reciprocity morality that encompasses the virtues of mutual respect and social equality as their ideal. That "all men (sic) are created equal" and should be treated equally infuses official governmental documents and legal codes.

At the risk of condemnation by postmodernists and poststructuralists, I tout social reciprocity as a universal human ethic that should always guide people's lives (Brantlinger, 2001, 2004a). I contend that critical theorists and disability studies scholars hold the same view, although they rarely state this explicitly. At the macrolevel, Rawls (1971) extols the benefits of a distributive justice in which resources are divided equally, except he insists that the greatest portion should go to those with the greatest needs. In terms of basing public policy on reciprocity principles, societies would have universal health care, free public education from daycare through university, equivalent funding for all schools and school districts, desegregation and inclusion at all levels, Social Security and Medicare for the elderly and infirm, accessible public transportation (perhaps similar to the efficient interurban streetcar system that was bought and then closed down by capitalists intent on selling cars), and fairly equalized salaries for all workers. Reciprocity morality encompasses protection of the natural environment, which would require immediate and drastic change in human/material relations to combat global warming and vanishing habitats for creatures at risk of harm and extinction, including human beings.

Societal systems that promote democracy and social justice are built on social reciprocity ideals. Social justice requires a shared worldview that recognizes that peaceful and productive social interdependence is built on mutual respect, fairness, recognition of self-defined identity, and sense of community (Kittay, 1999; Koggel, 1998). Observing teachers who effectively created inclusive and supportive learning communities, we found the following shared attitudes and behaviors: they facilitated student self-determination and social-responsibility; enabled success and positive identity; supported inclusive and respectful social relations; were sensitive to feelings and expressed needs; provided space for the expression of diverse opinions; engaged interest in local to global issues; created opportunity to articulate opinions and defend personal positions; enhanced group goal-setting and sense of accomplishment; inspired students to seek solutions to authentic social problems; enhanced literacy and knowledge; and developed commitment to democratic ideals (Brantlinger, Morton, & Washburn, 1999). Emancipatory pedagogy encourages students to engage—rather than avoid—the controversial (Brantlinger & Danforth, 2006).

Although socialism, the political system most aligned with social reciprocity morality, is dismissed as un-American, religious faiths are more consistent with socialism's social reciprocity morality[1] than with the competitive and divisive ethos of capitalism. Unfortunately, prevailing hegemonic ideology reinforces neoliberals' fantasy that unfettered capitalism will automatically and wisely regulate the market and shape policy for the public good; as a result, even people who receive piddling amounts of trickle-down rewards appear convinced of the validity of capitalism. Capitalism, in turn, constructs desire for status as well as resource and opportunity hoarding; that is, the enactment of social hierarchy.

Disability Studies: Endorsing People's Right to Name Themselves and Tell Their Stories

Disability studies, in contrast to special education, was founded on collective opposition to imposed labels and social segregation. Disability study scholarship centers on preventing the damage caused by disability constructs and hierarchical and segregating practices in schools. Ferri and Connor (2006) "problematize soft labels" that have "expanded the meaning of disability and facilitated containment and exclusion" (p. 176, 179). Disability studies scholars eschew the technical-rational science of mainstream special educators who pursue practices that continue to label and separate children on the grounds of disability. A rule that arose from African-American, feminist, and queer studies initiatives is that people have the right to name themselves and have their names respected by others. Similarly, disability studies scholars advocate for children's and adults' right to declare whether or not they have a disability and participate in determining how their needs might be met.

Related to the idea of self-determination, Moyers (2007, January 12) claims that people are entitled to tell their own stories. In regard to learning to understand oneself and speak one's own stories, I fondly recall my senior English class in a rural Minnesota high school in 1957. Mrs. Deutsch had students envision the "good life" and describe it to classmates. She was a strict, no-nonsense teacher, so we had to be honest, respectful, and supportive in sharing our identities and ideas about the future. It is odd that we were comfortable doing this with Mrs. Deutsch, a product of East coast Ivy League schools and generally intimidating due to her style and high expectations. My class of almost 40 had attended school together in the same building for 12 years. At least two classmates could not read at all and others were not academically accomplished, nevertheless, they were included in the activity and everyone listened to, and respected, their stories and dreams. After imagining our futures, we spent the year deciphering what various authors conveyed about their ideas, or their character's ideas, of living a good life. It was a much-needed consciousness-raising experience that forced us to think about our values and goals. The activity brought the class closer together, perhaps falling into the category of "dialogue" (encounter of true words between people) envisioned by Freire, who argues, "dialogue cannot exist in the absence of a profound love for the world" and "cannot exist without humility and hope" (cited in Hudak, 2001, pp. 70–73). Based on that brief overview of the implications of social reciprocity morality, I next discuss the current tendencies that interfere with its realization.

The Mechanisms and Purposes of Hierarchy Production

Apfelbaum (1999) theorizes about the mechanisms of, and rationale for, the creation of hierarchy. She observes that dominant groups shore up distinction and advantage by creating myths about features related to race, class, gender, ability, and competency. They promote their own traits as superior by circulating evidence (often based on science) that only members of the mainstream embody important standards. Outsiders, and their attributes, are *marked, labeled, branded, and stigmatized.* Apfelbaum points out that names imply within-group homogeneity and between group difference. Dominant groups hold maximum power when the distinction between "us" and "them" is perceived as a fundamental, irreversible asymmetry, with groups having little in common. Yet, hierarchies are not purposeless, passive rankings but, rather, are based on interdependent status relationships. Domination depends on subordination. Winners need losers. Superiority needs inferiority. The status, role, and perhaps even raison d'être of dominant groups depend on the existence of subordinate others. In creating imaginary, symbolic distinctions that reify difference, powerful insiders project onto outsiders what they disdain. If the central group considers itself normal and able, "Others" become abnormal and disabled. Said (1978) posits the "Orient" portrayal of Muslims as a phobic projection of Western imaginary. Similarly, Nietzsche (1967) observes that "one becomes good by constructing the Other as evil" (cited in McCarthy & Dimitriadis, 2001, p. 225).

Capitalism structures societal hierarchy, but schools are the key institution that reproduces social stratification (Bowles & Gintis, 1976). Meritocractic schools[2] are instrumental in producing merit (social capital valued for future exchange) and structuring privilege. For example, creating advanced courses for advantaged students means Others with less power are relegated to an oppressive substructure of low tracks and special education segregation. The damaging impact of meritocracy's subordinate creation is generally underestimated and ignored (Young, 1965). As with other critical theorists and disability studies scholars, I maintain that the lessons learned about self and Others within meritocratic schools are so lethal to the involved individuals and to democratic community that they are not justifiable.

Researchers who confront school stratification tend to focus on victims—the children shunted aside and devalued. Although I agree that children from nonadvantaged families suffer most in meritocracies, the winning typically associated with elite students must be questioned. Intense within-class competition is debilitating. Regardless of their own insistence on privilege, school hierarchy poses risks for dominant class students (see Brantlinger, 1993, 2003, 2004b, forthcoming a, b). To understand why meritocracies develop despite not benefiting anybody, I look at how science, perhaps unwittingly, provides the framework and tools for school stratification.

My discussion in this chapter relates mostly to students in "high-incidence" or "mild" disability categories (learning disabilities, mild mental retardation, emotional disturbance, attention deficit disorder, and attention deficit hyperactivity disorder; that is, LD, MiMH, ED, ADD, ADHD). As Mercer (1973) observes, children with these labels tend not to be seen as disabled by their families, so their "disability" surfaces primarily within the school context. It is no coincidence that children classified as failures are disproportionately from families who are poor and of color (Artiles & Trent, 1994; Oakes, 2005). While the negative repercussions of imposing damaging labels and school segregation of special education must be recognized, it is not the only stratifying system that inflicts harm. Ability grouping, tracking, ethnocentric curriculum, personal prejudice, and lack of enforcement of prosocial behavior also interfere with the creation of inclusive, democratic learning communities. Furthermore, despite the lack of evidence of academic and social gains from student sorting and ranking, these have intensified over time (Caplan, 1995; McNeil, 2000). Because schools are structured to produce differentiated outcomes for diverse students, the resulting failure cannot be considered unintentional (Varenne & McDermott, 1998).

Earlier I stated that everyone has the right to name themselves and tell their own stories (determine their life conditions). Yet, anyone who has watched students resist labels understands that social justice is not served by a special education system that bases "services" (educational funding) on "disability" classification. I recently witnessed an adolescent, whose care-provider tactfully suggested that she be tested for a learning "condition," scream at the top of her lungs "I am *not* ADHD!" During years of teaching special education and supervising field settings, I noticed the pain and humiliation experienced by classified children. I watched them sneak into special education classes early or late so their destination could not be detected by schoolmates, insist that teachers cover windows to the room so that nobody could see them there, and carry big wrapper-covered books in the hallway so they would appear smart—not stupid and "special education."

Nevertheless, instead of seeing this rejection and disgrace, professionals and policymakers—middle class people generally—see special education as beneficial for classified students. I argue that it is the people who gain employment by "meeting Others' needs" who are the primary beneficiaries of the system (Brantlinger, 2006). While labeled students tell of personal shame and ineffective self-contained (segregated) programs, individuals with the power to create categorical labels, classify children, and determine their treatment and placement are rarely positioned to identify with, or even listen to, labeled children and their families (Hudak & Kihn, 2001; Stoughton, 2006). Just as powerful individuals evade fighting in wars they create, those who structure stratified schooling are rarely positioned at the bottom rung of school hierarchy.

In *Successful Failure: The School America Builds*, Varenne and McDermott (1998) explore how the failure identity built into a [meritocratic] school structure inflicts systemic cruelty and symbolic violence. Davies (2004) identifies the "maldistribution of resources that effects psychological, emotional, cultural, and intellectual integrity" as political violence (p. 11). It is puzzling—and unforgivable—that in a purportedly democratic country, children are forced to take part in compulsory schooling that begins to bestow the status of winner and loser on them from an early age. Students struggle to deflect the failure identity imposed on them during their school years. Interviews indicate that years after leaving school low-income parents are still intensely emotional in describing their resentment of disparaging labels, rejection, and isolation from "respectable kids" (Brantlinger,

1985). Kaufman (2001) poignantly recalls her own struggle to retrieve a positive identity years after she suffered the indignity of being held back in first grade. The reach of disability classification is not restricted to the school years—it has "staying power" (Hudak, 2001, p. 9). It is likely that classification "continues to have meaning after the label is no longer relevant" because disability identity is "construed as innate and stable," something inherent in individuals rather than a by-product of school structure (Taubman, 2001, p. 186).

Official Imposition of Damaged Identity

Identity formation is both "voluntary and involuntary" (Fuss, 1995, p. 10). When voluntary, "people tell Others who they are, but even more important, they tell themselves and try to act as though they are who they say they are" (Holland, Lachicotte, Skinner, & Cain, 1998, p. 3). When identity is voluntary, people experience autonomy and control, however, the imposition of negative identity causes various reactions. The healthiest response may be to reject the despised label, its implications, and even the educational system responsible for producing the label. In contrast, those who internalize the involuntary identity and passively comply with "the system" often succumb to self-hate and loss of agency. Either way, labeled students are alienated from the settings where naming takes place. Clearly, identity develops in the midst of power relationships: "Most struggles over social justice are about the domination, silencing, oppression, and marginalization of specific identity groups" (Dimitridis & Carlson, 2003, p.18). Focusing on colonialism's neurotic structure, Fanon (1952) notes the ravages a racist society inflicts on Black Americans' identity. In racial classification, minority status inevitably equates with inferiority and stigma (Peshkin, 1991). "Many constructs [labels], unreflected upon, carry the messages of power: they demean; they exclude; they create stereotypes (Greene, 2001, p. xvi). In *Stigma* (1963) and *Asylum* (1961), Goffman was among the first to describe the profound impact of disability labels and institutionalization. Although the application of derogatory labels and ostracizing placement translates into emotional trauma and social stress for a large number of children, Apple (2001) claims, "the 'helping' language of schools at times makes it hard to see the very real hidden social effects of the social and psychological labels used by educators" (p. 261).

That school routinely imposes unflattering and counterproductive identities on students is evident in an inspection of grading and testing practices. As I read Kate Atkinson's (2004) novel, *Case Histories*, I was struck by an observation of a main character, Jackson, a private eye, when someone used red ink to designate males in a report of a criminal investigation. He mused, "It made the boys stand out and look more dangerous, or incorrect somehow" (p. 149). The red ink triggered a "sudden image of his essays at school, spider-webbed with the angry red-ink annotations of his teachers." Jackson confides that it was "only after he left school and joined the army that he discovered he was intelligent" (p. 149). Fortunately, Jackson overcame the stigma of failure and avoided the lasting effects that damaged identity usually has on postschool life.

Science's Tight Grasp on Social Life

Disability studies is replete with accounts of personal suffering, so my aim is to show how dominant individuals depend on science to structure school and societal hierarchy. In addition, I address how science-driven practice refuses ethics as a grounding principle for practice. Specifically regarding special education, I discuss how societal hierarchy, school meritocracy, the nature of science, and unquestioning faith in (special) education science result in a proliferation of problematic classifications for a burgeoning number of students.

The Eminence and Overreach of Science

In the past few decades, a host of scholars have contributed to knowledge about the nature of science and the results of various scientific enterprises (Aronowitz, 1988; Burroughs, 1912/2007; Danforth, 1999; Feyerabend, 1976; Foucault 1978, 1979; Gallagher, 1998, 2001; Harding, 1987; Kuhn, 1962; Popkewitz, 2004; Willinsky, 2005). Because my overview must be brief, I refer readers to these scholars for a fuller understanding of the nature and influences of science. It is clear that "science is the big game in town" that has "amassed social capital as a marker for what it means to be modern" (Styers, 2001, p. 235). One cannot fail to appreciate the comforts and conveniences of modern life that result from science and invention, yet there is increasing recognition that advances are counterbalanced with such repercussions as dwindling supplies of fossil fuel, pollution and destruction of natural resources, global warming, and problematic side-effects of medical treatment. My concern here is with the human waste incurred by a social science that imitates hard science's thinking and overgeneralizes its techniques to encompass human domains.

The Drift to Technical-Rational Agendas for Social Life

In 1912, Burroughs predicted that the growing primacy of science would be accompanied by an increasingly mechanistic view of the world. In reference to psychology, Capshew (1999) explains that although the study of the mind began as a humanistic enterprise, it has become so objectified and decontextualized that subjects' humanity is scarcely recognizable. Intentionally abstract and complex rhetoric (jargon) distracts attention from, or obfuscates, a humanistic—and realistic—portrayal of people's lives. Foucault (1978) argues that disciplinary discourse and technologies of power (examination, hierarchical observation, normalizing judgment) *produce* certain identities. In special education, *examination* is enacted through formal testing, and disability is reified through *hierarchical observation* as children are matched with disability categories. *Normalization* is enforced by prescribing appropriate cures for "abnormal" students.

Social Position of Scientists and Science's Objects

Because education, science, and progress are conflated in people's minds in modern society, problems result from (undue) respect for the educated. Situated squarely in the middle class, most scientists are further endowed with White and male privilege. This "determinate societal position" organizes their conceptualization of problems and choice of subject matter methods (Smith, 1987, p. 91). Scientists/professionals see themselves as singularly enlightened, intelligent, and informed as they monopolize the production of "objective and universal" truth. They feel entitled to make decisions for themselves and Others. Despite thinking themselves morally superior, Davies (2004) reminds us that highly educated people have been responsible for a host of major atrocities. Indeed, considerable wrong has transpired through scientists' intention to improve society by fixing, or eliminating, individuals.

Power discrepancies are evident in who (scientists, professionals, educated people) make decisions and the poor children and children of color who are the objects of naming. Local knowledge is disregarded and replaced by scientific evidence. Scientists, most obviously those who directly influence institutional treatment, are implicated in a reductionism that only recognizes their own findings and points of view. Yet, traffic between the scientific and the institutional, and the scientific and the popular, belies the possibility that social scientists could be the noninterfering, truth-telling, outside observers they claim to be (Holland et al., 1998). Naming the source and sustenance of power, Aronowitz (1988) observes: "The scientific community ritualistically denies it alliance with economic/industrial and military power even though the evidence of links is overwhelming" (p. 20). I address these connections later.

Special education expertise has produced and maintained a hierarchy between those providing services and those served (Brantlinger, 2004b). Special education scientists tend not to respect the subjectivity (feelings and preferences) of children who struggle in meritocratic schools. The view that science is neutral allows insiders' perspectives to be ignored and ethics dismissed on the grounds that attending to such factors contaminates research. For example, when labeling a child, only the fit between individual traits as measured by objective tests and the label definitions are considered. Given the deliberate suppression of subjective or moral factors, subordinate children are bound to receive subtractive schooling (Valenzuela, 2005). Identities, and school careers, are spoiled by imposing disability classifications on a burgeoning mass of poor children and children of color and relegating them to lesser school circumstances.

Epistemology is a "theory of knowledge" that Harding (1987) examines as she questions "what passes as legitimate knowledge" and "whose knowledge counts" in science (p. 3). Her observations of "the virulence of white men's hostility to women learning how to speak and organize" (p. 5) is reminiscent of mainstream special education scholars' ridicule of TASH[3] and inclusion advocates as being singularly subjective and ideological (Brantlinger, 1997). Practice in the field of special education is, and always has been, grounded in demands that scientific evidence be used to cure or control certain individuals. However, recently pressure to fund, disseminate, and utilize only scientific evidence-based research has intensified.

Science Is As Science Does

Unfortunately, special education science has been implicated in providing rationale for various inhumane practices. Since the science of disability first emerged, proclamations based on scientific grounding (validated tests, verified classifications) rendered some children to be uneducable—a status that justified exclusion from public schools. After these children broke the exclusion barrier to become a legal part of public schools, scientists developed sorting mechanisms to declare who did and did not belong in mainstream schools and classrooms. Experts coined terms and attached them to objects (children), thus exacerbating educational disparities. Regardless of students and families' resistance to derogatory and ostracizing labels, scientists rarely focus on the feelings of those classified. To some extent, labeling and treatment evolved in response to educators' concerns about children who do not respond to instruction with "normal" progress or to discipline with good behavior—special education science does provide the magic of a disappearing act for undesirable children.

One scientific enterprise that is touted as an advancement is the development of objective tests to identify disability. From the turn of the 20th century, scientists have created tests that magically distinguish superiority in public school students from mediocrity and inferiority. In turn, derived scores justify giving children humiliating names and educating them in lesser circumstances. It is important to acknowledge that constructing certain Others as outside the norm has never been based on radical humanism or a social reciprocity morality. Such differentiation is part of a scientific technical–rational agenda based on the assumption that experts know what is best for Others (Brantlinger, 2004b). The history of disability reveals that immoral actions often rely on the justification of science.

Concern about the overrepresentation of poor children and children of color among the ranks of the disabled has existed at least since Dunn (1968) wrote that special education might have a negative impact. Yet, despite rhetoric of "meeting needs" and providing an "appropriate education," the impact on those receiving labels has never been a major concern of those who determine professional practice. Ferri and Connor (2006) document that after *Brown vs. Board of Education* mandated racial desegregation, schools maintained racial separation by placing huge numbers of students of color in special education classrooms and low tracks. This practice was rationalized by tacit acceptance of the belief that Black children are less able than their White schoolmates and by knowledge of inferiority/disability demonstrated by objective tests. Ferri and Connor conclude that, "special education played a role in the failure of *Brown* to achieve racially desegregated classrooms" (p. 4) and that "tracking and special education inevitably resegregate children along racial lines" (p. 43).

School level choices may seem naive and unrelated to science; however, the decision making of local personnel is shaped by their training and it takes place within the elaborated classification framework designed by scientists. The array of specific tests and treatments are endorsed—but rarely verified—by science. Efficacy studies are nonexistent and the few that exist do not confirm the positive social and academic impact claims of traditional special education professionals. Regarding disability's reification, Gallagher (2001) observes, "it is the meaning we collectively bring to difference and the social, physical, and organizational arrangements built on our interpretations that make a person's difference a disability" (p. 3). Again, these meanings are produced in the scientific discourse of the times by the powerful, educated people who control schools. The blatantly insulting classifications of imbeciles, idiots, defectives, and retardates have been replaced by such euphemisms as "children with substantial needs" or "children with cognitive disabilities." "Person-first" language is meant to convey respect for those labeled; however, harmful naming and sorting practices continue regardless of new and improved classifications.

Science has also caused havoc outside school doors. Medical expertise justified placing young children in institutions by advising parents to give disabled children up at birth so they would "not get attached" and so "knowledgeable state hospital personnel could provide special care for children." Eugenics science established a hierarchy of human traits and societal values that were evoked to justify incarceration and sterilization in the United States, and genocide, euthanasia, and use of disabled people as human guinea pigs in experiments here and abroad. From the slavery era to the present, science condoned unethical medical experimentation on African Americans and various institutionalized populations (Washington, 2006).

Reliance on scientific expertise is part of the American history of disability. Goddard (1914) draws on his own scientific wisdom to denigrate lay people's perceptions:

> Mary is a splendid illustration of that type of girl that is most dangerous in society. Pretty and attractive and with just enough training to enable her to make a fair appearance she deceives the very elect as to her capacity. [If left at large] Responsibilities would be placed on her which she could never carry. In institutional life she is happy and useful. Unprotected she would be degraded, degenerate, and the mother of defectives. (p. 93)

Fernald (1896), founder of an institution for "dysgenic" individuals, clarifies:

> The feebleminded are a parasitic, predatory class, never capable of self-support, or of managing their own affairs. Feebleminded women are almost invariably immoral and if at large usually become carriers of venereal disease or give birth to children who are as defective as themselves. Every feebleminded person, especially the high grade imbecile, is a potential criminal, needing only the proper environment and opportunity for the development and expression of his criminal tendencies. (p. 67)

These are dramatic examples and, granted, a century old. Nevertheless, scientists still call the shots. A blatant example is the push to restrict funding and dissemination only to random sample research and mandate that only evidence-based practices be implemented in schools. This movement affects academia in distinguishing individuals who use the "right" scientific methods from those who supposedly do not. Another hierarchy in higher education divides scientists' knowledge from that of school personnel. Scientists eschew the contextualized and practical knowledge produced by teachers, school administrators, and parents.

Struck Dumb by Science and Overachievement

People are ranked according to whether they are among the highly educated, with advanced degrees from distinguished institutions, or among the least educated who drop out of failing urban schools. The process of interpersonal comparisons is perpetual and purposeful in meritocratic systems. The extent of affiliation with science is part of the picture in hierarchy development. Mathematics, chemistry, and physics professors are judged to be brighter and more important to progress than faculty in the social sciences and humanities (Hatch, 2006). In their ties to education's failures, special education teacher educators are among the lowest of the low. Perhaps to improve their status and sense of worth, (special) educational professionals strive to imitate the discerning and labeling habits of the "hard" sciences—hard in this case might mean either "difficult" or "as dense as a rock." Aware that word usage is significant in identifying and discussing disability, critical scholars study the meanings of language, including their underside or reverse interpretation of terminology; semantics are essential when studying special education.

Critical thinking and expression of agency in behalf of personal ideals are the responsibility of all citizens; nevertheless, various pressures constrain those activities. Referring to academia's "disciplined minds," Schmidt (2000) equates the "system" with "hierarchical organization" of bosses and employees in the production of social, economic, and political practices (p. 12). According to Schmidt, closed systems "require strict adherence to an assigned point of view," hence are not intellectually challenging and constrain creativity (p. 15). Schmidt argues:

> Professional education and employment push people to accept a role in which they do not make a significant difference, a politically subordinate role. These working professionals face intense pressure to compromise their ideals and sideline their commitment to work for a better world. (p. 2)

In discussing the role of the "shrink," Schmidt notes that: "Many mental problems originate not in diseases of the brain but in deficiencies of society" (p. 34). These deficiencies include "the arduousness of living with unfulfilling work, financial insecurity, arbitrary bosses, lack of solidarity and insufficient personal power, together with the anguish caused by racism, sexism, ageism, lookism, ableism, and all the other oppressive hierarchies that plague this society" (p. 35). Hence, Schmidt argues, attempting to adjust people to the unhealthy society that caused the problems is not the best approach for the individuals or society.

Schmidt claims that it is *"on the job* that professionals display ideological caution." They are "very much at home playing by the rules," and feel "no pressing need to question the social structure in which they do their work," indeed, they "fear any suggestion of not playing by the rules" (p. 12). Schmidt criticizes "liberal professionals [who] smugly conclude that they are the force for social progress," yet because they like the prominence and control related to professional status, they "will not hear a word in favor of a more democratic distribution of power in society" (p. 13). Schmidt contends that professionals are "fundamentally conservative" although "liberalism is the dominant ideology in the professions" (p. 4). He observes that left-leaning or oppositional professionals have remained relatively small (5%), while the "vast majority continue to share the views of corporate business executives on most basic issues" (p. 15).

Dweck (2002) adds a twist to the story of dumbing down elites, claiming that current practice, "makes people dumb by telling them they are smart." If people think they are smart, "they give up trying to learn and understand" (p. 87). Her argument is in line with White privilege theory that maintains that powerful people are guided by a sense of entitlement and consider themselves to be immune from the consequences of their behavior. Sternberg (2002) conceptualizes stupidity as the oppositive of rationality, claiming that a continuum of mindfulness to mindlessness exists in human thinking (p. 3). He posits stupidity at the level of individuals and social systems. Grigorenko and Lockery (2002) characterize special education as "an indicator of society's thinking 'stupidly' about problems of those who have a temporal, content, and/or sequential difficulty with learning" (p. 160). They contend that the field is riddled with overidentification (p. 161), the fallacy of intuition (pertains to judgments made without preliminary reasoned cogitation or ones that are counterintuitive) (p. 163), and the cure fallacy (p. 171). Feyerabend (1976) compares socialization in science to training a pet to obey, claiming "well-trained rationalists" obey the mental image of their master as they conform to the standards of argumentation learned. Apparently, they are incapable of realizing that what is regarded as the "voice of reason" is but a causal after-effect of the training received (p. 25). Feyerabend concludes that habits of mind and the reductions they permit become natural sources of blindness into the reality of circumstances.

Rethinking Science

Aronowitz (1988) observes that science actually does rely on local knowledge and that "scientific norms can be traced to...historical and discursive presuppositions" (p. viii). Certainly the "science" of the eugenics movement was influenced by personal worries about the dangers presented by diverse Others as well as on the discourse of what constitutes good families, worthy people, and healthy races/ethnic groups (Gould, 1996). Aronowitz illustrates how science is embedded in or infused with the myths and magic that scientists (and their followers) bring to their practice. Pursuit of profit and the absence of humanistic interests also are evident in various scientific pursuits. Certainly, the creation of disability sells pharmaceutical products. It is no coincidence that the growth of the organization Children with Attention Deficit Disorders (CHADD), sponsored by drug companies that prescribe their pills as a cure, evolved along with the burgeoning identification of ADD and ADHD children. As I peruse magazines and watch popular television shows, I see ads that describe symptoms for new diseases and recommend medicines to cure these manufactured ailments. In examining such phenomena, it is necessary to ask Antonio Gramsci's (1929–1935/1971) essential question: "Who benefits?"

Neoliberal Ideology and Hierarchy

One response to the question of who benefits from the exclusion of morality and local knowledge in determining social life is the corporate world. The corporate-controlled media's successful dissemination of neoliberal (atavistic faith in the free market) and neo-conservative (belief in the superiority of European-American traditions and knowledge) ideologies, means that professionals and the general public see the purpose of school as centered around strategies that contribute to the economy or at least do not threaten corporate control of social life. The public is socialized to see the particular knowledge produced through schooling as necessary to themselves and society. Moore and Young (2004) criticize both the neoconservative tradition in which curriculum is a given body of knowledge that schools are to transmit and the "technical-instrumentalists [neoliberals] whose interest is the needs of the economy" but operate "under the guise of promoting the employability of all students" (p. 238). People are subject to positioning by the powerful discourses they encounter (Holland et al., 1998, p. 27). Promotion of capitalism and class distinction dominates American discourse. As a result of rightist trends, school structures have become increasingly stratified and conditions for children of different social classes more and more disparate (Apple, 2001; Gabbard, 2003; Giroux, 2003). "Neo-liberals view students as human capital—as future workers who need the requisite skills and dispositions to work efficiently and effectively" (Apple, p. 263). Apple claims that neoliberal and neoconservative ideological movements have transformed America's common sense so that egalitarian ideals are threatened.

Luke and Luke (1995) argue from a structuralist and neo-Marxist perspective "premised on the assumption that systematic distortions and misrepresentations of social facts and economic and political realities serve identifiable class interests" (p. 368). They argue that under rightist reform, "children are socialized into a regime of boredom, mapped onto a psychometric grid of classification, and relegated to deskilled, classed, and gendered occupations" (p. 272). Beane (2005) identifies an emerging (technical-instrumental) literature that is "dominated mostly by ways to work with(in), adapt to, or address things like standardized testing, scripted curriculum packages, overly prescriptive content standards, and other policies that are actually antithetical to a progressive vision of education" (p. xiv). Writing about his teaching career in New York City schools, McCourt (2005) asks: "What is education, anyway? What are we doing in this school?" (p. 253). McCourt's questions are in line with Beane's concern that only a few progressive educators "attach themselves to any large and compelling social vision that might elevate its sense of purpose, attract more advocates, and help sustain the concept against its critics" (p. xiv).

Faith in Science, Capitalism, and Progress

In contrast to science's purported reliance on observable evidence and verification of findings, faith consists of beliefs not necessarily grounded in any hard reality. Faith typically is spoken of as relating to organized religions. Indeed, those who believe in religious tenets often deny the need for the backing of scientific rationality. Some dismiss scientific evidence, as is the case with evolution—the "intelligent design" that Darwin delineated is garnered as evidence of creation by a supreme being. Faith also comes in secular forms that allow people to affiliate with certain political parties and endorse particular public figures. Political faith typically expresses itself uniquely in people who occupy various strata in the social hierarchy. As noted earlier, neoliberals, who tend to be well-healed, put faith in the "free market," or an economic agenda. Due to the circulation of hegemonic ideologies, people in Other social positions may be duped into supporting the neoliberal agenda even if they have little to gain from their faith.

It is not the negative aspects of religious and political faith that concern me here, rather it is the faith that extends outside spiritual and political boundaries. Contention between people of various religious faiths and political loyalty is ubiquitous; however, most Americans are part of the faith community that worships science and education. Since the Enlightenment, when faith in science caught up with religious faith, modern people trust that a trajectory of social improvement necessarily results from the discoveries in science and the accumulation of academic knowledge. An important legacy that dominates social thought is, "the inscription of progress as a foundational assumption of intellectual knowledge" (Popkewitz & Brennan, 1998, p. 6). The mainstream faith community has confidence in the efficacy of education, including the validity of tests and current school practices. Their faith in disability labels and traditional special education services is so deep that disability is reified to the status of being an essential, all-encompassing aspect of particular human existence. To return to the topic of this chapter—the lack of justice for people identified as having disabilities—it is clear that most people are part of the faith community that sees special education as helpful and benevolent, regardless of evidence to the contrary.

One aspect of faith is that it is always accompanied by doctrine and texts. The science of disability classification has become increasingly inscribed in local and federal law. Faith in the system undergirds *Introduction to Exceptionality* and other special education textbooks (Brantlinger, 2006). These texts construct what appears to be a credible matrix of disability classifications and offer a smorgasbord of services that socialize unsuspecting preservice teachers into thinking classifications are real and it is necessary to know about specialized treatments to effectively educate children. Textbooks are packaged in an authoritative style that is replete with facts based on scientific evidence. There are no caveats that suggest the reality that disability categories fluctuate and are rarely blessed with clear-cut parameters. Special education is grounded in a legal language, hence labels, treatments, and placements appear not only justified but mandated. The assuredness of textbook presentation indicates that school personnel should not defy the system by avoiding labels or using their own choice of pedagogies and, most importantly, should not challenge the wisdom of the scientific and professional system.

My experience with the Council for Exceptional Children (CEC) and special education colleagues is that their ideologies center around the assumption that the development of new disability classifications and specialized treatments mean progress in the field. This observation is consistent with what is revealed in an inspection of the presentations at annual CEC conferences, the manuscripts published in special education journals, and the textbooks faculty select for their special education courses. Special educators are not alone in accepting prescriptive, but unjust, systems, almost all school personnel perpetually rank and sort by grading, testing, and complying with tracking arrangements.

After teaching in low-income schools, and having studied the impact of social class status on the nature and quality of students' schooling, I have a clear mental image of school hierarchies and their confluence with racial and ethnic status. I try not to despair about the resilience of within-school sorting of students and between-school disparities in educational resources. Hence, I was puzzled by an exchange with a colleague who asked me to provide feedback on her "critical ethnography" manuscript. Her main concern was the leveling phenomenon in the Mexican school she studied. She was bothered at the school's lack of academic push and that students of differing abilities were all treated as equals and educated together—a goal I have always desired. As I read her manuscript, it was evident that her ideological perspective endorsed meritocratic schooling replete with its ubiquitous competition between students and internal stratification. However, when I suggested that her study was not grounded in a critical perspective so it would be wise to take that claim out of the introduction, she took offense. That she thinks in terms of competition and hierarchy also is evident in her descriptions of certain colleagues as "exceptionally bright" and "rising stars," and her dismissal of others as not worthy of association. A conversation with a special education faculty member with a declared interest in social justice, revealed that his professional goal was to bring the United States' special education system to Mexico. When I asked if that meant he would transport all the testing, labeling, and segregating routines, he seemed surprised that I did not share his goal. To him "the system" means progress, whereas to me it means oppression.

Rethinking Science, Progress, Hierarchy, and Disability

Disability study scholars, parents, and students join a quest to *quit* assigning disparaging names to individuals and *stop* excluding them from mainstream settings. Gallagher (2001) observes "an impasse between the empiricists, who champion [what they call] a neutral and scientific resolution to the [inclusion] debate" and those for whom inclusion is a "struggle of conscience [to be achieved] through free, open, and informed moral discourse" (p. 651). Although the American Educational Research Association (AERA) Disability Studies in Education Special Interest Group has grown considerably since its creation in 2001, it still would match Schmidt's (2001) conclusion that oppositional groups represent minority status in most fields. Perhaps this is because disability studies scholars have the audacity to challenge the themes of scientific expertise and social progress that dominate special educators' thinking. According to disability studies scholars, Ferri and Connor (2006), "because we are studying *exclusion* rather than inclusion, our work runs counter to traditional progress stories of the field. Our approach focuses on what was left unsaid, masked, obscured, and silenced in stories of inclusion and desegregation" (p. 6). Dimitriadis and Carlson (2003) suggest that schools return to an earlier mission "to socialize [students] into a common culture and a common conception of the public good" (p. 22).

Due to the unshakeable faith in science, the outsider status of those who receive services, and the intractability of deeply ingrained stratifying systems, meritocracy retains a tight hold on schooling. It is laudable that the editors of this volume include disability as a social justice issue. Like the field of special education generally, disability studies scholars have mainly been isolated from others who are concerned about inequities in education. They have worked on their own as outsiders to both general and special education professional communities. It is clear, however, that formation of disabling identities is only one of the many damaging consequences of meritocratic schooling. Therefore, it is essential that progressive educators from all subject area backgrounds join hands, heads, and hearts to combat all dimensions of hierarchical schooling and engage in collective efforts to democratize schools and establish a social reciprocity morality to bring social justice within schools' doors.

Notes

1. A social reciprocity moral code appears in world religions: "What is hateful to you, do not to your fellow man. That is the entire Law; all the rest is commentary" (Judaism). "Hurt not others in ways that you yourself would find hurtful" (Buddhism). "No one of you is a believer until he desires for his brother that which he desires for himself" (Islam). "Do unto others as you would have them do unto you" (Christianity). "Blessed is he who preferreth his brother before himself" (Baha'i Faith).
2. Meritocracies are competitive systems that seek to identify merit in some so they can advance in school and post-school life. As they select the worthy, by default or intention, those judged less worthy are given derogatory names and are relegated to lesser school circumstances.
3. TASH (The Association for Severely Handicapped) is a disability organization that tried to see things from the perspective of labeled children and their families. It was among the first professional organizations to endorse full inclusion.

References

Apfelbaum, E. (1999). Relations of domination and movements for liberation: An analysis of power between groups. *Feminism & Psychology, 9*(3), 267–272.

Apple, M. (2001). Afterword: The politics of labeling in a conservative age. In G. M. Hudak & P. Kihn (Eds.), *Labeling: Pedagogy and politics* (pp. 261–283). New York: RoutledgeFalmer.

Aronowitz, S. (1988). *Science as power: Discourse and ideology in modern society.* Minneapolis: University of Minnesota Press.

Artiles, A. J., & Trent, S. (1994). Overrepresentation of minority students in special education: A continuing debate. *Journal of Special Education, 27,* 410–427.

Atkinson, K. (2004) *Case histories.* New York: Back Bay Books.

Beane, J. A. (2006). Foreword. In E. R. Brown & K. J. Saltman (Eds.), *The critical middle school reader* (pp. xi–xv). New York: Routledge.

Bowles, S., & Gintis, H. (1976). *Schooling in capitalist America.* New York: Basic Books.

Brantlinger, E. (1985). Low-income parents' perceptions of favoritism in the schools. *Urban Education, 20,* 82–102.

Brantlinger, E. (1993). *The politics of social class in secondary school: Views of affluent and impoverished youth.* New York: Teachers College Press.

Brantlinger, E. (1997). Using ideology: Cases of non-recognition of the politics of research and practice in special education. *Review of Educational Research, 67,* 435–460.

Brantlinger, E. (2001). Poverty, class, and disability: A historical, social, and political perspective. *Focus on Exceptional Children, 33*(7), 1–19.

Brantlinger, E. (2003). Who wins and who loses? Social class and student identities. In Michael Sadowski (Ed.), *Adolescents at school: Perspectives on youth, identity, and education* (pp. 107–121). Cambridge, MA: Harvard Education Press.

Brantlinger, E. (2004a). *Dividing classes: How the middle class negotiates and rationalizes school advantage.* New York: RoutledgeFalmer.

Brantlinger, E. (2004b). Confounding the needs and confronting the norms: An extension of Reid and Valle's Essay. *Journal of Learning Disabilities, 37*(6), 490–499.

Brantlinger, E. (2006). "The big glossies" How textbooks structure (special) education. In E. Brantlinger (Ed.), *Who benefits from special education? Remediating [fixing] other people's children* (pp. 45–76). Mahwah, NJ: Erlbaum.

Brantlinger, E. (forthcoming a). Playing to middle class self-interest in pursuit of school equity. In L. Weis (Ed.), *The way class works.* New York: Routledge.

Brantlinger, E. (forthcoming b). (Re)Turning to Marx to understand the unexpected anger among "winners" in schooling: A critical social psychology perspective. In J. Van Galen & G. Noblit (Eds.), *Late to class.* Buffalo: State University of New York Press.

Brantlinger, E., & Danforth, S. (2006). Critical theory perspective on social class, race, gender, and classroom management. In C. M. Evertson & C. S. Weinstein (Eds.), *Handbook of classroom management: Research, practice, and contemporary issues* (pp. 157–180). Mahwah, NJ: Erlbaum.

Brantlinger, E., Morton, M. L., & Washburn, S. (1999). Teachers' moral authority in classrooms: (Re)structuring social interactions and gendered power. *The Elementary School Journal, 99*(5), 491–504.

Brown, D. E. (1991). *Human universals.* Philadelphia: Temple University Press.

Burroughs, J. (Sept, 1912/January/February, 2007). Science. *The Atlantic, 299*(1), 50–51.

Caplan, P. J. (1995). *They say you're crazy: How the world's most powerful psychiatrists decide who's normal.* Reading, MA: Perseus.

Capshew, J. H. (1999). *Psychologists on the march: Science, practice, and professional identity in America, 1929–1969.* Cambridge, UK: Cambridge University Press.

Danforth, S. (1999). Pragmatism and the scientific validation of professional practices in American special education. *Disability and society, 14*(6), 733–751.

Davies, L. (2004). *Education and conflict: Complexity and chaos.* New York: Routledge.

Dimitriadis, G., & Carlson, D. (2003). Introduction. In G. Dimitriadis & D. Carlson (Eds.), *Promises to keep: Cultural studies, democratic education, and public life* (pp. 1–35). New York: RoutledgeFalmer.

Dunn, L. M. (1968). Special education for the mildly retarded: Is much of it justifiable. *Exceptional Children, 35,* 5–22.

Dweck, C. S. (2002). Beliefs that make smart people dumb. In R. J. Sternberg (Ed.), *Why smart people can be so stupid* (pp. 24–41). New Haven, CT: Yale University Press.

Fanon, F. (1967). *Black skin, white masks.* New York: Grove Press.

Fernald, W. E. (1896). Some methods employed in the care, and the training of feeble-minded children of the lower grades. In *forty-eighth annual report of the trustees of the Massachusetts School for the Feeble-Minded at Waltham year ending 1895.* Boston: Wright & Potter.

Ferri, B. A., & Connor, D. J. (2006). *Reading resistance: Discourses of exclusion in desegregation and inclusion debates.* New York: Peter Lang.

Feyerabend, P. (1976). *Against method.* London: New Left Books.

Foucault, M. (1978). *The history of sexuality: An introduction* (Vol. 1). New York: Vintage.

Foucault, M. (1979). *Discipline and punish: The birth of the prison.* New York: Vintage.

Fuss, D. (1995). *Identification papers.* New York: Routledge.

Gabbard, D. A. (2003). Education IS enforcement! The centrality of compulsory schooling in market societies. In K. J. Saltman & D. A. Gabbard (Eds.), *Education as enforcement: The militarization and corporatization of schools* (pp. 61–78). New York: RoutledgeFalmer.

Gallagher, D. (1998). The scientific knowledge base of special education. Do we know what we think we know? *Exceptional Children, 60,* 294–309.

Gallagher, D. (2001). Neutrality as a moral standpoint, conceptual confusion and the full inclusion debate. *Disability and Society, 16*(5), 637–654.

Giroux, H. (2003) Series foreword. In Z. Leonardo (Ed.), *Ideology, discourse, and school reform* (pp . ix–xi). Westport, CT: Praeger.

Goddard, H. H. (1914). *Feeble-mindedness, its causes and consequences.* New York: Macmillan.

Goffman, E. (1961). *Asylum.* New York: Penguin.

Goffman, E. (1963). *Stigma: Notes on the management of spoiled identity.* Englewood Cliffs, NJ: Prentice-Hall.

Gould, S. J. (1996). *The mismeasure of man.* New York: W.W. Norton.

Gramsci, A. (1971). *Selections from the prison notebooks* (Q. Hoare & G. N. Smith, Eds.). New York: International Publishers. (Original work published 1929–1935)

Greene, M. (2001). Foreword. In G. M. Hudak & P. Kihn (Eds.), In *Labeling: Pedagogy and politics* (pp. xvi–xvii). New York: RoutledgeFalmer.

Grigorenko, E., & Lockery, D. (2002). Smart is as stupid does: Exploring bases of erroneous reasoning of smart people regarding learning and other disabilities. In R. J. Sternberg (Ed.), *Why smart people can be so stupid* (pp. 159–186). New Haven, CT: Yale University Press.

Harding, S. (1987). Introduction: Is there a feminist method? In S. Harding (Ed.), *Feminism and methodology* (pp. 1–15). Bloomington: Indiana University Press.

Hatch, J. A. (2006). Qualitative studies in the era of scientifically-based research: Musings of a former QSE editor. *International Journal of Qualitative Studies in Education, 19*(4), 403–407.

Holland, D., Lachicotte, W., Jr., Skinner, D., & Cain, C. (1998). Preface. In D. Holland, W. Lachicotte, D. Skinner, & C. Cain (Eds.), *Identity and agency in cultural worlds* (pp. vii–ix). Cambridge, MA: Harvard University Press.

Hudak, G. M. (2001). On what is labeled "playing": Locating the "true" in education. In G. M. Hudak & P. Kihn (Eds.), *Labeling: Pedagogy and politics* (pp. 9–26). New York: RoutledgeFalmer.

Hudak, G. M., & Kihn, P. (2001). *Labeling: Pedagogy and politics.* New York: RoutledgeFalmer.

Kaufman, J. S. (2001). The classroom and labeling: "The girl who stayed back." In G. M. Hudak & P. Kihn (Eds.), *Labeling: Pedagogy and politics* (pp. 41–54). New York: RoutledgeFalmer.

Kittay, E. F. (1999). *Love's labor: Essays on women, equality, and dependency.* New York and London: Routledge.

Koggel, C. M. (1998). *Perspectives on equality: Constructing a relational theory.* Lanham, MD: Rowman & Littlefield.

Kuhn, T. (1962). *The structure of scientific revolutions.* Chicago: University of Chicago Press.

Luke, C., & Luke, A. (1995). Just naming? Educational discourses and the politics of identity. In W. T. Pink & G. W. Noblit (Eds.), *Continuity and contradiction: The futures of the sociology of education* (pp. 357–380). Cresskill, NJ: Hampton.

McCarthy, C., & Dimitriadis, G. (2001). Labeling resentment: Re-narrating difference. In G. M. Hudak & P. Kihn (Eds.), *Labeling: Pedagogy and politics* (pp. 225–232). New York: RoutledgeFalmer.

McCourt, F. (2005). *Teacher man.* New York: Scribner.

McNeil, L. M. (2000). *Contradictions of school reform: Educational costs of standardized testing.* New York: Routledge.

Mercer, J. R. (1973). *Labeling the mentally retarded.* Berkeley: University of California Press.

Moore, R., & Young, M. (2004). Knowledge and the curriculum in the sociology of education. In M. Olssen (Ed.), *Culture and learning: Access and opportunity in the classroom* (pp. 235–256). Greenwich, CT: Information Age.

Moyers, B. (2007, January 12th). *Big media is ravenous. It never gets enough. Always wants more. And it will stop at nothing to get it. These conglomerates are an empire, and they are imperial.* Paper presented at the National Conference on Media Reform, Memphis, TN.

Oakes, J. (2005). *Keeping track: How schools structure inequality* (2nd ed.). New Haven, CT: Yale University Press.

Peshkin, A. (1991). *The color of strangers: The color of friends.* Chicago: University of Chicago Press.

Popkewitz, T., & Brennan, M. (1998). *Foucault's challenge: Discourse, knowledge and power in education.* New York: Teachers College.

Popkewitz, T. S. (2004). Is the National Research Council Committee's Report on Scientific Research in Education scientific? *Qualitative Inquiry, 10*(1), 62–78.

Rawls, J. (1971). *A theory of justice.* Cambridge, MA: Harvard University Press.

Said, E. (1978). *Orientalism.* New York: Vintage Books.

Schmidt, J. (2000). *Disciplined minds: A critical look at salaried professionals and the soul-battering system that shapes their lives.* Lanham, MD: Rowman & Littlefield.

Smith, D. E. (1987). Introduction: Is there a feminist method? In S. Harding (Ed.), *Feminism and methodology* (pp. 84–96). Bloomington: Indiana University Press.

Sternberg, R. J. (Ed.). (2002). *Why smart people can be so stupid.* New Haven, CT: Yale University Press.

Stoughton, E. (2006). Marcus and Harriet: Living on the edge in school and society. In E. Brantlinger (Ed.), *Who benefits from special education? Remediating (fixing) other people's children* (pp. 145–164). Mahwah, NJ: Erlbaum.

Styers, R. (2001). The "magic" of "science": The labeling of ideas. In G. M. Hudak & P. Kihn (Eds.), *Labeling: Pedagogy and politics* (pp. 235–249). New York: RoutledgeFalmer.

Taubman, P. M. (2001). The callings of sexual identity. In G. M. Hudak & P. Kihn (Eds.), *Labeling: Pedagogy and politics* (pp. 179–200). New York: RoutledgeFalmer.

Valenzuela, A. (2005). Subtractive schooling and divisions among youth. In E. R. Brown & K. J. Saltman (Eds.), *The critical middle school reader* (pp. 357–373). New York: Routledge.

Varenne, H., & McDermott, R. (1998). *Successful failure: The school America builds.* Boulder, CO: Westview.

Washington, H. A. (2006). *Medical apartheid: The dark history of medical experimentation on Black Americans from colonial times to the present.* New York: Doubleday.

Willinsky, J. (2005). Scientific research in a democratic culture: Or what's a social science for? *Teachers College Record, 107*(1), 38–51.

Young, M. F. D. (1965). *Rise of the meritocracy.* Baltimore: Penguin.

26 Doing a (Dis)Service

Reimagining Special Education from a Disability Studies Perspective

Beth A. Ferri

They don't really want to hear the truth. (Isis, cited in Jones, 2004, p. 72)

Which is the greater right, treatment or freedom? Judging from our journals and our rhetoric, one can make the case that our field [of special education] has decided that it's more important for the individual to be treated than to be free. (Burton Blatt, 1984, p. 170)

The field of special education has historically situated itself within either a humanistic discourse of care and support or within an advocacy-based orientation of civil rights, espousing "ideologies of cure, care, benevolence, charity, control, [and] professionalism" (Ware, 2004, p. 2). Special education in the United States can also be linked to advocacy efforts, oftentimes on the behalf of parents, who rallied against the widespread discrimination, marginalization, and outright exclusion of their children with disabilities. Given its roots in advocacy and educational rights, special education can be thought of as having social justice aims.

Nonetheless, despite even its best intentions, there is much to be gained by looking at how special education specifically, and the category of disability more generally, has served to justify the exclusion of certain groups of students in schools (Erevelles, 2005, p. 75). As Brantlinger (2004) writes, it is time to turn the gaze inward and actively work to eliminate oppressive educational practices and structures to which we participate. In other words, as the late Burton Blatt would remind us, "What is needed in the field of special education is not merely more research, more presentations, or more publications, but regular and thoughtful [and I would add critical] analyses of our works" (1984, p. ix).

Taking seriously these calls for self-reflexivity and critique, requires that we cast a critical eye on both the history and current practices of special education—particularly focusing on the mechanisms that turn student differences into pathologies and that result in the overrepresentation of students from minority racial groups in special education. Taken together these critiques highlight how special education ultimately functions not so much as a service to students with special needs, but also as a tool to shore up the exclusivity of general education—allowing it to maintain a false sense of homogeneity and a rigid set of normative practices that disempower an ever-increasing number of students. Thus, I am arguing that what on the surface seems to support educational rights and access, paradoxically upholds social injustice and exclusion.

In the following sections of this chapter I highlight some of the major critiques of special education, first from scholars in disability studies in education and then from current and former special education students, whose bodies and histories bare the effects of current practices. These voices, drawn from a several sources, remind us that it is not enough for scholars to talk to us about social justice, but that we must also put ourselves in a position where we can hear from those most disaffected by our current state of affairs. As Bell (1997) writes, "social justice education begins with people's lived experience and works to foster a critical perspective and action directed toward social change" (p. 14). If we take student voices seriously, they point us toward a reimagining dis/ability and recasting special education practice in ways that are more fully informed by an expanded notion of social justice.

Reframing Special Education Practice

Special education was originally conceptualized as a set of specialized *services* designed to ensure educational equity and access for students with disabilities; however, over the years, special education has come to be (mis)understood as a *place* to send students who cannot or will not assimilate into general education's rigid "demands for conformity and rationality" (Erevelles, 2005, p. 72). Designed as a parallel system to general education, the dual system of education privileges certain groups by separating and marginalizing students that general education casts as problematic or difficult (Artiles, 2005). Once students are separated out and marked, they are assumed to be *"fundamentally different"* [italics in original] from their nondisabled peers (Brantlinger, 2004, p. 20). In this way, the category of disability itself constitutes these students as "special." Thus, disability labels function as a discursively produced system of social othering that creates divisions between students who are considered normal and regular and those who are seen as deficient and disordered (Slee, 2004).

Once a student is defined as a "problem," the mechanisms that label, rank, and exclude him or her are assumed to be neutral and valid—a rational and necessary response to student difference (Brantlinger, 2004, p. 11). But not everything falls under the diagnostic gaze. In its hyperfocus on etiology, diagnosis, and specialized interventions directed at individual learners, general education practice, which is often inflexible, rigid, and ineffective for an increasingly wide range of learners, falls conveniently outside the clinical gaze (Slee, 2004; Wedell, 2005). When a child is referred for special education, the "classroom context is seldom taken into account" because disability is presumed to be intrinsic to the child (Harry & Klingner, 2006, p. 67). In this decontextualized view of disability, it is only the student, not the system or larger educational context, which is deemed deficient and in need of intervention. In other words, when traditional models of instruction fail students, it is the student who is seen as deficient rather than the instructional model (Gallagher, 2005). Even under the recent changes to the way schools diagnose learning disabilities, called Response to Intervention (RTI), when a child does not respond to an intervention, the problem is still assumed to be intrinsic to the child. Thus, under RTI the student is considered to have a learning disability when he or she does not "respond" to research-based academic interventions. In other words, if clinical research says an instructional approach *should* work, then a child who does not benefit from that intervention must be deficient in some way. Therefore, although RTI will make interventions available to a wider group of students who are struggling, it remains a tool for determining eligibility for special education and ultimately labeling the child, not the educational context, as deficient. Moreover, the model does not challenge the efficacy of the intervention itself, which, because it is research-based, is not called into question. Thus, regardless of the model, it is telling that we label students rather than classroom practices (or teachers) as deficient, disordered, disabled.[1] Likewise our intervention efforts are typically directed at individual students, rather than at instructional practices. In other words, the object of remediation is the student, because it is the student who is deemed deficient.

Critiques of special education in recent years have questioned the efficacy of and the moral and ethical justification of segregated special education placements. As Linton (2006) argues, "special education is not a solution to the 'problem' of disability, it *is* the problem, or at least one of the major impediments to the full integration of disabled people in society" (p. 161, italics in original). Other critics have focused on the over-representation of students from racial minorities in special education (Ferri & Connor, 2006; Harry & Klingner, 2006; Losen & Orfield, 2002). Rather than viewing these critiques as *either* about race *or* about disability, I would argue that they underscore the interconnected forms that exclusion and discrimination take in schools. In other words, each of these critiques highlights a failed commitment to teach everyone, to value everyone, and to exclude no one (Kugelmass & Ainscow, 2004). They are at core about the complicated ways that race, ethnicity, social class, and gender intertwine with dis-ability status, which leads to interlocking forms of exclusion and marginalization. These include practices such as academic tracking, special education placements, disciplin-ary policies and practices, as well as gifted/talented programs and advanced placement options given to students.

The practice of sifting out "deficient" students often segregates the very students who are *already* marginalized on the basis of social class, race, or ethnicity. Schools enact a form of "ability profiling" by relying on "cultural narratives and deficit discourses," identifying, labeling, and sorting students based on their perceived risk rather than their potential or promise (Collins, 2003, p. 192). This practice relies on a dovetailing of racism and ableism and underscores how firmly entrenched special education is in the ever-present "quagmire of educational segregation" (Kliewer & Raschke, 2002, p. 43). In fact, questioning the disproportionate placement of students from racial minority groups in special education is one of the most longstanding critiques of the field (Dunn, 1968; Sleeter, 1987). Recent data confirms that students from racial minorities are as much as two to three times as likely to be labeled mentally retarded or emotionally dis-turbed as White children (Losen & Orfield, 2002). Once labeled, students from racial minorities are also more likely to be placed in segregated classrooms (Fierros & Conroy, 2002).

History shows us that the moment segregated special classes came into being they were populated with students from racial and ethnic minority groups, from immigrant populations, and from lower social classes and statuses (Erevelles, 2005; Ferri & Connor, 2006; Franklin, 1987). Coinciding with the eugenics movement, these nongraded classes and facilities flourished in the first half of the 20th century. Designed for children who were deemed "slow," "retarded," or "feebleminded," these classes were precursors to today's self-contained special education classrooms. Thus, the relationship between seg-regation based on race and segregation based on disability is not a recent phenomenon, but it came into particularly high relief after the historic *Brown v. Board of Education* (1954) decision made segregating students based on racial categories unconstitutional. As I argue elsewhere, special education, like tracking and gifted/talented programs, functioned as a way to subvert desegregation orders after *Brown*—creating a way to segregate students *within* schools once it was impossible to segregate them *between* schools (Ferri & Connor, 2006). Ultimately serving the needs of general education, spe-cial education became a "clearinghouse" for children deemed defective, disordered, or simply difficult (Kliewer & Raschke, 2002, p. 54). This practice proved so effective that by the early 1970s, disability categories served as the "chief metaphor" for explaining and highlighting differences between students and for justifying their exclusion (Harry & Klingner, 2006).

Of course, as Roger Slee (2004) argues, "schools were never really meant for everyone" (pp. 47–48) and special education simply masks general education's need for conformity and homogeneity (Baker, 2002). It could, therefore, be said that special education simply provides an exceptionally effective buffer zone between the children of the dominant group and those who would be relegated to the margins of the educational system. It provides a way to remove "challenging students from view" creating a "perverted" form of democratic education (Jones, 2004, p. 190). Thus, we should not be surprised that like all low status placements in schools (i.e., remedial and vocational tracks), special education is likewise marked by an overrepresentation of historically marginalized students (Brantlinger, 2005; Harry & Klingner, 2006; Losen & Orfield, 2002). In recent years, even "the special education population has become increasingly segregated along racial lines" (Artiles, 2005, p. 92) students from different racial backgrounds with similar educational profiles receive different diagnostic labels, according to race.

When one considers who benefits from these arrangements, it becomes obvious that general education has a large stake in maintaining the status quo of a dual system of education (Brantlinger, 2004). We should not expect general education to give up its *special need* for keeping its "clearing house" for the children it deems defective (Kliewer & Raschke, 2002, p. 54). Perhaps, then, it should be acknowledged that special education is neither simply a set of *services* for students with particular learning needs nor is it a neutral *place* to serve these students. Instead, special education must be seen as a dubious mechanism for the maintenance of an exclusionary general education system. Thus, meaningful reform and a more just educational system will require nothing less than a complete rethinking of the entire system. Likewise, if social justice is our goal then our policies of inclusion cannot simply be focused on students with disabilities, but rather must encompass the goal of supporting and welcoming all learners and eliminating all forms of social exclusion (Kugelmass & Ainscow, 2004). Socially just education cannot be limited to "softening the blow" of a rigid general education system. It must acknowledge that our current system is not working for a wide range of learners (Wedell, 2005). As the numbers of students in special education continue to expand in unprecedented numbers, perhaps we are near the point of recognizing that we cannot label everyone—at some point we have to begin to question our own practices. This questioning will require schools to move away from a medical model approach to thinking about disability as a deficit or pathology within the individual child, toward a social model conceptualization of disability as socially and politically constructed. In other words, disability must be primarily understood as one of the ways that we have organized difference in schools (Erevelles, 2005).

The taken-for-granted "normative practices, beliefs, and assumptions about disability" are being rewritten by scholars in the area of disability studies in education (DSE), who are both rewriting and critiquing the discourse of dis/ability[2] (Ware, 2005, p. 104). DSE distinguishes itself from traditional approaches to disability by rejecting medical model understandings of disability and by aligning itself with other identity-based studies. As Gabel (2005) writes, "the disability-as-deficit [model]...is rejected as the basis for understanding the lived experience of disabled people because it tends to pathologize difference and rely solely on expert knowledge" (p. 2). As a field of inquiry, DSE positions itself as critical rather than clinical, social rather than individualist. It assumes competence (Biklen, 2005) where traditionalists only see deficit, and views all students as diverse in their abilities, interests, and needs. Scholars in DSE have cast a critical eye on traditional practice, and along with people with disabilities, they are forging new ways of reimagining dis/ability and difference in schools and society.

Reimagining Dis/ability and Special Education Practice

Traditional special education methods are "rooted in deficit-bound psycho-medical paradigms" that transmogrify different ways of moving, learning, behaving, and being into individual pathologies (Slee, 2004, p. 47). Steeped in medical and deficit models of disability, special education positions disabled students as objects of a clinical and diagnostic gaze that leaves little room for alternative ways of knowing about disability experience. Because students are positioned as objects of study—as problems to correct or remediate—their voices and perspectives remain silenced and devalued just as their bodies remained segregated and marginalized. Any cursory survey of special education journals yields a mountain of quantitative studies examining every possible nuance of the assessment profiles of students with disabilities. There remains a dearth of research that focuses on the voices or perspectives of disabled people themselves. But what happens when we shift the object of the gaze from students with disabilities to special educational practice—what do students and former students have to say about the practices that have been set up to serve them and about the labels that they have been given? In the next section I focus on what can be learned from taking seriously what students have to say about our existing practices.

The following quotes are taken from several recent studies that prominently feature the voices of current and former students who received special education services. Although these are certainly not exhaustive of research that includes student voice, I attempted to represent a range of student experiences, as informed by race, ethnicity, gender, social class, and disability label. I also included only studies that that quote directly from the individuals themselves. Unfortunately, special education research continues to be dominated by positivist research, which limits the number of studies published that focus so intently on the lived experience of students. Thus, studies like the ones that I include continue to be the exception to the rule. As Reid and Valle (2004) persuasively argue, because students with disabilities are not seen as subjects of their own meaning making, their voices are often authorized or mediated by a clinical or diagnostic gaze, which leads to an absence of insider perspectives on special education practice.

Representing a range of races, ethnicities, genders, and social classes, the individuals that I include in this chapter have also been given a variety of special education labels, from learning disabled to autistic to emotionally disturbed. Despite these and other differences there are surprising similarities among the group, particularly related to the construction of dis/ability and the efficacy of special education services. Their insights offer important critiques of current educational practices and point the way toward greater reform.

In the first group of excerpts I include examples of individuals questioning the label of disability itself. In these examples, individuals are actively rejecting the dominant understanding of disability, which cast it as a deficit or deficiency. They instead point to a more social model of disability, defining it as something that is constructed and arbitrary. As Biklen (2005) notes, disability is not "knowable in any definitively objective sense…[it] can be studied and discussed, but it is not knowable as a truth. It must always be interpreted" (p. 3). In these quotes, we hear students negotiating alternative ways of knowing about disability:

- I have a disability, but I am capable. (student in Lipsky & Gartner, 1997, p. 149)
- They think you don't have any intelligence. (student in Fleischer, 2001, p. 115)
- I hated to go to the "dummy room." I'm not dumb. (student in Lipsky & Gartner, 1997, p. 150)

- I have limitations. So do many other people. (Frugone, in Biklen, 2005, p. 196)
- Mental retardation is the most disgraceful label...[and it] does not prove that the mind is incapable of thinking. (Mukhopadhyay, in Biklen, 2005, p. 136)
- If I were to say anything about autism, it would be how fascinating it is.... More importantly I have to admit that other people's attitude toward autism and to its various attributes are even more fascinating. (Blackman, in Biklen, 2005, pp. 148–149)
- No one's behavior is naturally bad—other people make it that way. (Air, in Jones, 2004, p. 177)

If disability is always a construction, however, the question becomes whose construction is privileged? In the field of special education it is not the "subjugated knowledges" (Bell, 1997, p. 13) of individuals who have been labeled, but the clinical view of disability that reigns. Alterative understandings that would call into question these dominant notions of disability remain marginalized in traditional special education discourse.

Another area of consensus among the individuals in these studies involved their views of the diagnostic process, which redefined their particular differences into categories of deviance (Apple, 2001). Many of the individuals in this sampling were highly critical not only of the labels they received, but also of the procedures and mechanisms involved in assessment.

- I became the child that was disabled, the one who went to a school for children with disabilities. (Attfield, in Biklen, 2005, p. 209)
- The psychologist and the other people decide...I couldn't stand those people. They would get into my business about everything. (Michelle, in Connor, 2008, p. 180)
- I had hundreds of tests...everyone wanted to know what was wrong with me rather than just seeing the energy and passion that I had for so many things. (O'Connor, in Rodis, Garrod, & Boscardin, 2001, p. 72)
- The whole testing procedure is somehow actually constructed on whether the tester observed the person to socialize in the way the tester understood to be socialization. (Blackman, in Biklen, 2005, p. 149)

Wary of the power inherent in the ability to assign disability labels, many described the process of testing and labeling as invasive. Still others question why individuals should be held to such rigid and inflexible norms. As Mukhopadhyay writes, "Students are not pieces of a jigsaw puzzle who could be forced inside to form a desired pre-planned picture" (quoted in Biklen, 2005, p. 134). Another finds it "ridiculous" to expect all children "to learn the same way" (O'Connor, in Rodis et al., 2001, p. 71). Instead, they argue that all students are different and all students have needs that are fluid and contextual (Reid & Valle, 2004). They locate disability in inflexible school structures and the low expectations that teachers have once they learn of a child's disability. Contrary to how their teachers and peers view them, however, individuals see themselves as capable and intelligent, even fascinating.

It is instructive that students feel mystified about the process of being labeled and placed in special education. As Vanessa (in Connor, 2008) asks, "Who put me in special education? I never knew nothing, it just happened...I think it's unfair" (p. 242). Another student in the same study explains how parents are often coerced into putting their children into special education. He says that parents end up signing the papers because school officials threaten to retain their child unless they agree to the placement. He goes on to say,

- [When] parents sign that paper, you just lost your rights right there. And once you're in there it's just like Hell.... Getting in is easy, but getting out is hard. Any kid can get into special education. To get out of special ed., it takes Hell to get out of special education. (Michael, in Connor, 2008, p. 149)

Another 16-year-old African-American male questions the limited access students in special education get to the general education curriculum. He notices that in special education, "All you see is Black faces" (Jesse, in Smith, 2001, p. 113). Because he believes he's getting an inferior education and less of a chance in life he comes to view the situation as a crisis, exclaiming: "I want out! Get me outta' here" (p. 110)! Other students share similar stories:

- As I see it, I was not given a fair chance. No one at the time thought to ask me where I would like to go to school. (Attfield, in Biklen, 2005, p. 203)
- [That] label followed me for a long time. (O'Connor, in Rodis et al., 2001, p. 64)
- Whenever I had trouble with a class they immediately took me out of there and stuck me in resource.... They kept pulling me out and putting me in resource again... [but] we didn't do anything about the class [I was missing]. We didn't learn about social studies in resource; we played games. All we did was play games. (Rose, in Ferri, Keefe, & Gregg, 2001, pp. 25–26)

Here students recognize how little control they and even their parents have in the process. Pushed and pulled from general education classes to special education and back, students feel powerless over the decision making process. As Harry and Klingner (2006) write, "once the discourse of disability is set in motion, it becomes a very difficult mechanism to interrupt" (p. 7). "Social forces intertwine to construct an identity of 'disability,'" which constitutes certain student types that general education "finds too difficult to serve" (p. 9). In the process students are made to feel powerless over decisions that will impact their lives for years. When we consider how students feel about the process, we must question our taken-for-granted notions of special education needs and ask, "Whom does the current system serve? Who feels empowered/disempowered by the current model of service provision?"

Another issue brought up in these and other examples involved the ineffective instruction students received in special education. Many talked about unchallenging curriculum and days of playing games. The following examples focus on the actual instruction provided in resource rooms and other special classes.

- Instead of giving you challenging work, they just teach you the same thing, over and over, every year.... You basically have to learn on your own. (Michael, in Connor, 2008, p. 146)
- ...[T]he assignments at this school suck! They don't have anything to do with anything and we learn absolutely nothing from them. Its all just work to keep us busy and out of trouble. We do the same things everyday.... It's senseless! (Isis, in Jones, 2004, p. 72)
- The work will be all too easy, you won't learn anything. (Chanell, in Connor, 2008, p. 84)
- All we did was play games. [We] played computer games. [We] played board games.... I would come home with all sorts of toys...from winning stuff from games...but I felt stupid because I had to leave the class. (Rose, in Ferri et al., 2001, p. 25)

- The [special education] teachers were kind, but...they underestimated me. (Pelkey, in Rodis et al., 2001, p. 21)
- When you're in there you ain't doin' nothin'. You're doin' basics...for example, when I was in fifth grade, I was doin' first grade work. (Jesse, in Smith, 2001, p. 111).
- School was a big disappointment and the work was never challenging. (Attfield, in Biklen, 2005, p. 209)

Believing that the instruction they were receiving in segregated settings was inferior led many to favor inclusion. Some have very specific suggestions of what would have been helpful to them:

- I don't live in an isolated society; I shouldn't learn in an isolated classroom.... Other students benefit from the insight I have...I can sometimes perceive things that other students miss. (Lipsky & Gartner, 1997, p. 149)
- I would have liked to have seen someone try to help me, you know, get through those classes instead of taking me out. (Rose, in Ferri et al., 2001, p. 26)
- The special ed system is dumb...it teaches you nothing. (Jesse, in Smith, 2001, p. 112)
- Sometimes I think the teachers make things worse with kids by riding them when they are already having a bad day. They should leave us alone when we are like that. (Air, in Jones, 2004, p. 42)
- Teachers must be willing to not just give me a desk and then leave me to fill the chair. I need to be asked questions, and given time for my thoughtful answers. Teachers need to become a conductor, and guide me through the many places I may get lost. (Burke, in Biklen, 2005, p. 253)

Regrettably, special education, like all low status educational placements (such as remedial or low tracked classes and underresourced urban schools), is characterized by low expectations and traditional skill-based direct instruction (Brantlinger, 2005; Harry & Klingner, 2006). Although general educators continue to believe in the efficacy of segregated special education classes, the reality of these classes is often marked by large class sizes, increasing teacher shortages, undifferentiated and ineffective instruction, inappropriate curriculum, undue restrictiveness, stigma, and disappointingly low graduation rates (Harry & Klingner, 2006). It is a fact that many resource rooms are not much more than "supervised study halls" (Brantlinger, 2005, p. 127). As a result, those who come to school with the least cultural capital and who are in the most need of progressive and effective instruction are given the least opportunity to learn from highly qualified and engaged teachers (Gallagher, 2005; Harry & Klingner, 2006).

In the next set of examples, I focus on how special education labels change the way students are perceived by others, leading to a form of "social othering" (Slee, 2004, p. 49).

- It sounds to me like they [teachers] gave up on me. (Rose, in Ferri, et al., 2001, p. 27)
- [Teachers] didn't really set high expectations for me...That's where I lost some...confidence, academically, especially. (John, in Ferri et al., 2001, p. 27)
- Cuz of my reputation, I'm sure they'll try to get me angry so they can throw me out again. It won't even have to be a big thing, just something stupid, and they'll use it as an excuse to kick me out like they did in middle school. (Isis, in Jones, 2004, p. 70)

- [Teachers] underestimated me...[and] I was rarely asked to really think. (Pelkey, in Rodis et al, 2001, p. 21)
- Of course, coming from this [special] school doesn't help when you're trying to find a job. (Air, in Jones, 2004, p. 34)
- My teacher gave up on me within weeks of my beginning school. She went through the motions but she had no great expectations of my achieving. I felt like I was being denied an education. (Attfield, in Biklen, 2005, p. 209)
- Since the [the Art teacher] new [sic] I was in special education...he was treating me differently.... Hmm, it's a special education thing...how he treated me. (Chanell, in Connor, 2005, p. 121)
- Once they find out, girls don't want to date you, no one wants to talk to you. Because you're labeled as a special education kid. Not attractive. (Michael, in Connor, 2008, p. 155)
- When I was in [special education], I really wanted to kill myself, because that's the most embarrassing thing to a kid. (Michael, in Connor, p. 141)
- Segregation made me a social outcast. I made no friends. (Attfield, 2005, p. 209)

In these excerpts students highlight some of the personal, social, and educational costs of being labeled. Rejected by peers and diminished by teachers, students who are labeled must learn to cope with a stigmatized identity. Labels "confer a lesser status on those labeled," although they are seen by professionals as necessary in order to provide students with services (Apple, 2001, p. 261). Conveying that they feel like "social outcasts" or pariahs, students communicate the degree to which being labeled creates a form of social stigma (Goffman, 1963). It is no surprise, therefore, that students who receive these services are "less likely to evaluate them as helpful and necessary" than students who do not receive these services (Brantlinger, 2005, p. 134). It was telling that many of the students in these studies made references to confinement, prison, and even death in describing special education classrooms and services.

- At fifteen years of age I was drafted into "Life Skills." It was like a deathblow. (Attfield, in Biklen, 2005, p. 210)
- It's like prison, once you learn your lesson, you should be released. (Michael, in Connor, 2008, p. 148)
- It was like jail. (Chanell, in Connor, 2008, p. 75)
- Ten years of my life has been wasted in special education. (Jesse, in Smith, 2001, p. 113)
- [It was] standard practice for the district, locking their embarrassing students away so as not to be embarrassed by them and tossing enough food down so they'd survive, not so much that they might grow and thrive. (Queen, in Rodis et al., 2001, p. 4)
- I knew the doors of education would always remain closed for me.... So, when one school said "sorry" and the next school referred me to a school for the mentally retarded, mother did not even try to ask a third. (Muklopadhyay, in Biklen, 2005, p. 128)
- My parents refused to send me to a school for children with severe learning difficulties, which was the only offer on the table. (Attfield, in Biklen, 2005, p. 203)
- In the back of the building...we were kind of hidden away. (Rose, in Ferri et al., 2001, p. 28)
- Because I feel so closed up in there. It feels like a prison. I can't stand that. (Isis, in Jones, 2004, p. 178)

Based on these examples it is difficult to view much of our current special education practices as either effective or moral (Brantlinger, 2004). It is stunning to hear students speak not of services, but of confinement, incarceration, and punishment. Like many disability studies scholars and activists, these students reject deficit views of disability as well as the traditional approaches to instruction that are based on these views. Instead, they actively forge alternative conceptualizations of disability, defining it "as a symbol of oppression, as a marginal social status, as membership in a minority group, as an embodied experience" (Gabel & Danforth, 2002, p. 3).

If we want to enact meaningful reform, we would do well to listen carefully to the voices that are positioned on the furthest margins of our schools. Drawing insights that resonate with social justice education, their voices call for a complete dismantling of the "underlying [ableist] assumptions that produce and reproduce structures of domination," which disadvantage students with disabilities (Bell, 1997, p. 11).

In the final section of the chapter I propose various ways to reimagine dis/ability from a disability studies perspective. I examine the need to shift the object of remediation from disabled bodies and lives to inaccessible educational structures and ableist attitudes. I draw on the above voices of disabled people to help us imagine dis/ability otherwise. Finally, I conclude that when we view disabled people as sources of knowledge, we can begin to reconfigure practice in ways that honors different ways of knowing and being and that seamlessly integrates supports for all students.

Reforming Schools for Everyone

Despite the history of overrepresentation in special education, advocates of inclusion and scholars working on issues of overrepresentation have not engaged in any sustained dialogue regarding the complex ways that exclusion and discrimination work in today's schools. Likewise, the social model of disability is also "conspicuously missing in the scholarship of prominent educational theorists," who write about other ways that students are marginalized in schools (Erevelles, 2005, p. 67). As Jones (2004) writes, *ableism* is too often ignored when scholars are critiquing "other *isms* such as racism or sexism" (p. 15). This lack of engagement with more critical understandings of disability signals an "unquestioned support of the dominant paradigm pertaining to disability" (Erevelles, 2005, p. 67) and a failure to identify with the struggles of disabled people to dismantle such ableist notions of dis/ability.

In our reform efforts, we must take a stand against all forms of segregation and marginalization in schools, whether based on racism or ableism or any other ism (Ferri & Connor, 2006). This will require that we take responsibility for all students and reject deficit models of disability and ethnocentric views of culture, ethnicity, and race. Anything short of this will fail to address how a dual system of education depends on the practice of marginalizing students based on perceived difference and will fall short of developing a "socially just educational system in a democratic society" (Artiles, 2005, p. 86). The dialogue that Artiles (2005) and others (Erevelles, 2005; Ware, 2005) call for must also include the perspectives of those most invested in reform—those students whose bodies and histories "bear the weight" of segregation (Kliewer & Raschke, 2002, p. 43). Paying close attention to the voices of students themselves provides us with insider knowledge about how to make schools more democratic and just.

For example, the focus of our efforts should be on modifying our instructional practices and institutional structures, rather than requiring students to adjust to arbitrary norms. Instead of rushing to label a child as deficient when they do not learn the way that we teach, we must teach students the way that they learn (Kluth, Straut, & Biklen,

2003, p. 18). This shift in the object of remediation requires that we honor different ways of reading, writing, perceiving, and moving through space as equally valid (Hehir, 2005; Reid & Valle, 2004). It requires us to adopt a "presumption of competence" rather than a deficit orientation (Biklen, 2005, p. 1). Instead of locating our failures within students, it demands that we look inward and ask, "What other approach can I try" (p. 73)?

Rather than viewing students with diverse learning needs as a drag on resources, we must begin to value what students with disabilities bring to the classroom. Honoring diversity requires that we view students with disabilities as valued members of our schools and classrooms—not because we are charitable, but because students with disabilities, like all students, have a lot to offer. If the students cited in this article have anything at all to say, it is that we are missing out on what they have to teach us—both about themselves and our practices. Their words demand that we question our taken-for-granted assumptions about disability—recognizing the ways that they are smart, "capable" (Lipsky & Gartner, 1997, p. 149), and even "fascinating" (Blackman, in Biklen, 2005, p. 149)! By revaluing disability and difference, they ask us to reject ableist assumptions that it is "better for a child to walk than roll, speak than sign, read print than read Braille" or listen to an audio book (Hehir, 2005, p. 15). In other words, they demand that we refuse hegemonic notions of literacy and learning and being in the world. They also ask us to think carefully about the efficacy of labels and special education services that come to feel like a form of imprisonment. They show us how when we label kids we rob them of their "energy and passion" for learning (O'Connor in Rodis et al., 2001, p. 72) as well as their rights (Michael, in Connor, 2005, p. 197).

Because all students are different and all students have needs, learning supports must be embedded seamlessly into the general education classroom, not tacked on or subcontracted out. When supports are embedded and integrated into the general education classroom, they can be made available to support any or all students who need them, *whenever* they need them. By embedding services we also stop giving students and parents a false choice between general education settings offering little or no supports or flexibility or segregated special education classes offering little access to a challenging or meaningful curriculum. It also shows that we understand that disability is contextual and reflects a lack of fit between one's particular body or brain and one's environment. Instead of thinking about disability as an either/or category, by embedding supports in inclusive classrooms, we recognize the fluid nature of disability and provide supports when they are needed. Rather than thinking of disabilities as severe or mild—as if impairment related needs are static across settings—we understand that it is the setting and the availability of supports, resources, accommodations that determine the level of impact of any disability. Of course, ideally our classroom structures and instructional practices would be universally designed[3] to maximize the degree of fit between all students and the learning context—providing students with differentiated, meaningful, and challenging curriculum, along with high-access instruction, targeted supports structures, and choice.

In closing, a social justice approach to special education services must move away from structures and practices that dehumanize and marginalize students (Jones, 2004). There is no excuse for students or their parents to feel mystified (or imprisoned) by the services set up to support them. We need to recognize that students have something to teach us about their learning styles and needs. In shifting our attention from the center to the margin, we gain important insights about how to make our educational practices better not just for students who are labeled, but for everyone. We begin to see that *all* students need real choices, authentic curriculum, and appropriate levels of control over their school lives (Jones, 2004). Finally, by repositioning our ideas about where expertise about disability is located, a social justice approach to disability honors a foundational motto of the disability rights movement, "Nothing about us, without us."

Additional Resources

Disability Studies in Education (Special Interest Group) of American Educational Research Association (AERA). http://www.aera.net/Default.aspx?id=1297

Disability Studies for Teachers of Syracuse University's Center on Human Policy. http://www.disabilitystudiesforteachers.org/

Universal Design for Learning, website of the *Center for Applied Special Technology* (CAST). http://www.cast.org/pd/index.html

Building pedagogical curbcuts: Incorporating disability into the university classroom and curriculum. Available in pdf download through Syracuse University's Graduate School. http://gradschpdprograms.syr.edu/resources/publications-books.php

Notes

1. I often have a somewhat tongue-in-cheek conversation with my teacher education students about changing who gets labeled in schools. Inverting the gaze, we shift labels from students to classrooms or even individual teachers. In our new system the most inclusive teacher gets the label of "gifted" and the least inclusive classroom or teacher gets the label of "pedagogically delayed or instructionally disordered."

2. Scholars in disability studies sometimes use dis/ability to highlight how what we think of as normalcy or "ability" is every bit as constructed as disability. So, the use of dis/ability simultaneously calls both disability and ability into question. Another example that is particularly useful in illustrating the doubleness of words is reflected in the terms *dis/ease* (which can mean illness, but also discomfort) and *in/valid* (which can mean incapacitated, but also illegitimate). Similarly, I use *(Dis)Service* in the title to demarcate ways that special education considers itself as a service and yet, in practice, this so-called service can be very disempowering to the individuals it proposes to serve. Likewise terms like *(mis)understood* signal the ways that taken for granted assumptions and understandings are called into question by a more critical framework.

3. Universal Design for Learning is an approach to instructional design that borrows from the concept of universal design in architecture. Its goal is to design instruction that meets the needs of the widest possible range of learners. The Center for Applied Special Technology (CAST) has been at the forefront of this approach to instructional design. See their website at http://www.cast.org/research/udl/index.html.

References

Apple, M. W. (2001). Afterword: The politics of labeling in a conservative age. In G. M. Hudak & P. Kihn (Eds.), *Labeling: Pedagogy and politics* (pp. 261–283). New York: Routledge/Falmer.

Artiles, A. J. (2005). Special education's changing identity: Paradoxes and dilemmas in views of culture and space. In L. Katzman, A. G. Gandhi, W. S. Harbour, & J. D. LaRock (Eds.), *Special education for a new century. Harvard Educational Review* (pp. 85–120) (Reprint Series, No. 41).

Attfield, R. (2005). The color of rich. In D. Biklen (Ed.), *Autism and the myth of the person alone* (pp. 199–248). New York: New York University Press.

Bell, L. A. (1997). Theoretical foundations for social justice education. In L. Adams, L. A. Bell, & P. Griffin (Eds.), *Teaching for diversity and social justice: A sourcebook* (pp. 3–15). New York: Routledge.

Biklen, D., with Attfield, R., Bissonnette, L., Blackman, L., Burke, J., Frugone, A., et al. (2005). *Autism and the myth of the person alone.* New York: New York University Press.

Blatt, B. (1984). *In and out of books: Reviews and other polemics on special education.* Baltimore, MD: University Park Press.

Brantlinger, E. (2004). Ideologies discerned, values determined: Getting past the hierarchies of special education. In L. Ware (Ed.), *Ideology and the politics of (In)exclusion* (pp. 11–31). New York: Peter Lang.

Brantlinger, E. (2005). Slippery shibboleths: The shady side of truisms in special education. In S. Gabel (Ed.), *Disability studies in education: Readings in theory and method* (pp. 125–138). New York: Peter Lang.

Brown v Board of Education, 347 U.S. 438 (1954).

Collins, K. M. (2003). *Ability profiling and school failure: One child's struggle to be seen as competent.* Mahwah, NJ: Erlbaum.

Connor, D. J. (2005). *Labeled "learning disabled": Life in and out of school for urban, Black and/ or Latino(a) youth from working-class backgrounds.* Unpublished doctoral dissertation, Teachers College, Columbia University, New York.

Connor, D. J. (2008). *Urban narratives, portraits in progress: Life at the intersections of learning disability, race, and social class.* New York: Peter Lang.

Dunn, L. M. (1968). Special education for the mildly retarded: Is much of it justifiable? *Exceptional Children, 35,* 5–22.

Erevelles, N. (2005). Rewriting critical pedagogy from the periphery. In S. Gabel (Ed.), *Disability studies in education: Readings in theory and method* (pp. 65–83). New York: Peter Lang.

Ferri, B. A., & Connor, D. J. (2006). *Reading resistance: Discourses of exclusion in desegregation and inclusion debates.* New York: Peter Lang.

Ferri, B. A., Keefe, C. H., & Gregg, N. (2001). Teachers with learning disabilities: A view from both sides of the desk. *Journal of Learning Disabilities. 34*(1), 22–52.

Fierros, E. G., & Conroy, J. W. (2002). Double jeopardy: An exploration of restrictiveness and race in special education. In D. J. Losen & G. Orfield (Eds.), *Racial inequality in special education* (pp. 39–70). Cambridge, MA: Harvard Education Press.

Fleischer, L. E. (2001). Special education students as counter-hegemonic theorizers. In G. M. Hudak & P. Kihn (Eds.), *Labeling: Pedagogy and politics* (pp. 115–126). New York: Routledge/ Falmer.

Franklin, B. M. (1987). The first crusade for learning disabilities: The movement for the education for backward children. In T. Popkewitz (Ed.), *The foundation of the school subjects* (pp. 190–209). London: Falmer.

Gabel, S., & Danforth, S. (2002). Disability studies in education: Seizing the moment of opportunity. *Disability, Culture and Education, 1*(1), 1–3.

Gabel, S. L. (2005). Introduction: Disability studies in education. In S. L. Gabel (Ed.), *Disability studies in education: Readings in theory and method* (1–20). New York: Peter Lang.

Gallagher, D. (2005). Searching for something outside ourselves: The contradiction between technical rationality and the achievement of inclusive pedagogy. In. S. Gabel (Ed.), *Disability studies in education: Readings in theory and method* (pp. 139–154). New York: Peter Lang.

Goffman, E. (1963). *Stigma: Notes on the management of spoiled identity.* New York: Simon & Schuster.

Harry, B., & Klingner, J. (2006). Why *are so many minority students in special education?* New York: Teachers College Press.

Hehir, T. (2005). *New directions in special education: Eliminating ableism in policy and practice.* Cambridge, MA: Harvard Education Press.

Jones, M. M. (2004). *Whisper writing: Teenage girls talk about ableism and sexism in school.* New York: Peter Lang.

Kliewer, C., & Raschke, D. (2002). Beyond the metaphor of merger: Confronting the moral quagmire of segregation in early childhood special education. *Disability, Culture, and Education, 1*(1), 41–62.

Kluth, P., Straut, D. M., & Biklen, D. P. (Eds.). (2003). *Access to academics for ALL students: Critical approaches to inclusive curriculum, instruction, and policy.* Mahwah, NJ: Erlbaum.

Kugelmass, J., & Ainscow, M. (2004). Leadership for inclusion: A comparison of international perspectives. *Journal of Research in Special Education Needs, 4*(3), 133–141.

Linton, S. (2006). *My body politic: A memoir.* Ann Arbor: University of Michigan Press.

Lipsky, D. K., & Gartner, A. (1997). *Inclusion and school reform: Transforming America's classrooms.* Baltimore, MD: Paul H. Brookes.

Losen, D. J., & Orfield, G. (Eds.). *Racial inequality in special education.* Cambridge, MA: Harvard Education Press.

Reid, D. K., & Valle, J. (2004). The discursive practice of learning disability: Implications for instruction and parent school relations. *Journal of Learning Disabilities, 37*(6), 466–481.

Rodis, P., Garrod, A., & Boscardin M. L. (Eds.). (2001). *Learning disabilities and life stories.* Boston, MA: Allyn & Bacon.

Slee, R. (2004). Meaning in the service of power. In L. Ware (Ed.), *Ideology and the politics of (in)exclusion* (pp. 46–60). New York: Peter Lang.

Sleeter, C. E. (1987). Why is there learning disabilities? A critical analysis of the birth of the field with its social context. In T. S. Popkewitz (Ed.), *The foundations of the school subjects* (pp. 210–237). London: Palmer Press.

Smith, A. (2001). The labeling of African American boys in special education. In G. M. Hudak & P. Kihn (Eds.), *Labeling: Pedagogy and politics* (pp. 109–114). New York: Routledge/Falmer.

Ware, L. (2004). Introduction. In L. Ware (Ed.), *Ideology and the politics of (in)exclusion* (pp. 1–8). New York: Peter Lang.

Ware, L. (2005). Many possible futures, many different directions: Merging critical special education and disability studies. In S. Gabel (Ed.), *Disability studies in education: Readings in theory and method* (pp. 103–124). New York: Peter Lang.

Wedell, K. (2005). Dilemmas in the quest for inclusion. *British Journal of Special Education, 32*(1), 3–11.

27 "The Tell-Tale Body"

The Constitution of Disabilities in School

Ray McDermott and Jason Duque Raley

The tell-tale body is all tongues. Men are like Geneva watches with crystal faces which expose the whole movement.... The face and eyes reveal what the spirit is doing, how old it is, what aims it has. The eyes indicate the antiquity of the soul, or, through and how many forms it has already ascended. (Emerson, 1860, p. 154)

...a culture [is] not a community basket weaving project, nor yet an act of god; [is] something neither desirable nor undesirable in itself, being inevitable, being nothing more or less than the recorded effects on a body of people of the vicissitudes with which they had been forced to deal. (Baldwin, 1955, p. 140)

A popular but risky way to play nature and nurture[1] with children comes in two parts: the first describes what they cannot do at an early age; the second assumes that the identified limitations predict directly what they cannot do as adults. A more reliable way to predict what children will do as adults is to describe the roles available in the social structure that will acquire them regardless of their abilities. The analytic view from adult roles is most revealing and corrective in a society with a systematic and unjust misfit between the likely potentials of children and the jobs ready to reward them with position and status. The possibility of an unjust misfit requires, as Emerson might say, that we listen to "the tell-tale body" of the children to see what they have been through, to see what their "face and eyes reveal" about getting squeezed into lives smaller than promised at birth.

In the United States, the tight fit between race, class, and school failure signals an unjust system that assures the reproduction of biased individual outcomes over collective potential. Schooling, as Baldwin said of culture, is "not a community basket weaving project, nor yet an act of god," but it does divide a population and leaves its "recorded effects" on the bodies of a people's children: Make that, says this paper, *recorded literally*. The well-funded apparatus for diagnosing the problems of young children, as nice as it sounds, has become a guidance system for reproducing a divided and often unjust social structure, no less racist and class biased in outcomes than before, but now phrased in terms of embodied psychological traits, for example, ability, intelligence, attention span, problem solving skills, speed of reasoning, language capacity, and so on. These traits have been isolated from the potentials of real children and have become institutional labels: Learning Disability, Low IQ, Attention Deficit Disorder, Hyperactivity, English Language Learner,[2] and so on. They dictate limits on the best a child can be. Professional testers can add to the list with every new budget for more children to be diagnosed.

In the last 300 years, with the rise of nation-states, industrial capitalism, democracy, individualism, science, and university systems, words for various positive activities or events have been newly nuanced as kinds of persons. The medieval genius, for example, was not a person who was invariably smart across a range of situations, but a medium, a person only momentarily chosen by God, to perform some great breakthrough; by the 18th century that same person was complete with copyright powers over his[3] artistic and scientific achievements. This celebration of individual types is part of a larger package institutionalizing (you can't do without one) and commodifying (you can buy one) not only the genius, but the expert, the scientist, the scholar, the tycoon, and the creative artist. The inherently intelligent entered the fray in the late 19th century, and the idea of the gifted 10-year old (and his, yes, mostly male at first, and later his or her LD counterpart) come to the fore in the late 20th century.

This seems positive enough, in a survival of the smartest sordid sorting sort of way, but for two dissenting traditions. First, the new terms for individuals were immediately followed by complaints that they are better treated as names for situations that happen to turn out productively for individuals in the right place at the right time. Second, the new terms were followed by measures of all those who, for reasons of an unfortunate constitution, could never succeed or make a difference. The negative extension of the new terms, along with racism, colonialism, and class bias, has filled our lives for the past 150 years with reports of illiterates, the hopelessly dull and stupid, the primitive, the uneducated, the uneducable, the criminal, the merely normal, and, for the past 50 years, the disabled of many kinds (LD, ADD, and even ELL, etc.). If you or yours haven't been caught and labeled yet, just you wait.[4]

This chapter expands the first line of dissent by treating achievement as situational and uses the second to critique the unjust degradation of those not achieving in expected ways. We seek a more political phrasing, not just to complain about the school disability industry, but to disrupt it. Two questions lurk in the background. By what perverse arrangements among persons variously situated in relation to opportunity and power would a society misdirect the tools of science to make children less than they are? How, if only at the level of research, can we intervene?

The point is *not* that there is no such thing as individual differences among learners; *nor* do we think differences among learners might not constitute difficult situations as the world is currently organized. Our point is rather that differences are better thought of as opportunities, and that a democracy intent on justice and equality should do more than just talk about equal opportunity. When the United States prepared for war in early 1942, potentials were put to use. People locked out from becoming machinists, pilots, and nurses before Pearl Harbor were suddenly given a chance. Arbitrary barriers were momentarily removed, the better to make war more efficiently. The same words, rearranged, state the pressing issue for American education today. How can we make war more effectively on the arbitrary barriers to everyone getting access?

To insure its own survival, a democracy must make the most of everyone's potential. The current situation in the United States is poised to go in two directions: on the plus side, huge financial and institutional commitments for special education, all in the name of helping and appreciating individual differences, and, on the minus side, an ever growing sorting apparatus of diagnoses, tests, and labels for excluding more children from success (Varenne & McDermott, 1998). Together they make a contradictory logic: yes, everyone can learn, and yes, because everyone can learn, those who do not learn better than others must have something, uhm, seriously wrong with them. So goes American common sense—step on others to climb on the shoulders of giants—to which everyone has to ascribe, or pay the price.

Emotionally, we take a lead from Christopher Nolan, an Irish writer trapped from birth by a cerebral palsy that kept him out of touch even with those close about him. At 12, his family noticed he could send messages by dropping his head, with a stick attached to it, in the direction of typewriter keys. At 15, he wrote an acclaimed book of poetry and at 21 an autobiography that outlined his plight and offered a hope—his plight of fancy:

> Century upon century saw crass crippled man dashed, branded and treated as dross in a world offended by their appearance, and cracked asunder in their belittlement by having to resemble venial human specimens offering nothing and pondering less in their life of mindless normality. So [he] mulled universal moods as he grimly looked back on the past, but *reasons never curb but rather create new gleeful designs.* (Nolan, 1987, p. 3; italics added)

This is the way to see all children and not just the dramatic case. Every situation should be built for children to create "new gleeful designs," and educational institutions should make the best of what children can do, and not just diagnose their problems. It takes a great democracy to live up to this promise and great promises to enliven a democracy. The American educational system is less a contributor to democracy of late. One reason is that it is getting harder to promise that children will be educated to their full potential.

We proceed in three main parts. The first offers an approach to the learning body in a democratic state promising equal opportunity and justice for all. Current theories of school and society have been captured by a cynicism won in hindsight, accurate perhaps, but we prefer to begin with an optimism, the better to reroute our disappointments and to state a new direction. We begin early in American democracy when hope was still easy, but not naïve. We begin with Emerson, who was a disruptive observer of the use of intellect in a democracy. Almost a half-century after Emerson's essay on "The American Scholar," Oliver Wendell Holmes (1885, p. 115) called it "our intellectual Declaration of Independence," something much needed by both children and adults in schools today.[5] Emerson appreciated that education by books could be a stimulus to the development of great thinkers and in turn great wisdom, but he also understood that learning at its best comes from all the people working together. "The greatest genius," he warned, "is the most indebted man" (1995, p. 127). In a posthumous book on the *Natural History of Intellect*, Emerson called for "a Farmer's Almanac of mental moods" (1894, p. 10). Farmers, he thought, are bedrock to the collective wisdom people, scientists among them, accustomed as they are to think with nature and culture. The body would certainly be a chapter in his Almanac, but imagine his surprise that a contemporary version would have to include a chapter on the labeled and disabled, maligned and misaligned, bodies of schoolchildren.

Emerson appreciated the body as a nexus of the person's experience in a wider world of forces. We can read a person's experience in a society by the marks recorded on the body:

> A main fact in the history of manners is the wonderful expressiveness of the human body. If it were made of glass, or of air, and the thoughts were written on steel within, it could not publish more truly its meaning than now.... The tell-tale body is all tongues. (1860, p. 154)

For those called disabled, for those with a dissed-ability, a missed-ability, their bodies show less what they cannot do and more the marks put upon them by circumstances, by those seemingly not disabled at the time, by the Temporarily Able Bodied without the means or willingness to see strength and wisdom where it is easier to see absence. Remember Baldwin on culture: "nothing more or less than the recorded effects on a body of people of the vicissitudes with which they had been forced to deal" (1955, p. 140). As for everybody, so for every body![6] This section begs for a more representative democracy in which all citizens, young and old, established and just starting out, hyperliterate or just learning to read, would take their place in a larger whole, as Emerson urged, as representative of the wider wisdom of the society. In Emerson's democracy, everyone—including Emerson's genius: the "most indebted man"—works in service of a less bruising society with a less bruising school.

Our second and third parts recast accounts of disabled children into accounts of their others who might be inhibiting and, more evocatively, inhabiting their bodies: their *inhabitus*. By others, we mean both those immediately around them and those who have brought them together given social and political arrangements both near and far. As every new generation of parents learns to fear, the socialization of children can involve millions of others who set agendas, model desires, offer resources, and limit outcomes. We describe a clumsy child and a hyperactive child, the first mostly overlooked and the second impossible to overlook, and show how both develop with a precise attunement to an unnecessarily consequential issue at deep play and hard work around them: the attribution of inherent intelligence and of the lifelong promise of early literacy.

The Body Politic

Two important arguments have stood against the march of disability labels: first, that the "truly" disabled are often more able than their labels imply, and, second, that many if not most of the children called LD have been "falsely" labeled. The contrast set of "truly" and "falsely" in the last sentence is proposed in the most mutually relevant sense, both traits—true and false—being defined in terms of each other. By "truly," adults usually mean visible, particularly to those on the look out for disabilities. Children who cannot see or hear, or children with Down syndrome or severe cerebral palsy (Christopher Nolan, always), are in some sense visible. Even if visible, they can still be "falsely" labeled relative to a fit between what they can do and the environments others create for them (Christopher Nolan, if treated as only a "crass crippled man" when, after all, he could communicate beautifully). For a nice example, consider a society in which both hearing and deaf populations use a signed language; under such circumstances, to label a person as deaf says only that they cannot hear, and says nothing else about them.[7] In a more divided community in which a hearing population controls the media of participation and cannot use the relevant sign language, the label of deaf invites conditions for unjust condemnation. The more "truly" visible the deaf, or any other labeled group in an inhospitable society, the more "falsely" they are labeled relative to their potential.

By the same analytic turn, children with LD are not "truly" visible, except in situations requiring particular skills on unique tasks (often necessary on psychological tests only), and whether they are "falsely" labeled depends on the ecological validity of the test and, more importantly, the institutional adequacy of the pedagogy used to address the problem. Children without LD, but labeled as such, are also not visibly LD, not "truly" LD, but the truth value of their diagnosis is more complex. They have been "falsely" labeled by their diagnosis, but if it works to everyone's advantage—that their family stops calling them stupid, that more time on formal tests allows them to display their learning more fully—then, given the conditions of the system, we may want to say they have not been "falsely" labeled, while reserving the right to say that under different conditions, under better conditions, *under conditions encouraging the most learning by everyone in all situations*, labeled and labelers alike have been "falsely" played by the diagnosis and the system that invited it.

This difficult account of the double life of labels allows the key point. Without a careful description of the environments in which a disability becomes visible, to whom, why, under what circumstances, by what mix of "truly" and "falsely," and with what outcomes, true and false are neither rigorous categories, nor rigidly contrasted categories.

In selecting a clumsy and a hyperactive child, we seek a midpoint in the true–false continua (yes, the plural form is accurate). The conditions are there to be seen—clumsy is clumsy if anyone bothers to look and hyperactive is overbearingly present—yet we can show that the symptoms do not belong to the identified child alone. It takes a few people to make a problematic situation and a whole society to arrange a diagnosis. Remember Emerson: "...you must take the whole society to find the whole man" (2004, p. 51). Watching the bodies of people in interaction affords a partial vision of the whole society at work, and so the other way round. Christopher Nolan after age 12 was not just, or not at all, a disabled person, but a poet using words to create "new gleeful designs." A theory of disability requires not just a description of children facing a problem, but an analysis of their environment and a critique of the people who call them names.

We can start with the behavior of a child in school. Cancel that. We must start with a report of what is missing in the behavior of a child in school, for this is how schools establish a focus. American education is taken with, and held accountable for, the interpretation of what is wrong with individual children. Misbehavior and missing behavior are the institutionally well-paid pre/occupations of consequence, the stuff of a child's school records, the stuff of the institutional biographies that record a child's problems in school files forever. To account for missing behavior, to interpret, say, a child *not* learning to read as quickly as others, schools do not look out to the larger world of inequalities of which they are a part. They go in the opposite direction. What counts, what is counted, is the missing behavior, and, to make it visible and recordable, tests are given and the results treated as real, more real than the child to the extent that the tests claim to have gotten inside the child's head, into the throne room of cognitive abilities and disabilities. The problem with global norming is that our kids are getting toasted by tests.

Many problems offered children in American schools are not worth having. They must relentlessly arrange not to get caught not knowing something, constantly to do better than others, show off what is learned elsewhere as if it were learned in school—these are not productive problems for children to overcome. Some are crushed by the pressures, and those who survive are not always kinder and gentler persons for their competitive success. Without schools obsessed by what is wrong with children, everyone might be better off. Without schools and parents looking for LD and ADD children, the diagnoses of moment, we might be better able to ask questions about the conditions that have encouraged such problems. If Emerson is right that we can "read very sharply all your private history in your look and gait and behavior" (1860, p. 154), perhaps we can read in "the tell-tale bodies" of children their private histories and the social milieu that has staged the problems they must confront.

Many societies have developed strong literacy traditions without LD labels, MRI images, ADD worries, or ELL programs (McDermott, Goldman, & Varenne, 2006; McDermott & Varenne, 1995). Traditional societies rarely develop such notions, although a century of anthropology, from Franz Boas (1911) and Paul Radin (1927) to Charles Frake (1980) and Harold Conklin (2007), has shown that they make extraordinary cognitive and intellectual demands on both children and adults. Even most contemporary state societies have developed literacy without theories of cognition and intelligence dividing up the population. It is more than possible, and maybe preferable, to build education systems that demand effort and responsibility more than intelligence. Japan might be the most prominent example of a society with an inclusive skill base answerable to questions about responsibility. In contrast, the United States was the first society to institutionalize a narrow definition of intelligence as measured on IQ tests (Raftery, 1988), and it has followed that mistake as the first society to institutionalize the search for LD (although the trouble, as if LD were on sale at Wal-Mart, has been spreading around the globe).

Without a bipolar distribution of wealth and power, no one would need such a diagnosis. Children could be what they are without fear of being looked down upon or pushed aside without school credentials. We are all, said Karl Marx (1963) most famously,[8] responsible for creating the social world, albeit under conditions others have arranged for us. If the full history of the world can be read in the sensuous organization of working bodies, as Marx (1852/1963) also said, then we can ask how historical circumstances have been beating children into the appearance of disability. The world has its way with bodies. We wear the bodies of others, of those long before us and those now around us. Our bodies are designed, as Emerson said, by the responses of others to fate, their struggles with power and wealth, and their place in the culture of interpretations that has them, never according to their own schedule, alternately terrified and ennobled, disabled and enabled, hiding and showing off. Of all the things that could be said, and have been said, about children in various eras and cultures, what kind of society would make LD the description of choice? And can we reorganize society so children's bodies would not have to bear the weight of social structure?

A Clumsy Child

> Under a commanding thought all people become graceful. (Emerson, 1855/1990, p. 123)

Detailed studies in three fields have delivered summative conclusions about the resources and constraints available to people moving about with each other. Physiological studies have shown that walking is organized by trajectories that connect every beginning with an end, every whither with a whence. Sociological studies of the organization of people walking have shown them to be vehicular units sensitive to the role of others in the maintenance and disruption of the guiding trajectory (Goffman, 1971). Cultural studies have revealed constant in situ and post facto interpretations of people walking as a key to how they can be interpreted and talked about to others.

We examine the vehicular behavior of a child in a preschool classroom. Our analysis begins as she takes aim, sets her sights, her rights, and her lefts and rights, and lays out a trajectory in which she and others will engage. The others react and build an instruction system for the child to follow. If they give divided directions, like two people in a face-off trying to pass each other on a crowded sidewalk, they can thwart the path of the walker (in our case: first a sitter, then a walker). The walker can be made to look clumsy. The thwarted person can be talked about and talked to as a clumsy person.

Clumsy Crystal has hands and feet and arms and legs and a voice, and they all get in the way. She says she's clumsy. Her teachers agree. In the summer before kindergarten, the classroom filled with students new to school, and Crystal's body seemed the least accustomed: lying on the floor while others sat, taking her shoes off while others tucked their feet crisscross, tripping over the edge of a carpet while others stepped over her. Videotapes from her kindergarten and first grade are filled with Crystal and other children bumping into or tripping over each other. Here comes Clumsy Crystal.

We followed Crystal through a series of classroom episodes. Her body is there, out-of-place, in the middle of a group reading activity. Crystal's clumsiness was not the reason we started looking at the tape, but the teacher's strong responses to it bewildered us. Mrs.

Pomeroy's strong scolding seemed, in our minds, sudden and disproportionate to Crystal's transgression. We saw only Crystal's body, first leaning sideways and then forward into the center of the circle of students, and we heard Crystal's voice murmuring something to her neighbors. Other students were, at various times, more out-of-place, louder, more in the way than Crystal, but without anyone saying anything about them. But there Crystal is, getting yelled at, first at 5 and then at 19 minutes into a 22-minute activity. This paper details only the second scolding, when we find Crystal bent over, head turned to her neighbor, and asking what sounds like a question. "Crystal," the teacher says strongly, "I'm not going to accept that." Crystal leans back, sits up straight, covers her mouth with both hands, and the beat goes on.

The recording begins after the morning recess. Students enter the classroom, find their places around the perimeter of the rug on the floor, and arrange their bodies for the group reading activity to follow. The teacher announces that they will read a story, *The Mitten*. As several students comment she had already read the book to them, Mrs. Pomeroy explains that today the students will read the book to her. There is a break in the action, and instead of reading, the teacher begins a five-minute exchange on Carl's demand that other students return the "fake money" he had given out at recess. The exchange is more public rebuke than dialogue, and punctuated by the teacher's mostly unsuccessful effort to turn the exchange into a group lesson on citizenship. A successful transition to what looks like story time happens in the 20 seconds between two utterances, the first an announcement they are now "back to the story," and the second a request for students to reorient their bodies by "sitting crisscross applesauce *first*" and then "raising your hand to answer the questions." The explicit reorganization of bodies into a new configuration marks the shift to the new kind of activity. After 12 minutes, Mrs. Pomeroy refuses to accept Crystal's body and voice.

We offer three versions of Crystal's wrongly placed behavior. The first focuses directly on Poor Crystal tipping over and mumbling, out of control in body and voice. Because she is working with wiggly children, a fake money economy, and a slow-moving book, we could also focus on Poor Mrs. Pomeroy. The teacher directs a question, sees Crystal tipping and talking (again), scolds her (again), and moves back to questioning. The scolding has an effect. Crystal sits upright and covers her mouth. Students across from her call for a turn. Story time affords an explanation of Crystal's scolding and a chance to exercise our sympathies. This feels good, but cannot stand as an analysis.

A second version focuses more carefully on Crystal's interaction with her environment over the course of the activity, and we get to report a pattern. Crystal is not alone in the circle. She is sitting next to Bonita, a 3-year-old child who is spending part of her day in the kindergarten (she is the daughter of a teacher at the school). Bonita has been in the class before, but she is not up to the ways and means of kindergarten. Five times during the book reading (the one at 19 minutes is the fourth of the five), Crystal reaches to rearrange Bonita or the space around her: once as the group is just getting started, three times in the course of questions and answers, and again as the group moves to another activity. Each time, Bonita is in violation of the visible normative order. From this angle, Crystal is less a violator than an enforcer of the classroom order.

This version is appealing. Poor Crystal is still in trouble, but with a competent and well-intentioned sensorium under conditions that might be too much for any mind/body to handle gracefully. Crystal must monitor both her own and Bonita's body. Crystal's body and voice may *look* out of control, but she is only suffering from competing commitments. The teacher seems to know from past experience that Crystal is clumsy and loud, but a second look shows Crystal is living for two, with what Emerson called commanding thoughts coming from two directions. With one small accusation, we can add a villain to the sympathy story: Poor Crystal, yes, but no longer the Poor Teacher, but the Insensitive Teacher. If only she could see what we see. Crystal is misunderstood.

A few minutes after the scolding, the circle of students gives way to an alphabet-sing-ing conga line snaking around desks and bookshelves. Crystal is late off the floor and late into line. We might have predicted her delayed arrival, but we can now offer a reason. As before, Crystal has to organize two bodies—her own and Bonita's—and it is a task that keeps Crystal's body in the wrong place and at the wrong time.

The first account is limited to Clumsy Crystal on her own, and the second adds the teacher and Bonita into the mix with Crystal, her body and mind. The third version takes a wider angle view of what everyone is doing and treats the actions of both child and teacher as only two links in a sequence chain of activities made relevant over time.

The third version asks us to look away from Crystal and Bonita. We hear Carl, from his seat at Mrs. Pomeroy's left knee, doing his best to make reading into a two-party conversation. He leans into her field of vision, he wiggles, he touches her knee, he raises his voice, he talks in a whisper. We see the teacher, working with the means available to make reading into something the whole group can be seen doing. She asks questions and scans the group, and she turns the book so Carl can't see. Meanwhile, the other students struggle to determine whom this reading is for and how to manage their participation. They sit quietly, legs crisscross, exchanging glances with each other (but not with the teacher); or they lean into the center of the circle, wave their hands, and monitor the circle for competitors. In the middle of this finely tuned mayhem, Crystal's body is in the right place at the right time for the teacher to have a reason to stop paying attention to Carl, to scold Crystal, and to give a moment for everyone else to place themselves into the core or the periphery of the group. The third version reveals a teacher struggling to keep a handful of fidgety 5-year-olds attending to a book they have already read, and it shows students (not Crystal) trying to figure out how to show off that they have an answer to any question officially put to the group.

In the third account, Crystal's body is no less contorted or in the wrong place, but perhaps at the right time for others to get their interactional work done. While Crystal divides her time and rhyme between Bonita and the group, the teacher can reengage her students in question-answer chains. Andy and his neighbors can call for a turn, and Carl can raise his hand. Some students get to look better than others. The third account makes it harder to see victims and villains, unless we are willing to have undue sympathy or condemnation for ordinary kids and adults doing ordinary things. For a moment at least, the classroom seems to be a simple case of ordinary people using the materials, resources, and structures available to them to make it from one moment to another.

By the third analysis, Crystal is made comparatively invisible, but she is not trans-formed into a normal person as a result. Even if she does not look clumsy, even if no one responds to her on the spot as clumsy, she does not get time off from being labeled. The first account makes clumsiness a problem in the relation between Crystal's head and body. The second account makes clumsiness a problem in the relation between Crystal's body and those who pay immediate attention to her. With too much to think about, or with a mind divided by the attention of others, no wonder Crystal looks clumsy. In the third account, Crystal is not called clumsy while others are paying attention. If not quite the property of the group pushing and pulling on Crystal's intentions and extensions, clumsiness is still in the group's range of jurisdiction for description, critique, and com-plaint either after a clumsy move or, and this is crucial, even if a clumsy move never takes place. Crystal's clumsiness is one way the group—and even the analyst—can explain what might be going on in ways consequential to their ongoing activities. Crystal's clum-siness is an opportunity for everyone else to appear, or claim to appear, graceful. If Crystal is not just clumsy on occasion, she can still be called clumsy on call. Her clumsiness is a constant occasion for a "status degradation ceremony" (Garfinkel, 1956). Crystal's clumsiness is a constant opportunity for others to look, or to claim to look, elegant and graceful. Clumsy Crystal Makes Graceful Group.

Crystal's body is an opportunity for others to do local interactional work, and her recognized clumsiness makes the opportunities regular. This is not the kind of opportunity we had in mind when we wrote that differences are better thought of as opportunities than as difficulties, and that a democracy must make the most of everyone's potential. Our first statement was more political than descriptive. What we meant was that *persons who are different* should provide for *a differently construed, more diversely imagined* society and structure, with room for new "gleeful designs." This is not what happens when Crystal's behavior creates only an opportunity for more broadly distributed involvement, but all of the conforming kind. Crystal leans, talks, and arranges Bonita, and the rest of the group can remember, and organize again into a circle of students sitting crisscross applesauce waiting to be called on to give answers the teacher and the book already know. The easy acknowledgement of Crystal's clumsy body makes for the easy recovery of the group's involvement without forcing a demand that reading become something people do to learn things together and not just a measure of the *individual child*.

A Hyperactive Child

Peter was a busy boy around the classroom. He followed everyone else's behavior carefully, and he was quick to give advice to others about how they should behave. He was often calling out to the teacher, mostly to tell what he was doing and how well he was doing it. The teacher in turn paid attention to him as quickly as possible and struggled to get him back on task. There were three difficult boys in the first grade classroom, all of them given to the best and most experienced teacher, who in turn rarely went five minutes without attending to each of the boys personally, if only for a few seconds of contact, physical adjustment, encouragement, reprimand, or threat. Two of the boys were labeled and placed in special classes for the second grade. Peter was not labeled, although all adults agreed he was hyperactive and might have to be reclassified later. There was an important behavioral difference between the two labeled boys and Peter: the first two had to be monitored carefully, and Peter hardly at all; as the teacher walked around the classroom, she would constantly check on the first two boys, whereas Peter could be counted on to show up often and loudly. Peter was easier than the first two boys, but still the hyperactive label followed him.

For a major part of every morning, the class was organized into three independent reading groups and three individual children who were in no group, one because she was far ahead of the other children in reading, one because he had been put out of the group for misbehavior, and one because he was still wetting his pants and was a constant source of complaint and degradation. In the morning, the teacher would work with each group while keeping an eye on the rest of the class, and in the afternoon she would work with the three group-orphaned individuals. The groups were organized by skill level, and everyone in the room seemed to know that there was a top, middle, and bottom group. The three difficult boys started in the bottom group where two of them, Peter and James, remained for the year; the third boy, Simon, became one of three orphaned children.

We offer three findings on Peter's hyperactivity and use them to raise questions about the diagnosis and the society that invited it. First, hyperactivity is well tuned to the situations of which it is a part. Certainly Peter was noticeable to even a casual classroom observer. He seemed to be everywhere, calling for this and that and butting into everything. And yet, he was rarely singled out as a problem. The first hint came from a videotape that surveyed the entire room while the teacher was with the reading groups. Peter had just finished working with the teacher and the bottom group, where he had greeted most every turn change with loud offers to read and loud complaints when he did not get a turn. While the teacher worked with the top group, Peter sat at his desk watching them work through their turns to read. For 25 minutes, he did not move or say anything. Impulse control was not a problem. Just what was this thing called hyperactivity and why was the label applied to Peter?

A second doubt developed with a second kind of data. As part of wider inquiry into the behavior of reading groups in the classroom, we used the Benesch dance notation system to record the movements of children and the teacher during a reading group session; we recorded torso shifts and arm, leg, and head movements—the information that Benesch, watching a dance in Paris, could send on paper to a director in New York and expect a reasonable replication. At this level of detail, finger, mouth, and eye movements were not recorded. In the bottom group, Peter could be seen making dramatic moves and a great deal of noise. The slow motion record of the movements told a different story. Our appointed hyperactive child was not first on the list of who moved the most. Actually, the teacher moved the most, then two other children, then Peter. Again, we were left wondering what it means to be called hyperactive.

A third kind of data offers a partial answer. Beyond the question of who moves the most, we recorded when different people moved and in what directions. Peter's movements seemed well coordinated with times for getting a turn to read, often at the same time the teacher was moving, and, perhaps most strikingly, often in the opposite direction from the teacher. The plot thickens. Peter was a pivotal member of the group, literally so. Whenever the group would switch activities, say, from chatting about a book to reading a book, or from one person reading aloud to another person reading aloud, Peter was sure to be involved. When the first turn to read was given to Anna, Peter read the first words on the page before Anna did, and when it was moved next to Maria, Peter first pounded on the table calling for a turn and then complained that he didn't get it. The next two turns were rejected by those called on, leaving the teacher in a difficult situation and mumbling to herself, and in both cases Peter was there to make a claim for the turn. Even after he had a turn to read, he called immediately for the next turn. When the teacher arranged for a next reader, Peter moved with her. He was always available for a turn, but when he did not get one, he complained and moved away from the teacher. When the first four turns went to other children, in each case, he sulked to the left, and in each case the teacher took her first free moment to reach out to him, to adjust his book. Not amazingly, although there are six children neatly distributed around a small rectangular table, the teacher's legs and torso were usually turned to Peter. When other children got her attention, she would divide her top half away from Peter and leave her bottom half pointing in his direction. Peter, it seems, took work, and so did the teacher's job of organizing the group and assigning turns to read while at the same time overseeing the rest of the class. The teacher seemed to rely on Peter being available to take a turn, to offer an answer, or to direct others to what is happening.

The Peter–teacher drama was at its clearest at turn-relevant moments, but played out in small and quicker ways at disruptions and other junctures within a given child's turn. For example, if the teacher turned from the bottom group to pay attention to someone from another group, Peter, guaranteed, would turn away from her until she returned to the group. It is easy to understand why adults might call this hyperactivity: because Peter cannot sit still, as soon as the teacher looks elsewhere, he's gone. But from the perspective of the group, Peter can just as easily be understood as the child in charge of the teacher paying attention to his group. When the teacher is not with the group, if a child from another group enters, Peter is the border guard, and he will chase the visitor away. When the teacher is with the group and an outsider gets her attention, Peter can do that same job, but in a way appropriate to handling a teacher: he turns away from the group until the teacher notices and reaches out for him until they are refocused inside the reading group and the visitor leaves. Who is in charge here? And what can we say about seeming hyperactivity when it seems to be exquisitely well timed at the level of milliseconds with the teacher's behavior and has the consequence of getting the teacher to behave appropriately for the bottom group getting back to work reading?

Peter's body is an opportunity for others to interact, and his recognized busyness makes the opportunities regular. This is not the sense of opportunity we called for when we wrote that differences are better thought of as opportunities than as difficulties and that a democracy must make the most of everyone's potential. Our first statement was more political than descriptive. What we meant was that *persons who are different* should provide for *a differently construed, more diversely imagined* society and structure, with room for new "gleeful designs." This is not what is happening when Peter's behavior creates an opportunity for the teacher to return to the reading lesson as a place to show off and compete. Peter bangs about, and screams, and arranges the teacher, and the rest of the group can organize again into a circle of students waiting to be called on to show off how much they can read better than others. The easy recognizability of his pouncing body makes for the easy recalibration of the group without an insistence that reading become more than just a measure of the individual child; that reading become an opportunity for people to learn together.

Democracy Disabled

In 1880, two years before the death of Emerson (and Darwin, and Marx only another year later), Henry Adams published a small novel called *Democracy*. Based on his years as a political journalist in Washington, Adams explored the vast darkness of strategy and duplicity that had become crucial to success in the young capital, but he also had one of his characters, named in a prescient fit, Gore, state the hope of a democracy in terms still thrilling to anyone working in education:

> I believe in democracy. I accept it. I believe in it because it appears to me the inevitable consequence of what has gone before it. Democracy asserts the fact that the masses are now raised to a higher intelligence than formerly. Our civilization aims at this mark…I grant it is an experiment, but it is the only direction society can take that is worth its taking; the only conception of its duty large enough to satisfy its instincts; the only result that is worth an effort or risk. (1880/2003, p. 45)

The experiment is not over, but it is getting more difficult to state the promise without a sense of defeat, without an embarrassment at how it has gone wrong. Intelligence, at least the sort defined by school and academic degrees, is the new property. So-called high intelligence comes at the price of a so-called low intelligence and its disabilities, the result being a so-called democracy with the chosen few climbing ladders of information and skill at the expense of the many. Measured, attributed, and certified down to and even inside the body, down to the level of answers to arbitrary questions, useless knowledge, and partial skills, intelligence has become high and haughty, a term for what some people own that most others do not and cannot own. The others—the masses, each one labeled as a kind of problem child in school: Low IQ, LD, ADD, ELL, slow, clumsy, and generally nonreactive—have less access than before, and their intelligence is under assault, downgraded, degraded, and erased. Their abilities are disabled. The narrow range of intelligence demanded, acknowledged, and given formal degrees by the psychometric industrial complex is increasingly available for a price only a few can afford. In a double pun, the new intelligence, like property, comes with an alienation of rights, with an alienation of reads and writes (Lave & McDermott, 2002). The disinherited have become the "disinherented." When pressed with evidence that the masses cannot be high first priority in postbellum Washington, Adams has Gore defend his faith in democracy: "I have faith; not perhaps in the old dogmas, but in the new ones; faith in nature; faith in science; faith in the survival of the fittest" (2003, p. 46).

The new dogmas have not done well. The rise of Reaganomics has brought a revival of the fittest, the financially fittest, and a consequent decline of the middle class and worsening conditions for the working and poor classes. The survival of the fittest in which Adams placed his hopes has given way to the fetish of the fittest at the local gym, the presence of which is nicely correlated with school performance; parents with money live in neighborhoods with gyms, Starbucks, athletic leagues, and tutoring centers, all crucial to the well-rounded (but sleek), well-founded (but lost), and well funded individuals who make it institutionally (Pope, 2001). The gait keepers rule. The schools that were to protect children from any increasing division between the classes have been kidnapped into certifying class differences by academic degrees, and, worse, science at its most mechanical and disingenuous has been paid off to produce the tests that make the sorting look legitimate (McDermott & Hall, 2007).

We started this paper with a question about the perverse arrangements among persons that would force a society to misdirect the tools of science against its own children. The situation has become simple. It is old-time politics around class and race, but with the difference that political hegemony is now phrased and scientifically confirmed, make that infirmed, in terms of cognitive abilities and disabilities. Adams was writing at the beginning of the Gilded Age, and we are writing at the beginning of its second coming. We also asked about how we can intervene. For starters, we can look to the bodies of the children to find the pushes and pulls of the wider system played out on their sensuous engagements and entanglements with the world we have given them. We should look less inside their bodies, where we cannot see as much as we gain license to make up our own models, abjectively verified, of what might be happening. We should look more to their active relations with the world, to their bodies in the world. We should try to articulate their attentions and intentions, of course, and their retentions, why not, but most of all we have to define and confront the tensions, extensions, and detentions we have offered them. We should study them, yes, but with an eye to how they negotiate their places and suffer our symptoms and consequences.

Imagine then an intervention at the level of research and policy: that every description of what is wrong with children must come complete with a description of the society that has invited the diagnosis; that every description of what is wrong with children must come complete with a prescription for a confrontation with the political and economic circumstances that are going to use and abuse the disabilities. It is easy to appreciate perhaps how Christopher Nolan's loving family, before they discovered Christopher's responsiveness, might have missed the new gleeful designs he was creating in his mind. But it should not be easy to excuse a whole society for searching out disabilities and using them in the competitive wars that mark a child's pathway through school. So what if Crystal is clumsy if she can be shown to be taking care of others? What kind of society would look for the minor things she cannot do well and not notice the important things she can do well? So what if Peter is hyperactive if he can be shown to be bringing order to others? What kind of society would be on the lookout for the ways he is wild and not notice what he sacrifices and accomplishes with his movements? Who gets served by each documentation of disability and failure, but those with the resources to avoid the consequences of being labeled and disabled and those who make a career out of diagnosis and treatment without acknowledging how they are a part of the problem?

Democracy is not easy. Even the new dogmas—"faith in nature; faith in science; faith in the survival of the fittest," said Adams—have been subverted into doing the work of the old order: nature delivers individual differences, science documents them, and an ideology of the survival of the fittest provides the justification for conditions of birth being the best predictor of school success and failure. It won't do. Democracy has to create the best conditions for every skill, every preoccupation, yes, and every kindness. Crystal for Secretary of State and Peter for Speaker of the House, please. Let kindness, however clumsy, reign. Let order, however hyper, find its mark for the better.

Notes

1. Most cultures do not divide children by nature versus nurture. The false opposites were used by Shakespeare to talk about the moral order from the view of a frustrated teacher:
    Prospero: A devil, a born devil, on whose nature
    Nurture can never stick; on whom my pains,
    Humanly taken, all, all lost, quite lost;
    And as with age his body uglier grows,
    So his mind cankers. (*The Tempest*, IV.i.188–192)
   A survey of proverbs available to Shakespeare shows two main choices on nature and nurture: "Nature passes nurture" and "Nurture passes nature" (Tilley, 1950, pp. 491, 509). Francis Galton (1865) dragged this phrasing into contemporary debates on inherited intelligence and genius. His analysis of nature, nurture, and eugenics is undeniably racist, but with a nice twist: that he uses it to distinguish Northern and Southern Europeans, a split that leaves the rest of the world unscathed.

2. Although knowing another language is clearly not a sign of a disability, it might just as well be if classroom teachers are asked to sort children who "cannot learn" from those who simply do not know the language of instruction. Teachers should be allowed to ignore this divide. The situation has become silly enough that teachers at one end of a district must get the same Spanish into heads that teachers at the other end must suppress.

3. Yes, yes, always male genius back then, and for a long time after; see Battersby (1989) on the gonadal genius. On the very idea of genius, see McDermott (2006).

4. On LD as an institution, see Mehan (1993, 1996) and McDermott (1993), McDermott and Varenne (1995), and McDermott, Goldman, and Varenne (2006).

5. On the importance of 19th century thought for rethinking American education, see the excellent study by Maxine Greene (1965).

6. Highlights from a large literature: On culture, bodily movement, and symbolism, see Mauss (1951), Turner (1980), and the dazzling volume on the Dogon by Calame-Griaule (1973); on the behavioral mechanisms involved, see Kendon (2003) and Schegloff (1996); on philosophical accounts of the communicative body, see Bentley (1941) and Merleau-Ponty (1964). Of particular relevance to this paper are Bateson and Mead (1942) on child training for balance in Bali and Efron (1941/1971) on bodily movement tied to stereotypes of intelligence.

7. For an important account of a 19th century community of kind, and kindness, on Martha's Vineyard, see Groce (1985).

8. The sentiment was well expressed in two 18th century novels: *Tristram Shandy*, by Lawrence Sterne, and *Jacques, the Fatalist*, by Denis Diderot. The former was the model for Marx's only attempt, at age 19, at writing a novel (Wheen, 2001).

References

Adams, H. (2003). *Democracy*. New York: Modern Library. (Original work published 1880)

Baldwin, J. (1955). *Notes of a native son*. Boston: Beacon.

Bateson, G., & Mead, M. (1942). *Balinese character*. New York: New York Academy of Science.

Battersby, C. (1989). *Women and genius*. Bloomington: Indiana University Press.

Bentley, A. (1941). The human skin: Philosophy's last line of defense. *Philosophy of Science, 8,* 1–19.

Boas, F. (1911). *The mind of primitive man*. New York: Macmillan.

Calame-Griaule, G. (1985). *Words and the Dogon world*. Philadelphia: ISHI. (Original work published in 1965)

Conklin, H. C. (2007). *Fine description* (J. Kuipers & R. McDermott, Eds.). Monograph 56. New Haven, CT: Yale Southeast Asia Studies.

Efron, D. (1971). *Gesture, race, and culture*. The Hague: Mouton. (Original work published as *Gesture and environment* 1941)

Emerson, R. W. (1860). *The conduct of life*. Boston: Ticknor & Fields.

Emerson, R. W. (1894). *Natural history of intellect and other papers*. Boston: Houghton, Mifflin.

Emerson, R. W. (1990). *Topical notebooks of Ralph Waldo Emerson* (Vol. 1, S. S. Smith, Ed.). Columbia: University of Missouri Press.

Emerson, R. W. (1995). *Representative men*. New York: Marsilio. (Original work published in 1850)

Emerson, R. W. (2004). *Essays and poems by Ralph Waldo Emerson*. New York: Barnes & Noble.

Erickson, F. (2002). *Talk and social theory*. New York: Routledge.

Frake, C. O. (1980). *Language and cultural description*. Stanford, CA: Stanford University Press.

Galton, F. (1865). Hereditary talent and character. *Macmillan's Magazine, 12,* 157–166, 318–327.

Garfinkel, H. (1956). Conditions of a successful status degradation ceremony. *American Sociological Review, 61,* 420–424.

Goffman, E. (1971). *Relations in public*. New York: Harper.

Greene, M. (1965). *The public school and the private vision*. New York: Random House.

Groce, N. (1985). *Everyone here spoke Sign Language*. Cambridge, MA: Harvard University Press.

Holmes, O. W. (1885). *Ralph Waldo Emerson*. Boston: Houghton.

Kendon, A. (1990). *Conducting interaction*. Cambridge, UK: Cambridge University Press.

Kendon, A. (2004). *Gesture: Visible activity as utterance*. Cambridge, UK: Cambridge University Press.

Lave, J., & McDermott, R. (2002). Estranged labor learning. *Outlines, 4,* 19–48.

Marx, K. (1963). *The 18th Brumaire of Louis Bonaparte*. New York: International Press. (Original work published in 1852)

Marx, K. (1964). *Economic and philosophical manuscripts of 1844*. New York: International Press.

Mauss, M. (1951). Les techniques du corps. In C. Lévi-Strauss (Ed.), *Sociologie et anthropologie* (pp. 362–386). Paris: Presses Universitaires de France. (Original work published in 1936)

McDermott, R. (1993). Acquisition of a child by a learning disability. In S. Chaiklin & J. Lave (Eds.), *Understanding practice* (pp. 269–305). New York: Cambridge University Press.

McDermott, R. (2006). Situating genius. In Z. Bekerman, N. Burbules, & D. Silverman-Keller (Eds.), *Learning in places* (pp. 185–202). New York: Peter Lang.

McDermott, R., Goldman, S., & Varenne, H. (2006). The cultural work of learning disabilities. *Educational Researcher, 35*(6), 12–17.

McDermott, R., & Hall, K. (2007). Scientifically debased research on learning, 1854–2006. *Anthropology of Education Quarterly, 38*(1), 82–88.

McDermott, R., & Varenne, H. (1995). Culture as disability. *Anthropology of Education Quarterly, 26,* 324–348.

Mehan, H. (1993). Beneath the skin and between the ears. In S. Chaiklin & J. Lave (Eds.), *Understanding practice* (pp. 241–269). New York: Cambridge University Press.

Mehan, H. (1996). The construction of an LD student. In M. Silverstein & G. Urban (Eds.), *Natural histories of discourse* (pp. 253–276). Chicago: University of Chicago Press.

Merleau-Ponty, M. (1964). *The phenomenology of perception.* New York: Routledge & Kegan Paul. (Original work published 1944)

Nolan, C. (1987). *Under the eye of the clock.* New York: St. Martin's Press.

Pope, D.C. (2001). *Doing school.* New Haven, CT: Yale University Press.

Radin, P. (1927). *The mind of primitive man.* New York: Dover.

Raftery, J. (1988). Missing the mark: Intelligence testing in the Los Angeles Public Schools, 1922–32. *History of Education Quarterly, 28,* 73–93.

Schegloff, E. (1998). Body torque. *Social Research, 65,* 535–596.

Tilley, M. P. (1950). *A dictionary of proverbs in England in the sixteenth and seventeenth centuries.* Ann Arbor: University of Michigan Press.

Turner, T. (1980). The social skin. In J. Sherfas & R. Lewin (Eds.), *Not work alone* (pp. 112–140). Beverly Hills, CA: Sage.

Varenne, H. & McDermott, R. (1998). *Successful failure.* Boulder, CO: Westview.

Wheen, N. (2001). *Karl Marx.* New York: Norton.

Response to Part 5

Bodies, Disability, and the Fight for Social Justice in Education

Jim Ferris

The autumn wind is running hard today through the trees: long-needled pines, maples, and oaks, mostly, and the leaves are holding on, except for the occasional one which lets go and runs with the wind, for a moment, until gravity takes it down to the ground. How long will the other leaves hold on? In Wisconsin, where I live, winter is inevitable, inexorable, cold and clear, harsh, austere, fully beautiful in its different way—but it does not spare the leaves. And falling off the branch is part of being a leaf, isn't it?

I do not want to make too much of this fact of nature—leaves are part of an organism, rather than individual living things in themselves, and the odds are very good that there will be another bounty of leaves in the spring. I do want to note, though, that all of the human conditions that in this time and place we call *disability*—this vast and remarkable profusion of different ways of being human in the world—are, like leaves, facts of nature. But they are also facts of culture. People differ in a whole host of ways—facts of nature— but it is we humans ourselves who decide which of those human differences we think are significant and which not—facts of culture. In the world that existed just a few hundred years ago, only a small number of people knew how to read, and there was no such thing as 20/20 vision. And in a world of instrument flight and voice command, screen readers and talking books, standards and expectations seem likely to shift again—and again. The ability to run, to jump, to throw a spear or shoot an arrow, to track game, to drive a wagon or a station wagon, to sit still, to focus on a linear progression of tasks, to perform detailed mathematical computations in one's head, to evaluate and respond to a complex and constantly changing set of circumstances, to adapt to changes in the world, and in our bodies—that old saw "the only constant is change" is at least as true tomorrow as it was in the time of Heraclitus.

And it is especially true for disabled people. They are the face of humanity; they show us the wide range of shapes and colors that make up our woodland. And they show us how to adapt. One of the enduring images of the disability rights movement is Anna Stonum's illustration of the stages of human evolution from small monkey to great ape to upright human. The last figure is a person in a wheelchair going up a ramp. The legend: Adapt or perish.

Disabled people have been living all their lives in a world which only recently has begun to make meaningful accommodations to them. Living in this world requires adaptability and imagination. The world asks that of all of us, but it *demands* those characteristics from disabled people. And they know well that the most powerful things they must work against are the discrimination, stigmatization, and marginalization that are at the heart of the oppression of disabled people right up to today. When we are applauded for overcoming our disability, what we are overcoming is oppression—physical and attitudinal— from a world that likes to think of itself as "normal"—whatever *that* means.

446

There is much holding on to do to counter that force. I'm glad that the leaves are mostly holding on—I want to see them turn all their colors. But I'm glad for the ones that fall, too; whether I pick them up and save them, these moments of difference, these harbingers, these heralds remind us of our inevitable changes, our surprising differences. Is it more leaflike to hold on, or to let go? The answer, of course, is both. Leaves are where the life of the tree comes clear; disabled people, at once vulnerable, adaptable, and strong, are humanity writ large, writ plain. Disabled people are where humanity comes clear.

Part 6

Youth and Social Justice in Education

Edited and Introduced by Jeffrey Duncan-Andrade

> We must clasp hands—not just with young people, as we did here, but also with older people, the elderly and the children—so we become a single will. We must clasp hands to avoid the most terrible of wars threatening humanity today, as well as to achieve everyone's most cherished desires.
>
> (Guevara, 2000, p. 60)

> I know you don't want to hear about the pain and suffering that goes on in "that" part of the city. I know you don't want to hear about the kids getting shot in "that" part of the city. But little do you know that "that" part of the city is your part of the city too. This is our neighborhood, this is our city, and this is our America. And we must somehow find a way to help one another. We must come together—no matter what you believe in, no matter how you look—and find some concrete solutions to the problems of the ghetto.
>
> (Jones & Newman, 1997, p. 200)

Academic failure in urban schools persists despite increasing attention to the problem. This failure is most pronounced in urban high schools where dropout rates are consistently above 50% and college going rates are below 10% (Harvard Civil Rights Project, 2005). Strategies aimed at addressing these issues are debated in and across research, policy, and practice circles, but have made little impact on the educational attainment of poor, non-White children in the last 40 years. In recent years, major reform plans like those funded by the Carnegie Corporation (Carnegie Corporation, 2001) and the Gates Millennium Foundation (The American Institutes for Research, 2003), have allocated millions of dollars toward innovative programs that have not substantially improved achievement in urban schools.

As we consider new ways to improve urban schools, we must consider where such plans have missed the mark. While efforts that increase fiscal resources to urban schools should be lauded, it has become increasingly clear that this formula for urban school reform is not a panacea. Rothstein (2004) suggests these efforts fail because the resources they produce are not used to directly address pressing social and systemic issues that result from poverty and urban life (nutrition, health, violence, housing). Instead, new school resources are used to supplement a wide range of institutional measures aimed at raising test scores: high stakes testing and test preparation programs, decreasing school/class sizes, increasing the number of computers per student, increasing the number of textbooks per student, implementing scripted literacy and math programs, and improving facilities. Sadly, these efforts have not produced notable gains in urban school student engagement or achievement at state or national levels.

The failure of increased material resources to produce commensurate academic growth should not be misinterpreted to mean that material resources are unimportant.

Several studies (Ferguson & Ladd, 1996; Greenwald, Hedges, & Laine, 1996) challenge economist Eric Hanushek's (2001) argument that "there is no clear systematic relationship between resources and student outcomes." One need look no further than the unwavering commitment of wealthy communities to the maintenance of highly resourced schools to understand the importance of money for the successful operation of schools. Resource models for urban school improvement have missed the mark in the way they have outlined the purpose of these resources and the measurement of their impact. To date, most resource-based efforts have focused on improving instruction and learning conditions to help students "escape" their communities by attending college. Valenzuela (1999) has called this a subtractive model of schooling, one where urban students are asked (tacitly or explicitly) to exchange the culture of their home and community for the "higher culture" of the school in order to gain access to college. This approach reduces the life choices for urban youth of color into a false binary: stay behind as a failure or "get out" as a success. Faced with the prospects of leaving their communities behind in order to be successful, many urban youth opt out of school. They choose to retain an identity that they perceive to be in conflict with schools' expectations of them, even if the cost of that choice is educational marginalization (MacLeod, 1987; Valenzuela, 1999).

Urban education reform movements must begin to develop partnerships with communities that help young people succeed and maintain their identities. This additive model of education focuses on the design of urban school cultures, curricula, and pedagogies that identify urban students' cultures and communities as assets, rather than as deficits (Moll, Amanti, Neff, & Gonzalez, 1992; Valenzuela, 1999). Urban youth's unique lives and conditions deserve an education system that accomplishes two complementary goals. Education should prepare them to confront the conditions of social and economic inequity in their daily lives and give them access to the academic skills that make college attendance an option.

This approach to urban education reform is a double investment in urban communities. It provides pedagogy and curricula that make school immediately relevant in urban youth's lives. It also breaks the cycle of disinvestment in human capital in urban communities by cultivating graduates who recognize their capacity to improve urban centers, rather than seeing them as places to escape. These prospects offer urban youth a renewed sense of purpose with regard to school, and provide the community the necessary human and institutional capital to contribute to its social, economic and political revitalization.

Confronting the "Urban" in Urban Schools

While a new vision for urban school reform must continue insisting on the presence of equitable material resources in all schools, the studies done by the American Institutes for Research and the Carnegie Foundation suggest that these resources must be used to directly address the context of urban life and poverty. In the few places where there have been consistent successes with urban students, this approach has been the clear epistemological pattern. In efforts like those represented in the individual practices of successful urban educators (Duncan-Andrade, 2007), as well as institutional efforts such as UCLA's Institute for Democracy Education and Access (IDEA) Summer Seminar (Morrell, 2004), Tucson's Social Justice Project (Cammarota & Romero, 2006), and Chicago's Batey Urbano (Flores-González, Rodriguez, & Rodriguez-Muñiz, 2006) the focus remains on pedagogies that challenge the social and economic inequities that confront urban youth. These successes can be expanded if more attention is paid to developing teachers that can implement pedagogies which address the conditions of urban life and develop a sense of agency among students for altering those conditions.

Pedagogical reform efforts must move beyond the failed multicultural education movement and implement this more critical pedagogy. Teachers and school administrators need support in developing and implementing pedagogy that draws from urban youth's social contexts. Moll (1992) has referred to these contexts as a student's "funds of knowledge". Rather than perceiving the community as a place to rise above, schools must draw from knowledge that students bring with them to school, knowledge that is acquired from the streets, family cultural traditions, youth culture, and the media. Ladson-Billings (1994) has referred to this as "culturally relevant pedagogy." Lee (2004) suggests that teachers must be better equipped to investigate what is going on in the lives of their students so that their curriculum and pedagogy can be reflective of those lives. This deeper understanding of students' lives better positions school officials to appreciate and positively influence how these social contexts affect the educational outcomes for urban youth.

Beyond Critique: A Modest Plan for Educational Equity

There is virtually no disagreement that access to quality teachers can level the educational playing field. Thus, more attention must be paid to the recruitment, training, development, and support given to urban teachers and school leaders. This is particularly important if educators are to develop pedagogies, curricula, and school cultures that are more attentive to the most pressing community needs. Thus far, the social justice community has lacked the strategic planning to address these challenges. This lack of deliberate planning is due, in part, to a presumed alliance amongst educators committed to social justice. This alliance is presumed because of our shared recognition that there are widespread inequalities in our society (e.g., education, housing, employment, safety, legal justice, citizenship). However, social justice educators disagree on how to respond to these inequalities. Worse yet, rather than creating a strategic plan, social justice educators have tended to critique and undermine each other's work. Instead of a collective plan of action, we have a penchant for affirmation through negation. We affirm our position by negating the position of others. These critiques without solutions are mostly aimed at neoconservative arguments that attempt to rationalize social inequalities. Occasionally, they are also fired at other members of the social justice community.

Using critique to negate a position does not, in and of itself, affirm a more socially just position. One must deconstruct the logic of the opposing position *and* provide an alternative proposition that incorporates a stronger logic. Ideally, one's position is supported by practice-based evidence that the proposed ideas will work for the targeted communities. The need for the documentation and dissemination of effective practice models for urban youth poses a real challenge for the social justice community. To meet the challenge, we must heed Althusser's (2001) extension of Marx's challenge to all critical theorists: "the *ultimate* reality of the union of theory and practice [is when] philosophy ceases...to interpret the world. It becomes a weapon with which to change it: *revolution*" (p. 7). Until our social justice theories are supported by successfully tested models we will not change the world, we will only critique it.

Among all that we critique and debate in education, there is one fact on which we have relative consensus. From child psychology to pedagogical theory, studies show that positive self-identity, hope, and a sense of purpose are essential prerequisites for academic achievement. The test score fetish of the high-stakes era has turned us away from prioritizing these elements of teaching, even though gains in these areas are the key to raising test scores. It seems a plausible conclusion that no small part of the gaps in school achievement are attributable to the fact that most successful students enter school with a positive self-identity, a clear purpose for attending school, and a justifiable hope that school success will be rewarded in the larger society. For most low-income children, particularly low-income children of color, there is little in the history of school or the broader society that would concretely justify any of those three beliefs.

Of course, it is much easier to develop a test preparation program in a corporate laboratory than to develop effective teachers. Developing effective urban educators is hard work and some argue that it is not as cost-effective as scripted curriculum, test prep manuals, and one-day trainings. However, a program cannot be cost effective if it does not produce results. We will never develop some ideal instructional program that can be exported from classroom to classroom. Great teaching will always be about relationships and programs do not build relationships, people do. The truth of the matter is that we have the know-how to make achievement in urban schools the norm, as it is in high-income communities. There are successful teachers in every school even where failure is rampant. We should be spending more time figuring out who they are, collaborating with them, and studying what they do and why it works. That work should guide teacher-credentialing programs and school-based professional support structures so that more teachers can develop those effective practices.

This decade will usher in upwards of one million new teachers, mostly into urban schools (National Commission on Teaching and America's Future [NCTAF], 2003). This brings with it an unprecedented opportunity to swing the pendulum toward educational equity. We can, if we so desire, invest heavily in refocusing our efforts to recruit, train, and develop urban educators that will be highly effective. We can know what makes effective urban educators. We can name the characteristics of their practices. We can link those characteristics to increases in engagement and achievement. If we fail to significantly invest in the support and development of these characteristics in this new wave of teachers, as we have with their predecessors, we will almost certainly end up as the nation that James Baldwin foreshadowed over 45 years ago:

> [this] nation has spent a large part of its time and energy looking away from one of the principal facts of its life.... Any honest examination of the national life proves how far we are from the standard of human freedom with which we began.... If we are not capable of this examination, we may yet become one of the most distinguished and monumental failures in the history of nations. (Baldwin, 1961, p. 99)

Our continued failure to provide a quality education to large percentages of poor and working class children will eventually bankrupt this nation, economically and morally. If this failure continues, it is not because we lack the know-how to effectively educate all our children, it is because we lack the resolve to do it.

References

Althusser, L. (2001). *Lenin and philosophy and other essays*. New York: Monthly Review Press.

American Institutes for Research. (2003). *High time for high school reform: Early findings from the evaluation of the National School District and Network Grants Program*. Menlo Park, CA: Author.

Baldwin, J. (1961). *Nobody knows my name*. New York: Dell.

Cammarota, J., & Romero, A. (2006). A critically compassionate intellectualism for Latina/o students: Raising voices above the silencing in our schools. *Multicultural Education*, 14(2), 16–23.

Carnegie Corporation. (2001). Whole-district school reform. *Carnegie Reporter*, 1(2), 1–2.

Duncan-Andrade, J. (2007, November–December). Gangster, canastas, and ridas: Defining, developing, and supporting effective teachers in urban schools. *International Journal of Qualitative Studies in Education, 20*(6), 617–638.

Flores-González, N., Rodríguez, M., & Rodríguez-Muñiz, M. (2006). From hip-hop to humanization: Batey Urbano as a space for Latino youth culture and community action. In *Beyond resistance: Youth activism and community change* (pp. 175–196). New York: Routledge.

Greenwald, R., Hedges, L. V., & Laine, R. D. (1996). The effect of school resources on school achievement. *Review of Educational Research, 66*(3), 361–396.

Guevara, E. (2000). *Che Guevara talks to young people.* New York: Pathfinder.

Hanushek, E. A. (2001, Spring). Efficiency and equity in education. *National Bureau of Economic Research Reporter,* 15–19.

Harvard Civil Rights Project. (2005). *Confronting the graduation rate crisis in California.* The Civil Rights Project. Cambridge, MA: Harvard University.

Jones, L., & Newman, L. (1997). *Our America: Life and death on the South Side of Chicago.* New York: Washington Square Press.

Ladson-Billings, G. (1994). *The dreamkeepers: Successful teachers of African American children.* San Francisco: Jossey-Bass.

Lee, C. (2004). Literacy in the academic disciplines and the needs of adolescent struggling readers. *Adolescent Literacy, 3,* 14–25.

MacLeod, J. (1987). *Ain't no makin' it: In a low-income neighborhood.* Boulder, CO: Westview.

Moll, L. C., Amanti, C., Neff, D., & Gonzalez, N. (1992). Funds of knowledge for teaching: Using a qualitative approach to connect homes and classrooms. *Theory into Practice, 31,* 132–141.

Morrell, E. (2004). *Becoming critical researchers: Literacy and empowerment for urban youth.* New York: Peter Lang.

National Commission on Teaching and America's Future (NCTAF). (2003). *No dream denied: A pledge to America's children (Summary report).* Washington, D.C: Author.

Rothstein, R. (2004). *Class and schools: Using, social, economic, and educational reform to close the black-white achievement gap.* Washington, D.C.: Economic Policy Institute.

Valenzuela, A. (1999). *Subtractive schooling.* Albany, NY: SUNY Press.

28 For and Against

The School–Education Dialectic in Social Justice

K. Wayne Yang

"I shall create! If not a note, a hole./If not an overture, a desecration."[1] Gwendolyn Brooks's (1968/1992) poem, "Boy Breaking Glass,"captures a fundamental dialectic in human agency: that between constructive and destructive action. Nowhere is this more relevant than in considering the agency of oppressed peoples when facing institutions that ostensibly benefit them, such as youth of color vis-à-vis schools in the divested urban ghettos of the United States. The school–education dialectic refers to how social justice efforts must simultaneously deconstruct oppressive school systems while constructing emancipatory projects of education. Given that schooling in the United States more often reproduces than disrupts class-based inequalities (Bowles & Gintis, 1976, pp. 125–126), inculcates racist and misogynist ideologies rather than critiques them (hooks, 1994), and promotes a colonial agenda over one of self-determination (Woodson, 2000), human agency, that is, the ability to transform these very structures of social reproduction (Giddens, 1979), becomes an obligatory focal point in any discussion of social justice.

Therefore, any struggle by, with, for youth in education raises the question of whether human agency, in the context of an inequitable education system, serves to create overtures or desecrations of mainstream schooling institutions.

Schooling is a peculiar form of education. That is, if the term *education* describes all forms of learning in general, then *schooling* is a peculiar institution that formally conditions young people to legitimated systems of knowledge reproduction. In this respect, schools may not educate but instead inure students to a pedantic culture (Freire, 1970/2000); likewise, a person may be highly schooled, yet remain miseducated (Woodson, 2000). The core contradiction lies in the juncture where formal education diverges from the fundamental project of humanization (Freire, 1970/2000). Put simply, it is the vocation of all humans to struggle for education even if it means to work against schooling (Woodson, 2000).

School is a dialectical space wherein both education and miseducation are possibilities. This school–education dialectic summons some very practical questions. In my own experience, I have engaged in schooling institutions from various stances: as a teacher within a mainstream, comprehensive, urban high school; as a reform officer in the superintendent's cabinet; and as the founder of a social justice school. In each of these settings, practitioners must grapple with how to work for the school system, and yet work against its repressive features. A number of theoretical propositions also emerge from this dialectic, and help frame the educational literature in social justice. At the macrolevel of institutions, should social movements build schools or work to unschool? At the microlevel of classroom curriculum, is critical curriculum a deconstruction of society or an inculcation of skills necessary for society? This final question not only challenges the role of youth agency in relationship to education, but also that of pedagogy to social justice, movement making, and human rights. This chapter refuses to stay in a polemic position of writing "for" social justice, and rather engages a critical questioning of "how" social justice might be engaged through schooling, particularly within the context of U.S. urban education.

Two Freires: Pieces of a Social Justice Literature

In the United States, the development of social justice literature is yet immature, and the next few decades will reveal a deeper understanding of this as a serious area of inquiry. As a result, current research on social justice is syncretic; that is, it draws selectively, it erases selectively, and remembers selectively from a hybrid genealogy of educational efforts within and without the United States. As we glue together these pieces, we begin to notice gaps and shadows in the way social justice in education is discussed.

This progressive agenda in U.S. education syncretically misremembers Paulo Freire as a promoter of institutional critique and student-centered classrooms, and forgets the realities of his educational practices from Brazilian camponês adult literacy. In effect, there are two Freires in social justice literature. One is a philosopher delving into the abstract principles of humanization through "conscientization" and dehumanization through "banking education." One is a literacy strategist, who appropriated the capital of the Brazilian university for the struggle of the camponês, and navigated the unresolvable complexities of his own class, race, and privilege to do so. Together, they form a binary that must be studied holistically and dialectically in any consideration of social justice work. However, in typical Western fashion, Friere has been dichotomized, and his two halves have been hierarchized in U.S. education. In semiotics, we call this presence and absence (Derrida, 1978), whereby Freire the philosopher is given an idealized, benign, and Whiter presence that overshadows his darker twin. By implication through exclusion, the second Freire is imperfect, violent, and Black. Nonetheless, this second Freire, the strategist, is obfuscated but still nearby, waiting for his insurgence in the U.S. world of education.

The two Freires play out in schooling with dramatic consequences. Idealized democracy can generate naive attempts at deregulating schooling spaces, whereby "equal voice" privileges acritical reproductions of racist, sexist, and violent thought, as Ellsworth (1989) illustrated through pitfalls she faced in her own teaching of U.S. college students in a classroom environment rooted in student voice and dialogue.

By contrast, the Cuban literacy campaign translated both Freire's philosophies and strategies to the Cuban context of a newly found revolutionary state under the shadow of U.S. imperialism, and to national scale (Kozol, 1978). Although similar in addressing adult literacy, Cuba's campaign was in many ways dissimilar to Freire's work in San Recife. Where Freire abhorred reading primers, Cuba implemented one, based on the understanding that the literacy brigadistas, many of whom were young children, needed tools. The Cuban methods involved unmistakably nationalistic and counterimperialistic generative themes, such as the impact of U.S. policy on Cuban farmers. Such discourses were not benign, and silenced counterrevolutionary dissent as well as socialized a revolutionary identity.

The recovery that must be made is to return the historical specificity of Freire's work, the practical aspects that ground his philosophies, and thereby the real, rather than ideal, aspects that could be translated to U.S. urban schools and youth of color. Most importantly, we have to start considering the exercises of power in Freire and Freirian-inspired work. Once such exercise of power lies in the workings of pedagogy, especially in the socialization of youth through schooling. The second Freire suggests to us that schooling, or the formal conditioning of youth to legitimated knowledge systems, could yet be a valid method of emancipatory education. Often, this possibility is obscured by the fear of "banking education"—the inculcating of learners to a depository of information and to a colonial relation between student and teacher—a process that Freire (1970/2000) so eloquently critiqued. However, its opposite, "problem-posing education," is not the absence of pedagogical power, nor the absence of authority, nor a benign activity. Rather, it is a form of socialization that requires difficult examination of worldly conditions, by teacher and student, through rigorous, even painful literate endeavor (Freire & Macedo, 1987, p. 77). The question facing social justice educators is not whether to socialize youth, but how, and to what?

Social justice literature in education is also syncretic in its selective forgetting of traditions in educational thought. One of the grand erasures that hopefully scholarship in the upcoming decades will recover are the writings of postslavery, pre-Civil Rights Black educators, such as Ana Julia Cooper and Carter G. Woodson who are situated in a broader "diaspora" of Black thought from Black Americanists to Black nationalists to pan-African internationalists. These educator-intellectuals are regularly omitted in the curricula in schools of education, yet their work offers invaluable insights to effective struggle within mainstream institutions that were literally founded upon a hypothesis of Black subordination. The tradition of Black educational thought, when viewed through the window of post-Reconstruction writers, offers a complex perspective for and against schooling. On one hand, Woodson (2000) decried schools as colonizing institutions that sap intellectual resources from the community, and teach a Eurocentric curriculum. The expansion of public schooling then is an expansion of the colonial project. On the other hand, these same Black educators viewed schools as a possible institutional structure for community "uplift" (Cooper, 2000), and for the development of an educated class of community servants (Woodson, 2000).

These gaps in theory manifest as uncertainties in practice for a coherent social justice vision. This chapter proceeds with several illustrations of these practical dilemmas. These short vignettes are not meant to be in-depth analyses of complex phenomena; I use them to raise fallacies and insights into how youth and their education communities negotiate the school–education dialectic. Most significantly, they point to critical directions for much needed research in social justice literature. The first vignette asks the question, what is the role of pedagogy in moving youth walkouts and protests from "crisis behavior" (Melucci, 1980) to sustainable and strategic social movements? The second asks, what is appropriate discipline in a school for social justice? The third poses the question, how can grassroots movements in schooling effectively implement a socially just education within the state project of mass education? In this respect, this chapter proceeds with a problem-posing orientation.

A Pedagogical Strategy for Youth Organizing?

Subaltern groups, including youth of color in divested urban areas of the United States, have always found ways to subvert spaces toward countercultural practices, often contrary to the intention of their architects. For example, in the enormous protests for immigrant rights in Paris and the United States in 2006, youth exploited the corporate technologies of text messaging in cellular phones and Internet social networking sites (Yang, 2007). In universities, designed often to promote a docile technocratic class and to produce elites who will reproduce social inequality (Bourdieu & Clough, 1996), students are often the main fomenters of dissent. In urban public schools, despite curriculum and authoritarian systems to the contrary (Apple, 2004), youth have consistently mobilized around a diverse set of issues (Noguera, Ginwright, & Cammarota, 2006). In many ways, walkouts, protests, and other direct confrontations with institutional authorities have become the imagined modus operandi of the American political dissenter.

During the short life of the school that I founded, East Oakland Community High School (EOC), I witnessed youth mobilize their entire student body in an unusual display of Black–Brown solidarity for immigrant rights. Not quite a year later, these youth, their families, and teachers walked eight miles from the school to the state-run district offices. Their action was part of a yearlong battle with the state over the future of their school, ultimately resulting in the closure of EOC. They also organized school lunch boycotts, and participated in rallies against the high school exit exam. Furthermore, our youth were frequently solicited to attend rallies for affirmative action on college campuses, walkouts for teacher contracts, marches against the war in Iraq; flyers for political actions were so ubiquitous that they often littered school hallways. Interested news reporters would even inquire when the next walkout might take place. These strategies of dissent are so conventional that youth have difficulty imagining social justice outside of the spectacle of protest. What then, should be the relationship of social justice educators to youth organizing? The choice should not be framed as a simple, "Should I walkout with the youth or not?" A serious examination of solidarity must pose the question: by what pedagogy could youth move from performances of dissent to strategic, enduring social change?

EOC moved from a standard of exposing youth to political actions to analyses of political power. At first, youth learned about the atrocities in Darfur, discussed the cultural bias in textbooks, and studied the lives of revolutionary heroes. They read the biography of Stan "Tookie" Williams (the founder of the Los Angeles Crips), and protested outside the prison walls on the night of his execution. Youth community action research projects were exposé-oriented, and concluded with predictable political stances. Outside of fairly polemic position-statements, youth could articulate very little about the workings of power. Arguably, this kind of political education, although relevant, were not "generative themes" (Freire, 1970/2000) from their own daily existence. Rather, they were imposed political imperatives. By the second year, youth were analyzing how various social actors struggle for political dominance through culture-producing institutions of church, family, media, and school. As generative themes, they traced the economic genealogies of consumer products in their neighborhoods, and studied the semiology in popular media forms from video games to magazines to music. They then applied their understanding in an original analysis of a social phenomena, culminating in a public lecture to a community audience. Similarly, EOC moved from a curriculum of featuring political dissent to one of producing rigorous skills in academic, new media, and critical literacies (Morrell, 2004).

Our goal was to train youth to become producers of strategic public texts, rather than consumers of political education. Youth were trained to: produce their own films; apply social theory to everyday media; debate through legal discourse; deconstruct and reconstruct academic texts; write research papers, literary analyses, and statistical reports; design websites; operate statistical software for the social sciences; and present to diverse audiences from academic researchers, to congressional policy-makers, to peers. In other words, youth developed skill sets to speak authoritatively in both mainstream and subaltern spheres. In the case of the immigrant rights march, I argue that Black–Brown youth solidarity was rooted neither in ideological consensus nor in common political interests, but rather in a shared cultural space carried out in popular media: Internet and cellular phone social networks (Yang, 2007). This directs educators to think about what rigorous training in new media and popular culture would look like, starting from existing research including Morrell (2001), Morrell and Duncan-Andrade (2002), and Ginwright and NetLibrary (2004). This emerging body of work on popular culture demands that we see youth as human beings, and not economically conceived Marxist actors. The latter case essentially imagines students as rational decision makers who trade in a currency of critical theory—that the only relevant currency is ideological partisanship.

Social justice, so ill-conceived, will continue to be politically relevant, but culturally irrelevant and theoretically stunted. Youth actors condense to form larger movements not only in response to the structural inequalities, but also to trade in pleasure, in post-colonial differences. Youth participate in postmodern, yet highly ancient, sign-systems that signaled human concerns long before the advent of capitalism. Any clear social justice agenda must address the fundamental humane concerns of popular culture in youth movement. In the case of the eight-mile march, youth managed for a time to redirect the question from schooling to education.

While the state focused on whether or not to close a school, the community asked the question of how a school might provide a just education. They marched not to keep their school open, nor to smash the state, but rather on the platform of quality education, achieved through self-improvement and self-critique. They employed print and multimedia research materials, alongside personal narratives, all nested within a broader discourse of educational quality (Arredondo, 2007). The marchers violated all depictions manufactured by the state propagandists to characterize the youth as violent, the school as acritical and self-defensive, and the teachers as subversive commandos in a terrorist organizing camp. After eight miles in the rain, five hours of peaceful waiting, dozens of presentations of articulate self-critique and plans to move forward, the state-appointed administrator nonetheless closed the school. After the Administrator's decision that night, even the police (hired in extra numbers to protect the state from the marchers) held hands with the youth and wept in the hallways outside the school board chambers. This moment of empathy showed the winning of hearts and minds through moral compulsion, and the influence of revolutionary subjects (the youth, teachers, and families) over nonrevolutionary classes (police, media, public officials). The youth and those adults who worked alongside them were able to construct a public consensus for their cause, or at least, fracture the state consensus against it. Such tactics reveal how subaltern actors collude with supposed adversaries, operating for and against, and elude a priori assignments of political affiliations.

Although it is important to recognize youth as an important political category and agential social group distinct from adults, we must avoid the fallacy of idealizing youth as an isolated, independent social category. Any effective practice in youth organizing enacts a sophisticated understanding of how adults, particularly teachers and other adult authorities, work in solidarity with youth groups. This involves a rigorous conceptualization of the politics of solidarity, but especially the role of adult pedagogues, leaders, and mentors. This give and take between adult guidance and youth self-determination is reflected in sociological examinations of social movements, in effective youth participatory action research (Morrell, 2004), in learning theory on the role of apprenticeship and guided participation (Schieffelin & Ochs, 1986), in critical pedagogy in the U.S. urban schooling context, and in the voices of youth organizers themselves. To answer the question of how pedagogy could transform youth dissent to organized social movement, future research must critically analyze the forms of adult authority, solidarity, and curricular strategies.

Disciplined for Justice?

Because of its institutional nature, schooling is a regulatory process that conditions the minds and bodies of both students and teachers (Foucault, 1979). Highly regulated schools provide apt conditioning environments and tend to discourage a liberatory education. The most profound consequence of this is how the ghetto conditions of urban schools acritically help to construct the prison-industrial complex and a docile workforce (Davis, 1998). However, one ideological fallacy is to presume that deregulation is the natural agenda for social justice in schools. Instead, an effective social justice strategy must consider how these systems of regulation can favor an emancipatory movement in schooling at large. The liberal mentality is discomfited by the regulatory function of schooling. Accordingly, the liberal response is to either deny or obfuscate the regulatory systems in a school (Yang, 2008). The inaugural year at East Oakland Community High School (EOC) was characterized by a deregulatory culture: there were no bells, no hallway passes, no security guards, and conventional punishment systems like suspensions were avoided. However, no alternatives to orthodox regulatory measures were constructed—the assumption was that explicit ideology, democratic culture, and caring adults would counteract years of conditioning. The result was an unleashing of a schooled habitus (Bourdieu & Clough, 1996; Willis, 1977), or habituation of youth to become docile under repression yet self-destructive once unbound. The "hidden curriculum" of schools (Apple, 2004) not only trains compliance by inuring youth to a factory setting of structured authoritarianism, but also conditions a dependency on those very systems of regulation.

By the middle of the second year, EOC was in a cultural and academic crisis, where physical and symbolic violence among the youth became common and little academic discipline was in place for students to be successful at the school's accelerated curriculum. At this point, a group of core teachers strategized to take over the culture of the school, with the explicit theory that the school's mission was not to create a liberal environment, but rather a disciplined space for training youth leaders, similar to the Black Panther Party's Oakland Community School. The resulting discipline intervention, called the "redemption plan," was rooted in the moral authority of a "young elders circle" of the most respected adults on campus. The circle identified a long-list of 50 youth, or approximately one-third of the student body, who in their estimation had been miseducated by our school to consistently disrespect adults and each other. The young elders circle became the regulating body, imposing a set of contractual expectations on the youth as a parallel system to conventional district punishments of suspension and expulsion. The objectives, in a very Foucauldian sense, were for youth to internalize the moral order of the teachers, all couched within a reformist discourse. By the third year, fights became virtually nonexistent on campus. From the new cultural paradigm emerged a youth leadership group called the NSurGentes, who would intervene when racist/misogynist language and other forms of symbolic violence arose. An academic presentations curriculum became the norm for all 11th grade coursework, and every youth defended academic presentations across subjects twice per year. The school demonstrated the largest increase on the state Academic Performance Index of any high school in Oakland. Although still far from the purported vision of academic and moral rigor, the school undeniably had accomplished a major shift in culture.

However, this process of seizing the regulatory functions of the school and instituting a culture of discipline was nonbenign. As with any exercise of power, conflict preceded consensus and the new dominant group sought acquiescence from those who dissented. Of the second year faculty, three of 10 were either requested to leave or willingly departed. Of the 50 students identified for the redemption plan, at least three left the school. In selecting words such as *regulation* and *authority*, I have intended to make transparent the nonbenign mechanisms of the redemption plan. Furthermore, this example of regulation is a window into a cultural direction that EOC was taking across school arenas—including teacher development and youth training in academics, arts, and organizing. This kind of work raises questions about how power, although appropriated toward emancipatory interests, still contains repressive operations. A critical conceptualization of power, as exercised by groups engaged in social change, needs to be developed as the social justice literature in education progresses. To effectively answer the question of authority and discipline within a social justice schooling agenda, one body of literature yet to emerge are studies that cover the strategies, exercises of power, and forms of regulation in social justice schools.

Institutionalizing a Just State?

My direct work in district reform took place on top of two crashing waves. The first was a grassroots takeover of the district, a reform movement to generate small, community-based schools mobilized by thousands of families in the most economically and educationally divested parts of the city (Yang, 2004). The second was a highly repressive state takeover of the school district, resulting in relegation of the elected school board to advisory status, firing the superintendent, and the appointment of a state administrator as an absolute authority to govern the district. Both "takeovers" illustrate that competition exists among elite state agents, and how influencing these elites can provide or restrict space for more revolutionary activity.

This small schools movement was led and mobilized largely by a faith-based organization, which I call Oakland United Congregations (OUC) in my writings. OUC had an explicit theory of power, which was to consolidate their own power through a large grassroots constituency, and to influence those in power through winning consent rather than antagonistic confrontation (Yang, 2004). Furthermore, their efforts enabled them to construct their own elites with high positional authority, including the superintendent and his reform officers (Yang, 2004). In contrast to other movements for community control of schools (e.g., Podair & Ebrary, 2002), OUC did not establish community boards or oversight committees. Community power was predicated on constructing state authorities who were obligated to grassroots constituencies, rather than institutions that were micromanaged by community groups. OUC's power thesis provided a large degree of effectiveness within circuits of power—and also earned them constant criticism from more militant activist groups. However, the small schools provided space for more radical endeavors, such as the School for Social Justice (now closed), as well as the school that I founded, East Oakland Community High School (now closed). When state takeover of Oakland Unified seemed likely, but not yet imminent, I met with various community organizers, elected officials, and unionists, to advise them of the dramatic shift in authoritarianism that would occur once the legislature voted to take over OUSD, and of the possible scenarios under which takeover could be avoided.

The response from nearly all these parties was that the current Oakland administration was just as bad, if not worse, than the state. Some union activists said they were too busy fighting for the pending contract. Other activist groups, although locally powerful in school district wranglings, were too busy in more global political engagements, such as the U.S. invasion of Iraq and affirmative action on college campuses. The teacher's union president publicly supported state takeover, claiming that contract negotiations would be easier because there would only be one person to meet with. Even when the union took a stance against state takeover, they made it clear that this did not imply support for the current administration. In short, city schools' political bodies took all administrators to be natural enemies of teachers, and were unconcerned about different regime changes. As a result, little solidarity within these powerful groups was achieved against (or even in preparation for) state takeover. Some exceptions were the community groups most engaged with direct reform in Oakland, who together managed to redirect some of the authoritarianism of the state takeover into continuation of community initiated reforms—at least for a few years. However, the overall apathy helped to herald an easy administrative takeover.

Unfortunately, regime change had a profound impact. Under the superintendent, the teachers' union had enjoyed a 24% increase in salaries—the largest pay raise in decades. Community power was at an unprecedented level, with actual representatives at the highest level of decision making in the district. The new small schools enjoyed a modest set of autonomies, free from district micromanagement. Whether or not these gains were at the behest or despite the efforts of the current superintendent was immaterial—the facts remained that a "permissive context" (Meeks, 1993) facilitated unprecedented shifts toward community power. By contrast under state takeover, teacher salaries were immediately cut by 4%. The small schools lost their autonomy and became a mechanism for punishment—whereby low-performing schools were closed and then reopened. Doublespeak state agents, such as the ironically named "Chief of Community Accountability" whose main job was to hold the community accountable to the state, replaced hard-won community allies in positions of power.

Future research on social movements in schooling must dispel the reductionist concept of a monolithic state, engaged in an innate adversarial relationship with grassroots communities. As U.S. schooling continues to tread down the path of state policing of school test performance, and diminishing state investment in education, this kind of reasoning may appear ideologically abhorrent. However, it is all the more relevant to distinguish between state institutional resources and state authoritarianism, in order to answer how communities may yet organize for a socially just education system.

Synthesis: A Nonbenign Theory of Empowerment

One possible synthesis to the school–education dialectic is to imagine a strategic radicalism rather than a polemic one, a strategic education rather than political education, and education that is socially just instead of schools of social justice. In the area of social justice curriculum, we have seen the developments of a cultural–linguistic radicalism (what counts is how one is taught), an epistemological radicalism (what counts as knowledge), and a functionalism radicalism (what is the purpose of education). However, an effective social justice agenda must begin to consider a strategic radicalism. As social justice literature advances, we should think beyond political education, and toward a strategic education.

Much as schooling has been a training ground for workers for a capitalist economy (Bowles & Gintis, 1976; Willis, 1977), social justice curriculum must be wary not to simply become a training ground for the rank and file in a political cause. One insight lies in understanding the difference between promoting a specific political critique, and promoting critical a framework (Solorzano & Delgado Bernal, 2001) that leads to original application and new analyses. The second insight lies in developing the skill sets for youth to speak authoritatively in both public and subaltern spheres.

Strategic education requires an explicit teaching of codes of power (Delpit, 1988), not to submit to the dominant or hegemonic reading of codes (Hall, 1973) but rather to understand how to negotiate reading and indeed oppositional readings of these codes— what I term a "critical code fluency" (Yang, 2004). In this respect, "access" (Collatos, Morrell, Nuno, & Lara, 2004) to higher education takes on a more radical meaning, a radical "detracking" of courses (Oakes, 2005) subverts current systems of academic capital to construct transformative agents with full credentials in institutions of power.

The vignettes in this chapter illustrated urgent areas of research into the dilemmas of social justice education within the urban U.S. context. Across these three areas of youth organizing, social justice discipline, and state–community schooling projects, a common thread of analysis is how power may serve emancipatory interests. Whereas critical theory offers a critique of the repressive aspects of power (Foucault, 1979), by contrast, "empowerment" in educational literature is treated as a largely benign process (e.g., Maldonado, Rhoads, & Bienavista, 2005; McQuillan, 2005). In actuality, the processes by which marginalized people come into social, economic, cultural, or discursive power are rarely benign, but rather decolonizing acts of symbolic and sometimes literal violence (Fanon, 1965).

For any realistic analysis of social justice efforts in education, we must develop a critical theory of empowerment, a term which refers to the construction of power, and moving from being a subjugated to a dominant group in social conflict. We must examine how empowerment itself is not a benign process, but a revolutionary one constituted by its own particular forms of violence and domination. Any social justice agenda with teeth will admit that conflict is unavoidable in radical change, and how we come to predict, and shape conflict is of great import.

Note

1. Reprinted by consent of Brooks Permissions.

References

Apple, M. W. (2004). *Ideology and curriculum* (3rd ed.). New York: RoutledgeFalmer.

Arredondo, G. (2007). *Village Unido: Building multicultural school based movement to improve urban schooling.* Paper presented at the American Anthropological Association 2007 Annual Meeting, Washington, DC.

Bourdieu, P., & Clough, L. C. (1996). *The state nobility: Elite schools in the field of power* [*Noblesse d'Ètat*]. Stanford, CA: Stanford University Press.

Bowles, S., & Gintis, H. (1976). *Schooling in capitalist America: Educational reform and the contradictions of economic life.* New York: Basic Books.

Brooks, G. (1992). Boy breaking glass. In *Blacks*. Chicago: Third World Press. (Original work published 1968)

Collatos, A., Morrell, E., Nuno, A., & Lara, R. (2004). Critical sociology in K-16 early intervention: Remaking Latino pathways to higher education. *Journal of Hispanic Higher Education, 3*(2), 164–179.

Cooper, A. J., & University of North Carolina at Chapel Hill, Library. (2000). *A voice from the south.* Chapel Hill, NC: Academic Affairs Library, University of North Carolina at Chapel Hill.

Davis, A. Y. (1998). Masked racism: Reflections on the prison industrial complex; what is the prison industrial complex? Why does it matter? *Colorlines, 1*(2), 11.

Delpit, L. D. (1988). The silenced dialogue: Power and pedagogy in educating other people's children. *Harvard Educational Review, 58*(3), 280–298.

Derrida, J. (1978). *Writing and difference* [*Ecriture et la diffèrence*]. Chicago: University of Chicago Press.

Ellsworth, E. (1989). Why doesn't this feel empowering? Working through the repressive myths of critical pedagogy. *Harvard Educational Review, 59*(3), 297–324.

Fanon, F. (1965). *The wretched of the earth* [*Damnés de la terre*]. New York: Grove Press.

Foucault, M. (1979). *Discipline and punish: The birth of the prison* [*Surveiller et punir*]. New York: Vintage Books.

Freire, P. (2000). *Pedagogy of the oppressed* [*Pedagog'a del oprimido*] (30th anniversary ed.). New York: Continuum.

Freire, P., & Macedo, D. P. (1987). *Literacy: Reading the word and the world*. South Hadley, MA: Bergin & Garvey.

Giddens, A. (1979). *Central problems in social theory: Action, structure, and contradiction in social analysis*. Berkeley: University of California Press.

Ginwright, S. A., & NetLibrary, I. (2004). *Black in school*. New York: Teachers College Press.

Hall, S. (1973). *Encoding and decoding in the television discourse*. Birmingham, UK: Centre for Cultural Studies, University of Birmingham.

hooks, B. (1994). *Teaching to transgress: Education as the practice of freedom*. New York: Routledge.

Kozol, J. (1978). *Children of the revolution: A Yankee teacher in the Cuban schools*. New York: Delacorte Press.

Maldonado, D. E. Z., Rhoads, R., & Buenavista, T. L. (2005). The student-initiated retention project: Theoretical contributions and the role of self-empowerment. *American Educational Research Journal, 42*(4), 605–638.

McQuillan, P. J. (2005). Possibilities and pitfalls: A comparative analysis of student empowerment. *American Educational Research Journal, 42*(4), 639–670.

Meeks, B. (1993). *Caribbean revolutions and revolutionary theory: An assessment of Cuba, Nicaragua and Grenada*. London: Macmillan Caribbean.

Melucci, A. (1980). The new social movements: A theoretical approach. *Social Science Information, 19*(2), 199–226.

Morrell, E. D. (2001). *Transforming classroom discourse: Academic and critical literacy development through engaging popular culture*. PhD dissertation, University of California, Berkeley. Retrieved July 23, 2008, from Dissertations & Theses @University of California data base. (Publication No. AAT 3044604)

Morrell, E. (2004). *Becoming critical researchers: Literacy and empowerment for urban youth*. New York: Peter Lang.

Morrell, E., & Duncan-Andrade, J. (2002). What do they learn in school: Using hip-hop as a bridge between youth culture and canonical poetry texts. In J. Mahiri (Ed.), *What they don't learn in school: Literacy in the lives of urban youth* (pp. 247–268). New York: Peter Lang.

Noguera, P., Ginwright, S. A., & Cammarota, J. (2006). *Beyond resistance! Youth activism and community change: New democratic possibilities for practice and policy for America's youth*. New York: Routledge.

Oakes, J. (2005). *Keeping track: How schools structure inequality* (2nd ed.). New Haven, CT; London: Yale University Press.

Podair, J. E., & Ebrary, I. (2002). *The strike that changed New York*. New Haven, CT: Yale University Press.

Schieffelin, B. B., & Ochs, E. (1986). *Language socialization across cultures*. New York: Cambridge University Press.

Solorzano, D. G., & Bernal, D. D. (2001). Examining transformational resistance through a critical race and LatCrit theory framework: Chicana and Chicano students in an urban context. *Urban Education, 36*(3), 308–342.

Willis, P. E. (1977). *Learning to labour: How working class kids get working class jobs*. Farnborough, UK: Saxon House.

Woodson, C. G. (2000). *The mis-education of the Negro*. Chicago: African American Images.

Yang, K. W. (2004). *Taking over: The struggle to transform an urban school system system*. PhD dissertation, University of California, Berkeley. Retrieved July 23, 2008, from Dissertations & Theses @University of California data base. (Publication No. AAT 3165613)

Yang, K. W. (2007). Organizing MySpace: Youth walkouts, pleasure, politics and new media. Paper presented at the American Anthropological Assocation 2007 annual meeting, New York.

Yang, K. W. (2008). Discipline or punish? Building rigorous learning communities in urban schools. Paper presented at the American Educational Research Association 2008 annual meeting, New York.

29 The Social Justice Education Project

A Critically Compassionate Intellectualism for Chicana/o Students

Julio Cammarota and Augustine F. Romero

In the fall semester of 2001, 1,805 Chicana/o students began their freshman year in the Tucson Unified School District (TUSD). Four years later, the graduating class of 2005 consisted of only 1,133 Chicanas/os. Over the course of four years, the district had lost 37.3% of these students. This decrease in Chicana/o students is not an aberration. Every graduating class—throughout the last several years—reveals this pattern of attrition.

The district and national policy response to this situation might best be called the "Leave No Chicana/o Untested." The logic behind this approach seems to reside in some hope that high stakes testing will improve academic performance, thereby augmenting graduation rates. However, research shows that high stakes tests may exacerbate Chicana/o student attrition (Valenzuela, 2005). The standard strategies of rote instruction, remediation, and grade level retention are more likely to make students uninterested in education than they are to raise test scores. Once they lose interest, students are sucked into a downward spiral of decreasing academic performance, diminishing expectations, and declining school perseverance. In TUSD's previous six graduating classes, the average loss within the Chicana/o student enrollment has been 41%.

Given the high attrition of Chicana/o students within the district and a national high-stakes testing policy that seems to create more problems than solutions (Boger, 2002; Reardon & Galindo, 2002; Tippeconnic, 2003; Valenzuela, 2005), we decided to develop an educational program for TUSD that would generate success for Chicana/o youth. Our program, entitled the Social Justice Education Project (SJEP), embraces a three-prong educational philosophy that emphasizes cooperative learning, compassionate student–educator relationships, and social justice content. We call this educational approach *critically compassionate intellectualism*, as it aims to raise students' critical awareness and their academic performance (Cammarota & Romero, 2006). Since the program began in 2003 it has demonstrated consistently positive results.

This chapter has three objectives. First, we discuss the theoretical underpinnings that inform critically compassionate intellectualism in the SJEP classroom. Second, we introduce aspects of the SJEP curriculum, which help to transform this theory into practice. Third, we demonstrate how the SJEP has increased the academic performance and educational attainment of the students in the program. We draw from a series of indicators to reveal the program's effectiveness, including student interviews, student course evaluations, standardized test results, and graduation rates. The data from these indicators suggest a strong correlation between SJEP's critically compassionate intellectualism and the academic achievement of the participants. We conclude the chapter by reflecting on our experiences as educators and defining the theoretical advancements required to enhance educational practices for Chicana/o students.

Toward a Theory of Critically Compassionate Intellectualism

A critically compassionate intellectualism approach combines three educational perspectives into one framework. Each perspective—cooperative learning, compassionate educator–student relationships, and social justice consciousness—carries a set of principles about learning and human advancement. Each of these is enhanced by the simultaneous presence and implementation of the others. We begin this section by examining the educational principles behind cooperation, then move to compassion, followed by consciousness. This sequence reveals the interrelationship among the three parts of critically compassionate intellectualism and the complicated wholeness to the theoretical framework.

Cooperation

Our perspective on cooperative learning is centered on principles derived from critical pedagogy (Darder, 2002; Freire, 1967/1994; McLaren, 1994). Although a variety of treatments and expressions of critical pedagogy exist, the core principle strives to level out hierarchy in the classroom to create greater equality in the production and exchange of knowledge between educators and students. The required first step toward engendering equality involves a critique of the traditional lecture style of instruction. This traditional style assumes that the educator possesses all the knowledge in the classroom while students are ignorant subjects passively waiting to receive this knowledge. The resulting dynamic from these assumptions is a classroom in which the educator is the sole authority of power while students lack any voice or input in their learning process. This classroom social organization reflects an undemocratic and hierarchical structure of the powerful and the powerless.

By encouraging students to create and pose questions as the basis for learning, this traditionally unjust power dynamic is challenged and dissolved. Thus, the use of questioning is a significant principle behind critiquing the traditional lecture style and generating a just classroom dynamic. Within the questioning mode, what Freire (1967/1994) calls the "problem-posing method," lessons start with questions that originate from students' concerns or experiences—posed by either the educator or students, or sometimes by everyone. The attainment of knowledge should never occur from the distribution of an absolute, irrefutable fact, but rather as process of discovery in which educator and students work collectively and democratically. The problem-posing method infers a collective—not single—authority in the construction and attainment of knowledge. The intended consequence of sharing authority in knowledge production is a classroom that models a democratic social organization.

The sharing of authority in the classroom is not easily accomplished. Many students, particularly adolescents, have numerous years of experience with the traditional lecture style and have learned to be passive observers. The objective of collective learning is for students to become active citizens. Sharing authority and encouraging students to expand their roles in the classroom meets this objective. Role redefinition requires the students' liberation from the narrow confines of passive dependency and ascendance into the endless possibilities of active leadership.

However, students, especially students of color, rarely have leadership opportunities in classrooms and thus have limited knowledge of how to take on leadership roles inside the classroom. Furthermore, the common model of leadership in this country, and possibly around the world, centers on leading by domination and oppression. When asked to lead, some students might draw from this common model and act in ways that sustain uneven power relations within the classroom. Freire (1998) describes the causes of people reproducing oppression during their quest for freedom:

> The oppressed, having internalized the image of the oppressor and adopted his guidelines, are fearful of freedom. Freedom would require them to eject this image and replace it with autonomy and responsibility. (p. 48)

Students, therefore, should learn how to lead by unlearning oppressive ideologies and epistemologies that persuade them to believe they cannot lead or they can only accomplish leadership through domination. A democratic and collective learning involves a new form of leadership based on compassion and responsibility for self and others. Since few examples of this type of leadership exist, students are often hesitant to adopt this role, because they are "fearful" (Freire, 1967/1994) of claiming it.

Compassion

To teach students to overcome their fears of liberation, educators must model a democratic leadership that embraces compassion as a means of fostering liberation. Education literature rarely addresses "compassion" as an important pedagogical element. However, "caring," an analogous principle, is represented in the literature (Noddings, 1984, 1992; Valenzuela, 1999). Our experiences within the SJEP have revealed many important lessons regarding caring, particularly that trust emerges only when teachers continuously demonstrate a deeply profound sense of caring for students. The development of these caring relationships introduces greater avenues of leadership for both students and teachers.

Valenzuela (1999) shows that students tend to mistrust their teachers when they believe they do not care. Within a trusting environment, students have greater opportunities to learn new lessons, while unlearning the lessons of dehumanization and oppression that sustain an unquestioned reality (Haney Lopez, 2003). Specific to this process, students recognize that they can create and transform knowledge (Delgado Bernal, 2002), and as leaders, it is critical that they engage in a praxis that promotes social justice for their families and communities.

In the classroom, showing compassion not only for the student's academic progress but also his or her life circumstances engenders a caring environment. Thus, the educator must express compassion for the challenges that stifle academic performance inside of schools, as well as the broader social and economic forces that make learning difficult (poverty, racism, sexism, homophobia, etc.). Compassion involves acknowledging the student as a complete human being by recognizing the problems in his or her life that impede well-being. Compassionate educators reveal the capacity to mentor students through these challenges, and embrace the responsibility to facilitate a resolution to some of the most pressing issues facing students. It has been our experience that this type of compassion and commitment fosters an expanded sense of hope within students.

It is through the educator's compassion that the student feels acknowledged, validated, and most importantly, supported in his or her journey through life's difficulties. Listening to the student, taking note of his or her personal struggles, and allowing him or her to express frustrations, and then finding different ways to advocate for students becomes the foundation for developing a compassionate educator–student relationship. Once compassion is evident in the relationship between the educator and students, trust within the classroom will increase. The educator attains an enhanced capacity to lead, and can therefore facilitate the students' ascendance into leadership roles. Trust allows the educator to mitigate the students' fears and motivate them to redefine their roles in the classroom.

It is important to note that compassion toward students of color is not simply defined as a concern for their individual suffering. What happens to an individual student should be a matter of concern. However, an educator's compassion should not end there; students' experiences and struggles as members of a larger social group must be recognized and addressed. The struggles of students of color extend beyond individual crisis to community-wide oppression. Racism, along with other forms of oppression, can hurt them as individuals and harm their families, peers, neighborhoods, and communities. A student's entire world, including historical struggles that have positioned him or her as socially, economically, or politically subordinate, are primary focal areas for the critically compassionate educator.

Consciousness

To achieve a humanizing compassion, educational content should elevate students' critical consciousness. A real demonstration of compassion for students of color involves centering coursework on analyzing and addressing the various forms of oppression that confront them. However, understanding the true complexity and parameters of oppression is a challenging educational matter, one which takes considerable time and knowledge to comprehend. Some students recognize the real forces of oppression constraining their life experiences; others, however, lack the critical consciousness to perceive what truly holds them down.

Freire (1970) asserts that at least three significant types of consciousness (magical, naive, and critical) are apparent throughout the general population, representing successive stages in human development. The first stage is termed *magical consciousness* in which people believe God predetermines their fate. They assume they have no control over circumstances and therefore accept that their lot in life is given and immutable. When reflecting on the reason for poverty, those with a magical consciousness will most likely assert that it is God's will. The danger with this type of consciousness is that oppressed populations will find little room to change their status. God determines and fixes reality to the point in which people feel they have no other choice but to accept their subordination.

The second stage of development, according to Freire, is *naive consciousness* in which people assume that their situation in life is the result of family upbringing and culture. Thus, an individual's success or failure is perceived as directly related to how they have been raised and the kinds of cultural beliefs they have been exposed to while growing up. In American society, naive consciousness is quite prevalent and informs a dominant explanation for the low academic attainment of students of color. Those embracing this consciousness believe that many students of color fail because they originate from families or cultures that do not value education, resulting in a lack of motivation to succeed in school. In this regard, naive consciousness parallels "deficit thinking" (Valencia, 1997) in that failure is understood as a problem of deficiency on the part of the students and their families. In other words, it presumes certain communities lack the "right" family and cultural values for academic success.

The final stage of development is *critical consciousness*. Those adhering to this type of consciousness will understand that living conditions derive from social and economic systems, structures, and institutions. God, family, and culture have little to do with the circumstances of one's environment. Rather, it is individual and collective agency, along with the structures that result from that agency, that have the most significant influence over peoples' living situations. God, family, and culture do not directly engender wealth or poverty; structures of privilege, oppression, and exploitation do. The primary benefit of critical consciousness is that it clarifies that reality is not fixed and immutable, but rather the product of human construction. Therefore, if humans create social conditions, they also have the power to alter those conditions. Individuals who attain critical consciousness, perhaps the highest stage of human development, feel capable and confident they can change the material conditions of their lives and the lives of those around them.

A key objective of educators, therefore, should be to facilitate the attainment of critical consciousness. This progress is achieved through the educator modeling critical consciousness in his or her instruction. Educational content must center on a critical perspective relevant to the student's social, cultural, and historical realities. This contextualization comes about when historically marginalized students learn subjects, such as history or social studies, in ways that prioritize discussions of injustice and oppression. Ultimately, modeling critical consciousness facilitates students' awareness of the social and economic forces bearing down on their lives, and the potential for disrupting those forces.

The Cycle of Critically Compassionate Intellectualism

Critically compassionate intellectualism flows more in a cyclical than in a linear fashion, with the effects of each element running both clockwise and counterclockwise through the cycle. For instance, the attainment of critical consciousness supports cooperative learning because students will be circumspect about the dynamics that might sway the pedagogy toward an authoritarian lecture style; thus, the classroom processes that are undemocratic will be quickly recognized and addressed. Cooperative learning promotes critical consciousness because students must put their conceptions of justice into practice to sustain a democratic classroom. Likewise, compassion facilitates cooperation in that working collectively and democratically requires a true concern for others. Compassion also elevates critical consciousness by encouraging a comprehensive perspective of human suffering.

A critically compassionate intellectualism in full cycle secures the intellectual development of students of color. The ultimate goal of this tripartite educational approach is to assist students in recognizing their intellectual abilities and how to use them. Students are provided with the opportunity to reflect what Gramsci (1992) calls "organic intellectualism" such that they study and learn to lead their communities in the struggle for social justice. Intellectualism, in this case, is connected to a greater purpose––to serve in the interest of liberating people from the shackles of oppression. With this purpose in mind, students will strive to educate themselves in order to educate others.

The Social Justice Education Project

The Social Justice Education Project (SJEP) started as a collaboration between the University of Arizona and Tucson Unified School District at Cerro High School. The district had previously established a social science curriculum based on Chicano studies ("U.S. History through a Chicano Perspective") that provided students with a course that counted for their required U.S. history credits. We proposed to the principal a subcurriculum that would be folded into the school's U.S. history course. The proposed class would include Chicana/o studies, critical race theory, and a participatory action research project. To make sure the course material was covered thoroughly, we asked the principal if we could work with a cohort of students through their junior and senior years of high school.

The administration approved, and the class began in the spring semester of 2003. For four straight semesters—from 2003 through 2005—students were introduced to advanced-level social science material such as critical race theory, critical pedagogy, and social theory. Simultaneously, they learned participatory action research methodologies for assessing and addressing everyday injustices facing them and their communities.

Cerro High School

Cerro High School (CHS) is located in the southwestern portion of Tucson, in the second largest school district in Arizona. Cerro has a majority Chicana/o student population with a high concentration of low-achieving Chicana/o students. The socioeconomic statuses of the neighborhoods that surround CHS are among the lowest in the city's greater metropolitan area. A May 2006 report revealed that of the city's 32 zip code areas, the one in which CHS is ranked 26th. The median income per zip code in Tucson was $48,612 as compared to $30,082 in zip codes within CHS's attendance area. The majority of CHS's neighborhoods have traditionally been home to Chicano families, which helps to explain CHS's 63.2% Chicana/o student population. Furthermore, 55.3% of the students at CHS receive free lunch, considerably higher than the district average of 35.2%.

In the fall of 2002, there were 315 Chicanas/os enrolled in the freshman class at CHS and at the end of their senior year in the spring of 2006 that number had dwindled to 151. Over the last seven graduating classes Chicana/o four-year matriculation rates at CHS ranged from 37% for the class of 2004 to 60% for the class of 2002. In the 2003 to 2004 school year, CHS had the lowest percentage of students meeting mastery in all three areas of the Arizona Instruments for Measuring Standards (AIMS) test. Over the last five years, Cerro has had the lowest Advanced Placement Student Access Indicator (APSAI) (Solórzano & Ornelas, 2002, 2004) in the district, which is a figure used to measure access to the highest level academic courses in high schools. During the 2005 to 2006 academic year, Cerro's APSAI was 217, placing it at the bottom of all TUSD high schools. In comparison, the school with the best APSCI is TUSD's academic flagship school, College Preparatory High School (63% Anglo and 20% Chicana/o), had an APSCI of 9.9. The short of it is that Cerro has one advanced placement course for every 217 students, while College Prep has one advanced placement course for every 10 students.

Social Justice Education: Critically Compassionate Intellectualism in Practice

As a response to these unequal schooling conditions, the SJEP was designed to practice critically compassionate intellectualism by placing the intellectual development of Chicana/o students as its top priority. It provides students with the opportunity to investigate social and economic problems that undermine their potential to excel academically as well as impede the welfare and prosperity of their families and communities. The teachers in the program do not tell students what these problems are; they simply "problem-pose" by stating questions that prompt them to think about the complexities and tensions within their social context.

For example, a research assignment that prompted students into thinking about their social world involved photo documentation of their school and neighborhood environments. Students were given a disposal camera and then asked to document the environments in which they live. They were asked to take photographs that would help answer the following question: What are some problems you see in your life? Students spent about two weeks with the camera, ready to capture the various challenges they encountered in their day-to-day activities.

Some students had difficulty deciding what to photograph because they had not yet attained the critical consciousness necessary to "see" problems. Others surpassed the magical and naive stages of consciousness and recognized the deep-rooted structures fomenting injustice in their communities. These students became critical agents for their peers because they were able to use their intellectual capacities to help those still walking down the path of human development toward critical consciousness. Their photos and attendant explanations fostered a class dialogue that opened all eyes to the day-to-day challenges facing many Chicana/o students in the Tucson area.

One student shared some photos he had taken around his neighborhood. The photos showed major cracks in the streets and sidewalks, garbage piles rotting in an empty dirt lot, public bathrooms deteriorating in the local park, and families living in substandard housing. He explained that these impoverished conditions have a negative effect on a student's attitude. He argued that young people make judgments about their value to the society based largely on the conditions of their neighborhoods. When a young person sees that the neighborhood where he or she lives is in a perpetual state of squalor, it is understood as an indicator that society and the people with the power to rectify such conditions do not care about that individual.

Another student furthered these sentiments saying that unequal treatment in the larger society often undermines the Chicanas/os' trust in schools:

> …it's like the same thing, they were all taught the same things, to do certain things, to be in the same positions in life…my mom was telling me that they were forced to learn, the women, they were taught typing classes so that they could move up in the world as secretaries. And, my dad was tracked into auto mechanics. Neither [was] on the college track, they were on a track that the racist system believed was right. Like today, my parents, like today's [Chicanos] most…really don't have a chance. Look at our school, look at the ones in the AP classes, there are twice as many Chicanos as Whites in our school, but do they have twice as many Chicanos in the AP classes? No!

As the students collectively reflected on their own neighborhoods in comparison to other areas of Tucson, they concluded that the local government adequately maintains the parts of the city that are inhabited by Whites. Their Chicana/o neighborhoods, in comparison, have been underserved for years. An explanation of "why" this happens involved a lengthy discussion about local politics and activism and analysis of the fact that elected officials tend to respond more empathetically to the demands of White communities than to issues raised by Chicana/o communities. However, students did not want to ignore the fact that their communities can be more proactive. This turned the discussion to investigations of solutions that could come from within their communities. This led students to conclude that the perseverance of poverty in their neighborhoods is at least partially the result of community fatalism, something that can be overcome through access to education and their generation's participation in change-making efforts. One student, Rolando Yanez, explained that these kinds of conversations helped students understand their potential to change the conditions in the community: "The class, the project…showed the students that we could say something; we didn't have to be scared. We know that we need to stand up. We are conscious, and we need to use our conscience for justice, and to fight racism."

Along these lines of acting on their budding critical awareness, students continued to document the conditions of poverty by conducting field observations and taking photos. They also interviewed peers about the effects of poverty on motivation to see whether their theory held any water in reality. The students' research constructed a strong case about the negative impacts of poverty on the academic achievement of Chicana/o students (Delgado-Gaitan, 1990; Delgado-Gaitan & Trueba, 1988; Rumberger, 1995; Rumberger & Rodriguez, 2002).

To make sure that their voices were heard, students arranged a presentation of their research with the county board of supervisors. After the presentation, the board recommended that SJEP youth work closely with the county department of health and human services to assess neighborhood conditions and develop ideas to resolve these issues. This has since led to the planning and development of a new youth center in Tucson, and has sparked a number of dialogues aimed at addressing the needs of Chicano and other marginalized youth in the city.

Chicana/o Academic Identity

Another resolution offered by the students was the expansion of the SJEP. One of the main reasons students requested an expansion of the SJEP program was its value in developing their academic identity and increasing their academic proficiency. Examples of students' newly developed academic identity and their elevated levels of academic proficiency are reflected in numerous programmatic assessments: SJEP student performance on the AIMS Test, student surveys, and student testimonials regarding the transformations that have taken place as a result of their participation the SJEP.

Entering the 2004 to 2005 school year, eight of the 12 SJEP students needed to pass at least two sections of the AIMS test, with 6 of 12 needing to pass all three sections. At the end of the 2005 to 2006 school year, the SJEP students had 100% pass rates in both the reading and writing sections, and a 91% pass rate in the math section. An equivalent comparison between Anglos or Chicanas/os who needed to pass any or all sections of the AIMS is difficult; especially, given the significant decline in the Class of 2006's Chicana/o enrollment between the end of its sophomore year and the end of its senior year (266 to 151 = 44% loss of Chicana/o enrollment).

In addition, over the course of the two years of the SJEP program (2004–2005 SY to 2005–2006 SY), 100% of the students who entered the project in the 2004 to 2005 school year with a deficiency in any test areas passed all phases of the AIMS test. More impressive are the results without augmentation[1] for this same group of students. Without augmentation, 34 out of 36 students passed the reading section, 35 of 36 students passed the writing section, and 27 of 35 students passed the math section.

Further evidence of the impact of the pedagogical approached used in SJEP can be seen by comparing the success of the SJEP students to their Anglo peers that also needed to pass sections of AIMS after their sophomore year. During this same time period (2004–2006), the number of Anglo Cerro students that failed to pass the reading section was 6 of 28 or 21%; for writing 10 of 32 or 31%; and for math 9 of 50 or 18%. The sample sizes are close enough to justify comparison, and what this data reveals is that the SJEP students outperformed their similarly situated White peers on two sections of the AIMS and were close to equal on the third section.

Another example of the strong academic identity that was built in the program can be seen in the graduation rate of the students in SJEP. Over its four graduating classes, the combined SJEP graduation rate exceeds the Anglo graduation rates at schools where SJEP is offered (SJEP rate v. school site rate for Anglos): Class of 2004: 94% SJEP vs. 81% site; Class of 2005: 96% SJEP vs. 83% site; Class of 2006: 97% SJEP vs. 82% site; and the Class of 2007: 99% SJEP vs. 84% site.

Perhaps the most telling data about the effectiveness of the SJEP are the students' responses on the program's exit survey. On the program's most recent exit survey, 100% of the students strongly believed that participation in the SJEP led to the improvement of their writing and reading skills. Moreover, 100% strongly believed that their readiness for college was better because of their participation in the SJEP. Lastly, 100% strongly believed that after participating in the SJEP they could make valuable contributions to their community and society in general.

Student interviews were equally as revealing about the program's level of positive influence on students' lives. Veronica Alvarez, a freshman at Arizona State University stated:

> People need to know that these classes (SJEP classes) are the reason why me and probably all of us have done good in school and on the AIMS test. These classes gave me confidence; I knew I would feel smart at least once a day. And then Lopez (Lorenzo Lopez is the SJEP teacher of record) was right, I realized that these classes were really, really hard, and if I could do good in these classes, I could get As in my other classes too. This class also helped me believe that I could go to a university. Nobody in my family even went to Pima [local community college] and most of them didn't even graduate from high school. I am going to graduate from college and a big part of that will be these classes and the project.

Another student, Yolanda Martinez, a freshman at Pima Community College said:

> I have thought I wasn't going to graduate from Cerro because I didn't think I was going to pass the AIMS. This project, the classes and you guys helped me to pass the AIMS. If I didn't take these classes or have you, Lopez and Kim (what is her title) for my teachers I would not be graduating. My life would be different, next year I am going to Pima and then to the U of A. I remember one day you were talking about the other class (cohort one) and how they said the project saved their lives. That made me think, I was wondering if that could be true. I didn't think you were lying, but I was not sure how this would be for me. For me and Jairo this class did change our lives. It helped us to understand that... Nos vemos el mundo con ojos critico, you know like you say we see the world different. We see ourselves different, I see myself different, and I believe different things. Now I believe that things can change, I can help change things, and the things can be just. It hard, and sometimes it feels like too much, but I know Mexicanos or Chicanos can be strong, we do have power, and unless we speak up and take action nothing will change. I am going to help.

These testimonials, in combination with the surveys and the test scores, lead us to conclude that there is a strong correlation between students' participation in the SJEP and the development of an academic identity, increases in academic proficiency, and improvement on the AIMS test.

The Future of Critically Compassionate Intellectualism: Toward Antiracist Pedagogy

Racism is the sum of programs, practices, institutions, and structures deeply rooted within social life that maintain a social and racial order wherein White domination is perpetuated and intensified (Delgado & Stefancic, 2001; Ladson-Billings & Tate, 1995; Pine & Hilliard, 1990). In schools, racism is reflected in entrenched policies, practices, biased curricula, and standardized testing. The ideology of racism creates, maintains, and justifies the continual production of injustice, inequality, and oppression. These products lead to the creation of a system of ignorance wherein Chicanas/os and other people of color are exploited and oppressed (Solórzano & Yosso, 2000). Social scientists have effectively documented the fact that these conditions benefit White students and victimize students of color (Haymes, 2003; Pine & Hilliard, 1990; Yosso, 2002).

Omi and Winant (1994) state, "The hallmark of [American] history has been racism.... The U.S. has confronted each racially defined minority with a unique form of despotism and degradation" (p. 1). The American reality for people of color has been one of inequality, injustice, and exclusion. These experiences include, but are not limited to, slavery, invasion, occupation, colonization, genocide, and extermination. Given the racist reality of America's past, present, and likely future, it is essential that critically compassionate intellectualism confronts racism as something that is not a mistake, not periodic, not irrational, but rather is a social construction that maintains White domination and advances injustices and inequalities experienced by people of color in the United States (Delgado & Stefancic, 1997).

Given that racist structures hinder the intellectual development of students of color, a critically compassionate intellectualism must deal with racism head on. The future of critically compassionate intellectualism must include its evolution into a comprehensive antiracist praxis that addresses all forms of racism in American society, including White privilege, White supremacy, language and cultural oppression, uneven resource distribution, differential treatment, and disparities in academic outcomes.

The success of critically compassionate intellectualism in the SJEP allows us to say with certainty that educational programs are most effective for Chicana/o students when they prepare them to confront and overcome racism. Anything short of this will perpetuate patterns of educational marginalization for Chicana/o youth.

Note

1. Augmentation is a process whereby students can use successful academic coursework to add points to their AIMS scores.

References

Boger, J. C. (2002). *Education's "perfect storm?" Racial resegregation, "high stakes" testing, and school inequities: The case of North Carolina.* Paper presented at The Resegregation of Southern Schools? A Crucial Moment in the History (and the Future) of Public Schooling in America Conference, Chapel Hill, NC.

Cammarota, J., & Romero, A. (2006). A critically compassionate pedagogy for Latino youth. *Latino Studies, 4,* 305–312.

Darder, A. (2002). *Reinventing Paulo Freire: A pedagogy of love.* Boulder, CO: Westview Press.

Delgado, R., & Stefancic, J. (1997). *Must we defend Nazis? Hate speech, pornography, and the new first amendment.* New York: New York University Press.

Delgado, R., & Stefancic, J. (2001). *Critical race theory: An introduction.* New York: New York University Press.

Delgado Bernal, D. (2002). Critical race theory, Latino critical theory, and critical raced-gendered epistemologies: Recognizing student of color as holders and creators of knowledge. *Qualitative Inquiry, 8*(1), 105–126.

Delgado-Gaitan, C., & Trueba, E. (1988). *School and society: Learning content through culture.* New York: Praeger.

Delgado-Gaitan, C. (1990). *Literacy for empowerment: The role of parents in children's education.* New York: Falmer.

Freire, P. (1970). *Education for critical consciousness.* New York: Continuum.

Freire, P. (1994). *Pedagogy of the oppressed.* New York: Continuum. (Original work published 1967)

Freire. P (1998). *The Paulo Freire Reader* (A. Freire, A. Maria, & D. Macedo, Eds.). New York: Continuum.

Gramsci, A. (1992). *Prison notebooks.* New York: Columbia University Press.

Guillaumin, C. (1992). Une societé en ordre: De quelques-unes des former d'ideologie raciste [Social order: Some of the foundations of racist ideology]. *Sociologies' et Sociétés, 24*(2), 13–23.

Haney Lopez, I. (2003). *Racism on trial: The Chicano fight for justice.* Cambridge, MA and London: Belknap Press of Harvard University Press.

Haymes, S. (2003). Toward a pedagogy of place for black urban struggle. In S. May (Ed.), *Critical multiculturalism: Rethinking multicultural and antiracist education* (pp. 42–76). London and Philadelphia: Falmer Press.

Ladson-Billings, G., & Tate, W., IV (1995). Toward a critical race theory of education. *Teachers College Record, 97*(1), 47–63

McLaren, P. (1994). *Life in schools: An introduction to critical pedagogy in the foundations of education.* White Plains, NY: Longman.

Noddings, N. (1984). *Caring: A feminine approach to ethics and moral education.* Berkeley: University of California Press.

Noddings, N. (1992). *The challenge to care in schools: An alternative approach to education.* New York: Teachers College Press.

Omi, M., & Winant, H. (1994). *Racial formation in the United States.* New York: Routledge.

Pine, G., & Hilliard, A. (1990). Rx for racism: Imperative for America's schools. *Phi Delta Kappan, 71*(8), 593–600.

Reardon, S. F., & Galindo, C. (2002). *Do high-stakes tests affect students' decisions to drop out of school? Evidence from NELS* (Working Paper). University Park, PA: Pennsylvania State University, Population Research Institute.

Rumberger, R. (1991). Chicano dropouts: A review of research and policy issues. In R. Valencia (Ed.), *Chicano school failure and success: Research and policy agenda for the 1990s* (pp. 64–89). New York: Falmer.

Rumberger, R. (1995). Dropping out of middle school: A multilevel analysis of students and schools. *American Educational Research Journal, 32,* 583–625.

Rumberger, R., & Rodriques, G. M. (2002). Chicano dropouts: An update of research and policy issues. In R. Valencia (Ed.), *Chicano school failure and success: Past, present, and future.* (pp. 118–130). London: Routledge/Falner.

Solórzano, D., & Ornelas, A. (2002). A critical race analysis of advanced placement classes: A case of educational inequality. *Journal of Latinos & Education, 1*(4), 215–229.

Solórzano, D., & Ornelas, A. (2004, February/March). A critical race analysis of Latina/o and African American advanced placement enrollment in public high schools. *High School Journal, 87*(3), 15–26.

Solórzano, D., & Yosso, T. (2000). Toward a critical race theory of Latina and Chicano education. In C. Tejada, C. Martinez, & Z. Leonardo (Eds.), *Charting new terrains: Latina(o) education* (pp. 35–65). Cresskill, NJ: Hampton Press.

Tippeconnic, J. W. (2003). *The use of academic achievement tests and measurements with American Indian and Alaska native students.* Washington, D.C.: Institute of Education Sciences.

Valencia, R. (1997). *The evolution of deficit thinking: Educational thought and practice.* Washington, D.C.: Falmer.

Valencia, R. (2002). *Chicano school failure and success: Past, present, and future.* London, New York: RoutledgeFalmer.

Valenzuela, A. (1999). *Subtractive schooling: US-Mexican youth and the politics of caring.* Albany: State University of New York Press.

Valenzuela A. (Ed.). (2005). *Leaving children behind: Why Texas-style accountability fails Latino youth.* Albany, NY: SUNY Press.

Yosso, T. (2002). Toward a critical race curriculum. *Equity and Excellence in Education, 35*(2), 93–107.

30 Social Justice Youth Media

Elisabeth Soep, Belia Mayeno Saavedra,
and Nishat Kurwa

Like any radio feature, this story contains multiple characters, and the full version, the one we really want to tell, won't fit the prescribed format. It's a story about stories—narratives young people produce for broadcast on local and national media outlets, through an organization called Youth Radio in Oakland, California. Youth Radio was founded in 1992 by broadcast journalist Ellin O'Leary. Students are recruited from economically abandoned, heavily tracked, and rapidly resegregating public schools. They come to Youth Radio after school to write commentaries and news features, produce and DJ music segments, host panel discussions and community events, and create videos and web content. They arrive at Youth Radio on a Wednesday and, by Friday of that same week, they're on the air for a live public radio show, *Youth in Control*. After six months of introductory and advanced classes, students can move into paid positions in Youth Radio's various departments. At any given time, approximately 35 young people ages 14 to 24 are on payroll. Their teachers are peers who've graduated from the program, and their circle of collaborators, producers, and editors includes adult media professionals attached to some of the world's most influential broadcast outlets.

We focus here on a single Youth Radio story produced in 2004, called *Picturing War*, reported by Belia Mayeno Saavedra. In the story, young U.S. Marines respond to reports that detainees were being tortured at Abu Ghraib prison in Iraq. The reports featured photographs from the prison that pictured male Iraqi detainees, many naked, simulating sex acts, piled on top of one another, and attached to leashes and wires, with U.S. soldiers looking on, sometimes posing, sometimes with cameras. At the time, debates in the United States raged over who deserved blame for the acts pictured in those photographs—young prison guards or their higher-ups. It seemed like an ideal Youth Radio story—especially because we had already developed relationships with several young vets through our ongoing *Reflections on Return from Iraq* series, exploring the experiences of young military personnel adjusting to life back home. National Public Radio's Morning Edition aired *Picturing War* in April of 2004.

In this chapter, Belia Mayeno Saavedra, the story's reporter, is joined by two Youth Radio producers, News Director Nishat Kurwa, and Education Director/Senior Producer Elisabeth (Lissa) Soep. Belia and Nishat are both Youth Radio graduates who participated as high school students, and Lissa started working at the organization as a doctoral student in 1999. Through our positions in Youth Radio's newsroom, we mentor young people through every stage of story production, and there's one bit of advice we give again and again. Express yourself conversationally. Don't write the story like an English class essay. Tell it like you're talking to a friend. In this chapter, we aim to follow our own advice. We offer this story about the relationship between youth media production and social justice as a conversation among the three of us. Two years after *Picturing War* aired, we dug out the old interview logs, booked our own studio, and recorded our reflections on what it was like to coproduce that story. We discussed moments that stood out to us as especially challenging and important, and we considered how this story relates to Youth Radio's larger mission and model.

Why This Story?

There are stories in Youth Radio's archive that have a much more straightforward relationship to social justice than *Picturing War*. A young man describes his deportation to Mexico immediately upon release from a U.S. prison. Young producers use slam poetry and street-corner interviews to comment on the effects of Oakland's rising homicide rate. A high school senior contemplates whether to grow out her wavy hair or get it locked before heading off to a predominantly white college.

Each of these stories would seem a perfect candidate for a chapter like this one, examining how young people and adults practice social justice by making media. And yet stories like these make it too easy for us to side-step some uncomfortable but critical questions that reveal why social justice education is so hard (see Fleetwood, 2005).[1] And so we chose a story that continues to challenge us, several years after broadcast. As the world struggled to make sense of the prison abuse scandal at Abu Ghraib, Youth Radio sought out perspectives from young people who had lived and fought their way through the war in Iraq. But the views they shared were disturbing and difficult to hear. What does it take, this story made us ask, to engage "youth voice" in a meaningful way, when some youth voices are shaped by structures and policies that destroy young people's lives?

Framing the Story

When the Abu Ghraib scandal hit, Youth Radio had already produced a commentary for NPR with a young Marine who went to UC Riverside. During that process, he told us about two college classmates who, like him, had recently returned from war, and he also talked about the archives of digital photographs they had taken throughout their deployments and circulated among fellow troops, family members, and friends. We contacted this young Marine, to see if he and his fellow vets could help us understand how widespread detainee torture was, what they saw as the root causes and ripple effects of the abuse, and how military personnel throughout Iraq were using digital photography to document their deployments.

Like any Youth Radio story, we approached this one with an audience in mind. Youth Radio has multiple broadcast partnerships, ranging from web radio shows with maybe 10 or 20 listeners to massive international outlets like iTunes and NPR, with its 27 million listeners. This story was an obvious contender for national broadcast, and Belia Mayeno Saavedra, the reporter, had filed several stories over the years for NPR. At the time, she occupied a dual status at Youth Radio. At the age of 23, her primary role by that point was as an associate producer and peer educator teaching younger students in the program. But occasionally she continued to report stories for the newsroom—especially stories like *Picturing War*, which required midday interviews and an incredibly fast turnaround time, two factors not hospitable to high school schedules.

Lissa and Belia headed down to UC Riverside to hook up with the three young Marines we hoped to feature in the story. We sat around a table in one of the dorms and started talking about what had gone down at Abu Ghraib. At the time, the Bush Administration was framing the detainee abuse as an unauthorized aberration carried out by a handful of misguided soldiers. There were many in the United States and elsewhere who balked at this argument, countering that torture is an inevitable byproduct of an imperialist war (Puar, 2005). While the Marines we interviewed went to great lengths to distance themselves from the young Abu Ghraib prison guards, they seemed to endorse arguments that framed the guards' actions as anything but exceptional, in what became the opening scene of Belia's story.

Picturing War, by Belia Mayeno Saavedra

Part 1

Belia: A year ago, Former Marine reservist Ed [last name] returned from Iraq, after taking part in the U.S. invasion. Now he's back at the University of California at Riverside, a 26-year-old art student. Here's what he says about the stories of prison abuse coming out of Iraq.

Ed: It's like Chris Rock said, I wouldn't do it, but I understand. I'm not saying I approve of it, but I understand the conditions that led up to them doing it.

Belia: Ed's buddy Luis [last name], a shy 21-year-old, resumed his freshman year at Riverside when he returned from Iraq a year ago.
(Sound comes up... bit of quiet laughter, Luis: "Oh yeah, I remember that, but you know what happened...")

Belia: Luis was a field radio operator for a logistics unit in Iraq.... He says sometimes they had to round up Iraqis and detain them. And that when you see someone as your enemy, and you feel like they're going to kill you, you start to look at them with hate. At some point, Luis says, you're going to lose your judgment, even if it's just for a minute or two. And it's up to you to know how to manage it, he says. He tells this story.

Luis: I think we picked up prisoners, and put barbed wire around them. I recall one of the corporals offering me an opportunity to go in there and abuse some of them. I think it was Corporal—

G.: No, don't name him.

Female Voice: No. Don't.

G.: Don't name him.

Luis: He said, Hey, [last name], look, there's one of those Iraqi guys. Wanna go in there and kick 'em? I thought about it for a split second, but then I guess my judgment came into play, and I said, that's not the right thing to do. Just go back to my five ton, and if I'm called upon to do something, gotta do my job.

Belia: When you ask him about what happened at Abu Graib, Luis says the soldiers responsible should be treated harshly, possibly including higher ups. But like his buddy Ed, Luis says the abuses don't really surprise him.

Luis: People see it on TV, they're not living it, so they find it surprising, "Oh, this is obscene." But then, you tell me one thing that happens during war that is not obscene.

Just weeks after the first pictures of prison torture came out, here the young Marines said that detainees were encircled behind barbed wire throughout Iraq, not only inside walled prisons, and that prisoner abuse was by no means isolated to Abu Ghraib or carried out by low-level renegades. At many points, Belia's interview with the three young Marines felt more like a casual conversation, flitting among references to politics, masturbation, danger, fear, adventure, tourism, and popular culture. Belia sensed that the young Marines talked differently about what they had done in Iraq with her than they would have with an adult reporter:

Belia: In terms of how he (Ed) explained it, and how open he felt, and the language he used to express—like the stuff about Chris Rock—that came out of me being in a similar age group, with a similar idiom, similar experience with pop culture. I was in between Luis and Ed, in terms of age. Clearly Lissa, you had a lot of assets and skills that I didn't have, but inversely, I had some skills that I could offer in terms of my age and way of talking to them, and that's a model for how people can be teachers and students at the same time.

Lissa: Right. And it's not about, we as adults are mentors and the young people are apprentices, which in itself is progressive compared to a didactic instructor and passive student. But it really is more than that. As you're saying, Belia, if an adult went in and did that story alone, we could not have pulled it off. Likewise, if a young person had done that story alone, they couldn't have pulled it off. So we depend on each other in nuanced ways. Now that can be misinterpreted to mean the kids have access and the adults have the analysis and wisdom. It's not just that the young people use the same slang. It goes back to knowing how to ask the right questions, and knowing how to frame this whole set of issues and from where to build an analysis.

Belia: One of the things I noted looking over the log is that my job wasn't simply to act as an inside "youth" agent to get the story. There's a section of the tape that didn't air. They (the Marines) spent all this time talking about how there was a whole lot of masturbation going on in Iraq, all the porn they brought...I think they were trying to scandalize us. I don't know what your friendships are like, Lissa, but I was used to being around dudes that age who were constantly talking about that stuff. And I said, "Okay, you guys are saying it's really hypocritical they don't let you have porn there, but everybody has it. How does that link to other things, like the torture, that really happen, but nobody acknowledges?" And I think that because my initial response to them was rooted in an understanding of, "Okay they're trying to scandalize us, but I get it, and it's not something that's freaking me out," and I could then move on to make a connection between that and the larger conversation about hidden behavior in the military.

In the midst of that conversation, Luis was just about to reveal the name of the corporal who reportedly invited him to "go in there" and kick "one of those Iraqi guys." G., his fellow Marine, stopped him: "No, don't name him." No surprise there—Luis was still on active duty. But that male voice is not the only one you hear if you listen closely to this moment in the story. You can also pick up a female voice—Lissa's. She, too, is stopping him from naming names.

Lissa: I had to listen back to the tape a couple times to believe I had actually done that. We decided to keep that full bit of tape in the final story, unedited, so listeners could hear Luis being stopped from outing his corporal by name. But that doesn't explain why I did what I did in the first place, and to be honest, I'm still trying to figure that out myself. I think I was afraid that as soon as Luis implicated someone else by name, he might get scared and pull out. I'd seen that happen before. And also, in other *Reflections on Return* stories, we'd had soldiers decide that they needed approval to participate, and then the public affairs office killed the story.

Still, Lissa inadvertently helped protect a corporal who reportedly invited Iraqi detainee abuse. Maybe she thought she was somehow protecting Luis himself. In Youth Radio's production model, we approach young people as agents whose voices should be amplified, not vulnerable populations in need of our benevolent protection. But if the media production process itself creates risk for young participants—whether they are sources, as was the case here, or reporters like Belia—that complicates the question of responsibility. If an organization's mission is to "serve" and "promote" youth voice, to what extent do we need to anticipate and prevent negative consequences for young people drawn into any given media story? It goes back to Youth Radio's larger media production methodology:

Nishat: Our first consideration is, what is the potential effect of doing this story on this particular student, whether on their personal life, their family, their community. And then beyond that, then, the second level is the media literacy, where it's like, I'm gonna try to find a way for you to do the story you want to do, but not without asking you to reflect on and question your motivations, and what informs your perspective. I try to communicate to the student, if you put something like this out in the world, the audience might not perceive it in the way you meant it. I ask them, what will bring a fuller view to show that you're not blindly writing this opinionated story, without acknowledging that there might be people who feel differently? I just try to provide a framework for critical thought with any story that a young person wants to do.

Sometimes, that critical thought can revolve around a single word. After all, in a four minute radio story, every utterance counts. In preparing this story, we struggled to find the right adjective to describe the photographs Ed brought back from Iraq. In the popular discourse, "horrifying" seemed to be the word of choice to characterize the Abu Ghraib photos. Ed described his own pictures in the second half of Belia's story:

Picturing War, by Belia Mayeno Saavedra

Part 2

(Bring up computer sound...)

Belia: And as we've seen over the past weeks, the graphic images of war are not only televised, they're digitized. After Ed was called to Iraq, one of the first things he did was stock up on camera supplies.

Ed: We spent a lot of time patrolling, driving around, so I'd whip out the camera, real quick, take a picture. I mean, we wouldn't be taking out the camera when we were doing anything mission critical or important. But I mean, half the time we spent on the road, we got to see a lot of Iraq.... But I just took the pictures as a record of my travels, I guess. Because me going to Iraq, going to war and back, was the only real adventure I'll ever have. (laugh)

Belia: These reservists say, when they come home from Iraq, it's normal for them to scan their pictures onto a computer, e-mail them around, or burn them onto a CD. It's a digital yearbook of a military unit's shared experience in Iraq. Ed put *his* photos on the web.

(Bring up sound...Ed, "Here's—okay, we're gonna go in, and it says—and here's a link to it...")

Belia: Some of the pictures are just pretty shots of the desert, and the ruins in Babylon. But many of them are graphic shots of charred dead bodies, or truncated torsos lying in the sand. The photos show us *what* he saw, and the captions he added tell us *how* he saw it. Ed and his fellow Marines nicknamed one burnt corpse "Mr. Crispy."

Ed: When I first saw dead bodies, I was like, I've never seen dead bodies like that before, so out of curiosity, I whipped out the camera and stuff. I was in the car, we were still driving the whole time, I didn't get out and say, oh, Kodak moment. Just gave it to my driver, my guy on top, the gunner, take pictures, basically what it was, you find your photo ops when you can....

Belia: Ed points to another shot, one of Americans in camouflage giving candy to Iraqi children, and his caption reads "Hey kids, here's some candy. Now make sure you don't sneak up on me tonight or I'll have to shoot you."
(*Bring up sound:* Ed, "So here's a picture of blown up tanks, big old statue of AK 47s on an Iraqi flag, that's pretty good...")

Belia: Ed's grisly photos and captions are disturbing. And what may have started as a personal travelogue is now part of a growing stream of images soldiers are bringing home, changing the way the world sees this war.

Even with the deadline of a morning broadcast bearing down on us, it probably took more than an hour to compose the story's final paragraph.

Belia: The thing that was hard for us was, that they (the Marines) did have responsibility for the words they used, the pictures they put up, the way they behaved. But in the interview, Ed kept saying, "You have to love the war, because if you don't love the war, you're gonna go crazy." And I kept hearing that over and over in my head as I was looking at the things he did and his website, and the ways he talked about the war. His perspective was disturbing, it did disturb us. But the use of "horrifying," something about that felt very removed, like, "Oh, look at that horrible thing that person is doing over there that I have nothing to do with." Because even though I didn't send him to Iraq, in the larger scheme of things, living as an American citizen and benefiting in certain ways from the military–industrial complex and all the "isms" and crazy things we're all pulled into just by virtue of where we live ànd who we are, I think that "horrifying," and other words that were more removed or felt more distant were maybe a little too passive. But we did have to choose something that showed [that] it's not like this was okay with us.

Implications for Social Justice Education

As evident in this last comment from Belia, a whole lot of process hides behind youth media products—moments of fraught deliberation about how to tell a meaningful story that has the potential to upset assumptions and raise generative questions. As we noted in the opening paragraphs of this chapter, *Picturing War* is by no means the ultimate shining example of a Youth Radio story with a clean social justice message. Some of the ideas conveyed in this story conform to rather than challenge systems and institutions that make life more dangerous for young people who are already marginalized. And yet, at Youth Radio, we are not in the business of soliciting stories we agree with. The ones that challenge our own personal politics are among the most important we can produce:

Belia: The reason why those stories are so important is because they really illuminate the fact that our multiple identities allow us many different degrees of power and privilege. A lot of times, the way people understand things is, we're the marginalized ones, and those people over here are the ones who have power. But when somebody comes out and they are marginalized in all these ways, like, "I'm Black from a working class family," but they also say, "and I'm homophobic, and this is why," admitting that they feel this way is very, very enriching to the dialogue about homophobia or racism. If we were just to say, "You can't say that, that's not the right thing to say," if we didn't let that get out, we can't really tackle these issues in any substantive way, because nobody's acknowledging and being accountable for the fact that they hold these views.

Our goal, of course, is not to allow young people to express whatever biases they hold, and then leave it at that. Difficult stories are valuable not only because they articulate the complex relationships among our different identities, but also because they provide a valuable opportunity to perform perhaps the most crucial work of the social justice educator—the cocreation of critical thinking in a reflexive environment.

And yet, as important as the learning environment can be for the individuals involved, the product is what circulates through the world in a very concrete sense. In the old days, a radio story like *Picturing War* essentially evaporated after it aired. Now, Belia, Luis, and Ed will likely come across this story years and years from now—and so might their friends, parents, love interests, teachers, and potential employers. As educators, then, we carry serious responsibility for helping young people feel confident about what they want to put out into the world, knowing that it won't go away. That said, we also have the opportunity to recontextualize our products, to consider what more there is to say. At Youth Radio, our website now routinely features converged media "build-outs" with photographs; links to research, resources, and referrals; and even free curriculum ideas as part of our "Teach Youth Radio" initiative to integrate high quality youth-produced content into school- and community-based classrooms.[2] While we can never control how an audience hears the voices we broadcast, we can and do continually revisit stories like *Picturing War* long after they've aired. These stories keep us thinking, forcing us sometimes to clarify and transform our own instincts, as producers and educators, based on opportunities like this one, to question ourselves.[3]

Notes

1. In developing the concept of "social justice youth media," we are indebted to Ginwright and Cammarota (2002).
2. Please see http://www.youthradio.org/fourthr/index.shtml.
3. Our discussion of the making of this story draws from a chapter to appear in Soep and Chávez, forthcoming.

References

Fleetwood, N. (2005). Authenticating practices: Producing realness, performing youth. In. S. Maira & E. Soep (Eds.), *Youthscapes: The popular, the national, the global* (pp. 155–172). Philadelphia: University of Pennsylvania Press.

Ginwright, S., & Cammarota, J. (2002). New terrain in youth development: The promise of a social justice approach. *Social Justice, 29*(4), 82–96.

Puar, J. (2005). On torture: Abu Ghraib. *Radical History Review, 93,* 13–38.

Soep, E., & Chávez, V. (forthcoming). *Drop that knowledge: Youth radio stories.* Berkeley: University of California Press.

Youth Radio. (n.d.). http://www.youthradio.org/fourthr/index.shtml

31 The 5 E's of Emancipatory Pedagogy

The Rehumanizing Approach to Teaching and Learning with Inner-City Youth

Laurence Tan

Framing the Problem: The Dehumanization of Teaching and Learning

Many people, especially parents, see schools as the grand equalizer to inequality, yet the reality is that the institution of schooling has contributed to social stratification. Public education is in a state of crisis, particularly the education system in poor communities that are permeated by racism, poverty, violence, and oppression. In many urban centers, like the South Los Angeles elementary school where I teach, schools respond to the societal and community issues with dehumanizing control mechanisms aimed at both students and teachers. These mechanisms of control include, but are not limited to, school uniforms, zero tolerance discipline policies, scripted curriculum programs, and excessive emphasis on standardized testing. All these forms of school control are done in the vain pursuit of academic achievement on standardized tests on which schools like mine have historically failed. In turn, many administrators and teachers end up using student performance on tests to discuss student potential and to develop strategic plans with the primary goal of making the greatest numerical gains on the next set of tests.

The dehumanizing elements of our current education system have a ripple effect on teachers and students. Teachers become disenchanted with teaching and struggle to maneuver through the bureaucracies of teaching. Students begin to resist explicitly by disobeying and challenging school employees, as well as implicitly by disengaging and not caring about school (Freire, 2003; Giroux, 2001; Means & Knapp, 1991). As an educator I cannot overlook these conditions and their impacts. Understanding the realities of teaching in this day and age, through readings, critically analyzing historical trends, and more importantly, through my experiences with urban education as a student myself and now as a teacher, I am intentional about approaching my profession in a way that is often at odds with the current norms of the institution of school.

To respond to the dehumanizing conditions in urban schools and communities, I have committed myself to develop pedagogical practices aimed at preparing students to change those conditions. These kinds of students will emerge from our classrooms only if we are willing to develop emancipatory educational programs that use counterhegemonic pedagogies. In an attempt to describe my efforts at developing this sort of practice, this chapter will describe core elements of my educational philosophy, provide examples of those elements in my practice, and narrate the impact this approach has had on the achievement and critical consciousness of my students.

The Five E's in Emancipatory Education

The success I have experienced in the classroom can be largely attributed to my efforts to develop a humanizing pedagogy, one which values caring for students and the pursuit of social change. This pedagogy has always been guided by my experience as an immigrant urban youth of color that grew up participating in many aspects of urban youth culture (hip hop, graffiti art, and video games). It has also been deeply influenced by critical educational theories and my own notions of social justice. To describe the approach that has resulted from these various influences, I created the "5 E's of Emancipatory Education": engage, educate (enable), experience (through exposure), empower (through knowledge of self), and enact. These five concepts guide my teaching, curriculum design, and community building. Everything I do as a teacher, inside and outside of the classroom, naturally encompasses them.

Engage: Building Trust, Respect, and Buy-In with Students, Families, and Communities

Engagement is a crucial component in building trust, respect and "buy-in" with students and families. In order for engagement to occur, I recognize that I must truly know the realities faced by my students, their families, and their communities. Although I am committed to engaging each of the aforementioned groups, the limits of this chapter will only permit me to focus on my use of strategies that incorporate youth culture and critical media literacy to engage students. By utilizing youth culture, students are often positioned as content experts and I am repositioned as a learner. When used effectively, this can help balance the power structure in the classroom.

Youth culture and media are powerful tools of engagement because there is a "pervasiveness of media in the lives of urban youth" (Duncan-Andrade, 2004). Cornell West (2004) argues that media provides young people with "distractive amusement and saturates them with pleasurable sedatives that steer them away from engagement with issues of peace and justice...[and] also leaves them ill equipped to deal with the spiritual malnutrition that awaits them after their endless pursuit of pleasure" (pp. 174–175). While many of my colleagues might use a popular cartoon character in a mathematical word problem, or have students write stories using youth culture centered topics, I try to use popular culture to develop critical thinking in addition to traditional academic skills. This development of critical skills helps students deconstruct the desensitization and apathy, while not devaluing their engagement in the media.

Regardless of how we might feel as educators about youth culture, we must realize that young people are heavily invested and influenced by it. Oftentimes what students are learning in the media is in direct conflict with the lessons they receive in school, which can lead to internal and external conflicts with teachers and the curriculum. We can mitigate these conflicts, and even capitalize on them, when we use the media in our classrooms to help students make sense of the sensory stimuli with which they are bombarded. As Morrell (2004) states, teachers must invest themselves in an understanding of youth culture through the eyes of the students they represent:

> [I]t is important to attempt to understand why certain elements of popular culture, such as films, television shows, songs, or magazines might be appealing to young people. The voyage of understanding and empathizing with students enough to make sense of their interests and out-of-school literacy practices will demand that teachers exit their comfort zone and see, as much as possible, through the eyes of the students. (p. 118)

Creating culturally responsive curriculum (Gay, 2000) through the use of youth culture (Duncan-Andrade, 2004; Morrell, 2004) is a central element of my classroom efforts to engage students toward a journey of critical intellectualism and action.

Educate: Developing Academic and Critical Competencies

The buy-in that results from engaging curriculum encourages active participation from both the student and the teacher. This participation is critically important for the development of academic and critical competencies, which ultimately allow students to become self-sufficient in their endeavors. To increase personal and academic self-sufficiency in students, educators must develop two sets of skills in students: (1) the foundational skills for academic competencies, and (2) the critical skills that allow students to analyze society and what they can do to make it more democratic and socially just.

In my first year of teaching I naively believed that as long as my students were critically aware of social issues, then the foundational academic skills would fall into place. As an example, when I first taught writing I focused so much on valuing student voice that I neglected to effectively teach writing structures and conventions. So, although my students were able to identify and write about their experiences with injustice, they were not equipped with the foundational writing skills that would allow them to truly convey their messages. I came to realize that it was not good enough for me to see the brilliance of my students when others would not see it because they lacked the basic skills I was supposed to be teaching them. My students had to become solid academically and critically in order to create changes for themselves and for others.

I learned from my mistakes and spent my second year focusing on using writing as a tool to become an effective communicator. We talked about how frustrating it was when others did not understand us and consequently misinterpreted our message when we spoke. We transferred those experiences to how we wrote. Writing became a way to express truth, instead of an assignment for a grade. The standard curriculum provided the frameworks for developing basic writing skills and genres (expository, persuasive, and narrative). In order to avoid over overcompensating on writing conventions at the expense of engagement and critical thinking, I often modified the writing prompt provided by the mandated curriculum. These modifications allowed students to write on things that were meaningful to them, like a letter to the principal making suggestions for changes in the school. As another example, I replaced the standard research project on astronomy, with a research project on marginalized people of color who have impacted communities similar to those of my students. Those biographies and lessons about struggle and resistance were then reaffirmed by providing students with firsthand experiences at demonstrations and rallies for issues of justice in the community.

Education has to be about merging the foundational academic skills that allow students to be self-sufficient with critical thinking and problem solving skills. Freire (2003) states that "[t]o surmount the situation of oppression, people must first critically recognize its causes, so that through transforming action they can create a new situation, one which makes possible the pursuit of a fuller humanity" (p. 47). In order for that to occur, the students must be equipped with the critical skills to identify oppression and its causes and have access to the institutional skills to create the "new situation" he references. I am not ashamed to admit that it took some time to learn the importance of combining these two skill sets. That growth, much like the growth that happens with students, came through experience, mistakes, self-reflection, and a commitment to getting better every day.

Experience: From Exposure to Lived Experience

People that are victimized by oppressive conditions can end up perpetuating those conditions because they have not been able to conceptualize a different model. To counter this, my teaching exposes students to different models of social possibility that exist beyond the classroom, school, and local community. Many teachers do this by scheduling a field trip to a university or by promoting college as the ultimate option for individual liberation. The problem with this as the model for social change is that it can lead students to believe that success lies exclusively outside of their neighborhood. Fanon (2004) refers to this as the paradigm of the "colonized intellectual," and cautions that this person will likely "forget the very purpose of the struggle—the defeat of colonialism" (p. 13).

Exposure to college and other mainstream opportunities can be a great tool for opening doors for students that are traditionally denied access to those options. However, simply exposing students to possibilities falls short of helping students develop into people who will take up the challenge of creating social change. To develop students that will challenge the status quo, critical educators must also go beyond reading, talking, and learning about the protests and demonstrations of the Civil Rights era (which falls in line with simple exposure). Students must also have the opportunity to act on what they learn by engaging in social action, which might include participating in social actions that promote peace, police accountability, immigrant rights, workers' rights, or educational justice. This helps to connect past struggles they learn about in class with the current issues, allowing them to understand the systemic elements that have allowed conditions of injustice to persist throughout history.

I will not tell my students what battles to take up, but I will use my position to expose them to the historical and present-day structures that have led to conditions of inequality. Indeed, Freire (2003) argues that the struggle for liberation among the oppressed cannot happen without this awareness:

> In order for the oppressed to be able to wage the struggle for their liberation, they must perceive the reality of oppression not as a closed world from which there is no exit, but as a limiting situation which they can transform. (p. 47)

My students are not too young to experience injustice, poverty, violence, inequity, and hardship, yet they lack the words, tools, and experience with taking action to know how to respond to those oppressive conditions. Therefore, a major part of my pedagogy is a commitment to exposing students to ideas and methods for social action, despite their young age, so that they can contemplate more constructive ways to direct the angst which comes from their experiences growing up in South Los Angeles.

As their teacher, my role is "to help students learn how to problem-pose or 'problematize' their reality, in order to critique it and discover new ways to both individually and collectively work to change their world" (Darder, 2002, p. 33). I can also play the role of "institutional agent" (Stanton-Salazar, 1997) helping my students navigate through the system, exposing them to various forms of cultural capital, social networks, and outlets for their thoughts and actions. By experiencing these various possibilities students start to realize that there are numerous ways to channel themselves toward hope and change.

The opportunity to act on a developing critical consciousness is imperative for the creation and maintenance of hope among students. Whether through their spoken words, writing, organizing community events, or just entering spaces with people to dialogue, students must come to realize their importance and power as youth. Giroux (2001) argues for the development of this consciousness in adults, and I have extended this same sensibility to much younger people:

> [T]he task of radical educators must be organized around establishing the ideological and material conditions that would enable men and women from oppressed classes to claim their own voices. This would enable the development of a critical discourse of the wider society. (p. 116)

Through the development of academic and critical skills students develop the capacity to name, contextualize, analyze, and act upon their oppression. As this realization of the problems and of their potential agency develops, the students become more transformative in their intellectualism. They become empowered with a set of skills that allow them to navigate within the current system knowing that they are trying to get into a position to change it.

Empowerment of Self: Knowing That There Is Hope

To develop students' knowledge of self and sense of self-worth, my pedagogy focuses heavily on communicating to my students that they are genuinely accepted and cared for in our class. It is easy for students living through the oppressive conditions in urban centers to hate themselves and their dispositions. Recently, I had a student that would regularly break down in class saying that she hated her life and herself. She would constantly ask out loud why life was so tough on her. As the year progressed, she learned that she was not alone in those thoughts and that there were actual societal forces causing her to feel those frustrations. This awareness that her suffering was not her own fault led her to change her self-perception, as well as her feelings about her family and community. She came to the realization that she could be active in her community, supporting causes that would directly impact the conditions that frustrated her. She became particularly adept at utilizing her literacy skills to express herself through poetry, and through that medium she also learned to express the love she had for her family, home, community, and more importantly, herself. Ultimately, her budding knowledge of self has motivated her to become active in community organizing and artistic creations that positively influence the community. In the end, success as an urban educator is heavily dependent on one's ability to help students realize their worth and potential agency. Fanon (2004) suggests that when oppressed peoples develop a strong sense of self, "they discover their humanity, they begin to sharpen their weapons to secure its victory" (p. 8). Once they make that discovery they are ready for emancipatory action.

Enact: What Are You Going to Do About It?

Ultimately, the goal is to have students use the critical academic skills that they develop in the classroom to create change outside of the classroom. Without action the cycle of inequity and injustice continues. Freire (2003) argues that oppressed people, like my students and their families, "will not gain this liberation by chance but through the praxis of their quest for it, through their recognition of the necessity to fight for it" (p. 45). Freire's argument is that liberation will come from the people who are oppressed, which suggests that as an educator of oppressed people my pedagogy and practice should be preparation to participate in that struggle for freedom. Part of my responsibility in that endeavor is to provide opportunities for students to realize, through participation, the possibility that their efforts can change the circumstances in which they live. By taking part in opportunities to use the skills we have developed in class to participate in action for social change, students become increasingly aware of their potential to use their education to positively impact the community.

These grounded experiences with direct action do not always have to equate to frontline community organizing and action. More subtle ways students can enact their critical sensibilities can come from them shifting from consumers of knowledge to producers of knowledge. For example, one of our final class projects requires students to create their own documentaries. In this act, the students become producers by utilizing their skills to create share narratives that are often not heard. In addition to these kinds of production activities, students' are given opportunities to organize a variety of direct actions for social justice. It is these actions, ones that my students directly control, that are the most worthwhile. These include petitions, letter writing, and demonstrations in support of issues that they felt need to be addressed. A number of my students have also participated in rallies and used the media to show solidarity and support for issues that directly affect them and their communities.

Maneuvering Through the Madness: The 5 E's in a Mandated Scripted Curriculum

The mandates of a scripted curriculum can make it seem difficult to implement pedagogy that deviates from district standards. It is possible to implement this type of pedagogy, but it requires determination, planning, and the courage to try (Friere, 1998). The key is to find the crossover between one's expectations as a social justice educator and the expectations of the district or the state. District and state mandates tend to be broad and interpretable, which makes some room for social justice pedagogy. In my case, I weave in "what I have to do" with "what I know is the right thing to do." This allows my students to be successful in traditional ways, but also as social justice scholars.

To demonstrate how I balance these sometimes competing agendas, the following section outlines an Open Court unit that meets both sets of standards (state and social justice). Open Court is a district mandated, scripted reading program broken into six-week units. The success of the program is measured by mandatory district assessments at the end of each unit. In 5th grade, the theme for the third unit is "Heritage." The stories in the unit revolve around cultures and traditions that are mostly foreign to my students. Over the course of the unit, students are expected to create a "Heritage" album/scrapbook and produce a written narrative about a tradition in their family. Taking those expectations, as well as the state required literacy standards, I modify the unit to the following projects:

- a poetry unit
- a cultural zine
- biographies on people of color that positively influenced/affected communities of color
- ethnographic documentaries
- the first stages of a community research project (see appendix 1).

The five E's of emancipatory pedagogy are present in the projects and activities outlined throughout the unit. Students become engaged in various ways, including through popular media, technology, and other culturally engaging materials. These materials are used to develop academic, critical, and technological competencies as students go through various processes to complete the projects that range from writing samples to the creation of a video on DVD. The unit concludes with formal presentations from students, which gives them a chance to showcase what they have learned and teach others. The presentations and multimedia products provide a critical investigation of the historical conditions people of color have faced and the heritage of resistance and activism that are part of those histories. These outcomes are supported, at least tacitly, from my administration because this approach produces some of the best test scores in the school. This is an important point to make because many teachers committed to social justice feel that they must choose between pursuing traditional measures of success and social justice pedagogy. My experience suggests that we can do both.

Outcomes: Measuring Your Effectiveness

In both the language arts and math sections of the California Standards Test (CST), my students consistently meet or exceed state averages (see appendix 2 for recent examples). Across the board, my students' averages were above the local district's averages. Due to the fact that achievement is so low in our local district, our administration developed a protocol where they asked teachers to create and track strategies for increasing the test scores of select students throughout the year. This process began in the first few days of the school year, before the students returned, by having our entire teaching staff examine test scores from the previous year. We were trained how to select a few students who were in a "strategic range" that would allow us to move them up quickly and gain the most points on their test scores. The process required teachers to submit names of the students so that progress could be monitored by the principal and the district director.

This approach to raising a school's test scores is not a phenomenon isolated to my school. In fact, it is an approach used throughout the city of Los Angeles to demonstrate that schools serving poor children are getting "better." What it actually demonstrates is the dehumanization of students and teachers. Nevertheless, this is the system that teachers have to confront. One way we can confront these conditions is to understand that test score gains are not mutually exclusive of social justice pedagogy. In an effort to show that this is possible, I have also included the state test scores for the target students in my class this past year (see Table 31.1).

It is important to understand that this sampling is based on a criterion set by my school and district. According to district policies, I am a successful teacher because most of my students experienced similar gains. At some level, it is this level of success on standardized measures that has allowed me to continue to operate with relative flexibility in my pedagogy and curriculum. This is an important point to make in our discussions of what

Table 31.1 Sampling of Target Students CST Test Scores Before and During My Class

Student	Language arts		Math	
	Before	*During*	*Before*	*During*
V.R.	320B	386P	394P	476A
D.A.	374P	390A	386P	557A
M.C.	239FBB	319B	264BB	294BB

A = Advanced; FBB = Far Below Basic; BB = Below Basic; B = Basic;
P = Proficient
*This sampling shows academic growth over time, but more importantly, doing so by implementing an Emancipatory Pedagogy and developing critical thinking and action skills.

it means to be a social justice educator. We can be critical of the excessive focus on testing, but we must also realize that our students can perform on those tests. The testing craze certainly reduces some of our freedom as educators, but it should not preclude us from developing pedagogical strategies that incorporate elements of critical thinking and social justice. We can raise test scores without seeing students as numbers on a statistical sheet.

It is important to point out that I do not use test scores as the sole measure of my effectiveness or my students' progress. To illustrate some of the other measures I use, I will share a brief story about Gero, who struggled to complete the work assigned in my class. He would take inordinate amounts of time in everything he did, oftentimes holding back the rest of the class an extra 30 to 60 minutes during our assessment periods. Regardless of what the assignment was, how challenging or easy, he would not be successful at completing it.

Gero was particularly opposed to writing, until we got to our poetry unit, and then something clicked. He had finally found a form of literacy where he felt he could express himself. When we got to our next district mandated writing assessment, one where students were responsible for writing a persuasive essay on slavery, I saw a breakthrough for him. I told the class that they were allowed to choose their own persuasive topic (war, community issues, immigration issues, etc.) as long as it followed the guidelines for a persuasive essay. Fifteen minutes after giving the assessment, Gero dropped a sheet of paper down on my desk. After I asked him what he put on my desk, he responded that he had placed his "prewrite" there and that he was now ready to write the "real" essay. As he went back to his seat I began to read this prewrite only to discover a lengthy and complex poem on immigration. The following is the poem he wrote:

Immigration Issues by Gero

Now I know that there's a lot of people in the United States
and a lot of those people are the ones that hate
being mistreated and a lot of those people are being looked at with disgrace
and a lot of those people are being spit in their face
its a hard case
of misjudgement

Get to know us before you get to throw us out
Now how the [heck] are you going to say this is your land
I demand that you do the research and know that we were here first
And you came to us with thirst
Of land so we gave you a hand and you bit it
Now do you get it
This was our land till the Spaniards came and stole it
And then they sold it
to you and you already knew that we were here
But your people didn't care they just wanted us out so they threw us out
Anywhere

But we came back crossing a lot of struggles and tossing our selves over the border
in order to have a better life and we came with a dream
and back then it used to seem that that dream was unreachable

some immigrants were able to accomplish their dream even in
the toughest times when it seemed that they couldn't
They wouldn't give up
They didn't give a [crap]
They wouldn't stop they would keep going and take the lead
and that's how we all succeed when we're in need
So when you're in need don't give up
Don't give a [crap]
Just keep going and you'll be showing the whole world
that you can and then they'll understand to treat us better
whenever they see us
Maybe one little kid will want to be us
Now do the research and know that we were here first
and you came to us with thirst
of land and we gave you a hand and you bit it
Now do you get it?

Gero's growth was not immediately quantifiable on state test scores. What I learned from him was that the use of an emancipatory pedagogy does not always yield immediate results. Sometimes it takes time for young people to find their voice in such a way that they feel they can use the concepts that we are learning in the class. What is different about an emancipatory pedagogy and a test-driven pedagogy is that the former does not give up on students. It is a persistent pedagogy that aims to strike a balance between challenging and supporting students until they find the room to express their thoughts and ideas. When Gero finally found his voice, he also found the confidence to tackle other forms of writing like the persuasive essay, on which he eventually did quite well. Gero has continued writing poetry and now enjoys performing his pieces at conferences and for community organizations.

Longitudinal Impacts: The Watts Youth Collective

Perhaps the most significant outcome of an emancipatory pedagogy is the longstanding relationships that develop between students and myself, and between the students themselves. As one example, some of my former students created an organization called the Watts Youth Collective (WYC). It started when several of my former students became involved in community organizations around Los Angeles after leaving my class. When those organizations started moving in directions that did not include the interests of my students, they decided to create their own organization. They formed the WYC, a collective of youth who would meet in the homes of the various members to work on projects that would positively affect their community.

Of primary concern to them has been the growing tension between "Black and Brown" community members. As a response, they created documentaries to dispel the stereotypes that plague their community, challenging viewers to get to know their neighborhood before passing judgment or being influenced by the media's interpretation of their community. They have also challenged themselves to educate each other by confronting their own personal issues and prejudices. As a supporter, I aided by setting up workshops on racism, college access, and provided the resources to conduct their projects (video cameras, editing assistance, transportation, etc). As an educator, I cannot take credit for these transformative behaviors, but I can see the lessons that we shared in class are developing and spreading from my former students to other young people in the community. The following poem from Jojo suggests that the pedagogy he experienced in our fifth grade class shaped his current commitments to the WYC and social change in the community:

> 5th grade...the grade where my eyes were opened
> where I got to see the real history of Watts
> the real history of America
> where I have learned to fight
> for freedom, justice, and my rights...
> ...I believe we can solve anything
> so lets unite as we have
> united in our Watts Youth Collective
> and to know you can make change...in unity is a feeling of
> POWER...JUSTICE... FREEDOM...and LIBERATION.

These shifts in consciousness should not be held as separate objectives from traditional academic achievement because they are the precursors for social change in the community.

Another outcome of the WYC has been the development of a mentorship model, where students return to my classroom each year to act as mentors to my current students. This continues the cycle of community building as my current students get to hear stories and get advice from my former students. These mentoring relationships reinforce the importance of the things being taught in the class, and reassure my current students that our relationship will extend well beyond this one year of their schooling. For my former students, this mentorship model allows them to feel that they have a safe space to continue learning, building, and organizing. Since its inception in 2004, the WYC has gone from six members to its current membership of 30 students, ranging in age from 7th to 12th grade.

Parting Thoughts

My story is not unique. I have seen and heard about effective urban teachers from all over the nation, from a variety of backgrounds (single parents, people with families, teachers not from the "hood"). These counternarratives are important stories of success that occur in spite of the repressiveness of the conditions in urban schools. We must continue to share these stories because they offer a glimpse of hope for a better educational system and world. We must also be careful about how we tell these stories because successful teachers in urban schools are often looked upon as exceptional, something that cannot become the norm. It is my hope that by sharing stories of our pedagogy and its impact, that others will be inspired to generate their own counternarratives. Such a series of counternarratives can help us connect to one another, while also building momentum for changing the perspectives of our colleagues in this effort to achieve educational justice. The challenge for an emancipatory education for all children is arduous, but through critical hope and continually challenging ourselves to do better, we can find the fortitude to stay the course.

References

Darder, A. (2002). *Reinventing Paulo Freire: A pedagogy of love*. Boulder, CO: Westview Press.

Duncan-Andrade, J. (2004). Your best friend or your worst enemy: Youth popular culture, pedagogy, and curriculum in urban classrooms. *The Review of Education, Pedagogy, and Cultural Studies, 26,* 313–337.

Fanon, F. (2004). *Wretched of the earth.* New York: Grove Press.

Freire, P. (2003). *Pedagogy of the oppressed.* New York: Continuum.

Gay, G. (2000). *Culturally responsive teaching: Theory, research, and practice.* New York: Teachers College Press.

Giroux, H. (2001). *Theory and resistance in education: Toward a pedagogy for the opposition.* Westport, CT: Bergin & Garvey.

Means, B., & Knapp, M.S. (1991). Introduction: Rethinking teaching for disadvantaged students. In B. Means, C. Chelemer & M. S. Knapp (Eds.), *Teaching advanced skills to at-risk students: Views from research and practice* (pp. 2–22). San Francisco: Jossey-Bass.

Morrell, E. (2004). *Linking literacy and popular culture: Finding connections for lifelong learning.* Norwood, MA: Christopher-Gordon.

Stanton-Salazar, R. (1997). A social capital framework for understanding socialization of racial minority children and youth. *Harvard Educational Review, 67*(1), 1–40.

Stanton-Salazar, R. (2001). *Manufacturing hope and despair: The school and kin support networks of U.S. Mexican youth.* New York: Teachers College Press.

West, C. (2004). *Democracy matters: Winning the fight against imperialism.* New York: Penguin Press.

Appendix 31.1

The following is a chart that shows the activities we conduct in our class and the description of those activities during our Open Court Unit 3: Heritage section.

Activity	Description
Biography of a Person of Color who positively affected Communities of Color	This research project challenged students to look at an overshadowed and underrepresented person whose contributions created a positive legacy for others to follow. The Students had to research using the internet and books, delving into very challenging expository texts. More importantly, they began to understand a broader sense of a true People's History, struggles of a people for a people, as well as connecting their legacies to their lives and current experiences. They are also supposed to connect the group work those individuals They become the expert and are responsible for teaching others (in the class and in the school) through their PowerPoint presentations.
Poetry Unit	While we are learning about cultures, heritage, traditions, and legacies we get into poetry as an option to deliver their narratives in a different way. This expressive writing allows students to write about them, their families, community, and issues affecting them. It gives the students another way to give a voice to the voiceless. They analyze poetry (Tupac's "The Rose that Grew from Concrete," Maya Angelou's "I Rise", and Sandra Cisneros' "House on Mango Street", etc...), learn to deconstruct the messages and the context that created these messages, and transform their learning by creating and performing their own poems.
Zines	The students learn about the power of images and design through this medium. They partake in a history of zines and show how some can be used to inspire and create change. They then work collaboratively to create a Community/Cultural Zine of their own on a topic of their choosing (some have done zines on cultural hairstyles, foods, games, etc...). This project allows the students to transcend consumers of media like magazines by becoming producers of positive and community oriented media.

(*continued*)

Appendix 31.1 Continued

Ethnographic Documentaries	With the whole unit revolving around stories on culture and traditions, the students are required to produce a narrative. The students are responsible for taking that narrative beyond pencil and paper towards a more visual aspect. They conduct interviews of their families and share stories. They take those stories and create a 3-5 minute documentary that they learn to put together. Using basic video editing skills which I teach a few students who are responsible for teaching the rest of the class, the students make their crude videos and show them to the school and community. Some of the stories that they have captured revolve around coming to this country and the struggles their families have encountered.
Community Research and Action Project	During this unit, the students tie in Math by conducting a Community Research Project. As a class they generate a couple questions for which to conduct their research ("What are the problems that affect the community?" and "What are the problems that affect the school?"). Once they spend some time interviewing family, neighbors, and community members they bring back the data and design an action project to help address the results of their research. Their action project is carried through oftentimes resulting in a Community Action Night where they have presented their research findings and solutions to the community, created teatro/theatre skits, and written poetry to inform and influence the community. They have also used their research to present at places like UCLA.

Appendix 31.2 California Standards Test (CST) '06

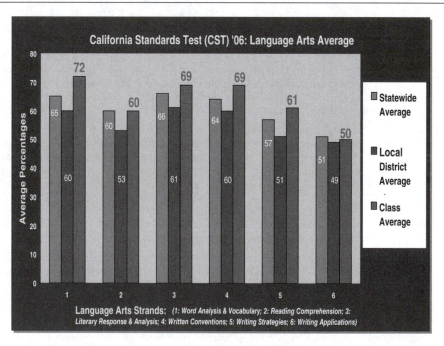

32 *Real Talk*[1]

Transformative English Teaching and Urban Youth

Patrick Camangian

Before I began teaching high school English in South Los Angeles, I did not know the extent to which youth of color in urban communities were underserved and disenfranchised. After seven years, I have witnessed a crisis in urban youth culture. Too many young people continue to use violence as a means for solving their problems, internalize their resentment of familial and social conditions that are unjust, and uncritically consume and reproduce dispositions that value what they have and how they look (external), over what they think and how they feel (internal). The realities of these struggles for my students made sitting in professional development sessions difficult because there we were trained to emphasize "state-approved" standardized curriculums which foreground academic content and assessment tools that overlooked the material conditions and needs of our students. In an effort to transform my English teaching I sought to develop pedagogy that would be responsive to the confusion and anger I saw in my students. I did this by drawing from the very text that was most relevant to them, their lived experiences. Transformative education, in this case, meant increasing students' level of academic engagement and achievement, and critically shifting students' perceptions about themselves and the world around them.

When I was a student in the Los Angeles public schools, I experienced irrelevant classroom curriculum and poorly trained, impersonal teachers. These learning conditions were major contributors to my own sense of academic marginalization that ultimately resulted in my dropping out of high school. A full generation later, I was seeing the same substandard state of urban schooling and similar self-defeating responses from students. The resulting academic failure of many students has spawned increasing questions about whether there might be a "school to prison pipeline" facing many urban youth (Christle, Jovilette, & Nelson, 2005; Wald & Losen, 2003). Recognizing the consequences of unengaging curriculum and pedagogy from my own school experiences, and my fortune in having avoided the school to prison pipeline, I set out to become the type of teacher I wished I had when I was in high school.

By writing about my use of critical pedagogy, I hope to contribute to the growing body of work that challenges the deficit-thinking perspective that views the realities and struggles of urban youth as apart from, if not irrelevant to, a rigorous academic program (see Solórzano & Yosso, 2004). I adhere to the research that suggests teachers should draw from their students' rich funds of prior knowledge to increase academic engagement (Moll, Amanti, Neff, & Gonzalez, 1992). Teaching at a predominantly Black (70%) and Latino (30%) high school with a statewide rank in the lowest percentile, I came into the 2004 to 2005 school year drawing from social theory to create a critical and culturally relevant English composition curriculum to mediate the frustrations youth were having in their communities.

Teaching Their Word and Their World

By identifying the needs of learners as relative to their social contexts, Freire and Macedo (1987) frame literacy as a correlating practice of "reading the word and the world." They argue that young people first learn to decipher the universe around them before accessing and developing the language to describe it. To effectively develop the literacy capacity of our students, Freire and Macedo state, "I have always insisted that words used in organizing a literacy program come from what I call the 'word universe' of people who are learning, expressing their actual language, their anxieties, fears, demands, and dreams..." (p. 35). In other words, to effectively engage youth in the process of literacy development, teachers must scaffold student learning from the contexts from which their youth draw their notions of reality. Recognizing the agency of teachers to accomplish this task, Freire and Mecedo claim:

> Educators have to invent and create methods in which they maximize the limited space for change that is available to them. They need to use their students' cultural universe as points of departure, enabling students to recognize themselves as possessing a specific and important cultural identity...[this] requires respect and legitimation of students' discourses... which are different but never inferior. (p. 127)

In essence, Freire and Macedo remind us that our literacy teaching practices must remain dynamic, culturally relevant, and responsive to the destabilizing social conditions that undermine a critical democracy. The role of a critical literacy teacher is to help students become socially conscious of how they construct their realities. Thus, the critical literacy teacher must facilitate a learning space that allows students to reknow what they think they already know.

Taking Freire and Macedo at their word, I found it necessary to develop in my students a set of active communication skills and literacy practices to help prepare them for transcending and transforming the struggles they experience in their everyday lives. Instead of overlooking the interrelated conditions that shaped my students' worldviews, I developed curricular units that were inclusive of both school content and students' lived experiences. The course reported on here was one semester in length and was divided into four curriculum units, following the format of the school district's pacing plan: narrative, expository, research, and persuasive. For each unit, students adhered to the following three steps:

1. Choose a topic drawing from their lived experience to interrogate an immediate condition that shaped many of the lives of local youth.
2. Write an essay that analyzes that condition as it relates to them personally, but also as it relates to the interests of their community.
3. Prepare and deliver a speech based on their essay that shares the analysis with the class.

What follows are a series of excerpts taken from student presentations during these four units in a detracked 12th grade expository composition class. Interviews with students are used toward the end of the chapter to discuss the impact of the pedagogy on student identities. Both the student work and the interviews offer glimpses into a classroom community built with the explicit intent of using literacy to develop knowledge-of-self and critical social consciousness among urban youth. To select the student samples used here, I first sorted students into quartiles using grade point averages to rank their academic achievement prior to being in my class. Next, I randomly selected class work from two students that appeared in the bottom achievement quartile, students that normally would be categorized as "at risk" and "low achievers."

Auto-Ethnography Unit: When Students Have a Chance for *"Real Talk"*

To culminate the narrative unit that began the semester, students shared critical auto-ethnographies, which reflected their development of narratives that examined significant personal experiences in relation to larger cultural phenomenon. Students were expected to write and perform a narrative essay that fulfilled the following three requirements: (1) examined the oppressive effects of society; (2) connected their experiences with other oppressed social groups; and (3) offered a strategy for social change (see Carey-Webb, 2001).

The opportunity for the young people in the class to examine, write, and speak about their lived experiences proved a powerful way to begin the semester. It was particularly engaging for those students whose voices had been marginalized in some of their other classrooms. As one example of this intensified engagement among students, we can look at what happened with Max.[1] Max had never fared well in his English classes, but he had chosen to invest himself in this assignment and volunteered to be one of the first students to read his essay. When his turn came to read, he handed me his narrative essay, strolled to the front of the classroom, pulled his long white t-shirt upwards off of his black sweat pants, and rubbed his hands together. The following excerpt is the introduction to the auto-ethnography that he recited, entitled "Our Past, My Present, Our Future":

> To destroy one's culture is to destroy one's past, present, and future. And to destroy one's past, present, and future is to destroy one's soul. Now my culture is known as the African-American culture. It's known as the Black. It's known as the Negro. It's known as the man who has to depend on another man for survival. The woman that must depend upon welfare. The teenage boy and girl that must depend upon athletics. The infant boy or girl that must depend upon child support. But, I don't see us as a dependent race. I see us as the mended race. From the almost ended race to the fourteenth amendment race. Ironically, I learned to understand our purpose through being a victim of cultural genocide by committing the worst crime of all, cultural homicide.

Max's introduction is thick with repetition and parallel structures, which he uses to frame the historical complexity, collective spirit, and immortality of African-American people. He draws from varied African experiences in the United States to point to the struggles and strengths of a devalued and self-determined people. Varying his descriptors from African-American, Black, and Negro subtly captures the multiple ways the group has been publicly defined and denied access to equitable citizenship. Max cites the different ways African peoples have survived their marginalization using both concrete and abstract understandings of their lived experiences. Equally as impressive is the fact that Max performed this introduction from memory, which coupled with his effective use of expressions, gestures, and tones, made for a powerful opening to his presentation. The quality of the writing and the effort Max put forth in preparing for his presentation are both indicative of the power of these personalized kinds of writing assignments to engage young people that are typically silenced in classrooms.

After his powerful introduction, Max went on to tell the class a story from his experiences with Black-on-Black violence in South Los Angeles. He used this assignment to embrace the opportunity to accept responsibility for participating in self-defeating Black agency. Through this critical self-reflection, he examined how his actions affected his cultural community as a whole, emerging with a narrative of hope:

> I felt as if I was empty now. It felt like something just happened where I betrayed my God, I betrayed my beliefs, I betrayed everything. I betrayed my mother. I let down my father. I let down myself. I let down my people…. Our time is now. A new era is in place…. We have finally been given the opportunity to be respected as human beings in this society, on this earth, in this day…. This opportunity shall and will be applied by us, all of us, to one day redeem our ancestors the true compensation that they deserve.

Over the next several days, 28 more students in Max's class performed their auto-ethnographies. Afterwards, we had a class discussion to allow students to make connections across the various stories in order to construct a collective narrative. The similarities of the students' experiences were eye opening for many of the students that had shared classrooms with these peers but had never had the opportunity to hear about their lives. This allowed students to see how their individual experiences were not isolated, but part of a phenomenon larger than themselves. The strength of the individual stories, combined with the developing collective narrative of the class, set the tone for even more powerful writing and public speaking as the school year progressed. In Max's case, his future writing focused on gender-relationships in the school and local youth community, the urgency of Black activism, and the importance of African-American history in the context of a school where it was largely ignored.

Expository Unit: An Exposé on Gang Life

Another student, Marcus, shared an auto-ethnography that explored the connection between being deprived of one's father, youth violence, and gang membership in the context of his neighborhood. Marcus's work in the second unit is a good example of how students were able to build on the personalized elements of the auto-ethnography for their future writing. During the expository writing unit, Marcus conducted a micro-ethnography on his street gang, and wrote about their socially constructed notions of masculinity (see Morrell, 2004, for curricular ideas). His writing challenges the idea that gangs are altogether destructive and delinquent by humanizing gang members and exploring the complexity of the circumstances that lead them to join the gang.

When it came time for Marcus to read his expository piece, he stood with his chest out in the front of class, sporting a navy colored Seattle Mariners[2] hat and a royal blue t-shirt. He delivered a presentation he called "Masculinity in the Hood" using Power Point slides. On one slide, titled "Organized Unity," he discussed themes of community and culture in the gang, attempting to humanize the young men in his gang as strong and intelligent:

> If organized correctly, to White Supremacists, a gang member's mind-set is a threat. A gang's physical power is still extremely organized, with determination, but is exercised on the wrong enemy. Their physical power has a lot of potential cuz' they fight for what they want…. Gangs are also strong because of their unity…. We lose a homie like every other week, but it makes us stronger. That's what brings us together…. We some soldiers. We some [young men] you don't come across everyday…. It's just some direction we need so that, instead, it's justice that would bring us together….

Marcus also talked the class through the sometimes harmful contradictions of gang life, particularly the pride and the drive for power that inform many of the gang's activities that can result in violence within community:

> Power plays an important role in the hood. Since we don't have [power] as a community, it is often misused in many ways and results in self-destruction.... The roots of this power can be summed up as pride.... A gang-member's pride is a very fragile thing; it's real easy to be hurt.... Like, if you say the wrong thing to us, we'll go off. That's just pride. We don't like to be disrespected...

Marcus concluded his analysis by describing the complex ways young men in the gang construct their collective identity of manhood:

> To conclude, when you think of masculinity in the hood, there's both negative and positive aspects.... As far as I've seen in the negative, I seen somebody get shot and die over it. [There's also a lot of] betrayal, like I showed. And a lot of time [is] wasted.... But there are also positive effects...a lot of [young men] get a sense of identity out of it. You get a sense of who you could become...and what you're capable of doing. But, people always want to look at how we construct masculinity in the hood as just a negative aspect.... So, basically, it's both positive and negative, and it's like now that my knowledge is changing, I'm more interested in using the positive aspects....

Marcus's presentation was special for its academic adherence, but even more significant because of who the speaker was, the topic, and the context in which he shared this work. Marcus's open membership and relatively high rank as a younger member in a notorious local street gang marked him as an intimidating young man whose academic history was one of extreme disengagement. The opportunity afforded him by these writing assignments and the open and critical culture of the class, allowed him to use his gang membership to conduct an "insider" study that validated those experiences as worthy of academic discussion. At the same time, critically analyzing his lifestyle and those of this peers challenged him to be critical of the practices of the gang. Marcus's presentation made for profound levels of organic intellectualism (Gramsci, 1971), as he engaged in study that helped him better understand himself and his social group, without having to denounce that group as altogether evil. The class also benefited from hearing Marcus's presentation because he helped to present the complexities of a group of people whose behaviors are often reduced in analysis to simple self-destruction. The limits of this chapter do not permit a broader analysis of the work produced in these literature units, but the small samples from Max and Marcus hint at the academic capacity of urban youth when they are permitted and challenged to think critically about their lived experience, and then supported to format their knowledge into genres that fit with the expectations of academic contexts.

Poetry as a Persuasive Literary Device

Part of the final unit on persuasive writing used poetry to tap into the fact that many urban youth find spoken word poetry as a viable outlet to articulate the obstacles presented by their social realities (see Jocson, 2005, for curricular ideas). Students drew from prior writing assignments to create and perform poems reflecting their work over the semester. Since their poems were to be informed by the analytical lens we had been developing, students were expected to offer complex interpretations of their often underexamined realities. Max had found his stride in the class after the auto-ethnography unit and had emerged as one of the finest speakers in the group. As in the first unit, he volunteered to be one of the first presenters. To begin his reading, he lowered his black Pittsburgh Pirates baseball hat over his face and performed an interpretation of the complex issues facing urban Black communities today:

"We've Got a Gun to Our Head"

> It's got a gun to my head
> Its fingers are on the trigger
> Its words are the bullets that's breakin me down
> I'm tryin' to figure
> If my history is my Teflon[3]
> Then why should I bet on the teachings of Uncle Tom's step-son....

The multilayered meaning of "its" in this poem used personification and figure of speech to place accountability for the conditions of violence and inequality on two groups; members of the community that participate in their own self-destruction ("we've got a gun to our head") and the nefarious history of miseducation that has confronted African Americans in schools ("the teachings of Uncle Tom's step-son"). The main character in Max's poem was meant to represent African Americans as a group who are threatened by death from two sides: from members of their own community and from Eurocentric descriptions of Black history.

Max used a similar critical sociohistorical critique in this second poem, which he entitled "Historical Property":

> Why can't we make straight our place?
> Stop jokin' around and make straight our face
> So they don't degrade and delay our race
> So they don't make haste and delay our pace
> 1492 is when they lied to you
> When they tried to sneak by the truth
> But it wasn't just the West Indies
> Not just the Caribbean
> Cause South Africa was rewired too
> Now it's 2005 and it's we who do it
> The red or the bluest
> Who are you shootin'?

Here Max used a number of literary devices (repetition, rhyme, assonance, and consonance) to emphasize key ideas of social responsibility throughout the poem. He connected the colonial domination of people of color (referencing 1492) to modern day street gangs (Bloods ["red"] and Crips ["blue"]) to describe a holocaust-like condition for Black communities in 2005.

A couple of days later, Marcus performed one of his poems. In it, Marcus analyzed the role of psychological violence in the schooling process he experienced in South Los Angeles. "The title of this poem is, Weapons of Mass Destruction," he said, smirking at me as he began reading:

I'm trapped in this system
That's constructed much like this dope game
LAUSD
Havin' me hooked to their cocaine teaching
And drug paraphernalia textbooks
Cuz' school is the most dangerous place I've been
Where the ones we trust to teach us
Are incarcerating our minds
And demonstrating social reproduction
I return from my blind abduction
With weapons of mass destruction
Blue Chucks, S dome, white T, blue khakis
And a bomb education are my Teflon

The power of this poem was not so much in its form, content, or delivery, but more in the credibility that Marcus had amongst his peers in the class to make this kind of critique of school. His poem expressed a disdain for urban schools and a celebration of street sensibilities. This was important because gangs were often the targets of derision from school officials and Marcus was someone that was no longer perceived as someone with an uncritical allegiance to street life. Thus, the poem becomes a commentary on the relationship between an ineffective school system and the choice to join a street gang. Marcus's peers understood his desire to tell the truth about schools and the potential of young gang members seeking to educate themselves even when that was not expected of them.

Transformed Lives

If we can adapt the academic literacy skills students are expected to learn so that they are relevant to the lives of young people, then we will be more likely to get the classroom engagement that will result in increased achievement. The use of traditional academic writing standards to draw out the personal stories of young people is a strategy that has led many students to shift from participating in self-defeating behaviors into more transformative actions in their lives (Solorzano & Delgado Bernal, 2001). In individual interviews at the end of the semester students described the processes of critical thinking, writing, and speaking in the class as an enjoyable process of self-improvement. They contrasted this to other English classes where they felt that these skills were academic chores. As one example, Max made the following comment during his interview: "When [our class] first started touching into the critical teaching, it was fun because we actually touched into our own lives. Things that really, really affect us."

The impact that this had on Max's academic engagement and achievement was extraordinary. Although course grades are clearly subjective measures of academic growth (as are test scores), Table 32.1 clearly reflects a shift in Max's investment in his English class once he entered our expository composition class. He rarely missed a day, was a stellar

Table 32.1

Course	Eng 9A	Eng 9B	Eng 10A	Eng 10B	American Literature (11A)	Contemporary Composition (11B)	Expository Composition (12A)
Grade	F	F	F	F	F	Not enrolled	A

Table 32.2

Course	Eng 9A	Eng 9B	Eng 10A	Eng 10B	American Literature (11A)	Contemporary Composition (11B)	Expository Composition (12A)
Grade	C	C	D	D	C	B	A

contributor to classroom activities, and completed virtually every assignment with attention to detail and rigor.

Marcus's improvement in English courses was not as stark, but his growth over time in my classes was impressive. He enrolled in my 11th grade American literature class in the Fall semester. He enrolled quite late in the semester because he had just been released from the California Youth Authority, but he was able to keep up with the work in the class and earned a "C" grade. From there he showed steady improvement, earning a "B" in the second semester of his 11th grade year, and eventually joining Max as on of the top students in the 12th grade expository composition class (see Table 32.2).

This approach to literacy instruction was not just effective with Max and Marcus. In comparison to the rest of the English department, students found much more success in my class. Again, I recognize that the chart below could just reflect vastly different grading policies between myself and my colleagues. In some cases this was true, in others it was not. However, what is undeniable is the level of investment students were willing to make in my classes, both in their attendance and in their work ethic. These are the prerequisite conditions for academic success and they go a long way to explaining the disparity in academic achievement seen in Table 32.3.

In Max's interview, he explained the importance of the value placed on oral communication skills as a primary reason for these higher levels of student engagement in the class:

> Speaking…made us closer because some of my classmates and I found out that we were closer to each other than we thought. Speaking about personal problems. And that made us know them, made us understand them better. Made us closer. It was one of the best feelings I ever had. It was the best class I've ever been into.

In communities where many youth rightfully distrust institutions such as schools, it is critical that we use pedagogical strategies that allow students to form personal relationships with each other and with the teacher. In schools and communities where resources are scarce, it is not hard to imagine how students can come to view one another through the eyes of skepticism and prejudice. To disrupt these divisive conditions, we must develop in youth the tools necessary for articulating and listening to the complexity of each other's humanity, which is often embodied in the way young people perform their personalities and express their interests. In his interview, Marcus makes this very same point:

> We were bonding because we all gave each other a chance to humanize ourselves…let us know each other's stories…after that we looked at each other different. If some-

Table 32.3

	A's	B's	C's	D's	F's
All Eng. Classes (2746 students)	238 / 9%	549 / 20%	684 / 25%	484 / 17%	791 / 29%
My English Class (114 students)	54 / 45%	34 / 29%	23 / 19%	2 / 1.7%	1 / 1%

body look at me like, "oh, he a gang banger." After I told my narrative I humanized myself. "Oh, he's more than a gang banger. That [man's] smart." You feel me? They stopped looking at me as just a gang banger and start looking at me as a smart Black man, which I always want you to look at me as.

It is important to note that an overemphasis on personal struggles in classroom discussions can potentially isolate students from the larger phenomenon facing marginalized people. This is why it is essential to move students' analyses from the personal to the interpersonal, and to address cross-cultural and gendered differences. These connections across difference push the parameters of compassion from individual moments of understanding to collective bonds among students that might otherwise see themselves as different from one another. For Marcus, these connections became clear the more he had the opportunity to connect his own condition to that of his classmates:

Latino struggles, you know, the female struggles that was in the classroom and all that, it was still beautiful because a struggle is a struggle. And whether it's different… when it all boils down to it we're all struggling…. We all in here struggling. I mean I would rather we all in here struggling, you know, helping each other than half of us struggling, half of us not, and they not helping me to get to where they're at.

Max also found the commitment of the class to identify collective struggles empowering:

In this class, it was the whole class. We were together. We were forming a bond. We were forming a unity and this unity formed, it just formed, a big fist that could just knock anything down…. It felt like we had power. We felt like we had power and we know that we had power. And I wish that everyone could understand that having this whole unity in the classroom can roll over to the community and just have the community, you know, together and then we could make [change] happen.

To this point, these pedagogical strategies have been discussed for their importance to my students' curricular engagement and academic achievement. However, they were equally important in the expansion of their interpersonal and cross-cultural relationships. This extension of the range of their relationships came in part as the result of their own identity reformation, which helped them to understand their capacity for critical self-reflection and growth. For instance, Max became more conscious that his actions impact society and that society, including many of its injustices, continue to affect him:

You start opening your mind to all kinds of things. And you start thinking outside the box. You start thinking about other things that you would never, ever think about before…. You start evaluating everything that goes on. You start thinking about, not only am I an African-American young teenage male in this society, period. It's also me, having a positive or negative effect on this society. Me being oppressed. I never thought I was oppressed.

Marcus interpreted this transformative process similarly, but through his own newly constructed reality:

I realized that I was a slave, but I broke those shackles though. I started to look at life critically…. Like, "damn, this [is] crazy. My mind is trapped…. I'm incarcerated mentally...I've got to break free." You just basically opened my eyes, you know, just found out who I was, you know, what I'm about. Really.

It would be disingenuous of me to suggest that every one of my students transformed themselves into change agents in their communities. Some simply wanted to join the work force, others chose to pursue college hoping to escape the community. It is safe to say, though, that every student was challenged to think further than they had before, specifically about issues young people were facing in the communities. It can also be said that a good number of students found a voice in themselves like the one Marcus found. He was able to transfer the survival skills he developed as a gang member to finish high school and move on to begin his college education. He realized that it was necessary for him to change his life, but also to become a force for transformative change in his community:

> Like I told myself, "I'm not about to get caught up in this [trouble] no more. I'm not going to jail. I'm about to use *the game*, I'm about to use the system to win the system. You feel me? I'm about to go to school, and I'm going to stay in *the hood* so I'ma just educate myself. I'ma do this, and I'ma grind here. If I could grind in the hood, then you know for sure I could go to school and grind. Cuz in the hood, it's harder....

He did not find the transition out of street life easy and he continued to participate in gang related activities after high school. However, he became much more conflicted about his role in the community and slowly reduced his affiliation with his old lifestyle. He maintained a job at a local train yard for a couple of years, passed an African-American history class at a local community college, and continues to work toward fulfilling requirements to attend a California State University. He recently moved out of state in order to recreate a life for himself more suitable for a student, away from the local tensions and temptations of his past. We have maintained a friendship and mentored relationship and continue to dialogue about his potential to use those street informed leadership qualities to benefit, instead of compromise, the good of his community.

Max took the semester and summer after our class to retake courses he had failed earlier in high school. Impressed by the quality of his growth, leadership, and academic work in my class, a local California State University accepted him through special admissions. Max has since received his high school diploma and enrolled in a four-year university where he currently holds a 3.0 cumulative grade point average.

Conclusion

Significant modifications were made to the ideology of the course content in order to deal with the social and economic urgencies facing my students. In spite of these changes, the course fulfilled writing and oral convention components for both the 11th and 12th grade California English-language Arts Content Standards. It is important that educators know that they can modify the content of their lessons to reflect the needs of their students and still meet the standards they are expected to teach. There is value in meeting the standards, but the more significant learning outcomes appear when our pedagogy allows students to connect to one another by sharing their familiar struggles. In the case of the class discussed here, this was particularly important because many of the students had no relationship with one another before the class, and some even had antagonistic relationships before the class. As Max noted, the class became a family that modeled for students ways to interact better with one another in their own communities.

When we do not normalize critically relevant pedagogies, we effectively sanction self-defeating ideologies and practices that inhibit individual and collective growth among our students. The process toward self-actualization often begins by articulating the anger and frustration that traps whole communities in vicious cycles of self-destruction. Thus, with pedagogical approaches such as these, we must be willing to embrace the discomfort that may arise when listening to urban youth articulate their interpretations of reality. The willingness on our part to move through these uncomfortable spaces with our students, allows them to develop the analytical and academic skills to better navigate the unjust social conditions they must face. This class taught me that there is a double value to this approach to teaching; it allows young people to develop the academic literacy skills necessary to maneuver through the schooling system, while also arming them with the critical literacy to transform their lives and the lives of others in the community.

Notes

1. "Real talk" is an urban interpretation for terms more simply stated as "honestly" or "to tell you the truth." It is used in the title to privilege honest examinations of local urban phenomenon oftentimes ignored in formal academic contexts. In other words, this article attempts to argue for the inclusion of urban youths' community realities inside of schools that do otherwise.
2. Pseudonyms are used for students.
3. Referred to as an "'S' Dome," the Mariners' logo signifies a local street gang. Though this uniform serves as an unintended visual aid for his presentation, the student is consistently wearing a combination of blue and a corresponding hat as everyday attire. This goes against school sanctioned uniform policies intended to prevent students from open gang affiliated proclamations, but monitoring this is not my priority so long as students participate in intellectual engagement.
4. Referenced repeatedly, "Teflon" is street slang alluding to firearms or bullet-proof vests, sometimes used when describing the need to deflect or deny some sort of attack.

References

Carey-Webb, A. (2001). *Literature and lives: A response-based approach to teaching English.* Urbana, IL: National Council of Teachers of English.

Christle, C. A., Jovilette, K., & Nelson, M. C. (2005). Breaking the school to prison pipeline: Identifying school risk and protective factors for youth delinquency. *Exceptionality, 13*(2), 69–88.

Freire, P., & Macedo, D. (1987). *Literacy: Reading the word and the world.* Westport, CT: Bergin & Garvey.

Gramsci, A. (1971). *Prison notebooks.* New York: International Publishers.

Jocson, K. (2005). "Taking it to the Mic": Pedagogy of June Jordan's poetry for the people and partnership with an urban high school. *English Education, 37*(2), 44–60.

Moll, L., Amanti, C., Neff, D., & Gonzalez, N. (1992). Funds of knowledge for teaching: Using a qualitative approach to connect homes and classrooms. *Theory into Practice, 31,* 132–141.

Morrell, E. (2004). *Becoming critical researchers: Literacy and empowerment for urban youth.* New York: Peter Lang.

Solorzano, D. G., & Delgado Bernal, D. (2001). Transformational resistance through a critical race and Latcrit theory framework: Chicana and Chicano students in an urban context. *Urban Education, 36*(3), 308–342.

Solorzano, D., & Yosso, T. (2004). From racial stereotyping and deficit discourse toward a critical race theory of teacher education. In W. De la Torre, L. Rubalcalva, & B. Cabello (Eds.), *Urban education in America: A critical perspective* (pp. 67–81). Dubuque, IA: Kendall/Hunt.

Wald, J., & Losen, D. (2003). *Defining and redirecting a school-to-prison pipeline.* The Civil Rights Project. Cambridge, MA: Harvard University.

33 Critical Race Theory Meets Participatory Action Research

Creating a Community of Black Youth as Public Intellectuals

A. A. Akom

Introduction

Time, Newsweek, Vogue, Cosmo, and other news and entertainment conglomerates have contributed to the hypervaluation of Whiteness and in doing so have attempted to create a collective memory of Black people as social problems rather than social partners. Movies, TV shows, and print ads romanticize Whiteness, pathologize Blackness and Raza, while rendering Asian and indigenous populations as invisible. In the post-Civil Rights era this has held constant, even during the 1990s and into the 21st century, when a remarkable thing happened: Aspects of youth culture in general, and aspects of White and Asian youth culture in particular, underwent a Black reincarnation via the hip hop aesthetic. Yet through it all, the visible and invisible representations of Whiteness remain quite remarkable; perhaps best symbolized by the "White House" and who occupies it, Disney world's light skinned/mainly blue-eyed "heroes" and "sheroes" (Disney gives creatures blue eyes even when depicting the animal kingdom), Wall Street, or advanced placement classes (Akom, 2001). Collectively these images, representation, and lived experiences have created a world where it "pays" to look (and act) like Snow White or Cinderella—even if your name is Pocahontas.

And yet representations of Whiteness are more than simply products of the corporate imagination (Kelley, 1998). Color-coded public and private spaces signify our country's commitment to what Kozol (2006) refers to as: "Apartheid Schooling in America." Abandoned housing stock, environmental racism, neighborhoods without grocery stores and an overabundance of liquor stores, barbed wire fences, and railroad tracks; stand in stark contrast to green spaces, white picket fences, Whole Foods, and Trader Joe's (Akom, 2006, 2007). However, the most striking element of this human spectacle is the people who occupy these urban and suburban spaces. Prisons and jails are full of Black and Brown bodies whose incarceration has left them plenty of time to contemplate the role that a White supremacist capitalist partriarchical heteronormative society has played in the reproduction of social inequality (Akom, 2004; Torre & Fine, 2007).

In other words, while obscuring unemployment, underemployment, and rising environmental racism, commercial representations of Whiteness powerfully underscore the link between color-coded access to institutional resources and the ways in which the electronic media have become a powerful pedagogical force in shaping the racial imagination of students and teachers with respect to how they view themselves, others, and the larger society. At the same time they highlight the historic development of Whiteness as a commodity, as Du Bois pointed out in his classic *Black Reconstruction* (1935)—skin color privilege advanced the interest of both White elites (materially) and the White working class (psychically) so that "it actually paid to be White." According to Du Bois, "Whiteness yielded a 'public and psychological wage' vital to white workers" (Harris, 1995, p. 325). Specifically, Du Bois discussed how Whites:

Were given public deference...because they were white. They were admitted freely with all classes of white people, to public functions. To public parks...the police were drawn from their ranks, and the courts, dependent on their votes, treated them with...leniency.... Their vote selected public officials, and while this had small effect upon the economic situation, it had great effect on their personal treatment.... White schoolhouses were the best in the community, and conspicuously placed, and they cost anywhere from twice to ten times as much per capita as the colored schools. (pp. 700–701)

Indeed, historically a central mobility strategy for many White teachers lay in their ability to converge "White" and "teacher" in a way that evaded rather than confronted class exploitation, while at the same time, protecting their racial privilege. Although not afforded the same economic and social privileges of the White ruling class, many White teachers reconciled their lower rank in the class hierarchy by erecting an equally virulent racial hierarchy and championing themselves as "not Black" (Harris, 1995, p. 325). By fashioning their American identity as oppositional to the Black "other" Andrew Hacker (1992) and Cheryl Harris (1995) suggest that "the question was not so much "who is white" but, rather, "who may be considered white," for the historical pattern was that various immigrant groups of different ethnic origins were accepted into White identity "shaped around Anglo-American norms" (Hacker, 1992, p. 155; Harris 1995, p. 325). Despite appearing as a choice, evasive and complicated forms of resistance and accommodation such as "passing" painfully illustrate the power of Whiteness in the reproduction of racial hierarchy. Harris explains:

> The decision to pass as white was not a choice, if by that word one means voluntariness or lack of compulsion. The fact of race subordination was coercive, and it circumscribed the liberty to define oneself. Self–determination of identity was not a right for all people but a privilege accorded on the basis of race. (p. 285)

The overarching effect of this hypervaluation of Whiteness, both historically and contemporaneously, has had a powerful effect on public schools, teacher education programs, and the dispositions necessary to effectively teach an increasingly diverse student population. Recognizing skin color privilege as a powerful force that impacts access to institutional resources and privileges requires that we substantially reassess the role of race in the development of political consciousness among urban and suburban youth and the ways in which critical pedagogy shapes oppositional cultures at school and in our communities. More specifically, some of the central challenges that continue to face urban and suburban educators are: How do we integrate a theory of race that ameliorates opportunity gaps in educational space? How do prospective teachers learn to courageously confront differences of race, culture, and language diversity? How do we prepare a disproportionately White teaching force to become more culturally relevant learners and teachers?[1]

The purpose of this essay, then, is to offer some suggestive observations about the ways in which critical race theory can inform a critical race methodology in an effort to foreground the impact of race and racism in all aspects of teacher education (Duncan, 2003; Foster, 1997). The approach I take challenges the ways that critical race theory (CRT) and youth participatory action research (YPAR) have been dichotomized in the literature on race and racism in teacher education (Cammarota & Fine, 2007; Kincheloe, 2004; Smith-Maddox & Solorzano, 2002). In much of this literature critical race theory is depicted, in part, as a form of storytelling; a place to provide words, and valuable insight on racial inequality in America and beyond. However, the theory by itself does not prevent someone from dying, or from the "same old shit happening again and again" as one community expert reported. It is with this sense of reality and purpose that this article attempts to merge CRT with YPAR in an effort to address issues of social justice within a wider framework of self-determination, decolonization, and democratization. Having stated the essential outlines of my argument the rest of the discussion will offer an analysis of the linkages between CRT and YPAR and the ways in which a critical race methodology was used by students of color as a theoretical, methodological, and peda-gogical tool to challenge racism, sexism, and classism in the realm of teacher education and beyond (Duncan, 2002; Parks, 2007; Yosso & Solorzano, 2002).

Critical Race Theory and Education

Over a decade ago, a quiet and important theoretical revolution began in the United States in the study of race and education. In 1995, Gloria Ladson-Billings and William Tate published an article, entitled "Toward a Critical Race Theory of Education," Pub-lished in the *Teachers College Record*. This important article detailed how the intersec-tion of race and property rights could be used to better understand inequities in the American educational system. If we are to locate the origins of the opportunity gap, the authors argued, it is important to examine Cheryl Harris's construct of "Whiteness as property" in the realm of education. For Harris (1993), Whiteness was not solely a dimension of self-identity and personhood, rather skin-color privilege has legal ramifica-tions connected to property rights, class status, and citizenship.

Conceived of in this way, Harris goes on to highlight how one of the key privileges of "Whiteness as property" is the absolute right to exclude "others." Building from her framework, Ladson-Billings and Tate (1995) discuss how the right to exclude has mani-fested in the educational realm. First, the authors argue, exclusion was demonstrated by attempting to deny Blacks access to schooling altogether (Dixon & Rousseau, 2006).[2] Second, it was demonstrated by the creation and maintenance of an apartheid-like edu-cational system under the guise of "separate but equal." More recently, forms of exclu-sion have been demonstrated by the growing insistence on vouchers, public funding of private schools, and schools choice (Dixon & Rousseau, 2006; Savas, 2000).[3] Finally, the absolute right to exclude within schools is demonstrated by the ongoing problem of racial profiling in education—or what is more benignly referred to as tracking—and the rolling back and lack of meaningful enforcement of civil rights gains (Akom, 2001; Darling-Hammond, 1997; Oakes, 1995; Oakes, Muir, & Joseph, 2000).

According to Ladson-Billings and Tate (1995) there are at least five elements that form the basic perspective of CRT in education: (1) the centrality of race and racism and their intersectionality with other forms of subordination; (2) the challenge to dominant ideolo-gies (for example, patriarchy, neutrality, objectivity, colorblindness, and meritocracy); (3) the commitment to social justice and working toward the end of eliminating racial oppression as part of the broader goal of ending all forms of oppression; (4) a transdisci-plinary perspective that values and includes epistemological frameworks from Africana studies, ethnic studies, women's studies, etc.; and (5) the centrality of experiential knowl-edge of people of color.

These five themes are not new; however, collectively they represent a challenge to the existing models of examining racial inequality in education (Solorzano & Yosso, 2002, p. 68). Since the publication of their article, several other scholars have written about the application of CRT to education (Solorzano & Bernal, 2001). However, the linkages between CRT and YPAR as an alternative methodology aimed at creating emancipatory knowledge and schools as liberatory institutions is currently undertheorized (Solorzano & Yosso, 2002). In the following pages I begin to address these empirical oversights.

Theory as Liberatory Practice[4]: Repositioning Students as Subjects and Architects of Research

> Necesitamos teorias (we need theories) that will rewrite history using race, class, gender, and ethnicity as categories of analysis, theories that cross borders, that blur boundaries—new kinds of theories with new theorizing methods.... We are articulating new positions in the "in between," Borderland worlds of ethnic communities and academies...social issues such as race, class, sexual difference are intertwined with the narrative and poetic elements of a text, elements in which theory is embedded. In our mestizaje theories we create new categories for those of us left out or pushed out of existing ones. (p. 26)

Gloria Anzaldua (1987, 1990) challenged us to develop new theories because she was hurting and desperately trying to find a place of her own belonging. Her lived experience of critical thinking, reflecting, and analysis, became a place where she could heal, transform, repair her hurt in an effort to transcend the pain. What I have learned from Gloria Anzaldua, bell hooks, Paulo Freire, and Franz Fanon is that theory can be a place to heal—a place to retrieve ourselves and remake what we are (hooks, 1994).

Freire's work in particular provides us with the foundations for a theory of democratic schooling that is linked to serving the most marginalized groups in our society. His critical praxis starts from the premise that all education is political and thus schools are never neutral institutions (Smith-Maddox & Solorzano, 2002, p. 69).[5] Freire (1967/1970) firmly believed that one of the ways that schools maintain and reproduce the existing social order is by using the "banking method of education." This approach often leads to: (1) students being viewed as passive receptacles waiting for knowledge to be deposited from the teacher; (2) mono-directional pedagogical formats whereby students do not feel their thoughts and ideas are important enough to warrant a two-way dialogue with teachers; (3) "cradle classrooms" in which students are dependent on teachers for the acquisition of knowledge; and (4) students viewing schools as key mechanisms in the reproduction of inequality rather than places where education is seen as a practice of freedom, a place to build critical consciousness, and social mobility (Ginwright & Cammrotta, 2002).

In contrast to the banking method, Freire suggested a method of social inquiry known as the pedagogy of the oppressed—a social praxis where we learn to perceive social, political, and economic contradictions, and to take action against the oppressive elements of reality. At the core of Freire's work was the desire to understand the ways in which *adults* "read" the world's existing political and economic stratifications, as these stratifications organize the system we call education. However, even though Freire's pedagogical techniques revolutionized adult education and literacy programs world wide, absent from Freire's analysis was an explicit commitment to understanding how *young* people "read" existing racial and socioeconomic stratification in the realm of education.

These empirical and theoretical oversights raise a number of questions that need to be explored by critical educators interested in amplifying youth voice, while at the same time, addressing the impact of processes of racialization on educational achievement. For instance, how can youth initiated research be used as a tool to advocate for racial justice in urban and suburban schools? What would a standards-based racially just curriculum look like when informed by racially conscious youth and adults? How does race (in terms of meaning and identity) and merit (in terms of access to institutional resources and privileges) interact in public and educational space in a way that enables White youth and adults to maintain racial privileges without claiming overt racial superiority (Lewis, 2003)?

In order for Freire's message to remain relevant to today, we must reposition students as subjects and architects of research. Enabling youth to deconstruct the material and ideological conditions that oppress them inspires a process of community building and knowledge production. As Freire (1982) eloquently argued, "the silenced are not just incidental to the curiosity of the researcher but are the masters of inquiry into the underlying causes of the events in their world. In this context research becomes a means of moving them beyond silence into a quest to proclaim the world" (p. 34). For example, "Eronne," a 17-year-old Black American student revealed her understanding of race, identity, and what makes an effective teacher:

> The problem here isn't only that the White teachers are racist...I mean...lots of them are...but that is not the only problem that I see.... Another problem is that even when you "luck out" and get a Black teacher they aren't always that good at teachin'...I mean...the young Black teachers I've had can't seem to make up their mind whether they want to be our friends or be our teachers.... They start off bein' real kool and then they want to get real strict all of a sudden...I mean...it's like they have a form of teacher schizophrenia or somethin'.... Make up your mind, man....Are you my friend or are you my teacher?... The Latino and Asian teachers...they kinda kool but they don't really kick it with us Black girls...And the White teachers...they just don't care.... It's their way...that White way...or the highway...Simple as that.... And then they wonder why we don't try in school...part of the problem is you don't give a shit or you don't know how to teach...either way I lose...except for when I'm in this class...I love this class because the curriculum is about me...about my life...my problems...my history.... Why can't we learn about the positive contributions Black people make in regular (read White) history class.... Why is all they teach us about is how Black people were slaves and stuff.... What about all of the inventions Black people have made?... Why can't we talk about that in "regular" history class.... And they wonder why I don't try and don't come to class...I remember they were all laughin' at me because I didn't know who Hitler was...and I was like...I don't give a damn about who Hitler is.... Why do you think the Jewish Holocaust is more important than the African Holocaust? Why should I care who Hitler is? What does Hitler have to teach me about my community?

Eronne's testimony reveals how critical race methodology is an explicit process of self-reflection and critical inquiry (Smith-Maddox & Solorzano, 2002, p. 76). Her comments provide a comprehensive description of her notions of difference and diversity. At the same time, they show how she is deeply aware of the subtle ways in which race, racism, and teacher efficacy are organized and their impact on student performance.

By repositioning youth such as Eronne as researchers, rather than the researched, the popular conception of young people as problems, pathology, and prevention shifts to viewing young people as agents, achievers, and assets (Akom, 2003; Ginwright & Cammarotta, 2007).[6] Such a position stands in sharp contrast to the current conceptualizations of young people, particular Black youth, as dangerous, disengaged, and disinterested consumers who lack any type of connection to mainstream funds of knowledge, forms of capital, and literacies of power (Morrel, 2006). By legitimating democratic inquiry within schools and outside of schools, YPAR "excavates knowledge 'at the bottom' and 'at the margins'" (Matsuda, 1995) and signifies youths fundamental right to ask, investigate, and contest policies and practices that reenforce social injustice (Torre & Fine, 2006, p. 272).

Merging CRT and YPAR: Creating Emancipatory Knowledge for Urban and Suburban Educators

Because of its commitment to social justice and action as part of the research process, YPAR represents an orientation to inquiry that is highly consistent with the principles of CRT (Minkler, 2004, p. 684). As a collaborative approach that breaks down the barriers between the researcher and the researched and values community members as equitable partners in the research enterprise, YPAR also underscores the liberatory principles of agency, equity, and self-determination. At the same time, YPAR identifies research as a significant site of struggle between the interest and ways of knowing of traditional Western research and decolonizing frameworks that reflect the inherent belief in the ability of people of color to accurately assess our own strengths and needs and our right to act upon them in this world (Smith, 1999).

Although differing in some of their goals and strategies, CRT and YPAR approaches may be "seen to share a set of core values and principle and have as their centerpiece three interrelated elements: participation, research, and action" (Minkler, 2004, p. 685). Borrowing and extending the work of Smith-Maddox and Solorzano (2002), Fals-Borda (1987), Minkler (2004), Camarotta and Fine (2007), Fanon and others, below I outline the essential elements of combining CRT with YPAR as a form of resistance to oppressive social elements in race and education. My goal is to inform the training of prospective and existing teachers with a fresh innovative approach that avoids the pitfalls of cultural deficit models. The fundamental elements of this approach are as follows:

- it is participatory and youth driven;
- it is cooperative, engaging teachers and youth in a joint research process in which each contributes equitably;
- it foregrounds race, racism, gender, and other axis of social difference in the research design, data collection, and analysis;
- it helps prospective teachers focus on the racialized and gendered experiences of communities of color;
- it challenges the traditional paradigms, methods, and texts as a way to engage in a discourse on race that is informed by the actual conditions and experiences of people of color;
- it is committed to colearning, cofacilitating, and bidirectionality;
- it is transdisciplinary, drawing on Black/Africana studies, Raza studies, ethnic studies, and women's studies, to name a few;
- it involves local capacity building;
- it is an empowering process through which all participants can increase control of their lives;
- it seeks a balance between critical thinking, reflection, analysis, and action;
- it emphasizes a union of mind, body, and spirit rather than a separation of these elements.

It is important to note that where my work differs from Maddox-Smith and Solorzano's conceptualization of "critical race methodology" is that the approach I am proposing is not a method per se, but rather, an orientation to educational research that may employ any number of qualitative and quantitative methodologies. According to Linda

Tuhawai Smith (1999), what is distinctive about decolonizing research methodologies is not the methods used but the methodological context of their application. What is new is not the research itself but who is leading the research, who owns the research, who carries it out, who writes it up, who benefits from it, and how the results are disseminated (Smith, 1999, p. 10).

Educators need to find ways to identify the resources and strengths of youth of color and place them in the center of their research, curriculum, and teaching practicum's (Smith-Maddox & Solorzano, 2002, p. 71). Indeed, by combining CRT with YPAR a critical race methodology can be developed that challenges the dominant mind-set, increases academic engagement and achievement, and builds new understandings of the strength and assets of youth of color and the communities in which we come from.

Bridging Theory with Practice: Creating a Community of Black Youth as Public Intellectuals

For the past four years I have been infusing Black/Africana studies curriculum into urban and suburban high school classrooms. Utilizing Black history, philosophy, social science, and spirituality as weapons in the fight for racial justice is consistent with the mission of Black/Africana studies, which was born in 1968 at San Francisco State University and from its inception has been committed to linking theory with praxis and community service (Kunjuku, 1986; Woodson, 1933). Thus, in an effort to address issues of race and racism in the "liberal" Bay area, in 2004 I began a Step-to-College/Urban Teacher Pipeline Project with mostly Black and multiracial youth from the cities of Berkeley, Oakland, and Richmond, California.[7]

Although there are multiple goals to this ongoing project, four emerge as primary and are important to share here. They are as follows: (1) to infuse Africana curriculum into high schools in an effort to increase the pool of available teachers from a broader and more diverse background;[8] (2) to increase college access for students of color; (3) to use YPAR to increase literacies of power (academic literacies, critical literacies, civic literacies, and new media literacies), conduct professional development trainings with teachers, and make programmatic changes in local schools and communities; and finally (4) to create an explicit teacher pipeline for students of color to return to communities of color as teachers. Overall, the Step-to-College/Urban Teacher Pipeline Project, founded and originated by my colleague Jeff Duncan-Andrade with the help of Dean Jacob Perea in the School of Education, is an 8-year project committed to supporting young people living in Berkeley, Oakland, and Richmond through high school and the university, while encouraging them to return to community based schools as K–12 public education teachers.

Creating a Youth Bill of Rights

In Fall 2005, The Research Collaborative on Youth Activism (RCYA), a three-tiered, national partnership between youth activists, direct service providers, and researchers approached our Step-to-College program to participate in researching, developing, and implementing a Youth Bill of Rights to improve the quality of life for young people in the city of Berkeley and beyond.[9] At the invitation of RCYA, and in conjunction with Berkeley High Schools' Communication and Arts and Science Academy and Berkeley Tech, we began to create a multigenerational, multisite team of researchers—youth and adult, urban and suburban—to consider the following questions that we felt central to building more effective schools for all youth in general and youth of color in particular:

- In what ways do young people of color conceptualize their rights?
- What constitutes collective rights for young people?
- What are the social and economic conditions that limit possibilities and opportunities for young people in our community?
- How do state institutions (city governments, schools, police, etc) impede the progress and healthy development of young people in our communities?
- What is the relationship between racial justice, youth rights, and teacher efficacy in the city of Berkeley?
- How do young people perceive the processes and consequences of the opportunity gap in this community?
- What are the organizations or processes that empower young people to become agents of community change?

Against this backdrop, a coalition of high school and undergraduate students directed by myself, and working with a corps of graduate students, and professional film-makers—began conducting surveys, interviews, and focus groups that helped us grapple with the reality of racism in the heart of liberalism and the ways that race still impacts access to institutional resources and privileges in what is arguably the most liberal region in the United States (Fine, Roberts, & Torre, 2004).

Following in the footsteps of the important work conducted by the Participatory Action Research Collective pioneered by Michelle Fine and Maria Torre at CUNY, the first phase of our project involved intensive "research camps" where students were trained in local civil rights history, critical race theory, feminist thought, and indigenous knowledge (to name a few). Students were also immersed in qualitative and quantitative research methods including: survey design and observational research strategies. At this stage we also divided into four student research teams each focused on one core condition of examining teaching and learning as a civil right—quality teachers, a rigorous curriculum, adequate learning materials, issues of immigration and language diversity, and a healthy and positive physical and social environment (Morrel, 2006, p. 116).

During the second phase of our project we crafted research questions pertaining to a Youth Bill of Rights, interrogated each other for potential bias, and worked through the specifics of research design and data collection (Torre & Fine, 2006). In this phase we also began thinking about how Freire's work influenced our thinking about teaching and learning as a civil right. Freire's work taught us that in spite of obvious and important power differentials students are in a strategic position to invite their teachers to liberate themselves and transform their present realities. One of our goals, then, became to help teachers see their students, families, and the communities where we come from as assets and sources of strength (Smith-Maddox & Solorzano, 2002, p. 73). By applying CRT we recognized that in order for teachers to no longer be "colorblind" and "culture-blind" they "had to learn how to talk about race, to understand how the knowledge of race has been constructed and reconstructed through time, and to unlearn racism" (Smith-Maddox & Solorzano, 2002, p. 73). In our third phase young people investigated and denaturalized the conditions of their everyday lives by exploring various research and pedagogical tools such as Geographic Information Systems mapping, participatory surveys, participant observation, photo-voice, focus groups, web research, identity maps, individual interviews, archival research, oral histories, policy analyses, and participatory videos (i.e., short films and feature length documentary movies). Youth researchers also conducted open-ended interviews with teachers about the dominant ideology of color-blindness and its impact on teacher recruitment, teacher development, teacher efficacy, and educational outcomes. During this phase we were concerned about the quality of instruction for all students, particularly, low-income youth, linguistically gifted students, and students of color.

Our fourth and final phase is an action phase where we continue modeling Freirean pedagogy by having students facilitate "critical inquiry groups" with other students about pressing social issues such as race, poverty, police brutality, fratricide, homicide, and teacher efficacy (this occurred at the end of the Fall semester). At the end of the Spring semester, these same students facilitated youth driven professional development "critical inquiry groups" with teachers with the explicit goal of providing continuous feedback loops to improve the practice of teaching and learning. In this manner, the authority of the critical teacher becomes dialectical; as teachers relinquish the authority of the "banking system," they assume the mature authority of facilitators of student inquiry and problem posing (Kincheloe, 2004). "In relation to such teacher authority, students gain their freedom—they gain the ability to become self-directed human beings capable of producing their own knowledge" (Kincheloe, 2004, p. 17). Our youth driven critical inquiry groups have 11 central aims as follows:[10]

- Youth driven professional development should deepen and broaden content knowledge.
- Youth driven professional development should provide a strong foundation in the pedagogy of particular disciplines.
- Youth driven professional development should provide knowledge about the teaching and learning processes.
- Youth driven professional development should be rooted in and reflect the best available research.
- The content of youth driven professional development should be able to be aligned with the standards and curriculum teachers use as well as augment those standards.
- Youth driven professional development should contribute to measurable improvement in student achievement.
- Youth driven professional development should be intellectually engaging and address the complexity of teaching and learning.
- Youth driven professional development should be implemented in a way that provides sufficient time, support, and resources to enable teachers to master new content and pedagogy and to integrate this knowledge and skill into practice.
- Youth driven professional development should be designed by students in cooperation with teachers and/or other experts in the field.
- Youth driven professional development should take a variety of forms, including some we have not typically considered.
- Youth driven professional development should be site specific but can also be used comparatively across sites.

Disseminating Research Findings and Advocating for Social Change

Reporting and disseminating our research findings is an important part of our critical race methodology. It follows our first form of research dissemination targeted visual learners (many young people today) by showing our documentary films at the annual Berkeley High Film festival. The festival was attend by hundreds of community residents, teachers, staff, and administrators from the Berkeley Unified School District, SFSU faculty, members of the school board and other elected officials. All films were so well received that a series of conversations are now taking place with the Berkeley mayor's office and city manager's office about having a youth summit with the explicit goal of Berkeley becoming the first city in the United States to adopt our Youth Bill of Rights. Our second form of research dissemination consists of our student projects being uploaded to the KPFA radio station web site and disseminated to thousands of listeners across the Greater Bay area through youth radio blogs. The website is accessed by tens of thousands of people worldwide, many of them aspiring teachers and researchers. Our third form of research dissemination consists of sending teams of student representatives to present at major conferences around the country. In 2006 we sent a team to the Alex Haley Farm in Tennessee, and in 2007 we sent a team of student representatives to present our Youth Bill of Rights to the Black and Latino Caucus in Washington D.C. as well as the annual American Anthropological Association conference also held in Washington D.C. Finally, and perhaps most importantly, our greatest achievement is that in our first year six students from the original 75 enrolled in our Urban Teacher Pipeline Project at SFSU. Their story is to be continued.

Conclusion

In this chapter I have argued that by combining CRT with YPAR it is possible to create a new methodological orientation that Smith-Maddox and Solorzano (2002) refer to as "critical race methodology" (p.80). The most important contribution of this framework is that it is youth driven and that it directly confronts and challenges ideologies of color-blindness, racelessness, and meritocracy that many teachers develop as a result of their own cultural and educational experiences. The framework that I propose attempts to get at these deeply rooted ideologies by introducing students to critical race theory, Africana studies, Women's studies, and so on, and by utilizing professional development—"critical inquiry groups"—whereby students help teachers unlearn stereotypical knowledge of race while analyzing, problem solving, theorizing what it means to teach a diverse student population (Smith-Maddox & Solorzano, 2002, p. 80). Deeply embedded within this framework is a pedagogical approach that uses Freire's critical praxis as a tool for helping students identify and name systemic and institutionalized problems that students of color face, analyze the cause of these problems, and find solutions to them (Bonilla-Silva, 2001; Omi & Winant, 1993).[11]

By employing this methodology students and teachers are able to exchange experiential knowledge about their communities that is critical to understanding systemic processes of racialization that students confront on an everyday basis (Smith-Maddox & Solorzano, 2002, p.80). Critical inquiry groups also create the conditions for students and teachers to "examine the moral and ethical dilemmas of teaching and learning while challenging their own intrinsic assumptions and learning to talk about race" (Smith-Maddox & Solorzano, 2002, p.80).

By engaging young people whose voices are too often marginalized in teacher training and professional development, a critical race methodology provides an innovative way for challenging the status quo and pushing scholarship in new directions by asking new questions and questioning old assumptions (Cahill, 2007). Because the theory of action is developed from within the YPAR process and combined with the critical race literature, there are embedded opportunities for challenging the tacit beliefs, understandings, and worldviews that students and teachers bring with them into educational space (Cahill, 2007). Implementation of this approach in high schools and in teacher education programs around the country is an important way for students and teachers to consistently reflect upon their "epistemological orientation and understand the values and practices of students and their families as well as the racial, cultural, and language difference they represent" (Smith-Maddox & Solorzano, 2002, p. 80). Failure to do so may limit the possibilities of eradicating racialized opportunity gaps and ensure that many students of color continued to be "left behind" and pushed into the growing prison industrial complex (Torre & Fine, 2007). To interrupt this process we need to be successful in attracting youth of color into our classrooms and engaging them in a combination of critical thinking and social action. The political potential of critical race methodology lies in its role in the development of future teacher-leaders, who, as they graduate from college, have the social, cultural, and economic capital to transform not only their community but also the world beyond (Flores-Gonzalez, Rodriguez, & Rodriguiz-Muniz, 2006). As always I am hopeful!

Acknowledgments

I would like to thank Sabaa Shoraka, Analena Hassberg, Aaron Nakai, Dawn Williams, Nick James, Rekia Mohammod-Jibrin, Assata Harris, Ayesha Abdut-Tawaab, Kai Crowder, Justine Fossett-Cunningham, and Shanice Kiel for their assistance in putting together this chapter.

Notes

1. Although these issues tend to be systematically neglected they have obvious and major consequences for new ways of understanding "racialized opportunity gaps," shifting demographic patterns, and the reconstitution of urban and suburban educational spaces occurring nation wide. For example, according to the 2000 Census, the United States is becoming increasing racially and ethnically diverse; yet a new survey of teachers' attitudes, training, and practices regarding teaching in multiracial schools indicates that "White teachers have very little interracial experience in their own school experiences, little training for diversity and tend to believe that they can effectively educate across racial lines." While teachers of color—despite having more training and experience for diverse settings, are less likely to believe that other teachers and administrators effectively handle diversity issues (Orfield & Lee, 2006).
2. This was unsuccessful, however, because Blacks have always had a firm commitment to racial and social uplift through liberatory education and autonomous Black freedom schools (Perry, Steele, & Hillard, 2003).
3. This was unsuccessful, however, because Blacks have always had a firm commitment to racial and social uplift through liberatory education and autonomous Black freedom schools (Perry et al., 2003).
4. See b. hooks, *Teaching to Transgress: Educations as a Practice of Freedom* (1994, chap. 5).
5. Amanda Lewis and Loic Wacquant go one step further arguing that schools are "race-making institutions" that socialize students into accepting the dominant ideology and existing racial hierarchies (Lewis, 2003).
6. Significantly and problematically, the research about young people too often conceptualizes young people as separate from their communities. They are either constructed as innocent children who need to be saved from dangerous communities—this is particularly true in the literature on urban working class youth and youth of color—or youth are constructed as being a danger to their community. In both cases young people are often assumed to be "at risk" aka in need of reform in order to become productive citizens who will give back to their community instead of dropping out of high school, becoming pregnant, doing drugs, and so on. The focus in the literature upon youth behavior loses sight of structural constraints. What's missing is the understanding of young people as part of communities; a transactional perspective in which youth development equals community development, which is the emphasis of this project.
7. "Less than 28% of California's public school teachers are people of color. However, more than 70% of the state's K-12 public school enrollees are students of color. Two likely causes

for this glaring and persistent disparity are: 1) the lack of college access for students of color; and 2) the absence of an explicit teacher pipeline for students of color to return to their communities as teachers" (see Duncan-Andrade, 2007). The Urban Teacher Pipeline is an 8-year project, started by professor extraordinaire Jeff Duncan-Andrade, committed to supporting young people living in Berkeley, Oakland, and Richmond through high school and the university, while encouraging them to return to community based schools as K-12 public education teachers (see the Cesar Chavez Institute website under Jeff Duncan-Andrade's listed projects for more information).

8. Many students in the program come from underserved, socioeconomically disadvantaged, and environmentally at risk communities. However, others come from elite zip codes. The overall racial and socioeconomic diversity of the project can help other school districts around the country address practical questions of segregation and integration within their schools and communities.

9. Under the guidance of Dr. Shawn Ginwright the purpose of the Research Collaborative on Youth Activism is to facilitate youth led initiatives that will allow students, direct service providers, and university researchers to produce more democratic, just, and critical ways to evaluate and improve schools and communities in the cities across the United States including Berkeley, Oakland, Chicago, Denver, New York, and Tucson. The intent of the collaborative is to train, organize, and facilitate the dissemination of relevant research findings to policy makers, practitioners, and researchers in order to increase support for social change activities that impact educational achievement and youth development locally and nationally (see the Cesar Chavez Institute website under Shawn Ginwright's listed projects for more information).

10. These 11 standards for youth driven professional development were adopted from the American Federation of Teachers.

References

Akom, A. A. (2001). Racial profiling at school: The politics of race and discipline at Berkeley High. In W. Ayers, B. Dohrn, & R. Ayers (Eds.), *Zero tolerance: Resisting the drive for punishment in our schools: A handbook for parents, students, educators, and citizens*. New York: New Press.

Akom, A. A. (2003). Reexamining resistance as oppositional behavior: The Nation of Islam and the creation of a Black achievement ideology. *Sociology of Education, 76*(4), 305–325.

Akom, A. A. (2004). *Ameritrocracy: The racing of our nation's children*. Unpublished doctoral dissertation, University of Pennsylvania, Philadelphia.

Akom, A. A. (2006). The racial dimensions of social capital: Toward a new understanding of youth empowerment and community organizing in America's urban core. In S. Ginwright, P. Noguera, & J. Cammarotta (Eds.), *Beyond resistance: Youth activism and community change* (pp. 81–92). New York: Routledge.

Akom, A. A. (2007, November–December). Cities as battlefields: Understanding how the Nation of Islam impacts civic engagement, environmental racism, and community development in a low income neighborhood. *International Journal of Qualitative Studies in Education, 209*(6), 711–730.

Anzaldua, G. (1987). *Borderlands/La frontera: The new mestiza*. San Francisco: Aunt Lute Press.

Anzaldua, G. (1990). *Making face, making soul, Haciendo Caras—Creative and critical perspectives by feminists of color*. San Francisco: Aunt Lute Press.

Bonilla-Silva, E. (2001). *White supremacy and racism in the post-civil rights era*. London: Lynne Rienner.

Cahill, C. (2007). Doing research with young people: Participatory research and ritual of collective work. *Children's Geographies, 5*(3), 297–212.

Cammarota, J., & Fine, M. (2007). *Revolutionizing education: Youth participatory action research in motion*. New York: Routledge.

Darling-Hammond, L. (1997). The right to learn: A blueprint for creating schools that work. San Francisco: Jossey-Bass.

Dixon, A. D., & Rousseau, C. K. (Eds.). (2006). *Critical race theory in education: All God's children got a song.* New York: Routledge.

Du Bois, W. E. B. (1935) *Black Reconstruction in America, 1860–1880.* New York: New Press. (Original work published 1935)

Duncan, G. (2002). Beyond love: A critical race ethnography of the schooling of adolescent Black males. *Equity and Excellence in Education, 3*(2), 131–143.

Duncan, G. (2003). Critical race theory and method: Rendering race in urban ethnographic research. *Qualitative Inquiry, 8*(1), 85–104.

Duncan-Andrade, J. (2007, November-December). Gangstas, wankstas, and ridas: Defining, developing, and supporting effective teachers in urban schools. *International Journal of Qualitative Studies in Education, 209*(6), 617–638.

Fals-Borda, O. (1987). The application of participatory action-research in Latin-America. *International Sociology, 2,* 329–347.

Fine, M., Roberts, R. A., & Torre, M. E. (2004). *Echoes of Brown: Youth documenting and performing the legacy of Brown vs. Board of Education.* New York: Teachers College Press.

Flores-Gonzalez, N., Rodriguez, M., & Rodriguiz-Muniz, M. (2006). From hip-hop to humanization: Batey Urbano as a space for Latino youth culture and community action. In S. Ginwright, P. Noguera, & J. Cammarotta (Eds.), *Beyond resistance: Youth activism and community change* (pp. 175–196). New York: Routledge.

Foster, M. (1997). *Black teachers on teaching.* New York: New Press.

Freire, P. (1970). *Pedagogy of the oppressed.* New York: Continuum. (Original work published 1967)

Freire, P. (1982). Creating alternative research methods: Learning to do by doing it. In B. Hall, A. Gillette, & R. Tandon (Eds.), *Creating knowledge: A monopoly* (pp. 29–37). New Delhi: Society for Participatory Research in Asia.

Ginwright, S., & Cammarotta, J. (2002). New terrain in youth development: The promise of a social justice approach. *Social Justice, 29*(4).

Ginwright, S., & Cammarotta, J. (2007, November-December). Youth activism in the urban community: Learning critical civic praxis within community organizations. *International Journal of Qualitative Studies in Education, 20*(6), 693–711.

Hacker, A. (1992). *Two nations: Black and White, separate, hostile, unequal.* New York: Ballantine Books.

Harris, C. (1993) Whiteness as property. *Harvard Law Review, 106,* 1716–1738.

Harris, C. (1995). Whiteness as property. In K. Crenshaw, N. Gotando, G. Peller, & K. Thomas (Eds.), *Critical race theory: The key writings that formed the movement* (pp. 276–291). New York: New Press.

hooks, b. (1994). *Teaching to transgress: Education as a practice of freedom.* New York: Routledge.

Kelley, R. G. D. (1998). Playing for keeps: Pleasure and profit on the post-industrial playground. In W. Lubiano (Ed.), *The house that race built* (pp. 195–321). New York: Vintage Books.

Kincheloe, J. L. (2004). *Critical pedagogy.* New York: Peter Lang.

Kozol, J. (2006). *The shame of a nation: The restoration of apartheid schooling in America.* New York: Crown.

Kunjufu, J. (1986). *Motivating and preparing Black youth for success.* Chicago: African American Images.

Ladson-Billings, G., & Tate, W. (1995). Toward a critical race theory of education. *Teacher College Record, 97*(1), 47–68.

Lewis, A. (2003). *Race in the schoolyard: Negotiating the color line in classrooms and communities.* New Brunswick, NJ: Rutgers University Press.

Matsuda, M. (1995). Looking to the bottom: Critical legal studies and reparations. In K. Crenshaw, N. Gotanda, G. Peller, & K. Thomas (Eds.), Critical race theory: The key writings that formed the movement (pp. 63–79). New York: The New Press.

Minkler, M. (2004). Ethical challenges for the "outside" researcher in community-based participatory research. *Health Education & Behavior, 31*(6), 684–697.

Morrel, E. (2006). Youth-initiated research as a tool for advocacy and change in urban school. In S. Ginwright, P. Noguera, & J. Cammarotta (Eds.), *Beyond resistance: Youth activism and community change* (pp. 111–128). New York: Routledge.

Oakes, J. (1995). Two cities' tracking and within-school segregation. *Teachers College Record, 96*, 681–690.

Oakes, J., Muir, K., & Joseph, R. (2000). Course taking and achievement in mathematics and science: Inequalities that endure and change. Madison, WI: National Institute of Science Education.

Omi, M., & Winant, H. (1993). On the theoretical concept of race. In C. McCarthy & W. Crichlow (Eds.), *Race, identity, and representation in education* (pp. 3–10). New York: Routledge Falmer.

Orfield, G., & Lee, C. (2006). *Denver public school: Resegregation, Latino style*. The Civil Rights Project. Cambridge, MA: Harvard University.

Parks, G. S. (2007). Critical race realism: Towards an integrative model of critical race theory, empirical social science, and public policy. *Cornell Law School Working Papers Series, 23*, 3–70.

Perry, T., Steele, C., & Hilliard, A. G., III (2003). *Young, gifted, and Black: Promoting high achievement among African-American students*. Boston: Beacon Press.

Savas, E. S. (2000). *Privatization and public private partnerships*. New York: Chatham House.

Smith, L. T. (1999). *Decolonizing methodologies: Research and indigenous people*. New York: Zed.

Smith-Maddox, R., & Solorzano, D. (2002). Using critical race theory, Paulo Freire's problem-posing method, and case study research to confront race and racism in education. *Qualitative Inquiry, 8*(1), 66–84.

Solorzano, D. G., & Bernal, D. D. (2001, May 3rd). Examining transformational resistance through a critical race and Latcrit theory framework: Chicana and Chicano students in an urban context. *Urban Education, 36*, 308–342.

Solorzano, D. G., & Yosso, T. J. (2002). A critical race counterstory of race, racism, and affirmative action. *Equity and Excellence in Education, 35*(2), 155–168.

Torre, M. E., & Fine, M. (2006). Researching and resisting: Democratic policy research by and for youth. In S. Ginwright, P. Noguera, & J. Cammarotta (Eds.), *Beyond resistance: Youth activism and community change* (pp. 269–285). New York: Routledge.

Torre, M. E., & Fine, M. (2007). Don't die with your work balled up in your fists: Contesting social injustice through participatory research. In B. J. Ross Leadbeater & N. Way (Eds.), *Urban girls revisited: Building strengths*. New York: New York University Press.

Woodson, C. G. (1933). *The mis-education of the Negro*. Washington, D.C.: Associate Publishers.

Yosso, T., & Solorzano, D. (2002). Critical race methodology: Counter-storytelling as an analytical framework for education research. *Qualitative Inquiry, 8*(1), 23–44.

Response to Part 6

Youth and Social Justice in Education

Grace Lee Boggs

In the last three years of his life Dr. Martin Luther King Jr., seeking a way to overcome the despair and powerlessness that exploded into the streets during unprecedented urban rebellions, said that what our young people needed "in our dying cities" was "direct action programs," programs to change themselves and, at the same time, programs that would revitalize their environments.

Just imagine how much safer and livelier and more peaceful our neighborhoods would be almost overnight if we reorganized education along the lines King proposed—if instead of trying to keep our children isolated for 12 years and more, we engaged them in community-building activities right now with the same audacity with which the Civil Rights Movement engaged them in desegregation activities 40 years ago: planting community gardens, recycling waste, organizing neighborhood arts and health festivals, rehabbing houses, painting public murals. By giving our children and young people a better reason to learn than just the individualistic one of making money, by encouraging them to exercise their Soul Power, we would also deepen and strengthen their intellectual engagement. Learning would come from practice, which has always been the best and most powerful way to learn.

Instead of trying to bully young people to remain in classrooms isolated from their communities and structured to prepare them to become cogs in the existing decaying economic system, we need to recognize that huge numbers of young people are dropping out of city schools, voting with their feet against an educational system which sorts, tracks, tests, and rejects or certifies them like products of a factory created for the age of industrialization. They are crying out for another kind of education, another way of being that gives them opportunities to exercise their creative energies because it values them as human beings.

A new approach is urgently needed in all our educational institutions. Instead of viewing the purpose of education as giving students the means for upward mobility to become the technological elites that will enable the United States to compete on the world market, we need to recognize that formal education bears a large part of the responsibility for our present crisis because it produces morally sterile technicians who have more know-how than know-why. At a time when we desperately need to heal the earth and build durable economies and healthy communities, our schools and universities are stuck in the processes and practices used to industrialize the earth in the 19th and 20th centuries.

We need to create a vision and develop strategies to help children transform themselves from angry rebels into positive change agents. To do this we need to go beyond the issue of power, or who controls our schools, and begin grappling with fundamental questions about the purpose of education, how children learn, and what kind of education we need in the world today. The time has come to go beyond the top-down factory model of education, which was created at the beginning of the 20th century to supply industry with a disciplined work force, and begin creating a new model which empowers young people to make a difference.

In the spring of 1963 the Southern Christian Leadership Conference led by Dr. King launched a "fill the jails" campaign to desegregate downtown department stores and schools in Birmingham. But few local Blacks were coming forward. Black adults were afraid of losing their jobs, local Black preachers were reluctant to accept the leadership of an "outsider," and city police commissioner Bull Conner had everyone intimidated. Facing a major defeat, King was persuaded by his aide, James Bevel, to allow any child old enough to belong to a church to march. So on D-Day May 2nd, before the eyes of the whole nation, thousands of school children, many of them first graders, joined the movement and were beaten, fire-hosed, attacked by police dogs, and herded off to jail in paddy wagons and school buses. The result was what has been called "The Children's Miracle." Inspired and shamed into action, thousands of adults rushed to join the Movement. All over the country rallies were called to express outrage against Bull Connor's brutality. Locally the power structure was forced to desegregate downtown stores, hire Blacks to work downtown, and begin desegregating the schools. Nationally the Kennedy administration, which had been trying not to alienate white Dixiecrat voters, was forced to begin drafting civil rights legislation as the only way to forestall more Birminghams.

The next year as part of Mississippi Freedom Summer, activists created Freedom Schools because the existing school system (like ours today) had been organized to produce subjects, not citizens. To bring about a "mental revolution," reading, writing, and speaking skill were taught through discussion of Black history, the power structure, and the need to build a Movement to struggle for positive change. In 1963 and 1964 the creative energies of children and young people were tapped to win the battle for desegregation and voting rights, and today they need to be tapped to rebuild our communities and our dying cities and to create a vibrant society and a democratic citizenry.

School and colleges dedicated to this new kind of education would look and act differently from today's educational institutions. For example, much more learning would take place *outside* school walls, while *inside* an integral part of the educational process would be the design and operation of the building—classes would audit resource flows of food, energy, water, material waste, and investments. Recognizing that education is about learning to be helpful and responsible citizens and that children don't learn only from books, segregation in schools based upon abilities would be ended. And more.

To resolve our deepening school crisis and to rebuild our society we need this paradigm shift in our approach to education, a shift that Martin Luther King anticipated. Let's make it happen.

Part 7

Globalization and Social Justice in Education

Edited and Introduced by Pauline Lipman and Karen Monkman

> The Futurists thought that the machine was God. Take a walk along any river in any country and one can see that the machine is almost defunct. God is rusting away leaving a fragile shell.
>
> (Wojnarowicz, 1999, p. 205)

> An autocratic state is no acceptable substitute; nor can the militarized state capitalism evolving in the United States or the bureaucratized, centralized welfare state be accepted as the goal of human existence. The only justification for repressive institutions is material and cultural deficit. But such institutions, at certain stages of history, perpetuate and produce such a deficit, and even threaten human survival. Modern science and technology can relieve people of the necessity for specialized imbecilic labor. They may, in principle, provide the basis for a rational social order based on free association and democratic control, if we have the will to create it.
>
> (Chomsky, 1970, p. 17)

Global economic and social processes are redefining the purposes and practices of education. Any serious discussion of social justice in education must address these processes. In this section of the Handbook, we focus on globalization as contested, ways in which that contestation is playing out in the field of education, and its implications for the struggle for social justice. The chapters examine ways in which globalization is undermining public education as a terrain of democracy and critical thought and action and ways in which critical educators, progressive social movements, and educational projects can and are challenging dominant educational and social agendas. Our selection of topics is necessarily partial. Many important issues are only briefly discussed or omitted altogether, including global environmental degradation as a social justice education issue; the various impacts of globalization on the education of women and girls; antiracist education; new immigrations, particularly from the global South to the global North; the role of education in the defense and preservation of languages and cultures; indigenous ways of knowing (Fals Borda & Mora-Osejo, 2003); the role of education in labor and community struggles (Novelli, 2004); and there are many others. The chapters are meant to be illustrative of the complex implications of globalization for education and social justice.

When we talk about globalization we have in mind economic, political, and cultural processes that liberalize trade and global flows of capital, labor, information, and culture. This is not a neutral process but, as Rizvi and Engel argue in the first chapter in this section, "globalization represents a deliberate, ideological project of economic liberalization [neoliberalism] that subjects states and individuals to more intense market forces." Neoliberal globalization is an ensemble of global economic and social policies that promote the primacy of the market in all social spheres, the ideology of individual competition and entrepreneurship, and the reduction of the government's role to promote collective social welfare. However, globalization is contested ideologically and politically at all spatial scales—from the local to the national and transnational. Boaventura de Sousa Santos reminds us that we must talk about "globalizations"—not just the globalization of capital, globalization from the center (the advanced capitalist economies of the North), globalization from above, but also globalization from below, globalization of social struggles against injustice initiated by marginalized peoples (Dale & Robertson, 2004). Neoliberal globalization produces its antithesis—a global politics of resistance and a demand for a more just world order. Bolivian peasants, Korean farmers, Indian workers, West African cotton producers, U.S. environmentalists, and British teachers find common ground against a nexus of oppressive and exploitative economic, cultural, and political forces. These movements are multifaceted, diverse, and local but they are also coalescing globally in the World Social Forum and protests against the World Trade Organization, summits of the leading capitalist countries, and global conferences to impose treaties in the interest of transnational capital. Declaring "another world is possible," these diverse movements challenge the inevitability of a world governed by the drive for capital accumulation resulting in vast disparities in wealth and the quality of daily life (Jomo & Baudot, 2007). The popular movements that have swept anti-neoliberal governments into power across Latin America testify to growing sentiment against this global neoliberal agenda. Beyond opposition, through local struggles and global networks, people are asserting more collective and just ways of producing and living together and with the earth. Stephen Gill (2003) summarizes this global dialectic—the present social conjuncture is defined by global neoliberalism and resistance to it. It is this conjuncture that we hope to illuminate in relation to education.

The idea of globalization as a contested process frames all the papers in this section. As a whole, the chapters demonstrate that education is central to neoliberal globalization *and* to struggles for global social justice. In the opening chapter Fazal Rizvi and Laura Engel analyze ways in which neoliberal globalization is redefining education and undermining educational equity, and they outline the role of intergovernmental organizations in this process. The ideology of neoliberal globalization links education to the requirements of the global knowledge economy. It reframes education in economic terms (human capital development), undermining other educational aims, including holistic human development, the creation of democratic communities, and social justice. As the neoliberal logic of market efficiency penetrates education systems, corporate-style governance, accountability, standards, and efficiency have become the global model. Education itself has become a global commodity with international trade agreements, such as the General Agreement on Trade in Services (GATS), and global education markets in privatized educational services. These neoliberal policies are profoundly affecting the nature of teachers' work, school organization and governance, what students learn, and how we talk and think about education.

Although neoliberals claim that expansion of access to education will reduce inequalities, the papers in this section make it clear that any discussion of social justice in education must also address structural inequalities in global, national, and local economies that are at the root of economic and social inequities. Susan Robertson extends this point by examining the global rescaling of educational provision and governance from the national level to global, regional, and local bodies, and its implications for "citizenship" and social justice. Robertson argues that since the early 1980s four intertwined shifts have taken place that undermine the role of national education systems and education as an arena in which social classes and marginalized groups can make claims for equity and justice. She argues the result is a significant democratic deficit. As globalization fragments the institutions and processes of government and rights are redefined in consumer terms, education is depoliticized as an important site of power/knowledge. At the same time, there are no adequate framings for making claims for equity and justice in education at the global or supraregional levels. Her chapter asks us to think more deeply about the multiple scales (e.g., local, supranational, regional, intergovernmental) in which to demand equity and justice in education and how we might do that.

Turning to resistance and "globalization from below" as a political and conceptual process, Jennifer Chan argues that, although the alternative globalization movement has not given much attention to education, antiglobalization movements are themselves educational. They produce counteranalyses, examples of possibility (alternatives to the existing global capitalist order), and the development of new subjectivities and conceptions of global, national, and local citizenship. We suggest that not only does this framework demonstrate that networks such as the World Social Forum are educative, it also offers a way of thinking about a broader conception of the connection between social justice and education.

This broader conception is central to Gustavo Fischman and Eric Haas's chapter as they consider the political and educational viability of critical pedagogy in the context of globalization. Fischman and Haas pose a crucial challenge: "How does one raise awareness without instilling a sense of hopelessness and loss of agency?" This chapter complicates the notion of critical pedagogy by arguing, first, that critical analyses of neoliberalism in education have to connect with the contradictory experiences of teachers and students. They also argue that proponents of critical pedagogy need to develop discourses of hope that go beyond heroic "narratives of redemption"—the critically conscious superteacher who transforms classrooms and schools. Instead they pose a more grounded notion of the teacher as a committed intellectual who concretely acts in classrooms, schools, and communities for social justice in alliance with others in an ongoing process of developing critical consciousness and working for educational change. Hope is grounded in the daily struggles of teachers and students.

The final chapter in the section, by Luis Armando Gandin, is an example of an anti-neoliberal educational project on the ground. In a case study of the Citizen Schools in Porto Allegre, Brazil, Gandin describes a local alternative to market-based educational policies that has taken on global significance—a "local action" with "global reach." The Citizen School project counters the marketization and economization of education discussed by Rizvi and Engel with a program of democratization of educational access, knowledge, and administration. Moreover, the Citizen School project also demonstrates that education can play a strategic role in the democratization of society when led by a progressive state. This possibility has, of course, expanded with the emergence of anti-neoliberal governments across Latin America. We are seeing the possibility of a proliferation of local models and conceptions of education that may, as they circulate in the discourses and networks of globalization from below, provoke new ways of thinking about the integral role of education in social justice.

Beyond the scope of this Handbook section lie a variety of educational policies and programs that also relate to globalization. Educational policy initiatives at the international and local levels are increasingly framed by human rights (see UNICEF's educational agendas, for example, and the work of many international NGOs), with intentions to challenge global and local inequities. Peace education is also a recognizable trend, as are environmentally focused educational programs. While these types of programmatic initiatives seek to situate human rights, global peace, or environmental sustainability as goals, they vary considerably in how they conceptualize globalization. We believe a more robust theorization of the forces of globalization would deepen their connection to global struggles for social justice.

The implications of immigration and transnationalism for social justice is another important topic not included in this section. With the restructuring of the global labor markets and economies in both the global South and the global North, new and diverse immigrations impact educational communities and systems. Life in schools is impacted by global labor restructuring, privatization, marketization, and the decreasing ability (or willingness) of nation-states to provide equitable education to the masses—an education that would serve the common good instead of particular interests. At the same time, however, immigrant communities have helped to build strong movements that are educational in themselves, and that promote social justice in schools. Immigration is yet another arena that demonstrates the contested nature of globalization. On the one hand, we see xenophobic anti-immigrant movements in schools in the United States and Europe in particular. On the other, immigrants and other marginalized communities are challenging Western-centric educational practices and epistemologies and broadening what counts as knowledge in educational settings.

De Sousa Santos argues that it is from the margins and the periphery of the global centers of power that "...the insights into our condition are more likely to come," from those "who on a daily basis experience domination, poverty, and social injustice" (Dale & Robertson, 2004, p. 147). We extend de Sousa Santos's claim to suggest that educational projects in the global South and liberatory educational work in marginalized communities in the heart of the centers of power are also stretching our understanding of possibilities and meanings of education and social justice.

Acknowledgments

We appreciate the original contributions of the authors in this section to a multifaceted discussion of the challenges and possibilities of education for social justice globally. Twelve colleagues have anonymously peer-reviewed these chapters. We also want to thank them for their very helpful comments and for deepening the dialog around globalization and education for social justice.

References

Chomsky, N. (1970). *Language and freedom.* Lecture presented at University Freedom and Human Sciences Symposium, Loyola University. Retrieved October 18, 2007 from, www.chomsky. info/books/state02.pdf

Dale, R., & Robertson, S. (2004). Interview with Boaventura de Sousa Santos. *Globalization, Societies, and Education, 2*(2), 147–160.

Fals-Borda, O., & Mora-Osejo, L. E. (2003). Eurocentrism and its effects: A manifesto from Colombia. *Globalization, Societies, and Education, 1*(1), 103–107.

Gill, S. (2003). *Power and resistance in the new world order.* New York: Palgrave Macmillan.

Jomo, K. S., & Baudot, J. (2007). *Flat world, big gaps: Economic liberalization, globalization, poverty and inequality.* New York: United Nations.

Novelli, M. (2004). Globalizations, social movement unionism and new internationalisms: The role of strategic learning in the transformation of the Municipal Workers Union of EMCALI. *Globalization, Societies, and Education, 2*(2), 161–190.

Wojnarowicz, D. (1999). *In the shadow of the American dream: The diaries of David Wojnarowicz.* New York: Grove Press.

34 Neo-Liberal Globalization, Educational Policy, and the Struggle for Social Justice

Fazal Rizvi and Laura C. Engel

Introduction

Since the mid- to late 1980s, educational policy has increasingly been incorporated around the world within the broader discourses about the changing nature of the global economy. It is argued that since the global economy is characterized as "knowledge-based," it requires greater levels of education and training than ever before. Educational systems are asked to produce a workforce more adequately prepared to meet the challenges of globalization. At the same time, it has been suggested that economic development is not possible without policies that encourage greater participation in education, especially by those who have traditionally been marginalized. Indeed, greater access to education is considered essential for success in the knowledge economy. In this way, a new rhetoric of access and equity in education seems to be emerging, inextricably tied to the assumptions about globalization's policy imperatives for education.

In this chapter, we want to argue that this construction of access and equity is fundamentally ideological because it assumes a minimalist understanding of the principles of social justice, is concerned only with formal access to educational institutions, and not with the broader issues of structural inequalities. Such an understanding of justice is predicted upon an overriding concern with capital accumulation. Furthermore, we want to suggest that this construction of access and equity is framed within a particular hegemonic characterization of globalization, which is not only reshaping economic and political relations around the world but is also transforming the discursive terrain within which educational policies are now developed and enacted. This terrain is informed by a range of neoliberal precepts, constituting a set of policy pressures which, increasingly, national systems of education now have to negotiate, and often embrace. These pressures emanate from a wide variety of sources, most notably intergovernmental organizations (IGOs), which now steer nation-states in various complex ways toward conceptions of educational governance and, more fundamentally, education's basic purposes in neoliberal terms.

We begin this chapter by arguing that while it is possible to imagine a range of different interpretations of globalization, it is the neo-liberal conception that has, in recent decades, become hegemonic. We then explore the role that IGOs have played in promoting the neo-liberal conception of globalization, and steering national systems towards embracing its prescriptions for educational reform. We suggest that it is a mistake to assume that neo-liberalism is not interested in issues of justice; but argue instead that its conception is based on a very "weak" and narrow notion of justice viewed largely as access to the existing institutions of education. Its focus on increasing levels of educational participation is based on capitalism's need for greater number of workers adequately prepared to work in the evolving knowledge economy. In this way, the idea of social justice is enveloped by the concerns of market efficiency, most notably through a predominantly economic framing of education. While we do not, of course, wish to deny the importance of providing marginalized populations institutional access, and indeed of preparing them for the world of work, we want to argue that the struggle for education and social justice needs to address the broader issues of structural inequalities, both pre-existing and those produced by neo-liberal globalization. Within this context, we want to suggest that mere access to education defined solely in terms of market efficiency is incapable of producing social justice, which, in our view, requires a more broadly based struggle against the disastrous consequences of neo-liberal globalization and corporate capitalism.

Interpreting Globalization

The concept of globalization has been widely used in recent years to characterize the imperatives driving educational changes, even if globalization remains poorly understood and highly contested. While there is little consensus or consistency over its meaning and implications, globalization does appear to name some of the social and economic changes that are currently taking place around the world. Most of these changes are driven by recent revolutions in information and communication technologies (ICT) and the rapid transnational flows of people, capital, ideas, and information, which have resulted in a world that is more interconnected and interdependent than ever before.

Paradoxically, these global processes have themselves created some of the conditions by which the idea of globalization has seemingly become ubiquitous, used widely in both policy and popular discourses to explain the nature of recent changes. As such, globalization has become what Anthony Nòvoa (2002) calls "planet speak." In general, it typically has been used to refer to a set of social processes that imply "inexorable integration of markets, nation-states and technologies to a degree never witnessed before—in a way that is enabling individuals, corporations and nation-states to reach round the world farther, faster, deeper and cheaper than ever before" (Friedman, 2000, p. 7). Such integration, however, is far from complete; and its nature can be understood in a variety of ways. Its impact is different from one place to another, clearly benefiting some communities more than others. While referring to a whole range of political, social, economic, and cultural processes, there are thus many different perspectives that can be used to interpret globalization. But what is beyond doubt is that these processes have transformed the nature of economic activity, changing the modes of production and consumption.

The global economy is now characterized as informational, networked, knowledge-based, postindustrial and service oriented (Castells, 2000). In his highly influential book, *The Condition of Postmodernity*, David Harvey (1989) provided perhaps one of the best descriptions of economic globalization. He argued that globalization describes "an intense period of time-space compression that has had a disorientating and disruptive impact on political-economic practices, the balance of class power, as well as upon cultural and social life" (p. 8). Improved systems of communication and information flows and rationalization in the techniques of distribution, he suggested, enabled capital and commodities to be moved through the global market with greater speed. The new post-Fordist organizational ideology, promoting flexibility and instantaneity, replaced the rigid structure and organization of the Fordist economy. This is expressed most explicitly in ideas of subcontracting, outsourcing, vertical disintegration, just-in-time delivery system, and the like.

Such economic globalization also has led to a new conception of governance, requiring a radically revised view of the roles and responsibilities of national governments, minimizing the need for their policy intervention, with greater reliance on the market

(Strange, 1996). Yeatman (1998) argued that this view suggested that the old centralized bureaucratic state structures had become too slow, sclerotic, and "out of sync" with the emergent needs of transnational capital, and that new devolved forms of governance were more compatible with the demands of the global economy. Indeed, theorists began to speak of the "retreat and erosion" (Strange, 1996), "the hollowing out" (Jessop, 1999), and the "changing architecture" (Cerny, 1990) of the state. This perspective of the state and global processes was rooted in the argument that "national boundaries no longer act as 'watertight' containers of the production process" (Dicken, 2003, p. 9). This interpretation of the declining state dislodged one of the central tenets of the modern nation-state system—the claim to distinctive symmetry and correspondence between territory and legitimacy.

It is now clear, however, that especially in the post-September 11 era, many of the claims about the demise of the state were overstated (Rizvi, 2004). We can now see how nation-states fiercely protect their sovereignty, even if it is equally true that the exclusive link between territory and political power has been broken, as a result not only of the globalizing economies and the operations of the transnational corporations but also of the changing political configurations that have made most arenas of public policy subject to global considerations. As Held and McGrew (2003) have argued, "the state has become a fragmented policy-making arena, permeated by transnational networks (governmental and non-governmental) as well as by domestic agencies and forces" (p. 11). So, while the modern state retains some of its authority, and indeed needs to perform some key functions, such as ensuring conditions necessary for capital accumulation, it now also needs to negotiate forces beyond its control—not only of transnational capital but also of policy ideologies emanating from IGOs. This applies to educational policy as much as it does to economic policy, as educational priorities have become thoroughly implicated within the global power configurations.

We are only beginning to appreciate how the accelerating political dynamics of globalization affect educational policy development at the national level in a range of complicated ways, most notably through the circulation of a particular set of educational ideas and ideologies, resulting in global educational policy networks, which have arguably become highly influential (Rizvi & Lingard, 2006). While these networks do not dictate or prescribe policy as such, they do constitute an informational terrain that steers national systems of education in a particular ideological direction. They have been enormously successful in creating a discursive framework within which a particular conception of globalization is now promoted, and within which its implications for education are now debated. Indeed, a discourse of "globalization's policy imperatives" appears to have become hegemonic.

In the constitution of global educational policy networks, the role of IGOs such as the Asia-Pacific Economic Cooperation (APEC), the European Union (EU), the Organization for Economic Cooperation and Development (OECD), the United Nations Educational, Scientific and Cultural Organization (UNESCO), the International Monetary Fund (IMF), and the World Bank has become highly significant (Dale & Robertson, 2002). They play an important role in the processes of educational policy formation and evaluation. This role is diverse, and may involve negotiating consensus and conventions, such as the Washington Consensus or the Bologna Declaration, to ensure coordinated policy action across national systems, or supporting international cooperation in education through the development of global indicators of performance and quality, such as Trends in International Mathematics and Science Study (TIMSS) and the Program for International Student Assessment (PISA). While the ultimate authority for policy development still remains with the national systems, participation in these international conventions and programs nonetheless ensures that nations are incorporated within the dominant ideological discourses that are promoted by IGOs, and circulate within the media and a global class of policy experts. These efforts lead to policy borrowing, modeling transfer, appropriation, and copying of ideas across national boundaries (Steiner-Khamsi, 2004). It is important to note, however, that the dominant ideological policy discourse promoted by IGOs does not affect every national system in the same way. While some "borrow" policies, others, developing countries, in particular, are often economically coerced into accepting its terms by IGOs that provide them with loans, grants, and aid, while others are able to resist some of their "advice."

These developments are eloquently elaborated by Bourdieu (2003), who has suggested that globalization represents a deliberate, ideological project of economic liberalization that subjects states and individuals to more intense market forces. This project, often referred to as neoliberal, is thus based on a politics of meaning that seeks to accommodate people and nations to a certain taken-for-grantedness about the ways the global economy operates and the manner in which culture, crises, resources, and power formations are filtered through its universal logic. It thus creates a global market mentality and global subjects who in turn view the world and the policy options they have through its conceptual prism. From this perspective, the term *globalization* designates certain power relations, practices, and technologies, playing a "hegemonic role in organizing and decoding the meaning of the world" (Scharito & Webb, 2003, p. 1). In this way, neo-liberalism is highly normative, and directs us toward a particular view of the collective consciousness of the world as a single space.

As a range of loosely connected ideas, neoliberal globalization specifies new forms of political–economic governance based on the extension of market relationships through which it suggests people and communities are becoming interconnected. In contrast to the earlier assumption that the state provision of goods and services was a way of ensuing social well-being of a national population, and as a way of forming communities, neoliberal globalization prescribes a new conception of social relations. It advocates a minimalist state, based on a "lean" government concerned to promote the instrumental values of competition, economic efficiency and choice, to deregulate and privatize state functions. As Peck and Tickell (2002) have argued, neo-liberalism promotes and normalizes a "growth-first approach" to policy, making social welfare concerns secondary (p. 394). It promotes market logics as natural, justifying them on the grounds of efficiency and even "fairness." It also preaches the principle of global "free trade," applying it to both goods and services, even to services such as health and education that were traditionally marked by their highly national character. Neo-liberal globalization thus represents a social imaginary that has become hegemonic (Rizvi, 2006).

Neo-Liberal Globalization and Shifts in Educational Policy

In recent years, educational policies have been deeply affected by this imaginary as national systems seek to realign their priorities to what they assume to be globalization's imperatives for education. As we have already noted, neo-liberal globalization demands a system-wide understanding of the global processes, not only of shifting economic processes but also of the changing nature of politics and cultural relations. In educational terms, such a context demands a new conception of education tied more closely to economic consideration but also the development of a range of cross-cultural skills and what is referred to as "global competence." These sentiments constitute a new discourse of education.

A part of this discourse is the concept of knowledge economy. In education, perhaps no other document has been more influential in promoting the idea of knowledge economy than the OECD's report, *The Knowledge Based Economy* (1996a). In this report, the economic goals of education are clearly given priority over its social and cultural purposes. In the knowledge economy, it is suggested, knowing about facts and theories is less important than an understanding of the world of social relations and the networks through which knowledge is converted into innovation and commercially viable products. In a flexible and dynamic economy, knowing how to find out relevant information and how to use it commercially is considered more important than formal, codified, structured, and explicit knowledge; as is the ability to work in culturally diverse contexts and possess generic skills of communication and problem solving. The idea of lifelong learning is linked to this objective. Its focus is on the dynamics of change—the changing nature of technologies, of work and the labor market, of the global markets, and of the demographic composition of organizations.

The idea of lifelong education was a major term of reference for UNESCO in 1994, and the OECD (1996b) adopted *Making Lifelong Learning a Reality for All* as a theme of its mandate for 1997 to 2001. However, the OECD attached a different meaning to the concept of lifelong learning. It was no longer linked to a humanistic conception of education, but to a neoliberalism that stressed the creation of the individualistic, self-capitalizing individual (Rose, 1999). Increasingly, the neo-liberal construction of the purposes of lifelong learning has become more dominant. It rearticulates the goals of education, placing a greater emphasis on preparing people for the world of work and a life of self-capitalization. In most of OECD's subsequent reports, the need to develop certain dispositions amongst all citizens toward ongoing learning across the life cycle is emphasized repeatedly. What are now required, it is suggested, are flexible, mobile, lifelong learners who are able to deal effectively with cultural diversity, endemic change, and innovation.

A similar neoliberal approach to education can also be found in documents produced by the EU, which in 2000 established a "strategic objective of becoming the most competitive and dynamic knowledge-based economy in the world." The European Commission (2001) has established a working group of experts to create a set of common indicators and benchmarks, in a strategy that has now become known as the Open Method of Coordination (OMC). As a new framework for comparison and consolidation of particular educational performance standards, the OMC gathers the "best" national education practices to design a set of common objectives for national education systems. Based on the objectives, represented European member states then compile and agree on a set of targeted yardsticks (statistics, indicators) for reaching the set objectives. Larsson (2002) has argued, "the dynamics of this [the OMC] have significant implications for national agenda setting. By identifying and making public best practice and by issuing recommendations to individual Member States the Commission and the Council can exert considerable pressure" (p. 13). Like the EU, most IGOs often insist that they are only providing forums for open and free exploration of educational ideas, but it has now become increasingly clear that they play a major hegemonic role in promoting neoliberal ideologies.

These ideologies are largely based on human capital theory (Becker, 1964), which postulates that expenditure on training and education should be considered as an investment undertaken with a view to increasing personal incomes. In the global economy, this investment is considered essential for individuals, corporations, and nations if they wish to secure competitive advantage. In its popular form, neo-liberalism thus assumes economic growth and competitive advantage to be a direct outcome of the levels of investment in developing human capital. This is clearly evident in an OECD (1998a) report, *Human Capital Investment: An International Comparison*:

The level of skills, knowledge and competencies held at any one time by individuals can be taken to represent the "stock" of human capital. The total stock within a country can influence its prosperity and international competitiveness. The distribution of knowledge and skills has an important bearing on social participation and access to employment and income. So, governments are interested in both the overall human capital stock and ways in which specific skills and competencies are distributed within the population. (p. 15)

The report goes on to suggest that, in a global economy, performance is increasingly linked to people's knowledge stock, skills level, learning capabilities, and cultural adaptability. It therefore demands policy frameworks that enhance labor flexibility not only through the deregulation of the market but also through reform to systems of education and training, better aligned to the changing nature of economic activity.

This does not mean that ethical and cultural issues are no longer relevant to education, but that they are now interpreted within the broader framework of education's economic ends. In this way, neoliberalism rests on what George Soros (1998) has called "economic fundamentalism," a kind of conceptual prism through which even notions like diversity and equity are rearticulated in economic terms.

In the process, a new discourse of educational purposes has emerged, not only sidelining education's traditional concerns with the development of individuals and communities but also rearticulating them. In educational systems, there has been a tension between its competing goals linked to social equity on the one hand and education's role in market efficiency on the other. In the next section, we want to argue that in the context of neoliberal globalization, the always-tenuous balance between equity and efficiency has been pushed firmly towards the latter. Education is now increasingly focused on the production of the self-capitalizing, flexible neoliberal subject. Perhaps even more significantly, we want to suggest that the very notion of equity has been rearticulated, becoming tied to the instrumentalist concepts of social capital and social cohesion, rather than to the stronger concerns about social justice.

Competing Conceptions of Equity in Education

Over the past two decades, much of what is now regarded as educational reform is based on an ideological belief that social and economic "progress" can only be achieved through systems of education geared more toward fulfilling the needs of the market. It also is assumed that educational systems have for far too long been inefficient and ineffective in ways that prevent them from meeting economic goals. Popular media and corporations have in particular propagated this view, and have called on governments to pursue reforms that are not only more socially and economically efficient but are also cognizant of the new "realities" of the knowledge economy in an increasingly globalized world. This has required the purposes of education to be more instrumentally defined, in terms of its capacity to produce workers who have grounding in basic literacy and numeracy, who are flexible, creative, and multiskilled, have good knowledge of new technologies, and are able to work in culturally diverse environments.

These aims of education are regarded as important for not only societies but also the individual. Indeed, societies are defined largely as a sum of individuals. Their economic well-being, health, employment, and productive citizenship are considered indicators of national success. A notion of access to education by individuals is therefore central to the neo-liberal ideology because it is argued that without access, chances of achieving social and economic mobility are negligible for individuals and detrimental to societies.

However, simple formal access to schools has never been sufficient to realize the potential of education, because unless families have an adequate economic base at home to support students attending schools, students are unlikely to be able to take advantage of formal access. This, of course, complicates the relationship between access to education and equity outcomes. While a commitment to formal access is entirely consistent with the idea of market efficiency, it is not enough to achieve social justice. For this to become a reality, attention needs be paid also to issues of the social conditions necessary for learning, of instructional quality, and of the resources that are necessary to support effective programs. Formal access to schooling does not always translate into effective equity outcomes.

Indeed, simple access can be counterproductive, setting up expectations which, if not realized, have the potential to create considerable social alienation among those who have invested time and effort in education, but without receiving the promised rewards. Without good teachers, who have adequate training and professional attitudes, access can undermine equity, even if it meets some of the standards of efficiency. Access can also be counterproductive if the curriculum and instruction is not linked to local cultures and traditions, and is inappropriate to the community in which it is offered. This requires a more complex view of equity than is suggested by the weak market efficiency view. Education has a whole range of purposes, and it is not simply about producing efficient workers for the changing global economy. If this is so, then efficiency has to be reconciled with the broader cultural concerns of education, linked to issues of class, gender, and ethnicity.

That simple access is not sufficient for achieving equity in education can be further demonstrated by addressing issues relating to the education of girls. In particular educational contexts, such as those of the developing countries, girls have had limited access to primary education. This has led to greater international attention on issues of educational access and opportunities for girls. In recent years, IGOs such as the OECD, the World Bank, UNESCO, and UNICEF have repeatedly emphasized the importance of gender equity in education. For example, UNICEF is the acting Secretariat and leading agency for the United Nations Girls' Education Initiative (UNGEI), which was launched in 2000 to focus on providing greater access to education, and to shrink the achievement gap between boys and girls in both primary and secondary education. Indeed much has been done to provide girls with greater access to education; and the number of girls attending school has never been greater. For example, as illustrated by the United Nations Statistical Division (2005), in most regions of the world, the ratio of girls to boys in primary education demonstrates that participation of girls is increasing, with large gains in Northern Africa, Eastern and Southern Asia, and least developed countries.

However, the neoliberal arguments for greater educational access of girls reveal a weak conception of equity, cast largely in terms of market efficiency, and the requirements of the global economy (Rizvi et al., 2005). According to the World Bank (2006), for example, "research has also shown that women and girls work harder than men, are more likely to invest their earning in their children, and are major producers as well as consumers." UNESCO (2003) has stated, "Educating girls yields the highest return in economic terms." Finally, the OECD (1998b) has urged that "Investing in women (with respect to education, health, family planning, access to land, etc.) not only directly reduces poverty, but also leads to higher productivity and a more efficient use of resources." Each of these views link gender equity to economic consumerism and efficiency, and views women as means to certain economic ends, rather than as people who participate in education for a wide variety of reasons, some economic, others social and cultural.

A stronger claim to gender equity in education, on the other hand, must address issues not only of their access to education but also of economic and social consequences of globalization for their lives. Here the picture is decidedly mixed. Recent data show that while girls are participating in education in larger numbers than ever before, the outcomes of their education are not socially and economically proportional to their efforts. For example, in recent years, there have been many more opportunities for women to utilize their education in paid work. However, this work has been predominantly in the service economy of global information, global communication, global retailing, and global finance (Scholte, 2000). Each of these areas has been characterized by "flexible" labor conditions and poorer career prospects, perpetuating and sometimes deepening gender hierarchies. Even the growing level of access of women to higher education indicates that their participation in the fields of the natural sciences and engineering is far from gender parity. With growing importance attached to these fields within the global economy, associated with technological innovation and technical expertise, this inequality is more significant than might first appear, because it suggests that the growing access of women to tertiary education is in areas that do not enjoy the same high economic rewards, social status, and prestige.

What this analysis indicates is that gender equity beyond access requires a more systematic focus on the social processes that perpetuate gender inequalities. This aspiration is clearly informed by a different view of the purposes of education. While the market efficiency view demands better utilization of the human resources that women represent, a stronger view of equity seeks a social transformation through which gender relations are reconfigured. This latter view highlights the importance of not only access and social inclusion, but also the need to rethink the terms of that inclusion. It envisages societies that have potentially been economically, politically, and socially transformed in gender terms. This requires changes not only to the ways in which education is administered but changes also to curriculum and pedagogy, especially in the context of globalization, with its potential to reshape patterns of both economic and social relations.

We have noted that the neoliberal emphasis on market efficiency has not entirely displaced concerns for social and educational equity. In fact, equity is readily incorporated within the broader discourse of market efficiency. For example, it has been argued by the OECD that a focus on market efficiency can in fact lead to greater equality and opportunities for social mobility. It is suggested that without workers who are able to perform effectively in the global labor market, the potential for social mobility is severely reduced; and that since the global economy requires appropriate social conditions for capital accumulation and economic growth, equity concerns cannot be overlooked by policymakers committed to market efficiency. As the OECD (1996b, p. 15) suggested:

> A new focus for education and training policies is needed now, to develop capacities to realize the potential of the "global information economy" and to contribute to employment, culture, democracy and, above all, social cohesion. Such policies will need to support the transition to "learning societies" in which equal opportunities are available to all, access is open, and all individuals are encouraged and motivated to learn, in formal education as well as throughout life.

Ultimately, what this discourse suggests is that market efficiency must now be regarded as a "meta-value," subsuming within its scope educational aspirations such as social equity, mobility, and even cohesion.

Equity, Efficiency, and Educational Governance

As a meta-value, the emphasis on market efficiency does not only suggest revisiting the basic purposes of education, which involves rearticulating the concept of equity, it also implies the need to reconfigure educational governance. With its emphasis on a more instrumental approach to education purposes, linked to the requirements of the knowledge economy, neo-liberal globalization demands a vigorous agenda for rethinking state structures and forms of educational governance. Incorporated within this agenda is the view that administrative reform is central to a nation's capacity to ensure accelerated economic productivity and growth. As a result, educational governance has been at the forefront of a wave of public sector reform that has seen the structures and practices of all public sector departments transformed under the rubric of "corporate managerialism" or "new public management." This transformation has been based upon private sector management practices, in which a greater emphasis is placed on outcomes achieved at the lowest possible costs.

The twin goals of greater efficiency (doing things at the lowest cost) and greater effectiveness (achieving the goals set) have underpinned the new structures that are less hierarchical and much flatter, with greater management prerogative for policy steering. The old top-down structure has thus been replaced by new governance arrangements, in which relations between the policy producing strategic center of the organization and the practice periphery have also been reset. The center establishes the strategic goals and desired policy outcomes, while the policy-practicing periphery is responsible for achieving these goals. As such, any new autonomy at the periphery is in relation to the means rather than policy ends, which are now set more tightly by the center as part of a new regime of outcomes accountability.

This new regime of governance is perhaps most clearly articulated in a highly influential OECD (1995) report, *Governance in Transition: Public Management Reforms in OECD Countries*. The report notes, in a not too muted criticism of old style state bureaucracies, that "highly centralised, rule-bound, and inflexible organizations that emphasise process rather than results impede good performance" and that the efficiency of the public sector "has a significant impact on total economic efficiency" (p. 7). This broadly ideological sentiment implies a new discourse of educational governance that has been promoted vigorously since the late 1990s. This discourse is constituted by such concepts as strategic planning, cost-efficiency, human resource allocation, competition and choice, optimizing information technology, performance management, and accountability.

Embodying these characteristics is the increasing rhetoric about "good governance," a phrase that masks an underlying shift in educational ideology. Debated under the rubric of good governance are issues concerning transparency of decision-making processes, forms of devolution, technologies of measuring educational performance, international benchmarking, mechanisms of quality assurance, appropriate accountability regimes, sources of educational funding, effective uses of public resources, and so on. Even this short list shows how most of these concerns relate to market efficiency, defined mostly in terms of the extent to which educational systems are responsive to the labor market needs of the global economy.

What we have thus witnessed in educational systems around the world, as a result of public sector restructuring in the name of good governance, is a centralization of policy setting and devolution of responsibility to achieve the goals set at the center. However, the idea of devolution can be, and has been, used in a number of different ways. In the 1995 report, the OECD itself recognized that it is frequently the case that devolution is used as "catch-all term for the granting of greater decision-making authority and autonomy" (p.

157). Traditionally, the democratic idea of devolution suggested that there was increased citizen participation, local control, "bringing the government to the people," and an overall enhancement of democratic principles, and that these principles were embodied within a broader conception of social justice.

Under the regime of neoliberal globalization, however, devolution has acquired a new meaning, and is now considered a strategy of governance, in which it is believed that less central bureaucracy enhances system efficiency (Engel, 2007). In this case, devolution signifies a transfer of central agency responsibilities, managerial tasks, and funding allocations to regional or local agencies. This global ideology of governance usurps any democratic meaning of devolution and promotes instead a more administrative and fiscal form. According to this definition, devolution involves a commitment to a set of corporate management principles and market ideologies. In this way, devolution involves considerations of how expenditure on education is allocated, distributed, and monitored. It is utilized to ease the financial burden of the central state, or to generate greater expenditure on education through the transfer of financial responsibilities to regional or local level agencies, or simply as means of achieving greater efficiency in fiscal matters. Local institutions are permitted to make decisions, but only in ways that are aligned to national goals and standards, which are increasingly linked to a broader technology of public administration.

In addition, an emphasis on fiscal devolution is linked to political conditions in which privatization is viewed as its logical outcome. In such a context, educational managers at local and district levels struggle to manage their own education programs and implement local priorities, particularly those that cannot be easily accommodated within the broader national frameworks directing performance-based funding regimes. The global trend toward privatization of education, not only at tertiary but also primary and secondary levels, has intensified inequalities in a number of ways. While governments around the world have highlighted the importance of higher levels of education, they have either been unwilling or unable to fund growth in demand for educational participation. The use of the rhetoric of privatization has thus become widespread around the world, along with an emphasis on the notions of quality, efficiency, and productivity. With the scaling back of government funding igniting a rise in privatization, the role of the private sector in education has also grown, blurring the lines between government and private responsibilities over education. These developments have had major implications for educational equity, as private interests have increasingly assumed a greater significance in policy development in education.

What is clear then is that the conception of educational purposes advocated by neoliberal globalization and its preferred model of educational governance are closely aligned. Both are linked to the concerns of market efficiency. Both emphasize the importance of market dynamics in the organization of education around a view of educational purposes concerned with the formation of human capital to meet the requirements of the global economy. With greater policy focus on the knowledge economy, the market efficiency perspective on the aims of education has become hegemonic, undermining those aims that are dedicated to the goals of social justice. While equity remains on the agenda, it has been rearticulated away from a strong definition of social justice towards the concerns of social and cultural formations. Concerns about class, gender, and race inequalities are less evident in this rearticulated equity agenda concerned largely with economic ends for individuals and societies alike.

Of course, efficiency and equity purposes of education need not be viewed as mutually exclusive: it is possible both to promote equity and to ensure that education is efficiently and effectively organized to serve the changing conditions in which it takes places. The balance, however, as we have argued in this paper, has tilted educational policy toward market efficiency because it has promoted a particular ideological view of educational aims linked to the requirements of a global knowledge economy and a range of ideas about educational governance derived from the new theories of public management, which increasingly promote corporatized and privatized administration of education, outcome measures, and knowledge as commodity. In this way, a fundamental tension between efficiency and equity has been left intact.

It also has given rise to a range of contradictions that can no longer be ignored. For example, the promotion of devolved systems of governance has left many educators and educational systems feeling disenfranchised, especially when they are expected to conform to unrealistic accountability regimes, and deliver outcomes for which they have not been adequately funded or resourced. Their professionalism has been sapped of any real meaning because they are now required to become efficient and effective in contexts that are culturally, economically, and politically complex. At the same time, the policy shift toward privatization, in particular, has compromised the broader goals of social justice and has widened inequalities not only across nations but also within the same communities. It has made the goals of gender and racial equity more difficult to realize.

Conclusion

In this chapter, we have discussed how a particular interpretation of globalization that is neo-liberal in orientation, has, in recent years, reconfigured the discursive terrain within which educational policy is developed and enacted; and how this reconfiguration has undermined, in various ways, the goal of equity and social inclusion in education. Led primarily by IGOs, this neo-liberal conception of globalization has become hegemonic, resulting in the dominance of market efficiency goals of education and the ascendancy of symbolic forms of access and equity. In relation to these goals, we have argued, there has been an emergence of new forms of educational governance that are aligned with the rhetoric of good governance. Consequently, administrative and fiscal forms of devolution have been readily employed in national systems of education around the world, often without an increase in local or regional autonomy, and in some cases, a decrease in educational financial resources.

Throughout our discussion of these developments, we have argued the rhetoric of access and equity couched in terms of market efficiency has often worked against the stronger claims of justice in and through education. It has also left many educators and educational systems feeling disenfranchised, especially when they are expected to conform to unrealistic accountability regimes, and deliver outcomes for which they have not been adequately funded or resourced. The policy shifts driven by neo-liberal globalization have compromised their broader social and political commitment, as they have widened inequalities across gender, class, and nations. Without a stronger notion of equity and access, the excessive emphasis on efficiency has resulted in greater focus on the operational requirements of the systems rather than upon lives of the people and their communities, thus undermining aims of education for social justice.

References

Becker, G. (1964). *Human capital.* New York: National Bureau of Economic Research.
Bourdieu, P. (2003). *Firing back: Against the tyranny of the market.* London: Verso.

Castells, M. (2000). *The rise of the network society*. Oxford: Blackwell.

Cerny, P. G. (1990). *Changing architecture of politics: Structure, agency and the future of the state*. London: Sage.

Dale, R., & Robertson, S. (2002). The varying effects of regional organizations as subjects of globalization on education. *Comparative Education Review, 46*(1), 10–36.

Dicken, P. (2003). *Global shift: Reshaping the global economic map in the 21st century* (4th ed.). New York: Guilford.

Engel, L. C. (2007). 'Rolling back, rolling out': Exceptionalism and neoliberalism of the Spanish state. *Critical Studies in Education, 48*(2), 213–277.

European Commission. (2001). *European report on the quality of school education: Sixteen quality indicators: Report based on the work of the working committee on quality indicators*. Luxembourg: Office for Official Publications of the European Communities.

Friedman, T. (2000). *Lexus and the olive tree: Understanding globalization*. New York: Farrar, Straus & Giroux.

Harvey, D. (1989). *The condition of postmodernity*. Oxford: Blackwell.

Held, D., & McGrew, A. (Eds.). (2003). *The global transformation reader: An introduction to the globalization debate*. Cambridge, UK: Polity Press.

Jessop, B. (1999). The changing governance of welfare: Recent trends in its primary functions, scale and modes of coordination. *Social Policy and Administration, 33*(4), 348–359.

Larsson, A. (2002, March 4th). *The new open method of co-ordination: A sustainable way between a fragmented Europe and a European supra state: A practitioner's view*. Lecture presented at Uppsala University.

Nóvoa, A. (2002). Ways of thinking about education in Europe. In A. Nóvoa & M. Lawn (Eds.), *Fabricating Europe: The formation of an education space* (pp. 131–156). Dordrecht, Netherlands: Kluwer.

Organisation for Economic Co-operation and Development [OECD]. (1995). *Governance in transition: Public management reforms in OECD countries*. Paris: Author.

Organisation for Economic Co-operation and Development [OECD]. (1996a). *The knowledge based economy*. Paris: Author.

Organisation for Economic Co-operation and Development [OECD]. (1996b). *Lifelong learning for all*. Paris: Author.

Organisation for Economic Co-operation and Development [OECD]. (1998a). *Human capital investment: An international comparison*. Paris: Author.

Organisation for Economic Co-operation and Development [OECD]. (1998b). *Gender and economic development: The work of Diane Elson. Summary and Comments, Introduction: Women and development*, Retrieved April 6, 2005, http://www.oecd.org/LongAbstract/0,2 546,en_2649_37419_2755271_1_1_1_37419,00.html

Peck, J., & Tickell, A. (2002). Neoliberalizing space. *Antipode, 34*(3), 341–624.

Rizvi, F. (2004). Rethinking globalization and education after September 11. *Comparative Education, 40*(2), 157–171.

Rizvi, F. (2006). Imagination and the globalization of educational policy research. *Globalization, Education and Societies, 4*(2), 193–206.

Rizvi, F., Engel, L., Nandyala, A., Rutkowski, D., & Sparks, J. (2005). Globalization and recent shifts in educational policy in the Asia Pacific: An overview of some critical issues. APEID/UNESCO Bangkok Occasional Paper Series No. 4, 1–59.

Rizvi, F, & Lingard, B. (2006). Globalization and the changing nature of the OECD's educational work. In H. Lauder, P. Brown, J. Dillabough, & A. H. Halsey (Eds.), *Education, globalization and social change* (pp. 247–260). Oxford: Oxford University Press.

Rose, N. (1999). *Powers of freedom reframing political thought*. Cambridge, UK: Cambridge University Press.

Scharito, T., & Webb, J. (2003). *Understanding globalization*. London: Sage.

Scholte, J. A. (2000). *Globalization: A critical view*. London: St. Martin's Press.

Soros, G. (1998). *The crisis of global capitalism*. Boston: Little, Brown.

Steiner-Khamsi, G. (2004). *The global politics of educational borrowing and lending.* New York: Teachers College Press.

Strange, S. (1996). *The retreat of the state: The diffusion of power in the world economy.* Cambridge, UK: Cambridge University Press.

UNESCO. (2003). *All for girls' education! Why it is important.* Retrieved May 8, 2005, from http://portal.unesco.org/education/en/ev.php-URL_ID=14091&URL_DO=DO_TOPIC&URL_SECTION=201.html

United Nations Statistics Division. (2005). *World and regional trends.* Retrieved September 7, 2006, from http://unstats.un.org/unsd/mi/mi_worldregn.asp

Williamson, J. (1990). *Latin American adjustment: How much has happened?* Washington, D.C.: Institute for International Economics.

World Bank. (2006). *Gender and development.* Retrieved December 7, 2006, from http://web.worldbank.org/WBSITE/EXTERNAL/TOPICS/EXTGENDER/0,,menuPK:336874~pagePK:149018~piPK:149093~theSitePK:336868,00.html

Yeatman, A. (1998). Trends and opportunities in the public sector: a critical assessment. *Australian Journal of Public Administration, 57(4),* 138–147.

35 Globalization, Education Governance, and Citizenship Regimes

New Democratic Deficits and Social Injustices

Susan L. Robertson

Introduction

In the past two decades, education systems[1] around the globe have undergone dramatic changes. In large part this is because of changes within and between nation-states, as the stakes increase in the competitive race between nations and regions in the global economy (cf. Cerny, 1997; Held, McGrew, Perraton, & Dicken, 1999). It is also because there has been a reconceptualization of the role of education across the developed and developing world: on the one hand, to tie education more closely to the economy in order to drive economic growth; and on the other, to develop the formal education sectors in such a way that they directly generate income for institutions, national economies, and for-profit firms who are moving into providing services in particular sectors.

Throughout this period there have been major changes in the structures and systems of governance of nation-states, with national states ceding some of their powers of governing to new or reinvigorated "scales" of activity—by scale I am referring to what Collinge (1999) calls "the vertical ordering of social formations"—as in concepts like the *national*, *regional*, *global*, and *local* (Jessop, 2000). New and invigorated global and regional institutions and structures, such as the World Trade Organization (WTO), the European Union (EU), the Free Trade Area of the Americas (FTAA), and New Partnership for Africa's Development (NEPAD), have emerged, all with important implications for education (Dale & Robertson, 2002; Robertson, Bonal, & Dale, 2002), while the decentralization and dispersal of the state's functions to local communities and private actors has considerably complicated the terrain of education provision, funding and its regulation (Dale, 1997). In sum, national/subnational education systems—at all levels—from schools to higher education establishments, are being transformed.

These transformations in the governance of education systems, however, raise important questions about how education systems now mediate citizens' claims-making and thus the terrain of social justice, particularly as education has been such an important institution in attempting to mediate the tensions between capitalism and democracy through redistribution and, more recently, recognition politics (see Carnoy & Levin, 1985). Education has been a key institution for nation-states in constructing *citizens*, not only in terms of identity, but also as potential workers and members of a polity—often referred to as "nation building" (Kymlicka & Norman, 1994). Education is an important political arena of struggle for members of a polity around who gets taught what, as well as matters of access and equal opportunity. It is also a central strategic platform for political actors, including political parties and the wider public—particularly because of its discursively constructed "public good" ethos.[2] Finally, education systems have been a core mechanism in generating legitimacy and societal cohesion for the capitalist state, in part through the knowledge that is transmitted, but also because of the capacity of education systems to propagate ideas like meritocracy, and the values of market economies and societies.

If, however, national systems of education are being transformed as a result of processes of globalization, the questions we must ask ourselves now are these: What form are these transformations taking? How do they alter the nature of national citizenship regimes? And, what are the implications of these shifts for citizens and claims-making in nation-states, particularly for the constitution of rights, responsibilities, identities, and social justice? In this chapter I want to address these questions by first outlining what I mean by 'citizenship' and the idea of a 'citizenship regime'. I will then develop four linked shifts that chart the nature of the transformations taking place in education that both directly and indirectly impinge on citizenship regimes. These shifts, I will argue, are re/constituting citizenship regimes and citizens at multiple scales and, as a result, the sites and parameters for claims-making and social justice. Specifically, I will suggest that as a result of neoliberal policies, programs and practices at multiple scales—from the global to the local—there is a diminution, if not an absence, of possibilities for political claims by citizens, giving rise to a significant democratic deficit.

Defining Citizenship and Citizenship Regimes

"In its narrowest definition, citizenship describes the legal relationship between the individual and the polity" (Sassen, 2005, p. 81). Until recently, the idea of citizenship was commonly associated with the Westphalian system of nation-states, with nationality a key component. This meant that two distinct ideas, that of citizenship and of nationality, tended to fuse. Until more recently, for example, a citizen could normally only be a passport holder in one nation, while dual or multiple passports were firmly discouraged. This reinforced the idea that nationality, such as "United States of America" or "Germany," and citizenship were the same.

However, while related to each other, nationality and citizenship reflect different legal frameworks. While both identify the legal status of an individual in terms of state membership, until more recently citizenship was largely confined to the national dimension (as in the right of access to state assistance, liability to conscription), while nationality referred to the international legal dimension of citizenship in the context of an interstate system (such as being a passport holder of a particular nation). In other words, being a passport holder (nationality) might not qualify an individual for all of the rights that a citizen of that nation (national and nonnational) might have access to. An example here might be when a UK national, who has been absent from the country for some time, has no recourse to public funds immediately on arrival back in the country, while a nonnational resident might have access to public funds as a result of meeting certain residency requirements. Alternatively, being a national of New Zealand until recently entitled individuals to access public funds in Australia.

These two brief examples make a wider point; that there is considerable variation across nation-states as to how citizenship is articulated, how noncitizens are defined, and what rights citizens are entitled to. We can also see that "citizenship is a social construction" (Jenson, 2000, p. 232). That is, how citizenship is understood and practiced varies with place and over time. Where these constructions develop some degree of stability and coherence, and are the foundation for widely understood and endorsed claims-making within a social formation, we can refer to these paradigmatic encodings as a *citizenship regime*. For Jenson, a citizenship regime can be seen as:

...the institutional arrangements, rules and understandings that guide and shape con-current policy decisions and expenditures of states, problem definitions by states and citizens, and claims making by citizens. A citizenship regime encodes within it a paradigmatic representation of identities, of the "national" as well as the "model citizen", the "second class citizen", and the non-citizen. It also encodes representa-tions of the proper and legitimate social relations among and within these categories, as well as the borders of "public" and "private". It makes, in other words, a major contribution to the definition of politics which organizes the boundaries of political debate and problem recognition in each jurisdiction. (Jenson, 2000, pp. 232–233)

Jenson (2001, pp. 4–5) develops four elements of a citizenship regime, each contrib-uting to the setting of boundaries and the constitution of citizenship. The first element concerns the expression of basic values about the *responsibility mix*; that is, by defin-ing the boundaries of responsibility, differentiating them from those of states, markets, families, and communities. Second, through the formal recognition of particular *rights* (civic, political, social and cultural, individual and collective), a citizenship regime estab-lishes the *boundaries of inclusion and exclusion* of a political community. In doing so, it identifies those entitled to full citizenship status and those who, in effect, hold second-class status. Third, a citizenship regime prescribes the *boundaries around democratic rules of the game* for a polity. Included in these are rules around access to the state, the modes of participation in civic life and public debates, and the legitimacy of specific types of claims-making. Fourth and finally, a citizenship regime contributes to the *definition of nation*, in both the narrow passport sense of nationality, and the more complicated notion of *national identity* and its geography. It therefore establishes the *boundaries of belonging*. Changes in the wider society challenge and change the encodings of citi-zenship regimes. However, Jenson's concept of citizenship regimes is implicitly assumed to be "national/nation"—which takes me to the core of my argument. New dynamics and developments, broadly referred to as processes of globalization, have challenged the primacy of the national scale and the supremacy of the nation-state as sole actor in the governance of education and producer of knowledgeable citizens, so that the citizenship regime of postwar national states is now being re/constructed and transformed.

Enter Globalization

As John Urry notes, when the discourse of globalization really took off "...exponential growth in the analyses of the global began to suggest that there was a putative global reconstruction of economic, political and cultural relationships" (Urry, 1998, p. 2) with transformations in the nature of the state, in turn, transforming the parameters of citi-zenship (Held et al., 1999; Sorensen, 2004).

Processes of globalization have laid bare the embedded, and socially constructed and produced nature of "citizenship" and the "national state" (Sassen, 2005, p. 80), as each has been challenged and transformed by internal and external pressures, processes, proj-ects, and practices associated with globalization. Key characteristics of this new regime include the liberalization of trade, the freer movement of finance capital around the globe, greater competition within the public and private spheres, increased levels of private sec-tor activity in formerly state dominated monopolies, the privatization of risk, the with-drawal of the state from various spheres of citizenship entitlement, and the reformulation of state-citizen rights/responsibilities relation (Cerny, 1997; Peck & Tickell, 2005; Sassen, 2005; Sorensen, 2004). Politically, the development of new supra- and subregional spaces, projects, and politics, such as the European Union (EU) or new structures of global governance, have opened up opportunities for rights (political and human) to be negotiated at these different scales. For instance, some indigenous communities and activist groups have sought the support of global and supranational actors in order to progress claims,[3] while citizens in particular national polities have moved to variously use the legal and social structures of the United Nations (UN), the International Labour Organization (ILO), and the European Union, to advance claims around labor rights, human rights, or social welfare and legal protection.

Globalization and the Transformation of Education

There are differing views as to how much education systems have changed as a result of processes of globalization[4] and different accounts as to the form that this is taking (for example, the extent of the globalization of ideas like devolution, internationalization and so on). There is nevertheless broad agreement that there have been significant changes in the rights/responsibilities mix, the borders around public and private, and the nature of the boundaries around education—particularly its public good/public sector and service nature. However, surprisingly, little attention is paid to the way in which these processes are re/constituting citizens and their politics,[5] along with citizenship and citizenship regimes. It is true that in the wake of concerns over the social order attention has reemerged regarding the creation of the entrepreneurial subject, or rather descriptive and normative analyses of citizenship programs, but analysis seems not to have gone further (cf. Lockyer, Crick, & Annette, 2003). It seems to me that four interlinked processes are implicated here in reorganizing the boundaries of political debate and problem recognition, at the level of the national, as well as at other scales of activity (global, regional, local) where education is being constituted.

First, there is a transformation taking place in the *mandate* and *governance* of education systems (Dale, 1997). The new mandate for education has been significantly influenced by human capital theory, and by neoliberal (economic competitivism, investing in knowledge producers, lifelong learning) and neoconservative ideas (Apple, 2004), while choice, diversity, and markets have emerged as the dominant ideas to guide the new structures of governance. In some countries, more and more of the various activities that comprised the "education services sector" have been unbundled and outsourced, including inspection and audit, curriculum writing, research, management services, special education services, and so on (Mahony, Hextall, & Mentor, 2004). In Britain these developments have been promoted under Public Private Partnerships (PPPs),[6] and given legal impetus under the Private Finance Initiative (PFIs). In spite of widespread and longstanding concerns, PPPs are now found in the public domain of many countries, including the United States, Britain, in national industrial policies in France, as well as in economic development policies in Italy and the Netherlands (Boviard, 2004). In the United States the establishment of charter schools legislation at the state level, and more recently the No Child Left Behind (NCLB) legislation, which has given the federal government an unprecedented role in determining education practices across the country, has opened the floodgates to a range of new providers of education services (Apple, 2004; Lipman, 2006). Trends at the EU level suggest a similar pattern, with PPPs being heavily promoted by the European Commission as the means for involving the private sector in delivering a competitive European knowledge-based economy. Similarly, PPPs are the World Bank's preferred solution to delivering the Millennium Development Goals for universal primary education and expanding the secondary sector. In sum, education is now becoming much more closely tied to the economy as a sector for industry investment and development (World Bank, 2003), while citizens are being constituted by the state as economic actors and choosers.

Second, education is being constructed as a *private good* and a *commodity*. This process is taking place at all levels of education, from primary to higher. Universities (Marginson & Considine, 2000) and schools (Lewis, 2005) have gone global in search of opportunities for raising revenues and recruiting foreign fee-paying students, while new for-profit firms have moved into the sector (Sachman, 2007; Henschke, 2007). A new language has emerged to talk about this development, and it is the language of importing and exporting education services, while education is increasingly presided over by departments of trade in nation-states. Trade in services is now estimated to be one of the most dynamic growth sectors for the developed economies and a critical means for ensuring continued growth. Importantly for my argument here, industry analysts estimate that the education market is valued to be upward of U.S.$2 trillion (Oxfam, 2002). Spurring on this development is the World Trade Organization, created in 1995 with the specific mandate to promote free trade and to regulate global trade (Peet, 2003). The innovative feature of the World Trade Organization's mandate was that, for the first time, services (including education) were brought into the ambit of the global trading regime (Robertson et al., 2002). This move has been highly controversial since services like education continue to be regarded by the public as "public goods."

A third development is the emergence of a new *functional and scalar division in the labor of education* (Dale, 2003; Robertson, 2002). In other words, education and its governance is being reallocated across scales, from the local to the global, now involving a new array of actors—public and private, including for-profit actors. A series of examples can be instanced here: the Bologna Process (BP) within the European Union, which intended to harmonize the structure and content of undergraduate and graduate degrees across the member states of the EU and beyond, so that institutional and national differences between systems were minimized (Dale, 2003; Keeling, 2006); Singapore's Global Schoolhouse—an initiative that seeks to provide a range of education services across the region and which has assembled in Singapore a range of globally competitive university departments (Olds & Thrift, 2005); the rise of personalized learning in Britain, which is intended to provide community-based rather than institutionally-based learning (Robertson, 2005); Brand New Zealand, which stamps a mark of quality on education providers within the region (Lewis, 2005); and neuroscience research on brains and learning (see OECD, n.d.). The control of learners and definitions of what counts as valuable knowledge is also being distributed across scales, with systems of benchmarking and other forms of assessment (for instance, national league tables, EU benchmarking, and global Programme for International Student Assessment [PISA][7] scores). An array of old and newer actors are now present at all these scales engaged in promoting these developments (e.g., Microsoft, IBM, Cisco Systems, Sylvan Learning Systems) and who are keen to promote digital learning technologies and new virtual approaches to learning (Robertson, 2002).

Fourth, the pluralizing of *identity* or identities is a reflection, in part, of the rise of identity politics, and, in part, of the breakdown of older forms of hegemonic identity (around social class and nation; e.g., British working class). A new terrain of identity claims has opened up (for example, in the United Kingdom by the Welsh, Scottish, and Northern Irish), while old identity claims are being reformulated. New political projects, such as the creation of the European Union (EU) and the "European citizen," are being advanced by the structures of the EU (European Commission, Council and Parliament), so that identity projects and claims are operating at multiple scales. In this latter case, education systems located at the national scale, as well as a parallel sector of learning at the European scale, are explicitly charged with the creation of the European citizen (Dale & Robertson, 2006). Identity claims are increasingly turning on cultural particularity rather than principles of universalism, as in the challenge by the French North African community that their young women have the right to wear the "foulard" (veil) in school, or where particular groups have asserted the right to state funding to establish schools which protect and promote their cultural and political interests. The upshot, however, of this process has been to privilege identity claims over redistribution (Fraser, 2005)—a matter I will come back to when assessing the implications of these transformations for education and citizenship regimes.

Education, National Citizenship Regimes, and Claims-Making

Globalization and the transformation of education continue to have important consequences for national citizenship regimes, claims-making, and the possibilities for social justice. To begin, the combination of changes in governance, processes of rescaling (global, national, and local), and commodification mean that citizenship regimes are being encoded at a multiplicity of scales, and that it is no longer exclusively the provenance of the national state. This does not mean that transformations being driven by processes of globalization are exclusively taking place out there, which is what David Held is suggesting with the idea of global governance (2002), or Nancy Fraser's press for new forms of global dialogue and political representation (2005). Rather, I am arguing that there have been significant transformations of education and the ways in which it is encoded in each of the four elements of contemporary citizenship regimes, as they operate *within* as well as *beyond* the boundaries of the nation-state. As Jayasuriya argues, "the changing architecture of power both globally and within the state serves to rupture and fragment the institutions and processes of governance; from this perspective, globalization is as much an internally as an externally driven process" (2001, p. 442).

As I have been suggesting, there has been a dispersion and dissolution of powers of governing into institutions in civil society, as well as the economy, within the boundaries of the nation-state as a result of the move from government to governance, for instance, with public–private partnerships, quangos (a UK regulatory agency outside the civil service, but financed and appointed by the government), outsourcing, and so on. However, there is also greater porosity in the boundaries around scales of governing and contestation over jurisdictions (for instance with the European Union, the principle of subsidiarity, and its interventions into national education systems with the Bologna process).

Recall Jenson's (2001) first element of a citizenship regime; that is, the nature of the boundaries around the responsibility mix between the state, market, community, and family. As I have argued, a mix reflects a particular set of values about social and political life. At present this mix is shaped by neoliberal ideas as to the precise role of the state, market, community, and family. Processes of globalization have also significantly altered the sites and scales at which actors might be located, including whether some scales take precedence over others. This has resulted in new struggles over all four boundaries and the terms of political debate.

Two consequences have followed from this. One is that neoliberalism has dispersed greater power and responsibility to the market, rather than the state, in the coordination of public goods and services, signaling the dominance of economism. The result of this is "...a form of economic constitutionalism that gives a juridical cast to economic institutions, placing these institutions beyond politics" (Jayasuriya, 2001, p. 443). Jayasuriya argues that not only is sovereignty transformed, but that the very nature of these governance changes results in a transition from political constitutionalism to a kind of economic constitutionalism (p. 443). Put another way, contracting out public education services to the private sector and community not only constructs them as economic relationships, thus depoliticizing them; but they are legally protected "beyond" politics. Mahony et al.'s (2004) research on the way private contractors in the education sector in Britain claim commercial sensitivity, thereby blocking public scrutiny, is an example here of this.

Second, economic constitutionalism is not confined to the national level. The World Trade Organization's General Agreement on Trade in Services (GATS), by transforming education into a global service industry and locating its governance in global regulations that protect investors and profits rather than citizens and knowledge, also constitution-alizes the economic over the political at the global scale. Similar processes have taken place at the regional scale, for instance with the North American Free Trade Agreement (NAFTA) and the Free Trade Area of the Americas (FTAA). Not only is education and its transformation into a commodity removed and insulated from popular scrutiny or demo-cratic accountability within the political realm, but the regulatory instruments, such as the dispute settlement processes, work in favor of particular agents and their projects (Gill, 2003, p. 132); that is, the transnational for-profit firms, and the powerful countries or blocs such as the United States and European Union, as well as those countries with a vested interest in trading education services globally.

The transformation of education through commoditizing and rescaling has direct implications for the rights of citizenship. On the one hand, rights are constructed in con-sumer terms; for example, as information in the marketplace to facilitate choices about which education provider to choose in the local, global or regional marketplace. The only "right" that can be protected by nation-states is the right to choose, not an equal ability to realize this choice (Ball, 2003). Paradoxically, while the right to (free primary) educa-tion is recognized in several international instruments, including the Universal Declara-tion on Human Rights (1948) to which all countries are signatories, there is no way to force a particular government to meet its commitments. However, if a company trading in education services were to lose the right to trade in a particular country (e.g., because it was renationalized or because of a change in policy at the level of the nation-state), the country where the company is based will have, according to the WTO rules, the right to compen-sation. These kinds of global initiatives have thus narrowed the policy space for national states and their economies, in turn reducing the scope for national actors and nationally located citizens to determine policies and programs. It would seem that rules concerning free trade are much stronger in international law than rules concerning human rights (Fre-drikssen, 2004, p. 422) or laws that might protect national sovereignty.

Finally, transformations in education as a result of globalization also affect identity construction/production, particularly national identity. The picture is complex because the processes of rescaling generate not only possibilities of multiple postnational identi-ties (Welsh, British, European, cosmopolitan), but also an array of means of identification following the collapse of class and nationality as the primary identities. The acceleration of processes of migration, together with issues of security as a result of September 11, have given rise to new or renewed efforts at generating identification. New curriculum initiatives are being mobilized, such as "My Europe," a European Schoolnet initiative funded by the European Commission and available to the member states of Europe to help create and embed a European set of values and identity. The nongovernmental orga-nization Oxfam has been promoting its global citizenship curriculum in those countries where it funds education. Finally, Microsoft has been developing its own global learner initiatives. However, generating a coherent "identity" and securing forms of identifica-tion will be much more complicated in this new regionalizing and globalizing era. If we take the European Union and the idea of European citizenship as a specific case, two developments may well mediate the success of these initiatives. First, there has been rapid cultural diversification as a result of the growing multiethnicity of European societies due to the breaking down of old identification structures and migratory flows. Imposing a single identity is likely to be resisted, especially if the imposed identity appears to deny issues of religion and religious rights. Second, there is increased cynicism directed at the European project, in part because of a popular perception that the EU structures are not sufficiently open and democratic (Smith, 2004), but also because of the increasingly neoliberal nature of the EU's project.

However, these are dynamic processes, and there is emerging evidence that the growing economic competition between regional blocks (European Union, the United States, and Japan) and emerging nations (India, China) that is driving the integration of higher education across Europe (under the Bologna Process and also the Lisbon Agenda, which work to promote Europe as a globally competitive region (Corbett, 2005), and responses in other nations[8] will have important consequences for forming identities. At the more global level, it is not yet clear the extent to which the accelerating globalization of education under GATS (in particular through the expansion of e-learning and cross-border supply) will mediate ideas of citizenship and identity production. However, it is a matter of serious concern for nations like South Africa, whose fledgling democracy is dependent upon using its systems of education to promote national interests and national identities. Despite this fluidity and the potential for contradiction in identity projects, there is an evident convergence in the discourses and projects to construct the model citizen across these scales. The model (private) citizen is conceived of through the lens of neoliberalism and human capital theory. These citizens are responsible for their own welfare through workfare, their success through entrepreneurialism and competitivism, and their future through lifelong learning for the knowledge-based economy and society (Kuhn & Sultana, 2006). However, this model is being contested, not only at the global level (for instance, progress of the GATS has been very slow because of organized campaigns), but also through new sites of innovation in education, such as Venezuela's higher education reforms and the creation of Bolivarian Universities enabling all citizens to attend university free.

Neo-Liberal Citizenship Regimes and Spaces of Social Justice

So far I have argued that four intertwined shifts have taken place since the early 1980s, as a consequence of processes of globalization, that challenge the role of education systems in the re/production of postwar national citizenship regimes. These were (1) shifts in the mandate and governance of education; (2) the growing commoditization of education; (3) rescaling the labor of education; and (4) the pluralizing of identities. Taken together, these shifts have disturbed the embedded and once tightly bound categories of the national state and notions of national citizenship, in turn reconstituting citizenship and citizenship claims in new ways. However, what I have also argued is that, though there is a pluralizing of identities and processes of identity production, citizenship regimes have become dominated by neoliberal discourses and projects, and that this has resulted in the constitutionalization of the economic at multiple scales. This depoliticizes education as an important site of power/knowledge and a resource that is mobilized by particular social classes. However, there are no adequate framings for claims-making at the global or supraregional levels (aside from ideas like global cosmopolitanism, references to education as a human right, and a weak, if not unconstitutional, mandate for education at scales like the European Union). Nor are there sites of legally institutionalized power that might enable a system of multiscalar claims—corresponding to the encoding of citizenship regimes across scales. For the moment, then, the current state of affairs is more likely to privilege transnational capital and other powerful political actors at the expense of citizens, or those citizens who are successfully able to reconstitute themselves as entrepreneurial subjects. There has in response been a call for reclaimed citizenship (Magalhaes & Stoer, 2006).

Sassen (2005) and others are confident there has been an opening up of citizenship and thus possibilities for claims-making through the unraveling of the nationality–citizenship relation. Indeed, Fraser (2005) has gone so far as to call for new transnational politics of representation, arguing that claims-making is still largely located in nation-states. However, given that there has been a redistribution of the labor of education across scales, moving claims-making upward to the transnational scale simply relocates the space for claims-making to the global. This would overlook the distribution and transformation of the elements of citizenship regimes across scales. What follows from this insight is the importance of interrogating more closely the politics of the reconstituted spaces for claims-making that are now emerging, for these seem to me to be rather limited in their possibilities for delivering social justice and democracy.

In conclusion, I want to argue that what is important here is that we are able to reveal the way neoliberal governance and processes of rescaling have enabled new boundaries to be drawn, and new encodings to be constitutionalized that will depend on more than calls to action. It will require a new level of juridical literacy amongst sociologists of education (especially given the complex legal architecture of global and regional agreements), as well as a more global outlook on questions of education, and sites of knowledge production, distribution and consumption. Furthermore, in the development of a multiscalar chain of spaces for claims-making that could be at the heart of this project, the ideological content and the mechanisms of governance must be shaped by dialogue and debate in order to generate a stronger sense of the conditions for realizing social justice, and a remix of the boundaries around state, market, family and individual in order to move it away from excessive economism and the poverty of neo-liberalism. This would offer a far more robust platform for citizenship and social justice, and might provide both the content and the impetus for such a program in education.

Notes

1. By education systems, I am referring to the formal education sector—elementary/primary and secondary/high schools, along with further and higher education.
2. Newman (2006) argues that in the postwar period, the state has been regarded as the traditional embodiment of public values and the defender of a common conception of public interest (in opposition to the market)—reproduced as an ethos of public good. See Newman (2006) for a valuable discussion of the difficulty, as a result of changes in governance, in defining the public realm.
3. Margaret Keck and Kathryn Sikkink, in their book *Activists Across Borders* (1998), provide numerous examples of activist groups targeting actors who operate beyond the boundaries of the national state in order to advance claims for social justice. Makere Stewart-Harawira (2005) provides an excellent account of the way indigenous Maori tribes in New Zealand were able to use the UN Declaration of Human Rights to advance their case against the New Zealand government.
4. For example, Hargreaves (2001) argues that schools have changed little in more than two centuries, while there is a huge literature on the transformation of education systems since the early 1980s.
5. For interesting work that looks at the discursive, practical, and performed aspects of this, see Pykett (2006).

6. Boviard (2004, p. 201) notes that in the UK the Private Finance Initiative accounted for over £8 billion of capital works contracts signed between 1997 and 1999 (HM Treasury, 2000, cited in Boviard, 2004).

7. The Programme for International Student Assessment (PISA) is a triennial worldwide test of 15-year-old schoolchildren's scholastic performance, developed by the Organisation for Economic Co-operation and Development (OECD) in 1997.

8. For instance, Australia has responded to the Bologna Process by reviewing its own higher education structures to bring them more into line with the EU's Bologna Process, while the EC has been promoting the Bologna Process in Latin America as part of an initiative called Tuning America Latina.

References

Apple, M. (2004). Creating difference: Neo-liberalism, neo-conservatism and the politics of educational reform. *Educational Policy, 18*(1), 12–44.

Ball, S. (2003). *Class strategies and the education market: The middle class and social advantage.* London & New York: RoutledgeFalmer.

Boviard, T. (2004). Public private partnerships: From contested concepts to prevalent practice. *International Review of Administrative Science, 70,* 199–215.

Carnoy, M., & Levin, H. (1985). *Schooling and work in a democratic state.* Stanford, CA: Stanford University Press.

Cerny, P. (1997). The paradoxes of the competition state: The dynamics of political globalization. *Government and Opposition, 32*(2), 251–274.

Collinge, C. (1999). Self-organisation of society by scale: A spatial reworking of regulation theory. *Environment and Planning D: Space and Society, 17,* 557–574.

Corbett, A. (2005). *Universities and the Europe of knowledge: Ideas, institutions and policy entrepreneurship in European Union higher education policy 1955–2005.* New York: Palgrave.

Dale, R. (1997). The state and the governance of education: An analysis of the restructuring of the state–education relation. In A. H. Halsey, H. Lauder, P. Brown, & A. Stuart Wells (Eds.), *Education: Culture, economy, and society* (pp. 273–282). Oxford: Oxford University Press.

Dale, R. (2003, March 20). *The Lisbon Declaration, the reconceptualisation of governance and the reconfiguration of European educational space.* Paper presented at Institute of Education, RAPPE Seminar on Governance, Regulation and Equity in European Education Systems, London.

Dale, R., & Robertson, S. (2002). The varying effects of regional organisations as subjects of globalisation of education. *Comparative Education Review, 46*(1), 10–36.

Dale, R., & Robertson, S. (2006). The case of the UK: *Homo Sapiens Europoeus vs. Homo Questuosus Atlanticus*? European learning citizen or Anglo-American human capitalist. In M. Kuhn & R. Sultana (Eds.), *Homo sapiens Europoeus? Creating the European learning citizen* (pp. 21–46). New York: Peter Lang.

Fraser, N. (2005, November–December). Reframing justice in a globalizing world. *New Left Review, 56,* 69–88.

Fredrikssen, U. (2004). Studying the supra-national in education: GATS, education and teachers' unions' policies. *European Education Research Journal, 3*(2), 415–439.

Gill, S. (2003). *Power and resistance in the new world order.* New York: Palgrave Macmillan.

Hargreaves, D. (2001). Teachers' work. In OECD (Ed.), *Knowledge management for learning societies* (pp. 219–238). Paris: OECD.

Held, D. (2002). Cosmopolitanism: Ideas, realities and deficits. In D. Held & A. McGrew (Eds.), *Governing globalization* (pp. 305–324). Cambridge, UK: Polity.

Held, D., McGrew, A., Perraton, J., & Dicken, P. (1999). *Global transformations.* Cambridge, UK: Polity.

Hentschke, G. (2007). Characteristics of growth in the education industry—illustrations from U.S. education businesses. In K. Martens, A. Rusconi, & K. Leuze (Eds.), *New arenas of*

552   Susan L. Robertson

global goverance: The impact of international organisations and markets on educational policymaking. Basingstoke, UK: Palgrave Macmillan.

Jayasuriya, K. (2001). Globalization, sovereignty and the rule of law: from political to economic constitutionalism. *Constellations, 8*(4), 442–460.

Jenson, J. (2000). Restructuring citizenship regimes: The French and Canadian women's movements in the 1990s. In J. Jenson & B. de Sousa Santos (Eds.), *Globalizing institutions: Case Studies in regulation and innovation* (pp. 230–245). Aldershot, UK: Ashgate.

Jenson, J. (2001, March 8th–10th). *Changing citizenship regimes in Western Europe.* Paper presented at the University of Toronto, Re-inventing Society in a Changing Global Economy Conference. Toronto.

Jessop, B. (2000). The changing governance of welfare: Recent trends in its primary functions, scale and models of coordination. *Social Policy and Administration, 33*(4), 346–359.

Keck, M., & Sikkink, K. (1998). *Activists across borders.* Ithaca, NY: Cornell University Press.

Keeling, R. (2006). The Bologna process and the Lisbon research agenda: The European Commission's expanding role in higher education discourse. *European Journal of Education, 41*(2), 203–223.

Kuhn, M., & Sultana, R. (Eds.). (2006). *Homo sapiens Europoeus? Creating the European learning citizen.* New York: Peter Lang.

Kymlicka, W., & Norman, W. (1994). Return of the citizen: A survey of recent work on citizenship theory. *Ethics, 104*(2), 352–381.

Lewis, N. (2005). Code of practice for the pastoral care of international students: Making a global industry in New Zealand. *Globalisation, Societies and Education, 3*(1), 5–48.

Lipman, P. (2006) Chicago school reform: Advancing the global city agenda. In J. P. Koval, L. Bennett, F. Demissie, & M. Bennet (Eds.), *The new Chicago: A social and cultural analysis.* Philadelphia: Temple University Press.

Lockyer, A., Crick, B., & Annette, J. (2003). *Education for democratic citizenship: Issues of theory and practice.* Aldershot, UK: Ashgate.

Magalhaes, A., & Stoer, S. (2006). Knowledge in the bazaar: Pro-active citizenship in the learning society. In M. Kuhn & R. Sultana (Eds.), *Homo sapiens Europoeus? Creating the European learning citizen* (pp. 83–104). New York: Peter Lang.

Mahony, P., Hextall, I., & Mentor, I. (2004). Building dams in Jordan, assessing teachers in England: a case study of edu-business. *Globalisation, Societies and Education, 2*(2), 277–296.

Marginson, S., & Considine, M. (2000). *The enterprise university: Power, governance and reinvention in Australia.* Cambridge, UK: Cambridge University Press.

Newman, J. (2006). Rethinking "The Public" in troubled times. *Public Policy and Administration, 22*(91), 27–47.

Olds, K., & Thrift, N. (2005). Cultures on the brink: Re-engineering the soul of capitalism on a global scale. In A. Ong & S. Collier (Eds.), *Global assemblages: Technology, politics and ethics as anthropological tools.* Oxford: Blackwell.

Organisation for Economic Co-operation and Development (OECD). (n.d.).Brains and learning initiative of the Organisation for Economic Co-operation and Development (OECD). Retrieved January 22, 2007, from http://www.oecd.org/department/0,2688,en_2649_1493 5397_1_1_1_1_1,00.html

Oxfam. (2002). *Speaking notes for the World Social Forum event: GATS and the future of public services.* London: Oxfam.

Peck, J, & Tickell, A. (2005). Making global rules: Globalization or neoliberalism? In J. Peck & H. W-C Yeung (Eds.), *Remaking the global economy* (pp. 163–182). London: Sage.

Peet, R. (2003). *Unholy trinity: The IMF, World Bank and the WTO.* London: Zed.

Robertson, S. (2002, October 3–5). *Changing governance, changing equality? Understanding the politics of public-private partnerships in Europe.* Paper presented at ESF/SCSS: Exploratory Workshop on Globalisation, Education Restructuring and Social Cohesion in Europe. Barcelona.

Robertson, S. (2005). Re-imagining and re-scripting the future of education. *Comparative Education, 41*(2), 151–170.

Robertson, S., Bonal, X., & Dale, R. (2002). GATS and the education service industry: The politics of scale and global territorialisation. *Comparative Education Review, 46*(4), 472–496.

Sackman, R. (2007). Internationalization of markets for education? New actors in nations and increasing flows between nations. In K. Martens, A. Rusconi, & K. Leuze (Eds.), *New arenas of global goverance: The impact of international organisations and markets on educational policymaking.* Basingstoke, UK: Palgrave Macmillan.

Sassen, S. (2005). The repositioning of citizenship and alienage: Emergent subjects and spaces of politics. *Globalizations, 2*(1), 79–94.

Sorensen, G. (2004). *The transformation of the state: Beyond the myth of retreat.* Basingstoke, UK: Palgrave Macmillan.

Smith, A. (Ed.). (2004). *Politics and the European commission: Actors, interdependence and legitimacy.* London & New York: Routledge.

Stewart-Harawira, M. (2005). *The new imperial order: Indigenous responses to globalization.* London: Zed.

Urry, J. (1998, July–August). *Globalisation and citizenship.* Paper presented at the International Sociological Association, World Congress of Sociology. Montreal.

World Bank. (2003). *Lifelong learning for the global knowledge economy.* Washington, DC: World Bank Group.

36 The Alternative Globalization Movement, Social Justice, and Education

Jennifer Chan

Introduction: Constructing an Alternative Globalization

> There is the belief that the economy is untouchable because of the rule of the market, globalisation, the decline of nation states, etc. It is principally this which has led them to this consensus politics. The most important task for the left today is to find alternatives to neoliberalism. (Interview with Chantal Mouffe in Castle, "Hearts, Minds, and Radical Democracy," 1998)

It would not be an exaggeration to assert that much of the energy of the Left in the past decade has been spent on searching for alternatives against the existing global capitalist order. Inherited from the postwar international economic policy framework centered on the "unholy trinity" (Peet, 2003)—the International Monetary Fund avoiding balance of payment problems, the World Bank promoting economic development through international lending, and the General Agreement on Trade and Tariffs facilitating international trade through tariff reduction—the current model of corporate capitalism has been critiqued by many as undemocratic in its representation, inhuman in ignoring basic freedoms, and inequitable (Bello, 2002; Mertes, 2004; Yuen et al., 2004). A global resistance movement has emerged to demand not only redistributive justice, but also "a seat at the table" to reform the existing global governance structure. Although education is at the very center of the formation and expansion of this movement, it has received little theoretical and empirical attention.

This chapter looks at the emergence of the alternative globalization movement by focusing on its educational roles. The next section begins with a paradox, that is, while education is constitutive of this movement, it is often assumed and subsumed under the larger political agenda. I attribute this "abundant invisibility" both to the methodological limits within the fields of radical adult education and critical pedagogy, and to the theory-activism tension within the movement. The following sections move on to examine three main conceptualizations of education—as counteranalyses, possibilities, and new subjectivities/citizenships—in the alternative globalization movement. Broadening the conceptions of and methodological approaches to education to understand this global network entails asking new questions: Who are the actors in this pedagogic project for global justice? What are the multiple ways of knowing and doing beyond the World Bank or World Trade Organization way? In turn, how do counteranalyses and new possibilities constitute new subjectivities? I conclude the chapter by suggesting avenues for future research.

The Educational Paradox in the Alternative Globalization Movement: Abundant Yet Invisible

The alternative globalization movement finds its roots in the protest struggles in the global South against the Structural Adjustment Programs of the International Monetary Fund (IMF) since the late 1970s, peaking in the uprising in Caracas in 1989, and gaining political visibility after the failed ministerial meeting of the World Trade Organization (WTO) in Seattle in 1999 (Katsiaficas, 2004). Behind each "discontent" in the long protestography (Collins, 2004)—whether it targets the World Bank, IMF, WTO, G8, North America Free Trade Agreement (NAFTA), Asia-Pacific Economic Cooperation (APEC), or Asian Development Bank—lies an educational effort to elucidate the impact of regional and international organizations on people's lives. From debt to agricultural liberalization, to water privatization, to access to basic medicines, each issue-focused member organization/network researches and debunks the metanarrative of the growth-through-trade paradigm.[1] Since 2001, the alternative globalization movement has been organizing an annual World Social Forum (WSF) as an alternative to the World Economic Forum.[2] Under the overarching frame of "another world is possible," participants (from 13,000 in 2001 to 120,000 in 2004) self-organize panels, workshops, and cultural events that challenge "a process of globalization commanded by the large multinational corporations and by the governments and international institutions at the service of those corporations' interests, with the complicity of national governments" (World Social Forum, 2002, Principle B). Although common protest action like demonstrations and solidarity marches are often part of the program, the WSF could be considered first and foremost a mega pedagogical site. Through diverse ways of engaging in this "open meeting place," the goal of the WSF is to reinvent democracy such that "the mode of economic production, the structures of global governance, the dissemination of scientific innovation, the organization of the media, social relations and the relationships between society and nature, are subjected to a radical, participatory and living democratic process" (Fisher & Ponniah, 2003, p. 13).

Despite its centrality and abundance, education rarely figures center stage in the theoretical and empirical literature on the alternative globalization movement. This, I argue, is related both to the methodological limits within the fields of radical adult education and critical pedagogy, as well as to the theory versus action/intellectualism versus activism tension within the movement. There is a strong connection between radical adult education—defined as "adult education theory and practice dedicated to significant social transformation within the left-wing political tradition" (Holst, 2002, p. 4)—and social movements. Eyerman and Jamison (1991) argue that a defining characteristic of a social movement is its cognitive praxis; that is, the production of knowledge is central to the development of collective identities within social movements. Seen from this angle, social movements target not only societal transformation through educating the public, but also personal transformation through education that is internal to the movements (Holst, 2002). The past decade saw the flourishing of environmental, antiracist, feminist, and anticorporate globalization adult education that is centered on (1) an "activist-based political pedagogy" (Clover, 2004); (2) interlocking oppressions; and (3) an imperative linkage between education and social change.[3] In parallel, critical educational theorists who have traditionally focused on national formal educational systems have also begun to look at the relationships between global capitalism and critical pedagogy.[4] Though deeply concerned with social justice, neither the field of radical adult education nor critical pedagogy has paid much attention to the educational work within the alternative globalization movement. Radical adult education theorists have largely stayed within their issue and community focus while critical pedagogues remain primarily concerned with the impact of neo-liberalism on the national school setting.

In addition to the current methodological impasses in critical educational theories, the question of how and how much the movement should theorize itself also makes it difficult to discern the underlying educational currents of the alternative globalization movement. On one hand, as some have charged, academic social movement theory may not always be useful to the activists (Dixon & Bevington, 2003). On the other, "anti-intellectualism" (or as one activist puts it, "we can't get bogged down in analysis") often gives easy ground for critics to attack the movement as an "inchoate, 'postideological' mass of do-gooders, pragmatists, and puppeteers" (Featherstone, Henwood, & Parenti, 2004, p. 309). Despite the presence of movement intellectuals who occupy leadership positions in articulating the cognitive identity and interests of the movement, a sort of division of labor is apparent, a tension that has long been pointed out by critical feminist scholars including Chandra Mohanty and Gloria Anzaldua on power relations in knowledge production. Leading left intellectuals, such as Michael Hardt, Antonio Negri, Noam Chomsky, Immanuel Wallerstein, Ernesto Laclau, and Chantal Mouffe, provide theoretical elaborations while activists do the groundwork to construct grassroots globalism.[5] Although there is no unified theoretical position, many such theorists search for a postliberal and postsocialist political project as an alternative to neoliberalism; Postliberal because the organizing democratic principles of freedom and equality in liberal capitalism have proven to be an inadequate strategy for the Left; postsocialist because "traditional socialist thought failed to understand what were then called the new social movements: feminism, the anti-racist struggle, the environmental movement. It tried to absorb them into the model of class struggle rather than respecting them as inherently different forms of resistance arising from different modes of oppression" (Mouffe quoted in Castle, 1998). Hardt and Negri (2004), for example, propose the concept of the "multitude" that is beyond the working class, an "open and expansive network in which all differences can be expressed freely and equally, a network that provides the means of encounter so that we can work and live in common" (p. xiv). Laclau and Mouffe (2001) advocate for a radicalization of democratic values and an alliance of diverse movements through a logic of difference that allows various demands to coexist without losing the power of creating a broad anti-capitalist movement. Although members of the alternative globalization movement often readily adopt these radical pluralist perspectives, some activists are wary of a theoretical monopoly by intellectuals because, according to them, "ideas don't belong to pedestals. They belong in the street, at work, in the home, at the bar, and on the barricades" (Featherstone et al., 2004, p. 314). Subsumed by theorists who are concerned with the broader viable political project of the Left and assumed by activists who weave their educational work almost naturally into their daily organizing, education becomes an invisible pillar of the alternative globalization movement. In the following sectoins, I provide three conceptualizations of education—as counternarratives, alternatives, and new subjectivities/citizenships—as central to the building of this movement.

Education as Counteranalysis

The fundamental problem therefore lay with the very notion of the self-regulating market. (Holmes, 2004, p. 351)

The movement has won its most clear-cut victories, however, on the plane of ideas. (Yuen, 2004, p. xxv)

For the alternative globalization movement, a key part of the educational agenda is to provide a credible counteridea to the Thatcherite–Reagan dogma of TINA (There Is No Alternative to economic neo-liberalism). It is in the "cultural struggles" for the very definition of life, economy, nature, and society that education plays the role of counteranalyses (Escobar, 1995, p. 16). Weis and Fine (2004) propose counteranalyses as a working method for social justice research, in which "principle fracture lines" (an interior analysis of the key institutions through lines of difference and power) are juxtaposed with other lines of analyses to challenge well established facts and suggest where radical change can begin (p. xx).

The "well-established fact" of the existing capitalist order built upon a self-regulating market, free trade, and corporate control is that it is the best and only efficient global system that brings economic growth to everyone. A recent example of counteranalysis by the alternative globalization movement could be found in a public statement by more than 140 nongovernmental organization (NGO) representatives as a response to the growth-through-trade metanarrative put forward by the chief executives of over 60 multinational corporations just before the latest WTO ministerial meeting opened in Hong Kong in December 2005.

Metanarrative

We strongly believe that the WTO-based multilateral trading system is one of the central pillars of international co-operation. Multilateral initiatives to liberalise world trade and improve market access for goods and services are a strong driving force for global economic growth, job creation, and wider consumer choice—as well as keeping in check the ever-present threat of protectionism. We underline our conviction that a successful Doha round is vital to enable business to continue to play a leading role in the eradication of poverty and the raising of global living standards. (Asia Pacific Forum on Women, Law and Development, *Financial Times,* November 15th, 2005)

Counteranalysis

Although we have no illusions about why the corporations are so eager to see the round concluded, their argument that trade liberalisation is a "strong driving force for global economic growth, job creation and wider consumer choice" is utterly misleading. Their first claim about growth is questionable. A recent report from the Center for Economic Policy Research (CEPR) compares average growth rates in 175 countries between 1960–1979 and 1980–2000, divided into five groups according to their per capita income at the start of each period. In the top four groups, average growth rates fell by more than half.... Second, they claim that trade liberalisation will lead to job creation. Again, if we look at the research, between 1990 and 2002, unemployment increased in 7 out of 9 regions.... We realise that the WTO and trade liberalisation has been good for the corporate bottom-line. (People's Response to Asia Pacific Forum on Women, Law and Development, *Financial Times,* November 15th, 2005)

The current neoliberal globalization paradigm has been critiqued by many as undemocratic, inequitable, imperialist, and unsustainable (see Rizvi and Engel in this section). It privileges certain scientific knowledges while discrediting, concealing, and trivializing the knowledges that inform counterhegemonic practices and agents (De Sousa Santos,

2003). It is intolerant not only of diverse human cultures and value systems, but also of biodiversity. One of the most striking examples of undemocratic, inequitable, imperialist, and unsustainable practice is the imposition of a Western intellectual property rights regime in the Uruguay Round negotiations of the General Agreement on Trade and Tariffs, predecessor of the WTO. In an incisive analysis, an international legal scholar, Susan Sell (2003), recounts the tale of how a dozen leading U.S. pharmaceutical multinational corporations managed to shape the Trade Related Intellectual Property Rights (TRIPS) agreement:

> In March 1986, six months before the Punta del Este meeting launching the Uruguay Round of GATT negotiations, twelve corporate executives of US-based multinational corporations formed the Intellectual Property Committee (IPC). The IPC sought to develop international support for improving the international protection of intellectual property (patents, copyrights, trademarks, and trade secrets). The IPC, in conjunction with its counterparts in Europe and Japan, crafted a proposal based on existing industrialized country laws and presented its proposals to the GATT Secretariat. By 1994, the IPC had achieved its goal in the Trade Related Aspects of Intellectual Property (TRIPS) accord of the Uruguay Round... These private sector actors succeeded in getting most of what they wanted from an IP agreement, which now has the status of public international law. In effect, twelve corporations made public law for the world. (Sell, 2003, p. 96)

Patents protected under TRIPS, on seeds or drugs especially, have proven to be extremely costly to the majority world. Ninety-nine percent of Africans living with HIV/AIDS do not have access to the antiretroviral drugs because of patent restrictions. Part of the educational task of the alternative globalization movement is to expose the assumptions behind the hegemonic criteria of efficiency. The Western intellectual property regime, for example, has largely been developed through bioprospecting and biopiracy, made possible by colonialism (Schiebinger, 2004; Shiva, 2001).

Education as Possibilities

> The utopian dimension of the WSF consists in claiming the existence of alternatives to neoliberal globalization. (de Sousa Santos, 2003)

> Another world is not only possible; she is on her way. On a quiet day, I can hear her breathing. (Roy, 2004)

A common critique and misconception of the alternative globalization movement pinpoints the deconstructive rather than constructive nature of the movement. It is, however, important to underline the fact that network members are not against globalization per se. More than just resistance, the movement aims at alternative models of globalization based on transparency, democracy, and participation. In tandem with counteranalyses, the painstaking educational efforts of the movement in the past two decades consist of researching into and practicing alternative possibilities based on "globalization from below" (Brecher, Costello, & Smith, 2000). The ideas are necessarily diverse. For the sake of analysis, I group them into three broad categories: alternative development approaches, core principles, and global governance reform proposals.

The first ideological intervention of the alternative globalization movement is to insist that the free market/free trade approach is not the only one available. For the first four postwar decades, the international institutional arrangement was marked by global rules of economic integration while reserving room for national economic management, commonly referred to as the "Bretton Woods compromise" (Rodrik, 2002). The deregulation of financial and investment flows on the one hand, and the rapid expansion of free trade into areas such as agriculture and services on the other have an extremely short history. Several alternatives to free trade have been proposed. The Nobel Laureate Amartya Sen (1999), for example, advocates a human development approach that puts human capacity expansion at the center of a free trade regime. According to him, development can be seen "as a process of expanding the real freedoms that people enjoy. Focusing on human freedoms contrasts with narrower views of development, such as identifying development with the growth of gross national product" (p. 3). Yet another approach focuses on community sovereignty where "economic policies should be set in ethical, ecological, people-centered spiritual frameworks, that development goals should entail small-scale, decentralized communities" (Dunkley, 2004, p. 16).

Another set of alternatives pertains more to general principles rather than economic models. In an interesting analytical exercise after the Seattle meeting in 1999, John Cavanagh and Jerry Mander (2004) summarized 10 core principles from the publications and protest materials of various social movement organizations: (1) living democracy, (2) subsidiarity, (3) ecological sustainability, (4) common heritage, (5) economic and cultural diversity, (6) human rights, (7) jobs, livelihood, employment, (8) food security and safety, (9) equity, and (10) the precautionary principle. The core idea is that in a living democracy, people organize to "create governance systems that give a vote to those who will bear the costs when decisions are being made" (p. 80). Decisions are made as close as feasible to the level of the individuals who will bear their consequences. Hence, subsidiarity respects the notion that sovereignty resides in people, communities, and nations. An alternative economic system must take into consideration biodiversity on the one hand, and common heritage including water, land, air, forests, fisheries, culture and knowledge, and public services on the other. Other core principles include the respect for economic and cultural diversity, human rights, food sovereignty, equity, and the precautionary principle in applying biotechnology. Many concrete proposals have arisen from these principles. One idea, pushed by the Paris-based international NGO, Association pour la Taxation Financières pour l'Aide aux Citoyens/ATTAC, is the Tobin tax on international financial speculation. Another example, drawing upon the principle of the basic rights to health, is the public health clause, demanded by a global campaign on access to basic medicines, in the TRIPS Agreement (that is, TRIPS "can and should be interpreted and implemented in a manner supportive of WTO members' right to protect public health, and in particular, to promote access to medicines to all"), opening at least the theoretical possibility of patent exemption in cases of HIV/AIDS and malaria etc.[6] Yet another example, drawing upon the principles of diversity and human rights, is the 2005 UNESCO Convention on the Protection and Promotion of the Diversity of Cultural Expression—that affirms the "recognition of equal dignity of and respect for all cultures, including the cultures of persons belonging to minorities and indigenous peoples"—to put "sand in the wheels" in the incursion of the WTO into culture through the General Agreement on Trade in Services (for a full analysis see Chan-Tiberghien, 2004).[7]

A third set of alternatives proposed by the alternative globalization movement consists of a complete overhaul of the existing global governance system. There are some similar core principles—equitable representation, accountability, transparency, and subsidiarity/devolution of power (Woods, 2001)—but reform proposals diverge. For some, a new global governance structure needs to be embedded within a human rights framework, whether it concerns the rights of labor, women, children, migrant workers, or indigenous peoples (UBUNTU, 2003; World March of Women, 2004). For others, the issue of "democratic deficit" in the decision-making structures of global institutions needs to be addressed and redressed through the creation of more representative mechanisms such as a people's parliamentary assembly (Charter 99, 2000); a UN Economic Security Council to coordinate if not oversee the Bretton Woods institutions and the WTO (Commission on Global Governance, 1995); a new framework on international insolvency based on an ad hoc court to determine the legitimacy of debts (Jubilee, 2002); a financing facility for trade-related capacity building to enhance the negotiating capacity of developing countries at the WTO (Oxfam, 2002); or a "truth commission" to investigate the actions and impacts of the IMF and the World Bank (Fifty Years is Enough, 2002).

Education as New Subjectivities/Citizenships

> The production of ideas, knowledges, and affects, for example, does not merely create means by which society is formed and maintained; such immaterial labor also directly produces social relationships. Immaterial labor is biopolitical in that it is oriented toward the creation of forms of social life; such labor, then, tends no longer to be limited to the economic but also becomes immediately a social, cultural, and political force. Ultimately, in philosophical terms, the production involved here is the production of subjectivity, the creation and reproduction of new subjectivities in society. Who we are, how we view the world, how we interact with each other are all created through this social, biopolitical production. (Hardt & Negri, 2004, p. 66)

The alternative globalization movement has not only generated counteranalyses and alternatives, but also, very importantly, new subjectivities. Variously named as the "Seattle generation," "cosmopolitan *bricoleurs* of resistance and cooperation," and the "multitude" (Hardt & Negri, 2004; Losson & Quinio, 2002), movement activists have been performing and constructing global citizenship beyond its traditionally national juridical boundaries. While world citizenship could be understood as one that "embraces the need for some effective form(s) of supra-national political authority and for political action beyond the nation-state" (Heater, 2002, pp. 11–12), it does not replace local and national forms of civic participation. According to Held (2003), cosmopolitan/multiple citizenships mean that people would have access to a variety of political engagements on a continuum from the local to the global. Their actions over the past two decades—research, seminars, conferences, polycentric world social forums, teach-ins, popular theaters, documentaries, people's tribunals, and popular summer schools—demonstrate that activists can "self-organize across significant differences without a blueprint" (Conway, 2004, p. 260). This learning-by-doing social movement practice produces a shared new cultural identity, which becomes a sustaining vector in the construction of a "counter-empire" (Hardt & Negri, 2001). It is in this sense that Hardt and Negri consider such immaterial labor of knowledge production as an important social, cultural, and political force.

Conclusion

> Resistance lies in self-conscious engagement with dominant, normative discourses and representations and in the active creation of oppositional analytic and cultural spaces. Resistance that is random and isolated is clearly not as effective as that which is mobilized through *systemic politicized practices of teaching and learning*. Uncovering and reclaiming subjugated knowledge is one way to lay claims to alternative histories. (Chandra Mohanty, quoted in hooks, 2004, p. 32 , emphasis added)

I have attempted in this chapter to offer some conceptualizations of education within the alternative globalization movement. The alternative globalization movement is pedagogical in exposing the assumptions behind the hegemonic criteria of efficiency, putting forward alternative knowledges, and constructing global citizenship. To argue that education is constitutive of the political project for global justice requires reenvisioning educational praxis as counterweight to corporate globalization. I have elsewhere proposed a "global educational justice" research paradigm that recognizes the important connections between education and global social justice (Chan-Tiberghien, 2004). In such an expansive research agenda, educational researchers focus on the conditions of possibility for diverse knowledges to be recognized. Global educational justice requires us to expand our inquiry beyond the classroom to encompass all the new relevant educational actors in the streets, world summits, corporate boardrooms, world trade negotiation tables, and myriad social movement actions. It also involves the restoration and revitalization of subjugated non-Western knowledges/ways of knowing, so as to ensure no single metanarrative—that of the market—prevails. If much of the energy of the Left in the past decade has been spent in locating alternatives to the neo-liberal order, it is time we, as educational researchers and practitioners, took leadership and participated in this global pedagogic project for living democracy.

Notes

1. To cite just a few examples, on debt (Dano, 2003; George, 1992; Rudin, 2002; Toussaint & Zacharie, 2001); on agricultural liberalization (Glipo et al., 2003; Shiva, 2000; Shiva et al., 2003); on water privatization (International Consortium of Investigative Journalists, 2003; Olivera & Lewis, 2004; Shiva 2002); on access to basic medicines (Médecins Sans Frontières [MSF], http://www.accessmed-msf.org/campaign/campaign.shtm).
2. For origins, principles, and development of the WSF. Retrieved from http://www.forumsocialmundial.org.br/index.php?cd_language=2&id_menu=.
3. See, for example, Conway (2004), Clover (2004, 2003), and Dei and Calliste (2000).
4. See, for example, Fischman et al. (2005); McLaren and Farahmandpur (2005); and Stromquist and Monkman (2000).
5. There are exceptions to this sharp delineation of division of labor. See, for example, the works of Sonia Alvarez (1997, 1998).
6. See Médecins Sans Frontières at http://www.accessmed-msf.org/campaign/campaign.shtm.
7. For the full text, see UBESCO. Retrieved July 16, 2008, from http://portal.unesco.org/culture/en/ev.php-URL_ID=11281&URL_DO=DO_TOPIC&URL_SECTION=201.html.

References

Agreement on Trade-Related Aspects of Intellectual Property Rights,. Retrieved July 16, 2008, from http://www.wto.org/english/tratop_e/trips_e/t_agm0_e.htm

Alvarez, S. (1997). Reweaving the fabric of collective action: Social movements and challenges to "actually existing democracy" in Brazil. In R. G. Fox & O. Starn (Eds.), *Between resistance and revolution: Cultural politics and social protest* (pp. 83–117). New Brunswick, NJ: Rutgers University Press.

Alvarez, S. (1998). Latin American feminisms "go global": Trends of the 1990s and challenges for the new millennium. In S. E. Alvarez, E. Dagnino, & A. Escobar (Eds.), *Cultures of politics/ politics of cultures: Re-visioning Latin American social movements* (pp. 293–324). Boulder, CO: Westview.

Anzaldua, G., & Moraga, C. (Eds.). (1983). *This bridge called my back: Writings by radical women of color.* Albany, NY: Kitchen Table Press.

Asia Pacific Forum on Women, Law and Development. (2005, November 15th). Last and best chance to move Doha to a successful conclusion. [Letter to the editor]. *Financial Times*. Retrieved from http://www.apwld.org/doha_letter.htm

Bello, W. (2002). *Deglobalization: Ideas for a new world economy*. London and New York: Zed.

Brecher, J, Costello, T., & Smith, B. (2000). *Globalization from below: The power of solidarity*. Boston: South End.

Castle, D. (1998, June). Hearts, minds, and radical democracy—Adapting to the global market, managing public opinion. *Red Pepper*. Retrieved June 15th, 2006, from http://www.redpepper.org.uk/natarch/XRADDEM.HTML

Chan-Tiberghien, J. (2004). Towards a global educational justice research paradigm: Cognitive justice, decolonizing methodologies and critical pedagogy. *Globalisation, Societies and Education, 2*(2), 191–213.

Charter 99. (2000). A charter for global democracy. Retrieved February 25th, 2005, from http://www.oneworldtrust.org/pages/download.cfm?did=97

Clover, D. (2004). *Global perspectives in environmental adult education*. New York: Peter Lang.

Collins, T. (2004). A protestography. In E. Yuen et al. (Eds.), *Confronting capitalism: Dispatches from a global movement* (p. xxxiv). Brooklyn, NY: Soft Skull.

Commission on Global Governance. (1995). *Our global neighborhood*. Oxford and New York: Oxford·University Press.

Conway, J. (2004). *Identity, place and knowledge: Social movements contesting globalization*. Black Point, Nova Scotia: Fernwood.

Dano, E. (2003, February). Biodiversity, biopiracy and ecological debt. *Jubilee South Journal, 1*(2), 7–11.

Dei, G., & Calliste, A. (Eds.). (2000). *Anti-racism education: Theory and practice*. Halifax, Nova Scotia: Fernwood.

Dixon, C., & Bevington, D. (2003). *An emerging direction in social movement scholarship: Movement-relevant theory*. Unpublished manuscript.

Dunkley, G. (2004). *Free trade: Myth, reality and alternatives*. New York: Zed.

Escobar, A. (1995). *Encountering development: The making and unmaking of the Third World*. Princeton, NJ: Princeton University Press.

Eyerman, R., & Jamison, A. (1991). *Social movements: A cognitive approach*. University Park: Pennsylvania State University Press.

Featherstone, L., Henwood, D., & Parenti, C. (2004). Activism: Left anti-intellectualism and its discontents. In E. Yuen et al. (Eds.), *Confronting capitalism: Dispatches from a global movement* (pp. 309–314). Brooklyn, NY: Soft Skull.

Fifty Years is Enough: Network Platform. (2002). *Fifty years is enough*. Retrieved February 25th, 2005, from http://www.50years.org/about/

Fischman, G., McLaren, P., Sunker, H., & Lankshear, C. (Eds.). (2005). *Critical theories, radical pedagogies, and global conflicts*. Lanham, MD: Rowman & Littlefield.

Fisher, W., & Ponniah, T. (Eds.). (2003). *Another world is possible: Popular alternatives to globalization at the World Social Forum*. London & New York: Zed Books.

George, S. (1992). *The debt boomerang: How third world debt harms us all*. London: Pluto.

Glipo, A., Carlsen, L., Sayeed, A. R., de Rindermann, R. S., & Cainglet, J. (2003). *Agreement on agriculture and food sovereignty*. Paper presented at the WTO Conference, Cancun.

Hardt, M., & Negri, A. (2001). *Empire*. Cambridge, MA: Harvard University Press.

Hardt, M., & Negri, A. (2004). *Multitude: War and democracy in the age of empire*. New York: Penguin.

Heater, D. (2002). Competence and education. In *World citizenship: Cosmopolitan thinking and its opponents*. London and New York: Continuum.

Held, D. (2003). From executive to cosmopolitan multilateralism. In D. Held & M. Koenig-Archibugi (Eds.), *Taming globalization* (pp. 160–186). Cambridge, UK: Polity.

Holst, J. (2002). *Social movements, civil society, and radical adult education*. Westport, CT: Greenwood.

Holmes, B. (2004). "The revenge of the concept". In E. Yuen et al. (Eds.), *Confronting capitalism: Dispatches from a global movement* (pp. 347–366). Brooklyn, NY: Soft Skull.

hooks, b. (2004). *Teaching to transgress.* New York: Routledge.

International Consortium of Investigative Journalists. (2003). *The water barons: How a few powerful companies are privatizing your water.* Washington, D.C.: Center for Public Integrity.

Jubilee 2000. (2002). Resolving international debt crises—The Jubilee framework for international insolvency. Retrieved February 25th, 2005, from http://www.jubileeplus.org/analysis/reports/jubilee_framework.html

Katsiaficas, G. (2004). Seattle was not the beginning. In E. Yuen et al. (Eds.), *Confronting capitalism: Dispatches from a global movement* (pp. 3–10). Brooklyn, NY: Soft Skull.

Laclau, E., & Mouffe, C. (2001). *Hegemony and socialist strategy: Towards a radical democratic politics.* New York: Verso.

Losson, C., & Quinio, P. (2002) *Génération Seattle: Les rebelles de la mondialisation* [*Generation Seattle: The rebels of globalization*]. Paris: Grasset.

Médecins Sans Frontières (MSF). Retrieved July 16, 2008, from http://www.accessmed-msf.org-

Mertes, T. (Ed.). (2004). *A movement of movements: Is another world really possible?* New York: Verso.

Mohanty, C. (2003). *Feminism without borders: Decolonizing theory, practicing solidarity.* Durham, NC: Duke University Press.

Olivera, O., & Lewis, T. (2004). *Cochabamba: Water war in Bolivia.* Boston: South End.

Oxfam. (2002). *Rigged rules and double standards: Trade, globalization and the fight against poverty.* London: Oxfam.

Peet, R. (2003). *Unholy trinity: The IMF, World Bank and WTO.* New York: Zed.

People's Response. (2005, November 15th). Last and best chance to move Doha to a successful conclusion [Letter to the editor]. *Financial Times.* Retrieved from http://www.apwld.org/doha_letter.htm

Rodrik, D. (2002). *Feasible globalizations.* (Kennedy School of Government Faculty Research Working Papers Series). Cambridge, MA: Harvard University.

Roy, A. (2004, January). Speech at the Fourth World Social Forum, Mumbai, India.

Rudin, J. (2002, February). Odious debt revisited. *Jubilee South Journal, 1*(1), 11–21.

Schiebinger, L. (2004). *Plants and empire: Colonial bioprospecting in the Atlantic world.* Cambridge, MA: Harvard University Press.

Sell, S. (2003). *Private power, public law: The globalization of intellectual property rights.* Cambridge, UK: Cambridge University Press.

Sen, A. (1999). *Development as freedom.* Oxford: Oxford University Press.

Shiva, V. (2000). *Stolen harvest.* Boston: South End.

Shiva, V. (2001). *Protect or plunder: Understanding intellectual property rights.* London & New York: Zed.

Shiva, V. (2002). *Water wars: Privatization, pollution, and profit.* Boston: South End.

Shiva, V., Jafri, A., & Jalees, K. (2003). *The mirage of market access: How globalization is destroying farmers lives and livelihoods.* New Delhi: Navdanya.

de Sousa Santos, B. (2003, March 27). *The World Social Forum: Toward a counter-hegemonic globalization.* Paper presented at the Latin American Studies Association, 24th International Congress, Dallas.

Toussaint, E., & Zacharie, A. (2001). *Afrique: Abolir la dette pour liberer le developpement* [Africa: Abolish debt to free up development]. Brussels: CADTM.

UBUNTU—World Forum of Civil Society Networks. (2003). *Restructuring the WTO within the UN.* Retrieved June 15, 2006, from http://www.ubuntu.upc.es/

Weis, L., & Fine, M. (2004). *Working method: Research and social justice.* New York: Routledge.

Woods, N. (2001). *Governing the world economy: The challenges of globalization.* Retrieved June 15th, 2006 from, http://www.globalcentres.org/html/docs/Post%20Seattle%20Angst/Vision%20Papers-August15.pdf

World March of Women. (2004). *Women's global charter for humanity*. Retrieved February 25th, 2005 from, http://www.marchemondiale.org/news/mmfnewsitem.2005-03-04.1396677141/en/base_view

World Social Forum. (2002). *Charter of principles*. Retrieved July 16, 2008, from http://www.forumsocialmundial.org.br/main.php?id_menu=4_2&cd_language=2

Yuen, E. (2004). An introduction. In E. Yuen et al. (Eds.), *Confronting capitalism: Dispatches from a global movement*. Brooklyn, NY: Soft Skull.

37 Critical Pedagogy and Hope in the Context of Neo-Liberal Globalization

Gustavo E. Fischman and Eric Haas

I appreciate your efforts.... I understand that it is good to have access to those ideas. I mean it. Now at least I know what neoliberalism is, how it operates, and how it affects my personal and professional life. Perhaps...I don't think that I am a naïve teacher that doesn't know about exploitation, racism and oppression...and also the criticisms that should be made to bad schools, but...after reading and discussing all these books, I don't know but I am feeling sad, I am feeling that no matter what, we cannot win.

Those were the thoughts and emotions that Nancy shared with the class during the evaluation of a seminar on Paulo Freire and critical pedagogy conducted by one of the authors, Gustavo Fischman.[1] At that moment, Nancy was 32 years old. She was the first one in her family to attend college, a proud Mexican American, a self-described "caring and competent" fourth grade math teacher pursuing her doctoral degree. Nancy often expressed a tremendous sense of pride about her work in an urban school in Phoenix. Nancy was a straight A student, and during the semester she did not hide her difficulties and disagreements with some of the texts. As the student who most frequently and consistently defended what she called "the perspective of the teachers in the trenches," Nancy's opinions were very important for the group. For the first time during the whole semester, she concluded, "we cannot win."

As the instructor, I did not expect this conclusion to the seminar. Yet, Nancy had voiced some of my own fears and concerns. I had worked as a grassroots educator before moving into formal education and the world of schools, and so I have personally experienced the frustration of trying to improve an education system. Thus, I have continually looked for ways to incorporate into my teaching the necessary criticisms of the actual functioning of schools, administrators, and teachers with the ideas that will empower teachers to change schools, not scare them away. I concluded that, at least in this seminar, I didn't accomplish that goal.

The class was silent. I looked for a student who could add another perspective to Nancy's reflections, but I felt that the rest of the class was avoiding my attempts to make eye contact. To me, the silence was a robust indication that the students shared Nancy's opinions.

A feeling of despair and self-doubt began to inundate me. I counted to 60, or maybe to 100, and then asked,

I have the impression that reading about and discussing Freire and critical pedagogy had the emotional effect of creating a sense of despair and hopelessness in the group. Am I right?

Several in the group shook their heads. Paula, who was one of the youngest in the group and usually not very talkative, said with a laugh, "Don't worry, you didn't Ellsworthize us...well, maybe a little, but not too much and we can handle it."[2]

Paula's remark recuperated notions from previous discussions which the group debated and after a few minutes of dialogue, Nancy's words grabbed the group's attention:

> I would like to say something. I don't want to be misunderstood. No, I don't feel hopeless. I don't think that you hammered us with the "bad schools-oppressive teachers" message or "Ellsworthized" or even tried to "Freireized" or "brain-washed" us....
>
> I've been thinking about this since the beginning of this class, but I didn't have the words to express myself. I said that we couldn't win. I was sad, but that is not all. It was also...I was ashamed...it is just that I realized that my hopes, were "easy hopes," kind of "Hello Kitty hopes"...and then...working with all of you I have to give up the idea that by being the "super-caring-knowledgeable-efficient" teacher—and you know that I am all of that—I was going to first, fix my grade, then my school, later the district and so on. Please, don't laugh...that may have been unrealistic but it was my dream. That was my goal...I was sad not because I felt hopeless about what we can do as teachers. I think that I was sad because I realized I was trying to convince myself that teachers can win without pissing off people, without making enemies...I was sad of letting my "Hello Kitty Hopes" go. That is sad...that is scary, but it's not hopeless.

The class was silent. I couldn't tell if the new silence that greeted Nancy's words was an expression of respectful agreement or disagreement. But I clearly remember that when the students left the room saying, "I hope to see you again," I felt that they meant it.

We begin with the recollection of what happened in one of the authors' classes, not because we give to these testimonies some sort of magical power, or because we think that this example illustrates that critical pedagogy is effective and we need more of it. In fact, it is just the opposite. We share Nancy's reflections and reactions because we think that her words and thoughts encapsulate the limitations, and possibly even the dangers, of how critical pedagogy is practiced in the United States during this period of global neo-liberalism. In this chapter, we provide an overview of globalization and neo-liberalism, and then we describe their relationship to critical pedagogy. In setting forth this relationship, we argue that in order for critical pedagogy to become a viable educational–political discourse three developments should take place:

- the use of a thorough and teachable analysis of globalization, that includes an acknowledgment that aspects of global neo-liberal policies and practices have made, and can make, some positive contributions to school reform;
- the articulation of discourses of hope that go beyond notions of individual superteachers and "narratives of redemption"; and
- the implementation of pedagogical practices that both recognize and support educators as committed intellectuals, more than heroic critical ones.

Globalization, Neo-Liberalism, and Education

Doubtless, globalization has resulted in increased levels of capital accumulation, information dissemination, and technological discoveries, but it has also created disparities and inequalities between and within nations (Hill, 2005). These gains, disparities, and inequalities are reflected in differences in the top and bottom perspectives of globalization (Tabb, 2006). In financial terms, the benefits of globalization have disproportionately gone to the top of society (Stiglitz, 2002; Tabb, 2006; United Nations, 2005).[3]

At the same time, it is undeniable that processes associated with globalization have produced other benefits even for those who are considered the weakest economic actors in the global landscape (Friedman, 2005; Hardt & Negri, 2000). For example, globalization has increased access to technological innovation, expanded global networks for human rights and social activism, and developed alternative forms of communication and information, which have the potential to benefit most people in the world (Kellner, 2005).

Recognizing the complexity and contradictory features of these processes does not imply, however, that one should overlook the totalizing features and power of those discourses, which naturalize globalization and advocate it as new gospel.[4] Among those discourses, one of the strongest perspectives and most cohesive arguments about the benefits of globalization has been elaborated by institutions and individuals associated with the neo-liberal school of thought (Ball, Fischman, & Gvirtz, 2003; Hursh, 2006). Neoliberal discourses both theoretically and ideologically rest on a set of beliefs in the self-correcting qualities of the corporatist logic of the free market, as part of a self-proclaimed ideologically neutral discourse of efficiency and accountability (Fischman et al., 2003).

A central feature of the neo-liberal argument as applied to education is that schools must align their policies and practices with the notion of knowledge as a regular tradable commodity. Based on this perspective, it is easier to understand the two main criticisms of neoliberal educationalists: (1) state monopoly and "producer capture" cannot but create educational inefficiencies; and (2) educational inefficiencies resulting from public intervention stifle productivity, waste resources, and prevent economic, as well as social and even moral, improvements. The argument goes that in the post-9/11 and restructured global economy, for any society to remain competitive it will need to implement educational reforms emphasizing the development of a flexible, entrepreneurial teaching workforce (i.e., broadly educated, specifically trained, and without tenure), and a teacher-proof, standards-based, and market-oriented curriculum (Fischman & McLaren, 2005; Peters, 2005). Education is held to account. Its efficiency is measured. But this is not simply a process of measurement and comparison; it also affects and changes what it measures, driven by the reductionist idea that everything is a matter of accounting (Readings, 1996) and the only things that are worthwhile are those than can be counted or measured.

Within the neo-liberal discourse, institutions associated with the market and loosely defined notions, such as private sector, choice, and businesslike, are sanitized and romanticized. Market failings, as well as corrupt operations (such as Enron and World Com) and potentially disastrous policies (such as ignoring global warming, or neglecting to implement adequate "public policies" as demonstrated during the Hurricane Katrina evacuation), are minimized or erased, while the "perfections" of competition are set over and against the "conservatism" of state bureaucracies. The role of the state in regulating the corporate sector and in implementing policies aimed at promoting basic social fairness, or even timidly redistributing forms of social capital (such as education, health, and retirement benefits), are glossed over as the "nanny state" in the enthusiasm for neoliberal politics (Cato, 2005; Huntington, 2005). In this sense, the world is facing what the late Pierre Bourdieu (1998) referred to as the "'gospel of neoliberalism' a conservative ideology which thinks itself opposed to all ideology" (p. 126). This gospel is one that serves as a clarion call to combat "by every means, including the destruction of the environment and human sacrifice, against any obstacle to the maximization of profit" (p. 126).

This ideology without ideology is set over and against the "failures" of social democracy, and the inability of welfare systems to meet the needs of all citizens. Neo-liberalism gathers discursive strength and political influence from both its promises of a new kind of nonideological freedom, and a telling critique of democratic failures. It represents, in its own terms, a move beyond politics and back to a state of nature, back to the "natural" impulses of individualism and competition. It is important to emphasize that our criticisms of neo-liberalism in schools are not based on a nostalgic longing for a golden era, where supposedly a truly democratic public school system existed, but in the assessment that after more than 10 years of implementing neo-liberal inspired reforms they are far from delivering good educational results (Hursh, 2006).

Even if the measures of educational achievement do not produce the expected good results, it is undeniable that neo-liberalism as an educational discourse has been very influential not only in changing school practices, but also in defining the educational commonsense, what can be thought or imagined about schools.[5] The hegemonic position of these discourses is easy to perceive. In most schools, it is nearly impossible to find discourses that emphasize the need for greater democracy or improvement of the quality of life not measured in economic terms. There is a hegemonic inevitability about the logic of neo-liberal reforms, particularly because they are presented as simply rational–technical solutions to the problems of underachievement, separated off from their ideological and philosophical origins (Fischman, Ball, & Gvirtz, 2003; Haas, 2006).

For many teachers, such as Nancy, the neo-liberal emphasis on individualism, measurement, and technical solutions can fit well with a commonly accepted (and also carefully and constantly monitored) characterization of schooling within the parameters of a redemptive function: teaching and learning are individual acts that when properly performed will solve most problems associated with the lack of formal education (poverty, productivity, morality among many more social ills). The neo-liberal educational discourse is also articulated as a redeeming narrative, and thus, schools should be apolitical institutions, implementing scientifically verified "best practices" which will be assessed through standardized testing (e.g., Elmore, 1996). Taken against public schools' constant challenges and mixed record of success and failure, and the strong associations between notions of the "public" with authoritarianism, bureaucracy, inefficiency, and the paucity of truly democratic schools, neo-liberal perspectives reinforce educators' common sense about their individual roles and the need for politics to be kept out of the classroom. In sum, neo-liberalism is a powerful educational discourse because some of the elements associated with the perceptions of "public = failure" are real and felt by countless students and teachers.

The experience of teachers like Nancy demonstrates that neoliberal globalization is a mixed experience. There are many educators who are entrepreneurial, upwardly mobile professionals, who benefit from their own hard work, while teaching students who, despite great effort, continue to be economically and socially left behind. What we want to note is the importance of trying to understand and deconstruct the neoliberal perspective and the arguments of its supporters in light of these strongly differing experiences.

There is little doubt that globalization has not delivered all the benefits its public defenders have promised; however, the dynamics associated with it have impacted many and positively impacted at least some individuals in all sectors of society. "Globalization is not about what we all or at least the most resourceful and enterprising among us wish or hope to do. It is about what is *happening to us all*" (Baumann, 1998, p. 39, italics in original). Nancy's experience in a critical pedagogy class gave her the opportunity to reflect on the limits of the "equity and democratization" aspects of neoliberal globalization—the impacts she receives and transmits go well beyond her lived experience, and perhaps, her initial ability to affect change. Thus, some of the important challenges for teachers and teacher educators who want to use critical pedagogy become how to work on identifying and analyzing the effects of "naturalized" and oppressive dynamics (embedded in capitalism, racism, sexism, and other forms of oppression) on schooling, without instilling a sense of hopelessness and loss of agency. Moreover, how does one use CP with teachers like Nancy (ethnic minority, first generation college student) whose personal story illustrates that the neoliberal educational model offers, to at least a few individuals, so-called successful schooling? Why should Nancy be critical of neoliberalism and its schools?

Critical Pedagogy: Beyond the Narrative of Redemption

One of the strongest claims of most practitioners and supporters of critical pedagogy is that the concrete results of schooling are constructed in and through people's linguistic, cultural, social, and pedagogical specific interactions which both shape and are shaped by social, political, economic, and cultural dynamics (Darder, 2002; Giroux, 1988, 1994, 2000, 2003; Giroux & McLaren, 1989; McLaren, 2005; McLauren & Fischman, 1998; McLauren & Lankshear 1993; 1994; McLauren & Leonard, 1993). From this perspective, societies, communities, schools, teachers, and even students engage in oppressive practices, and thus understanding those practices needs to connect with transforming them. The connection of awareness to transformation, we believe, is an important contribution of critical pedagogy as an educational theory and as shared praxis that advances an agenda for educational change; it forces us to understand educational practices in broader sociopolitical contexts. By emphasizing the importance of understanding-transforming pedagogical-social realities, critical pedagogy also points to the intrinsic relationship between educational and social transformations, keeping in constant view new means of breaking down all forms of oppression.

A second strong claim of critical pedagogy is that educators have a central, but not exclusive, role in maintaining or challenging educational systems. For example, Giroux (1993), building upon the Gramscian concept of praxis and the Freirean notion of conscientization (Freire, 1989, 1997a, 1997b), has extensively discussed the possibility of teachers becoming "transformative intellectuals." Giroux contends that teachers need to engage in debate and inquiry, in order to open the spaces for taking critical stances toward their own practice and the practice of others. Through these activities, educators could begin reflexively and actively to shape their curricula and school policies. Transformative intellectuals are aware of their own theoretical convictions and are skilled in strategies for translating them into practice (Giroux, 1993, 2002).

Giroux's perspective is widely embraced by those associated with critical pedagogy (Darder, 2002; Giroux, 2005; McLaren, 2005). The social and political dimensions of schooling, the need to understand and transform schools and society, and the key role that educators in these processes play are core themes shared by many critical educators (Darder, Baltodano, & Torres, 2003; Fischman, McLaren, Sünker, & Lankshear, 2005). Although it is hard to quantify or even qualify the influence of critical pedagogues in North America, it would be hard to deny that, as a collective movement, it has produced one of the most dynamic and controversial educational schools of thought of the last 30 years. Nonetheless, it is also hard to deny that there are many educators like Nancy who react to the proposals of CP with great skepticism and despair.

We contend that a good deal of those reactions relate to the use of a *narrative of redemption* (NR) when arguing in favor of CP. NR involves a quasi-schizophrenic perspective in CP (as well as aspects of neoliberalism) in which schools are at present horrible and schools can be beautiful. The link between the horrible present and the beautiful future is the narrative of redemption with the superteacher as its hero. This is a common depiction in discourse about teachers not only in teacher training institutions but it is also especially strong in popular culture. The NR provides the basic discursive structure of most Hollywood characters from the films *To Sir with Love, Dangerous Minds,* and *Stand and Deliver* and the teachers of television's *Boston Public*. The NR works when an individual teacher overcomes all the systemic failures through the sheer force of his or her heroic and "organic" consciousness and deeds. When others follow the lead of the superteacher, the class or school as a larger system is redeemed. This process follows the biblical tradition of sin-crisis-failure-trauma and finalizes with archetypal myths of redemption-absolution-success-recovery. If accepted, the redeeming vision will, after the defeat of the enemy, create the ideal school, in which the perfect teacher and the model student will learn in individual harmony, separate from the chaos of the surrounding educational and social system.

The redemptive narrative is often used indiscriminately by both supporters and opponents of critical pedagogy, and one of its distinctive markers is that teaching appears as both the target of harsh social criticisms and the last space of hope. In that critical juncture of society's imaginary about teachers, they become the makers of terrible presents and hopeful futures. Further, the use of the NR in the teaching of critical pedagogy also contributes to the proliferation of gloom and doom. In fact, it often does so quite well. The references to Ellsworth (1989) and to Bullough and Gitlin (1995) by the students in the seminar on Paulo Freire are illustrative of the complexities of the tasks ahead. For these three scholars and for many teacher educators, there is a sense that critical pedagogy can be a self-defeating endeavor, in part because its "rationalist assumptions" and difficulties in analyzing power imbalances between critical pedagogues and their students. Critique of public schools, and of our own roles as teachers and teacher educators, is essential, but it can become debilitating, we believe, if not informed by a vision of hope not structured in the NR fashion.

A remarkable characteristic of the NR is the normative presentation of conflicts and struggles as expressions of hope in connection with educational and social change. Yet, only within the redemptive mythology of heroic teachers and students, is it possible to find "hope" inherent in racism, poverty, discrimination, and other conflicts, for to do so requires one often to minimize or ignore the real-life risks and suffering associated to those struggles.

We do not see any "natural connection" between struggle and hope, or even between schooling and hope. Our position is to recognize that conflicts and struggles are part of the everyday life of schools and societies, sometimes explicit and clear, often implicit and confusing, but always anchored in complex manners and expressing multiple dynamics of class, race, sexuality, language, and ethnicity relationships. It is in this unavoidability of the educational conflicts that committed teachers "must speak for hope, as long as it doesn't mean suppressing the nature of the danger" (Williams, 1989, p. 322). It is for these reasons that we find the intersection of critical pedagogy with the narrative of redemption as expressed in Nancy's Hello Kitty hopes to be counterproductive to the development of critically aware teachers who are effective in developing socially just school reform.

We contend that the concrete results of schooling, as understood through the lived experience of the pedagogical relationship between teachers and students, cannot be simply reduced to absolute and universal terms of either complete failure or total success. For Nancy and for countless teachers, assessing the results of their/our pedagogical intervention is constrained by conflictive relationships and the ways in which each of us, as members of multiple and specific social groups, recognizes, perceives, believes, and acts upon complex and contradictory realities. We contend that this "lived irreducibleness" of most educational processes, confronts teachers and students with unavoidable tensions, and underlies the sense of hopelessness and loss of agency that many progressive educators can feel at the end of a semester of critical pedagogy that focuses too strongly on binary opposition and a simplistic understanding of conscientization.

We propose that schools do not need and cannot sustain superteachers or critically super-conscious "organic intellectuals." Instead, schools need teachers that can recognize their intellectual function and can then assume the role of "committed intellectuals" (Fischman, 1998). The committed intellectual is more of an orientation or a process than a final state of being, and perhaps more importantly, commitment likely precedes or at least develops with concientization (Fischman & McLaren, 2005). Thus, the teaching of CP should begin here as well. Paulo Freire (1989) has noted:

> Concientization is not exactly the starting point of commitment. Concientization is more of a product of commitment. I do not have to be already critically self-conscious in order to struggle. By struggling I become conscious/aware. (p. 46)

In other words, an educator who is a committed intellectual is sometimes critically self-conscious and actively engaged in social networks, but at other times is confused, or even unaware of his or her limitations or capacities to be an active proponent of social change. They will continue to be both oppressed and oppressor, even as they struggle to become less of both.

Freire came to recognize that a deep understanding of the complex processes of oppression and domination is not enough to guarantee personal or collective praxis. Commitment is central, but the commitment to struggle against injustice is not "organic" and is more natural for some people than for others (Fischman & McLaren, 2005). Further, this commitment is not just to an individual struggle, but also to a developing community of similarly committed fellow activists. Only by developing an understanding that is born of a commitment to social justice in cooperation with others can such an understanding lead to both the type of concientization and the countersystemic networks necessary to challenge the hegemonic structures of domination and exploitation. The inequities of the globalization of capital can be challenged and even defeated, but not simply by understanding its formation and toiling individually; rather, it requires developing the will and the courage—the commitment— to struggle against it in cooperation with others.

The notion of the teacher as a committed intellectual is exactly the opposite of the teacher as the superagent of educational change, where he or she is able to do all the heroic tasks and thus everything is possible. Following Badiou (2001), we assume that the accomplishments of the committed intellectual will be a lot more humble:

> The conception of politics that we defend is far from the idea that "everything is possible". In fact, it is an immense task to try to propose a few possibles, in the plural—a few possibilities other than what we are told is possible. It is a matter of showing how the space of the possible is larger than the one we are assigned—that something else is possible, but not that everything is possible. (p. 115)

We contend that potentially all teachers could be committed intellectuals, based on the functions that they perform and not on any essential virtue or characteristic. For such a teacher it is not enough to understand how the multiple forms of exploitation are affecting their students, their families and communities; they are committed to reflectively act in their classroom (and beyond) as one of the focal points to transform the world. As Foucault (1980) convincingly indicates,

The essential political problem for the intellectual is not to criticize the ideological contents supposedly linked to science, or to ensure that his own scientific practice is accompanied by a correct ideology, but that of ascertaining the possibility of constituting a new politics of truth. The problem is not changing people's consciousness— or what's in their heads—but the political, economic, institutional regime of the production of truth. (p. 133)

The teacher as a committed intellectual recognizes that the Freirean notion of praxis and the capacity to engage in critical self-consciousness are not enough to transform both the repressive and integrative functions of the hegemonic orders. Nevertheless, they are necessary to finding ways to actively intervene in the world order in ways that have the potential to transform that world.

Contrary to the all-powerful "heroic-teacher" or the all-knowing "superconscious critical-teacher" of the NR, the teacher as committed intellectual that we propose is committed and oriented by the goals of educational and social justice without succumbing to essentialist positions or easy rhetorical discourses of good versus evil, populist nostalgia, possessive parochialism, or militant cultural particularism (Glass, 2004). We acknowledge that labor–capital antagonism is a fundamental dialectical contradiction within capitalist society, but reject as self-defeating the reduction of educational conflicts to simplistic binaries such as evil neoliberalism versus good social democracy.

Conclusions

Hope for a better and fairer future for our schools and societies is not problematic per se; however, hope that relies on a redemptive narrative of individual superteacher heroism, whether wrapped in neoliberal ideology or critical discourses, is ineffectual hope. Learning from Nancy's example implies the recognition that using critical pedagogy to inform our work as teachers requires that our classrooms offer not only consistent theoretical analyses, but also the commitment to value and aid the concrete practical experiences of our students.

To this end, we present three main ideas to guide the practice of teaching critical pedagogy so that it confronts the complex influences of globalization and neo-liberalism with the lived experiences of successful teachers in a manner that results in an empowered agency more than feelings of sadness and defeat. First, teachers and practitioners of CP should develop pedagogies that understand why the discourse of neoliberal globalization has become so dominant in educational spaces. Second, CP and especially the concept of pedagogical hope should not be structured as narratives of redemption that cannot help but get trapped in a cycle of self-defeating demands that teachers perform ever more challenging, heroic tasks. Third, CP should focus on the development of the notion and practices for educators to be committed intellectuals first, rather than ones that are primarily superconscious, always and purely resisting global and neoliberal policies and practices as part of a system of school reform. Teachers as committed intellectuals can engage in individual and collective actions as an integral part of the always contradictory and conflictive on-going processes of conscientization and educational change.

Freire (1997a) believed that hope is a historical and ontological need and not an external characteristic of the pedagogical situation, alien to the daily struggle of teachers and students. Critical pedagogues have developed a great repertoire of concepts and practices alternative to the oppressive educational systems (be they neo-liberal or not), but in order to be effective CP should recognize that the starting point of many teachers is similar to Nancy's original Hello Kitty hopeful attitude. As Freire vehemently stated "Just to hope, is to hope in vain" (1997b, p. 9), but it is nonetheless a better starting point that a cynical or hopeless perspective. We are committed to rethinking our students' as well as our own categories of analysis, and reflecting on the differences between hope in the individualistic heroic narrative of redemption and hope in a Freirean sense, which requires hope to be put in a concrete, practical experience of collective struggle, dialogue, and conflict. Then, critical pedagogy will attain its hopeful goals.

Notes

1. This seminar was taught by Gustavo E. Fischman at Arizona State University during the Fall 2005 semester.
2. Elizabeth Ellsworth's "Why Doesn't This Feel Empowering" (1989) was one of the required readings for the class. Ellsworth's article is considered one of the most poignant criticisms to the theory and practice of CP because she concluded that far from providing a discourse of hope and transformation and the abilities needed to make reforms, CP made things worse. *When participants in our class attempted to put into practice prescriptions offered in the literature [of critical pedagogy] concerning empowerment, student voice, and dialogue, we produced results that were not only unhelpful, but actually exacerbated the very conditions we were trying to work against, including Eurocentrism, racism, sexism, classism, and "banking education."... Far from helping to overcome relations of oppression in the classroom, the "discourses of critical pedagogy"...had themselves become vehicles of repression.* (p. 298)
3. The United Nations (2005) report on the world social situation concluded that "Surveys conducted in Africa, East Asia, Europe and Latin America indicate that a growing majority of individuals feel they have no control or influence over the economic, political and social factors that affect their lives. Economic and security concerns are causing a great deal of anxiety, and there is little confidence in the ability or commitment of State institutions to manage these growing problems" (p. 113).
4. We are not attempting to minimize the impact of the extensive use of information technologies and cyberspace in the transformation of everyday life, which is undoubtedly enormous, but to avoid considering cyberspace and IT as the new redeeming tool. As Wertheim (1997) noted, "Today's proselytizers of cyberspace proffer their domain as an ideal 'above' and 'beyond' the problems of the material world. While early Christians promulgated heaven as a realm in which the human soul would be freed from the frailties and failings of the flesh, so today's champions of cyberspace hail it as a place where the self will be freed from the limitations of physical embodiment" (p. 296, cited in Bauman, 1998, p. 19).
5. Bauman (1998) points out that the public no longer dominates the private: "The opposite is the case: it is the private that colonizes the public space, squeezing out and chasing away everything which cannot be fully, without residue, translated into the vocabulary of private interests and pursuits" (p. 107). Similarly, Lipsitz (2000) rightly argues that these discourses were very effective to "hide public concerns while foregrounding private interests—to encourage people to think of themselves as taxpayers and homeowners rather than as citizens and workers, to depict private property interests and the accumulated advantages accorded to white men as universal while condemning demands for redistributive justice by women, racial and sexual minorities, and by other aggrieved social groups as the 'whining of special interests'" (p. 84).

References

Apple, M. (2004). *Ideology and curriculum* (3rd ed.). Oxford: Taylor & Francis.
Badiou, A. (2001). *Ethics: An essay on the understandings of evil.* London: Verso.
Ball, S. J. (2003). *Class strategies and the education market.* London and New York: Routledge-Falmer.

Ball, S. J., Fischman, G., & Gvirtz, S. (Eds.). (2003). *Education, crisis and hope: Tension and change in Latin America*. New York: Routledge-Falmer.

Bauman, Z. (1998). *Globalization: The human consequences*. New York: Columbia University Press.

Bourdieu, P. (1998). *Acts of resistance: Against the tyranny of the market*. New York: The New Press.

Bullough, J., R. V., & Gitlin, A. (1995). *Becoming a student of teaching*. New York: Garland.

Cato, I. (2005). *Handbook on policy* (6th ed.). Washington, D.C.: Cato Institute.

Colin, C., & Streeck, W. (1997). *Political economy and modern capitalism: Mapping convergence and diversity*. London: Sage.

Darder, A. (2002). *Reinventing Paulo Freire: A pedagogy of love*. Boulder, CO and Oxford: Westview.

Darder, A., Baltodano, M., & Torres, R. (Eds.). (2003). *The critical pedagogy reader*. New York: Routledge-Falmer.

Ellsworth, E. (1989). "Why doesn't this feel empowering?" Working through the repressive myths of critical pedagogy. *Harvard Educational Review, 59*(3), 297–324.

Elmore, R. (1996). Getting to scale with good educational practice. *Harvard Educational Review, 66*(1), 1–26.

Fischman, G., & McLaren, P. (2005). Rethinking critical pedagogy and the Gramscian legacy: From organic to committed intellectuals. *Cultural Studies ↔ Critical Methodologies, 5*(4), 425–447.

Fischman, G., McLaren, P., Sünker, H., & Lankshear, C. (Eds.). (2005). *Critical theories, radical pedagogies and global conflicts*. Lanham, MD: Rowman & Littlefield.

Fischman, G. E., Ball, S., & Gvirtz, S. (2003). Towards a neoliberal education? Tension and change in Latin-America. In *Education, crisis and hope: Tension and change in Latin-America* (pp. 1–19). New York: Routledge-Falmer.

Fischman, G. E., & McLaren, P. (2000). Schooling for democracy: Toward a critical utopianism. *Contemporary Sociology, 29*(1), 168–180.

Foucault, M. (1980). *Power and knowledge: selected interviews and other writings*. New York: Pantheon.

Fischman, G. E. (1998). Donkeys and Superteachers: Popular education and structural adjustment in Latin-America. *International Journal of Education, 44*(2-3), 191–213.

Fischman, G. E., & McLaren, P. (2005). Rethinking critical pedagogy and the Gramscian legacy: From organic to committed intellectuals. *Cultural Studies ↔ Critical Methodologies, 5*(4), 425–447.

Freire, P. (1989). *Education for the critical consciousness*. New York: Continuum.

Freire, P. (1997a). *Pedagogy of hope: Reliving the pedagogy of the oppressed*. New York: Continuum.

Freire, P. (1997b). *Pedagogy of the heart*. New York: Continuum.

Friedman, T. L. (2005). *The world is flat: A brief history of the twenty-first century*. New York: Farrar, Straus & Giroux.

Giroux, H. (1988). *Teachers as intellectuals*. New York: Bergin & Garvey.

Giroux, H. (1993). *Border crossings*. New York: Routledge.

Giroux, H. (1994). *Disturbing pleasures: Learning popular culture*. New York: Routledge.

Giroux, H. (2000). *The mouse that roared*. Lanham, MD: Rowman & Littlefield.

Giroux, H (2002) Rethinking cutural Politics and radical pedagogy in the work of Antonio Gramsci. In C. Borg, J. Buttiegieg, & P. Mayo (Eds.), *Gramsci and education* (pp. 41–66). Lanham, MD: Rowman & Littlefield.

Giroux, H. (2003). Thinking politics and resistance as a form of public pedagogy. In G. Fischman, P. McLaren, & H. Sunker (Eds.), *Critical theories, radical pedagogies and global conflicts* (pp. 1–12). Lanham, MD: Rowman & Littlefield.

Giroux, H., & McLaren, P. (1989). *Critical pedagogy, the state and cultural struggle*. Albany, NY: SUNY Press.

Glass, R. (2004). Moral and political clarity and education as a practice of freedom. In M. Boler (Ed.), *Democratic dialogue and education: Troubling speech, disturbing silence* (pp. 15–32). New York: Peter Lang.

Haas, E. (2006). Civil right, noble cause, and Trojan horse: News media portrayals of think tank initiatives on urban education. In J. Kincheloe, P. Anderson, K. Rose, D. Griffith, & K. Hayes (Eds.), *Urban education: An encyclopedia* (pp. 439–450). Westport, CT: Greenwood Press.

Hardt, M., & Negri, A. (2000). *Empire*. Cambridge, MA: Harvard University Press.

Hill, D. (2005). Globalisation and its educational discontents: Neoliberalisation and its impacts on education workers' rights, pay and conditions. *International Studies in Sociology of Education, 15*(3), 256–288.

Huntington, R. (2005). *The nanny state: How New Labor stealthed us*. London: Artnik.

Hursh, D. (2005). The growth of high-stakes testing in the USA: Accountability, markets and the decline in educational equality. *British Education Research Journal, 31*(5), 605–622.

Hursh, D. (2006). The crisis in urban education: Resisting neoliberal policies and forging democratic possibilities. *Educational Researcher, 35*(4), 19–25.

Kellner, D. (2005). The conflicts of globalization and restructuring of education. In M. Peters (Ed.), *Education, globalization, and the state in the age of terrorism* (pp. 31–70). Boulder, CO: Paradigm.

McLaren, P. (2005). *Red seminars: Radical excursions into educational theory, cultural politics, and pedagogy*. Cresskill, NJ: Hampton Press.

McLaren, P., & Fischman, G. (1998). Reclaiming hope: Teacher education and social justice in the age of globalization. *Teacher Education Quarterly, 25*(4), 125–133.

McLaren, P., & Lankshear, C. (1993). Critical literacy and the postmodern turn. In P. McLaren & C. Lankshear (Eds.), *Critical literacy*. Albany, NY: SUNY Press.

McLaren, P., & Lankshear, C. (Eds.). (1994). *Politics of liberation: Paths from Freire*. London: Routledge.

McLaren, P., & Leonard, P. (Eds.). (1993). *Paulo Freire. A critical encounter*. New York: Routledge.

Peters, M. (Ed.). (2005). *Education, globalization, and the state in the age of terrorism*. Boulder, CO: Paradigm.

United Nations Development Project. (UNDP). (1996). *Human development report*. New York: UNDP.

Readings, B. (1996). *The university in ruins*. Cambridge, MA: Harvard University Press.

Robbins , C. G. (2006). *The Giroux reader*. Boulder, CO: Paradigm.

Stiglitz, J. E. (2002). *Globalization and its discontents*. New York: Norton.

Tabb, W. K. (2002). *Unequal partners: A primer on globalization*. New York: New Press.

Tabb, W. K. (2006). Trouble, trouble, debt, and bubble. *The Monthly Review, 58*(1). Retrieved from http://www.monthlyreview.org/0506tabb.htm.

United Nations. (2005). *The inequality predicament: Report on the world social situation*. New York: United Nations.

Wertheim, M. (1997). *Pythagoras' trousers: God, physics, and the gender wars* New York: W.W. Norton.

Williams, R. (1989). *Resources of hope*. New York: Verso.

38 Creating Local Democracy, Nurturing Global Alternatives

The Case of the Citizen School Project in Porto Alegre, Brazil

Luis Armando Gandin

When talking about the experiences of participatory democracy in the city of Porto Alegre, and more specifically about the World Social Forum and the World Education Forum held in that city for some years, the Portuguese sociologist Boaventura de Sousa Santos would say that the Forum and the Porto Alegre experiences were not antiglobalization initiatives but rather a form of "globalization from below" (Santos, 1995). This chapter will show an educational reform that did not have the intention of becoming a global experience but rather a local progressive alternative to market-based educational policies. Nevertheless, because of its innovations in terms of access to schools, curriculum, and educational governance, it has achieved (together with other local participatory democracy initiatives) a high degree of global interest. According to Michael Apple, in a lecture at the 2004 World Education Forum, Porto Alegre, being the "city of the Citizen School and the Participatory Budgeting," can "teach the world how to stop neoliberalism and neoconservativism" (World Education Forum, 2004). The World Social Forum and the World Education Forum (spaces created to think about alternatives to neo-liberalism in economy, culture, social life, and education) started in the city of Porto Alegre exactly because of the policies implemented by the local government.

The goal of this chapter is to describe and analyze the Citizen School project, the urban educational reform implemented in Porto Alegre, and its potential global lessons from the South.

Contextualizing the Citizen School Project

Porto Alegre is a city of almost 1.4 million people, situated in the southern region of Brazil. It is the capital of the state of Rio Grande do Sul and the largest city of the region. From 1989 to 2004, it was governed by a coalition of leftist parties (the Popular Administration), under the general leadership of the Workers' Party (*Partido dos Trabalhadores* or PT, formed in 1979 by a coalition of unions, social movements, and other leftist organizations). The Popular Administration was reelected three consecutive times, thus giving it and its policies even greater legitimacy. Despite the recent electoral loss that replaced PT in 2005 after 16 years in the municipal administration,[1] the basic structures of the project are still in place. The fact that the winning coalition of parties (a centrist alliance) had to promise not to change the major set of policies put in place by the PT government in order to be elected, is a clear indicator of how organic these policies became in the daily life of Porto Alegre's citizens.

The Citizen Schools are almost exclusively located in the *favelas* of Porto Alegre, serving a population that lives in extreme poverty. A significant number of schools were built as a concrete result of the Participatory Budgeting process (part of the participatory democracy structures created by the Popular Administration, where delegates vote on where the city should invest part of its budget; for more see Abers, 1998; Baiocchi, 2005; Santos, 1998). A number of neighborhoods prioritized the construction of schools in their assemblies. The fact that the schools were constructed in those neighborhoods is both a victory of the organization of those communities and a political commitment of the Popular Administration.

The Citizen School project was constructed explicitly as an alternative to the global marketization ideology around education—one that claims that education should operate as a market—and it is clear that the notion of citizenship was used overtly as a way of opposing the process that views knowledge as a commodity and students as consumers. The goal of the Citizen School project is to create citizens, which are defined as the ones who have material goods necessary for survival, symbolic goods necessary for their subjectivity, and political goods necessary for their social existence (Azevedo, 1999, p. 16).

Constructing the Project

An important contribution of the Citizen School project to the idea of a participatory democracy is the way its principles were created. In order to decide on the goals and principles of the municipal schools a democratic, deliberative, and participatory forum was created called the School Constituent Project. This project was constituted through a long process of mobilization of the school communities (using the invaluable lessons learned in the mobilization for the Participatory Budgeting), and it had the goal of generating the principles that would guide the policy for the municipal schools in Porto Alegre.

The process of organization of the School Constituent Project took a good deal of time. The whole process lasted 18 months, and involved thematic groups in the schools, regional meetings, and eventually the Constituent Assembly. The themes that guided the discussion were school governance, curriculum, principles for living together, and evaluation. The Constituent Assembly elected the radical democratization of the education in the municipal schools as the main normative goal of the Citizen School project. This radical democratization would have to occur in three dimensions: democratization of access to school, democratization of knowledge, and democratization of governance. These three principles would be the ones guiding every action in the municipal system of Porto Alegre. These three principles would have the impact of changing the structure of the schools and of the relationship between schools and the SMED.

Democratization of Access to Schools

If the schools were to have an impact on the lives of the children living in the most impoverished neighborhoods of Porto Alegre—where the municipal schools are situated—initial access to schools had to be a priority. For the Popular Administration, guaranteeing this access was, therefore, the first step to promoting social justice to communities historically excluded from social goods.

Granting access to all children of school age is not as easy as it might sound. Historically, Brazil has had an enormous number of children who did not attend school. National statistics show that this has been changing rapidly, but in 1991, when the Popular Administration was just starting, and even in 1994, when the Citizen School project had only been in existence for one year, the situation was grave in terms of initial access to schooling. Almost 17% of the Brazilian children of school age were not being formally educated in 1991; in 1994 this number had dropped to almost 13%.

When the Workers' Party was elected in 1988, the city of Porto Alegre had only 19 primary (K–8) schools ("fundamental education," as it is called in Brazil), with 14,838 students and 1,698 teachers, curriculum coordinators, and educational supervisors. Under the Popular Administration the number of students grew at a remarkable rate. Between 1988 and 2000, the number of students in fundamental education increased by 232%. This number shows how profound the impact of the actions of the SMED has been in Porto Alegre, and, although the comparison is not between equal circumstances, it is worth pointing out that between 1991 and 1998 the number of school-age children in Brazil increased by only 22.3% (Sistema de informações, pesquisas e estatísticas educacionais [INEP], 2000, p. 53).

The number of fundamental education schools increased by 126% under the Popular Administration government (and if we consider all the schools under the municipal government—including the schools geared toward early childhood, adolescents and young adults, and special education—the rate of increase is actually 210%). It is important to point out again that these schools were all constructed in very impoverished areas of the city and that the majority of new schools were actually built inside or around *favelas*. This means that the schools are not only bringing back students who drop out of state schools, but they are also creating a space for many children who have never attended school and possibly never would have were it not for the new municipal schools.

But guaranteeing initial access to school does not guarantee that these children will benefit from school. In order to really democratize the access to schools, in 1995 the SMED started to propose a new organization for the municipal schools. Instead of keeping the traditional structure of grades with the duration of one year (first to eighth in fundamental education), the idea was to adopt a new structure called Cycles of Formation. It is important to note that the idea of reorganizing the curriculum and the space-time of the schools in cycles instead of grades does not originate in Porto Alegre. What the Citizen School was implementing was not new per se, but a new configuration that, according to the SMED, would offer a substantially better opportunity for dealing with the need for democratization of access and knowledge.

In this new configuration, the traditional deadline—the end of each academic year—when the students had to "prove" that they had "learned," was eliminated in favor of a different time organization. The establishment of the cycles is a conscious attempt to eliminate the mechanisms in schools that perpetuate exclusion, failure, and dropouts, as well as the blaming of the victim that accompanies these. The idea is that by using a different conception of the equation learning/time, the Citizen School would not punish students for allegedly being "slow" in their process of learning

The schools now had three cycles of three years each, something that adds one year to the "fundamental education" (one year of early childhood education inside the schools, expanding "fundamental education" to nine years). This made the municipal schools responsible for the education of kids from 6 to 14 years old. The three cycles are organized based on the cycles of life: each one corresponds to one phase of development (i.e., childhood, preadolescence, and adolescence). The idea is to group together students of the same age in each of the years of the three cycles. This aims at changing the reality in the majority of public schools that cater to popular classes in Brazil and the one the SMED was faced with when the Popular Administration started to govern the city: students with multiple failures (and therefore much older) inside classrooms intended for much younger children. By having students of the same age in the same year of the cycle, the SMED claims to remotivate the kids who have failed multiple times.

In the schools using these cycles, students progress from one year to another within one cycle; the notion of "failure" is eliminated. Despite this victory, the SMED understood that the elimination of mechanisms of exclusion was not enough to achieve the goal of democratization of knowledge. Because of this, the Citizen School created several mechanisms that aim at guaranteeing the inclusion of students. It established Progression Groups for the students that have discrepancies between their age and what they have learned. The idea is to provide students who have experienced multiple failures in the past with a stimulating and challenging environment where they can learn at their own pace and fill the gaps in their academic formation that exist because of the multiple failures they have experienced. Furthermore, the Progression Groups are also a space for the students who come from other school systems (from other city or state schools, for example) and have experienced multiple failures to be given more close attention so that they are ultimately integrated into the cycles, according to their age. The idea here is that the school has to change its structure to adapt to the students, and not the reverse, which has been historically the case (Souza et al., 1999, pp. 24–25).

This idea of constructing a new structure to better respond to students' needs led to the creation of another entity: the Learning Laboratory. This is a space where students with more serious learning problems get individual attention, but also a place where teachers conduct research in order to improve the quality of the regular classes. For the students with special needs, there are the Integration and Resources Rooms, which "are specially designed spaces to investigate and assist students who have special needs and require complementary and specific pedagogic work for their integration and for overcoming their learning difficulties" (SMED, 1999a, p. 50).

With all these mechanisms, the Citizen School project not only grants initial access, but also intends to guarantee that the educational space occupied by the subaltern children is one that treats them with the dignity, respect, and quality necessary to keep them in the school and educate them to be real citizens.

Democratization of Knowledge

Curriculum transformation is a crucial part of Porto Alegre's project to build active citizenship. It is important to say that this dimension is not limited to access to traditional knowledge. What is being constructed is a new epistemological understanding about what counts as knowledge as well. It is not based on a mere incorporation of new knowledge within the margins of an intact "core of human wisdom," but a radical transformation. The Citizen School project goes beyond the mere episodic mentioning of cultural manifestations or class, racial, sexual, and gender-based oppression. It includes these themes as an essential part of the process of construction of knowledge.

In the Citizen School project, the notion of "core" and "periphery" in knowledge is made problematic. The starting point for the construction of curricular knowledge is the culture(s) of the communities themselves, not only in terms of content, but in terms of perspective as well. The whole educational process is aimed at inverting previous priorities and instead serving the historically oppressed and excluded groups. The starting point for this new process of knowledge construction is the idea of *thematic complexes*. This organization of the curriculum has the whole school working on a central generative theme in an interdisciplinary effort, whereby the disciplines and areas of knowledge will structure the focus of their content.

The schools are encouraged to follow steps for the construction of the thematic complex and for the translation of the macrodiscussions into curriculum. These steps involve acknowledging and studying the context where the school is situated, through participatory research conducted by the school collective in the community, selecting statements gathered in the research that are significant and representative of the aspirations, interests, conceptions, and cultures of the community, and elaborating principles that can guide the curriculum building process in the school.

The thematic complex provides the whole school with a central focus that guides the curriculum of that school for a period of time that can be one semester or an entire academic year. After having the principles—the larger contribution of each knowledge area for the discussion of the thematic complex—and the conceptual matrix—a web of concepts from the knowledge area, rather than isolated facts or information that the teachers understand are essential to use when dealing with the thematic complex—teachers have meetings organized by their knowledge areas and by each year in the cycles, to elaborate and plan the curriculum. Teachers have to "study" their own knowledge areas and elect the concepts that would help to problematize the thematic complex. They also have to work collectively with teachers of other areas in order to assemble a curriculum that is integrated and dense enough to simultaneously address the issues listed in the thematic complex.

Because the starting point for the thematic complex is popular knowledge or common sense, teachers are also forced to think about the relation between official knowledge and this common sense. Therefore, this approach deals simultaneously with three problems of traditional education: the fragmentation of knowledge, the "apparent" neutrality of school content, and the absolute supremacy that traditional schools grant to scientific/erudite knowledge over local community knowledge, especially very impoverished communities—as is the case in Porto Alegre.

The students are not studying history or social and cultural studies using books that never address their real problems and interests. Through the organization in thematic complexes, the students learn history by beginning with the historical experience of their families. They study important social and cultural content by focusing on and valorizing their own cultural manifestations. It is important to note that these students still learn the history of Brazil and the world, including the so-called high culture, but these will be seen through different lenses. Their culture will not be forgotten in order for them to learn "high status" culture. Rather, by understanding their situation and their culture and valuing it, these students will be able to simultaneously learn *and* will have the chance to transform their situation of exclusion. By studying the problems (rural exodus, living in illegal lots, etc.) and not stopping there, but studying the strengths of self-organization (in neighborhood associations and in cultural activities and groups), and connecting these issues to school knowledge such as geographical notions of space, historical events, mathematical competence, and many more, the Citizen School helps to construct real knowledge and alternatives for communities living in terrible conditions.

This shift of what is considered the core or the center of knowledge affects not only the pedagogical conception that guides the daily life in the classrooms; it also transforms how the school itself functions as a whole. This conception of knowledge now is spreading throughout the entire school system. The project not only serves the "excluded" by generating a different formal education for students, but also serves them by creating an innovative structure that makes it possible for the community of those who have historically been excluded to regain their dignity (both material and symbolic).

Democratization of Governance

The first mechanism that guarantees the democratization of governance is the Constituent Assembly. It not only provided a space to decide on the administration of the project, but also allowed for real participation in the definition of the goals of the Citizen School. Educational structures have, nevertheless, many levels of governance and democratization of these spaces demands the creation of new mechanisms.

Among the mechanisms created to democratize the governance of the educational system in Porto Alegre, the School Council is a central element. Its role is to promote the democratization of the decision-making process and governance in education in Porto Alegre. A product of the political will of the Popular Administration and the demands of social movements involved in education in the city, the school councils, established by a municipal law in December of 1992 and implemented in 1993, are the most important institutions in the schools. They are formed by elected teachers, school staff, parents, students, and by one member of the administration, and they have consultive, deliberative, and monitoring functions.

The task of the school council is to deliberate about the global projects for the school, the basic principles of administration, to allocate economic resources, and to monitor the implementation of the decisions. The principal and her or his team are responsible for the implementation of these policies defined by the school council.

In terms of resources, it is important to say that, before the Popular Administration took office, there was a practice (common in Brazil) of a centralized budget. Every expense (even the daily ones) had to be sent to the central administration before it was approved, and then, the money was sent to the school, or a central agency would purchase the product or the service necessary. In such a system, the school council would have "their hands tied," with no autonomy at all. The SMED changed this structure and established a new policy to make the amount of money available to each school every three months. According to the SMED, this was the measure that instituted the financial autonomy of the schools, which allowed the schools to manage their expenditures according to the goals and priorities established by the school council. At the same time that it creates autonomy, this measure gives parents, students, teachers, and staff who are present in the council a notion of social responsibility in administering public money, and it teaches them to hierarchize the investments with solidarity in mind (SMED, 1999b).

The school council also has the power to monitor the implementation, through the principal and her or his team, of its decisions (SMED, 1993, p. 3). In fact, the school council is an empowered structure in the schools. It is the main governance mechanism inside the schools, and its limitations are only the legislation and the policy for education collectively constructed in democratic forums. Decisions about the curriculum can be part of the deliberation, and the inclusion of parents, students, and staff (or even teachers, if we consider the traditional school) in this process is a great innovation of the model.

Along with the school council, another mechanism guarantees democratic spaces in the Citizen School: in the municipal schools of Porto Alegre, the whole school community elects the principal by direct vote. The one responsible for the implementation of the decisions of the school council, that is, the principal, is her- or himself elected after defending a particular project of administration for the school. There is a legitimacy that comes from this fact. The principal is not someone that necessarily represents the interests of the central administration inside the school councils, but someone that was voted by a majority of supporters inside that particular educational community. Principals have a great degree of embeddedness and, because of this, the SMED feels that it is possible to avoid the potential problem of having someone responsible for the concretization of the deliberations occurring in the school councils who is not connected with the project. But the responsibility of the community does not stop there: through the school council, the school community has a way of monitoring the activities of the principal and holding her or him responsible for implementing its democratic decisions.

The direct election of the one responsible for implementing the directives created by the school council, which is also elected directly by the school community, represents a mechanism that aims at generating the principle of democratic management at the local school level.

Potential Problems

The Citizen School project represents a clear advance toward the democratization of access to schools, of knowledge, and of governance. Nevertheless, as any other reform, it faces challenges that have to be addressed if the project wants to remain democratic and a viable progressive alternative to current conservative reforms.

The cycles represent an advance in the right direction: they allow students to stay in school, thereby combating the serious problem of dropouts. However, in order for them to provide students with continuous evaluation of their work, all the mechanisms created must be in place. This means that the new supporting structures (the close assessment of students' progress, the Learning Laboratories, etc.) must be in place. In times of budget constraints, these tend to be the first structures to be cut back. In a school that eliminated grade failure, the close monitoring of student progress and the supporting structures have to be there, otherwise there is a good chance students will not get the academic skills they need to continue their education. This is a serious issue and there are signs that some teachers are starting to doubt the universal elimination of grade failure, which could end up recreating the grade mentality in a cycle structure.

Another potential problem of the Citizen School project is related to the issue of class. The Workers Party has historically had its roots in a Marxist understanding of the primacy of class. Parts of the Marxist tradition have been accused (correctly, we think, in many cases) of choosing class as not just the central, but often the only, category of analysis, thus subordinating other forms of oppression to class (see Apple, 1988; Apple & Weis, 1983). Thus, in the material produced by the Popular Administration there are several explicit references to class oppression—and rightly so; but there are fewer references to racial or gender oppression. This could potentially lead to a position that ignores the specificities of oppressions other than those that are class-based. There are, therefore, reasons to believe that there are open spaces for popular organizations, such as the growing activist movement among Afro-Brazilians, women's social movements, and gay and lesbian organizations, to operate and demand from the educational state agencies the inclusion of issues that should be part of the agenda of every citizen who fights oppression, at either a local or global level.

In terms of the governance structures, a special attention has to be directed at the school councils. In the schools, there are different interests at play and, more importantly there is a specific technical knowledge that only teachers possess. When decisions in the school council, involve themes where this technical knowledge is part of the issue, teachers tend to have an important advantage. Therefore, in the decisions that involve pedagogical issues, parents may feel that they do not have the language or the convincing capability that teachers have because when teachers talk, they do it with a jargon that is often unfamiliar to the parents. There is certainly a learning process that will have to take place in the school councils. The technical knowledge that teachers have will eventually be faced with responses and arguments of those who will have learned how to better propose ideas and how to fight for the interest of parents. One of the great challenges for the Citizen School project is to intensify and extend the already existent process of education of parents in terms of what constitutes their rights and their space in the school. It requires the creation of a space where parents feel welcomed, where their knowledge about the community and their children is respected and valued as knowledge necessary to create better schools, and where parents get the discursive and intellectual tools to discuss these issues with teachers in a democratic manner. This process also has to involve educating teachers, people who had historically to get used to making all the decisions. Teachers and administrators will have to learn from the communities how to listen and how to establish a level of trust where parents feel that they do not need to use a specific jargon to be heard.

Finally, the fact that the PT is not in power in Porto Alegre represents a challenge to the integrity of the experience. Even with the current administration embracing some of the core principles of the Citizen School experience, there are fears that the grade failure might be reintroduced, representing a serious threat to the principles of the experience. Nevertheless, the fact that the main mechanisms are still in place after two years, might teach us something about the importance of making new understandings about education engrained in the school and community culture. The state was the agency that initiated the process of change, but the continuation of the changes does not depend on the state. The fact that they remained even after a new administration tells us something about the strength and the level of embeddedness of the Citizen School in Porto Alegre.

Local Action: Global Reach

Perhaps one of the most interesting aspects of the project is the fact that the Citizen School project and the Popular Administration as a whole have been establishing connections between the educational process of the city as a whole, not only with local issues and progressive initiatives, but also with global movements.

Since January of 2001, Porto Alegre has been hosting the World Social Forum and the World Education Forum. The city administration has paid part of the costs and provided the infrastructure for the meetings and assemblies. The World Social Forum was conceived of as a space for exchanging experiences and building networks of collaboration among counterhegemonic movements around the world and building what Santos and others have called "globalization from below" (Evans, 2000; Santos, 1995).

The first World Social Forum, in January of 2001, had 4,000 delegates from various countries of the world. The second forum, also held in Porto Alegre in January of 2002, attracted 15,000 delegates from 131 countries and 25,000 more people who participated without registering (Whitaker, 2002). There were also 1,500 journalists officially registered to cover the event (Klein, 2001). The third forum, again in Porto Alegre, had nearly 100,000 participants (20,000 delegates, 25,000 participants in the Youth Camp, 4,000 journalists plus nearly 50,000 general audience) (World Social Forum, 2003). In 2004 the organizers decided to have the Forum in India. In 2005 the World Social Forum returned to Porto Alegre with 155,000 registered participants.

The organization that the Popular Administration and the SMED are promoting with the World Social Forum and the World Education Forum are the attempt to build what Evans (2000) calls "transnational networks" (p. 230). In this sense, the experiences of Porto Alegre may also have considerable importance not only for Brazil, but also for people who are deeply concerned about the effects of the neoliberal and neoconservative restructuring of education and of the public sphere in general and struggle for finding alternatives. There seems to be a great deal to be learned from the successful alternative-creation and from the challenges and contradictions encountered by the Citizen School project.

Hosting events like the World Social Forum and the World Education Forum are a great step towards the construction of a "language of translation," or a step toward building a new common sense around education and creating alternative models, not only locally but also on a global scale (Pedroni & Gandin, 2007). With schools that dramatically improve access and decrease dropout rates, with a curriculum that challenges what knowledge should be taught, and with democratic governance structures that stimulate participation and community involvement, the Citizen School project can provide a concrete example of alternative to reforms based on the introduction of markets as the ultimate arbiters.

Perhaps the greatest lesson is the fact that the Citizen School project is coherently linked to larger dynamics of social transformation and to a coherent set of practices that aim to change the mechanisms of the state and the rules of participation in the formation of state policies. All of this has crucial implications for how we might think about the politics of education policy and its role in social transformation. Being formed by schools that center their life on how to address exclusion and how to create state policies that address this exclusion (avoiding "quick fixes"), the Citizen School project represents a real life experience of how difficult it is to construct radical democracy. The accomplishments and the challenges created by the experience are lessons to be learned not only by the citizens of Porto Alegre, but also by global citizens struggling for local and global transformations in their locales.

Notes

1. The PT loss in Porto Alegre has been attributed by many to a decline in middle class support of the municipal administration. The current administration was elected in a runoff election with 57% of the votes (the PT candidate received the remaining 43% of the votes).

References

Abers, R. (1998). From clientelism to cooperation: Local government, participatory policy and civic organizing in Porto Alegre, Brazil. *Politics & Society, 26*(4), 511–537.

Apple, M. W. (1988). *Teachers and texts*. New York: Routledge.

Apple, N. W., & Weiss, L. (Eds.). (1983). *Ideology and practice in schooling*. Philadelphia: Temple University Press.

Azevedo, J. C. (1999). Escola, Democracia e Cidadania. In C. Simon, D. Busetti, E. Viero, & L. W. Ferreira (Eds.), *Escola Cidadã: Trajetórias* (pp. 11–33). Porto Alegre, Brazil: Prefeitura Municipal de Porto Alegre—Secretaria Municipal de Educação.

Baiocchi, G. (2005). *Militants and citizens: The politics of participatory democracy in Porto Alegre*. Stanford, CA: Stanford University Press.

Evans, P. (2000). Fighting marginalization with transnational networks: Counter-hegemonic globalization. *Contemporary Sociology, 29*(1), 230–241.

Klein, N. (2001, March 19). A fete for the end of the end of history. *The Nation*. Retrieved May 17, 2002, from http://www.thenation.com/doc.mhtml?i=20010319&s=klein

Pedroni, T. C., & Gandin, L. A. (2007). *Building cosmopolitan solidarity across borders: Educational movements for the dispossessed in Brazil and the United States*. Paper presented at the CUFA Conference. Washington, D.C.

Sader, E. (2003). *Porto Alegre, até logo!* Zero Hora.

Santos, B. S. (1995). *Toward a new common sense: Law, science and politics in the paradigmatic transition*. New York: Routledge.

Santos, B. S. (1998). Participatory budgeting in Porto Alegre: Toward a distributive democracy. *Politics and Society, 26*(4), 461–510.

Secretaria Municipal de Educação (SMED). (1993). *Projeto Gestão Democrática—Lei Complementar no. 292*. Unpublished text.

Secretaria Municipal de Educação (SMED). (1999a). Ciclos de formação—Proposta político-pedagógica da Escola Cidadã. *Cadernos Pedagogicos, 9*(1), 1–111.

Secretaria Municipal de Educação (SMED). (1999b). Home page. Retrieved December 15, 1999 from, http://www.portoalegre.rs.gov.br/smed

Sistema de informações, pesquisas e estatísticas educaciionais [INEP]. (2000). *Education for all: Evaluation of the year 2000.* Brasilia, Brazil: INEP.

Souza, D. H., Mogetti, E. A., Villani, M., Panichi, M. T. C., Rossetto, R. P., & Huerga, S. M. R. (1999). Turma de progressão e seu significado na escola. In S. Rocha & B. D. Nery (Eds.), *Turma de progressão: a inversão da lógica da exclusão* (pp. 22–29). Porto Alegre, Brazil: SMED.

Whitaker, F. (2002). *Lessons from Porto Alegre.* Retrieved June 6, 2002 from, http://www.forum-socialmundial.org.br/eng/balanco_ChicoW_eng.asp

World Education Forum. (2004). *Lecturer stresses the importance of the Citizen School and of the Participatory Budgeting in the Education Forum.* Retrieved January 10, 2007 from, http://www.portoalegre.rs.gov.br/fme/interna.asp?mst=5&m1=23695

World Social Forum. (2000). *Goals of the World Social Forum.* Retrieved December 6, 2000 from, http://www.forumsocialmundial.org.br

World Social Forum. (2003). *Background: The events of 2001, 2002 and 2003.* Retrieved July 30, 2006 from, http://www.forumsocialmundial.org.br

Response to Part 7

Globalization and Social Justice in Education

David Gillborn

Globalization is everywhere; Google reveals in excess of 27 million references in the blink of an eye. Politicians and journalists are especially keen on the term, not least because it lends their views a sense of importance and intellectual weight. By invoking "globalization" they sound profound (as if they have a deep understanding of epochal shifts) *plus* they can present their chosen political ideology as if it were a necessary, even unavoidable path of survival. An additional attraction is that the term is so flexible that it can be applied to numerous different agendas.

Globalization is frequently used as a rationale for particular economic and social policies which force through neoliberal reforms that prioritize the market and attack state provision. Consequently we are told that globalization—by definition a force too big to be resisted—means that traditional protections for workers are now outdated and unsustainable. Globalization, we are told, means that the education system must produce high skill workers fit for the 21st century. A premium is placed on the highest attainers and "gifted and talented" programs are promoted on the eugenic grounds that "Today's gifted pupils are tomorrow's social, intellectual, economic and cultural leaders and their development cannot be left to chance" (National Academy for Gifted and Talented Youth, 2007). These programs are proclaimed as the height of meritocracy despite (or is it because of?) the fact that their students are overwhelmingly White and middle class. But, we are assured, this is necessary for everyone's sake because we must compete in a newly globalized world.

And if this feels unfair or exploitative, globalization has an answer for that too. Because, we are told, globalization is challenging the identity of states and individuals like never before. In particular, policymakers in the West link these assertions to supposed threats to security and national identity—a deployment that allows the speaker to insist on *his* or *her* chosen view of national identity as threatened and in need of strong defensive measures. Hence, the UK government insists on the importance of the English language and frowns on "excessive" use of religious dress among Muslim people because, *it says*, the cohesion of the nation is at stake. Hence a narrow disciplinary obsession with the expectations and beliefs of the White majority is dressed up as common sense and asserted as in the interests of all. In the words of a British Prime Minister:

> It is a matter both of cohesion and of justice that we should set the use of English as a condition of citizenship…we are not on our own in trying to find the right balance between integration and diversity. There is a global agonising on the subject…. Our tolerance is part of what makes Britain, Britain. So conform to it; or don't come here. (Blair, 2006)

So a "global agonizing" about identity and the nation-state is swiftly translated into new citizenship restrictions that prioritize the English language (and therefore people from predominantly White countries) while discriminating against people from South Asian countries seeking to reunite with family members already resident in Britain: all in the name of "cohesion," "justice," and "tolerance."

But critical scholars have pointed out that globalization has a longer history than most contemporary commentators choose to remember. Ricky Lee Allen (2001) argues that globalization is hundreds of years old and, although capitalism is its chosen *economic* form, its dominant *cultural* trope has always been White Supremacy. The murderous slave trade that built the economies of the "West" was truly global, brought incalculable cultural change in their path, and traded in Black bodies as if they were a commodity like any other. And when the United States proclaimed its independence, including the self-evident truth that "all men [sic] are created equal," it was understood that people of color were not included (Bell, 1987).

Meanwhile the hyperdiversity of contemporary cultures is accelerating not only through greater migration but also through the proliferation of media that serve migrant populations, such as satellite TV and radio stations dedicated to diverse communities beamed directly from their homelands, in their own languages, wherever they currently live on Earth.

Amid all this, nation-states are more than ever working to sustain the fiction that they are an ethnos— a single people based on a mythic cultural, pseudobiological lineage (Anderson, 2006). In the United States, Australia, and Britain, for example, the government and media maintain a view of the nation as unified around a set of beliefs that sustain race inequality and White Supremacy whilst espousing a superficial and empty version of multiculturalism. These tensions grow stronger all the time and are increasingly found in the school yard and the classroom; where the neat and tidy version of history taught through the formal and the hidden curricula rub up against the reality of racial oppression in the school, the locale, the nation-state, and the global.

References

Allen, R. L. (2001). The globalization of White supremacy: Toward a critical discourse on the racialization of the world. *Educational Theory, 51*(4), 467–485.

Anderson, B. (2006). *Imagined communities: Reflections on the origin and spread of nationalism* (Rev. ed.). London: Verso.

Bell, D. (1987). *And we are not saved: The elusive quest for racial justice.* New York: Basic Books.

Blair, T. (2006). *The duty to integrate: Shared British values.* Retrieved December 10, 2006, from http://www.pm.gov.uk/output/Page10563.asp#content

National Academy for Gifted and Talented Youth (NAGTY). (2007). *Gifted education: The English model in full.* Retrieved April 29, 2007, from http://www.nagty.ac.uk/about/english_model_full.aspx

Part 8

The Politics of Social Justice Meets Practice

Teacher Education and School Change

Edited and Introduced by Joel Westheimer
and karen emily suurtamm

> Can we, somehow, bring teachers and students together, not through the artificial sieve of certification and examination but on the basis of their common attraction to an exciting social goal? Can we solve the old educational problem of teaching children crucial values, while avoiding a blanket imposition of the teacher's ideas? Can this be done by honestly accepting as an educational goal that we want better human beings in the rising generation than we had in the last, and that this requires a forthright declaration that the educational process cherishes equality, justice, compassion and world brotherhood? Is it not possible to create a hunger for those goals through the fiercest argument about whether or not they *are* worthwhile? And cannot the schools have a running, no-ideas-barred exchange of views about alternative ways to those goals?
>
> (Zinn, 1997, p. 539)

> …give up teaching and go to digging ditches before bowing to the new American slavery of thought….
>
> (DuBois, 2002, p. 203)

Recent years have seen increased attacks on teacher education programs in general, and especially those that articulate the aim of promoting social justice. Most notably, in June 2006, the National Council for the Accreditation of Teacher Education (NCATE) submitted to pressure by conservative groups, removing brief mention of social justice from their accreditation standards (Wasley, 2006). Organizations like the American Council of Trustees and Alumni, the National Association of Scholars, and the Foundation for Individual Rights have helped to generate a climate where it is reasonable to label teacher educators "fanatics" on the grounds that they "believe that all teachers ought to strive to inculcate in their students a 'literacy for social equity and social justice'" (Stern, 2006).

Reclaiming the debate will entail dismantling the most common illusory assumptions: that social justice education is distinctly political; and that social justice educators stand in opposition to academic knowledge and rigor. Because social justice educators politicize the classroom in ways that are counter to the status quo, their methods become visibly and explicitly political. But the call of many conservatives, for a "solid academic and politics-free education" (Stern, 2006, p. 53), must be answered by voices who demonstrate that "teacher education is fundamentally a political enterprise, which must be analyzed and understood as such" (Cochran-Smith, 2005, p. 179), and, moreover, that a politicized education can, and must, be solidly academic. It should be clear to all that these attacks on social justice education differ in important ways from attacks on indoctrination. Few educators suggest that teachers advocate particular policy positions with regard to challenging social problems. Rather, the idea that teachers and students might tie knowledge to social ends is under siege. It doesn't have to be this way. A document produced by the Bank Street College of Education underscores several principles that guide their teacher education programs. It is imperative, they note, that teachers recognize that "education is a vehicle for creating and promoting social justice and encouraging participation in democratic processes," and also that they develop "deep knowledge of subject matter areas and [are] actively engaged in learning through formal study, direct observation, and participation" (Nager & Shapiro, 2007, p. 9).

Teacher education constitutes the foundation of efforts to build a strong teaching force that is prepared to teach diverse learners and equipped to teach for social justice. A thoughtful response to criticisms "from the outside," involves defending our programs, but also honestly and critically examining the project, strengthening our sense of what social justice teacher education entails, and working to develop programs that fulfill our goals (Fraser, 2005; Ladson-Billings, 2005). For example, Butin (2007) calls for an "anti-anti-social justice" orientation to service learning that constantly questions and disrupts the settling of our ideas. In this vision, the struggle for social justice is ongoing, where students work *with* others, rather than *for* others, and resist wrapping their ideas in neat packages that climax with concrete revelations.

This section of the handbook aims to continue the dialogue about the appropriate goals and methods of social justice teacher education, as well as the ways it can be defended. Marilyn Cochran-Smith and her colleagues identify different critiques of social justice education, arming us with the concepts and language to both consider and confront these discourses. Richert, Donahue, and LaBoskey engage in a rich discussion of the ways that White teacher candidates can grapple with racial identity, in order to teach culturally, racially, and linguistically diverse students. McDonald and Zeichner warn against purely symbolic efforts toward introducing social justice to teacher education programs and trouble the sometimes facile relationship between multicultural education and social justice-oriented education. Sleeter paints a compelling (and frightening) portrait of the current political climate in which this work must take place, and outlines her ideas for developing teacher education programs that more holistically embrace social justice.

The arguments presented in this section (and in the literature in general) reveal at least two important ways of conceptualizing social justice-oriented education. The first understands teachers as agents of social justice, who teach diverse learners so that all can achieve. This mission seeks to alter current inequalities in society by equipping marginalized communities with strong future leaders who are able to succeed. The second understands students themselves as agents (rather than instruments) of social change. In this vision, the teacher's role is to equip students with the knowledge, behavior, and skills needed to transform society into a place where social justice *can* exist. Of course, both visions are needed in a comprehensive and effective program, where teacher candidates understand how schooling is a political activity, which enables them to teach *for* social justice, but also to understand the larger political picture, which enables them to teach *about* social justice, so that others are empowered to continue the struggle.

This distinction may help us clarify several further issues that arise in this section. First, for some, social justice education becomes synonymous with multicultural education. As several of the authors point out, there is a great disparity between the demographic makeup of teachers and that of their students. Many novice teachers are unaware of the realities their students face, and the tools they, their families, and their communities may need to succeed. Indeed, failure to promote these tools in teacher education programs serves to work against social justice goals. For example, if we follow this line of reasoning, it might make sense to focus greater attention on teaching White teachers to teach diverse students. At the same time, if one believes society is structured along relations of power, in which those with privilege systematically and systemically alienate those without—or if one believes that capitalism would not survive if everyone "succeeded"—there is indeed more work to be done. Recognition of this culture of power, then, simultaneously reveals the need to implement social justice-oriented programs in *all* schools, and perhaps especially those filled with the children of those that gain privilege from the culture of power. Richert, Donahue, and LaBoskey invoke Milner, who reminds us that "students of color are *not* the problem. Race and the historical legacy of racism, and what these issues have meant for our schools and students in the United States, are essentially the problems" (Milner, 2003, p. 176). So-called disadvantaged kids are not preventing social justice from taking shape; rather, their marginalization is what prevents it. As such, the students who gain privilege from our power structures—those who may grow up to reinforce, assert, and defend them—are ideal candidates to learn about antiracism and social justice. As Ladson-Billings (2005) reminds us, the aim of creating a more diverse teaching force is not simply so that children will have teachers with more similar racial/cultural identities, but also "to ensure that all students, including White students, experience a more accurate picture of what it means to live and work in a multicultural and democratic society" (Ladson-Billings, 2005, p. 231). Moreover, Richert, Donahue, and Laboskey rightly argue that White teachers must first understand their own racial identity and privilege before they recognize that discussing racism in the classroom is their responsibility.

A second issue relates to a complaint often heard from students and novice teachers: that the "theory" about social justice that they've learned in school is not "practical" for the classroom (Williams, Connell, White, & Kemper, 2003). It is especially important that new teachers are able to see the importance *and* applicability of social justice education, lest they leave it at the academy doors upon certification. Teacher educators can help bridge the disconnect between teacher education and practice by building strong links in the K-12 community, and teaching social justice in a way that clearly connects it with practice.

A third issue that appears in several of the chapters in this section concerns the current political climate of education reform and the obstacles this climate poses for implementation of social justice teacher education programs. A myopic focus on test-based accountability has diverted attention from examination of social issues. Many educators assert that they want students to learn so that they can work effectively to make the world a better place, but the push for math and literacy training, to the exclusion of social studies, arts, and extracurricular programs, has made it difficult to think about the strengths of our democratic society and the challenges it faces at all educational levels. Indeed, a study by the Center on Education Policy (2006) found that 71% of districts reported cutting back time on other subjects to make more space for reading and math instruction. Social studies was the part of the curriculum most frequently cited as a place where these reductions took place. No one doubts the importance of literacy or math, but the demands of education and the development of effective democratic citizens require more than just these disciplinary skills.

Conclusion

Teaching teachers how to be concerned for and advance social justice in their classrooms should not be a controversial commitment. To say that one supports education for social justice is simply to say that one supports the idea of preparing students to use the knowledge and analytic skills they develop in school to identify ways in which society and societal institutions can treat people more fairly and more humanely. The words themselves are straightforward. *Social* implies that educators are talking about concepts and practices that relate to human society and how it is organized. *Justice* implies fairness or reasonableness in the way people are treated and decisions are made (Westheimer & Kahne, 2007).[1]

Since the inception of public schooling, educators have frequently sought to offer educational programs that would reduce the gaps between the haves and the have-nots in society by ameliorating poverty, providing broader employment opportunities to underserved populations, ensuring that students care about those with need and treat all individuals with respect, and—to use the current phrase—creating policies so that "no child is left behind." These efforts, like all educational and social policies, work with varying levels of effectiveness, but few doubt the value of these goals. Indeed, public schooling itself could be considered one of the greatest experiments in social justice, based on the idea that all children, regardless of their socioeconomic background, are entitled to quality education. Nobody denies that teacher education programs should teach teachers how to develop students' knowledge and skills such as reading and doing arithmetic. But knowledge and skills alone are not enough. As John Dewey so often asserted, a large part of what makes knowledge important is that it enables citizens to participate in the life of the community, to work both individually and collectively to make our society better (Dewey, 1916, 1938). And there should be no doubt that society always needs improving. The U.S Bureau of the Census reports that almost one out of five children (under the age of 18) is living in poverty. Some 44 million Americans live without health insurance, at least 9 million of them children. Hunger, homelessness, and violence plague many communities, making abundantly clear that there is much work that needs to be done to improve our society. The needs throughout the rest of the world are even more immense. The best ways to address these needs—both foreign and domestic—are understandably a matter for debate. What should be clear, however, is that we are better off when students learn to care about the needs of others and when they learn to analyze, discuss, and act on important social issues in thoughtful, caring, and informed ways. Such noble goals require "a much wider and richer dialogue about what needs to be defended in teacher preparation and at least as much, what is wrong and needs to be fixed" (Fraser, 2005, p. 282). Teaching is not just about individual successes of students, but rather about preparing them to work together to create a more equal, just world. Teacher education programs, as the chapters in this section make abundantly clear, have a critical role to play.

Note

1. These points are adapted from earlier writing by Westheimer and Kahne (2007).

References

Butin, D. (2007). Justice-leaning: Service-learning as justice-oriented education. *Equity & Excellence in Education, 40*, 177–183.

Cochran-Smith, M. (2005). The politics of teacher education. *Journal of Teacher Education, 56*(3) 179–180.

Dewey, J. (1916). *Democracy and education*. New York: Macmillan.

Dewey, J. (1938). *Experience and education*. New York: Macmillan.

DuBois, W. E. B. (2002). *DuBois on education* (E. F. Provenzo, Ed.). Walnut Creek, CA: Altamira Press.

Fraser, J. W. (2005). Notes toward a new progressive politics of teacher education. *Journal of Teacher Education, 56*(3), 279–284.

Ladson-Billings, G. J. (2005). Is the team all right? Diversity and teacher education. *Journal of Teacher Education, 56*(3), 229–234.

Milner, H. (2003). Teacher reflection and race in cultural contexts: History, meanings, and methods of teaching. *Theory into Practice, 42*(3), 173–180.

Nager, N., & Shapiro, E. K. (2007). *A progressive approach to the education of teachers: Some principles from Bank Street College of Education.* (Occasional Paper Series No. 18). New York: Bank Street College of Education.

Stern, S. (2006, April 14). "Social justice" and other high school indoctrinations. *Front Page Magazine.* Retrieved April 24, 2007, from http://www.psaf.org/archive/2006/April2006/SolSternSocialJusticeandotherIndoct041306.htm

Wasley, P. (2006). Accreditor of education schools drops controversial "social justice" standard for teacher candidates. *Chronicle of Higher Education.*

Westheimer, J., & Kahne, J. (2007). Introduction: Service learning and social justice education. *Equity & Excellence in Education, 42*(2), 97–100.

Williams, N. L., Connell, M., White, C., & Kemper, J. (2003). Real boats rock: A transdisciplinary approach for teacher preparation. *Action in Teacher Education, 24*(4), 95–102.

Zinn, H. (1997). *The Zinn reader: Writings on disobedience and democracy.* New York: Seven Stories Press.

39 Social Justice Teacher Education

Morva McDonald and Kenneth M. Zeichner

Increasingly, teacher education programs of all stripes claim to prepare teachers from a social justice perspective. For example, a self-proclaimed liberal teacher education program aims to prepare teachers from a social justice perspective—one in which they become "aware of the ways schools may reproduce hierarchies based on race, class, gender, and sexuality. Awareness should lead to action as teachers embrace their roles as student advocates and active community members."[1] Likewise, a Christian-centered program also aims to prepare teachers to promote justice[2] and develop a commitment to "providing a classroom where their students learn about and experience compassion and justice." This program acknowledges that such an effort requires "students' commitment, reflection, discernment and hard work, and above all, the transforming power of God's spirit." Although the social justice emphasis in these two programs may not necessarily conflict, the lack of clarity in the field at large about what constitutes social justice teacher education, and the lack of knowledge regarding the practices that support such an effort make it possible for institutions with differing perspectives, political agendas, and strategies to lay claim to the same vision of teacher preparation.

Ambiguous definitions are not new to teacher education. For example, beginning in the 1980s, many teacher education programs began to adopt the rhetoric of preparing teachers to be reflective practitioners. These efforts often remain symbolic and signal to administrators, accrediting agencies, students, and the public the innovative, state of the art practice of the program (Valli, 1992; Zeichner & Liston, 1996). In many cases however, programs adopt the notion of "reflective practice" to name existing practices and do not substantially challenge the status quo of program structures, curriculum, or pedagogy.[3]

Social justice teacher education may follow a similar path. On this path, programs will highlight a social justice mission, adopt the language of social justice in conceptual frameworks, program descriptions, and course syllabi, and perhaps tinker with course content, pedagogy, or field placements. A program may, for example, adopt a social justice mission to signal their explicit intention to prepare teachers to work with students from diverse backgrounds. In many ways, the term *social justice* will simply highlight existing practices such as a course on multicultural education or placements with students in diverse schools, and may do so without significantly considering how such offerings support a programmatic social justice mission. Previous trends in teacher education reform suggest that social justice efforts will largely remain symbolic and fall short of fundamentally changing the content, structure, and quality of teacher preparation (Grant & Secada, 1990).

If social justice teacher education is to become more than rhetoric and more than merely a celebration of diversity, we argue that it must strive to take a different path. On this path, teacher educators would be challenged to further conceptualize social justice teacher education, to negotiate difficult political differences both within and outside the teacher education community, and to develop and identify specific program practices that prepare teachers to teach from a social justice perspective. This path requires both a fundamental rethinking of program content and structure, and an expanded notion of who the relevant participants are in such redesign efforts. Social justice redesign efforts, if they are to embody a democratic process consistent with a social justice mission, must look to all those concerned with improving children's educational opportunities, including K–12 educators, college and university faculty and staff, community members, and parents to participate and make decisions about how teachers are prepared. While it is not necessarily true that socially just decisions will emerge from these inclusive and democratic deliberations (Zeichner, 1991), we believe that you cannot have a social justice oriented program without such inclusive social relations.

Implementing social justice teacher education that challenges oppressive social, political, and economic structures will be particularly difficult given the current political climate of the United States as well as the climate surrounding teacher education. Increasingly, schools of education and in particular teacher education programs are increasingly under attack and asked to substantiate their contribution to improving K–12 students' academic achievement as the warrant for their existence. This may not be an unreasonable standard, however, in the current atmosphere in which scores on standardized achievement tests are the sole measure of learning, producing such evidence will require a tremendous amount of resources and will likely lead teacher educators to focus on the narrower, more technical aspects of teacher preparation than those like social justice that demand prospective teachers to consider broader educational aims and purposes (Sleeter, 2007). Additionally, K–12 educators—critical partners of teacher education programs—are also under increased pressure as a result of high stakes accountability and in many cases are less likely to engage in the seemingly ambiguous work of social justice. Despite these conditions, we find teacher education programs across the country negotiating this difficult terrain and attempting to prepare teachers from a social justice perspective.

In this chapter, we aim to support the work of social justice teacher education. In the first section, we identify connections between multicultural teacher education and social justice teacher education, as well as distinctions that may refine the conception and implementation of social justice teacher education. In the second section, we consider two perspectives on social justice and explore how they might frame the efforts of teacher educators. We also argue that social justice teacher education programs might benefit from connecting their work with other social movements locally, nationally, and/or globally and provide some historical and international examples of such efforts. In the final section, we identify program policies and practices that would enable programs to implement a social justice orientation and offer brief descriptions of programs making such strides. These are not meant as proscriptions, but rather as examples of what is and could be in teacher education.

Multicultural and Social Justice Teacher Education

Social justice teacher education in part grows out of almost 30 years of effort within teacher education to include multicultural education. Since 1978, NCATE has required programs to include multicultural education as part of the preservice curriculum and over 80% of institutions reviewed by NCATE from 1988 to 1993 incorporated multicultural education into the curriculum (Gollnick, 1995).[4] The majority of efforts in multicultural teacher education have focused on preparing teachers to improve the educational opportunities and experiences of students of color, low-income students, and more recently, English language learners (Lucas & Grinberg, 2008). Social justice teacher education shares this goal, but differs from the implementation of multicultural education on two fronts—one conceptual and one structural (Feiman-Nemser, 1990; Tom, 1997).[5] Below, we highlight these conceptual and structural differences.

Conceptual Distinctions

Conceptually, social justice teacher education shifts the focus from issues of cultural diversity to issues of social justice, making social change and activism central to the vision of teaching and learning promoted. Social justice programs explicitly attend to societal structures that perpetuate injustice, and they attempt to prepare teachers to take both individual and collective action toward mitigating oppression. Although multicultural education is not a monolithic movement, the predominant practice of multicultural education tends to celebrate cultural diversity and the experience of the individual while paying less attention to societal structures and institutionalized oppression (Kailin, 2002). Many scholars, including individuals committed to antiracist education, have voiced strong critiques of this predominant notion of multicultural education (e.g., Mattai, 1992; McCarthy, 1988; Olneck, 1990). For example, Mattai and Olneck both suggest that multicultural education gives priority to the individual and the concept of culture over the institutionalized relationships among groups. As a result, some forms of multicultural education do not pay adequate attention to issues such as institutional racism or classism. Additionally, multicultural education as typically implemented focuses on content, values, and beliefs and remains disconnected from social activism aimed at changing the institutional structures that lead to inequity (Kailin, 2002; Sleeter, 1996).

Some strands of multicultural education do emphasize notions of justice and social activism and we suggest that social justice teacher education build on and expand these notions, particularly as they are enacted in practice. Banks (2002) identifies four approaches to multicultural education: contributions, additive, transformative, and social action. The transformative and social action approaches move beyond a celebratory notion of diversity to one that focuses on change and action. The transformative approach insists that the internal structure of the content and course material must be changed to include the experiences, perspectives, and knowledge of diverse groups, and the social action approach extends the transformative approach by requiring students to partake in social action—to actually engage in efforts of social change. Similarly, Sleeter and Grant (1993) identify five perspectives of multicultural education including one—education that is multicultural and reconstructionist—that reflects a social justice emphasis and challenges institutionalized forms of oppression. Others identify reconstructionist traditions within teacher education more generally that incorporate notions of justice (e.g., Grant & Secada, 1990; Liston & Zeichner, 1991). The more justice-oriented traditions—from Banks' social action approach to reconstructionist teacher education—have existed on the periphery of most efforts within teacher education, including those focused on multicultural teacher education. Sleeter reminds us, however, of the importance of justice being central to multicultural education:

> …multicultural education came out of the civil rights movement. It wasn't just about, "let me get to know something about your food and I'll share some of my food." The primary issue was one of access to a quality education. If we're not dealing with questions of why access is continually important, and if we're not dealing with issues like why we have so much poverty amid so much wealth, we're not dealing with the core

issues of multiculturalism. I know it may sound trite, but the central issue remains one of justice. (Sleeter, 2000–2001)

Social justice teacher education, as an extension of the social action approaches within multicultural education, aims to heed Sleeter's call, taking a perspective on justice in which both celebrating diversity and attending to structural inequities are central themes in the preparation of teachers. In addition to refocusing the conceptual foundation of programs, this effort will require redesigning the structural components in order to come to terms with the roadblocks encountered in the implementation of multicultural teacher education.

Structural Challenges

The history of multicultural teacher education highlights a number of challenges that social justice teacher education will likely face and need to overcome. The implementation of multicultural education within teacher education has been constrained by the fragmented structure of programs (Cochran-Smith, Davis, & Fries, 2004; Goodlad, 1990; Grant, 1994; Grant & Secada, 1990; Howey & Zimpher, 1987), which is, in part, the consequence of the culture and reward structure of higher education. As a result, the majority of programs respond to demands to address the increasing diversity of students by adding on a single course in multicultural foundations or requiring a placement in schools serving learners from diverse backgrounds[6] (Banks, 1995; Gay, 1994; Goodwin, 1997b; Grant, 1994; Ladson-Billings, 1995). Research suggests that add-on efforts have had a limited impact on prospective teachers' beliefs and attitudes about and practices with students of color, low-income students, and English language learners (Cochran-Smith, Davis, & Fries, 2003; Ladson-Billings, 1995; Tom, 1997; Villegas & Lucas, 2002). Rarely, however, have programs integrated multicultural content across the curriculum.

As currently implemented, issues such as race, class, and language diversity are primarily addressed in foundations courses, perhaps providing prospective teachers with important conceptual knowledge of teaching students from diverse backgrounds, but with few strategies for enacting that knowledge in their classroom practice (McDonald, 2005). As a result, this add-on approach maintains a dangerous dichotomy—a separation between preparing teachers with subject matter and pedagogical content knowledge and preparing them with knowledge of students from diverse backgrounds and commitments to social justice (Grossman, McDonald, Hammerness, & Ronfeldt, 2008). Lessons from practice teach that such dichotomies are false and in fact, that providing students traditionally disadvantaged by the system with high quality opportunities to learn requires teachers who can integrate subject matter expertise with knowledge of and commitments to social justice (e.g., Gutstein, 2003; Lee, 2001; Moses & Cobb, 2001).

The implementation pitfalls of multicultural teacher education provide a number of lessons for social justice teacher education programs. Such programs must take up the challenge of clarifying the vision(s) of justice orienting their work, which will require grappling with differing political views of social justice and teacher education both amongst program faculty and with other members of the community. Teacher educators must also fundamentally change the structure of programs that tend to marginalize concerns for justice and diversity and separate such foundational concerns from the actual practice of teaching. Such efforts will require a rethinking of existing program policies and practices, and potentially will require changing them in order to unseat the strongholds in teacher education that resist efforts at integration.

Connecting with Other Efforts

As suggested in the introduction, social justice efforts within teacher education programs have remained largely unarticulated, despite the rise in the number of programs that claim a social justice orientation. In this section, we examine ways in which social justice teacher education might consider conceptions of social justice based in other fields as well as how it might connect to other types of social movements in an effort to better clarify the work of social justice in teacher education.

Conceptual Possibilities

What individual programs mean when they suggest they prepare teachers from a social justice perspective is, in most cases, left implicit and as a result open to a broad array of interpretations. In this section, we suggest social justice teacher education would benefit from (1) considering how individuals in other disciplines such as philosophy, political science, or sociology have conceptualized notions of justice and (2) connecting with other social movements aimed at achieving justice.

Social justice efforts, as articulated in teacher education, generally draw from the conceptual work of multicultural education, and link to the larger goal of preparing teachers to work with students from diverse backgrounds.[7] In some cases, the move toward implementing social justice relies on teacher educators' conceptions of what constitutes social justice and rarely draws explicitly from broader theories of justice (McDonald, 2007). This lack of connection to other work regarding conceptions of justice perhaps constrains teacher educators and programs as they strive to develop missions and visions that include ideas of justice.

Differing conceptions of justice establish different kinds of aims, goals, and strategies. Dominant distributional theories of justice suggest that a primary means of achieving justice is to fairly distribute goods such as economic wealth, social position, and access to opportunity (Sturman, 1997). A central tenet of this concept is to slice the pie into equal parts, with the aim of giving everyone the same size piece, particularly if doing so leads to the greatest benefit of the most disadvantaged (Rawls, 1971). Critics argue, however, that distributional theories overemphasize individuals as independent of institutional arrangements and social structures, thereby overlooking the vast ways in which both individuals and social groups encounter oppression (Young, 1990).

A teacher education program that conceptualizes justice as distributed might for example focus prospective teachers' attention on ensuring that students have equal opportunities to participate or equal access to class materials and resources. For example, prospective teachers might learn to label Popsicle sticks with each student's name and then draw a stick to call on students to ensure fairness. From this perspective, equality is achieved by evenly distributing resources. Likewise, this conception would downplay the potential impact of a student's status in an oppressed group; for example, the impact of the student's race on his or her classroom experiences and levels of achievement. In some ways, this conception of justice maps fairly easily onto dominant conceptions of teaching in which the primary goal is to address the needs of the individual learner. Returning to our earlier discussion of multicultural education, this conception of justice reflects the philosophical perspective of predominant approaches to multicultural education (Banks, 2002; Sleeter, 1996).

Teacher educators could look to other perspectives on justice to challenge a distributional view and shift the focus away from the individual and toward a greater understanding and awareness of how institutional arrangements and social structures shape the opportunities available to individuals. This shift would address many of the critiques of multicultural education discussed earlier. For example, teacher educators might consider the perspective of Young (1990) who suggests that a concept of distribution cannot be accurately applied to nonmaterial goods. Simply put, one cannot divide respect, honor, or power. From this perspective, an individual's affiliation with particular social groups often significantly shapes his or her access to and experiences of nonmaterial and material goods. Such affiliations constrain and enable people's ability to participate in determining their actions and their ability to develop and exercise their capacities. Thus, addressing injustice requires developing respect for group differences without reaffirming or reestablishing aspects of oppression.

A teacher education program conceptualizing justice in this way, then, would provide prospective teachers with opportunities to think about how social structures such as race and racism, class and classism, shape the experiences of individual students. It would also suggest that justice within the context of a classroom may require teachers to attend to students' needs differentially—that, in fact, being just is not simply a matter of divvying up the pie evenly, but rather taking into consideration which individuals at the table might need more pie, or a different pie entirely, in order to be successful.

As suggested, the underlying conceptions of justice either explicitly or implicitly at play in a teacher education program work to frame the decisions and actions of the participating individuals. Drawing from more general theories and perspectives of justice might help teacher educators to clarify program aims and goals. From this standpoint, teacher educators would be challenged to discuss the following questions: Is justice about providing equal opportunity, but not necessarily equal outcomes? Is it about recognizing how individuals' connections to oppressed groups shape their experiences? Is it about reducing the impact of oppression? Does it require connecting to other efforts, within and outside of education, aimed at minimizing the affects of oppression? To answer these questions, teacher educators might benefit from grappling with theories of justice and their underlying assumptions. These efforts would also help the field of teacher education clarify the ambiguity present in current discussions of what constitutes social justice teacher education.

Connecting to Social Movements

Teacher education programs have a unique opportunity to improve the educational opportunities of students; however, they cannot go it alone. Social justice teacher education efforts must join with other levels of the educational system as well as organizations in the public and private sector to improve the educational opportunities and current realities of students of color, low-income students, and English language learners, and their families. Recent social justice efforts within education generally and teacher education more specifically have been isolated from other movements aimed at achieving justice, such as those focused on economic equality, political justice, neighborhood renewal, or health care reform. To some extent, envisioning social justice teacher education as part of other efforts aimed at improving the conditions of students' lives requires a reframing of the problem. The disparity in educational opportunities and outcomes between students of color, low-income students, or English language learners is not simply a result of an unjust educational system, but of a whole network of injustices that disadvantage such students and restrict their opportunities both in and out of school (Anyon, 2005; Children's Defense Fund, 2005). From this perspective, low achieving schools and low achieving students and their families are embedded in a broader social structure—one that requires change on economic and political fronts in order to improve the realities for many students and their families.

Examples of Programs Connected to Broader Social Justice Movements

One might argue that teacher education has enough already on its plate and that programs cannot join, in any practical sense, the efforts of other justice movements. However, historical and international examples offer some possibilities. Below we briefly describe three such possibilities: New College (1932–1939), The Putney School (1950–1964), and the Landless Workers Movement teacher education program in Brazil.

New College (1932–1939)

New College, an experimental teacher education program at Teachers College Columbia, aimed to move beyond the experiences provided by most colleges and normal schools.[8] According to Kirkpatrick, "ordinary college and normal schools can hardly have any other result than turning out teachers ignorant in our social situation and with no intelligent concern about it" (as quoted in Liston & Zeichner, 1991, p.29). A primary goal of New College was to counteract this complacency and prepare teachers to be leaders of societal reconstruction. New College faculty believed that a fundamental aspect of professional preparation was the broadening of prospective teachers' understanding of their role so that they would begin to view their job in light of broader societal needs and problems. New College set out to prepare teachers with this perspective through a number of activities. For example, teachers were expected to live and work for a summer at a student-operated farm in North Carolina, to work in industry for a term, and to study and travel abroad for at least a summer. Teachers also had multiple opportunities to debate political issues with students and faculty in organized assemblies. In the end, program faculty strived to ensure that no student was allowed to graduate if he or she remained politically illiterate or indifferent.

The Putney School (1950–1964)

The Putney Graduate School of Education (1950–1964), a small school affiliated with the Putney School of Putney, Vermont, aimed to support its students to develop commitments to social justice, racial equality, and environmental sustainability (Rodgers, 2006). Rodgers writes that "through a program that included living together in a mixed-race residence, studying and meeting leading voices in the Civil Rights movement, travelling together in a van over a period of several weeks to various sites of civil action in the deep South, and reflecting regularly on all these experiences, the program aimed to graduate 'transformed' individuals, ready to act in the world to change it" (p. 1267). Students were challenged to connect educational issues with civil rights issues and to connect their individual actions and efforts to broader social action.[9] Notably, the Putney School helped reframe students' views of education as solely work within classrooms to an understanding of how classroom life could relate to other concerns such as civil rights and racial justice.

Teacher Education in the Landless Workers Movement in Brazil

The Landless Workers Movement (MST)—one of the most important social movements in contemporary Latin America—struggles for social and economic justice in addition to agrarian reform. Diniz-Pereira (2005) points out that the MST views the struggle for land and economic justice as requiring an emphasis on education.[10] Three main principles ground the work of MST teacher education: technical and professional education, political preparation, and cultural preparation. Similar to the Putney School, political preparation emphasizes the development of an historical and class consciousness to support teachers in understanding how their practices connect to larger societal change efforts. Moreover, cultural preparation emphasizes developing teachers' ability to organize and build a culture of cooperation and solidarity (Dinize-Pereira, 2005). During the program, teachers increase their involvement in the community in an effort to learn more about the life conditions of the encampment and to develop a deeper commitment to the goals of the movement and the community (Diniz-Pereira, 2005).

All three examples suggest ways in which teacher education programs might work in conjunction with broader social movements. Notably, in each example, programs explicitly challenged teachers to expand their understanding of the current realities of students' lives and their role as teachers, and to become politically active by participating directly with efforts beyond classroom and school walls. These cases illustrate possibilities for how programs today might reorganize the structures, pedagogy, and curriculum to better provide prospective teachers with opportunities to develop the knowledge, practices, and dispositions necessary to work for social justice. Some might argue that these cases are exceptional, their efforts enabled by their time period or context, and that they illustrate practices difficult to replicate in the current context of U.S. teacher education. However, a number of programs across the U.S. currently employ a wide array of practices that one might characterize as supporting social justice, even though a limitation of such efforts is that they rarely connect to broader social movements. In the following section, we highlight specific practices to offer examples of the range of ways in which teacher education programs strive to address social justice.

Practices in Social Justice Teacher Education

Two types of strategies have been commonly reported in the literature on teacher education programs that claim to be driven by social justice goals: First are the efforts by teacher educators to recruit more students and faculty of color. The second set of strategies is concerned with the social relations, instructional, strategies, and structures within programs.

Admissions and Recruitment

First, the goal of recruiting more students and faculty of color into teacher education programs has been defended on the grounds that a more diverse teaching force is needed in order to provide an increasingly diverse public school population with a high quality education. This view stems from a desire to provide all students with teachers of color as role models and provide more equitable outcomes to students in terms of learning and graduation rates. It has also been asserted that diverse cohorts of teacher education students and faculty will create the learning conditions needed to educate teachers to be successful in today's public schools (Sleeter, 2007). Two general approaches have been utilized to recruit more diverse teacher education student cohorts. One type of intervention has involved changing admission requirements for traditional undergraduate and postgraduate college and university-based programs away from a system that relies exclusively on academic criteria to one that maintains high academic standards but is also more holistic, taking into account a variety of personal factors and life experiences.

A second approach to recruiting more teachers of color has been to create various types of alternative teacher education programs that focus on teaching in high needs urban and rural areas. These programs are structured in ways to make it attractive to prospective teachers of color and offer supports that make it more likely that students will complete the programs once admitted. One prominent example of such efforts was the Dewitt Wallace–Reader's Digest Fund programs that were initiated at over 40 sites in the United States in the late 1990s (Clewell & Villegas, 2001).

Another strategy for recruiting more students of color into teacher education programs is for four-year colleges and universities to initiate articulation agreements with two-year community colleges and technical colleges, which traditionally have enrolled more than one half of all racial/ethnic minority students who are in higher education (Villegas & Lucas, 2004). These agreements are designed to ease the transition of students from the two-year colleges into teacher education programs in colleges and universities and to support students to successfully complete these programs. Despite the above mentioned efforts, the U.S. teaching force remains predominately White and monolingual English speaking (Wirt et al. 2005; Zumwalt & Craig, 2005).

Along with the goal of creating more ethnic–racial diversity in teacher education student cohorts, a number of the changes in admissions policies in teacher education programs with a social justice focus have been aimed at recruiting students who are disposed toward becoming successful teachers who work for social justice. Recognizing the limited power of preservice teacher education to influence prospective teachers' worldviews and commitments toward equity and social justice (Haberman & Post, 1992), teacher educators sometimes choose to work with prospective teachers with whom they think they might be able to make a difference. This pragmatic stance of choosing to work with prospective teachers who arrive wanting to learn how to teach for social justice, and showing some potential to teach in this way, is supported by the evidence on teacher learning (Hammerness, Darling-Hammond, & Bransford, 2005).

In addition, a number of institutions across the United States have instituted policies that especially try to recruit faculty of color to campuses, and education units have utilized these policies to attempt to bring more faculty of color into their teacher education programs. These efforts have sometimes been part of more general efforts on some campuses to improve the climate and concrete support regarding diversity in all aspects of campus life (Melnick & Zeichner, 1997).

In-Program Initiatives

In addition to recruitment and admissions strategies, there are a number of actions that teacher educators have taken within their programs to further their social justice goals. One strategy, developed in the face of recent state mandates of performance-based assessment in teacher education programs, has been to modify and sharpen standards and assessments to explicitly reflect a commitment to social justice goals. Even in some programs that identify themselves as working toward social justice goals, the standards and assessments are often very generic and a social justice focus is not evident.

Evergreen State College is one example of a program with standards and assessments that explicitly reflect a commitment to social justice goals (Vavrus, 2002). For example, one of the standards for student teachers at Evergreen is concerned with assessing knowledge of multicultural, antibias curriculum planning. Different levels of development on this standard are identified, ranging from curriculum plans which do not incorporate multicultural perspectives and advance antibias goals to those which transform the conventional curriculum with multicultural and antibias goals (see Vavrus, 2002, p. 47). This explicit incorporation of social justice elements into the assessments that are used in the program reinforces the message that these are areas of importance for prospective teachers.

Probably the most common approach that can be found in the social justice teacher education literature is the required courses and parts of courses that focus on social justice issues. These courses go beyond the celebration of diversity to address such issues as racism and White and English language privilege (e.g., McIntyre, 2002) and, in some cases, focus on the development of various elements of "equity pedagogy" (Banks, 2003). A variety of instructional strategies and course assignments have been employed inside these courses such as story telling, autobiography, dialogue journals, literature, films, portfolios, and case studies (e.g., Florio Ruane, 2001; Garmon, 1998; Gomez, 1996; Noordhoff & Kleinfeld, 1993; Obidah, 2000; Pleasants, Johnson, & Trent, 1998). It is important to note that all of these instructional strategies can be used to work toward other visions of teaching and learning, and they are not in and of themselves evidence that a program is attempting to prepare teachers to teach for social justice.

One goal that is often present in the use of these various instructional strategies in teacher education courses is to expand the sociocultural consciousness of prospective teachers, to help them understand that "one's worldview is not universal but is profoundly influenced by a variety of factors, chief among them race/ethnicity, social class and gender" (Villegas & Lucas, 2002, p. 27). It has often been argued that achieving this greater understanding of one's self as a cultural being is a key aspect of preparing teachers to teach for social justice. In addition to this and other aspects of personal growth[11] that are sought in course-based efforts, teacher educators also focus on preparing teachers to be able to develop culturally relevant curriculum and use teaching and assessment practices that are sensitive to cultural variations and enable all students to demonstrate what they know and can do (Goodwin, 1997a; Irvine & Armento, 2001; Villegas & Lucas, 2002).

Another important element in social justice teacher education practices is the field experiences that are provided for prospective teachers in schools and communities. Although research is largely inconclusive about the characteristics of these school-based experiences that further the goal of preparing teachers to teach for social justice, it is clear from studies to date that it is the particular quality of these experiences that matters rather than merely placing student teachers in schools with diverse learners (Hollins & Guzman, 2005; Lane, Lacefield-Parachini, & Isken, 2003). These experiences can sometimes serve to strengthen and reinforce negative stereotypes held by student teachers rather than challenging them (Haberman & Post, 1992).

In addition, some programs have begun to incorporate community-based field experiences that focus on helping student teachers learn about the funds of knowledge and structures and social networks that exist in the communities where their pupils live. Although some of this work has focused on community experience as service learning (Boyle-Baise, 2002) and on the service element as a way to develop the cultural teaching competence of prospective teachers, there are a number of examples that position prospective teachers more as learners in communities, focusing on how these experiences support the preparation of teachers who teach for social justice (Boyle-Baise & McIntyre, 2008). Sometimes these experiences are linked to particular courses, engage prospective teachers in a form of participatory action research in communities or employ adults in communities to educate prospective teachers about particular aspects of community life (e.g., Buck & Sylvester, 2005; Burant & Kirby, 2002; Mahan, 1982; McIntyre, 2003; Seidel & Friend, 2002). Sometimes community experience for prospective teachers includes a cultural immersion experience of a semester or longer (Zeichner & Melnick, 1996). In one case, the focus of contact with community members in teacher education was on educating university teacher educators about particular communities so that they could incorporate this knowledge into the teaching of their campus courses (Koerner & Abdul-Tawwab, 2006). The assumption in many of these community-based teacher education efforts is that prospective teachers will see communities and neighborhoods as potential resources in their teaching and that teachers will see themselves as part of the communities in which they work (Ladson-Billings, 1994).

This last example raises the general issue of whose voices and knowledge need to be present in a teacher education program that claims to prepare teachers to teach for social justice. We have been quite critical of the tendency of so called social justice oriented teacher education programs that either exclude or marginalize the voices of K–12 teachers and community members in the teacher education process and have argued that these elitist social relations are a direct contradiction of the values that underlie any conception of social justice (e.g., Zeichner, 2006). It seems to us that by definition a social justice oriented teacher education program needs to include the genuine participation of K–12 teachers and community members in addition to college and university faculty and staff.

A key issue in understanding the efforts of teacher educators to incorporate teaching for social justice into a preservice teacher education program is the extent to which this goal has been infused throughout a program. This issue includes who on the teacher education faculty is engaged in this work (Moule, 2005). Recent research has indicated that the impact of teacher education programs on prospective teachers is much more powerful when there is a unified vision of teaching and learning that permeates a program than when attention to a goal exists in only some program components (Darling-Hammond, 2006). Infusion of social justice into the teacher education curriculum includes attention to the general education and content preparation of teachers in addition to professional education courses. For example, various campuses across the country have implemented ethnic studies and international/global requirements that are intended to contribute to enhancing the cultural competence of students.

In her study of two elementary teacher education programs in California that emphasize teaching for social justice, McDonald (2005) developed a framework for understanding the nature and quality of the infusion of social justice issues into a teacher education program. She found that opportunities to learn about teaching for social justice in these programs varied in terms of their emphasis on conceptual and practical tools.[12] In addition, she identified four types of teachers' learning opportunities related to social justice. These included opportunities to focus on individuals as independent of their affiliations with broader social groups; individuals as identified by membership in an educational category (e.g., special education student); individuals as identified by their membership in an oppressed group (e.g., their status as influenced by race, ethnicity, gender, class, or sexual orientation); and justice as attending to issues of oppression embedded in institutional structures. McDonald employed this framework to illuminate the specific nature of the attention to preparing teachers for social justice in each program and offers some potential for helping teacher educators think about the meaning of social justice in their own and others' programs.

Another important issue that has emerged in the literature on preparing teachers to work for social justice is that it tends to emphasize the preparation of White monolingual English teachers to teach students of color, while the preparation needs of prospective teachers of color are not adequately addressed (Montecinos, 2004; Sleeter, 2000–2001). This lack of attention to the backgrounds and cultures of prospective teachers of color and their needs for a culturally responsive education for teaching is often a direct contradiction of what teacher educators are encouraging their students to do in elementary and secondary schools and serves to weaken the impact of teacher education (Zeichner, 2003).

A final issue that has emerged in the literature on social justice teacher education is the lack of attention in many areas of the United States outside of English as a second language (ESL) and bilingual teacher education programs to preparing teachers to teach English language learners. This lack of attention is evidenced by the lack of research on the preparation of teachers to teach English language learners (Hollins & Guzman, 2005; Lucas & Grinberg, 2008) and by follow up surveys of teacher education program graduates even in so-called exemplary programs (Darling-Hammond, 2006).

In sum, a variety of practices have emerged in programs that claim to focus on preparing teachers to teach for social justice that include both recruitment and admissions efforts and efforts within programs to develop knowledge, skills, and dispositions that will enable teachers to teach for social justice. A number of issues have arisen in these efforts to implement social justice teacher education programs including the nature and degree to which social justice is infused throughout a program, who carries out the teacher education effort (just university academics or also teachers and community members), whether the preparation takes into account the background and experiences of all teacher candidates or focuses solely on preparing White teachers to teach students of color, and finally whether language diversity is addressed, in addition to other forms of diversity. In addition to such issues, the array of practices employed by programs suggests that attending to issues of social justice requires a programmatic investment—one that examines and likely reforms policies related to recruitment, admissions, and standards for prospective teachers as well as practices associated with the curriculum and pedagogy of courses and field placement experiences. Without such investment, efforts to address social justice will likely become peripheral to the core work of teacher preparation.

Conclusion

In this chapter, we have argued that social justice teacher education must learn from the history of other reform and redesign efforts in teacher education. First, social justice teacher education programs and the field of teacher education at large must explicitly grapple with the following questions: What is social justice teacher education? What are the program structures, policies, and practices that constitute social justice teacher education? As other teacher education reform efforts suggest, without the consideration of such questions, programs will likely simply adopt the label of social justice without challenging or changing existing practices. In addition, the ambiguity in terms of the concept and practice of social justice teacher education will allow a wide range of programs, some with very different agendas to lay claim to such a vision of teacher preparation.

We are not arguing that the field of teacher education should develop a prescriptive or narrow notion of social justice teacher education given that the context of individual programs and the communities in which they are situated will inform the nature of the work. However, we do urge teacher educators engaged in such work to challenge themselves and the field to develop a range of conceptions and practices that would provide some guidance in terms of the vision of teaching and learning and the practices of such a reform effort. The practices described above are a start in this direction, but further documentation and research of such efforts is critical to the ongoing development and conceptualization of social justice teacher education.

Finally, we argue that social justice teacher education programs may benefit from looking beyond conceptions of multicultural teacher education as typically implemented toward conceptions of justice as described by those in other fields. As we suggested, the conception(s) of justice a teacher education program adopts frames the work of teacher preparation and influences how prospective teachers develop ideas and practices associated with equity and justice. Social justice teacher education must also learn from the implementation pitfalls of multicultural teacher education and strive to overcome the barriers of program fragmentation and marginalization. This, as indicated above, requires a programmatic investment in social justice teacher education and cannot rest solely on the shoulders of individual teacher educators or on the backs of specific courses in multicultural education. The goal of preparing teachers to engage in efforts of justice, in addressing the inequities of the educational system, and in improving the living conditions and life opportunities for many students of color, low income students, and English language learners requires programs to fully and intentionally engage in redesigning programs at all levels, from policies to practices.

Notes

1. These descriptions of programs' conceptual frameworks come from documents submitted to the National Council for Accreditation of Teacher Education (NCATE; 2001). We would like to thank Art Wise of NCATE for allowing us to review a wide range of conceptual frameworks submitted by teacher education programs.
2. In this chapter we use the term *social justice* interchangeably with *justice*. We recognize that in the field of teacher education *social justice* is the more common term while scholars in the fields of political science and philosophy, for example, more commonly use the term *justice*.
3. Other innovative practices in teacher education such as professional development school partnerships have also lacked clarification regarding the conceptual and practical dimensions of what might constitute such a partnership. Ultimately, this lack of clarity has diminished the fundamental value of this concept and in many cases, left existing practices with K–12 schools unchanged.
4. Gollnick (1995) noted that NCATE accredited only 500 out of a total of 1,200 teacher education programs, but that these 500 programs prepared over 70% of the teachers entering teaching.
5. Feiman-Nemser (1990) and Tom (1997) suggest that teacher education programs engaged in redesign efforts must consider conceptual and structural reform. Conceptual reform requires the development of a vision of teaching and learning that gives direction to the practical activities of teacher education. Structural reform refers to a program's efforts to redesign the procedures and process for carrying out the preparation of prospective teachers, such as the course sequence and types and duration of field placements.
6. A major reason that teacher education programs remain fragmented is because of the institutional reward structures in colleges and universities that do not value the extra work it takes to develop greater program coherence.
7. While the focus in social reconstructionist oriented programs has been on preparing teachers to teach in schools attended by underserved students, the social justice work of teachers is important in schools serving students of all backgrounds.
8. All of the information regarding New College comes from Liston and Zeichner (1991).
9. For a full description of the Putney School see Rodgers (2006).
10. For a full description of the Landless Workers Movement's teacher education efforts see Diniz-Pereira (2005).
11. Other examples of personal growth goals that are sometimes sought include developing high expectations of teachers for the learning of all students, prejudice reduction, and dealing with the lack of awareness of White and English language privilege (Hollins & Guzman, 2005).
12. Conceptual tools (e.g., scaffolding) embody particular pedagogical strategies and practical tools (e.g., teaching methods for scaffolding instruction for English language learners) are the representation of more general concepts.

References

Anyon, J. (2005). *Radical possibilities: Public policy, urban education, and a new social movement*. New York: Taylor & Francis.

Banks, J. (1995). Multicultural education: Historical development, dimensions, and practice. In J. Banks & C. Banks (Eds.), *Handbook of research on multicultural education* (pp. 3–24). New York: Simon & Schuster Macmillan.

Banks, J. (2002). *An introduction to multicultural education* (3rd ed.). Boston, MA: Allyn & Bacon.

Banks, J. (2003). Multicultural education: Characteristics and goals. In J. Banks & C. Banks (Eds.), *Multicultural education: Issues and perspectives* (pp. 3–30). New York: Wiley.

Boyle-Baise, L. (2002). *Multicultural service learning: Educating teachers in diverse communities*. New York: Teachers College Press.

Boyle-Baise, L., & McIntyre, D. J. (2008). What kind of experience? Preparing teachers in PDS or community settings? In M. Cochran-Smith, S. Feiman-Nemser, & D. J. McIntyre (Eds), *Handbook of research on teacher education* (3rd ed., pp. 307–330). Mahwah, NJ: Erlbaum.

Buck, P., & Sylvester, P. S. (2005). Preservice teachers enter urban communities: Coupling funds of knowledge research with critical pedagogy in teachers' education. In N. Gonzalez, L. Moll, & C. Amanti (Eds.), *Funds of knowledge: Theorizing practices in households, communities, and classrooms* (pp. 213–232). Mahwah, NJ: Erlbaum.

Burant, T., & Kirby, D. (2002). Beyond classroom early field experiences: Understanding an educative practicum in an urban community. *Teaching and Teacher Education, 18*, 561–575.

Children's Defense Fund. (2005). *The state of America's children*. Washington, D.C.: Author.

Clewell, C. B., & Villegas, A. M. (2001). *Ahead of the class: A handbook for preparing new teachers from new sources: Design lessons from the Dewitt Wallace-Reader's Digest Fund's Pathways to Teaching initiatives*. Washington, D.C.: The Urban Institute.

Cochran-Smith, M., Davis, D., & Fries, M. K. (2004). Multicultural teacher education: Research, practice, and policy. In J. Banks & C. M. Banks (Eds.), *The handbook of research on multicultural education* (2nd ed., pp. 931–975). San Francisco: Jossey-Bass.

Darling-Hammond, L. (2006). *Powerful teacher education programs: Lessons from exemplary programs*. San Francisco: Jossey-Bass.

Diniz-Pereira, J. (2005). Teacher education for social transformation and its links to progressive social movements: The case of the Landless Workers Movement in Brazil. *Journal of Critical Education Policy Studies, 3*(2). Available online at http://www.jceps.com

Feiman-Nemser, S. (1990). Teacher preparation: Structural and conceptual analysis. In R. Houston, M. Haberman, & J. Sikulka (Eds.), *Handbook of research on teacher education* (pp. 212–233). New York: Macmillan.

Florio-Ruane, S. (2001). *Teacher education and the cultural imagination*. Mahwah, NJ: Erlbaum.

Garmon, M. A. (1998). Using dialogue journals to promote student learning in a multicultural teacher education course. *Remedial and Special Education, 19*(1), 32–45.

Gay, G. (1994). *NCREL monograph: A synthesis of scholarship in multicultural education*. Naperville, IL: North Central Regional Education Laboratory.

Gollnick, D. (1995). National and state initiatives for multicultural education. In J. Banks & C. Banks (Eds.), *Handbook of research on multicultural education* (pp. 44–64). New York: Simon & Schuster.

Gomez, M.L. (1996) Telling stories of our teaching: Reflecting on our practices. *Action in Teacher Education, 28*(3), 1–12.

Goodlad, J. (1990). *Teachers for our nation's schools*. San Francisco, CA: Jossey- Bass.

Goodwin. A. L. (1997a). (Ed.). *Assessment for equity and inclusion*. New York: Routledge.

Goodwin, A. L. (1997b). Historical and contemporary perspectives on multicultural teacher education: Past lessons, new directions. In J. King, E. Hollins, & W. Hayman (Eds.), *Preparing teachers for cultural diversity*. New York: Teachers College Press.

Grant, C. (1994). Best practices in teacher education for urban schools: Lessons from the multicultural teacher education literature. *Action in Teacher Education, 16*(3), 2–18.

Grant, C., & Secada, W. (1990). Preparing teachers for diversity. In R. Houston, M. Haberman, & J. Sikula (Eds.), *Handbook of research on teacher education* (pp. 403–422). New York: Macmillan.

Grossman, P., McDonald, M., Hammerness, K., & Ronfeldt, M. (2008). Dismantling dichotomies in teacher education. In M. Cochran-Smith, S. Feiman-Nemser, J. McIntyre, & K. Demers (Eds.), *The handbook of teacher education: A project of the Association of Teacher Educators* (3rd ed., pp. 243–248). New York: Macmillan.

Gutstein, E. (2003). Teaching and learning mathematics for social justice in an urban, Latino school. *Journal for Research in Mathematics Education, 34*(1), 37–37.

Hamerness, K., Darling-Hammond, L., & Bransford, J. (2005). How teachers learn and develop. In L. Darling-Hammond & J. Bransford (Eds), *Preparing teachers for a changing world* (pp. 358–389). San Francisco: Jossey-Bass.

Hollins, E., & Guzman, M. T. (2005). Research on preparing teachers for diverse populations. In M. Cochran-Smith & K. Zeichner (Eds.), *Studying teacher education* (pp. 477–548). Mahwah, NJ: Erlbaum.

Kailin, J. (2002). *Antiracist education.* Lanham, MD: Rowman & Littlefield.

Koerner, M., & Abdul-Tawwab, N. (2006). Using community as a resource for teacher education: A case study. *Equity and Excellence in Education, 39*, 37–46.

Ladson-Billings, G. (1994). *The dreamkeepers: Successful teachers of African-American children.* San Francisco: Jossey-Bass.

Ladson-Billings, G. (1995). Multicultural teacher education: Research, practice, and policy. In J. Banks & C. Banks (Eds.), *Handbook of research on multicultural education* (pp. 747–759). New York: Simon & Schuster Macmillan.

Lane, S., Lacefield-Parachini, N., & Isken J. (2003). Developing novice teachers as change agents: Student teacher placements against the grain. *Teacher Education Quarterly, 30*(2), 55–68.

Lee, C. (2001). Is October Brown Chinese? A cultural modeling activity system for underachieving students. *American Educational Research Journal, 38*(1), 97–141.

Liston, D., & Zeichner, K. (1991). *Teacher education and the social conditions of schooling.* New York: Routledge.

Lucas, T., & Grinberg, J. (2008). Responding to the linguistic reality of mainstream classrooms. In M. Cochran-Smith, S. Feiman-Nemser, & J. McIntyre (Eds.), *Handbook of research on teacher education* (3rd ed., pp. 606–636). Mahwah, NJ: Erlbaum.

Mahan, J. (1982). Community involvement components in culturally oriented teacher preparation. *Education, 103*(2), 163–172.

Mattai, P. R. (1992). Rethinking *multicultural education: Has it lost its focus or is it being misused?* Journal of Negro Education, 67(1), 65–77.

McCarthy, C. (1994). Multicultural discourses and curriculum reform: A critical perspective. *Educational Theory, 44*(4), 81–98.

McDonald, M. (2005). The integration of social justice in teacher education: Dimensions of prospective teachers' opportunities to learn. *Journal of Teacher Education, 56*(5), 418–435.

McDonald, M. (2007). The joint enterprise of social justice teacher education. *Teachers College Record, 109*(8), 2047–2081.

McIntyre, A. (2003). Participatory action research and urban education: Reshaping the teacher preparation process. *Equity and Excellence in Education, 36*(1), 28–39.

Melnick, S., & Zeichner, K. (1997). Teacher education for cultural diversity: Enhancing the capacity of teacher education institutions to address diversity issues. In J. King, E. Hollins, & W. Hayman (Eds.), *Meeting the challenge of diversity in teacher preparation* (pp. 23–39). New York: Teachers College Press.

Montecinos, C. (2004). Paradoxes in multicultural teacher education research: Students of color positioned as objects while ignored as subjects. *International Journal of Qualitative Studies in Education, 17*(2), 167–181.

Moses, R., & Cobb, P. (2001). *Radical equations: Math literacy and civil rights.* Boston: Beacon Press

Moule, J. (2005). Implementing a social justice perspective: Invisible burden for faculty of color. *Teacher Education Quarterly, 32*(4), 23–42.

National Council for Accreditation of Teacher Education. (2001). *Standards for professional development schools*. Washington, D.C.: Author.

Noordoff, K., & Kleinfeld, J. (1993). Preparing teachers for multicultural classrooms. *Teaching and Teacher Education, 91*(1), 27–39.

Obidah, J. (2000). Mediating boundaries of race, class and professional authority as a critical multiculturalist. *Teachers College Record, 102*(6), 1035–1060.

Olneck, M. (1990). The recurring dream: Symbolism and ideology in intercultural and multicultural education. *American Journal of Education, 98*, 147–183.

Pleasants, H., Johnson, C., & Trent, S. (1998). Reflecting, reconceptualizing and revising: The evolution of a portfolio assignment in a multicultural teacher education class. *Remedial & Special Education, 19*(1), 46–58.

Rawls, J. (1971). *A theory of justice*. Cambridge, MA: Harvard University Press.

Rodgers, C. (2006). "The turning of one's soul"—Learning to teach for social justice: The Putney graduate school of teacher education (1950–1964). *Teachers College Record, 108*(7), 1266–1295.

Seidel, B., & Friend, G. (2002). Leaving authority at the door: Equal status community-based experiences and the preparation of teachers for diverse classrooms. *Teaching and Teacher Education, 18*, 421–433.

Sleeter, C. E. (1996). *Multicultural education as social activism*. Albany, NY: SUNY Press.

Sleeter, C. E. (2000–2001). Diversity vs. white privilege. *Rethinking Schools, 15*.

Sleeter, C. E. (2007, April). *Equity, democracy, and neo-liberal assaults on teacher education*. Vice presidential address presented at the annual meeting of the American Educational Research Association, Chicago.

Sleeter, C. E., & Grant, C. (1993). *Making choices for multicultural education: Five approaches to race, class, and gender* (2nd ed.). New York: Merrill.

Sturman, A. (1997). *Social justice in education* (Vol. 40). Melbourne, Australia: The Australian Council for Educational Research.

Tom, A. (1997). *Redesigning teacher education*. Albany, NY: SUNY Press.

Valli, L. (1992). *Reflective teacher education: Cases and critiques*. Albany, NY: SUNY Press.

Vavrus, M. (2002). *Transforming the multicultural education of teachers: Theory, research, and practice*. New York: Teachers College Press.

Villegas, A. M., & Lucas, T. (2002). *Educating culturally responsive teachers*. Albany, NY: SUNY Press.

Villegas, A. M., & Lucas, T. (2004). Diversifying the teacher workforce: A retrospective and prospective analysis. In M. Smylie & D. Miretzky (Eds.), *Developing the teacher workforce* (pp. 70–104). Chicago: University of Chicago Press.

Wirt, J. G., Choy, S., Rooney, P., Hussar, W., Povasnik, S., & Hampden-Thompson, G. (2005). *The condition of education*. Washington, D.C.: National Center for Education Statistics.

Young, I. M. (1990). *Justice and the politics of difference*. Princeton, NJ: Princeton University Press.

Zeichner, K. (1991). Contradictions and tensions in the professionalization of teaching and the democratization of schools. *Teachers College Record, 92*(3), 363–379.

Zeichner, K. (2003). The adequacies and inadequacies of three current strategies to recruit, prepare and retain the best teachers for all students. *Teachers College Record, 105*(3), 490–515.

Zeichner, K. (2006). Reflections of a university teacher educator on the future of college and university-based teacher education. *Journal of Teacher Education, 57*(3), 326–340.

Zeichner, K., & Liston, D. P. (1996). *Reflective teaching: An introduction*. Mahwah, NJ: Erlbaum.

Zeichner, K., & Melnick, S. (1996). The role of community field experiences in preparing teachers for cultural diversity. In K. Zeichner, S. Melnick, & M. L. Gomez (Eds.), *Currents of reform in preservice teacher education* (pp. 176–196). New York: Teachers College Press.

Zumwalt, K., & Craig, E. (2005). Teachers' characteristics: Research on the demographic profile. In M. Cochran-Smith & K. Zeichner (Eds.), *Studying teacher education* (pp. 111–156). Mahwah, NJ: Erlbaum.

40 Teacher Education, Neoliberalism, and Social Justice

Christine E. Sleeter

Social justice in teacher education can be conceptualized as being comprised of three strands: (1) supporting access for all students to high-quality, intellectually rich teaching that builds on their cultural and linguistic backgrounds; (2) preparing teachers to foster democratic engagement among young people; and (3) preparing teachers to advocate for children and youth by situating inequities within a systemic sociopolitical analysis. These strands resonate with dilemmas that Delpit (1995) discussed regarding teaching other people's children. For communities that have been historically subordinated, gaining access to the dominant culture of power is of paramount importance. Reflected in the first strand above, teachers must be able to teach such children effectively so they can master that culture. At the same time, as the third strand suggests, the culture of power must also be critiqued, particularly for processes by which oppressive relationships are perpetuated. All of this must involve dialogue—the second strand—in which those who occupy positions of privilege, including teachers and teacher educators, learn to listen to, hear, and work with those who do not.

Although possibilities for building teacher education around social justice are rich, it is becoming increasingly difficult to enact them because the culture of power, embedded in global capitalism, is pressing away from social justice. Ironically, a history of weak relationships between teacher education and historically marginalized communities means that many communities do not see teacher educators as allies, even though teacher educators purport to serve them. After discussing global capital assaults on teacher education, I will suggest some lines of work that are urgently needed for teacher education to build alliances for social justice through collaborative relationships with historically underserved communities.

Assaults on Teacher Education and Social Justice

As a field, teacher education has never been a bastion of social justice, although many teacher educators have worked tirelessly and creatively to create strong social justice-oriented teacher education programs, and some states and accrediting agencies have had social justice requirements. But the field as a whole has always tended to be fairly traditional, mainly oriented toward preparing young White women for established missions and practices of schools. Teacher education faculty are overwhelmingly White, most having little experience teaching diverse populations (Zeichner, 2003).

Currently, teacher education and social justice are under active assault from "the parallel universe from which the business reform agenda springs" (Gelberg, 2007, p. 52). In the context of downsizing public services, the entire education enterprise has become much more firmly harnessed to serve corporate interests. "Corporatocracy," the form oligarchy now takes, characterizes today's political landscape. According to Perkins

(2004), corporatocracy is a linkage of three powerful institutions that are run by a small elite whose members move "easily and often" across them: major corporations, government, and major banks (p. 26). By gradually becoming more directly connected, these linked institutions have facilitated an increasingly powerful elite in building a global empire and accelerating elite wealth accumulation (Harvey, 2005).

Corporatocracy is the institutionalization of neoliberalism, a reworking of classical liberalism. As McChesney (2001) explained, neoliberalism assumes that markets, supporting free choice, entrepreneurial competition, and personal initiative, have the best potential to solve social problems and generate wealth, particularly when unfettered by government regulations. As McLaren and Farahmandpur (2005) put it more starkly, neoliberalism

> refers to a corporate domination of society that supports state enforcement of the unregulated market, engages in the oppression of nonmarket forces and antimarket policies, guts free public services, eliminates social subsidies, offers limitless concessions to transnational corporations,…and permits private interests to control most of social life in the pursuit of profits for the few. (pp. 15–16)

Neoliberals have joined with conservatives to restructure the global order and increase their power over it. As Hursh (2005) explains, "influential conservative and neoliberal foundations and think tanks aim to radically transform education through market competition, choice and privatization" (p. 617). These foundations are pressing teacher education in the following ways: (1) away from social justice teacher preparation and toward preparing teachers as technicians to raise student test scores; (2) away from being linked with teacher professional knowledge and teacher quality; and (3) toward becoming shorter or by-passed altogether.

Teacher Education as Preparation of Technicians

Teacher education should be directly linked to K–12 schooling. At their best, teacher education programs and schools collaborate to develop high quality teaching and strengthen democratic participation (Darling-Hammond, 2006). But pressures originating in global capitalism are pushing schools away from democratic participation and even away from rich conceptions of teaching. In the process, they are pushing teacher education away as well. In response to high-stakes testing, school districts across the United States, especially those serving low-income or culturally diverse students, have adopted increasingly prescribed curricula that are aligned with state standards and tests. Much prescribed curriculum emphasizes memorization much more than critical thinking. Increasingly, in schools that serve historically underserved communities, teaching means implementing prescribed curriculum packages "with fidelity" rather than responding to students, let alone developing teacher-made curricula (Achinstein, Ogawa, & Speiglman, 2004). In this context, teacher education programs are being compelled to reduce or eliminate not only explicit social justice teacher preparation, but also learner-centered teaching in general.

Standards for teacher preparation are under pressure to reduce or eliminate reference to social justice, multicultural education, or bilingual education. For example, in 2002 Iowa replaced the requirement of a multicultural education course with more reading methods coursework. California used to offer certification for general education teachers emphasizing Culture, Language and Academic Development (CLAD) and Bilingual Education (BCLAD). California's revised standards, however, "make clear repeatedly that the role of teacher education is to prepare teachers to teach the state-adopted content standards using state adopted materials" (Sleeter, 2003, p. 20). The phrase "state-adopted academic content standards" appears throughout the teacher preparation standards documents, but terms such as *culture*, *bilingual*, and *culturally relevant* do not. To investigate the impact of this change on teacher education programs, Montaño and colleagues (2005) surveyed faculty members in 16 California teacher education programs, finding that content addressing culture and language, formerly taught in designated courses, had now been "infused" or reduced. In 2006, National Council for the Accreditation of Teacher Education (NCATE), following a complaint by the National Association of Scholars and other conservative organizations, withdrew the term *social justice* as a possible desirable teacher disposition. While NCATE does not explicitly discourage member institutions from incorporating social justice into teacher education programs, this move undercuts a source of support that many teacher educators had used on their own campuses.

School districts are also pressuring teacher education programs. For example, Selwyn (2005–2006), a teacher educator at Antioch College, commented that it is increasingly difficult to find classroom field placements serving low-income students that model anything except scripted teaching. Recently a colleague who has long been active in social justice teacher education told me that school principals now insist that they need teachers trained to use the highly scripted elementary reading package *Open Court* rather than multicultural social justice education. New teachers who resist routinized, scripted teaching in order to teach in student-centered ways are subject to being pushed out, even when their students score very well on tests (Achinstein & Ogawa, 2006).

The shift away from support for critical, multicultural, and social justice perspectives and toward technical training reinforces an ideological shift away from education as preparation for democratic participation, toward education as work preparation and nothing else. It also reflects a narrowing of how equity is to be understood, away from addressing high poverty communities' chronic lack of basic resources, including education resources (e.g., Anyon, 2005; Berliner, 2005; Gándara, Rumberger, Maxwell-Jolly, & Callahan, 2003), and toward focusing on test scores only. Programs that build awareness of a larger view of equity disrupt attempts to directly address a much narrower, test-score driven conception of it.

Disconnecting Teacher Education from Teacher Quality

Teacher quality has been redefined in a way that allows teacher education to be regarded as unnecessary. Zeichner's (2003) three conceptions of teacher quality help to clarify what has happened. A professional conception, reflected in the work of professional groups such as the National Commission on Teaching and America's Future and the National Board for Professional Teaching Standards, emphasizes teachers' professional pedagogical knowledge base and ability to use that knowledge in the classroom. A social justice conception, reflected in the work of organizations such as the National Association for Multicultural Education, emphasizes teachers' knowledge of and ability to use culturally responsive instructional strategies. Both conceptions link teachers' professional pedagogical knowledge with subject matter competence.

A deregulation conception, reflected in reports by conservative think tanks such as the Fordham and Abel Foundations, emphasizes subject matter preparation only, seeing little or no professional pedagogical knowledge of value that can be learned other than through experience. This conception is supported by statistical research that correlates increases in students' test scores with teachers' verbal ability and the proportion of teachers in a school who hold subject matter rather than education degrees (Johnson, 2000; Monk,

1994). No Child Left Behind made the deregulation conception law by defining a highly qualified teacher as: "one who has full state certification as a teacher (including certification through alternative routes); or passed state teacher licensing exam and holds a license in that state" (Norfolk Public Schools, n.d.). The law places a premium on teachers' demonstrated subject matter knowledge aligned to the state's content standards, and on teacher testing. The Bush family has long-standing ties to McGraw-Hill, one of the main corporations selling curriculum packages and tests, and thus has a vested interest in pressing toward test-based systems for judging quality (Trelease, 2006).

Shifting conceptions of teacher quality away from professional knowledge and toward traditional measures of academic content knowledge enables any agency to certify teachers as long as it tests them according to state standards. This shift elevates testing as a way of determining teacher quality over other means, reducing the significance of that which is not testable, such as racial dispositions, expectations for student learning, or ability to connect academics with culturally diverse students. Defining teacher quality through testing also ignores social justice problems connected with testing. A long history of disproportionate failure rates among teachers of color is due to a variety of factors, including biases in whose knowledge is valued on tests and whose is not (Alberts, 2002; Epstein, 2005), the arbitrariness of cutoff scores and their relationship to the racial composition of who passes and who does not (Memory, Coleman, & Watkins, 2003), and connections between testing and perception of stereotype threat (Bennett, McWhorter, & Kuykendall, 2006; Steele & Aronson, 1995). Increased testing undercuts attempts to diversify the teacher population, tacitly dismissing the value of teacher diversity (Epstein, 2005; Flippo, 2003).

In addition, testing shifts power to determine what it means to learn and teach away from educators, and toward legislatures and the corporations that produce and sell tests. Harrell and Jackson (2006), based on an analysis of science teacher testing in Texas, for example, noted that although higher education was still expected to provide content knowledge, it was "the state legislature partnered with test companies" that defined what teachers should know; the greatest beneficiary appeared to be test companies.

Shortening Professional Teacher Education

Assaults on teacher education have juxtaposed teachers' content knowledge against pedagogical knowledge, arguing teachers need the former but not the latter. This, coupled with cuts in state spending on higher education, has led to a shortening of professional teacher education, reducing and in some cases squeezing out preparation for social justice.

Preservice teacher education programs had gradually lengthened from the 1970s through the early the 1990s. For example, between 1973 and 1983, required semester hours for elementary teachers in general studies increased from an average of 41 to 62, and in clinical experiences from 10 to 17 (Feistritzer, 1999). During that time, programs developed more intentional series of field experiences and added coursework that reflected changes in schools, such as mainstreaming exceptional children, working with technology, and teaching diverse learners. By 1999, required semester hours in general studies for elementary teachers had dropped to 51, in clinical experiences to 15, and in professional studies from a high of 38 down to 31 (Feistritzer, 1999). Keep in mind that while teacher education was shrinking, student diversity was growing rapidly; for example, it was becoming increasingly likely that teachers would have English learners in their classrooms that they would be expected to know how to teach.

Teacher education has been shortened through several venues. One venue has been the emergence of test-based programs with minimal professional preparation and no contact with a college of education. The American Board for Certification of Teacher Excellence (ABCTE) program Passport to Teaching, for example, is a test-based system in which holders of a bachelor's degree can complete certification exams online, to teach in states that accept this form of teacher certification. Teachers certified through test-based systems receive no training in any form of social justice education.

Most teachers are still certified through university-based programs, but many such programs have shrunk as colleges of education have been pressured to reduce time to degree in the wave of financial pressures on university budgets. As Jones (2003) explained, reduction in taxes coupled with rising costs of public services, in the great majority of states, has resulted in reductions of public expenditures on higher education. Cuts in teacher education programs, along with the other pressures described above, have squeezed curricular space for social justice work in teacher education. Rather than complementing methods coursework, increasingly coursework in multicultural and social justice education now competes with it. Shortened teacher preparation fits with a "trickle down" theory of teaching and learning in which what children should know is codified into standards and tests, to be delivered using materials that detail each concept and step for teaching it, and teachers need minimal preparation to deliver that content. Darling-Hammond (2006) explains, historically, "Limited training for teachers was seen as an advantage for the faithful implementation of newly designed 'scientific' curricula" (p. 78).

Managing Dissent through Science

It is in the interest of the corporatocracy to manage dissent while building consensus for its expansion. Science has emerged as a useful tool for this purpose. Martin (1999) pointed out that, "Because scientific knowledge is widely believed to have an authority derived from nature, undisputed scientific knowledge claims can play a powerful legitimating role" (p. 105). In several fields, the Bush administration has been charged with using science as a political tool, promoting findings that support its agenda while suppressing those that do not. Based on an examination of the administration's political interference with science, the Government Reform Minority Office (2003) noted that misleading statements, suppressed reports, and the like benefit mainly "important supporters of the President, including social conservatives and powerful industry groups"—the corporatocracy.

In education, a drastically narrowed conception of what counts as science is being used to support education reforms and suppress dissent. Renaming what had been the Office of Educational Research and Improvement as the Institute for Education Sciences, signaled this shift. The Institute defines "scientifically based research" as involving "a randomized controlled trial or a quasi-experiment (including quasi-experiments with equating, regression discontinuity designs, and single-case designs)" (What Works Clearinghouse, 2006). Other ways of framing and conducting research, such as phenomenological research, do not count. This conception of science affirms testing as a primary measure of success, while removing from consideration a huge amount of knowledge derived through research processes other than experimental research.

This redefinition casts most social justice work as irrelevant, since the only "legitimate" question left on the table is: What teaching strategies have been found to raise student test scores, using experimental or quasi-experimental research? Using that question and research so defined, the government is then able to identify schools in which test scores have risen, highlighting those to show that neoliberal reform is working, and which "scientifically based" teaching strategies to promote. Teacher educators who question this framing of knowledge, or who value teaching strategies that have not been validated as "scientifically based," are then cast as impediments to school improvement. Newspaper articles that appear periodically, for example, affirm the suspicion that "those who can, do; those who can't, teach; and those who can't teach, train teachers."[1]

Teacher education has for too long, in general, failed to serve historically underserved communities well. Currently, many historically underserved communities see neoliberal reforms that focus on the achievement gap as doing more to improve education for their children than teacher educators have been doing. In a letter to Congress, over 100 African-American and Latino superintendents emphasized their support for accountability reforms that focus directly on the achievement gap, writing that underachievement of students of color and students who live in poverty "has been swept underneath overall averages for too long" ("Don't Turn Back the Clock," 2003). The broader sociopolitical restructuring that is occurring under corporatocracy is probably detrimental to historically underserved communities in the long run, by rapidly widening gulfs between rich and poor and dismantling public services (Harvey, 2005). If we take social justice seriously in teacher education, what can we be doing, recognizing that the landscape has become much more difficult?

Teacher Education for Social Justice

A wide repertoire of existing practices and programs illustrate ways in which teacher education can help to ensure diverse communities equitable access to quality teaching, prepare teachers to advocate for diverse children, and prepare all students for democratic participation in a diverse society. From recruiting diverse candidates who demonstrate commitment to equity, to constructing fieldwork and professional coursework to build capacity for social justice education, there are many intervention points and strategies that are supported in the research.

Below I suggest a few of these. Possibilities in teacher education for social justice work are summarized in Table 40.1. Across the top are the three social justice strands I am using in this chapter. Down the left-hand side are three areas of teacher education that will be discussed: recruitment and admission, professional coursework, and guided fieldwork.

Recruitment and Admission

Teacher education can help to ensure that all students, and particularly those in historically underserved communities, have equitable access to high quality teachers who believe in them, are committed to working with them, are convinced they have cultural and linguistic resources on which academic learning and democratic participation can be built, and know how to facilitate that learning. Although in part this is a teacher preparation challenge, it is also a recruitment and admission challenge. It is widely recognized that the demographic gap between students and teachers is large and growing. In 2004, enrollment in U.S. public schools was a little more than half White (58%), and a little under half students of color; 20% of students spoke a language other than English at home (National Center for Education Statistics, 2007). Yet, the teaching force remains about 84% White.

Although many studies have found most White teacher candidates bring deficit-oriented stereotypes and very little cross-cultural background, knowledge, and experience (Sleeter, 2008), admission to teacher education is rarely denied on the basis of unwillingness to learn to teach diverse students well. Preservice teachers of color tend to bring a

Table 40.1 Teacher Education and Social Justice Themes

	Build equitable access to high-quality, intellectually rich, culturally affirming teaching	*Prepare teachers to foster democratic engagement among children and youth*	*Prepare teachers as equity advocates for children and youth*
Recruit, admit:	More diverse teacher candidates	Candidates committed to multicultural democracy	Candidates who believe in equity advocacy
Professional coursework that includes:	Self analysis, Socio-cultural framework for teaching and learning Teaching strategies linking what students bring to academics	Strategies for building multicultural democracy in classroom	Nature of institutional discrimination in society and schools
Guided fieldwork:	In culturally diverse and/or low-income settings. Inquiry-based to disrupt deficit theorizing, In communities to learn culture of students	In classrooms that support democratic decision-making	Inquiry into school and community patterns of inequity.

richer multicultural knowledge base than their White counterparts, and are more likely to bring a commitment and sense of urgency to multicultural teaching, social justice, and providing children of color with an academically challenging curriculum (Dee & Henkin, 2002; Knight, 2004; Rios & Montecinos, 1999; Su, 1997). Teachers who are willing to stay in challenging urban schools are more likely to be older adults who are from the community in which they are teaching, rather than young White teachers (Haberman, 1996).

It is possible for teacher education to recruit, admit, and prepare a significantly more diverse mix of prospective teachers than is currently the case. For example, the Pathways program at Armstrong Atlantic State University in Savannah, Georgia certified about 90 African-American teachers. It used a rigorous screening process to ensure that candidates (mainly paraprofessionals) were both academically and personally well-suited to teaching. The program offered candidates various forms of support through their professional preparation, reworked the teacher education course schedule to accommodate paraprofessionals' schedules, offered its students intellectual and cultural enrichment while in the program, and built an adult-oriented support network for them (Lau, Dandy, & Hoffman, 2007). Alverno College in Milwaukee, Wisconsin recruits from city high schools and paraprofessionals, attracting an older adult student population, about 25% of whom are of color (Darling-Hammond, 2006).

Such efforts are not intended to replace White teachers with teachers of color, but rather to build a teaching force that not only looks more like today's students, but also brings more knowledge from their communities into the profession. If teacher education seems irrelevant to many historically underserved communities, working actively with them to bring more members of such communities into teaching, via well-conceived teacher preparation programs, would be a start in making change.

Professional Coursework

Although social justice coursework should be woven through the entire professional prep-aration program, commonly it is added on without addressing the rest of the program as a whole. Quite often such additions are made by a small number of faculty members who have a commitment to teaching for social justice. Holistic, coherently planned programs, that thoughtfully weave multicultural and social justice coursework throughout, have much more impact on teacher candidates than single courses (Darling-Hammond, 2006; Villegas & Lucas, 2002).

Professional coursework that develops social justice begins by having teacher candi-dates examine their own backgrounds and experiences to identify assumptions, beliefs, and values they hold, as well as cultural contexts in which they have grown up that impact their understandings of schooling, children, and families (Feiman-Nemser, 2001). Gaining awareness of these powerful filters through which teacher candidates interpret students and teaching opens candidates to learning. Many teacher educators have teacher candidates write autobiographies or personal cultural histories (Lea, 1994) that discuss who was present and absent in communities where they grew up, core values they learned in their families, beliefs they hold about people who differ from themselves, and their conceptions of what "good teaching" looks like. For example, Kumashiro (2004) begins teaching about sexual orientation by having candidates write anonymously about how they honestly feel about issues involving sexual orientation, so that teaching can begin with their questions and concerns. As coursework then moves outward from candidates' lives, experienced teacher educators systematically use interactive, reflective processes that continue to engage candidates in examining their beliefs and experiences in relation-ship to analytical frameworks and key concepts.

In professional coursework, teacher candidates can learn a sociocultural framework of learning and teaching strategies that offers equitable access to quality education for diverse learners, such as scaffolding, using instructional conversations, and differentiat-ing instruction. As Gutiérrez and Rogoff (2003) explain, learning occurs through intel-lectual participation in cultural practices. The classroom is one site of cultural practice; so also are communities and homes in which children live. As teacher candidates gain understanding of language use and cultural practices that are familiar to the students, coursework can help them learn by building on the language, frames of reference, and patterns of relationships with which students are familiar.

Professional coursework focusing on multicultural democracy lays the foundation for building community in the context of diversity and developing children's awareness of complexities of culture, difference, and equity. Teacher candidates can learn to guide stu-dents in open and constructive conversations about differences they see and experience, and help them learn to make collective decisions that balance competing interests and demands. Reading the work of theorists such as Freire (1998), Apple (1996), and Banks (2003) can prompt candidates to distinguish between democracy and the marketplace, in which the concept of "freedom" has migrated from meaning political and cultural free-dom to meaning freedom to buy and make money. *Rethinking Schools* regularly features articles that help teacher candidates envision what it looks like to build democracy in diverse contexts. Professional coursework is most powerful when teacher candidates are diverse, and not only read about, but also experience building democratic communities in the context of diversity.

Learning to address barriers encountered by students from historically oppressed com-munities in schools requires teacher candidates to understand the nature of institutional discrimination. Without this understanding, teachers too often attribute students' difficulties to home or community "cultural deficiencies," rather than to institutionalized socio-political factors that can be addressed. Andrzejewski's (1995) comprehensive framework links macrolevel systems of oppression with local, everyday inequalities, and connects diverse forms of oppression, including racism, sexism, heterosexism, and classism. In the context of studying systems of oppression, she also has teacher candidates examine how media shape belief systems, juxtaposing social analyses embedded in alternative media with those in mainstream media. She emphasizes identifying and acting on local issues, while situating those within larger issues that require organizing in order to change.

As teacher candidates identify school and classroom barriers to equitable student learning, they can learn to construct alternative inclusive practices. For example, curricula, including state standards and textbooks, still reflect mainly the experiences and perspectives of White, middle class, heterosexual Americans, although diverse peoples are usually sprinkled throughout. In professional coursework, teacher candidates can explore the relationship between who is in curriculum and how students respond, then create multicultural curricula that teach core academic concepts through diverse groups' experiences (Sleeter, 2005).

Promising Practices in Guided Fieldwork

Various forms of fieldwork throughout teacher education is essential. An extensive, carefully designed mix of field experiences can have several purposes, including: helping candidates to decide whether they actually want to teach diverse students; helping them examine their assumptions about children and teaching; exposing them to varied models of teaching; teaching them to identify the intellectual resources students bring to school; helping them gather and use data to guide instruction and to examine schools as institutions; and providing guided teaching practice. Most fieldwork in teacher education, however, encourages replication of the status quo rather than critically questioning and transforming it (Feiman-Nemser, 2001). And simply requiring an experience in a low-income or minority school is just as likely to reinforce negative stereotypes (e.g., Marx, 2000; Tiezzi & Cross, 1997; Wiggins & Follo, 1999) as to challenge them (e.g., Chance, Morris, & Rakes, 1996; Fry & McKinney, 1997; Lazar, 1998).

One promising practice that is used far too little is guided inquiry in cross-cultural community-based learning. Such fieldwork has tremendous potential for building familiarity with diverse students and adults in their lives, investigating institutional discrimination, and learning to view schooling from another point of view. In cross-cultural community-based field experiences, candidates learn how to learn in a community that is culturally different from their own, using strategies such as active listening and nonjudgmental observation. In classrooms, teacher candidates see students reacting to school, but often attribute their reactions to students' lives outside school. By learning from their community contexts, teacher candidates can gain a much better understanding of students' capabilities, strengths, and interests.

Field experiences can vary widely in intensity and duration. Immersion experiences involve living in another cultural context for a period of time, ranging from days or weeks (e.g., Aguilar & Pohan, 1998) to a semester (e.g., Mahan & Stachowski, 1993–1994). In less-intensive experiences (which often take the form of service learning), teacher candidates visit neighborhoods or communities where they have a role to play (such as tutoring) or a specific guided learning activity (such as interviewing senior citizens or constructing a community portrait) (Boyle-Baise, 2002). For example, teacher candidates can work in an agency such as a community center, ethnic club, church, or homeless shelter, in connection with coursework addressing culture and community. Guided inquiry activities might explore why people come to the agency, what kinds of needs people have, what the local community is proud of, what its residents do well, what its children do when not in school, and so forth. In well-structured experiences, candidates see functioning communities and everyday cultural patterns first-hand, form relationships with people, confront stereotypes, and hear stories of lives that reflect abstractions they may have read about in textbooks.

Ultimately, this provides a basis for learning to construct culturally relevant teaching in the classroom. For example, Noordhoff and Kleinfeld's (1993) case study of the impact of a semester-long immersion experience in a small indigenous Alaskan community demonstrated this potential. The teacher candidates lived in the community and became involved in activities such as sewing or beading groups, or local church activities. The researchers videotaped them student teaching three times over the semester, documenting their shift from teaching as telling, to teaching as engaging the children with culturally relevant knowledge connected with academic knowledge.

Guided inquiry projects can investigate patterns of discrimination in the community context that impacts on families. For instance, teacher candidates can compare the prices of gasoline and groceries in low-income and upper-income neighborhoods, then the type of transportation available to a low-income resident who might want to shop outside his or her neighborhood. Or, they might investigate availability and accessibility of medical care to immigrants who are not yet fluent in English and who live in low-income neighborhoods. The notion of institutional discrimination begins to take on substance during such investigations. Numerous case studies have found teacher candidates to question prior stereotypes and become familiar with cultural strengths and community resources they had not seen before as a result of community-based learning (e.g., Bondy & Davis, 2000; James & Haig-Brown, 2002; Melnick & Zeichner, 1996; Moule, 2004; Olmedo, 1997; Seidl & Friend, 2002).

In classrooms, teacher candidates need cooperating teachers who can support inquiry-based, democratic, social justice-oriented practice. Programs that are able to provide this support generally involve close collaboration between schools, universities, and communities. The Bilingual/Multicultural Department at Sacramento State University, for example, has produced enough graduates that it now has a deep network of cooperating teachers who understand, model, and support social justice teaching. In addition, the department has forged Professional Development School relationships with several local schools. Faculty members engage in professional development there, which improves "coherence between practices in the student teaching placements and the theory and practices highlighted in coursework" (Wong, et al., 2007).

Conclusion

Quality teacher education is a valuable public resource. However, to be a quality resource to communities that have historically had least access to excellent teaching, teacher education must be relevant. Relevance requires that teacher educators collaborate directly with such communities, and social justice demands it. In the process of collaborating with communities, teacher educators can forge strategies to recruit and prepare a more culturally and linguistically diverse cadre of teacher candidates who reflect local communities more than is currently the case. Through collaboration that is build on dialogue across communities of difference, teachers can be prepared to advocate for children and youth and to foster democratic engagement, taking into account how local inequities are embedded within systems of oppression as well as movements for action.

Neoliberalism is actively dismantling public services, including teacher education. Based on a comprehensive analysis of its track record globally, Harvey (2005) finds that "the universal tendency [is] to increase inequality and to expose the least fortunate elements in any society ... to the chill winds of austerity and the dull fate of increased marginalization" (p. 118). The fate of teacher education is directly linked with fates of broad segments of the public, particularly those who can least afford the impact of massive privatization. For that reason, teacher educators must take social justice seriously.

Note

1. The original source of this phrase is unknown. The phrase appears on several websites, attributed to an unknown original source.

References

Achinstein, B., & Ogawa, R. T. (2006). (In)fidelity: What the resistance of new teachers reveals about professional principles and prescriptive educational policies. *Harvard Educational Review, 67*(1), 30–63.

Achinstein, B., Ogawa, R. T., & Speiglman, A. (2004). Are we creating separate and unequal tracks of teachers? The effects of state policy, local conditions, and teacher characteristics on new teacher socialization. *American Educational Research Journal, 41*(3), 557–603.

Aguilar, T. E., & Pohan, C. A. (1998). A cultural immersion experience to enhance cross-cultural competence. *Sociotam, 8*(1), 29–49.

Alberts, P. (2002). Praxis II and African American teacher candidates (or, "Is everything Black bad"?). *English Education, 34*(2), 105–125.

Andrzejewski, J. (1995). Teaching controversial issues in higher education: Pedagogical techniques and analytical framework. In R. J. Martin (Ed.), *Practicing what we teach* (pp. 3–26). Albany, NY: SUNY Press.

Anyon, J. (2005). *Radical possibilities.* New York: Routledge.

Apple, M. W. (1996). *Cultural politics and education.* New York: Teachers College Press.

Banks, J. A. (Ed.). (2003). *Diversity and citizenship education: Global perspectives.* San Francisco: Jossey-Bass.

Bennett, C. I., McWhorter, L. M., & Kuykendall, J. A. (2006). Will I ever teach? Latino and African American students' perspectives on PRAXIS I. *American Educational Research Journal, 43*(3), 531–575.

Berliner, D. C. (2005). Our impoverished view of educational review. *Teachers College Record.* August 2nd, 2005. Retrieved August 20th, 2005, from http://www.tcrecord.org

Bondy, E., & Davis, S. (2000). The caring of strangers: Insights from a field experience in a culturally unfamiliar community. *Action in Teacher Education, 22*(2), 54–66.

Boyle-Baise, M. (2002). *Multicultural service learning.* New York: Teachers College Press.

Chance, L., Morris, V. G., & Rakes, S. (1996). Fostering sensitivity to diverse cultures through an early field experience collaborative. *Journal of Teacher Education, 47*(5), 386–389.

Darling-Hammond, L. (2006). *Powerful teacher education.* San Francisco: Jossey-Bass.

Dee, J. R., & Henkin, A. B. (2002). Assessing dispositions toward cultural diversity among preservice teachers. *Urban Education, 37*(1), 22–40.

Delpit, L. (1995). *Other people's children.* New York: The New Press.

"Don't turn back the clock!" (2003). *The Education Trust.* Retrieved July 17th, 2004, from http://www2.edtrust.org

Epstein, K. K. (2005). The whitening of the American teaching force: A problem of recruitment or racism? *Social Justice, 32*(3), 89–102.

Feiman-Nemser, S. (2001). From preparation to practice: Designing a continuum to strengthen and sustain teaching. *Teachers College Record, 198*(6), 1013–1055.

Feistrizter, E. (1999). *The making of a teacher: A report on teacher preparation in the U.S.* National Center for Education Information. Retrieved September 18th, 2006, from http://www.ncei.com/MakingTeacher-rpt.htm

Flippo, R. F. (2003). Canceling diversity: High-stakes teacher testing and the real crisis. *Multicultural Perspectives, 5*(4), 42–45.

Freire, P. (1998). *Pedagogy of freedom.* Boulder, CO: Rowman & Littlefield.

Fry, P. G., & McKinney, L. J. (1997). A qualitative study of preservice teachers' early field experiences in an urban, culturally different school. *Urban Education, 32*(2), 184–201.

Gándara, P., Rumberger, R., Maxwell-Jolly, J., & Callahan, R. (2003, October 7th). English learners in California schools: Unequal resources, unequal outcomes. *Education Policy Analysis Archives, 11*(36). Retrieved October 8th, 2003, from http://epaa.asu.edu/epaa/v11n36/

Gelberg, D. (2007). The business agenda for school reform. *Teacher Education Quarterly, 34*(2), 45–58.

Government Reform Minority Office. (2003, August). *About politics & science: The state of science under the Bush administration.* Retrieved September 25th, 2006, from http://democrats.reform.house.gov/features/politics_and_science/index.htm

Gutiérrez, K. D., & Rogoff, B. (2003). Cultural ways of learning: Individual traits or repertoires of practice. *Educational Researcher, 32*(5), 19–25.

Haberman, M. (1996). Selecting and preparing culturally competent teachers for urban schools. In J. Sikula, T. J. Buttery, & E. Guyton (Eds.), *Handbook of research on teacher education* (2nd ed., pp. 747–760). New York: Macmillan.

Harrell, P. E., & Jackson, J. K. (2006, May). *Teacher knowledge myths: An examination of the relationship between the Texas examinations of educator standards and formal content area coursework, grade point average and age of coursework.* Paper presented at the Science, Technology, Engineering and Mathematics Education Institute, University of Massachusetts, Amherst. Retrieved September 21st, 2006, from http://www.stemtec.org/act

Harvey, D. (2005). *A brief history of neoliberalism.* Oxford: Oxford University Press.

Hursh, D. (2005). The growth of high-stakes testing in the USA: Accountability, markets, and the decline in educational quality. *British Educational Research Journal, 31*(5), 605–622.

James, C. E., & Haig-Brown (2002). "Returning the dues." Community and the personal in a university-school partnership. *Urban Education, 36*(2), 226–255.

Johnson, K. A. (2000). *The effects of advanced teacher training on student achievement.* Washington, D.C.: The Heritage Foundation.

Jones, D. (2003, February). State shortfalls projected through the decade. *Policy Alert.* San Jose, CA: The National Center for Public Policy and Higher Education.

Knight, M. G. (2004). Sensing the urgency: Envisioning a Black humanist vision of care of teacher education. *Race Ethnicity and Education, 7*(3), 211–228.

Kumashiro, K. K. (2004). Uncertain beginnings: Learning to teach paradoxically. *Theory into Practice, 93*(2), 111–115.

Lau, K. F., Dandy, E. B., & Hoffman, L. (2007). The Pathways Program: A model for increasing the number of teachers of color. *Teacher Education Quarterly, 34*(4), 27–40.

Lazar, A. (1998). Helping preservice teachers inquire about caregivers: A critical experience for field-based courses. *Action in Teacher Education 19*(4), 14–28.

Lea, V. (1994). The reflective cultural portfolio: Identifying public cultural scripts in the private voices of white student teachers. *Journal of Teacher Education, 55*(2), 116–127.

Mahan, J. M., & Stachowski, L. (1993–1994). Diverse, previously uncited sources of professional learning reported by student teachers serving in culturally different communities. *National Forum of Teacher Education Journal, 3*(1), 21–28.

Martin, B. (1999). Suppression of dissent in science. *Research in Social Problems and Public Policy, 7,* 105–135.

Marx, S. (2000). An exploration of preservice teacher perceptions of second language learners in the mainstream classroom. *Texas Papers in Foreign Language Education, 5*(1), 207–221.

McChesney, R. W. (2001, March). Global media, neoliberalism, and imperialism. *Monthly Review,* 1–19.

McLaren. P., & Farahmandpur, R. (2005). *Teaching against global capitalism and the new imperialism.* Boulder, CO: Rowman & Littlefield.

Melnick, S., & Zeichner, K. (1996). The role of community-based field experiences in preparing teachers for cultural diversity. In K. Zeichner, S. Melnick, & M. L. Gome (Eds.), *Currents of reform in preservice teacher education* (pp. 176–196). New York: Teachers College Press.

Memory, D. J., Coleman, C. L., & Watkins, S. D. (2003). Possible tradeoffs in raising basic skills cutoff scores for teacher licensure: A study with implications for participation of African Americans in teaching. *Journal of Teacher Education, 54*(3), 217–227.

Monk, D. H. (1994). Subject area preparation of secondary mathematics and science teachers and student achievement. *Economics of Education Review, 13,* 125–145

Montaño, T., Ulanoff, S., Quintanar-Sarellana, R., & Aoki, L. (2006). California Senate Bill 2042: The debilingualization and deculturalization of prospective bilingual teachers. *Social Justice, 32*(2), 103–121.

Moule, J. (2004). Safe and growing out of the box: Immersion for social change. In J. Romo, P. Bradfield, & R. Serrano (Eds.), *Working in the margins: Becoming a transformative educator* (pp. 147–171). Upper Saddle River, NJ: Merrill Prentice-Hall.

National Center for Education Statistics. (2007). *The condition of education 2000–2007.* Retrieved June 1st, 2007, from http://nces.ed.gov/programs/coe

Noordhoff, K., & Kleinfeld, J. (1993). Preparing teachers for multicultural classrooms. *Teaching and Teacher Education, 9*(1), 27–39.

Norfolk Public Schools. (n.d.). Glossary of terms from the No Child Left Behind Act of 2001. Retrieved August 15th, 2006 from, http://www.nps.k12.va.us/NCLB/NCLB_glossary.htm

Olmedo, I. M. (1997). Challenging old assumptions: Preparing teachers for inner city schools. *Teaching and Teacher Education, 13*(3), 245–258.

Perkins, J. (2004). *Confessions of an economic hit man.* San Francisco: Berrett Koehler.

Rios, F., & Montecinos, C. (1999). Advocating social justice and cultural affirmation. *Equity & Excellence in Education, 32*(3), 66–77.

Seidl, B., & Friend, G. (2002). Leaving authority at the door. *Teaching and Teacher Education, 18*(4), 421–433.

Selwyn, D. (2005–2006). Teacher quality: Teacher education left behind. *Rethinking Schools, 20*(2). Retrieved June 2, 2007, from http://www.rethinkingschools.org/archive/20_02/left202.shtml

Sleeter, C. E. (2003). Reform and control: An analysis of SB 2042. *Teacher Education Quarterly, 30*(1), 19–30.

Sleeter, C. E. (2005). *Un-standardizing curriculum: Multicultural teaching in standards-based classrooms.* New York: Teachers College Press.

Sleeter, C. E. (2008). Preparing white teachers for diverse students. In M. Cochran-Smith, S. Feiman-Nemser, & J. McIntyre (Eds.). *Handbook of research in teacher education: Enduring issues in changing contexts* (3rd ed., pp. 559–583). New York: Routledge.

Steele, C. M., & Aronson, J. (1995). Stereotype threat and the intellectual test performance of African Americans. *Journal of Personality and Social Psychology, 69*(5), 797–811.

Su, Z. (1997). Teaching as a profession and as a career: Minority candidates' perspectives. *Teaching and Teacher Education, 13*(3), 325–340.

Tiezzi, L. J., & Cross, B. E. (1997). Utilizing research on prospective teachers' beliefs to inform urban field experiences. *The Urban Review, 29*(2),113–125.

Trelease, J. (2006). The Bushes and the McGraws. *Trelease on Reading.* Retrieved May 29th, 2007, from http://www.trelease-on-reading.com/whatsnu_bush-mcgraw.html

Villegas, A. M., & Lucas, T. (2002). *Educating culturally responsive teachers.* Albany, NY: SUNY Press.

What Works Clearinghouse. (2006). *Evidence standards for reviewing studies.* Retrieved September 25th, 2006, from http://whatworks.ed.gov/reviewprocess/standards.html

Wiggins, R. A., & Follo, E. J. (1999). Development of knowledge, attitudes, and commitment to teach diverse student populations. *Journal of Teacher Education, 50*(2), 94–105.

Wong, P. L., Murai, H., Berta-Ávila, M., William White, L., Baker, S., Arellano, A., et al. (2007). The M/M center: Meeting the demand for multicultural, multilingual teacher preparation. *Teacher Education Quarterly*.

Zeichner, K. (2003). The adequacies and inadequacies of three current strategies to recruit, prepare, and retain the best teachers for all students. *Teachers College Record, 105*(5), 490–519.

41 Teacher Education for Social Justice
Critiquing the Critiques

Marilyn Cochran-Smith, Joan Barnatt,
Randall Lahann, Karen Shakman, and Dianna Terrell

As discussant for a recent American Educational Research Association (AERA) symposium on assessing teacher education, Tom Lasley (2007), Dean of the School of Education at the University of Dayton, commented that all too often, teacher educators make sure teacher candidates know things like Jonathan Kozol's (1991) analysis of the "savage inequalities" among America's rich and poor schools, but don't make sure they know how to teach kids to read. In a commentary for the alumni newsletter of the School of Education at Stanford University, Lee Shulman (2005), President of the Carnegie Foundation for the Advancement of Teaching, called for a consistent professional approach to teacher education based on deep preparation in the content areas and the practice of teaching and rigorous assessment of teaching outcomes. In conclusion, he wrote, "Commitment to social justice is insufficient; love is not enough" (¶ 5).

Both Lasley and Shulman are insiders in the teacher education community with distinguished histories in the field. It is precisely their insider status, however, that makes their comments both so important and so excoriating. They reflect the critique made by some people inside the community and many people outside it: teacher education for social justice centers on kids feeling good and teachers being politically correct, while nobody pays attention to learning. Within the current political climate—where neoliberal, market-based analyses of education have become "common sense" (Apple, 2006, p.15), and where accountability has shifted from resources to bottom line outcomes (Cuban, 2004)—this critique of teacher education for social justice is particularly damning.

In this chapter, we analyze four overlapping, but distinguishable, critiques of teacher education for social justice that are prevalent in the discourse: *the ambiguity critique, the knowledge critique, the ideology critique,* and *the free speech critique.* The chapter begins with discussion of the ambiguity critique, which sometimes stands alone, but is often a preface to other criticisms of social justice in teacher education. Then we take up the other three major critiques, explicating core ideas and assumptions and identifying the major players in the debates. Finally we re-examine these three critiques, blending our rejoinders with analysis of the larger agendas to which they are attached. We argue that although the critiques claim to be apolitical and value-free, they are, in fact, neither. Rather, many of the critiques of teacher education for social justice are part of a larger political ideology based on a narrow view of learning, an individualistic notion of freedom, and a market-based perspective on education that substitutes accountability for democracy. What most of the critics want is not a value-free teacher education, but one that matches their values, not an apolitical teacher education, but one with a more hegemonic and therefore invisible politics.

Teacher Education for Social Justice and the Ambiguity Critique

The idea of preparing teachers to teach for social justice is prevalent in a collection of teacher preparation programs and other initiatives in the United States and elsewhere. Local efforts have been loosely linked through national organizations such as the National Association for Multicultural Education (NAME), the Urban Network to Improve Teacher Education (UNITE),[1] and several committees and special interest groups of the American Association of Colleges for Teacher Education (AACTE) and the American Education Research Association (AERA). Institutional efforts have been encouraged by AACTE, which promoted attention to diversity in teacher education in the early 1970s, and the National Council for the Accreditation of Teacher Education (NCATE), which incorporated preparing teachers for diversity in its 1976 standards and included social justice as a desirable professional disposition in its 2000 standards.

Despite national attention, however, there is considerable variation in meanings of the term *teacher education for social justice*. Some programs with this label emphasize teachers' and students' cultural and ethnic identity, teaching prospective teachers how to provide culturally appropriate curriculum and pedagogy and how to build social supports for the learning of all students. Others focus on teachers' and students' activism regarding the social, economic, and institutional structures that maintain unearned privilege and disadvantage for particular racial, cultural, language, socioeconomic, and gender groups. Some programs that use the language of social justice emphasize civic education, focusing on teaching teachers how to prepare the future participants of a democratic society to deliberate, disagree and act in ways that are socially responsible. Some programs feature innovative community-based sites where teachers learn alongside community activists and parents, while others focus primarily on changing the curriculum within traditional university programs.

Many teacher education programs that take the social justice label emphasize some combination of the above and other ideas about how teaching is related to justice, diversity, access to learning opportunities, the distribution of social and economic resources, and the tensions in civil societies between self interest and the common good. However, the application of this language to disparate projects and programs, coupled with the absence of a fully developed definition or theory, has been a source of sharp criticism, which we refer to here as *the ambiguity critique*. This critique holds that teacher education for social justice is an ambiguous and vague slogan with multiple instantiations, no clear and consistent professional definition, and inadequate theoretical grounding. Interestingly, this critique has been made by both advocates and opponents of teacher education for social justice. Introducing a review of the meanings of social justice in education, for example, North (2006) asserted:

> [T]he label "social justice" is appearing throughout the field—in teacher education program discourses and policies, teacher-activist organization statements…, educational conference programs, and scholarly articles and books. Unfortunately, educators, educational researchers, and educational policymakers frequently employ this catchphrase without offering an explanation of its social, cultural, economic, and political significance. (p. 507)

Along similar lines, Grant and Agosto (2008) have argued that attention to social justice has increased over the past two decades "more in name than substance," and Zeichner (2006) asserted it was "difficult to find a teacher education program in the United States that [did] not claim to have a program that prepares teachers for social justice" (p.

328). These quotations represent the "anything and everything" version of the ambiguity critique, which emphasizes that the notion of social justice is undertheorized and the field lacks shared definitions. In addition, from this perspective, teacher educators only occasionally acknowledge the philosophical and historical roots of the notion of teaching for social justice, which increases the likelihood that it will be diluted, trivialized, or co-opted. Although we are advocates of teacher education for social justice, we must admit we agree with the "anything and everything" version of the ambiguity critique; it is rightly intended to push the field forward by demanding clarity, consistency, and incisiveness.

Strong opponents of teacher education for social justice also use the ambiguity critique. However, for some of the staunchest critics, although ambiguity is ostensibly an issue, it is actually nearly always either a cover for, or a prelude to, larger critiques of schooling, politics, and ideology. For example, in the debate about NCATE's inclusion of social justice as a desired disposition for teachers (discussed below), the National Association of Scholars (NAS) challenged the "constitutional propriety" of social justice as an accreditation criterion because of its lack of a definitive meaning, or what they termed its "contested ideological significance" (Balch, 2005, p. 1). Similarly the Foundation for Individual Rights in Education (FIRE; 2005) challenged social justice as a required disposition for teacher candidates, referring to it as "an entirely abstract concept...that can represent vastly different things to different people" (¶ 3). In these cases, as we show below, the real issue was not ambiguity, but the particular politics and the larger social movements to which social justice was attached.

Teacher Education for Social Justice: The Knowledge Critique

The *knowledge critique*, which focuses on the content and purposes of teacher education for social justice, is the most prominent of the current critiques and has, arguably, both the deepest roots and the sharpest teeth. In the context of the current accountability movement, where high stakes test results are broadly accepted as the final arbiter in debates about teacher preparation and teacher quality, the knowledge critique is particularly deadly.

In a nutshell, the knowledge critique holds that teacher education for social justice is about teachers being nice, children feeling good, and everybody blissfully ignoring knowledge. Citing Heather MacDonald's (1998) article, "Why Johnny's Teacher Can't Teach," which was broadly circulated in the Manhattan Institute's *City Journal*, *Newsweek* columnist George Will (2006) commented on the then-emerging controversy prompted by NCATE's inclusion of social justice in its list of desirable teacher dispositions. He said:

> Today's teacher education focus on "professional disposition" is just the latest permutation of what MacDonald calls the education schools' "immutable dogma," which she calls "Anything but Knowledge." The dogma has been that primary and secondary education is about "self-actualization" or "finding one's joy" or "social adjustment" or "multicultural sensitivity" or "minority empowerment" But is never about anything as banal as mere knowledge. (p. 98)

Throughout the column, Will hammered home the chasm between social justice and knowledge: he juxtaposed teacher education's stated commitment to preparing individuals "to promote social justice" with what he asserted was almost never the commitment in education schools—preparing individuals "to read, write and reason." He characterized the education school curriculum in terms of its "vacuity," its "progressive political catechism," and as "today's progressive patois," in contrast to "rigorous pedagogy," attention to "accomplishments measured by tests," and "teacher-centered classrooms where knowledge is everything" (p. 98). In short, although George Will is certainly not the major foe of teacher education for social justice, his column succeeded in bringing the critique to the *Newsweek* national readership. Below we look beneath the surface of the knowledge critique by identifying its major arguments and assumptions.

Major Arguments in the Knowledge Critique

The knowledge critique is based on two arguments about teacher education for social justice, one the mirror image of the other: (1) Teacher education programs with social justice goals place far too much emphasis on progressive and political educational goals, particularly respecting pupils' cultural identity and bolstering their self-esteem, on one hand, and promoting equity and social change, on the other. (2) At the same time, teacher education programs with social justice goals place far too little emphasis on traditional educational goals directly related to conveying subject matter knowledge and basic skills. From this perspective, the first of teacher education's failings—its progressive focus—is the cause of its second—lack of attention to basic knowledge and skills.

The first argument is an old one and is consistent with the positions of many conservative critics of progressive education. From this perspective, multicultural curriculum, culturally appropriate pedagogy, and the like, which are core aspects of teaching for social justice, are regarded as condescending, divisive, and anti-intellectual. Likewise, cultural critiques of school knowledge are regarded as mere political correctness, which are soft on substance and rigor. These aspects of teacher education for social justice are often wrapped up in one package by the critics and labeled as helping students "feel good about their racial or ethnic identity" (Ravitch, 2001, p. 426) or as mere "therapy" (Thernstrom & Thernstrom, 1997, p. 373).

From this perspective, teacher education programs for social justice inappropriately characterize teaching as a political activity and emphasize that teachers should be part of larger social movements. From this perspective, historical critiques of the education system as a reproducer of social and economic inequities are regarded as unsubstantiated and misguided. Nowhere is this application of the knowledge critique more visible than in the last decade's attacks on social studies education. The Fordham Foundation's monograph, *Passion Without Progress* (Leming, Ellington, & Porter-Magee, 2003), for example, reflected the decade's conservative analysis of "what went wrong with the social studies," as suggested in Chester Finn's (2003) foreword:

> Why is social studies education in such deep trouble?...one reason is the dominant belief systems of the social studies education professoriate who train future teachers in colleges and departments of education....The theorists' passion for radical social change and their propensity to use the public schools as a tool to do so, is undoubtedly one reason social studies is in crisis. It has resulted in a field that eschews substantive content and subordinates a focus on effective practice to educational and political correctness. (pp. i–ii)

This quotation illustrates both arguments of the knowledge critique, suggesting that teacher education's wrong-headed goals preclude their ensuring that teacher candidates can transmit important knowledge and skills.

Leming, Ellington, and Porter-Magee (2003) referred to this as "the kinds of basic knowledge ordinary Americans think important for their children to learn" and "traditional history and social science content" (p. ii). Likewise, in her excoriating explanation of why teachers can't teach, Heather MacDonald (1998) called this "plain old knowledge" (p.14), sarcastically pointing out that the "Anything But Knowledge" credo leaves education professors and their acolytes free to concentrate on "far more pressing matters than how to teach the facts of history or the rules of sentence construction" (p. 18). Ravitch's (2001) argument that the culprit in the 20th century's failed school reforms was progressive education is also helpful here. She contrasted initiatives that challenged the idea of a canon of agreed-upon knowledge that all citizens should have (e.g., constructivism, multiculturalism, and the self-esteem movement) with reform proposals like E. D. Hirsch's "cultural literacy" (Hirsch, 1987).

Assumptions Underlying the Knowledge Critique

A number of closely related assumptions underlie the major arguments of the knowledge critique. First, and perhaps most important, is the assumption that contemporary versions of teacher education for social justice are part of the long lineage of American progressive education, which historically has been anti-knowledge, anti-intellectual, and yoked to the idea that education can promote social and political change. Second is the assumption that there is an utter dichotomy between justice and knowledge. Simply put, this means that if teacher preparation programs are promoting social justice, then they are not promoting pupils' learning of academic knowledge and skills, which is the rightful and major purpose of schooling in society.

Most of the knowledge critiques of teacher education for social justice rely on both of these assumptions, which are usually entangled rather than discrete. Crowe's (2008) commentary on accountability and teacher education illustrates:

> As a substitute for empirically-based and scientifically-acceptable knowledge, the set of values loosely coupled into "social justice" may be best understood as the latest manifestation of "pedagogical romanticism" (Sedlak, in press) to beset the field. And the connection between these values and student learning is unclear...NCATE's "dispositions" give great emphasis to teacher attitudes and self-efficacy concepts that have no empirically demonstrable bearing on whether students in the classroom are learning anything that can be measured objectively...
>
> The endless argument about the "moral basis of education" undercuts claims of legitimacy and professional status.... The academy may revel in discussions about knowledge and truth and morality, but schools and policy leaders have real world problems to solve. (p. 992)

In this commentary, Crowe connected teacher education for social justice with beliefs, values, romanticism, self-efficacy, and morality. On the other hand, he contrasted teacher education for social justice with empirically based and scientifically acceptable knowledge, student learning, learning that can be measured objectively, legitimacy, professional status, and solving problems in the real world. In doing so, Crowe linked teacher education for social justice to previous romantic and progressive reforms at the same time he decoupled it from contemporary emphases on scientifically based research and evidence-based education. In doing so, he divorced social justice from knowledge, emphasizing instead their mutual exclusivity.

The quotations in this section reveal a number of somewhat different ideas that are usually rolled into the presumed dichotomy between justice and knowledge in teacher education: Unimportant information and activities monopolize the teacher education curriculum so there is no time or space for attention to subject matter knowledge. Teaching and teacher education for social justice, by definition, focuses on something other than academic subject matter and high standards, which is trivial and limited in intellectual substance. And, perhaps most important, "true" knowledge—the kind that ought to be the centerpiece of schooling and the kind that is testable on standardized tests—is objective and apolitical and thus cannot be coupled with, taught at the same time as, or in conjunction with, the overtly political knowledge that promotes activism and social justice. In short, from the perspective of the knowledge critique, teacher education for social justice does not, does not want to, and could not even if it wanted to, promote pupils' learning of subject matter knowledge and skills.

Teacher Education for Social Justice: The Ideology Critique

The *ideology critique* of teacher education for social justice is closely related to the knowledge critique in that it makes many of the same assumptions about the neutrality and the apolitical nature of academic knowledge and about the knowledge transmission role of the school. It is different, however, in that rather than focusing on the content and purposes of teacher education, the ideology critique focuses on the criteria and standards according to which prospective teachers are admitted into or barred from entering the profession.

In short, the ideology critique holds that evaluating prospective teachers on the basis of moral values, political perspectives, and certain dispositions, such as social justice, is a blatant misuse of the gate-keeping powers of professional accreditors. Although the ideology critique both pre- and postdates the NCATE dispositions controversy, it gained prominence when NCATE's (2001) inclusion of social justice as an example of a desirable disposition in teacher candidates became a flashpoint in contentious debates about how teachers should be assessed and who should decide whether they were admitted to the profession.

Backed by national conservative organizations, students at a number of colleges and universities complained that in order to be recommended for teaching certification, they had to have certain ideological beliefs. In December 2005, the *Chronicle of Higher Education* ran a story (Wilson, 2005), with the headline, "'We Don't Need That Kind of Attitude,'" and the subhead, "Education Schools Want to Make Sure Prospective Teachers Have the Right 'Disposition'" (p. A8). The article described a number of instances, like this one first reported in the *New York Sun* (Gershman, 2005):

> Brooklyn College's School of Education has begun to base evaluations of aspiring teachers in part on their commitment to social justice, raising fears that the college is screening students for their political views... teacher candidates could be ousted from the School of Education if they are found to have the wrong dispositions. (p. 1)

The *Chronicle* article also reported that some teacher education institutions had developed ways to assess the dispositions of teacher candidates and that there were grievances regarding these criteria pending at some institutions.

Major Arguments in the Ideology Critique

Two major arguments, closely tied to one another and almost always made in tandem, comprise the ideology critique: (1) Moral values, beliefs, and political ideologies vary according to the worldviews and traditions of families, communities, and religious and other groups; these values and ideologies are dynamic and contested rather than consensual in our society. (2) Institutions that prepare professionals and the accrediting agencies that monitor them are gatekeepers to the professions; they should judge candidates on their knowledge and performance as professionals, not on their politics, personality traits, or ideological perspectives. From this perspective, evaluating potential teachers on their dispositions for social justice is tantamount to controlling entry into the profession on the basis of partisan and controversial ideological positions rather than according to what is rightfully the business of teacher certification and accreditation—ensuring that only persons who can effectively convey academic knowledge to pupils are admitted into the profession.

The first argument here is deceptively straightforward—if and when the enterprise of teacher certification/accreditation focuses on beliefs, moral values, or dispositions, it becomes inappropriately political and ideological. Once this premise is accepted, the second follows easily and logically: the teacher certification/accreditation enterprise should be based on the assessment of potential teachers' knowledge and skills, not on their politics or ideology. The 2000 NCATE standards and the ensuing efforts of NCATE-accredited institutions to develop assessment tools to evaluate candidates' dispositions flew in the face of both the first and the second of these arguments and gave organizations and individuals already opposed to the social justice agenda the opportunity to challenge NCATE's gate-keeping criteria.

For example, in November 2005, the National Association of Scholars (NAS), an organization long opposed to social justice agendas, filed a formal letter with the U.S. Department of Education's Assistant Secretary for Post-Secondary Education. NAS requested that the DOE inquire into the "educational and constitutional propriety of the accreditation criteria used by NCATE," in particular challenging its reference to social justice, which, as noted above, they asserted was a term "necessarily fraught with contested ideological significance" (Balch, 2005, p. 1). In the same letter, NAS challenged the professional standards of a school of social work, based on the statement of the school that a purpose of social work education was "preparing social workers to alleviate poverty, oppression, and other forms of social injustice," an assumption NAS decried as "progressive political activism" (Balch, 2005, p. 3).

Some months later and following intense political pressure and media attention, NCATE withdrew the language of social justice from its standards. It is worth noting that although much of the NCATE debate seemed on the surface to be about the issue of professional dispositions, the fact is that the notion that good teaching is supported by certain "dispositions" was not invented with NCATE's 2000 performance standards (Wise, 2006). Rather this was consistent with other widely used teaching standards, which had not created any uproar. It is also worth noting that no public debate ensued about teacher candidates' dispositions toward caring, fairness, or honesty, which were the qualities in addition to social justice that had been listed as examples in NCATE's glossary entry for the term *disposition*. There is little doubt that it was social justice—rather than debate about whether dispositions should be a criterion for admitting teachers into the profession—that incited the critics.

The ideology critique is primarily about teacher education's accountability processes. Unlike the knowledge critique, which focuses on the content of the curriculum, the ideology critique zeroes in on certification and accreditation, in particular, the professional standards according to which potential teachers are judged fit to enter the field. The ideology critique, at least as it played out around NCATE's dispositions, held that the accreditation standards were unduly political.

Assumptions Underlying the Ideology Critique

Many of the assumptions that underlie the knowledge critique—assumptions about the neutrality and objectivity of core academic knowledge and the knowledge transmission purpose of schooling—also underlie the ideology critique. We do not rehash these here except to note that they apply. The central assumption animating the ideology critique, however, is that professional accreditation—and thus professional education—can be and ought to be apolitical, value-free, and neutral when it comes to moral and ethical issues. This presumes, of course, that there is a choice in education—as in all social institutions—between politics and no politics and that it is possible to engage in practice and policymaking in teacher preparation, certification, and program accreditation without being political.

The ideology critique works from the assumption that candidates ought to be selected for the teaching profession on grounds that are neither political nor ideological. In a commentary on the politics of teacher education, for example, Frederick Hess (2005), Resident Scholar at the American Enterprise Institute for Public Policy Research, expressed great concern that "leading voices in teacher preparation...ha[d] unapologetically argued that teacher education is inescapably about championing certain values" (p. 195).

From Hess's perspective, the problem was not only that teacher education's leaders linked values and ideology to teacher education, but also that they asserted that this was unavoidable. Hess rejected a teacher education system where the viewpoints and values of "the establishment" were allowed to govern who is permitted to teach. In contrast, Hess favored the "common sense" approach of deregulation, which opens up entry into teaching to many more would-be teachers and lets the market decide who should teach with pupils' test scores the ultimate arbiter of success. Hess's commentary illustrates that although the ideology critique ostensibly focuses on the gate-keeping function of teacher certification and accreditation, this critique is also linked to larger political agendas that favor market-based reforms of teacher education and neoliberal perspectives on the connection between education institutions and the economy.

Teacher Education for Social Justice: The Free Speech Critique

The third major critique of teacher education for social justice is the *free speech critique*, which focuses on the intellectual climate and civic environment of colleges and universities where teachers are prepared. Although it zeroes in on institutional climate rather than accountability criteria, the free speech critique shares many of the arguments and assumptions of the ideology critique. Like the ideology critique, the free speech critique became prominent in the teacher education discourse at about the same time that the NCATE dispositions controversy erupted. Neither the ideology critique nor the free speech critique, however, was simply a response to NCATE's inclusion of social justice language in its standards. Rather both of these critiques emerged as part of mounting concern among neoconservatives that universities, which they alleged had privileged liberal perspectives for years, had become so liberal that they were ostracizing students with conservative viewpoints and attempting to indoctrinate everybody into one orthodox—and liberal—viewpoint.

Simply put, the free speech critique holds that teacher education programs that promote social justice circumscribe teacher candidates' freedom to think and say whatever they wish and to adhere to whatever moral principles they choose. This critique has been promulgated by the Foundation for Individual Rights in Education (FIRE) (2007) and other groups whose purpose is to "defend and sustain individual rights at America's colleges and universities...and educate the public and concerned Americans about the threats to these rights on our campuses and about the means to preserve them" (¶ 1).

Major Arguments in the Free Speech Critique

The free speech critique of teacher education for social justice is comprised of two closely related arguments: (1) Teacher education courses or programs with social justice standards, requirements, assignments, curricula, or assessments amount to a political litmus test for would-be teachers and thus circumscribe their first amendment rights to hold whatever beliefs and moral principles they choose. (2) Promoting social justice in teacher education is anathema to the mission and traditions of the modern university, which is intended to foster an open intellectual atmosphere of free thought and speech.

The free speech critique puts these two arguments together, concluding that colleges and universities cannot simultaneously make social justice a central part of a professional program and, at the same time, foster the appropriate educational environment. An editorial in the *Chronicle of Higher Education,* written by Greg Lukianoff (2007), the President of FIRE, illustrates:

> At the heart of the modern liberal university is an ideal simultaneously grand and humble: None of us are omniscient, none can know what strange paths can lead to wisdom and understanding, and it is arrogant for any institution to assume the role of final arbiter of truth. Official orthodoxies impede rather than facilitate education and lead to dogma rather than living, organic ideas. One would hope that we are long past the time when education was viewed as an opportunity to inculcate "correct" and unchallengeable answers to philosophical, moral, and societal questions. (p. B8)

Lukianoff cited incidents from education and other professions, such as social work and law, where FIRE had supported students' efforts to file suit or bring grievances about social justice programs. He described teacher education for social justice as part of larger trends at universities to establish "mandatory political orthodoxy," to promote "dogma," and to promulgate "enforced conformity of thought." He juxtaposed these with the ideals he claimed should be at the heart of the university—"living, organic ideas," "liberal education," and "freedom" (p. B8). Lukianoff concluded that teacher education programs committed to social justice unavoidably infringed on students' civil rights and threatened the open intellectual atmosphere that is central to the university community.

Those who use the free speech critique regard teacher education for social justice as a process that compromises the intellectual freedom that is at the heart of civil society. Along similar lines, in a *U.S. News & World Report* column entitled, "Classroom Warriors," John Leo (2005) suggested that by focusing on social justice, the "cultural left" of education schools, was enforcing "political conformity" and imposing "groupthink" with dire consequences for both students and faculty:

> [T]he ed schools, essentially a liberal monoculture...require support for diversity and a culturally left agenda, including opposition to what the schools sometimes call "institutional racism, classism, and heterosexism." Predictably, some students concluded that thought control would make classroom dissent dangerous.... Five students filed written complaints and received no formal reply from the college. One was told to leave the school and take an equivalent course at a community college. Two

of the complaining students were then accused of plagiarism and marked down one letter grade....

K. C. Johnson, a history professor at the school who defended the dissenting students, became a target himself. After writing an article in *Inside Higher Ed* attacking dispositions theory as a form of mind control, Johnson faced a possible investigation by a faculty Integrity Committee. (p. 75)

Leo characterized FIRE as the legal champion in situations where the free speech rights of students and faculty were threatened. From this perspective, the university is a microcosm of larger society—both depend for their life's blood on the open exchange of ideas where disagreement and deliberation are encouraged, and orthodoxy is properly regarded as dangerous.

Assumptions Underlying the Free Speech Critique

There are two major assumptions underlying the free speech critique. The first is that teacher preparation courses and programs can and ought to be apolitical and, when it comes to morals and values, broadly ecumenical rather than parochial. Because this assumption is similar to one underlying the ideology critique, we do not elaborate further here. Second, the free speech critique assumes that universities are currently dominated by liberal—and in some cases, radical—faculty members whose views are privileged and who threaten the intellectual freedom of faculty and students with different ideas. Here, freedom is defined as an individual's right to express his or her own ideas freely and without fear coupled with freedom from exposure to particular ideas.

The free speech critique of teacher education for social justice underscores the perceived mounting disparity between liberal academics, on one hand, and a growing population of conservative college students and a relatively smaller number of conservative faculty, on the other. This critique is part of much larger efforts by conservative groups nationwide to ensure that universities—and in some cases K–12 schools—refrain from advocating particular views on issues that are deemed partisan or give "equal time" to opposing viewpoints. Along these lines, for example, a number of state legislatures are considering new "academic freedom" or "academic bill of rights" legislation. The American Federation of Teachers "Academic Freedom Forum" (2007) recently opened an article with this provocative example:

> The Arizona state legislature is considering a bill that could levy a $500 fine on professors who advocate "one side of a social, political or cultural issue that is a matter of partisan controversy," the *Arizona Daily Start* reports. K-12 teachers could face three hours of re-education or the loss of their teaching certificate for doing the same. (¶ 1)

The article reported that bills of this type were also being considered in Kentucky, West Virginia, Georgia, and New York, and in some places, like Virginia, legislators had even sponsored bills proposing that colleges and universities be required to prove they had "intellectual diversity" or "ideological balance" on campus (¶ 3). (Virginia's bill, which was criticized by opponents as having more to do with forwarding conservative viewpoints than promoting a true exchange of ideas, was subsequently rejected.)

The free speech critique of teacher education assumes that when teacher education programs have social justice in their standards, requirements, assignments, curricula, or assessments, this is tantamount to a mandatory "honor code" or "loyalty oath," which is inconsistent with the open intellectual atmosphere that is integral to universities. This amounts to indoctrination, limits individual freedom, and compromises the university as an open intellectual environment. From this perspective, critics want to ensure that college students have the right to express opinions that differ from those of their professors and supervisors as well as freedom from exposure to certain ideas about social justice that are considered partisan and ideological.

Conclusion: Reexamining the Critiques/Reframing Social Justice

As we have shown, the critiques of teacher education for social justice are overlapping but distinguishable. The knowledge critique targets content and purpose, the ideology critique aims at gate-keeping, and the free speech critique focuses on intellectual climate. Although these critiques are not the same, they are consistent and are often blended together. Further, each is sometimes introduced by the ambiguity critique, which holds that *social justice* is a fuzzy term, leaving it open to contested ideological and political interpretations. It is important to note that these critiques are not purveyed by the lunatic fringe of academia or by peripheral cultural groups. Rather they represent powerful— and increasingly widespread—arguments about teacher preparation, the educational environments that support learning, and the purposes of schooling in a democratic society. Although we are strong supporters of teacher education for social justice, we also think the critiques should be taken seriously. Because space limitations prevent us from thoroughly rejoining each argument we have identified, we conclude with cross-cutting points that reexamine the critiques and reframe our ways of thinking about teacher education for social justice.

Teacher Education for Social Justice and Learning

The alleged dichotomy between teacher education programs focused on social justice and programs focused on knowledge is the crux of some of the most damning critiques. Stated in its starkest terms, this implies that there is a choice about the goal of teacher education: either knowledge and learning *or* social justice. From the perspective of this dichotomy, then, social justice by definition precludes knowledge and learning. But this conclusion turns on a classic rhetorical move on the part of the critics—creating a Hobson's choice between "knowledge" and "little or no knowledge"—since no reasonable person would choose a teacher education program *not* dedicated to knowledge and improving pupils' learning. As political scientist Deborah Stone (2002) points out, a Hobson's choice wears "all the verbal clothing of a real choice, when in fact the very list of options determines how people will choose by making one option seem like the only reasonable possibility" (p. 246).

As teacher educators, we must expose the fact that the choice between knowledge and social justice is artificial and based on an utterly false dichotomy. On the other hand, we must also take a hard look at ourselves and our programs to ensure that teacher education for social justice really does have at its heart an explicit focus on pupils' learning and their life chances. But the notions of "learning" and "knowledge" central to teacher education for social justice are different from, and bigger than, the notions implicit in the critiques. From the perspective of social justice, promoting pupils' learning includes teaching much of the traditional canon, but it also includes teaching pupils to think critically about and challenge the universality of that knowledge. Along similar lines, we must be sure that teacher education for social justice focuses on accountability (e.g., evidence-based strategies, testing, using data to improve practice) while, at the same time, it critiques narrow understandings of "education science" and challenges the current testing regime, which constricts the curriculum, deprofessionalizes teaching, and leaves behind the same children as always.

This point must be loud and clear: teacher education programs with the goal of social justice do not give short shrift to teachers' subject matter knowledge nor do they fail to accept accountability for pupils' learning. Social justice programs do not do one or the other of these things; they concentrate on knowledge and accountability *and* they critique their embedded inequities. In contrast to the criticism noted in this chapter's opening lines, we must make it crystal clear that when teacher education programs focus on social justice, teacher candidates know how to teach kids to read, and they also know that the inequities of schooling and society make it much easier for some groups of kids to learn to read than others. Knowledge and justice are not dichotomous, but complementary, goals. In fact, many would suggest that attention to social critique and to improving society motivates students and stimulates knowledge acquisition. This means that it is not only the case that both social critique and subject matter knowledge can be taught, but also that pursuing the former can often further the goals of the latter.

Teacher Education for Social Justice and Freedom

As we have shown, critics make the argument that teacher education for social justice is tantamount to an ideological litmus test for teacher candidates that curtails their intellectual freedom and interferes with the open atmosphere of the universities they attend. Unchallenged, this is as deadly a critique of teacher education for social justice as is the claim that it eschews knowledge.

Characterizing teacher education for social justice as infringement on individual freedom is a powerful strategy, since freedom is among the rights Americans hold most dear. As Stone (2002) reminds us, however, freedom itself is a contested and continuously constructed concept, not a given. The critiques presume that freedom is upholding the rights of individuals to adhere to whatever beliefs and values they wish concerning education and schooling. Embedded in the idea of teacher education for social justice, on the other hand, is the presupposition that teaching is a profession with certain inalienable purposes, among them challenging the inequities in access and opportunity that curtail the freedom of some individuals and some groups to obtain a high quality education. With the former, freedom is defined as the prevention of outside interference with the ideas of individuals. From this perspective, which is fundamental to the critiques, it follows that teacher candidates should not only have freedom to express their own views, but also freedom from exposure to ideas about education with which they do not agree and from definitions of teaching that are inconsistent with their views. When teaching is conceptualized as challenging educational inequities so that everybody has rich learning opportunities, however, freedom is defined in a way that links individual freedom with social responsibility. From this perspective, freedom is the removal of those social, economic, and institutional barriers that are within the scope of human agency and that constrain individuals' or groups' access to educational opportunities and resources.

To respond to the critics, we must again be loud and clear. Contrary to the claim that teacher education for social justice limits freedom, the goal of teaching for social justice is indeed freedom—not the sort of freedom that protects individuals from certain ideas, but the freedom that unites the efforts of individual teachers with broader educational goals related to the common good. From this perspective, teaching is rightfully defined as helping to alleviate the inequities that curtail the freedom of all participants in our society to gain a quality education. This goal is integral to the very idea of learning to teach. In short, something like the sentiments regarding the preservation of human life in modern day versions of the Hippocratic Oath to which prospective doctors in nearly all medical schools ascribe, teaching for social justice is not an option, but a crucial and fundamental part of teaching.

Behind the Critiques of Teacher Education for Social Justice

As we have shown throughout this chapter, although they explicitly claim to be apolitical and "unideological," the viewpoints underlying all three of the major critiques of teacher education for social justice are in fact part of a larger political ideology. Michael Apple (2006) refers to this as the "rightward turn" in educational policy. He argues that this has come about through the "successful struggle by the right to form a broad-based alliance," which has won "the battle over common sense" (p. 31). Apple explains that:

> [This new alliance] has creatively stitched together different social tendencies and commitments and has organized them under its own general leadership in issues dealing with social welfare, culture, the economy, and…education…. [T]his alliance contains four major elements…sutured into the more general conservative movement. These elements include neoliberals, neoconservatives, authoritarian populists, and a particular fraction of the upwardly mobile professional and managerial new middle class. (p. 31)

Apple argues that the first two of these groups, especially the neoliberals, are the leaders of the conservative alliance and their efforts to "reform" education.

Applying Apple's analysis to the critiques of teacher education for social justice, we can see that the knowledge critique couples the neoconservative desire to return to the traditional knowledge and discipline of the canon with the neoliberal insistence on market-based education reforms that encourage private enterprise and consumer choice and make test score accountability the bottom line. Both the ideology and free speech critiques presuppose the neoliberal view of freedom as individual choice. The ideology critique links this perspective to the neoliberal disdain for regulation by characterizing teacher education certification, accreditation, and licensure as unproven policies and unnecessary roadblocks to improving teacher quality. The free speech critique links this perspective to the neoconservative characterization of the modern university as a hotbed of liberal, if not radical, perspectives that are anti-American, anti-White, and anticonservative. All three of these critiques skillfully use the rhetorical strategy Stone (2002) calls "the story of decline" (p. 138) to persuade the audience that if something is not done to change the situation (here, the proliferation of teacher education programs with social justice goals), our system of producing teachers for the nation's schools will continue to deteriorate.

In short, although they claim otherwise, the critiques of teacher education for social justice are very political and ideological. From the perspective of the critiques, the ultimate freedom is the freedom of the market, and democracy is narrowly defined in terms of market-based, bottom-line accountability coupled with the deregulation of schools, teacher preparation routes, and other educational services. From the perspective of social justice, however, freedom couples individuals' rights with social responsibility for the public good that ensures that everybody has freedom of access to rich opportunities to learn and to the resources that make that possible.

We are strong supporters of teacher education for social justice. In our judgment, there is no more pressing problem facing the schools—or society in general—than ensuring that all of the nation's schoolchildren have deep and rich learning opportunities, easy and truly equitable access to educational resources, and legitimate prospects following K–12 schooling for either further education or employment that pays a living wage. As we noted above, the bottom line of teacher education for social justice must be improving students' learning and their life chances. To make this happen, we need carefully worked-out theories of teacher education for social justice that take into account the social, historical, and philosophical moorings of the term and carefully apply them to the educational scene. We also believe, however, that critiques of teacher education for social justice must be taken seriously; their powerful arguments about teaching, learning, and schooling must be incisively unpacked, and their links to the dominant political and economic paradigm of neoliberalism must be exposed.

Note

1. UNITE existed as a spin-off or subgroup of the Holmes Partnership, explicitly focused on the preparation of teachers for urban schools, for just over a decade from 1994 to 2003.

References

American Federation of Teachers. (2007). Academic Freedom Forum. Retrieved May 17, 2007 from, http://www.aft.org/higher_ed/aff/marchapril07.htm

Apple, M. (2006). *Educating the "right" way: Market, standards, God, and inequality.* New York: Routledge.

Balch, S. (2005). National Association of Schools' letter to Sally Stroup requesting NCATE Investigation. Retrieved May 17, 2007 from, http://www.nas.org/aa/DoEd_ltr_EdSchPoliticization.pdf

Crowe, E. (2008). Teaching as a profession: A bridge too far? In M. Cochran-Smith, S. Feiman Nemser, J. McIntyre, & K. Demers (Eds.), *Handbook of research on teacher education: Enduring questions in changing contexts.* Mahwah, NJ: Erlbaum.

Cuban, L. (2004). Looking through the rearview mirror at school accountability. In K. Sirotnik (Ed.), *Holding accountability accountable* (pp. 18–34). New York: Teachers College Press.

Finn, C. (2003). Foreword. In J. Leming, L. Ellington, & K. Porter-Magee (Eds.), *Where did social stidies go wrong?* Retrieved May 19, 2007, from http://www.edexcellence.net/institute/publications/publication.cfm?id=317

Foundation for Individual Rights in Education. (2005). Letter to Columbia University President Lee Bollinger. Retrieved May 19, 2007 from, http://www.thefire.org/index.php/article/5100.html

Foundation for Individual Rights in Education. (2007). About FIRE. Retrieved May 17, 2007 from, http://thefire.org/index.php/article/4851.html

Gershman, J. (2005, May 31st). "Disposition" emerges as issue at Brooklyn College. *The New York Sun.* Retrieved May 17, 2007 from, http://www.nysun.com/article/14604?page_no=2

Grant, C., & Agosto, V. (2008). Teacher capacity and social justice in teacher education. In M. Cochran-Smith, S. Feiman Nemser, J. McIntyre, & K. Demers (Eds.), *Handbook of research on teacher education: Enduring questions in changing contexts.* Mahwah, NJ: Erlbaum.

Hess, F. (2005). The predictable, but unpredictably personal, politics of teacher licensure. *Journal of Teacher Education, 56,* 192–198.

Hirsch, E. D. (1987). *Cultural literacy: What every American needs to know.* New York: Houghton Mifflin.

Kozol, J. (1991). *Savage inequalities: Children in America's school.* New York: HarperCollins.

Lasley, T. (2007, April). *Rethinking teacher education: From teacher learning to student learning.* Discussant at symposium presented at American Educational Research Association Annual Meeting, Chicago.

Leming, J., Ellington, L., & Porter-Magee, K. (2003). Where did social studies go wrong? Retrieved May 19, 2007 from, http://www.edexcellence.net/institute/publication/publication.cfm?id=317

Leo, J. (2005, October 24th). Class(room) warriors. *U.S. News & World Report, 139,* 75.

Lukianoff, G. (2007). Social justice and political orthodoxy. *The Chronicle of Higher Education, 53*(30), B8. Retrieved May 17, 2007, from Academic OneFile database.

MacDonald, H. (1998). Why Johnny's teacher can't teach. *City Journal, 8*(2), 14–26.

National Council for Accreditation of Teacher Education. (2001). Professional standards for the accreditation of schools, colleges, and departments of education. Retrieved May 19, 2007 from, http://www.ncate.org/2000/2000stds.pdf

North, C. (2006). More than words? Delving into the substantive meaning(s) of "social justice" in education. *Review of Educational Research, 76*(4), 507–535.

Ravitch, D. (2001). *Left back: A century of battles over school reform.* New York: Simon & Schuster.

Shulman, L. (2005, Fall). Teacher education does not exist. *Stanford Educator,* 7.

Stone, D. (2002). *Policy paradox: The art of political decision making.* New York: W.W. Norton.

Thernstrom, S., & Thernstrom, A. (1997). *America in black and white: One nation, indivisible.* New York: Touchstone.

Will, G. (2006, January 16). Ed schools vs. education: Prospective teachers are expected to have the correct "disposition," proof of which is espousing "progressive" political beliefs. *Newsweek,* 98.

Wise, A. (2006). A statement from NCATE on professional dispositions. Retrieved on June 4, 2007 from, http://216.139.214.92/public/0616_MessageAWise.asp?ch=150

Wilson. R. (2005, December 16). We don't need that kind of attitude: Education schools want to make sure teachers have the right "disposition." *The Chronicle of Higher Education, 52*(17), A8.

Zeichner, K. (2006). Reflections of a university-based teacher educator on the future of college- and university-based teacher education. *Journal of Teacher Education, 57*(3), 326–340.

42 Preparing White Teachers to Teach in a Racist Nation

What Do They Need to Know and Be Able to Do?

Anna E. Richert, David M. Donahue, and Vicki K. LaBoskey

John: Since becoming a public school teacher two years ago as a White male in my mid-30s, I have been surprised at the degree to which race has been a factor in my relationships with my students (particularly with my African-American students). I had previously worked in different racially mixed settings and I did not perceive much tension with coworkers of different racial backgrounds. Once I entered the classrooms of inner city public schools, however, I quickly felt my White racial background to be an obstacle in developing positive relationships with my African-American students. Early on in my classroom experience, I found my students labeling me racist in response to what I felt was reasonable behavior. Having completed a teacher education program that emphasized personal inquiry, I wanted to explore how my African-American students perceived my behavior as racist.

John is a middle school history teacher in Oakland, California. Most of his students are African American. Though committed to teaching underserved students in an urban setting, John wondered if doing so effectively as a White person was possible. For his master's project he initiated a study that became a two-year journey of self-discovery about his White identity.

* * *

All across this nation, teachers like John are working diligently to do a better job of teaching the African-American, Latino, and other children of color in their classrooms. And yet as a nation we have made little progress in accomplishing that goal. Rather than closing the achievement gap, evidence points to a persistent disparity in achievement between children of color and their White peers (English, 2002; Lee, 2002). The National Assessment of Educational Progress (NAEP) reports, for example, that achievement levels for African-American and Hispanic students in mathematics and reading "are consistently and markedly lower than levels for white students as are high school graduation rates" (Banks et al., 2005, p. 237).

One factor that impacts student achievement and success in school is poverty. Whereas the United States is supposedly the "land of plenty," it is not so for many children, having the highest rate of childhood poverty among Western democratic nations (UNICEF, 2005)—a reality that affects African-American and Hispanic children at alarmingly disproportionate rates (U.S. Census Bureau, 2003).

Poverty creates conditions that are associated with low achievement in school: poor nutrition, inadequate health care, unsafe living conditions, and limited opportunities for out-of-school learning. The "in-school" opportunities for learning for children of poverty are typically not conducive to high achievement either. Schools serving poor communities are more likely to have fewer curricular offerings, lower access to technology and other resources, and greater numbers of underprepared teachers than schools serving more affluent communities (Darling-Hammond, 2004; Oakes & Saunders, 2002; Shields et al., 2001). But poverty alone cannot explain inequities in school success. Independent of socioeconomic status, White children out perform their peers of color on the standardized measures used in classrooms today (Aronson, Fried, & Good, 2002; Singham, 1998; Steele & Aronson, 1995).

Whereas standardized tests are important given their role in determining school opportunities for students, they reflect only one measure of our inability to meet the learning needs of children of color in this country. Dropout, suspension, and expulsion rates for students of color exceed those of White and Asian students (Kaufman, Alt, & Chapman, 2002; Skiba, Michael, Carroll Nardo, & Peterson, 2002; Townsend, 2000; Verdugo, 2002). For students who stay in school, the picture is not much less bleak. Black and brown children are much more likely than their White peers to be taught by underprepared/noncredentialed teachers (Darling-Hammond, 2004); be assigned to special education (Donovan & Cross, 2002); and attend schools that are underresourced in terms of libraries, technology, and other services that would enhance the children's academic preparation and success (Oakes & Saunders, 2002). Additionally, they are less likely to complete high school, whether through a diploma or GED (Kaufman, Alt, & Chapman, 2002) and if they do complete high school and are admitted to college, they are less likely to graduate from there as well (Cross & Slater, 2001). There is no shortage of evidence that our educational system in the United States is not serving well our children of color. The question we must ask ourselves is "why?"

Asa Hilliard (1991) posits will as another factor that obstructs our ability to achieve excellent outcomes for all children. He asks, "Do we truly will to see each and every child in this nation develop to the peak of his or her capacities?" If we do, he argues, "the highest goals that we can imagine are well within reach for those who have the will to excellence" (Hilliard, 1991, p. 22). Given what we know about national priorities and expenditures on education, a lack of will seems a reasonable hypothesis about why schools consistently fail to serve all students well. Kozol (2005) describes apartheid schooling in the United States and notes the segregation of schools by race and the predictable inequality of resources for schools serving African-American and Hispanic students.

While national priorities suggest a lack of concern for teaching all children toward high levels of academic success, we have substantial evidence that will might be less a factor for teachers—at least teachers such as John. A lack of know-how is more likely than a lack of concern. Like many others across this nation, John is determined to build a practice that serves the needs and builds the academic success of the children of color in his classroom. He is looking for knowledge about how to do so and the skills to do it.

This suggests a third factor that contributes to the achievement gap between White children and their peers of color: the race and ethnicity differences between White teachers and their students. In a recent review of research on the demographic profile of U.S. public school teachers, Zumwalt and Craig (2005) report that while the student population in the United States is becoming increasingly diverse, the teaching population remains predominantly White. Drawing on the 2003 findings from the National Center for Educational Statistics (NCES), a branch of the U.S. Department of Education, they report that in 1999 and 2000, 84% of the public school teaching force was White. Of the remaining 16%, "7.8% were African American, 5.7% Hispanic, 1.6% Asian and .8% Native American" (p. 114). Hollins and Guzman (2005) draw on the NCES (2003) data as well and report that "the percentage of all public school students from ethnic minority groups increased dramatically from 22% in 1972 to 39% in 2000" (p. 477). They also report that by the year 2035 students of color will constitute the statistical majority in U.S. public schools (p. 478).

The argument underlying this last factor, which we believe contributes to the disparities in academic achievement between White children and their peers of color, is that White teachers do not adequately understand the experiences, perspectives, and learning needs of children whose racial and ethnic backgrounds are different from their own. Coupled with this is the idea that White privilege blinds teachers to the ways in which schools function to support White students' success while simultaneously discouraging similar success for students of color.

We focus our attention for this literature review on race and its role in teaching all students toward academic success. As teacher educators, we must prepare and support teachers like John who are determined to teach their students to high levels of academic achievement. John is White, most of his students are not, and for teachers like him, race raises challenges as they try to understand their students. For this review, therefore, we looked to see what the literature tells us about preparing teachers to teach students of color. We framed our literature review to answer two questions: What do White teachers who strive for equal and excellent outcomes for every student need to know and be able to do to accomplish their equity goals? How can teacher preparation and professional development better support these teachers to do this important work?

What White Teachers Need to Know to Teach about Race and Racism

Whether out of ignorance, fear, indifference, or the mistaken belief that it is someone else's job, most White teachers do not address race and racism with their students, even though students in school are eager to talk about the subject (Lawrence, 1997; Lewis, 2004; Tatum, 1992a). Teacher educators such as Gay and Howard (2000) and Ladson-Billings (2001), among others, make the case that White teachers can and must learn culturally relevant ways of teaching to students of color, including teaching about race and racism. To do so, they must learn about how race and racism shape the lives of people in the United States (Ladson-Billings, 2000; Leavell, Cowart, & Wilhelm, 1999; Solorzano, 1997).

Understanding Race and Racism

Writing about preparation for teaching African-American students, Ladson-Billings (2000) describes the importance of understanding the pervasiveness of racism in U.S. history, the U.S. racial hierarchy with White and Black at opposite extremes, how everyone is placed along this continuum, and how moving toward Whiteness on that continuum confers privilege.

In addition to history, language plays a key role in learning and being able to teach about racism. Ladson-Billings (2000) speaks about grasping concepts of "equivalent" and "analogous" to avoid the "hierarchy of oppression" where discussions of racism degenerate into contests of who has suffered the most. Solorzano (1997) deconstructs stereotypes about intelligence, personality, and physical appearances used to denigrate people of color, how those stereotypes have been used to justify racist actions, and the connection between stereotypes and language. He writes, "when we think of welfare, crime, drugs, immigrants, and educational problems, we racialize these issues by painting stereotypic portraits of People of Color" (p. 10). To his list, we might add "inner city school," "English learner," or "special ed student." He calls for continually examining the racial stereotypes in the language of popular and professional media.

Understanding Whiteness, Privilege, and One's Own Racial Identity Development

A substantial body of literature (Banks, 2001a; Berlak & Moyenda, 2001; Causey, Thomas, & Armento, 2000; Gay & Howard, 2000; Howard, 1999; Ladson-Billings, 2001; Lawrence, 1997; Valli, 1995) argues that before White teachers can successfully take on the task of teaching about race and racism, indeed before they can even imagine that it is part of their responsibility, they must first understand their own racial identity. When White teachers reflect on their racial identity, they can begin to understand racism as more than personal prejudice, a condition they do not attribute to themselves. When White teachers see themselves as lacking prejudice, they believe racism has nothing to do with them. By contrast, when White teachers see that their Whiteness enmeshes them in experiences and ideology that privilege them, they understand how they participate in perpetuating racism and oppression of people of color. They also begin to understand how non-Whites perceive them (Lawrence, 1997).

Whiteness, like race more generally, is socially constructed and developmental. Helms (1990, 1994) describes a six-stage process of White racial development that includes recognizing and overcoming one's racism as well as building a positive nonracist racial and cultural identity. As with any stage theory, the stages are not entirely linear or exclusive. At the final stage of their development, White teachers internalize a new racial identity, acknowledge personal and institutional racism, and engage with allies—both White and people of color—to undo racism. This final stage represents a continual struggle, not an end point, for White people committed to antiracism. Towards developing this understanding of Whiteness, teacher educators may require future teachers to write and read personal racial autobiographies (Berlak & Moyenda, 2001; Causey et al. 2000; Ladson-Billings, 2000). Such strategies allow teachers to "consciously re-experience their own subjectivity when they recognize similar or different outlooks and experiences" (Ladson-Billings, 1990, p. 26).

Understanding the Identity Development and Experiences of People of Color

At the same time that White teachers must understand their own racial development, they must work with others, including students of color who may be in various places in their own racial development. White teachers must be prepared to incorporate students' racial identity development into judging students' readiness for certain conversations about race and when selecting materials, planning curriculum, and implementing lessons about race and racism (Gay, 1985). They must be ready for the challenges of facilitating classroom dialogue as they manage their own and others' identities (Tatum, 1992b).

Cross (1991) describes a five-stage theory of Black identity development that is analogous for people from other marginalized groups. In the preencounter stage, African Americans, having absorbed negative messages about Blackness in the larger society distance themselves from their own racial identity and minimize the importance of race in daily life. An experience with racism, for example, in school or from law enforcement, leads the individual to encounter a new stage where race takes on relevance in an African-American person's life. The resulting anger from experiencing White racism leads to immersion/emersion. At this stage, African-American persons are committed to exploring the multiple layers of Black history and experience and often dismiss or avoid anything White. The next step, internalization, is characterized by developing a positive, open, less defensive attitude toward Blackness and a willingness to work with others, including Whites. In the final stage, internalization-commitment, African-American persons are secure in their racial identity, engaged in work to support the African-American community, and participate in multicultural efforts against racism.

How do teachers use knowledge about racial identity development to bring race as a subject for learning to their classrooms? Knowledge about racial identity does not provide answers, only the challenge of figuring out what to do with such understanding, how to manage new dilemmas, and how to reframe practice. Valli (1995) suggests that in classrooms where the teacher is White and the students are not, teachers must learn to manage the dilemma of being color blind and color conscious at the same time. Learning to be color blind would seem to fly in the face of frequent admonitions to White teachers that if they don't see color, they don't see the child. In this case, being "color blind" means color "no longer function(s) as a barrier and cease(s) to be a reified, essentialist construct, signifying only hostility and otherness" (Valli, 1992, p. 122). Becoming a color conscious White teacher means understanding students' race and culture. It also means knowing that students view White teachers as racial beings and understanding, in a reversal of previous beliefs for most, that one's White racial identity is not neutral.

Banks (2001a) adds several additional dimensions to understanding identity formation by encouraging teachers and their students to balance cultural, national, and global identifications. In his view, national identification does not take on the assimilationist cast common in classrooms where White teachers do not see color or believe in the inferiority of other races and cultures. "...[I]ndividuals can attain healthy and reflective national identifications only when they have acquired healthy and reflective cultural identifications, and...individuals can develop reflective and positive global identifications only after they have realistic, reflective, and positive national identifications" (Banks, 2001a, p. 9). To accomplish this, teachers need to "challenge the metanarrative" (Banks, 2001a, p. 12) that defines learning in classes that look at U.S. history and culture.

Conversations about experiences of persons of color, both historically and currently, necessarily become part of the school agenda and allow White teachers to see that "students of color are *not* the problem. Race and the historical legacy of racism, and what these issues have meant for our schools and students in the United States, are essentially the problems" (Milner, 2003, p. 176). This conception of learning and teaching about race challenges preexisting notions by the majority of White teacher education students who see teaching students different from themselves as a problem (Vavrus, 1994) that can be solved solely through pedagogy (Bartolome, 1994), not by looking critically at self or others.

Gay and Howard (2000) describe the need for "critical cultural consciousness" which results when White teachers analyze "their own ethnic heritages;...the assumptions and beliefs they hold about other ethnic groups and cultures; and compare their assumptions about cultural diversity with other groups' versions of knowledge, truth, and reality" (pp. 7–8). This self-knowledge can then be translated into practices such as effective communication across racial lines and pedagogical skills for discussing issues of race and racism. It also serves as the first step away from unthinkingly centering Whiteness and marginalizing experiences and knowledge of people of color.

The road to critical cultural consciousness and inquiry into racism is not without stumbling blocks: White teachers' fears about teaching students of color and resistance to addressing race and racism, which can be manifest through silence, diversion, guilt, benevolent liberalism, and neoconservatism (Gay & Howard, 2000; Gay & Kirkland, 2003; King, 1991). Elementary teachers may exhibit fear of teaching students of another race or fear making race and racism part of subject matter because they believe it is not age-appropriate or promotes racial separatism locally and threatens national unity. Secondary teachers, particularly in math and science, may question the relevance of race and racism to their disciplines. Across grades, White teachers fear they do not know enough about other groups and will say something to offend others or perpetuate stereotypes.

Another stumbling block is what King (1991) calls "dysconscious" racism. She warns the problem is not "the *absence* of consciousness...but an *impaired* consciousness or distorted way of thinking about race" that results from "an uncritical habit of mind...that justifies inequity and exploitation by accepting the existing order of things as given" (p. 135). Dysconscious White teachers deplore racism but defend or are blind to White privilege, meaning their reflection must be focused on the ideology and history of oppression so they "re-experience the way dysconscious racism and miseducation victimize them" (p. 143).

Yet another obstacle is White teachers' insistence on a "safe" environment" for talking about racism and oppression. These "'safe places' usually are not clearly defined, but they seem to imply conversations that are devoid of controversy, conflict, confrontation, and contention" (Gay & Howard, 2000, p. 5). By contrast, hooks (1994) maintains that safety precludes critical learning about racism and Freire and Macedo (1995) point out the unexamined White privilege of insisting on preconditions for discussing race.

Creating Positive Learning Environments and Teaching Content

In addition to explicit engagement with issues of race and racism, student teachers need to learn the pedagogical approaches that have resulted in high achievement for students of color, but not in a rote fashion. If new teachers are to employ these strategies appropriately, they must understand their philosophical, theoretical, and empirical justifications. As Dewey (1938) emphasized, educational endeavors need to be guided by a well-articulated "end-in-view." Teachers must have a clear sense of the purposes, aims, and outcomes toward which their work is directed, if they are to make beneficial decisions about the nature of that activity. As Perry (2003) has noted, there are "extra" and particular competencies required of students of color in a racist nation that need to be understood and incorporated into the achievement visions of their teachers and schools. Nieto (1999) has used the phrase "academic success with cultural integrity" (p. 116) to describe the bimodal nature of this conceptualization. On the one hand, these students need to construct *powerful subject matter knowledge*. In addition, they must develop the orientations, often characterized as *positive racial identity development*, that will both allow them to succeed despite existing structural barriers and participate in the elimination of those racist-based impediments.

Powerful subject matter knowledge includes skills and deep understanding, as well as the ability to apply and extend that knowledge in innovative ways. As Ladson-Billings (1994) has noted, "If students are to be equipped to struggle against racism they need excellent skills from the basics of reading, writing, and math, to understanding history, thinking critically, solving problems, and making decisions; they must go beyond merely filling in test sheet bubbles with Number 2 pencils" (pp. 139–140). Such knowledge is best acquired or constructed, according to Delpit (1995), if skills are situated "*within the context of* critical and creative thinking" (p. 19). But powerful subject matter knowledge is only a part of the goal for students of color in a racist nation; it is necessary but not sufficient. They must also learn to question "the structural inequality, the racism, and the injustice that exist in society" (Ladson-Billings, 1994, p. 128) and "acquire the data, skills, and values needed to participate in civic action and social change" (Banks, 2001b, p. 197).

Learning Communities

In order to accomplish these goals, teachers need to be able to construct for their students of color "identity safe" (Steele, 2003) learning communities. According to Steele, identity safety can be created with a "simple relational strategy of using high standards and ability affirmation" (pp. 126–127). Many other scholars support this notion of combining "high expectations with unequivocal support; challenging instruction with personal caring" (Gay, 2006, p. 363). Although there can be many advantages to contexts where the teachers constructing these learning communities are of the same race as the students (Foster, 1997; Lee, 2001; Tatum, 1997), some research has found that White teachers can also be successful (e.g., Haberman, 1995; Steele, 2003). To do so, they need to truly believe that students of color are intelligent and capable and be able to convey that to them, as well as have the appropriate content knowledge and pedagogical skills.

Culturally Relevant Teaching

To create such an antiracist context, teachers must pay "attention to all areas in which some students might be favored over others" (Nieto, 1999, p. 169), which means attending to both the *interpersonal* and the *instructional* aspects of classroom life and the relationship between the two. Indeed there is substantial consensus in the literature on the need to conceptualize the desirable teaching of students of color in a holistic manner. A number of different terms have been used to describe this approach, but the most widely employed label at present is CRT, which stands for either culturally relevant teaching (Ladson-Billings, 1994; Milner, 2006) or culturally responsive teaching (Gay, 2006; Irvine, 2003), often used interchangeably.

According to Ladson-Billings (2001), culturally relevant teaching or pedagogy is "based on three propositions about what contributes to success for all students, especially African American students: Successful teachers focus on students' academic achievement; Successful teachers develop students' cultural competence; and Successful teachers foster students' sense of sociopolitical consciousness" (p. 144). Noteworthy here is that it is defined in terms of aims or outcomes rather than particular programs or strategies. Again, many scholars in this field support the notion that White teachers can learn CRT but since they are less likely to have previous knowledge of the social realities and cultural histories of their students of color, they need particular help in developing those understandings, in addition to the *attitudes* that will support them.

One of the more debated features of this process is related to the content of the cultural/racial information that White student teachers need to acquire. One danger regularly emphasized has to do with over-generalization or stereotyping. To mitigate this problem, Gutiérrez and Rogoff (2003) draw upon cultural-historical theory to advocate for familiarizing prospective teachers with historical "regularities" in various cultural communities, while also developing the expectation that individual students will vary in their involvement in and response to the multiple communities of which they are a part. The intent is to prevent the "pigeonholing" of particular students and instead expand the teachers' pedagogical repertoires so that they will be better equipped to assist children of color in drawing upon both familiar and new approaches to ensure powerful learning (p. 23).

The implications of CRT for the preparation of White teachers who will be teaching students of color is that teacher education programs need to take a holistic approach. Teacher educators must conceptualize the endeavor not as the acquisition of discrete content knowledge or pedagogical skills, but rather as the development of a "principled approach" (Kroll et al., 2005) to teaching that will result in a lifelong engagement in context-specific, inquiry-based practice committed to ensuring powerful learning for all students. Nonetheless, within that overall structure, it is possible to also gain from the literature more specific guidance as to what *classroom management approaches* and *instructional interventions* might best be added to the repertoires from which they will draw.

Interpersonal (Classroom Management)

The literature is consistent in acknowledging the close interconnection between the interpersonal and the instructional aspects of teaching. All those who wrote reviews of the literature related to successful classroom management for urban students, poor students, and students of color for the *Handbook of Classroom Management* (2006) emphasized this point: Critical theorists support "the constructivist philosophy that students learn best when actively engaged in meaningful, interesting, and important work. An authentic (relevant and engaging) curriculum is central to diminishing the need for behavior control strategies" (Brantlinger & Danforth, 2006, p. 168; see also, Gay, 2006; Milner, 2006). At the same time, however, these scholars and others in the field agree that the quality and nature of interpersonal interactions between teachers and students need specific attention. Research like that done by Ferguson (2001), Obidah and Teel (2001), and Lewis (2005) help us to understand why. Lewis makes clear that even the day-to-day, moment-to-moment interchanges can have a powerful influence on the development, or not, of a student's positive racial identity.

The main implications for the education of White teachers are, first and foremost, for them to develop a critical cultural consciousness. Second, they must become more familiar with "the cultural values, orientations, and experiences" (Gay, 2006, p. 343) of their students of color, because "Cultural differences in discourse, performance, and self-disclosure styles are among the most problematic impediments to effective instruction and management in culturally diverse classrooms" (p. 354).

Most of the recommendations with regard to positive classroom management in racially diverse classrooms are situated in the notion of community—in the classroom, in the school, and beyond. If students feel themselves to be a valued part of a caring, democratic community where they share responsibility for its successful functioning, and where competition and hierarchies are minimized, they will be more likely to commit to a positive involvement in that domain. In addition, they will be more inclined to help keep their fellow students constructively engaged as well. This notion of placing community at the center of classroom interactions is also quite relevant to recommended instructional processes.

Instructional Processes

As a result of her research into successful teachers of Native Alaskan students, Delpit (1995) concludes that what we need to bring to schools where we are teaching "other people's children" are "experiences that are so full of the wonder of life, so full of connectedness, so embedded in the context of our communities, so brilliant in the insights that we develop and the analyses that we devise, that all of us, teachers and students alike, can learn to live lives that leave us truly satisfied" (p. 104).

Pedagogy

Highlighted here is the need to employ instructional strategies that foster active, indeed joyful, engagement with people, as well as with relevant materials and ideas. Groupwork, designed in ways that will minimize the potentially racist social phenomenon of "status generalization" (Cohen, 1994), has been found by many to be particularly successful in that regard (e.g., Au & Kawakami, 1985; Lotan, 2006).

Also implied in Delpit's statement is the need to "begin where the students are" (Nieto, 1999), utilizing existing strengths as both the basis and means for further knowledge development and interrogation. White student teachers should thus become familiar with any research regarding noteworthy cultural regularities, always accompanied, of course, by the aforementioned caveats regarding individual variation. Even more importantly, White student teachers must be equipped with strategies for getting to know the cultural competencies of their particular students and their communities if they are to act as the "sociocultural mediators" they need to be; teachers who can "bridge between students' differences and the culture of the dominant society" (Nieto, 1999, p. 115).

What is particularly apparent in this literature is the recognition that White teachers will only be able to do this if they have at their disposal as many different instructional strategies as possible, as well as the ability and freedom to select and adapt them appropriately: "Competent teachers know how to employ multiple representations of knowledge that use students' everyday lived experiences to motivate and assist them in connecting new knowledge to home, community, and global settings" (Irvine, 2003, p. 46). The implication for teacher education is to provide candidates with both the abilities and the willingness to utilize a wide range of teaching strategies, including those sometimes seen to be in opposition to one another, like the whole-language versus basal-text techniques for early literacy education (Ladson-Billings, 1994). They must also become knowledgeable about how to determine which of these to use when and for whom, decisions that need to be influenced by the needs and interests of their students and families, as well as by the ongoing assessment and analysis of student learning. The form such assessment takes, according to the same authors, also needs to vary, in relation to the learners, the context, and the subject matter knowledge under construction—something else they need to learn to do.

Content

The virtually universal proposal for teaching students of color in a racist nation is for the expansion and sophistication of the curriculum in a number of important ways. First regards the inclusion of multicultural experiences, interpretations, and contributions via the literature students read (e.g., Gay, 2006; Lee, 2001) and the histories they study (e.g., Brantlinger & Danforth, 2006; Sleeter & Grant, 2003). Some essential qualifiers that accompany this admonition include the avoidance of what Banks (2001b) has referred to as the "heroes and holidays" approach. Instead, he and others propose a focus on the "*life-chances* [of various cultural groups] rather than on their *life-styles*" (p. 233). Furthermore, it would happen on a regular basis with all curricular topics, not just during Black History month or only with the subject matters of reading, English, and social studies, which is related to a second frequently supported means for transforming the curriculum.

Kumashiro (2001, 2002) asserts that antioppressive education "involves constantly *looking beyond* what it is we teach and learn" (p. 6). By this he means that while students are learning new knowledge they should simultaneously be engaged in critiquing that knowledge, since all, including science and mathematics, has been deeply influenced by the political and social context in which it was formulated. In doing so, they can also develop the understanding that they too can participate in the knowledge-generation process. The implication for teacher education is that candidates need to "be given the opportunity to construct concepts, generalizations, and theories so that they can develop an understanding of the nature and limitations of knowledge" (Banks, 2001b, p. 212), which represents a very particular way in which White student teachers can become the "pedagogical-content specialists" they need to be for students of color (Irvine, 2003).

A third suggestion for the expansion of the curriculum has to do with Delpit's (1995) notion of the "culture of power" or the codes or rules for participating in power, which "relate to linguistic forms, communicative strategies, and presentation of self; that is, ways of talking, ways of writing, ways of dressing, and ways of interacting" determined by those currently in power (p. 25). She argues that children of color need to be taught these codes if they are going to be able "to participate fully in the mainstream of American life" (p. 45). At the same time, however, they must be helped to understand the arbitrariness of those codes, thus demonstrating that the codes they already possess are just as valuable; but given the current power realities in the United States, they need to know both, which is relevant to a fourth curricular endorsement.

Students of color need to develop a sociopolitical consciousness that will enable and encourage them to participate in the transformation of society in ways more consistent with the ideals of democracy and social justice. In addition to the previously described curricular revisions, they must be provided with the tools for political engagement, best accomplished by providing students with "opportunities to practice democracy and decision making" (Sleeter & Grant, 2003) and with engagements in "dangerous discourses" (Nieto, 1999, p. 120) where issues of race and racism in society and in the curriculum are made explicit and critiqued.

Concluding Thoughts

So, where does this leave us when it comes to preparing White teachers to teach children of color? We find ourselves cautiously hopeful. Every day in our work we encounter many new and veteran teachers like John—with whom we began—who clearly demonstrate determination to become excellent teachers of all children. They give us hope. We also realize there is much we can do to help prepare and support these teachers as they do their important work. Whereas there is considerable evidence that supports Hilliard's contention that as a nation we lack the will to serve all children well—and we can see that there is much work to be done to address what Ladson-Billings (2006) calls the "education debt"—we feel we have school-based colleagues who have the will and commitment to do the work and make the changes we have described here. In addition, there is a substantial knowledge base that can inform the teacher preparation curriculum and agenda in this country. We can—and we must—draw on this knowledge base and incorporate into teacher preparation and teacher support ideas and strategies that will help teachers bring their African American and other students of color to high levels of academic success.

We are clear from our review of the literature that this process must begin with significant "race work" designed to help both White teachers and teacher educators understand and embrace their White identity and acknowledge their White privilege. Until teachers and teacher educators grapple honestly with the reality of race, racism, and racial politics in the United States—and own their role in perpetuating systems of oppression—we will not be able to dismantle these systems and create others that will lead students of color to experience more success in school. John can be a model for us in this way. He openly and honestly acknowledged what he did not know about teaching African-American students and owned his role in their lack of engagement and success in his class. He began by struggling with how to account for the role of race in his ability or inability to do his job. His journey directed him to rethink where race fits into the professional he was able to be, and the one he wanted to become.

Essential to a holistic orientation to teaching students of color in a racist nation is the need to attend to the overall school–district context and not just the behaviors and beliefs of particular teachers in individual classrooms. Many emphasize—and we agree—that systemic transformation is essential. We recognize that we must not overrely on the will and skill of what Haberman (1992) has referred to as "star" teachers. At the same time, we know that at the heart of what matters to children and their potential success in schools, are the teachers with whom they work every day. We have learned from this review that there is much we can do in teacher education to prepare and support White teachers—and White teacher educators—to work successfully within these transforming contexts. Our role as teacher educators is a necessary but not sufficient component of the larger change we are arguing for here. Teacher educators must help their students and themselves to understand how race and racism function to diminish the learning opportunities and academic attainment of children whose skin is black or brown. Only then will we have a real chance of "leaving no child behind."

References

Aronson, J., Fried, C., & Good, C. (2002). Reducing the effects of sterotype threats on African American college students by shaping theories of intelligence. *Journal of Experimental Social Psychology, 38*, 113–125.

Au, K., & Kawakami, A. (1985). Research currents: Talk story and learning to read. *Language Arts, 62*(4), 406–411.

Banks, J. (2001a). Citizenship education and diversity: Implications for teacher education. *Journal of Teacher Education, 52*(1), 5–16.

Banks, J. (2001b). *Cultural diversity and education: Foundations, curriculum, and teaching* (4th ed.). Boston: Allyn & Bacon.

Banks, J., Cochran-Smith, M., Moll, L., Richert, A. E., Zeichner, K, LePage, P., et al. (2005). Teaching diverse learners. In L. Darling Hammond & J. Bransford (Eds.), *Preparing teachers for a changing world* (pp. 232–274). San Francisco: Jossey-Bass.

Bartolome, L. (1994). Beyond the methods fetish: Towards a humanizing pedagogy. *Harvard Educational Review, 64*(2), 173–194.

Berlak, A., & Moyenda, S. (2001). *Taking it personally: Racism in the classroom from kindergarten to college.* Philadelphia: Temple University Press.

Branlinger, E., & Danforth, S. (2006). Critical theory perspectives on social class, race, gender, and classroom management. In C. M. Evertson & C. S. Weinstein (Eds.), *Handbook of classroom management: Research, practice, and contemporary issues* (pp. 157–180). Mahwah, NJ: Erlbaum.

Causey, V., Thomas, C., & Armento, B. (2000). Cultural diversity is basically a foreign term to me: The challenges of diversity for preservice teacher education. *Teaching and Teacher Education, 16*, 33–45.

Cohen, E. (1994). *Designing groupwork: Strategies for heterogeneous classrooms.* New York: Teachers College Press.

Cross, T., & Slater, R. (2001). The troublesome decline in African-American college student graduation rates. *The Journal of Blacks in Higher Education, 33*, 102–109.

Cross, W. (1991). *Shades of black: Diversity in African-American identity.* Philadelphia: Temple University Press.

Darling Hammond, L. (2004). What happens to a dream deferred? The continuing quest for equal educational opportunity. In J. A. Banks & C. A. M. Banks (Eds.), *Handbook of research on multi-cultural education* (2nd ed., pp. 607–630). San Francisco: Jossey-Bass.

Delpit, L. (1995). *Other people's children: Cultural conflict in the classroom.* New York: New Press.

Dewey, J. (1938). *Experience and education.* New York: Macmillan.

Donovan, S., & Cross, C. (2002). *Minority students in special and gifted education.* Washington, D.C.: National Academies Press.

English, F. (2002). On the intractability of the achievement gap in urban schools and the discursive practice of continuing racial discrimination. *Education and Urban Society, 34*(3), 298–311.

Ferguson, A. (2001). *Bad boys: Public schools in the making of black masculinity.* Ann Arbor: University of Michigan Press.

Foster, M. (1997). *Black teachers on teaching.* New York: New Press.

Freire, P., & Macedo, D. (1995). A dialogue: Culture, language, and race. *Harvard Educational Review, 65*(3), 377–402.

Gay, G. (1985). Implications of selected models of ethnic identity development for educators. *The Journal of Negro Education, 54*(1), 43–55.

Gay, G. (2006). Connections between classroom management and culturally responsive teaching. In C. M. Evertson & C. S. Weinstein (Eds.), *Handbook of classroom management: Research, practice, and contemporary issues* (pp. 343–370). Mahwah, NJ: Erlbaum.

Gay, G., & Howard, T. (2000). Multicultural teacher education for the 21st century. *Teacher Educator, 36*(1), 1–16.

Gay, G., & Kirkland, K. (2003). Developing cultural critical consciousness and self-reflection in preservice teacher education. *Theory into Practice, 42*(3), 181–187.

Gutierrez, K., & Rogoff, B. (2003). Cultural ways of learning: Individual traits or repertoire of practice. *Educational Researcher, 32*(5), 19–25.

Haberman, M. (1995). Selecting "star" teachers for children and youth in urban poverty. *Phi Delta Kappan, 76*(10), 777–781.

Helms, J. (Ed.). (1990). *Black and white racial identity: Theory, research, and practice.* Westport, CT: Greenwood.

Helms, J. (1994). Racial identity and "racial" constructs. In E. Trickett, R. Watts, & D. Birman (Eds.), *Human diversity* (pp. 285–311). San Francisco: Jossey-Bass.

Hilliard, A. (1991, September). Do we have the *will* to educate all children? *Educational Leadership, 49*(1), 31–36.

Hollins, E., & Guzman, M. T. (2005). Research on preparing teachers for diverse populations. In M. Cochran-Smith & K. M. Zeichner (Eds.), *Studying teacher education* (pp. 477–548). Mahwah, NJ: Erlbaum.

hooks, b. (1994). *Teaching to transgress: Education as the practice of freedom.* New York: Routledge.

Howard, G. (1999). *We can't teach what we don't know: White teachers, multiracial schools.* New York: Teachers College Press.

Irvine, J. (2003). *Educating teachers for diversity: Seeing with a cultural eye.* New York: Teachers College Press.

Kaufman, P., Alt, M., & Chapman, C. (2002). Dropout rates in the United States: 2000. *Education Statistics Quarterly, 3*(4). Retrieved April 16, 2007, from http://nces.ed.gov/programs/quarterly/Vol_3/3_4/q3-3.asp

King, J. (1991). Dysconscious racism: Ideology, identity, and the miseducation of teachers. *The Journal of Negro Education, 60*, 133–146.

Kozol, J. (2005). *The shame of the nation: The restoration of apartheid schooling in America.* New York: Three Rivers Press.

Kroll, L., Cossey, R., Donahue, D., Galguera, T., LaBoskey, V., Richert, A., et al. (2005). *Teaching as principled practice: Managing complexity for social justice.* Thousand Oaks, CA: Sage.

Kumashiro, K. (2001). "Posts" perspectives on anti-oppressive education in social studies, English, mathematics, and science classrooms. *Educational Researcher, 30*(3), 3–12.

Kumashiro, K. (2002). Against repetition: Addressing resistance to anti-oppressive change in the practices of learning, teaching, supervising, and researching. *Harvard Educational Review, 72*(1), 67–92.

Ladson-Billings, G. (1994). *The dreamkeepers: Successful teachers of African American children.* San Francisco: Jossey-Bass.

Ladson-Billings, G. (2000). Fighting for our lives: Preparing teachers to teach African American students. *Journal of Teacher Education, 51*(3), 206–214.

Ladson-Billings, G. (2001). *Crossing over to Canaan: The journey of new teachers in diverse classrooms.* San Francisco: Jossey-Bass.

Ladson-Billings, G. (2006). From the achievement gap to the education debt: Understanding achievement in U.S. schools. *Educational Researcher, 35*(7), 3–12.

Lawrence, S. (1997). Beyond race awareness: White racial identity and multicultural teaching. *Journal of Teacher Education, 48*(2), 108–117.

Leavell, A., Cowart, M., & Wilhelm, R. (1999). Strategies for preparing culturally responsive teachers. *Equity and Excellence in Education, 32*(1), 64–71.

Lee, C. (2001). Is October Brown Chinese? A cultural modeling activity system for underachieving students. *American Educational Research Journal, 38*(1), 97–141.

Lee, J. (2002). Racial and ethnic achievement gap trends: Reversing the progress toward equity? *Educational Researcher, 31*(1), 3–12.

Lewis, A. (2004). *Race in the schoolyard: Negotiating the color line in classrooms and communities.* New Brunswick, NJ: Rutgers University Press.

Lotan, R. (2006). Managing groupwork in the heterogeneous classroom. In C. M. Evertson & C. S. Weinstein (Eds.), *Handbook of classroom management: Research, practice, and contemporary issues* (pp. 525–539). Mahwah, NJ: Erlbaum.

Milner, H. (2003). Teacher reflection and race in cultural contexts: History, meanings, and methods in teaching. *Theory into Practice, 42*(3), 173–180.

Milner, H. R. (2006). Classroom management in urban classrooms. In C. M. Evertson & C. S. Weinstein (Eds.), *Handbook of classroom management: Research practice and contemporary issues* (pp. 491–522). Mahwah, NJ: Erlbaum.

Nieto, S. (1999). Who does the accommodating? Institutional transformation to promote learning. In *The light in their eyes: Creating multicultural learning communities* (pp. 72–102). New York: Teachers College Press.

Oakes, J., & Saunders, M. (2002). *Access to textbooks, instructional materials, equipment, and technology: Inadequacy and inequality in California's public schools.* Los Angeles: University of California at Los Angeles.

Obidah, J. E., & Teel, K. M. (2001). *Because of the kids: Facing racial and cultural differences in school.* New York: Teachers College Press.

Perry, T. (2003). Up from the parched earth: Toward a theory of African-American achievement. In T. Perry, C. Steele, & A. G. Hilliard III (Eds.), *Young, gifted and black: Promoting high achievement among African American students* (pp. 1–108). Boston: Beacon Press.

Shields, P., Humphrey, D., Weschler, M., Riel, L., Tiffany-Morales, J., Woodworth, K., et al. (2001). *The status of the teaching profession, 2001.* Santa Cruz, CA: The Center for the Future of Teaching and Learning.

Singham, M. (1998). The canary in the mine: The achievement gap between Black and White students. *Phi Delta Kappan, 80*(1), 8–15.

Skiba, R., Michael, R., Carroll Nardo, A., & Peterson, R. (2002). The color of discipline: Sources of racial and gender disproportionality in school punishment. *The Urban Review, 34*(4), 317–342.

Sleeter, C., & Grant, C. (2003). *Making choices for multicultural education: Five approaches to race, class, and gender* (4th ed.). Hoboken, NJ: Wiley.

Solorzano, D. (1997). Images and words that wound: Critical race theory, racial stereotyping, and teacher education. *Teacher Education Quarterly, 24*(3), 5–19.

Steele, C. (2003). Stereotype threat and African-American student achievement. In T. Perry, C. Steele, & A. G. Hilliard III (Eds.), *Young, gifted and black: Promoting high achievement among African American students* (pp. 109–130). Boston: Beacon Press.

Steele, C., & Aronson J. (1995). Stereotype threat and the intellectual test performance of African Americans. *Journal of Personality and Social Psychology, 69,* 797–811.

Tatum, B. (1992a). African-American identity, academic achievement and missing history. *Social Education, 56*(6), 331–334.

Tatum, B. (1992b). Talking about race, learning about racism: The application of racial identity theory in the classroom. *Harvard Educational Review, 62*(1), 321–348.

Tatum, B. (1997). *Why are all the Black kids sitting together in the cafeteria?* New York: Basic Books.

Townsend, B. (2000). The disproportionate discipline of African American learners: Reducing school suspensions and expulsions. *Exceptional Children, 66*(3), 381–391.

UNICEF. (2005). *Child poverty in rich countries 2005: Report card no. 6.* Florence, Italy: UNICEF Innocenti Research Centre.

U.S. Census Bureau. (2003). *Poverty in the United States, 2002.* Retrieved April 15, 2007, from www.census.gov/prod/2003pubs/p60-222.pdf

Valli, L. (1995). The dilemma of race: Learning to be color blind and color conscious. *Journal of Teacher Education, 46*(2), 120–129.

Vavrus, M. (1994). A critical analysis of multicultural education infusion during student teaching. *Action in Teacher Education, 16*(3), 45–57.

Verdugo, R. (2002). Race-ethnicity, social class, and zero-tolerance policies. *Education and Urban Society, 35*(1), 50–75.

Zumwalt, K., & Craig, E. (2005). Teachers' characteristics: Research on the demographic profile. In M. Cochran-Smith & K. M. Zeichner (Eds.), *Studying teacher education* (pp. 111–156). Mahwah, NJ: Erlbaum.

Bottom-Up Struggle
for Social Justice
Where Are the Teachers?

Carl A. Grant

Off the top on my head, every major struggle for social justice I can identify was initiated and maintained by the ordinary people, often people living on the margins of mainstream society. The impetus for social justice does not initially come from the top-down efforts of established institutions or individuals who are at the highest levels of the power pyramid. It comes about because some individual decides to rock the boat and stand-up for equity and equality. Socrates, Martin Luther, Mahatma Gandhi, Mother Jones, Sojourner Truth, W.E.B. DuBois, Jane Addams, Anna Julie Cooper, Martin Luther King, Jr., Paulo Freire, and Cesar Chavez were all boat rockers. These women and men refused to be compliant within their geographical and political context. They stood up and spoke truth to power and took action to bring about social equality.

Teachers (and here I am including teacher educators), with a few exceptions, do not seem fully engaged in an active struggle for social justice. In addition, the future is not very hopeful, because too many teacher candidates who claim they want to teach because they "love kids" seem to have in their mind a certain kind of student, rather than a classroom filled with a diverse group of students. Furthermore, they too often run away from teaching in two or three years if they are assigned to an urban school or a school where the students are unlike them or are burdened by problems and challenges not of their making. Similarly, those who take positions as teacher educators at the college level seem so concerned about doing the promotion and tenure dance—and consequently adhering to the status quo—that attention to social justice becomes secondary.

Of course teaching is very hard work, and perhaps too much is being asked of teachers when we argue that they should be soldiers for social justice. Or perhaps we should do a better job of selecting teacher candidates and teacher educators, including informing them about the social problems and issues that are endemic to most school settings, particularly in urban areas. Additionally, teacher candidates should be encouraged to do a better job of researching who they will probably be teaching and where they will most likely teach once they are licensed.

I know that social justice problems and issues such as distributive and material inequality and equity, as well as the absence of fairness in cultural recognition in urban schools, are not caused by teachers alone; nor can they be resolved by teachers alone. Nevertheless, I see too few teachers and teacher educators—and here I am speaking of both teachers of color and White teachers—demanding social justice for their students. Count the number of teachers at your school or who are a part of your faculty who actively stand up for the social justice their students need. I am not talking about "fairness" or equity, when, for example, the fight is for the students to have a spring dance, or a change in the cafeteria menu at the high school level. Nor am I talking about the "fairness" or equity issues that may arise at the college level with regard to, for instance, bringing a controversial speaker to campus. Yes, that is fighting for the students, but that fight has only a little to do with the students' future life opportunities.

Teachers, I believe are a key, but muted voice in the struggle for social justice in schools. Here, I am reminded of an event in 1963. It was during the height of the Intercultural Movement and the ascendance of the Civil Rights Movement when the curriculum and pedagogy of those movements included a call for public intellectuals, poets, novelists, and others to speak to teachers about the impact of racism and poverty in urban and rural areas and how these characteristics of social inequality affected the students who lived in those depressed areas. Both of these movements understood the major role teachers play in bringing about the successful education of African Americans and children from low income families.

James Baldwin was a major figure in these movements and was invited to tell his story—about the challenges he faced growing up and being a Negro in the United States—to a group of teachers. His talk, originally titled "The Negro Child—His Self-Image," and now commonly referred to as "A Talk to the Teachers"—was delivered to approximately 200 teachers in New York City. Subsequently, it was published in the *Saturday Review* in 1963 and republished in several anthologies. Since that time, his speech has been read by countless numbers of people.

In his talk, Baldwin challenged teachers at a personal level to become what are now referred to as workers for social justice. He spoke adamantly about their responsibility in the struggle for social justice. He did not mince any words and did not to let teachers off the hook regarding their responsibility to students. During the talk, Baldwin issued the following challenges to his audience:

> It is your responsibility to change society if you think of yourself as an educated person.... Now if I were a teacher in this school, or any Negro school, and I was dealing with Negro children, who were in my care only a few hours of every day and then would return to their homes and to the streets, children who have an apprehension of their future which with every hour grows grimmer and darker. I would try to teach them. I would try to make them know—that those streets, those houses, those dangers those agonies by which they are surrounded, are criminal.
>
> I would try to make each child know that these things are the results of a criminal conspiracy to destroy him. I would teach him that if he intends to get to be a man, he must at once decide that he is stronger than this conspiracy and that he must never make his peace with it. (1963/1985, p. 331)

Baldwin goes on to make several other excellent points, but my argument here is that he, too, saw teachers as a critical mass in the fight for social justice. Gandhi reminds us to be "the change we wish to see," and at this time I am concerned about the nature of the change teachers and teacher educators wish to see. If they don't want to see changes, or are slow to engage in the struggle to achieve the change for social justice, then the hope for social justice in schools and teacher education programs is bleak.

References

Baldwin, J. (1985). A talk to teachers. In *The price of the ticket: Collected nonfiction 1948–1985* (pp. 325–332). New York: St. Martin's Press. (Original work published 1963)

Part 9

Classrooms, Pedagogy, and Practicing Justice

Edited and Introduced by Rick Ayers

> Struggle is par for the course when our dreams go into action. But unless we have the space to imagine and a vision of what it means fully to realize our humanity, all the protests and demonstrations in the world won't bring about our liberation.
>
> (Kelley, 2003, p. 198)

> The classroom, with all its limitations, remains a location of possibility. In that field of possibility we have the opportunity to labor for freedom, to demand of ourselves and our comrades an openness of mind and heart that allows us to face reality even as we collectively imagine ways to move beyond boundaries, to transgress. This is education as the practice of freedom.
>
> (hooks, 1994, p. 207)

In this section we present classroom stories. Created by teachers and students together, these social justice education projects fit equally well in history courses as in math, English, science, or art. They are powerful experiences in high school, middle school, and elementary school. Sometimes they are part of officially sanctioned curriculum, in small schools with powerful social justice themes; sometimes they are subversive projects, lurking in the margins of impersonal, bureaucratic schools. Always they challenge and inspire us all, pushing beyond what the teacher initially had in mind, creating ripples beyond the lesson to the whole classroom community, beyond the classroom community to the whole school, and beyond the school to the larger society.

Powerful social justice education is found all over the country and the world—sometimes led by inspired teachers, other times initiated by students, parents, and other community members. We all know what it feels like when it is working, but we have not been able to put our fingers on exactly the elements that go into a powerful social justice curriculum.

Here are a few things it is not: First, social justice curriculum does not mean dogma, it does not mean cramming the teacher's opinions into the students. We all know teachers who do this. But they undermine their own goals and function as ineffective organizers. Students must be respected as thinking beings and they must be given opportunities to examine their own identities and the world they live in. Students should learn to entertain multiple points of view and to exercise critical thinking in making a difference in the world. Working with students with a social justice perspective demands that we understand that each person is an entire universe, each can develop as a full and autonomous person engaged with others in a fair and just community.

Second, social justice education does not mean academicizing the project of critical theory and social justice. While critical studies propose to empower the marginalized in the discourse and to shine a light on the real world from the perspective of the former

657

"other," a new round of curriculum books propose critical studies as a "new AP," another performance required of rich white kids to get by in high school and college. In such a teaching atmosphere, the students may go along, reluctantly, because after all they can do whatever they are told. But it is a weak bow to the real work of critical (and social justice) approaches—it misses the main insight, the centrality of the point of view of the marginalized. For this frozen version of critical studies, social justice is just a conversation, just another intellectual performance.

Social justice education must have meaning for the student population. It engenders transformative insights by everyone in our classrooms, from those born to traditional privileges to those who are marked as outsiders. And, most importantly, social justice education must be enacted through transformative action in the classroom, the school, and the wider community. This does not mean that the direction of every social justice education project is action. The key is that students learn to critically examine their world, to read their world, and then to take such action as they understand is needed.

We look to some of the outposts of consistent reflection and agitation for social justice education, such as *Rethinking Schools*, which puts out a teaching journal, books, and website. In their introduction to the collection *Rethinking the Classroom*, Linda Christensen and Stan Karp (2003) maintain that "schools and classrooms should be laboratories for a more just society than the one we now live in.... Accordingly, to be truly successful, school reform must be guided by democratic social goals and values that provide a deeper context for more traditional academic objectives" (p. i)

They argue that a social justice classroom should demonstrate a curriculum and classroom practice that is

- Grounded in the lives of our students;
- Critical in its approach to the world and itself;
- Multicultural, antibias, projustice;
- Participatory and experiential;
- Hopeful, joyful, kind, visionary;
- Activist;
- Academically engaging and challenging;
- Culturally competent.

Finally, a social justice classroom demands that the teacher challenge received wisdom about what students can learn as well as the ritual of assessment and evaluating students. Our schools have an abysmal record in teaching students to read, write, and think. But unless schools are "animated by broad visions of equity, democracy, and social justice, they will never be able to realize the widely proclaimed goal of raising educational achievement for all children" (Christensen & Karp, 2003, p. 1). A social justice classroom examines and undermines the achievement gap and celebrates powerful engagement and success for all students.

You will see in these stories a bit of all these elements. This does not mean that every classroom is so transformed, every week. Teachers are faced with frustrations, setbacks, and the deadening routines of the institution as well as the passive habits acquired by students over the years in such institutions. But a social justice classroom always teems with possibilities, always seeks out relevance, deeper meaning, and connections. Where most schools are focused on sorting students and on building an ethic of me-first competition, a social justice classroom sees students start to make their educational work part of their project in life, part of what they care about. And this is the kind of work we see blossoming everywhere.

References

Christensen, L., & Karp, S. (2003). *Rethinking the classroom*. Milwaukee, WI: Rethinking Schools Press.

hooks, b. (1994). *Teaching to transgress: Education as the practice of freedom*. New York: Routledge.

Kelley, R. D. G. (2003). *Freedom dreams: The Black radical imagination*. Boston: Beacon Press,

43 Playing in the Light

Experiential Learning and White Identity Development

Gretchen Brion-Meisels

> You never really understand a person until you consider things from his point of view.... Until you climb inside of his skin and walk around in it. (Harper Lee, 1960)

In September, I ask my eighth graders to explain what it means to be a student of their race at our diverse middle school. We barely know each other, and this is a complicated introduction to the study of American history. It is a complication I welcome.

My African-American students tend to answer this question with a real sense of clarity. Many of them talk about being proud of their ancestors; others speak of racism that continues to exist today. A former student, reflecting on popularity, explained:

> ...Here are some Black girl rules. (1) Have each other's back. (2) Never back down from a fight. (3) Don't show off in front of your friends. (4) If new people come around, don't change your attitude or do too much.... (11) Be real. Don't talk about your friends behind their back.... Most of the time if you decide that you want to be in a Black girl clique, you have to go by these rules. Trying to join a Black girl clique can sometimes be hard and have a lot of problems.

In sharp contrast, my White students often struggle to answer the question. Their answers are generally more vague and rarely racialized. This year, one writes simply: "It's fine, normal.... We don't much talk about race."
Another reflects:

> I was born and raised in the South.... I have been made fun of a little bit because I am from there. People [think] just because I'm from the South that I'm a cowboy or redneck.... Although I am of European descent, I do not feel connected to the culture.

Young White students rarely consider explicitly the experience of being White. Although issues of identity are equally important to them, the tendency is to focus on other social markers such as gender, geography, or personal style. Most White students interpret their experiences as completely outside the realm of race. In our society, Whiteness is defined largely by what it is not; to be White is to be "normal." Because Whiteness is not talked about explicitly, we are encouraged to pretend it does not exist.

These student writings testify to the ways in which public institutions make Whiteness invisible. While all of the students are engaging in the same curriculum and lunch period, their interpretation of the importance of race is drastically different. As a White educator, I can choose to ignore this difference in experience, allowing Whiteness to remain invisible at our school. Or, I can try to position myself as an ally to African-American students and colleagues for whom issues of race cannot be ignored. What do my African-American students need from me, their White teacher? How can I validate their experiences, and at the same time provide my White students with a safe space to explore their own racial identity? How do I open up conversations about race so that the students in my class can challenge their own assumptions and create new possibilities in their own identities?

Many educators today counter racism in their classrooms by preventing the symptoms (slurs, slang, put-downs, and segregation, to name a few), but this act does not transform students' understanding of race. Often, White students learn to avoid common manifestations of racism without challenging the assumptions that underlie them; similarly, African-Americans students internalize negative messages about their academic potential without questioning the fallacy of them. A symptomatic approach to antiracism is dangerous because it creates a world where White people know to hide their stereotypes but never think to question them. Of course, this latent racism is even more dangerous for African-American students. These young people are doubly oppressed by the inability of schools to meet their needs (as evidenced in the achievement gap) and the propagation of a political climate where test scores are used to judge academic potential.

In order to unpack the assumptions that underlie racism in schools, students must be given an opportunity to see the historical progression of institutionalized racism. For White students, this means learning to acknowledge the existence of Whiteness, and its link to privilege in our society. Because acknowledging Whiteness as privilege can lead to feelings of guilt and immobility, it is helpful to provide White students with alternative models of Whiteness. Exploring examples of White antiracism is one way to help students discover the possibility of alternative and complex identities. This article will attempt to provide one method of engaging White students in thinking about their own racial identity development. In doing so, it will inevitably be a reflection of my own racial identity as a White, female teacher in a diverse classroom.

* * *

To racial identity development theorists, the writings of my students would be far from surprising (Fine, Weis, Powell, & Wong, 1997; Tatum, 1997). Most African-American students at our diverse middle school are in what psychologist William Cross refers to as the *encounter* stage of Black racial identity development (Cross. 1991). After years of encountering images of Blackness from both White and non-White communities, these students are integrating racialized experiences into their own sense of self. In our "liberal" school culture, young African-American students experience countless events that encourage, if not force, them to understand the effect of racism on their identity. Many of these students have grappled consciously with conflicting images of what it means to be Black in our society.

Interestingly, the same diverse school culture has not effected a change in the racial identity development of many White students. In her work, Janet Helms highlights six statuses of racial identity development among White students: *contact, disintegration, reintegration, pseudo-independent, immersion/emersion* and *autonomy* (Helms, 1990). Helm's model takes into account the differing experiences of students whose race is *invisible* in American institutions. Briefly summarized, these stages range from essential colorblindness—or an inability to identify the impact of race in our personal lives—to the discovery of a positive White identity. In September, White students in my class appear to be in the *contact* stage of Helm's model. They interact in a racialized world—they even identify the effect of race and racism on others—but they have yet to acknowledge the importance of race in their own identities.

* * *

By October, our class is finishing its first history unit about the meeting of three worlds. I have randomly assigned the students to research one racial group in early America: Africans, Europeans, or American Indians. We've watched a few videos, looked at primary sources, and read secondary texts. The students have worked in small "race-similar" groups to research the experiences of their assigned race. It is an overambitious unit, really. One in which there is too much information crammed into too little time. In an institution of standards and testing that assumes eighth graders will remember what they learned at age 9, this is our way of reviewing *America's Roots*. The role of race in this unit is particularly complicated; it is in this period of history that the laws change and "African" becomes synonymous with "slave."

As the activity progresses, I notice an interesting phenomenon. There is an increasing pride among the African expert group. As they read about the horrors and struggles of slavery, they become progressively more attached to each other. I hear them talk about acts of resistance with honor. They are focused, sincere, and inquisitive. Of course, the students in this group are not all African American; there are Latinos, Asians, and a number of White students. It is with great sincerity that a White student yells, "Black power!" across the room.

I watch these moments play out from an observational standpoint. As a young White woman myself, I am still struggling through my own stages of racial identity development. Seeing students "play" Black power does not seem upsetting at first; I forget about how much this has to do with the commercialization of Blackness, and revel in a moment of interracial, racial pride.

The exercise ends with students presenting their own material to experts from other groups. The students, working in new groups, are supposed to share out the information from their expert group, allowing everyone to learn about each identity. It's a jigsaw activity, intended to teach kids about sharing information cooperatively. It is not intended to be a role-play. So, when a student politely pokes me, and whispers, "Ms. Brion, Jeffrey is crying," race is the last thing on my mind.[1]

But Jeffrey, one of my White students, *is* crying. The tears are streaming down his face, and he is tense with frustration. When I approach he responds unselfconsciously, "I will *not* do this activity anymore! I refuse! I will *not* take this abuse!" I still don't understand. "Sean has been insulting me for the past 15 minutes. I have been called slave master, plantation owner, and oppressor. I have asked him to stop, but he won't. I have had it!"

I look around. Jeffrey is sitting in a group of three White boys. One, Sean, is an African expert and a vocal participant in the Black power pride. The other, an expert in matters of the American Indian, seems baffled and amused.

Sean is horrified. "I'm sorry," he says immediately. This is uncharacteristic for middle school students, and it checks my angry response. "It's my fault. I was just kidding. I didn't mean it. I'm sorry." His sincerity is moving, actually, as he admits to a mistake of human relationship few adults can acknowledge. But Jeffrey continues to cry.

Shanice, an African-American student representing Africans in the group at the adjacent table jumps up. "He was just kidding, Jeffrey," she says. She is trying to help, and offers to "hug on it." But Jeffrey has already checked out. I try to process with him, try to get him to understand the misunderstanding. I want to utilize this moment to talk about the real cause of his pain. But this is too much for Jeffrey. More tears, and he is quickly hiding behind a book.

Ominous thoughts circulate through my head. I am a bad teacher. I have opened a can of worms. I have created imaginary race riots in early America. I have destroyed Jeffrey's sense of self, and perhaps that of every other White student in the room. Clearly, I am not equipped to run this classroom. But, these thoughts are pushed aside by the more immediate need to find some sense of resolution before the bell rings and they all move on. How do I help my students understand the transformative potential of this pain? How do I free them from the brambles of racism and privilege that they did not create?

My immediate response is far from transformative. I do what I often do in moments of panic and confusion: I speak my own truth. I talk about my own experiences being White and learning about slavery; I talk about finding examples of White antiracists in our history. Most adults, I tell them, avoid conversations about race or struggle through them. The students acknowledge different ways that people deal with pain—humor, sadness, anger. The class agrees to keep trying to understand each other.

* * *

In her essays, *Playing in the Dark*, Toni Morrison outlines the ways in which White American authors have implicitly defined Whiteness through their portrayal of Blackness. Morrison highlights literature as one realm through which Americans have been able to imagine and define race (Morrison, 1992). Like other intellectual leaders, she analyzes the dangers of an identity built on the back of an "other." Whiteness is empty, defined only by what it is not. This phenomenon hurts all of us by preventing the true development of our identities. For Whites, "it is a terrible paradox, [because] those who believe that they [can] control and define Black people [end up divesting] themselves of the power to control and define themselves" (Baldwin, 1984, p. 180).

For my African-American students, the process of imagining and defining racial identity is a daily occurrence. It happens on the way to school, in the corner store, in classrooms and lunchrooms and bus stations. It happens on television, in magazines, in the simple act of saying, "hello." My White students have the privilege of choosing to ignore race; however, the invisibility of Whiteness in our culture is debilitating for them. They come to understand their identities as completely separate from their skin color. When asked to identify their "culture," these students stumble and hesitate. When pushed, they name ancestral ethnicity, religion, region, or even sexuality, all of which allow them to avoid acknowledging White privilege. This is what institutionalized racism expects them to do. It is the very principle on which our power structure is based.

Without realizing it, the jigsaw activity has allowed my White students to "play" a different race, to experience belonging to a different culture. In the process of becoming an expert, my White students have begun to identify with their adopted racial group. For those who experience being African or American Indian, this exercise engenders feelings of pride and empowerment. But those who experience being White are forced to feel privilege in a new way. This activity is particularly transformative for students whose actual identity matches that of their role.

Even for those who play themselves, "playing" race, is a unique view into our own understanding of it. The typically invisible concept of Whiteness as privilege is quickly revealed in the context of early America. All of us, no matter what race, are forced to confront the effect of race on our own racial identity. But for my White students, many of whom are confronting this reality consciously for the first time, there is anonymity in the game.

When White Americans begin to see Whiteness as socially constructed privilege, they are often left with troubling questions about their racial identity. What is White, if not privilege? If privilege is invisible, then how can we effect change? And, does identifying as White mean identifying as racist? For many, these questions are debilitating.

"Playing race" allows students to ask these questions from a safe distance. Sean can escape his feelings of guilt and discomfort by "playing" African, while Jeffrey is able to mourn his character's Whiteness in place of his own Whiteness. Still, both boys clearly demonstrate the beginnings of Helm's second stage: *disintegration* (Tatum, 1997). They begin to consciously identify the effects of racism on their own lives, as well as the lives of non-White Americans.

Furthermore, the experience gives both boys the chance to problematize Whiteness as privilege. By "acting" White privilege, Jeffrey gets to step away from prepackaged ideas about Whiteness and identify himself as a White person in opposition to this privilege. Sean, playing an African, has a similar opportunity. Both boys are able to wear their Whiteness physically while rejecting their Whiteness ideologically. In so doing, they create an alternative and complex model of Whiteness for the other students in our class.

Even for adults, it is quite complicated to identify ideologically as antiracist, while identifying physically as White. Becky Thompson and her colleagues eloquently discuss this challenge in their article, "Home/Work: Antiracism Activism and the Meaning of Whiteness." They write:

> Whiteness is confusing and complex, partly because white people are symbols and individuals at the same time.... We identify that we are white (as description) and we experience privilege (based on racial hierarchy) as we confront the absurdity of an invented ideological system that bases power on descriptive differences. We must claim a reality (that we have white skin) and deal with the unearned privileges as we show that the hierarchy is, itself, an invention. (1997, p. 357)

To deal with this multiplicity of experience, the women choose to identify different realms of their Whiteness: Whiteness as description (skin color), Whiteness as experience (unearned privilege), and Whiteness as ideology (a system of exploitation based on White supremacy).[2] Some group members begin to refer to themselves as "antiracist racists."[3] This term qualifies their experiences as institutionally privileged Whites (a racism we cannot escape) with the ideology of wanting to fight this racism.

Sean and Jeffrey, lacking the language and experience that they need, identify themselves as antiracist racists by their sheer acceptance of frustration. In their willingness to feel, act, confront, and "play," these young men grapple with a problem that the rest of us have spent years simply trying to name.

* * *

What happens when all of the people involved in a racial misunderstanding are White? In our classroom, this experience allowed the African-American students to step in as the experts. Having felt and thought about race carefully, these students came forward to try to facilitate the healing. Shanice, for example, brought reality back into our "game" when she offered to help Sean (playing African) resolve the conflict. In addition, the experience gave our classroom community the opportunity to imagine Whiteness in new ways.

By mid-November, we are ready to discuss this experience more openly. We have all had some distance, a chance to breathe. There have been many more moments of courage and sensitivity in our classroom. It seems an appropriate time to revisit the issue. I ask the students to think about the experience of our first unit. Already, we are deep into the American Revolution; we have spent several days mulling over the hypocrisy of slave owners fighting for freedom.

In their reflections, White students share their own feelings of sadness and confusion. Sean writes, "I did not feel proud at all, knowing that my people owned slaves." Jeffrey is more literal, "I felt like everyone who wasn't in my group was against me." A third White student writes, "I felt proud that some White people were fighting against slavery. I believe I would have been one of those people."

Their honesty makes me want to share my own experiences growing up in a diverse school. Perhaps, this is selfish. I talk about feeling ashamed and not knowing how to be White. Some of my African-American students are fascinated. "Why did you feel bad?" they ask. "It wasn't your fault." I try to explain in a way that will not further isolate my White students. I am careful; I know that my experiences with race are, inevitably, affecting these stories. I am afraid of my power, but also excited by their honesty. I talk about my own search for White antiracist role models.

We read about Thomas Jefferson. They know his name, but are shocked to find out that Jefferson himself was a slave owner riddled with guilt and confusion about the issue of slavery. Jefferson (1788) wrote,

> Indeed I tremble for my country when I reflect that God is just.... But it is impossible to be temperate and to pursue this subject through the various considerations of policy, of morals, of history natural and civil. We must be contented to hope they will force their way into every one's mind. (p. 173)

The first step is to know that there are others who have struggled, White and Black. Racism hurts all of us; pain can be transformative.

Throughout the year, we will talk about different models of Whiteness in history. I will tell them about Whiteness as description, experience, and ideology. When we talk about slavery, we will also talk about examples of interracial activism: slaves and indentured servants who run away together or resist; individuals who collaborate to write newspapers. We will spend some time looking at the ways in which different Americans, White and Black, became involved in the Underground Railroad. While conductors risked their lives, station masters risked jail time, and sponsors remained completely anonymous. These examples provide multiple models of antiracism with differing levels of personal involvement. I hope my students will use them to think critically about the kind of ideologies that they want to embrace.

* * *

Giving students the opportunity to think critically about race and racism in the context of school is not an easy task. The ability to question structures of power is not a skill-set written into our curriculum or standards. Furthermore, even when we provide students with opportunities to change their attitude, we are not directly changing the outcomes that play out in their lives. Many educators would argue it is more important to strengthen the academic performance of African-American students than to broaden the perceptions of those around them. While I acknowledge that changing attitudes does not change structures of power, I believe deeply that both are necessary for urban youth to understand their place in the context of race. Supporting self-reflection and critical thinking among young people opens up doors of possibility; possibility is necessary for change.

In a letter written to his nephew, James Baldwin once suggested that White Americans are scared to lose their sense of identity. He wrote:

> [White people] are in effect still trapped in a history they do not understand; and, until they understand it, they cannot be released from it. They have had to believe for many years, and for innumerable reasons, that Black men are inferior to white men. Many of them, indeed, know better, but as you will discover, people find it very difficult to act on what they know. To act is to be committed, and to be committed is

to be in danger. In this case, the danger, in the minds of most white Americans is the loss of their identity. (Quoted in Groot & Marcus, 1998, p. 5)

As educators, it is our responsibility to provide young White Americans with alternative and hybrid identities. Otherwise, fear will overpower their youthful desire for justice. By giving students the freedom to experience and imagine different models of Whiteness, we create the possibility for multifaceted identities. Using American history to explore Whiteness, perhaps my students will be able to better piece together their own ideas about privilege and power in our society.

Notes

1. All student names have been changed to protect privacy.
2. These labels can be credited to group member Patti DeRosa (Thompson, 1997, p. 357).
3. Ibid.

References

Baldwin, J. (1984). On being "white"…and other lies. In D. R. Roediger (Ed.), *Black on white: Black writers on what it means to be white* (p. 177–180). New York: Schocken Books.

Cross, W. E. (1991). *Shades of Black: Diversity in African-American identity*. Philadelphia: Temple University Press.

Fine, M., Weis, L., Powell, L., & Wong, L. (1997). *Off white: Readings on race, power and society*. New York: Routledge.

Groot, M., & Marcus, P. (1998, March/April). Digging out of the white trap. In C. Hartman (Ed.), *Challenges to equality: Poverty and race in America, part I* (pp. 15–19). Armonk, NY: Sharpe.

Helms, J. E. (Ed.). (1990). *Black and white racial identity: Theory, research and practice*. Westport, CT: Greenwood.

Jefferson, T. (1788). *Notes on the State of Virginia*. Philadelphia: Prichard & Hall.

Lee, H. (1960). *To kill a mockingbird*. Philadelphia: J.B. Lippincott.

Morrison, T. (1992). *Playing in the dark: Whiteness in the literary imagination*. New York: Vintage Books.

Tatum, B. (1997). *"Why are all the black kids sitting together in the cafeteria": A psychologist explains the development of racial identity*. New York: Basic Books.

Thompson, B. (1997). Home/work: Antiracism activism and the meaning of whiteness. In M. Fine, L. Weis, L. Powell, & L. M. Wong (Eds.), *Off white: Readings on race, power, and society* (pp. 354–366). New York: Routledge.

44 Teaching Poetry Workshop

Rafael Casal

What can I say about teaching writing workshops that hasn't already been said about—scuba diving? It's dangerous, always an adventure, and the deeper you go, the more rewarding it can be. When working with young writers, you're never short of a few challenges, but when you unlock a young person's ability to articulate him- or herself, you do more than just get them to turn something in on time, you revolutionize the way they'll interact with the world for the rest of their lives. The gift of language is truly priceless. It can pull even the worst cases out of the dark, by giving them the ability to communicate their frustrations and challenges during a time in life (like high school) where your learning conditions and needs are so vital.

She was in the back of the room of 15 students talking, laughing, playing, flirting, arguing, and text messaging, all waiting for the workshop to begin. Buried in her journal, reading something that could have been a death threat by how intensely she was scanning its contents. She couldn't have been a day over 16, Latina, dressed a bit overly sophisticated for her age. One eyebrow firmly raised as if her journal told her something about herself she disagreed with. In front of her, a girl and her boyfriend argued about their inability to communicate, which seemed to be getting nowhere. I interrupted the social carnival in my normal way:

"Ooooooooooooooo kkkkkkkkkkkkkkkkkkkkkk!"

People finished up their last fragments of conversations with whispers as everyone took there seats and grabbed for something to write with. The girl in the back didn't break a moment of concentration from her journal, as if she wasn't even here for my workshop.

It's 4:00 pm, one hour after school's out, and she is still on campus. She is definitely here for my workshop.

I asked everyone to take five minutes and do a freewrite exercise, starting with the first line, "How could you do this to me/us/them." Everyone but her began to write frantically, trying to come up with something FRESH to share within the five minutes given. I heard a slight sucking of the teeth from her corner of the room, and looked up to find that her pen wasn't moving.

I decided to wait until the prompt was over to see if her story unfolded during the quick sharing rotation before the full workshop began. She stared into the screen of her phone for the full five minutes until I called everyone's attention back to me.

"Ok, that's five minutes, finish your last thoughts and put it to bed. Anyone have anything they want to share before we begin?"

Another teeth-sucking sound from her corner of the room.

A few people raise their hands, a few beginner poems are shared, and I get a good sense of what the room's writing experience is. A great tool for me, but clearly not the prompt to get Ms. Phone-a-lot in the back's intellectual mind racing.

We proceeded with an hour workshop dissecting the idea of freedom of speech, based on a story I told about a colleague of mine who performed a very "anti-American poem" as some would call it, on an HBO television program that was based on the very idea of free speech. Following his performance he was investigated and dissected by the FBI for quite some time, for his radical opinions and ambitious method of expressing them on such a public forum. The workshop consists of hearing the poem, telling the story, then reading the Bill of Rights, and getting the room to a place of understanding between what is promised, and what often becomes the reality of our freedom of speech policy. Much of the conversation is referenced back to other American icons that were terrorized by our government for expressing an opinion that countered the existing narrative: The radio station that opposed McCarthy, John Lennon, MLK, the Black Panther Party, etc. etc.

We review the idea of the ripple effect. Many students question whether or not his actions did anything but get him inconvenienced by the government. We talk a bit about drawing a line in the sand.

It may seem pointless, something anyone can come along and kick over, brush away, make disappear, but if there is always someone there to draw it again, persistence will prevail. This colleague of mine was an inspiration for other people to draw lines where they witnessed injustice. A man/woman willing to sacrifice a bit of him- or herself for the betterment of his or her community and country. Anti-American? In many ways the epitome of American to me.

What I'd like everyone to do is to think of a time where you saw a line that needed to be drawn, and draw it for me now. Draw me your line in the sand. Somewhere you feel an injustice that must stop where you draw this line of yours. Write for…the next 30 minutes. Don't let your pencil leave the paper. If you can't think of anything…tell me why, but once you begin, don't stop.

Pencils touch bottom lips. Eyes look toward the sky. People stare at pages. For a minute nothing happens. At this point it is very important for me to be as silent as possible. My mood sets the tone for the atmosphere of the next 30 minutes. One by one pens begin to shake on their desks. Some slow at first, then enthusiastic at moments. Some ignore my instruction to keep writing at all costs and pause for long periods of time to think of the next line. My perfectionists.

Ms. Phone-a-lot is bored. She writes not a word for the entire period. She opens a book and reads instead.

Can't complain.

When I ask for people to wrap up their thoughts, deep sighs of relief are mixed in with requests for more time. Either way, it's over. I give all of the eager participants a chance to showcase anything clever they may have discovered in the last half an hour. The quiet ones share last. My rappers and slam veterans' hands are up first. They are both wonderful. The slammers' writing is both well pieced together and ready for performance, but usually there are many filler words placed in for style purposes that we will filter out over time. The rappers can't do anything but rhyme in bar form, although as a "rapper" myself I can somewhat peer through the constraints of the style they've chosen and hear the clever undertone they have yet to fully unleash. This is such a gift to receive. A model I have to help put together but I can see what it could be like the cover of the box is buried in the moments in their freewrites where they truly let go. They stopped judging themselves. They ignored who they had told their peers who they were for a moment and allowed themselves to be bigger than high school.

Ms. Phone-a-lot in the back raises her hand.

"Yes?"

> What is it about people and poetry and needing to fuckin' complain about everything all the time? Like what's the deal with raggin' on the government all the time and all this fight the power bullshit? Its crap. People write all these things just to get some applause or whatever but it's so empty. If you're gonna draw in the sand with a line or whatever then go do it don't write about going to do it, that's bullshit.

I can't help but smile enthusiastically. I think I might have said that very same thing the day before to a friend.

"Are you asking me personally?"

"Well, YEAH."

> Tupac said something that really stayed with me. "I won't be the one to change the world, but will definitely spark the brain that WILL change the world." Do you think the phrase "I have a dream" is any less powerful than the LA riots? One of physical action and one speech of action? I feel them both to be equally as important. And those with the gift to inspire with language must practice such inspiration, not ONLY to write what you feel but live it in practice. This is not to have us in this room breeding supercitizens by any means, I sure as hell know I'm no freedom fighter, but I definitely view my writing as a way to speak up for people who have yet to speak up for themselves. Giving voice to the voiceless. That is every writer's....power.

I don't think I satisfied her with that at all.

The workshop sharing continues, and before I know it is 6 pm and time to close up shop. I mingle for a bit with different students before the room is just this young woman and I. On her way out the door I ask her if we will ever hear some of that writing in the book she clutches to her chest as she walks out.

"Oh no. I'm no good."

"Somehow I doubt that"

"Goodnight."

"Goodnight."

She doesn't come back to my workshop the following week.

A month or so later I get a myspace message from her out of the blue. I recognize the face and open curiously. She writes something to the extent of:

> So.... I saw you on TV the other day at my aunt's house. You did this poem...about women's body image...anyway I just thought I'd tell you that I really loved what you said and it was...very refreshing to hear. It.... I needed it. Anyway I'm still writing a lot sorry I haven't been at your workshop. Are you still doing them?—Candace

"Hey Candace, I'm glad you enjoyed the poem. Just...drawing a line in the sand. You never know who they help. Workshops are starting back next Monday, 4 to 6 like last time. Maybe I'll see you there and finally hear a bit of that writing of yours. Rafael Casal"

She came back. Shared.

Her writing was amazing.

45   A Soft Approach to Hard Teaching[1]

Avi Lessing

Act 1

By my second year of teaching, my theater classes that met on the old, raised stage at Dawson High, a school north of Chicago, were packed, and sometimes the auditorium filled with visitors as well. Visitors consisted of other students who either wanted to watch my class or to miss their own. When the classes functioned, kids did credible work that went beyond acting. One student, Lily, said to me, "In your class people can be themselves, it's like a home." My belief that students should be themselves had drawbacks too. In my afternoon acting class, on a Friday in the dead of winter, Antonio LeBlanc mooned me and I, enraged, charged after him down a series of hallways. Later, he and I ended up in a meeting with the dean and his parents in The Office. In my first year of teaching, I had the strange feeling that it was not Antonio who was in trouble, but me.

After all, I reasoned in my head, hadn't I caused this? Sitting next to Antonio in under-sized puke green chairs waiting to be called in, I wondered how we arrived at this place? If I only knew how to discipline properly, this would never have happened. This kind of thinking began at different starting points, but always ended the same way, with resounding finality. I am not a real teacher. What was I even thinking getting into the profession in the first place? We were called in. Antonio said, "I didn't ever know you were mad, Mr. Lessing. You're always grinning." Really? I felt dumbstruck. I thought I had been mad as hell at this kid many times before, and yet here he was saying the opposite. The message came through only after yelling at the top of my lungs like a madman, disrupting classroom after classroom like a tidal wave as we ran by.

That kid taught me a something I would never glean from formal teacher education. Previously, I had thought I should develop a teacher–student relationship so that I can teach my students. Getting to know you exercises should not just be first day events but sprinkled throughout the year. Now I am convinced that the relationship *itself* is the teaching. For me, getting to know each other is the teaching. The teacher–student relationship must be authentic or else the student's relationship to the material the teacher presents sours. The implicit message we teach students when our teaching identity differs from our real life identity is that their school person should be different from who they are at home. We are essentially modeling that school matters in only one sense—going to college, getting a good job—but not at all in other ways—as in the important business of figuring who one is and what one's life means. The 13th century mystical poet, Rumi, spoke to this divide in the poem "Two Kinds of Intelligences":

> There are two kinds of intelligence: One acquired,
> as a child in school memorizes facts and concepts
> from books and from what the teacher says,

collecting information from the traditional sciences
as well as from the new sciences.

With such intelligence you rise in the world.
You get ranked ahead or behind others
in regard to your competence in retaining
information. You stroll with this intelligence
in and out of fields of knowledge, getting always more
marks on your preserving tablets.

There is another kind of tablet, one
already completed and preserved inside you.
A spring overflowing its springbox. A freshness
in the center of the chest. This other intelligence
does not turn yellow or stagnate. It's fluid,
and it doesn't move from outside to inside
through the conduits of plumbing-learning.

This second knowing is a fountainhead
from within you, moving out.

—Rumi[2]

As teachers, I wish we could teach from this place of intuition, passion, the right brain thinking. Moreover, I wish this kind of talk wouldn't elicit derisive laughter among colleagues.

With Antonio, I had the choice either to predetermine our relationship through a series of rules and expectations that I had largely stolen—this being my first year—from other teachers' syllabi or trust that Antonio was speaking the truth when he said that he did not know I was angry until the chasing incident, and that it was our mutual responsibility to negotiate this relationship. This did not mean that I needed to change my teaching so that I frowned and yelled all of the time. The fact is, I do grin a lot. It also did not mean abdicating equal power to him; after all I was the leader of the class. What it did mean is that Antonio and I had to establish a genuine relationship by working through what I thought of him and what he thought of him, not between a list of expectations that I did not believe in, and which made no sense to him. A much stronger, but more complicated choice is to be open to my students, to be transparent about the way I teach, to say why I am doing what I am doing, and when I think I am right, and when I may have acted falsely or with less integrity than I would have liked. True, it would have been easier to silence Antonio through a series of rules. Fearing that he wouldn't graduate, Antonio would probably shrink back into a corner. But *easier to manage* frequently deadens the soul of why I teach in the first place. I would never have gotten to see him improvise, or lead a class in a warm-up, or do hilarious, cruel things within the appropriate context of an improv scene. I have kept in touch for many years with Antonio. He was the most talented student improviser I have ever met and went on to study at Second City, the comedy training center in Chicago.

This kind of self-discovery, or self-admitting of my own ineptitude, fear, and doubt about teaching became a powerful tool for me, acknowledging that I did not have to have all of the answers was far more useful than pretending that I did. Despite all of my intentions to do good in the classroom, there was a great possibility for doing harm, and that possibility increased when I made assumptions about who students were, and the ways they should act toward me. The possibility for misunderstanding increased when I taught students with backgrounds that were different from my own. I undoubtedly connected more easily to Jewish students that, like myself, grew up upper middle class; however, most of my students did not fit that narrow description. And yet, I realized early on that I saw color, and if people said they did not, I was suspicious of them. How do you not see color with the history of our country, with the present predicament of our cities, of the way our schools are de facto segregated? How can teachers and students cross the real divides that separate us?

Teaching theater was a way to opt out of a structure that seemed to grant the teachers all of the power and the students none. Kids like Antonio, who were on the edge of huge trouble, but were also hugely talented, fascinated me—their power, intelligence, and talent went widely unnoticed in a school structure that demanded compliance. It was a structure that could not risk even being perceived as not in control. I wanted to choose a play for the fall production of my second year of teaching that shifted power to the students and captured the voices of students who did not have a place in the school. The students that did care about grades were far more difficult to teach, because threats about grades made no difference, but I couldn't help but admire their honesty, their insubordination in a system that historically held no promise.

Act 2

Anna Deavere Smith's play, *Twilight*, followed the aftermath of the 1991 Rodney King riots, which followed a not guilty verdict of five White police officers, filmed beating a defenseless Black man on the side of the road. Devised entirely through interviews conducted with those most affected by or involved in the violence, the play speaks to this divide that separates those in power and those without, and how that line, especially in a crisis, gets blurred. The first line of the play, spoken by a mixed student at Stanford, is "Who's they?" This little pronoun, *they*, indicates a serious problem we have with language. Especially explosive is its use when we apply it to race. And how about when we apply it to education? Who are we talking about when we talk about raising up *their* scores, or finding better ways to discipline *them*? If we keep lamenting that *they* are the source of problems in Los Angeles, and *their* test scores are not where they should be, aren't we also saying that it's *their* fault?

The play explores the way people are categorized, and yet in their voices, how each individual is peculiarly unique. Reading Ms. Smith's play is like seeing people that have been hidden for centuries. The idea in her work is to discover a fuller version of *We the People*, and toward that end, the characters in her play are not characters, they are real people, who speak in their own language, no longer censored.

The play offers wonderful opportunities for a school with a diverse population of kids—the chance for Black and Latino students to act in a distinctly modern play, about issues we rarely talked about that mattered at our school. There also existed considerable obstacles—for one thing, for students of color, especially Black boys, it was taboo to act in a play. Also, the theater department largely consisted of White students even though they were the minority population at our school. Not to mention that as a White teacher directing a play with mostly non-White characters, I had to be sensitive not to step in and be the voice for a group that I could not claim membership in. Finally, the town had a race riot in the late 60s that had led to deep unspoken fault lines in the town. Many White families fled when the Latino population surged in the 80s, and many people thought the school, in general, was going nowhere. The school was suburban geographically, but essentially urban, meaning, we worked with too many marginalized students with not nearly enough resources.

After each performance, we generated a dialogue with the audience and invited guests—a representative from the NAACP, social workers, scholars, the head of the police department, activists, and poets to begin a conversation with the audience and the actors. The intensity of the student performers (who, in many cases could directly relate to the text) forced the audience to turn the lens toward themselves about the issues in the play. They engaged in a conversation they wouldn't normally enter with people they did not know. The students, in attendance, began to talk about their experience in the school, their feelings of exclusion, blame, and guilt. Nothing was solved by a play—this was no movie—but people spoke, at great risk, despite their uncertainty, and this uncertainty far from feeling threatening, actually offered a way to begin a larger dialogue. It was not about solving problems but rather admitting there was a problem in the first place.

After the play, the principal, Laurie Shula, who winced noticeably when one of the characters used profanity, came up to me and offered heartfelt praise. "This was special, Mr. Lessing." I felt pretty good for about two weeks. The first day of theater class, second semester that year, only three minutes into class, I gestured over to a group of Black boys who wore Starter jackets, and said, "Guys, could you quiet down," and then later, "Guys!" to which one responded, "What do you mean, *you guys*?" What did I mean? Here I was directing Twilight with an opening monologue asking the provocative question, "Who's they?" and I essentially had labeled these three boys. But weren't they disturbing the class? Hadn't I merely tried to get order? That rationalization blanketed an implicit assumption, however, that I had made prior to class even beginning. In truth, I came in with the expectation that those three students, the darkest and most typically male, the biggest in size, would be trouble. They had walked in the room, and I had shrunk back. That realization carries some shame for me even now, but it was also an open door to walk in. If I couldn't see those boys properly, how could I teach them? And how much had their experiences been shaped by other adults who, in one way or another, also shrunk back, and thought, here comes trouble.

I did not have to look outside of the school for racism; it was right there, smack dab in the middle of myself. The next day, I apologized to those boys in front of the whole class. That did not clear me of my actions, and initially we all felt a little uncomfortable with my admission. One of my current students best describes that moment as "the time where you ask us to lean into our discomfort…it's like we're used to being hard in the world, but you want us to be soft in this classroom, and so the rules out there don't apply here." My vision of a perfect school is a place where teachers get to be human beings, students get to see teachers make errors, be sad, even go grocery shopping, without surprise or shock or embarrassment. A bad school is where teachers behave like automatons, or worse, classroom managers, which sounds like something out of Orwell, that dispense information to students. We're inundated with information, but starving for experience. We can be real human beings not in despite of our work, but because our work demands it. What students most need—our humanness, our own moral dilemmas, our very real struggles, we somehow feel obligated to deny the opportunity to share. It is an untellable loss to the students and teachers.

One of those kids that I singled out for talking that first day of class, a talented football player named Tony Warren, ended up doing theater for the next two years, even appearing in the musical *Guys and Dolls*, as one of the gangsters, and later in a Beckett play. Another boy, D.C. Fryman, really was a tough kid, who had been arrested for carjacking, but he was also sweet, playful, and eager to please. Eugene Lincoln was the biggest kid in the class but also the shyest. I don't want to exaggerate or clean up these boys' lives: they weren't teacher's pets. They were Black boys mostly in lower tracked classes in a public school system. Of course they weren't ready to drink the Kool-Aid that I was serving. Yet, they were also not thugs, or troublemakers, or not interested in school. They were not they.

Each had a story to tell just as the people who suffered in the LA riots and populated Anna Deavere Smith's play had stories to tell. My apology was a way of admitting that I make mistakes, a risk that makes teaching messier, but also richer. It meant that they got status, so they no longer had to play into the role of disinterested, bored students, and I did not have to be their programmatic, knowing teacher.

Of course, it wasn't a perfect world: my classes frustrated students, some kids wanted me to take control, kick people out of class when things got out of hand, but better than any system were the real relationships I could now claim. Tony, D.C., and Eugene emerged as distinct separate people, who I got to know, whose lives became real to me, whose faces took on specificity beyond their race. Their names evoke their faces and their faces make me remember their mannerisms and their stories, and perhaps at the heart of teaching is a kind of caring, a tenderness for others.

Act 3

Of course, as often happens in teaching, you don't just get your feet wet, you get drenched. My teaching tends to go that way, burst of praise followed by a torrent of intense scrutiny. My department head, at the school I now teach at, Barry Allison, told me that I'm the most polarizing teacher in the department. "Far more good than bad, though," he added diplomatically. Of course, without Barry, I would have no chance to offer the elective course that I created—Experiments in Reading Literature and the World. I'm always thanking him, and he's always laconically reminding me that I've thanked him enough.

Sometimes I'm amazed that he hired me at all. I showed up to our interview 45 minutes late, smelling like a campfire from the night before, wearing an orange colored button-down that I noticed midinterview had a large mustard stain on the right elbow. The week before I had spent way too much money on new clothes for a different interview, at a job that I coveted and prepared for, and didn't get. Now, here was Barry, practically awaking me from my slumber to offer me a job. I think it was an instinctual decision that he could later justify. Our teaching styles are completely different: in more than 20 years of teaching he's never received a complaint about his teaching. In six years, I am probably averaging three or four every year. I'm often more provocative than he bargained for.

At a casual glance, my second semester seventh period Experiments class, in now my sixth year of teaching has a similar demographic to my seventh period, first semester class. Both had a higher percentage of students of color than the two other classes combined; in both, about half the students did not identify as White. In the previous semester that class had been occasionally the hardest to direct, and the most unruly, but undoubtedly had the richest experience as well.

The challenging discussions we had about race the semester before were of little help to me the following semester. For one, in that first semester class, around half of the students of color occupied a middle or upper-middle class status in the school. They were in AP classes, they had mixed group of friends. They had enough status to venture into uncomfortable topics without risking everything. In the second semester class, there existed a class divide as well as a race divide. Attempting to acknowledge this divide, let alone bridging it, seemed like a foolish endeavor at times.

This particular class divided itself from the beginning. A friend of mine guest taught, and he aptly nailed the group as fragile. Midsemester, I was out sick on a Friday and the class got into a discussion about whether Barack Obama would be president someday. That ended with one kid storming out in tears and the rest of the class left with deep divisions.

Later in the semester, I brought in an exercise called the "Race to High Paying Jobs." The exercise offered a series of statements that related to race and class, where students had to either step forward toward the finish line or backward further away from it. At the end of 50 statements, I pointed to the wall, and said this is the race to high paying jobs, "GO!" Two girls, one Puerto Rican, the other Black, found themselves all the way in the back, with their other classmates scattered in front of them. The students near the front, mostly White raced to the wall in front of them. The students in the back, mostly of color, either walked to the wall, or did not even bother touching it at all. The exercise, I thought, was a success. We could finally bust open this mythology that we all have an equal chance in our society. We could begin to deconstruct institutional racism. My ignorance to some important factors led to a series of missteps that dug the students in a deep hole regarding their conversation about difference. One, the students who were most affected by these obstacles, who found themselves backing up again and again, boiled with anger that the class and especially I had essentially humiliated them. Letrice Washington and Angelica Fuentes found themselves taking step after step after step backwards, until, as Angelica reminded the class many times in the weeks that followed, "I was completely out the door, out of the room!"

Obviously, the disparity in their starting positions for the race to high paying jobs was contrived. I thought its effect as a kinesthetic, silent activity, however, would trigger the students to challenge the notion that "we are all equal." Instead, the students began to question my leadership, each other, and furthermore, refused, along with the frightened class, to question or even discuss the validity of the exercise.

What I did not count on was the explosiveness of responses. As is so often the case with my teaching practice, in theory or as a vision, I welcome discourse, discontent, and provocation in the attempt to create a genuine engagement in the classroom. When this reality hits, it's often complex, scary, and leaves you, the teacher, in the ignominious position of feeling like an idiot. When this happens, my teacher alarm clock goes off, and the ever-present inner-critic inside me seems to self-implode. Great, now what, Avi? The kids you want to engage, you alienate. Why can't you be a normal English teacher? When are you ever going to be prepared? Why weren't you ready for this? How are you going to fix it? Perhaps I should become something else, start over, as say, a sports agent. Letrice, in particular, vented her anger with laserlike aim.

> That exercise doesn't tell you anything. I'm not behind anyone. And I'm tired of coming into the classroom and seeing that poster-board that your students from last semester made. Why do you always have to be talking about the achievement gap at this school? And Black students this. And Black students that. How do you know those statistics are even right? And even if they are right, how is that supposed to help me?

I had no answers for her—I did not know—and doubt, this trait I secretly admired in myself and encourage in students—did not inspire confidence in the room. I had admired Buddhist teachers who talked about the ability to rest in crisis moments. And yet I did not feel restful; I felt awful and conflicted and at the end of each day, until I dragged myself into the swimming pool for some much needed change in energy, utterly spent.

Wasn't Letrice right? I hadn't thought it through properly. An exercise like stepping forward and backwards was relatively easy for a White, upper-middle class male to lead. Had I done the exercise with the students, I would find myself near the front of the line. For those kids in the back, the exercise is not a game, it is their life, and to admit to its truth would be crushing. It could debilitate them in their quest to beat the very odds that I insisted in pointing out to them. And what was my purpose? Under the watch of their wary eyes, my noble ideas felt suddenly without merit, and utterly removed from their every day struggles.

Another dynamic that I would only grasp much later, is that Letrice and Angelica had also been incensed by one of the other students, Lisa, who they thought had given them a dirty look during the exercise. For weeks they harbored anger toward Lisa, who, perhaps not coincidentally, was the Whitest student in my class, and in addition, played violin. Skin color, no matter how much we all want to wish it away, still tears apart families, determines alliances between friends, and often influences the way human beings interact. Letrice talked in class about having a lighter skinned relative who wouldn't speak to her because she was ashamed that she was so dark. Angelica thought of herself as Black in a school culture that often did not register the nuances of race, skin color, and ethnicity.

Yet, the trouble with skin color is that it only tells part of a story. Lisa was deeply troubled in her own way. Her boyfriend's parents hated her, her mother had suffered a stroke that left her confined to the house, and she was getting rejected from colleges left and right, that, even had they had admitted her, she would not be able to afford to go.

Act 4

These were some of the confluences that played out one day when Lisa gave an oral presentation investigating the phenomena of the world of ice-skating. In this particular project, students probed how people within certain worlds or phenomena made meaning in those places. Lisa belonged to the world she was looking at; she was a top-notch figure skater. In the course of her presentation, she lamented the lack of African Americans who skated. She cited the high cost of skates as one of the reasons for the lack of diversity.

During the presentation, I felt some discomfort from the class, but I would be lying if I said that I understood how the Black students, or poor students, might feel from the presumption underlying Lisa's comment, or even that I checked in with students such a comment might affect after class. As so often happens in the case of dynamics that occur between students, I was almost completely blind to what was happening.

I did notice in the ensuing days that Letrice and Angelica became even more distant than usual. Andre, a mutual friend of theirs, increased the amount of times he checked his cell phone for text messages during class. And Kendrick, a student who initially wanted to understand the divide in the class, and had been a leader, now came in late with a great show of languor, and remained silent throughout class. It felt like the whole class, including myself, was slipping into quicksand.

The middle of the school year feels like the middle of your life: you're too close to it to understand it properly. You desperately want to relax, and yet you can't quite let anything go: it all wore heavily on me. I tried to focus on my other classes, lamenting that my seventh period was simply difficult, not motivated, and all of the other deferrals that we teachers are taught to dispense when conflict arises. The daily chime at twelve o'clock, 15 minutes before class would start, now sounded like a death knell.

Letrice meanwhile was steaming. She always had other books from other classes out. She said she didn't like the class. She talked only with Angelica; her circle of vision seemed to blot out everyone else around her. When I pressed her in class to talk about what was bothering her, she said, "Fine you want to know? One student in this class is a racist." Then the bell rang.

The next day the class was tense; everyone was on edge. Who was it? Was there really a racist in the class? Reading Malcolm Gladwell, James Baldwin, Bill Ayers, and Peggy McIntosh could not prepare us for a moment quite like this. When Letrice finally recalled what Lisa had said during her skating report, the dam broke. Letrice directed her pointed criticism right at Lisa without looking at her. Lisa began to sob, Letrice looked sickened, and the class quickly scrambled to take one side or the other. I bumbled my way through something utterly diplomatic and neutral: "I can see why Letrice is angry and I can see why Lisa is upset right now and perhaps what we should do is...." Letrice interrupted: "Stop protecting everyone. She said it, OK she said it, she said it!" When the class rallied to Lisa's defense, Letrice walked right out the door.

The next day, as we tried to reassemble what had happened, Letrice packed up early again and left again, this time deliberately, slowly, almost as if part of funeral processional. This time I followed her.

"What are you doing," she said, whirling on me.

"I just wanted to see how you are."

"Not good, if you can't tell!"

"Yeah, I can see that. This was not my intention, to make your second semester of your senior year a total misery."

"Well it is."

"I'm sorry."

"I can't tell you," she said, some tears beginning to roll down her face, "how much I wish that I was Lisa, with everyone gathering around me to see how I'm doing. But no, instead, I get kids staring at me. 'Why is Letrice such a bitch?' 'Why is Letrice so fucking mean?' Nobody knows how hard it is. I have to be hard. Nobody is going to mess with me." She sat huddled, nodding her head up and down, as if saying yes to all of the resistance she needed just to make it through her days.

Something like a cold peace now descended upon the class. People exhaustively came in, and waited for class to be over. I helplessly muddled through. I brought in students from the semester before to talk about how valuable—"leaning into discomfort"—could be. The current class promptly told my former students to leave. *Who are they to condescend to us* seemed to be the general sentiment. At a total loss, I turned toward the more academic aspects of the class to focus on hoping a break from communicating with each other would help.

When we finally returned to storytelling, the main focus of the class, I thought we had achieved a small victory. The final project, inspired by Anna Deavere Smith, was a collection of their stories, acted out, with members of the class portraying each other. My first semester classes had produced startling results, with accolades from their audiences, and the students forging truly empathetic relationships with each other. One student had said that as she was performing the part of an exchange student from Thailand, she looked out at the audience and locked eyes with the girl who told the story. "And at the moment, I was her, Mr. Lessing. I have never felt that way in my whole life." The difficulty with teaching this way though is that it is unpredictable and what happened first semester could not help me with what was happening in my class now.

Andre put away his cell phone long enough to tell his story. He talked about coming out to his mother and trying to balance the gay scene in Chicago with school and church. Students were visibly uncomfortable, not just by the admission that he was gay, but by the detail in which he discussed his forays in the particular gay scene he felt attached to. After his story concluded, few students came up to acknowledge him. Lisa, who knew

Andre strongly sided with Letrice in their previous encounter, was among the throng of students who left the room without looking at him.

The next day Andre unleashed a torrent of expletives on Lisa and others who he felt scorned him. His fury astonished the class and the oblivious observing education graduate school student who was visiting that day. What must he be thinking? I surmised he thought something along the lines of—*is this teaching*? And if this is teaching, then I want none of it. But this was more my projection than truth. Andre cursed, he threatened, he yelled. The fragile, cold truce had cracked and again the class, once again, lost its footing.

The following day, Andre felt remarkably better. He was smiling openly.

"You feel better today?" I asked.

"Oh, yeah, I'm straight. Why?"

"I don't know, maybe because 24 hours ago you looked ready to attack me," I half-jokingly poked at him.

"Oh that. That's just how we talk. I was just talking."

It's difficult to generalize, but Andre again was echoing something that my mooning student, Antonio LeBlanc, years earlier had hinted at. I had thought Andre had lost control the previous day. I was close to telling him to settle down or even question whether I should be kicking him out of class. This was in direct proportion to my fear that I had let him take too much power. Yes, in the classroom, it is our job to make sure our students are safe, but too often our zero tolerance for swearing, misbehavior, and noncompliance also stops us allowing the students to actually grow up and solve problems that they have the ability to work through.

Act 5

From that day on, a state of grace seemed to fall on us. We all did acknowledge Andre the following day, and though it was slightly forced, he accepted Lisa's hug. Letrice remained aloof and Angelica had bouts of disenchantment, but even those two would stage a remarkable recovery at the end of the year.

The first breakthrough occurred when Letrice, along with Angelica and others, insisted that I tell a story as well. "What story should I tell?" I asked, suddenly put on the spot. "Like you say to us," another student, Anna, chimed in, "something that teachers don't usually share, something that makes you feel safe, but maybe uncomfortable." "In intensity, from 1 to10, pick a 5," another student chimed in mocking my elicitations. I talked about how I had a bad temper and how it was embarrassing how it would sometimes come out. This surprised the class—the identity that I cultivated in front of them was one of laid back, rebel, an easy going, self-knowing, if not strange teacher. After class, I said to Letrice, "So, I'm curious. Does hearing my story deepen or lessen your respect for me."

"Deepens," she whispered.

"But what about what you said about being hard."

"Yes, but of course what I want is to be soft too." She paused and jabbed a finger into my chest. "Don't tell nobody."

I assigned Letrice to tell back Anna's story and vice versa. Both told difficult stories about their fathers. In rehearsal, Anna was reticent, given the class's history, to take on Letrice's mannerisms—her gestures, cadence, volume, and accent. Presumably she did not want anyone to accuse her of mocking Letrice's voice, afraid, no doubt, of being pegged as a racist. I urged her to listen to the tape, to let her story be her guide. Letrice moaned about having to memorize Anna's whole story, and vowed to do the minimum required.

On the day of Anna's performance, and the last day of the semester, Letrice sat in front of me. Her back began to quiver slightly when Anna first began to tell her story back to her. She beautifully conveyed the emotion of Letrice's story, and, for the most part, nailed the intonation, pitch, and pace of her voice. Anna had obviously memorized and rehearsed the whole thing. Letrice's reaction was unexpected: Anna's portrayal moved her, and she cried openly. The fact that Anna saw her, and was able to become her, without judgment and little interpretation, made Letrice's troubles seem more real, more shared by the rest of the class.

The most surprising event came last: Letrice returned the favor in a stunning performance of Anna's story that left the two embracing each other at the end. Andre, too, not to be outdone, nailed his ending performance as well. The bell rang and the year ended; as seniors their high school careers were over.

This time Andre hugged Lisa whole-heartedly. Letrice was in line right behind him. They smiled and hugged and cried, and I hadn't directed any of it. Frankly, I was too exhausted to do much more than watch.

Note

1. Except in the case of well-known figures introduced by first and last names, I have changed names of people and schools and other details in order to protect privacy.
2. Permission was granted by Coleman Barks Essential Run.

46 Keeping It Real

Milton Reynolds

This story begins near the dawn of my teaching career when I was teaching at Nueva Middle School in Hillsborough, a school dedicated to the education of gifted children. Not an unreasonable need, but certainly a concept that requires close examination because it is rooted in a troubling history. Seeing myself as a person who is committed to the goals and principles of social justice and equitable access, I struggled with myself a great deal before deciding to eventually take the job at Nueva. Part of my internal struggle was gaining some clarity about what it meant to be an educator as the term is most expansively defined and in that, *who* would I serve?

Having decided to take the job, the story I told myself to salve my inner conflict was that I'd be an advocate for the few students of color that attended the school. I'd be a touchstone, a place of potential refuge for them. I knew the experience of being the "visible visitor" all too well; it was a lived experience. Since I was the only full time teacher of color at the school it seemed a reasonable stance. There were a couple of other folks of color on campus; the gardeners, janitors, and two, maybe three support staff, but I felt it important that the students had other models. After all, this was at a school for the "gifted," so the absence of teachers of color presented a real dilemma, but for me it also reeked of possibility.

By virtue of circumstances, I had the ticket to the show; for most of my life I was raised in communities in which I'd been the visible visitor. As difficult as that aspect of my upbringing had been at times, it provided me with the skills needed to navigate this community. I'd discovered long ago how to read the cues present in my social environment, so that "the large shadow I cast," as my father often refers to it, didn't work against me. These lessons were hard in coming and often painful, but if I could spare some of my students the indignities and slights I'd suffered through sharing my experiences and strategies then it seemed a noble goal.

As it turned out, many of the students who were most affected by my presence were actually the White students. Most of them had never had an opportunity to interact with any people of color in a meaningful way, outside of the "traditional" superordinate/subordinate patterns that typified their lives, so the sustained engagement w/me was a real eye opener for some. While this isn't the thrust of my piece I must say that many of those interactions are still with me, as I'm sure they are for many of my former students.

The primary story I want to convey is about a student of mine, Rahman Jamaal McCreadie. I was aware of Rahman before he came to the middle school in seventh grade. I'd seen him on campus, he was one of those kids with that twinkle in their eye; he was obviously very bright, if not a little squirrelly. When time allowed I would walk down to the lower school and check in with the younger kids; it gave me a chance to get to know them and they me, so I was familiar with Rahman and knew that I wanted to engage him once he got to the middle school. When that time came I inherited him after a bit of lobbying. In looking at his previous reports, it was clear that he was coming with some "baggage," but it was also clear that folks didn't really "see" him.

When I began to review his cumulative reports, they seemed to represent a very different student from the one I had come to know. In my mind it had a great deal to do with the way his previous teachers had seen him; the way they interpreted his behaviors. For the record, Rahman is biracial, but looks "identifiably" African American. Rahman was raised by his mother and by and large the community that he navigated in and out of school was predominately White, as were the social norms that he internalized.

Rahman wasn't your "average" kid, by seventh grade he'd already earned a Black belt in karate; he was an accomplished trumpet player, an exceptional mathematician, had strong writing skills, and was becoming an accomplished actor. He was literally bursting with talent. Needless to say it was troubling to me that many of his previous teachers viewed him as problematic. I don't think that anybody would say he was horrible and he was generally well liked, but little things are big.

Halfway into our first year together, in seventh grade, he was still struggling with some of the behavioral issues and was experiencing some frustration about the situation. As his advisor I started up a conversation with him about the situation saying, "Well, Rahman, as a young Black man...." He stopped me midsentence. It was apparent by the look on his face and his actions that I had clearly upset him. Maybe upset isn't the right word, but clearly I'd put him in a place of great dissonance. This was disconcerting to me, as I'd always prided myself on being attuned to my students and attentive to their needs. I was always available to them and felt I really connected with all of them, especially Rahman. It was also shocking to me that I had done to him what some of the others had; I hadn't seen him as he saw himself.

He proceeded to tell me, "Well, I see myself as both White and Black and I need you to see both sides of me...." I had to pause for a second and think of what to say. The immediate response of just about anybody would be to defend themselves and say, "Well, no, that's not what I meant to say...." But somehow I knew that this wasn't the time or the place for that. What was important at that moment was for me to allow Rahman to tell me what he needed me to hear, simply for me to listen. Quite frankly, a defensive response had never seemed sufficient for me either in thinking back on some of the racialized moments of my trajectory through childhood. Fortunately, for our relationship I kept quiet and was able to hear him. In that moment I demonstrated to him that our relationship was more important than me being right.

It's still an emotionally weighty event for me; recounting that frozen snapshot still brings up lots of feelings. It was one of those moments everyone has in their teaching careers when we become the student and our student becomes the teacher. We are still very close and communicate often. On more than one occasion we've reflected on that experience and we both view that as a defining moment in our relationship.

Rahman knew that I was invested in him. We were tight and we talked a lot; sometimes it was about school, but other times it was about life in general. In some ways, he would say I was a "surrogate" father for him because his dad really wasn't in the picture early on. So as you might imagine I was shaken in the moment he revealed his chosen identity to me. Fortunately, I did bite my tongue. I allowed him to teach me; it's one of the wisest things I've done in my teaching career. In retrospect it wasn't much, I just had to be willing to accept the important lesson that my student bravely provided me with and I was able to as he says, "keep it real."

The conversation we started years ago still continues between us. As he told me later, that was the first time he began to think of himself as Black, even as he said he wasn't, at least not entirely so. In retrospect it shouldn't have been all that surprising, as the extended family he was surrounded by were all European Americans and that was the case for the community he lived in. Nevertheless, our interaction started an internal process of inquiry about his identity that has been ongoing.

Our conversations about identity and place deepened and as it did the process pulled us together and opened doors to other conversations. Even though I'd botched my first attempt, we eventually got to what I was trying to communicate to him in the first place. That was the notion that there were a series of social circumstances that were at the root of his frustrations and that they were largely a function of the way in which other people were seeing him and interpreting his actions. The upshot of the situation was that those were things we could work on together, as I'd had to figure out similar strategies myself. My task as his advisor became one of helping him learn how to navigate the social norms of that community and how to avoid the conflicts that arose from interpretations of his behavior. It wasn't that his behavior was any worse than anyone else's it was just that he was more "visible."

Our conversations helped to illuminate the context he was struggling to see and lacked the language to articulate, as he hadn't really thought of himself "racially" prior to our conversation, at least not in a way that was connected to how he was viewed. Once we were able to surface the social context, everything changed. It was a very short period of time until he got his "behavioral issues" sorted out and became quite skilled at navigating the school environment. There was carryover outside of school as well.

When it came time for him to go to high school we had another hurdle to surmount, where to go? Rahman had already told me that he wanted, "to be around his people" and to attend a high school where he would not be the visible visitor. We went back and forth on this he, his mother, and me. My advice to him was that I wanted him to be in a position to get what he needed out of school. Foremost in my mind was the desire to keep him focused on his education, but also to set the stage for college. I encouraged him to think about the matter, but to do so in broader terms. I understood his desire to be at a bigger school where he wouldn't be so visible and would have a larger peer group, but I also didn't want him to get lost in the mix or sidetracked by some of the social aspects of school.

There were many schools interested in him and some were offering substantial scholarships. I knew that even though the "price of admission" to some of these schools would be both economic and social and that he would yet again have to endure the rigors of being the visible visitor, that in the long haul it would afford him a greater set of options at the end of four years. The other major concern his mother and I shared was the question of whether the behaviors that might afford him membership in the community at the school he voiced a desire to attend, might ultimately run counter to his academic needs. Fortunately he trusted me enough to weigh in heavily on this decision.

He ultimately decided to go to one of the schools that had been working hard to recruit him and as we had surmised, the opportunities there would soon reveal themselves. He got to travel to Africa during his freshman year and in subsequent years went to Cuba and Iceland. He won the lead role in nearly all the school plays. He practically owned the school by the time he left. The benefit was really twofold, as he really helped that school and his peers to grow and in doing so, helped challenge some of their traditional practices like the "senior slave auction" and other problematic traditions. To his credit, he was able to apply his now well-honed social skills such that he was able to get his needs met and to be heard in the process.

To bring this to an end, he went on to graduate near the top of his class, was overwhelmingly selected as their graduation speaker, and had an array of colleges to choose from as we had hoped. He settled on USC, where he graduated from the School of Cinematic Arts and now enjoys a growing audience for his music and a successful film career.

While this story has a happy ending, Rahman's behavior in middle school was not egregious in comparison to his peers; in fact it wasn't any different. He was simply more visibly obvious. A major dilemma in education is that there's a big intersection between who's in front of the class and who's in the seat. This fragile intersection has elements of social class and aspects of gender and race often loom large. A friend of mine used to say that "Everyone likes puppies but some folks are afraid of dogs." Not to compare people with animals, but I see his saying as rather descriptive of the journey that many youth and especially young men of color make at they move from elementary school to middle school and one that continues as they matriculate into high school.

These young men enter the classroom hoping to be seen as good kids, as open to learning and hoping, like most of us, that their teachers will like them. While it's fair to say that many students do encounter similar classrooms from time to time, too often, they encounter just the opposite. As they grow older and bigger in stature they often encounter fear and distrust from adults and frequently find themselves in positions where folks expect the least of them. In my life this procession of experiences translated to hurt, from hurt to frustration, and from frustration to anger. In the absence of staff that I trusted, those who'd simply "keep it real with me" my anger and alienation festered until I was eventually expelled from school in my junior year.

Sadly, most of the penalties and the consequences that accrue around this dynamic weigh heavily on students, usually long before they had the chance to figure it out. When I look at the dropout/expulsion rates of young Latino and African-American males in particular, I can't help but think that so much of it has to do with them reacting to their environments and interactions within those environments as I had reacted to mine. None of this needs to happen.

I firmly believe that any teacher can effectively teach any student. And while it's true that "race" can present a hurdle it doesn't have to. Learning, like many things in life is a largely social process. One's ability to work effectively with students is contingent upon one's ability to communicate the importance of that relationship to that student. True, teachers have other responsibilities as it relates to the transmission of knowledge, but I feel it's largely the relational aspects of the equation that are lacking.

What was important for Rahman was that he knew that I cared about him and I was invested in him as a person. Our initial conversation was one of those moments where the student became the teacher and I was open to the lesson. I now often work w/preservice or new teachers and I make a point to tell them that among other things, teaching is largely about relationships. It is important to have content mastery, it's important to be able to scaffold information so students can navigate it, but if the students believe that you don't care about them or you're not invested in them, you can be a pedagogical wizard and end up falling flat.

47 Renaming the Moon
Learning English in Middle School

Julie Searle

How does language join us together, or thrust us into a terrible loneliness? Can school be a sane place for preteens in culture shock? What is it that allows us the freedom to write? How do we write with exigency? While we are waiting for our common language to cohere, how can we be a community of thinkers?

These are some of the questions I have grappled with this year—my first as one of the humanities teachers for beginning English language learners in a middle school in Berkeley, California. I was asked a week before school began to take on the level one and two seventh and eighth grade class in English and history for a year. There would be 20 students—and eight home languages. I could not resist.

The day before classes began, I was talking to a few colleagues about my unexpected assignment. A teacher who had worked with many of my students last year looked down my student list. "Oh man,…low…low…low…really low—he really struggles…she's really low, too. Wow…." Already I was made aware of a view I would need to resist: students as problems.

On the contrary, one of the most powerful concepts that make a classroom a place worth being in is "welcome." We often write this word with an optimistic exclamation point on day one, but fail to make it manifest during the year. Minute by minute, the welcome must be restated, refelt. You are welcome to be confused! You are welcome to try again! You are welcome, just as you are!

I thought a great deal about my new class, and felt an overwhelming urgency about their language acquisition. Still, teaching that honors the students must be a matter of regular invention, and I realized I would need to create the curriculum with clues from the students themselves. On the first day of class, I held up an index card with the word *door* written on it. I taped it to the door and asked, "What other words do you know that are in this room?" The kids went to town. They knew *telephone, window, wall*. By the time we ran out of cards, someone had climbed on a stool to make sure the Rousseau poster way up on the wall had a sign that said, "lion." Shakespeare's mysterious face was labeled "man." Above my desk the photo of Malcolm X had two cards that succinctly named both his inner light and intelligence: "smile" and "glasses."

It was clear from the first day that our most powerful shared language was the language of gestures—our faces and hands. By the second week, I felt I was acting out verbs and nouns like a desperate player of the Commedia del'arte. Nothing written in any of the workbooks was working well for me: Sheltered English Language Instruction, also known as Improvisational Theater. Handing out strips of paper to each table group one Tuesday, I said, "Write a good sentence describing what you see. Help each other!" I staggered around the room, clutching a tissue box. I grabbed the classroom phone and had a fake conversation with my mom. Voices buzzed; hands shot up. The first strip nailed it: "The teacher is so sick! She is trying to call her mother." Our classroom hall pass is a stuffed toy, a monkey. I grabbed him next and gestured with a pair of student scissors. The students consulted each other, wrote, and announced confidently, "Crazy Mr. Monkey is cutting the air."

On day two this Fall, I happened to be stepping out during a prep to make some photocopies. Aminah came running down the hall to me. She is my only student from Yemen. I heard she was here last year but made "little progress." This year she is my only student who covers her head. At this moment she was out of breath. When I realized she was near tears, I found myself choking up too. Clearly, the world is too big and strange. We went over her schedule and decided she should be in a computer class, her elective. I, a reluctant driver who has been lost on so many freeways and in so many neighborhoods, walked her to the building where the teacher was expecting her. Ok, deep breath. We smiled at each other—navigational success!

From the beginning, I looked for others to talk with about silent Aminah and all the rest of the kids. Gina, an insightful 20-year-old tutor from UC Berkeley who is a native Spanish speaker from Michoacán, appeared like an angel in September to volunteer in my class. Gina is lovely with the kids, patient, approachable, and practical. When I asked her a few questions about her sense of the students, she said simply, "Well…y'know—they're traumatized." Her matter of fact yet dramatic choice of words surprised me, but made me think about the strain of being a preadolescent in an unfamiliar cultural setting. On days when half the class arrived late and without a pencil, Gina's point was particularly helpful to me.

By October, I encountered another version of "support" for my students. On Tuesdays volunteers came by bus from a wealthy retirement community to work one on one with students learning English. Four of my slightly more advanced students were invited to meet with tutors. This program has been going on for a few years, usually focused on volunteers talking to students about the books they're reading, and on building vocabulary. This year, the dedicated director of the newcomer program at our school confided in me that she was rethinking how effective some of the tutors were in their interactions with students.

In an orientation meeting, one woman pressed for state reading scores. "It would help to know how far below grade level these students are." My heart sank. Was this really the most interesting question she could think of? I explained to the tutors that all the students they work with will score "below basic" in standardized grade level tests, but as tutors they would have the opportunity to gain insight into the kinds of literacy skills the students have in their native languages. They would also have the chance to get to know what the kids were curious about, and what they were beginning to understand.

The volunteers assumed that as tutors they had plenty to offer since they were "educated." I felt there was an essential element of curiosity and imagination missing. After a few weeks, I became frustrated by the lack of enthusiasm the participating students expressed when I sent them off to the library on Tuesdays. Plus, I missed their voices. At about that time, the program was cut back and no longer had places for my four.

Meanwhile, I was searching for a text that would begin to get at U.S. history curriculum, but would also be a good fit for language development. I wanted to read something that mattered. There was comfort in the concreteness of

"Yesterday I called my cousin.

Today I will call my cousin.

Tomorrow I am going to call my cousin."

But what else?

In a textbook, I found a full-page portrait of Chief Joseph with his "I Will Fight No More Forever" speech, after his effort to lead Nez Percé families to Canada. I found notes about the characteristics of a speech: "short, clear sentences; simple, clear structure; strong, memorable words"—good.

When class started, I stood on one of the green desk chairs, waved my arm and said, "Listen, my people!"

I asked the class, "Would you talk like that to borrow a pencil?"

"No." scoffed Yoshi, "For something important!"

First, I asked everyone to look at the portrait. Students began to argue.

"He is Chinese?"

"No! Indian!"

"What ? Indian?!"

"No—Native American."

I came back into the conversation.

"Right—OK everyone, he is also a chief. What does that mean to you?"

Someone ventured, "Like Bush?"

(Big laugh from the others...")

I asked them, "I mean, who do you think of as a leader?"

"More like Vicente Fox?"

At this point we paused, and talked more about the Nez Perce and historical background. Then I read the speech. I asked everyone to stand up and read the last few lines together. After three tries, we sounded pretty good.

After the recitation I asked, "So— why is Chief Joseph speaking this way?"

As I stood in front of the class at that moment I asked myself, "Just what am I thinking? Where am I going with this after all?" Though I work the long hours of any teacher in an urban middle school, all too often I still feel absurdly unprepared.

Out of my confusion, a sudden inspiration...I noticed the big black and white photo of Dr. King on my door. He is standing next to a set of microphones in front of UC Berkeley's Sproul Hall, Of course, I thought gratefully, a connection.

We ended up creating a Venn diagram on the board about Martin Luther King and Chief Joseph. As a student I resented the use of these awkward overlapping circles that didn't quite accommodate my ideas. I've learned to teach my students to make the "both" section a generous center for commonalities. Big space for big thoughts.

"Both—had discrimination by White people!"

"One guy—he was talking about blankets and food...."

"The other one was African American—and more from our time."

"Both—worried about children!"

"Both—human!"

After weeks of disjointed lessons, a mixture of grammar lessons and simple sentences, I was hungry for some shared literature. I found an anthology of folktales which we began to read together. We read about jealous Pablo and Charon, the banished son. We talked about why they were called "folktales." People just told these stories to each other. As the kids observed, "Nobody really wrote them or made money."

After three months of working with the Earphone English (books on tape) program, a collaboration with the public library, I sent an update to the librarian who meets with the kids every other week: "Mira is going back to India because of her new baby brother, and Emanual is going to finish high school in Morelia." As I typed the news, I felt the loss of these two memorable students. So much of what I feel on a daily basis is frustration and inadequacy. All Fall, every lesson, every transition, every move with this class took so much time. When I was at my worst, I told them "It's like being in boring stop-and-go traffic."

By early December I came in excited about a new plan. Come hell or high water, we would write together. We would take baby steps, but with enthusiasm. I had just returned from a workshop about teaching writing. My vision: comfortable, familiar content coupled with academic language and formal organization. My opening question was, "How do you wake up in the morning?" Soon we were acting out an impatient mom shaking her child, and the disruptive buzz of an alarm clock. "Any other ideas?" My wonderful volunteer patted her head and chest. I understood. "Oh, right...some people have the clock inside!" Together we wrote "procedural paragraphs," starting with "How to Stay in Bed When You Should Get Up." According to my class, here's how: First, tell yourself you have lots of time. Next, plan to get up in just five more minutes. Finally, just pull up the blanket and close your eyes."

On another foggy morning, the copier was broken so I decided we would read the William Carlos Williams poem, "This Is Just to Say," an extended apology which was included in an anthology we had many copies of. We read it aloud, with each student taking one short line. We talked about whether or not a person who read the poem would be likely to forgive the theft of plums. I asked all the students to write excuses. Some just copied my example. Juan wrote, "I'm sorry I read your diary. I thought it was about me."

Veronica wrote, "I apologize for missing your party. I was very, very dead."

After asking for some spelling help, Fernando wrote, "I'm sorry I was in a fight and got suspended. I am in love."

Just before winter break. I was discouraged. Several of my students had been getting in trouble: Jesus was suspended for bringing superglue to school and smearing it on door handles. Aminah and Jasmin were fighting in a miserable tangle of Arabic and Spanish. "She said madre!" Miguel had been referred to counseling for drawing obscene pictures on other kids' notebooks. Omar was having a hard time listening to his audiotape of Stuart Little. The last lesson before winter break unfolded when I realized the next folktale from China in our anthology was too confusing. Oh, fine. I could at least give the students a dictation with words from the text. Just then I heard Miguel mumble some magic words under his breath, "Oh yeah—the moon speaks Spanish."

It was time for us to write a poem, and we did, everybody together, with a dying blue pen on the overhead.

Moon Poem in December, Room 201

The moon speaks Spanish.
It says
buenas noches!
In Russia, it follows you
down a snowy road.
It speaks
but no one listens,
In India, the moon is round
and white,
It is shining yellow in Thailand,
The moon in Norway wears a hat
and sings
about tomorrow, It is called
The Blue Cheese.
The moon is a rabbit,

a man.
From the sky it
looks at you
with
sleepy eyes.
In Spanish, says your grandmother,
it is telling you good night,
I will come back.

48 Developing Social Justice Mathematics Curriculum from Students' Realities

A Case of a Chicago Public School

Eric (Rico) Gutstein

Well we should protest and use mathematics, showing them our reasoning. We should fight for this school to stay integrated. As an individual I think I can't do anything because in order to make change you have to be with a bunch of people to make it happen. That's how this school was built. (Mirta,[1] Latina student, ninth grade)

I learned that Black kids ain't wanted and you're not supposed to be anywhere where you're not wanted. (Alice, African-American student, ninth grade)

In May 2001, fed up with what they perceived as evasive stalling tactics from city officials about their promise of a new high school for Chicago's Little Village community, 14 neighborhood residents started a hunger strike (Russo, 2003; Stovall, 2005). Nineteen days later, they called off the strike for health reasons. Within weeks, Chicago Public Schools (CPS) administration found the funds they had allocated and promised to Little Village in 1998. At that time, the CPS Board was also committed to building two college-prep, selective-enrollment high schools in whiter, more affluent Chicago communities. CPS built those schools, on time and without community struggle, leading many in Little Village (and elsewhere) to view the situation as the "rich getting richer." But activists in this Mexican immigrant community did not let up easily; the hunger strike culminated a decade-long struggle for a new school in the densely populated neighborhood where many students attended a nearby, overcrowded high school.

The resulting school, the Little Village/Lawndale High School (LVLHS), cost $68 million and is the most expensive public school ever built in Chicago. It houses four small schools that opened in fall 2005. Each has a separate administration and its own two-story corridor that opens on both ends into an outer ring with shared spaces (lunch room, auditorium, library, gyms, pool, etc.). Residents were surveyed by community activists to determine what they felt was important in the new school. Based on the responses, organizers and community members decided to have four small schools with separate emphases and 350 to 400 students each. The four schools are the World Language High School; the Multicultural Arts High School; Infinity: Math, Science, and Technology High School; and Social Justice High School. This article is about the mathematics program at Social Justice High School (known informally as "SoJo").

I am a university mathematics educator and have been a member of Sojo's design team since December 2003. I currently work with the school's mathematics (and other) teachers, and am considered part of the staff. As I write this in September 2008, Sojo, like the other LVLHS schools, just enrolled its fourth class of a little less than 100 ninth graders and currently has about 375 students. Thus, there are about 1500 students in the building.

Despite the community victory, things rarely go as planned—especially in Chicago. The hunger strikers fasted for a new school in overcrowded Little Village. When CPS fulfilled its promise, residents expected the new school would serve their neighborhood. However, larger political forces interceded. Because Chicago has an ugly history of racist exclusion, the federal government sued CPS in 1980 for its segregated schools. The ensuing "consent decree" mandated that new schools be racially balanced, if possible, which meant mixing white students and students of color (CPS schools are currently less than 9% white).[2] However, the Board's interpretation was to change the campus' attendance boundaries to include parts of North Lawndale, the African-American community immediately north of Little Village (in fact, Little Village is South Lawndale). The hunger strikers and others had demanded the school be nonselective and have open enrollment for students in its attendance boundaries. But to do this and include North Lawndale students, the Board narrowed the boundaries to exclude part of Little Village. This caused divisions in Little Village because some children would be "displaced" from LVLHS by African Americans. While the hunger strikers, many residents, and other community activists argued that the schools should be for both communities, others were upset. Complicating the situation is Chicago's historical neighborhood and turf issues and an ambivalent relationship between the two parts of the greater Lawndale community.

Complicating the Mix: Mathematizing Students' Social Realities

The schools opened in Fall 2005 with an enrollment that was 30% African American and 70% Latina/o. Relationships between Black and Brown students are generally good. Students work and play sports together, there is virtually no violence, and students occasionally sit together across racial lines in settings where they can choose seats (e.g., the cafeteria). We have observed much physical affection between students of different races, although there are language, style, and cultural differences to which students sometimes react. Sojo staff have tried to create a safe, welcoming space for African-American students and orchestrated a series of conversations about race in the 2005 to 2006 school year to emphasize that commonalities between the students and their communities outweighed differences. However, despite relatively harmonious surface relationships, African-American staff reported that Black students say that they feel isolated, marginalized, and excluded. The school clearly has a long way to go. And staff's efforts inside the building cannot easily overcome the hostility outside. If they stay after school, Black students have to navigate a half-mile walk in Little Village to the bus to North Lawndale (city buses come to the building but only right after school ends). Tensions between racially divided, rival neighborhood gangs affect students as well, even if only a few students are gang affiliated.

This complex mix surfaced in January 2006 when a local Latino politician (Mr. Sandoval) held a press conference and proposed that a nonbinding referendum to reinstate the original school boundaries be on the March 2006 (regular) ballot—in essence, eliminating African-American students. That day, Black Sojo students began asking teachers if they were going to be kicked out. Although the Sojo principal took a strong public stand that the school would continue to be for all of Lawndale (and was castigated in a local Latino newspaper), Black students were scared, angry, and unmollified. One of the Sojo mathematics teachers suggested that students do a week-long mathematics project in which the central question was: What is a fair solution for both communities? In the rest of this article, I examine this project (the "Boundaries Project") and situate it within a framework on teaching and learning mathematics for social justice.

Teaching and Learning Mathematics for Social Justice

A central part of our framework (the mathematics team at Sojo is myself and the three mathematics teachers) is a dual set of goals. One set concerns mathematics: the goal is for students to learn mathematics in rich, connected ways and develop mathematical power, conceptual understanding, and procedural proficiency. We want students to have the mathematical competencies to pass "gate-keeping" tests (like the ACT) and have the opportunities to pursue advanced mathematics courses and mathematically based careers. We also want them to reorient their views about mathematics away from the traditional one of mathematics as a decontextualized series of disconnected, discrete pieces of knowledge to be rotely memorized and regurgitated upon demand. Instead, we want students to view mathematics as a way to make sense out of the world. Sojo teaches the *Interactive Mathematics Program* (IMP) (Fendel, Resek, Alper, & Fraser, 1998), an NCTM-aligned, National Science Foundation-funded, "reform" curriculum. These goals about mathematics learning comprise what Ernest Morrell (2005) referred to as a "pedagogy of access." In these ways, the mathematics program at Sojo is similar to that of many other schools that have equity as a central part of their framework.

What makes Sojo different from many other schools, however, is its social justice emphasis. In the mathematics program, we also have social justice goals (Gutstein, 2006). These goals are that students use mathematics to begin to develop (1) critical sociopolitical knowledge of their local and broader social realities ("reading the world" with mathematics); (2) a sense of *social agency*, that is, a view of themselves as capable of effecting meaningful change for social justice ("writing the world" with mathematics); and (3) strong cultural and social identities. These constitute what Morrell (2005) called a "pedagogy of dissent" whose ultimate purpose is to prepare youth to take on their role as change agents toward a more just society. It is insufficient that students have access and opportunities, even if necessary to more toward equity. Ultimately, this is an individual solution because a pedagogy of access may not challenge the institutional structures that create inequality and injustice in the first place. Thus we advocate for the unity of both sets of goals, mathematics and social justice, for pedagogies of both access and dissent.

However, teaching mathematics for social justice is complex. Not only do mathematics teachers need strong, conceptually grounded content knowledge, they also need pedagogical content knowledge (Shulman, 1986); general pedagogical knowledge; knowledge of human development; and most importantly, knowledge of their students and their cultures, languages, and communities as well (Ladson-Billings, 1994). On top of all this, to effectively teach for social justice, in any subject, teachers need strong knowledge of history, politics, and social movements (Camangian & Yang, 2006; Christensen, 2000; Gutstein, 2008).

Nor is social justice curriculum a simple matter. Although examples of social justice mathematics units and projects exist, there is no connected, comprehensive curriculum (e.g., like IMP) for students to achieve the above social justice mathematics goals. At Sojo, we have adopted a framework related to Paulo Freire's (1970/1998) insistence that an education oriented toward reading and writing the world should start from "the present, existential, concrete situation, reflecting the aspirations of the people" (p. 76). Freire wrote this about adults in community-based literacy settings in Latin America in the 1960s, but his ideas have deeply influenced educators around the globe for decades. His perspective involves acknowledging that learners have valuable, valid knowledge about their lives and social realities. Freire advocated that teachers investigate and then use what he called "generative themes" (key social contradictions in students' lives and how they understand them) from which to develop curriculum. These themes are part of what

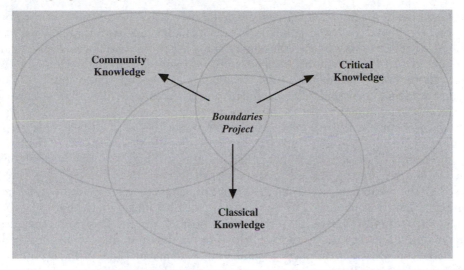

Figure 48.1   The intersection of community, critical, and classical knowledge.

we call "community knowledge," which also includes informal mathematical knowledge (Mack, 1990); other informal, out-of-school knowledge; knowledge and perspectives about everyday life; and also students' language and culture. The issues of the Boundaries Project constituted a generative theme in our students' lives, and their fears, understandings, prejudices, and uncertainties about their neighborhoods, identities, and interrelationships with others were all part of their community knowledge.

Figure 48.1 presents how students' community knowledge relates to developing "critical knowledge" of mathematics (Frankenstein, 1987, 1998) and our mathematics goals, which we collectively refer to as learning "classical knowledge" (of mathematics). The lines between the knowledges are meant to be permeable and vague, and their separations often unclear, for they can transform into each other. Utilizing a Freirean-like approach, we aim to build on students' community knowledge (i.e., generative themes) and, from that starting point, attempt to have students use mathematics to develop deeper critical knowledge of their sociopolitical realities as well as the mathematical competencies they need for various life opportunities. However, it is our experience that synthesizing and honoring these three knowledges in meaningful ways is quite difficult. To our knowledge, there are few examples of this being done in mathematics classrooms (for reports from Brazil see Gandin, 2002; O'Cadiz, Wong, & Torres, 1998).

The Boundaries Project

The project took a week (we had 400 minutes a week of mathematics the first year of school) and was quite intricate. We used the 70:30 ratio of Latinas/os to African Americans as a central idea from which to explore other issues. Each school had about 100 students at the time, and we asked students what the school and campus would look like in subsequent years if the ratio stayed the same or changed in various ways. With the full-capacity campus estimate of 1,400, there would be 420 African Americans and 980 Latinas/os. Using census data, students then investigated the probability of a Little Village or North Lawndale student getting into the school by lottery, given different ratios. This was complicated because although we had an estimate of 4,000 high school age students in Little Village, we had none for North Lawndale. The Census gave the number of 15- to 19-year-olds (a 5-year cohort) so students had to adjust to find how many high school-aged students were in the community. This led to discussions and investigations of dropout rates of local schools because students knew not all high-school-age youth were in school. Furthermore, more youth drop out in earlier high school grades than later ones, and students knew that older Lawndale youth were more likely than younger ones to be out of the community—in the military, prison, or even the grave. This harsh reality affects how one creates a model to find the number of 15- to 18-year-olds given the number of 15- to 19-year-olds. Students eventually simplified, found 80% of the five-year total, and decided that North Lawndale had about 4,150 high-school age youth—while also mathematizing the oppressive conditions of their lives.

Based on the 70:30 ratio, we asked the chance of being accepted for students from each community. This was about a 24.5% chance for Little Village youth, but only about a 10.1% chance for North Lawndale—something most felt unfair. This raised the question of how to determine the ratio so that students from both communities had equal chances since there were different numbers of potential students in Little Village (4,000) and North Lawndale (4,150). Some students also examined dropout rates and capacities in neighborhood schools and tried to determine how many spots were actually needed for the students who still attended high school.

Analyzing the Project: What Did Students Learn, What Did We Learn?

A primary goal of the project was that students develop mathematical power. A large majority of the students were able to answer some simpler questions (e.g., if the ratio were 20:80 or 40:60, what would be the chance of being accepted for students from each community). To determine probabilities, many students used a *percent bar,* an intuitive, conceptual tool from a percentage unit in the middle-school *Mathematics in Context* curriculum (National Center for Research in Mathematical Sciences Education & Freudenthal Institute [NCRMSE & FI], 1997–1998). We taught parts of this unit previously because the teachers felt that students' conceptual understanding of percentages was weak. But most students had difficulty with challenging problems. Few solved what was arguably the most convoluted: having found the number of 15- to 18-year-olds (in both communities), students then found the percentage of people who were in that age range (7.5% of all Lawndale residents). We gave them a census map with the number of residents for 16 sample North Lawndale blocks—they found the mean number of residents (171), then computed the average number of high school age youth per block using the 7.5% percentage (~13). Finally, they were to find how many of these "average" North Lawndale blocks the school boundaries would need to be extended by so that the chances of a North Lawndale student would be equal to that of a Little Village student—given their own personal ratio of choice (which ranged between 30:70 to 50:50 for most students, but did include 35:65 and 40:60). This was an extremely difficult problem to handle, and very few completed it.

This messy mathematics was quite challenging for students. We asked ourselves if students were doing high school mathematics because proportional reasoning is essentially middle-school work, although the probability and data analysis were more high school level. Their work provided evidence that they could mainly apply ideas in these content areas only when the problems were relatively straightforward. However, we would argue that to assess their mathematical growth, one has to consider that the mathematical complexity came not so much from the actual computations or algorithms students used but rather from mathematizing, understanding, setting up situations, and estimating, with simplifying assumptions. While our analysis suggests that what they may have learned with respect to actual content was limited, they gained experience in a number of sophisticated mathematical processes—representation, reasoning, communicating, and problem solving.

Because our goals also included that students develop sociopolitical consciousness (i.e., critical knowledge of their social context) as well as a sense of social agency, we examined our observations and students' writings for evidence. Our analysis was that students became more knowledgeable and clearer about the situation. They understood the (mathematical) reasons why CPS changed the racial composition (and boundaries), they heard some of the hunger strikers and their school principal support African-American students, and they also observed divisions in Little Village. Furthermore, their sense of agency was strongly evident. Students' written responses to the question, "What do you think we should do about the situation?" were quite clear. Over two thirds answered that action should be taken to "fight," "petition," "march," "protest," "bring this to the board," "speak out," and more. Only five students wrote that nothing could be done. Fabiola (a Latina), gave a typical response that suggested agency: "Something other than math I learned was that LVLHS and especially SJ will continue to fight against Sandoval's referendum so that our school will not be segregated…. We should continue to fight against this referendum…[and]…investigate to make the boundary fair."

We also learned, or relearned, as Alice's opening quote demonstrates, that the issues were volatile and close to students' hearts. This was evident in how students addressed the central question. The issue emerged of whether Sojo (and the campus) should remain at the 70:30 ratio. We had students write and justify their views on that point. Most Latina/o students advocated that the ratio stay the same while many African Americans wanted the building to be 50:50. Almost no one suggested that African-American students leave and the school be segregated—at least not aloud or in writing. In one class, students heatedly discussed the ratio. Amara, an African-American student, argued that "fair" meant that the schools should be half Black, half Brown, but Virginia, a Latina, countered that because the school was physically in a Latina/o community, the current ratio made sense. She pressed Amara on what ratio she would propose if the school was in North Lawndale, to which Simon, a Latino, quipped that they (Latinas/os) would be chased if it was. Amara insisted on a 50–50 ratio regardless of where the school was. The discussion continued for a while and cooled off, but the emotionality was evident. An English class also took up this theme, and some students expressed their views in letters to Mr. Sandoval and the media. Almost all the letters supported the current boundaries with the ratio remaining the same or increasing to 50–50 (which some African-American students advocated).

We know that, in general, it is difficult to attribute responsibility to one particular aspect of a school when there are interacting, interrelated goals. This element surfaces when researching social justice mathematics pedagogy and curriculum in a setting with a whole school effort toward social justice. In that sense, we learned that the above lesson applied to our situation because students discussed the issues in other classes, the principal took a public stand, the story was in the news, and conversations occurred in both communities. Thus, the controversy was in the air. We do have evidence that students mathematized their social realities in several ways, such as the above discussion about finding the number of 15- to 18-year-olds, and that students began to develop critical knowledge and social agency in mathematics class. However, we do not suggest that this occurred solely through mathematics, nor do we claim that their mathematical analyses were necessarily decisive in the process. But because of the overlapping and interconnected processes in the school, we do not consider it productive to spend too much time trying to tease out the role that each aspect played in the development of critical knowledge—we are satisfied with the position that mathematics class contributed and that we see evidence of reading and writing the world with mathematics.

We also learned that it is complicated to connect community, critical, and classical knowledges. For example, it was difficult to ensure students developed classical mathematical knowledge while simultaneously holding debates about what ratio was fair (i.e., critical knowledge). Conversely, we also saw instances in which some students' difficulty with proportional reasoning, for example, hampered their capacity to answer questions about equity and fairness—that is, insufficient classical knowledge impeded the development of their critical knowledge. And when we consider the relationship of community to classical knowledge, while we were relatively successful in starting from students' generative themes, our analysis suggests that students' mathematics learning could have been stronger. Finally, although in this particular situation we were able to tie into students' community knowledge, we are clear that in general it is not simple to grasp students' generative themes, nor are they guaranteed to be the same as those of the adults in their communities. In a sense, we view these all as research areas to address and attempt to untangle as we move forward.

Conclusion

The project and what we learned need to be contextualized within a larger program of teaching and learning mathematics for social justice at Sojo. We present this not as an exemplar of what students learned but rather of some of the challenges, complexities, and potential in connecting students' community knowledge to their critical awareness, while supporting their development of classical mathematical knowledge. The limitations and uncertainties present us with ongoing areas of research as well as of pedagogical and curricular development. We created the project in two days because the issue was immediate—we did not have the luxury of creating a well-thought out, cohesive unit connected to what students were already learning. We needed to seize the teachable moment, even though the work challenged and sometimes frustrated students because of its difficulty and open-ended, messy nature. We would argue that some of this is inevitable because of the ill-defined nature of daily and community life, but are working to minimize any incoherency. However, we also emphasize that, overall, most students were substantially more engaged in this project than at almost any other time during the year.

In the 2008 to 2009 school year, we aim to address several conceptual and practical issues we discuss here, such as strengthening students' mathematical learning on these types of projects, creating more cohesive projects, and building on generative themes. We have planned an extended multiweek unit on the theme of displacement affecting both communities—North Lawndale, because the rampant Chicago gentrification is now displacing people from there to far reaches of the city or to desperately poor suburbs, and Little Village, because immigration policies threaten to displace people back to Mexico. The opportunity to politically connect both communities and emphasize the unified struggle is unfortunately present in the reality of common exclusion.

Of the various justice-oriented mathematics projects students completed that year, this stands out because of how well it connected to, and built on, a generative theme. In general, without comprehensively investigating students' lives, it is hard to create authentic curriculum based on those realities. We had the opportunity to create this project because of the school and community political context—and we would have been remiss not to pursue it. Furthermore, generative themes are linked to genuine problems that are not easily answered. No one individual can answer the essential question we posed of what was a fair solution—not a teacher, student, parent, community member, administrator, or politician. To resolve this issue will take concerted, collaborative efforts by all of these groups because ultimately this is a question of the allocation of resources. That is, as some students discovered, there are not enough quality schools for *all* Lawndale students, North and South, even with the new campus. Because of injustices like this, the fundamental purpose of teaching (mathematics) for social justice is to create opportunities for youth to become participants in solving the real problems of their communities and change agents who will stand up and fight for justice using mathematics and every other means with which to do so.

Acknowledgments

Although this article is single authored, the teaching, planning, assessment, and analysis involved in this story were collaboratively shared among three other people besides the author: Joyce Sia (teacher), Phi Pham (teacher), and Patricia Buenrostro (mathematics support staff).

Notes

1. All students' names are pseudonyms.
2. According to the decree (Chicago Public Schools, 2008):
   ...the District currently applies specified racial goals to the extent practicable, in selecting applicants for admission in magnet schools and programs. The goal of each magnet school and program is to have an enrollment between 65-85 percent minority (Black, Hispanic, Asian/Pacific Islander, or American Indian/Alaskan Native) and 15–35 percent non-minority (White) (p. 3).

References

Camangian, P., & Yang, K. W. (2006, March 30). *Transformative teaching and youth resistance.* Talk given at DePaul University, Chicago.

Chicago Public Schools. (2008). Chicago public schools policy manual: Magnet schools and programs. Chicago: Author. Retrieved June 23rd, 2008, from http://policy.cps.k12.il.us/documents/602.2.pdf

Christensen, L. (2000). *Reading, writing, and rising up: Teaching about social justice and the power of the written word.* Milwaukee, WI: Rethinking Schools.

Fendel, D., Resek, D., Alper, L., & Fraser, S. (1998). *Interactive mathematics program.* Berkeley, CA: Key Curriculum Press.

Frankenstein, M. (1987). Critical mathematics education: An application of Paulo Freire's epistemology. In I. Shor (Ed.), *Freire for the classroom: A sourcebook for liberatory teaching* (pp. 180–210). Portsmouth, NH: Boyton/Cook.

Frankenstein, M. (1998). Reading the world with math: Goals for a critical mathematical literacy curriculum. In E. Lee, D. Menkart, & M. Okazawa-Rey (Eds.), *Beyond heroes and holidays: A practical guide to K-12 anti-racist, multicultural education and staff development* (pp. 306–313). Washington D.C.: Network of Educators on the Americas.

Freire, P. (1998). *Pedagogy of the oppressed.* (M. B. Ramos, Trans.). New York: Continuum. (Original work published 1970)

Gandin, L. A. (2002). *Democratizing access, governance, and knowledge: The struggle for educational alternatives in Porto Alegre, Brazil.* Unpublished doctoral dissertation, University of Wisconsin, Madison.

Gutstein, E. (2006). *Reading and writing the world with mathematics: Toward a pedagogy for social justice.* New York: Routledge.

Gutstein, E. (2008). Building political relationships with students: An aspect of social justice peda-gogy. In E. de Freitas & K. Nolan (Eds.), *Opening the research text: Critical insights and in(ter)ventions into mathematics education* (pp. 189–204). Albany, NY: SUNY Press.

Ladson-Billings, G. (1994). *The dreamkeepers.* San Francisco: Jossey-Bass.

Mack, N. K. (1990). Learning fractions with understanding: Building on informal knowledge. *Journal for Research in Mathematics Education, 21,* 16–32.

Morrell, E. (2005, February 3rd). *Doing critical social research with youth.* Talk given at DePaul University, Chicago.

National Center for Research in Mathematical Sciences Education & Freudenthal Institute (NCRMSE & FI). (1997–1998). *Mathematics in context: A connected curriculum for grades 5–8.* Chicago: Encyclopedia Britannica Educational Corporation.

O'Cadiz, M., Wong, P., & Torres, C. (1998). *Education and democracy: Paulo Freire, social movements, and educational reform in São Paulo.* Boulder, CO: Westview Press.

Russo, A. (2003, June). Constructing a new school. *Catalyst.* Retrieved March 3rd, 2004, from http://www.catalyst-chicago.org/06-03/0603littlevillage.htm

Shulman, L. S. (1986). Those who understand: Knowledge growth in teaching. *Educational Researcher, 15,* 4–14.

Stovall, D. O. (2005). Communities struggle to make small serve all. *Rethinking Schools, 19,* 4. Retrieved September 1st, 2006, from http://www.rethinkingschools.org/archive/19_04/stru194.shtml

49 Robles' Dilemma

Armando Torres

My career did not begin the first day I stepped into the classroom. It began in an English class, or maybe the day of my graduation from high school, when my English teacher asked me a most sincere question: "They (the school) are going to let you speak in front of the whole graduation class?" Or maybe my career began when my Teacher Cadet teacher made it clear to me that according to the way I get along with people, I could make a good teacher. Perhaps my real passion for teaching became clear when I realized for myself the effect, both negative and positive that teachers can have on their students (a lot of my memories are negative, along with moments when I really wanted to learn and my teachers did not fulfill their responsibility in terms of the academic learning that should have taken place).

Through many years, and as a teacher still, I have flashbacks to the times my English teacher ignored me in class when I made comments related to the lesson; my Algebra teacher called me out in front of the whole class for scoring last on chapter tests (regardless of how hard I tried); my Government teacher gave me detention for sleeping in class (after working eight-hour shifts five days a week at my job—and I had to wake up to be at my 7:30 am class); or another English teacher made me do push-ups in class for speaking a language other than English. Now, I find myself teaching in the same class where the students were placed on lock-down because of a gang affiliated shooting that took the life of a fellow classmate in front of the school building. But sometimes I feel that the teaching I am doing is the teaching I would have liked my teachers to have done with me. I make a major effort to eliminate any pessimistic vocabulary when I am talking to students.

The realization of my dream began many years later as I applied for teaching jobs in various school districts. After succumbing to rejection letter after rejection letter, I took a short, a very short vacation in southern California. Just as I was settling in, I got a call from the dean of Richmond High School, my alma mater back in the Bay Area. "Mr. Torres, we have an opening for an 80% teaching position. We would like for you to join us if you are available." The next day I was on a return flight to the Bay Area. Excitement accompanied me all the way. Just the bare image of me, Armando Torres, soon to be Mr. Torres, standing in front of a classroom as I would finally get a chance to do what I had been aspiring to do since my years as a high school student—teach. By the time we hung up the phone, I realized that I had not even asked what subject. Yet, it didn't matter at the time. What mattered was the fact that I would finally get a chance to step into a classroom, the very classroom that I had sat in as a student many years before. However, this time it would be different. This time, I would be in control of the environment within the classroom. This time, I would establish the positive and nurturing relationship that needs to occur between teacher and student. This time, I would be sure that my new introduction to these classrooms would be different from what I had myself experienced as a high school student at Richmond High, and that many of the students were currently experiencing.

Ironically, my teaching career would begin at the same school from which, 10 years earlier, I had been expelled. Many teachers still remembered me. While a few teachers were happy to see me, others were cold and bitter at having me, their "trouble maker" on their teaching staff. Despite this, I was proud. I was proud that the same teachers that once upon a time asked me to leave the class because I was "unteachable," now had to put up with me as a member of the faculty. I would also be among the same staff with those teachers that reminded me of what an amazing teacher I would be one day.

"So you sure you want to do this?" said Mr. Crozzley, as I stepped into his office. "Would you be willing to teach full time if the opportunity arose?" he continued. Without hesitation, I gladly nodded and welcomed the challenge. Little did I know what was coming my way. He broke down the scenario. "Since you're not full-time staff, we cannot get you a classroom for yourself so you'll be teaching in three different classrooms, three different subjects." All of a sudden the enthusiasm that I felt two days before left me, as if it was also taking my dream, the opportunity to teach in my own personal space. Having a personal space is important to me because it allows for full control and stability in one's teaching. He asked me with concern, "Will that be OK for you?" Was it OK? What was my other choice? Of course it was. It would be a great opportunity for me to tough it up my first year and maybe work my way up and hope to one day have my own classroom. In retrospect, I don't think it was so much toughing it up; I really think it was a silly decision on my part, and one that I regretted for a while but learned to accept as a great lesson.

This was the scenario: First period I would be in the east wing of the school. For the second period I would have to collect my teaching materials and drag them to the west wing of the school. I needed to get to that classroom before the teacher, who had the only key for the room, had left. Third period I would run back to the previous classroom, which had been used by a teacher that only utilized the room for three periods, yet wasn't willing to hand over the room for someone he once taught, or at least thought he taught. Fourth and fifth periods, I would be able find refuge in the social science lounge. I had initially considered using this underutilized space as my classroom; however, it was too small to teach in and full of abandoned teacher lockers. It wasn't exactly my ideal setting for what my classroom should look like. Sixth period I would work my way to the north wing and teach a world history class of 43 students. From east wing to west wing to north wing would be my pilgrimage through the masses of hundreds of bodies attempting to work their way to class, to their lockers, to their friends, bathrooms, to the large body of students congregating to see a fight. Students moving behind me, in front of me, next to me, blocking my right of way to a classroom. And in that classroom I would find an able body of students who expected something new from their teacher, or at least something that would keep them academically interested in school.

Based on the students' attendance, I was keeping them academically interested in school. Class size varied from 24 ninth grade students in my second period social science sheltered class, to 43 bilingual tenth, eleventh, and twelfth grade students in my sixth period world history class. Just as students feel exhausted at the end of the day, so do teachers, and I was no exception.

Never to forget that back-to-school night: as fatigued as I was, so were the parents from their long day of work. The parents came only to find their children's teacher without a classroom. Instead, their teacher was behind a table in the middle of a hallway looking like an army recruiter at a college recruitment center. The only things accompanying the teacher behind the table were his students' grades and a few brochures on "How to Help Your Son/Daughter Learn." I was armed with a smile demonstrating that everything was just fine. And it was! I was enjoying my job. I had a wonderful group of students that had made the decision to show up to class. Now while the simple act of attending class may not be a huge accomplishment, for the students that I work with, the simple act of just showing up to class is a struggle and a success all in one. This is especially so for those students who are considering leaving school, which at Richmond High were far too many students. I was convinced that my success as a teacher began with my ability to connect with my students. The connection I made with my students was because of my attitude toward them. It was this attitude that allowed me to keep my head above water, along with their interest to learn. Despite these conditions, I continuously questioned my reason for sticking with this job. It wasn't long before my pilgrimage from class to class began to take a toll on me. Plus, class size began to increase as the school year progressed.

Don't get me wrong, some great lessons where taking place during my busy moments at Richmond High School. I will never forget the lack of interest my students first had about the subject of steroids. It was around the time Arnold Schwarzenegger was running for governor of California. The press quickly began to circulate articles on steroids. An article the students and I found interesting was on "Steroids and High School Athletes." Students voiced their opinion and were up front, "Those are problems rich white kids have. We don't have them problems here," said Ruby. This was a great opportunity to use this controversial topic as a teachable moment in class. The students and I divided the class in half—debating for and against steroids. Having students walk out of class saying, "I don't even agree on using steroids yet having to defend them was fun." or "We should do more of that, Mr. Torres," reaffirmed for me that as a teacher I have to be flexible enough to take advantage of the unplanned teachable moments. Through this activity, I was able to see the importance of student interaction and student voices. Little did I know that during her junior year, Ruby would be on the cover of the local newspaper sharing her experience on Richmond High's Debate Team and how it had encouraged her to seek a career in law.

While many students leave memorable moments in the lives of teachers, only a few are actually the ones that make teachers decide whether they return the next school year or not. I could never forget the presence of *Panda*. Panda was a 5 feet 2 inches, dark skin Mexican-American kid who could go anywhere he wanted and would always be noticed by students and teachers alike. The young ladies at school didn't find him attractive, he was too cute. His constant and unbreakable smile was impossible not to notice. Soccer was his passion and even though he was part of the junior varsity soccer team, he often rode the bench for the varsity team. Playing on the varsity team was his aspiration, especially since he was a freshman. Who wouldn't want to play on Richmond High's varsity soccer team? It has been nationally recognized as an elite team placing fourth in the state of California and 13th in the United States. The varsity players looked on Panda as the little brother everyone wanted to have. He was funny, sincere with his words, immaturely talkative, made everyone laugh; he was cute and always the center of attention.

In the classroom, Panda participated in all classroom activities except one, reading. We did current event articles with a KWLH chart to go with it. When time permitted, we debated some issues. He enjoyed debating against the use of steroids amongst high school athletes. Panda was often selected as the speaker/representative of the group when it was time for presentations. One time, while teaching the lesson on the Native American experience in the Bay area, I had asked Panda to read. It was no wonder why Robles talked so much.

As a ninth grader, Robles was reading at second grade level! Words like *the, they, a*, and *if* were easy for him to read, but *became, plagues*, and *instinct* became words that were torturous to him. The discomfort of his reading was obvious to the entire class, yet there were still a few giggles in the class that just couldn't be held back. I constantly reminded the class to "Respect others' right to learn and my right to teach." It so happened that Panda had compensated for his lack of reading ability with verbal participation. Just as the blind develop a keen sense of hearing, Panda developed a skill at talking that became his defense mechanism to make up for his inability to read.

As his teacher, I sought out support from other high school staff. I learned from his counselor that Panda had been kicked out of previous classes due to behavior issues such as excessive use of profanity, talking too much, and not respecting others' opinion. I stood in awe! I could never have guessed that Robles had these issues. I mean, he did talk out of place a few times, maybe twice, I pulled him out of class to speak to him about his language, but I assumed (never assume) every teacher when having discipline issues with their students did the same—talk to them individually without calling them out in front of the class. Whereas other teachers had negative experiences with Panda, I did not, well maybe twice, but no more than that! Robles and I worked well together. There was mutual respect between teacher and student and even though I would discipline him on occasion, he always knew it came from a sincere desire to see him succeed. We even spent a few nights going over his reading skills at the local Barnes & Noble in order for him to feel a bit more comfortable reading in class. He was happy to have me offer extra assistance and I was equally as happy to be able to provide it. If you would have asked me to guess which were his books of choice, I would have never guessed, and you wouldn't have either: *The Life of Selena* and *The Titanic*. It was evident he knew the history behind Selena—her childhood, the life of her family, her career as a singer, and other topics I wasn't aware of in her life.

Hearing the counselor describe to me other teachers' experiences with Panda, caused me to ask, "Is that the reason why Robles has been placed in my class?" You see, Panda was at the point where no one wanted him in their class. In many teachers' eyes, Panda had become an "unteachable" student, just as I had been labeled, many years before. However, I believe there are no "unteachable" students and Panda proved this to me. It seemed like every time I spoke about Robles in department meetings, no one was sure who I was talking about, kind of like a rare species. One teacher expressed something that I hated the most, "He shouldn't even be in this school. It is impossible to teach him." Those words have haunted me for years. The same words that had been used against me years before were being used on Panda: Words that degrade a student. Words that didn't break my bones, but damn, how they did and do cause psychological pain. Unfortunately for me, and for many students as well, we begin to believe judgments like that, especially when we lack the positive reinforcement that can easily make a difference to students' performance.

I've noticed that many teachers do not have the attitude of "all students can triumph," or "they are all teachable." And if they do have that attitude, it's positive effects can easily be lost due to the excess work placed on teachers in underprivileged communities. Being underpaid, working with oversized classrooms, disciplinary issues, adjunct duties, and being surrogate parents for many of the students are common experiences all teachers face. However, at schools like Richmond High, located in low income, high crime communities that are known to be in one of the nation's most violent cities, these experiences are multiplied. Unfortunately, this extra burden manifests itself in the attitude the teachers have toward the students most vulnerable to their behavior: low income students, first generation students whose parents are immigrants, English language learners, "unteachable" students, those students that have been marginalized within our educational system and have no other options as to where they attend high school. These teachers have taught me a very important lesson: Don't be like them. Don't assume that students are "unteachable," don't marginalize students, don't take your frustrations out on the students. A few other lessons learned were to avoid the teachers' cafeteria; do not listen to the negative feedback they share about students; and most definitely, do not follow in their footsteps, regardless of how many years they have been in the teaching field or how many degrees they possess.

Despite having to migrate from class to class, my policy has been to always greet students at the door. Why greet them you may ask? It is important for me to greet each student because in doing so I am acknowledging that individual's presence: and the funny thing is that they will get used to it and will greet you when you forget. Also, don't take frustrations out on them—they too are victims of the system. Do not be afraid of wishing them a good day when leaving your classroom—those might be the last and only positive words they may hear before walking out into the streets when they leave Richmond High at the end of the school day.

One afternoon, Panda walked into my sixth period class. "I've been looking all over for you Mr. Torres," he said in a playful angry voice. Excitement was glowing everywhere. It appeared as if he was walking on air! In one hand he held a piece of paper I couldn't figure out why he was so excited. He couldn't believe he had the grades that would allow him to play on Richmond High's varsity soccer team. "Torres! I made it!" "You made what?" I asked pretending to not know what he was talking about. "I made the grades! I'm going to play for Richmond High!" he expressed with an unforgettable enthusiasm.

Soccer season wasn't in full effect when rumors were being spread in the district of losing extracurricular activities due to budget cuts, and this would include sports. Soon, the rumors turned to debate at the school board and quickly began to worry many members of team sports and athletes like Robles, for whom, unfortunately, the only reason for going to school was to play team sports. Robles was not at Richmond High to earn his high school diploma, or get an education to attend college, he was there because he wanted to play soccer. The funding situation began to draw media attention, both in Spanish and English. The media contacted the coaches and asked to make a special segment on students who relied on school sports for motivation in continuing to go to school. Coaches agreed that in fact, if they had ever seen a change in any student's academics and attitude toward school, it had been Robles. Upon this recommendation, Robles was followed in school by a camera crew who wanted to capture the experience of this once troubled kid who now had found an interest in academics through team sports. He walked into my class with the camera crew and astonished me! "Mr. Torres, they want to talk to you." Out of all his teachers and counselors, Robles wanted me to talk about the improvement he had experienced ever since his acceptance by the soccer team. After hesitating to appear on the Bay Area news, I unwillingly agreed to participate with Robles. Why not? This was a great opportunity for me to share with a larger community what a motivated teacher can accomplish when moving beyond student stereotypes. What astonished me the most is that in my classes, I had, and continue to have, many students like Robles, students other teachers find "unteachable" and "unwilling to learn."

You see, I am continually given students, just like Robles, that are "unteachable." Students that other teachers hope will not show up to class. It is these very same teachers that are amazed to find out how well these students perform with me and to see that I am able to capture what the students really know. Students that literally live on the other side of the tracks and struggle greatly with the task of being a student, I don't have a problem with them. I am able to connect with them and be that positive teacher that they need— like the very few positive teachers that I had when I was a student at the same school. I also have self-motivated students who regardless of how distracting the classroom is, will still finish their assignment, whether it is at home, or at school. They will finish it.

My biggest dilemma is finding that academic balance where I can contain the Robles, the self-motivated students, and the state mandated standards, as well as maintaining a healthy balance for myself where I will avoid a career change due to teacher burnout—the career that I so much desire to follow until I retire. I continually question whether I am finding the adequate balance necessary in order to educate the students that have made the decision to show up to class. Is it what I do that is different from other teachers that continues to draw the students to class? If so, where does that come from? Does it come from experiences of teachers having low expectations of me? Does it come from living in the same 'hood as the students? Is it because I am a teacher of color? Or is it because of the respect I give my students and the high expectations I have for them? I don't have an answer for these questions, what I do have is the sincere commitment to continue educating the students that walk through my classroom door.

50 Teaching in the Undertow
Resisting the Pull of Schooling-as-Usual

Gregory Michie

As a child, I was amazed by the ocean. I remember being awed as I looked out at the vast expanse of blue-green water off the South Carolina coast. And I recall the cautionary words my mother used each time I tried to wade in deeper than my waist: "Be careful of the undertow," she'd say.

According to my mom, the undertow was an invisible current beneath the ocean's surface that, if you weren't careful, could pull you down the coastline or out to sea before you knew what was happening. It tugged you along almost imperceptibly, she said, so you had to consciously keep your bearings: Pick a recognizable landmark and don't lose sight of it.

I could've used her advice when I began teaching seventh and eighth grade on Chicago's south side two decades later. I went in with no formal preparation or credentials, and as a White male transplanted from the South, I was an outsider to my students in many ways. My approach at the time grew mostly out of what made sense to me. I thought classrooms should be active spaces where kids had regular opportunities to do and make things. I thought students should be encouraged to creatively express themselves, that their voices should be not only heard, but valued. I believed kids should feel a connection between what they studied in school and their lives outside it, and should be pushed to think critically about the world around them. Most of all, I recognized that a meaningful, quality education was crucial for the young people I would be teaching, whose communities had been largely neglected and abandoned by those in power.

But having beliefs or guiding principles is one thing. Figuring out how to put them into practice, I learned, is another matter altogether, especially if you're teaching at a struggling urban school where the "pedagogy of poverty," as Martin Haberman (1996) calls it—characterized by "constant teacher direction and student compliance"—is in widespread use. In that sort of environment, it's easy to lose your footing as a novice teacher, to begin to drift from your anchorage, to be seduced by the pull of convention or expediency or outside demands. The undertow of schooling, you quickly figure out, can be as strong and stealthy as any ocean's—maybe even more so.

So, how do you resist? The first thing to know is, as much as it may seem otherwise at first, you're not alone. I've spent significant time in dozens of Chicago schools over the years, and while many have their share of adults who have become, at least on the surface, jaded or resigned to mediocrity, I've also found dedicated, caring, even visionary teachers almost everywhere I've been. This is important to understand as a new teacher because it makes it less likely that you'll fall into the trap of seeing yourself as the anointed one, the lone crusader working for justice in an unjust school and world. Heroic teacher memoirs and Hollywood movies notwithstanding, that is rarely, if ever, the way things are.

While the organizational structures and scheduling at your school may not support alliance-building among teachers (and may, in fact, implicitly encourage you to isolate yourself), one of the best things you can do for yourself as a beginning teacher is to seek out allies—both within your school and in the broader community of educators. Fellow teachers with whom you are aligned philosophically and politically can be vital sources of both emotional support and practical ideas, and even those who don't seem to share your views can sometimes prove helpful. A colleague who's been teaching in your building for 25 years, even if "traditional" or "burned out" at first glance, may still have lessons to impart and useful advice to offer, and may, in time, turn out to be not as one-dimensional as you originally thought.

That's not to say that you should expect to be surrounded by hopeful and forward-thinking educators. Cynicism can be deeply entrenched in big-city public schools, and also wildly contagious. One of the first temptations for a new teacher is to join this chorus of negativity and begin, however reluctantly, to recite the sorts of excuses you were certain you'd never make: that you can't really get to know your students because there are too many of them, that you can't engage students in group work because they get out of control, that you can't focus on building critical thinking skills when your kids are having a hard enough time just finding a vocabulary word in the dictionary. I've heard myself say or think all those things at one time or another, and they're all legitimate dilemmas. But Bill Ayers, longtime educator and author of *To Teach* (2001), points out that focusing on all the impediments to your work, while perhaps therapeutic in the short term, is ultimately a dead-end for the committed teacher. Ayers suggests turning each obstacle around and viewing it from a more hopeful perspective by saying, "OK, this is my situation, these are the realities. Given that, what *can* I do?" Maybe you can't do everything you'd planned or imagined—at least not right away—but you can always do something.

It may be that you have to start with something small and seemingly insignificant—like bulletin boards, for instance. In many elementary and middle schools, bulletin boards simply become part of the scenery, wallpapered with routine announcements or seasonal messages that rarely provoke thought or cause anyone—adults or kids—to stop and take notice. But bulletin boards can be to teachers and students what blank walls are to graffiti artists: an opportunity—the most visible one of all in many schools—to make a statement, to pose questions, to speak out on an issue, to bring kids' lives into classrooms or hallways. In one school I visited, I saw a bulletin board that featured the words THEY WERE HERE FIRST at its center, with the names of a number of American Indian tribes radiating around the outer edges. At another school, seventh graders recognized the Day of the Dead by displaying letters they'd written to loved ones who had passed away. Still another teacher put up a thought-provoking quote along with an invitation for students to attach quotes they found challenging or inspiring.

Those may not sound like such radical acts when placed alongside the more elaborate proposals of education's critical theorists. But once you're in a classroom of your own, you begin to realize that it's in the details, as much as in the big-picture theorizing, that critical conceptions of teaching find life. Kids can learn about equity and justice from the way community is formed in a classroom, how decisions are made, who is represented on the walls and bookshelves, what sorts of interactions are encouraged and discouraged, whose thoughts and ideas are valued, and, yes, even what's on the bulletin boards. Teaching for social justice, in practice, is as much about the environment you create as it is about the explicit lessons you teach.

Content does matter, though, and it's another area in which, as a new teacher, you'll be challenged to hold true to your beliefs. For one thing, it's likely that you'll feel the ominous cloud of high-stakes testing looming over every curricular decision you make. One of the many tragic consequences of this is that the basic curriculum question—What knowledge and experiences are most worthwhile for my students?—can seem either beyond your purview as a teacher or entirely moot. When you're handed a booklet of state goals or district guidelines, loaded down with textbooks and teachers' guides, and told what sequence of lessons to follow, it's easy for curriculum to become not something you wrestle with or debate, but something you unwrap: a social studies series called "Discoveries," let's say, that gives kids few opportunities and little inspiration to actually make any.

Beyond that, you may be further overwhelmed by all you need to do to make what you teach more meaningful and to lend it a critical perspective: limiting the use of biased and oversimplified textbooks, bringing in primary source documents, connecting topics to real-world issues, reading whole novels instead of chopped-up basal selections, giving students opportunities to write about their lives, weaving the arts throughout your subject areas, inviting your kids to help decide what they want to study, and so on. The colossal size of the challenge can be truly paralyzing: because you can't do everything, you delay doing anything, and instead fall back on using textbooks and following directives until you get your feet more firmly on the ground.

But the ground is always shifting when you're a teacher, so your feet may never be fully planted. Instead of waiting for that to happen, take on something more manageable: Start with one subject and commit yourself to bringing it to life for your students, even if you're temporarily relying on canned curricula for other subjects. Or, if you teach only one or two subjects to several groups of kids, try putting your own spin on things one day a week, and then build from there. Again, you may not be able to do everything you'd hoped all at once—but you can do something.

If you're coming into the classroom with an orientation toward teaching for social justice, you already understand that public schools too often serve as an oppressive force in the lives of poor children and students of color. I had that reality in mind when I started out as a new teacher, and I wanted to do my part to interrupt it. But my approach, at least initially, was naïve: if schools were oppressive, I figured, then the antidote to that was freedom, so in my classroom students would be "free." It sounded great in my head, but since I hadn't thought out the specifics of what freedom really meant within the context of a public school—or how I might create the conditions where it could happen—I quickly found myself in the midst of absolute chaos in my classes.

The problem with chaos is not only that it makes you crazy, but it directs all your energy toward anticipating and addressing student misbehavior. Other concerns, such as whether your kids are learning anything of value, tend to fall by the wayside. These skewed priorities are often reinforced by administrators who place a premium on order and control, and who hold up as exemplary those teachers who keep the tightest reins on their students. If you're not careful, you can find yourself falling into a similar pattern of thinking: classifying your days as good or bad based solely by how quietly your students sit at their desks or how straight they line up in the hallways.

Many young teachers are confident they'll be able to rise above such pressure once they have a classroom of their own, or delude themselves with the belief that they'll be viewed as such cool teachers that they won't have to worry about disciplinary issues. Progressive approaches to teaching often encourage such an attitude by glossing over classroom management concerns, or by suggesting that if teachers simply come up with engaging lessons, management issues will largely take care of themselves. But my experience is that, in many urban classrooms, it's far more complicated than that, and if you're blindsided by serious discipline concerns, as I was, it can be tempting to adopt draconian corrective measures. The point is not to obsess over order and control as a beginning teacher, but to go in with a specific plan of action for building community among your students rather than vague notions about "freedom." If you really want to have a collaborative and democratic environment in your classroom, you have to be thoughtful and purposeful in creating structures that support it.

These details of practice—creating an environment for learning, rethinking your curriculum, and fostering a democratic community—can all provide opportunities for bringing a social justice perspective into your classroom. But it's also possible to become lost in the everyday details, to get so caught up in the immediacy of your teaching that you don't pay enough attention to its larger contexts. Indeed, the undertow may pull you in such a direction: Professional development seminars and in-service workshops frequently encourage tunnel vision in new teachers by focusing narrowly on specific methods, strategies, or one-size-fits-all approaches.

That's why it's important to remind yourself that methods and other practical matters mean little unless placed within larger social, economic, and political contexts. For beginning teachers at urban schools—especially for those who are coming in as "outsiders" to the communities where they're teaching—committing to continued efforts at self-education on issues of race, culture, and poverty is vital (and also something you're not likely to get at an in-service). Middle-class teachers who lack a personal understanding of poverty and the many ways it can impact children, families, and neighborhoods need to do all they can to increase their awareness. Likewise, White teachers need to work hard to learn about the cultural histories and current struggles of their students of color and, at the same time, to examine their own privilege.

If they don't, the result can be teachers who, consciously or not, see the world exclusively through their own racial, cultural, and class-based lenses—a tendency which may lead them to interact with students and families in detrimental ways. A teacher friend once told me of a White colleague's advice to a Mexican immigrant student who was having trouble getting his homework completed: "Just go in your room, close the door, shut out all the noise, and focus on your work." That the student didn't have a room of his own or a door to close apparently never occurred to the teacher. More recently, another teacher I know listened as a White counselor expressed her dismay at what she perceived as the limited experiences of some of her school's Mexican American students. "I can't believe these kids haven't been to Navy Pier," the woman said, referring to a downtown Chicago tourist attraction. "Their parents don't take them places. When I was little, my mom would pack up the car and take us to Grant Park." She added, "And we weren't rich, either. But she still took us places."

Such responses grow out of an often subconscious worldview that takes for granted a White, middle-class, English-speaking frame of reference. Examining previously unrecognized social advantages and privileges can help White, middle-class teachers question such notions and recognize, as anthropologist Wade Davis (2004) has said, that the "world in which [they] were born does not exist in some absolute sense, but is just one model of reality." Understanding the limitations of their own perspectives may in turn help them work with students of color and their families in more authentic and respectful ways. But like learning to teach, the process of confronting one's class privilege and redefining one's Whiteness is a continual one (Howard, 2005; Tatum, 1997). For the committed White teacher—myself included—it's an ongoing project.

Still, no matter what you do to buoy yourself as a new teacher, you're almost certain to have moments—probably more than a few of them—when you question the value and effectiveness of what you're doing. One of the most persistent early challenges for a socially conscious teacher, at least it was for me, is fighting the feeling that your work isn't making a difference, or at least not the sort of difference you'd imagined. When your goals are expansive and hopeful, when you believe that teaching is potentially a world-changing act, it can become discouraging to feel as if your efforts are falling far short of that vision. As one young teacher I know put it, "You feel like you should be seeing light bulbs going off in kids' heads every day, like they're suddenly seeing the world differently. But a lot of times, you think, 'This whole week—nothing! I'm not teaching for social justice!'"

At times like those, the undertow pulls in the direction of fatalism, despair, and emotional disengagement. It beckons you to stop trying so hard, to be more "realistic" about the kids you teach, to abandon your belief that public schools can be transformed in any meaningful or lasting way. Resisting that suffocating pull, and instead, holding onto hope requires a delicate balancing act: acknowledging the grim systemic realities and personal limitations you face as a teacher, but at the same time recommitting yourself to working toward something better. You have to forgive yourself for your failings, then turn around and try to use them to refocus and reenergize your teaching the next day. You also have to allow yourself to appreciate the good moments that do take place in your classroom, no matter how small they may seem in the grand scheme of things. In doing so, you should keep in mind the words of poet and essayist Audre Lorde: "Even the smallest victory is never to be taken for granted. Each victory must be applauded, because it is so easy not to battle at all, to just accept and call that acceptance inevitable" (1999, p. 152). I think every new teacher should have that quote taped to her desk, her classroom door, her rearview mirror, her alarm clock—to any spot where she might need a little extra strength for the journey.

Becoming a teacher is a journey, after all, one in which you're always learning. One thing I learned while writing this piece is that there's actually no such thing as an undertow. The force of water that pulls you down the beach is, in fact, called a longshore current, and the one that pulls you out to sea is known as a rip current. Undertow, it turns out, is a colloquialism. Considering that my mother was born on a farm in Georgia and raised in rural Kentucky, it makes perfect sense that that's the term she's always used. Longshore currents and rip currents will probably always be "the undertow" to me.

I learned one more thing, too. If you ever find yourself caught in a real rip current, the best approach is not to try to swim directly against it. You'll exhaust yourself, and the current's force will end up pulling you out anyway. Instead, say those who are knowledgeable in the science of wave motion, you should avoid panicking, swim with the current for a little while, and eventually you'll be free.

The undertow of schools, in my experience, doesn't release teachers from its pull quite so easily. Still, burnout being what it is, there is something to be said for new teachers not trying to fight it at every turn. The best advice, I think, is to choose your battles early on, pace yourself, swim with the current when you have to, and never lose sight of that spot on the shore.

References

Ayers, W. (2001). *To teach: The journey of a teacher* (2nd ed.). New York: Teachers College Press.

Davis, W. (2004, February 9). Interview with John Burnett. National Public Radio. Retrieved April 25, 2006, from http://news.kusp.org/templates/story/story.php?storyId=3809815

Haberman, M. (1996). The pedagogy of poverty versus good teaching. In W. Ayers & P. Ford (Eds.), *City kids, city teachers: Reports from the front row* (pp. 118–130). New York: New Press.

Howard, G. (2005). *We can't teach what we don't know: White teachers, multiracial schools* (2nd ed.). New York: Teachers College Press.

Lorde, A. (1999). A burst of light: Living with cancer. In J. Price & M. Shildrick (Eds.), *Feminist theory and the body: A reader* (pp. 149–162). New York: Routledge.

Tatum, B. D. (1997). *"Why are all the Black kids sitting together in the cafeteria?" and other conversations about race.* New York: Basic Books.

51 Radical Walls

Classrooms that Celebrate Activism and Social Justice

An Interview with Josh MacPhee

Nicolas Lampert and Josh MacPhee

Josh MacPhee is a street artist, designer, curator, author, and activist. His first book was *Stencil Pirates: A Global Survey of the Street Stencil* (2004). A street stenciler and poster maker for over a decade, MacPhee also helps run JUSTSEEDS, a radical art distribution project as a way to develop and distribute t-shirts, posters, and stickers with political content. Since 2000 he has curated the *Celebrate People's History* poster series, a collection of inexpensive educational posters focused on suppressed and little known histories of social justice movements.

Lampert: What inspired you to start the *Celebrate People's History* series?

MacPhee: I first started producing the posters in 1998, soon after I had moved to Chicago. I noticed that there was a lot to look at on the street, but that 99% of it was advertisements of one form or another, either for corporate movies or records, or for independent music shows, or even for protests or meetings. It's not that all of this was necessarily so bad, but it was striking how everything was a directive, it all expected the audience to buy something or go somewhere. I wanted to put something on the street that was a little more generous than that. In conversations with my roommate, who was a teacher, I decided to produce a poster for Malcolm X's birthday and to cover the streets with it. This was the first People's History poster, and the beginning of the idea of producing posters around people, groups and events in history that were extremely important for social justice movements but have been erased or hidden by mainstream history.

Lampert: Now that the poster series is well established and has been wheatpasted in the streets, are you aware of any teachers hanging the Celebrate People's History posters in classrooms?

MacPhee: Yes, a lot of teachers hang them in their classes. Teachers from around the country have e-mailed me and told me they use them; many have even sent me photos of them on their classroom walls.

Lampert: What age group was it for?

MacPhee: In most cases it appears that they are for middle school to high school age kids, but I know of some elementary school teachers that use the posters, as well as college professors.

Lampert: What has been the reaction from teachers to your poster series?

MacPhee: For the most part teachers seem really excited that the posters are available and financially accessible. There seem to be very few high quality visual resources for teachers about alternative or "people's" history. There are a number of books that have been cropping up, but very little in terms of graphic materials

Figure 51.1 The
Occupation of Alcatraz by
Josh MacPhee.

to hang in the classroom or to use with students that respond better to visuals than straight text.

Lampert: Have any of the posters in the series to date focused on people's movements within creating schools and alternative forms of education?

MacPhee: Although used by teachers, the posters themselves have not been overly focused on education. Some of the people celebrated by the posters were scholars and educators, for instance Elisé Reclus, the 19th century geographer and anarchist, and more recently I printed a poster about the Highlander Folk School. Highlander originally opened its doors in the 1930s as a place for Southern poor and working class people to educate themselves in order to radically change society. In the 1950s Highlander became a prime training ground for the early Civil Rights Movement, hosting workshops and providing space for groups to meet and organize.

Lampert: Have any teachers assigned their students to work on their own posters that celebrate people's history?

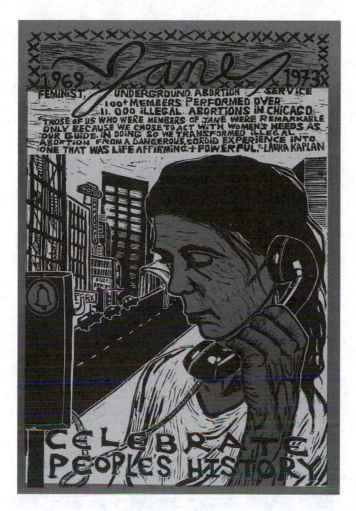

Figure 51.2 Jane Collective by Meredith Stern.

MacPhee: I have had a number of teachers tell me that they were integrating people's history poster making into their curriculums. The one example I am most familiar with is in Pittsburgh, where Tresa Varner, a printmaking teacher at CAPA, the Pittsburgh arts high school. Tresa did a People's History unit in which each of her students produced a two-color linoleum block people's history print. A selection of these student prints were then hung at an exhibition called *Small Acts* at the Space Gallery in downtown Pittsburgh alongside a selection of the Celebrate People's History posters I organized and created.

Lampert: From your own past experience as a student (K–12) do you recall any similar types of posters within the classroom that inspired you?

MacPhee: I have no memory at all of any liberatory visual materials in school. I know from research that there were some materials that came out in the 1970s, but they weren't in use in the schools I went to. Most of my friends that are teachers didn't experience any either, which is in large part why I think educators appreciate the posters so much.

Lampert: Much of the curriculum in K–12 in history is looking at a very standard, top-down, European-American version of American history. Rarely do students learn about people's struggles or in many cases, their own ethnic history. How

Figure 51.3 Highlander Folk
School by Lindsay.

do you see the CPH posters challenging this? Are the posters a window for
people to learn more about various individuals and events? Are they meant to
inspire?

MacPhee: First of all, the posters are not intended to be full history lessons in and of
themselves. They are created with the hope to educate and inspire people
enough to learn more about certain subjects on their own. In addition, when
I began the series almost 10 years ago, most of the posters being produced
were about specific individuals, a set of alternative heroes so to speak. At some
point in the process I decided that even though the posters were important,
this approach of celebrating people's heroes was doing a disservice to our
understanding of history. If the posters are truly to be an alternative to mainstream history, they need to be more than just our version of great men and
great battles, but need to help illustrate how history really happens, through
the hard work of groups of people, and lots of them. So I've refocused the project away from individuals and onto groups and collectives as well as specific
events and activities. I feel this is a more honest look into our history and also
values the collective aspects that are most important for moving forward and

Figure 51.4 Sylvia Ray Rivera
by John Gerken.

creating a future we want to live in. I also have moved more and more toward producing posters that focus on events and groups outside of the United States. Our culture is already so myopic, with everything "American" always held up as the most important, and I think the posters can start opening windows into history outside the United States.

Lampert: The theme of many of your recent presentations and talks has been on "Taking Control of Your Visual Landscape," a critique of just how corporate the public landscape has become and the impact this has had on culture and people's attitudes toward what is possible and what is not. In regard to students, the K–12 age group, why is it essential that a critique of the visual landscape begin at this age?

MacPhee: The earlier students learn to understand that their visual landscape is not a natural product, but specifically created with specific intentions in mind, the earlier they will be able to understand what those motivations are, and if they agree with them or not, and therefore intellectually interact with the landscape by choice, rather than default. It is really about choice and autonomy, without an understanding of how people are trying to influence you, it is

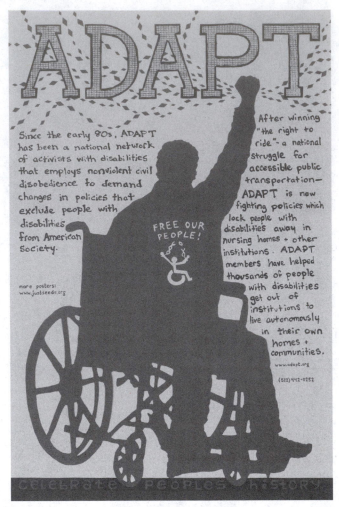

Figure 55.5 ADAPT by Anonymous Artist.

nearly impossible to make educated choices about whether you want to be influenced, and influenced by whom for what purposes.

Lampert: Images have a very profound impact on society, yet visual literacy (and the arts for that matter) is downplayed in most educational curriculums. In your opinion, why is it essential that students learn about and engage in the arts?

MacPhee: Every day our world becomes a more and more complex web of images and signs, many of which are not neutral or benign, but specifically intended to make us speak, move, act in certain specific ways. Increasingly it is not simply written language, but text in concert with images that information is transferred, whether this is on television, the Internet, magazines, billboards, or just about any other information transfer point in our society. Unless we are taught the skills necessary to decipher this complex web, then we are at the mercy of the image-makers. The more students engage in arts education, the deeper their understanding of visual language, and the higher their level of what I like to call "meta-literacy," and understanding of the language that is laid on top of standard written language.

Acknowledgment

Josh MacPhee was interviewed by Nicolas Lampert in February 2006. For more on Josh MacPhee's work please visit: http://www.justseeds.org.

For more on Nicolas Lampert's work (including a previous interview with Josh MacPhee) please visit: http://www.machineanimalcollages.com.

Reference

MacPhee, J. (2004). *Stencil Pirates: A global survey of the street stencil.* Brooklyn, NY: Soft Skull Press.

MacPhee, J. (2007). *Realizing the impossible: Art against authority.* Oakland, CA: AK Press.

52 Teaching Teachers to Teach Queerly

Kevin K. Kumashiro

I write this chapter as a new academic year gets underway. Three weeks into the fall and I am still struggling to learn the names of the dozens of prospective teachers in my under-graduate, introductory course on urban education. I love teaching this course, perhaps because my attempts at troubling their assumptions and perspectives on what schools should and could look like often lead to my own awakenings.

We have spent the first few weeks developing several themes or "lenses" that we will revisit throughout the semester as we examine a range of ways that schools perpetuate social inequities. One such lens is that of the hidden curriculum, which was the topic of my class session just days ago. I began by dividing the chalkboard in half, asking the students to brainstorm: When does gender or sexual orientation come up in schools? That is, when do we see or learn something about gender or sexual orientation? Going around the room, I asked each student to share one instance, and I recorded their responses on either half of the board. The left side of the board was much fuller, and included such instances as: lining up for separate restrooms, less resources for girls' sports teams, dress codes, calling on boys more often, encouraging boys to study science (and discouraging them from the arts), boy–girl couples at dances, name calling (like "fag") and the failure of adults to intervene, permission forms for "mother or father," more male figures in history textbooks. The right side was fleshed out only after some prompting by me: celebrating Women's History Month, lessons on women writers, lessons on gender discrimination, lessons on family diversity, guest speakers on lesbian, gay, bisexual, and transgender (LGBT) issues.

We then discussed differences between the two lists. The left list is longer. The left-hand items take place all the time while the right-hand items occur occasionally if at all. The left-hand items often reflect messages that we hear in popular culture or our com-munities about gender and sexual differences, while the right-hand items are often trying to challenge such messages. The left-hand items often go unobserved because they have become commonplace in schools and society, while the right-hand items are often the result of teachers intentionally trying to raise these issues.

Indeed, researchers have distinguished between these two categories, the right side being the formal or official curriculum (what we are intentionally teaching), the left side, the hidden curriculum (what we teach indirectly, unintentionally, and often, unknow-ingly). The hidden curriculum is often in stark contrast to the formal curriculum, result-ing in a form of education that is permeated with multiple and contradictory teachings. Because the hidden curriculum is more commonplace and pervasive, because it echoes the messages that students hear from outside of schools, because it rarely goes challenged, and because it is more *what we actually do* versus *what we say that we should do*, it arguably has more educational significance than the formal curriculum. This helps us to see why the occasional lectures about, say, the importance of treating girls in the same ways that we treat boys will mean little if students observe that the teacher calls on boys to move tables and girls to sweep, or that the textbooks highlight men in history much more so than women. Challenging gender and sexual bias, in other words, requires more than teaching lessons about gender and sexual differences—it also requires addressing the many hidden ways that such lessons already occur.

I pointed out several key issues that are raised by this activity. First, every school and every classroom will have a unique set of hidden lessons, and no school or classroom is without them. Even in our course, taught by someone who thinks a lot about hidden curriculums, there will likely be messages that students are learning that I did not intend or even do not support. Second, in a school that is teaching multiple and contradictory messages, different students will likely "learn" very different things. We brainstormed a number of factors that influence what and how students learn: what they learned from their parents and the media;, what they are interested in or have come to value; how they feel about the teacher; and whether they were even paying attention at any given moment. The identities, life experiences, learning styles, and past learnings all create unique "lenses" through which students make sense of the world around them, and because we all have different lenses, we should expect that we will learn and react to lessons in unpredictable, unique ways.

As we debriefed this activity, my students voiced a range of responses. They spoke, for example, of the presumption that schools should focus on the "academic" subjects and remain neutral or silent on such social, controversial issues as gender bias and sexual orientation. Such a presumption is problematic when we see that schools can never be neutral on such issues, given the myriad and pervasive ways in which such issues arise. Students also spoke of the importance of doing an activity like this with teachers as a way to raise awareness of the many ways that schools can indirectly teach about gender and sexual orientation. They shared memories of teachers claiming that bias did not exist in their schools because they did not see it manifest in obvious ways, or worse yet, teachers remaining silent in the face of such instances. Silence can be instructive, as when adult silence around antigay name-calling indirectly teaches that such action is acceptable in schools.

But where my students seemed troubled was in their questions about the implications of this activity, particularly regarding the multiple lessons coming from schools and the multiple "lenses" being used by students. Can teachers ever be aware of all of the hidden lessons in their school? Does the hidden curriculum make the formal, intentional lessons on bias pointless? If students are all using unique "lenses," how do we ensure that they are learning what we want them to learn?

I was reminded of a lesson I once taught to prospective teachers several years ago. As is commonly the case in workshops for teachers on homophobia in schools, I centered my workshop on a litany of statistics and quotations that reflected the many challenges experienced by LGBT youth, particularly regarding high rates of bullying and harassment, alcohol and other drug use, family tensions and homelessness, even depression and suicide. Such statistics provoked in me deep sympathy and anger, and I assumed that others would respond similarly and with a commitment to act. But after reading through the statistics, one person's response revealed the problem with my assumption. She asked how it was that people have responded to these statistics in other situations where I have shared them. Although she personally felt disturbed and motivated to address these problems, she said that she could imagine someone saying, "See, I always felt there was something wrong with being homosexual, and here's the proof—look at all the problems they experience."

The lenses that students bring to the classroom can lead them to respond to any lesson in multiple, unpredictable ways, which means that information meant to challenge bias can actually serve to reinforce that bias, as was the case in this student's imagined response. I shared this experience with my students as an illustration of how the students' lenses can indeed take lessons in counterproductive directions. As we explored alternative ways of teaching that lesson, at least three considerations emerged.

First, there was the development of a shared lens. The notion that multiple lenses can lead students to "learn" in ways that directly contradict the goals of the lesson suggest that teachers must find ways to help students to develop alternative lenses, particularly shared or common lenses that allow the various individuals in the classroom to hear one another through common language and shared perspectives. When teachers speak of "scaffolding" their lessons, or sequencing their lessons "progressively," they are, in a sense, altering their students' lenses such that they respond to their lessons in productive ways. Were I to reteach my lesson with the litany of statistics, it would be important to engage in pre- or postactivities that invite students to "read" those statistics in antioppressive ways and not in ways that merely reinforce existing homophobia.

Of course, teaching should not consist merely of teachers insisting that everyone end up in the same place, which means that the development of shared lenses cannot be the only goal. This leads to the second consideration, the encouragement of taking unbeaten paths. Yes, it was a problem that I had not anticipated the many ways that students could have responded to the statistics. But it is equally problematic for me now to expect that all students "should" respond in only certain ways, namely, in ways that I have already determined to be the better ones. We often define teaching as a demand to conform: we say where we want students to end up (the objectives), we plan a lesson to get them there (the activities), and then we assess whether or not they got there, and if they did, we conclude that our teaching was effective, and their learning, accomplished. But if we acknowledge that any lens is partial and has both strengths and weaknesses, including the lenses of the teachers, then such a demand to conform is problematic. In fact, such a demand is what is commonly criticized about some forms of multicultural education, as when arguing that we are simply replacing one perspective (the hegemonic one) with another (the politically correct one). Learning must involve going where neither the student nor the teacher could have foretold and, as a class, taking the unbeaten path.

But this is not to say that every way of reading is equally antioppressive, which leads to the third consideration, the paradoxes of teaching and learning. Some ways of reading support and perpetuate bias, and other ways of reading explicitly challenge bias. A fundamental goal for teachers, then, should be neither to insist on learning the one "best" lens, nor to value all lenses equally. Rather, the goal should be to articulate a variety of lenses and examine what each one makes possible and impossible. Students might ask, How does this lens reinforce stereotypes or challenge them? What does this lens highlight, and what does this lens make difficult to see? What questions does this lens invite us to ask, which emotions does this lens touch, and on whom does this lens call to act?

Such questions make teaching and learning paradoxical precisely because they call into question the very things being taught and learned. As teachers, we often have a difficult time acknowledging the assumptions, gaps, and political implications of our own teaching, and an even harder time making such partialities a central part of our lesson. Yet, perhaps it is precisely when students ask such critical questions about our teaching that they think critically about what they are learning, how they are learning it, and how any learning, even the "antioppressive" ones, cannot help but be partial and political.

Often, as I teach prospective teachers, I confront a strong desire for very concrete strategies to address homophobia in schools, or as they often put it, "What do I do when someone says 'fag'?" Such a demand is understandable—teaching is not easy, and we need tools to make antioppressive teaching doable. Furthermore, asking students to raise critical questions about the necessarily partial and political nature of what and how they are learning requires a level of vulnerability and unpredictability for which we as educators have rarely been prepared. But perhaps the desire for certainty and control is what has prevented us from imagining and engaging in ways of teaching that can help us to address the contradictions inherent in antioppressive change. Ironically, by acknowledging the problems with trying to control what and how students learn, and by illustrating what it could mean to center the gaps in our own teaching, my students and I seemed to feel less stressful about the challenges of antioppressive teaching, and more hopeful in our abilities to enact it in our classrooms. With these questions lingering, we ended the class session, and I left with the hope that such work has only just begun in the classrooms of these future teachers and in my own.

Response to Part 9

Classrooms, Pedagogy, and Practicing Justice

Héctor Calderón

> People should be the subject of education, not the object, as they are the subject of their own destiny.
>
> (Freire, 1970, p. 59)

In the fall of 1991 I had been hired at El Puente as the senior tutor of a new educational program. The program was designed to help students improve their reading, writing, and math skills. With a team of five tutors, I assisted members of El Puente with their homework, tests, reports, and any other school-related tasks. On one particularly hot, agonizing summer day, just before the mandated RCT and Regents exams, a member walked in and collapsed on a chair as if her knees had given way to the weight of her frustrations. She propped her chin in her hands and began in a soft but desperate voice to spill her guts: "Why do we have to take tests? Who the hell invented school? What's the point of all these classes? Why are my teachers so boring?" I tried to offer some hollow words of comfort. "Well, you know, that if you don't pass these tests or do well in your classes, you can't graduate. And if you don't graduate, you can't apply to college. And if you don't go to college, you can't...." "But what the hell is the point, school has nothing to do with me," she hollered at me. "Is this the way it's going to be, me doing crap I don't care about in order to 'make it.' Nah, I don't think so, this ain't for me. I wanna find my soul." Her words made me stop dead in my tracks. I had rehearsed and spoken my words of advice a million times before. But today, Yesenia had made me pause. Yesenia's words resonated with my own private quest and really, a collective quest we all share to make meaning of our existence and of our world. That day, I realized that institutions of learning never address the question of the soul—the essence of a human being. They pontificate about a prescribed course of life, which is devoid of meaning, in order to achieve "success." And unfortunately everybody plays the role, teachers, administrators, guidance counselors, and me, with my "pithy" words of advice.

This became a critical realization as I began thinking about how I would address learning and eventually, help create the El Puente Academy for Peace and Justice. In my learning process, I sought to undo years of schooling that had been inculcated into my consciousness. I needed to let go of many notions and practices I associated with learning. At the time I was introduced to Paulo Freire, the renowned Brazilian educator, he became a pivotal figure in giving voice and vision to what I was searching for. I remember reading one sentence in particular in his classic book, *Pedagogy of the Oppressed*: "Learners are the subject of the learning process and not the object, as they have to be the subject of their destiny." With that single sentence, Freire had transformed my whole outlook on education. This was precisely what Yesenia was talking about. She wanted learning to reflect her questions, her aspirations, her stories, her world! Throughout her years of schooling, she had been taught "important skills," but in the service of what? The question "for the sake of what?" was completely left out of the picture. After that fateful day, Yesenia and I talked. I shared with her what she had provoked in me. "I was angry at my life that day," she said as she exhaled a breath of relief. I told her that she was right, school should be meaningful. Yesenia looked at me intently and said "I think I like that." We have been friends in the service of learning ever since.

As we try to make sense of our lives, we can draw on the power of community to help us. We discover ourselves in the context of community. My conversations with Yesenia and countless other young people became the basis for the types of curriculums I cocreated with young people and the body of work that eventually became the El Puente Academy for Peace and Justice.

The school that understands itself as a community-creation celebrates the community's cultures and histories, as well as addressing its concerns and well-being. In an article titled "The Spirit of Transformation: An Education Reform Movement in a New York City Latino/a Community," M. Rivera and P. Pedraza articulated that idea this way (2000):

> The goal of community development as an educational objective is implicit in pedagogical approaches that consider the socio-historical contexts of students, particularly their daily life experiences, to be of paramount importance. Centering pedagogical practices on issues of language, culture and identity is an attempt to integrate these two levels, individual and communal, through a program of activities and actions that fosters individual Latino/a student development.

The purpose of education, especially within marginalized communities, is critically and explicitly attached to developing the community and connecting learning to essential skills that students will need for their survival and success within their community and the larger society. I believe in a vision of school that does not separate the world from the world of school. The responsibility of schools to families and communities is to work together in the process of liberating our minds and souls. If schools do not fulfill its mission, it is the right of the people to demand and insist they do. "Education, as Che Guevara put it, "is the property of no one as a whole. And if education is not given to the people, they will have to take it" (Walters, 2000, p. 69).

References

Freire, P. (1970). *Pedagogy of the oppressed*. New York: Herder & Herder.

Rivera, M., & Pedraza, P. . (2000). The spirit of transformation: An education reform movement in a New York City Latino/a Community. In S. Nieto (Ed.), *Puerto Rican Students in U.S. Schools*. Mahwah, NJ: Erlbaum.

Walters, M-A. (Ed.). (2000). Che Guevara talks to young people. New York: Pathfinder Pess.

Editors' Conclusion

I—who have "gone the gamut" from an almost angry rejection of my dark skin by some of my brainwashed brothers and sisters to a surprised queenhood in the new black sun—am qualified to enter at least the kindergarten of new consciousness now. New consciousness and trudge-toward-progress. I have hopes for myself.

(Brooks, 1972, p. 86)

The road from study to action was short.

(Zinn, 2001, p. 206)

Bertolt Brecht asked this question in his poem "Motto": "In dark times, will there also be singing?" And his answer: "Yes, there will be singing./About the dark times." Brecht knew something about the dark times—hounded and attacked and driven from the United States in the 1950s.

Our work here and now is to sing about the dark times, for the dark times are all around us. And in these times it is essential to begin with a particularly precious ideal—the belief that education at its best is an enterprise geared to helping every human being reach the full measure of his or her humanity, inviting people on a journey to become more thoughtful and more capable, more powerful and courageous, more exquisitely human in their projects and their pursuits. That ideal—always revolutionary, and never more so than today—is central to achieving a democratic and open society. And like democracy itself it is an ideal that is never quite finished, never easily or finally summed up—it is neither a commodity with readily recognized features nor a product for consumption. No. Rather democracy, like education, is an aspiration to be continually nourished, engaged, and exercised, a dynamic, expansive experiment that must be achieved over and over again by every individual and each successive generation if it is to live at all.

As we near the end of this collective book project we note that this is but a draft of a draft, incomplete and unfinished. We were able to assemble a small temporary community of educators and thinkers, artists and activists and writers who have helped to identify, name, and represent an array of issues that matter when we think about teaching and schooling and social justice. But the effort is still sketchy, and that is surely the permanent condition of the thing: in this dynamic, forward-charging, imperfect human endeavor, there is always more to know, more to uncover, more to expand and embrace. So we offer this now as an utterance in a conversation, a call that requires the response of readers to come even partially to life.

The first issue of Antonio Gramsci's newsletter, *The New Order,* featured this hopeful call-to-arms on its masthead: "Instruct yourselves because we shall need all our intelligence. Agitate because we shall need all our enthusiasm. Organize yourselves because we shall need all our power."

We note that educators face a contradiction at the heart of their efforts: the humanistic ideal, the democratic injunction tell us that every person is an entire universe, that each can develop as a full and autonomous person engaged with others in a common polity and an equality of power; the capitalist imperative insists that profit is at the center of economic and political progress, and develops then a culture of competition, elitism, and hierarchy. An education for capitalism fails as a humanizing exercise; an education for democracy and justice fails as an adjunct to capitalism—either the schools or the system must die.

Teaching aims both to guide and to set free, to initiate *into* as well as to liberate *from*. Teaching is part prescription, part permission. Great teachers walk this fault line consciously, with courage and confidence, working to move their students into thinking for themselves, awakening in them new awarenesses, igniting their imaginations and encouraging them to live a while in possibility, spurring them to go further and further. And teachers simultaneously provide students with access to the tools of the culture, the structures of the disciplines, the various languages and literacies that will allow them to participate fully and freely. This is only possible when teachers present themselves as incomplete, questioning, fallible, searching human beings themselves—identical in this regard to those they teach.

We don't know really how to change the world, of course; we don't know when our efforts are in vain—but we do know that change in small places can gesture toward larger transformations, and that changing a single mind can unleash a universe of possibilities. We can all act for small changes rather than waiting for some monumental movement when everything will magically fall into place; we can all act for larger changes even as we attend to needs and demands in the particular.

Schools and classrooms have always been contested spaces, sites of hope and struggle—hope for a transformed future or a unique possibility, struggle over everything from what that future might entail to who ought to be invited to participate and to shape our common world. Every wave of official "school reform"—every initiative, every impulse, every opportunity—must, then, be met with skepticism, agnosticism, and doubt by those of us who work toward a more democratic future, a more just social order. Even when we embrace particular strategies and tactics, even as we join particular struggles, we must consciously resist orthodoxy and certainty, the seduction of easy belief, the descent into dogma.

The triumph of a fierce and relentless market fundamentalism is everywhere apparent, on the street, of course, but penetrating our homes as well, our families, our places of worship—our vaunted private lives. Privatization redefines everything from health care to criminal justice, from mercenary armies to private prisons, from waste management to elections, from safety to the distribution of water. In this bizarrely misshapen world, hierarchy rules, competition of every kind is always good, profit an undisputed virtue, efficiency and standardization a given, advertising a fine art, individual consumption the pinnacle of participation.

The current iteration of the school wars mirrors all this: the marketeers are in full eruption, leading the retreat from the dream of a robust, diverse, and well-funded public educational system in the hands of the many (the reality includes, of course, significant exclusions) toward a system of private schools for the benefit of a few. The Edison schools are only one egregious example—steeped in the rhetoric of freedom and the market, these proudly for-profit McSchools produce nothing and sell nothing, relying instead on a neat shell game whose chief accomplishment seems to be to transfer public monies to private hands under the banner of "free choice." The dismantling of public education for all is under way.

In less than full-blown mode the skirmishes are widespread, and so are the markers: vast resources directed to the simplistic task of sorting youngsters into camps of winners and losers; intolerant school cultures that reward obedience and conformity while punishing initiative and courage; a curriculum that is fragmented, alienating, and irrelevant; layers of supervision and regulation that reduce the role of the teacher to that of a clerk or a functionary, and constitute a dagger in the intellectual and ethical heart of teaching.

To question the tenets of the marketeers, to wonder if our schools, for example, or our children are being well-served by any of this is to be relegated to the margins of polite or serious policy discourse.

There is a deep need to rethink in fundamental terms the whole purpose and larger meaning of school in light of the end of work as we know it—we are witnessing massive displacement, with all manner of attendant pauperization and alienation. What will this mean for human survival or happiness and well-being for all? What are our choices? Schooling as job training and career preparation is an anachronism, and yet that reductive goal is preached repeatedly from the White House to the state house. Schools need to radically reconsider and restructure in a way that connects to the reality of the modern world.

We know that the fight for democratic schools cannot be fully achieved within a profoundly undemocratic social order. A classroom built on equality and community, shared power, the right to humane treatment, full participation and access, will always live in sharp conflict with a society of hierarchy, elitism, and concentrated wealth and power. The ideal of education as humanization—an enterprise in which opportunities and resources are organized to overcome embedded and historical injustices and to allow everyone to realize herself or himself in the full participation in political, social, cultural, and economic life—stands in direct contradiction to the demands of a system that objectifies everyone and enforces the acquiescence of each to the demands of the corporate body.

In our society the democratic charge, the egalitarian injunction, clashes with the corporate/market imperative. Schools as democratic outposts and islands of decency—places of equity, inclusion, access, respect for the humanity of each—undermine elitism and are worth fighting for. They can become both a call and a springboard for action. But democratic school reform by itself is all but impossible—the more things change, the more they stay the same. When reforms have been achieved at all they have been linked in coalitions with larger communities of concern—parents, citizens, committed persons. Teachers at these moments do not defend their turf as teachers per se, nor as union members exclusively, but recast themselves as educators-workers-parents-citizens-artists-activists. Here they have expanded power and purpose. Here is where the possibility of exposing the contradiction of democracy and capital exists in all its exquisiteness. The schools cannot (even if they dare) create a new social order—at least not alone. There is something more that is needed.

Market fundamentalism today parades under the rubric of the "*Ownership Society*," with ownership supposedly the common national goal, shared by Enron executives, factory workers, and public housing residents alike. It is apparent everywhere these days, penetrating our schools, our homes, our families, our places of worship—our private lives. The "Ownership Society" is enforcing a narrowly reimagined and redefined public space, cannibalizing everything from health care to retirement benefits, criminal justice, waste management, elections, public safety, water rights. Any area that has traditionally been part of the "common good" and publicly administered is now part of the "open sector," up for grabs, and public schools are at the center of this reactionary reversal. Public space is divided into sectors to be sold off or privately managed.

On Mothers Day, 2001, a group of mothers and grandmothers in the mainly Mexican community of Little Village began a hunger strike demanding that the Chicago Public Schools leadership fulfill its commitment to build a new high school in the community. Funds set aside for the new school had been spent on new exclusive enrollment schools on the north side. The hunger strike drew widespread support form church and community groups leading to a victory when new superintendent Arne Duncan announced that the money had been "found" to build the most expensive high school in Chicago in Little Village. But the parents didn't stop there. After much discussion, the community group decided that the new school for 1,450 students should be designed as a campus of four small, themed, autonomous high schools sharing a common space.

In the spring of 2002 a group of teachers at Chicago's Curie High School sent an open letter to the school board announcing that they planned as a group to refuse to administer a standardized test that they found "not in the best interests of our students." This was, for them, one test too many, and their planned disobedience was big news locally. Teachers from other schools took up the challenge and soon a public debate was under way about standards and the educational value of tests, and momentum began to build against this specific measure. Within months the board announced it would discontinue the test, but not before a wider effort to rethink the entire testing business had begun.

Sometimes students lead the way, and wide-awake teachers—students of their students—can learn a thing or two about courage and integrity. A group of college-bound kids at Whitney Young High School boycotted the SATs, claiming that the tests undermined any notion of a thoughtful or engaged education. This rebellion of the privileged against a system that they claimed hurt all students challenged their teachers to speak out publicly for or against the SATs, and for or against supporting the students' action. Students made the call, teachers heard it and acted; that moment resonates and encourages.

Yes, we can sing about the dark times. At the same time—hear the chorus of these bright possibilities, the mothers, the students, the teachers and neighbors who drew together and changed the world, or a piece of it. These are stirrings, awakenings, openings. Each is a cry for justice. Each is a step along the way. We are taking the journey together.

References

Brooks, G. (1972). *Report from part one*. Detroit: Broadside Press.

Zinn, H. (2001). *Howard Zinn on history*. New York: Seven Stories Press.

Resources

The work is long, but many are involved. What follows is a snapshot, a moment in time, a gathering of what we know about and love right now—some online sources of information and inspiration, starting with the arts.

Arts and Activism

Adbusters

www.adbusters.org

A global network of artists, activists, writers, pranksters, students, educators and entrepreneurs who want to advance the new social activist movement of the information age. Their aim is to topple existing power structures and forge a major shift in the way we will live in the 21st century.

AREA Chicago

areachicago.org

Art/Research/Education/Activism. The irregular newsletter of events, actions, and gatherings taking place throughout Chicago.

Beehive Design Collective

http://www.beehivecollective.org/

An arts and activist collective that *creates collaborative, anticopyright images that can be used as educational and organizing tools.*

Docs Populi: Documents for the Public

http://www.docspopuli.org/

This is the site of Lincoln Cushing, a librarian and archivist of digital imagery. The site is a fantastic source of, as Cushing notes, "significant graphic material" including Chinese and Cuban poster art, a history of the clenched fist image, and labor and library artifacts. It also includes links to other great sources of imagery, including a site on student activism in the 1930s, the Center for the Study of Political Graphics, and the Chicago Women's Graphics Collective.

Graphic Witness: Visual Arts and Social Commentary

http://graphicwitness.org/ineye/index2.htm

A site dedicated to social commentary through graphic imagery by artists working from the turn of the 20th century to the present, with related bibliographic and biographic data. The site includes a photographic history of the Mexican Revolution, a complete 1934 edition of Karl Marx's *Capital* in lithographs by Hugo Gellert, and indices of artists.

Hip-Hop Association

http://www.hiphopassociation.org

The Hip-Hop Association community building organization with national headquarters in Harlem. The Association's mission is to utilize Hip-Hop culture as a tool to facilitate critical thinking, foster social change and unity, by empowering communities through the use of media, technology, education, and leadership development; while preserving Hip-Hop culture for future generations.

The Institute for Figuring

http://www.theiff.org/

The Institute For Figuring is an organization dedicated to the poetic and aesthetic dimensions of science, mathematics, and the technical arts. The site includes a "history of kindergarten."

Justseeds

http://www.justseeds.org/

Justseeds/Visual Resistance Artists' Cooperative is a decentralized community of artists who have banded together to both sell their work online in a central location and to collaborate with and support each other and social movements. The website is not just a place to shop, but also a destination to find out about current events in radical art and culture. Their blog covers political printmaking, socially engaged street art, and culture related to social movements. The Association believes in the power of personal expression in concert with collective action to transform society. People's History Posters can be purchased at the site (see chapter 51 for examples).

Radical Art Caucus

http://www.radicalartcaucus.org

The Radical Art Caucus (RAC) has as its primary mission the promotion of art and art historical scholarship that addresses historical and contemporary problems of oppression and possibilities for resistance. RAC brings together scholars and artists who ground their work in the material knowledge of cultural conditions and practices related to critiquing fundamental issues of unequal distribution of resources, social hierarchies, and unjust political authority which affect disenfranchised populations in all periods of history. The site has links to artist sites and a newsletter.

RTMark

http://www.rtmark.com

RTMARK receives project ideas from Internet users, then lists them online. Each listed project has its own discussion list (linked from the project). When a project requires a bit of funding to be accomplished, sometimes investors will step up to the plate and offer their help. Even more often, people will offer nonfinancial help or feedback. These are the folks that brought the world the Barbie Liberation Organization, Phone in Sick Day 2002, and The Yes Men—see below.

The Yes Men

http://www.theyesmen.org/

This organization impersonates big-time criminals in order to publicly humiliate them. Their targets are leaders and big corporations who put profits ahead of everything else.

Part 1: Historical and Theoretical Perspectives

Civic Engagement Research Group

http://www.civicsurvey.org/Civic_Engagement_Mission_Statement_.html

This group's mission is to provide an evidence base that informs the design of policies and programs that promote the development of citizens for an effective, just, and humane democratic society. The site has downloadable reports and papers and links to organizations focused on civic engagement and education.

Democratic Dialogue

http://www.democraticdialogue.com/

Democratic Dialogue is committed to the critical exploration of democratic ideals in education and society through a program of international collaborative research and dissemination. The organization engages educators, political scientists, sociologists, philosophers, teachers, policymakers, and cultural workers (e.g., artists, curators, and critics) as well as the broader public community who are concerned with ideals, tensions, policies, and practices of education for democracy. Democratic Dialogue reaches across disciplinary, institutional, and national boundaries through innovative research projects and methods of dissemination, community dialogues and events, and the pursuit of creative approaches to projects that engage themes of democracy, education, and society. The site includes links to publications and descriptions of research projects.

Highlander Research and Education Center

http://www.highlandercenter.org/index.html

The Highlander Center was founded in 1932 to serve as an adult education center for community workers involved in social and economic justice movements. The goal of Highlander was and is to provide education and support to poor and working people fighting economic injustice, poverty, prejudice, and environmental destruction. The founding principle and guiding philosophy of Highlander is that the answers to the problems facing society lie in the experiences of ordinary people.

Social Justice

http://www.socialjusticejournal.org

This is a quarterly nonprofit educational journal that seeks to promote human dignity, equality, peace, and genuine security. Its early focus on issues of crime, police repression, social control, and the penal system has expanded to encompass globalization, human and civil rights, border, citizenship, and immigration issues, environmental victims and health and safety concerns, social policies affecting welfare and education, ethnic and gender relations, and persistent global inequalities. The site has a "teacher resource" center that includes a variety of journals/articles that educators can use, such as:

United for Peace and Justice

http://www.unitedforpeace.org

United for Peace and Justice is a coalition of more than 1,300 local and national groups throughout the United States who have joined together to protest the immoral and disastrous Iraq War and oppose our government's policy of permanent warfare and empire-building.

Part 2: International Perspectives on Social Justice in Education

Activities of the E.U., Summaries of Legislation—Rights in Third Countries

http://europa.eu/scadplus/leg/en/lvb/r10107.htm

This site contributes to the work of the World Conference against Racism, Racial Discrimination, Xenophobia, and Related Intolerance.

Colours of Resistance

http://colours.mahost.org/

Colours of Resistance (COR) is a grassroots network of people who consciously work to develop antiracist, multiracial politics in the movement against global capitalism. COR is committed to helping build an antiracist, anti-imperialist, multiracial, feminist, queer and trans liberationist, antiauthoritarian movement against global capitalism.

UN Charter of Human Rights

http://www.un.org/Depts/dhl/resguide/spechr.htm#

Human rights are recognized as fundamental by the United Nations and, as such, feature prominently in the Preamble of the Charter of Human Rights: "...to reaffirm faith in fundamental human rights, in the dignity and worth of the human person, in the equal rights of men and women and of nations large and small...." The Organization's prominent role in this area is carried out by a number of human rights bodies (described here), some of which date back to the very foundation of the United Nations.

United Nations Universal Declaration of Human Rights

http://www.un.org/Overview/rights.html

On December 10th, 1948 the General Assembly of the United Nations adopted and proclaimed the Universal Declaration of Human Rights, the full text of which appears on this site. Following this historic act the Assembly called upon all member countries to publicize the text of the Declaration and "to cause it to be disseminated, displayed, read and expounded principally in schools and other educational institutions, without distinction based on the political status of countries or territories."

European Parliament—Committee for Civil Liberties, Justice, and Home Affairs

http://www.europarl.europa.eu/activities/expert/committees/presentation.do;jsessionid=4178AC1F60B68BA67A936EDFBE03E847.node2?committee=2362&rewritten&language=EN

This site details the work of the committee responsible for the protection within the territory of the Union of citizens' rights, human rights, and fundamental rights, including the protection of minorities, as laid down in the Treaties and in the Charter of Fundamental Rights of the European Union, and more, as noted here.

The European Union Agency for Fundamental Rights

http://fra.europa.eu/fra/index.php

The European Union Agency for Fundamental Rights (FRA) is a body of the European Union (EU), established through Council Regulation (EC) No 168/2007 of February 15, 2007. It is based in Vienna and is being modeled on the European Monitoring Centre on Racism and Xenophobia (EUMC). FRA carries out its tasks independently. It cooperates with national and international bodies and organizations, in particular with the Council of Europe. It also works closely with civil society organizations. The first report of this body, *Report on Racism and Xenophobia in the EU Member States* (2006), is available here: http://fra.europa.eu/fra/material/pub/racism/report_racism_0807_en.pdf

Part 3: Race, Ethnicity, and Language: Seeking Social Justice in Education

Black Radical Congress

http://www.blackradicalcongress.org/

This is the homepage of the Black Radical Congress. Any individual who identifies her- or himself as Black (African or African-descended), and agrees with the BRC Principles of Unity is eligible for membership in the Black Radical Congress. Any individual regardless of identity may become a BRC Supporter.

Challenging White Supremacy

http://www.cwsworkshop.org/

Challenging White Supremacy (CWS) workshop organizers believe that the most effective way to create fundamental social change in the United States is by building mass-based, multiracial grassroots movements led by radical activists of color.

Greensboro Justice Fund

http://www.gjf.org/

Born in the tragedy of the 1979 Greensboro Massacre, the Greensboro Justice Fund is dedicated to the service of all those fighting for human dignity against bigotry in the South today. The Greensboro Justice Fund assists grassroots organizations in the South working for racial justice, political and economic empowerment, and an end to racist, religious, and homophobic violence.

La Unidad Latina Foundation

http://foundation.launidadlatina.org/

The La Unidad Latina Foundation was established in 1999 to serve as an independent, nonprofit, charitable organization dedicated to educational achievement and civic empowerment in the Latino community.

National Association for Bilingual Education

http://www.nabe.org_

One of the leading bilingual/EAL education advocates around. They are very accessible and have lots of resources for those new to bilingual/EAL education, as well as long-time activists and educators. The site also includes information on bilingual/EAL education advocacy.

Terralingua

http://www.terralingua.org

Terralingua supports the integrated protection, maintenance, and restoration of the biocultural diversity of life—the world's biological, cultural, and linguistic diversity —through an innovative program of research, education, policy, and on-the-ground action.

Znet.org: Racewatch

http://www.zmag.org/racewatch/racewatch.cfm

Znet hosts a collection of essays around various issues of social justice/social change. This is the race watch page, which has a very diverse and well written archive of essays on everything from antiracism, White privilege, institutional organizing, and youth work.

Part 4: Gender, Sexuality, and Social Justice in Education

Advocates for Youth

http://www.advocatesforyouth.org/

Has a lot of material for lesson plans around sex ed, as well as various campaigns to get involved in. They also have sections particularly for youth of color, and have a new affiliate website—www.MySistahs.org—for womyn of color. They are queer friendly. The website is also in Spanish and French.

Beyondmedia Education

http://www.beyondmedia.org/

Beyondmedia Education's mission is to collaborate with underserved and underrepresented women, youth, and communities to tell their stories, connect their stories to the world around us, and organize for social justice through the creation and distribution of alternative media and arts. Beyondmedia Education works with communities most in need of media education and services because of economic or social exclusion. Since 1996, Beyondmedia Education has partnered with over 100 community-based organizations and schools to produce media arts on subjects ranging from girls' activism to women's incarceration. The site includes a catalogue of videos (for purchase) made by women and girls on topics ranging from disability to home birth.

Coalition for Positive Sexuality

http://www.positive.org/

This is a grassroots organization that is based in Washington, D.C. The website has material dedicated to queer issues. It also has online and national resources from a sex positive perspective, as well as information on parental consent laws in regards to teen abortions. The website is English/Spanish.

Gay Lesbian Straight Education Network (GLSEN)

www.glsen.org/cgi-bin/iowa/all/home/index.html

An organization for students and teachers who are working for safe schools for all people, regardless of sexual orientation. They have a lot of information on how to start a Gay/Straight Alliance for your school. GLSEN also has information on a number of different campaigns and laws related to queer friendly schools.

Gay Shame

http://www.gayshamesf.org

"GAY SHAME is a Virus in the System. We are committed to a queer extravaganza that brings direct action to astounding levels of theatricality." The organization states that it will not be satisfied with a commercialized gay identity that denies the intrinsic links between queer struggle and challenging power. Gay Shame seeks nothing less than a new queer activism that foregrounds race, class, gender, and sexuality, to counter the self-serving "values" of gay consumerism and the increasingly hypocritical left. Gay Shame is dedicated to fighting the rabid assimilationist monster with a devastating mobilization of queer brilliance.

Intersex Society of North America

http://www.isna.org

The Intersex Society of North America (ISNA) is devoted to systemic change to end shame, secrecy, and unwanted genital surgeries for people born with an anatomy that someone decided is not standard for male or female.

National Coalition to Support Sexuality Education

http://www.siecus.org

"Consists of over 135 national nonprofit organizations, many of which are noted role models and initiators in promoting health, education, and social justice for our nation's youth." The Unitarian Universalist Association is one of these organizations. They not only have resources relating to sexuality education in schools, they also have a section devoted to religion and sexuality.

The National Women's Law Center

http://www.nwlc.org/

The mission of this organization is to protect and advance the progress of women and girls at work, in school, and in virtually every aspect of their lives.

The Public Education Regarding Sexual Orientation Nationally (P.E.R.S.O.N)
Project

http://www.personproject.org/
An activist network that works for fair, accurate, and unbiased information on queer and trans people in public schools. They have an awesome organizing handbook on their website as well as links to a lot of great organizing resources.

The Lambda Legal Defense and Education Fund
http://www.lambdalegal.org/
Lambda Legal is the oldest national organization pursuing high-impact litigation, public education, and advocacy on behalf of equality and civil rights for lesbians, gay men, bisexuals, transgender people, and people with HIV. The work Lambda does has an impact on the way we live—Lambda works to change laws, policies, and ideas. From their national headquarters in New York and four regional offices in Atlanta, Chicago, Dallas, and Los Angeles, their legal and public education experts select the cases and issues that will have the greatest impact in protecting and advancing the rights of LGBT people and those with HIV.

Sex Etc.

http://www.sexetc.org/
An extensive website on multiple issues relating to sex ed including pregnancy, sexually transmitted infections, abortion, abuse and violence, emotional health, and many other topics. It has message boards, articles, and sex ed related Q & A. Another plus—its editorial board consists of teenagers.

Spiritual Youth for Reproductive Freedom
http://www.syrf.org/
Spiritual Youth for Reproductive Freedom (SYRF) educates, organizes, and empowers youth and young adults (ages 16–30) to put their faith into action and advocate for pro-choice social justice.

Part 5: Bodies, Disability, and the Fight for Social Justice in Education

American Association of People with Disabilities

http://www.aapd.com/index.php
AAPD is the largest national nonprofit cross-disability member organization in the United States, dedicated to ensuring economic self-sufficiency and political empowerment for the more than 56 million Americans with disabilities.

AIDS Coalition to Unleash Power (ACT UP)

http://www.actupny.org/
A diverse, nonpartisan group of individuals united in anger and committed to direct action to end the AIDS crisis.

The Disability Social History Project

http://www.disabilityhistory.org/dshp_about.html

The Disability History Project is a community history project that welcomes your participation. It offers an opportunity for disabled people to reclaim their history and determine how they want to define themselves and their struggles. People with disabilities have an exciting and rich history that should be shared with the world. E-mail anything that you would like to see become part of the Disability Social History Project, including your disabled heroes, important events in disability history, and resources.

The Ragged Edge (formerly Disability Rag)
http://www.ragged-edge-mag.com/
The Disability Rag started publishing in 1980. In 1997 it went from print to online, under a new name, The Ragged Edge. This site offers an archive of some early disability rights movement material as well as current reporting, blog links, poetry and personal essays.

UIC Society for Disability Studies

http://www.uic.edu/orgs/sds/generalinfo.html
The Society for Disability Studies is an international nonprofit organization that promotes the exploration of disability through research, artistic production, and teaching.

Part 6: Youth and Social Justice in Education

Freechild

http://www.freechild.org/
The Freechild Project works across the United States and Canada, providing tools, training, and expert consultation in the fields of youth development, youth empowerment, and youth involvement.

Inner City Struggle (also known as "Schools Not Jails")

http://www.innercitystruggle.org/
InnerCity Struggle promotes safe, healthy, and nonviolent communities by organizing youth and families in Boyle Heights and East Los Angeles to work toward economic and social justice.

The National Network Opposing Militarization of Youth

http://www.youthandthemilitary.org/
The National Network Opposing Militarization of Youth (NNOMY) is integral in bringing groups together so they can help the nation understand that providing youth with peaceful and viable alternatives to achieve success in life is an important sign of a civilized society.

Social Justice Education

http://www.socialjusticeeducation.org/
Social Justice Education is an agency based in Boston's African American, Caribbean, and Latino communities, devoted to developing youth leadership.

Youth On Board

http://www.youthonboard.org/site/c.ihLUJ7PLKsG/b.2039165/k.BE6D/Home.htm

Youth on Board prepares youth to be leaders and decision makers in their communities and strengthens relationships between youth and adults through publications, customized workshops, and technical assistance.

Youth Restorative Action Project

http://www.yrap.org/

The Youth Restorative Action Project (YRAP) is a Youth Justice Committee as sanctioned under section 18 of the Youth Criminal Justice Act. YRAP is the first committee of its kind mandated to work in Youth Court with young people who have caused harm as a result of racism, intolerance, and significant social issues. YRAP meets with young offenders to discuss the harm that has been caused by criminal action, and comes up with creative, effective resolutions to repair the harm and address the actions of the youth, in a way both educational and rehabilitative.

Part 7: Globalization and Social Justice in Education

Campus Antiwar Network

http://www.campusantiwar.net/

Campus Antiwar Network is the largest and leading independent, democratic, grassroots network of students opposing the occupation of Iraq and military recruiters in our schools at campuses all over the country.

Food Not Bombs

http://www.foodnotbombs.net

This website is designed to help the community connect with the global Food Not Bombs movement. This is a small, all-volunteer collective that is dedicated to helping people start and maintain local Food Not Bombs groups. The organization's goal is to encourage people to join Food Not Bombs in taking direct action for peace and social justice.

Globalization and Education

http://globalizationandeducation.ed.uiuc.edu/

Globalization and Education is an Internet resource aimed at providing diverse perspectives on ways in which education is being shaped by global processes. The site was developed by a collective of research students at the University of Illinois, Urbana-Champaign.

Human Rights and Social Justice Organizations

http://www.bfsr.org/hr.html

This site has over 25 different links to other organizations that promote social justice and human rights.

Human Rights Video Project

http://www.humanrightsproject.org

The *Human Rights Video Project* is a national library project created to increase the public's awareness of human rights issues through the medium of documentary films.

Independent Media Center

http://www.indymedia.org

The Independent Media Center is a network of collectively run media outlets for the creation of radical, accurate, and passionate tellings of the truth. The Center works out of a love for and to inspire people who continue to work for a better world, despite corporate media's distortions and unwillingness to cover the efforts to free humanity.

MADRE

http://www.madre.org

As a human rights organization, MADRE does much more than document and condemn abuses. MADRE works with women who are affected by violations to help them win justice and, ultimately, change the conditions that give rise to human rights abuses.

Mobilization for Global Justice

http://www.globalizethis.org/

Information on major antiglobalization protests and solidarity actions can be found on this website. The main focus of this site is around the International Monetary Fund (IMF) and World Bank.

Not In Our Name (NION)

http://www.notinourname.net

NION was initiated at a meeting in New York City in March of 2002 proposing ways to strengthen and expand resistance to our government's course in the wake of September 11, 2001. On this site are Regional Contacts, an Events Calendar, Resources and Links, and other useful information around antiwar/antiglobalization.

The Ruckus Society

http://www.ruckus.org/

The Ruckus Society provides environmental, human rights, and social justice organizers with the tools, training, and support needed to achieve their goals.

School of the Americas Watch

http://www.soaw.org/

SOA Watch is an independent organization that seeks to close the U.S. Army School of the Americas, under whatever name it is called, through vigils and fasts, demonstrations and nonviolent protest, as well as media and legislative work.

Part 8: The Politics of Social Justice Meets Practice: Teacher Education and School Change

The Alternative Education Resource Organization

http://www.educationrevolution.org/

AERO provides information, resources, and guidance to families, schools, and organizations regarding their educational choices. AERO disseminates information, both nationally and internationally, on topics such as: home schooling, public and private alternative schools, and charter schools.

Educators for Social Responsibility

http://www.esrnational.org

Educators for Social Responsibility (ESR) helps educators create safe, caring, respectful, and productive learning environments. We also help educators work with young people to develop the social skills, emotional competencies, and qualities of character they need to succeed in school and become contributing members of their communities.

The International Association for Learning Alternatives

http://www.learningalternatives.net/

The IALA mission signals our interest in seeing that parents and students have choices of educational programs to meet their needs, interests, learning styles, and intelligences. We believe that a one-size education program does not fit everyone and that education is best served by having choices for all.

The Nation Center for Fair and Open Testing

http://www.fairtest.org/

An organization that works to reform/end standardized testing and promote other methods of evaluation. They focus on trying to eliminate the racial, gender, cultural, and class barriers within testing. They have a lot of articles and facts/statistics related to testing.

National Association for Multicultural Education

http://www.nameorg.org/

The Founders of NAME envisioned an organization that would bring together individuals and groups with an interest in multicultural education from all levels of education, different academic disciplines, and diverse educational institutions and occupations.

The North Dakota Study Group (NDSG) on Evaluation

http://learn.aero.und.edu/pages.asp?PageID=43095

A diverse network of progressive educators dedicated to advocacy for useful, fair, and democratic ways to document and assess children's learning and offering a criticism of educational reform and practice in the light of an enduring concern with democracy and the estate of childhood. Online discussion forum: http://groups.yahoo.com/group/ndsgroup/

School Funding Equity

http://www.geocities.com/~schoolfunding/

This site is intended to give visitors an overview of the funding disparities that plague this country's schools.

Students Against Testing

http://www.nomoretests.com

This site was created to be a strong force against the score-obsessed education machine known as standardized testing. At the same time, SAT also exists as an advocate for bringing positive, creative, and real-life learning activities into the schools. SAT believes that urgent action from the student body itself is the most direct way to counteract the boredom and petty competition that currently plagues the schools. The site offers a range of resources.

Working to Improve Schools and Education

http://www.ithaca.edu/wise/

This is a website for educators and those interested in issues related to education on a variety of topics. This website is mostly a compilation of amazing resources on topics from school uniforms to Waldorf education to gender issues in schools. Many issues that are often not covered when discussing education reform are covered here. The website is coordinated by Jeff Claus, an Ithaca College Professor in the Center for Teacher Education.

Part 9: Classrooms, Pedagogy, and Practicing Justice

EdChange

http://www.edchange.org/

EdChange is dedicated to equity and justice in schools and society. They *act* to shape schools, organizations, and communities in which the full diversity of people have opportunities to live, learn, and thrive free from oppression.

Education for Liberation

http://www.edliberation.org

This is a national coalition of teachers, community activists, youth, researchers, and parents who believe a good education should teach people—particularly low-income youth and youth of color—to understand and challenge the injustices their communities face.

Holistic Education, Inc.

http://www.holistic-education.net/

The mission of Holistic Education, Inc. is to help people develop their individual strengths and capacities to the fullest possible extent through holistic education.

New York Collective of Radical Educators

http://www.nycore.org

New York Collective of Radical Educators (NYCoRE) is a group of public school educators committed to fighting for social justice in our school system and society at large, by organizing and mobilizing teachers, developing curriculum, and working with community, parent, and student organizations. We are educators who believe that education is an integral part of social change and that we must work both inside and outside the classroom because the struggle for justice does not end when the school bell rings.

Radical Math

http://www.radicalmath.org

Radical Math Teachers are educators who work to integrate issues of economic and social justice into math classes, and seek to inspire and support other educators to do the same. Radical Math Teachers believe that math literacy is a civil right, and that our nation's failure to provide students, especially low-income youth of color, with a high-quality math education is a terrible injustice.

Radical Teacher—A Socialist, Feminist, and Antiracist Journal on the Theory and Practice of Teaching

http://www.radicalteacher.org

Radical Teacher is an independent magazine for educational workers at all levels and in every kind of institution. The magazine focuses on critical teaching practice, the political economy of education, and institutional struggles.

Rethinking Schools

http://www.rethinkingschools.org/

An organization made up of educators, administrators, parents, activists, and others who want to revision our schools. It was founded in the 1980s as a magazine in response to issues surrounding Milwaukee public schools. While Rethinking Schools started out as a quarterly magazine (which still exists) its website not only has past articles on a variety of subjects but also links to related websites.

Teaching for Change
http://www.teachingforchange.org/

Teaching for Change provides teachers and parents with the tools to transform schools into centers of justice where students learn to read, write, and change the world.

Teachers for Social Justice (Chicago)
http://www.teachersforjustice.org/

An organization of teachers, administrators, preservice teachers, and other educators working in public, independent, alternative, and charter schools and universities in the Chicago area. We have come together based on our commitment to education for social justice. We are working toward classrooms and schools that are antiracist, multicultural/multilingual, and grounded in the experiences of our students. We believe that all children should have an academically rigorous education that is both caring and critical, an education that helps students pose critical questions about society and "talk back" to the world. We share ideas and curriculum, and support each other in our work. We are also an activist organization, working to get the voices of educators into the public discussion of school policies.

Teachers for Social Justice (San Francisco)

http://www.t4sj.org

Teachers 4 Social Justice is a grassroots nonprofit teacher support and development organization. Their mission is to provide opportunities for self-transformation, leadership, and community building to educators in order to effect meaningful change in the classroom, school, community, and society. T4SJ organizes teachers and community-based educators and implements programs and projects that develop empowering learning environments, more equitable access to resources and power, and realizing a just and caring culture.

Teachers Unite

http://www.teachersunite.net

Teachers Unite is building a community of educators who work in solidarity with students and parents to demand social, economic, and educational justice. Teachers Unite's political education forums and collaborative projects with advocacy organizations are designed to help teachers examine the roots of public education's challenges and take action. The idea driving Teachers Unite is one where public schools graduate visionary leaders and their teachers fight with them to challenge power structures and demand equity.

Unschooling.com

http://www.unschooling.com/

The website offers a variety of unschooling resources including news articles and information on relevant laws.

Contributors

A. A. Akom examines the relationship between critical race theory and youth participatory action research. Akom's scholarship focuses on how youth and adults struggle to overcome racialized social practices as they structure local meanings of culture, class, privilege, and power in everyday life. He is an Assistant Professor of Urban Sociology and Africana Studies and Codirector of Educational Equity at the Cesar Chavez Institute at San Francisco State University.

Ricky Lee Allen is Assistant Professor of Educational Thought and Sociocultural Studies at the University of New Mexico. He specializes in the role of White identity politics in various forms of educational thought.

Anthony Arnove is a writer, activist, and public intellectual.

Dennis Attick is a doctoral candidate in Social Foundations of Education at Georgia State University. Dennis is also the Education Director at The Bridge, an alternative school and treatment center for incarcerated adolescents in Atlanta.

Rick Ayers is in advanced studies in the Language, Literacy, and Culture program of the UC Berkeley Graduate School of Education. He is coeditor of the series *Between Teacher and Text* (Teachers College Press) and cocreator (with students) of the *Berkeley High Slang Dictionary*.

William Ayers teaches at the University of Illinois at Chicago.

Joan Barnatt is a doctoral candidate in Curriculum and Instruction at Boston College's Lynch School of Education. Her research interests include practitioner inquiry, mentoring and induction, global education, and school reform.

Zvi Bekerman teaches anthropology of education at the School of Education and The Melton Center, Hebrew University of Jerusalem. He is also a Research Fellow at the Truman Institute for the Advancement of Peace, Hebrew University. His main interests are in the study of cultural, ethnic, and national identity, including identity processes and negotiation during intercultural encounters and in formal/informal learning contexts.

Wanda. J. Blanchett is Associate Dean for Teacher Education and Outreach at the University of Colorado at Denver and Health Sciences Center. Dr. Blanchett's research focuses on issues of inequity including urban teacher preparation, issues of race, class, culture, and gender, disproportionate representation of students of color in special education, severe disabilities, and issues of sexuality for students with disabilities.

Grace Lee Boggs is a writer and political activist who has been an advocate for social justice for over 60 years.

Deron Boyles is Professor of Educational Policy Studies in the College of Education at Georgia State University. His research interests include school–business partnerships, epistemology, pragmatism, and the philosophy of John Dewey.

Ellen Brantlinger is retired from the Curriculum and Instruction Department at Indiana University, Bloomington. She has written about social class, disability studies, sexuality issues pertaining to people with disabilities, qualitative inquiry, and teacher education.

Gretchen Brion-Meisels grew up in Cambridge, MA, where she struggled to understand her own privilege in a diverse social context. After writing her senior thesis on positive models of White antiracism, she began teaching middle school humanities. In a Baltimore City classroom, she encountered the devastating effects of institutionalized inequity. Her work continues to be driven by her desire to create equitable schools. In 2007, she began doctoral studies.

Enora R. Brown is Associate Professor in the School of Education at DePaul University. Her work in critical human development studies focuses on sociocultural and psychological processes, interpersonal dynamics, and institutional hierarchies that frame human development and the construction of identity. Her publications address the intersections amongst the construction of youth and teacher identities, educational policy and reform, and the sociohistorical dynamics of race and social class in school contexts.

Héctor Calderón is the principal at the El Puente Academy for Peace and Justice.

Patrick Camangian is Assistant Professor at the University of San Francisco's School of Education and Teacher Education Department.

Julio Cammarota is Assistant Professor in the Bureau of Applied Research in Anthropology and the Mexican-American Studies and Research Center at the University of Arizona. His research focuses on participatory action research with Latina/o youth, institutional factors in academic achievement, and liberatory pedagogy. He has published articles on family, work, and education among Latinas/os and on the relationship between culture and academic achievement.

Tony Carusi is a teacher educator and doctoral candidate in Educational Policy Studies at Georgia State University focusing on philosophy of education. His main research includes ideology criticism of positivistic notions of education that provide economistic justifications for schooling and define the public of public education accordingly.

Rafael Casal is a poet-activist who has won numerous awards including the National Teen Poetry Slam. He is an independent music producer and works for Youth Speaks in San Francisco.

Jennifer Chan is Associate Professor at the University of British Columbia. Her research focuses on issues of global governance, especially human rights and educational multilateralism; transnational social movements; Japanese civil society; and development of multiculturalism in Japan and France. Her latest publications include *Gender and Human Rights Politics in Japan: Global Norms and Domestic Networks,* and *Another Japan is Possible: New Social Movements and Global Citizenship Education in Japan.*

Marilyn Cochran-Smith is the John E. Cawthorne Millennium Chair in Education and directs the Doctoral Program in Curriculum and Instruction at Boston College's Lynch School of Education. Winner of AERA's 2007 Research to Practice award for *Policy, Practice and Politics in Teacher Education,* Cochran-Smith's research interests include research on teaching and teacher education, social justice education, and practitioner inquiry.

David J. Connor is Associate Professor in the School of Education at Hunter College, City University of New York. His interests include disability studies, learning disabilities, and issues of race, class, and gender in education.

Kimberly Cosier teaches Art Education Theory and Practice, Art and Visual Learning, and 3D Concepts and supervises student teachers in Art Education as an Associate Professor at the University of Wisconsin-Milwaukee.

Hillary Dachi is Senior Lecturer, Head of Department of Educational Planning and Administration, Chair of the Faculty of Education Strategic Planning Committee, and a member of the Senate at the University of Dar es Salaam. His research interests include financing education; education administration and planning; education of working children; and globalization and education policy.

David M. Donahue, Associate Professor of Education at Mills College, Oakland, California, teaches in the secondary teacher credential program. Previously, he was the Director of Mills College's service learning program. He has worked with Amnesty International's Human Rights Education program and the Equitas International Centre for Human Rights Education over the past 15 years, developing and leading training programs on human rights for teachers and activists around the world.

Jeffrey Duncan-Andrade is Assistant Professor in Raza Studies and the College of Education and Co-Director of the Educational Equity Initiative at San Francisco State University's Cesar Chavez Institute. He also teaches a 12th grade English literature course in East Oakland, California.

Laura C. Engel is a Research Fellow in the School of Education at the University of Nottingham, United Kingdom. She is a member of the Centre for Research into Equity and Diversity in Education and the UNESCO Centre for Comparative Educational Research. Currently, Engel is working on two EU Framework Programme 6 research projects, which explore intersecting issues of inclusion, education policy, citizenship, and lifelong learning across Europe. Her research interests also include globalization, multilevel governance, and education policy.

Beth A. Ferri is Associate Professor at Syracuse University, where she coordinates the Doctoral Program in Special Education and the Master's Program in Inclusive (Special)

Education (grades 7–12). She is also core faculty in the Disability Studies program and associate faculty in Women's Studies. She recently published the book *Reading Resistance: Discourses of Exclusion in Desegregation and Inclusion Debates* with coauthor David J. Connor.

Jim Ferris is a past president of the Society for Disability Studies, the leading international scholarly organization in Disability Studies. Author of the award-winning book *The Hospital Poems*, his work has appeared in many journals, including *The Georgia Review* and the *Michigan Quarterly Review*. A former newspaper reporter and television producer, he holds the Ability Center Endowed Chair in Disability Studies at the University of Toledo, where he directs the Disability Studies Program.

Gustavo E. Fischman is Associate Professor of Curriculum and Policy Studies in the Mary Lou Fulton College of Education at Arizona State University. His areas of specialization are comparative education, gender studies in education, critical pedagogy, and the use of image-based methodologies in educational research. He is the author of *Imagining Teachers: Rethinking Teacher Education and Gender* and *La Ley y La Tierra: Historia de un Despojo*.

David Gabbard has earned national and international recognition for his work in critical educational policy studies and democratic educational theory. Along with five published books, his record of scholarly production includes over 50 articles and book chapters. The first edition of his *Knowledge and Power in a Global Economy: Politics and the Rhetoric of School Reform* received the Critic's Choice Award from the American Educational Studies Association in 2001.

Susan L. Gabel is Professor of Special Education in the National College of Education at National-Louis University where she teaches courses in disability studies in education, special education, and the foundations of education. Her research focuses on the social and political contexts of disability in education. She is the editor of *Disability Studies in Education: Readings in Theory and Method* and the co-editor, with Scot Danforth, of *Vital Questions Facing Disability Studies in Education*.

Luis Armando Gandin is a Professor of Sociology of Education in the School of Education of Federal University of Rio Grande do Sul in Porto Alegre, Brazil. He is one of the editors of the journal *Currículo sem Fronteiras* (Curriculum without Borders, http://www.curriculosemfronteiras.org), an open-access, peer-reviewed educational publication and editor of the journal *Educação & Realidade* (Education and Reality). Professor Gandin has been researching and writing on the areas of sociology of education, international and comparative education, critical education and pedagogy, educational policy, and progressive educational reforms. He has published six books (as main author or editor) and is working as one of the editors on two international handbooks: on critical education and sociology of education.

David Gillborn is Professor of Education at the Institute of Education, University of London and editor of the journal *Race Ethnicity & Education*.

Carl A. Grant is Hoefs-Bascom Professor of Teacher Education in the Department of Curriculum and Instruction at the University Wisconsin-Madison and Professor in the Department of Afro-American Studies. He has written or edited 25 books or monographs in multicultural education or teacher education and more than 135 articles, chapters in books, and reviews.

Eric (Rico) Gutstein teaches mathematics education at the University of Illinois, Chicago. His areas are teaching mathematics for social justice, Freirean approaches to teaching and learning, and urban education. He has taught middle and high school mathematics. Rico is a founding member of *Teachers for Social Justice* (Chicago) and is active in social movements. He is author of *Reading and Writing the World with Mathematics: Toward a Pedagogy for Social Justice*.

Eric Haas is a Senior Fellow at the Rockridge Institute.

Horace R. Hall is Assistant Professor at DePaul University in the Department of Educational Policy Studies and Research. He is also founder and director of a Chicago-based youth program called REAL (Respect, Excellence, Attitude, and Leadership). REAL offers students an in-school space to artistically express themselves while gaining insight into how social, political, and economic dynamics shape the world around them.

Annette Henry is Professor of Multicultural Education at the University of Washington, Tacoma. Her scholarship examines Black women teachers' practice in the United States and Canada as well as race, language, gender, and culture in sociocultural contexts of teaching and learning. Her interests include alternative epistemologies and methodologies. She has written extensively about conceptual and methodological issues regarding research with Black women and girls.

Anna Hickey-Moody is Lecturer in Creative Arts Education at Monash University, Australia. Her forthcoming monograph, *Unimaginable Bodies*, will be published in 2008. Anna has taught in universities since 1999 and in community settings since 1996. Her research brings together creative arts and cultural studies, via a focus on social justice for marginalized youth.

Patricia Hulsebosch is Professor of Education and Assistant Dean at Gallaudet University where she teaches courses in curriculum and early childhood education. Her research focuses on relationships among home, school, and community and the influences of culture on teaching and learning.

David Hursh is Associate Professor at the Warner Graduate School of Education at the University of Rochester. His recent research examines the rise of high-stakes testing and accountability within the context of neoliberal ideologies and changing forms of governmentality. Some of his recent publications have appeared in the *American Educational Research Journal*, *Policy Futures in Education*, and *Race, Ethnicity, and Education*.

Amanda Keddie is a Postdoctoral Research Fellow at the University of Queensland. Her teaching areas, research, and publications focus on issues of pedagogy, gender, masculinity, schooling, and social justice. She has recently published her first coauthored book with Martin Mills entitled *Teaching Boys: Developing Classroom Practices that Work*.

Jane Kenway is Professor of Education at Monash University in Australia. Her research expertise is in the politics of educational change in the context of wider social, cultural, and political change. Her recent jointly written books are *Masculinity Beyond* *the Metropolis, Haunting the Knowledge Economy,* and *Consuming Children: Education—Advertising—Entertainment.*

Kevin K. Kumashiro is Associate Professor of Policy Studies at the University of Illinois, Chicago and the founding director of the Center for Anti-Oppressive Education. He has worked as a teacher and teacher educator in schools and colleges across the United States and abroad, and has served as a consultant for school districts, educational organizations, and government agencies. He has authored or edited seven books, including *Troubling Education,* which received the 2003 Gustavus Myers Outstanding Book Award.

Nishat Kurwa leads Youth Radio's newsroom and International Desk, working with reporters in the Bay Area and internationally to produce stories for Youth Radio's local and national outlets. A graduate of Youth Radio's core class of Fall 1995, she moved on to become the producer of KMEL's public affairs show *Street Knowledge with Davey D* and is currently also a news producer at KCBS Radio in San Francisco. In 2004 Ms. Kurwa was named a Salzburg Seminar Fellow.

Vicki K. LaBoskey, Professor of Education at Mills College, Oakland, California teaches in and coadministers the elementary portion of the Teachers for Tomorrow's Schools Credential Program. Her research and consulting work has focused on supporting teacher educators and preservice and inservice teachers in the transformation of their practice and their institutions according to the goals of equity and social justice through reflective teaching, narrative inquiry, and self-study.

Randall Lahann is a doctoral student in Curriculum and Instruction at the Lynch School of Education at Boston College. His research interests include teacher education for social justice and alternate-route teacher preparation programs.

Nicolas Lampert is a Milwaukee/Chicago based interdisciplinary artist and writer. He works collectively with Justseeds/Visual Resistance (http://www.justseeds.org), the Street Art Workers (http://www.streetartworkers.org), and the Cut and Paint e-zine project (http://www.cutandpaint.org). His visual art website is: http://www.machineanimalcollages.com

Lisa Lee is Director of the Jane Addams Hull House Museum on the campus of the University of Illinois at Chicago.

Pepi Leistyna is Associate Professor of Applied Linguistics Graduate Studies at the University of Massachusetts, Boston, where he coordinates the research program and teaches courses in cultural studies, media literacy, and language acquisition. Speaking internationally on issues of democracy, public education, and social justice, he has published articles in a wide range of journals and his books include: *Breaking Free: The Transformative Power of Critical Pedagogy.*

Zeus Leonardo is the author of *Ideology, Discourse, and School Reform* (Praeger) and he is editor of *Critical Pedagogy and Race* (Blackwell), and co-editor (with Tejeda and Martinez) of *Charting New Terrains of Chicano(a)/Latino(a) Education* (Hampton). His articles have appeared in *Educational Researcher*; *Race, Ethnicity, and Education*; and *Educational Philosophy and Theory.*

Avi Lessing is a high school teacher outside of Chicago. He teaches an elective English class called Experiments in Reading Literature and the World. He uses theater, storytelling, meditation, and therapeutic models in the classroom to engender a greater sense of self and community.

Amanda Lewis is Associate Professor of Sociology at Emory University in Atlanta, Georgia. Her research focuses on how race shapes educational opportunities from kindergarten through graduate school and on how our ideas about race get negotiated in everyday life. Her research on these topics has appeared in a number of books and journals including *Sociological Theory, American Educational Research Journal, American Behavioral Scientist*, and the *Du Bois Review*.

Pauline Lipman is Professor of Policy Studies and Director of the Collaborative for Equity and Justice in Education, College of Education, University of Illinois-Chicago. Her research focuses on race and class inequality in schools, globalization, and political economy and cultural politics of race in urban education. She is the author of *Race, Class, and Power in School Restructuring; High Stakes Education: Inequality, Globalization, and Urban School Reform;* and is an education activist in Chicago.

Josh MacPhee is an artist, curator, and activist currently living in Brooklyn, NY. His work often revolves around themes of radical politics, privatization, and public space. His most recent book is Reproduce & Revolt/Reproduce Y Rebélate (Soft Skull Press, 2008, co-edited with Favianna Rodriguez). He also organizes the *Celebrate People's History* Poster Series and is part of the political art collective Justseeds.org.

Sandra Mathison is Professor of Education at the University of British Columbia. Her research focuses on the potential and limitations of evaluation as a democratizing practice in schools, and currently emphasizes a critique of the pernicious practice of evaluating schools through simplistic outcomes-based accountability strategies.

Belia Mayeno Saavedra is the Workshop Coordinator and a Facilitator at Voices UnBroken, a South Bronx nonprofit which provides creative writing and poetry workshops for incarcerated women and girls. She is currently studying English and Africana/Latino studies at Hunter College in Manhattan. She graduated from Youth Radio's core program in 1997, and won the Radio and Television News Directors Ed Bradley Scholarship and a Gracie Award from American Women in Radio and Television.

Cris Mayo is Associate Professor in the Department of Educational Policy Studies and the Gender and Women's Studies Program at the University of Illinois at Urbana-Champaign. Her publications in the areas of gender studies and philosophy of education include *Disputing the Subject of Sex: Sexuality and Public School Controversies*, as well as articles in *Educational Theory, Philosophy of Education*, and *Philosophical Studies in Education*.

Lance T. McCready is Assistant Professor of Urban Education at the Ontario Institute for Studies in Education at the University of Toronto. He received his doctorate in Social and Cultural Studies with a Designated Emphasis in Women, Gender, and Sexuality Studies from the University of California, Berkeley. Dr. McCready's research and writing focuses on curricular and pedagogical issues in urban education, specifically the "troubles" facing Black male students in urban schools.

Ray McDermott is a grade school teacher turned cultural anthropologist. For 40 years, he has been applying the tools of cultural analysis to how children learn, how schools work, and why Americans have invested so heavily in a misfit between the two. More recently, he has been working on the intellectual history of ideas about learning, genius, justice, logic, and the body. He is the author of *Successful Failure: The Schools America Builds* (with Hervé Varenne) and an editor of *Fine Description* (with Joel Kuipers).

Morva McDonald is Assistant Professor of Education in the University of Washington's College of Education. Her research focuses on teacher education and the preparation of teachers for diversity as well as students' opportunities to learn in and out of school. She uses sociocultural theories of learning to frame and understand teacher preparation and students' opportunities to learn.

Erica R. Meiners, Associate Professor of Education and Women's Studies at Northeastern Illinois University, is involved with a number of local social justice initiatives in Chicago linked to prison resistance, queer organizing, and educational equity. Since 1999, she has been teaching at, and coordinating, an alternative high school for formerly incarcerated men and women, and she is the author of *Right to Be Hostile: Schools, Prisons and Making of Public Enemies* (2007).

Gregory Michie teaches in the Department of Curriculum and Instruction at Illinois State University, where he coordinates a year-long student-teaching internship program in Chicago Public Schools. He is the author of *Holler if You Hear Me: The Education of a Teacher and His Students*, a memoir of his experiences teaching in Chicago.

Martin Mills is Associate Professor in the School of Education, The University of Queensland, Australia, and Visiting Professor at Roehampton University, London, UK. He teaches and researches in the areas of gender and education, violence, and school reform and pedagogy. His recent books include *Challenging Violence in Schools: An Issue of Masculinities* (2001); and the coauthored *Leading Learning: Making Hope Practical in Schools* (2003).

Karen Monkman, Associate Professor of Education Policy Studies and Research, and Director of the doctoral program in education at DePaul University, teaches courses in comparative education, anthropology and sociology of education, and qualitative research methods. Her research focuses on relationships between education and globalization, immigration, and gender, within the United States and in low income regions of the world.

Jennifer Mueller is Assistant Professor in the Department of Curriculum and Instruction at the University of Wisconsin, Milwaukee. Her research is focused in teacher education, particularly in policy, pedagogy, and programming to create learning environments that prepare teachers for effective, equitable teaching in urban and diverse schools.

Salim Muwakkil is a senior editor of *In These Times*, a magazine dedicated to informing and analyzing popular movements for social, environmental, and economic justice. He is currently a Crime and Communities Media Fellow of the Open Society Institute, examining the impact of ex-inmates and gang leaders in leadership positions in the black community. Muwakkil is working on a documentary titled Chicago Gangs: An American

Story and writing the text for a book of photographs documenting the tenure of Harold Washington, Chicago's first black mayor.

Carla O'Connor is Arthur F. Thurnau Professor and Associate Professor of Education at the University of Michigan. Her research focuses on the racial identity, academic experience, and educational resilience of Black youth.

Elizabethe C. Payne is an education sociologist in the Cultural Foundations of Education Department at Syracuse University. She is also the founding director of The Q Center, a youth center supporting LGBT young people in the Central New York area. Elizabethe's research focuses on the life histories of adolescent lesbians, school experiences of LGBT youth, and HIV and sex education in schools. She teaches courses in qualitative research methodology, Youth Culture, and Queer Youth Experiences in schools.

Therese Quinn is Associate Professor of Art Education at The School of the Art Institute of Chicago. She is writing a book with Erica Meiners about the effects of privatization on queer teachers and students in public schools.

Jason Duque Raley, of the University of California, Santa Barbara, takes a broad interest in the local structuring of social relations, the analysis of improvisation, and the special possibilities (and problems) offered by schooling. His current work includes studies of trust and authority in face-to-face encounters, the interactional organization of momentum in school talk, and work on the intellectual history of motivation.

Milton Reynolds is a Program Associate with Facing History and Ourselves, an international educational professional development and curriculum development organization. He currently presides over the board of Literacy for Environmental Justice, a Bayview/Hunters Point-based youth leadership/environmental justice organization and also serves on the board of The Working Group, in addition to holding a commissioner's seat on the San Mateo County Juvenile Justice and Delinquency Prevention Commission.

Anna E. Richert is Professor of Education in the School of Education at Mills College in Oakland, California where she is Director of the MA/Credential Program, Teachers for Tomorrow's Schools. Recently a Carnegie Teacher Education Scholar, Richert's current research looks at the potential of multilayered web-based representations of practice for the preparation of urban school teachers. Her work focuses at the intersection of teacher learning and school reform.

Fazal Rizvi is Professor in Educational Policy studies at the University of Illinois at Urbana-Champaign where he directs its global studies in education program. His new book, *Globalizing Educational Policy*, will be published in 2008.

Susan L. Robertson is Professor of Sociology of Education at the University of Bristol, United Kingdom. Her current research interests include processes of globalization, regionalization, and education, with a particular focus on the relationship between economic strategies and social justice. She is coordinator of the Centre for Globalisation, Education and Societies at the University of Bristol and cofounding editor of the journal *Globalisation, Societies and Education.*

Augustine F. Romero is Tucson Unified School District's Senior Academic Director for Ethnic Studies. He is a doctoral candidate in the University of Arizona's Language, Reading and Culture Department. Augustine's research focuses on movement toward Critical Compassionate Intellectualism and its impact upon children of color.

Kenneth J. Saltman is Associate Professor of Educational Policy Studies and Research at DePaul University in Chicago. His work considers educational politics and policy in relation to broader political, cultural, and economic matters. His books include *Capitalizing on Disaster: Taking and Breaking Public Schools*, *The Edison Schools*, and *Collateral Damage*.

Mara Sapon-Shevin is Professor of Inclusive Education at Syracuse University and a community peace activist. Her areas of commitment include teaching for social justice, music and movement in education, antiracism and antihomophobia work, and teacher education. She is actively involved in Middle East peace issues, antiwar activism, and singing for social justice. Her most recent book is *Widening the Circle: The Power of Inclusive Classrooms*.

Julie Searle teaches English and history in Berkeley, California. She has written articles on arts-based education and language development, and was on the steering committee for the Edible Schoolyard. A parent of three daughters, she was a cofounder of Oakland-based Parents Against the War. Previously, she worked at The Poetry Center at San Francisco State University.

Karen Shakman is a doctoral candidate at Boston College Lynch School of Education. She is a primary researcher in a longitudinal qualitative case study of learning to teach. Her research interests include teacher education for social justice, teacher induction, and the impact of school context on teachers.

Laurene E. Simms is Professor in the Department of Education at Gallaudet University. She is also the director of graduate programs at that institution.

Tove Skutnabb-Kangas, Emerita, University of Roskilde, Denmark, and Åbo Akademi University, Finland, has written or edited around 50 books and almost 400 articles and book chapters, in 31 languages, about minority education, linguistic human rights, linguistic genocide, subtractive spread of English, the relationship between biodiversity and linguistic diversity. She was the Linguapax award recipient in 2003.

Christine E. Sleeter is Professor Emerita in the College of Professional Studies at California State University, Monterey Bay. Her research focuses on antiracist multicultural education and teacher education. She has received several awards including the California State University Monterey Bay President's Medal, the National Association for Multicultural Education Research Award, and the AERA Committee on the Role and Status of Minorities in Education Distinguished Scholar Award.

Andrew P. Smiler is Assistant Professor of Psychology at the State University of New York (SUNY) at Oswego. His research focuses on the ways in which individuals, both male and female, define and enact masculinity, as well as cultural influences (activity options, media) that influence those definitions and enactments. He also studies the romantic and sexual behaviors of adolescents and young adults.

Elisabeth Soep is Education Director and Senior Producer at Youth Radio, a national youth development organization and independent production company, where she collaborates with youth reporters on stories for NPR and other outlets. Lissa holds a doctorate in education from Stanford University, and she writes and teaches about youth, media culture, and education. Lissa's research has been published in journals including the *Harvard Educational Review* and *Teachers College Record*.

David Stovall is Associate Professor of Educational Policy Studies and African-American Studies at the University of Illinois at Chicago. He also works as a volunteer social studies teacher at the Greater Lawndale Little Village Social Justice High School.

karen emily suurtamm is Project Director of Democratic Dialogue, an Education Research Unit in the Faculty of Education, University of Ottawa.

Laurence Tan is a full-time teacher at 122nd Street Elementary School. Drawing upon his experiences as an immigrant growing up by the border in San Diego, he works with youth and families toward social change and community building. Involved in many community and justice-based grassroots organizations, Laurence is currently most invested and proud of his work with his former fifth grade students in their formation of the Watts Youth Collective (WYC) to positively change their Watts community.

Shelley K. Taylor teaches in the Faculty of Education at the University of Western Ontario. She teaches courses in English and French on second/multilingual language education, and minority language issues, and conducts microlevel (classroom-based), ethnographic research seen in macro (sociopolitical) perspective. She currently holds an IS leadership position in TESOL.

Dianna Terrell is a doctoral student in the Curriculum and Instruction program at the Lynch School of Education, Boston College. Her research interests include secondary history and civic education, social justice, and education policy.

Helen R. Thumann is Associate Professor and Undergraduate Program Director in the Gallaudet University Department of Education. Areas of interest include education of deaf and hard of hearing children, adolescent and adult literacy, the transition from school to work, bilingual education, and teacher preparation.

Leon Tikly is Professor in Education at the University of Bristol and Director of the Research Programme Consortium on Implementing Education Quality in Low Income Countries (EdQual). His research interests include the impact of globalization on social justice and education in Africa and the achievement of Black and Minority Ethnic learners in the UK.

Armando Torres teaches social science in the same school that he graduated from, Richmond High School in Richmond, California. His goals are to bring dignity and compassion into his classroom of diverse learners and teach them how to lead independent, successful lives.

Marc A. VanOverbeke is Assistant Professor in the College of Education at Northern Illinois University, where he teaches courses in history of education and foundations of education. He earned his doctorate in Educational Policy Studies from the University of Wisconsin, Madison.

K. Wayne Yang is Assistant Professor of Ethnic Studies at the University of California at San Diego.

Joel Westheimer is University Research Chair in Democracy and Education and Professor in the Social Foundations of Education at the University of Ottawa where he also directs www.DemocraticDialogue.com. His most recent book is *Pledging Allegiance: The Politics of Patriotism in America's Schools* (Teachers College Press, 2007).

Kenneth M. Zeichner is Hoefs-Bascom Professor of Teacher Education at the University of Wisconsin, Madison.

Index

Multiple masculinities, characteristics, 341
Multiracial schools, African–American students, 62
Muslims, gender equity, 112–115

N

Narrative of redemption, critical pedagogy, 569–573
Nation-state machinery, education, 139
National Assessment of Educational Progress, 7–8
National Council on Education Standards and Testing, 9
National Education Goals Panel, 9
National identity, American frontier, 15
National school system, Native Americans, 72
National security, 112–115
Native Americans
  cultural imperialism, 64
  education
    cultural genocide, 81–82
    forced boarding schools, 81–82
    racialized system, 80–82
  land acquisition, 63–65, 68
    acculturation-acquisition plan, 69–70
    Dawes Severalty Act, 79–80
    final conquest, 78–80
    General Allotment Act, 79–80
    Peace Commission, 79
  national school system, 72
  racialized displacement, 74–76
  slavery, 63–65
  sovereignty, 68
  Spanish colonization, 63–65
  syncretism, 64
  U.S. Constitution, 70
  westward expansion, 72–73
Naturalization Act of 1790, 69
Nature vs. nurture, 431
Neoliberal citizenship regimes, spaces of social justice, 549–550
Neoliberal globalization, 108–110, 565–573
  critical pedagogy, 569–573
  educational policy, 529–539
  efficiency, 537–539
  equity, 537–539
  governance, 537–539
  shifts, 532–534
  hope, 565–573
Neoliberalism, 10–12
  Africa, 123–124
  characterized, 154–156
  combating neoliberal educational discourse, 152–162
  competition, 155
  education, 110–112, 156–161
    social justice, 156–161
  educational inequality, 159–160
  gender equity, 108–112
    critical pedagogy, 569–573
  ideals inherently masculinist, 109
  market, 155
  objectives, 155–156
  social democratic liberalism, 156–161

  societal hierarchy, 410
New College, social justice teacher education, 601
New Dawn Alternative High School, 285, 292–293, 296–297
New Partnership for Africa's Development, 124, 128, 129, 131
New racism, 231
New York State
  standardized testing regime, 158
  standards-based assessment, 158
No Child Left Behind Act, 7
  adequate yearly progress, 158–159
  criticism, 52–53
  educational inequality, 159–160
  evaluation
    annual yearly progress, 8
    narrowed scope, 8–9
    prescriptive, 8
  Linguistic Language Rights, 183–184
Nolan, Christopher, 432–433
Non–White racism, 239, 240
Nonviolent civil disobedience, 55
North American Free Trade Agreement, 548
North West Kurdistan, educational language rights, 172–174, 180–186
  Kurds, 172–174, 180–186
Novice teachers, 705–709

O

Obedience, 727
  kindergarten, 52
Obscenity, Gay–Straight Alliances, 322–324
Open Method of Coordination, 533
Oppression, 1
  poor White people, 221–222
  women's position, 107
Order, 707
Out, defined, 300
Overrepresentation, special education, 419, 426
Ownership society, 727

P

Palestinian–Jewish education, in Israel, 138–149
Panoptical time, 101
Paradigmatic gaze, educational reform, 139–141
Parental notification, Gay–Straight Alliances, 322–324
Participant observation, 265
Participatory action research, critical race theory, 508–517
  advocating for social change, 516–517
  disseminating research findings, 516–517
  emancipatory knowledge for urban and suburban educators, 513–514
  merging, 513–514
  repositioning students as subjects and architects of research, 511–513
  theory as liberatory practice, 511–513
Passing, 509
Perceived to be bisexual youth, 286
Perceived to be gay youth, 286